BROWNLIE'S PRINCIPLES OF PUBLIC

INTERNATIONAL LAW

BROWNLIE'S PRINCIPLES OF

PUBLIC INTERNATIONAL LAW

Eighth Edition

BY

JAMES CRAWFORD, SC, FBA

OXFORD

UNIVERSITY PRESS

OXFORD
UNIVERSITY PRESS

Great Clarendon Street, Oxford OX2 6DP,
United Kingdom

Oxford University Press is a department of the University of Oxford.
It furthers the University's objective of excellence in research, scholarship,
and education by publishing worldwide. Oxford is a registered trade mark of
Oxford University Press in the UK and in certain other countries

Fifth Edition published in 1998
Sixth Edition published in 2003
Seventh Edition published in 2008
Impression: 1

British Library Cataloguing in Publication Data
Data available

Library of Congress Control Number: 2012944652

ISBN Hbk 978-0-19-965417-8
ISBN Pbk 978-0-19-969969-8

Printed in Great Britain by
CPI Group (UK) Ltd, Croydon, CR0 4YY

OUTLINE CONTENTS

CONTENTS

PART II PERSONALITY AND RECOGNITION

PART III TERRITORIAL SOVEREIGNTY

PART IV LAW OF THE SEA

PART V THE ENVIRONMENT AND NATURAL RESOURCES

PART VI INTERNATIONAL TRANSACTIONS

PART IX THE LAW OF RESPONSIBILITY

PART X THE PROTECTION OF INDIVIDUALS AND GROUPS

AUTHOR BIOGRAPHIES

Ian Brownlie (1932–2010) was born on 19 September 1932 in Liverpool and was educated at Alsop High School, Liverpool and Hertford College Oxford, before undertaking a doctorate at Oxford under Humphrey Waldock. He spent a year (1955–56) at Kings College Cambridge as Humanitarian Trust Student in Public International Law. He taught at Nottingham Law School (1957–63) before becoming a tutorial fellow and university lecturer in law at Wadham College (1963–76). Following a period as Professor of International Law at the LSE, from 1980 to his retirement in 1998 he was Chichele Professor of Public International Law in the University of Oxford and a Fellow (later Distinguished Fellow) of All Souls College. He was a member of the International Law Commission from 1997–2008, and its Chairman in 2007. He was knighted in 2009 for services to international law. He was the author of numerous books on international law, including *International Law and the Use of Force by States* (1963), *African Boundaries* (1979), *State Responsibility (Part I)* (1983), and his 1995 Hague lectures, *The Rule of Law in International Affairs* (Martinus Nijhoff, 1998). A member of Blackstone Chambers, he was a leading advocate before the International Court of Justice, the European Court of Justice, the European Court of Human Rights, and other international tribunals, as well as before the English courts. He was an arbitrator in a number of important cases including *Barbados/Trinidad & Tobago* (2006).

James Crawford is Whewell Professor of International Law and a Fellow of Jesus College, Cambridge and concurrently Research Professor of Law at LaTrobe University. He is a Senior Counsel (NSW) and a member of the English bar, practising from Matrix Chambers. He was the first Australian member of the United Nations International Law Commission and was responsible for the ILC's work on the International Criminal Court (1992–94) and for the second reading of the ILC Articles on State Responsibility (1997–2001). A graduate student of Ian Brownlie's, he has appeared before the International Court of Justice and other international tribunals and was, for many years, Director of the Lauterpacht Centre for International Law in the University of Cambridge.

PREFACE

It is difficult to overestimate the importance of successive editions of Ian Brownlie's *Principles* for the teaching of international law over the last 45 years. It is not too much to say that several generations of Anglophone international lawyers have absorbed their sense of the structure of their subject from *Principles*.

That is certainly true in my case. I first used this work (in its first edition of 1966) when studying international law at the University of Adelaide in 1968. My undergraduate lecturer, DP O'Connell, was less than pleased to see me carrying the 'radical' Brownlie around in that year of student unrest. In fact I had also bought (but did not carry around) O'Connell's much heavier work.

In 1972, I began a doctorate at Oxford. My supervisor was Brownlie, as I had hoped. Despite expressing considerable reserve when I announced that my doctoral subject was statehood (not one aspect but all of it), he eventually warmed to the idea. I realize once again, in reviewing closely the relevant chapters of the 7th edition, how much I owe the 'insights' of that thesis to *Principles*.

It was thus both an honour and a responsibility to be asked to undertake the 8th edition of *Principles*, following Ian's tragic death in January 2010.[1]

It turned out to be a more difficult commission than I had thought. The text was in need of an overhaul, and there were many new developments to be taken into account. The Press stipulated that this all had to be done within the same length as the 7th edition, so that for every insertion there had to be an equal excision. While it has proved possible to preserve much of Brownlie's text and, I hope, the general spirit and tone of the work, it proved necessary to engage not only in updating, but also in some restructuring. A determined effort has been made to review the footnotes so as to include the best recent literature of the subject, while not losing sight of the literature of the period 1945–75 to which so much reference was made in successive editions.

I am only too aware of the warning against '"ancestor worship" in text-book literature ... the tyranny of mortmain'.[2] There has been a cottage industry of renovating texts,[3] prompting calls for 'another book, rather than a new edition of this one'.[4] Robert Jennings made the same complaint of the 6th edition of Oppenheim,[5] before going on to co-edit the 9th. Whether the present effort was worth it is for others to judge; but in my view Brownlie still speaks perceptively about international law as law, about its systematic character,

---

[1] A biographical memoir of Brownlie is in British Academy, XI *Biographical Memoirs* (in press). See also Owada (2010) 81 *BYIL* 1; Lowe, ibid, 9.

[2] J M[ervyn] J[ones] (1944) 21 *BY* 242, 243.

[3] On the British textbook tradition: Crawford, in Beatson & Zimmermann (eds), *Jurists Uprooted. German-speaking Emigré Lawyers in Twentieth Century Britain* (2004) 681.

[4] Warbrick (2000) 11 *EJIL* 621, 632. I am indebted to this best of Brownlie reviews, and have taken much of its advice.

[5] RY J[ennings] (1947) 24 *BYIL* 512, 513.

about sovereignty as a value, about the relations of nationality, and the implications of peremptory norms outside the field of treaties, among many other things.

A more fundamental question is whether *any* single volume can account in a meaningful way for the scope and content of modern international law, or even cope with its general principles. The subject is now too large, too diverse, too ramified to permit such treatment. We do not produce—except for foreign audiences—single volume works on English law (still less British) law. Why should international law be any different?

There are a number of answers. First of all, international law is still normally studied as such, especially at first degree level. In studying it students approach it as a foreign law, foreign at least to their experience of law; many doubt that it *could* be law—though with every second problem in our world an international one, they have no difficulty seeing that it *should* be. It is a function of a single volume handbook, among other things, to address both this 'should' and this 'could'.

Secondly, international law has been and remains a *system*, based on and helping to structure a system of relations among states and other entities. Yet this systemic aspect is lost or obscured if one studies only the law of the sea, the law of the environment, the law of human rights. For these presume, and are configured by, the law of the land, the anthropocene environment, the powers of states. The sea, the environment would not be problems if not for ourselves and our associations.

Thirdly, we need international law as a whole, not a set of parts attracting differential affiliation or disrespect. Trade notoriously suffers in wars; children suffer from misrule; the environment suffers from misguided production because of subsidies. Things are *connected*. This is not to suggest that international law is a universal solvent or solution. But it is an indispensable method—the world being as it is—for exploring and implementing solutions.

Note on the text

The first edition of *Principles* (1966) contained 26 chapters in 11 parts, some parts consisting only of one or two chapters. Some new chapters were later added, as follows: immunities (2nd edition), environmental law (5th edition), international criminal law (6th edition), and the use or threat of force by states (6th edition). In this edition I have restructured the parts and chapters to some extent, while trying not to alter the overall conception of the book as, first, an advanced text for students, undergraduate and graduate, treating core issues from a lawyer's perspective, and secondly, a useful guide to the components of the subject for scholars and practitioners. I have added an introduction and rewritten certain chapters. Internal numbering of sections and sub-sections has been introduced. Cross-referencing is to chapters only and each chapter is as far as possible self-contained (at the expense of a limited amount of duplication between chapters). Instead of cross-referencing, there is a very full index.

Despite these changes, the text of the 8th edition is still essentially Brownlie's. But I have not hesitated to modify it where this seemed to be appropriate in the interests of clarity, concision, current priorities, or the need to reflect developments. The danger of editions of classic texts (both Brierly and Oppenheim are examples) is that they atrophy by interpolation, become encrusted. The other strategy—the assumption of ownership of the text—seems to me the only course, while preserving a decent respect for the original author's known views. Otherwise one ends up with a text which no-one—author or editor—can be held to accept or believe. In our online days—the days of the splendidly recursive *Max Planck Encyclopedia*—we need not more detail, more fragments, but a coherent account of the core. That is what *Principles* always promised. For this attempt at fulfilling the promise I take full responsibility.

* * *

Acknowledgements

My thanks are due to the institutions and the many people within them who made this edition possible: to the Lauterpacht Centre for International Law under its Director, Professor Marc Weller; to my associates at LCIL who assisted with this project (notably Tiina Pajuste, Juliette McIntyre, Cameron Miles, Anna Cowan, and Rumiana Yotova), and to the Cambridge graduate cohort of 2010–11 who spent many hours checking references and gathering materials for the revision. They were: Daniel Barton, Fernando Bordin, Sophie Chapman, Daniel Costelloe, Riddhi Dasgupta, Michail Dekastros, Berk Demirkol, Ali El-Haj, Henner Goett, Caroline Henckels, Luis Jardón Piña, Jonathan Ketcheson, Apurba Khatiwada, Belinda McRae, Jasmine Moussa, Thang Nguyen Dang, Agnieszka Paszcza, Kate Purcell, Cecily Rose, Andrew Sanger, Geraldo Vidigal Neto, and Helen Worsnop.

Individual chapters, once completed in draft, were read by colleagues and friends, whose help and suggestions I greatly appreciate. They were: Pierre Bodeau-Livinec, Rodman Bundy, William Butler, Matthew Craven, John Crook, Zachary Douglas, John Dugard, Malcolm Evans, Malgosia Fitzmaurice, Guy Goodwin-Gill, Tom Grant (multiple chapters), Christine Gray, Douglas Guilfoyle, Kaj Hober, Ben Juratowitch, Jan Klabbers, Pierre Klein, Martti Koskenniemi, Stephen McCaffrey, John Merrills, Sarah Nouwen (multiple chapters), Roger O'Keefe, Simon Olleson (multiple chapters), Alain Pellet, Philippe Sands, Danesh Sarooshi, William Schabas, Nico Schrijver, Malcolm Shaw, Ivan Shearer, Bruno Simma, Stefan Talmon, Christian Tams, Tullio Treves, Colin Warbrick, and Xiaodong Yang. The illustrative map of maritime zones in chapter 12 I owe to Dr Robin Cleverly, Head, UK Hydrographic Office, Taunton, with whom I have spent many happy cartographic hours.

At Oxford University Press I must thank Jacqueline Senior, John Louth, and Helen Davis.

The text is, as far as possible, current as at 1 January 2012. All websites cited were current on that day. Opportunity was taken to add references to a few major developments between January and June 2012.

JRC
Lauterpacht Centre for International Law
University of Cambridge
1 June 2012

PREFACE TO THE SEVENTH EDITION

Changes have occurred in many areas of the law since the last edition of this book. Care has been taken to renovate the treatment of a number of topics, including jurisdictional immunities, the responsibility of states, indirect expropriation, international criminal justice and informal extradition.

At the same time, the procedure of renovation has been accompanied by certain inhibitions stemming from the inherent nature of a single volume treatment of the principles of public international law. The temptation to include a detailed treatment of recent complex events (the invasion and occupation of Iraq, for example) has been resisted. To deal adequately with such events would involve excursions well beyond the ambit of a legal handbook. If the situation of Iraq be taken as an example, the limitations can be seen immediately. In the first place, the determination of the material facts would involve considerable difficulty. Secondly, there is the central problem which is the tendency of the State actors to adopt convenient suppositions of fact, this tendency leading to the risk of positing a State practice based upon fiction.

The recent episodes of unilateralism have usually involved law-breaking rather than the development of the law, and it is inappropriate to appear to characterise law-breaking actions as 'precedents' or 'practice'. The book continues to present an analysis of the principles of public international law when the law is being applied in a framework of normality.

The new text reflects the substantial case law of the International Court of Justice and the recent work of the International Law Commission.

I would thank the Hague Academy of International Law and Mr Steven van Hoogstraten for his permission to make use of some passages of my General Course delivered in 1995 and published by the Academy under the title *The Rule of Law in International Affairs* (pp. 65–74) in 1998. I would also like to thank the staff of Oxford University Press, and in particular Rebecca Gleave and Rekha Summan, for their care and consideration. I am grateful for assistance received from Lavonne Pierre and Adam Sloane of Blackstone Chambers.

Finally, my thanks go to my wife for her assistance.

IAN BROWNLIE, Q.C.
Blackstone Chambers
Temple
2008

TABLE OF TREATIES

TABLE OF CASES

ABBREVIATIONS

NOTE: UK and international law reports appear in the following list without reference to their jurisdiction of origin (e.g. Weekly Law Reports, International Law Reports). The origin of all other report series may be determined from their title (e.g. Australian Law Reports) or a reference to jurisdiction in parentheses (e.g. Federal Reporter, Second Series (US)).

A.2d	Atlantic Reporter (Second Series) (US)
ABS	*American Behavioral Scientist*
AC	Appeal Cases
AdV	*Archiv des Völkerrechts*
Af & Asian S	*African and Asian Studies*
Af HRLJ	*African Human Rights Law Journal*
Af JICL	*African Journal of International and Comparative Law*
Af JLS	*African Journal of Legal Studies*
AFDI	*Annuaire français de droit international*
AHRLR	African Human Rights Law Reports
Air & Space L	*Air and Space Law*
AJCL	*American Journal of Comparative Law*
AJIL Supp	*American Journal of International Law, Supplement*
AJIL	*American Journal of International Law*
Akron LR	*Akron Law Review*
ALJ	*Australian Law Journal*
ALR	Australian Law Reports
ALRC	Australian Law Reform Commission
Ann ASL	*Annals of Air and Space Law*
Ann de l'Inst	*Annuaire de l'Institut de droit international*
Ann Suisse	*Annuaire Suisse de Droit International*
APSR	*American Political Science Review*
AR En Res	*Annual Review of Environmental Resources*
Arb Int	*Arbitration International*
ARSIWA	Articles on the Responsibility of States for Internationally Wrongful Acts

AU	African Union
AUJIL & Pol	American University Journal of International Law and Policy
AUILR	American University International Law Review
AULR	American University Law Review
Austrian JPIL	Austrian Journal of Public and International Law
Austrian RIEL	Austrian Review of International and European Law
AYIL	Australian Year Book of International Law
BD	British Digest of International Law
Berkeley JIL	Berkeley Journal of International Law
BFSP	British and Foreign State Papers
BIT	Bilateral Investment Treaty
Boston Col ICLR	Boston College International and Comparative Law Review
Boston UILJ	Boston University International Law Journal
BPIL	British Practice in International Law
Brooklyn JIL	Brooklyn Journal of International Law
BVerfGE	Bundesverfassungsgerichts (Germany)
BvR	Verfassungsrechtliche Beschwerde (Germany)
BY	British Year Book of International Law
C&SLJ	Company and Securities Law Journal
California WJIL	California Western Journal of International Law
Cam RIA	Cambridge Review of International Affairs
Can BR	Canadian Bar Review
Can JEPS	Canadian Journal of Economics and Political Science
Cardozo JICL	Cardozo Journal of International and Comparative Law
Cardozo LR	Cardozo Law Review
Case WRJIL	Case Western Reserve Journal of International Law
CEDAW	Convention on the Elimination of All Forms of Discrimination against Women
CEPMLP	Centre for Energy, Petroleum and Mineral Law and Policy Internet Journal
CETS	Council of Europe Treaty Series

Ch	Law Reports, Chancery Division
Chicago JIL	*Chicago Journal of International Law*
ChiKentLR	*Chicago-Kent Law Review*
Chin JIL	*Chinese Journal of International Law*
CJIELP and Policy	*Colorado Journal of International Environmental Law*
CLF	*Criminal Law Forum*
CLJ	*Cambridge Law Journal*
CLP	*Current Legal Problems*
CLR	Commonwealth Law Reports (Australia)
Cmd, Cmnd	United Kingdom, Command Papers
CMLR	*Common Market Law Review*
Col HRLR	*Columbia Human Rights Law Review*
Col J EurL	*Columbia Journal of European Law*
Col JEL	*Columbia Journal of Environmental Law*
Col JTL	*Columbia Journal of Transnational Law*
Col LR	*Columbia Law Review*
Comm L Bull	*Commonwealth Law Bulletin*
Conn JIL	*Connecticut Journal of International Law*
Cornell ILJ	*Cornell International Law Journal*
CP Rep	Civil Procedure Reports
Crawford, *Selected Essays*	Crawford, *International Law as an Open System: Selected Essays* (2002)
CTS	Consolidated Treaty Series
CYIL	*Canadian Yearbook of International Law*
Den LJ	*Denver Law Journal*
DePaul LR	*DePaul Law Review*
Dir Int	*Diritto Internazionale*
DJILP	*Denver Journal of International Law and Policy*
DLR (4th)	Dominion Law Reports, Fourth Series (Canada)
Dods	Dodson's Admiralty Reports
DRC	Democratic Republic of the Congo
DSB	*Department of State Bulletin*

Duke JCIL	*Duke Journal of Comparative and International Law*
Duke LJ	*Duke Law Journal*
ECHR	European Convention for the Protection of Human Rights and Fundamental Freedoms
ECLR	*European Constitutional Law Review*
ECOMOG	Economic Community of West African States Monitoring Group
ECOWAS	Economic Community of West African States
ECR	European Court Reports
ECtHR	European Court of Human Rights
EECC	Eritrean-Ethiopian Claims Commission
EEZ	Exclusive Economic Zone
EHRLR	*European Human Rights Law Review*
EJIL	*European Journal of International Law*
ELJ	*European Law Journal*
ELR	*European Law Review*
EPIL	*Max Planck Encyclopedia of International Law,* paper edition
ETL	*European Transport Law*
ETS	European Treaty Series
EWCA	England and Wales Court of Appeal
EWHC	England and Wales High Court
Ex D	Law Reports, Exchequer Division
F	Federal Reporter (US)
F.2d	Federal Reporter, Second Series (US)
F.3d	Federal Reporter, Third Series (US)
F.Supp 2d	Federal Supplement, Second Series (US)
F.Supp	Federal Supplement (US)
FCR	Federal Court Reports (Australia)
Fed Comm LJ	*Federal Communications Law Journal*
Fin YIL	*Finnish Yearbook of International Law*
Florida JIL	*Florida Journal of International Law*
FLR	Family Law Reports

FLR	*Federal Law Review*
Fordham ILJ	*Fordham International Law Journal*
Fordham LR	*Fordham Law Review*
FRUS	*Foreign Relations of the United States*
FRY	Federal Republic of Yugoslavia
G Wash ILR	*George Washington International Law Review*
G Wash LR	*George Washington Law Review*
Ga JICL	*Georgia Journal of International and Comparative Law*
GAOR	General Assembly Official Records
GCCS	Geneva Convention on the Continental Shelf
GCHS	Geneva Convention on the High Seas
GCTS	Geneva Convention on the Territorial Sea and Contiguous Zone
Geneva Convention I	Geneva Convention for the Amelioration of the Condition of the Wounded and Sick in Armed Forces in the Field
Geneva Convention II	Geneva Convention for the Amelioration of the Condition of the Wounded, Sick and Shipwrecked Members of the Armed Forces at Sea
Geneva Convention III	Geneva Convention Relative to the Treatment of Prisoners of War
Geneva Convention IV	Geneva Convention Relative to the Protection of Civilian Persons in Time of War
Genocide Convention	Convention on the Prevention and Punishment of the Crime of Genocide
Geo J	*GeoJournal*
Geo LJ	*Georgetown Law Journal*
Geo Rev	*Geographical Review*
GG	*Global Governance*
GIELR	*Georgetown International Environmental Law Review*
GLJ	*German Law Journal*
GST	*Transactions of the Grotius Society*
Guggenheim	Guggenheim, *Traité de droit international public* (2 vols, 2nd edn, 1967)
GYIL	*German Yearbook of International Law*

Hackworth	Hackworth, *Digest of International Law* (1940–44)
Hague JJ	*Hague Justice Journal*
Hague *Recueil*	*Recueil des cours de l'Académie de droit international*
Hague YIL	*Hague Yearbook of International Law*
Harv HRJ	*Harvard Human Rights Journal*
Harv ILJ	*Harvard International Law Journal*
Harv LR	*Harvard Law Review*
Harv NSJ	*Harvard National Security Journal*
Hastings ICLR	*Hastings International and Comparative Law Review*
HCA	High Court of Australia
HCR	Scott (ed), Hague Court Reports
Higgins, *Development* (1963)	Higgins, *The Development of International Law through the Political Organs of the United Nations* (1963)
Hitotsubashi JLP	*Hitotsubashi Journal of Law and Politics*
Hous JIL	*Houston Journal of International Law*
HRLR	*Human Rights Law Review*
HRQ	*Human Rights Quarterly*
Hudson, *Int Legis*	Hudson (ed), *International Legislation* (9 vols, 1931–50)
Hyde	Hyde, *International Law Chiefly as Interpreted and Applied by the United States* (3 vols, 2nd edn, 1947)
IACHR	Inter-American Commission on Human Rights
IACtHR	Inter-American Court of Human Rights
ICC Statute	Rome Statute of the International Criminal Court
ICCPR	International Covenant on Civil and Political Rights
ICERD	International Convention on the Elimination of all Forms of Racial Discrimination
ICESCR	International Covenant on Economic, Social and Cultural Rights
ICJ Pleadings	International Court of Justice: Pleadings, Oral Arguments, Documents
ICJ Reports	Reports of Judgments, Advisory Opinions and Orders of the International Court of Justice
ICLQ	*International and Comparative Law Quarterly*

ICRC	International Committee of the Red Cross
ICSID Rev-FILJ	*ICSID Review – Foreign Investment Law Journal*
ICSID	International Centre for the Settlement of Investment Disputes
ICTY Statute	Statute of the International Tribunal for the Prosecution of Persons Responsible for Serious Violations of International Humanitarian Law Committed in the Territory of the Former Yugoslavia since 1991
ICTY	International Criminal Tribunal for the Former Yugoslavia
Idaho LR	*Idaho Law Review*
IDI	Institut de Droit International
IELR	International Environmental Law Reports
IHRR	International Human Rights Reports
IJMCL	*International Journal of Marine and Coastal Law*
ILA	International Law Association
ILC *Ybk*	*Yearbook of the International Law Commission*
ILC	International Law Commission
ILDC	Oxford Reports on International Law, International Law in Domestic Courts
ILM	International Legal Materials
ILQ	*International Law Quarterly*
ILR	International Law Reports (continuation of the *Annual Digest*)
ILSA JICL	*International Law Students Association Journal of International & Comparative Law*
Imm & Nat LR	*Immigration and Nationality Law Review*
Indian JIL	*Indian Journal of International Law*
Indiana JGLS	*Indiana Journal of Global Legal Studies*
Int Comm LR	*International Community Law Review*
Int Crim LR	*International Criminal Law Review*
Int Environ Agreements	*International Environmental Agreements: Politics, Law and Economics*
Int Lawyer	*International Lawyer*
Int Org LR	*International Organizations Law Review*

Int Org	*International Organization*
IR	Irish Reports
Iran–US CTR	Iran–US Claims Tribunal Reports
IRRC	*International Review of the Red Cross*
Is LR	*Israel Law Review*
Is YBHR	*Israeli Yearbook of Human Rights*
It YIL	*Italian Yearbook of International Law*
ITBL	*International Tax and Business Lawyer*
ITLOS	International Tribunal for the Law of the Sea
J Marshall LR	*John Marshall Law Review*
J Space L	*Journal of Space Law*
J Trans LP	*Journal of Transnational Law and Policy*
JAIL	*Japanese Annual of International Law*
JCCP	*Journal of Commonwealth and Comparative Politics*
JCP	*Juris-Classeur Périodique*
JCSL	*Journal of Conflict & Security Law*
JDI	*Journal du droit international*
JEL & P	*Journal of Environmental Law and Practice*
JEL	*Journal of Environmental Law*
JEMIE	*Journal on Ethnopolitics and Minority Issues in Europe*
JIA	*Journal of International Arbitration*
JIANL	*Journal of Immigration Asylum and Nationality Law*
JICJ	*Journal of International Criminal Justice*
JIDS	*Journal of International Dispute Settlement*
JMLC	*Journal of Maritime Law and Commerce*
JORF	*Journal officiel de la République Français*
JWIT	*Journal of World Investment and Trade*
JWT	*Journal of World Trade*
JYIL	*Japanese Yearbook of International Law* (continuation of *JAIL*)
KB	Law Reports, King's Bench
Lauterpacht, *Development* (1958)	H Lauterpacht, *The Development of International Law by the International Court* (1958)

Lauterpacht, *Function of Law* (1933, repr 2011)	H Lauterpacht, *The Function of Law in the International Community* (1933, repr 2011)
LCP	*Law and Contemporary Problems*
LDD	*Law, Democracy & Development*
Lewis & Clark LR	*Lewis & Clark Law Review*
LJIL	*Leiden Journal of International Law*
LJN	Landelijk Jurispr Nr (Netherlands)
Lloyd's Rep	Lloyd's List Law Reports
LLR	*Liverpool Law Review*
LNOJ	League of Nations, *Official Journal*
LNTS	League of Nations, Treaty Series
Lowe & Fitzmaurice (eds), *Jennings Essays* (1996)	Lowe & Fitzmaurice (eds), *Fifty Years of the International Court of Justice: Essays in Honour of Sir Robert Jennings* (1996)
Loyola LA ICLJ	*Loyola of Los Angeles International & Comparative Law Journal*
Loyola LA ICLR	*Loyola of Los Angeles International & Comparative Law Review* (continuation of *Loyola LA ICLJ*)
Loyola LR	*Loyola Law Review*
LPIB	*Law and Policy in International Business*
LPICT	*Law & Practice of International Courts and Tribunals*
LQR	*Law Quarterly Review*
Mar Policy	*Maritime Policy and Management*
McGill LJ	*McGill Law Journal*
McNair, *Opinions*	McNair, *International Law Opinions* (3 vols, 1956)
McNair, *Treaties* (1961)	McNair, *The Law of Treaties* (1961)
Md LR	*Maryland Law Review*
Mélanges Reuter	*Mélanges offerts à Paul Reuter: le droit international, unité et diversité* (1981)
Melb JIL	*Melbourne Journal of International Law*
Melb ULR	*Melbourne University Law Review*
MES	*Middle Eastern Studies*
Mich JIL	*Michigan Journal of International Law*
Mich LR	*Michigan Law Review*

Millenium	*Millennium: Journal of International Studies*
Minn JIL	*Minnesota Journal of International Law*
Minshu	*Saikou Saibansho Minji Hanreishu* (Japan)
MLR	*Modern Law Review*
Moore, *Digest*	Moore, *A Digest of International Law* (8 vols, 1906)
Moore, *Int Arb*	Moore, *History and Digest of the International Arbitrations to which the United States Has Been a Party* (6 vols, 1898)
MPEPIL	*Max Planck Encyclopedia of International Law,* online edition
MPUNYB	*Max Planck Yearbook of United Nations Law*
MSU JIL	*Michigan State University College of Law Journal of International Law*
NAFTA	North American Free Trade Agreement
NATO	North Atlantic Treaty Organization
NELR	*New England Law Review*
NILR	*Netherlands International Law Review*
NJ	*Nederlandse Jurisprudentie* (Netherlands)
NJA	*Nyutt Juridiskt Arkiv* (Sweden)
NJW	*Neue Juristische Wochenschrift*
Nordic JIL	*Nordic Journal of International Law*
Notre Dame LR	*Notre Dame Law Review*
NQHR	*Netherlands Quarterly of Human Rights*
NRG 2nd Ser	*Nouveau Recueil Général de traités et autres actes relatifs aux rapports de droit international,* Second Series
NRJ	*Natural Resources Journal*
Nw JIHR	*Northwestern Journal of International Human Rights*
Nw ULR	*Northwestern University Law Review*
NY	New York Reports (US)
NYCLR	*New York City Law Review*
NYIL	*Netherlands Yearbook of International Law*
NYLJ	*New York Law Journal*
NYS.2d	New York Supplement (Second Series) (US)

NYUJILP	*New York University Journal of International Law and Politics*
NZLJ	*New Zealand Law Journal*
NZYIL	*New Zealand Yearbook of International Law*
OAS	Organization of American States
OAU	Organization of African Unity (now African Union)
Ocean Ybk	*Ocean Yearbook*
OCLJ	*Ocean and Coastal Law Journal*
OCM	*Ocean and Coastal Management*
ODIL	*Ocean Development & International Law*
Ohio NULR	*Ohio Northern University Law Review*
Ohio St LJ	*Ohio State Law Journal*
OJEU	*Official Journal of the European Union*
OJLS	*Oxford Journal of Legal Studies*
Oppenheim	Oppenheim, *International Law* (9th edn, 1992), edited by Sir Robert Jennings and Sir Arthur Watts
OZföR	*Österreichische Zeitschrifi fur öffentliches Recht*
P	Probate, Divorce and Admiralty Division
P.2d	Pacific Reporter, Second Series (US)
Palestine YIL	*Palestine Yearbook of International Law*
PAS	*Proceedings of the American Society of International Law*
PCA	Permanent Court of Arbitration
PCIJ	Publications of the Permanent Court of International Justice
PLO	Palestine Liberation Organization
Pol YIL	*Polish Yearbook of International Law*
PRC	People's Republic of China
Public LR	*Public Law Review*
QB	Law Reports, Queen's Bench
RBDI	*Revue Belge de Droit International*
RCEEL	*Review of Central and Eastern European Law*
RDI (La Pradelle)	*Revue de droit international* (Paris, ed La Pradelle)
RDI	*Revue de droit international*

Rdi	*Rivista di Diritto Internazionale*
RDILC	*Revue de droit international et de législation comparée* (Brussels)
RDISDP	*Revue de Droit International, de Sciences Diplomatiques et Politiques*
Rec Dalloz	Recueil Dalloz (France)
Rec Lebon	Recueil des arrêts du Conseil d'État (France)
Rec	Recueil des décisions du Conseil constitutionnel (France)
Restatement Third	American Law Institute, *Restatement of the Law Third: The Foreign Relations Law of the United States* (2 vols, 1987)
Rev Arb	*Revue de l'Arbitrage*
Rev crit DIPriv	*Revue critique de droit international privé*
RG	*Rossiiskaia gazeta*
RGDIP	*Revue générale de droit internaional public* (Paris)
RIAA	United Nations, *Reports of International Arbitral Awards*
RITD	*Revue internationale de la théorie du droit*
S Af YIL	*South African Yearbook of International Law*
San Diego ILJ	*San Diego International Law Journal*
Satow	Satow, *Satow's Diplomatic Practice* (6th edn, 2009), edited by Sir Ivor Roberts
Scan SL	*Scandinavian Studies in Law*
SCR	Supreme Court Reports (Canada)
Seoul LJ	*Seoul Law Journal*
SFRY	Socialist Federal Republic of Yugoslavia
Sørensen, *Les Sources* (1946)	Sørensen, *Les Sources du droit international: Étude sur la jurisprudence de la Cour Permanente de Justice Internationale* (1946)
Soviet YIL	*Soviet Yearbook of International Law*
Sp YIL	*Spanish Yearbook of International Law*
Stanford JIL	*Stanford Journal of International Law*
Stanford LR	*Stanford Law Review*

SWJL & Tr Am	*Southwestern Journal of Law and Trade in the Americas*
Syracuse JILC	*Syracuse Journal of International Law and Commerce*
Syracuse LR	*Syracuse Law Review*
TDM	*Transnational Dispute Management*
TEE	*Trends in Ecology and Evolution*
Temple ICLJ	*Temple International and Comparative Law Journal*
Texas ILJ	*Texas International Law Journal*
Texas LR	*Texas Law Review*
TFEU	Treaty on the Functioning of the European Union
Times LR	Times Law Reports
Trans L	*Transnational Lawyer*
Tul Mar LJ	*Tulane Maritime Law Journal*
U Chic LR	*University of Chicago Law Review*
U Chic LSR	*University of Chicago Law School Roundtable*
U Miami IA LR	*University of Miami Inter-American Law Review*
U Miami ICLR	*University of Miami International and Comparative Law Review*
U Penn JIL	*University of Pennsylvania Journal of International Law*
U Penn LR	*University of Pennsylvania Law Review*
U Pitt LR	*University of Pittsburgh Law Review*
UBCLR	*University of British Columbia Law Review*
UC Davis JILP	*University of California, Davis Journal of International Law & Policy*
UCLA JILFA	*UCLA Journal of International Law and Foreign Affairs*
UKHL	United Kingdom House of Lords
UKMIL	UK Materials on International Law (in BY)
UKTS	United Kingdom Treaty Series
UN Charter	Charter of the United Nations
UNCLOS I	First United Nations Conference on the Law of the Sea, 1956

UNCLOS II	Second United Nations Conference on the Law of the Sea, 1960
UNCLOS III	Third United Nations Conference on the Law of the Sea, 1973–82
UNCLOS	United Nations Convention on the Law of the Sea
UNMIK	United Nations Interim Administration Mission in Kosovo
UNTAET	United Nations Transitional Administration in East Timor
UNTS	United Nations Treaty Series
US Digest	*Digest of United States Practice in International Law*
US	United States Supreme Court Reports
USC	United States Code
UST	United States Treaties
Utah LR	*Utah Law Review*
Utrecht LR	*Utrecht Law Review*
Va JIL	*Virginia Journal of International Law*
Va LR	*Virginia Law Review*
Vand JTL	*Vanderbilt Journal of Transnational Law*
VCCR	Vienna Convention on Consular Relations
VCDR	Vienna Convention on Diplomatic Relations
VCLT II	Vienna Convention on the Law of Treaties between States and International Organizations or between International Organizations
VCLT	Vienna Convention on the Law of Treaties
Villanova ELJ	*Villanova Environmental Law Journal*
VKS	*Vestnik Konstitutionnogo Suda Rossiskoi Federatsii* (Russian Federation)
Wayne LR	*Wayne Law Review*
Wheaton	Wheaton's Supreme Court Reports (US)
Whiteman	Whiteman, *Digest of International Law* (1963–73)
Wisconsin ILJ	*Wisconsin International Law Journal*
WLR	Weekly Law Reports
WRD	*Water Resources Development*

WTAM	*World Trade & Arbitration Materials*
Yale JIL	*Yale Journal of International Law*
Yale JWPO	*Yale Journal of World and Public Order*
Yale LJ	*Yale Law Journal*
Ybk Air & Space Law	*Yearbook of Air and Space Law*
Ybk ECHR	*Yearbook of the European Convention on Human Rights*
Ybk IEL	*Yearbook of International Environmental Law*
Ybk IHL	*Yearbook of International Humanitarian Law*
Ybk Space P	*Yearbook of Space Policy*
YBWA	*Yearbook of World Affairs*
ZaöRV	*Zeitschrift für Ausländisches Öffentliches Recht und Völkerrecht*
Zemanek Festschrift	Ginther & Hafner (eds), *Festschrift für Karl Zemanek zum 65. Geburtstag* (1994)

GLOSSARY

acquis communautaire. From the French 'that which has been agreed upon by the Community'; the accumulated body of case-law, treaties, and legislation that comprise the laws of the European Union.

acta iure imperii; iure imperii. An act characteristic of or unique to a state, e.g. involving governmental authority (as opposed to *acta iure gestionis*).

acta iure gestionis; iure gestionis. An act not characteristic of or unique to a state, e.g. a commercial transaction (as opposed to *acta iure imperii*).

ad hoc. Formed or derived for a particular purpose; lacking in generality.

amicus curiae. A person permitted to present arguments bearing upon issues before a tribunal yet not representing the interests of any party to the proceedings.

aut dedere aut iudicare. A principle usually embodied in a treaty requiring a state to either try an accused or extradite him or her to another state willing to do so.

casus foederis. The preconditions contained within a treaty (usually regional) for the formation of an alliance. Commonly contained within pacts of collective self-defence.

causa sine qua non. A necessary cause of the event.

compromis. A special agreement between states to submit a particular issue either to an arbitral tribunal or to the International Court.

conflict of laws (private international law). A part of the law of each state which provides rules for deciding cases involving foreign factual elements, e.g. a contract made abroad.

cujus est solum usque ad caelum et ad inferos. He who owns the surface has title both to the airspace above and the subsoil.

culpa. The civil/Roman law term employed to refer to negligence, lack of reasonable care.

de facto. A situation arising in fact, whether recognized legally or not; as opposed to *de iure*.

de iure. According to law or by right; as opposed to *de facto*.

de lege ferenda. Relating to the law as it should be if it were to accord with good policy (cf *de lege lata*, concerning the law as already laid down).

delicta iuris gentium. Wrongs recognized by public international law.

détournement de pouvoir. A term of French administrative law originally, meaning abuse of administrative powers by public officials.

dicta. Propositions of law stated by tribunals not directed to the principal matters in issue; not the grounds of decision (cf *ratio decidendi*).

dies ad quem. The day to which.

diligentia quam in suis. The standard of care normally exercised by a person in the conduct of his or her own affairs.

dolus. The intention to inflict harm.

dominium. Title or ownership.

equity infra legem. Equity defined by legal principles.

erga omnes. Opposable to or valid against 'all the world', i.e. all other legal persons, irrespective of specific consent on the part of those thus affected.

ex aequo et bono. Equity at large, unconstrained by law (cf *equity infra legem*).

ex gratia. As a matter of discretion (e.g. a compensation payment made *ex gratia*).

ex hypothesi. In accordance with or following from a hypothesis stated.

ex injuria non oritur jus. The principle that no right can be arise from an unlawful act.

ex officio. By virtue of office; a right derived by virtue of holding a particular position.

ex post facto. Occurring after the fact.

ex proprio motu. See *proprio motu*.

force majeure. The occurrence of an irresistible force or unforeseen restraint.

forum non conveniens. A common law doctrine used at the discretion of the court to deny jurisdiction where there is a more appropriate forum for the resolution of a dispute elsewhere.

forum prorogatum. Jurisdiction on the basis of tacit consent after a case has been submitted.

imperium. Governmental authority; a governmental interest.

in absentia. Used ordinarily in relation to a civil or criminal trial conducted without the presence of the accused.

in limine. At the outset.

in statu nascendi. In the process of formation.

in pari delicto. Equally at fault; equally implicated in wrongful conduct.

in personam. Applicable to an individual, natural or juridical; a personal action (cf *in rem*).

inter alia. Among other things.

inter se. Between the parties to a specific agreement or other transaction.

intuitu personae. By virtue of the person concerned.

ipso facto. By the fact itself; the direct consequence of an action.

iura in re aliena. Rights in another property.

iura novit curia. The principle that a court or tribunal is presumed to know the law.

ius cogens. Peremptory norms of general international law.

ius gentium. Those rules of law common to all nations; the law of nations. Originally a Roman term preceding the modern formulation 'international law'.

jurisprudence constante. A consistent jurisprudence or line of authority.

lato sensu/stricto sensu. The broad sense/the narrow sense.

lex ferenda. See *de lege ferenda.*

lex lata. The law as it exists; as opposed to *de lege ferenda.*

lex specialis. The principle that a particular law that may displace a more general law in the event of a conflict between the two.

lis alibi pendens; lis pendens. Dispute pending elsewhere; a doctrine of private international law to obviate or otherwise reduce the risk of parallel proceedings in the same matter.

locus delicti. The state or jurisdiction where a tort or civil wrong was committed.

locus standi. The existence of a sufficient legal interest in a case; title to sue.

mala in se. Recognized as inherently wrong.

mutatis mutandis. Applicable to an analogous situation with necessary modifications.

nemo dat quod non habet. The principle that a donor cannot give a greater interest than he or she already has.

ne bis in idem. The principle that no person should be proceeded against twice over the same matter.

nullum crimen sine lege. The principle that a crime cannot be committed unless it was considered as such under an applicable system of law at the time of its commission; also called the principle of legality.

obiter; obiter dicta. See *dicta.*

opinio iuris sive necessitatis. The element in the practice of states which denotes that the practice is required by international law.

pacta sunt servanda. The principle that agreements are binding and are to be implemented in good faith.

pacta tertiis nec nocent nec prosunt; pacta tertiis. The principle that an agreement or treaty is only binding on those who are party to it.

persona non grata. One who is not welcome; term of art in diplomatic relations used to formally proscribe a person from entering or remaining within the receiving state.

petitio principii. An argument or assertion which begs the question.

prima facie. In principle; presumptively.

proprio motu. Of the court's s own motion.

qua. Considered as; in the character or capacity of.

quid pro quo. A reciprocal exchange, e.g. consideration for acts performed or to be performed.

ratio; ratio decidendi. The principal proposition or propositions of law determining the outcome of a case, or necessary for the decision of a particular case (cf *dicta*).

ratione materiae. By reason of the subject-matter; thus an immunity *ratione materiae* is an immunity accorded by reference to the subject-matter of the claim.

ratione personae. By reason of the person; thus an immunity *ratione personae* is accorded by reason of a person's status (e.g. a serving head of state).

ratione temporis. By reference to time; thus an objection to jurisdiction *ratione temporis* is an objection by reference to the time at which a claim arose.

rebus sic stantibus. The implication that the obligations under a treaty are terminable in the event of a fundamental change of circumstances.

res communis. Objects or areas held in common, not subject to the sovereignty of a single state (e.g. high seas, outer space).

res inter alios acta. A matter affecting third parties and not opposable to the legal persons between whom there is an issue.

res iudicata. The principle that an issue actually decided by a court should not be reopened.

res nullius. An asset susceptible of acquisition but presently under the ownership or sovereignty of no one.

siège social. French legal concept for determining corporate domicile; may be loosely rendered as 'head office' or 'predominant place of administrative activity'.

stare decisis. The principle that a tribunal should follow its own previous decisions and those of other tribunals of equal or greater authority.

stipulation pour autrui. Contractual stipulation in favour of a third party.

sui generis. Not falling within normal legal categories; unclassifiable.

travaux préparatoires. Preparatory work; preliminary drafts, minutes of conferences, and the like, relating to the conclusion of a treaty.

ultra vires. Unauthorized by legal authority; invalid as beyond power.

uti possidetis iuris; uti possidetis. The presumption that the boundaries of a new state or entity follow those that existed under the previous (colonial) regime.

PART I

PRELIMINARY TOPICS

1

INTRODUCTION

'Then felt I like some watcher in the skies
When a new planet swims into his ken...'
Keats[1]

1. DEVELOPMENT OF THE LAW OF NATIONS

The law of nations, now known as (public) international law,[2] developed out of the tradition of the late medieval *ius gentium*.[3] Through an influential series of writers—Vitoria,[4] Gentili,[5] Grotius,[6] Pufendorf,[7] Wolff,[8] Vattel,[9] and others—it came to be seen as a specialized body of legal thinking about the relations between rulers, reflective of

---

[1] 'On First Looking into Chapman's Homer' (1816), reproduced in Strachan, *Routledge Literary Sourcebook on the Poems of John Keats* (2003) 79–82.

[2] The term 'international law' was invented by Jeremy Bentham in 1789 and established itself in the 19th century in preference to the older 'law of nations', itself a translation of the *ius gentium* of Grotius and the *droit des gens* of Vattel: Janis (1984) 78 *AJIL* 405. For the history of international law: Grewe, *The Epochs of International Law* (1984, tr Byers 2000); Koskenniemi, *The Gentle Civilizer of Nations* (2002); Neff, in Evans (ed), *International Law* (3rd edn, 2010) 3; Simpson, in Crawford & Koskenniemi (eds), *Cambridge Companion to International Law* (2012) 25; Koskenniemi, ibid, 47; Jouannet, *The Liberal-Welfarist Law of Nations* (2012).

[3] Though antecedents may be identified e.g. in the rules-based system of diplomacy of New Kingdom Egypt (1550–1069BCE) and the Bronze Age world system of the Near East: Liverani, in Cohen & Westbrook (eds), *Amarna Diplomacy* (2000) 15; Westbrook, ibid, 28; Moran, *The Amarna Letters* (1992). Generally: Bederman, *International Law in Antiquity* (2001).

[4] *c*1492–1546. Vitoria's lectures at the University of Salamanca were transcribed by his students: e.g. *De Indis* (1532); *De Iure belli Hispanorum in barbaros* (1532). Further: Pagden & Lawrance (eds), *Vitoria: Political Writings* (1991); Scott, *The Spanish Origin of International Law* (1934, repr 2000).

[5] 1550–1608. *De Legationibus Libri Tres* (1585); *Hispanicae advocationis libri duo* (1613). With the emergence of Grotius, Gentili's contribution to international law was forgotten until his 'rediscovery' by Holland: Haggenmacher, in Bull, Kingsbury & Roberts (eds), *Hugo Grotius and International Relations* (1990) 133. Further: Kingsbury (1998) 92 *AJIL* 713; (2008) 79 *BY* 1.

[6] 1563–1645. *Mare Liberum* (1609); *De iure belli ac pacis* (1625). Generally: Tuck, *The Rights of War and Peace* (1999) ch 3; Miller, in Zalta (ed), *The Stanford Encyclopedia of Philosophy* (2011), available at www.plato.stanford.edu/entries/grotius/.

[7] 1632–1694. *De iure naturae et gentium* (1672). Further: Tuck (1999) ch 5.

[8] 1679–1754. *Ius naturae methodo scientifica pertractatum* (1740–1748); *Ius gentium methodo scientifica pertractatum* (1750). Further: Hettche, in Zalta (ed), *The Stanford Encyclopedia of Philosophy* (2008), available at www.plato.stanford.edu/entries/wolff-christian/#HumSci.

[9] 1714–1767. *Le Droit des gens* (1758). Further: Tuck (1999) ch 6.

custom and practice in such matters as treaty-making, the status of ambassadors, the use of the oceans, and the modalities of warfare. It was not continuous with the *ius gentium* of the Romans, but the thirteenth-century rediscovery of Roman or civil law by figures such as Thomas Aquinas[10] reinforced the idea that law could structure or at least moderate the relations between kingdoms, principalities, and republics.[11] The Thomist conceptualization of such relations owed much to the notion of the 'just war' that was later to preoccupy Grotius and others. At that time, international law—if the term was even applicable—was essentially a moral question (resulting in the elevation of the 'just war' to a matter of Christian doctrine); but it was engaged with issues familiar to a modern practitioner, such as territorial claims, treaties, the right of legation, and related matters.[12] A signal development hinting at advances yet to come was that war was seen as the prerogative of the sovereign:

For it is not the business of a private individual to declare war, because he can seek for redress of his rights from the tribunal of his superior. Moreover it is not the business of a private individual to summon together the people, which has to be done in wartime. And as the care of the common weal is committed to those who are in authority, it is their business to watch over the common weal of the city, kingdom or province subject to them.[13]

In terms of intellectual history, international law was thus European in origin, although the Europe in question was large, extending to the whole Mediterranean, to Russia and the Near East; thence international law travelled with the colonizers to the Americas, to Asia, to Africa and eventually to Oceania.[14] At this time Europe was not chauvinistic in defining membership of the international system.[15] For example, the Ottoman Empire was accepted as a valid participant as early as 1649.[16]

In the Far East, a number of states such as Siam/Thailand, China, and Japan survived the colonial onslaught and continued to assert their independence, as demonstrated by Macartney's embassy to China in 1792 and his acid reception by the Qianlong Emperor.[17] By the mid-nineteenth century China had been largely cowed

---

[10] 1225–1274. Principally: *Summa Theologia* (1274) and the *Summa contra Gentiles* (c1264–1274).

[11] Further: Kingsbury & Straumann, in Besson & Tasioulas (eds), *The Philosophy of International Law* (2010) 33.

[12] Draper, in Bull et al (1990) 177, 181–5. On the concept of 'just war': chapter 33.

[13] Aquinas, *Summa Theologia* (1274, tr English Dominican Province 1974), Question 4, Art 1.

[14] Generally: Anghie, *Imperialism, Sovereignty and the Making of International Law* (2005).

[15] Brownlie, in Bull & Watson (eds), *The Expansion of International Society* (1984) 357.

[16] E.g. Instrument for the Prolongation of the Peace between the Emperor of the Holy Roman Empire and the Sultan of Turkey, 1 July 1649, 1 CTS 457. The idea that the Ottoman Empire was only accepted into international society with the Treaty of Paris, 30 March 1856, 114 CTS 409 is a solecism.

[17] Generally: Peyrefitte, *The Collision of Two Civilizations* (1993). The Qianlong Emperor refused Macartney's embassy and later wrote to King George III explaining in greater detail the reasoning behind his rejection of the English request. He concluded with the threat that any attempt by English merchants to exceed the minimal freedoms already granted would be met with instant expulsion ('[i]n that event your barbarian merchants will have had a long journey for nothing') and the injunction that the English king was to '[t]remblingly obey and show no negligence'.

by the use of gunboat diplomacy, leading to the Treaties of Beijing in 1860.[18] Japan, by contrast, engaged in a controlled opening to the west, with British naval advisers and an early translation of Wheaton's *International Law*.[19] A few Asian nations were able to maintain their autonomy, either because it was convenient for the colonial powers (as in the case of Siam/Thailand) or because the state succeeded in internal modernizing (as in the case of Japan, whose navy crushed Russia's at the battle of Tsushima in 1905). Similarly, Ethiopia was able to maintain its independence at the expense of Italy following the latter's defeat at the battle of Adowa in 1896. The remainder of the African continent, however, was subjugated: following the Berlin Conference of 1884 and the 'Scramble for Africa'[20] it was divided between Great Britain, France, Belgium, Germany, Spain, Portugal, and Italy to create a political landscape that would last until after the Second World War.[21]

By this stage, the 'modern structure' of the law of nations was recognizably in place. The system of diplomatic relations, recognition, international organizations, treaties, and customary international law had taken on essentially modern contours. At the same time, colonialism had reshaped the world in a Eurocentric image. By the 1920s, the number of states in the world had been reduced to some 64, of which 16 were former Spanish and Portuguese colonies in South and Central America. Of the non-European nations, only seven—Ethiopia, Liberia, the Ottoman Empire (Turkey), Thailand, China, Japan, and Afghanistan—had managed to retain independence without formal qualification of their sovereignty.

Perhaps as a concomitant of this reduction, sovereignty was assigned unique value in the international sphere. By the 1920s, it was widely thought that international law was entirely dependent on the consent—express or implied—of states,[22] and was applicable to states alone: 'Since the Law of Nations is based on the common consent of individual States, and not of individual human beings, States solely and exclusively are the subjects of International Law'.[23] But the influence of earlier eras was not entirely expunged. Even at this point in time—the crest of the positivist wave—the Permanent Court of International Justice had indicated that rights under international law could be conferred on individuals.[24]

---

[18]   24 October 1860, 123 CTS 71 (China–Great Britain); 25 October 1860, 123 CTS 79 (China–France); 14 November 1860, 123 CTS 125 (China–Russia).

[19]   Generally: Yamauchi (1996) 24 *Hitotsubashi JLP* 1.

[20]   Generally: Packenham, *The Scramble for Africa* (1991); Anghie, 'Berlin West Africa Conference (1884–5)' (2007) *MPEPIL*. The Conference was capped by the General Act concerning the Congo, 26 February 1885, 165 CTS 485, which in effect formalized the terms of the Scramble. Also: chapter 9.

[21]   Liberia, a free settlement of former slaves, was never colonized. Morocco was divided into Spanish and French zones but maintained a certain identity: *Nationality Decrees Issued in Tunis and Morocco* (1923) PCIJ Ser B No 4; *Rights of Nationals of the United States of America in Morocco (France v US)*, ICJ Reports 1952 p 176.

[22]   *The SS Lotus* (1927) PCIJ Ser A No 10, 18.

[23]   1 Oppenheim (1st edn, 1904) 18. Further: chapter 4.

[24]   *Polish Postal Service in Danzig* (1925) PCIJ Ser B No 11, 32–41. Also: *Steiner and Gross v Polish State* (1928) 4 ILR 291; Parlett, *The Individual in the International Legal System* (2010) ch 2.

At around this time, international legal personality gained an added dimension with the emergence of international organizations. In the nineteenth century states moved from the bilateral treaty and reliance on diplomatic contact to other forms of co-operation. The Congress of Vienna (1814–15) heralded an era of international conferences and multilateral treaties: later there appeared river commissions such as the European Commission of the Danube (1856) and administrative unions such as the International Telegraph Union (1865). After 1919 the League of Nations and then the United Nations provided a more developed attempt at universal peacekeeping arrangements, and many specialized institutions concerned with technical, economic, and social co-operation were established. Permanent organizations with executive and administrative organs paralleled but did not completely replace the system of ad hoc diplomacy and conferences.[25]

Over the course of the twentieth century, international law underwent a profound process of expansion. Developments included, *inter alia*, the creation of international organizations of universal membership with treaty-making powers (see chapter 7), a detailed elaboration of the law of the sea (see chapters 11–13), the establishment of permanent bodies (or at least permanently available institutions) for the settlement of international disputes, including 'mixed' disputes between states and private parties (see chapter 32), the prohibition on the use of force by states (see chapter 33); the emergence of various sub-disciplines or specialist areas of work and study; notably, human rights (see chapter 29), international environmental law (see chapters 14, 15), international economic law,[26] international criminal law (see chapter 30), and progress towards the codification of international law, principally through the work of the International Law Commission.[27]

2. INTERNATIONAL LAW AS LAW

At an elementary level, the normative system of international law is derived from four sources, enumerated in Article 38(1) of the Statute of the International Court of Justice: (1) treaties; (2) customary international law; (3) general principles of law; and (4) 'judicial decisions and the teachings of the most highly qualified publicists of the various nations, as a subsidiary means for the determination of rules of law'.[28] But

---

[25] On the history of international organizations: Klabbers, *An Introduction to International Institutional Law* (2nd edn, 2009) ch 2; Reinalda, *Routledge History of International Organizations* (2009).

[26] For public regulation of monetary, trade and economic issues: Ruiz-Fabri, in Crawford & Koskenniemi (2012) 352. For protection of foreign investment: chapter 28.

[27] For the ILC's work: Watts, Pronto & Wood, 1–4, *The International Law Commission, 1949–1998* and *1999–2009* (1999, 2010).

[28] Further: Pellet, in Zimmerman, Tomuschat & Oellers-Frahm (eds), *The Statute of the International Court of Justice* (2006) 677. On the sources of international law: chapter 2.

these, important in their own right, tell us little about the wider intellectual history of the field or its normative underpinnings.

(A) NATURAL LAW ORIGINS

The early development of international law saw its gradual separation from natural law, a process spurred on by the Reformation and the wars of religion, notably the Thirty Years War which ended with the Peace of Westphalia (1648). Natural law as a school of thought had emerged from the philosophical traditions of Roman law and the Roman Church, which conceived of a universal *ius naturale* (natural law properly speaking) of which the *ius gentium* (the law of peoples) was a subset.[29] Natural law, thus conceived, was universal; this was the background from which emerged Vitoria, Grotius, and other early theorists. Their contribution, willingly or not, was the separation of the *ius gentium* from the *ius naturale* and its modulation into a *law of nations*, which applied specifically to the rulers of states. This was particularly evident in the work of Grotius, who depicted international law as the gradual development of universal principles of justice which could be deciphered through human agency (independent of received religion):

But as the Laws of each State respect the Benefit of that State; so amongst all or most States there might be, and in Fact there are, some Laws agreed on by common Consent, which respect the Advantage not of one Body in particular, but of all in general. And this is what is called the Law of Nations, when used in Distinction to the Law of Nature. ...

Let it be granted then, that Laws must be silent in the midst of Arms, provided they are only those Laws that are Civil and Judicial, and proper for Times of Peace; but not those that are of perpetual Obligation, and are equally suited to all Times. For it was very well said ... That between Enemies, Written, that is, Civil Laws, are of no Force, but Unwritten are, that is, those which Nature dictates, or the Consent of Nations has instituted. ... [T]here are some Things, which it would be unlawful to practise even against an Enemy.[30]

Thus understood, the law of nations was a system of norms whether derived from a universally applicable, 'natural' morality or attested by 'the Consent of Nations'. But over time, thinking on the subject became progressively more concerned with a limited agenda of legal issues external to the state, as can be seen from a side-by-side comparison of Grotius' *De iure belli ac pacis* (1625) and Vattel's *Le Droit des gens* (1758). The bridge between the two was Wolff, who attempted a description of the *ius gentium* according to scientific principles.[31] Wolff argued that collective society could

---

[29] Further: Gierke, *Political Theories of the Middle Age* (1900, tr Maitland 1938) 73, 167, 172. Also: Neff, in Evans (3rd edn, 2010) 3, 6–8.

[30] Grotius, *De iure belli ac pacis* (1625, ed Tuck 2005) I.Prelim.§§XVIII, XXVII.

[31] During the 1740s, Wolff published a vast work attempting to describe natural law according to science. The last volume applied these principles to the law of nations: Wolff, *Ius Gentium Methodo Scientifica Pertractatum* (1749, tr Drake & Hemelt 1934).

not be promoted unless states formed a universal political entity, a 'supreme state' from which would proceed the law of nations:[32]

[A]ll the nations scattered throughout the whole world cannot assemble together, as is self-evident, that must be taken to be the will of all nations which they are bound to agree upon, if following the leadership of nature they use right reason. Hence it is plain, because it has to be admitted, that what has been approved by the more civilized nations is the law of nations.[33]

Wolff was the progenitor of Vattel's *Le Droit des gens*, which could claim to be the first international law textbook.[34] But Vattel's text was at odds with many of Wolff's conclusions, most notably with the concept of the 'supreme state', preferring instead to see the (European) state system as a collective capable of acting in the common interest.[35] Thus Vattel asserted that the continent formed...

a political system in which the Nations inhabiting this part of the world are bound by their relations and various interests into a single body. It is no longer, as in former times, a confused heap of detached parts, each of which had little concern for the lot of the others, and rarely troubled itself over which did not immediately affect it. The constant attention of sovereigns to all that goes on, the custom of resident ministers, the continual negotiations that take place, make of modern Europe a sort of Republic, whose members—each independent but all bound together by a common interest—unite for the maintenance of order and the preservation of liberty. Hence arose that famous scheme of the political balance, or the equilibrium of power.[36]

But greater minds than Vattel's were at play. Immanuel Kant (1724–1809)[37] sought to re-characterize the binding character of international law, proposing an international federation of republican states (*foedus pacificum*)—along substantially similar lines to Wolff's 'supreme state'[38]—backed by coercive rules, as the only method by which a secure and lasting peace could be achieved:

There is only one rational way in which states coexisting with other states can emerge from the lawless condition of pure warfare. Just like individual men, they must renounce their savage and lawless freedom, adapt themselves to public coercive laws, and thus form an *international state* (*civitas gentium*), which would necessarily continue to grow until it

---

[32] Tuck (1999) 187–8.

[33] Wolff (1749, tr Drake & Hemelt 1934) §20.

[34] The influence of Vattel was perhaps strongest in the newly formed United States of America. Alongside Grotius and Pufendorf, Jefferson referred to Vattel frequently: Sears (1919) 13 *APSR* 379; Cohen & Jefferson (1971) 119 *U Penn LR* 823. George Washington borrowed a copy of *Le Droit des gens* from the New York public library in 1789 and failed to return it: AFP, 'George Washington's library book returned, 221 years later' (*The Guardian*, 20 May 2010). Generally: Janis, *The American Tradition of International Law* (2004).

[35] Tuck (1999) 191–2. Also: Allott, *The Health of Nations* (2002) 412–16, lamenting Vattel's victory over Wolff.

[36] Vattel, *Le Droit des gens* (1758) III.iii.§47.

[37] On Kant and international law: Tuck (1999) ch 7; Perreau-Saussine, in Besson & Tasioulas (2010) 53. For Kant's own work see the polemic 'Perpetual Peace: A Philosophical Sketch' (1795), reproduced in Reiss (ed), *Kant: Political Writings* (2nd edn, 1992) 93.

[38] Perreau-Saussine, in Besson & Tasioulas (2010) 53, 59 n33; cf Tuck (1999) 219–20.

embraced all the peoples of the earth. But since this is not the will of the nations, according to their present conception of international right ... the positive idea of a *world republic* cannot be realised. If all is not to be lost, this can at best find a negative substitute in the shape of an enduring and gradually expanding *federation* likely to prevent war. The latter may check the current of man's inclination to defy the law and antagonise his fellows, although there will always be a risk of it bursting forth anew.[39]

(B) FROM POSITIVISM TO THE PRESENT DAY

The early modern period also saw the emergence of 'sovereign' states from the claims of Empire, secular or religious. States emerged as material, independent entities and international law was one of the ways they developed of managing their relations. The apparent paradox of how law could operate between sovereigns is resolved by the priority given to consent in the formation of legal obligation and the role of co-operation in interstate affairs—combined with the insight that sovereignty includes the capacity to make commitments not merely temporary in character.[40] Indeed the law itself begins to say what it takes to become a state and what, as a matter of law, it means to be a state.

Since the law of nations developed within a system wholly lacking in other institutions, international law is highly state-centric, a position reinforced from the early nineteenth century by the development and subsequent dominance of positivism as an account of law and legal obligation. Applied to jurisprudence, positivism was distinguished by the notion that *only* positive law—that is, law which had in some form been enacted or made by authority—could be considered true law. International law, which could only with difficulty be seen to be made—and then in a diffuse way—was caught up in this.

Positivism saw the law as a creation of power, a command of a sovereign enforced by a sanction. International law was not law *above* states, but law *between* states, enforceable, short of war, by way of moral opprobrium or by reciprocal denial of benefits. Indeed according to some positivists, notably John Austin (1790–1859), international law was only 'law improperly so called'.[41] In this sense, Austin conjectured:

[T]he law obtaining between nations is not positive law: for every positive law is set by a given sovereign to a person or persons in a state of subjugation to its author ... [T]he law obtaining between nations is law (improperly so called) set by general opinion. The duties which it imposes are enforced by moral sanctions: by fear on the part of nations, or by fear on the part of sovereigns, of provoking general hostility, and incurring its probable evils, in case they shall violate maxims generally received and objected.[42]

Austin's attitude to international law arose from its not complying with his positivist axiom: in the international system there was no sovereign, thus no command, and

---

[39] Kant (1795) 105.
[40] *The SS Wimbledon* (1923) PCIJ Ser A No 1, 25.
[41] Austin, *The Province of Jurisprudence Determined* (1832, 1995 edn) 123.
[42] Ibid, 171.

sanctions were decentralized and sporadic. This was an extreme position, not inherent in positivism as such but in the dogma of a single sovereign as the fount of all law. Austin's friend and intellectual predecessor—Jeremy Bentham (1748–1832)—had no such issue with international law, principally because he thought that national sovereigns, just as they could proclaim laws for the benefit of their own communities, could also together promulgate international law: they were not disabled from collective action.[43] Bentham, unlike Austin, also believed that a real law might be enforced by a religious or moral sanction:

When a foreign state stands engaged by an express covenant to take such a part in the enforcement of such a law as that in question, this is one of the cases in which a foreign state is said to stand with reference to such law in the capacity of a guarantee. Of a covenant of this sort many examples are to be met with in the history of international jurisprudence.[44]

A more refined version of positivist legal theory was elaborated by HLA Hart (1907–92). Drawing on Kelsen, Hart distinguished three categories of rules: (a) primary rules, concerning human action and interaction; (b) secondary rules (rules of adjudication, enforcement, and change) which underpin and operate in relation to the primary rules; and (c) the master 'rule of recognition', which enables the observer to identify the components of the system and to treat them as legal. It was the internal attitude, mainly of the officials, those responsible for the application of the secondary rules, which marked the system as legal and not merely a set of social rules. What mattered was not their acceptance of primary rules but their acceptance of the *system* by which those rules were generated and applied: it was the combination of primary and secondary rules which was the essence of law.[45]

Measured by this more complex standard, Hart saw international law as a marginal form, possessing some but not all the characteristics of a developed legal system and then only imperfectly.[46] It had only rudimentary institutions of adjudication, enforcement, and change—no courts of compulsory jurisdiction, no legislature, a frail internal attitude on the part of officials: 'no other social rules are so close to municipal law as international law',[47] but social rules they remained.

This position was the subject of critical scrutiny by Brownlie,[48] who argued that whatever the theoretical overlay of law/not law imposed by Hart (and positivists in general), the reality of international law told a different story:

The lack of compulsory jurisdiction and a legislature is regarded by Hart not as the special feature of a system which operates in conditions of a certain kind, but as the marks of an outcast, of a butterfly which is not wanted for a pre-determined collection. Yet ... the stability of international relations compares quite well with internal law, given the grand

---

[43] For an analysis of Bentham in this respect: Janis (1984) 78 *AJIL* 405, 410–15.
[44] Bentham, *An Introduction to the Principles of Morals and Legislation* (1789, 1970 edn) 68–70.
[45] Hart, *The Concept of Law* (2nd edn, 1994) ch 5.
[46] Ibid, ch 10.
[47] Ibid, 237.
[48] Brownlie (1981) 52 *BY* 1.

total of municipal systems ruptured by civil strife since 1945. And whilst it may be said that international law lacks secondary rules, this matters less if one accepts the view that secondary rules do not play such a decisive role in maintaining the more basic forms of legality in municipal systems.[49]

(C) THE BASIS OF OBLIGATION

In fact there are many examples of public order systems which lack an identifiable sovereign but manage to function—ranging from the customary laws of indigenous societies to the law of the European Union. The classification of a system as legal does not predetermine its effectiveness: witness various national law systems in greater or lesser disarray. The question is whether the rules, traditions and institutions of a given system enjoy at least some salience within the relevant society, meet its social needs, and are applied through techniques and methods recognizably legal—as distinct from mere manifestations of unregulated force. There is no reason to deny to such systems the classification of being legal—recognizing however that this leaves many questions open.

During the twentieth century, understanding of international law has been further articulated through sociological theories,[50] as well as, latterly, by the resurgence of a more rigorous and pragmatic natural law approach.[51] In particular, John Finnis has defended the idea of an international law—particularly customary international law—able to emerge without being made by anyone with authority to make it, and without the benefit of Hart's secondary rules for the authorized generation and alteration of rules:

[A]lthough there are direct 'moral' arguments of justice for recognizing customs as authoritative...the general authoritativeness of custom depends upon the fact that custom-formation has been *adopted* by the international community as an appropriate method of rule creation. For, given this fact, recognition of the authoritativeness of particular customs affords all states an opportunity of furthering the common good of the international community by solving interaction and co-ordination problems otherwise insoluble. *And this opportunity is the root of all legal authority, whether it be the authority of rulers or (as here) of rules.*[52]

---

[49] Ibid, 8.

[50] Notably through the work of Myers McDougal and the 'Yale' or 'New Haven' school of international legal thinking: e.g. McDougal & Burke, *The Public Order of the Oceans* (1962); McDougal, Lasswell & Chen, *Human Rights and World Public Order* (1980); McDougal (ed), *Studies in World Public Order* (1987); McDougal & Felciano, *The International Law of War* (1994). Further: Reisman (1992) 86 *PAS* 118.

[51] Neff, in Evans (3rd edn, 2010) 3, 18–19. Further: Orakhelashvili, 'Natural Law and Justice' (2007) *MPEPIL*.

[52] Finnis, *Natural Law and Natural Rights* (2nd edn, 2011) 244 (emphasis added); the whole passage (ibid, 238–45) should be read.

3. THE REALITY AND TRAJECTORY OF INTERNATIONAL LAW

(A) THE STATE AND SOVEREIGNTY[53]

States are 'political entities equal in law, similar in form . . . the direct subjects of international law'.[54] Despite the manifest historical contingencies involved, once statehood is generally recognized, a new situation arises: the new state *is* 'sovereign', *has* 'sovereignty'; and this is true no matter how fragile its condition or diminutive its resources. In this respect, sovereignty has not evolved much from the position described by Vattel in the eighteenth century:

Since men are naturally equal, and a perfect equality prevails in their rights and obligations . . . nations composed of men and considered as so many free persons living together in a state of nature, are naturally equal, and inherit from nature the same obligations and rights. Power or weakness does not in this respect produce any difference. A dwarf is as much a man as a giant; a small republic is no less a sovereign state than the most powerful kingdom.[55]

The state monopoly of sovereignty—and the capacity to act on the international plane that it brings with it—is on occasion the subject of criticism, to the point that it is suggested that the word be avoided entirely.[56] A stronger challenge is the opposition to sovereignty as the key organizing concept of the international community. With the emergence of privatization and globalization as influential forces within the world economy, it is argued, sovereignty bears less resemblance to the way things are, a perception heightened when viewed against a background of anti-formalism and rule scepticism:[57] from that perspective, sovereign equality, a formal rule if ever there was one, is an obvious target.

These criticisms call for a response. For example Kingsbury emphasizes the disadvantages of any normative transformation:

State sovereignty as a normative concept is increasingly challenged, especially by a functional view in which the state loses its normative priority and competes with supranational, private and local actors in the optimal allocation of regulatory authority. But discarding sovereignty in favour of a functional approach will intensify inequality, weakening restraints on coercive intervention, diminishing critical roles of the state as a locus of identity as an autonomous zone of politics, and redividing the world into zones.[58]

---

[53] Generally: Crawford, in Crawford & Koskenniemi (2012) 117.
[54] *Reparation for Injuries suffered in the Service of the United Nations*, ICJ Reports 1949 p 174, 177–8.
[55] Vattel, *Le Droit des gens* (1758) I.Prelim.§18.
[56] '[T]he sovereignty of states in international relations is essentially a mistake, an illegitimate offspring': Henkin (1999) 68 *Fordham LR* 1, 2.
[57] E.g. Kennedy (2008) 34 *Ohio NULR* 827.
[58] Kingsbury (1998) 9 *EJIL* 599, 599.

But it is also important to stress the flexibility of the concept of sovereignty and its capacity to provide a common denominator for the world's manifold cultures and traditions such that an international society is possible. As a concept, sovereignty carries limited substantive consequences and is consistent with a range of internal forms of government. It is also capable of responding to developments on the international plane, as seen with the rise of international organizations. The relationship there, however, is a symbiotic one, with institutions such as the International Criminal Court bolstering the internal competence of sovereignty through the principle of complementarity, at least in theory.[59]

Despite repeated suggestions of the 'death' of sovereignty—or its irrelevance—its normative basis within international law remains. Indeed, the system is ordered such that entrenched ideas are unlikely to succumb, as distinct from being modified through practice or through the accretion of new ideas and values. Such modification or accretion is at the present time dependent on the will of states, and it is not difficult to predict that sovereignty will retain its hold on the international plane for the foreseeable future.[60]

(B) THE INSTITUTIONAL STRUCTURE

One of the major developments of international law in the past century has been the emergence of international organizations with universal membership that seek to regulate the use of force between states.[61] Two such organizations may be identified, each the product of a World War. The first, the League of Nations, largely conceived by United States President Woodrow Wilson,[62] was established as part of the Peace of Versailles in 1919;[63] it disintegrated with that peace over the course of the 1930s. The second, the United Nations, was established by the Charter of the United Nations in 1945.[64] Despite many tribulations, it still occupies the field as the general purpose forum on the international plane.

Although the two organizations are superficially similar, they chose different strategies to regulate the interaction of states. The Covenant of the League of Nations[65] did not outlaw war per se, as distinct from limiting the circumstances of resort to war

---

[59] ICC Statute, 17 July 1998, 2187 UNTS 3, Art 17. Further: Benzing (2003) 7 *Max Planck UNYB* 591. For complementarity in practice: Nouwen, *Complementarity in the Line of Fire* (2012).

[60] Skinner, in Kalmo & Skinner (eds), *Sovereignty in Fragments* (2010) 26, 46.

[61] Further: Crawford, in Fox (ed), *The Changing Constitution of the United Nations* (1997) 3. On the history of international organizations: Claude, *Swords into Plowshares* (4th edn, 1984).

[62] Schwietzke, 'Fourteen Points of Wilson (1918)' (2007) *MPEPIL*.

[63] Generally: Fleury, in Boemeke, Feldman & Glaser (eds), *The Treaty of Versailles* (1998) 507. This association with Versailles was to ultimately undermine the Covenant and the League, as both became synonymous with the 'Carthaginian peace' of massive reparations and the war guilt clause: Keynes, *The Economic Consequences of the Peace* (1920); Mantoux, *The Carthaginian Peace, or The Economic Consequences of Mr Keynes* (1946).

[64] 26 June 1945, 892 UNTS 119.

[65] 28 June 1919, 225 CTS 195.

(Articles XII, XIII, XV). Indeed, it sought to use the institution of war as a response to the violation of its provisions (Article XVI).

1. Should any Member of the League resort to war in disregard of its covenants under Articles XII, XIII or XV, it shall *ipso facto* be deemed to have committed an act of war against all other Members of the League, which hereby undertake immediately to subject it to the severance of all trade and financial relations, the prohibition of all intercourse between their nationals and the nationals of the covenant-breaking State, and the prevention of all financial, commercial and personal intercourse between the nationals of the covenant-breaking State and the nationals of any other State, whether a Member of the League or not.

Article XVI sought to guarantee the key commitments or covenants which positioned the League as a system for collective security and as guarantor of the performance of obligations under international law. A central procedural requirement was that of unanimity or qualified unanimity within the League Council, with guarantees for representation of any Member 'during the consideration of matters specifically affecting the interests of that Member' (Articles IV and V). In practice the idea of 'automaticity' of sanctions was watered down—but automaticity was one of the factors which kept an isolationist United States outside the League.[66]

The United Nations is a very different construct. It was created independent of any peace treaty, avoiding the unfortunate associations with a punitive peace that had dogged the League. The close connection between commitment and sanction that characterised the Covenant was ruptured and replaced by a broad discretionary power of the Security Council. Where the Covenant overtly attempted to guarantee international law, backed by a system of collective security, the Charter outlawed the unilateral use of force outright save in defined and limited circumstances (Articles 2(4) and 51). Articles 39 and 42 of the Charter give the Security Council power to respond or not respond limited by the deliberately vague need to identify a 'threat to or breach of the peace or act of aggression' (see chapter 33). Where the League required consultation and unanimity in the decision making process, the Charter *withdrew* the veto from all except the five Permanent Members (Article 27(3))—the US, the UK, France, the People's Republic of China (formerly the Republic of China), and Russia (formerly the USSR). The veto ceased to be a concomitant of sovereignty and became a guarantee that the five major powers could not be outvoted on key issues.[67]

A distinction might perhaps be drawn between the UN as an international organization—a piece of legal machinery with its own international personality (Articles 100, 104, and 105)—and its capacity to give effect to the common policies of the members within broad areas of competence. No trace of such a 'constitutional' aspect may be found in the language of the Charter. But such an understanding may be hinted at in subsequent interpretations. In *Reparation for Injuries*, for example, in

---

[66] E.g. Walters, 1 *History of the League of Nations* (1952) 66–74.

[67] On proposals for the reform of the Security Council: Fassbender, *UN Security Council Reform and the Right of Veto* (1998); Bourantonis, *The History and Politics of UN Security Council Reform* (2005); Blum (2005) 99 *AJIL* 632.

according to the United Nations claim-bringing capacity analogous to that of a state, the Court said that the founding members of the UN 'represent[ed] the vast majority of the members of the international community'.[68] But it is too much to say that the UN is pre-eminent within the international system; we are only at the beginning of developments which might justify such a conclusion.[69] Notably, for the UN to function in such a manner would require the better institution of democratic accountability and respect for individual human rights at a global level.

(C) A *SYSTEM* OF INTERNATIONAL LAWS

The reality of international law—whatever its theoretical underpinnings—is clearly that of a system of laws, albeit one that cannot be uncritically analogized to domestic legal systems.[70] Moreover it is a system which, day in and day out, is generally effective: millions of people are transported daily by air and otherwise across state boundaries; those boundaries are determined and extended; the resources so allocated are extracted and sold across boundaries; states are represented and committed. In Henkin's words, 'almost all nations observe almost all principles of international law and almost all of their obligations almost all of the time'.[71] International law provides—in significant part—not merely the vocabulary of interstate relations but its underlying grammar.

[T]he reality of international law, that is to say, the actual use of rules described as rules of international law by governments, is not to be questioned. All normal governments employ experts to provide routine and other advice on matters of international law and constantly define their relations with other States in terms of international law. Governments and their officials routinely use rules which they have for a very long time called 'the law of nations' or 'international law'... The law delimits the competence of States. No journey by air could take place in reasonable limits if it were not for a network of legal structures involving the jurisdiction of States, the agreements of States and various [International Civil Aviation Organization] procedures and standards. The law also provides tools for constructing institutions. Typically, what is, in effect, the *loi cadre* of the EEC is a multilateral treaty.[72]

In the absence of any formal hierarchy—the negation of which is the point of the established doctrine of the equality of states—the basis of obligation in international law is found in the practice of states, which regard certain processes as generating legal rights and obligations and conduct themselves with international legal rules in

---

[68] ICJ Reports 1949 p 174, 185.

[69] Further: Lavalle (2004) 41 *NILR* 411; Talmon (2005) 99 *AJIL* 175; Bianchi (2006) 17 *EJIL* 881; Joyner (2007) 20 *LJIL* 489; Hinojosa Martinez (2008) 57 *ICLQ* 333; Orakhelashvili, *Collective Security* (2011) 220–2.

[70] The value of municipal law analogies was proclaimed (to the point of overstatement) by Hersch Lauterpacht (1897–1960): Lauterpacht, *Private Law Sources and Analogies of International Law* (1927); Lauterpacht, *Function of Law* (1933, repr 2011) ch 6.

[71] Henkin, *How Nations Behave* (2nd edn, 1979) 47; cf Koh (1997) 106 *Yale LJ* 2599.

[72] Brownlie (1981) 52 *BY* 1, 1–2.

mind: obtaining legal advice about making and complying with the law; instructions to state officials about their obligations under international law; applying international law domestically (including making multiple modifications of domestic law).[73]

International law has the characteristics of a system, not just a random collection of rules: the basic constructs of personality, sources (including treaties), interpretation, and responsibility, provide a framework within which rules may be generated, applied and, increasingly, adjudicated upon. The system is, though, institutionally deficient. The absence of a legislature with universal authority and the consensual basis for judicial jurisdiction reinforce the voluntarist and co-operative character of most international law most of the time.

(D) THE TRAJECTORY OF INTERNATIONAL LAW

As demonstrated, the history of international law has been unusually tumultuous, though perhaps not more so than any other system of law developing over a comparable length of time. Have its fundamentals changed? There is no legal reason why they should not. Indeed, the system itself exists in a persistent and even necessary state of flux.

At a fundamental level, the power structures within the international system are such that sovereignty and statehood remain the basic units of currency. Thus, states may use their power to modify the law to make rules about statehood itself—and they have done, notably about colonial self-determination (chapter 5). They may qualify aspects of their sovereignty of an institutional basis by becoming members of international organizations (chapter 7) or accepting the jurisdiction of international tribunals (chapter 32). And such undertakings are no longer exceptional; there is no longer a presumption against commitment. These developments (and others not supported by any institutional apparatus) have greatly expanded the content of international law and in so doing have diminished the sphere of domestic jurisdiction. The demands of international co-operation to give effect to the widening range of international obligations has both enhanced the rights of states and given them more obligations to fulfil. But they have not altered the character of the state nor the basis for the obligation to comply with international law.

The standard international legal relation remains that bilateral right and duty between two states (and this is often true even though the formal basis of the relationship is found in a multilateral treaty). It corresponds to a simple civil obligation (whether in contract or tort (delict) or property) in domestic legal systems. However, this simplified version of international law is beginning to change. In part this is because of the commitment of states to international organizations, in part to the use of international law to create obligations in the general interest (at least of those states which accept the obligations), such as for the protection of human rights or of

---

[73] Cf Crawford (1979) 73 *AJIL* 628. A generation later the picture would be the same.

the environment. But there is no legal manifestation of the 'international community', the interests of which are promoted in this way. Where there is an international organization, it may have rights as against state members to implement (or even to enforce) accepted standards. Where there is not, the burden falls upon other states to take action to secure the implementation in the general interest of another state's obligations, without themselves being direct victims of any breach of the law. It is not too much of an exaggeration to detect the development of a limited system of rules of public law in modern international law (and, for international organizations and tribunals, a similar development of administrative law) (see further, chapter 27). There is no international criminal law which applies to states as accused, but there is an increasing body of rules, administered in part by international tribunals, which subjects the conduct of individuals (potentially including state officials) to international criminal law.

These developments, particularly in the field of human rights, have added another category of personality (albeit heavily qualified) to those within the international legal system, namely individuals and sometimes corporations created by national law. It is no longer possible to deny that individuals may have rights and duties in international law; but what rights and duties they do have depends upon the operation of particular rules of international law and not on any notion of natural personality operating with the legal system. The importance attached to international human rights within many modern constitutions has added another dimension to the international legal system, an element of constitutional law where identified values give a category of rules hierarchical authority. Thus, it is maintained, egregious violations of fundamental rules of human rights have constitutional consequences for an errant state, beyond those prescribed by the standard law of state responsibility.

There are difficulties with this concept, both in identifying the particular rules and in isolating the legal consequences of their violation. The possibility has encouraged recent speculation about the 'constitutionalization' of international law, a concept which would appear to imply that statehood is something which is conferred by the international system (and which could be taken away), rather than predominantly the consequence of material facts of which the law takes account. But there is little evidence, even from the most progressive perspective, that the foundation of international legal obligation and the basic character of the legal system which is its product have been significantly modified. Proposals for judicial review of Security Council resolutions, for 'global administrative law' and so forth look fragile, given the persistence of the institutional limitations of the international system.[74]

---

[74] E.g. Alvarez (1996) 90 *AJIL* 1; Martenczuk (1999) 10 *EJIL* 517; Petculescu (2005) 52 *NILR* 167; Hinojosa Martinez (2008) 57 *ICLQ* 333. On the emergence of a 'global administrative law': Kingsbury, Krisch & Stewart (2005) 68 *LCP* 15; Stewart (2005) 68 *LCP* 63; Dyzenhaus (2005) 63 *LCP* 127; McLean (2005) 63 *LCP* 167. Further: chapter 27.

(E) SCEPTICISM AND IDEALISM

This is not to say that the institutions of international law have not given rise to undesirable outcomes. Wealth and power are extremely unequally divided, within and between states, and the inequalities may be growing. The absence of anything approaching an international constitution based on democratic principles allows tyrants to safely graze, sometimes for decades.[75] Open breaches fester. But critics of international law have tended to approach the subject in extreme ways—by dismissing the project entirely,[76] or by attributing to the agencies of reform almost magical powers.[77] Koskenniemi has seen the progress of international law as the function of an irresolvable duality between apology and utopia:

A law which would lack distance from State behaviour, will or interest would amount to a non-normative apology, a mere sociological description. A law which would base itself on principles which are unrelated to State behaviour, will or interest would seem utopian, incapable of demonstrating its own content in any reliable way. To show that international law exists, with some degree of reality, the modern lawyer needs to show that the law is simultaneously normative and concrete—that it binds a State regardless of that State's behaviour, will or interest but that its content can nevertheless be verified by reference to actual State behaviour, will or interest.[78]

It is easy to be sceptical of the claims of international law given the discrepancies between the power of states, the complexity of modern military systems and, more generally, the scope of the enterprise of international relations. It is also facile. No doubt we should be critical—and even sceptical—in our approach to particular questions and proposals. The fact remains however that there are things which manifestly need to be done which can be done only by collective action. There is no point in one state ceasing to produce chlorofluorocarbons if other states continue to do so. The solution to the global problem precipitated by the hole in the ozone layer was achieved by co-ordinated action.[79] Political decolonization, which changed the face of the globe, would not have happened so quickly or comprehensively without international law's articulation of priorities.[80] The moratorium on the hunting of the great whales has saved some species from extinction and led to the substantial recovery

---

[75] Brownlie (1981) 52 BY 1, 2 (admitting that at any one time 'international society contains a certain number of dangerous eccentrics').

[76] Notably within the US academy: e.g. Goldsmith & Posner, *The Limits of International Law* (2005).

[77] E.g. Pogge, in Crawford & Koskenniemi (2012) 373. For a more hesitant 'utopian' view: Allott, *The Health of Nations* (2002).

[78] Koskenniemi, *From Apology to Utopia* (2nd edn, 2005) 17. For a potential 'third way': Bowring, *The Degradation of the International Legal Order* (2008).

[79] Vienna Convention for the Protection of the Ozone Layer, 22 March 1985, 1513 UNTS 324; Montreal Protocol on Substances that Deplete the Ozone Layer, 16 September 1987, 1522 UNTS 28. Further: Held, Hervey & Theros (eds), *The Governance of Climate Change* (2011). For international environmental law generally: chapter 15.

[80] Generally: Pahuja, *Decolonising International Law* (2011).

of others.[81] The examples could be multiplied. In sum, international law provides a set of techniques for addressing the huge collective action problems presented by the co-existence of nearly 200 sovereign states. There is no large stock of available replacements for it. Despite its critics, it provides a normative structure for a rules-based system of international society. At present it is being tested, possibly to destruction.[82] But if it is destroyed we shall all be the worse for it.

---

[81] International Convention for the Regulation of Whaling, 2 December 1946, 161 UNTS 72, Art VIII and Schedule I, §10(d–e). Further: Gillespie, *Whaling Diplomacy* (2005).

[82] Generally: Pellet, in Crawford & Nouwen (eds), 3 *Select Proceedings of the European Society of International Law* (2010) 81.

2

THE SOURCES OF
INTERNATIONAL LAW

1. INTRODUCTION

International law provides a normative framework for the conduct of interstate relations. In this sense, international society is no exception to the maxim of *ibi societas, ibi ius*: where there is social structure, there is law. The sources of international law define the rules of the system: if a candidate rule is attested by one or more of the recognized 'sources' of international law, then it may be accepted as part of international law. Simultaneously, the diffuse character of the sources highlights the decentralization of international law-making.

The formally recognized sources of international law are reflected in Article 38 of the Statute of the International Court of Justice.[1] These sources are often presented—as in Article 38—as separate, but they influence each other in practice.

It is common for writers to differentiate between formal and material sources of law. Formal sources are those methods for the creation of rules of general application which are legally binding on their addressees. The material sources provide evidence of the existence of rules which, when established, are binding and of general application. In the context of international relations, however, the use of the term 'formal source' is misleading since it conjures up notions associated with the constitutional machinery of law-making within states. No such machinery exists for the creation of international law. Decisions of the International Court, unanimously supported resolutions of the General Assembly concerning matters of law, and important multilateral treaties seeking to codify or develop rules of international law are all significant to varying degrees. Nonetheless they are not binding on states generally. In this sense 'formal sources' hardly exist in international law. As a substitute, and perhaps as a 'constitutional' equivalent to formal sources, international law works on the basis that the general consent or acceptance of states can create rules of general application. The definition of custom in international law is essentially a statement of this principle, and not a reference to ancient custom as in English law.

---

[1] 26 June 1945, 892 UNTS 119.

In international law the distinction between formal and material sources is consequently difficult to maintain. The former reduces to a quasi-constitutional principle of inevitable but unhelpful generality. What matters more is the variety of material sources. These are the all-important *evidence* of a normative consensus among states and other relevant actors concerning particular rules or practices. Decisions of the International Court, resolutions of the General Assembly, and 'law-making' multilateral treaties are evidence of the attitude of these actors toward particular rules and of the presence or absence of consensus. Moreover, there is a process of interaction which gives these a status somewhat higher than other 'material sources'. Neither an unratified treaty nor a report of the International Law Commission (ILC) to the General Assembly has any binding force as a matter of treaty law or otherwise. However, such documents stand as candidates for public reaction, approving or not as the case may be. They may approach a threshold of consensus and confront states which wish to oppose their being given normative force in a significant way.

The law of treaties concerns the content of specific obligations accepted by the parties (states and other persons with treaty-making power), that is, it concerns the incidence of obligations resulting from express agreement. Treaties may be bilateral or multilateral,[2] but even if multilateral the obligations they create may run primarily between the two parties concerned—for example, the sending state and the receiving state in the case of diplomatic relations. But even if genuinely multilateral, the constraints of the treaty form still apply: in principle, treaties neither oblige nor benefit third parties without their consent. Thus the incidence of particular conventional obligations is a matter distinct from the sources of general international law, which is made by more diffuse processes. Treaties *as such* are a source of obligation and not a source of rules of general application. Treaties may however form an important material source in that they may be reflective of, or come to embody, customary international law.[3]

2. THE STATUTE OF THE INTERNATIONAL COURT OF JUSTICE

Historically the most important attempt to specify the sources of international law was Article 38 of the Statute of the Permanent Court of International Justice,[4]

---

[2] VCLT, 22 May 1969, 1155 UNTS 331, does not define 'bilateral' or 'multilateral'. However, Art 60(1) assumes that a bilateral treaty is between two parties. Likewise, Arts 40–1, 55, 58, 60, 69, and 70 assume that a multilateral treaty is between three or more. Further: Crawford (2006) 319 Hague *Recueil* 326.

[3] Thirlway, in Evans (ed), *International Law* (3rd edn, 2010) 95, 97.

[4] 16 December 1920, 112 BFSP 317.

taken over nearly verbatim[5] as Article 38 of the Statute of the International Court of Justice:

1. The Court, whose function is to decide in accordance with international law such disputes as are submitted to it, shall apply:

   (a) international conventions, whether general or particular, establishing rules expressly recognized by the contesting States;

   (b) international custom, as evidence of a general practice accepted as law;

   (c) the general principles of law recognized by civilized nations;

   (d) subject to the provisions of Article 59, judicial decisions and the teachings of the most highly qualified publicists of the various nations, as subsidiary means for the determination of rules of law.

2. This provision shall not prejudice the power of the Court to decide a case *ex aequo et bono*, if the parties agree thereto.

Article 59 provides that decisions 'have no binding force except between the parties and in respect of that particular case'.

These provisions are expressed in terms of the function of the Court. However they reflect the previous practice of arbitral tribunals, and Article 38 is often put forward as a complete statement of the sources of international law.[6] Yet the article makes no reference to 'sources' and, on close inspection, cannot be regarded as a straightforward enumeration.

The first question is whether paragraph 1 creates a hierarchy of sources. There is no express hierarchy, but the draftsmen stipulated an order, and in one draft the word 'successively' appeared.[7] In practice sub-paragraphs (a) and (b) are the most important: we can explain the priority of (a) by the fact that it refers to a source of obligation which will ordinarily prevail as being more specific.[8] But it is unwise to think in terms of hierarchy as dictated by the order (a) to (d) in all cases. Source (a) relates to *obligations*; in some circumstances a treaty does not give rise to a corresponding

---

[5] The clause in the first paragraph 'whose function is to decide in accordance with international law' was added in 1946 in order to emphasize that the application of the enumerated sources was the application of international law: Thirlway, in Evans (3rd edn, 2010) 95, 98–9.

[6] Generally: Hudson, *The Permanent Court of International Justice* (1943) 601–12; Pellet, in Zimmermann, Tomuschat & Oellers-Frahm (eds), *The Statute of the International Court of Justice* (2006) 677. Also: the Revised General Act for the Pacific Settlement of International Disputes, 28 April 1949, 71 UNTS 101, Art 28; ILC Model Rules on Arbitral Procedure, Art 10, ILC *Ybk* 1958/II, 78, 83; Scelle, ILC *Ybk* 1958/II, 1, 8. Art 38 has often been incorporated textually or by reference in the *compromis* of other tribunals.

[7] Cf Quadri (1964) 113 Hague *Recueil* 245, 343–4; Akehurst (1974–75) 47 *BY* 273, 274–5. But see *South West Africa (Ethiopia v South Africa; Liberia v South Africa)*, Second Phase, ICJ Reports 1966 p 6, 300 (Judge Tanaka, diss). In general: Kennedy (1987) 2 *AUJIL & Pol* 1, 20–45; Mendelson, in Lowe & Fitzmaurice (eds), *Fifty Years of the International Court of Justice* (1996) 63; Villiger, *Customary International Law and Treaties* (2nd edn, 1997); Charney, in Delbrück (ed), *New Trends in International Lawmaking* (1997) 171; Meron (2003) 301 Hague *Recueil* 9, 373.

[8] In accordance with the *lex specialis* principle: see Fragmentation of International Law, Report of the Study Group of the ILC, A/CN/4/L.702, 18 July 2006, esp 8–11; Vranes (2006) 17 *EJIL* 295. For special custom as a *lex specialis*: *Right of Passage over Indian Territory (Portugal v India)*, ICJ Reports 1960 p 6, 39–40.

obligation of a state party, notably when it is contrary to a peremptory norm of international law;[9] and in all cases the *content* of a treaty obligation depends on the interpretation of the treaty, a process governed by international law.[10] A treaty may even be displaced by a subsequent rule of customary international law, at least where its effects are recognized in the subsequent conduct of the parties.[11]

Dating back to 1920, Article 38 has been described, *inter alia*, as out of date, narrow and ill-adapted to modern international relations.[12] But in practice it is malleable enough, and its emphasis on general acceptance is right: customary law is not to be confused with the last emanation of will of the General Assembly.[13]

3. INTERNATIONAL CUSTOM[14]

(A) THE CONCEPT OF CUSTOM

Article 38 refers to 'international custom, as evidence of a general practice accepted as law'. The wording is prima facie defective: the existence of a custom is not to be confused with the evidence adduced in its favour; it is the conclusion drawn by someone (a legal adviser, a court, a government, a commentator) as to two related questions: (a) is there a general practice; (b) is it accepted as international law? Judge Read has described customary international law as 'the generalization of the practice of States',[15] and so it is; but the reasons for making the generalization involve an evaluation of whether the practice is fit to be accepted, and is in truth generally accepted, as law.

Although the terms are sometimes used interchangeably, 'custom' and 'usage' are terms of art with different meanings. A usage is a general practice which does not reflect a legal obligation: examples include ceremonial salutes at sea and the practice of granting certain parking privileges to diplomatic vehicles.[16] Such practices are carried on out of courtesy (or 'comity') and are neither articulated nor claimed as legal

---

[9] Indeed this is the *definition* of a peremptory norm, at least according to VCLT, Art 53. Further: chapter 27.

[10] Cf VCLT, Arts 31–3. Further: chapter 16.

[11] *Air Transport Services Agreement* (1963) 38 ILR 182, 248–55.

[12] Thirlway, in Evans (3rd edn, 2010) 95, 99.

[13] Ibid, 115.

[14] Séfériadès (1936) 43 *RGDIP* 129; de Visscher (1955) 59 *RGDIP* 353; Lauterpacht, *Development* (1958) 368–93; D'Amato, *The Concept of Custom in International Law* (1972); Thirlway, *International Customary Law and Codification* (1972); Akehurst (1974–75) 47 *BY* 1; Bernhardt (1976) 36 *ZaöRV* 50; Haggenmacher (1986) 90 *RGDIP* 5; Stern, *Mélanges Reuter* (1981) 479–99; Kirgis (1987) 81 *AJIL* 146; Thirlway (1990) 61 *BY* 1, 31–110; Wolfke, *Custom in Present International Law* (2nd edn, 1993); Mendelson (1995) 66 *BY* 177; ILA, Report of the Sixty-Ninth Conference (2000) 712; Thirlway (2005) 76 *BY* 1, 92–108; Perreau-Saussine & Murphy (eds), *The Nature of Customary Law* (2007); Orakhelashvili (2008) 68 *ZaöRV* 69; d'Aspremont, *Formalism and the Sources of International Law* (2011) 162–70; Kammerhofer, *Uncertainty in International Law* (2011) 59–85. For approaches to custom that draw on economic theory: Goldsmith & Posner (1999) 66 *U Chic LR* 1113; Norman & Trachtman (2005) 99 *AJIL* 541.

[15] *Fisheries (UK v Norway)*, ICJ Reports 1951 p 116, 191 (Judge Read).

[16] *Parking Privileges for Diplomats* (1971) 70 ILR 396; Roberts (ed), *Satow's Diplomatic Practice* (6th edn, 2009) §9.15.

requirements. International comity is a species of accommodation: it involves neigh-bourliness, mutual respect, and the friendly waiver of technicalities.[17] However, par-ticular rules of comity, maintained consistently without reservation, may develop into rules of customary law.[18]

The material sources of custom are manifold and include: diplomatic correspondence, policy statements, press releases, the opinions of government legal advisers, official man-uals on legal questions (e.g. manuals of military law), executive decisions and practices, orders to military forces (e.g. rules of engagement), comments by governments on ILC drafts and accompanying commentary, legislation, international and national judicial decisions, recitals in treaties and other international instruments (especially when in 'all states' form),[19] an extensive pattern of treaties in the same terms, the practice of interna-tional organs, and resolutions relating to legal questions in UN organs, notably the General Assembly. The value of these sources varies and will depend on the circumstances.

(B) THE ELEMENTS OF CUSTOM

(i) Duration and consistency of practice

The question of uniformity and consistency of practice is very much a matter of appre-ciation. Complete uniformity of practice is not required, but substantial uniformity is, and for this reason in *Anglo-Norwegian Fisheries* the Court refused to accept the existence of a 10-mile rule for the closing line of bays.[20]

Provided the consistency and generality of a practice are established, the formation of a customary rule requires no particular duration. A long practice is not necessary, an immemorial one even less so: rules relating to airspace and the continental shelf have emerged following a fairly quick maturation period.[21] In *North Sea Continental Shelf* the Court said:

Although the passage of only a short period of time is not necessarily, or of itself, a bar to the formation of a new rule of customary international law on the basis of what was originally a purely conventional rule, an indispensable requirement would be that within the period in question, short though it might be, State practice, including that of the States whose interests are specially affected, should have been both extensive and virtually uniform in the sense of the provision invoked;—and should moreover have occurred in such a way as to show a general recognition that a rule of law or legal obligation is involved.[22]

---

[17] See the *Alabama* (1872), in Moore, 1 *Int Arb* 653; *The Paquete Habana*, 175 US 677, 693–4, 175 (1900); *Parking Privileges for Diplomats* (1971) 70 ILR 396, 402–4.

[18] E.g. some diplomatic tax exemptions were originally granted as a matter of comity but are now con-solidated as legal requirements in Art 36 of the VCDR, 18 April 1961, 500 UNTS 95. See further Roberts (6th edn, 2009) §§8.4–8.5.

[19] E.g. references to 'every State' or 'all States' in UNCLOS, Arts 3, 17, 79, 87, etc.

[20] ICJ Reports 1951 p 116, 131.

[21] On the rapid evolution of key rules concerning the continental shelf: Crawford & Viles, in Crawford, *Selected Essays* (2002) 69.

[22] *North Sea Continental Shelf (Federal Republic of Germany/Netherlands; Federal Republic of Germany/Denmark)*, ICJ Reports 1969 p 3, 43.

This sets a high standard: it was met in the case of some of the rules concerning the continental shelf articulated in the Truman Proclamation, but not the delimitation rule which the ILC had proposed as a matter of convenience and which was not contained in that Proclamation.[23]

(ii) Generality of practice

Complete consistency is not required; often the real problem is to distinguish mere abstention from protest by a number of states in face of a practice followed by others. Silence may denote either tacit agreement or a simple lack of interest in the issue. It may be that the Permanent Court in the *Lotus* case misjudged the consequences of absence of protest and the significance of fairly general abstention from prosecutions by states other than the flag state.[24] In the event the Geneva Convention on the High Seas adopted the rule which the Court had rejected—a rare example of the overruling by treaty of a decision of the Court on a point of custom.[25]

In *Fisheries Jurisdiction (UK v Iceland)* the International Court referred to the extension of a fishery zone up to a 12nm limit 'which appears now to be generally accepted' and to 'an increasing and widespread acceptance of the concept of preferential rights for coastal states' in a situation of special dependence on coastal fisheries.[26] But while refusing to 'render judgment *sub specie legis ferendae*, or [to] anticipate the law before the legislator has laid it down',[27] the Court did in fact articulate a rule of preferential coastal state rights, a transitional step towards the Exclusive Economic Zone regime which would be included in the United Nations Convention on the Law of the Sea (UNCLOS).[28]

(iii) 'Accepted as law': *opinio iuris sive necessitatis*

The Statute of the International Court refers to 'a general practice accepted as law'. Some writers do not consider this psychological element to be required for custom,[29] but something like it must be necessary.[30] It is ordinarily expressed in terms of the Latin neologism *opinio iuris sive necessitatis*, a phrase which has, perhaps regrettably,

---

[23] (1946) 40 *AJIL Supp* 45. For the Court's reasons for rejecting the 'equidistance/special circumstances' rule, see ICJ Reports 1969 p 6, 43–6. For maritime delimitation see further chapter 12.

[24] *SS Lotus* (1927) PCIJ Ser A No 10, 16; cf Lauterpacht (1958) 384–6. Also *The Paquete Habana*, 175 US 677 (1900).

[25] 29 April 1958, 450 UNTS 11, Art 11; UNCLOS, Art 97.

[26] ICJ Reports 1974 p 3, 23–6. For reliance on the practice of a limited number of states, see the *SS Wimbledon* (1923) PCIJ Ser A No 1, 15, 25–8.

[27] ICJ Reports 1974 p 3, 23–4.

[28] UNCLOS, Part V, and further: chapter 11.

[29] See Guggenheim, 1 *Études Scelle* (1950) 275. For Kelsen *opinio iuris* is a fiction to disguise the creative powers of the judge: Kelsen (1939) 1 *RITD* 253. Cf Kelsen, *Principles of International Law* (2nd edn, 1967) 450–1. But analytically the judge is in no different position than any other evaluator of custom, except that the judge's decision may bind the parties (ICJ Statute, Art 59).

[30] Further: Kirgis (1987) 81 *AJIL* 146, arguing that custom operates on a 'sliding scale', along which the level of *opinio iuris* required to substantiate an assertion of custom is directly relative to the manifestation of state practice. Also Roberts (2001) 95 *AJIL* 757.

become established.[31] But the idea of normativity—the articulation of a practice as binding—is not new: as a necessary requirement of a customary rule it goes back to Isidore of Seville (c540–636CE) and beyond.[32]

The International Court will often infer the existence of *opinio iuris* from a general practice, from scholarly consensus or from its own or other tribunals' previous determinations.[33] But in a significant minority of cases the Court has displayed greater rigour. Examples include the *Lotus*, where France asserted that the flag state has exclusive criminal jurisdiction over accidents occurring on the high seas. The Permanent Court rejected the French claim:

Even if the rarity of the judicial decisions to be found among the reported cases were [established] ... it would merely show that States had often, in practice, abstained from instituting criminal proceedings, and not that they recognized themselves as being obliged to do so; for only if such abstention were based on their being conscious of having a duty to abstain would it be possible to speak of an international custom. The alleged fact does not allow one to infer that States have been conscious of having such a duty; on the other hand ... there are other circumstances calculated to show that the contrary is true.[34]

Presumably the same principles should apply to both positive conduct and abstention, yet in the *Lotus* the Court was not ready to accept continuous conduct as evidence of a legal duty and required a high standard of proof of *opinio iuris*.[35]

Again in *North Sea Continental Shelf* Denmark and the Netherlands argued that the equidistance–special circumstances method of delimiting the continental shelf had become accepted as law by the date of the Convention on the Continental Shelf.[36] The Court declined to presume the existence of *opinio iuris* based on the practice as at that date. Nor did it accept that the *subsequent* practice of states based upon the

---

[31] Lit, 'an opinion of law or necessity'. The first appearance of the term seems to have been in von Liszt, *Das Völkerrecht* (1st edn, 1898) 6; von Liszt, *Das Völkerrecht* (3rd edn, 1925) 16; also Rivier, *Principes de droit des gens* (1896) 35, who refers to the idea but does not use the term. It is implicit in the judgment in the *Lotus* (1927) PCIJ Ser A No 10, 28, but was not actually used by the Court until *North Sea Continental Shelf*, ICJ Reports 1969 p 3, 43–4; thence (spuriously) *Military and Paramilitary Activities in and against Nicaragua (Nicaragua v US)*, ICJ Reports 1986 p 14, 96–8. Cf Mendelson (1995) 66 *BY* 177, 194.

[32] Isidore of Seville, *Etymologiae, Liber V: De Legibus et Temporibus*, reproduced in Barney, Lewis & Berghof, *The Etymologies of Isidore of Seville* (2011) ch 3, §§3–4 ('Custom is law established by moral habits, which is accepted as law when written law is lacking: it does not make a difference whether it exists in writing or reason, since reason too commits to law ... Custom is so called also because it is in common usage').

[33] *North Sea Continental Shelf*, ICJ Reports 1969 p 3, 44; *Delimitation of the Maritime Boundary in the Gulf of Maine Area (Canada/US)*, ICJ Reports 1984 p 246, 293–4; *Nicaragua*, ICJ Reports 1986 p 14, 108–9; *Legality of the Threat or Use of Nuclear Weapons*, ICJ Reports 1996 p 226, 254–5; *Armed Activities on the Territory of the Congo (Democratic Republic of the Congo v Uganda)*, ICJ Reports 2005 p 168, 226–7, 242; *Legal Consequences of the Construction of a Wall in the Occupied Palestinian Territory*, ICJ Reports 2006 p 136, 171–2; *Pulp Mills on the River Uruguay (Argentina v Uruguay)*, Judgment of 20 April 2010, §§203–6. Also: *Prosecutor v Furundžija* (1998) 38 ILM 317; *Responsibilities and Obligations of States Sponsoring Persons and Entities with Respect to Activities in the Area*, ITLOS Case No 17 (Advisory Opinion, 1 February 2011) 41, 44–6.

[34] (1927) PCIJ Ser A No 10, 28; also ibid, 60 (Judge Nyholm, diss); 97 (Judge Altamira, diss).

[35] For criticism: Lauterpacht (1958) 386. See, however, MacGibbon (1957) 33 *BY* 115, 131.

[36] 29 April 1958, 499 UNTS 311.

Convention had produced a customary rule. However, the decision is not incompatible with the view that existing general practice raises a presumption of *opinio iuris*. Before 1958, there was little practice concerning the equidistance principle apart from the records of the ILC, which revealed the experimental aspect of the principle at that time.[37] As to post-1958 practice, the Court's rejection of the argument rested primarily on two factors: (a) Article 6 was directed at agreement and was not of a norm-creating character;[38] (b) the convention having been in force for less than three years, the state practice was inadequate 'to show a general recognition that a rule of law or legal obligation is involved'.[39] But the tenor of the judgment is hostile to the presumption of *opinio iuris*.[40]

In *Nicaragua*,[41] the Court expressly referred to *North Sea Continental Shelf*:

In considering the instances of the conduct … the Court has to emphasize that, as was observed in the *North Sea Continental Shelf* cases, for a new customary rule to be formed, not only must the acts concerned 'amount to a settled practice', but they must be accompanied by the *opinio juris sive necessitatis*. Either the States taking such action or other States in a position to react to it, must have behaved so that their conduct is 'evidence of a belief that this practice is rendered obligatory by the existence of a rule of law requiring it. The need for such a belief, i.e., the existence of a subjective element, is implicit in the very notion of the *opinio juris sive necessitatis*'.[42]

Likewise, the Court in *Diallo* took the more exacting approach to custom, and to the requirement of *opinio iuris* in particular. The Court noted the inconclusiveness and insufficiency of mere practice:

The fact … that various international agreements, such as agreements for the promotion and protection of foreign investments and the Washington Convention, have established special legal régimes governing investment protection, or that provisions in this regard are commonly included in contracts entered into directly between States and foreign investors, is not sufficient to show that there has been a change in the customary rules of diplomatic protection; it could equally show the contrary.[43]

The choice of approach appears to depend on the character of the issues—that is, the state of the law may be a primary point in contention—and on the discretion of the Court. The approach may depend on whether practice is largely treaty-based (in which case *opinio iuris* is sufficient to expand application of the treaty norms as custom), or whether the law on the question is still developing.

---

[37] ICJ Reports 1969 p 3, 28, 32–41.

[38] Ibid, 41–2.

[39] Ibid, 43.

[40] Ibid, 43–5. For contemporary comment: Baxter (1970) 129 Hague *Recueil* 31, 67–9; D'Amato (1970) 64 *AJIL* 892; Marek (1970) 6 *RBDI* 44. Also *Nuclear Tests (Australia v France)*, ICJ Reports 1974 p 253, 305–6 (Judge Petrén).

[41] ICJ Reports 1986 p 14, citing ICJ Reports 1969 p 6, 44.

[42] ICJ Reports 1986 p 14, 108–9. Also ibid, 97–8, 97–103, 106–8.

[43] *Ahmadou Sadio Diallo (Guinea v Democratic Republic of the Congo)*, Preliminary Objections, Judgment of 24 May 2007, §§30–1.

(C) THE RELATIVITY OF CUSTOM

The term 'general international law' should not be taken to require universal acceptance of a rule by all subjects of international law. True, there are rules of international
law which are universally accepted, and the *system* of international law is daily reaffirmed by states in making and responding to claims of right. But the principles of the
system—consent, the requirements for custom, the persistent objector—mean that
particular rules may have less than universal acceptance, yet still form part of international law. Similarly a rule of international law to which a state has not expressly or by
implication accepted may not be opposable to that state.

(i) The persistent objector

The reduction of custom to a question of special relations is illustrated by the rule that
a state may exempt itself from the application of a new customary rule by persistent
objection during the norm's formation.[44] Evidence of objection must be clear, and there
is a rebuttable presumption of acceptance. Whatever the theoretical underpinnings of
the persistent objector principle, it is recognized by international tribunals,[45] and in the
practice of states. Indeed given the majoritarian tendency of international relations the
principle is likely to have increased prominence.[46] However, with the increasing emergence of communitarian norms, reflecting the interests of the international community
as a whole, the *incidence* of the persistent objector rule may be limited.[47] More common
may be disagreement as to the meaning or scope of an accepted rule, as to which the
views of particular disputing states will not be decisive.[48] Nonetheless the persistent
objector rule reinforces the principle of state consent in the creation of custom.

[44] The principle was recognized by both parties, and by the Court, in *Anglo-Norwegian Fisheries*, ICJ
Reports 1951 p 116, 131. Also: *North Sea Continental Shelf*, ICJ Reports 1969 p 3, 26–7, 131 (Judge Ammoun);
235, 238 (Judge Lachs, diss); 247 (Judge ad hoc Sørensen, diss); *Asylum (Colombia/Peru)*, ICJ Reports 1950
p 266, 277–8; and cf the central finding of non-opposability of exclusive fisheries zone claims in *Fisheries
Jurisdiction (UK v Iceland)*, ICJ Reports 1974 p 3, 29–31.

[45] Examples include the US and Japan's refusal to accept territorial sea claims of more than 3nm
(1 O'Connell (1982) 156, 163–4), and the PRC's refusal to accept the restrictive doctrine of sovereign immunity (*Democratic Republic of Congo v FG Hemisphere Associates LLC*, Hong Kong Court of Final Appeal,
Judgment of 8 June 2011).

[46] See esp Charney (1985) 56 *BY* 1; Charney (1993) 87 *AJIL* 529. Further: Fitzmaurice (1957) 92 Hague
Recueil 5, 99–101; Waldock (1962) 106 Hague *Recueil* 5, 49–53; Schachter (1982) 178 Hague *Recueil* 21, 36–8;
Lau (2005) 6 *Chicago JIL* 495; Elias, 'Persistent Objector' (2006) *MPEPIL*; Quince, *The Persistent Objector
and Customary International Law* (2010); Dumberry (2010) 59 *ICLQ* 779.

[47] *Seabed Advisory Opinion*, ITLOS Case No 17, op §2 (B) referring to the obligations of states in general
with respect to activities in the deep seabed. Also ibid, §180 on 'the *erga omnes* character of the obligations
relating to preservation of the environment of the high seas and in the Area.'

[48] E.g. the disagreement between the US and many other states as to the definition of torture: United
States Reservation upon ratification of the Convention against Torture, 21 October 1994, and objections
by Finland, 27 February 1996; Netherlands, 26 February 1996; Sweden, 27 February 1996; Germany, 26
February 1996. Cf further criticism in Report of the Committee against Torture, A/55/44 (2000) §§179–80;
Murphy, 1 *US Digest* (2002) 279–80, 289–98; Nowak & McArthur (eds), *The United Nations Convention
against Torture* (2008), §§A1:10, 20, 24–5, 50–4.

(ii) The subsequent objector

In *Anglo-Norwegian Fisheries* part of the Norwegian argument was that even if the 10nm closing line for bays and certain rules were part of general international law, they did not bind Norway which had 'consistently and unequivocally manifested a refusal to accept them'.[49] The UK admitted the general principle, while denying that Norway had manifested its supposed refusal to accept the rules. Thus it regarded the question as one of persistent objection. The Court did not deal with the issue in this way, however. Its *ratio* was that Norway had departed from the alleged rules, if they existed, *and that other states had acquiesced* in this practice. But the Court was not explicit with respect to the role of acquiescence in validating a subsequent contracting-out.[50] Here one must face the problem of change in a customary rule.[51] If a substantial group of states asserts a new rule, the momentum of increased defection, complemented by acquiescence, may result in a new rule,[52] as was the case concerning the continental shelf. If the process is slow and neither the new nor the old rule has an overwhelming majority of adherents, the consequence is a network of special relations based on opposability, acquiescence and even perhaps historic title. This situation will normally be transitional in character—though in affairs of state, transitions can take some time.

(iii) Bilateral relations and local custom

Some customary norms may be practised only within a particular region, creating a 'local' customary law. Such a norm is reducible to the level of a bilateral relation, as in the *Right of Passage* case.[53] There, Portugal relied on such a custom to establish a right of access to Portuguese enclaves in Indian territory inland from the port of Daman. The Court held:

It is difficult to see why the number of States between which a local custom may be established on the basis of long practice must necessarily be larger than two. The Court sees no reason why long continued practice between two States accepted by them as regulating their relations should not form the basis of mutual rights and obligations between two States.[54]

---

[49] ICJ Reports 1951 p 116.

[50] The dictum requiring explanation is: 'In any event the ten-mile rule would appear to be inapplicable as against Norway inasmuch as she has always opposed any attempt to apply it to the Norwegian coast.' ICJ Reports 1951 p 116, 131. See Fitzmaurice (1957) 92 Hague *Recueil* 5, 99–101; Sørensen (1960) 101 Hague *Recueil* 5, 43–7.

[51] E.g. *Lauritzen v Chile* (1956) 23 ILR 708, 710–12.

[52] Since a delict cannot be justified on the basis of a desire to change the law, the question of *opinio iuris* arises in a special form. In the early stages of change this can amount to little more than a plea of good faith.

[53] ICJ Reports 1960 p 6, 39–43; cf 62–3 (Judge Wellington Koo); 82–4 (Judge Armand-Ugon, diss); 110 (Judge Spender, diss). Also: *Jurisdiction of the European Commission of the Danube* (1927) PCIJ Ser B No 14, 6, 114 (Deputy-Judge Negulesco, diss); *Nottebohm (Liechtenstein v Guatemala)*, Second Phase, ICJ Reports 1955 p 4, 30 (Judge Klaestead, diss).

[54] ICJ Reports 1960 p 6, 39. Further: Thirlway, in Evans (3rd edn, 2010) 95, 107.

When considering the formation of bilateral custom, general formulae concerning custom will not supplant the need for case-by-case analysis. Where a party seeks to vary the general law on a bilateral basis, the proponent of the special right has to give proof of a sense of obligation on the part of the territorial sovereign. In such circumstances the notion of *opinio iuris* merges into the principle of acquiescence.[55] In *Right of Passage*, the transit arrangement dated back to the Mughal period, and went unquestioned by the British and later independent Indian governments.[56]

The best-known example of a regional custom is that of diplomatic asylum in Latin-America, concerning the right of the embassies of other states to give asylum to political refugees.[57] Specifically Columbia relied against Peru on 'an alleged regional or local custom peculiar to Latin-American States'.[58] The Court observed:

> The Party which relies on a custom of this kind must prove that this custom is established in such a manner that it has become binding on the other Party. The Colombian Government must prove that the rule invoked by it is in accordance with a constant and uniform usage practised by the States in question, and that this usage is the expression of a right appertaining to the State granting asylum and a duty incumbent on the territorial State.[59]

The Court went on to remark that 'even if such a custom existed between certain Latin-American States only, it could not be invoked against Peru which, far from having its attitude adhered to it, has on the contrary repudiated it'.[60] Other attempts to establish a norm of local custom before an international court or tribunal have likewise failed.[61]

4. TREATIES

Treaties are the most important source of obligation in international law.[62] 'Law-making' treaties moreover have a direct influence on the content of general international law, an influence not conveyed adequately by their designation as material sources.

---

[55] Generally: D'Amato (1969) 63 *AJIL* 211; Antunes, *Estoppel, Acquiescence and Recognition in Territorial and Boundary Dispute Settlement* (2000); Marques Antunes, 'Acquiescence' (2006) *MPEPIL*.

[56] Thirlway, in Evans (3rd edn, 2010) 95, 107.

[57] Ibid, 106.

[58] *Asylum*, ICJ Reports 1950 p 266, 276.

[59] Ibid, 276–7.

[60] Ibid, 277–8.

[61] E.g. *Rights of Nationals of the United States of America in Morocco (France v US)*, ICJ Reports 1952 p 176, 199–200 (emphasis added), citing *Asylum*, ICJ Reports 1950 p 266, 276–7. Also: Lauterpacht (1958) 388–92; Thirlway, in Evans (3rd edn, 2010) 95, 107.

[62] Generally: McNair, *The Law of Treaties* (1961); Rosenne, *The Law of Treaties* (1970); Baxter (1970) 129 Hague *Recueil* 27; Elias, *The Modern Law of Treaties* (1974); Sinclair, *Vienna Convention on the Law of Treaties* (2nd edn, 1984); Bastid, *Les Traités dans la vie internationale* (1985); Rosenne, *Breach of Treaty* (1985); Gaja (1987) 58 *BY* 253; Rosenne, *Developments in the Law of Treaties 1945–1986* (1989); Combacau, *Le Droit des traités* (1991); Menon, *The Law of Treaties between States and International Organizations* (1992); Buergenthal (1992) 235 Hague *Recueil* 303; Reuter, *Introduction to the Law of Treaties* (2nd edn, 1995):

Bilateral treaties may provide evidence of customary rules,[63] and indeed there is no dogmatic distinction between 'law-making' treaties and other treaties. If bilateral treaties, for example those on extradition, are habitually framed in the same way, a court may regard the standard form as law even in the absence of a treaty obligation in that case.[64] However, caution is necessary in evaluating treaties for this purpose.

(A) 'LAW-MAKING' TREATIES

So-called 'law-making' treaties create legal obligations, the one-time observance of which does not discharge the obligation. Thus a treaty for the joint carrying-out of a single enterprise is not law-making, and fulfilment of the treaty's objects will discharge the obligation. Law-making treaties create *general* norms, framed as legal propositions, to govern the conduct of the parties, not necessarily limited to their conduct *inter se*— indeed the expression of an obligation in universal or 'all states' form is an indication of an intent to create such a general rule. The Declaration of Paris of 1856 (on neutrality in maritime warfare), the Hague Conventions of 1899 and of 1907 (on the law of war and neutrality), the Geneva Protocol of 1925 (on prohibited weapons), the General Treaty for the Renunciation of War of 1928, the Genocide Convention of 1948, and the four Geneva Conventions of 1949 (on the protection of civilians and other groups in time of war) are examples of this type. Moreover, those parts of the UN Charter that do not spell out the constitutional competence of the organization's organs, and other organizational questions, have the same character—notably the principles set out in Article 2 and further articulated in the Friendly Relations Declaration of 1970.[65] UNCLOS is a more recent example.[66] Although treaties are as such binding only on the parties, the number of parties, the explicit acceptance of these rules by states generally and, in some cases, the declaratory character of the provisions combine to produce a powerful law-creating effect.[67] Non-parties may by their conduct accept the provisions of a convention

---

Klabbers, *The Concept of Treaty in International Law* (1996); Gowlland-Debbas (ed), *Multilateral Treaty-Making* (2000); Fitzmaurice (2002) 73 BY 141; Wolfrum & Röben (eds), *Developments of International Law in Treaty Making* (2005); Fitzmaurice & Elias, *Contemporary Issues in the Law of Treaties* (2005); Corten & Klein (eds), *Les Conventions de Vienne sur le Droit des Traités* (2006); Dinstein (2006) 332 Hague *Recueil* 243; Aust, *Modern Treaty Law and Practice* (2nd edn, 2007); Ulfstein (ed), *Making Treaties Work* (2007); Villiger, *Commentary on the 1969 Vienna Convention on the Law of Treaties* (2009); Orakhelashvili & Williams (eds), *40 Years of the Vienna Convention on the Law of Treaties* (2010); Canizzaro (ed), *The Law of Treaties beyond the Vienna Convention* (2010); Fitzmaurice, 'Treaties' (2010) *MPEPIL*.

[63] See the *Wimbledon* (1923) PCIJ Ser A No 1, 25; *Panevezys–Saldutiskis Railway* (1939) PCIJ Ser A/B No 76, 51–2 (Judge Erich); *Nottebohm*, ICJ Reports 1955 p 4, 22–3. See also Baxter (1970) 129 Hague *Recueil* 31, 75–91; Sørensen, *Les Sources du droit international* (1946) 96–8.

[64] Cf *Re Tribble* (1953) 20 ILR 366; *N v Public Prosecutor of the Canton of Aargau* (1953) 20 ILR 363.

[65] GA Res 2625(XXV), 24 October 1970, as to which see Arangio-Ruiz (1972) 137 Hague *Recueil* 419.

[66] 10 December 1982, 1833 UNTS 3.

[67] McNair (1961) 216–18 describes Art 2, §§3–4 of the Charter as the 'nearest approach to legislation by the whole community of States that has yet been realised'.

as representing customary international law.[68] This has been the case with Hague Convention IV of 1907[69] and the annexed rules on land warfare. In special circumstances even an unratified treaty may be regarded as evidence of generally accepted rules.[70]

In *North Sea Continental Shelf*[71] the principal issue was the extent to which, if at all, Germany was bound by the provisions of the Geneva Convention on the Continental Shelf (GCCS) which it had signed but not ratified. The Court concluded that only the first three articles represented emergent or pre-existing customary law.[72] The basis on which the Court distinguished between articles included reference to the faculty of making unilateral reservations, a faculty which applied to some articles but not to those which, by inference, had a more fundamental status. That was a case where the treaty itself made the distinction; by contrast the mere existence of reservations where no provision for reservations is made in the treaty will not by itself annul the probative value of its provisions.[73] The Court concluded, further, that the provision on delimitation of shelf areas in Article 6 of the Convention had not become a rule of customary law by virtue of the subsequent practice of states and, in particular, of non-parties.[74] The six dissenting judges regarded the Convention as having greater potency, particularly with respect to the generation of rules after the conclusion of the Convention.[75] In both *Gulf of Maine*[76] and *Continental Shelf (Libya/Malta)*,[77] considerable weight was accorded to aspects of UNCLOS, although it was not yet in force.

According to Baxter, after *North Sea Continental Shelf* it became clear that 'the treaty-making process may also have unwelcome side-effects': this is the so-called 'Baxter paradox'.[78] In particular, he notes that treaties declaratory or constitutive of custom may 'arrest' its further development and that until 'the treaty is revised or amended, the customary international law will remain the image of the treaty as it was before it was revised.'[79]

---

[68] There must be evidence of consent to the extension of the rule, particularly if the rule is found in a regional convention: *European Human Rights Convention* (1955) 22 ILR 608, 610. Cf the treatment of a European regional convention in *Pulp Mills*, Judgment of 20 April 2010, §§203–19.

[69] E.g. *In re Goering* (1946) 13 ILR 203.

[70] See *Nottebohm*, Second Phase, ICJ Reports 1955 p 4, 23; *Legal Consequences for States of the Continued Presence of South Africa in Namibia (South West Africa) notwithstanding Security Council Resolution 276 (1970)*, ICJ Reports 1971 p 16, 47. Cf *North Sea Continental Shelf*, ICJ Reports 1969 p 3, 41–3; Baxter (1970) 129 Hague *Recueil* 31, 61.

[71] ICJ Reports 1969 p 3.

[72] Ibid, 32–41, 86–9 (Judge Padilla Nervo); 102–6, 123–4 (Judge Ammoun).

[73] ICJ Reports 1969 p 3, 182 (Judge Tanaka, diss); 198 (Judge Morelli, diss); 223–5 (Judge Lachs, diss); 248 (Judge Sørensen, diss). Cf Baxter (1970) 129 Hague *Recueil* 31, 47–51.

[74] *North Sea Continental Shelf*, ICJ Reports 1969 p 3, 41–5.

[75] Ibid, 56 (Judge Bengzon); 156–8, 163, 169 (Vice-President Koretsky, diss); 172–80 (Judge Tanaka, diss); 197–200 (Judge Morelli, diss); 221–32 (Judge Lachs, diss); 241–7 (Judge Sørensen, diss).

[76] ICJ Reports 1982 p 246, 294–5.

[77] ICJ Reports 1985 p 13, 29–34.

[78] Baxter (1970) 129 Hague *Recueil* 27, 92. Further: Baxter (1965–66) 41 *BY* 275.

[79] Baxter (1970) 129 Hague *Recueil* 27, 97.

(B) RELATION OF TREATIES TO CUSTOM

When norms of treaty origin crystallize into new principles or rules of customary law, the customary norms retain a separate identity even where the two norms may be identical in content. Thus a state which fails to become a party to a law-making treaty may find itself indirectly affected by the norms contained in the treaty—unless its opposition rises to the level of persistent objection. Even then its position may be awkward: it will be unable to invoke the new rule itself but unable also to secure from other states continued adherence to the old. This was the experience of the US and Japan in continuing to assert a maximum 3nm territorial sea once it became clear that most states rejected that standard in favour of 12nm.[80] More generally the US has sought to rely on provisions of UNCLOS—for example in the field of maritime transit—despite its repeated failure to ratify.

In the long run, one significant effect of non-participation in a law-making treaty is inability to invoke its dispute settlement provisions: a dispute can only arise under a treaty as between parties to the treaty. This may not matter if there is a separate basis for jurisdiction, for example under the Optional Clause or a free-standing dispute settlement treaty,[81] and if the customary law rule is arguably the same as that contained in the treaty. In *Nicaragua*, the position was unusual: the US relied on an Optional Clause reservation that excluded the Court from applying the Organization of American States (OAS) Charter, under which the dispute arose, in the absence of other affected states. The Court avoided the effect of the jurisdictional reservation by holding that it was free to apply customary international law (the content of which was, it held, the same as the OAS Charter).[82] But this was to confuse jurisdiction and applicable law: states do not cease to have disputes under a treaty merely because the Court has, in consequence, no jurisdiction over those disputes. The views of the dissenting judges on this point are to be preferred.[83]

As a general rule, the requirements of duration, consistency, and generality of practice, as well as *opinio iuris*, means that customary law is often outpaced by specific treaties. But this is not always the case; in the longer term, customary law may be called on to mould and even modify treaty texts which cannot realistically be amended, however desirable amendment might be. A case in point is the law of self-defence as expressed in Article 51 of the UN Charter.[84] This parallels the right of self-defence that existed in customary international law prior to the Charter, but makes no mention

---

[80] *Nicaragua*, ICJ Reports 1986 p 14, 92–6, 152–4 (President Nagendra Singh); 182–4 (Judge Ago); 204–8 (Judge Ni); 216–19 (Judge Oda, diss); 302–6 (Judge Schwebel, diss); 529–36 (Judge Jennings, diss).

[81] E.g. American Treaty on Pacific Settlement, 30 April 1948, 30 UNTS 55; European Convention for the Pacific Settlement of Disputes, 29 April 1957, 320 UNTS 243.

[82] *Nicaragua*, ICJ Reports 1986 p 14, 92–6, 152–4 (President Nagendra Singh).

[83] Ibid, 216–19 (Judge Oda, diss); 302–6 (Judge Schwebel, diss); 529–36 (Judge Jennings, diss). Further: Crawford, 'Military and Paramilitary Activities in and against Nicaragua (Nicaragua v United States of America)' (2006) *MPEPIL*. It is only fair to record that this was one of Ian Brownlie's outstanding wins before the Court (as counsel for Nicaragua).

[84] Jia (2010) 9 *Chin JIL* 81, 98–100. On self-defence in international law: chapter 33.

of necessity and proportionality. Despite the absence of these words in Article 51, the International Court has read them in.[85] The principle does not, however, cut both ways, and the requirement in Article 51 that any exercise of the right be reported to the Security Council has not been imported into custom.[86]

5. GENERAL PRINCIPLES OF LAW[87]

Article 38(1)(c) of the Statute of the International Court refers to 'the general principles of law recognized by civilized nations'.[88] This source is listed after treaty and custom, both of which depend more immediately on state consent. Nonetheless, these general principles are not considered 'subsidiary means', a term confined to Article 38(1)(d). The formulation appeared in the *compromis* of arbitral tribunals in the nineteenth century, and similar formulae appear in draft instruments on the functioning of tribunals.[89] In the Committee of Jurists that prepared the Statute there was no consensus on the significance of the phrase. Descamps (Belgium) had natural law concepts in mind; his draft referred to 'the rules of international law recognized by the legal conscience of civilized peoples'. Root (US) considered that governments would mistrust a court that relied on subjective concepts associated with principles of justice. However, the Committee realized that the Court must have a certain power to develop and refine such principles. In the end a joint proposal by Root and Phillimore (UK) was accepted, and this became the text we now have.[90]

Root and Phillimore regarded these principles as rules accepted in the domestic law of all civilized states, and Guggenheim held the firm view that paragraph (c) must be applied in this light.[91] However, Oppenheim's view is preferable: '[t]he intention is to

---

[85] *Nuclear Weapons*, ICJ Reports 1995 p 226, 244–5.

[86] *Nicaragua*, ICJ Reports 1986 p 14, 105.

[87] Generally: Lauterpacht, *Private Law Sources and Analogies of International Law* (1927). See further Fitzmaurice (1957) 92 Hague *Recueil* 1; Herczegh, *General Principles of Law and the International Legal Order* (1969); Cheng, *General Principles of Law as Applied by International Courts and Tribunals* (2nd edn, 1987); Raimondo, *General Principles of Law in the Decisions of International Criminal Courts and Tribunals* (2007); Gaja, 'General Principles of Law' (2007) *MPEPIL*.

[88] The adjective 'civilized' was introduced by the Committee of Jurists in 1920. The Committee apparently considered all nations 'civilized', though it is easy to see that how term could possess an unfortunate colonialist connotation. 'It can be firmly admitted that, for the time being, all States must be considered as "civilized nations"': Pellet, in Zimmermann et al (2006) 789.

[89] See Art 7 (on general principles of justice and equity) of Convention XII Relative to the Establishment of an International Prize Court, 18 October 1907, 3 NRG (3d) 688 (signed but never entered into force). Also: ECHR, 4 November 1950, 213 UNTS 222, Art 7(2), providing for 'the trial and punishment of any person for any act or omission which, at the time when it was committed, was criminal according to *the general principles of law recognized by civilized nations*' (emphasis added).

[90] Descamps, *Procés-verbaux* (1920) 316, 335, 344. Sørensen remarks that the compromise formula has an inherent ambiguity which is inimical to any rational interpretation of the provision: Sørensen (1946) 125.

[91] Guggenheim (1958) 94 Hague *Recueil* 6, 78.

authorize the Court to apply the general principles of municipal jurisprudence, in particular of private law, insofar as they are applicable to relations of States'.[92] The latter part of this statement is significant. Tribunals have not adopted a mechanical system of borrowing from domestic law. Rather they have employed or adapted modes of general legal reasoning as well as comparative law analogies in order to make a coherent body of rules for application by international judicial process. It is difficult for state practice to generate the evolution of the rules of procedure and evidence as well as the substantive law that a court must employ. An international tribunal chooses, edits, and adapts elements from other developed systems. The result is a body of international law the content of which has been influenced by domestic law but which is still its own creation.[93]

(A) GENERAL PRINCIPLES OF LAW IN THE PRACTICE OF TRIBUNALS

(i) Arbitral tribunals

Arbitral tribunals have frequently resorted to analogies from municipal law. In the *Fabiani*[94] case between France and Venezuela the arbitrator had recourse to municipal public law on the question of state responsibility for the state's agents, including judicial officers, for acts carried out in an official capacity. The arbitrator also relied on general principles of law in assessing damages. The Permanent Court of Arbitration applied the principle of moratory interest on debts in *Russian Indemnity*.[95] Since the Statute of the Permanent Court was concluded in 1920, tribunals not otherwise bound by it have generally treated Article 38(1)(c) as declaratory.[96]

In practice tribunals show considerable discretion in matters involving general principles. Decisions on the acquisition of territory tend not to reflect domestic derivatives of real property, and municipal analogies may have done more harm than good here. The evolution of the rules on the effect of duress on treaties has not depended on changes in domestic law.[97] In *North Atlantic Fisheries* the tribunal considered the concept of servitude but refused to apply it.[98] Moreover, in some cases, for example those

---

[92] 1 Oppenheim, §12.

[93] See Tunkin (1958) 95 Hague *Recueil* 5, 23–6; de Visscher, *Theory and Reality in Public International Law* (3rd edn, 1968) 400–2. Cf *South West Africa*, ICJ Reports 1950 p 128, 158 (Judge McNair, diss).

[94] (1902) 10 RIAA 83. The claim was based on denial of justice by the Venezuelan courts.

[95] (1912) 1 HCR 297. See also *Sarropoulos v Bulgaria* (1927) 4 ILR 263 (extinctive prescription).

[96] See e.g. *US v Germany* (1923) 2 ILR 367; *Roumania v Germany* (1927) 4 ILR 542; *Lena Goldfields* (1929) 5 ILR 3; *Greek Powder & Cartridge Co v German Federal Republic* (1958) 25 ILR 544, 545; *Arbitration between Newfoundland and Labrador and Nova Scotia* (2002) 128 ILR 425, 534–5; *Feldman v Mexico* (2002) 126 ILR 26, 42; *Waste Management v Mexico* (2002) 132 ILR 146, 171–2; *Abyei Arbitration* (2009) 144 ILR 348, 504.

[97] Nineteenth-century writers took the view that duress directed against the state had no vitiating effect. Since 1920 the contrary view has been accepted, under the influence not of domestic analogy but developments in the law relating to the use of force: VCLT, Arts 51–2, and further: chapters 16, 33.

[98] (1910) 1 HCR 141.

involving the expropriation of private rights, reference to domestic law might yield uncertain results, and the choice of model reveal ideological predilections.

(ii) The International Court and general principles

The Court has used Article 38(1)(c) sparingly. 'General principles' normally enter judicial reasoning without formal reference or label. However, the Court has on occasion referred to general notions of responsibility. In *Chorzów Factory* the Court observed that 'one Party cannot avail himself of the fact that the other has not fulfilled some obligation or has not had recourse to some means of redress, if the former Party has, by some illegal act, prevented the latter from fulfilling the obligation in question, or from having recourse to the tribunal which would have been open, to him'.[99] The Court went on to observe that 'it is a principle of international law, and even a general conception of law, that any breach of an engagement involves an obligation to make reparation'.[100] The Court has relied on occasion on the principle of estoppel or acquiescence.[101] At other times references to abuse of rights and to good faith may occur.[102] But the most frequent and successful use of domestic law analogies has been in the field of evidence, procedure, and jurisdiction. Thus there have been references to the rule that no one can be judge in his own suit,[103] to litispendence,[104] to *res iudicata*,[105] to various 'principles governing the judicial process',[106] and to 'the principle universally accepted by international tribunals ... to the effect that the parties to a case must abstain from any measure capable of exercising a prejudicial effect in regard to the execution of the decision to be given'.[107] In *Corfu Channel* the Court considered circumstantial evidence

---

[99] *Factory at Chorzów,* Jurisdiction (1927) PCIJ Ser A No 9, 31.

[100] *Factory at Chorzów,* Merits (1928) PCIJ Ser A No 17, 29.

[101] *Legal Status of Eastern Greenland* (1933) PCIJ Ser A/B No 53, 52–4, 62, 69; *Arbitral Award Made by the King of Spain on 23 December 1906 (Honduras v Nicaragua)*, ICJ Reports 1960 p 192, 209, 213; *Temple of Preah Vihear (Cambodia v Thailand)*, ICJ Reports 1962 p 6, 23, 31–2, 39–51 (Judge Alfaro). Also ibid, 26, where the Court said: 'It is an established rule of law that the plea of error cannot be allowed as an element vitiating consent if the party advancing it contributed by its own conduct to the error'. Further: *Barcelona Traction, Light and Power Company, Limited (Belgium v Spain)*, Preliminary Objections, ICJ Reports 1964 p 6, 24–5; *North Sea Continental Shelf,* ICJ Reports 1969 p 3, 26; *Gulf of Maine,* ICJ Reports 1984 p 246, 308–9; *Land and Maritime Boundary between Cameroon and Nigeria,* Preliminary Objections, ICJ Reports 1998 p 275, 303–4; *Legality of Use of Force (Serbia and Montenegro v Canada)*, Preliminary Objections, ICJ Reports 2004 p 429, 444–7.

[102] E.g. *Free Zones of Upper Savoy and the District of Gex,* Second Phase (1930) PCIJ Ser A No 24, 12; (1932) PCIJ Ser A/B No 46, 167. For references to individual judges' use of analogies: Lauterpacht (1958) 167. Also *Right of Passage,* ICJ Reports 1960 p 6, 66–7 (Judge Wellington Koo); 90 (Judge Moreno Quintana, diss); 107 (Judge Spender, diss); 136 (Judge Fernandes, diss).

[103] *Interpretation of Article 3, Paragraph 2, of the Treaty of Lausanne* (1925) PCIJ Ser B No 12, 32.

[104] *Certain German Interests in Polish Upper Silesia,* Preliminary Objections (1925) PCIJ Ser A No 6, 20.

[105] *Effect of Awards of Compensation Made by the United Nations Administrative Tribunal,* ICJ Reports 1954 p 47, 53.

[106] *Application for Review of Judgment No. 158 of the United Nations Administrative Tribunal,* ICJ Reports 1973 p 166, 177, 181, 210; *Application for Review of Judgment No. 273 of the United Nations Administrative Tribunal,* ICJ Reports 1982 p 325, 338–40, 345, 356.

[107] *Electricity Company of Sofia and Bulgaria* (1939) PCIJ Ser A/B No 79, 199.

and remarked that 'this indirect evidence is admitted in all systems of law, and its use is recognized by international decisions'.[108] In his dissenting opinion in *South West Africa (Second Phase)*, Judge Tanaka referred to Article 38(1)(c) of the Court's Statute as a basis for grounding the legal force of human rights concepts and suggested that the provision contains natural law elements.[109] The Court's reasoning in *Barcelona Traction* relied on the general conception of the limited liability company in municipal legal systems,[110] a position repeated in *Diallo*.[111]

(B) GENERAL PRINCIPLES OF INTERNATIONAL LAW

The rubric 'general principles of international law' may alternately refer to rules of customary international law, to general principles of law as in Article 38(1)(c), or to certain logical propositions underlying judicial reasoning on the basis of existing international law. This shows that a rigid categorization of sources is inappropriate. Examples of this type of general principle of international law are the principles of consent, reciprocity, equality of states, finality of awards and settlements, the legal validity of agreements, good faith, domestic jurisdiction, and the freedom of the seas. In many cases these principles may be traced to state practice. However, they are primarily abstractions and have been accepted for so long and so generally as no longer to be *directly* connected to state practice. Certain fundamental principles of international law enjoy heightened normativity as peremptory norms (see chapter 27).

6. JUDICIAL DECISIONS[112]

(A) JUDICIAL DECISIONS AND PRECEDENT IN INTERNATIONAL LAW

Judicial decisions are not strictly a formal source of law, but in many instances they are regarded as evidence of the law. A coherent body of previous jurisprudence will have important consequences in any given case. Their value, however, stops short of precedent as it is understood in the common law tradition.

Article 38(1)(d) starts with a proviso: '[s]ubject to the provisions of Article 59, judicial decisions ... as subsidiary means for the determination of rules of law'. The significance of the word 'subsidiary' here is not to be overstated.[113] Article 59 provides that a decision of the Court has 'no binding force except as between the parties and

---

[108] ICJ Reports 1949 p 4, 18. Also: *Right of Passage*, Preliminary Objections, ICJ Reports 1957 p 125, 141–2; *German Interests*, Preliminary Objections (1925) PCIJ Ser A No 6, 19.

[109] ICJ Reports 1966 p 6, 294–9 (Judge Tanaka, diss).

[110] *Barcelona Traction*, ICJ Reports 1970 p 3, 33–5.

[111] *Diallo*, Judgment of 30 November 2010, §47.

[112] Generally: Lauterpacht (1958) 8–22. Further: Pellet, in Zimmermann et al (2006) 784–90.

[113] Fitzmaurice, in *Symbolae Verzijl* (1958) 153, 174 (criticizing the classification).

in respect of that particular case'. Lauterpacht argued that Article 59 does not refer to the major question of judicial precedent but to the particular question of intervention.[114] Article 63 provides that if a third state avails itself of the right of intervention, the construction given in the judgment shall be equally binding on the intervening third state. Lauterpacht concludes that 'Article 59 would thus seem to state directly what Article 63 expresses indirectly'. However, the debate in the Committee of Jurists indicates clearly that Article 59 was not intended merely to express the principle of *res iudicata,* but rather to rule out a system of binding precedent.[115] In *Polish Upper Silesia* the Court said: '[t]he object of [Article 59] is simply to prevent legal principles accepted by the Court in a particular case from being binding on other States or in other disputes'.[116] In practice, however, it has not treated earlier decisions in such a narrow spirit.[117]

It is true that the Court does not observe a doctrine of precedent, except perhaps on matters of procedure. But it strives to maintain judicial consistency. In *Exchange of Greek and Turkish Populations*, the Court referred to 'the precedent afforded by' the *Wimbledon*, reflecting the principle that treaty obligations do not entail an abandonment of sovereignty.[118] In *Reparation for Injuries*,[119] the Court relied on a pronouncement in a previous advisory opinion[120] for a statement of the principle of effectiveness in interpreting treaties. Such references are often a matter of 'evidence' of the law, but the Court aims for consistency and thus employs the technique of distinguishing previous decisions.[121] In *Peace Treaties,* for example, the questions submitted to the Court concerned the interpretation of dispute settlement clauses in the peace treaties with

---

[114] Lauterpacht (1958) 8.

[115] See Descamps (1920) 332, 336, 584. Also: Sørensen (1946) 161; Hudson (1943) 207; Waldock (1962) 106 Hague *Recueil* 5, 91. Waldock observes: 'It would indeed have been somewhat surprising if States had been prepared in 1920 to give a wholly new and untried tribunal explicit authority to lay down law binding upon all States'.

[116] *German Interests* (1926) PCIJ Ser A No 7, 19.

[117] Generally: Lauterpacht (1931) 12 *BY* 31, 60; Lauterpacht (1958) 9–20. Further: Shahabuddeen, *Precedent in the World Court* (1996); Rosenne, 1–3 *The Law and Practice of the International Court 1920–2005* (4th edn, 2006); Brown, *A Common Law of International Adjudication* (2007). See also *Diallo*, Judgment of 30 November 2010, §§67–8, where the Court referred expressly to the case-law of other international courts and treaty bodies, namely the ECtHR and the African Commission on Human and Peoples' Rights.

[118] *Exchange of Greek and Turkish Populations* (1925) PCIJ Ser B No 10, 21.

[119] *Reparation for Injuries Suffered in the Service of the United Nations*, ICJ Reports 1949 p 174, 182–3.

[120] *Competence of the ILO to Regulate, Incidentally, the Personal Work of the Employer* (1926) PCIJ Ser B No 13, 7, 18.

[121] Also: *Interpretation of Peace Treaties with Bulgaria, Hungary and Romania*, First Phase, ICJ Reports 1950 p 65, 89 (Judge Winiarski, diss); 103 (Judge Zoričič, diss); 106 (Judge Krylov, diss); *South West Africa*, Preliminary Objections, ICJ Reports 1962 p 319, 328, 345; *Northern Cameroons*, Preliminary Objections, ICJ Reports 1963 p 15, 27–8, 29–30, 37; *Aerial Incident of 27 July 1955 (Israel v Bulgaria)*, ICJ Reports 1959 p 127, 192 (Judges Lauterpacht, Wellington Koo & Spender, diss); *South West Africa*, Second Phase, ICJ Reports 1966 p 6, 240–1 (Judge Koretsky, diss); *North Sea Continental Shelf*, ICJ Reports 1969 p 3, 44, 47–9; 101–2, 121, 131, 138 (Judge Ammoun); 210 (Judge Morelli, diss); 223, 225, 229, 231–3, 236, 238 (Judge Lachs, diss); 243–4, 247 (Judge Sørensen, diss); *Namibia*, ICJ Reports 1971 p 16, 26–7, 53–4; *Kasikili/Sedudu Island*, ICJ Reports 1999 p 1045, 1073, 1076, 1097–100; *Land and Maritime Boundary between Cameroon and Nigeria (Cameroon v Nigeria)*, ICJ Reports 2002 p 303, 353–4, 359, 415–16, 420–1, 440–7, 453.

Bulgaria, Hungary, and Romania. In fact the request arose from other parties' allegations against these three states of breaches of treaty provisions on the maintenance of human rights, allegations of substance. The Court rejected arguments that it lacked the power to provide an opinion. It said:

Article 65 of the Statute is permissive. It gives the Court the power to examine whether the circumstances of the case are of such a character as should lead it to decline to answer the Request. In the opinion of the Court, the circumstances of the present case are profoundly different from those which were before the Permanent Court of International Justice in the *Eastern Carelia* case.[122]

Attempts have sometimes been made to have the Court depart explicitly from an earlier decision: the Court has either declined to do so[123] or has by-passed the point entirely.[124] But there is no doubt as to the Court's power to depart from or qualify the effect of an earlier decision, something which it is more inclined to do tacitly.[125] The position may be different when there is a line of concordant decisions (a *jurisprudence constante*), in which case reversal is not to be expected.

(B) DECISIONS OF INTERNATIONAL TRIBUNALS

The literature contains frequent reference to decisions of arbitral tribunals. The quality of such decisions varies considerably. However, certain arbitral awards have made notable contributions to the development of the law.[126]

Much depends on the status of the tribunal and of its members, and on the conditions under which it conducts its work. The judgment of the International Military Tribunal for the Trial of German Major War Criminals,[127] the decisions of the Iran–United

---

[122] *Peace Treaties*, First Phase, ICJ Reports 1950 p 65, 72, referring to *Status of Eastern Carelia* (1923) PCIJ Ser B No 5, 27. See Lauterpacht (1958) 352–7, for criticism of the distinction between procedure and substance. See further Fitzmaurice (1952) 29 BY 1, 50–2. Cf *South West Africa*, Preliminary Objections, ICJ Reports 1962 p 319, 471–3 (Judges Spender & Fitzmaurice, diss); *Cameroons*, Preliminary Objections, ICJ Reports 1963 p 15, 35, 37–8; 62–4 (Judge Wellington Koo); 68–73 (Judge Spender); 108, 125–7 (Judge Fitzmaurice); 140–1 (Judge Morelli); 150–1 (Judge Badawi, diss); 156–9, 170, 182 (Judge Bustamante, diss); 187–91, 194–6 (Judge Beb a Don, diss). *Eastern Carelia* was also distinguished in *Namibia*, ICJ Reports 1971 p 16, 23, and in *Wall*, ICJ Reports 2004 p 136, 161–2.

[123] E.g. *Cameroon v Nigeria*, Preliminary Objections, ICJ Reports 1998 p 275, 291, following the decision in *Right of Passage*, Preliminary Objections, ICJ Reports 1957 p 125, 146, on the immediate effect of an Optional Clause declaration.

[124] E.g. *Application of the Convention on the Prevention and Punishment of the Crime of Genocide (Croatia v Serbia)*, Preliminary Objections, ICJ Reports 2008 p 412, 434–5, avoiding applying the decision in *Legality of Use of Force (Serbia and Montenegro v Belgium)*, Preliminary Objections, ICJ Reports 2004 p 279, 318–24, on the interpretation of Art 35(2) of the Statute.

[125] E.g. the development of obligations *erga omnes* in *Barcelona Traction*, Jurisdiction, ICJ Reports 1970 p 3, 32 tacitly reversing *South West Africa*, Second Phase, ICJ Reports 1966 p 6, in which standing was denied to Liberia and Ethiopia.

[126] E.g. *The Alabama* (1872), in Moore, 1 *Int Arb* 653; *Behring Sea Fisheries* (1893), in Moore, 1 *Int Arb* 755.

[127] *In re Goering* (1946) 13 ILR 203.

States Claims Tribunal, and the decisions of the International Criminal Tribunal for the Former Yugoslavia, among others, contain significant findings on issues of law. The International Court has referred to arbitral decisions on many occasions;[128] it also refers compendiously to the jurisprudence of international arbitration.[129]

(C) DECISIONS OF THE INTERNATIONAL COURT AND ITS PREDECESSOR

In theory the Court applies the law and does not make it, and Article 59 of the Statute reflects a feeling on the part of the drafters that the Court was intended to settle disputes as they came to it rather than to shape the law. Yet a decision, especially if unanimous or almost unanimous, may play a catalytic role in the development of the law. The early decisions and advisory opinions in *Reparation for Injuries*, *Reservations*, and *Anglo-Norwegian Fisheries* had a decisive influence. However, some discretion is called for in handling decisions. The much-criticized *Lotus* decision for instance, the outcome of the casting vote of the President, was rejected by the ILC, a position endorsed in 1958 and again in 1982.[130] At its third session, the ILC refused to accept the principles emerging from the *Reservations* advisory opinion (a stance which was reversed at its fourteenth session).[131] Moreover, it may display a lack of caution to extract general propositions from opinions and judgments devoted to a specific problem or to the settlement of a dispute entangled with the special relations of two states.[132]

---

[128] E.g. *Polish Postal Service in Danzig* (1925) PCIJ Ser B No 11, 30 (referring to *Pious Funds of the Californias* (1902) 9 RIAA 11); *Lotus* (1927) PCIJ Ser A No 10, 26 (referring to *Costa Rica Packet*, in Moore, 5 *Int Arb* 4948); *Legal Status of Eastern Greenland* (1933) PCIJ Ser A/B No 53, 45–6 (referring to *Island of Palmas* (1928) 2 RIAA 828); *Nottebohm*, Preliminary Objections, ICJ Reports 1953 p 113, 119 ('since the *Alabama* case, it has been generally recognized, following the earlier precedents, that in the absence of any agreement to the contrary, an international tribunal has the right to decide as to its own jurisdiction and has the power to interpret for this purpose the instruments which govern that jurisdiction'); *Gulf of Maine*, ICJ Reports 1984 p 246, 302–3, 324 (referring to *Anglo–French Continental Shelf* (1979) 54 ILR 6); *Land, Island and Maritime Frontier Dispute (El Salvador v Honduras)*, ICJ Reports 1992 p 351, 387 (referring to the Swiss Federal Council's award in *Certain Boundary Questions between Colombia and Venezuela* (1922) 1 RIAA 228); *Sovereignty over Pedra Branca/Pulau Batu Puteh, Middle Rocks and South Ledge (Malaysia/Singapore)*, ICJ Reports 2008 p 12, 32 (referring to the *Meerauge Arbitration (Austria v Hungary)* (1902) 8 *RDI* 2nd Ser, 207), 80 (referring to *Territorial Sovereignty and Scope of the Dispute (Eritrea v Yemen)* (1998) 22 RIAA 209); *Maritime Delimitation in the Black Sea (Romania v Ukraine)*, ICJ Reports 2009 p 61, 109 (referring to *Eritrea/Yemen (Maritime Delimitation)* (1999) 22 RIAA 367), 125 (referring to *Barbados v Trinidad and Tobago* (2006) 27 RIAA 214).

[129] *Factory at Chorzów*, Jurisdiction, (1927) PCIJ Ser A No 9, 31; *Factory at Chorzów* (1928) PCIJ Ser A No 17, 31, 47; *Anglo-Norwegian Fisheries*, ICJ Reports 1951 p 116, 131. Also: *Peter Pázmány University* (1933) PCIJ Ser A/B No 61, 243 (consistent practice of mixed arbitral tribunals); *Barcelona Traction*, Second Phase, ICJ Reports 1970 p 30, 40. The Court has also referred generally to decisions of other tribunals without specific reference to arbitral tribunals. E.g. *Legal Status of Eastern Greenland* (1933) PCIJ Ser A/B No 53, 46; *Reparation for Injuries*, ICJ Reports 1949 p 174, 186.

[130] See GCHS, 29 April 1958, 450 UNTS 82, Art 11; ILC *Ybk* 1982/II, 41–2.

[131] ILC *Ybk* 1951/I, 366–78; ILC *Ybk* 1962/I, 229–31, 288–90.

[132] On *Genocide*: McNair (1961) 167–8. On *Nottebohm*: Flegenheimer (1958) 25 ILR 91, 148–50.

In practice open defiance of the Court's authority is rare.[133] Although its judgments are only binding between the parties, and not binding at all in the case of an advisory opinion, the Court's uninterrupted history, stated preference for consistency and wide jurisdiction *ratione materiae* have resulted in its pronouncements on issues of substance being given great weight.

Moreover, the Court has proved influential in defining the procedural law of international courts and tribunals, such that some commentators have now begun to refer to 'a common law of international adjudication'.[134] Whilst it is correct to state that in international law 'every tribunal is a self-contained system (unless otherwise provided)',[135] the Court's lengthy period of operation—throughout much of which it was the only international tribunal of any significance—has enabled it to lay down a body of procedural case-law which was and is a natural source of inspiration for later tribunals.

(D) DECISIONS OF NATIONAL COURTS[136]

Article 38(1)(d) of the Statute of the International Court is not limited to international decisions. Decisions of national courts also have value. Some decisions provide indirect evidence of the practice of the forum state on the question involved. Others involve an independent investigation of a point of law and a consideration of available sources, and thus may offer a careful exposition of the law. Municipal judicial decisions have been an important source of material on the recognition of governments and states, state succession, sovereign immunity, diplomatic immunity, extradition, war crimes, belligerent occupation, the concept of a 'state of war', and the law of prize.[137] However, the value of these decisions varies considerably, and individual decisions may present a narrow, parochial outlook or rest on an inadequate use of sources. A further problem arises from the sheer number of domestic decisions touching on international law. While the most significant of these may be widely circulated,[138] others go unnoticed.

---

[133] Cf the decision of the ICTY in *Prosecutor v Tadić* (1999) 124 ILR 61, 98–121, which disagreed with the International Court's requirement of effective control when attributing the conduct of private actors to a state under the rules of state responsibility, as laid down in *Nicaragua*, ICJ Reports 1986 p 14, 61–5. The International Court reasserted the view in *Nicaragua* in *Genocide (Croatia v Serbia)*, ICJ Reports 2007 p 43, 209–11. Further: Cassese (2007) 18 *EJIL* 649.

[134] Generally: Brown, *A Common Law of International Adjudication* (2007).

[135] *Prosecutor v Tadić* (1995) 105 ILR 419, 458 (Jurisdiction).

[136] Generally: Lauterpacht (1929) 10 *BY* 65. Further: Falk, *The Role of Domestic Courts in the International Legal Order* (1964); Nollkaemper, *National Courts and the International Rule of Law* (2011).

[137] See *The Scotia*, 81 US 170 (1871); *The Paquete Habana*, 175 US 677 (1900); *The Zamora* [1916] 2 AC 77; *Gibbs v Rodríguez* (1951) 18 ILR 661; *Lauritzen v Government of Chile* (1956) 23 ILR 708.

[138] E.g. *Minister of State for Immigration and Ethnic Affairs v Teoh* (1995) 104 ILR 460; *Reference re Secession of Quebec* (1998) 115 ILR 536; *R v Bow Street Metropolitan Stipendiary Magistrate, ex parte Pinochet Ugarte (No 3)* [2000] 1 AC 147; *Gaddafi* (2000) 125 ILR 490; *Sosa v Alvarez-Machain*, 542 US 692 (2004); *Hamdan v Rumsfeld*, 548 US 557 (2006). See generally the cases in the ILR and the ILDC.

7. OTHER MATERIAL SOURCES

(A) THE CONCLUSIONS OF INTERNATIONAL CONFERENCES

The 'final act' or other statement of conclusions of a conference of states may be a form of multilateral treaty, but, even if it is an instrument recording decisions not adopted unanimously, the result may constitute cogent evidence of the state of the law on the subject. Even before the necessary ratifications are received, a convention embodied in a Final Act and expressed as a codification of existing principles may be influential.[139]

(B) RESOLUTIONS OF THE GENERAL ASSEMBLY

General Assembly resolutions are not binding on member states except on certain UN organizational matters. However, when they are concerned with general norms of international law, acceptance by all or most members constitutes *evidence* of the opinions of governments in what is the widest forum for the expression of such opinions.[140] Even when resolutions are framed as general principles, they can provide a basis for the progressive development of the law and, if substantially unanimous, for the speedy consolidation of customary rules. Examples of important 'law-making' resolutions include the General Assembly's Affirmation of the Principles of International Law recognized by the Charter of the Nürnberg Tribunal;[141] the Declaration on the Granting of Independence to Colonial Countries and Peoples;[142] the Declaration of Legal Principles Governing Activities of States in the Exploration and Use of Outer Space;[143] the Rio Declaration on Environment and Development,[144] and the UN Declaration on the Rights of Indigenous Peoples.[145] In some cases a resolution may have effect as an authoritative interpretation and application of the principles of the Charter: this is true notably of the Friendly Relations Declaration of 1970.[146] But each resolution must be assessed in the light of all the circumstances, including other available evidence of the states' opinions on the point or points in issue.

(C) THE WRITINGS OF PUBLICISTS[147]

The Statute of the International Court includes, among the 'subsidiary means for the determination of rules of law', 'the teachings of the most highly qualified publicists

---

[139] See *Re Cámpora* (1957) 24 ILR 518, *Namibia*, ICJ Reports 1971 p 16, 47.

[140] *Nicaragua*, ICJ Reports 1986 p 14, 98–104, 107–8.

[141] GA Res 95(I), 11 December 1946, adopted unanimously.

[142] GA Res 1514(XV), 14 December 1960 (89–0:9).

[143] GA Res 1962(XVIII), 13 December 1963, adopted unanimously.

[144] GA Res 47/190, 22 December 1992, adopted without a vote.

[145] GA Res 61/295, 13 September 2007 (144–4:11).

[146] Declaration on Principles of International Law Concerning Friendly Relations, GA Res 2625(XXV), 24 October 1970, adopted without vote.

[147] Generally: Lauterpacht (1958) 23–5; Allott (1971) 45 *BY* 79; Cheng (ed), *International Law* (1982); Westberg & Marchais (1992) 7 *ICSID Rev-FILJ* 453; Jennings, in Makarczyk (ed), *Theory of International Law*

of the various nations' or, in the French text, 'la doctrine'. The phrase 'most highly qualified' is—fortunately or otherwise—not given a restrictive effect, but authority naturally affects weight. In some areas individual writers have had a formative influence. However, subjective factors enter into any assessment of juristic opinion and individual writers will tend to reflect national and other prejudices; further, some publicists see themselves to be propagating new and better views rather than providing a presentation of the existing law, a tendency the more widespread given increasing specialization.

Whatever the grounds for caution, the opinions of publicists enjoy wide use. Arbitral tribunals and national courts make sometimes copious reference to jurists' writings. National courts are generally unfamiliar with state practice and are ready to rely on secondary sources as a substitute. Ostensibly the International Court might seem to make little or no use of jurists' writings.[148] However this is because of the process of collective drafting of judgments, and the need to avoid an invidious selection of citations. The fact that the Court makes use of writers' work is evidenced by dissenting and separate opinions,[149] in which the 'workings' are set out in more detail, and which reflect the Court's actual methods. There are many references to writers in pleadings before the Court.

(D) CODIFICATION AND THE WORK OF THE INTERNATIONAL LAW COMMISSION

A source analogous to the writings of publicists, and at least as authoritative, is the work of the ILC, including its articles and commentaries, reports, and secretariat memoranda. Also in the same category are the bases of discussion of the 1930 Hague Codification Conference, and (though to a lesser extent) the reports and resolutions of the Institute of International Law and other expert bodies.[150]

---

at the Threshold of the 21st Century (1996) 413; Rosenne, *The Perplexities of Modern International Law* (2004) 51–3; Wood, 'Teachings of the Most Highly Qualified Publicists' (2010) *MPEPIL*.

[148] But see the *Wimbledon* (1923) PCIJ Ser A No 1, 28 ('general opinion'); *German Settlers in Poland* (1923) PCIJ, Ser B No 6, 6, 36 ('almost universal opinion'); *Question of Jaworzina* (1923) PCIJ Ser B No 8, 37 ('*doctrine constante*'); *German Interests,* Preliminary Objections (1925) PCIJ Ser A No 6, 20 ('the "teachings of legal authorities"', 'the jurisprudence of the principal countries'); *Lotus* (1927) PCIJ Ser A No 10, 26 ('teachings of publicists', 'all or nearly all writers'); *Nottebohm,* Second Phase, ICJ Reports 1955 p 4, 22 ('the writings of publicists'). Also: *Application of the Convention on the Prevention and Punishment of the Crime of Genocide (Bosnia and Herzegovina v Serbia and Montenegro),* ICJ Reports 2007 p 43, 125, referring to Lemkin, *Axis Rule in Occupied Europe* (1944) 79.

[149] *Diversion of Water from the Meuse* (1937) PCIJ Ser A/B No 70, 76–7 (Judge Hudson); *South West Africa,* ICJ Reports 1950 p 128, 146–9 (Judge McNair); *Peace Treaties,* Second Phase, ICJ Reports 1950 p 221, 235 (Judge Read, diss); *Asylum,* ICJ Reports 1950 p 266, 335–7 (Judge Azevedo, diss); *Temple,* ICJ Reports 1962 p 6, 39–41 (Vice-President Alfaro); *Gabčíkovo-Nagymaros Project (Hungary/Slovakia),* ICJ Reports 1997 p 7, 88–119 (Judge Weeramantry); *Pulp Mills,* Judgment of 20 April 2010, Joint dissenting opinion of Judges Al-Khasawneh & Simma, §§3, 12, 14.

[150] E.g. the reference to ALRC 24, *Foreign State Immunity* (1984) in *KPMG Peat Marwick v Davison* (1997) 104 ILR 526, 616 (NZCA) and *Zhang v Jiang* (2008) 141 ILR 542 (NSWCA).

Narrowly defined, codification involves the comprehensive setting down of the *lex lata* and the approval of the resulting text by a law-determining agency. The process has been carried out historically at international conferences, beginning with the First and Second Hague Peace Conferences of 1899 and 1907, and by groups of experts whose drafts were the subjects of conferences sponsored by the League of Nations or by the American states. However, the ILC, created as a subsidiary organ of the General Assembly in 1947 on the basis of Article 13(1)(a) of the Charter, has had more success in the process of codification than the League bodies had.[151] Its membership combines technical qualities and civil service experience, so that its drafts may reflect solutions acceptable to governments. Moreover, it reflects a variety of political and regional standpoints. In practice the ILC has found it impossible to maintain a strict separation of its tasks of codification and of 'progressive development' of the law. Its work on various topics, notably the law of the sea, has provided the basis for successful conferences of plenipotentiaries and for the resulting multilateral conventions. In 2001 it adopted its Articles on Responsibility of States for Internationally Wrongful Acts following nearly four decades of work, but expressed the view that there was no immediate need to convene a conference for their adoption as a treaty.[152] They have been relied upon extensively by international courts and tribunals as an authoritative statement of the law on state responsibility.[153]

8. OTHER CONSIDERATIONS APPLICABLE IN JUDICIAL REASONING

(A) EQUITY IN THE JURISPRUDENCE OF THE INTERNATIONAL COURT

'Equity' refers to considerations of fairness and reasonableness often necessary for the application of settled rules of law. Equity is not itself a source of law, yet it may be an important factor in the process of decision-making. Equity may play a significant role in supplementing the law, or may unobtrusively enter judicial reasoning. In *Diversion of Water from the River Meuse* Judge Hudson applied the principle that equality is equity, and stated as a corollary that a state requesting the interpretation of a treaty must itself have fulfilled its treaty obligations. He observed that under 'Article 38 of the Statute, if not independently of that Article, the Court has some freedom to consider

---

[151] GA Res 174(II), 21 November 1947. On the ILC's work: Briggs, *The International Law Commission* (1965); United Nations, *International Law on the Eve of the Twenty-first Century* (1997); Watts (ed), 1–4 *The International Law Commission 1949–1998* (1999–2010); Morton, *The International Law Commission of the United Nations* (2000); Rao, 'International Law Commission' (2006) *MPEPIL*; United Nations, *The Work of the International Law Commission* (7th edn, 2007).

[152] ILC *Ybk* 2001/II, 31.

[153] Also: Crawford, Pellet & Olleson (eds), *The Law of International Responsibility* (2010). Further: chapters 25–7.

principles of equity as part of the international law which it must apply'.[154] For its part the Court focused on the interpretation of the relevant treaty.

In *North Sea Continental Shelf*[155] the Court had to resort to the formulation of equitable principles concerning the lateral delimitation of adjacent areas of the continental shelf. This was a consequence of its opinion that GCCS Article 6 did not represent customary law. In *Fisheries Jurisdiction (UK v Iceland)* the International Court outlined an 'equitable solution' to the differences over fishing rights and directed the parties to negotiate accordingly.[156] In *Frontier Dispute (Burkina Faso/Mali)* the Chamber of the Court applied the principle of 'equity *infra legem*' to the division of a frontier pool.[157]

Reference should also be made to Article 38(2),[158] which provides: '[t]his provision shall not prejudice the power of the Court to decide a case *ex aequo et bono*, if the parties agree thereto'. The power of decision *ex aequo et bono* involves elements of compromise and conciliation, whereas equity in the general sense ('equity *infra legem*') finds application as part of the normal judicial function. In *Free Zones* the Permanent Court, under an agreement between France and Switzerland, was asked to settle the questions involved in the execution of a provision in the Treaty of Versailles.[159] While the Court had to decide on the future customs regime of the zones, the agreement contained no reference to any decision *ex aequo et bono*. Switzerland argued that the Court should work on the basis of existing rights, and, by a technical majority including the vote of the President, the Court agreed. It said:

... even assuming that it were not incompatible with the Court's Statute for the Parties to give the Court power to prescribe a settlement disregarding rights recognized by it and taking into account considerations of pure expediency only, such power, which would be of an absolutely exceptional character, could only be derived from a clear and explicit provision to the effect, which is not to be found in the Special Agreement ...[160]

The majority doubted the Court's power to give decisions *ex aequo et bono*, but it would be unwise to draw general conclusions since much turned on the nature of the agreement. Additionally, the majority regarded the power to decide cases *ex aequo et bono* as distinct from the notion of equity. However, the terminology is not well settled. The

---

[154] *Diversion of Water from the Meuse* (1937) PCIJ Ser A/B No 70, 73 (Judge Hudson). Also *Wimbledon* (1923) PCIJ Ser A No 1, 32 (on the currency in which the damages are to be paid). Instances of equity in arbitral jurisprudence include *Orinoco Steamship Co* (1910) 1 HCR 228; *Norwegian Shipowners* (1922) 1 ILR 189; *Eastern Extension, Australasia and China Telegraph Company, Limited* (1923) 6 RIAA 112; *Trail Smelter* (1941) 9 ILR 315.

[155] ICJ Reports 1969 p 3, 46–52, 131–5 (Judge Ammoun); 165–8 (Vice-President Koretsky, diss); 192–6 (Judge Tanaka, diss); 207–9 (Judge Morelli, diss); 257 (Judge Sørensen, diss).

[156] ICJ Reports 1974 p 3, 30–5.

[157] ICJ Reports 1986 p 554, 631–3. Also: *Review of UNAT Judgment No 273*, ICJ Reports 1982 p 325, 536–7 (Judge Schwebel, diss).

[158] Judge Kellogg thought otherwise but was in error. *Free Zones*, Second Phase (1930) PCIJ Ser A No 24, 39–40 (Judge Kellogg). See *North Sea Continental Shelf*, ICJ Reports 1969 p 3, 48.

[159] *Free Zones* (1930) PCIJ Ser A No 24, 4. Cf the earlier phase (1929) PCIJ Ser A No 22. Also: Lauterpacht, *Function of Law* (1933) 318; Lauterpacht (1958) 213–17.

[160] *Free Zones* (1930) PCIJ Ser A No 24, 10.

drafters of the General Act of Geneva of 1928[161] apparently regarded a settlement *ex aequo et bono* as synonymous with equity. The converse, where 'equity' refers to settlement *ex aequo et bono*, has arisen in some arbitration agreements. On occasion equity is treated as the equivalent of general principles of law.[162]

(B) CONSIDERATIONS OF HUMANITY

Considerations of humanity will depend on the judge's subjective appreciation, a factor which cannot be excluded. However, these considerations may relate to human values already protected by positive legal principles which, taken together, reveal certain criteria of public policy and invite analogy. Such criteria are connected with general principles of law and equity, and need no particular justification. References to principles or laws of humanity appear in preambles to conventions,[163] in GA resolutions,[164] and in diplomatic practice. The classic reference is a passage from *Corfu Channel*,[165] in which the Court relied on certain 'general and well-recognized principles', including 'elementary considerations of humanity, even more exacting in peace than in war'. On occassions the provisions of the UN Charter concerning the protection of human rights and fundamental freedoms have seen use as a basis for the legal status of considerations of humanity.[166]

(C) 'LEGITIMATE INTERESTS'

In particular contexts the applicability of rules of law may depend on criteria of good faith, reasonableness, and the like. Legitimate interests, including economic interests, may in these circumstances be taken into account. Recognition of legitimate interests explains the extent of acquiescence in the face of claims to the continental shelf and to fishing zones. In this type of situation it is, of course, acquiescence and recognition that provide the formal bases for the development of the new rules. In *Anglo-Norwegian Fisheries* the Court did not purport to be doing anything other than applying existing rules, but it had to justify this special application of the normal rules to the Norwegian

---

[161] General Act for the Pacific Settlement of International Disputes, 26 September 1928, 93 LNTS 343, Art 28. The provision was copied in other treaties.

[162] E.g. *Norwegian Shipowners* (1922) 1 ILR 189, 370.

[163] See especially preamble to the Hague Convention Concerning the Laws and Customs of War on Land, 18 October 1907, 36 Stat 2227: 'Until a more complete code of the laws of war has been issued, the High Contracting Parties deem it expedient to declare that, in cases not included in the Regulations adopted by them, the inhabitants and the belligerents remain under the protection and the rule of the principles of the law of nations, as they result from the usages established among civilized peoples, from the laws of humanity, and the dictates of the public conscience'. This is known as the Martens clause.

[164] E.g. Declaration on the Prohibition of the Use of Nuclear and Thermo-nuclear Weapons, GA Res 1653(XVI), 24 November 1961.

[165] ICJ Reports 1949 p 4, 22. The statement referred to Albania's duty to warn of the presence of mines in its waters. See also *Nicaragua*, ICJ Reports 1986 p 14, 112–14; Thirlway (1990) 61 BY 1, 6–13.

[166] In *South West Africa*, Second Phase, ICJ Reports 1966 p 6, 34, the Court held that humanitarian considerations were not decisive. But see ibid, 252–3, 270, 294–9 (Judge Tanaka, diss).

coastline. In doing so it referred to 'certain economic interests peculiar to a region, the reality and importance of which are clearly evidenced by a long usage'.[167] It also referred to traditional fishing rights buttressed by 'the vital needs of the population' in determining particular baselines.[168]

Judge McNair, dissenting, expressed disquiet:

In my opinion the manipulation of the limits of territorial waters for the purpose of protecting economic and other social interests has no justification in law; moreover, the approbation of such a practice would have a dangerous tendency in that it would encourage States to adopt a subjective appreciation of their rights instead of conforming to a common international standard.[169]

This caution is justified, but the law is inevitably bound up with the accommodation of different interests, and the application of rules usually requires an element of appreciation.

---

[167] ICJ Reports 1951 p 116, 133. Also ibid, 128: 'In these barren regions the inhabitants of the coastal zone derive their livelihood essentially from fishing'. Further: Fitzmaurice (1953) 30 BY 1, 69–70; Fitzmaurice (1957) 92 Hague Recueil 5, 112–16; Thirlway (1990) 61 BY 1, 13–20.

[168] ICJ Reports 1951 p 116, 142.

[169] ICJ Reports 1951 p 116, 169 (Judge McNair, diss).

3

THE RELATIONS OF INTERNATIONAL AND NATIONAL LAW

1. THEORETICAL APPROACHES[1]

The relationship between international and national law[2] is often presented as a clash at a level of high theory, usually between 'dualism' and 'monism'. Dualism emphasizes the distinct and independent character of the international and national legal systems.[3] International law is perceived as a law between states whereas national law applies within a state, regulating the relations of its citizens with each other and with that state. Neither legal order has the power to create or alter rules of the other. When international law applies in whole or in part within any national legal system, this is because of a rule of that system giving effect to international law. In case of a conflict between international law and national law, the dualist would assume that a national court would apply national law, or at least that it is for the national system to decide which rule is to prevail.

Monism postulates that national and international law form one single legal order, or at least a number of interlocking orders which should be presumed to be coherent and consistent. On that basis international law can be applied directly within the national legal order. This position is represented by jurists whose views diverge in significant respects. Hersch Lauterpacht was a forceful exponent of a version of monism; he emphasized that individuals are the ultimate subjects of international law, representing both the justification and moral limit of the legal order.[4] The state

---

[1] Triepel (1923) 1 Hague *Recueil* 77; Kelsen, *Principles of International Law* (2nd edn, 1967) 290, 551; Lauterpacht, 1 *International Law: Collected Papers* (1970) 151; Santulli, *Le statut international de l'ordre juridique étatique* (2001); Nijman & Nollkaemper (eds), *New Perspectives on the Divide Between National and International Law* (2007); cf Denza, in Evans (ed), *International Law* (3rd edn, 2010) 411, 417–18.

[2] Terminology is not consistent; the terms 'national', 'municipal', 'domestic', and 'internal' are all used to refer to the legal order of or within the state, although the terms have slightly different connotations. Here the term used is 'national', but it includes local or regional as well as central laws and institutions.

[3] Gaja, in Nijman & Nollkaemper (2007) 52.

[4] Lauterpacht, *International Law and Human Rights* (1950) 70.

is disliked as an abstraction and distrusted as a vehicle for maintaining human rights. International law is seen as the best available moderator of human affairs, and also as a condition of the *legal* existence of states and therefore of the national legal systems.[5]

Hans Kelsen developed monist principles on the basis of formal methods of analysis dependent on a theory of knowledge.[6] According to Kelsen, monism is scientifically established if international and national law are part of the same system of norms receiving their validity and content by an intellectual operation involving the assumption of a single basic norm (*Grundnorm*). Only that assumption makes sense of the shared normativity of law. This basic norm he formulates, with nice circularity, as follows: 'The states ought to behave as they have customarily behaved'.[7] International law in turn contains a principle of effectiveness, which allows revolution to be a law-creating fact and accepts as legitimate the historically first legislators of a state. This, as if by delegation, provides the basic norm of national legal orders; the whole legal ordering of humanity is at once presupposed and integrated: 'Since the basic norms of the national legal orders are determined by a norm of international law, they are basic norms only in a relative sense. It is the basic norm of the international legal order which is the ultimate reason of validity of the national legal orders, too'.[8]

Thus Kelsen developed a monist theory of the relation between international and national law.[9] Law is a hierarchical system whereby each legal norm derives its validity from a higher norm. This chain of validity can be traced to the *Grundnorm*, which is not a norm of positive law but rather a 'hypothesis of juristic thinking'.[10] International and national law form a single system of norms because they receive their validity from the same source:[11] the *Grundnorm* evidently has a lot to answer for. But Kelsen's theory is complicated in that he considered it equally possible that the relationship between legal orders could be conceived on the basis of the primacy of national law

---

[5] 1 Oppenheim (8th edn, 1955) 38: '… it is only by reference to a higher legal rule in relation to which they are all equal, that the equality and independence of a number of sovereign States can be conceived. Failing that superior legal order, the science of law would be confronted with the spectacle of some sixty sovereign States, each claiming to be the absolutely highest and underived authority'.

[6] Kelsen, *General Theory of Law and State* (1945) 363; Kelsen (2nd edn, 1967) 553. For views related to but not identical with those of Kelsen: Verdross (1927) 16 Hague *Recueil* 247, 287; Kunz (1924) 10 *GST* 115; Starke (1936) 17 *BY* 661. On Kelsen: Kammerhofer (2009) 22 *LJIL* 225; von Bernstorff, *The Public International Law Theory of Hans Kelsen* (2010); Kammerhofer, *Uncertainty in International Law* (2011); Kammerhofer, in Orakhelashvili (ed), *Research Handbook on the History and Theory of International Law* (2011) 143.

[7] Kelsen (2nd edn, 1967) 564. This was Kelsen's second attempt at the basic norm; the first was *pacta sunt servanda* (Kelsen, *Das Problem der Souveränität und die Theorie des Völkerrechts* (2nd edn, 1928) 217), which was later subsumed within the *Grundnorm*: Kelsen, *Reine Rechtslehre* (1934) 130. Further: Koskenniemi, *The Gentle Civilizer of Nations* (2001) ch 3; Koskenniemi, *From Apology to Utopia* (2nd edn, 2005) 226–40.

[8] Kelsen (1945) 367; Kelsen (2nd edn, 1967) 562.

[9] Kelsen (1945) 363; Kelsen (2nd edn, 1967) 553. For criticism of Kelsen's theory of the unity of all law: Hart, *Essays in Jurisprudence and Philosophy* (1983) 309.

[10] Kelsen (2nd edn, 1967) 559.

[11] Ibid, 564.

rather than of international law.[12] The choice between these alternatives is to be made on political rather than legal grounds.[13]

Faced with this apparent impasse, it seems natural to seek to escape from the dichotomy of monism and dualism. Above all, neither theory offers an adequate account of the *practice* of international and national courts, whose role in articulating the positions of the various legal systems is crucial. Fitzmaurice attempted to by-pass the debate by arguing that there was no common field of operation: the two systems do not come into conflict *as systems* since they work in different spheres, each supreme in its own field.[14] However, there could be a conflict of *obligations*, an inability of the state on the domestic plane to act in the manner required by international law in some respect: the consequence of this will not be the invalidity of state law but the responsibility of the state on the international plane.[15] Rousseau propounded similar views, characterizing international law as a law of co-ordination which does not provide for automatic abrogation of national rules in conflict with obligations on the international plane, instead international law deals with incompatibility between national and international law through state responsibility.[16]

In considering these and later contributions to the debate about the relations between legal systems, it seems desirable to leave behind the glacial uplands of juristic abstraction. In fact legal systems are experienced by those who work within them as having relative autonomy (how much autonomy depends on the power and disposition of each system, and varies over time). The only theory which can adequately account for that fact is some form of pluralism.[17] Each legal system has, almost by definition, its own approach to the others (though in practice there is much borrowing). To talk of 'national law' is to generalize; but as soon as one asks what approach a given system (international law, English law, French law ...) takes to another, the mist clears: it is possible to state the position with clarity and to understand that each system reserves to itself the authority to determine for the time being the extent and terms of interpenetration of laws and related issues of the separation of powers.

---

[12] Ibid, 580.

[13] Ibid, 587–8.

[14] Fitzmaurice (1957) 92 Hague *Recueil* 1, 68.

[15] Ibid, 79. Anzilotti, 1 *Cours de droit international* (1929) 57, puts forward this view, but is often classified as a dualist.

[16] Rousseau (1958) 93 Hague *Recueil* 369, 473. Rousseau asserts the primacy of international law—but by this means primacy in its own field.

[17] To talk simply of dualism is to imply that national legal systems all have the same features. Why should this be? The US is not the Federal Republic of Germany; their relation is international not constitutional, but international law holds them apart; it does not unify them: e.g. Cohen, in Besson & Tasioulas (eds), *The Philosophy of International Law* (2010) ch 12. For EU law, which unifies to a degree: Slaughter & Burke-White, in Nijman & Nollkaemper (2007) 110.

2. RELATIONS OF INTERNATIONAL AND NATIONAL LAW: AN OVERVIEW

(A) INTERNATIONAL LAW'S APPROACH TO NATIONAL LAW[18]

(i) In general

Here the position is not in doubt. A state cannot plead provisions of its own law or deficiencies in that law in answer to a claim against it for a breach of its obligations under international law.[19] This principle is reflected in Article 3 of the ILC's Articles on Responsibility of States for Internationally Wrongful Acts which provides that:

The characterization of an act of a State as internationally wrongful is governed by international law. Such characterization is not affected by the characterization of the same act as lawful by internal law.[20]

Arbitral tribunals,[21] the Permanent Court,[22] and the International Court[23] have consistently endorsed this position. It goes back to *Alabama Claims*,[24] where the US recovered damages from Great Britain for breach of its obligations as a neutral during the Civil War. The absence of legislation to prevent the fitting out of commerce raiders in British ports or to stop them leaving port to join the Confederate forces provided no defence to the claim. In *Free Zones* the Permanent Court observed '... it is certain that France cannot rely on her own legislation to limit the scope of her international obligations ...'.[25] The same principle applies where the provisions of a state's constitution are relied upon. In the words of the Permanent Court:

a State cannot adduce as against another State its own Constitution with a view to evading obligations incumbent upon it under international law or treaties in force. Applying these

---

[18] Dupuy, in Crawford, Pellet & Olleson (eds), *The Law of International Responsibility* (2010) 173; Denza, in Evans (3rd edn, 2010) 411, 412–17; Lauterpacht, *Development* (1958) 262, 314, 332; Fitzmaurice (1957) 92 Hague *Recueil* 1, 85.

[19] VCLT, 22 May 1969, 1155 UNTS 331, Art 27, referring to justification for failure to perform a treaty. Cf VCLT, Art 46, permitting a state to argue the invalidation of consent by reason of the violation of its internal law where the violation was 'manifest and concerned a rule of its internal law of fundamental importance'. Further: chapter 16.

[20] Appended to GA Res 56/83, 12 December 2001. Also: Draft Declaration on Rights and Duties of States, GA Res 375(IV), 6 December 1949, Art 13.

[21] *Shufeldt* (1920) 2 RIAA 1081, 1098; *Norwegian Shipowners* (1922) 1 RIAA 309, 331.

[22] *SS Wimbledon* (1923) PCIJ Ser A No 1, 29; *Jurisdiction of the Courts of Danzig* (1928) PCIJ Ser B No 15, 26; *Free Zones of Upper Savoy and the District of Gex* (1930) PCIJ Ser A No 24, 12.

[23] The leading cases are *Fisheries (UK v Norway)*, ICJ Reports 1951 p 116, 132; *Applicability of the Obligation to Arbitrate under Section 21 of the United Nations Headquarters Agreement of 26 June 1947*, ICJ Reports 1988 p 12, 34; *Elettronica Sicula SpA (ELSI) (US v Italy)*, ICJ Reports 1989 p 15, 51, 74; *Avena and Other Mexican Nationals (Mexico v US)*, ICJ Reports 2004 p 12, 65.

[24] Moore, 1 *Int Arb* 653.

[25] *Free Zones of Upper Savoy and the District of Gex* (1932) PCIJ Ser A/B No 46, 96, 167. Also: *Greco-Bulgarian Communities* (1930) PCIJ Ser B No 17, 32.

principles to the present case, it results that the question of the treatment of Polish nationals or other persons of Polish origin or speech must be settled exclusively on the basis of the
rules of international law and the treaty provisions in force between Poland and Danzig.[26]

An associated question is whether the mere enactment of legislation can give rise
to international responsibility, or whether an obligation is only breached when the
state implements that legislation. There is a general duty to bring national law into
conformity with obligations under international law,[27] but what this entails depends
on the obligation in question. Normally a failure to bring about such conformity is
not in itself a breach of international law; that arises only when the state concerned
fails to observe its obligations on a specific occasion.[28] But in some circumstances
legislation (in its absence) could of itself constitute a breach of an international obligation, for example where a state is required to prohibit certain conduct or to enact a
uniform law.

(ii) National laws as 'facts' before international tribunals

In *Certain German Interests in Polish Upper Silesia*, the Permanent Court observed:

From the standpoint of International Law and of the Court which is its organ, national laws
are merely facts which express the will and constitute the activities of States, in the same
manner as do legal decisions or administrative measures. The Court is certainly not called
upon to interpret the Polish law as such; but there is nothing to prevent the Court's giving
judgment on the question whether or not, in applying that law, Poland is acting in conformity with its obligations towards Germany under the Geneva Convention.[29]

Thus a decision of a national court or a legislative measure may constitute evidence of
a breach of a treaty or of customary international law.[30] However, the general proposition that international tribunals take account of national laws only as facts 'is, at
most ... debatable'.[31]

The concept of national law as 'merely facts' has at least six distinct aspects.

(a) National law may itself constitute, or be evidence of, conduct in violation of a
rule of treaty or customary law.

(b) National law may be part of the 'applicable law' either governing the basis of a
claim or more commonly governing a particular issue.

(c) Whereas the principle *iura novit curia* applies to international law, it does not
apply to matters of national law. International tribunals will generally require proof of

---

[26] *Treatment of Polish Nationals in the Danzig Territory* (1932) PCIJ Ser A/B No 44, 24. Also: *Georges
Pinson (France) v United Mexican States* (1928) 5 RIAA 327.

[27] *Exchange of Greek and Turkish Populations* (1925) PCIJ Ser B No 10, 20. The principle applies to both
unitary and federal states.

[28] McNair, *Treaties* (1961) 100. Cf Fitzmaurice (1957) 92 Hague *Recueil* 1, 89.

[29] (1926) PCIJ Ser A No 7, 19.

[30] *India—Patents*, WTO Doc WT/DS50/AB/R, 15 December 1997, §65.

[31] Jenks, *The Prospects of International Adjudication* (1964) 552, 548.

national law, although they may also (subject to due process constraints) undertake their own researches.[32]

(d) When called upon to apply national law an international tribunal should seek to apply that law as it would be applied in the state concerned.[33] It is for each state, in the first instance, to interpret its own laws.[34] International tribunals are not courts of appeal and they do not have the authority to substitute their own interpretation of national law for those of the national authorities, especially when that interpretation is given by the highest national courts. In many situations an international tribunal must simply take note of the outcome of a domestic decision and then deal with its international implications.[35] It will only be in exceptional circumstances that an international tribunal will depart from the construction adopted by a national authority of its own law, such as where a manifestly incorrect interpretation is put forward in the context of a pending case.[36]

(e) International tribunals cannot declare the unconstitutionality or invalidity of rules of national law as such.[37] Only if it is transparently clear that a national law would be treated as unconstitutional or invalid by the national courts should an international tribunal follow suit.

(f) The proposition that an international tribunal 'does not interpret national law as such'[38] is open to question. When it is called on to apply rules of national law, an international tribunal will interpret and apply domestic rules as such.[39] This may occur in a variety of circumstances. First there is the case of *renvoi*: in *Lighthouses*, for example, the special agreement required the court to decide if the contracts had been 'duly entered into' under Ottoman law.[40] Or international law may designate a system of domestic

---

[32] *Brazilian Loans* (1929) PCIJ Ser A No 21, 124–5; *Nottebohm (Liechtenstein v Guatemala)*, Second Phase, ICJ Reports 1955 p 4, 35 (Judge Read, diss), 51 (Judge Guggenheim, diss); *United States—Carbon Steel*, WTO Doc WT/DS213/AB/R, 28 November 2002, §157.

[33] *Serbian Loans* (1929) PCIJ Ser A No 20, 46; *Brazilian Loans* (1929) PCIJ Ser A No 21, 125: 'It is French legislation, as applied in France, which really constitutes French law.'

[34] *Ahmadou Sadio Diallo (Republic of Guinea v Democratic Republic of the Congo)*, Judgment of 30 November 2010, §70. Also: *Panevezys-Saldutiskis Railway* (1939) PCIJ Ser A/B No 76, 19.

[35] *Anglo-Norwegian Fisheries*, ICJ Reports 1951 p 116, 181 (Judge McNair); *Certain Questions of Mutual Assistance in Criminal Matters (France v Djibouti)*, ICJ Reports 2008 p 177, 230.

[36] *Diallo*, Judgment of 30 November 2010, §70. Also: *Fraport AG Frankfurt Airport Services Worldwide v Philippines*, 23 December 2010, §§236, 242, available at www.italaw.com.

[37] *Interpretation of the Statute of the Memel Territory* (1932) PCIJ Ser A/B No 49, 294, 336; *International Responsibility for the Promulgation of Laws in Violation of the Convention (Article 1 and 2 of the American Convention on Human Rights)* (1994) 116 ILR 320, 332.

[38] The PCIJ in *Upper Silesia* was not unequivocal in its remark that the Court was 'not called upon to interpret the Polish law as such': (1926) PCIJ Ser A, No 7, 19. Also: *Nottebohm*, Second Phase, ICJ Reports 1955 p 4, 36 (Judge Read, diss), 52 (Judge Guggenheim, diss); *Application of the Convention of 1902 governing the Guardianship of Infants (Netherlands v Sweden)*, ICJ Reports 1958 p 55, 108 (Judge Moreno Quintana).

[39] *Guardianship of Infants*, ICJ Reports 1958 p 55, 91 (Judge Lauterpacht); *Southern Pacific Properties (Middle East) Limited v Arab Republic of Egypt* (1988) 3 ICSID Reports 131, 141.

[40] *Lighthouses in Crete and Samos* (1934) PCIJ Ser A/B No 62, 19.

law as the applicable law in respect of some claim or transaction.[41] Where relevant issues (whether classified as 'facts' or otherwise) require investigation of national law, the Court has made the necessary findings.

(iii) Treatment of national law by international tribunals

Cases where a tribunal dealing with issues of international law has to examine the national law of one or more states are by no means exceptional.[42] The spheres of competence claimed by states, represented by territory, jurisdiction, and nationality of individuals and legal persons, are delimited by legislation and judicial and administrative decisions. International law sets the limits of such competence, but in order to decide whether particular acts are in breach of obligations under treaties or customary law, the Court has had to examine national law relating to a wide range of topics including expropriation,[43] fishing limits,[44] nationality,[45] guardianship and welfare of infants,[46] the rights of shareholders in respect of damage suffered by corporations,[47] and the arbitrary arrest and expulsion of aliens.[48] National law is very frequently implicated in cases concerning individuals, including those relating to the protection of human rights and the exhaustion of local remedies.

A considerable number of treaties contain provisions referring directly to national law[49] or employing concepts which by implication are to be understood in the context of a particular national law.[50] Many treaties refer to 'nationals' of the contracting parties,[51] and the presumption is that the term connotes persons having that status under the internal law of one of the parties. Similarly, treaties often involve references to legal interests of individuals and corporations existing within the cadre of a given national law. Treaties having as their object the creation and maintenance of certain standards of treatment of minority groups or aliens may refer to a national law as a method of describing the status to be created and protected.[52] The protection of rights may be stipulated as being 'without discrimination' or as 'national treatment' for the

---

[41] *Serbian Loans* (1929) PCIJ Ser A No 20; *Brazilian Loans* (1929) PCIJ Ser A No 21.

[42] Marek (1962) 66 *RGDIP* 260; Stoll, *L'application et l'interprétation du droit interne par les juridictions internationales* (1962); Jenks (1964) 547; Santulli, *Le statut international de l'ordre juridique étatique* (2001).

[43] *Upper Silesia* (1926) PCIJ Ser A No 7.

[44] *Anglo-Norwegian Fisheries*, ICJ Reports 1951 p 116, 176 (Judge McNair, diss).

[45] *Nottebohm*, Second Phase, ICJ Reports 1955 p 4.

[46] *Guardianship of Infants*, ICJ Reports 1958 p 55.

[47] *Barcelona Traction, Light and Power Company Limited (Belgium v Spain)*, Second Phase, ICJ Reports 1970 p 3.

[48] *Diallo*, Judgment of 30 November 2010.

[49] E.g. the treaty considered in *Tokios Tokelés v Ukraine* (2004) 11 ICSID Reports 313.

[50] *Exchange of Greek and Turkish Populations* (1925) PCIJ Ser B No 10, 20.

[51] E.g. Convention on the Settlement of Investment Disputes between States and Nationals of Other States, 18 March 1965, 575 UNTS 159, Art 25(1), (2) (ICSID Convention).

[52] *Jurisdiction of the Courts of Danzig* (1928) PCIJ Ser B No 15; *Statute of the Memel Territory* (1932) PCIJ Ser A/B No 49.

categories concerned.[53] Controversy has been generated in relation to the meaning and scope of the so-called 'umbrella clause'[54] including the circumstances in which breach of a contract between an investor and a host state will also amount to a breach of such a clause contained in an investment treaty.[55] The better view is that, if the obligation in question is one which arises under national law, for example under a contract, it is only if in truth the obligation is breached that the umbrella clause has anything to operate upon: that clause does not 'internationalize' the contract.[56]

On occasion an international tribunal may be faced with the task of deciding issues solely on the basis of national law. *Serbian Loans*[57] concerned a dispute between the French bondholders of certain Serbian loans and the Serb-Croat-Slovene government, the former demanding loan service on a gold basis, the latter holding that payment in French paper currency was permissible. The French government took up the case of the French bondholders and the dispute was submitted to the Permanent Court. The Court emphasized its duty to exercise jurisdiction duly conferred by agreement, in the absence of provision to the contrary in the Statute.[58] On the merits the Court held that the substance of the debt and the validity of the clause defining the obligation of the debtor state were governed by Serbian law, but, with respect to the method of payment, the law applicable was that of the place of payment, in this case French law.

(B) INTERNATIONAL LAW BEFORE NATIONAL COURTS: GENERAL CONSIDERATIONS

(i) Establishing international law before national courts

An initial issue is whether the jurisdiction considers international law to be 'part of' (in the sense of generally available to) national law, a question that is often constitutional in character, and which may be answered differently for customary law and

---

[53] *German Settlers in Poland* (1923) PCIJ Ser B No 6; *Minority Schools in Albania* (1935) PCIJ Ser A/B No 64, 4. The Permanent Court did not regard formal equality as the only criterion of equal treatment. Further: Fitzmaurice (1959) 35 *BY* 183, 191.

[54] A typical formulation of such a clause is found in Art 7(2) of the German Model BIT (2008): 'Each Contracting State shall fulfil any other obligations it may have entered into with regard to investments in its territory by investors of the other Contracting State.'

[55] Crawford (2008) 24 *Arb Int* 351, 366. On the history of umbrella clauses: Sinclair (2004) 20 *Arb Int* 411.

[56] *SGS Société Générale de Surveillance SA v Philippines* (2003) 129 ILR 444, 490; *CMS Gas Transmission Company v Argentine Republic*, 25 September 2007, §§89–100; *Duke Energy Electroquil Partners & Electroquil SA v Republic of Ecuador*, 18 August 2008, §§317–25, both available at www.italaw.com. Outside the field of umbrella clauses, *Sandline International v Papua New Guinea* (1998) 117 ILR 552, 560–3, in holding a domestic contract internationalized was wrongly decided; also *Ioannis Kardassopoulos v Georgia*, 6 July 2007, §§171–94, available at www.italaw.com, which was really a case of estoppel.

[57] *Serbian Loans* (1929) PCIJ Ser A No 20. Also: *Brazilian Loans* (1929) PCIJ Ser A No 21; *Consistency of Certain Danzig Legislative Decrees with the Constitution of the Free City* (1935) PCIJ Ser A/B No 65; *Illinois Central Railroad Company (USA) v United Mexican States* (1926) 4 RIAA 21; *Norwegian Shipowners* (1922) 1 RIAA 309, 330.

[58] *Serbian Loans* (1929) PCIJ Ser A No 20, 19.

treaties.[59] Thus, the 1949 German *Grundgesetz* provides in Article 25 that '[t]he general rules of public international law shall be an integral part of federal law'. Where such a position is adopted, a national court will go about establishing the content of international law as a matter of legal argument.[60] Once a court has ascertained that there are no bars within its own legal system to applying the rules of international law or provisions of a treaty, the rules are accepted as rules of law and are not required to be established by evidence, as in the case of matters of fact and foreign law.[61] But in the case of international law, this process of judicial notice has a special character. In the first place, there is a serious problem involved in finding reliable information of international law, especially customary law, in the absence of formal proof and resort to expert witnesses. Secondly, issues of public policy and difficulties of obtaining evidence on larger issues of state relations combine to produce a procedure whereby the executive may be consulted on certain questions of mixed law and fact, for example, the existence of a state of war or the status of an entity claiming sovereign immunity.

Thus in France, for example, the Minister of Foreign Affairs may give an interpretation of a treaty to a court, which may then be relied upon in later cases involving the same provision.[62] Detailed research is normally out of the question, and counsel cannot always fill the gap. In these circumstances it is hardly surprising that courts have historically leaned heavily on the opinions of writers, though modern practice—at least in England—has tended to steer away from academic commentaries as a source of law.[63] It can happen that a national court itself makes a full investigation of all the legal sources,[64] including treaties and state practice—yet here also works of authority may be relied upon as repositories and assessors of state practice. Reference may also be made to decisions of international tribunals[65] and the work of the ILC.[66]

---

[59] Generally: Shelton (ed), *International Law and Domestic Legal Systems* (2011). Also: Denza, in Evans (3rd edn, 2010) 411, 417–24.

[60] *Trendtex Trading Corporation v Central Bank of Nigeria* [1977] QB 529, 569 (Stephenson LJ).

[61] Fentiman, *International Commercial Litigation* (2010) ch 6.

[62] E.g. *Barbie*, 20 December 1985, *JCP* 1986 II 20655 (1988) 100 ILR 330. Likewise, under US judicial practice, great weight is given to opinions on international law given by the executive by way of *amicus curiae* briefs, interventions as party or non-party, or 'executive suggestions': Denza, in Evans (3rd edn, 2010) 411, 422.

[63] They may, however, provide structure and focus to more direct sources (i.e. the decisions of international courts and tribunals): Fatima, *Using International Law in Domestic Courts* (2005) 50–1. Further: *R v Keyn* (1876) 2 Ex D 63, 202 (Cockburn J); *West Rand Central Gold Mining Co v R* [1905] 2 KB 391, 407 (Lord Alverstone CJ); *R (European Roma Rights Centre) v Immigration Officer at Prague Airport* [2005] 2 AC 1, 38 (Lord Bingham).

[64] *R v Keyn* (1876) 2 Ex D 63; *In re Piracy Jure Gentium* [1934] AC 586; *State (Duggan) v Tapley* [1952] IR 62; *Haw Pia v China Banking Corp* (1951) 18 ILR 642; *Lauritzen v Government of Chile* (1956) 23 ILR 708.

[65] E.g. *R (on the application of Al-Jedda) (FC) v Secretary of State for Defence* [2008] 1 AC 332.

[66] *Jones v Ministry of Interior Al-Mamlaka Al-Arabiya AS Saudiya (Kingdom of Saudi Arabia)* [2006] UKHL 26, §12 (Lord Bingham).

(ii) International law as the applicable law in national courts

Once a national court has determined that international law is in some way applicable to a matter before it, it falls to the court to determine how that law is to sit alongside any national law that may also be applicable. Indeed, the increasing penetration of international law into the domestic sphere has to an extent muddied the distinction between the two.[67] Thus, international law is increasingly finding its way into national courts, and judges are increasingly finding themselves called upon to interpret and apply it—or at least to be aware of its implications.

Again, the approach of a national court to international law will be largely determined by the rules of the jurisdiction in question. But certain issues common to many or all jurisdictions may be identified.

(a) Courts may be called upon to adjudicate in conflicts between a municipal law on the one hand, and a rule of customary international law on the other. Many municipal systems now appear to have in one way or another accepted customary international law as 'the law of the land', even where no constitutional provision is made,[68] but questions remain as to how it fits within the internal hierarchy of a national system. As a general (but by no means absolute) rule, an extant statute will prevail over a rule of customary international law if no reconciliation is possible by way of interpretation.[69]

(b) The question also arises with respect to treaties, but will take on a more overtly constitutional flavour. 'Monist' systems may expressly provide that duly signed and ratified treaties take precedence over national legislation.[70] In other ('dualist') systems where the conclusion of a treaty is an executive act, it will be for the legislature to implement the treaty as part of domestic law—insofar as this may be required. In such a system the treaty is applied by the courts as mediated by the legislation, and legislation will prevail, again unless the issue can be resolved by interpretation.[71]

(c) When applying international law rules, municipal courts may find it necessary to develop the law, notably where it is unclear or uncertain.[72] This will include consideration of how the international rule is applicable in a domestic context, a process

---

[67] Brölmann, in Nijman & Nollkaemper (2007) 84.

[68] Shelton, in Shelton (2011) 1, 6–7.

[69] Ibid, 7.

[70] Thus, in monist systems the parliament will usually play a much more active role in the debate prior to adoption of the treaty: e.g. Constitution of the Netherlands, Arts 91, 94; Constitution of the Russian Federation, Art 15.3. Further: Shelton, in Shelton (2011) 1, 6.

[71] Shelton, in Shelton (2011) 1, 6–7. E.g. *Minister for Immigration and Ethnic Affairs v Teoh* (1995) 104 ILR 460, 471 (Mason CJ & Deane J).

[72] E.g. *Lord Advocate's Reference No 1, 2000* [2000] SLT 507, where a Scottish court had to determine the legality of the UK's Trident nuclear missile programme, despite the fact that the International Court had earlier avoided answering the question of whether the mere *holding* of nuclear weapons was in breach of international law: *Legality of the Threat or Force of Nuclear Weapons*, ICJ Reports 1996 p 226. Further: Neff (2002) 51 *ICLQ* 171.

which has been notable, for example, in the field of state immunity.[73] The question is particularly vexed in the US due to the so far unique provisions of the Alien Tort Statute[74] and subsequent efforts to define its scope.[75]

(d) Even in monist systems, the court may need to determine the extent to which a rule of international law may be directly applied. For example, a treaty (even if duly ratified and approved in accordance with constitutional processes) may be held 'non-self-executing', that is to say, inapplicable without further specification or definition by the legislature.[76]

(e) A further question is the extent to which the executive may intervene in the court's application of international law. One consideration may be the need for the judiciary and the executive to speak with one voice with respect to the foreign policy of the country in question. Thus, when considering issues such as the recognition of states and governments, state immunity and diplomatic immunity the courts may accept direction from the executive.[77] Caution must be exercised, however, particularly in the European context, with the European Court of Human Rights holding in *Beaumartin v France* that the practice in extreme forms is incompatible with the right of access to 'an independent and impartial tribunal'.[78] There, the practice scrutinized was the French procedure of referring preliminary questions on matters of treaty interpretation to the Minister for Foreign Affairs, and treating any opinion given as binding.[79] The revised French practice does not attribute binding effect to such opinions and indeed does not require them to be given at all.[80]

(f) A court may be called upon under the rules of private international law to apply foreign law. If it is alleged that the applicable law is in conflict with international law, the court may be required to determine whether the act or law of a foreign state is contrary to its international obligations. In many jurisdictions—notably in the US—such issues have given rise to the 'act of state' doctrine, whereby a court will, as an organ of a sovereign, refuse to pass judgment on the acts of another, formally equal, sovereign. The scope of the doctrine varies from one jurisdiction to another.

---

[73] E.g. *Nulyarimma v Thompson* (1999) 96 FCR 153; *Rasul v Bush* 542 US 466 (2004); *Ferrini v Federal Republic of Germany* (2004) 128 ILR 658; *R v Jones (Margaret)* [2007] 1 AC 136. Also: Guilfoyle (2001) 29 *FLR* 1. On state immunity: chapter 22.

[74] 28 USC §1350 (initially enacted in 1789). Also: the Torture Victims Protection Act 1991, 106 Stat 73. Further: chapter 21.

[75] *Filartiga v Pena-Irala*, 630 F.2d 876 (2nd Cir, 1980); *Sosa v Alvarez-Machain*, 542 US 692 (2004). Further: Roth (2004) 98 *AJIL* 798.

[76] Paust (1988) 82 *AJIL* 760; Vásquez (1995) 89 *AJIL* 685; Crootof (2011) 120 *Yale LJ* 100.

[77] E.g. *Arantzazu Mendi* [1939] AC 256; *Gur Corporation v Trust Bank of Africa Ltd* [1987] QB 599; *GITSI* [1990] Rec Lebon 171, 111 ILR 499; *Agyepong* [1994] Rec Lebon 523, 111 ILR 531; *British Arab Commercial Bank plc v National Transitional Council of the State of Libya* [2011] EWHC 2274.

[78] ECHR, 4 November 1950, 213 UNTS 222, Art 6.

[79] *Beaumartin v France* (1994) 107 ILR 50, 56.

[80] Further: *Difference Relating to Immunity from Legal Process of a Special Rapporteur of the Commission on Human Rights*, ICJ Reports 1999 p 62, 87–8.

(g) Finally, the court, confronted with an intricate issue of international law, may simply concede that it is beyond its capacity to decide, that is, is non-justiciable. As will be seen, the doctrine exists in England and in other common law jurisdictions.[81]

A further suite of issues emerges with respect to federal states:[82] the capacity of entities other than the federal government to deal with questions of foreign affairs; the place of international law in the components of the federal system,[83] and the capacity of courts other than those at a federal level to apply international law.

(C) RES IUDICATA AND THE TWO SYSTEMS[84]

(i) National res iudicata before international courts

From a formal point of view, res iudicata is a general principle within the meaning of Article 38(1)(c) of the Statute, applied in tandem by international and national courts.[85] But there is no effect of res iudicata from the decision of a national court so far as an international jurisdiction is concerned. Even if the subject-matter may be substantially the same, the parties may well not be, at least in the context of diplomatic protection and possibly outside that context also.[86] Other considerations also play a role, not least the principle that international law is (in its own terms) supreme. But an international tribunal may be bound by its constituent instrument to accept certain categories of national decisions as conclusive of particular issues.[87]

Some international tribunals afford natural and juridical persons standing against states, including decisions of state courts. For example the European Court of Human

---

[81] Denza, in Evans (3rd edn, 2010) 411, 435.

[82] Shelton, in Shelton (2011) 1, 20–2.

[83] E.g. the adoption of legislation based on international human rights standards by the Australian Capital Territory and the state of Victoria, where no comparable bill of rights exists on a constitutional or federal level: Human Rights Act 2004 (ACT); Charter of Human Rights and Responsibilities Act 2006 (Vic); *Momcilovic v R* [2011] HCA 34.

[84] Reinisch (2004) 3 *LPICT* 37; Shany, *Regulating Jurisdictional Relations Between National and International Courts* (2007).

[85] Cheng, *General Principles of International Law* (1953) 336; Reinisch (2004) 3 *LPICT* 37, 44; Shany (2007) 159; Schreuer, Malintoppi, Reinisch & Sinclair, *The ICSID Convention* (2nd edn, 2009) 609. Also: *Interpretation of Judgments No 7 and 8 (Factory at Chorzów)* (1927) PCIJ Ser A No 13, 27 (Judge Anzilotti, diss); *Trail Smelter* (1938) 3 RIAA 1905, 1950; *Waste Management Inc v United Mexican States* (2002) 41 ILM 1315, 1322; *Effects of Awards of Compensation made by the UN Administrative Tribunal*, ICJ Reports 1954 p 47, 53; *Amco Asia Corp v Indonesia* (1988) 1 ICSID Reports 543, 549; *Application of the Convention on the Prevention and Punishment of the Crime of Genocide (Bosnia and Herzegovina v Serbia and Montenegro)*, ICJ Reports 2007 p 43, 90–1. Some scholars go so far as to elevate it to the status of custom: Reinisch (2004) 3 *LPICT* 37, 44; Shany (2007) 159–60.

[86] *Upper Silesia* (1925) PCIJ Ser A No 6, 20; *Amco Asia Corp v Indonesia* (1984) 89 ILR 366, 459.

[87] Cf *Georges Pinson (France) v United Mexican States* (1928) 5 RIAA 327, 348 (the commission held that it would give great weight to factual findings made by the national claims commission). Under NAFTA, 17 December 1992, 32 ILM 289. Art 1131(2), decisions of the Free Trade Commission (an intergovernmental executive body) are binding on tribunals: e.g. *Mondev International Ltd v United States of America* (2002) 6 ICSID Reports 181, 223–4.

Rights functions as a court of final resort on human rights issues; it is only accessible once local remedies have been exhausted and does not re-examine any questions of fact already dealt with by a municipal court.[88] In the case of investor-state arbitration tribunals, the default position is that the decisions of national court create no *res iudicata* insofar as the work of the tribunal is concerned,[89] but the parties to the bilateral or multilateral treaty granting the tribunal jurisdiction may incorporate procedural roadblocks into the bargain, such as the so-called 'fork in the road' clause.[90] Such a clause requires the claimant to elect investor-state arbitration or litigation before the courts of the host state of the investment as its preferred method of dispute resolution. Once an election is made, other ways of bringing the original claim are closed to the claimant.

(ii) International *res iudicata* before national courts

In principle decisions by organs of international organizations are not binding on national courts without the co-operation of the national legal system,[91] which may adopt a broad constitutional provision for 'automatic' incorporation of treaty norms or require specific acts of incorporation or implementation. On the other side of the equation, however, municipal courts may seek to circumvent the finality of such decisions without engaging the question of *res iudicata* through interpretive legerdemain. In recent times this has been a feature of US practice, which links the effect of a judgment to the status of the relevant international court or tribunal's constitutive instrument within municipal law.[92]

Leaving aside such arguments, a decision of the International Court, even one concerning substantially the same issues as those before a national court, does not of itself create a *res iudicata* for the latter.[93] However, it does not follow that a national court should not recognize the validity of the judgment of an international tribunal of manifest competence and authority, at least for certain purposes.[94] For this reason, states often accord *res iudicata* effect to international and domestic arbitral awards.[95] On the one hand, this is desirable as a matter of common sense, and the arguments

---

[88] ECHR, Art 26.

[89] *Amco Asia Corp v Republic of Indonesia* (1984) 89 ILR 366, 459.

[90] E.g. *Occidental Exploration and Production Company v Republic of Ecuador* (2004) 138 ILR 35, 48–53.

[91] Schreuer, *Decisions of International Institutions before Domestic Courts* (1981); Skubiszewski (1968–69) 2 *Pol YIL* 80; Shany (2007) 161. Also: *Diggs v Richardson*, 555 F.2d 848 (DC Cir, 1976) (Security Council resolution non-self-executing); *Bradley v Commonwealth of Australia* (1973) 128 CLR 557; *Medellin v Dretke*, 544 US 660 (2005).

[92] E.g. *Medellin v Texas*, 552 US 491 (2008).

[93] *Socobel v Greek State* (1951) 18 ILR 3; *Committee of United States Citizens Living in Nicaragua v Reagan*, 859 F.2d 929 (DC Cir, 1988); *Breard v Greene*, 523 US 371 (1998), and generally Schulte, *Compliance with Decisions of the International Court of Justice* (2004) 77.

[94] *Messina v Petrocacchino* (1872) LR 4 PC 144; *Dallal v Bank Mellat* [1986] 1 QB 441, 457 (Hobhouse J). For comment: Fox (1988) 37 *ICLQ* 1, 24; Crawford (1986) 57 *BY* 410.

[95] E.g. Arbitration Act 1996 (UK) ss58, 66; 9 USC §13; International Arbitration Act 1974 (Cth) ss16, 33; UNCITRAL Model Law on International Commercial Arbitration 2006, Art 17H(1).

from a policy perspective are well known; parties to litigation are at a certain point in time entitled to draw a line under a dispute and be free of continued legal harassment. On the other, it may be the subject of a treaty obligation, for example under the New York Convention[96] or the ICSID Convention.[97] Outside those areas with specific treaty obligations, state practice is extremely variable, with a number of countries not affording *res iudicata* effect to foreign judgments,[98] or even those judgments arising from a different federal unit of the same country.[99]

(iii) *Res iudicata* and third parties

In international law *res iudicata* includes issue estoppel, but does not extend to the US doctrine of collateral estoppel (binding upon third parties).[100] But the decisions of an international court or tribunal may carry evidentiary weight even vis-à-vis third parties. For example national courts, in dealing with cases of war crimes and issues arising from belligerent occupation, the validity of acts of administration, of requisition and of transactions conducted in occupation currency have relied upon the findings of the International Military Tribunals at Nuremberg and Tokyo as evidence, even conclusive evidence, of the illegality of the war which resulted in the occupations.[101]

Quite aside from this, the legal reasoning employed by international tribunals may carry weight. In *Mara'abe v Prime Minister of Israel*, the Supreme Court of Israel found that the International Court's *Wall* advisory opinion[102] did not constitute *res iudicata* but that the Court's interpretation of international law (as opposed to factual determinations) should be given 'full appropriate weight'.[103]

---

[96] Convention on the Recognition and Enforcement of Foreign Arbitral Awards, 10 June 1958, 330 UNTS 38, Art III.

[97] ICSID Convention, Arts 53, 54.

[98] The same may be said of its correlative in the criminal law, *ne bis in idem*: van den Wyngaert & Stessens (1999) 48 *ICLQ* 779, 781–90.

[99] E.g. *United States v Lanza*, 260 US 227 (1922); *United States v Wheeler*, 435 US 313 (1978). Further: Shany (2007) 160.

[100] On estoppel: *Legal Status of Eastern Greenland* (1933) PCIJ Series A/B No 5. Cf Bowett (1957) 33 *BY* 176; Martin, *L'estoppel en droit international public* (1979); Tams, in Crawford, Pellet & Olleson (2010) 1035, 1044–5, 1047–8. Also: the ILA committee reports on *lis pendens* and *res iudicata* in international commercial arbitration: (2009) 25 *Arb Int* 35 (Interim Report); (2009) 25 *Arb Int* 67 (Final Report); (2009) 25 *Arb Int* 83 (Recommendations), and chapter 18.

[101] Brownlie, *Use of Force* (1963) 185. Also: *N v B* (1957) 24 ILR 941; *B v T* (1957) 24 ILR 962. On the special relationship between the Allied military tribunals in occupied Germany and the IMT at Nuremberg: UN War Crimes Commission, 15 *Law Reports of Trials of War Criminals* (1949) 17.

[102] *Legal Consequences of the Construction of a Wall in the Occupied Palestinian Territory*, ICJ Reports 2004 p 136.

[103] (2005) 129 ILR 241, 285, 298.

3. INTERNATIONAL LAW IN THE
COMMON LAW TRADITION[104]

(A) DEVELOPMENT OF THE COMMON LAW APPROACH

The common law was initially seen, and saw itself, as the law of the land—of the king-dom of England. It was applied by the common law courts at Westminster and set over against the civil law which governed maritime matters, foreign trade and also, given its links to the *ius gentium*, the relations of princes and republics. The latter law was practised by the civilians before the civil law courts such as the Court of Admiralty, and before the Council. The Council's advice on the law of nations came from civilian-trained lawyers, not from the common lawyers.[105]

The situation changed to some extent in the eighteenth century, following the aboli-tion of the conciliar courts at the Restoration and the opening up to the common law courts of the field of international commercial litigation. Part of that opening was a greater willingness to be influenced by foreign and civil law, a trend personified by Lord Mansfield, who first recorded the principle of 'incorporation', that is, that inter-national law was 'part of the law of England', a tradition he attributed to Lord Talbot and handed on to Blackstone.[106] What the Court of Admiralty in its prize jurisdic-tion saw as a simple matter of applicable law became for the common law courts a deliberate choice.[107] But this open-minded approach was qualified in various ways: the supremacy of parliament meant that treaties (the conclusion of which were a royal prerogative) were *not* part of English law, and the old role of the Council in matters of external relations left a prototype of the act of state doctrine[108] together with a defer-ence to executive authority in matters of the foreign prerogative (notably recognition). The overall result was eclectic, reflecting a practical rather than theoretical policy in the courts. In the post-Judicature Act period (post-1875) there has been much by way of practical development, but the essential pattern has not changed and the various components of the tradition remain poorly integrated.

It is necessary to take the components in turn, beginning with the most straightforward.

---

[104] Westlake (1906) 22 *LQR* 14; Lauterpacht (1939) 25 *GST* 51; 1 Lauterpacht (1970) 154, 218; Crawford (1982) 76 *PAS* 232; Fatima (2005) 403.

[105] McNair, 3 *Opinions* Appendix II, and for a synopsis Crawford, in Zimmermann & Beatson (eds), *Jurists Uprooted* (2004) 681.

[106] *Barbuit* (1737) Cases *t* Talbot 281; *Triquet v Bath* (1764) 3 Burr 1478, 1481; *Heathfield v Chilton* (1767) 4 Burr 2015, 2016. Later: *De Wütz v Hendricks* (1824) 2 Bing 314, 315; *Emperor of Austria v Day* (1861) 30 LJ Ch 690, 702 (reversed on appeal on another point); *R v Keyn (The Franconia)* (1876) 2 Ex D 63. Further: O'Keefe (2008) 79 *BY* 7, 12–23.

[107] For an overview of the legal history: Baker, *An Introduction to English Legal History* (4th edn, 2002) 117–54. On the rise and fall of the civilians: Squibb, *Doctors' Commons* (1977) 1–22, 102–9.

[108] E.g. *Blad v Bamfield* (1674) 36 ER 992 (Ch); *Duke of Brunswick v King of Hanover* (1848) 9 ER 993.

(B) TREATIES IN ENGLISH LAW[109]

(i) Unincorporated treaties

In England the conclusion and ratification of treaties are within the prerogative of the Crown, and if a transformation doctrine were not applied, the Crown could legislate for the subject without parliamentary consent,[110] in violation of the basal notion of parliamentary sovereignty.[111] The rule does not apply in the very rare cases where the Crown's prerogative can directly extend or contract jurisdiction without the need for legislation.[112]

Thus, as a strongly dualist system, English law will not ordinarily permit unimplemented treaties to be given legal effect by the courts.[113] A concise statement of this rule was provided by the Privy Council in *Thomas v Baptiste*:

Their Lordships recognise the constitutional importance of the principle that international conventions do not alter domestic law except to the extent that they are incorporated into domestic law by legislation. The making of a treaty ... is an act of the executive government, not of the legislature. It follows that the terms of a treaty cannot effect any alteration to domestic law or deprive the subject of existing legal rights unless and until enacted into domestic law by or under authority of the legislature. When so enacted, the courts give effect to the domestic legislation, not to the terms of the treaty.[114]

Thus unimplemented treaties cannot create directly enforceable rights nor deprive individuals of legal rights previously bestowed; this is known as the principle of *no direct effect*. They similarly cannot prevail over statutes, are not ordinarily contracts capable of enforcement in domestic courts, and their infringement by the UK is domestically without legal effect.[115] Neither do decisions by international courts and

---

[109] The term 'English law' has been used here for the sake of concision, but the position in England broadly reflects that in other Commonwealth countries: McNair, *Treaties* (1961) 81; Mann (1958–59) 44 *GST* 29; Jacobs & Roberts (eds), *The Effect of Treaties in Domestic Law* (1987); Gardiner (1995) 44 *ICLQ* 620; Fatima (2005); Sales & Clement (2008) 124 *LQR* 388, 394–413; Aust, *Modern Treaty Law and Practice* (2nd edn, 2007) 178; Neff, in Shelton (2011) 620, 621–6.

[110] Sales & Clement (2008) 124 *LQR* 388, 399.

[111] 'The bedrock of the British constitution': *R (Jackson) v Attorney General* [2006] 1 AC 262, 274 (Lord Bingham).

[112] *JH Rayner (Mincing Lane) Ltd v Department of Trade and Industry* [1990] 2 AC 418, 500. Further: *The Parlement Belge* [1880] 4 PD 129, 150; *Post Office v Estuary Radio Ltd* (1968) 2 QB 740, 753.

[113] *JH Rayner (Mincing Lane) Ltd v Department of Trade and Industry* [1990] 2 AC 418, 499–500 (Lord Oliver). Also: *Rustomjee v R* [1876] 2 QB 69, 74 (Lord Coleridge); *The Parlement Belge* (1879) 4 PD 129, 150, 154–5 (Sir Robert Phillimore); *Walker v Baird* [1892] AC 491, 496–7 (Lord Herschell); *Mortensen v Peters* (1905–6) F (JC) 93, 100–1; *Hoani Te Heuheu Tukino v Aotea District Maori Land Board* [1941] AC 308 (PC), 324–5 (Viscount Simon LC); *Pan-American World Airways Inc v Department of Trade* [1976] 1 Lloyd's Rep 257, 260 (Lord Denning MR), 261–2 (Scarman LJ); *JH Rayner (Mincing Lane) Ltd v Department of Trade and Industry* [1989] Ch 72, 164 (Kerr LJ); *In re M and H (Minors) (Local Authority: Parental Rights)* [1990] 1 AC 686, 721 (Lord Brandon); *R v Director of Public Prosecutions, ex parte Kebilene* [2000] 2 AC 326, 340 (Lord Bingham MR); *R v Lyons* [2003] 1 AC 976, 987 (Lord Bingham), 995 (Lord Hoffmann).

[114] [2000] 2 AC 1 (PC), 23 (Lord Millett); ibid, 31–3 (Lords Hoffmann & Goff, diss).

[115] Fatima (2005) 283–8; Sands & Clement (2008) 124 *LQR* 388, 397–8.

tribunals which determine the UK to be in breach of unimplemented treaty obligations have any domestic effect. In *R v Lyons*,[116] Lord Hoffmann noted that despite the
fact that the judiciary is one of the three organs of state, it was not the responsibility of
the courts to uphold the UK's international obligations in such cases:

The argument that the courts are an organ of state and therefore obliged to give effect to
the state's international obligations is in my opinion a fallacy. If the proposition were true,
it would completely undermine the principle that the courts apply domestic law and not
international treaties. ... International law does not normally take account of the internal
distribution of powers within a state. It is the duty of the state to comply with international
law, whatever may be the organs which have the power to do so. And likewise, a treaty may
be infringed by the actions of the Crown, Parliament or the courts. From the point of view
of international law, it ordinarily does not matter. In domestic law, however, the position is
very different. The domestic constitution is based upon the separation of powers. In domestic law, the courts are obliged to give effect to the law as enacted by Parliament. This obligation is entirely unaffected by international law.[117]

(ii) Incorporated treaties

Once a treaty is implemented by Parliament,[118] the resulting legislation forms part of
UK law and is applicable by the courts as so implemented.[119] Accordingly, there is no
distinction in the law of the UK between self-executing and non-self-executing treaties; all treaties may be classified as non-self-executing as all require legislative action
to become law. An apparent exception to this rule arises in the case of treaties concluded by the institutions of the European Union, with the European Court of Justice
holding these to be directly enforceable within member states as part of the *acquis
communautaire*. But in UK law EU treaties have this effect because of the relevant
statute.[120]

Once enacted, the statute implementing the treaty will function as any other Act
of Parliament. Thus, for example, the words of a subsequent Act of Parliament will
prevail over the provisions of a prior treaty in case of clear inconsistency between the
two.[121]

---

[116] *R v Lyons* [2003] 1 AC 976, 987 (Lord Bingham). Also: *R v Secretary of State for the Home Department,
ex parte Brind* [1991] 1 AC 696, 747 (Lord Bridge); *Re McKerr* [2004] 2 All ER 409.

[117] [2003] 1 AC 976, 995.

[118] In some cases, ratification may take place through the executive order of a Minister who has previously been granted legislative authorization to do so: Neff, in Shelton (2011) 620, 622.

[119] *Maclaine, Watson & Co Ltd v Department of Trade and Industry* [1990] 2 AC 418, 500 (Lord Oliver).
Also: *British Airways v Laker Airways* [1985] AC 58. The most obvious example of this is the Human Rights
Act 1998 (UK), which gives qualified domestic effect to the European Convention on Human Rights.

[120] Case C-87/75, *Bresciani* [1976] ECR 128; Case C-104/81, *Kupferberg* (1982) 93 ILR 76. Also: the
European Communities Act 1972 (UK); Fatima (2005) ch 6.

[121] *IRC v Collco Dealings Ltd* [1962] AC 1; *Woodend (KV Ceylon) Rubber and Tea Co v IRC* [1971] AC
321.

Legislation to give effect in domestic law to treaty provisions may take various forms. A statute may directly enact the provisions of the international instrument, which will be set out as a schedule to the Act.[122] It may employ its own substantive provisions to give effect to a treaty, the text of which is not itself enacted. It may be that the enacting legislation makes no specific reference to the treaty in question, though there is extrinsic evidence to show that the statute was intended to give effect to it.[123] The result is a balancing act that requires the court to scrutinize the strength of the relationship between the enacting statute and its parent treaty, and determines the strength of the latter as an interpretative tool.[124]

(iii) Treaties and the interpretation of statutes[125]

Questions surrounding the interpretation of treaties and statutes in English law can generally be divided into two categories: the interpretation of enabling instruments, and the interpretation of other legislation in light of treaties entered into, both incorporated and unincorporated. As to the former, it is to be remembered that primary object of interpretation is the implementing statute, and only at one remove the treaty which implements or incorporates it.[126] Accordingly, although international courts and tribunals may rule on the interpretation of a treaty, their rulings are not binding.[127]

On the other hand the interpretation of treaty provisions is a matter of law. Unlike in some countries, the courts do not seek binding interpretations of treaties from the executive.[128] They will apply international rules of treaty interpretation, as reflected in the Vienna Convention on the Law of Treaties,[129] rather than the domestic canons of statutory interpretation (though these are less different than they were).[130] Furthermore,

---

[122] E.g. Diplomatic Relations Act 1964 (UK), giving direct effect to certain provisions of the VCDR, 18 April 1961, 500 UNTS 95.

[123] E.g. *In re Westinghouse* [1978] AC 547 (regarding the Evidence (Proceedings in other Jurisdictions) Act 1975, implementing the unmentioned Hague Convention on the Taking of Evidence abroad in Civil or Commercial Matters, 18 March 1970, 847 UNTS 241).

[124] For a case of an unimplemented treaty giving rise to domestic rights and obligations: *Ecuador v Occidental Exploration & Production* [2007] EWCA Civ 656 (BIT arbitration). For BIT arbitration: chapters 28, 32.

[125] Sinclair (1963) 12 *ICLQ* 508; Mann, *Foreign Affairs in English Courts* (1986) 97; Fatima (2005) 65–186; Gardiner (1995) 44 *ICLQ* 620; Gardiner, *Treaty Interpretation* (2008) 129; Neff, in Shelton (2011) 620.

[126] On the primacy of the incorporating statute: *Rey v Government of Switzerland* [1999] 1 AC 54 (PC), 63 (Lord Steyn); *R v Secretary of State for the Environment, Transport and the Regions, ex parte International Air Transport Association* [2000] 1 Lloyd's Rep 242, 244 (Jowitt J); *R (Al-Fawwaz) v Governor of Brixton Prison* [2001] 1 AC 556, 606–7 (Lord Rodger); *R (Al-Skeini) v Secretary of State for Defence* [2004] EWHC 2911 (Admin), §301 (Rix LJ).

[127] Though the courts will, as a general rule, follow them: Neff, in Shelton (2011) 620, 623. Further: *R v Lyons* [2003] 1 AC 976, 992.

[128] Absent a direction as to interpretation in the enacting statute itself: e.g. the Carriage by Air Act 1961, s4A. Cf Neff, in Shelton (2011) 620, 623.

[129] 22 May 1969, 1155 UNTS 331, Arts 31–2. Further: chapter 16.

[130] E.g. *Fothergill v Monarch Airlines Ltd* [1981] AC 251, 282 (Lord Diplock); *Republic of Ecuador v Occidental Exploration & Production* [2007] EWCA Civ 656, §26; *Czech Republic v European Media Ventures SA* [2007] EWHC 2851 (Comm), §51; *R v Asfaw* [2008] 1 AC 1061, 1114–15 (Lord Mance).

in the interests of coherent interpretation between states parties to the relevant agreement, the decisions of other domestic tribunals on the interpretation of treaties are
taken into account.[131]

Difficulties may arise where the implementing statute is ambiguous on its face as to
the extent to which it implements a treaty, or fails to mention the treaty entirely. But
where it is clear that Parliament intended to implement a treaty through the legislation, the terms of the legislation are to be construed if possible so as to conform to the
treaty.[132]

More generally, as noted by Diplock LJ in *Salomon*: 'Parliament does not intend to
act in breach of international law, including therein specific treaty obligations'.[133] This
presumption applies to unincorporated treaties as much as incorporated ones,[134] but
it only applies to legislation enacted *after* a treaty has been signed or ratified.[135] On the
other hand, it will apply even where there is no link between the treaty and the legislation in question.[136] In addition to legislation, the presumption may also apply to other
instruments or guidelines given domestic effect.[137]

The presumption itself will only act as an aid to interpretation where the statutory
provision is open to interpretation in that it is not clear on its face.[138] In *Ex parte Brind*,
Lord Bridge, having regard to the then-unimplemented European Convention for the
Protection of Human Rights and Fundamental Freedoms (ECHR), said:

But it is already well settled that, in construing any provision in domestic legislation which
is ambiguous in the sense that it is capable of a meaning which either conforms to or conflicts with the Convention, the courts will presume that Parliament intended to legislate
in conformity with the Convention, not in conflict with it. Hence, it is submitted, when a
statute confers upon an administrative authority a discretion capable of being exercised in
a way which infringes any basic human right protected by the Convention, it may similarly
be presumed that the legislative intention was that the discretion should be exercised within
the limitations which the Convention imposes.[139]

---

[131] *R v Immigration Appeal Tribunal, ex parte Shah* [1999] 2 AC 629, 657 (Lord Hoffmann) ('[a]s a general
rule it is desirable that international treaties should be interpreted by the courts of all states parties uniformly'). Also: *R v Asfaw* [2008] 1 AC 1061, 1095 (Lord Hope).

[132] *Garland v British Rail Engineering Ltd* [1983] 2 AC 751, 771 (Lord Diplock); *R v Secretary of State for
the Home Department, ex parte Brind* [1991] 1 AC 696, 748 (Lord Bridge); *A v Secretary of State for the Home
Department (No 2)* [2006] 2 AC 221, 255 (Lord Bingham); *R (Al-Skeini) v Secretary of State for Defence* [2008]
1 AC 153, 192 (Lord Rodger).

[133] *Salomon v Commissioners of Customs and Excise* [1967] 2 QB 116, 143.

[134] Fatima (2005) 296–316.

[135] *R (Hirst) v London Northern District Coroner* [2005] 1 AC 400, 415–16 (Lord Brown).

[136] *Salomon v Commissioners of Custom and Excise* [1967] 2 QB 116, 144 (Diplock LJ); *R v Secretary of
State for the Home Department, ex parte Brind* [1991] 1 AC 696, 747–8 (Lord Bridge).

[137] *Mirza v Secretary of State for the Home Department* [1996] Imm AR 314 (CA), 318 (Nourse LJ).

[138] *R v Secretary of State for the Home Department, ex parte Brind* [1991] 1 AC 696, 760 (Lord Ackner);
Attorney-General v Associated Newspapers [1994] 2 AC 238, 261–2 (Lord Lowry); *JA Pye (Oxford) Ltd v
Graham* [2003] 1 AC 419, 444 (Lord Browne-Wilkinson); *R v Lyons* [2003] 1 AC 976, 987 (Lord Bingham).

[139] *R v Secretary of State for the Home Department, ex parte Brind* [1991] 1 AC 696, 747–8; cf ibid, 760
(Lord Ackner).

(iv) Treaties and the determination of the common law

The presumption in favour of interpreting English law in a way which does not place the UK in breach of an international obligation applies not only to statutes but also to the common law.[140] Use may be made of unincorporated treaties particularly where the common law is uncertain or developing.[141] The English courts have regularly taken into account treaty-based standards concerning human rights in order to resolve issues of common law, including the legality of telephone tapping,[142] the offence of criminal libel,[143] contempt of court,[144] and freedom of association.[145] This development is not confined to human rights treaties: *Alcom Ltd v Republic of Colombia*, for example, involved reference to general international law for purposes of statutory interpretation in the context of state immunity.[146]

(C) CUSTOMARY INTERNATIONAL LAW[147]

(i) 'Incorporation'

It has become received wisdom that the common law approach to customary international law is that of 'incorporation',[148] under which customary rules are to be considered 'part of the law of the land' provided they are not inconsistent with Acts of Parliament. The following statement by Lord Denning MR in *Trendtex Trading Corp v Central Bank of Nigeria* is usually cited in support of the proposition:

Seeing that the rules of international law have changed—and do change—and that the courts have given effect to the changes without any Act of Parliament, it follows...inexorably that the rules of international law, as existing from time to time, do form part of English law.[149]

---

[140] *R v Lyons* [2003] 1 AC 976, 992 (Lord Hoffmann). Also: *Attorney-General v Guardian Newspapers Ltd (No 2)* [1990] 1 AC 109, 283 (Lord Goff).

[141] *A v Secretary of State for the Home Department (No 2)* [2005] UKHL 71, §27 (Lord Bingham); *Derbyshire County Council v Times Newspapers* [1992] QB 770, 812 (Balcombe LJ).

[142] *Malone v Metropolitan Police Commissioner (No 2)* [1979] 1 Ch 344, 379 (Megarry V-C); noted Crawford (1979) 50 *BY* 217, 232.

[143] *Gleaves v Deakin* [1980] AC 477.

[144] *Attorney-General v BBC* [1981] AC 303.

[145] *Cheall v Association of Professional Executive Clerical and Computer Staff* [1983] 2 AC 180.

[146] [1984] AC 580, 597 (Lord Diplock).

[147] O'Keefe (2008) 79 *BY* 7; Sales & Clement (2008) 123 *LQR* 388, 413–20; Neff, in Shelton (2011) 620, 626–30. Also: Bingham, *The Rule of Law* (2010) ch 10.

[148] The antagonist of incorporation is the doctrine of 'transformation', under which custom will only become part of the law of England once codified in statute or in prior authoritative judicial decision—a doctrine of stasis so far as the common law is concerned. English courts have subscribed to an incorporationist approach since the 18th century: O'Keefe (2008) 79 *BY* 7, 9–10; Lauterpacht (1939) 25 *GST* 51, 65, 75–6, 84, 86; Holdsworth, *Essays in Law and History* (1945) 266. Also: *R v Keyn* (1876) 2 Ex D 63; *West Rand Central Gold Mining Co v R* [1905] 2 KB 391; *Mortensen v Peters* (1906) 8 F (J) 93; *Commercial and Estates Co of Egypt v Board of Trade* [1925] 1 KB 271, 295.

[149] [1977] QB 529, 554; reiterated in *R (Campaign for Nuclear Disarmament) v Prime Minister of the United Kingdom* (2002) 126 ILR 727, 738; and as a general principle underlying *R (European Roma Rights*

But according to Lord Wilberforce, it may be wise to 'avoid commitment to more of the admired judgment of Lord Denning MR than is necessary'.[150] The position in England is not that custom forms *part* of the common law (how can foreign states of whatever legal tradition make the common law?), but that it is a *source* of English law that the courts may draw upon as required.[151] The doctrine is decisive only occasionally. According to O'Keefe, outside of immunities cases it has only twice had a decisive impact on the outcome,[152] although there are other cases where it has been influential.

As Lord Bingham said in *R v Jones (Margaret)*:

The appellants contended that the law of nations in its full extent is part of the law of England and Wales. The Crown did not challenge the general truth of this proposition, for which there is indeed old and high authority…I would for my part hesitate…to accept this proposition in quite the unqualified terms in which it has often been stated. There seems to be truth in Brierly's contention…that international law is not a part, but is one of the sources, of English law.[153]

In short, the relationship of custom and the common law is more nuanced than either the doctrines of incorporation or transformation would suggest.[154]

(ii) The process and limits of 'incorporation'

It is possible to discern a broad process in the way the common law adopts customary international law. There is an initial question of or akin to choice of law: is this a subject matter on which international law has something to say, and which it allows (or even requires) national courts to say. If (as with foreign state immunity) the answer to both questions is yes, there is a second, constitutional question: is this an area where the common law courts retain law-making power or (as with substantive criminal law) not.[155] Where it is appropriate to consider norms of international law, rather than the law of the forum or a foreign law, then the courts will take judicial notice of the applicable rules, whereas formal evidence is required of foreign (national) law.

Centre) v Immigration Officer at Prague Airport [2005] 2 AC 1. Cf *R v Secretary of State, ex parte Thakrar* [1974] QB 684, 701. Further: Neff, in Shelton (2011) 620, 627.

[150] *I Congreso del Partido* [1983] AC 244, 261–2. Also: *R v Jones (Margaret)* [2007] 1 AC 136, 155 (Lord Bingham).

[151] Brierly (1935) 51 *LQR* 24, 31.

[152] *Commercial and Estates Co of Egypt v Ball* (1920) 36 Times LR 526; *Commercial and Estates Co of Egypt v Board of Trade* [1925] 1 KB 271. Further O'Keefe (2008) 79 *BY* 7, 24–9. Also: *Rose Mary* (1953) 20 ILR 316; O'Connell (1955) 4 *ICLQ* 267.

[153] [2007] 1 AC 136, 155 (citations omitted).

[154] E.g. *R (Al-Haq) v Secretary of State for Foreign and Commonwealth Affairs* [2009] EWHC 1910, §40 ('[t]he issue of the incorporation of customary international law into domestic law is not susceptible to a simple or general answer'). Also: O'Keefe (2008) 79 *BY* 7, 60 ('[i]t pays to emphasize at this point that the terms "incorporation" (as conceptualized here), "transformation", "adoption", "translation", "transposition" and the like are no more than metaphors for what is actually going on, and like many metaphors, they tend to obscure as much as they promise to enlighten').

[155] *R v Jones (Margaret)* [2007] 1 AC 136.

However, the courts still have to ascertain the existence of the rules of international law and their effect *within the national sphere*: the latter task is a matter on which the rules of international law may provide limited guidance. Case-law suggests that four considerations are relevant to the question of incorporation.[156]

(a) The first question is whether the customary international law rule is susceptible to domestic application.[157] For example, is the rule in question of a strictly interstate character, or does it implicate the rights of private parties? Self-evidently, the former may be difficult to restructure as a norm within a domestic legal system, aside from cases where the common law has transposed the various state immunities directly from international law. In the case of the latter, individual rights may be more readily transposed.[158] Some courts have identified further limits that might be imposed on such an attempted transposition, based not on amenability for adoption, but on the character of the norm. In *Al-Saadoon*, Laws LJ said:

[T]he...proposition that the customary rule may be sued as a cause of action in the English courts is perhaps not so clear cut. It would of course have to be shown that the rule did not conflict with any provision of English domestic law...I apprehend the rule would also have to possess the status of *jus cogens erga omnes*...[159]

But whilst 'incorporation' as conceived here has existed since the eighteenth century, the concept of peremptory norms is much more recent. The combination of the two is ahistorical—but the insight that certain norms may imperatively call for implementation is a valuable one. Something similar may have been implied by Justice Souter's dictum for the Supreme Court in *Sosa* that norms of international law, to be given direct effect under the Alien Tort Statute, have to be 'specific, universal, and obligatory' (although *Sosa* concerned statutory, not common law incorporation).[160]

(b) The next question is whether the proposed common law rule is contradicted by any constitutional principle.[161] Thus in *R v Jones (Margaret)*, the issue was whether the crime of aggression in customary international law could be considered part of the law of England. Lord Bingham said that in order for a customary norm to be translated to the common law, it must conform to the constitution: 'customary international

---

[156] O'Keefe (2008) 79 *BY* 7, 63–6.

[157] *R v Secretary of State for the Home Department, ex parte Thakrar* [1974] QB 684, 702 (Lord Denning MR), 708–9 (Orr LJ); *JH Rayner (Mincing Lane) Ltd v Department of Trade and Industry* [1989] Ch 72, 184–5 (Kerr LJ), cf 219–20 (Nourse LJ). Also: *West Rand Central Gold Mining Co v R* [1905] 2 KB 391, 409–12 (Lord Alverstone CJ).

[158] O'Keefe (2008) 79 *BY* 7, 64.

[159] *R (Al-Saadoon) v Secretary of State of Defence* [2009] EWCA Civ 7, §59 (Laws LJ), noted by O'Keefe (2009) 80 *BY* 451, 463. Similar terminology may be found in *A v Secretary of State for the Home Department (No 2)* [2006] 2 AC 221, 262 (Lord Bingham); *R (Mohamed) v Secretary of State for Foreign and Commonwealth Affairs* [2008] EWHC 2048 (Admin), §171.

[160] *Sosa v Alvarez-Machain*, 542 US 692, 732 (2004), citing *Hilao v In re Estate of Marcos*, 25 F.3d 1467, 1475 (9th Cir, 1994).

[161] Sales & Clement (2008) 124 *LQR* 388, 414.

law is applicable in the English courts only where the constitution permits'.[162] As the constitution requires that only Parliament could be responsible for the creation of crimes in English law,[163] aggression could not be considered an element of the common law but was a matter for legislation.[164] Lords Hoffmann and Mance reached substantially similar conclusions.[165]

Within the consideration of constitutionality and custom is the principle that the common law is inferior to statute, a concept flowing directly from the doctrine of parliamentary sovereignty.[166] Thus, a customary norm may only be transposed into the common law to the extent that it does not conflict with an Act of Parliament. In *Chung Chi Cheung v R*, Lord Atkin said:[167]

The courts acknowledge the existence of a body of rules which nations accept amongst themselves. On any judicial issue, they seek to ascertain the relevant rule, and, having found it, they will treat it as incorporated into the domestic law, so far as it is not inconsistent with rules enacted by statutes or finally declared by their tribunals.

Thus, in *Ex parte Thakrar*, a statement in the Immigration Act 1979 that any exceptions to the rule that a non-patrial required leave to enter the UK were to be found within the Act itself prevented the introduction of an additional exception through the operation of customary international law.[168] Similarly, in *Al-Adsani v Government of Kuwait*, Mantell J would not accept the argument that a common law tort of 'torture' arising from custom (even if it could be said that one existed) would prevail over the provisions of the State Immunity Act 1978.[169]

(c) A third consideration is whether the proposed rule is itself contradicted by some antecedent principle of the common law. In *West Rand*, Lord Alverstone CJ accepted that custom could contribute to the common law insofar as it was not 'contrary to the principles of her laws as decided by her courts'.[170] Similarly, Lord Atkin in *Chung Chi Cheung v R* conditioned incorporation on consistency 'with rules... finally

---

[162] [2007] 1 AC 136, 160, quoting O'Keefe (2001) 72 *BY* 293, 335.

[163] Whilst the judiciary did have a common law power to create new crimes, this was surrendered in *Knuller (Publishing, Printing and Promotions) Ltd v Director of Public Prosecutions* [1973] AC 435.

[164] [2007] 1 AC 136, 160–3. Another persuasive consideration for Lord Bingham was the fact that the incorporation of aggression into the common law would grant the courts the capacity to review the executive's conduct of foreign affairs and the deployment of armed forces, areas traditionally considered non-justiciable: ibid, 162–3.

[165] Ibid, 170–1 (Lord Hoffmann); 179 (Lord Mance).

[166] Generally: Goldsworthy, *Parliamentary Sovereignty* (2010).

[167] [1938] 4 All ER 786, 790. Also: *Mortensen v Peters* (1906) 8 F (J) 93 (Court of Justiciary, Scotland); *Polites v Commonwealth* (1945) 70 CLR 60; *Roussety v The Attorney General* (1967) 44 ILR 108.

[168] *R v Secretary of State for the Home Department, ex parte Thakrar* [1974] QB 684, 708 (Orr LJ), 710 (Lawton LJ). The position was affirmed by the Divisional Court: [1974] QB 684, 690–2 (Lord Widgery CJ, with whom May and Bridge JJ agreed). Also: *Viveash v Becker* (1814) 3 M & S 284, 298 (Lord Ellenborough CJ).

[169] (1995) 103 ILR 420; upheld on appeal: (1997) 107 ILR 536. Also: *Jones v Saudi Arabia* [2007] 1 AC 270 (similar reasoning, though customary basis of proposed cause of action not explicit).

[170] *West Rand Central Gold Mining Co v R* [1905] 2 KB 391, 408 (Lord Alverstone CJ).

declared by…tribunals'.[171] A practical example of how extant principles may bar the expansion of the common law in this way occurred in *Chagos Islanders v Attorney General*.[172] The case concerned a claim for damages based in reliance on the UK's supposed breach of the international human right not to be prevented from returning to one's home state. Ouseley J denied the claim, noting that even if breach of the right in question could be said to violate a common law as well as customary right, this could not, in itself, give rise to an action for damages. To do so, His Honour noted, would be 'no more and no less than a particular example of a tort for unlawful administrative acts',[173] the possibility of which the House of Lords had previously excluded at common law.[174]

(d) A further problem is one of precedent. In *Trendtex*, Lord Denning said:

International law knows no rule of *stare decisis*. If this court is satisfied that the rule of international law on a subject has changed from what it was 50 or 60 years ago, it can give effect to that change—and apply the change in our English law— without waiting for the House of Lords to do it…After all, we are not considering here the rules of English law on which the House has the final say. We are considering the rules of international law.[175]

By contrast in *Thai-Europe Tapioca Service Ltd v Government of Pakistan* Scarman LJ said:

it is important to realise that a rule of international law, once incorporated into our law by decisions of a competent court, is not an inference of fact but a rule of law. It therefore becomes part of our municipal law and the doctrine of *stare decisis* applies as much to that as to a rule of law with a strictly municipal provenance.[176]

But it is excessively parochial to think that an incorporated rule of international law is entirely domesticated, any more than an incorporated treaty. It should be open to the courts to reconsider the rule if there are indications of material change in international law, and more generally to track developments in the law. On the one hand it was artificial to think that a House of Lords decision on absolute immunity of 1938[177] should be considered as preclusive in the very different state of affairs in 1978. On the other hand the decision in *Trendtex* was authority on the contemporary state of international law, and was in fact followed as such.[178]

---

[171] [1938] 4 All ER 786, 790

[172] [2003] EWHC 2222 (QB). Also (far earlier) *Emperor of Austria v Day & Kossuth* (1861) 3 De G F & J 217, 251 (Turner LJ).

[173] [2003] EWHC 2222 (QB), §379.

[174] *Three Rivers DC v Bank of England (No 3)* [2003] 2 AC 1, 190 (Lord Steyn), citing *X (Minors) v Bedfordshire County Council* [1995] 2 AC 633.

[175] *Trendtex Trading Corporation v Central Bank of Nigeria* [1977] QB 529, 554.

[176] [1975] 3 All ER 961, 969–70; ibid, 968 (Lawton LJ). Also: *The Uganda Co (Holdings) Ltd v Government of Uganda* [1979] 1 Lloyd's Rep 481, 487 (Donaldson J), criticized by Crawford (1980) 51 BY 303, 325–6.

[177] *Compania Naviera Vascongada v SS Christina* [1938] AC 485.

[178] Also: *I Congreso del Partido* [1978] 1 QB 500, 518 (Robert Goff J); *R v Metropolitan Stipendary Magistrate, ex parte Pinochet Ugarte (No 1)* [2000] 1 AC 61, 77 (Lord Slynn); *R v Jones (Margaret)* [2005] QB 259, 273.

(D) NON-JUSTICIABILITY AND ACT OF STATE

(i) Non-justiciability

It was a long-standing position in English law that the Crown's prerogative powers were immune from judicial control. That is no longer so,[179] although the extent of judicial review depends on the subject-matter.[180]

Despite these developments, several areas of government activity connected with international law remain generally off limits to the courts. In *Abassi* the Court of Appeal was asked to require the Foreign Secretary to make representations to the US government on behalf of British nationals detained in Guantanamo Bay. Although the Court was deeply concerned by what it saw as US intransigence, it declined to make the orders requested.[181]

The courts are also extremely reluctant to pronounce on issues connected to the deployment of armed forces.[182] In *R v Jones (Margaret)*, Lord Hoffmann acknowledged that whilst the House of Lords was in principle capable of examining the deployment of armed forces by the government, '[t]he decision to go to war, whether one thinks it was right or wrong, fell squarely within the discretionary powers of the Crown to defend the realm and conduct its foreign affairs'.[183]

Another area which remains within the traditional non-justiciable Crown prerogative is treaty-making:[184] this (in conjunction with the doctrine of no direct effect) precludes most adjudication on unincorporated treaties. As Lord Scott said in *A v Secretary of State for the Home Department*:

It is not, normally, the function of the courts to entertain proceedings the purpose of which is to obtain a ruling as to whether an Act of Parliament is compatible with an international treaty obligation entered into by the executive. ... The executive has extensive and varied prerogative powers that it can exercise in the name of the Crown but none that permit lawmaking. In being asked, therefore, to perform the function to which I have referred,

---

[179] Fatima (2005) 273; Sales & Clement (2008) 124 *ILQ* 388, 395–6; Masterman, *The Separation of Powers in the Contemporary Constitution* (2011) 89–114.

[180] *Council of Civil Service Unions v Minister for the Civil Service* [1985] AC 374, 398 (Lord Fraser), 408 (Lord Scarman), 411 (Lord Diplock), 418 (Lord Roskill); *R v Secretary of State for Foreign and Commonwealth Affairs, ex parte Everett* [1989] QB 811, 820 (Taylor LJ); *R (Abassi) v Secretary of State for Foreign and Commonwealth Affairs* [2002] EWCA Civ 1598, §106 (Lord Phillips MR).

[181] *R (Abassi) v Secretary of State for Foreign and Commonwealth Affairs* [2002] EWCA Civ 1598, §107; cf ibid, §§65, 67. Further: *R (Al Rawi) v Secretary of State for Foreign and Commonwealth Affairs* [2008] QB 289.

[182] *R (Gentle) v Prime Minister* [2008] 1 AC 1356; cf [2006] EWCA Civ 1689. Further: Masterman (2011) 100–1.

[183] [2007] 1 AC 136, 172; cf 163 (Lord Bingham).

[184] *Attorney-General v Nissan* [1970] AC 179, 216 (Lord Morris); *Blackburn v Attorney-General* [1971] 2 All ER 1380, 1382 (Lord Denning MR); *Ex parte Molyneaux* [1986] 1 WLR 331, 335–6 (Taylor J); *Council of Civil Service Unions v Minister for the Civil Service* [1985] AC 374, 398 (Lord Fraser), 407 (Lord Scarman), 441 (Lord Diplock); *Lonrho Exports Ltd v Export Credits Guarantee Department* [1999] Ch 158, 179 (Lightman J); *Lewis v Attorney-General of Jamaica* [2001] 2 AC 50 (PC), 77 (Lord Slynn).

the courts are … being asked to perform a function the consequences of which will be essentially political in character rather than legal.[185]

There is, however, a measure of flexibility here,[186] and the courts have sought to reduce the effects of non-justiciability, including in relation to unincorporated treaties. In the first place, courts are willing to interpret unincorporated treaties where it is necessary to do so in order to determine rights and obligations under domestic law and thereby 'draw the court into the field of international law'.[187] In *Occidental Exploration*, the Court of Appeal held that an award made in favour of the appellant under the bilateral investment treaty (BIT) between the US and Ecuador gave rise to justiciable rights in the UK, even though the BIT was (unsurprisingly) not part of English law.[188] The Court concluded:

We accept that the English principle of non-justiciability cannot, if it applies, be ousted by consent. We are however concerned with issues regarding its proper scope and interpretation in a novel context. The considerations which we have identified … all militate against an understanding of that principle … which would tend, if anything, to undermine the chosen scheme of those involved.[189]

Similarly, in *Al-Jedda*,[190] the claimant alleged that his detention in Iraq by British forces was in breach of the UK's obligations under the ECHR. In turn, the government asserted that the claimant's detention was not only justified by the need to ensure security in Iraq, but also by the terms of Security Council Resolution 1546 of 2004, which qualified the UK's ECHR obligations by way of Article 103 of the Charter. Neither the Charter nor the Resolution had been incorporated into English law. The necessary foothold came from the Human Rights Act 1998, which gave effect to the ECHR in UK law. As the Act provided that ECHR rights were only applicable to the extent they were recognized on the international law plane, the court was required to examine the effect of the Resolution to determine the scope of the ECHR in the particular circumstance.[191]

In the second place, courts have demonstrated that they are willing to consider unincorporated treaties as part of the process of finding the UK to be in breach of its

---

[185] [2005] 2 AC 68, 146. Also: *Cook v Sprigg* [1899] AC 572, 578; *West Rand Central Gold Mining Co Ltd v R* [1905] 2 KB 391, 408–9 (Lord Alverstone CJ); *Republic of Italy v Hambros Bank* [1950] Ch 314, 329 (Vaisey J); *Malone v Metropolitan Police Commissioner* [1979] Ch 344, 352–4 (Sir Robert Megarry V-C); *R v Ministry of Defence, ex parte Smith* [1996] QB 517, 558 (Sir Thomas Bingham MR); *R v Khan* [1997] AC 588, 581–2 (Lord Nolan); *R (Campaign for Nuclear Disarmament) v The Prime Minister* [2002] EWHC 2777 (Admin), §§36–7.

[186] Fatima (2005) 273–4.

[187] *R (Campaign for Nuclear Disarmament) v Prime Minister* [2002] EWHC 2777 (Admin), §§36–41 (Simon Brown LJ).

[188] *Occidental Exploration & Production Co v Ecuador* [2006] QB 432, 457.

[189] Ibid, 467.

[190] *R (Al-Jedda) v Secretary of State for Defence* [2008] 1 AC 332. Further: Sands & Clement (2008) 124 LQR 388, 397.

[191] [2008] 1 AC 332, 357 (Lord Rodger). Cf *R (Quark Fishing Ltd) v Secretary of State for Foreign and Commonwealth Affairs* [2006] 1 AC 529, 544 (Lord Bingham), 545–6 (Lord Nicholls), 559 (Lord Hope).

obligations under international law, though the determination of breach will have no legal effect of its own.[192] Its use is most notable when illuminating rights present in municipal law under the ECHR and particularly Article 15, which permits the UK to take measures derogating from the Convention provided that such measures are not inconsistent with its other obligations under international law. Thus, in *A v Secretary of State for the Home Department,* Lord Bingham—determining the validity of a derogation under ECHR Article 15[193] and the compatibility of the Anti-terrorism, Crime and Security Act 2001 with ECHR Article 5—said:

What cannot be justified here is the decision to detain one group of suspected international terrorists, defined by nationality or immigration status, and not another. To do so was a violation of [ECHR] article 14. It was also a violation of article 26 of the [International Covenant on Civil and Political Rights] and so inconsistent with the United Kingdom's other obligations under international law within the meaning of [ECHR] article 15...[194]

It is however very doubtful whether there is a broader exception to non-justiciability for unincorporated human rights treaties.[195]

Thirdly, where the decision-maker explicitly relies on a treaty in making a decision, the courts will apply normal standards of judicial review to the treaty as so relied on.[196]

(ii) Judicial restraint and act of state

Policy considerations of a similar kind have led courts to apply a further rule of non-justiciability, holding a claim to be barred if it requires determination of the lawfulness or validity of acts of a foreign state. This is a doctrine of English public law which, long familiar in a general way, still has very uncertain limits.[197]

Broadly, the doctrine prescribes that courts do not adjudicate on matters of international law arising in disputes between foreign states. The modern source of the doctrine is Lord Wilberforce's statement in *Buttes Gas* that:

[T]he essential question is whether...there exists in English law a more general principle that the courts will not adjudicate upon the transactions of foreign sovereign states. Though I would prefer to avoid argument on terminology, it seems desirable to consider this principle,

---

[192] Fatima (2005) 279, 281–2.

[193] Human Rights Act 1998 (Designated Derogation) Order 2001 (UK).

[194] [2005] 2 AC 68, 124. Also: *R (European Roma Rights Centre) v Immigration Officer at Prague Airport* [2005] 2 AC 1, 45–7 (Lord Steyn), 64–5 (Baroness Hale); *R (R) v Durham Constabulary* [2005] 2 All ER 369, 385 (Lord Bingham), 392–4 (Baroness Hale).

[195] *Re McKerr* [2004] 2 All ER 409, 425 (Lord Steyn), citing Hunt, *Using Human Rights Law in English Courts* (1998) 26–8; Collins (2002) 51 *ICLQ* 485, 496–7. Contra: Sales & Clement (2008) 124 *LQR* 388, 398–400.

[196] *R v Secretary of State for the Home Department, ex parte Launder* [1997] 1 WLR 839, 867 (Lord Hope); *R v DPP, ex parte Kebilene* [2000] 2 AC 326, 367 (Lord Steyn). But the treaty must be the basis of the decision, not simply mentioned in passing by the decision-maker: *R (Corner House Research) v Director of the Serious Fraud Office* [2009] 1 AC 756, 851.

[197] It is not to be confused with what is sometimes referred to as the domestic act of state doctrine: cf *Buron v Denman* (1848) 2 Ex D 167. Generally: Perreau-Saussine (2007) 78 *BY* 176.

if existing, not as a variety of 'act of state' but one for judicial restraint or abstention...In my opinion there is, and for long has been, such a general principle, starting in English law, adopted and generalized in the law of the United States of America which is effective and compelling in English courts. This principle is not one of discretion, but is inherent in the very nature of the judicial process...I find the principle clearly stated that the courts in England will not adjudicate upon acts done abroad by virtue of sovereign authority.[198]

Within this principle there are in fact two overlapping doctrines: judicial restraint on the one hand, and act of state on the other. The former is triggered by issues relating to the transactions of states,[199] and requires the court to exercise its discretion to determine whether it is sufficiently equipped to handle the dispute. In *Buttes Gas*, the Court would have been required to address vexed questions of international law arising from the actions of two emirates in the Arabian Gulf with regard to a contested island, Abu Musa, and two competing oil companies claiming concessions within its territorial sea.

Judicial restraint is a discretionary principle,[200] but where it applies it is a substantive bar to adjudication, reflecting the incapacity of a national court to deal adequately with certain issues on the international plane. Thus, it cannot be waived, even by the state(s) concerned.[201]

The concept of act of state forms the hard core of the principle:[202] it refers to the non-justiciability in a national court of the acts of a foreign state within its own territory[203] or, exceptionally, outside it.[204] Thus, in *Ex parte Johnson*, it was held that once consent to a re-extradition had been obtained by the UK from Austria under the European Convention on Extradition,[205] in the form of a diplomatic note, the court could not then proceed to inquire into the quality of the consent so offered.[206] As a domestic rule of law, it is distinct from the doctrine of state immunity, a rule of international law.[207] Justiciability in this context refers to the act of determining the lawfulness or validity

---

[198] *Buttes Gas & Oil Co v Hammer (No 3)* [1982] AC 888, 932–3. Also the well-known earlier statement of Lord Halsbury LC in *Cook v Sprigg* [1899] AC 572, 578 ('It is a well-established principle of law that the transactions of independent states between each other are governed by laws other than those which the municipal courts administer'). For criticism of the breadth of the dictum: Crawford (1982) 53 *BY* 253, 259–68.

[199] Fatima (2005) 385.

[200] E.g. *R v Bow Street Magistrate, ex parte Pinochet (No 1)* [2000] 1 AC 61, 104 (Lord Lloyd, diss).

[201] Ibid, 90.

[202] *Kuwait Airways Corporation v Iraqi Airways Co (Nos 4 and 5)* [2002] 2 AC 883, 1108 (Lord Hope). Thus, all acts of state will trigger judicial restraint, but not the reverse.

[203] *AM Luther v James Sagor & Co* [1921] 3 KB 532, 548 (Warrington LJ); *Buttes Gas and Oil Co v Hammer (No 3)* [1982] AC 888, 934 (Lord Wilberforce); *Kuwait Airways Corporation v Iraqi Airways Co (Nos 4 & 5)* [2002] 2 AC 883, 922 (Lord Hope); *Jones v Saudi Arabia* [2004] EWCA Civ 1394, §10.

[204] *R v Bow Street Magistrate, ex parte Pinochet (No 1)* [2000] 1 AC 61, 106 (Lord Nicholls); *Banca Carige v Banco Nacional de Cuba* [2001] 3 All ER 923, §29 (Lightman J).

[205] 13 December 1957, 359 UNTS 273.

[206] *R v Secretary of State for the Home Department, ex parte Johnson* [1999] QB 1174, 1186 (Bell J). Also: *Salaman v Secretary of State in Council of India* [1906] 1 KB 613.

[207] *R v Bow Street Magistrate, ex parte Pinochet (No 1)* [2000] 1 AC 61, 106 (Lord Nicholls); *R v Bow Street Magistrate, ex parte Pinochet (No 3)* [2000] 1 AC 147, 269 (Lord Millett). On state immunity: chapter 22.

of a foreign act of state performed within its own domain; the court is not prevented from taking note of its existence.[208]

As with the wider doctrine of non-justiciability, exceptions to the doctrine of act of state nonetheless exist.[209] The first is that the acts of a foreign state will be justiciable where their recognition would be contrary to English public policy. The exception arose originally with respect to gross human rights violations in *Oppenheimer v Cattermole*,[210] and was expanded in the decision of *Kuwait Airways Corporation v Iraqi Airways Company* to include acts of state done in clear violation of international law more generally.[211] The case concerned the seizure and removal of aircraft owned by Kuwait Airways during the illegal invasion of Kuwait by Iraq in August 1990. But the scope of this exception is uncertain. Lord Steyn stated that not every rule of public international law will create such an exception.[212] Lord Nicholls (with whom Lord Hoffmann agreed) stated that the points of law before them were 'rules of fundamental importance' and quoted *Oppenheim v Cattermole* more generally to the effect that '[i]nternational law, for its part, recognises that a national court may properly decline to give effect to legislative and other acts of foreign states which are in violation of international law'. Moreover, the exception was applied more broadly to the doctrine of judicial restraint as identified in *Buttes Gas*, based on the dictum by Lord Wilberforce that abstention was predicated on a lack of 'manageable standards'. As Lord Nicholls noted, the breach of international law was 'plain beyond dispute', and was acknowledged as such by Iraq with its acceptance of the Security Council-mandated ceasefire; accordingly, '[t]he standard being applied by the court [was] clear and manageable, and the outcome not in doubt'.[213]

Thus 'clearly established' rules of international law may be considered part of the public policy of the UK,[214] as are human rights more generally.[215]

The second exception arises where Parliament has rendered an issue which is ordinary beyond the competence of the court justiciable. In the first *Pinochet* case before the House of Lords, Lord Nicholls noted that 'there can be no doubt that the [act of state] doctrine yields to a contrary intention shown by Parliament'. In that case, the definition of 'torture' in section 134(1) of the Criminal Justice Act 1988 and section

---

[208] *R v Bow Street Magistrate, ex parte Pinochet (No 1)* [2000] 1 AC 61, 118 (Lord Steyn); cf ibid, 103 (Lord Lloyd, diss). Also: *Salaman v Secretary of State in Council of India* [1906] 1 KB 613, 639–40 (Fletcher Moulton LJ).

[209] Fatima (2005) 395–401.

[210] [1976] AC 249, 265 (Lord Hodson), 277–8 (Lord Cross).

[211] Ibid, 278, citing *In re Claim by Helbert Wagg & Co Ltd* [1956] Ch 323, 334 (Upjohn J).

[212] [2002] 2 AC 833, 1102; O'Keefe (2002) 73 *BY* 400. Also: *Jones v Saudi Arabia* [2005] EWCA 1394, §90 (Mance LJ); *R (Abbasi) v Secretary of State for Foreign and Commonwealth Affairs* [2002] EWCA Civ 1598, §§57–67 (Lord Phillips MR).

[213] *Kuwait Airways Corporation v Iraqi Airways Company (Nos 4 & 5)* [2002] 2 AC 833, 1081.

[214] *Oppenheim v Cattermole* [1976] AC 249, 265 (Lord Hodson), 277–8 (Lord Cross); *Kuwait Airways Corporation v Iraqi Airways Co (Nos 4 & 5)* [2002] 2 AC 883, 1081 (Lord Nicholls), 1103 (Lord Steyn).

[215] *Oppenheim v Cattermole* [1976] AC 249, 263 (Lord Hailsham), 278 (Lord Cross), 282–3 (Lord Salmon).

1(1) of the Taking of Hostages Act 1982 in terms required the investigation of foreign officials in certain cases.

(E) THE COMMON LAW TRADITION IN THE UNITED STATES[216]

(i) Treaties

Formally US law views treaties and other international agreements as a source of law, as described by Article VI§2 of the Constitution (the Supremacy Clause):

[A]ll Treaties made or which shall be made with the authority of the United States, shall be the supreme Law of the Land and the Judges in every state shall be bound thereby, anything in the Constitution of Laws of any state to the contrary notwithstanding.[217]

As such, treaties are on par with federal legislation, and will prevail over laws enacted by the states. As Justice Sutherland said in *United States v Belmont*:

Plainly, the external powers of the United States are to be exercised without regard to state laws or policies...And while this rule in respect of treaties is established by the express language of [Article VI] of the Constitution, the same rule would result in the case of all international compacts and agreements from the very fact that complete power over international affairs is in the national government and is not and cannot be subject to any curtailment or interference on the part of the several states...In respect of all international negotiations and compacts, and in respect of our foreign relations generally, state lines disappear.[218]

A principal point of difference between the common law tradition as developed in the UK and the tradition that subsequently emerged in the US is the method by which treaties are incorporated into municipal law. In *Foster v Neilsen*,[219] Justice Marshall adopted for the US a modified version of the UK's dualist model. At its heart was the distinction between self-executing treaties, which by their terms could be incorporated into municipal law without more, and non-self-executing treaties,[220] which required enabling legislation to be effective.[221]

Currently, the central question within US jurisprudence on treaties is the process by which a court determines that a treaty or other international agreement is self-executing. Here, vigorous debate has been prompted by the Supreme Court's decision in *Medellin v Texas*,[222] which concerned the domestic effect within the US of the

---

[216] 1 *Restatement Third* §§111–15; Paust, *International Law as Law of the United States* (2nd edn, 2003); Dubinsky, in Shelton (2011) 631.

[217] 1 *Restatement Third* §111, comment *(d)*; Dubinsky, in Shelton (2011) 631, 641–2.

[218] 301 US 324, 331 (1937).

[219] 27 US 253 (1829).

[220] E.g. Paust (1986) 82 *AJIL* 760; Iwasawa (1986) 26 *Va JIL* 635; Buergenthal (1992) 235 Hague *Recueil* 303; Vásquez (1995) 89 *AJIL* 695; Hathaway (2008) 117 *Yale LJ* 1236; Bederman (2008) 102 *AJIL* 528; Bradley (2008) 102 *AJIL* 540; Charnovitz (2008) 102 *AJIL* 551; Vásquez (2008) 102 *AJIL* 563; Wuerth (2009) 13 *Lewis & Clark LR* 1; Huang (2011) 79 *Fordham LR* 2211.

[221] Further: 1 *Restatement Third* §111.

[222] 552 US 491 (2008).

decision of the International Court in *Avena*.[223] There the International Court held that the US was in breach of its obligations under Article 36 of the Vienna Convention on Consular Relations (VCCR)[224] to provide consular notification to foreign nationals who are detained or arrested. The consequence was an order for the 'review and reconsideration' of the cases of 51 individuals so affected. The question for determination by the Supreme Court in *Medellin* was whether the Charter—which had not been the subject of an enabling statute issued by Congress—was in this respect self-executing.

Earlier US decisions starting in the 1970s had referred to a variety of factors to determine the self-executing status of the treaty under consideration.[225] The following list is indicative: 'the purposes of the treaty and the objectives of its creators, the existence of domestic procedures and institutions appropriate for direct implementation, the availability and feasibility of alternative enforcement methods, and the immediate and long-range consequences of self- or non-self-execution'.[226] In *Medellin*, the Court gave far greater weight to the text of the Charter. Chief Justice Roberts, speaking for the majority, said of Article 94 (requiring that each Member comply with decisions of the International Court to which it is a party):

The Article is not a directive to domestic courts. It does not provide that the United States 'shall' or 'must' comply with an ICJ decision, nor indicate that the Senate that ratified the UN Charter intended to vest ICJ decisions with immediate legal effect in domestic courts. Instead, '[t]he words of Article 94…call upon governments to take certain action.'[227]

On this basis, the majority concluded that as the Charter, the Optional Protocol to the VCCR, and the Statute had not been incorporated into US law by way of legislation and the treaties were not themselves self-executing, they could not be given judicial effect.[228]

As shown by *Medellin*, the Supreme Court's current approach utilizes predominantly the text of the treaty.[229] The ultimate issue is whether the text 'conveys an intention'

---

[223] *Avena*, ICJ Reports 2004 p 12.

[224] 22 April 1963, 596 UNTS 261.

[225] E.g. *People of Saipan v US Department of the Interior*, 302 F.2d 90, 97 (9th Cir, 1974); *United States v Postal*, 589 F.2d 862, 877 (5th Cir, 1979); *Frolova v Union of Soviet Socialist Republics*, 761 F.2d 370, 373–4 (7th Cir, 1985).

[226] *United States v Postal*, 589 F.2d 862, 877 (5th Cir, 1979), quoting *People of Saipan v US Department of the Interior*, 302 F.2d 90, 97 (9th Cir, 1974). This approach was favoured by the dissenters in *Medellin*, who urged reliance on a 'practical, context-specific' methodology to determining self-execution: 552 US 491, 549 (2008) (Justice Breyer, diss). This was rejected by the majority on the basis that it was indeterminate and would 'assign to the courts—not the political branches—the primary role in deciding when and how international agreements would be enforced': ibid, 516.

[227] 552 US 491, 508 (2008), citing *Committee of United States Citizens living in Nicaragua v Reagan*, 859 F.2d 929, 938 (DC Cir, 1989). Further: McGuinness (2008) 102 *AJIL* 622.

[228] 552 US 491, 511 (2008). Also: *Corus Staal BV v Department of Commerce*, 395 F.3d 1343, 1348–9 (Fed Cir, 2005); *Sanchez-Llamas v Oregon*, 548 US 311, 354 (2006). Cf *Medellin v Dretke*, 544 US 660, 693–4 (2005) (Breyer J, diss), arguing that Art 94 of the Charter *does* require internal compliance by US domestic courts with decision of the International Court. Also: *Torres v State of Oklahoma* (2004) 43 ILM 1227.

[229] Cf Bradley (2008) 104 *AJIL* 540, 542.

of self-execution.[230] In *Medellin*, the Court appears to have viewed the intention of US treaty-makers as dispositive.[231] In addition, although some commentators—and notably the *Restatement Third*[232]—had previously taken the position that there was, in cases of ambiguity, a strong presumption in favour of the self-execution of treaties, the Court in *Medellin* appears to have distanced itself from such a notion, instead requiring that each treaty be considered on its facts, with reference to text, structure, and ratification history.[233] However, notwithstanding *Medellin*, important lower courts continue to apply the more nuanced test for self-execution advocated in the *Restatement Third*.[234] In addition, the Supreme Court's emphasis on text in *Medellin* is not universally shared. The Senate Foreign Relations Committee, for example, was unhappy with *Medellin* and modified its procedures in response.[235] Moreover, it might be suggested that the Supreme Court's approach does not accord with the reality of international treaty-making, particularly in a multilateral context: it is not realistic to expect a multilateral treaty involving negotiators from a range of legal cultures to deliberately include in the text of their agreement express language to satisfy the Court's parochial requirements.[236]

The final question is the effect—if any—of an unimplemented non-self-executing treaty. As Bradley points out, *Medellin* is ambiguous on this point.[237] The Court rejected the argument that such a treaty merely fails to provide a private right of action within US law, but may still be applied where such a cause of action is not necessary,[238] but refused to comment further. As a basic rule, however, a non-self-executing treaty which has not been the subject of implementing legislation has no status in domestic law and is not judicially enforceable.[239] In *Medellin*, the dissent went so far as to imply that the conclusion of such a treaty is to be considered 'a near useless act'.[240]

But an analogue of the UK's presumption of compatibility is present in US law. In *Murray v Schooner Charming Betsy*, Marshall CJ wrote that 'an act of Congress

---

[230] *Medellin v Texas*, 552 US 491, 505 (2008).

[231] 552 US 491, 521 (2008). Cf Reisenfeld (1980) 74 *AJIL* 892; Vásquez (1995) 98 *AJIL* 695; Vásquez (2008) 83 *Notre Dame LR* 1601; Moore (2006) 75 *G Wash LR* 1.

[232] 1 *Restatement Third* §111, comment 5. Also: Henkin, *Foreign Affairs and the United States Constitution* (2nd edn, 1996) 201; Vásquez (1999) 99 *Col LR* 2154. Other commentators argue for a presumption *against* self-execution: e.g. Yoo (1999) 99 *Col LR* 1955, 2218.

[233] 552 US 491, 518, 520 (2008); Bradley (2008) 102 *AJIL* 540, 545–7; Crootof (2011) 120 *Yale LJ* 1784, 1787. Also: *Al-Bihani v Obama*, 619 F.3d 1, 15–16 (DC Cir, 2010) (Judge Kavanaugh).

[234] E.g. *Brzak v United Nations*, 597 F.3d 107 (2nd Cir, 2010). Further: Crook (2010) 104 *AJIL* 281.

[235] Since *Medellin*, the Senate has taken care to state in both its reports and in declarations included in all resolutions of advice and consent whether treaties (or specific provisions thereof) are or are not self-executing: Crook (2010) 104 *AJIL* 100; Crook (2011) 105 *AJIL* 124.

[236] The situation may be different with respect to bilateral arrangements: Crook (2011) 105 *AJIL* 124.

[237] Bradley (2008) 102 *AJIL* 540, 547–50.

[238] E.g. when invoked defensively in a criminal case: 552 US 491, 505 n2 (2008) ('a "non-self-executing" treaty does not by itself give rise to domestically enforceable federal law'); ibid, 506 n3. Also: 1 *Restatement Third* §111, comment *(a)*.

[239] *Foster v Neilson*, 27 US 253, 314 (1829). Further: Crootof (2011) 120 *Yale LJ* 1784, 1786.

[240] 552 US 491, 553 (Breyer J, diss). Also: Powell (2001) 150 *U Penn LR* 245.

ought never be construed to violate the law of nations if any other possible construction remains'.[241] In the *Restatement Third*, this is rendered as '[w]here fairly possible, a United States statute is to be construed so as not to conflict with international law or with an international agreement of the United States'.[242] The canon was developed to resolve situations in which a treaty or rule of customary international law conflicted with a statute passed later in time by Congress. Ordinarily, this would result in the latter impliedly repealing the former. *Charming Betsy* by contrast required later statutes to be interpreted, if possible, consistently with the earlier international law obligations of the US. As with the UK presumption of compatibility, the *Charming Betsy* canon is only applicable where the statute to be interpreted is ambiguous on its face.[243]

Neither the *Charming Betsy* nor the *Restatement Third* makes any distinction between self-executing and non-self-executing treaties. As such, courts have interpreted the canon to breathe life into non-self-executing treaties.[244] Such treaties may be held to have codified customary international law;[245] more broadly they represent international obligations entered into in good faith from which the US presumably does not wish to depart. Particularly influential is the International Covenant on Civil and Political Rights (ICCPR),[246] which was ratified by the US in 1992 with a declaration that Articles 1 to 27 were not self-executing. Despite this, the courts regularly utilize *Charming Betsy* in order to avoid conflicts with the non-self-executing provisions of the ICCPR.[247]

The *Charming Betsy* has been applied to treaties other than the ICCPR,[248] may be invoked in a purely domestic context with no international nexus,[249] and its relevance does not appear to have been diminished appreciably by the decision in *Medellin*.[250]

(ii) Customary international law

The traditional understanding is that the US relationship with custom is essentially monist in character. This position was formulated early on in the *Paquete Habana*:

---

[241] 6 US 64, 118 (1804).

[242] 1 *Restatement Third* §114

[243] E.g. *United States v Yousef*, 327 F.3d 56, 92 (2nd Cir, 2003). Cf Eskridge, Frickey & Garrett, *Statutes and the Creation of Public Policy* (4th edn, 2007) 884.

[244] An idea generally credited, at least in the modern era, to Vásquez (1995) 89 *AJIL* 695, 716 ('In countless cases, the vast majority of those raising treaty-based claims, the Court has resolved the case without even mentioning the self-execution issue').

[245] Crootof (2011) 120 *Yale LJ* 1784, 1796–801. Thus the VCLT, signed but not ratified by the US, is applied in US courts: e.g. *Weinberger v Rossi*, 456 US 25, 29 (1982); *Committee of US Citizens living in Nicaragua*, 859 F.2d 929, 940–1 (DC Cir, 1988).

[246] 16 December 1966, 999 UNTS 171.

[247] *Maria v McElroy*, 68 F.Supp 2d 206, 231–2 (EDNY, 1999), reversed on other grounds by *Restrepo v McElroy*, 369 F.3d 627 (2nd Cir, 2004).

[248] E.g. *Khan v Holder*, 594 F.3d 773 (9th Cir, 2009) (interpreting statute in accordance with the United Nations Protocol Relating to the Status of Refugees, 4 November 1967, 606 UNTS 267).

[249] E.g. *Kane v Winn*, 319 F.Supp 2d 162, 196 (D Mass, 2004). Cf *Serra v Lapin*, 600 F.3d 1191, 1198 (9th Cir, 2010).

[250] E.g. *Capitol Records Inc v Thomas*, 579 F.Supp 2d 1210 (D Minn, 2008).

International law is part of our law, and must be ascertained and administered by the courts of justice of appropriate jurisdiction as often as questions of right depending on it are duly presented for their determination. For this purpose, where there is no treaty and no controlling executive or legislative act or judicial decision, resort must be had to the customs and usages of civilized nations.[251]

The conventional view of custom[252] vis-à-vis the municipal law of the US is therefore that it is a source of law, first in the sense that state and federal courts may apply these rules to determine a dispute, and secondly in the sense that rules of custom, as per the *Charming Betsy*, are tools of interpretation.[253] Thus the *Restatement Third*:[254] '[c]ustomary international law is considered to be like common law in the US, but is federal law'. This basic position remains unchallenged: two recent Supreme Court decisions saw no reason to depart from the *Paquete Habana*.[255] But '[c]ustomary law does not ordinarily confer legal rights on individuals or companies, even rights that might be enforced by a defensive suit such as one to enjoin or to terminate a violation by the United States (or a State) of customary international law'.[256]

Customary international law, however, has recently been the cause of considerable scholarly friction,[257] with some critics arguing that the monist incorporation of custom into municipal law is inconsistent with principles of democratic governance.[258] Dubinsky links these concerns with emerging efforts to diminish the scope of custom in American municipal law, principally through the undermining of the *Charming Betsy* canon.[259] In *Serra v Lapin*, a case concerning the consistency of prison wages with customary international law, it was said that the *Charming Betsy* 'bears on a limited range of cases'[260] and could not apply to purely domestic matters that did not inject considerations of international comity.[261] In *Al-Bihani v Obama*,[262] the DC Circuit Court of Appeals was called upon to determine whether a foreign national was detained validly pursuant to the 2001 Congressional Authorization for the Use of Military Force (AUMF). Remarkably, Judge Brown, writing for the majority, held that international law could not limit the President's authority under the AUMF for three reasons. First, the AUMF contained no indication that the customary international

---

[251] 175 US 677, 700 (1900).
[252] E.g. Dickinson (1952) 101 *U Penn LR* 26; Henkin (1984) 82 *Mich LR* 1555; Koh (1998) 111 *Harv LR* 1824.
[253] Dubinsky, in Shelton (2011) 631, 642–3.
[254] 1 *Restatement Third* §111, comment *(d)*.
[255] *Sosa v Alvarez-Machain*, 542 US 692, 737–8 (2004); *Samantar v Yousuf*, 130 S Ct 2278 (2010).
[256] 1 *Restatement Third* §111, reporters' note 4.
[257] Dubinsky, in Shelton (2011) 631, 644–51. E.g. Maier (1989) 10 *Mich JIL* 450, 461, 475–6.
[258] E.g. Bradley & Goldsmith (1997) 110 *Harv LR* 815.
[259] Dubinsky, in Shelton (2011) 631, 644–51. Further: Bradley (1997) 86 *Geo LJ* 479, 536; and generally Alford (2006) 67 *Ohio St LJ* 1339.
[260] 600 F.3d 1191, 1198 (DC Cir, 2010).
[261] For criticism: Dubinsky, in Shelton (2011) 631, 648–9.
[262] 590 F.3d 866 (DC Cir, 2010).

humanitarian law constituted an extra-textual limiting principle,[263] an argument that cuts clear across the line of authorities beginning with the *Charming Betsy* that such an intention need not be expressed. Second, the laws of war had not been introduced directly into US law via enabling legislation and therefore could not be a source of authority for the court.[264] True it is, customary international law could not have provided the detainee in *Al-Bihani* with rights opposable against the US government,[265] but that was not what was sought; rather, Al-Bihani was relying on the AUMF as the source of his rights as interpreted in light of custom. Third, it was said that the laws of war were so vague that they were of limited use in determining the scope of the President's powers under the AUMF and that moreover, 'we have no occasion here to quibble over the intricate application of vague treaty provisions and amorphous customary principles'.[266] Leaving to one side questions as to the indeterminacy of international humanitarian law, this is—in the words of the separate opinion of Judge Williams—'hard to square'[267] with the decision of the Supreme Court in *Hamdin v Rumsfeld* which relied explicitly on the laws of war to determine that the AUMF included the authority to detain.[268]

The DC Circuit, sitting *en banc*, declined to rehear *Al-Bihani v Obama*,[269] but in refusing the application, the majority took the unusual step of simply issuing a short statement to the effect that the issues of the domestic legal status of the laws of armed conflict addressed in the panel's decision were not necessary for the disposition of the merits.[270]

(iii) The Alien Tort Statute (ATS)[271]

The ATS gives federal courts jurisdiction[272] over cases where the applicable law is customary international law where (a) the plaintiff is an alien, (b) the defendant[273] is responsible for a tort, and (c) the tort in question violates international law, including

---

[263] 590 F.3d 866, 871 (DC Cir, 2010).

[264] Ibid.

[265] Further: *Medellin v Texas*, 552 US 491, 505 (2008).

[266] 590 F.3d 866, 871 (DC Cir, 2010).

[267] Ibid, 885.

[268] 542 US 507, 519 (2004) (O'Connor J, plurality).

[269] 619 F.3d 1 (DC Cir, 2010).

[270] Ibid, 1. Cf ibid, 10–53 (Judge Kavanagh). Further: Crook (2010) 104 *AJIL* 656, 657.

[271] 28 USC §1350. Further: *Filartiga v Pena-Irala*, 630 F.2d 876 (2nd Cir, 1980). Also: the Torture Victims Protection Act 1991, which provides a cause of action for any victim of torture or extrajudicial killing wherever committed: 106 Stat 73. For a fuller account of the ATS and its operation in a jurisdictional sense: chapter 21.

[272] E.g. *Sosa v Alvarez-Machain*, 542 US 692, 720 (2004) ('[the ATS] furnished jurisdiction for a relatively modest set of actions alleging violations of the law of nations').

[273] There is no nationality requirement imposed on the defendant by the ATS; accordingly, US companies are named as defendants in most ATS cases, converting the statute into a corporate social responsibility tool: e.g. *Doe v Unocal*, 395 F.3d 932 (9th Cir, 2002) But a determination by the Supreme Court as to whether corporations can be held liable under the ATS has not yet been made: cf *Presbyterian Church of Sudan v Talisman Energy Inc*, 582 F.3d 244 (2nd Cir, 2009); *Kiobel v Royal Dutch Petroleum*, 621 F.3d 111 (2nd Cir, 2010) (*cert* granted); *Sarei v Rio Tinto* (9th Cir, Docket No 02–56256/02–56390/09–56381, 25 October 2011)

customary international law. Since the 'rediscovery' of the ATS in the 1980s, it has been extensively litigated, breathing life into custom as an element of domestic law in the US. Dozens of actions have been brought, some resulting in sizeable settlements. To date, the claims pursued have related largely to human rights abuses; courts have found that such norms include (but are not limited to) prohibitions on genocide and war crimes,[274] torture[275] and cruel, inhuman, or degrading treatment,[276] summary execution,[277] disappearances,[278] non-consensual medical experimentation on children,[279] and forced labour.[280] The Supreme Court in *Sosa v Alvarez-Machain*,[281] however, narrowed the scope of those customary international law rules the breach of which could grant a right of action under the ATS to 'norm[s] of an international character accepted by the civilized world' that are 'defined with a specificity comparable to the features of the 18th-century paradigms we have recognized',[282] being those norms with a definite content and similar international acceptance to the rules extant at the time the Act was passed (e.g. offences against ambassadors, violations of safe conduct, and piracy). Thus, in *Sosa*, the applicant failed in his claim based on 'the clear and universally recognized norm prohibiting arbitrary arrest and detention'.[283] The principles enunciated in *Sosa* were applied in *Sarei v Rio Tinto*, with the majority there holding that the plaintiffs' claims of genocide and war crimes fell within the ATS, whereas claims alleging crimes against humanity arising from a blockade and racial discrimination did not.[284]

(iv) Non-justiciability of political questions and acts of state

The doctrines of act of state and the non-justiciability of political questions are analogous to the similar doctrines that exist in the UK. Both are, however, in a state of considerable flux.

Like the English conception of non-justiciability, the political question doctrine seeks to remove from judicial scrutiny certain politically sensitive questions thought

---

slip op; cf Crook (2010) 104 *AJIL* 119. Following argument on the point, the Supreme Court has relisted *Kiobel* for argument as to its extra-territorial effect generally: Order of 5 March 2012.

[274] *Kadić v Karadžić*, 70 F.3d 232, 240 (2nd Cir, 1995).

[275] *Abebe-Jira v Negewo*, 72 F.3d 844, 847 (11th Cir, 1996).

[276] *Xuncax v Gramajo*, 886 F.Supp 162, 179 (D Mass, 1995).

[277] *Hilao v In re Estate of Marcos*, 25 F.3d 1467, 1472 (9th Cir, 1994); *Xuncax v Gramajo*, 886 F.Supp 162, 179 (D Mass, 1995).

[278] *Forti v Suarez-Mason*, 694 F.Supp 707, 720 (ND Cal, 1988).

[279] *Abdullahi v Pfizer Inc*, 562 F.3d 163, 176–7 (2nd Cir, 2009).

[280] *Doe v Unocal*, 395 F.3d 932, 957 (9th Cir, 2002).

[281] 542 US 692 (2004).

[282] Ibid, 725.

[283] Alvarez had previously succeeded in making out this cause of action before the 9th Circuit sitting *en banc*: 331 F.3d 604, 620 (9th Cir, 2003). For the Supreme Court reasoning dismissing the identified norm as a cause of action: 542 US 692, 731–8 (2004).

[284] (9th Cir, Docket No 02–56256/02–56390/09–56381, 25 October 2011) slip op 19332–3, 19358–80.

inappropriate for judicial resolution.[285] A judicial construct and not constitutionally required, it may be traced back to *Marbury v Madison*,[286] though the most authoritative modern statement was in *Baker v Carr*, which identified six factors that might render a dispute non-justiciable:

Prominent on the surface of any case held to involve a political question is found a textually demonstrable constitutional commitment of the issue to a coordinate political department; or a lack of judicially discoverable and manageable standards for resolving it; or the impossibility of deciding without an initial policy determination of a kind clearly for non-judicial discretion; or the impossibility of a court's undertaking independent resolution without expressing lack of the respect due coordinate branches of government; or an unusual need for unquestioning adherence to a political decision already made; or the potentiality of embarrassment from multifarious pronouncements by various departments on one question.[287]

Despite the litany of factors given in *Baker v Carr*, the doctrine has been applied only rarely and idiosyncratically by the Supreme Court and others in a few discrete domestic fields, including political apportionment and gerrymandering,[288] impeachment,[289] constitutional amendments,[290] the political status of foreign countries,[291] and most importantly for the purposes of the present discussion, foreign affairs and the deployment of armed forces.[292] Thus in *Greenham Women against Cruise Missiles v Reagan*,[293] the decision to deploy American cruise missiles in the UK was held non-justiciable.

As was emphasized in *Klinghoffer*, 'the doctrine is one of "political questions", not "political cases"'.[294] Similarly, in *Kadić v Karadžić*, it was said:

Although we too recognize the potentially detrimental effects of judicial action in cases of this nature, we do not embrace the rather categorical views as to the inappropriateness of judicial action…Not every case 'touching foreign relations' is nonjusticiable…and judges should not reflexively invoke these doctrines to avoid difficult and somewhat sensi-

---

[285] Henkin (1976) 85 *Yale LJ* 597; Redish (1984) 79 *Nw ULR* 1031; Charney (1989) 83 *AJIL* 805; Franck, *Political Questions/Judicial Answers* (1992); Seidman (2004) 37 *J Marshall LR* 441; Choper [2005] *Duke LJ* 1457.

[286] 5 US (1 Cranch) 137, 165–6 (1803).

[287] 369 US 186, 217 (1962). Also: *Schneider v Kissinger*, 412 F.3d 190 (DC Cir, 2005); *Bancoult v McNamara*, 445 F.3d 427 (DC Cir, 2006); *Gonzalez-Vera v Kissinger*, 449 F.3d 1260 (DC Cir, 2006). As a whole, the doctrine is linked to Jeffersonian considerations of the separation of powers: *US Department of Commerce v Montana*, 503 US 442, 456 (1992), quoting *Baker v Carr*, 369 US 186, 217 (1962).

[288] E.g. *Colgrove v Green*, 328 US 549 (1946).

[289] E.g. *Nixon v United States*, 506 US 224 (1993).

[290] E.g. *Coleman v Miller*, 307 US 433, 450 (1939).

[291] *Zivotofsky v Secretary of State*, 571 F.3d 1227 (DC Cir, 2010) (*cert* granted), concerning a statue passed by Congress requiring that 'Israel' be inserted as the place of birth for every American child born in Jerusalem. Further: Crook (2010) 104 *AJIL* 278; Crook (2011) 105 *AJIL* 814.

[292] E.g. *Goldwater v Carter*, 444 US 996 (1976).

[293] 591 F.Supp 1332 (1984). Also: *Gilligan v Morgan*, 413 US 1 (1973) (composition, training, equipping, and control of the National Guard non-justiciable) *Can v United States*, 14 F.3d 160 (2nd Cir, 1994) (issues of succession arising from assets of a foreign state non-justiciable); *Corrie v Caterpillar*, 503 F.3d 974 (9th Cir, 2007) (provision of military assistance by US to foreign states a political question).

[294] *Klinghoffer v SNC Achille Lauro*, 937 F.2d 44, 49 (2nd Cir, 1991).

tive decisions in the context of human rights. We believe a preferable approach is to weigh carefully the relevant considerations on a case-by-case basis. This will permit the judiciary to act where appropriate in light of the express legislative mandate of the Congress...without compromising the primacy of the political branches in foreign affairs.[295]

The doctrine of act of state[296] in the US developed alongside its UK counterpart, and to a certain extent influenced its development.[297] It is presented in the *Restatement Third* as follows:

In the absence of a treaty or other unambiguous agreements regarding controlling legal principles, courts in the United States will generally refrain from examining the validity of a taking by a foreign state of property within its own territory, or sitting in judgment on other acts of a governmental character done by a foreign state within its own territory and applicable there.[298]

The doctrine emerged in *Underhill v Hernandez*,[299] which rooted the concept in considerations of international comity, and presented it as an iron rule from which no derogation was permitted:

Every sovereign state is bound to respect the independence of every other sovereign State, and the courts of one country will not sit in judgment on the acts of the government of another done within its own territory. Redress of grievances by reason of such acts must be obtained through the mean open to be availed of by sovereign powers as between themselves.[300]

Over time, however, the rationale of the doctrine shifted and in the process it became more flexible.[301] In *Banco Nacional de Cuba v Sabbatino* the Supreme Court repositioned the act of state doctrine and abandoned the *Underhill* justification of state sovereignty as determinative, though sovereignty still 'bears on the wisdom of employing [it]'.[302] Rather, the court aligned act of state—like the political question doctrine—with considerations of the separation of powers, and concerns as to possible adverse effects on US foreign policy.[303] The *Sabbatino* Court listed three non-exclusive factors as relevant in applying the doctrine: (a) the greater the degree of codification or

---

[295] 70 F.3d 232, 249 (2nd Cir, 1995), citing *Baker v Carr*, 369 US 186, 211 (1962); *Lamont v Woods*, 948 F.2d 825, 831–2 (2nd Cir, 1991).

[296] Bazyler (1986) 134 *U Penn LR* 325; Chow (1987) 62 *Wash LR* 397; Fox (1992) 33 *Harv ILJ* 521; Born, *International Civil Litigation in United States Courts* (3rd edn, 1996) ch 9; Pearsall (2005) 43 *Col JTL* 999; Patterson (2008) 15 *UC Davis JILP* 111.

[297] *Buttes Gas & Oil Co v Hammer (No 3)* [1982] AC 888, 932–3 (Lord Wilberforce), citing *Underhill v Hernandez*, 168 US 250, 252 (1897), *Oetjen v Central Leather Co*, 246 US 297, 304 (1918), both of which influenced *AM Luther v James Sagor & Co* [1921] 3 KB 252.

[298] 1 *Restatement Third* §443(1).

[299] 168 US 250 (1897).

[300] Ibid, 251–2. Also: *Outjen v Central Leather Co*, 246 US 297, 300–4 (1918) (stressing the need to protect comity and 'the peace of nations'); *Ricaud v American Metal Co*, 246 US 304, 309 (1918) ('to accept a ruling authority and to decide accordingly is not a surrender or abandonment of jurisdiction, rather it is an exercise of it').

[301] 1 *Restatement Third* §443, comment *(a)*.

[302] 376 US 398, 401(1964).

[303] Ibid, 423.

consensus concerning a particular area of international law to which the act relates, the more appropriate it is for the judiciary to render decisions regarding it; (b) the greater the political controversy attending the matter, the more likely the doctrine is to be applied; and (c) where the government that committed the act still exists, the doctrine is more likely to be applied. In applying these factors, the court concluded that it was not competent to examine the validity of the nationalization of foreign property by the Cuban government within its own territory, even where the action was illegal under international law.[304]

The doctrine was significantly restricted in its operation when revisited by the Supreme Court in *Kirkpatrick*.[305] Two American contractors had bid for a construction contract with the Nigerian Air Force. The winner secured the contract through bribery, and the loser sued under US anti-racketeering laws. The Court held that the kind of balancing act set down in *Sabbatino* was only required where a plaintiff challenged the *legal effect* of the act of a foreign state. Thus the act of state doctrine will only apply where a US court is called upon squarely to assess the validity of the act in question under the sovereign's own laws. Peripheral engagement with acts of state will not frustrate a claim, nor will an assessment of whether the act took place in fact or the motivations behind it.[306] Moreover, the doctrine applies only to 'official' or 'public' acts of the sovereign (acts *iure imperii*);[307] thus it will apply to acts such as the passage of laws, governmental decrees, the creation of government agencies and military/police actions, but not to those things performed in a private capacity (acts *iure gestionis*).[308]

The act of state doctrine is also subject to a series of discrete further exceptions.[309] In the first place, as it is, in some sense, a choice of law issue, it will not apply where a US court can look to a treaty or other 'unambiguous instrument regarding controlling legal principles'.[310]

The second exception is sometimes referred to as the *Bernstein* exception,[311] and will arise where the State Department guides the courts as to the applicability of the act of state doctrine. The status of this exception is controversial, however; in *Bernstein* itself, a majority of the justices refused to accept the directive of the State Department as dispositive. In a later case, Justice Douglas warned that such a rule would make

---

[304] Ibid, 428. Further: *Alfred Dunhill of London Inc v Republic of Cuba*, 425 US 682 (1976).

[305] *WS Kirkpatrick & Co Inc v Environmental Tectonics Corporation International*, 493 US 400 (1990). Further: Bederman, *International Law Frameworks* (2001) 199 (arguing that *Kirkpatrick* took the act of state doctrine in the US 'to the vanishing point').

[306] 493 US 400, 405, 409 (1990).

[307] Ibid, 409–10.

[308] *Alfred Dunhill of London Inc v Republic of Cuba*, 425 US 682, 711 (1976). Also: *Malewicz v City of Amsterdam*, 362 F.Supp 2d 298, 314 (DDC, 2005).

[309] Born (3rd edn, 1996) 729–44.

[310] *Banco Nacional de Cuba v Sabbatino*, 376 US 398, 428 (1964); *American Intern Group Inc v Islamic Republic of Iran*, 493 F.Supp 522, 525 (DDC, 1980); *Kalamazoo Spice Extraction Co v PMG of Socialist Ethiopia*, 728 F.2d 422 (6th Cir, 1984). Further: Born (3rd edn, 1996) 738–4.

[311] *Bernstein v NV Nederlandsche-Amerikannsche Stoomvart-Maatschappij*, 210 F.2d 375 (2nd Cir, 1954).

the Supreme Court a 'mere errand boy for the Executive Branch which may choose to pick some people's chestnuts from the fire, but not others'.[312] The Supreme Court in *Kirkpatrick* placed special emphasis on the judiciary's responsibilities under Article III of the Constitution, placing the exception further in doubt.[313]

The third exception is similarly inchoate, and may arise where the act of state complained of is 'commercial' rather than 'official'.[314] This distinction can be seen as a continuation of the public/private discussion surrounding the scope of the original doctrine and has never been adopted squarely by the Supreme Court.[315] But the situation is characterized by divisions and debate between and even within the various Circuit Courts of Appeals.[316]

The fourth, fifth, and six exceptions to the act of state doctrine are statutory in origin. The fourth is relatively straightforward: the Federal Arbitration Act[317] provides expressly that '[e]nforcement of arbitration agreements...shall not be refused on the basis of the Act of State doctrine'.[318] The fifth was an amendment introduced by the outraged Senator Hickenlooper of Iowa in response to the decision in *Sabbatino*. The so-called 'Second Hickenlooper Amendment'[319] provides generally that the act of state doctrine shall not apply to claims concerning alleged expropriations in violation of international law. It has, however, been interpreted narrowly by the courts, which have held that the amendment applies only where specific properly directly involved in the unlawful act of state is located in the US.[320] Other courts have held that the amendment will only apply in relation to property rights, as opposed to rights arising in contract.[321] The sixth statutory exception may arise in the case of the Torture Victims Protection Act,[322] which allows the filing of civil suits against individuals who, acting in an official capacity for a foreign nation, have committed torture or extrajudicial killing.

---

[312] *First National City Bank v Banco Nacional de Cuba*, 406 US 750, 733 (1972).

[313] *WS Kirkpatrick & Co Inc v Environmental Tectonics Corporation International*, 493 US 400, 404–10 (1990). Further: Denza, in Evans (3rd edn, 2010) 411, 412–17.

[314] Born (3rd edn, 1996) 733–8.

[315] E.g. *Alfred Dunhill of London Inc v Republic of Cuba*, 425 US 682, 695 (1976) (White J, plurality); *WS Kirkpatrick & Co Inc v Environmental Tectonics Corporation International*, 493 US 400, 404–5 (1990); *United States v Giffen*, 326 F.Supp 2d 497 (SDNY, 2005) (declining to apply act of state doctrine where parties' contract made actions commercial, as opposed to governmental); *Government of the Dominican Republic v AES Corporation*, 466 F.Supp 2d 680, 695 (ED Va, 2006) ('The act of state doctrine does not cover private and commercial acts of sovereign states'); *Malewicz v City of Amsterdam*, 517 F.Supp 2d 332, 337–9 (DDC, 2007) (acquisition of painting by city official not a public act); but cf *Honduras Aircraft Registry Ltd v Government of Honduras*, 129 F.3d 543, 550 (11th Cir, 1997); *Glen v Club Mediterranee SA*, 450 F.3d 1251, 1254 n2 (11th Cir, 2006) (no commercial activity exception).

[316] Patterson (2008) 15 *UC Davis JILP* 111, 125–8.

[317] 9 USC §15.

[318] Further: *Republic of Ecuador v ChevronTexaco Corporation*, 376 F.Supp 2d 334, 367 (SDNY, 2005).

[319] 22 USC §2370(e)(2).

[320] E.g. *Banco Nacional de Cuba v Chase Manhattan Bank*, 658 F.2d 875, 882 (2nd Cir, 1981); *Compania de Gas de Nuevo Laredo v Entex Inc*, 696 F.2d 332 (5th Cir, 1982).

[321] *Hunt v Coastal States Gas Producing Co* (1979) 66 ILR 361. Further: Born (3rd edn, 1996) 744.

[322] 28 USC §1350.

4. INTERNATIONAL LAW IN THE CIVIL LAW TRADITION

It is misleading to speak of a civil law approach to the reception of international law; since no uniform approach can be identified. A few general observations may be made before moving on to consider six specific case studies (viz., France, Germany, Italy, Russia, the Netherlands, Sweden).

With some notable exceptions, such as the Netherlands, Italy, and Sweden, European jurisdictions approach customary international law from a monist perspective, and indeed many give it some form of constitutional standing. Europe is also emblematic of the monist approach to treaty law, with treaties—to the extent they are capable of standing alone—given direct effect. This is not to say that the executive is given a free hand to make treaties, but rather that the constitutions of states such as France, the Russian Federation, and the Netherlands provide that the legislature play a role in the treaty-making process *prior* to signature and/or ratification. Finally, with regard to judicial avoidance techniques, the European countries tend to view the non-justiciability of foreign acts of state as an Anglo-American doctrine. They do, however, practice varying degrees of judicial restraint with regard to the acts of their own governments, with France and Italy practicing a model of non-justiciability similar to UK and US practice, Germany and the Netherlands operating a more overtly constitutional model, Sweden coming close to seeing all legislative acts as non-justiciable, and Russia adopting the completely opposite view.

(A) CUSTOMARY INTERNATIONAL LAW IN THE EUROPEAN TRADITION

As a general rule, the civil law jurisdictions adopt a monist stance with regard to customary international law, with incorporation frequently occurring at a constitutional level.

(i) France

In France, this situation subsists despite the fact that the 1958 Constitution of the Fifth Republic makes no reference to custom. Rather, it contains in its preamble a *renvoi* to its predecessor,[323] the 1946 Constitution of the Fourth Republic, which had stated that 'the French Republic, true to its traditions, conforms to the rules of international public law'.[324] The only relevant substantive provision in the 1946 preamble states that: 'Subject to reciprocity, France shall consent to the limitations upon its sovereignty

---

[323] Constitution of the Fifth Republic, Preamble ('The French people solemnly proclaim their attachment to the Rights of Man and the principles of national sovereignty as defined by the Declaration of 1789, confirmed and complemented by the Preamble to the Constitution of 1946').

[324] Constitution of the Fourth Republic, Preamble, §14.

necessary to the organization and preservation of peace'.[325] These are ambiguous guidelines for the incorporation of custom.[326] But the *Conseil Constitutionnel* appears to have accepted the applicability of custom into the French system and attempts to ensure the compatibility of French legislation with it.[327] For example, by referring in its decision of 9 April 1992[328] on the Treaty of Maastricht[329] to the 'rules of public international law', the *Conseil* accepted 'the rule *pacta sunt servanda* which implies that all treaties that are in force bind the parties and must be executed by them in good faith'.

Some scholars seek to draw comparisons between the approach of the *Conseil Constitutionnel* and the supposedly negative approach of the *Conseil d'État*.[330] This is not entirely unfair: as noted by Decaux,[331] whilst the latter may recognize the existence of custom it tends to bestow on it an infra-legislative character, at least insofar as it cannot prevail over later domestic laws.[332]

(ii) Germany

The position is much more straightforward in Germany: the Basic Law provides in Article 25 that '[t]he general rules of public international law form part of the Federal law. They take precedence over the laws and directly create rights and duties for the inhabitants of the Federal territory'.[333] The first sentence of Article 25 establishes custom as part of German law; the second elevates it in the municipal hierarchy of norms, such that any internal legislation deemed inconsistent will be void. Custom is, however, subject to the provisions of the Basic Law itself. But the Federal Constitutional Court has developed an unwritten principle on the commitment of the Basic Law to international law,[334] requiring all municipal law—including the Basic Law itself—to be interpreted consistently with international law to the extent possible.

---

[325] Ibid, §15.

[326] Decaux, in Shelton (2011) 205, 235.

[327] E.g. *Re Self-Determination of the Comoros Islands*, 30 December 1975, Rec 41, 74 ILR 91; *Nationalization Law*, 16 January 1982, Rec 18, 75 ILR 700; *Nationalization Law (No 2)*, 11 February 1982, Rec 31, 75 ILR 700; *Law on the Evolution of New Caledonia*, 8 August 1985, Rec 63; *Law on the Evolution of New Caledonia (No 2)*, 23 August 1985, Rec 70.

[328] *Treaty on European Union*, 9 April 1992, Rec 55, 93 ILR 337.

[329] Treaty on European Union, 7 February 1992, *OJEU* C 191/1.

[330] E.g. Carreau, *Droit international* (9th edn, 2007) 447.

[331] Decaux, in Shelton (2011) 205, 236-7.

[332] E.g. *Paulin* [2000] Rec Lebon 317; *Zaidi* [2000] Rec Lebon 159; *Aquarone* [1997] Rec Lebon 206.

[333] 23 May 1949; amended by the Unification Treaty, 31 August 1990, 30 ILM 457. The most recent (58th) amendment occurred on 27 July 2010. On reunification: Harris (1991) 81 *Geo Rev* 170. Notable considerations of Art 25 by the Constitutional Court include: *Philippine Embassy*, 46 BVerfGE 342 (1977), 65 ILR 146; *National Iranian Oil Company*, 64 BVerfGE 1 (1983), 65 ILR 215; 75 BVerfGE 1 (1988) (further: decision of 4 December 2007, 2 BvR 38/06); *Diplomatic Immunity (Syria)*, 96 BVerfGE 68 (1997), 115 ILR 595; 117 BVerfGE 141 (2006); *Argentine Necessity*, 118 BVerfGE 124 (2007), 138 ILR 1.

[334] Pithily rendered in German as *Völkerrechtsfreundlichkeit des Grundgesetzes*: Folz, in Shelton (2011) 240, 245-6.

In general German judges may take judicial notice of the rules of customary inter-national law and apply them as such.[335] In case of doubt as to whether a customary rule exists or is capable of creating individual rights, Article 100(2) of the Basic Law requires the matter to be referred to the Federal Constitutional Court, which by tradi-tion includes a public international law specialist.

(iii) Italy

A similar position has been taken by Italy, with Article 10(1) of the Constitution of 1948 providing that '[t]he Italian legal system conforms to the generally recognized rules of international law'. This provides a vehicle for the incorporation of custom into munici-pal law, though the ordinary method of integration via legislation remains especially for those norms of customary international law which are considered to be non-self-executing. Within the domestic hierarchy, therefore, custom assumes the status of a constitutional directive, and municipal laws will be invalid to the extent of any incon-sistency. This leaves open the question whether custom is to be considered superior to the Constitution itself, an issue addressed by the Constitutional Court in *Russel v Societa Immobiliare Soblim*,[336] which concerned a possible conflict between diplomatic immunity and Article 24(1) of the Constitution guaranteeing an individual right of suit. There it was held that custom—by way of the *lex specialis* rule—could only prevail over the terms of the Constitution where the norm in question was formed prior to the entry into force of the Constitution. More recently, however, the Court appears to have adjusted this rigidly chronological rule, and has since stated that 'fundamental prin-ciples of the constitutional order' and 'inalienable rights of the human being' are the only limitations on the incorporation of custom.[337] Thus custom is considered a source of law that may override the Constitution as *lex specialis* to the extent that is does not conflict with a fundamental rule of the constitutional order concerning an inalienable human right.[338] In a more recent case the *Corte di Cassazione* said:

Article 10, paragraph 1, of the Constitution affirms that the Italian legal order must conform to the generally recognized rules of international law . . . However, even those scholars main-taining that customary rules incorporated by means of Article 10 enjoy a constitutional sta-tus . . . recognize that they must respect the basic principles of our legal order, which cannot be derogated from or modified. Fundamental human rights are among the constitutional principles which cannot be derogated from by generally recognized rules of international law.[339]

---

[335] Ibid, 245.

[336] Constitutional Court, 18 June 1979, Judgment No 48, 78 ILR 101.

[337] Constitutional Court, 23 March 2001, Judgment No 73. Earlier: Constitutional Court, 29 January 1996, Judgment No 15.

[338] Scholars differ on whether peremptory norms are subject to the same limitations. It seems arguable that they may be considered themselves as 'fundamental principles of the constitutional order': Cataldi, in Shelton (2011) 328, 346, 349–52. Also: Constitutional Court, 29 December 1988, Judgment No 1146; *Ferrini v Federal Republic of Germany*, *Corte di Cassazione*, 11 March 2004, Judgment No 5044, 128 ILR 659.

[339] *Corte di Cassazione*, 13 January 2009, Judgment No 1072.

Within the Italian system, Article 10(1) represents an unusually powerful method of direct incorporation with respect to custom; it has been said to be a 'permanent converter' of such norms.[340] It has been held to extend to peremptory norms as well as general principles of international law.[341] Thus all domestic legal institutions have jurisdiction to verify the content of customary international law and apply it to relevant municipal statutes. The courts are considered independent in this respect and intervention by legislature or executive is not permitted. Nor is the court required to seek proof from a party seeking to apply a customary rule any more than any other rule of Italian law.

(iv) Russian Federation

Perhaps the most unusual situation is that of the Russian Federation. On the surface, the Russian position owes much to the strongly monist attitude towards custom seen in Germany and Italy. Article 15(4) of the Constitution of the Russian Federation of 1993 provides that the 'commonly recognized principles and norms of the international law and the international treaties of the Russian Federation shall be a component part of its legal system'.[342] This is not an ordinary constitutional norm; it is part of the first chapter of the Constitution, which may only be amended via a complicated special procedure. Moreover, the rule has been replicated in all codes and Federal Laws adopted after the Constitution entered into effect.[343] This stands in marked contrast to the system as it stood under the Soviet Union, where the invocation of international law by the courts was rare.[344]

Nonetheless the reality differs very much from the theory of Article 15(4). Quite simply, Russian courts are ill equipped to determine the content of custom and the Supreme Court offers the lower courts very little in the way of useful direction. In the 10 October 2003 ruling of the Plenum of the Supreme Court, it was held that:

The commonly recognised principles of the international law shall imply the basic imperative norms of the international law accepted and recognised by the international community of States as a whole, the deviation from which is inadmissible. The commonly recognised principles of the international law, in particular, comprise the principle of universal respect for human rights and the principle of fair implementation of international obligations. The commonly recognised norm of the international law shall imply the rule of conduct

---

[340] Further: Cataldi, in Shelton (2011) 328, 342–4.

[341] On general principles: *Re Hartmann and Pude*, Constitutional Court, 18 April 1967, Judgment No 48, 71 ILR 232; *Zennaro*, Constitutional Court, 8 April 1976, Judgment No 69, 77 ILR 581; Constitutional Court, 27 April 1994, Judgment No 168. On peremptory norms: *Ferrini v Federal Republic of Germany*, *Corte di Cassazione*, 11 March 2004, Judgment No 5044, 128 ILR 659; *Lozano v Italy*, *Corte di Cassazione*, 24 July 2008, Case No 31171/2008, ILDC 1085 (IT 2008); *Corte di Cassazione*, 13 January 2009, Judgment No 1072.

[342] Butler, *Russian Law* (3rd edn, 2009) 693–6.

[343] Marochkin (2007) 6 *Chin JIL* 329, 330.

[344] On international law and the USSR: Gryzbowski, *Soviet Public International Law* (1970).

accepted and recognised as legally mandatory by the international community of States as a whole.[345]

The failure to articulate the procedure by which custom is to be received into Russian municipal law underpins Tikhomirov's observation that Russian courts tend not to apply customary international law, but prefer to have reference to the corpus of conventional law that Russia has accumulated.[346] Nonetheless, custom is applied on occasion, for example in *Re Khordodovskiy*,[347] where the applicant brought proceedings to have a portion of the Rules of Internal Discipline in Penitentiary Institutions invalidated. The provision prevented a prisoner from obtaining access to a lawyer or other representative within the prisoner's working hours, a position contrary to customary international law.[348] The Cassation Chamber of the Supreme Court held that by virtue of Article 15(4) of the Constitution, this norm had been integrated into the municipal law of the Russian Federation, and upheld the decision of the Supreme Court invalidating the offending regulation.[349]

(v) The Netherlands

In contrast to its position on treaties, the Constitution of the Netherlands is silent as to the municipal effect of custom.[350] In principle, it does not prevail over domestic legislation,[351] the Constitution or the 1954 Charter for the Kingdom.[352] But several domestic statutes seek to incorporate custom into municipal law on a *sui generis* basis; where this occurs and the norm in question is self-executing, it will prevail over other domestic laws.[353] In certain other instances, custom may be integrated without the need for implementing legislation,[354] though custom will only take priority over domestic delegated legislation. On those rare occasions where the Dutch courts make

---

[345] Plenum of the Supreme Court of the Russian Federation, Decree No 5, 10 October 2003, §1.

[346] Tikhomirov, in Shelton (2011) 517, 523. But cf Danilenko (1999) 10 *EJIL* 51, 57–9, identifying an emerging trend in the application of custom in the jurisprudence of the Russian Constitutional Court. Danilenko goes on to note, however, that 'ordinary' Russian courts have much less experience in applying custom, and are more likely to rely on treaties and 'commercial customs in the sphere of international trade' (ibid, 58–9). Further: Denza, in Evans (3rd edn, 2010) 411, 420–1. Marochkin (2007) 6 *Chin JIL* 329, 344, who despite his initial pessimism, nonetheless concludes 'we can speak [generally] about a positive attitude of the Court system towards international law'.

[347] *Re Khordodovskiy* (2006) 133 ILR 365.

[348] As reflected in the Body of Principles for the Protection of All Persons under any Form of Detention or Imprisonment, GA Res 43/173, 9 December 1988, Principle 18.

[349] (2003) 133 ILR 365, 370.

[350] The Constitution dates from 1848, but has been amended repeatedly, most recently in 2002. Further: Erades, in van Panhuys, Jitta, Sik & Stuyt (eds), 3 *International Law in the Netherlands* (1980) 388.

[351] NJ (1961) No 2.

[352] Alkema, in Shelton (2011) 407, 419. The Charter (*Statuut*) regulates the relationship between the Netherlands and its former colonial territories in the Caribbean. E.g. NJ (1974) No 361.

[353] Alkema, in Shelton (2011) 407, 419. This form of integration will generally concern the execution of court judgments, as well as certain matters of criminal and fiscal law. E.g. General Provisions Kingdom Legislation Act of 1829, Art 13(a): 'The courts' jurisdiction and the enforceability of judgments is subject to the exceptions recognised in international law'.

[354] E.g. NJ (1979) No 113, reported in Barnhoorn (1980) 11 *NYIL* 289, 326.

reference to custom, it is considered appropriate for them to take into account the views of the government, which represents the state in international affairs and is as such considered to be a law-making actor,[355] unless the custom in question is so clear that no further input is required.

(vi) Sweden

Of the systems analysed, the most strongly dualist (at least formally) is that of Sweden. Nowhere in the Swedish Constitution is customary law mentioned and no statute purports to integrate customary international law as a whole into Swedish municipal law. Aside from European Court of Human Rights and EU cases, *sui generis* examples of transformation of customary norms are largely confined to the criminal sphere.[356]

However, customary international law is not deprived of all legal effect within the Swedish legal system. In fact, the Swedish Supreme Court has applied principles of customary international law when such principles are not enshrined in statute.[357] Moreover, Swedish courts assume that the *Riksdag* and the executive do not intend to violate international law when enacting statutes or issuing regulations.[358] Ambiguous statutes will, where possible, be interpreted consistently with international law. Moreover, Swedish courts may go further still and assume a tacit reservation in favour of international law within Swedish legislation generally. In light of the above, Swedish courts have granted foreign states jurisdictional immunity despite the absence of any rule that permits it.[359] But where a principle of custom conflicts directly with Swedish law and permits no reinterpretation, the court is expected to follow the municipal directive.[360]

(B) TREATIES AND NATIONAL LAW IN THE EUROPEAN TRADITION

A relatively common theme between European jurisdictions is the supremacy of treaties over domestic law. For this reason, European constitutions will generally prescribe careful controls over the signature and ratification of international agreements.

---

[355] Alkema, in Shelton (2011) 407, 420.

[356] Bogdan (1994) 63 *Nordic JIL* 3, 4–6; Klamberg (2009) 9 *Int Crim LR* 395, 296–7. E.g. Swedish Criminal Code (*Brottsbalken*), ch 22.6: 'A person guilty of a serious violation of a treaty or agreement with a foreign power or an infraction of a generally recognised principle or tenet relating to international humanitarian law concerned armed conflict shall be sentenced for [a] crime against international law and imprisoned at most for four years'.

[357] E.g. *Anna B v Union of Soviet Socialist Republics* [1934] NJA 206; *The Crow v von Herder* [1964] NJA 65.

[358] Bogdan (1994) 63 *Nordic JIL* 3, 5.

[359] Ibid. Cf e.g. *In re Bolin* [1934] NJA 206, 7 ILR 186; *The Rigmor* [1942] NJA 65, 10 ILR 240; *Municipality of Västerås v Iceland* [1999] NJA 821, 128 ILR 705. Apart from a statute of 1938 which implements the 1929 Brussels Convention on state-owned vessels, Sweden does not have any general legislation on sovereign immunity. The Swedish Supreme Court has applied the rules and principles of customary international law in the area of state immunity: e.g. *Bostadsrättsföreningen x 13 v Kingdom of Belgium* [2009] NJA 905; *Sedelmayer v Russian Federation*, 1 July 2011, available at www.italaw.com.

[360] Bogdan (1994) 63 *Nordic JIL* 3, 5.

(i) France

This may be seen in the context of the French Constitution, which provides in Article 55 that:

Treaties or agreements duly ratified or approved shall, upon publication, prevail over Acts of Parliament, subject, with respect to each agreement or treaty, to its application by the other party.

This places treaties at a level superior to ordinary legislation but inferior to the Constitution.[361] But the *Conseil Constitutionnel* does not consider treaties to form part of the corpus of constitutionality (i.e., constitutional norms in their own right), meaning that it is spared the ordeal of assessing the conformity of every new treaty or international agreement with those that came before it.[362] Article 54 does provide some form of constitutional oversight by way of referral 'from the President of the Republic... the Prime Minister... the President of one or the other Houses or from sixty Members of the National Assembly or sixty Senators'. Where the *Conseil* declares a proposed agreement incompatible, revision of the Constitution prior to ratification under Article 52 or 53 is required or the treaty will need to be abandoned.[363]

Insofar as the actual incorporation of treaties is concerned, the Constitution distinguishes between ordinary treaties, which may be signed and ratified by the President under Article 52, and those treaties which require an additional act of Parliament in order for ratification to occur (Article 53):

Peace Treaties, Trade agreements, treaties or agreements relating to international organization, those committing the finances of the State, those modifying provisions which are the preserve of statute law, those relating to the status of persons, and those involving the ceding, exchanging or acquiring of territory, may be ratified or approved only by an Act of Parliament.

They shall not take effect until such ratification or approval has been secured.

The category of treaties defined by Article 53 is potentially broad, rendering France in respect of most significant agreements effectively dualist,[364] though it claims to be a monist jurisdiction in the sense that no directly implementing statute is required

---

[361] Decaux, in Shelton (2011) 207, 216. This much is confirmed by the *Conseil Constitutionnel: Treaty establishing a European Constitution*, 19 November 2004, Rec 173. The *Conseil d'État* only conceded that Art 55 applies to legislation that post-dates the treaty in question in 1989 (*Re Nicolo* [1989] Rec Lebon 748, 93 ILR 286): Denza, in Evans (3rd edn, 2010) 411, 420. In *Sarran*, the *Conseil* held that the superiority of treaties did not extend to provisions of a constitutional character: [1998] Rec Lebon 368. Also: *Syndicat national de l'industrie pharmaceutique* [2001] Rec Lebon 624.

[362] The sole exception to this rule is where a new treaty addresses directly a previously ratified treaty: *Treaty on European Union*, 9 April 1992, Rec 55, 93 ILR 337.

[363] The use of this procedure is not uncommon. The Treaty of Maastricht was the subject of three referrals: one presidential leading to *Treaty on European Union*, 9 April 1992, Rec 55, 93 ILR 337; a senatorial referral leading to *Treaty on European Union (No 2)*, 2 September 1992, Rec 76, 98 ILR 180; and one referral by the National Assembly on the referendum law authorizing ratification, leading to *Treaty on European Union (No 3)*, 23 September 1992, Rec 94. Further: Decaux, in Shelton (2011) 207, 217.

[364] Decaux, in Shelton (2011) 207, 212.

to give a duly concluded and published treaty domestic effect. The Article 53 division does not correspond to any taxonomy found elsewhere, and thus irrespective of whether ratification by Parliament is required prior to signature, France will incur an international obligation upon signature.

As stated in Article 55 of the Constitution, once a treaty has (as the case may be) been subjected to prior scrutiny by the *Conseil Constitutionnel*, prompted constitutional revision, been ratified by the required number of parties and been published in the *Journal Officiel*, it will prima facie have supremacy over domestic law. Treaties will ordinarily be held to be self-executing, save where (a) the treaty in question contains only obligations directed to and as between states or (b) it cannot be applied without legislative elaboration. The obstacle course does not end there, however: the *Conseil Constitutionnel* has proved curiously reticent when called upon to assess the conformity of domestic laws with published treaties.[365] This may be explained by the refusal of the *Conseil* to give constitutional status to international norms,[366] thus allowing for the *Cour de Cassation* and *Conseil d'État*, which have no jurisdiction to exercise constitutional control, to assess the conformity of later laws with treaties. The jurisprudence of the *Cour de Cassation* is accordingly more forthright: in *Cafés Jacques Vabre*[367] it was held that the EEC Treaty[368] was to be applied over the French Customs Code, even though the latter was later in time. The *Conseil d'État* went further still in the *Gardedieu* judgment, noting that the responsibility of the state is

...susceptible to being engaged...because of obligations that belong to it to ensure the respect for international conventions by public authorities, to make amends for all prejudices that result from the intervention of a law that is adopted in disregard of the international obligations of France.[369]

When applying this principle, French courts must continue to comply with the terms of the Constitution. A treaty that has not been published in the *Journal Officiel* cannot be invoked before a judge and will not have domestic effect, even if in force

---

[365] *Abortion Law*, 15 January 1975, Rec 19, 74 ILR 523; *1961 Supplementary Budget Amendment*, 20 July 1977, Rec 39; *Monthly Payment Law*, 18 January 1978, Rec 21; *Mutual Assistance in Criminal Matters*, 17 July 1980, Rec 36; *Finance Act 1990*, 29 December 1989, Rec 110; *Senate Rules Amendment*, 23 July 1991, Rec 81; *Economic and Financial Law*, 24 July 1991, Rec 82; *Planning and Building Law*, 21 January 1994, Rec 40; *Foreign Residence and Asylum Law*, 5 May 1998, Rec 245; *Finance Act 1999*, 29 December 1998, Rec 326; *Universal Healthcare Law*, 23 July 1999, Rec 100; *Equal Opportunity Law*, 30 March 2006, Rec 50. Further: Decaux, in Shelton (2011) 207, 223–5.

[366] *Abortion Law*, 15 January 1975, Rec 19, 74 ILR 523. When acting as electoral judge, however, the *Conseil* will assess the conformity of domestic laws to international treaties (*Elections of the Val d'Oise*, 21 October 1988, Rec 183, 111 ILR 496).

[367] *Administration des Douanes v Société Cafés Jacques Vabre* [1975] Rec Dalloz 497, 93 ILR 240, 263. This approach has been expanded beyond the Community sphere, most notably in the context of the criminal law: e.g. *Glaeser* [1976] Rec Dalloz 1, 74 ILR 700; *Barbie*, 20 December 1985, JCP 1986 II 20655, 78 ILR 124.

[368] Treaty establishing the European Economic Community, 25 March 1957, 298 UNTS 3.

[369] [2007] Rec Lebon 78.

internationally.[370] The court will also be required to assess the condition of 'reciprocity' in Article 55,[371] though the *Conseil Constitutionnel* has somewhat narrowed the scope of this caveat such that it does not have to apply to all treaties,[372] either on the basis of the subjective intention of the legislature in ratifying it or the objective character of the rights contained within the treaty.[373] Thus, when examining the ICC Statute,[374] the *Conseil* stated that the obligations that follow from it 'apply to each of the State parties independently from conditions for their execution by other parties; that thus the reservation of reciprocity mentioned in Article 55 of the Constitution is not to be applied'.[375] Where the issue is raised before the *Conseil d'État*, it must consult the Ministry of Foreign Affairs as to whether reciprocity exists.[376] It has generally confined application of the doctrine to bilateral treaties, presumably due to the difficulty of monitoring international participation in multilateral treaties of an objective character.[377] This traditional stance is subject to potential changes, however, as the European Court of Human Rights has considered it to be a violation of the right to fair trial.[378]

(ii) Germany

Again, the position in Germany is more direct. Article 59(2) of the Basic Law bestows on the legislature the capacity to regulate the treaty-making power of the executive as follows:

Treaties that regulate the political relations of the Federation or relate to subjects of federal legislation require the consent or participation, in the form of a federal statute, of the bodies competent in any specific case for such federal legislation.

Due to the broad wording of Article 59(2), most treaties concluded by Germany will require prior legislative ratification, published in the *Bundesgesetzblatt*.[379] Following entry into force of the treaty, the German courts will apply it as part of national law.[380] Thus a treaty stands on a similar footing to an ordinary statute and may be repealed

---

[370] *National Federation of Guardianship Associations* [2000] Rec Lebon 781; *Prefect of La Gironde v Mhamedi* [1992] Rec Lebon 446, 106 ILR 204 (suspension of application of treaty must also be subject to publication). Further: Decaux, in Shelton (2011) 207, 226.

[371] Further: Decaux, *La Réciprocité en droit international* (1980).

[372] *Finance Act 1981*, 30 December 1980, Rec 53; *Higher Education Framework Act*, 30 October 1981, Rec 31.

[373] Decaux, in Shelton (2011) 207, 227.

[374] 17 July 1998, 2187 UNTS 3.

[375] *Re ICC Statute*, 22 January 1999, Rec 29, 125 ILR 475.

[376] E.g. *GITSI* [1992] Rec Lebon 346, 106 ILR 198; *Mme Chevrol-Benkeddach* [1999] Rec Lebon 116.

[377] Decaux, in Shelton (2011) 207, 227.

[378] *Chevrol v France* [2003] EtCHR 49636/99, §§76–84.

[379] Paulus, in Sloss (ed), *The Role of Domestic Courts in Treaty Enforcement* (2009) 209, 214–18.

[380] There is some disagreement within the German authorities as to how this is brought about. Total incorporation is seen as too radical, whereas transformation tends to decontextualize the treaty from the international sphere. The approach most germane to Art 59(2) is that of 'execution' which characterizes the legislative ratification of the treaty as a legislative directive to follow the provisions of the treaty as international law within the domestic order: ibid, 217–18.

expressly or impliedly by later legislation, though there is a heavy presumption against this.[381] The views of the executive will not be taken into account due to a fairly strict separation of powers and the total absence of any *amicus curiae* procedure by which it might make itself heard.[382]

In applying treaties, German courts recognize the distinction between self-executing and non-self-executing treaties, though there is a certain tendency to assume the latter. A treaty provision will be considered non-self-executing where (1) the treaty excludes direct application, (2) the treaty refers to the necessity of further implementation by states parties, either nationally (by decree) or internationally (by further interstate agreements), and (3) the treaty provision in question cannot be applied directly as it (a) does not designate the responsible administration, (b) does not define a necessary administrative procedure, or (c) does not designate the jurisdiction of a specific court.[383] The Federal Constitutional Court has a special role to play in exercising judicial review of lower courts beyond what would be appropriate in ordinary domestic cases:

[T]he Federal Constitutional Court is also competent to prevent and remove, if possible, violations of public international law that consist in the incorrect application or non-observance by German courts of international law obligations and may give rise to international law responsibility on the part of Germany…In this, the Federal Constitutional Court is indirectly in the service of enforcing international law and in this way reduces the risk of failing to comply with international law. For this reason, it may be necessary, deviating from the customary standard, to review the application and interpretation of international law treaties by the ordinary courts.[384]

Under this system, problems may arise where a treaty requiring implementation via domestic legislation refers matters to an international tribunal which then issues a decision inconsistent with a pronouncement of the Federal Constitutional Court. This occurred in 2004, where the European Court of Human Rights ruled the developed approach of the Federal Constitutional Court with respect to the right to privacy inconsistent with ECHR Article 8.[385] As a result, the Court made a pronouncement as to the rank and role of the ECHR within the German legal order:[386] it held that while a constitutional complaint could only be based on an alleged violation of fundamental rights guaranteed in the *Grundgesetz*, and not on the ECHR as such, the ECHR nonetheless formed part of the legal order. Thus the German courts were required to take heed of the ECHR as interpreted by the European Court of Human Rights, with a failure to do so being grounds for a constitutional complaint.[387]

---

[381] Ibid, 209–10.

[382] Folz, in Shelton (2011) 240, 244; cf Paulus, in Sloss (2009) 209, 221–2.

[383] Folz, in Shelton (2011) 240, 242–3.

[384] 111 BVerfGE 307, 328 (2004).

[385] *Von Hannover v Germany* [2004] ECtHR 59320/00, overruling 101 BVerfGE 361 (1999).

[386] Generally: 111 BVerfGE 307 (2004).

[387] The Court upheld this realignment with Strasbourg in principle in 120 BVerfGE 180 (2008), which was then appealed (again) to the ECtHR (Application No 60641/08, pending). Similar developments have

(iii) Italy

The Italian Constitution makes no express provision for the incorporation of international treaties into municipal law; accordingly, a treaty will produce no direct effect unless it has been integrated via legislation.[388] Two methods for this are usually identified:[389] the 'special' method, which incorporates the treaty into law via a short statute with the treaty annexed; and the 'ordinary' method, which reformulates and interprets the treaty before amending national legislation in order to achieve implementation. The two are on occasion combined. The ordinary procedure is utilized wherever the treaty is incapable of standing on its own two feet as a national law, and therefore requires legislative elaboration, with the special method used where international norms 'have an inherent aptitude—to be ascertained on a case-by-case basis—to be directly applied in the domestic order'.[390]

Legislative ratification via the special method will usually contain two operative provisions: an article authorizing ratification, and an article ordering 'full implementation' of the treaty. The latter is not a constitutional requirement. The use of the special method will also indicate that the legislature and executive consider the treaty in question to be self-executing. In applying a treaty ratified through the use of the special method, the courts need not defer to the other organs of state, though they are bound to take into account treaty reservations that the executive or legislature may formulate.[391]

The Italian Constitution was amended by a Constitutional Law of 18 October 2003 which introduced, *inter alia*, a new Article 117(1). This states that 'The legislative power shall be exercised by the State and the Regions in compliance with the Constitution and with the constraints deriving from European Union legislation and international obligations'. This provision has been interpreted by the Constitutional Court as meaning that provisions of those treaties that are in conformity with the Constitution as regards their content and the procedure for their adoption have indirectly a constitutional status which makes them prevail over 'ordinary' laws. This result is obtained by a case-by-case mechanism: a judge who considers that a domestic law provision is incompatible with a treaty, or with a customary international rule, may submit to the Constitutional Court the question of non-conformity of that law with Article 117(1). The Constitutional Court has in various cases held legislation to be contrary to Article 117(1), and abrogated them because of their non-conformity with the ECHR.[392] Article 117 has not yet been applied to other treaties or to customary rules.

---

occurred in preventive detention cases: e.g. 109 BVerfGE 133 (2004), overruled in *M v Germany* [2009] ECtHR 19359/09, in turn implemented in 2 BvR 2933/08 (2011). Further: Kirchhof (2011) 64 *NJW* 3681.

[388] *Corte di Cassazione*, 22 March 1984, Judgment No 1920.

[389] Cataldi, in Shelton (2011) 328, 338.

[390] Ibid, 339.

[391] Ibid, 342.

[392] E.g. Constitutional Court, 24 October 2007, Judgment No 248; Constitutional Court, 24 October 2007, Judgment No 249.

(iv) Russian Federation

As with customary international law, treaties concluded by the Russian Federation are formally integrated into its municipal legal system by virtue of Article 15(4) of its Constitution.[393] Article 15(4) goes on to state that '[i]f other rules have been established by an international treaty of the Russian Federation than provided for by law, the rules of the international treaty shall apply'. This gives an international treaty priority over domestic law, at least as a matter of principle;[394] it does not, however state whether a treaty has to fulfil certain conditions to gain such priority.[395]

In order for a treaty to enter the Russian legal system, it must be signed and ratified. This was clarified by the Supreme Court as follows:

The courts shall take into consideration that an international treaty is applicable if the Russian Federation expressed by competent authorities its consent to be bound by the treaty through its action (signature, expressed of instruments constituting a treaty, ratification, acceptance or approval, accession or by any other means if so agreed) and on the assumption of entry into force for the Russian Federation.[396]

Under a federal law of 1995, a treaty which is self-executing and officially published has direct legal effect within the Russian legal system.[397] As Butler observes, however, substantial numbers of USSR treaties were in all likelihood never gazetted and are thus not subject to application by the Russian courts.[398] The Supreme Court gave some guidance in determining the self-executing character of a treaty, giving particular weight to 'indications, contained in the treaty, regarding obligations of Member States to amend national laws of these states'.[399] Where a treaty is not self-executing, municipal effect will be provided via legislative enactment and embellishment.

In interpreting and applying international conventions, Russian courts have proved punctilious in enforcing the above requirements.[400] Insofar as interpretation is concerned, the courts may have recourse to the views of the Ministry of Foreign Affairs,

---

[393] Further implementation is provided by Federal Law No 101-фз of 15 July 1995 on the International Treaties of the Russian Federation: Butler (3rd edn, 2009) 696–7.

[394] Further: Tikhomirov, in Shelton (2011) 517, 521.

[395] Plenum of the Supreme Court of the Russian Federation, Decree No 5, 10 October 2003, §8 ('The rules of the effective international treaty of the Russian Federation, the consent on the mandatory nature of which was issued in the form of a federal law, shall be given priority against the laws of the Russian Federation'). Also: Plenum of the Supreme Court of the Russian Federation, Decree No 8, 31 October 1995. If consent to a treaty was not given by way of ratification in the form of a federal law, then treaty rules will only have priority with respect to subordinate normative-legal acts issued by the governmental agency which concluded the treaty: Butler, in Sloss (2009) 410, 421.

[396] Resolution adopted by the Plenum of the Supreme Court of the Russian Federation, Decree No 5, 10 October 2003, §4. In 2007 Federal Law No 101-фз of 15 July 1995 was amended to give Rosatom, a state-owned corporation, treaty-making capacity: Butler (2008) 102 *AJIL* 310; Butler (3rd edn, 2009) 696.

[397] Plenum of the Supreme Court of the Russian Federation, Decree No 5, 10 October 2003, §3.

[398] Butler, in Sloss (2009) 410, 417. The period between entry into force and publication may be as long as several years: ibid, 434.

[399] Plenum of the Supreme Court of the Russian Federation, Decree No 5, 10 October 2003, §3.

[400] In particular the requirement of official publication: Butler, in Sloss (2009) 211, 436–8.

but will ordinary apply VCLT Articles 31 and 32. Their scope of review does not, however, extend to assessing the content or legitimacy of any reservations made by the government.[401] Failure to apply relevant treaty provisions, or error in their application, may be corrected on appeal.[402]

(v) The Netherlands

With respect to treaties, the system of incorporation described by the Netherlands sits the furthest towards the monist end of the spectrum. All treaties binding on the Netherlands as a matter of international law are automatically incorporated into the Dutch municipal legal system, without any need for implementing legislation. The rule is not constitutional per se,[403] but may be traced back to a 1919 decision of the Supreme Court.[404] The historical rationale for the principle is only partly satisfied by the democratic fact that treaties entered into by the Netherlands must be approved by Parliament. Rather, as Nollkaemper notes,[405] it is more a reflection of the Netherlands' generally accepting attitude towards international law, as reflected in the constitutional imperative that the Netherlands actively promote the development of the international legal order.[406]

Due to the unusual efficiency of the Dutch system, careful control is exercised over the treaty-making process by the bicameral legislature of the Netherlands, the States-General.[407] Although the government is directly responsible for the negotiation of treaties, the legislature must be kept informed throughout the process of negotiation and updated regularly.[408] It may also add interpretive declarations or reservations to the bill approving the treaty, which are then incorporated by the government once the treaty is formally concluded.[409] Once the text is finalized and approved by the Council of Ministers, it will be referred to the legislature prior to final signature or ratification and accompanied by an explanatory memorandum, consisting primarily of an

---

[401] Tikhomirov, in Shelton (2011) 517, 523. Also: Plenum of the Supreme Court of the Russian Federation, Decree No 5, 10 October 2003, §5. Further: Butler, in Sloss (2009) 411, 418–21.

[402] Butler, in Sloss (2009) 411, 418.

[403] Reference is sometimes made to Art 93 of the Constitution, which provides that 'Provisions of treaties and resolutions by international institutions that are binding on all persons by virtue of their contents shall become binding after they have been published' as providing a constitutional basis for the *validity* of treaties, but this is better characterized as going to their *direct effect* within municipal law: Nollkaemper, in Sloss (2009) 326, 331–3.

[404] NJ (1919) No 371.

[405] Nollkaemper, in Sloss (2009) 326, 332.

[406] Constitution of the Netherlands, Art 90 ('The Government shall promote the development of the international rule of law'). On this imperative: Besselink (2003) 34 *NYIL* 89.

[407] On the role of Parliament in the treaty-making process: Alkema (1984) 31 *NILR* 307; van Dijk & Tahzib (1991) 67 *ChiKentLR* 413.

[408] Law on the Approval and Promulgation of Treaties, Stb 1994, 542, Art 1 (Law on Treaties); also Klabbers (1995) 44 *ICLQ* 629. The government is not required to inform Parliament as the *content* of the treaty in question, merely its progress, though this does not prevent Parliament from requesting that further information be provided.

[409] Nollkaemper, in Sloss (2009) 326, 328.

article-by-article commentary. Article 91(1) of the Constitution provides that 'The Kingdom shall not be bound by treaties, nor shall treaties be denounced without the prior approval of Parliament'. It goes on to state, however, that 'cases in which approval is not required shall be specified by Act of Parliament', leading the Law on Treaties to create several significant loopholes by way of a list of exceptions contained in Article 7 thereof.[410] Treaties need not be the subject of prior approval where exemption from this requirement has already been provided by law,[411] where they concern exclusively treaties for which approval has already been granted,[412] where the treaty is for a period of less than one year and does not impose considerable financial obligations,[413] where the treaty (exceptionally) is secret and confidential,[414] where the new treaty merely extends an existing but expiring treaty[415] and, with respect to changes to execution, annexes that are already part of an approved treaty.[416] Furthermore, both the Constitution and the Law on Treaties provide for the facility of merely tacit approval.

Treaties will ordinarily be approved by a simple majority within the States-General. Where, however, a proposed treaty conflicts with a provision of the Constitution, Article 91(3) provides that a two-thirds majority in both the upper and lower houses will be required for approval to be granted. Once approved, the provisions of self-executing treaties will on a *sui generis* basis override the Constitution, making the Netherlands one of the few jurisdictions in the world that places international law obligations above its constitutional instrument within the domestic legal order. This much is provided in Article 94 of the Constitution, which provides that '[s]tatutory regulations in force within the Kingdom shall not be applicable if such application is in conflict with provisions of treaties or of resolutions of international organizations that are binding on all persons'. The inclusion of the caveat 'binding on all persons' is an important one, and has been interpreted as excluding those treaty provisions that require by virtue of their content further parliamentary action in order to take effect (i.e. non-self-executing provisions).[417] The question of direct effect is resolved by the courts first by reference to the intention of the states parties to the treaty, with the

---

[410] Further: Klabbers (1995) 44 *ICLQ* 629, 631–5.

[411] Law on Treaties, Art 7(a). E.g. the Act of Approval for the Convention on the Privileges and Immunities of the United Nations, 13 February 1946, 1 UNTS 15, states that the government has the right to enter into similar agreements with international organizations without the need for prior legislative approval. On immunities agreements and international organizations: chapter 7.

[412] Law on Treaties, Art 7(b).

[413] Ibid, Art 7(c).

[414] Ibid, Art 7(d).

[415] Ibid, Art 7(e).

[416] Ibid, Art 7(f). This loophole could permit changes to the fabric of existing treaties that rely on lengthy indexes for their substance. E.g. it would exclude from parliamentary approval changes in annexes to environmental treaties detailing prohibited or restricted substances unless Parliament has made a reservation precluding unapproved changes: Klabbers (1995) 44 *ICLQ* 629, 634–5; Nollkaemper, in Sloss (2009) 326, 328.

[417] The justification for this is rooted in the separation of powers; were vague or hortatory provisions given supremacy, this would give too much power to the courts to override the codified will of the legislature: Nollkaemper, in Sloss (2009) 326, 332–5.

court then resorting to a textual analysis where intention cannot be determined.[418] Even without direct effect, treaties may still play a role in the interpretation of legislation: 'Dutch courts should, as far as is possible, interpret and apply Dutch law in such a way that the State meets its treaty obligations'.[419]

(vi) Sweden

During the eighteenth century, the Swedish position on the direct validity and effect of treaties was similar to the current, liberal Dutch practice,[420] but in more recent times it has come to adopt the same rigidly dualist position that it displays formally with regard to custom: an international treaty will have no direct effect unless incorporated into municipal law via a legislative act.[421] Though the Constitution provides no direct support for this notion, some commentators point to Chapter 10, Article 3 of the Instrument of Government as indirectly confirming it. It provides:

The *Riksdag*'s approval is required before the Government concludes an international agreement which is binding upon the Realm:

1. if the agreement requires the amendment or abrogation of an act of law or the enactment of a new act of law;

2. or if it otherwise concerns a matter to be decided by the *Riksdag*.

This attitude was confirmed by leading cases decided by three of the highest courts in Sweden, the Supreme Court,[422] the Supreme Administrative Court,[423] and the Labour Court.[424] On the other hand there are examples of Swedish courts interpreting domestic laws so as to comply with unincorporated treaties in a manner that would appear to conflict with reasonably clear statutory wording.[425]

The legislative act itself that incorporates the treaties will depend largely on the form of the treaty in question. If it is capable of being applied by the Swedish courts, its text will usually be translated into Swedish and incorporated by reference. Where it is not, transformation and elaboration via statute will need to occur.[426] Where the

---

[418] See e.g. NJ (1995) No 619, reported in Barnhoorn (1997) 27 *NYIL* 336. On the process: Nollkaemper, in Sloss (2009) 326, 341–5.

[419] NJ (1992) No 107. The principle applies irrespective of whether the law so interpreted entered into force before or after the adoption of the treaty: Nollkaemper, in Sloss (2009) 326, 349–50.

[420] E.g. *Rundqvist v Montan* [1892] NJA 377.

[421] Bogdan (1994) 63 *Nordic JIL* 3, 6–11.

[422] *Swedish Engine Drivers' Union v The State* [1972] *Arbetsdomstolens Domar* No 5.

[423] *Sandström v The Crown* [1973] NJA 423.

[424] *Engquist v The School Board of Luleå Municipality* [1974] *Regeringsrättens Årsbock* No 61.

[425] This is especially the case with the ECtHR: e.g. *Prosecutor v Sulayman F* [1992] NJA 532; *Folke B v Navarsvikens jaktvårdsområdesförening* [1994] NJA 290. On the general doctrine that statutes should be interpreted consistently with Sweden's obligations under international law: *Ingela C v KFA* [1981] NJA 1205; *The Tsesis* [1983] NJA 3; *Prosecutor v Lennart A* [1988] NJA 572; *Prosecutor v Nezmi A* [1989] NJA 131.

[426] Bogdan (1994) 63 *Nordic JIL* 3, 10–11.

Swedish statute does not fully reflect the wording of the original treaty, the court is expected to attempt a reconciliation; if none is possible, the statute prevails.[427]

(c) NON-JUSTICIABILITY IN THE EUROPEAN TRADITION

As with customary and conventional international law, the question of judicial abstention or intervention in state affairs is the result of choices internal to each legal system.[428]

(i) France

In France, this is represented by the doctrine of *acte de gouvernement*, which will exclude judicial review of an executive decision where it either (a) 'project[s] onto the international plane the manifestation of the wishes of the French authorities and consequently only [has] meaning in the context of the relations between the French State and an international organization or another State'; or (b) 'exclusively [involves] an assessment of the appropriateness of action from the standpoint of foreign policy'.[429] The *Conseil d'État* has confirmed that the question is one of the competence of French tribunals and not the admissibility of the claim.[430] The doctrine has been applied, *inter alia*,[431] to the exercise of government powers to protect French nationals abroad,[432] the decision whether or not to publish an international agreement,[433] an alleged omission in the conduct of relations with a foreign government,[434] the vote of a Minister in the Council of the European Community,[435] the establishment of an international maritime exclusion zone,[436] a refusal to enter into international negotiations with a foreign state or institute proceedings before the International Court,[437] the suspension of an international agreement,[438] and the suspension of scientific co-operation with Iraq following the invasion of Kuwait.[439] It was applied to the decisions to deploy French

---

[427] Ibid, 10.

[428] For a comparative view of emerging trends: Benvenisti (1993) 4 *EJIL* 159; Amaroso (2010) 23 *LJIL* 933. Also: the (now slightly dated) overview of European attitudes towards non-justiciability given by Advocate-General Darmon in Case C-241/87, *Maclaine Watson & Co Ltd v Council & Commission of the European Communities* (1990) 96 ILR 201, 217–18.

[429] *United Kingdom and Governor of Hong Kong* [1993] Rec Lebon 267, 106 ILR 233 (*Commissaire du Gouvernement* Vigouroux).

[430] Ibid, 236. Also: *GITSI* [1992] Rec Lebon 346, 106 ILR 198, 200 (*Commissaire du Gouvernement* Kessler).

[431] Further: *United Kingdom and Governor of Hong Kong* [1993] Rec Lebon 267, 106 ILR 233, 238–40.

[432] *Delle Buttner* [1953] Rec Lebon 184.

[433] *De Malglaive* [1970] Rec Lebon 635, 72 ILR 236. However, if the treaty is published, the judge is competent to assess whether the act of publication is in conformity with constitutional provisions: *Commune of Porta* [2002] Rec Lebon 260.

[434] *Petit T* [1973] Rec Lebon 921.

[435] *The Greens Association* [1984] Rec Lebon 382.

[436] *Paris de Bollardière* [1975] Rec Lebon 423, 74 ILR 95.

[437] *Société Sapvin* [1988] Rec Lebon 133, 89 ILR 6.

[438] *Prefect of La Gironde v Mahmedi* [1992] Rec Lebon 446, 106 ILR 204.

[439] *GITSI* [1992] Rec Lebon 346, 106 ILR 198.

troops against Yugoslavia during the Kosovo War[440] and to allow US/UK aircraft to access French airspace during the Second Gulf War.[441]

The French judiciary will only consider an *acte de gouvernement* where it has a definable international flavour; where the act is based primarily on considerations relating to public policy or the national public services, whether carried out at home or abroad, it will be justiciable.[442] The withdrawal of a French co-operation assistant serving abroad was considered not so much a sovereign act as an act of management carried out by the national public services responsible for co-operation.[443] The same may be said of the allegedly inadequate protection of foreign diplomats by French police,[444] and the destruction by the French Navy of a ship abandoned on the high seas.[445]

The doctrine of *acte de gouvernement* has been the subject of erosion, however, under what Advocate-General Darmon referred to as the theory of 'detachable acts'.[446] On this approach, an act that might prima facie appear non-justiciable may nevertheless be subject to the courts' jurisdiction 'if the French authorities have some independent choice with regard to the procedure by which they perform their international obligations and can themselves take the initiative as regards the means by which they comply with those obligations'.[447] Decisions as to extradition have proved particularly susceptible to such separation, as seen in *United Kingdom and Governor of Hong Kong*. There, the British government applied to the *Conseil d'État* for the review of a decision by the French government not to extradite a Malaysian businessman accused of serious fraud and financial mismanagement in Hong Kong. *Commissaire du Gouvernement* Vigouroux argued that judicial review of extradition matters would not impede the government's freedom of action in foreign policy. Accordingly, a decision rejecting extradition was severable from the wider field of bilateral diplomatic relations and judicial review was permitted.[448]

(ii) Germany

The German constitutional model is characterized by a strong system of judicial review that virtually eliminates non-justiciability.[449] Judicial review of executive acts is not an implied right but a deliberate choice in a system that establishes a court for the purpose of assessing the conformity of executive acts and legislation with the Basic Law. Article 19(4) of the Basic Law provides that 'Should any person's right be violated

---

[440] *Mégret* [2000] Rec Lebon 291.

[441] *Committee against the Iraq War* [2003] Rec Lebon 707.

[442] *United Kingdom and Governor of Hong Kong* [1993] Rec Lebon 267, 106 ILR 223, 239–40.

[443] *Finance Ministry* [1966] Rec Lebon 476.

[444] *Yener and Erez* [1987] Rec Lebon 151, 89 ILR 1.

[445] *Société Nachfolger Navigation Company Ltd* [1987] Rec Lebon 319, 89 ILR 3.

[446] Case C-241/87, *Maclaine Watson & Co Ltd v Council & Commission of the European Communities* (1990) 96 ILR 201, 217–18.

[447] Ibid, quoting *Radiodiffusion française* [1950] Rec Lebon 652 (*Tribunal des conflits*).

[448] *United Kingdom and Governor of Hong Kong* [1993] Rec Lebon 267, 106 ILR 223, 240–3.

[449] For a comparison with the common law tradition of judicial review as practised in the US: Currie, *The Constitution of the Federal German Republic* (1999) 162–72; Quint (2006) 65 *Md LR* 152.

by public authority, recourse to the court shall be open to him'. Article 93(1)(1) further permits suits to be launched between different organs of the federal government on questions of competence.[450] The Federal Constitutional Court was created to sit outside the 'ordinary' court system and hear those matters associated with the enforcement of the Basic Law.[451]

Although *prima facie* applying only to those basic rights contained within the Basic Law itself (which, it must be remembered, are to be interpreted in accordance with international law, itself superior to domestic statute)[452] this limitation has been eroded through the breadth of the rights in question,[453] and subsequent judicial expansion through interpretation. An affected citizen may invoke the interests of third parties[454] and questions of federalism and the separation of powers in bringing a suit.[455] Even more remarkably, Article 93(1)(2) permits one-third of the members of the *Bundestag* to file an action directly in the Federal Constitutional Court challenging the constitutionality of a piece of legislation; thus, when a divisive piece of legislation is passed by a narrow majority, it can reasonably be expected to get a second airing before the Court.[456]

Within the German constitutional system, there is no tradition of automatic judicial deference to the executive in regard to foreign policy.[457] This potentially extends to questions surrounding the deployment of Germany's armed forces.[458] When the German government sought to join NATO forces charged with enforcing resolutions of the Security Council in Yugoslavia, this was challenged in *International Military Operations*.[459] The Federal Constitutional Court held that such action was permissible so long as it remained within the framework of a 'system of mutual collective security'.[460] The power of review further extends to the treaty-making power of the German state, with the court intervening to assess and provide texture to both the Basic Treaty[461] between the

---

[450] This form of jurisdiction is known as *Organstreit* or 'dispute between constitutional organs': Quint (2006) 65 *Md LR* 152, 156–7.

[451] Basic Law, Arts 92–4, 100.

[452] Folz, in Shelton (2011) 240, 245.

[453] Basic Law, Art 2(1) refers to 'freedom of personality'. The Federal Constitutional Court has interpreted this as including any and all things that a person might wish to do: 6 BVerfGE 32, 41 (1957). Further: Currie (1999) 165–6.

[454] E.g. 85 BVerfGE 191, 205–6 (1992) (employer permitted to argue that a ban on nocturnal employment discriminated against female employees).

[455] E.g. *Jurisdiction over Berlin*, 20 BVerfGE 257, 268–71 (1966), 75 ILR 113, 114–16 (excessive delegation); 26 BVerfGE 246, 253–8 (1969) (lack of federal authority).

[456] E.g. 39 BVerfGE 1 (1975) (challenging a statute relaxing the criminal penalties for abortion).

[457] Folz, in Shelton (2011) 240, 244.

[458] Quint (2006) 65 *Md LR* 152, 161–2.

[459] On the basis that German forces could only be deployed for the purposes of 'defence': Basic Law, Art 87a(2).

[460] 90 BVerfGE 286 (1994), 106 ILR 319, 327–30. Further: Quint, *The Imperfect Union* (1997) 290–6.

[461] Treaty concerning the basis of relations between the Federal Republic of Germany and the German Democratic Republic, 21 December 1972, *Bundesgesetzblatt* II (1973) 423.

German Democratic Republic (GDR)[462] and the Federal Republic of Germany (FRG) and the Maastricht Treaty.[463]

Confusingly, however, some hints of an aversion to 'political questions' may on occasion be detected.[464] In *Cruise Missiles (Danger to Life)*,[465] a number of FRG citizens launched a constitutional challenge against the deployment in the FRG of American medium-range missiles with nuclear warheads in accordance with a NATO resolution. The applicants alleged that the missiles violated the right to life and physical integrity under Article 2(2) of the Basic Law, and further argued that the deployment infringed Article 25 since it violated a general rule of international law prohibiting such weapons. The Court refused to hear the application for three reasons: (a) there was no data available by which the Court could ascertain the alleged risk to life and health and, in any case, the materialization of such a risk was wholly dependent on the future political and military decisions of the USSR;[466] (b) any infringement of the Basic Law on which such a claim could be based could only be actionable against the German state, with the direct threat here arising from the nuclear potential of the USSR;[467] and (c) it was the responsibility of the government to decide upon the foreign and defence policy of FRG, not the Court.[468]

According to Currie, in refusing to hear such matters the Court is doing nothing more than concluding that the Basic Law commits a certain issue to the discretion or determination of another branch of government.[469] A similar solution was hinted at in *Chemical Weapons*, linking the availability of judicial review to the particular character of national defence. The Court held that:

in order to comply with the requirements for the admissibility of constitutional complaints based on an alleged violation of the duty of protection enshrined as a basic right in Article 2(2)…the complainant must be able to prove conclusively that the public authorities either totally failed to take precautionary measures or that the regulations enacted and the measures actually taken were totally inappropriate or wholly insufficient to achieve the aim of providing protection…[470]

In such cases the Court has not excluded judicial review entirely, but imposed an evidentiary hurdle commensurate with the gravity of the issues under consideration. Formally, it remains the case that Germany has not yet developed a doctrine of non-justiciability.

---

[462] *Relations Treaty between the FRG and GDR*, 36 BVerfGE 1 (1973), 78 ILR 149. The Court gave a restrictive interpretation to the agreements so as to avoid the full recognition of the GDR in international law.

[463] *Maastricht Treaty 1992*, 89 BVerfGE 155 (1993), 98 ILR 196. The Court affirmed that any further derogation from German sovereignty would be met with extremely close scrutiny.

[464] Further: Currie (1999) 170–1; Quint (2006) 65 *Md LR* 152, 166.

[465] 66 BverfGE 39 (1983), 106 ILR 353.

[466] Ibid, 362.

[467] Ibid, 361.

[468] Ibid, 362.

[469] Currie (1999) 170–1.

[470] *Chemical Weapons Deployment (Danger to Life)*, 77 BVerfGE 170 (1987), 106 ILR 389, 395.

(iii) Italy

As with the French system, Italian doctrine provides that acts of government (*teoria dell'atto do governo*) are non-justiciable, basing its position on the notion that the exercise of government discretion is necessary in order to preserve certain constitutional or political imperatives.[471] Here, the point of reference is the Constitution, which reserves certain matters for the executive and legislature, most notably the capacity of Parliament to declare a state of war and vest the government with the necessary powers of prosecution.[472] Such acts, by reason of their inherently discretionary character but also due to separation of powers considerations, are non-justiciable.[473]

The leading decision is *Marković*, where the *Corte di Cassazione* ruled on the liability of the Italian government in claims brought by Serbian civilians whose relatives were killed during an aerial bombardment of Belgrade by NATO forces in 1999. Liability was premised on two alternative bases: that Italy was jointly liable for the airstrike as a NATO member; or the bombardment was carried out from bases located on Italian soil. In a concise judgment, the Court held that the acts in question were non-justiciable:

> The selection of a method for conducting hostilities is amongst those acts which are performed by the Government. All such acts are expressions of a political function which, under the Constitution, is envisaged as emanating from a constitutional organ. The nature of this function is that it is impossible to protect individual interest from its effects on the basis that those acts falling within its scope are incapable of precise definition... With regard to acts of this type, no court has the power to review the manner in which the function is exercised.[474]

Thus, the Italian approach sits within the same tradition as that of France, the UK, and the US.[475]

(iv) Russian Federation

The Russian system for judicial review is similar to its German counterpart. Article 46(2) of the Constitution provides that '[d]ecisions and actions (or inaction) of state bodies, bodies of local self-government, public associations and officials may be

---

[471] Frulli (2003) 1 *JICJ* 406, 410.

[472] Constitution of Italy, Arts 78 and 87.

[473] Further: Virga, 1 *Diritto amministravito* (6th edn, 2001) 280.

[474] *President of the Council v Marcović*, Corte di Cassazione, 5 June 2002, Judgment No 8157, 128 ILR 652, 655–6. Frulli argues that while the initial *declaration* of war may not be justiciable, those individual acts performed in the prosecution of armed conflict ought to be, with any other alternative depriving a plaintiff of his or her rights under Arts 2 and 24 of the Constitution. Moreover, this argument is consistent with representations previously made by the Italian government before the ECtHR: Frulli (2003) 1 *JICJ* 406, 412–14.

[475] There is here a certain tension with Art 2 of the Constitution, which provides that '[t]he Republic recognizes and guarantees the inviolable rights of man, as an individual, and in the social groups where he expresses his personality, and demands the fulfilment of the intransgressible duties of political, economic, and social solidarity'. This is paired with Art 24, which itself provides the right to an effective judicial remedy for the violation of fundamental rights and interests. Further: Frulli (2003) 1 *JICJ* 406, 412.

appealed in a court of law'. Courts tend to see any attempt to transgress this right as unconstitutional.[476] Moreover, administrative complaints are generally not subject to the defence of sovereign immunity.[477] A wider jurisdiction is posited by the Article 125 with respect to the Constitutional Court;[478] though its capacity to hear certain disputes is dependent on referral of the matter by a relevant government body,[479] it retains the general jurisdiction to hear complaints regarding the violation of the constitutional rights and freedoms of citizens on petition.[480]

The landscape of judicial review and non-justiciability in Russia is complicated by the fact that the current Constitutional Court is Russia's second since the break-up of the Soviet Union. The first was established in 1991, with its jurisdiction based in part on the 1978 Constitution of the Soviet Union combined with the 1991 Law on the Constitutional Court of the Russian Soviet Federative Socialist Republic, which did not exclude the court from involvement in political affairs.[481] The result was a highly destructive confrontation between the Court and President Yeltsin in the context of the 1993 Russian constitutional crisis. This ended with the introduction of the current 1993 Constitution and the 1994 Law on the Constitutional Court, Article 3 of which states that the court 'shall rule exclusively on questions of law'. The Court lost the right to examine cases *ex proprio motu* as well as its competence over non-normative acts of the president and other executive officials and agencies.[482]

Despite the imperative contained in Article 3 of the 1994 Law on the Constitutional Court, the Court has not refrained from addressing issues which would ordinarily be thought political in nature. For example in the *Chechnya* case,[483] the Court was asked by a minority in the Russian Parliament pursuant to Article 125(2) of the Constitution to assess the constitutionality of a decision by President Yeltsin to order troops to Chechnya. Although it refused to consider 'the political expediency of the [Government's] decisions or the validity of the actions carried out on that basis', the Court nonetheless considered itself competent to rule on the legality of the initial orders, which were upheld.[484]

It is to be remembered that Article 3 of the 1994 Law on the Constitutional Court is a jurisdictional limitation applicable to that court alone; there is no evidence of a

---

[476] Burnham, Maggs & Denilenko, *Law and Legal System of the Russian Federation* (4th edn, 2009) 640–1.

[477] Ibid, 645.

[478] Butler (3rd edn, 2009) 172–7. For a history of the Constitutional Court: Trochev, *Judging Russia* (2008).

[479] Constitution of the Russian Federation, Art 125(2).

[480] Ibid, Art 125(4).

[481] Burnham et al (4th edn, 2009) 72.

[482] Ibid, 73. Further: Trochev (2008) ch 3.

[483] Ruling No 10-P, VKS 1995 No 11, 3 (31 July 1995).

[484] Additionally, the court managed to avoid giving substantive consideration to the human rights issues raised by the case, by referring them to unspecified further proceedings before the criminal courts: Pomeranz (1997) 9 *RCEEL* 9, 26–8.

similar doctrine developing at other levels of the Russian judicial hierarchy, though its theory and practice remain relatively inchoate.

(v) The Netherlands

Judicial review in the Netherlands bears a passing similarity to German position, but is at the same time quite different owing first to the unusual position that treaty law holds within the jurisdiction, and secondly to the strictures of the Dutch Constitution. Article 120 of the Constitution provides that the 'constitutionality of Acts of Parliament and treaties shall not be reviewed by the courts'.[485] This automatically places a jurisdictional limitation—unique amongst liberal democracies—on judicial review that may only be resolved by the fact that Dutch law does not consider treaties to be 'constitutional' in nature, opening the possibility of assessing municipal statutes according to the yardstick of international conventions signed and ratified by the Netherlands.[486]

Dutch law does not know of a political question doctrine, in the sense that those issues intrinsically connected with the legislature are automatically removed from the competence of the courts.[487] Rather, it has in recent times begun to demonstrate—on a discretionary basis—an extreme deference towards the exclusive competence of the legislature with respect to political matters. This first arose in *Association of Lawyers for Peace* which again considered a pre-emptive application by a community group seeking a declaration that the deployment of nuclear weapons by the Netherlands would be illegal. Dismissing the application the Court held that:

[T]he applications instituted in the present action relate to questions concerning the policy of the State in the area of foreign policy and defence, which...will depend to a large extent on political considerations...This means that the civil courts should observe a large degree of restraint in assessing applications such as the one instituted in the present case, which are designed to designate in advance as unlawful...acts to implement political decisions in the area of foreign policy and defence...It is not, after all, the function of the civil courts to make political decisions of this nature.[488]

This doctrine of judicial restraint in matters of foreign policy and defence has been applied repeatedly since,[489] most notably in dismissing an application to have President Bush arrested for war crimes on an official visit to the Netherlands,[490] and

---

[485] Generally: van der Schyff (2010) 11 *GLJ* 275.

[486] Van der Schyff (2010) 11 *GLJ* 275, 279–81.

[487] E.g. *Foundation for the Prohibition of Cruise Missiles*, NJ (1991) No 248, 106 ILR 400, concerning an attempt by a community organization to pre-empt the Dutch government from permitting US cruise missiles to be based on Dutch soil. In Germany, the question was considered effectively non-justiciable: *Cruise Missiles (Danger to Life)*, 66 BVerfGE 39 (1983), 106 ILR 353. The Dutch court did not even refer to the doctrine when dismissing the application.

[488] *Association of Lawyers for Peace v Netherlands*, NJ (2002) No 217, §3.3.

[489] Generally: Fleurin (2010) 57 *NILR* 262.

[490] Here, the interlocutory judge paid particular attention to the effects that such an order, if granted, would have on US–Dutch relations and Dutch foreign policy as a whole: *Hague City Party v Netherlands*, ILDC 849 (NL 2005), §§3.4–5, 3.8.

in yet another pre-emptive application to prevent the deployment of Dutch forces in any attempt to support retributive measures by the US in the wake of the 9/11 terrorist attacks without the authorization of force by the Security Council.[491]

(vi) Sweden

In Sweden, judicial review of administrative and legislative action is a comparative latecomer owing to a strong belief in democratic sovereignty. Indeed, the institution has, until recently, been seen as 'undemocratic and not a natural part of a living, vital democracy'.[492] Nonetheless, a right to judicial review was accepted by the Supreme Court in 1964,[493] and was introduced to the Constitution in 1979, in the form of review for 'manifest' error.[494] Thus, non-justiciability was not determined by the subject-matter but by the magnitude of the perceived inconsistency.[495]

This limitation on review was in 2010 replaced with a vaguer requirement that 'In the case of review of an act of law...particular attention must be paid to the fact that the *Riksdag* is the foremost representative of the people and that fundamental law takes precedence over other law'. The wider effect of this amendment on Swedish jurisprudence is not yet apparent.

5. CONCLUSIONS

On the whole question of the relation between national and international law theoretical constructions have done much to obscure realities. If one had to choose between the theories considered earlier in this chapter, then the views of Fitzmaurice and Rousseau might be preferred as coming closer to the truth. Each system is supreme *in its own field*; neither has hegemony over the other. And yet any generalities offered can only provide a background to the complex relations between the national and international systems. Three factors operate. The first is organizational: to what extent are the organs of states ready to apply rules of international law internally and externally?[496]

---

[491] NJ (2004) No 329, §3.4. Also: NJ (2003) No 35 (concerning Kosovo).

[492] Nergelius, *Constitutional Law in Sweden* (2011) 121.

[493] [1964] NJA 471.

[494] The requirement was introduced in case-law prior to constitutional integration: [1951] NJA 39. Also: [1948] NJA 188. The resulting standard is steep. One former Swedish judge has stated that it required him to rule non-justiciable issues surrounding legislation he believed clearly unconstitutional where one of his colleagues could not detect a manifest error; if his colleagues were in disagreement, the error could by definition not be manifest: Nergelius (2011) 120.

[495] See Nergelius (2011) 117–20.

[496] Monists underestimate this aspect of the matter or gloss it over with conceptualism. The fact is that national law is more viable in terms of organization whereas international law is less of a system *in this sense*. From this perspective there is some substance in the view that international law derives from the activities of the constitutional organs of states. International law has often been dependent on state machinery for its enforcement. Although there has been a strengthening of international institutions, especially of

This seems to suggest a pluralist vision, in which it falls to each system to regulate its own relationship with other legal systems. The second factor is the difficulty of proving the existence of particular rules of international law. In case of difficulty national courts usually rely on advice from the executive or existing precedents, and the result may not accord with an objective appreciation of the law. Thirdly, courts, national and international, will often be concerned with the question of which is the *appropriate* system to apply to particular issues arising. The question of appropriateness emphasizes the distinction between organization, that is, the character of the jurisdiction as 'national' or 'international', and the character of the rules of both systems as flexible instruments for dealing with disputes and regulating non-contentious matters. An international court may find it necessary to apply rules of national law, while bodies, such as the United States Foreign Claims Settlement Commission, which are national in terms of organization and competence may find it appropriate, and be authorized, to apply rules of international law on a large scale. When a national court applies a rule of international law because it is appropriate, it is pointless to ask if the rule applied has been 'transformed', except insofar as 'transformation' describes a process required by a particular national system before certain organs are permitted, or are willing, to apply rules of international law.

dispute settlement (see chapter 32), international law remains largely dependent on state machinery for enforcement. Further, many aspects of international law are to be implemented primarily at a domestic level and international institutions play a secondary role. This view, characterized as monism-in-reverse, was supported by e.g. Decencière-Ferrandière (1933) 40 *RGDIP* 45. Critics have tended to caricature this position, but it accords with widely held views that international law is *international* and not dependent on a supranational coercive order.

PART II

PERSONALITY AND RECOGNITION

4

SUBJECTS OF
INTERNATIONAL LAW

1. INTRODUCTION[1]

A subject of international law is an entity possessing international rights and obligations and having the capacity (a) to maintain its rights by bringing international claims;[2] and (b) to be responsible for its breaches of obligation by being subjected to such claims.[3] This definition, though conventional, is unfortunately circular since, while the indicia referred to depend in theory on the existence of a legal person, the main way of determining whether the relevant capacity exists in case of doubt is to inquire whether it is in fact exercised. All that can be said is that an entity of a type recognized by customary law as *capable* of possessing rights and duties and of bringing and being subjected to international claims is a legal person. If the latter condition is not satisfied, the entity concerned may have legal personality of a very restricted kind, dependent on the agreement or acquiescence of recognized legal persons and opposable on the international plane only to those agreeing or acquiescent. The principal formal contexts in which the question of personality has arisen have been: capacity to make claims in respect of breaches of international law, capacity to make treaties and agreements valid on the international plane, and the enjoyment of privileges and immunities from national jurisdiction. States pre-eminently have these capacities and immunities; indeed the incidents of statehood as developed under customary law have provided the indicia for, and instruments of personality in relation to, other entities.

Apart from states, organizations may have these capacities and immunities if certain conditions are satisfied. The capacity to claim under international law, at least for organizations of a certain type, was established in *Reparation for Injuries*.[4] Waldock's first report on the law of treaties noted the capacity of international organizations to

---

[1] Especially Lauterpacht, 2 *International Law* (1975) 487; Barberis (1983) 179 Hague *Recueil* 145; Higgins, *Problems and Process* (1994) 39–55; Nijman, *The Concept of International Legal Personality* (2004); Crawford, *Creation of States* (2nd edn, 2006) 28–33; Portmann, *Legal Personality in International Law* (2010).

[2] *Reparation for Injuries Suffered in the Service of the United Nations*, ICJ Reports 1949 p 174, 179.

[3] For the ILC's rejection of the concept of 'delictual capacity' in the context of state responsibility: ILC *Ybk* 1998/I, 1, 31, 196.

[4] *Reparation for Injuries*, ICJ Reports 1949 p 174.

become parties to international agreements, and this reflected the existing practice.[5] Since *Reparation for Injuries* international organizations have joined states as a recognized category of legal persons, and this has facilitated acceptance of quite limited or marginal entities as such (for international organizations see chapter 7).

Thus it is states and organizations which represent the normal *types* of legal person on the international plane. However, the realities of international relations are not reducible to a simple formula. The 'normal types' have congeners which create problems, and various entities which are of neither type can have a certain personality—for example. the International Committee of the Red Cross (ICRC).[6] Moreover, abstraction of types of acceptable persons at law falls short of the reality, since recognition and acquiescence may sustain an entity which is in some respects anomalous and yet has a web of legal relations on the international plane.

In spite of the complexities, it is as well to remember the primacy of states as subjects of the law. As Friedmann observes:

The basic reason for this position is...that 'the world is today organized on the basis of the co-existence of States, and that fundamental changes will take place only through State action, whether affirmative or negative'. The States are the repositories of legitimated authority over peoples and territories. It is only in terms of State powers, prerogatives, jurisdictional limits and law-making capabilities that territorial limits and jurisdiction, responsibility for official actions, and a host of other questions of co-existence between nations can be determined...This basic primacy of the State as a subject of international relations and law would be substantially affected, and eventually superseded, only if national entities, as political and legal systems, were absorbed in a world state.[7]

2. ESTABLISHED LEGAL PERSONS

(A) STATES

This category is by far the most important, but it has its own problems, analysed in chapter 5. For instance, the existence of 'dependent' states with certain qualified legal

---

[5] ILC *Ybk* 1962/II, 31, 32, 35, 37. Also: Brierly, ILC *Ybk* 1950/II, 230; Lauterpacht, ILC *Ybk* 1953/II, 96; Fitzmaurice, ILC *Ybk* 1956/II, 117–18; 1958/II, 24, 32; Waldock, ILC *Ybk* 1962/II, 31, 35–7. At a later stage the Commission decided to confine the draft articles to the treaties of states: ILC *Ybk* 1965/II, 18; 1966/II, 187, Art 1, commentary. Instead a separate treaty was concluded, modelled on the VCLT: Convention on the Law of Treaties between States and International Organizations or between International Organizations, 12 March 1986, 25 ILM 543.

[6] E.g. Agreement between the International Committee of the Red Cross and the Swiss Federal Council to Determine the Legal Status of the Committee in Switzerland, 19 March 1993, GA Res 45/6, 16 October 1990, Rules of Procedure and Evidence for the Application of the Rome Statute of the International Criminal Court, Art 73; *Prosecutor v Simić* (1999) §46, available at www.icty.org/x/cases/simic/tdec/en/90727EV59549.htm.

[7] Friedmann, *The Changing Structure of International Law* (1964) 67, quoting Jessup, *A Modern Law of Nations* (1948) 17. Cf Anghie (1999) 40 *Harv ILJ* 1, 2; Cassese, *International Law* (2nd edn, 2005) 71.

capacities has historically complicated the picture, but, providing the basic conditions for statehood existed, the 'dependent' state retained its personality. In some federations (notably those created by a union of states at the international level), the constituent members retain certain residual capacities. In the constitutions of Switzerland[8] and Germany,[9] component states are permitted to exercise certain state functions, including treaty-making. Normally, the states, even when acting in their own name, do so as agents for the union.[10] The US Constitution enables the states of the Union to enter into agreements with other states of the Union or with foreign states with the consent of Congress.[11] But this happens rarely if at all, and in most federations, old and new, the federal government's power to make treaties with foreign states is exclusive.[12] The position of the International Court, set out in *LaGrand* and *Avena*, is that international obligations under the Vienna Convention on Consular Relations (VCCR) must be fully observed irrespective of constitutional limitations, and, though the means of implementation remain for it to choose, the federal state incurs responsibility for the wrongful acts of its subdivisions.[13]

(B) ENTITIES LEGALLY PROXIMATE TO STATES

Political settlements have from time to time produced entities, such as the former Free City of Danzig, which, possessing a certain autonomy, territory and population, and some legal capacities on the international plane, are more or less like states. Politically such entities are not states in the normal sense, yet legally the distinction is not very significant. The treaty origin of the entity and the existence of some form of protection by an international organization—the League of Nations in the case of Danzig—matter little if, in the result, the entity has autonomy and a nucleus of the more significant legal capacities, for example the power to make treaties, to maintain

---

[8] *Jenni v Conseil d'État* (1978) 75 ILR 99. The Swiss Cantons may 'conclude treaties with foreign countries within the domain relevant to their competencies' but these 'may not be contrary to the law and interests of the Federation nor to the rights of other Cantons': Swiss Constitution (as amended, entered into force 1 January 2000) Art 56.

[9] German Constitution, Art 32(3); Lindau Agreement regarding the Treaty Making Power of the Federation, 14 November 1957: (1957) *Bulletin des Bundesregierung* 1966.

[10] Waldock, ILC *Ybk* 1962/II, 31, 36–7; Wildhaber, *Treaty-Making Power and Constitution* (1971); Uibopuu (1975) 24 *ICLQ* 811; Di Marzo, *Component Units of Federal States and International Agreements* (1980) 48–9; Hocking, *Foreign Relations and Federal States* (1993); Opeskin (1996) 43 *NILR* 353; Rudolf, 'Federal States' (2007) *MPEPIL*; Grant, in Hollis (ed), *Oxford Guide to Treaties* (2012) ch 6.

[11] Constitution Art I (10)(3); 1 *Restatement Third*, §302(f); Hollis (2010) 88 *Texas LR* 741.

[12] The Australian federal executive has exclusive power to enter into treaties, which the federal Parliament can implement by legislation under the 'external affairs' power: *Koowarta v Bjelke-Petersen* (1982) 68 ILR 181; *Commonwealth v Tasmania* (1983) 68 ILR 266; *Queensland v Commonwealth* (1989) 90 ILR 115; *Victoria v Commonwealth* (1996) 187 CLR 416. In Canada, s132 of the Constitution Act 1867 (UK) vests the power to make treaties in the federal government, but the federal Parliament cannot legislate to implement in domestic law treaties falling within areas of provincial jurisdiction. See *Attorney-General for Canada v Attorney-General for Ontario and Others* [1937] AC 326.

[13] *LaGrand (Germany v US)*, ICJ Reports 2001 p 466, 514; *Avena and Other Mexican Nationals (Mexico v US)*, ICJ Reports 2004 p 12, 65–6.

order and exercise jurisdiction within the territory, and to have an independent nationality law. The jurisprudence of the Permanent Court recognized that Danzig had international personality proximate to that of a state, except insofar as treaty obligations created special relations in regard to the League and to Poland.[14] Under Articles 100 to 108 of the Treaty of Versailles, the League of Nations had supervisory functions and Poland had control of the foreign relations of Danzig.[15] The result was a protectorate, the legal status and constitution of which were externally supervised. To describe legal entities like Danzig as 'internationalized territories'[16] is not very helpful since the phrase covers a number of distinct entities and situations and elides the question of legal personality.[17]

The point is that a special status may attach without the creation of a legal person. An area within a state may be given a certain autonomy under treaty without this leading to any degree of separate personality on the international plane: this was the case with the Memel Territory, which had a special status in the period 1924 to 1939 yet remained part of Lithuania.[18] Another type of regime, more truly international, involves exclusive administration of a territory by an international organization: this was the regime proposed for Jerusalem by the Trusteeship Council in 1950 but never implemented.[19] In such a case no new legal person is established except insofar as an agency of an international organization may have a certain autonomy.

(C) ENTITIES RECOGNIZED AS BELLIGERENTS

In practice, belligerent or insurgent bodies within a state may enter into legal relations and conclude agreements on the international plane with states and other belligerents/ insurgents. Fitzmaurice has attributed treaty-making capacity to 'para-Statal entities recognized as possessing a definite if limited form of international personality, for example, insurgent communities recognized as having belligerent status—*de facto*

---

[14] E.g. *Free City of Danzig and the ILO* (1930) PCIJ Ser B No 18; *Polish Nationals in Danzig* (1932) Ser A/B No 44, 23–4. Germany occupied the Free City in 1939 and since 1945 the area has been part of Poland.

[15] Treaty of Peace, 28 June 1919, 225 CTS 188. On Danzig see further Crawford (2nd edn, 2006) 236–41; Stahn, *The Law and Practice of International Territorial Administration* (2008) 173–85.

[16] Ydit, *Internationalized Territories* (1961); Verzijl, 2 *International Law in Historical Perspective* (1970) 500–2, 510–45. A more recent label—hardly more informative—is 'international territorial administration', of which the type-case is Kosovo under SC Res 1244 (1999): e.g. Wilde, *International Territorial Administration* (2008) 114–27.

[17] The Italian Peace Treaty of 1947 provided for the creation of a Free Territory of Trieste with features broadly similar to those of the Free City of Danzig, but placed under the direct control of the UN Security Council. The Permanent Statute of Trieste was not implemented: the administration of the territory was divided by agreement in 1954 and the partition made definitive by the Treaty of Osimo, 1 October 1975, 1466 UNTS 25; Crawford (2nd edn, 2006) 235–6.

[18] *Interpretation of the Statute of the Memel Territory* (1932) PCIJ Ser A/B No 49, 313. Cf the complex legal status of the International Zone of Tangier, wound up in 1956: Gutteridge (1957) 33 *BY* 296; Ydit (1961) 154–84.

[19] GA Res 181(II), 29 November 1947. Further: Ydit (1961) 273–314; Cassese (1986) 3 *Palestine YIL* 13; Hirsch, Housen-Couriel & Lapidoth, *Whither Jerusalem?* (1995); Stahn (2008) 99–102.

authorities in control of specific territory'.[20] This statement is correct as a matter of principle,[21] but its application to particular facts requires caution. A belligerent community often represents a political movement aiming at secession: outside the colonial context, states have been reluctant to accord any form of recognition in such cases, including recognition of belligerency.[22]

(D) INTERNATIONAL ADMINISTRATION OF TERRITORIES PRIOR TO INDEPENDENCE

In relation to territories marked out by the UN as under a regime of illegal occupation and qualified for rapid transition to independence, an interim transitional regime may be installed under UN supervision.[23] Thus the final phase of Namibian independence involved the UN Transition Assistance Group, established by SC Resolution 435 (1978).[24]

In 1999 the long-drawn-out crisis concerning the illegal Indonesian occupation of East Timor was the subject of decisive action by the Security Council. SC Resolution 1272 (1999) established the UN Transitional Administration in East Timor (UNTAET) with a mandate to prepare East Timor for independence.[25] UNTAET had full legislative and executive powers and assumed its role independently of any competing authority. After elections, East Timor (Timor-Leste) became independent in 2002.[26]

Following the dissolution of the Socialist Federal Republic of Yugoslavia (SFRY), civil war broke out in the disputed, previously self-governing, territory of Kosovo, ending with NATO military intervention.[27] The Security Council in Resolution 1244 (1999) put in place the framework for an interim civil administration, further elaborated by regulations of the UN Mission in Kosovo (UNMIK). UNMIK regulation 2001/9 of 15 May 2001 set out a Constitutional Framework for Provisional Self-Government, dividing administrative responsibilities between UN representatives and the Provisional Institutions of Self-Government of Kosovo. Following unsuccessful

---

[20] ILC *Ybk* 1958/II, 24, 32; Fitzmaurice (1957) 92 Hague *Recueil* 5, 10. The draft articles on the law of treaties as initially adopted referred to 'States or other subjects of international law': ILC *Ybk* 1962/II, 161. This was intended to cover the case of insurgents.

[21] McNair, *Law of Treaties* (1961) 676; Kelsen, *Principles of International Law* (2nd edn, 1967) 252. Further: Chen, *The International Law of Recognition* (1951) 303–6; Crawford (2nd edn, 2006) 380–2.

[22] Under ARSIWA, Art 10, successful insurgents may be responsible (*qua* government of the old or new state, as the case may be) for conduct of the insurgent movement, but this is a rule of attribution, not a retrospective recognition of legal personality. Cf Cahin, in Crawford, Pellet & Olleson (eds), *The Law of International Responsibility* (2010) 247–55; Zegveld (2002) 160–4; and further: chapter 25.

[23] Generally: Chesterman, *You, The People: The United Nations, Transitional Administration and State-Building* (2004); Knoll, *The Legal Status of Territories subject to Administration by International Organisations* (2008); Ronen, *Transition from Illegal Regimes under International Law* (2011).

[24] See Berat, *Walvis Bay: Decolonization and International Law* (1990); Ronen (2011) 38–46.

[25] SC Res 1272 (1999). Further: Drew (2001) 12 *EJIL* 651.

[26] SC Res 1414 (2002); GA Res 57/3, 27 September 2002, admitting the Democratic Republic of Timor-Leste to UN membership.

[27] S/1999/648.

negotiations between Serbia and Kosovo regarding final status, on 17 February 2008 a declaration of independence of Kosovo was adopted, giving rise to a request by the General Assembly for an advisory opinion.[28]

On the one hand, the Court held, '[t]he Constitutional Framework derives its binding force from the binding character of resolution 1244 (1999) and thus from international law. In that sense it … possesses an international legal character'.[29] On the other hand '[t]he Constitutional Framework … took effect as part of the body of law adopted for the administration of Kosovo during the interim phase',[30] and it did not dispose of the territory beyond that phase. SC Resolution 1244 (1999) could not be interpreted as precluding all action aimed at resolving the impasse which the parties beyond question had reached.[31] Rather it was a matter for the UN Special Representative or the Security Council to prohibit (or to condemn after the fact) any unilateral declaration of independence. Neither had done so. In the circumstances 'the authors of that declaration did not act, or intend to act, in the capacity of an institution created by and empowered to act within that legal order but, rather, set out to adopt a measure the significance and effects of which would lie outside that order'.[32] There was thus no breach of the Constitutional Framework either. Apparently, guarantees of international territorial administration go only so far, as against claims to sovereignty.[33] The status of Kosovo remains unresolved.

(E) INTERNATIONAL ORGANIZATIONS

The conditions under which an organization acquires legal personality on the international plane are examined in chapter 7. The most important person of this type is the United Nations.

Entities, acting with delegated powers from states, may appear to enjoy a separate personality and viability on the international plane.[34] By agreement states may create joint agencies with delegated powers of a supervisory, rule-making, and even judicial character. Examples are the administration of a *condominium*, a standing arbitral tribunal, the International Joint Commission set up under an agreement concerning boundary waters between Canada and the US and the former European Commission

---

[28] GA Res 63/3, 8 October 2008.
[29] *Accordance with International Law of the Unilateral Declaration of Independence in Respect of Kosovo*, Opinion of 22 July 2010, §§88–9.
[30] Ibid, §§89, 99–100.
[31] Ibid, §§114–15, 118–19, and for the impasse in negotiations see the Ahtisaari Report: S/2007/168, 2 February 2007.
[32] Ibid, §105.
[33] For criticism: e.g. Kohen & LaMar (2011) 24 *LJIL* 109. Further on Kosovo see Weller, *Contested Statehood* (2009). Generally on secession: chapter 5.
[34] See Fitzmaurice, ILC *Ybk* 1952/II, 118. On the role of the chartered companies such as the English East India Company and the Dutch East India Company: McNair, 1 *Opinions* 41, 55; *Island of Palmas* (1928) 2 RIAA 829, 858–9.

of the Danube.[35] As the degree of independence and the legal powers of the particular agency increase it will approximate to an international organization.

(F) INDIVIDUALS

There is no general rule that the individuals cannot be 'subjects of international law', and in particular contexts individuals have rights *inuitu personae* which they can vindicate by international action, notably in the field of human rights and invest-ment protection.[36] At the same time to classify the individual as a 'subject' of the law is unhelpful, since this may seem to imply the existence of capacities which do not exist and does not avoid the task of distinguishing between the individual and other types of subject. Moreover while international human rights law recognizes a variety of rights for individuals (and even corporations), the norms of human rights law are not yet regarded as applying horizontally between individuals, in parallel to or substitution for the applicable national law. To the extent that some human rights instruments include provisions dealing with individual responsibilities as well as rights, international law provides no means for their enforcement. In practi-cal terms, human rights (and other obligations assumed for the benefit of individu-als and corporations) arise against the state, which so far has a virtual monopoly of responsibility.[37]

3. SPECIAL TYPES OF PERSONALITY

(A) CORPORATIONS, PUBLIC AND PRIVATE

Reference to states and similar political entities, to organizations, and to individuals does not exhaust the tally of entities active on the international scene. Corporations, whether private or public, often engage in economic activity in one or more states other than the state under the law of which they were incorporated or in which they have their economic seat. The resources available to the individual corporation may be greater than those of the smaller states, and they may have powerful diplomatic back-ing from their home government. Such corporations can and do make agreements,

---

[35] Baxter, *The Law of International Waterways* (1964) 103–7, 126–9.

[36] Parlett, *The Individual in the International Legal System* (2011). See also chapters 28 (investment arbi-tration), 29 (human rights).

[37] Similar considerations apply to international non-governmental organizations (INGOs), some of whom—e.g. Greenpeace, Medecins sans Frontières, Amnesty International—have become very influential, but without the need to claim international legal personality: Lindblom, *Non-Governmental Organizations in International Law* (2005); Dupuy & Vierucci (eds), *NGOs in International Law* (2008).

including concession agreements, with foreign governments.[38] In this connection in particular, some have argued that the relations of states and foreign corporations *as such* should be treated on the international plane and not as an aspect of the normal rules governing the position of aliens and their assets on the territory of a state.[39] In principle, however, corporations do not have international legal personality. Thus a concession or contract between a state and a foreign corporation is not governed by the law of treaties.[40] The question will be pursued further in chapter 24.

On the other hand conduct of corporations may sometimes be attributed to the state for the purposes of responsibility, and separate state-controlled entities may be able to plead state immunity before foreign courts. It will not always be easy to distinguish corporations which are so closely controlled by governments as to be state agencies for such purposes. The conferral of separate personality under national law is not conclusive of autonomy vis-à-vis the state for purposes of international law.[41]

Important functions are performed today by bodies which have been grouped under the labels 'intergovernmental corporations of private law' or '*établissements publics internationaux*'.[42] The point is that states may by treaty create legal persons whose status is regulated by the national law of one of the parties. At the same time, the treaty may contain obligations to create a privileged status under the national law or laws to which the corporation is subjected. The parties by their agreement may accord certain immunities to the institution created and confer on it various powers. Where the independence from the national laws of the parties is marked, the body concerned may simply be a joint agency of the states involved, with delegated powers effective on the international plane and with a privileged position vis-à-vis local law in respect of its activities.[43] Where there is, in addition to independence from national law, a considerable quantum of delegated powers and the existence of organs with autonomy in decision and rule-making, the body concerned has the characteristics of an international organization. It is when the institution created by treaty has a viability and special function which render the description 'joint agency' inappropriate, and yet has powers and privileges primarily within the *national* legal systems and jurisdictions of the

---

[38] E.g. the Channel Tunnel Concession of 1986 between an Anglo-French consortium and the British and French governments, analysed in *Eurotunnel* (2007) 132 ILR 1, 51–5.

[39] Seidl-Hohenveldern, *Corporations in and under International Law* (1987) 12–14. For a particularly egregious example: *Sandline v Papua New Guinea* (1998) 117 ILR 552.

[40] Waldock, ILC *Ybk* 1962/II, 32. Cf *Anglo-Iranian Oil Co (UK v Iran)*, Jurisdiction, ICJ Reports 1952 p 93, 112; *SGS v Philippines* (2004) 8 ICSID Reports 518, 553.

[41] McNair, 2 *Opinions*, 39. See *Noble Ventures v Romania*, 12 October 2005, §§68–86, available at www.italaw.com.

[42] Sereni (1959) 96 Hague *Recueil* 169; Goldman (1963) 90 *JDI* 321; Friedmann (1964) 181–4, 219–20; Adam, 1–4 *Les Organismes internationaux spécialisés* (1965–77); Angelo (1968) 125 Hague *Recueil* 482; Salmon, *Dictionnaire* (2001) 453, 1029.

[43] The treaty concerned may result in legal personality under the national law of the parties. See *Vigoureux v Comité des Obligataires Danube-Save-Adriatique* (1951) 18 ILR 1. For the Bank for International Settlements prior to its restructuring in 1993: Bederman (1988) 6 *ITBL* 92; Tarin (1992) 5 *Trans L* 839; *Reineccius v Bank of International Settlements* (2003) 140 ILR 1.

various parties, that it calls for use of a special category. An example of an intergovernmental enterprise of this kind is Eurofima, a company set up by a treaty involving 14 states in 1955, with the object of improving the resources of railway rolling stock. The treaty established Eurofima as a corporation under Swiss law subject to certain modifications.[44] The parties agreed that they would recognize this (Swiss) private law status, as modified by the treaty, within their own legal systems. The corporation is international in function and the 14 participating railway administrations provide the capital. The corporation is also given privileges on the international plane, including exemption from taxation in Switzerland, the state of domicile. However, useful as the category '*établissements publics internationaux*' may be, it is not an instrument of exact analysis, and does not reflect a distinct species of international legal person. This type of arrangement is the product of a careful interlocking of national and international legal orders on a treaty basis, and the product will vary considerably from case to case.

(B) NON-SELF-GOVERNING PEOPLES

Quite apart from the question of protected status and the legal effect of mandate or trusteeship agreements, it is probable that the populations of 'non-self-governing territories' within the meaning of Chapter XI of the Charter have legal personality, albeit of a special type. This proposition depends on the principle of self-determination (see chapter 29). Furthermore, practice in the course of the anti-colonial campaign conducted within the UN and regional organizations conferred legal status upon certain national liberation movements.[45] Most of the peoples represented by such movements have acquired statehood.

National liberation movements may, and usually do, have other roles, as *de facto* governments and belligerent communities. Political entities recognized as liberation movements have a number of legal rights and duties, the more significant of which are as follows:

(a) In practice liberation movements have the capacity to conclude binding international agreements with other international legal persons.

(b) There are rights and obligations under the generally recognized principles of humanitarian law. The provisions of the Geneva Protocol I of 1977 apply to conflicts involving national liberation movements if certain conditions are fulfilled.[46]

[44] Convention on the Establishment of 'Eurofima', European Company for the Financing of Railway Equipment, 20 October 1955, 378 UNTS 159.

[45] Wilson, *International Law and the Use of Force by National Liberation Movements* (1988); Ranjeva, in Bedjaoui (ed), *International Law* (1991) 107–10; David, *Principes de Droit des Conflits Armés* (2nd edn, 1999) 195–8; Younis, *Liberation and Democratization* (2000).

[46] Protocol Additional to the Geneva Conventions of 12 August 1949, and relating to the Protection of Victims of International Armed Conflicts (Protocol I), 8 June 1977, 1125 UNTS 3, Arts 1(4), 96(3).

(c) The legal capacity of national liberation movements is reflected in the right to participate in the proceedings of the UN as observers, this right being conferred expressly in various GA resolutions.[47]

(d) The designation of a non-self-governing people engaged in a process of national liberation has implications for the colonial (or dominant) power. Thus the colonial authorities do not have the capacity to make agreements affecting the boundaries or status of the territory which are opposable to the people concerned.[48]

(C) ENTITIES *SUI GENERIS*

Whilst due regard must be had to legal principle, the law cannot ignore entities which maintain some sort of existence on the international legal plane in spite of their anomalous character. The role played by politically active entities such as belligerent communities indicates that, in the sphere of personality, effectiveness is an influential principle. As elsewhere (and subject to compliance with any relevant peremptory norm), acquiescence, recognition, and the incidence of voluntary bilateral relations may prevail. Some special cases may be briefly considered.

In a Treaty and Concordat of 1929, Italy recognized 'the Sovereignty of the Holy See in the international domain' and its exclusive sovereignty and jurisdiction over the City of the Vatican.[49] Numerous states recognize the Holy See and have diplomatic relations with it and the Holy See is a party to many treaties. Functionally, and in terms of its territorial and administrative organization, the Vatican City is proximate to a state. However, it has no population, apart from resident functionaries, and its sole purpose is to support the Holy See as a religious entity. Some jurists regard the Vatican City as a state but its special functions make this doubtful. However, it is widely recognized as a legal person with treaty-making capacity.[50] Its personality rests partly on its approximation to a state, in spite of the peculiarities, including the patrimonial sovereignty of the Holy See, and partly on acquiescence and recognition by existing legal persons. More difficult is the question of the personality of the Holy See apart from its territorial base in the Vatican City.[51] Probably the personality of political and

---

[47] Thus the Palestine Liberation Organization was granted observer status in GA Res 3237(XXIX), 22 November 1974, granted the right to circulate communications without the need for an intermediate in GA Res 43/160, 9 December 1988, designated 'Palestine' in GA Res 43/77, 15 December 1988, and granted the right to participate in debate and certain additional rights in GA Res 52/250, 7 July 1998. Further: Kassim (1980) 9 *DJILP* 1; Shaw (1984) 5 *LLR* 19.

[48] See *Delimitation of the Maritime Boundary between Guinea-Bissau and Senegal* (1989) 83 ILR 1, 25–30; *Kasikilili/Sedudu Island (Botswana/Namibia)*, ICJ Reports 1999 p 1045, 1091–2.

[49] Lateran Pacts, Treaty of Conciliation, 11 February 1929, 130 BFSP 791. See Duursma, *Fragmentation and the International Relations of Micro-States* (1996) 374–419. Further: Kunz (1952) 46 *AJIL* 308; 2 Verzijl (1970) 295–302, 308–38; Crawford (2nd edn, 2006) 221–33.

[50] Fitzmaurice, ILC *Ybk*, 1956/II, 107, 118; *State of the Vatican City v Pieciukiewicz* (1982) 78 ILR 120; *Re Marcinkus, Mennini & De Strebel* (1987) 87 ILR 48; *Holy See v Starbright Sales* (1994) 102 ILR 163.

[51] The problem of personality divorced from a territorial base is difficult to isolate because of the interaction of the Vatican City, the Holy See, and the Roman Catholic Church: Duursma (1996) 386–96.

religious institutions of this type can only be relative to those states prepared to enter into relations with them on the international plane. Even in the sphere of recognition and bilateral relations, the legal capacities of institutions like the Sovereign Order of Jerusalem and Malta must be limited simply because they lack the territorial and demographic characteristics of states.[52]

Two other political animals require classification. 'Governments-in-exile' may be accorded considerable powers within the territory of most states and be active in various political spheres. Apart from voluntary concessions by states and the use of 'governments in exile' as agencies for unlawful activities against established governments and states, the status of a 'government-in-exile' is consequential on the legal condition of the community it claims to represent, which may be a state, belligerent community, or non-self-governing people. Its legal status will be established the more readily when its exclusion from the community of which it is an agency results from acts contrary to a peremptory norm.[53]

Lastly, there is the case of territory title to which is undetermined, which is inhabited and has an independent administration. Communities existing on territory with such a status may be treated as having a modified personality, approximating to that of a state. In one view, this is the situation of Taiwan. Since 1972 the UK, like most other governments, has recognized the Government of the People's Republic of China (PRC) as the sole government of China, and it acknowledges the position of the PRC that Taiwan is a province of China.[54] No government has managed to sustain a recognition policy based on two Chinese states. The question whether Taiwan is a 'country' may nevertheless arise within particular legal contexts;[55] it is also a 'fishing entity' for law of the sea purposes,[56] and as a separate customs territory it is a WTO member.[57] Though not recognized as a state, it has an international legal identity.

---

[52] In the law of war the status of the Order is merely that of a 'relief society' within the meaning of Geneva Convention III, 12 August 1949, 75 UNTS 135, Art 125. Cf Prantner, *Maltesorden und Völkergemeinschaft* (1974), reviewed by O'Connell (1976–77) 48 *BY* 433; Theutenberg, *The Holy See, the Order of Malta and International Law* (2003).

[53] Talmon, *Essays in Honour of Ian Brownlie* (1999) 499; and generally Talmon, *Recognition of Governments in International Law* (1998) 113–268.

[54] Official statements reported in (1986) 57 *BY* 509, 512; (1991) 62 *BY* 568; (1995) 66 *BY* 618, 620–1; Additional Articles to the Constitution of China, 25 April 2000, Art 11; White Paper Taiwan Affairs Office and the Information Office of the State Council 21 February 2000, 'The One-China Principle and the Taiwan Issue'; Anti-Secession Law of PRC, 14 March 2005. Also: Crawford (2nd edn, 2006) 197–221; Freund Larus (2006) 42 *Issues & Studies* 23.

[55] E.g. *Reel v Holder* (1981) 74 ILR 105, noted (1981) 52 *BY* 301.

[56] Serdy (2004) 75 *BY* 183.

[57] Marrakesh Agreement establishing the WTO, 15 April 1994, 1867 UNTS 3, Art XII; Cho, *Taiwan's Application to GATT/WTO* (2002); Mo (2003) 2 *Chin JIL* 145; Hsieh (2005) 39 *JWT* 1195.

4. CONCLUSIONS

This survey should carry with it a warning against facile generalizations on the subject of legal personality. In view of the complexity of international relations and the absence of a centralized law of corporations, it would be strange if the legal situation was simple or uniform. The number of entities with personality *for particular purposes* is considerable. Moreover, the tally of autonomous bodies increases if agencies of states and organizations with a quantum of delegated powers are taken into account. The listing of candidates for personality, as characters to be encountered in the practice of international law and relations, has a certain value. Yet such a procedure has its pitfalls. In the first place, a great deal depends on the relation of the particular entity to the various aspects of the substantive law. Thus individuals are in certain contexts regarded as legal persons, yet it is obvious that they cannot make treaties, nor (if only because of lack of any available forums) can they be subjected to international claims—outside the limited field of international criminal law applicable in international tribunals. The *context* remains paramount. Further, subject to the operation of peremptory norms, the institutions of acquiescence and recognition have been active in sustaining anomalous relations. Finally, the intrusion of agency and representation has created problems both of application and of principle. Thus it is not always easy to distinguish a dependent state with its own personality from a subordinate entity with no independence, a joint agency of states from an organization, or a private or public corporation under some degree of state control from the state itself.

Given the breadth and occasional vagueness of the concept of 'subjects of international law' (and the complete disappearance of the term 'objects', whose only function was denial of status)[58] it has been asked whether the concept has any value.[59] The answer must be in the affirmative. It matters whether an entity has direct access to international forums; it matters whether an entity is directly bound by the body of general international law. On the other hand, being so bound is a constraint that most entities such as INGOs do not need. States and international organizations, and by inference other subjects, are bound not to intervene in the domestic jurisdiction of another state (see chapter 20). The whole point of an NGO may be to do just that, in the pursuit of its aims. The 'international plane' is a construct, not a place—but it remains an arena to which, in most circumstances, one needs a ticket.

---

[58] Oppenheim, *International Law* (1st edn, 1905) 344–5 (individuals classed as 'objects' alongside rivers, canals, lakes, straits, etc).

[59] E.g. Higgins (1994) 49–50.

5

CREATION AND INCIDENCE OF STATEHOOD

1. INTRODUCTION

As noted in chapter 4, the state is a type of legal person recognized by international law. Yet, since there are other types of legal persons so recognized, the possession of legal personality is not in itself a sufficient mark of statehood. Moreover, the exercise of legal capacities is a normal consequence, rather than conclusive evidence, of legal personality: a puppet state may have all the paraphernalia of separate personality and yet be little more than an agency for another power. It is sometimes said that statehood is a question of fact, meaning that it is not a question of law.[1] However, as lawyers are usually asking if an entity is a state with a specific legal claim or function in view, it is pointless to confuse issues of law with the difficulties of applying the legal principles to the facts and of discovering the key facts in the first place. The criteria of statehood are laid down by the law. If it were not so, then statehood would produce the same type of structural defect that has been detected in certain types of doctrine concerning nationality. In other words, a state would be able at its own unfettered discretion to contract out of its obligations under international law simply by refusing to characterize the other party as a state. A readiness to ignore the law may be disguised by a plea of freedom in relation to a key concept, determinant of many particular rights and duties, like statehood or nationality. To some extent this position anticipates the results of the examination of recognition in chapter 6. Nevertheless, as a matter of presentation the question whether recognition by one or more other states is a determinant (as mandated by the 'constitutive theory' of recognition) will be ignored in the present chapter. The subject of state succession is also excluded from this discussion: the subject-matter conventionally described by that label is considered in chapter 19.

Despite the importance of the subject-matter, the literature is rather uneven.[2] Three factors have contributed to this. First, though the subject is important as a matter of

---

[1] Oppenheim, 1 *International Law* (1st edn, 1905) 99–101; cf 1 Oppenheim 120–3.

[2] Generally: 1 Whiteman 221–33, 283–476; Guggenheim (1952) 80 Hague *Recueil* 1; Higgins, *Development* (1963) 11–57; Fawcett, *The British Commonwealth in International Law* (1963) 88–143; Marek, *Identity and Continuity of States in Public International Law* (2nd edn, 1968); Verzijl, 2 *International Law in Historical*

principle, the issue of statehood does not often raise long-standing disputes. Secondly, much of the literature is devoted to broad concepts of sovereignty and equality of states and gives prominence to incidents of statehood rather than its origins and continuity. Finally, many rifts in relations between particular states concern issues of *government* rather than statehood.

2. LEGAL CRITERIA OF STATEHOOD

Article I of the Montevideo Convention on Rights and Duties of States provides: 'The State as a person of international law should possess the following qualifications: (a) a permanent population; (b) a defined territory; (c) government; and (d) capacity to enter into relations with the other States.'[3] This brief enumeration is often cited,[4] but it is no more than a basis for further investigation. Not all the conditions are necessary, and in any case further criteria must be employed to produce a working definition.[5]

(A) POPULATION

The Montevideo Convention refers to 'a permanent population'. This criterion is intended to be used in association with that of territory, and connotes a stable community. Evidentially this is important, since in the absence of the physical basis for an organized community, it will be difficult to establish the existence of a state.

(B) DEFINED TERRITORY

There must be a reasonably stable political community and this must be in control of a certain area. It is clear that the existence of fully defined frontiers is not required and that what matters is the effective establishment of a political community.[6] In 1913

Perspective (1969) 62–294, 339–500; Rousseau, 2 *Droit International Public* (1974) 13–93; Arangio-Ruiz, *L'État dans le sens du droit des gens et la notion du droit international* (1975); Crawford (1976–77) 48 *BY* 93; Lauterpacht, 3 *International Law* (1977) 5–25; Grant, *The Recognition of States* (1999); Crawford, *Creation of States* (2nd edn, 2006); Caspersen & Stansfield, *Unrecognized States in the International System* (2011). On UN membership: Grant, *Admission to the United Nations* (2009); Duxbury, *The Participation of States in International Organisations* (2011).

[3] Convention on Rights and Duties of States adopted by the Seventh International Conference of American States, 26 December 1933, 165 LNTS 19.

[4] E.g. Fitzmaurice (1957) 92 Hague *Recueil* 1, 13; Higgins (1963) 13; Fawcett (1963) 92.

[5] Grant (1999) 37 *Col JTL* 403.

[6] *Deutsche Continental Gas-Gesellschaft v Polish State* (1929) 5 ILR 11; *North Sea Continental Shelf (Federal Republic of Germany/Netherlands; Federal Republic of Germany/Denmark)*, ICJ Reports 1969 p 3, 32; *In re Duchy of Sealand* (1978) 80 ILR 683. Further: Badinter Commission, *Opinion No 1* (1991) 92 ILR 162; *Opinion No 10* (1992) 92 ILR 206.

Albania was recognized by a number of states in spite of a lack of settled frontiers,[7] and Israel was admitted to the UN in spite of disputes over its borders.[8]

There is no fixed lower limit either of population or territory, and some recognized states have tiny quantities of both. At one time it was thought that the UN admission of 'micro-states', in particular the European micro-states of Liechtenstein, San Marino, Monaco, and Andorra, was precluded because of their size, but the principle of universality of UN membership prevailed. In the 1990s, all were admitted to membership—in the case of Andorra after significant reforms which removed doubts as to its independence from France and Spain.[9]

(C) GOVERNMENT

The shortest definition of a state for present purposes is perhaps that it is a stable political community supporting a legal order to the exclusion of others in a given area. The existence of effective government, with centralized administrative and legislative organs, is the best evidence of a stable political community.[10] However, effective government is in certain cases either unnecessary or insufficient to support statehood. Some states have arisen before government was very well organized, as, for example, Poland in 1919[11] and Burundi and Rwanda, admitted to the UN in 1962.[12] The principle of self-determination—also discussed in chapter 29—was once commonly set against the concept of effective government, more particularly when the latter was used as an argument for continued colonial rule. The relevant question has become, instead, in whose interest and for what legal purpose is government 'effective'? Once a state has been established, extensive civil strife or the breakdown of order through foreign invasion or natural disasters are not considered to affect personality. Nor is effective government sufficient, since this leaves open the questions of independence and representation by other states, discussed below.

(D) INDEPENDENCE

In the Montevideo Convention's enumeration, the concept of independence is represented by the requirement of capacity to enter into relations with other states. Independence is the decisive criterion of statehood.[13] Guggenheim distinguishes the

---

[7] On Albania: Ydit, *Internationalized Territories* (1961) 29–33; Crawford (2nd edn, 2006) 510–12.

[8] See Jessup, US representative in the SC, 2 December 1948, quoted in 1 Whiteman 230; also SC Res 69 (1949), GA Res 273(III), 11 May 1949.

[9] On the European micro-states generally: Duursma, *Fragmentation and the International Relations of Microstates* (1996). On micro-states as UN members: Crawford (2nd edn, 2006) 182–5. On Andorra before the reforms of 1993: Crawford (1977) 55 *RDISDP* 259; on those reforms: Duursma (1996) 316–73.

[10] Guggenheim (1952) 80 Hague *Recueil 1*, 83; Higgins (1963) 20–5.

[11] Temperley, 5 *History of the Peace Conference at Paris* (1921) 158. Cf Chen, *The International Law of Recognition* (1951) 201. Further: Crawford (2nd edn, 2006) 530–1.

[12] Higgins (1963) 22.

[13] 2 Rousseau (1974) 68–73. Cf Marek (1968) 161–90.

state from other legal orders by means of two tests which he regards as quantitative rather than qualitative.[14] First, the state has a degree of centralization of its organs not found elsewhere. Secondly, in a particular area the state is the sole executive and legislative authority. In other words the state must be independent of other state legal orders, and any interference by such legal orders, or by an international agency, must be based on a title of international law.

In the normal case independence as a criterion may create few problems. However, there are sources of confusion. In the first place, independence may be used in close association with a requirement of effective government,[15] leading to the issues considered earlier. Again, since a state is, in part, a legal order, there is a temptation to rely on formal criteria. Certainly, if an entity has its own executive and other organs, conducts its foreign relations through its own organs, has its own system of courts and legal system, and a nationality law of its own, then there is strong evidence of statehood. However, there is no justification for ignoring foreign control exercised in fact through the ostensibly independent machinery of state. But the emphasis is on foreign *control* overbearing the decision-making of the entity concerned on a wide range of matters and doing so systematically and on a continuing basis. The practice of states has been to ignore—so far as issues of statehood are concerned—forms of political and economic blackmail and interference directed against weaker members. Further there is a distinction between agency and control, on the one hand, and ad hoc interference and 'advice', on the other.[16]

(i) 'Dependent states'

Foreign control of the affairs of a state may occur under a title of international law, for example as a consequence of a treaty of protection, or some other form of consent to agency or representation in external relations, or of a lawful war of collective defence and sanction leading to an occupation and imposition of measures designed to remove the sources of aggression. Allied occupation of Germany under the Berlin Declaration of 5 June 1945 is an example of the latter: supreme authority was assumed in Germany by the Allies jointly.[17] Providing that the representation and agency exist in fact and in law, then there is no formal difficulty in saying that the criterion of independence is

---

[14] Guggenheim (1952) 80 Hague *Recueil* 183, 96.

[15] In *Aaland Islands* the Commission of Jurists referred to the disorder existing in Finland and observed: 'It is therefore difficult to say at what exact date the Finnish Republic in the legal sense of the term actually became a definitely constituted sovereign State. This certainly did not take place until a stable political organization had been created, and until the public authorities had become strong enough to assert themselves throughout the territories of the State without the assistance of foreign troops': (1920) *LNOJ Sp Supp* No 3, 3. This sets the bar very high and would have embarrassing consequences if generally applied.

[16] On independence as a criterion for statehood: Crawford (2nd edn, 2006) 62–88.

[17] The occupation was not a belligerent occupation, nor was there a *debellatio* leading to extinction of Germany as a state: Protocol on Zones of Occupation in Germany, 12 September 1944, 227 UNTS 279; further: Jennings (1946) 23 BY 112; Sharp, *The Wartime Alliance and the Zonal Division of Germany* (1975); Hendry & Wood, *The Legal Status of Berlin* (1987); Piotrowicz & Blay, *The Unification of Germany in International and Domestic Law* (1997).

satisfied. Unfortunately, writers have created confusion by rehearsing independence as an aspect of statehood and then referring to 'dependent states', which are presented as an anomalous category.[18] Here the incidents of personality are not sufficiently distinguished from its existence. The term 'dependent' is used to indicate the existence of one or more of the following distinct situations:

(1) the absence of statehood, where the entity concerned is subordinated to a state so completely as to be within its control (and the origin of the subordination does not establish agency or representation);

(2) a state which has made concessions to another state in matters of jurisdiction and administration to such an extent that it has in some sense ceased to be sovereign;[19]

(3) a state which has legally conferred wide powers of agency and representation in foreign affairs on another state;[20]

(4) a state, which in fact suffers interference from another state and may be a 'client' state politically, but which quantitatively is not under the complete and permanent control of the 'patron';

(5) a legal person of a special type, appearing on the international plane for certain purposes only, as in the case of mandated and trust territories and some protectorates.

The category of independence (or sovereignty used synonymously) can only be applied concretely in the light of the legal purpose with which the inquiry is made and the particular facts. In *Austro-German Customs Union*[21] the Permanent Court was asked whether the proposed customs union was contrary to the obligations of Austria under a Protocol of 1922 'not to alienate its independence' and to 'abstain from any negotiations or from any economic and financial engagement calculated directly or indirectly to compromise this independence'.[22] By a majority of eight to seven the Court held that the customs regime contemplated would be incompatible with these obligations. Here the term 'independence' referred to a specialized notion of economic relations in a treaty, and the obligations were not confined to abstention from actual and complete alienation of independence. In *Nationality Decrees* the Permanent Court emphasized that protectorates have 'individual legal characteristics resulting from the special

---

[18] Hall, *International Law* (8th edn, 1924) 18, 20, 33; 1 Oppenheim 125–6 ('sovereignty' used as a synonym for 'independence').

[19] On the Gulf States: Al Baharna, *The Arabian Gulf States* (2nd rev edn, 1975); Al Baharna, *British Extra-Territorial Jurisdiction in the Gulf 1913–1971*(1998).

[20] This may occur without subordination. Since 1919 by agreement the Swiss Federal Council has conducted the diplomatic relations of Liechtenstein: Duursma (1996) 161–9. Also Busek & Hummer (eds), *Der Kleinstaat als Akteur in den Internationalen Beziehungen* (2004).

[21] *Customs Régime between Germany and Austria* (1931) PCIJ Ser A/B No 41, 37.

[22] Protocol No 1, 4 October 1922, 116 BFSP 851.

conditions...under which they were created, and the stage of their development'.[23] A protected state may provide an example of international representation which leaves the personality and statehood of the entity represented intact, though from the point of view of the *incidents* of personality the entity may be 'dependent' in one or more of the senses noted above. In *US Nationals in Morocco* the International Court, referring to the Treaty of Fez and the creation of a French protectorate in 1912, stated: 'Under this Treaty, Morocco remained a sovereign State but it made an arrangement of contractual character whereby France undertook to exercise certain sovereign powers in the name and on behalf of Morocco, and, in principle, all of the international relations of Morocco'.[24] In fact it appears that the relation was one of subordination and not agency.

Another aspect of dependency emerges in the context of former colonies. Postcolonial dependency has been analysed in the general framework of development economics and public administration. With regard to the latter, the colonial analogy is manifested in a state or other territorial unit being placed under partial or full administration by an international organization, thereby losing control over some or all aspects of governance and becoming dependent on the administrator.[25] The discourse of development, on the other hand, created a scalar system of states—dividing states into 'developed' or 'developing'—secured by positing an ostensibly universally attainable end point in the status of 'developed'. This division made it possible for the West to mediate the potentially disruptive effects of formal sovereign equality and prevent it from leading to substantive equality. The economic institutions created the possibility for ongoing surveillance and interventions to transform 'developing' states.[26] Numerous 'developing' states are reliant on foreign aid and loans from institutions such as the World Bank and the UN Development Programme. The economic assistance programmes usually have conditions attached to them. The conditions can relate, for example, to the use of the money, to the recipient's policies on matters such as human rights, expropriation, or democratization. The recipient has little choice but to comply if it wants to gain and retain access to these funds. Such 'developing' states

---

[23] *Nationality Decrees in Tunis and Morocco* (1923) PCIJ Ser B No 4, 7.

[24] *Rights of Nationals of the United States of America in Morocco (France v US)*, ICJ Reports 1952 p 176, 188. Also Guggenheim (1952) 80 Hague *Recueil* 1, 96. Cf the separate but dependent personality of India 1919–47; on which see McNair, *The Law of Treaties* (1938) 76; Poulose (1970) 44 *BY* 201; *Right of Passage over Indian Territory (Portugal v India)*, ICJ Reports 1960 p 6, 95 (Judge Moreno Quintana, diss). Cf also the position of Monaco in relation to France: Duursma (1996) 274–91. On the status of Hungary after German occupation in 1944: *Restitution of Households Effects Belonging to Jews Deported from Hungary (Germany)* (1965) 44 ILR 301, 334–42. On the status of Croatia in Yugoslavia during the German occupation: *Socony Vacuum Oil Company* (1954) 21 ILR 55, 58–62. On Morocco as a French protectorate: Treaty for the Organisation of the Protectorate, 30 March 1912, 106 BFSP 1032.

[25] The colonial analogy has been made in different ways e.g. in Helman & Ratner (1992) 89 *Foreign Policy* 3; Lyon (1993) 31 *JCCP* 96; Gordon (1995) 28 *Cornell ILJ* 301; Richardson (1996) 10 *Temple ICLJ* 1; Perritt (2004) 15 *Duke JCIL* 1. Cf Wilde, *International Territorial Administration* (2008) ch 8. For more on international administrations: chapter 4.

[26] Pahuja, *Decolonising International Law* (2011) 46–7.

are reliant on foreign resources and consequently prone to influence and interferences by the 'developed' world.

It has been suggested that some of the post-colonial states have 'failed' and now require supervision by the international community or select states. Brooks has even argued that post-colonial states 'rarely possessed the attributes of robust states in anything other than a purely formal legal sense'.[27] To address the problem of 'failed states', Helman and Ratner proposed 'United Nations Conservatorship', envisaging three options whereby the UN 'manages the affairs' of the 'failed state'.[28] Pfaff declared that '[m]uch of Africa needs, to put it plainly, what one could call a disinterested neo-colonialism' and suggested that the European Union should 'collectively assume such responsibilities in cooperation with Africans in an effort to arrest the continent's decline and put it on a progressive course'.[29] This remains a minority position. Moreover, some African states are exhibiting solid growth and poverty reduction, supporting the view that the causes of the persistence of severe poverty, and hence the key to its eradication, lie within those countries themselves.[30]

A different side of post-colonial dependency is exhibited by the fact that some states elect to stay associated with the former colonial power. Guam is an American dependency, Aruba is part of the Kingdom of the Netherlands, the British Virgin Islands is a Crown Colony, and Anguilla is an 'associated state' of Britain. In these cases local authorities are responsible for most internal affairs, while 'parent' states are responsible for defence and external relations.[31]

(ii) Associations of states

Independent states may enter into forms of co-operation by consent and on an equal footing. The basis for the co-operation may be the constitution of an international organization, such as the UN or the World Health Organization. However, by treaty or custom other structures for maintaining co-operation may be created. One such structure, the confederation, has in practice either disintegrated or been transformed into a federation. Membership does not affect the legal capacities and personality of member states any more than membership of an organization and has less effect than membership of some organizations, for example, the European Union, which has a certain federal element, albeit on a treaty basis.[32]

---

[27] Brooks (2005) 72 *U Chic LR* 1159, 1168.

[28] Helman & Ratner (1992) 89 *Foreign Policy* 3, 13.

[29] Pfaff (1995) 74 *Foreign Affairs* 2, 2, 6. Also Kreijen, *State Failure, Sovereignty and Effectiveness* (2004).

[30] Further: Pogge, in Crawford & Koskenniemi (eds), *Cambridge Companion to International Law* (2012) 373.

[31] Ehrenreich & Brooks (2005) 72 *U Chic LR* 1159, 1187.

[32] TFEU, 13 December 2007, *OJEU* C 115/47 2008. Generally: Gerven, *The European Union* (2005); Dashwood, *Law and Practice of EU External Relations* (2009); Hix, *The Political System of the European Union* (3rd edn, 2011).

(E) A DEGREE OF PERMANENCE[33]

If one relies principally on the concept of a stable political community, it might seem superfluous to stipulate for a degree of permanence. Time is an element of statehood, as is space. However, *permanence* is not necessary to the existence of a state as a legal order, and a state which has only a very brief life may nevertheless leave an agenda of consequential legal questions on its extinction.[34]

(F) WILLINGNESS TO OBSERVE INTERNATIONAL LAW

In the modern literature, this is not often mentioned as a criterion, and it has been subjected to trenchant criticism.[35] Delictual and other responsibilities, even though no longer exclusive to states, are consequences of statehood, and it is indefensible to express as a criterion of statehood a condition which the entity can only accept *because* it is a state.

A more fundamental issue is whether some degree of 'civilization' is inherent in statehood. For example Hyde adds a further criterion: 'the inhabitants must have attained a degree of civilization, such as to enable them to observe…those principles of law which are deemed to govern the members of the international society in their relations with each other'.[36] However, it is usually omitted from enumerations of criteria and is redolent of the period when non-European states were not accorded equal treatment by the European Concert.[37]

(G) SOVEREIGNTY[38]

The term 'sovereignty' may be used as a synonym for independence, an important element in statehood considered already. However, a common source of confusion lies in the fact that 'sovereignty' may be used to describe the condition where a state has not exercised its own legal capacities in such a way as to create rights, powers, privileges, and immunities in respect of other states. In this sense a state which has consented to another state managing its foreign relations, or which has granted extensive extra-territorial rights to another state, is not 'sovereign'. If this or a similar content is given to 'sovereignty' and the same ideogram is used as a criterion of

---

[33] Chen (1951) 59–60; Kelsen, *Principles of International Law* (2nd edn, 1966) 381–3; Waldock, ILC *Ybk* 1972/II, 34–5; 1 *Restatement Third*, §§201–2.

[34] Cf the anti-Jewish legislation of the Italian Social Republic of Sálo: *Mossé* (1953) 20 ILR 217; *Levi* (1957) 24 ILR 303; *Sonnino* (1956) 24 ILR 647; *Wollemborg* (1956) 24 ILR 654. British Somaliland became independent on 26 June 1960 but united with Somalia to form the Somali Republic on 1 July 1960. It remains formally unrecognized as a separate state: UKMIL (2010) 81 *BY* 453, 503–5.

[35] Chen (1951) 61.

[36] Hyde, 1 *International Law* (1922) 23; Chen (1951) 127–9. Also 1 Whiteman 223.

[37] Gong, *The Standard of 'Civilization' in International Society* (1984); Bull & Watson, *The Expansion of International Society* (1985); Fidler (2001) 2 *Chic JIL* 137. And see chapter 1.

[38] Generally: Crawford, in Crawford & Koskenniemi (2012) ch 5. Further: Chayes & Chayes, *The New Sovereignty* (1995); Krasner, *Sovereignty, Organized Hypocrisy* (1999); MacCormick, *Questioning Sovereignty* (1999); Kalmo & Skinner (eds), *Sovereignty in Fragments* (2010).

statehood,[39] then the incidents of statehood and legal personality are once again confused with their existence. Thus the condition of Germany after 1945 involved a considerable diminution of German sovereignty in this sense, and yet Germany continued to exist as a state. Considerations of this sort have led some to reject sovereignty as a criterion.[40]

An alternative approach is that of the International Court in *US Nationals in Morocco*, where the judgment described Morocco as a 'sovereign State', meaning that it had maintained its basic personality in spite of the French protectorate.[41] It would be possible for a tribunal to hold that a state which had granted away piecemeal a high proportion of its legal powers had ceased to have a separate existence as a consequence. But it may be difficult to distinguish granting away of capacities and the existence of agency or representation, and there is a strong presumption against loss of status.

(H) FUNCTION AS A STATE

Experience has shown that entities may exist which are difficult to regard as states but which have a certain, even considerable international presence. The Treaty of Versailles of 1919 created the Free City of Danzig, which had the legal marks of statehood in spite of the fact that it was placed under the guarantee of the League of Nations and Poland had the power to conduct its foreign relations.[42] The Italian Peace Treaty of 1947 provided for the creation of the Free Territory of Trieste, which was to be placed under the protection of the Security Council.[43] The type of legal personality involved in these two cases is a congener of statehood, and it is the specialized political function of such entities, and their relation to an organization, which inhibits use of the category of statehood.

(i) States *in statu nascendi*

A political community with considerable viability, controlling a certain area of territory and having statehood as its objective, may go through a period of travail before that objective has been achieved. In any case, since matters such as definition of frontiers and effective government are not looked at too strictly, the distinction between entities *in statu nascendi* and statehood cannot be very readily upheld.[44] States not

---

[39] Cf Badinter Commission, *Opinion No 1* (1991) 92 ILR 162: 'The Committee considers … that such a state is characterized by sovereignty'. But cf 1 Oppenheim (1st edn, 1905) 108.

[40] Rousseau (1948) 73 Hague *Recueil* 1, 178–80. Cf *Duff Development Co v Government of Kelantan* (1924) 2 ILR 124, 127 (Viscount Finlay); Judges Adatci, Kellogg, Rolin-Jaequemyns, Hurst, Schücking, van Eysinga & Wang (diss), *Austro-German Customs Union* (1931) PCIJ Ser A/B No 41, 37, 77. Further: Fawcett (1963) 88–93; *Lighthouses in Crete and Samos* (1937) PCIJ Ser A/B No 71, 94.

[41] ICJ Reports 1952 p 176, 185, 188. Also: Rolin (1950) 77 Hague *Recueil* 305, 326.

[42] Crawford (2nd edn, 2006) 236–41. But disputes between Danzig and Poland were referred to the PCIJ by means of its advisory jurisdiction in view of Art 34 of the Statute of the Court, which gives *locus standi* in contentious cases only to states. On Danzig: chapter 4.

[43] 49 UNTS 124.

[44] Cf the cases of Albania in 1913; Poland and Czechoslovakia in 1917–18; Estonia, Latvia, and Lithuania, 1918–20. See 1 Hackworth 199–222. Also the case of Indonesia, 1946–49: 2 Whiteman

infrequently first appear as independent belligerent entities under a political author-ity which may be called, and function effectively as, a provisional government. Once statehood is firmly established, it is justifiable, both legally and practically, to assume the retroactive validation of the legal order during a period prior to general recogni-tion as a state, when some degree of effective government existed. Leaving questions of state succession on one side, the principle of effectiveness dictates acceptance, for some legal purposes at least, of continuity before and after statehood is firmly established.[45]

In particular, the principle of self-determination may justify the granting of a higher status to certain types of belligerent entities and exile governments than would other-wise be the case. In exceptional circumstances, a people may be recognized by the inter-national community, and by interested parties, as having an *entitlement* to statehood, and thus as being a state *in statu nascendi*. Normally, this transitional status leads, without too much delay, to independence under the auspices of the UN. However, in the case of the Palestinian people, there has been an eccentric bilateral process in which the question of statehood has been in issue between the government of Israel and the Palestine Liberation Organization (PLO),[46] which, in turn, has given rise to problems in multilateral institutions.[47] The Palestine question is considered below.

3. SOME ISSUES OF STATEHOOD

Three major situations affecting world order provide insight into the issues of state-hood in our time.

(A) GERMANY SINCE 1945[48]

The termination of hostilities against the German *Reich* in June 1945 coincided with the disappearance of effective national government in its territory.[49] In response, the

---

165–7. Cf the observations of Lord Finlay, *German Interests in Polish Upper Silesia* (1926) PCIJ Ser A No 7, 4, 84.

[45] For the asserted continuity of the Palestine Mandate and Israel see *AG (Israel) v Eichmann* (1961) 36 ILR 5, 52–3; (1962) 36 ILR 277, 304. See further *ALB v Austrian Federal Ministry for the Interior* (1922) 1 ILR 20; *Poznanski v Lentz & Hirschfeld* (1924) 2 ILR 228; *Establishment of Czechoslovak State* (1925) 3 ILR 13; *HE v Federal Ministry of the Interior* (1925) 4 ILR 25; *Deutsche Continental Gas-Gesellschaft v Poland* (1929) 5 ILR 11.

[46] Oslo Accords (1993) 32 ILM 1542. Cassese, *Self-determination of Peoples* (1995) 230–48; Shehadeh, *From Occupation to Interim Accords* (1997); McDowall, *The Palestinians* (1998); Crawford (2nd edn, 2006) 434–48. Further: *Legal Consequences of the Construction of a Wall in the Occupied Palestinian Territory*, ICJ Reports 2004 p 136.

[47] E.g. the ICC: Shaw (2011) 9 *JICJ* 301, with citations to literature at 302 n2.

[48] Hendry & Wood (1987); Frowein (1992) 86 *AJIL* 152; Piotrowicz (1992) 63 *BY* 367; Crawford (2nd edn, 2006) 452–66.

[49] Berlin Declaration, 5 June 1945, 145 BFSP 796.

Allied Powers assumed 'supreme authority with respect to Germany', under which an Allied Control Council took the place of the German government.[50] Though the Allies affirmed the integrity of Germany in principle, they divided the country into four Zones of Occupation, and, instead of a single central government, the Commanders-in-Chief of the Four Powers acted separately in each Zone and jointly only with respect to 'Germany as a whole'. Difficult questions of interpretation arose for the courts of the states involved in zonal administration.[51] As for the subject-matter of joint administration, this was, evidently, a residue of the general governmental functions and of the rights and responsibilities of the one state which had existed as at the time of capitulation, though there, too, the arrangement was unusual and tended to defy formal categorization. That some authority was reserved under the rubric of 'Germany as a whole' was suggested in various instruments,[52] but the primacy of the separate zonal administrations remained, and it was from them that the post-war configuration of Germany emerged.

In particular, the failure of the four Powers to implement the Potsdam Agreement regarding reunification opened the way to the evolution of two separate governmental units—one in the Soviet Zone, one in the three Western Zones. The Federal Republic of Germany (FRG) began as a subordinate government of the Western Allies in their Zones, from 23 May 1949, though they quickly adopted the view that this was no mere delegate. Their Declaration of 19 December 1950 indicated as follows: 'The Three Governments consider that the Government of the Federal Republic is the only German Government freely and legitimately constituted and therefore entitled to speak for the German people in international affairs.'[53] A Tripartite Convention on Relations of 26 May 1952 enlarged the authority of the Federal Republic, though this was not an unlimited authority: the three Western Allies retained 'the rights and responsibilities, heretofore exercised or held by them, relating to Berlin and to Germany as a whole, including the reunification of Germany and a peace settlement.'[54] Soviet recognition of the FRG on 13 September 1955[55] retrospectively validated what was otherwise a series of *ultra vires* acts, for no Ally or group of Allies, save the four as a whole, had had the competence to relinquish quadripartite authority.[56]

The Soviet Union, in response to developments in the Western Zones, on 7 October 1949 declared the establishment of a German Democratic Republic (GDR). A treaty of 20 September 1955 indicated that the GDR held general freedom of action in respect of 'domestic and foreign policy,' reserving for the USSR the 'obligations of the Soviet

[50] Statement on Control Machinery in Germany, 5 June 1945, 145 BFSP 803.

[51] See *Brehm v Acheson*, 90 F.Supp 662 (SD Tex, 1950); *Recidivism (Soviet Zone of Germany)* (1954) 21 ILR 42.

[52] 1952 Tripartite Convention, Art 2: 331 UNTS 327; 1955 Convention (USSR–GDR), Art 1, 226 UNTS 201; 1972 Treaty on the Basis of Intra-German Relations, Art 9, 21 December 1973, 12 ILM 16.

[53] [1964] *BPIL* 276.

[54] 331 UNTS 327.

[55] Letter from Prime Minister Bulganin to FRG delegation, 13 September 1955: 162 BFSP 623.

[56] Mann, *Studies in International Law* (1972) 671.

Union and of the GDR under existing international agreements relating to Germany as a whole.'[57] The Western Allies resisted these developments. The principal arguments which they set out against the statehood of the GDR were (a) that the absence of general recognition of the GDR was a fundamental infirmity (even though this was a position already largely untenable by the 1950s); (b) that the lack of democratic institutions prevented the GDR from attaining independence; (c) that the GDR was subordinate to the USSR; and (d) that the putative independence of the GDR was in breach of the self-determination of 'Germany as a whole.'[58] Whatever the legal characterization of the process by which the GDR became consolidated as a state, its statehood eventually received general recognition. This was through a series of transactions, in particular a Non-Aggression Treaty between the FRG and the USSR of 12 August 1970, in which the frontier between the two German states was affirmed;[59] and a Treaty on the Basis of Inter-German Relations between the FRG and GDR of 21 December 1972 in which each acknowledged that neither 'can represent the other in the international sphere or act on its behalf'.[60] The Four Powers declared their acceptance of separate UN membership on 9 November 1972,[61] and the two German states were admitted unopposed the next year.[62]

It is clear enough that the Four Powers, in 1990, relinquished their remaining joint powers in respect of 'Germany as a Whole',[63] including, concretely, what remained of their territorial rights in Berlin, the eastern sector of which the Western Powers had never accepted as integral to the GDR.[64] But, by the same provision of the final settlement, 'the united Germany shall have accordingly full sovereignty over its internal and external affairs,'[65] which suggests a reversion of authorities and responsibilities, rather than their disappearance. So, while the two Germanies after 1945 were in some sense successor states,[66] a strong element of continuity persisted to 1990, and was thereafter reaffirmed in the form of the Federal Republic.

(B) PALESTINE

Since 1945 there has been a consolidation of the view that statehood is a question of law rather than just fact. Peremptory norms have influenced this process, but it has

---

[57] 226 UNTS 201. Also USSR–GDR Treaty of Friendship, Mutual Assistance and Co-operation, 12 June 1964, 553 UNTS 249, Arts 7, 9.

[58] Crawford (2nd edn, 2006) 456–7.

[59] 1972 UNTS 315, 9 ILM 1026, Art 3.

[60] 12 ILM 16, Art 6.

[61] 12 ILM 217.

[62] SC Res 344 (1973); GA Res 3060(XXVIII), 18 September 1973.

[63] Treaty on the Final Settlement with Respect to Germany, 12 September 1990, 1696 UNTS 123, Art 7(1).

[64] Three Powers note of 14 April 1975: A/10078. Further: (1977) 81 *RGDIP* 494, 613–14, 772–4. About Berlin generally: Hendry & Wood (1987).

[65] Treaty on the Final Settlement, Art 7(2).

[66] Ress, *Die Rechtslage Deutschlands* (1978) 199–228.

nonetheless been highly politicized in particular cases, the Israel–Palestine conflict presenting an acute example.[67]

The agenda between the government of Israel and the PLO has, since 1993, included 'the permanent status negotiations', which were (it was assumed) to lead to an independent Palestinian state. Article I of the Oslo Accords of 1993[68] provided as follows:

The aim of the Israeli-Palestinian negotiations within the current Middle East peace process is, among other things, to establish a Palestinian Interim Self-Government Authority, the elected Council (the 'Council'), for the Palestinian people in the West Bank and the Gaza Strip, for a transitional period not exceeding five years, leading to a permanent settlement based on Security Council Resolutions 242 and 338. It is understood that the interim arrangements are an integral part of the whole peace process and that the negotiations on the permanent status will lead to the implementation of Security Council Resolutions 242 and 338.[69]

A decade later, the Israelis and the Palestinians still had not reached a final-status peace agreement. In 2003, the Quartet co-ordinating the negotiations (the US, the EU, the Russian Federation, and the UN) proposed a performance-based Roadmap envisaging the emergence of a Palestinian state.[70] Phase III of the Roadmap required that the parties negotiate a final and comprehensive permanent status agreement based on SC Resolutions 242, 338, and 1397 and entailing 'two states, Israel and sovereign, independent, democratic and viable Palestine, living side-by-side in peace and security'. The Roadmap was endorsed by the Security Council in November 2003.[71] However, the parties still failed to agree on final status. In November 2007, the Israeli–Palestinian Joint Understanding declared the intent of the parties to 'immediately launch good-faith bilateral negotiations in order to conclude a peace treaty, resolving all outstanding issues, including all core issues without exception, as specified in previous agreements', '[i]n furtherance of the goal of two states, Israel and Palestine, living side by side in peace and security'.[72] The parties also committed to implement their respective obligations under the Roadmap.[73] Peace talks stalled after Israel refused to extend a 10-month freeze on settlement activity in the occupied Palestinian territory. That decision prompted the Palestinian Authority to withdraw from direct talks with Israel, which had only resumed a few weeks earlier after a two-year hiatus.

---

[67] And one giving rise to unusually sharp exchanges: Crawford (1990) 1 *EJIL* 307; Boyle (1990) 1 *EJIL* 301; Benoliel & Perry (2010) 32 *Mich JIL* 73; Quigley (2011) 32 *Mich JIL* 749.

[68] Declaration of Principles on Interim Self-Government Arrangements, 13 September 1993, 32 ILM 1527, and see Benvenisti (1993) 4 *EJIL* 542; Cassese, ibid, 564; Malanczuk (1996) 7 *EJIL* 485.

[69] SC Res 242 (1967) provided for the 'withdrawal of Israeli armed forces from territories occupied in the recent conflict'; SC Res 338 (1973) called upon the parties concerned to begin the process of implementation of SC Res 242 (1967).

[70] Performance-based Roadmap to a Permanent Two-State Solution to the Israeli–Palestinian Conflict, S/2003/529, 7 May 2003.

[71] SC Res 1515 (2003), op §1.

[72] Joint Understanding Read by President Bush at Annapolis Conference, 27 November 2007, released by the White House, Office of the Press Secretary, available at www.unispal.un.org.

[73] Ibid.

In November 2011, noting an agreement of the parties in October 2011 to make comprehensive proposals on territory and security, the UN called for an immediate resumption of peace talks.[74]

Though the parties had not reached a final status agreement, Palestine applied for admission to membership in the UN on 23 September 2011.[75] The Security Council Committee on the Admission of New Members was unable to recommend action to the Security Council and instead adopted a report noting deep divisions within the Council.[76] Palestine had previously been accepted into membership in the Non-Aligned Movement, the Organization of Islamic Cooperation, the Economic and Social Commission for Western Asia, the Group of 77, and UNESCO.[77] Some 130 states have recognized Palestine as a state.[78]

(c) KOSOVO

Another unresolved case is that of Kosovo. States submitting observations in the *Kosovo* advisory proceedings addressed, *inter alia*, the right to self-determination (outside the colonial context), and some posited that a state might be created under a right to 'remedial secession'.[79] However, the Court found that it was 'not necessary to resolve these questions in the present case', as the General Assembly had requested the Court's opinion on a narrower question—that is, whether the declaration of independence was in accordance with international law. The Court concluded that 'general international law contains no applicable prohibition of declarations of independence'. Accordingly, the 'declaration of independence of 17 February 2008 did not violate general international law'.[80] The Court found that SC Resolution 1244 (1999) did not address the authors of the declaration of 17 February 2008 and so did not constrain them from issuing a declaration of independence either. The authors of the declaration were not acting as one of the Provisional Institutions of Self-Government within the Constitutional Framework, but rather were representatives of the people of Kosovo acting outside the framework of the interim administration.[81] Nor did the resolution reserve the final determination of the status of Kosovo to the Security Council.[82] The Court chose not to address the consequences of such a declaration of independence—whether a new state had been

---

[74] 14 November 2011, UN calls for immediate resumption of peace talks, available at www.un.org/apps/news/story.asp?NewsID=40381&Cr=Palestin&Cr1=.

[75] Application of Palestine for Admission to Membership in the UN, A/66/371, 23 September 2011.

[76] Report of the Committee on the Admission of New Members concerning the application of Palestine for admission to membership in the UN, S/2011/705, 11 November 2011, §21.

[77] The latter occurred on 31 October 2011: 'General Conference admits Palestine as UNESCO Member State', 31 October 2011, Doc UNESCO_Pal-MemberState, UNESCO Press release.

[78] Ibid, §14.

[79] *Accordance with International Law of the Unilateral Declaration of Independence in Respect of Kosovo*, Opinion of 22 July 2010, §82.

[80] Ibid, §84.

[81] Ibid, §§109, 114, 118–19.

[82] Ibid, §114.

created or whether other states would be obliged to recognize (or to refrain from recognizing) it. As at 1 January 2012, some 85 states had recognized Kosovo.[83]

4. ACHIEVING INDEPENDENCE: SECESSION AND SELF-DETERMINATION[84]

If independence is the decisive *criterion* of statehood, self-determination is a principle concerned with the *right* to be a state.[85] A key initial development was the reference to 'the principle of equal rights and self-determination of peoples' in Articles 1(2) and 55 of the UN Charter.[86] Many saw these references as merely hortatory, but the practice of UN organs powerfully reinforced the principle—in particular the Declaration on the Granting of Independence to Colonial Countries and Peoples, adopted by the General Assembly in 1960 and referred to in a long series of resolutions since.[87] The Declaration treats the principle of self-determination as one of the obligations stemming from the Charter: it is in the form of an authoritative interpretation.[88] The right to self-determination of 'all peoples' was subsequently included as common Article 1 of the two human rights Covenants of 1966.[89]

Means of achieving self-determination include the formation of a new state through secession, association in a federal state, or autonomy or assimilation in a unitary (non-federal) state.[90] It is generally accepted that peoples subjected to colonial rule have a right to elect independence under international law, but the question of secession, and self-determination more generally, has been highly controversial outside the colonial context.[91] In practice a marked distinction has developed between full ('external') self-determination and qualified ('internal') self-determination. This was perhaps definitively formulated by the Canadian Supreme Court:

We have also considered whether a positive legal entitlement to secession exists under international law in the factual circumstances contemplated by Question 1, i.e., a clear democratic

---

[83] www.mfa-ks.net/?page=2,33.

[84] Cristescu, *The Right to Self-Determination* (1981); Higgins, *Problems and Process* (1994) 111–28; Cassese (1995); Franck, *Fairness in International Law and Institutions* (1995) 140–69; Quane (1998) 47 *ICLQ* 537; McCorquodale (ed), *Self-Determination in International Law* (2000); Ghanea & Xanthaki (eds), *Minorities, Peoples and Self-Determination* (2005); Crawford (2nd edn, 2006) 108–28.

[85] Crawford (2nd edn, 2006) 107.

[86] Also chapters XI (Declaration Regarding Non-Self-Governing Territories) and XII (International Trusteeship System).

[87] GA Res 1514(XV), 14 December 1960.

[88] Waldock (1962) 106 Hague *Recueil* 33; *Right of Passage*, ICJ Reports 1960 p 6, 95–6 (Judge Moreno Quintana, diss).

[89] ICESCR and ICCPR, GA Res 2200A(XXI), 16 December 1966; respectively 993 UNTS 3 and 999 UNTS 171.

[90] GA Res 1541(XV), 15 December 1960; GA Res 2625(XXV), 24 October 1970.

[91] See chapter 29.

expression of support on a clear question for Quebec secession. Some of those who supported an affirmative answer to this question did so on the basis of the recognized right to self-determination that belongs to all 'peoples'. Although much of the Quebec population certainly shares many of the characteristics of a people, it is not necessary to decide the 'people' issue because... a right to secession only arises under the principle of self-determination of peoples at international law where 'a people' is governed as part of a colonial empire; where 'a people' is subject to alien subjugation, domination or exploitation; and possibly where 'a people' is denied any meaningful exercise of its right to self-determination within the state of which it forms a part. In other circumstances, peoples are expected to achieve self-determination within the framework of their existing state. A state whose government represents the whole of the people or peoples resident within its territory, on a basis of equality and without discrimination, and respects the principles of self-determination in its internal arrangements, is entitled to maintain its territorial integrity under international law and to have that territorial integrity recognized by other states.[92]

Questions of internal self-determination and remedial secession are left open here and remain controversial. The International Court did not address submissions on remedial secession in the *Kosovo* opinion.[93]

5. IDENTITY AND CONTINUITY OF STATES[94]

The term 'continuity' of states is not employed with any precision, and may be used to preface a diversity of legal problems. Thus it may introduce the proposition that the legal rights and responsibility of states are not affected by changes in the head of state or the internal form of government.[95] This proposition can, of course, be maintained without reference to 'continuity' or 'succession', and it is in any case too general, since political changes may result in a change of circumstances sufficient to affect particular types of treaty relation. More significantly, legal doctrine tends to distinguish between continuity (and identity) and state succession. The latter arises when one international personality takes the place of another, for example by union or lawful annexation. In general, it is assumed that cases of 'state succession' are likely to involve important changes in the legal status and rights of the entities concerned, whereas if there is continuity, the legal personality and the particular rights and duties of the state remain unaltered. The distinction is examined in more detail in chapter 19.

---

[92] *Reference re Secession of Quebec* (1998) 115 ILR 536, 594–5. Also: Crawford (1998) 69 *BY* 115; Bayefsky (ed), *Self-Determination in International Law: Quebec and Lessons Learned* (2000).

[93] *Kosovo*, Opinion of 22 July 2010, §82.

[94] In particular: Kunz (1955) 49 *AJIL* 68; Kelsen (1966) 383–7; Marek (1968); O'Connell, 1–2 *State Succession in Municipal Law and International Law* (1967); Eisemann & Koskenniemi (eds), *State Succession* (2000); Crawford (2nd edn, 2006) 667–99; Craven, *The Decolonization of International Law* (2007).

[95] McNair, 1, 3 *Opinions*; 1 Hackworth 387–92; *Tinoco Concessions* (1923) 2 ILR 34.

6

RECOGNITION OF STATES AND GOVERNMENTS

1. RECOGNITION AS A GENERAL CATEGORY[1]

Whenever a state acts in a way which may affect the rights or interests of other states, the question arises of the significance of their reaction to the event. In *Legal Status of Eastern Greenland*, it was held that Norway had, through a declaration by its Foreign Minister, Nils Ihlen, accepted Danish title to the disputed territory.[2] There the acceptance by Norway of Denmark's claim was by informal agreement: in other instances formal treaty provisions will involve recognition of rights. However, apart from agreement, legally significant reactions may occur in the form of unilateral acts or conduct involving recognition or acquiescence. Unlawful acts of states may meet with protest from other states. Such acts are not in principle opposable to other states in any case, and protest is not a condition of their illegality. Conversely, the validity of a claim to territory is not conditioned on its acceptance by other states.

But acts of protest or recognition play a significant role. Furthermore, there is a spectrum of issues involving areas of uncertainty, novel, and potentially law-changing claims (cf the development of claims to continental shelf resources), or which arise in a context where issues are most sensibly settled on an ad hoc and bilateral basis.

---

[1] State practice and other materials: 2 Whiteman 1–746; 1 Hackworth 161–387; 1 Moore 67–248. Literature: Lauterpacht, *Recognition in International Law* (1947); Jessup, *A Modern Law of Nations* (1948) 43–67; Brown (1950) 44 *AJIL* 617; Chen, *The International Law of Recognition* (1951); Fitzmaurice (1957) 92 Hague *Recueil* 1, 16–35; Kelsen, *Principles of International Law* (2nd edn, 1967) 387; Jennings (1967) 121 Hague *Recueil* 323, 349–68; Lauterpacht, 1 *International Law: Collected Papers* (1970) 308; Salmon, *La Reconnaissance d'état* (1971); Verhoeven, *La Reconnaissance internationale dans la pratique contemporaine* (1975); Brownlie (1982) 53 *BY* 197; Dugard, *Recognition and the United Nations* (1987); Verhoeven (1993) 39 *AFDI* 7; Rich (1993) 4 *EJIL* 36; Hillgruber (1998) 9 *EJIL* 491; Talmon, *Recognition of Governments in International Law* (1998); Grant, *The Recognition of States* (1999); Murphy (1999) 48 *ICLQ* 545; Talmon, *Recognition in International Law: A Bibliography* (2000); Talmon (2004) 75 *BY* 101; Crawford, *Creation of States* (2nd edn, 2006) 12–28; Talmon, *La non reconnaissance collective des Etats illégaux* (2007); Fabry, *Recognizing States* (2010); Craven, in Evans (ed), *International Law* (3rd edn, 2010) 203.

[2] (1933) PCIL Ser A/B No 53, 73. The better view is that the facts disclosed an agreement rather than a unilateral act, the *quid pro quo* being Danish recognition of Norwegian sovereignty over Svalbard (Spitzbergen). On unilateral acts in general: chapter 18.

Disputes are often decided on the basis of facts, including elements of acquiescence, establishing a special content of legal relations between the parties, and this quite apart from treaty. Finally, protest and recognition may involve pure acts of policy not purporting to involve legal characterizations of other states' conduct.

More specifically, however, the term 'recognition' (if not exactly a term of art)[3] is commonly used to refer to two related categories of state acts: first, the recognition of another entity as a state; and second, the recognition of that entity's government as established, lawful or 'legitimate', that is as entitled to represent the state for all international purposes.[4] It further implies an undertaking by the recognizing state that it will treat the entity in question as a state (or as the government of an already recognized state).[5]

2. RECOGNITION OF STATES

(A) THEORETICAL OVERLAY[6]

In this context legal writing has adopted the emphasis and terminology of political relations, notably in relation to the fundamental issue of recognition of states. Indeed 'there is probably no other subject in the field of international relations in which law and politics appear to be more closely interwoven'.[7]

The dominance of the category 'recognition' has led to some perverse doctrine. When a state is in dispute over title to territory, a court or tribunal will examine all the available and legally significant conduct of either party. A declaration by one party that it does not 'recognize' the title of the other will not determine the issue, and will usually be worth very little. A statement registering the fact that at a certain date the opponent was in actual occupation may be evidence, but only within the context of the particular case will the statement have significance. When the existence of states and governments is in issue, by contrast, a sense of perspective seems to be elusive.

Indeed the complexity one may expect of legal issues in interstate relations has been compacted into a doctrinal dispute between the 'declaratory' and 'constitutive' views

---

[3] Brownlie (1982) 53 *BY* 197, 197–8.

[4] E.g. 1 *Restatement Third* §§202, 203. Recognition of a state may be independent of the recognition of its government, though the reverse is not true: ibid, §203, comment *(a)*.

[5] Ibid, §202, comment *(c)*. Also: Montevideo Convention on the Rights and Duties of States, 26 December 1933, 165 LNTS 19, Art 6 ('The recognition of a State merely signifies that the State which recognizes it accepts the personality of the other with all the rights and duties determined by international law').

[6] Generally: Brownlie (1982) 53 *BY* 197; Grant (1999); Talmon (2004) 75 *BY* 101; Crawford (2nd edn, 2006) 19–28.

[7] Lauterpacht (1947) v.

of recognition.[8] According to the declaratory view,[9] the legal effects of recognition are limited: recognition is a declaration or acknowledgement of an existing state of law and fact, legal personality having been conferred previously by operation of law. In a relatively objective forum such as an international tribunal, it would be entirely proper to accept the existence of a state although the other party to the dispute, or third states, do not recognize it.[10] This perspective appears to have been accepted (at least tacitly) by the International Court. In *Genocide (Bosnia and Herzegovina v Yugoslavia)*,[11] it was argued by the Socialist Federal Republic of Yugoslavia (SFRY) that the allegations of the breach of the Genocide Convention[12] made by Bosnia-Herzegovina were not admissible as the parties to the dispute had not recognized each other at the time of the events in question. The Court dismissed this argument on the basis that, as recognition had been given subsequently in the Dayton Accord,[13] any defect was merely procedural and could be remedied by re-filing the claim to relate to events of genocide occurring prior to 1995.

Substantial state practice supports the declaratory view.[14] Unrecognized states are quite commonly the object of international claims by the very states refusing recognition. An example is Israel, long held accountable under international humanitarian and human rights law by certain Arab states that persistently deny it recognition.[15]

The declaratory theory of recognition is opposed to the constitutive view, according to which the political act of recognition is a precondition of the existence of legal rights: in its extreme form this implies that the very personality of a state depends on the political decision of other states.[16] The most nuanced defence of this perspective

---

[8] Talmon helpfully characterizes the declaratory position as *status-confirming* and the constitutive position as *status-creating*: Talmon (2004) 75 *BY* 101, 101–2.

[9] Adherents include Chen (1951); Waldock (1962) 106 Hague *Recueil* 1, 147–51; Rolin (1950) 77 Hague *Recueil* 305, 326–37; Kunz (1950) 44 *AJIL* 713; Charpentier, *La Reconnaissance internationale* (1956); Duursma, *Fragmentation and the International Relations of Micro-States* (1996) 110–15; Talmon (2004) 75 *BY* 101; Crawford (2nd edn, 2006) 19–22.

[10] E.g. *Tinoco Concessions* (1923) 1 RIAA 369; *Deutsch Continental Gesellschaft v Polish State* (1929) 5 ILR 11.

[11] *Application of the Convention on the Prevention and Punishment of the Crime of Genocide (Bosnia and Herzegovina v Yugoslavia)*, Preliminary Objections, ICJ Reports 1996 p 595, 612–13.

[12] Convention on the Prevention and Punishment of the Crime of Genocide, 9 December 1948, 78 UNTS 277.

[13] General Framework Agreement for Peace in Bosnia and Herzegovina, 14 December 1995, 35 ILM 75.

[14] Montevideo Convention, Arts 3 ('The political existence of the State is independent of recognition by the other States'), 6. Also: 1 *Restatement Third* §202(1); Badinter Commission, *Opinion No 10* (1992) 92 ILR 206, 208; *Reference re Secession of Quebec* (1998) 115 ILR 536, 589–90. Further: Talmon (2004) 75 *BY* 101, 106–7.

[15] Craven, in Evans (3rd edn, 2010) 203, 244.

[16] Constitutive doctrine takes many forms; many jurists allow certain rights prior to recognition. Adherents include Anzilotti, 1 *Cours de droit international* (1929) 160; Kelsen (1932) 42 Hague *Recueil* 117, 260–94 (earlier he was a declaratist: (1929) 4 *RDI* 613, 617–18); Lauterpacht (1947). *Certain German Interests in Polish Upper Silesia* (1926) PCIJ Ser A No 7, 28 does not unequivocally support the constitutive view, since the issue was the existence of a contractual nexus between Germany and Poland: that

is that of Lauterpacht, who conceives of states as the gatekeepers of the international realm:

[T]he full international legal personality of rising communities…cannot be automatic… [A]s its ascertainment requires the prior determination of difficult circumstances of fact and law, there must be *someone* to perform the task. In the absence of a preferable solution, such as the setting up of an impartial international organ to perform that function, the latter must be fulfilled by States already existing. The valid objection is not against the fact of their discharging it, but against their carrying it out as a matter of arbitrary policy distinguished from legal duty.[17]

Taken to its logical conclusion, however, the constitutive view is as a matter of principle impossible to accept: it is clearly established that states cannot by their independent judgment remove or abrogate any competence of other states established by international law (as distinct from agreement or concession). Moreover, the constitutive theory of recognition leads to substantial difficulties in terms of practical application. How many states must recognize? Can existence be relative only to those states which recognize?[18] Is existence dependent on recognition only when this rests on an adequate knowledge of the facts? More vitally, does non-recognition by a state entitle it to treat an entity as a non-state for the purposes of international law, for example, by intervening in its internal affairs or annexing its territory?

One solution put forward is that of the 'collectivization' of recognition, under which statehood matures through membership of the United Nations, or at least a call by the UN that the new state be recognized.[19] Whilst this would circumvent what Lauterpacht called the 'grotesque spectacle'[20] of relative statehood, it has its own problems:[21] notably, it cannot account for the legal position of a state in the period between its declaration of independence and its admission to the UN, which in the case of the two Koreas lasted some 43 years.[22] Moreover, under Article 4 of the UN Charter statehood is a criterion for membership, not a consequence.

Poland could not invoke a treaty against Germany did not connote its non-existence as a state. For the view that UN Secretariat practice supported the constitutive position: Schachter (1948) 25 *BY* 91, 109–15.

[17] Lauterpacht (1947) 55. Lauterpacht tempers the severity of this position by reference to a 'duty' of recognition.

[18] Further: Kelsen (1941) 35 *AJIL* 605, 609; Lauterpacht (1947) 67, 88; Crawford (2nd edn, 2006) 21–2.

[19] E.g. Chen (1951) 222; Dugard (1987) 125–7; Duursma (1996) 110–12; Hillgruber (1998) 9 *EJIL* 491; Grant (2009) 256. Also and earlier: Lauterpacht (1947) 167–9.

[20] Lauterpacht (1947) 78.

[21] Talmon (2004) 75 *BY* 101, 105.

[22] The Republic of Korea was established on 15 August 1948 and the Democratic Republic of North Korea on 9 September 1948. Both states were admitted to the UN on 17 September 1991: SC Res 702 (1991); GA Res 46/1, 17 September 1991.

(B) THE VARIED LEGAL CONSEQUENCES OF RECOGNITION AND NON-RECOGNITION

There is no such thing as a uniform type of recognition or non-recognition.[23] The terminology of official communications and declarations is not very consistent: there may be '*de iure* recognition', '*de facto* recognition', 'full diplomatic recognition', 'formal recognition', and so forth. The term 'recognition' may be absent, taking the form instead of agreement to establish diplomatic relations or a congratulatory message on independence day. The typical act of recognition has two legal functions. First, the determination of statehood, a question of law: such individual determination may have evidential value.[24] Secondly, a condition of the establishment of formal relations, including diplomatic relations and the conclusion of bilateral treaties: it is this second function which has been described by some as 'constitutive', but it is not a condition of statehood. Since states are not legally required to make a public declaration of recognition nor to undertake optional relations such as the exchange of ambassadors, the expression of state intent involved is political in the sense of being voluntary. But it may also be political in a more obvious sense. An absence of recognition may not rest on any legal basis at all, there being no attempt to pass on the question of statehood as such. Non-recognition may simply be part of a general policy of disapproval and boycott. Recognition may be part of a policy of aggression involving the creation of a puppet state: the legal consequences here stem from the breaches of international law involved.[25]

Above all, recognition is a political act and is to be treated as such. Correspondingly, the term 'recognition' does not absolve the lawyer from inquiring into the intent of the recognizing government, placing this in the context of the relevant facts and law. Indeed, non-recognition (in the sense of a refusal to have formal relations) may carry with it the implicit *assumption* of recognition (in the sense of an acknowledgement of existence). Warbrick notes that a bare statement of non-recognition carries five possible meanings, only one of which is a definitive declaration that the entity in question is not regarded as a state. Under his taxonomy, non-recognition is: (a) a statement of neutrality, under which no view is taken deliberately as to the entity's statehood; (b) driven purely by political calculations (thereby implying recognition of statehood in law); (c) driven by the understanding that recognition would be unlawful or premature (genuine non-recognition); (d) issued on the basis that supervening obligations in custom or

---

[23] 1 *Restatement Third* §202, comment (*a*): 'States may recognize an entity's statehood by formal declaration or by recognizing its government, but states often treat a qualified entity as a state without any formal act of recognition'.

[24] Recognition is rarely 'cognitive' in a simple sense: the issue is one of law as well as fact, and cognition, which may involve no outward sign, occurs before, often long before, public recognition. Cf 2 Whiteman 13 (Secretary of State Dulles).

[25] E.g. the Japanese recognition of 'Manchukuo': Crawford (2nd edn, 2006) 78–9.

treaty prevent recognition; (e) issued on the basis of a supervening obligation imposed by the Security Council.[26]

This leads to a consideration of the *practicalities* of recognition: the existence of a state is of little worth unless it is accepted as such into the community of nations. It is of little value to assert that Taiwan or Somaliland is a state if nobody will engage with it on such a basis.[27]

(C) THE 'DUTY TO RECOGNIZE'

Lauterpacht[28] and Guggenheim[29] adopt the view that recognition is constitutive but that there is a legal duty to recognize. This standpoint has been vigorously criticized as bearing no relation to state practice and for its inconsistency, providing as it does that state consent is determinative of statehood whilst in the same breath narrowing its scope until only one option remains.[30] A constitutive argument dependent on a duty to recognize in order to reconcile theoretical inconsistency becomes the declaratory theory viewed from a different perspective.

In principle the legal duty implies that the entity in question already bears the marks of statehood and (although Lauterpacht does not express it thus) the duty would seem to be owed to the entity concerned. The argument postulates personality on an objective basis. Discussion of Lauterpacht's views often reveals a certain confusion among the critics. Recognition, *as a public act of state*, is an optional and political act and there is no legal duty in this regard. However, in a deeper sense, if any entity bears the marks of statehood, other states put themselves at risk legally if they ignore the basic obligations of state relations. Few, for example, took the view that its Arab neighbours could treat Israel as a non-entity. In this context of state *conduct* there is a duty to accept and apply certain fundamental rules of international law, a legal duty to 'recognize' for certain purposes at least.[31] But there is no duty to make an express, public determination or to declare readiness to enter into diplomatic relations by means of recognition: this remains political and discretionary. Non-recognition (in this sense) is not a determinant of diplomatic relations, and the absence of diplomatic relations is not in itself non-recognition of the state.[32]

---

[26] Warbrick, in Evans (ed), *Aspects of Statehood and Institutionalism in Contemporary Europe* (1997) 9, 1–11.

[27] Generally: Brenthurst Foundation, *The Consequences of Somaliland's International (Non) Recognition*, Discussion Paper 2011/05 (2011). Further: UKMIL (2006) 77 *BY* 597, 618–19; (2007) 78 *BY* 634, 682; (2008) 79 *BY* 565, 596–7; (2009) 80 *BY* 661, 709–10, 712–13; (2010) 81 *BY* 435, 503–5.

[28] Lauterpacht (1947) 73–5; 158–61; 1 Lauterpacht (1970) 308, 312–14.

[29] 1 Guggenheim 190–1.

[30] Kunz (1950) 44 *AJIL* 713; Cohn (1948) 64 *LQR* 404; Briggs (1949) 43 *AJIL* 113; Jessup (1971) 65 *AJIL* 214, 217; Brownlie (1982) 53 *BY* 197, 209; Talmon (2004) 75 *BY* 101, 103; Crawford (2nd edn, 2006) 22.

[31] E.g. 1 *Restatement Third* §202(1).

[32] Brownlie (1982) 53 *BY* 197, 209.

(D) IMPLIED RECOGNITION[33]

Recognition is a matter of intention and may be express or implied.[34] The implication of intention is a process aided by certain presumptions. According to Lauterpacht, in the case of recognition of states, only the conclusion of a bilateral treaty, the formal initiation of diplomatic relations, and, probably, the issue of consular exequaturs, justify the implication.[35] No recognition is implied from negotiations, unofficial representation, the conclusion of a multilateral treaty to which the unrecognized entity is also a party, admission to an international organization (at least in respect to those not supporting admission),[36] or participation with the entity concerned at an international conference. Confusion arises from two sources. First, the terminology of governmental statements may lead tribunals to give legal status to acts intended only to give a low level of recognition:[37] for example, an authority with which only informal and limited contacts have been undertaken may be accorded sovereign immunity by national courts.[38] Secondly, different considerations ought to apply to different aspects of recognition, yet doctrine tends to generalize about the subject. Thus, in terms of evidence in an international tribunal, informal relations, especially if these persist, may have probative value on the issue of statehood. However, as a matter of optional bilateral relations, recognition depends on intention.[39]

(E) RETROACTIVITY OF RECOGNITION[40]

British and American courts have applied the principle of retroactivity in following or interpreting the views of the executive in matters of recognition, but Oppenheim describes the rule as 'one of convenience rather than of principle'.[41] Once again one ought not to generalize except to say that on the international plane there is no rule of retroactivity. As to the basic rights and duties entailed by statehood, delayed recognition cannot be 'retroactive' because in a special sense it is superfluous. Optional and consensual relations it may or may not be, since the area is one of discretion.[42]

---

[33] Lauterpacht (1947) 369–408; Chen (1951) 201–16; Lachs (1959) 35 *BY* 252. US practice: 1 Hackworth 327–63; 2 Whiteman 48–59, 524–604; 1 *Restatement Third* §201.

[34] In some cases, a state may base its policy of recognition with respect to both states and governments around an approach of implied recognition: Talmon (2009) 7 *NZYIL* 1.

[35] Lauterpacht (1947) 406.

[36] Some international organizations are open to non-states: e.g. autonomous customs territories under the WTO (Hong Kong, Macao & Taiwan) and the World Tourism Organization. Further: chapter 7.

[37] Cf Talmon (2009) 7 *NZYIL* 1, 17.

[38] E.g. *Arantzazu Mendi* [1939] AC 256.

[39] Brownlie (1982) 53 *BY* 197, 208.

[40] E.g. *Haile Selassie v Cable And Wireless Ltd (No 2)* [1939] 1 Ch 182. Also: 2 Whiteman 728–45; 1 Hackworth 381–5; Chen (1951) 172–86; Brownlie (1982) 53 *BY* 197, 208–9.

[41] 1 Oppenheim 161 (9th edn, 1992).

[42] Cf *Polish Upper Silesia* (1926) PCIJ Ser A No 7, 27–39, 84 (Lord Finlay).

(F) RECOGNITION AND MEMBERSHIP OF INTERNATIONAL ORGANIZATIONS[43]

Collective recognition may take the form of a joint declaration, for example that of the Allied Supreme Council after the First World War, or an invitation to a new state to become a party to a multilateral treaty of a political character such as a peace treaty. The functioning of international organizations of the type of the League of Nations and United Nations provides a variety of occasions for recognition, of one sort or another, of states. Recognition of other members, or of non-members, may occur in the course of voting on admission to membership[44] and consideration of complaints involving threats to or breaches of the peace. Indeed, it has been argued that admission to the League and the UN entails recognition by operation of law by all other members, whether or not they voted for admission.

The position, supported by principle and practice, would seem to be as follows. Admission to membership is evidence of statehood,[45] and non-recognizing members are at risk if they ignore the basic rights of existence of an entity the object of their non-recognition.[46] However, there is nothing in the Charter, or customary law, which requires a non-recognizing state to enter into optional bilateral relations with other members.[47] In any event the test of statehood in general international law is not necessarily applicable to the issue of membership in the specialized agencies of the United Nations,[48] as demonstrated by the recent admission of Palestine to UNESCO.

There are other elements in the case of organizations, adequate treatment of which cannot be given here. Can the UN and its organs (including the Secretariat), *as such*, accord recognition? For the purposes of the Charter numerous determinations of statehood are called for: thus, for example, the UN Secretary-General acts as depositary for important treaties. Whether, and to what extent, such determinations provide evidence of statehood for general purposes must depend on the relevance to general international law of the criteria employed in a given case.[49] Attitudes of non-recognition

---

[43] Generally: Rosenne (1949) 26 *BY* 437; Aufricht (1949) 43 *AJIL* 679; Wright (1950) 44 *AJIL* 548; Higgins, *Development* (1963) 131–2, 140–4, 146–50; Dugard (1987); Crawford (2nd edn, 2006) ch 4; Grant, *Admission to the United Nations* (2009); Duxbury, *The Participation of States in International Organisations* (2011) 314–15.

[44] Cf *Northern Cameroons (Cameroon v UK)*, Preliminary Objections, ICJ Reports 1963 p 15, 119–20 (Judge Fitzmaurice).

[45] E.g. *Genocide (Bosnia and Herzegovina v Yugoslavia)*, Preliminary Objections, ICJ Reports 1996 p 595, 611. Also: Rosenne, *Developments in the Law of Treaties 1945–1986* (1989) 215; Grant (2009) 254. For UK state practice: UKMIL (2009) 80 *BY* 661, 706 (UK written intervention in the *Kosovo* advisory opinion).

[46] Grant (2009) 255 ('UN admission, entailing the participation of all members in a multilateral treaty, may be described as putting a formal frame around the opposability of statehood toward all other UN members'). E.g. the UN admission of Montenegro: SC Res 1691 (2006), GA Res 60/264, 12 July 2006.

[47] S/1466, 9 March 1950; Kelsen, *Law of the United Nations* (1951) 946.

[48] Morgenstern, *Legal Problems of International Organizations* (1986) 46–68.

[49] United Nations organs have been involved in varying degrees in the process of political creation of some states, viz., Indonesia, Israel, Libya, Republic of Korea, Somalia, Namibia, and Kosovo. On the UN role: Crawford (2nd edn, 2006) ch 12. See also chapter 8.

may depend on the political positions of individual members and the view that in any case the special qualifications for membership contained in Article 4 of the Charter are not fulfilled: statehood may be necessary but it is not sufficient.

3. RECOGNITION OF GOVERNMENTS[50]

The status of an entity as the government of a state raises somewhat different issues to those raised by recognition of statehood, although the differences were historically obscured by the practice of diplomatic recognition being applied to both states and governments. The legal entity in international law is the state; the government is in normal circumstances the representative of the state, entitled to act on its behalf. The consequences of an entity not being considered a state are potentially greater. The absence of a (recognized) state with respect to some area of the world raises the possibility of a legal vacuum, although in practice this may be mitigated in various ways.[51] By contrast the absence of a (recognized) government does not lead to a loss of title, and may simply require some form of curatorship.[52]

In short although recognition of government and state may be closely related, they are not identical. Non-recognition of a particular regime is not necessarily a determination that the community represented by that regime does not qualify for statehood. Non-recognition of a government may mean that it is not regarded as a government in terms of independence and effectiveness, or that the non-recognizing state is unwilling to have normal intergovernmental relations with it. Recognition in the context of voluntary relations may be made conditional on the democratic character of the regime, the acceptance of particular claims, or the giving of undertakings, for example on treatment of minorities.[53] Here, the European Community's Guidelines on the Recognition of New States, adopted in response to the breakup of the USSR and Yugoslavia, are instructive.[54] The sphere of optional relations and voluntary obligations is one of discretion and bargain. In terms of bilateral voluntary relations, an unrecognized government is little better off than an unrecognized state.

---

[50] Generally: Galloway, *Recognizing Foreign Governments* (1978); Ando [1985] *JAIL* 28, 29–46; Talmon (1992) 63 *BY* 231; Talmon (1998). Also: 1 *Restatement Third* §203; Pavot (2006) 14 *Rev Aff Eur* 297; Talmon (2009) 8 *Chin JIL* 135.

[51] Thus *de facto* control may continue while issues of succession are resolved: e.g. the continued involvement in Kosovo of UNMIK: S/2011/675, 31 October 2011, §2.

[52] E.g. *Government of Somalia v Woodhouse, Drake & Carey (Suisse) SA* [1993] QB 54.

[53] Kelsen (2nd edn, 1966) 403–4; cf Murphy (1999) 48 *ICLQ* 545. E.g. the Roosevelt–Litvinov Agreement, 16 November 1933, 11 TIAS 1248 (recognition of the USSR by the US dependent on the resolution of certain financial claims and an undertaking by the USSR not to take acts prejudicial to the internal security of the US). Also: Duxbury (2011) 101–3 on EC recognition of former-Soviet states.

[54] 16 December 1991, 31 ILM 1485. Further: Hillgruber (1998) 9 *EJIL* 491.

In *Tinoco Concessions*, Great Britain claimed on the basis of concessions granted by a former revolutionary government of Costa Rica which had not been recognized by some other states, including Great Britain itself. The arbitrator, Taft CJ, observed:

The non-recognition by other nations of a government claiming to be a national personality, is usually appropriate evidence that it has not attained the independence and control entitling it by international law to be classed as such. But when recognition *vel non* of a government is by such nations determined by inquiry, not into its *de facto* sovereignty and complete governmental control, but into its illegitimacy or irregularity or origin, their non-recognition loses something of evidential weight on the issue with which those applying the rules of international law are alone concerned. What is true of the non-recognition of the United States in its bearing upon the existence of a *de facto* government under Tinoco for thirty months is probably in a measure true of the non-recognition by her Allies in the European War. Such non-recognition for any reason, however, cannot outweigh the evidence disclosed by this record before me as to the *de facto* character of Tinoco's government, according to the standard set by international law.[55]

In the case of governments, 'the standard set by international law' is so far the standard of secure *de facto* control of all or most of the state territory. The Tinoco regime had that, and was thus the government for the time being of Costa Rica, irrespective of non-recognition.

(A) *DE IURE* AND *DE FACTO* RECOGNITION

The distinction between *de iure* and *de facto* recognition occurs exclusively in the context of recognition of governments: there is no such thing as a *de facto* state.[56] General propositions about the distinction are to be distrusted; everything depends on the intention of the government concerned and the general context of fact and law.[57] On the international plane a statement that a government is recognized as the '*de facto* government' of a state may involve a purely political judgment, involving a reluctant or cautious acceptance of an effective government, lawfully established in terms of international law and not imposed from without, or an unwarranted acceptance of an unqualified agency. On the other hand, the statement may be intended as a determination of the existence of an effective government, but with reservations as to its

---

[55] (1923) 1 RIAA 369, 381. Also: *Wulfsohn v RSFSR*, 234 NY 372 (1923); *Sokoloff v National City Bank*, 239 NY 158 (1924); *Salimoff v Standard Oil Co*, 262 NY 220 (1933); *Deutsche Continental Gas-Gesellschaft v Polish State* (1929) 5 ILR 11; *Socony Vacuum Oil Company* (1954) 21 ILR 55; *Standard Vacuum Oil Company* (1959) 30 ILR 168; *Clerget v Représentation Commerciale de la République démocratique du Viet-Nam* (1969) 96 JDI 894, 898; Badinter Commission, *Opinion No 1* (1991) 92 ILR 162; *Opinion No 8* (1992) 92 ILR 199; *Opinion No 10* (1992) 92 ILR 206.

[56] Frowein, *Das de facto-Regime im Völkerrecht* (1968) proposed the idea of a '*de facto* regime' to describe political entities that exercise control over territories, but which are not recognized as states. The concept is not reflected in state practice and appears chiefly in the German literature. Further: Talmon (2004) 75 *BY* 101, 103–5; Frowein, '*De Facto* Regime' (2009) *MPEPIL*.

[57] Briggs (1939) 33 *AJIL* 689; Brownlie (1982) 53 *BY* 197, 207–8; Talmon (1998) 59–111; Craven, in Evans (3rd edn, 2010) 203, 244–5.

permanence and viability. No doubt the legal and political reasons for caution may coincide, but they rarely affect courts, which, with or without the epithet *de facto,* accord recognition the same effect. It is sometimes said that *de iure* recognition is irrevocable while *de facto* recognition can be withdrawn. In the political sense recognition of either kind can always be withdrawn: legally it cannot be unless a change of circumstances warrants it.

Situations do occur where there is a serious legal distinction between *de iure* and *de facto* recognition. Thus some governments accepted certain legal consequences of German control of Austria, 1938–45, and Czechoslovakia, 1939–45, for example in the fields of nationality law and consular relations. Yet these same governments did not accept the lawfulness of German authority.[58] In documents relating to these matters '*de facto* recognition' may be used to describe acceptance of facts with a dubious legal origin: *de iure* recognition would be inappropriate and unjustifiable.[59] In this context it is hazardous to accept the full legal competence of an administration accorded only '*de facto* recognition'. Thus, in *Bank of Ethiopia v National Bank of Egypt and Liguori,*[60] the Court gave effect to an Italian decree in Ethiopia on the basis that the UK had recognized Italy as the *de facto* government. In truth Italy was no more than a belligerent occupant. Furthermore, in situations where rival governments were accorded *de iure* and *de facto* recognition in respect of the same territory, problems arise if the same legal consequences are given to both forms of recognition.[61]

(B) RECOGNITION OF GOVERNMENTS IN ABEYANCE

There is a school of thought supporting the automatic recognition of *de facto* governments, exemplified by the 'Estrada doctrine' enunciated by the Mexican Secretary of Foreign Relations in 1930.[62] As a means of reducing non-recognition as a source of interference in internal affairs this is laudable, but difficulties remain.

In 1980 the British government adopted the practice of no longer according recognition to governments. The statement read as follows:

Where an unconstitutional change of regime takes place in a recognised State, Governments of other States must necessarily consider what dealings, if any, they should have with the new regime, and whether and to what extent it qualifies to be treated as the Government of the State concerned. Many of our partners and allies take the position that they do not recognise Governments and that therefore no question of recognition arises in such cases. By contrast, the policy of successive British Governments has been that we should make and announce a decision formally 'recognising' the new Government.

---

[58] On UK and US policies: Brownlie, *Use of Force* (1963) 414–16.
[59] British *de iure* recognition in 1938 of the Italian conquest of Ethiopia in 1936 was avoided in 1941: Wright (1937) 31 *AJIL* 683; Talmon (1998) 102–3, 290; Crawford (2nd edn, 2006) 519–20.
[60] [1937] Ch 513.
[61] Further: *Carl Zeiss Stiftung v Rayner and Keeler Ltd (No 2)* [1967] 1 AC 853, 898–904 (Lord Reid), 950–78 (Lord Wilberforce). Also: *Hesperides Hotels Ltd v Aegean Turkish Holidays Ltd* [1978] QB 205, 218 (Lord Denning MR).
[62] Estrada (1931) 25 *AJIL Supp* 203; Jessup (1931) 25 *AJIL* 719.

This practice has sometimes been misunderstood, and, despite explanations to the contrary, our 'recognition' interpreted as implying approval...

We have therefore concluded that there are practical advantages in following the policy of many other countries in not according recognition to Governments. Like them, we shall continue to decide the nature of our dealings with regimes which come to power unconstitutionally in the light of our assessment of whether they are able of themselves to exercise effective control of the territory of the State concerned, and seem likely to continue to do so.[63]

The practical result of this change has been unfortunate. Executive certificates, like the one supplied in *Gur Corporation*,[64] may be indecisive and reflect the premise that the issues are unrelated to questions of general international law. Such a premise is especially inappropriate in cases where the legitimacy of the regime raises issues of validity in terms of general international law, for example, in case of foreign intervention, or there are competing administrations and their internal validity is linked to issues of international law. No doubt the facts are paramount in each case but the facts can only be assessed within the appropriate legal framework.[65]

When issues of international legality have been in question, however, the UK government has provided the necessary guidance, for example, in relation to the status of Kuwait under Iraqi occupation in 1990;[66] and the status of the 'Turkish Republic of Northern Cyprus' (TRNC).[67] Most recently, clarification as to the legitimate government of Libya was provided in the form of a certificate (apparently contrary to the announced policy) explicitly stating that the government considered the National Transitional Council (NTC) to be the legitimate government of Libya and did not recognize any other government in Libya, notably the former Qaddafi regime. This certificate permitted the NTC to obtain access to English bank accounts in Libya's name formerly under the control of Qaddafi and his supporters.[68]

(C) CREDENTIALS AND REPRESENTATION IN INTERNATIONAL ORGANIZATIONS

The approval of the credentials of state representatives by organs of the United Nations raises problems similar, but not identical, to those concerning admission, since in

---

[63] UKMIL (1980) 51 *BY* 355, 367–8. Also: Warbrick (1981) 30 *ICLQ* 568. Further: 1 *Restatement Third* §203, reporter note (1).

[64] *Gur Corporation v Trust Bank of Africa Ltd* [1987] 1 QB 599.

[65] For criticism: Brownlie (1982) 53 *BY* 197, 209–11; Crawford (1986) 57 *BY* 408; Talmon (1998) 3–14. Also: *Republic of Somalia v Woodhouse Drake and Carey (Suisse) SA* [1993] QB 54, noted Kingsbury (1993) 109 *LQR* 377; Crawford (1993) 52 *CLJ* 4.

[66] *Kuwait Airways Corporation v Iraqi Airways Company and the Republic of Iraq* (1999) 116 ILR 534, 580–1.

[67] *Caglar v Billingham* (1996) 108 ILR 510, 519; *Veysi Dag v Secretary of State* (2001) 122 ILR 529, 536.

[68] *British Arab Commercial Bank plc v National Transitional Council of the State of Libya* [2011] EWHC 2274 (Comm) [23]–[25] (Blair J).

practice the formal requirements for approving credentials have been linked with a challenge to the representation of a state by a particular government.[69]

4. COLLECTIVE NON-RECOGNITION AND SANCTIONS

One form of collective non-recognition seen in practice is the resolution or decision of an organ of the United Nations, based on a determination that an illegal act has occurred.[70] Support for the concept was provided by the International Court in the *Kosovo* advisory opinion.[71] Article 41(2) of the ILC Articles on the Responsibility of States for Internationally Wrongful Acts takes this further, providing that 'no State shall recognize as lawful a situation created by a serious breach' of an obligation arising under a peremptory norm of international law.[72] In the present context, this obligation entails two central duties of abstention: (a) not to recognize as lawful situations created by a serious breach of international law; and (b) not to render aid or assistance in maintaining the situation. Thus there is a duty not to recognize the illegal acquisition of territory, an obligation confirmed as customary international law in the *Wall* opinion.[73]

It is possible, though by no means necessary, to refer to such practice as collective non-recognition. There is no doubt a duty of states parties to a system of collective security or other multilateral conventions not to support or condone acts or situations contrary to the treaty concerned.[74] The duty of non-recognition is not, however, absolute. As the International Court stated in *Namibia*:

In general, the non-recognition of South Africa's administration of the Territory should not result in depriving the people of Namibia of any advantages derived from international co-operation. In particular, while official acts performed by the Government of South Africa on behalf of or concerning Namibia after the termination of the Mandate are illegal and invalid, this invalidity cannot be extended to those acts, such as, for instance, the registration of

---

[69] Higgins (1963) 131–2, 140–4, 146–50; Kelsen (2nd edn, 1967) 946.

[70] 1 Lauterpacht (1970) 308, 321; Kelsen (2nd edn, 1967) 415–16; Dugard (1987) 81–111; Crawford (2nd edn, 2006) 157–73; Talmon, in Talmon et al (eds), *Fundamental Rules of the International Legal Order* (2006) 99; Talmon (2007); Ronen, *Transition from Illegal Regimes under International Law* (2011) chs 2 and 3.

[71] *Accordance with International Law of the Unilateral Declaration of Independence in Respect of Kosovo*, Opinion of 22 July 2010, §81.

[72] On the aetiology of Art 41: Talmon, in Talmon et al (2006) 99, 102–3; Dawidowicz, in Crawford, Pellet & Olleson (eds), *The Law of International Responsibility* (2010) 677. See also chapter 27.

[73] *Legal Consequences of the Construction of a Wall in the Occupied Palestinian Territory*, ICJ Reports 2004 p 136, 171, cf ibid, 232 (Judge Kooijmans).

[74] Cf the Stimson Doctrine: League of Nations, *Official Journal*, Spec Supp No 101 (1932) 87–8 ('it is incumbent upon the members of the League of Nations not to recognize any situation, treaty or agreement which may be brought about by means contrary to the Covenant of the League of Nations or the Pact of Paris'). Further: 1 Lauterpacht (1970) 308, 337–48; Turns (2003) 2 *Chin JIL* 105; Fabry, *Recognizing States* (2011) 135–7; Grant, 'Doctrines (Monroe, Hallstein, Brezhnev, Stimson)' (2008) *MPEPIL*, §C. See further chapter 27.

births, deaths and marriages, the effects of which can be ignored only to the detriment of the inhabitants of the Territory.[75]

This formulation is very similar to the historical position adopted by the US and later by the UK, whereby the national courts of a non-recognizing state may continue to give effect to rights and liabilities of non-recognized regimes which are of an essentially internal and private law character.

In some contexts the duty of non-recognition will be carefully spelled out and may be associated with measures recommended or required as a form of sanction or enforcement. The Security Council resolutions of 1965 and 1966 characterized the Smith regime in Rhodesia as unlawful in terms of the UN Charter and called upon all states not to recognize it.[76] Similar issues arose in relation to the situation in Namibia (formerly South West Africa) following the termination of the Mandate,[77] the South African 'Bantustans',[78] the status of the Turkish-occupied area of Cyprus (the 'TRNC') after the Turkish invasion of 1974,[79] and in relation to the annexation of East Timor by Indonesia.[80] More recently, the obligation has arisen in relation to Israeli activities in the Occupied Territories as a consequence of the *Wall* advisory opinion, where the Court said:

Given the character and the importance of the rights and obligations involved, the Court is of the view that all states are under an obligation not to recognize the illegal situation resulting from the construction of the wall in the Occupied Palestinian Territory, including in and around East Jerusalem. They are also under an obligation not to render aid or assistance in maintaining the situation created by such construction.[81]

The General Assembly subsequently called on all Members 'to comply with their legal obligations as mentioned in the Advisory Opinion',[82] but the Security Council took no

---

[75] *Legal Consequences for States of the Continued Presence of South Africa in Namibia (South West Africa) notwithstanding Security Council Resolution 276 (1970)*, ICJ Reports 1971 p 16, 56. Also: *Loizidou v Turkey (Merits)* (1996) 108 ILR 443, 462. Generally: Ronen (2011) 80–100.

[76] SC Res 216 (1965); SC Res 217 (1965); SC Res 232 (1966); SC Res 253 (1968); SC Res 277 (1970). Later: SC Res 318 (1972); SC Res 320 (1972); SC Res 388 (1976); SC Res 409 (1977); SC Res 423 (1978). On the UN resolutions concerning Rhodesia: Fawcett (1965–66) 41 *BY* 103; McDougal & Reisman (1968) 62 *AJIL* 1; Dugard (1987) 90–8; Gowlland-Debbas, *Collective Responses to Illegal Acts in International Law* (1990); Ronen (2011) 27–37.

[77] Generally: *Namibia*, ICJ Reports 1971 p 16.

[78] SC Res 385 (1976); SC Res 402 (1976); SC Res 407 (1977); SC Res 417 (1977).

[79] SC Res 541 (1983); SC Res 550 (1984). Further: Case C-432/92, *R v Minister of Agriculture, Fisheries and Food, ex parte SP Anastasiou (Pissouri) Ltd* (1994) 100 ILR 257; *Loizidou v Turkey (Preliminary Objections)* (1995) 103 ILR 622; *Loizidou v Turkey (Merits)* (1996) 108 ILR 443; *Demopoulos v Turkey* [2010] ECtHR 46113/99. Generally: Ronen (2011) 38–54.

[80] GA Res 3485(XXX), 12 December 1975; GA Res 31/53, 1 December 1976; GA Res 32/34, 28 November 1977; GA Res 33/39, 13 December 1978; GA Res 34/40, 21 November 1979; GA Res 35/27, 11 November 1980; GA Res 36/50, 24 November 1981; GA Res 37/30, 22 November 1982; SC Res 384 (1975); SC Res 389 (1976). Further: Ronen (2011) 54–61. Also: *East Timor (Portugal v Australia)*, ICJ Reports 1995 p 90.

[81] *Wall*, ICJ Reports 2004 p 136, 200.

[82] GA Res ES-10/15, 20 July 2004, §3.

action with respect to the matter, and no state undertook to alter its behaviour towards Israel, even with respect to the provision of aid.[83]

5. ISSUES OF RECOGNITION BEFORE NATIONAL COURTS[84]

(A) OVERVIEW

Individual recognition may have important practical consequences on a domestic level. Where the local courts are willing or obliged to follow the advice of the executive, the unrecognized state or government cannot claim immunity from the jurisdiction, obtain recognition for purposes of conflict of laws of its legislative and judicial acts, or sue in the local courts. The attitude to questions of recognition adopted by municipal courts will thus reflect the policies of the forum state, and great caution is needed in using municipal cases to establish propositions about recognition in general international law. In particular, because of the constitutional position of many courts in matters concerning foreign relations, it is unjustifiable to treat the cases as evidence supporting the constitutive position.

(B) THE POSITION OF THE UNITED KINGDOM COURTS

In matters of recognition, the UK judiciary has historically adhered to two closely-related principles. The first, expressed in the *Arantzazu Mendi*, is that '[o]ur State cannot speak with two voices on such a matter, the judiciary saying one thing, the executive another.'[85] The second is that although both the executive and the judiciary are considered to be manifestations of the state, only the former is competent to determine foreign policy. It is accordingly not within the purview of the courts to, *sua sponte*, 'recognize' a state or

---

[83] Ronen (2011) 312 attributes the ineffectiveness of collective non-recognition to (a) non-uniform application of the duty (Soviet annexation of the Baltic states, Indonesian annexation of East Timor), (b) the internal strength of certain illegal regimes (the case of Rhodesia), or (c) the political consequences inherent in implementing non-recognition (the case of Israel and Palestine). Talmon, in Talmon et al (2006) 99, 125, is more sanguine, but believes the scope of the duty to be limited.

[84] Generally: Mann (1943) 29 *GST* 143; Merrills (1971) 20 *ICLQ* 476; Nedjati (1981) 30 *ICLQ* 388; Verhoeven (1985) 192 Hague *Recueil* 13; Talmon (1998) Appendix I; Fatima, *Using International Law in Domestic Courts* (2005) 388.

[85] [1939] AC 256, 264 (Lord Atkin). This principle still exists: *Adams v Adams* [1971] P 188, 198 (Simon P); *In re Westinghouse Electric Corporation Uranium Contract Litigation (Nos 1 & 2)* [1978] AC 547, 617; *Gur Corporation v Trust Bank of Africa Ltd* [1987] QB 599, 604 (Steyn J), on appeal, ibid, 625 (Nourse LJ); *Lonrho Exports Ltd v Export Credits Guarantee Department* [1999] Ch 158, 179 (Lightman J); *R (Sultan of Pahang) v Secretary of State* [2011] EWCA Civ 616, §14 (Maurice Kay LJ), [30] (Moore-Bick LJ); *British Arab Commercial Bank plc v National Transitional Council of the State of Libya* [2011] EWHC 2274 (Comm), §25 (Blair J).

government;[86] rather, they must follow the lead of the executive. Thus, in the early case of *The Annette*,[87] the courts refused to extend state immunity to ships of the unrecognized 'Provisional Government of Northern Russia'. Although the UK government has professedly ceased issuing formal statements of recognition of governments, it still does so on occasion, in which case its certificate will be taken by the courts as conclusive.[88]

In the absence of a certificate, the court may examine executive action to infer that recognition has taken place.[89] But the court is not required to guess at an unexpressed intent, and can look at the matter at large. In *Republic of Somalia v Woodhouse Drake and Carey (Suisse) SA*, Hobhouse J saw the following factors as determinative in the absence of a certificate: (a) whether the government in question is the constitutional government of the state; (b) the degree, nature, and stability of its administrative control; (c) whether the executive has had any dealings with the purported government and the nature of those dealings; and (d) in marginal cases only, the attitude of other states towards the purported government.[90] He added that mere statements by the Foreign and Commonwealth Office falling short of outright recognition, though highly persuasive as evidence, were not determinative.[91]

The question may be complicated where the executive chooses to qualify its recognition as *de facto* rather than *de iure*. In *AM Luther v James Sagor & Co* the Court of Appeal held that the fact that recognition was extended on a *de facto* basis alone did not diminish the legal rights available to the state.[92] This position was refined in the *Haile Selassie* case.[93] This was a claim by the Emperor of Ethiopia to assets located in England at a time when the UK recognized Italy as the *de facto* government, whilst Selassie remained *de iure* sovereign. At first instance, it was held that the Italian *de facto* authority did not impair the Emperor's capacity to recover the assets in question, but before the defendant appealed, the UK government extended *de iure* recognition to the Italian authorities in Ethiopia. The Court of Appeal held this to operate retroactively[94] from

---

[86] As noted by Mann (1943) 29 *GST* 143, 145: '[t]he Courts cannot *make* foreign policy' (emphasis in original).

[87] [1919] P 105. Also: *Luther v Sagor* [1921] 1 KB 456, on appeal [1921] 3 KB 532.

[88] E.g. *Mighell v Sultan of Johore* [1894] 1 QB 149, 158 ('When once there is the authoritative certificate of the Queen through her minister of state as to the status of another sovereign, that in the courts of this country is decisive'); *Carl Zeiss Siftung v Rayner and Keeler Ltd (No 2)* [1967] AC 853, 43 ILR 25; *Gur Corporation v Trust Bank of Africa Ltd* [1987] QB 599; *Veysi Dag v Secretary of State* (2001) 122 ILR 529, 535–6; *British Arab Commercial Bank plc v National Transitional Council of the State of Libya* [2011] EWHC 2274 (Comm), §25 (Blair J).

[89] [1987] QB 599, 625. Cf Mann (1987) 36 *ICLQ* 348, 349–50; Beck (1987) 36 *ICLQ* 350.

[90] [1993] QB 54, 68.

[91] Ibid, 65. Further *Sierra Leone Telecommunications Co Ltd v Barclays Bank* [1998] 2 All ER 821.

[92] [1921] 1 KB 456.

[93] *Haile Selassie v Cable & Wireless Ltd (No 2)* [1939] 1 Ch 182.

[94] But cf *Gdynia Ameryka Linie Zeglugowe AS v Boguslawski* [1953] AC 11 (recognition of the new *de iure* government's acts only retrospective 'in so far as those acts related to matters under its control at the time when the acts were done'); *Civil Air Transport Inc v Civil Air Transport Corporation* [1953] AC 70 ('retroactivity of recognition operates to validate acts of a *de facto* Government which has subsequently become the new *de iure* government, and not to invalidate acts of a previous *de iure* Government').

the date at which *de facto* authority was first extended. Thus, the Emperor's claim was displaced and any rights to property held vested in the King of Italy.

The *Haile Selassie* case gives texture to an obvious problem, that is when there is both a *de iure* and *de facto* government with respect to the same territory.[95] Historically, the practice of the British courts was 'uniform to the point of rigidity':[96] the acts of unrecognized states and governments were given no weight.[97] But the courts have adopted a number of devices by way of mitigation. The first, which is virtually a legal fiction, operates on the basis of an imputed agency: the acts of the unrecognized entity are considered to be performed under powers delegated to it by the legitimate sovereign. In the *Carl Zeiss* case,[98] the House of Lords interpreted the acts of the unrecognized government of the German Democratic Republic (GDR) as those of a subordinate organ of the Soviet Union, the *de iure* government of the relevant territory; the practical effect was that the acts of the GDR government could give rise to rights and liabilities ordinarily seen to emanate from a *de iure* government without offending the executive's policy of non-recognition. A similar situation emerged in *Gur Corporation*, where the Court of Appeal found the unrecognized 'Bantustan' of Ciskei to be a subordinate body of South Africa.[99]

A second device permits the recognition of private acts internal to the unrecognized states. Put simply, the English courts have endeavoured to recognize rights and obligations which are of a wholly private law character, unconnected to the grounds for non-recognition.[100] In *Hesperides Hotels*, Lord Denning MR expressed the view that the laws of a non-recognized entity could give rise to rights and obligations opposable in English courts insofar as they related to 'the day-to-day affairs of the people, such as their marriages, their divorces, their leases, their occupations and so forth'.[101] Lord Donaldson MR in *Gur Corporation* agreed, noting (again obiter) that:[102]

I see great force in this [private law] reservation, since it is one thing to treat a state or government as being 'without the law', but quite another to treat the inhabitants of its territory as 'outlaws' who cannot effectively marry, beget legitimate children, purchase goods on credit or undertake countless day-to-day activities having legal consequences.

The 'private acts' exception was actually applied by Sumner J in *Emin v Yeldag*,[103] who expanded Lord Denning's position to include all private acts done within a

---

[95] Generally: Mann (1987) 36 *ICLQ* 348.

[96] Lauterpacht (1947) 145.

[97] E.g. *City of Berne v Bank of England* (1804) 9 Ves Jun 346; *AM Luther v James Sagor & Co* [1921] 1 KB 456. Much later: *Adams v Adams* [1971] P 188.

[98] *Carl Zeiss Siftung v Rayner and Keeler Ltd (No 2)* [1967] AC 853. Also: Greig (1987) 83 *LQR* 96.

[99] *Gur Corporation v Trust Bank of Africa Ltd* [1987] 1 QB 599.

[100] Further: *Caglar v Billingham* (1996) 108 ILR 510, 534.

[101] *Hesperides Hotels Ltd v Aegean Turkish Holidays* [1978] QB 205, 218. Also: *Carl Zeiss Siftung v Rayner and Keeler Ltd (No 2)* [1967] AC 853, 954 (Lord Wilberforce).

[102] *Gur Corporation v Trust Bank of Africa Ltd* [1987] 1 QB 599, 622.

[103] [2002] 1 FLR 956; cf *B v B* [2000] FLR 707. Also: *Parent v Singapore Airlines & Civil Aeronautics Administration* (2003) 133 ILR 264. Further Ronen (2004) 63 *CLJ* 268.

non-recognized state, provided that (a) there was no statutory prohibition on the recognition of the act, and (b) the act of recognition did not undermine the political or diplomatic goals of the executive.[104]

The limits of the exception were demonstrated in *Kibris Türk*, where the court reviewed a decision by the Secretary of State for Transport refusing to permit a Turkish airline to operate flights between the United Kingdom and Northern Cyprus. Wyn Williams J held that the decision was correct for two reasons. In the first place, though it controlled only the south of the island, the government of Cyprus was the recognized government for the territory in question within the meaning of the Chicago Convention[105] and therefore had the capacity to regulate air traffic within the territory.[106] In the second, for the court to allow the granting of a permit would be to contradict the government's long-standing non-recognition of the TRNC; in this respect, the private acts exception could not be invoked:

[M]any of the acts of the Government of the TRNC as they relate to aviation are public and international in character. They are not properly described as laws which regulate the day to day affairs of the people who reside in the TRNC either as described by Lord Denning MR, or Sumner J ... This court is obliged to refuse to give effect to the validity of acts carried out in a territory which is unrecognized unless the acts in question can properly be regarded as regulating the day to day affairs of the people within the territory in question and can properly be regarded as essentially private in character.[107]

(C) THE POSITION OF THE UNITED STATES COURTS

Much of the jurisprudence concerning non-recognition arose from the US' refusal to recognize the Soviet Union from the latter's emergence in 1922[108] to the Roosevelt–Litvinov Agreements of 1933.[109] The US position on the recognition of governments generally is as set out in the *Restatement Third*:[110]

> (1) an entity not recognized as a state, or a regime not recognized as the government of a state, is ordinarily denied access to courts in the United States;

---

[104] The Foreign Corporations Act 1991 c 44 (UK) s1, provides that where a question arises as to the corporate status of a body under the laws of a non-recognized country, and those laws are applied by a settled court system, the question shall be determined as if the territory were a recognized state. Also: UKMIL (1991) 62 *BY* 535, 565–8.

[105] Convention on International Civil Aviation, 7 December 1944, 15 UNTS 295 (as amended).

[106] *R (on the application of Kibris Türk Hava Yollari & CTA Holidays) v Secretary of State for Transport* [2009] EWHC 1918 (Admin), §§44–67. The decision was affirmed on appeal: [2010] EWCA Civ 1093. Further: Talmon (2005) 43 *AdV* 1; Talmon (2009) 8 *Chin JIL* 135.

[107] *R (on the application of Kibris Türk Hava Yollari and CTA Holidays) v Secretary of State for Transport* [2009] EWHC 1918 (Admin), §89.

[108] E.g. *Wulfsohn v RSFSR*, 234 NY 372 (1923). On the early US cases: Dickinson (1931) 25 *AJIL* 214; Borchard (1932) 36 *AJIL* 261; Lauterpacht (1947) 145–50 (comparing early UK and US practice).

[109] Further: Kallis (1933) 20 *Va JIL* 1; Talmon (1998) 34–7; Grant (1999) 49–51.

[110] Generally: Fountain (1988–89) 29 *Va JIL* 473.

(2) a regime not recognized as the government of a state is not entitled to property belonging to that state located in the United States;

(3) courts in the United States ordinarily give effect to acts of a regime representing an entity not recognized as a state, or of a regime not recognized as a government of a state, if those acts apply to territory under the control of that regime and relate to domestic matters only.

In respect of principles (1) and (2) above, the situation in the US is similar to that of the UK: a non-recognized state[111] or government can neither appear before the forum courts, nor assert a right to property held in the US.[112] Although the courts have indicated that a mere *absence* of recognition is not determinative,[113] where the executive has indicated clearly that the courts are closed to an unrecognized state, the judiciary will normally comply.[114]

The prohibition on access, however, may be relaxed depending on the facts of the case, the practical consequences of granting or not granting access and the extent to which access is germane to the foreign policy goals of the United States.[115] Thus in *Upright v Mercury Business Machines Co*[116] non-recognition of the GDR did not prevent the assignee of a trade acceptance issued by a GDR instrumentality from bringing suit. By contrast in *Kunstsammlungen zu Weimar* a GDR government agency was converted into a purportedly separate legal person in an attempt to intervene in a case concerning the recovery of two valuable paintings. The court determined that the formal change had no effect on the GDR's control of the erstwhile agency, and denied it standing, noting that to do otherwise would be

---

[111] But cf the special provisions under the Taiwan Relations Act, 22 USC §3301 and further *Mingtai Fire and Marine Insurance Co Ltd v United Parcel Service*, 177 F.3d 1142 (9th Cir, 1999). Further: Lee, *The Making of the Taiwan Relations Act* (2010); Ahl, 'Taiwan' (2008) *MPEPIL*. More generally, non-recognized governments are still offered certain protections under the US Criminal Code in relation to, e.g. counterfeiting of currency or killing of officials and representatives: 18 USC §§11, 1116. Non-recognized states are also entitled to sovereign immunity: *Wulfsohn v RSFSR*, 234 NY 372 (1923); cf *Klinghoffer v SNC Achille Lauro*, 937 F.2d 44 (2nd Cir, 1991).

[112] E.g. *The Penza*, 277 F 91 (EDNY, 1931); *The Rogdai*, 276 F 294 (ND Cal, 1920); *RSFSR v Cibrario*, 235 NY 255 (1923); *Republic of Vietnam v Pfizer Inc*, 556 F.2d 892 (8th Cir, 1977). However, the courts remain open to recognized governments with which the US does not have diplomatic relations: *Banco Nacional de Cuba v Sabbatino*, 376 US 398, 408–12 (1964).

[113] E.g. *Ministry of Defence of the Islamic Republic of Iran v Gould Inc*, No CV 87–03673-RG, US Dist Ct, CD Cal, 14 January 1988 (1988) 82 *AJIL* 591; *Petrochemical v The M/T Stolt Sheaf*, 860 F.2d 551 (2nd Cir, 1988).

[114] E.g. *Republic of Panama v Republic National Bank of New York*, 681 F.Supp 1066 (SDNY, 1988); *Republic of Panama v Southern International Bank*, 682 F.Supp 1144 (SD Fla, 1988). Further: Fountain (1988–89) 29 *Va JIL* 473.

[115] E.g. *The Maret*, 145 F.2d 431, 439 (3rd Cir, 1944); *Transportes Aeros de Angola v Ronair*, 544 F.Supp 856, 863–4 (D Del, 1982) (corporations owned by non-recognized governments permitted to appear); *Russian Volunteer Fleet v United States*, 282 US 481, 492 (1931) (alien investor from non-recognized country entitled to compensation for expropriation). Further: 1 *Restatement Third* §205, comment (a).

[116] 213 NYS (2d) 417 (1961).

to 'render our government's non-recognition of the German Democratic Republic a meaningless gesture'.[117]

US courts since the Civil War[118] have acknowledged the acts of non-recognized states, provided that such acts '[deal] solely with private, local and domestic matters' and not 'matters extending beyond the borders' of the unrecognized entity.[119] This in effect presaged the private acts exception: Lauterpacht called it the doctrine of 'justice and public policy'.[120] The rationale was expressed in *Salimoff v Standard Oil Co of New York*: 'to refuse to recognize Soviet Russia as a government regulating the internal affairs of the country, is to give to fictions an air of reality which they do not deserve'.[121] The limits of the doctrine, however, may be seen in *The Maret*,[122] where the court refused to recognize the nationalization of a ship by the unrecognized Soviet Republic of Estonia.[123]

(D) THE POSITION IN EUROPE

(i) A 'pan-European' approach

The legal consequences of non-recognition in Europe vary from state to state, but some overarching framework is provided by pan-European institutions, especially the European Court of Justice. As a general rule (to which Switzerland and the Netherlands are notable exceptions)[124] non-recognized states have no right of appearance, and their acts will not be given effect by European courts.[125] This was seen in the early *Soviet Marriages* case, where the Royal Hungarian Court of Appeal refused to acknowledge a marriage concluded under the laws of the unrecognized Russian Soviet Federative Socialist Republic.[126] The position softened somewhat by the later

---

[117] *Kunstsammlungen zu Weimar v Elicofon*, 358 F.Supp 747, 757 (EDNY, 1972), affirmed on appeal 478 F.2d 231 (2nd Cir, 1973). The US later recognized the government of East Germany, after which it was permitted to intervene: *Federal Republic of Germany v Elicofon*, 358 F.Supp 747 (EDNY, 1972).

[118] *Texas v White*, 74 US 700 (1868).

[119] *Carl Zeiss Siftung v VEB Carl Zeiss*, 293 F.Supp 892, 900 (SDNY, 1968). Also: *Sokoloff v National City Bank of New York*, 239 NY 158 (1924); *Federal Republic of Germany v Elicofon*, 358 F.Supp 747 (EDNY, 1972); *Daniunas v Simutis*, 481 F.Supp 132 (SDNY, 1978); *Matter of Bielinis*, 284 NYS.2d 819 (1967); *Matter of Luberg's Estate*, 243 NYS.2d 747 (1963). Further: Lauterpacht (1947) 147; 1 *Restatement Third* §202, reporter note 6; ibid, §205, reporter note 3.

[120] Lauterpacht (1947) 147.

[121] 186 NE 679, 882 (1933); cf *Latvian State Cargo & Passenger SS Line v McGrath*, 188 F.2d 1000 (DC Cir, 1951). Further: Dickinson (1933) 27 *AJIL* 743.

[122] *Maret*, 145 F.2d 431 (3rd Cir, 1944).

[123] Further: *Autocephalous Church of Cyprus v Goldberg and Feldman Fine Arts Inc*, 917 F.2d 278 (2nd Cir, 1990).

[124] E.g. *Schinz v High Court of Zurich* (1926) 3 ILR 32; *Exportchleb Ltd v Goudeket* (1935) 8 ILR 117; *Mrs X v Y* (1946) 13 ILR 19; *South Moluccas v The Netherlands New Guinea* (1954) 21 ILR 48; *VEB Carl Zeiss Jena v Carl Zeiss Heidenheim* (1965) 72 ILR 550; *Billerbeck and Cie v Bergbau-Handel GmbH* (1967) 72 ILR 69; *Wang v Switzerland* (2004) ILDC 90.

[125] On the early European cases: Lauterpacht (1947) 151–3.

[126] (1925) 3 ILR 31. Further: *Soviet Government v Ericsson* (1921) 1 ILR 54; *In re Serventi* (1921) 1 ILR 294; *Bekker v Willcox* (1923) 2 ILR 50; *Soviet Representation in Czechoslovakia* (1925) 3 ILR 60; *Chiger v Chiger*

twentieth century, as suggested in the attitude of the Italian Court of Cassation towards the GDR:

In conformity with long-standing doctrine in Italy and throughout the European continent... where the question arises of establishing the effects in Italy of an act of private law executed abroad, it is irrelevant whether or not a State maintains diplomatic relations with another State whose rule of private international law is to be enforced, or whether or not the latter State is recognized by the former. The only prerequisite for the enforcement of a foreign legal rule is its effectiveness, provided that the particular legal provision does not also require reciprocity of treatment and so long as the principles of the foreign law to be enforced do not appear incompatible with the fundamental rules of the *lex fori*, in which case the foreign law is unenforceable for reasons of public policy.[127]

Differences in approach may depend on the readiness of national courts to apply international law. In some states, the judiciary treats the political question of recognition as distinct from statehood and assesses the capacity of an entity *proprio motu* rather than deferring to executive acts. This may be seen in *Fretilin v Netherlands*, in which an East Timorese resistance group attempted to halt the sale of three Dutch corvettes to the Indonesian government. The District Court of Amsterdam held the claim inadmissible on grounds that East Timor was not a state and the Fretilin Liberation Front therefore had no legal personality. It said, however, that 'this question must be decided independently by a court of law, irrespective of the question of recognition' and, further, 'on the basis of the factual criteria for statehood laid down by international law'.[128] A more recent example is the Italian Court of Cassation in *Djukanovic*, deciding that Montenegro was not then a state.[129]

In *Anastasiou I*,[130] the European Court of Justice heard questions referred to it by the English High Court regarding the importation of agricultural products from Northern Cyprus. Under the terms of an Association Agreement between the European Communities and the Republic of Cyprus in 1972 and a Protocol concluded in 1977, in order to obtain preferential tariff treatment each consignment of goods for export was to be accompanied by a certificate issued by the customs authorities of the exporting state as proof of origin. Northern Cypriot goods were exported into the UK and elsewhere[131] with certificates produced by TRNC authorities, prompting the question whether these were valid for the purposes of the Agreement and Protocol. Although

---

(1926) 3 ILR 26; *Digmeloff v State Civil Officer of St Josse-Ten-Noode* (1928) 4 ILR 69; *Krimtschansky v Officier de l'Etat Civil de Liège* (1929) 5 ILR 47; *Nonis v Federation of Seamen* (1930) 5 ILR 45; *Société Despa et Fils v USSR* (1931) 6 ILR 37; *Cibrario v Russian Trade Delegation* (1931) 6 ILR 54; *International Registration of Trade-Mark* (1959) 28 ILR 82.

[127] *Warenzeichenverband Regekungstechnik EV v Ministry of Trade and Industry* (1975) 77 ILR 571, 571.

[128] *Democratic Republic of East Timor & Fretilin v State of the Netherlands* (1980) 87 ILR 73, 74. Also: *FRG-GDR Relations Case* (1973) 78 ILR 149, 165–6.

[129] *Italy v Djukanovic* (2004) ILDC 74.

[130] Case C-432/92, *R v Minister of Agriculture, Fisheries and Food, ex parte SP Anastasiou (Pissouri) Ltd* (1994) 100 ILR 257.

[131] Belgium, France, Germany, Ireland, Italy, Netherlands: ibid, 270.

the question turned mainly on the interpretation of the relevant texts, the UK and the European Commission argued that to deny the validity of the certificates would be to deny the inhabitants of the TRNC the advantages granted by the Agreement and Protocol, and thus the *Namibia* exception applied.[132] The Court, adopting the position of Advocate-General Gulmann,[133] disagreed:

While the *de facto* partition of the territory of Cyprus, as a result of the intervention of the Turkish armed forces in 1974, into a zone where the authorities of the Republic of Cyprus continue fully to exercise their powers and a zone where they cannot in fact do so raises problems that are difficult to resolve in connection with the application of the Association Agreement to the whole of Cyprus, that does not warrant a departure from the clear, precise and unconditional provisions of the 1977 Protocol on the origin of products and administrative cooperation.[134]

(ii) Expanding the *Namibia* exception

Notwithstanding the judgment of the European Court of Justice in *Anastasiou I*, the *Namibia* exception arguably has expanded before the European Court of Human Rights.[135]

In *Loizidou v Turkey*, Turkey argued that in order to provide housing for displaced Turkish Cypriots fleeing from the south, the TRNC was justified in expropriating the houses of displaced Greek Cypriots. The majority did not reject this argument outright, but said that in the circumstances the expropriation was disproportionate.[136] The Court went further in *Cyprus v Turkey (Fourth Interstate Case)*, where it accepted that the remedies available in the TRNC were 'domestic' remedies provided by Turkey:[137]

It is to be noted that the International Court's Advisory Opinion…shows clearly that, in situations similar to those arising in the present case, the obligation to disregard acts of *de facto* entities is far from absolute. Life goes on in the territory concerned for its inhabitants. That life must be made tolerable and be protected by the *de facto* authorities, including their courts; and, in the very interest of the inhabitants, the acts of these authorities related thereto cannot be simply ignored by third States or by international institutions, especially courts, including this one. To hold otherwise would amount to stripping the inhabitants of the territory of all their rights whenever they are discussed in an international context, which would amount to depriving them even of the minimum standard of rights to which they are entitled.[138]

---

[132] (1994) 100 ILR 257, 276. Further: *Namibia*, ICJ Reports 1971 p 16, 56.

[133] (1994) 100 ILR 257, 281.

[134] Ibid, 297. But cf Case C-219/98, *R v Minister of Agriculture, Fisheries and Food, ex parte SP Anastasiou (Pissouri) Ltd* [2000] ECR I-5268.

[135] Ronen (2011) 88–98.

[136] *Loizidou v Turkey (Merits)* (1996) 108 ILR 443, 468; 474 (Judge Baka, diss), 481 (Judge Pettiti, diss). Further: *Foka v Turkey* [2008] ECtHR 28940/95; *Protopapa v Turkey* [2009] ECtHR 16084/90.

[137] (2001) 120 ILR 10, 42–6.

[138] Ibid, 44–5.

The Court built on this further in *Demopoulos v Turkey*, where access to the Court was barred under Article 35(1) of the European Convention for the Protection of Human Rights and Fundamental Freedoms[139] on the basis that domestic remedies in the TRNC had not been exhausted.[140]

---

[139] 4 November 1950, 213 UNTS 222.

[140] [2010] ECtHR 46113/99, §§68–129. Further: Ronen (2011) 95; Loucaides (2011) 24 *LJIL* 435, and see chapter 27.

7

INTERNATIONAL
ORGANIZATIONS

1. INTRODUCTION

As discussed in chapter 1, in the late eighteenth and nineteenth century states developed multilateral forms of co-operation, supplementing reliance on bilateral treaties and diplomacy. These included the first international organizations. Initially the mandates of such organizations were constrained, for example the European Commission of the Danube (1856) and the International Telegraph Union (1865). But after 1920 the League of Nations and then the United Nations provided a more developed notion of universal peacekeeping arrangements, and many specialized institutions concerned with technical, economic, and social co-operation were established. The study of international organizations and the multiplicity of institutions and agencies is a department of the political and social sciences: the present chapter can only indicate the main legal problems arising from interstate organizations.[1]

2. LEGAL PERSONALITY

(A) INTERNATIONAL ORGANIZATIONS AS SUBJECTS OF INTERNATIONAL LAW

Given the large number of international organizations extant,[2] it is difficult to find a catch-all definition that is neither under- nor over-inclusive. One possible starting point

---

[1] Generally: Klabbers, *An Introduction to International Institutional Law* (2nd edn, 2009); Sands & Klein, *Bowett's Law of International Institutions* (6th edn, 2009). Also: Morgenstern, *Legal Problems of International Organizations* (1986); Colliard, *Institutions des relations internationales* (9th edn, 1990); Kirgis, *International Organizations in Their Legal Setting* (2nd edn, 1993); White, *The Law of International Organisations* (1996); Dupuy (ed), *A Handbook of International Organizations* (2nd edn, 1998); Schermers & Blokker, *International Institutional Law* (4th edn, 2003); Amerasinghe, *Principles of the Institutional Law of International Organizations* (2nd edn, 2005); Sarooshi, *International Organizations and Their Exercise of Sovereign Powers* (2005); Alvarez, *International Organizations as Law-Makers* (2005); Diez de Velasco Vallejo, *Las organizaciones internacionales* (15th edn, 2008); Akande, in Evans (ed), *International Law* (3rd edn, 2010) 252.

[2] There is no definitive list of international organizations: Amerasinghe (2nd edn, 2005) 6. The *Yearbook of International Organizations 2009/10* states that there were at that point 241 'conventional'

is Article 2(a) of the ILC's 2011 Draft Articles on the Responsibility of International Organizations, which provides:

'[I]nternational organization' means an organization established by treaty or other instrument governed by international law and possessing its own international legal personality. International organizations may include as members, in addition to States, other entities.[3]

Whilst useful, this definition was developed in the context of international responsibility, which presupposes legal personality. It is possible for an international organization to have no such personality but still—by virtue of its treaty-based, interstate character and activity—be considered an international organization. Nonetheless, most international organizations will possess separate personality.

Although international organizations have existed since the mid-nineteenth century, attribution of legal personality to them is relatively new.[4] A shift began after 1919, though it was characterized by equivocation. The Covenant of the League of Nations made no reference to legal personality.[5] By 1926, however, its *modus vivendi* with Switzerland included recognition of its separate existence on the international plane.[6]

Then, in *Reparation for Injuries*[7] the International Court went a step further. Following the assassination of the United Nations' envoy Count Folke Bernadotte and his entourage by Zionist nationalists,[8] the Court was asked to advise on the capacity of the UN, as an organization, to bring an international claim for injury to its personnel on the lines of diplomatic protection, and in respect of injury to the UN caused by the harm to its agents. The Charter did not contain any explicit provision on the international legal personality of the UN,[9] but the Court drew on the implications of

---

intergovernmental organizations: Figure 2.9. Also: Blokker, in Blokker & Schermers (eds), *Proliferation of International Organizations* (2001) 1.

[3] A/CN.4/L.778, 30 May 2011. Akande draws on this definition to derive three primary attributes of an international organization: (1) the entity is composed predominantly of states and other international organizations; (2) the entity is established by an instrument recognized by international law, whether a treaty or some other mechanism; and (3) the entity possesses autonomous organs with a will separate from its members: Akande (2010) 252, 254.

[4] Bederman (1996) 36 *Va JIL* 275; Crawford, *Selected Essays* (2002) 19–22; Sands & Klein (6th edn, 2009) 474–6; Portmann, *Legal Personality in International Law* (2010) ch 5.

[5] The Covenant did however provide for the immunity of officials and representatives of the League (Art 7(4)) and the inviolability of League premises (Art 7(5)).

[6] *Communications du Conseil Fédéral Suisse concernant le Régime des Immunités Diplomatique du Personnel de la Société des Nations et du Bureau International du Travail*, 18 September 1926, 7 *OJLN* (1926) annex 911a, 1422. Further: Hill, *Immunities and Privileges of International Officials* (1947) 14–23; Gautier (2000) 4 *MPUNYB* 331, 341–2.

[7] *Reparation for Injuries suffered in the Service of the United Nations*, ICJ Reports 1949 p 174.

[8] SC Res 57 (1948).

[9] Art 104 of the Charter relates solely to legal capacity of the Organization in the municipal law of member states: Bridge (1969) 18 *ICLQ* 689; Seidl-Hohenveldern & Rudolph, in Simma (ed), 2 *The Charter of the United Nations* (2nd edn, 2002) 1302.

the instrument as a whole, noting that, if the UN was to fulfil its tasks, 'the attribution of international personality is indispensable.'[10]

The Court then analysed the Charter itself and identified those textual elements that implied that the UN was intended to possess such personality, noting, *inter alia*, the defined position of Members in relation to the UN and the requirement that they assist it (Article 2(5)), the obligation to comply with and enforce decisions of the Security Council (Article 25), the capacity of the General Assembly to make recommendations to Members (Article 10), the grant of legal capacity, privileges, and immunities to the UN in the territory of its Members (Articles 104 and 105), and the conclusion of treaties between the UN and its Members (e.g. Article 43). These, the Court held, indicated that:

the Organization was intended to exercise and enjoy, and is in fact exercising and enjoying, functions and rights which can only be explained on the basis of the possession of a large measure of international personality and the capacity to operate upon an international plane. It is at present the supreme type of international organization, and it could not carry out the intentions of its founders if it was devoid of international personality. It must be acknowledged that its Members, by entrusting certain functions to it, with the attendant duties and responsibilities, have clothed it with the competence required to enable those functions to be effectively discharged.

Accordingly, the Court has come to the conclusion that the Organization is an international person. That is not the same thing as saying that it is a state, which it certainly is not, or that its legal personality and rights and duties are the same as those of a state. Still less is it the same thing as saying that it is 'a super-state', whatever that expression may mean. ... What it does mean is that it is a subject of international law and capable of possessing international rights and duties, and that it has capacity to maintain its rights by bringing international claims.[11]

(B) INDICIA OF INTERNATIONAL LEGAL PERSONALITY

Two main theories have been offered to explain the decision.[12] The first is that it is the will of the founders that determines whether an international organization possesses international legal personality.[13] If international law is based on the freely expressed consent of states, they may breathe personality into an organization.[14] But some organizations are not expressly endowed with international legal personality forcing its generation via inference.[15] This problem was pronounced with organizations

---

[10] ICJ Reports 1949 p 174, 178–9.

[11] Ibid, 179.

[12] Further: Amerasinghe (2nd edn, 2005) 79–91; Akande (2010) 252, 256–7.

[13] E.g. Sands & Klein (6th edn, 2009) 479–80.

[14] Amerasinghe (2nd edn, 2005) 79.

[15] Tunkin argued that an international organization could only acquire international personality by express constitutional provision: (1966) 119 Hague *Recueil* 1, 20–5.

formed in the early years of the United Nations,[16] but has declined with respect to later institutions.[17] More substantial is the question how organizations created by some states interact with third parties, whose refusal to acknowledge personality could reflect upon the potential emptiness of the concept. One solution is to condition personality on recognition by third parties, but in practice the institution of recognition has not been extended to organizations.[18]

The alternative and better view is that international organizations are capable of attaining 'objective' legal personality independent of recognition by performing certain functions on the international plane.[19] This was the position taken, at least in part, by the Court in *Reparation for Injuries*.[20] The criteria for the possession of legal personality by an international organization may be summarized as follows:[21]

(1) a permanent association of states, or other organizations, with lawful objects, equipped with organs;

(2) distinction, in terms of legal powers and purposes, between the organization and its member states; and

(3) the existence of legal powers exercisable on the international plane and not solely within the national systems of one or more states.[22]

An organization may exist but lack the organs and objects necessary for legal personality. The Commonwealth of Nations was such an association initially: it is now regarded as a distinct legal entity, though lacking a formal constitution.[23] Similarly, a multilateral convention may be institutionalized to some extent with provision for regular conferences, yet not involve any separate personality.[24] On the other hand joint agencies of states,[25] for example an arbitral tribunal or a river commission, may

---

[16] E.g. Constitution of the United Nations Educational, Scientific and Cultural Organization, 15 November 1945, 4 UNTS 275, Art XII; Constitution of the World Health Organization, 22 July 1946, 14 UNTS 185, Art 66.

[17] E.g. UNCLOS, 10 December 1982, 1833 UNTS 3, Art 176 (International Seabed Authority); Agreement Establishing the World Trade Organization, 15 April 1994, 1867 UNTS 154, Art VIII.1; ICC Statute, 17 July 1998, 2187 UNTS 3, Art 4(1).

[18] The main counter-example was the initial non-recognition of the EEC by the USSR: Schermers & Blokker (4th edn, 2003) 1133, 1174–6, 1182–3. It was not a success and did not inspire imitation.

[19] Amerasinghe (2nd edn, 2005) 79. Also: Higgins, *Problems and Process* (1994) 47–8. The theory was first developed by Seyersted, *Objective International Personality of Intergovernmental Organizations* (1963); Seyersted (1964) 4 *Indian JIL* 53.

[20] ICJ Reports 1949 p 174, 178–9.

[21] Cf Amerasinghe (2nd edn, 2005) 82–3.

[22] Further: Jenks (1945) 22 *BY* 267; Ginther, *Die völkerrechtliche Verantwortlichkeit internationaler Organisationen gegenüber Drittstaaten* (1969); Dupuy (1960) 100 Hague *Recueil* 461, 467–88; Weissberg, *The International Status of the United Nations* (1961); Amerasinghe (1995) 47 *Austrian JPIL* 123.

[23] On the Commonwealth of Nations: Fawcett, *British Commonwealth in International Law* (1963); Dale (1982) 31 *ICLQ* 451.

[24] Cf the conflicting decisions of Italian courts on the status of the North Atlantic Treaty Organization (NATO): *Branno v Ministry of War* (1954) 22 ILR 756; *Mazzanti v HAFSE* (1954) 22 ILR 758.

[25] E.g. the International Joint Commission (US–Canada): Boundary Waters Treaty, 11 January 1909, USTS 548; MacKay (1928) 22 *AJIL* 292; Spencer, *The International Joint Commission Seventy Years On* (1981);

have restricted capacities and limited independence but be regarded as a separate legal person.[26] This applies also to agencies and subsidiary organs of organizations, such as the United Nations Conference on Trade and Development (UNCTAD), the High Commissioner for Refugees, and the Technical Assistance Board in relation to the United Nations.[27]

Secondly, if an organization has considerable independence and power to intervene in the affairs of member states, the arrangement may resemble a federal union. The EU is sometimes characterized in this way, though this is debatable, as it is only competent to exercise those powers attributed to it by its member states.[28]

Thirdly, while an organization with legal personality is normally established by treaty, the source could be the resolution of a conference of states or a uniform practice.[29] The constitutional basis of the United Nations Industrial Development Organization (UNIDO) is to be found in resolutions of the General Assembly,[30] whilst the Organization of the Petroleum Exporting Countries (OPEC) and the Organisation for Security and Cooperation in Europe (OSCE) derive from government consensus reached at international conferences.[31]

In short, at the international level there is no legal and administrative process comparable to the municipal concept of incorporation. Where there is no constitutional system for recognizing and registering associations as legal persons, the primary test is functional. Indeed, it would be fatuous to work from an abstract model in face of the existence of some 250 organizations of states, varying from the universal to the bilateral.

(C) OBJECTIVE PERSONALITY AND THIRD STATES

One attribute of the objective theory of legal personality for international organizations is that it renders that personality opposable to third states, even though the

Reardon, in Susskind et al (eds), *International Environmental Treaty Making* (1992) 125; International Joint Commission, *Annual Report for 2008: Boundary Waters Treaty Centennial Edition* (2008) available at www. ijc.org/php/publications/pdf/ID1629.pdf.

[26] In *Pulp Mills on the River Uruguay*, the ICJ affirmed that a river commission established by Argentina and Uruguay had 'a permanent existence of its own' and was an 'international organization with legal personality': ICJ Reports 2010 p 14, 52–3 (§§86–9).

[27] Morgenstern (1986) 23–6.

[28] Treaty on European Union, 7 February 1992, *OJEU* C 191/1, Arts 4, 5. The EU is thus a classic example of the *competences d'attribution*, as spoken of by the Permanent Court in *Jurisdiction of the European Commission of the Danube* (1927) PCIJ Ser B No 14, 64. Also: *Exchange of Greek and Turkish Populations* (1925) PCIJ Ser B No 10. Further: Amerasinghe (2nd edn, 2005) 77–8.

[29] E.g. the World Tourism Organization; it is unusual in having three tiers of membership: (a) full members (states); (b) associate members (dependencies of states); and (c) affiliate members (companies and NGOs): Gilmour (1971) 18 *NILR* 275. Cf *Zoernsch v Waldock* [1964] 1 WLR 675 (on the constitution of an organ of an organization).

[30] Gutteridge, *The United Nations in a Changing World* (1969) 75–85. UNIDO's legal status as a specialized agency has been the subject of an express treaty: Constitution of the United Nations Industrial Development Organization, 8 April 1979, 1401 UNTS 3, Art 21(1).

[31] Akande, in Evans (3rd edn, 2010) 252, 254.

organization in question is normally the creation of treaty. This is made clear in the ILC's commentary to Draft Article 2, where it is said that 'it would not be necessary to enquire whether the legal personality of an organization has been recognized by an injured State before considering whether the organization may be held internationally responsible according to the present articles'.[32] In this, the ILC saw as conclusive the decision in *Reparation for Injuries*, with its emphasis on 'objective legal personality'.[33] Although the Court conditioned its opinion on the quantity and standing of the founding Members of the United Nations, there are good reasons for applying this proposition to *all* international organizations, and in practice this has occurred.

3. PRIVILEGES AND IMMUNITIES[34]

In order to function effectively, international organizations require minimum standards of freedom and legal security for their assets, headquarters, and other establishments, and for their personnel and accredited representatives of member states. By analogy with diplomatic privileges and immunities, the necessary privileges and immunities of agents of international organizations, as well as of the organizations themselves. in respect of the territorial jurisdiction of host states (that is, those states which have agreed to house the headquarters or other activities of an organization) may be recognized. The analogy is not perfect, however, and three difficulties are apparent.[35] First, in contrast to diplomatic immunity, it is normal for officials of an organization to have the nationality of (and often a special relationship with) a member state, including the host state. A national of the receiving state who is a member of a foreign mission will only be extended diplomatic immunity on a narrow and highly conditioned basis.[36] Secondly, a diplomat, although immune from the jurisdiction of the receiving state, remains under the sending state's jurisdiction. Thirdly, whereas reciprocity provides an incentive for states to respect international diplomatic law, an international organization does not have access to an effective regime of sanctions.

---

[32] ILC Report 2011, A/66/10, 76.

[33] ICJ Reports 1949 p 174, 185.

[34] Secretariat Study, ILC *Ybk* 1967/II, 154–324; El-Erian, ILC *Ybk* 1967/II, 133–53; ILC *Ybk* 1968/II, 119–62; ILC *Ybk* 1969/II, 1–21; ILC *Ybk* 1970/II, 1–24; ILC *Ybk* 1971/II(1), 1–142; *Privileges and Immunities of International Organizations,* Res (69) 29 of the Committee of Ministers, Council of Europe (1970). Also: Lalive (1953) 84 Hague *Recueil* 205, 291–385; Jenks, *International Immunities* (1961); Schröer (1971) 75 *RGDIP* 712; Michaels, *International Privileges and Immunities* (1971); Dominicé (1984) 187 Hague *Recueil* 145; Glenn, Kearney & Padilla (1981–82) 22 *Va JIL* 247; Duffar, *Contribution à l'étude des priviléges et immunités des organisations internationales* (1982); Singer (1995–96) 36 *Va JIL* 53; Gaillard & Pingel-Lenuzza (2002) 51 *ICLQ* 1; Amerasinghe (2nd edn, 2005) ch 10; Robert, *Mélanges Salmon* (2007)1433; Miller (2007) 4 *Int Org* 169; Sands & Klein (6th edn, 2009) 489–516; Möldner, 'International Organization or Institutions, Privileges or Immunities' (2011) *MPEPIL*.

[35] Sands & Klein (6th edn, 2009) 490.

[36] VCDR, 18 April 1961, 500 UNTS 95, Arts 8(2), 38(1).

(A) SOURCES OF PRIVILEGES AND IMMUNITIES[37]

(i) Treaty law

The privileges and immunities of international organizations derive from multiple sources. In the first place, the constituent instrument of the organization will ordinarily contain at least a general provision[38] stating that the organization and its personnel are to be accorded immunity. Article 105 of the Charter is emblematic:

1. The Organization shall enjoy in the territory of each of its Members such privileges and immunities as are necessary for the fulfilment of its purposes.

2. Representatives of the Members of the United Nations and officials of the Organization shall similarly enjoy such privileges and immunities as are necessary for the independent exercise of their functions in connexion with the Organisation.[39]

A further source of privileges and immunities are separate multilateral agreements. The Convention on the Privileges and Immunities of the United Nations[40] is the example most frequently identified as such, having inspired other similar instruments, notably the Convention on the Privileges and Immunities of the Specialized Agencies.[41] These may be further cemented by headquarters agreements between the organization and host state, for example the agreement between the United Nations and the US with respect to the UN headquarters in New York.[42]

(ii) National law

National law, especially host state law, is central in ensuring the privileges and immunities of international organizations. It will generally be required to implement relevant international agreements.[43] It may add to these agreements, or act as substitute where the state in question has yet to enter into them.

---

[37] Sands & Klein (6th edn, 2009) 490–3; Ryngaert (2010) 7 *Int Org LR* 121.

[38] Other constituent instruments may establish privileges and immunities in detail: e.g. Articles of Agreement of the International Bank for Reconstruction and Development, 22 July 1944, 2 UNTS 134, Art VII (IBRD Articles); Convention on the Settlement of Investment Disputes between States and Nationals of Other States, 18 March 1965, 575 UNTS 159, Arts 18–24 (ICSID Convention).

[39] Further: Statute of the International Atomic Energy Agency, 26 October 1956, 276 UNTS 4, Art XV; Constitution of the International Labour Organization, 1 April 1919, 15 UNTS 40, Art 40; Agreement Establishing the World Trade Organization, 15 April 1994, 1867 UNTS 154, Art VIII.

[40] 13 February 1946, 1 UNTS 15 (General Convention).

[41] 21 November 1947, 33 UNTS 261. Also: General Agreement on Privileges and Immunities of the Council of Europe, 2 September 1949, 1337 UNTS 420 (Council of Europe Immunities Agreement); Agreement on Privileges and Immunities of the Organization of American States, 15 May 1949, 1438 UNTS 83; Agreement on the Privileges and Immunities of the International Criminal Court, 9 September 2002, 2271 UNTS 3 (ICC Immunities Agreement).

[42] 26 June 1947, 11 UNTS 11 (UN Headquarters Agreement). Also: Interim Agreement on Privileges and Immunities of the United Nations concluded between the Secretary-General of the United Nations and the Swiss Federal Council, 11 June 1946, 1 UNTS 164 (UN Immunities Agreement); Headquarters Agreement between the International Criminal Court and the Host State, 7 June 2007, ICC-BD/04-01-08; Sands & Klein (6th edn, 2009) 491.

[43] E.g. International Organizations 1968 (UK); International Organizations Immunity Act 1945, 59 Stat 669 (US); International Organizations (Privileges and Immunities) Act 1963 (Cth) (Australia).

(iii) Customary international law

Then there is the question of the role of customary international law in this context.[44] Some governments and municipal courts have adopted the view that immunity exists in custom.[45] The *Restatement Third* specifies that international organizations are entitled in custom to 'such privileges and immunities as are necessary for the fulfilment of the purposes of the organization, including immunity from legal process and from financial controls, taxes and duties'.[46] Immunity has occasionally been recognized by the courts of non-member states,[47] and aspects of the immunity may have the status of general principles of law, though it has been suggested that this may only extend to the United Nations system, due to its universal character.[48]

As to organizations of more limited membership, the question remains open.[49] Speaking of the International Tin Council, Bingham J said:

[I]nternational organizations such as the ITC have never so far as I know been recognized at common law as entitled to sovereign status. They are accordingly entitled to no sovereign or diplomatic immunity in this country save where such immunity is granted by legislative instrument, and then only to the extent of such grant.[50]

According to Amerasinghe[51] and Higgins,[52] this misses the point: immunity is necessary to allow these organizations to function, and there is no difference between organizations of limited and unlimited membership in this respect. It would seem churlish for a state to agree to house an organization but deprive it of those attributes that would allow it to function as intended.[53] This was observed by the International Court in *Privileges and Immunities of the UN*.[54]

A further question is whether international organizations are entitled to immunity with respect to non-member states. Practice suggests that there is no customary rule in point.[55] A Malaysian court held that comity did not require it to acknowledge immunity granted to an organization of limited membership by the

---

[44] Higgins (1994) 90–4; Amerasinghe (2nd edn, 2005) 344–8; Sands & Klein (6th edn, 2009) 492–3; Ryngaert (2010) 7 *Int Org LR* 121, 123–32.

[45] Generally: *Iran–US Claims Tribunal v AS* (1985) 94 ILR 321; *Eckhardt v Eurocontrol (No 2)* (1984) 94 ILR 331.

[46] All examples given by the Reporter are of universal organizations: 1 *Restatement Third* §467(i). For the view that immunity will not be extended to limited membership organizations to which the US does not belong: *International Tin Council v Amalgamet Inc*, 524 NYS.2d 971 (Supp, 1988).

[47] *ZM v Permanent Delegation of the League of Arab States to the United Nations* (1993) 116 ILR 643.

[48] Sands & Klein (6th edn, 2009) 493.

[49] Higgins (1994) 91; Reinisch, *International Organizations before National Courts* (2000) 145–57; Amerasinghe (2nd edn, 2005) 347–8.

[50] *Standard Chartered Bank v International Tin Council* [1987] 1 WLR 641, 648.

[51] Amerasinghe (2nd edn, 2005) 347–8.

[52] Higgins (1994) 91.

[53] This may also extend to situations in which non-member states have consented to host state operations within their territory: Akande, in Evans (3rd edn, 2010) 252, 272–3.

[54] *Applicability of Article VI, Section 22 of the Convention on the Privileges and Immunities of the United Nations*, ICJ Reports 1989 p 177, 192–6.

[55] E.g. Sands & Klein (6th edn, 2009) 493.

UK.[56] A Swiss court held that it lacked jurisdiction over an employment dispute between an organization and one of its officials,[57] though this may reflect a *sui generis* exception as distinct from a general rule.[58]

It may be argued, however, that if the personality of international organizations stems from an objective assessment of their functions and non-parties are required to accept their separate identity, then this personality must be populated with the attributes necessary for the organization to carry out its mandate, including as necessary the immunity of the institution and its personnel.[59]

(B) PRIVILEGES AND IMMUNITIES ATTACHING TO THE ORGANIZATION

As noted, the source of privileges and immunities of most organizations is a general treaty provision; some international organizations (notably the UN) have concluded additional treaties articulating these immunities.[60] But if they do not, the general provision in the original agreement will need to be given content. In that case reference may be had to the functional basis of privileges and immunities, with the extension of a particular protection predicated on necessity. Organizations vary, so may their immunities. As experience with UN peacekeeping forces shows, relations with the host state in particular will depend a great deal on the specific function involved and all the circumstances. Decisions of national courts on the immunities of agents of international organizations do not as yet produce a coherent body of principles. Some decisions rely by analogy on diplomatic immunities; others take a more rigorously functional view.[61] But four broad immunities and

---

[56] *Bank Bumiputra Bhd v International Tin Council* (1987) 80 ILR 24. Also: *International Tin Council v Amalgamet Inc*, 524 NYS.2d 971 (Supp, 1988) (international organization entered into an arbitration clause; held to have impliedly waived immunity).

[57] *ZM v Permanent Delegation of the League of Arab States to the United Nations* (1993) 116 ILR 643.

[58] Higgins (1994) 92; Amerasinghe (2nd edn, 2005) 324–8. Also: *International Institute of Agriculture v Profili* (1930) 5 ILR 413; *Weidner v International Telecommunications Satellite Organization*, 382 A.2d 508 (DC, 1978).

[59] Sands & Klein (6th edn, 2009) 493; cf Reinisch (2000) 146.

[60] Alternatively, they may be incorporated by reference: e.g. WTO Agreement, Art VIII.4.

[61] E.g. *Clarsfield v Office Franco-Allemand pour la Jeunesse* (1968) 72 ILR 191; *International Patents Institute Employee* (1969) 70 ILR 418; *M v United Nations and Belgium* (1969) 69 ILR 139; *Porru v Food and Agriculture Organization* (1969) 71 ILR 240; *Re Pisani Balestra di Mottola* (1969) 71 ILR 565; *International Atomic Energy Agency Representative Immunity* (1971) 70 ILR 413; *Stahel v Bastid* (1971) 75 ILR 76; *European Space Operations Centre Official Immunity* (1973) 73 ILR 683; *Bari Institute v Jasbez* (1977) 77 ILR 602; *M v Cantonal Appeals Commission of Berne* (1977) 75 ILR 85; *X v Department of Justice & Police of Canton of Geneva* (1977) 75 ILR 90; *Weidner v International Telecommunications Satellites Organization*, 382 A.2d 508 (DC, 1978); *Broadbent v Organization of American States*, 628 F.2d 27 (DC Cir, 1980); *Tuck v Pan-American Health Organization*, 668 F.2d 547 (DC Cir, 1981); *Food and Agriculture Organization v INDPAI* (1982) 87 ILR 1; *Cristiani v Italian Latin-American Institute* (1985) 87 ILR 20; *Girod de l'Ain* (1986) 82 ILR 85; *African Reinsurance Corporation v Abate Fantaye* (1986) 86 ILR 655; *Mininni v Bari Institute* (1986) 87 ILR 28; *Sindicato UIL v Bari Institute* (1986) 87 ILR 37; *Economic Community of West African States v BCCI* (1993) 113 ILR 472; *Sossetti v Multinational Force and Observers* (1994) 128 ILR 640; *Scimet v African Development*

privileges are generally identified as attaching to—and subject to waiver by[62]—the organization.[63]

The first is immunity from jurisdiction, that is, from all forms of legal process of the forum state. It includes immunity from execution, principally in the sense of judgments or arbitral awards.[64] An expanded example may be seen in the General Agreement Article II, section 2,[65] which provides that:

the United Nations, its property and assets, wherever located and by whomsoever held, shall enjoy immunity from every form of legal process, except and in so far as in any particular case it has expressly waived its immunity.

The key rationale for this immunity is that otherwise member state courts may purport to rule on the legality of acts of the organization. Some jurisdictions have sought to limit the scope of this immunity by reference to acts done *iure gestionis* as distinct from *iure imperii*, by analogy with state immunity.[66] But practice is limited to a few states. However a trend may be developing whereby national courts are willing to deny immunity with respect for claims for denial of justice before administrative tribunals internal to the organization,[67] due to the circumstantial inconsistency of the immunity with other supervening principles of international law. This is notable in the case of the European Court of Human Rights. In *Waite and Kennedy v Germany*[68] and *Beer and Regan v Germany*[69] the Court held that Germany's maintenance of the immunity of the European Space Agency (ESA) was consistent with its obligations under ECHR Article 6(1) regarding the right to a fair trial.[70] The Court held, however, that maintenance of the immunity could not be reflexive, and that access to the German courts with respect to actions against international organizations could only be refused to the extent that the organization possessed an internal process of review that could protect adequately the Article 6(1) rights of any claimants, a requirement fulfilled by the ESA Appeals Board.[71]

Bank (1997) 128 ILR 582; *League of Arab States v I* (2001) 127 ILR 94; *African Development Bank* (2005) 138 ILR 498. Further: Ryngaert (2010) 7 *Int Org LR* 121.

[62] E.g. *Shearson Lehman Bros Inc v Maclaine Watson & Co Ltd (No 2)* [1988] 1 All ER 116 (inviolability of official archives waived by communication of documents by member states to third parties).

[63] Sands & Klein (6th edn, 2009) 493ff.

[64] Ibid, 499–500. On the distinction between immunity from jurisdiction and execution: Ryngaert (2010) 7 *Int Org LR* 121, 144–6.

[65] Further: Council of Europe Immunities Agreement, Art 3; ICSID Convention, Art 20; ICC Immunities Agreement, Art 6. A constituent instrument may also narrow the scope of the immunity: e.g. IBRD Articles, Art VII(3). Also: Sands & Klein (6th edn, 2009) 495.

[66] E.g. the practice of the Italian courts: *Branno v Ministry of War* (1954) 22 ILR 756; *Indpai v Food and Agriculture Organization* (1982) 87 ILR 5. For the US approach: Oparil (1991) 24 *Vand JTL* 689.

[67] Reinisch (1999) 93 *AJIL* 933; Reinisch (2008) 7 *Chin JIL* 285; Sands & Klein (6th edn, 2009) 497–9.

[68] (1999) 118 ILR 121.

[69] [1999] ECtHR 28934/95.

[70] 4 November 1950, 213 UNTS 222.

[71] (1999) 118 ILR 121, 136 ('For the Court, a material factor in determining whether granting ESA immunity from German jurisdiction is permissible is whether the applicants had available to them a reasonable alternative means to protect their rights under the Convention').

The second common protection concerns the inviolability of the organization's premises and archives.[72] In practice, this mirrors the protection granted to diplomatic missions; the authorities may not enter the premises of the organization, even where effecting an arrest or serving a writ, without the consent of the administrative head of the organization. On rare occasions this protection has been breached: for example, schools administered by the United Nations Relief and Works Agency in the Gaza Strip were damaged severely through the actions of the Israeli Defence Force during 2009 operations against Hamas.[73]

The third protection afforded to international organizations pertains to currency and other fiscal matters.[74] Many international organizations administer considerable funds, often contributed by their membership, the mobility of which is crucial to their operation. General Convention Article II, section 5 provides:

Without being restricted by financial controls, regulations or moratoria of any kind,

(a) the United Nations may hold funds, gold or currency of any kind and operate accounts in any currency;

(b) the United Nations shall be free to transfer its funds, gold or currency from one country to another or within any country and to convert any currency held by it into any other currency.[75]

This protects the United Nations from municipal exchange control regimes. It is supplemented by Article II, section 7, which protects it from direct taxation and customs duties, except municipal taxes which are merely a charge for the use of public utilities.[76]

The fourth functional protection extended to international organizations is freedom of communication.[77] This is modelled on the similar freedom of diplomatic missions, and includes freedom from censorship, the right to use codes and couriers, the privilege of the diplomatic bag and its attendant inviolability, and, in the territory of each state, treatment of official communications in a manner as favourable as that accorded to diplomatic missions. The exemplar is General Convention Article III, sections 9 and 10.[78]

---

[72] Amerasinghe (2nd edn, 2005) 330–5; Sands & Klein (6th edn, 2009) 500–2. Also: e.g. Council of Europe Immunities Agreement, Arts 4–5; ICSID Convention, Art 23(1); ICC Immunities Agreement, Arts 4, 7.

[73] UN Office for the Coordination of Humanitarian Affairs, 'Field Update on Gaza from the Humanitarian Coordinator. 30 January–2 February 2009', available at www.ochaopt.org/documents/ocha_opt_gaza_humanitarian_situation_report_2009_02_02_english.pdf.

[74] Amerasinghe (2nd edn, 2005) 328–30; Sands & Klein (6th edn, 2009) 502–3.

[75] Further: Council of Europe Immunities Agreement, Arts 6, 7; ICSID Convention, Art 24; ICC Immunities Agreement, Arts 6, 8–10.

[76] For the regime of trust funds held by organizations: Bantekas (2010) 81 BY 224.

[77] Amerasinghe (2nd edn, 2005) 335–7; Sands & Klein (6th edn, 2009) 503.

[78] Also: e.g. Council of Europe Immunity Agreement, Art 8; ICC Immunity Agreement, Art 11.

(c) PRIVILEGES AND IMMUNITIES ATTACHING TO PERSONNEL

The privileges and immunities of personnel are again functional: international organizations require people to make decisions and carry them out.[79]

(i) Immunity attaching to organization officials

There is no general agreement on the scope of immunity in the absence of treaty. The minimum principle appears to be that officials of international organizations are immune from local jurisdiction and execution in respect of all official acts. Thus General Convention Article VII, section 18 provides:

Officials of the United Nations shall:

(a) be immune from legal process in respect of words spoken or written and all acts performed by them in their official capacity;

(b) be exempt from taxation on the salaries and emoluments paid to them by the United Nations;

(c) be immune from national service obligations;

(d) be immune, together with their spouses and relatives dependent on them, from immigration restrictions and alien registration;

(e) be accorded the same privileges in respect of exchange facilities as are accorded to the officials of comparable ranks forming part of diplomatic missions to the Government concerned;

(f) be given, together with their spouses and relatives dependent on them, the same repatriation facilities in time of international crisis as diplomatic envoys;

(g) have the right to import free of duty their furniture and effects at the time of first taking up their post in the country in question.

Whilst such provisions ordinarily extend such immunity to officials of the organization only, some institutions cast the net wider. The ICC Immunities Agreement and the agreement between the UN and Sierra Leone regarding the Special Court for Sierra Leone[80] both grant immunity to counsel and persons otherwise assisting,[81] witnesses[82] and victims.[83] The ICSID Convention provides for the immunity of parties, agents, counsel, advocates, witnesses, and experts (Articles 21 and 22).

---

[79] Amerasinghe (2nd edn, 2005) 337–40; Sands & Klein (6th edn, 2009) 508–16.

[80] Agreement between the United Nations and the Government of Sierra Leone on the Establishment of a Special Court for Sierra Leone, 16 January 2002, appended to Report of the Secretary-General on the Establishment of a Special Court for Sierra Leone, S/2000/915, 4 October 2000 (SCSL Agreement).

[81] ICC Immunities Agreement, Art 18; SCSL Agreement, Art 14.

[82] ICC Immunities Agreement, Art 19; SCSL Agreement, Art 15.

[83] ICC Immunities Agreement; Art 20; SCSL Agreement, Art 15 (to the extent that victims can be considered witnesses).

Difficulties can arise in determining whether an individual has committed an act in an official capacity.[84] The International Court has held that any determination of an official act made by the Secretary-General is binding,[85] a position not adopted with alacrity by states.[86]

Treaties may also require that certain officials be given the equivalent of full diplomatic immunity. Both the General Convention (Article V, section 19) and the Council of Europe Immunity Agreement (Article 16) require that such protection be extended to the Secretary-General and Assistant Secretaries-General, their spouses and minor children. The immunity given to judges of the International Court[87] and other holders of judicial or prosecutorial offices[88] is also equated to diplomatic privileges.

(ii) Immunity attaching to state representatives

The agreements that provide immunity to the officials of international organizations usually extend protection to state representatives to the organization.[89] General Convention Article IV, section 11 grants representatives to the United Nations an even broader set of immunities than those ordinarily granted to officials of the Organization. Indeed state representative immunity has much more in common with full diplomatic immunity[90] than the protections afforded to officials of the organization,[91] though the two do not completely align, notably in the frequent restriction that a state representative is only granted immunity from legal process with respect to acts done in an official capacity.[92]

State representatives to international organizations are not ordinarily accredited to the host state but to the organization itself.[93] A notable exception to this practice is contained within UN Headquarters Agreement, Article IX, section 25, which requires that apart from permanent representatives and certain other high-ranking officials, the staff of the mission must be agreed between the sending state, the US and the Secretary-General.

---

[84]   Sands & Klein (6th edn, 2009) 508.

[85]   *Difference Relating to Immunity from Legal Process of a Special Rapporteur of the Commission of Human Rights*, ICJ Reports 1999 p 62, 87.

[86]   E.g. *Westchester County v Ranollo*, 67 NYS.2d 31 (City Ct Ranollo, 1946) (State Department certificate required). Further: Preuss (1947) 41 *AJIL* 555. Cf *Curran v City of New York*, 77 NYS.2d 206 (Sup Ct, 1947). Some acts may never be considered official: e.g. espionage: *US v Coplon and Gubitchev*, 88 F.Supp 915 (SDNY, 1950).

[87]   ICJ Statute, Art 19.

[88]   E.g. ICC Immunities Agreement, Art 15. Further: *Zoernsch v Waldock* [1964] 2 All ER 256.

[89]   Sands & Klein (6th edn, 2009) 504–7.

[90]   Cf UN Headquarters Agreement, Art V, s15 granting full diplomatic immunity to state representatives attending the UN in the US.

[91]   Further: Council of Europe Immunities Agreement, Arts 9–10 (representatives to the Committee of Ministers) 13–15 (representatives to the Consultative Assembly); ICC Immunities Agreement, Arts 13–14 (representatives to the Assembly of States and ICC subsidiary organs).

[92]   E.g. ICC Immunities Agreement, Art 13(1)(b); General Convention , Art III, s11. Also: UN Immunities Agreement, Art IV, s9(a).

[93]   Amerasinghe (2nd edn, 2005) 338–9.

The question of privileges and immunities of state representatives is addressed by the Vienna Convention on the Representation of States in their Relations with International Organizations of a Universal Character,[94] adopted in 1975 in face of opposition from the major host states. It shows no sign of entering into force, and is an example of the futility of majoritarian processes in matters where a balance between the majority (sending states) and a controlling minority (host states) is essential.[95]

4. PERFORMANCE OF ACTS IN THE LAW

The analogue for the exercise of legal functions in international relations is the state, in spite of the obvious analogical dangers. The most viable type of organization will have legal powers similar to those normally associated with statehood. However, the individuality of each organization must be emphasized: in the first place the extent of legal capacity will be found in the constituent treaty of the organization.

(A) TREATY-MAKING POWER[96]

Although the capacity of international organizations to enter into treaties was originally doubted,[97] it is now accepted.[98] The Vienna Convention on the Law of Treaties between States and International Organizations or between International Organizations was adopted on 21 March 1986;[99] it is modelled, perhaps too closely, on the 1969 Vienna Convention on the Law of Treaties (VCLT).[100] It is open for accession 'by any organization which has the capacity to conclude treaties' (Article 84). It is not yet in force but acts as a legal and practical guide.

---

[94] 14 March 1975, A/CONF.67/16.

[95] Fennessy (1976) 70 *AJIL* 62.

[96] Dupuy (1960) 100 Hague *Recueil* 461, 489ff; Karunatilleke (1971) 75 *RGDIP* 12; Chiu, *The Capacity of International Organizations to Conclude Treaties* (1966); Zemanek (ed), *Agreements of International Organizations and the Vienna Convention on the Law of Treaties* (1971). Also: Draft Articles on Treaties Concluded between States and International Organizations or between International Organizations, ILC *Ybk* 1982/II(2), 17 (Reuter, Special Rapporteur). Further: Brölmann, *The Institutional Veil in Public International Law* (2007); Corten & Klein (eds), *Les Conventions de Vienne sur le Droit des Traités* (2006) 183–93.

[97] E.g. *South West Africa (Ethiopia v South Africa; Liberia v South Africa)*, Preliminary Objections, ICJ Reports 1962 p 319, 495–503 (Judges Fitzmaurice & Spender) (treaty-making capacity of League of Nations). Cf the majority, which appears to have tacitly accepted the capacity of the League to enter into treaties at 330–2.

[98] *Reparations for Injuries*, ICJ Reports 1949 p 174, 178–9. Also: Amerasinghe (2nd edn, 2005) 101–3; Sands & Klein (6th edn, 2009) 483.

[99] (1986) 25 ILM 543. Further: Gaja (1987) 58 *BY* 253.

[100] 22 May 1969, 1155 UNTS 331.

The existence of legal personality does not necessarily imply power to make treaties, though in practice organizations readily assume a treaty-making power. Additionally, the constituent instrument may limit the treaty-making powers of the organization to certain organs.[101] The competences of the organization as a whole provide a further limitation.[102] Where an agreement is entered into, however, the organization as a whole will be bound,[103] even, potentially, where the contracting organ is acting *ultra vires*.[104] On the other hand while the organization is bound by its organs, member states are not as such bound due to their separate legal personality.[105]

Constituent instruments do not normally confer a general treaty-making power, but this may be (somewhat problematically) established via the interpretation of the instrument as a whole or the doctrine of implied powers.[106] The UN Charter authorizes the conclusion of trusteeship agreements (Chapter 12), relationship agreements with the specialized agencies (Articles 57, 63), specialized agreements permitting national armed forces to be placed at the disposal of the Security Council (Article 43) and conventions concerning privileges and immunities (Article 105(3)). But it has concluded headquarters agreements and agreements on co-operation with other organizations, without express authorization. Thus a specific constrained power to enter into treaties is used to infer legal personality, which is in turn used to infer a general treating-making capacity.[107]

(B) CAPACITY TO ESPOUSE INTERNATIONAL CLAIMS

In *Reparation for Injuries*, the International Court held unanimously that the United Nations was a legal person with capacity to bring claims against both member and non-member states for direct injuries to the Organization.[108] The power to bring such claims was apparently regarded as concomitant with legal personality. However, the Court also expressed its conclusion in terms of implied powers and effectiveness.[109] Similar reasoning may apply to other organizations. The capacity to espouse claims thus depends (a) on the existence of legal personality, and (b) on the interpretation of the constituent instrument in the light of the functions of the particular organization.[110] In contrast, the existence of immunities is not conditioned on the separate legal personality of the entity concerned.

---

[101] E.g. Art 63 of the Charter, conferring power to conclude relationship agreements with specialized agencies on ECOSOC.

[102] E.g. Opinion 2/94, *Accession by the Community to the European Convention for the Protection of Human Rights and Fundamental Freedoms* [1996] ECR I-1759.

[103] Sands & Klein (6th edn, 2009) 486.

[104] Art 46(2) of the 1986 Convention.

[105] But on mixed agreements of the EU: Hillion & Kautrakos (eds), *Mixed Agreements Revisited* (2010).

[106] Amerasinghe (2nd edn, 2005) 102; Sands & Klein (6th edn, 2009) 483. Some early commentators were of the opinion that such powers needed to be conferred expressly: e.g. Kelsen, *Law of the United Nations* (1950) 330; Lukashuk (1960) *Soviet YIL* 144.

[107] Sands & Klein (6th edn, 2009) 484.

[108] ICJ Reports 1949 p 174, 184–5, 187.

[109] Ibid, 180. Cf Schermers & Blokkers (4th edn, 2004) 1183–4.

[110] Sørensen (1960) 101 Hague *Recueil* 1, 139, relates the capacity directly to legal personality.

As to functional protection of agents, the Court in *Reparation for Injuries* used similar reasoning to justify its opinion that the UN could espouse claims for injury to its agents.[111] On this point the Court was not unanimous,[112] and certainly this capacity cannot readily be invoked by other organizations, especially when their functions do not include peacekeeping.[113] The principle is now largely (but not entirely) uncontroversial.[114] The situation remains particularly delicate when a claim is made on behalf of an agent who is a national of the respondent state.[115] The Court addressed this difficulty, noting that:

The action of the Organization is in fact based not upon the nationality of the victim but his status as an agent of the Organization. Therefore it does not matter whether or not the State to which the claim is addressed regards him as its own national, because the question of nationality is not pertinent to the admissibility of the claim.[116]

A problem which remains to be solved is the determination of priorities between the state's right of diplomatic protection and the organization's right of functional protection.[117] Again by analogy with states, it may be that the right to espouse is concurrent but subject to a rule against double recovery.

(C) STANDING BEFORE INTERNATIONAL TRIBUNALS

When an organization has legal personality it has in principle *locus standi* before international courts and tribunals. But everything depends on the statute governing the adjudicatory body or the *compromis* concerned, and in many cases international organizations have no such access.[118] Notably while certain organizations have access to the International Court through its advisory jurisdiction, the Statute still limits standing to states (Article 34).[119] But international organizations may have standing before international tribunals where the jurisdiction of the tribunal may be activated through the treaty-making or contracting capacity of the organization.[120]

---

[111] ICJ Reports 1949 p 174, 181–4. Further: El-Erian, ILC *Ybk* 1963/II, 159, 181–3; Hardy (1961) 37 *BY* 516; Hardy, ILC *Ybk* 1967/II, 218–19; Carabot & Ubeda-Saillard, in Crawford, Pellet & Olleson (eds), *The Law of International Responsibility* (2010) 1073.

[112] ICJ Reports 1949 p 174, 189 (Judge Winiarski, diss), 196 (Judge Hackworth, diss), 205 (Judge Badawi, diss), 217 (Judge Krylov, diss).

[113] E.g. Pescatore (1961) 103 Hague *Recueil* 1, 219–21.

[114] Carabot & Ubeda-Saillard (2010) 1073, 1083.

[115] E.g. the *Alicja Wesolowska* case, where a Polish national in the employ of the UN was arrested and imprisoned by Polish authorities in 1979. The UN's claim and attempts to obtain a right of visit failed: ibid, 1082–3. Further: Meron (1980) 167 Hague *Recueil* 285, 336.

[116] ICJ Reports 1949 p 174, 186.

[117] Ibid, 185–6; Bowett, *United Nations Forces* (1964) 151, 242–8; Carabot & Ubeda-Saillard (2010) 1073, 1081–2.

[118] Schermers & Blokker (4th edn, 2003) 1185.

[119] Though Art 34(3) of the Statute obliges the Court to update international organizations on cases concerning their constituent instruments. Also: Jenks, *The Prospects of International Adjudication* (1964) 185–224; Schermers & Blokker (4th edn, 2003) 1185–6.

[120] E.g. UNESCO-France, *Question of the tax regime governing pensions paid to retired UNESCO officials residing in France* (2003) 25 RIAA 231.

(D) CAPACITY TO OWN PROPERTY

Another element of legal personality is the capacity for an international organization to own property under the municipal law of a state. This is a simple matter of functional necessity.[121] Conversely ownership of property may act as an indication of legal personality.[122] Any property so owned falls under the aegis of the organization's privileges and immunities.

(E) RESPONSIBILITY[123]

If an organization has a legal personality distinct from that of the member states, and performs functions which in the hands of states may give rise to responsibility, then it is in principle reasonable to impute responsibility to that organization.[124] Such claims are ordinarily predicated on the exhaustion of 'local remedies', that is, before any competent organ of the organization.[125] This follows generally from the Court's reasoning in *Reparation for Injuries*. The most notable development in the law of responsibility for international organizations is its codification in the ILC's Draft Articles of 2011, a project which owes much to the Commission's previous work on state responsibility. Under Draft Article 3, every internationally wrongful act by an organization entails its international responsibility (see also Draft Article 4). Similar rules have also been adopted with respect to attribution (Draft Articles 6 to 9), breach of international obligations (Draft Articles 10 to 13), circumstances precluding wrongfulness (Draft Articles 20 to 27), the content of international responsibility (Draft Articles 28 to 42) and its implementation (Draft Articles 41 to 57).

Moreover, separate legal personality presumptively prevents liability from attaching to an organization's members, as demonstrated in the *International Tin Council* cases. This litigation commenced as a consequence of the inability of the ITC to meet its liabilities; the issues of public international law (e.g. the question of the residual responsibility of the member states) were not faced head on by the English courts and the decisions turned to an extent on the construction of the International Tin Council (Immunities and Privileges) Order in relation to matters essentially of English law.[126]

---

[121] Akande, in Evans (3rd edn, 2010) 252, 259–60.

[122] Reinisch (2000) 44–5.

[123] Eagleton (1950) 76 Hague *Recueil* 318; Ginther, *Die völkerrechtliche Verantwortlichkeit internationaler Organisationen gegenüber Drittstaaten* (1969) 1336–40; Hirsch, *The Responsibility of International Organizations toward Third Parties* (1995); Klein, *La Responsabilité des organisations internationales dans les ordres juridiques internes et en droit des gens* (1998); Sands & Klein (6th edn, 2009) 516–30; Klein, in Crawford, Pellet & Olleson (2010) 297. Cf further the Report of Higgins (1995) 66 *Ann de l'Inst* 249; and the Resolution adopted in 1995 (1995) 66 *Ann de l'Inst* 445; ILA, Report of the 71st Conference (2004) 164–241.

[124] Schermers & Blokkers (4th edn, 2004) 1184–5.

[125] E.g. Convention on International Liability for Damage Caused by Space Objects, 29 March 1972, 961 UNTS 187, Art XXII(3).

[126] *International Tin Council Appeals* [1988] 3 All ER 257.

In the Court of Appeal in the 'direct actions' by creditors against the member states Kerr LJ concluded:

In sum, I cannot find any basis for concluding that it has been shown that there is any rule of international law, binding upon the member states of the ITC, whereby they can be held liable, let alone jointly and severally, in any national court to the creditors of the ITC for the debts of the ITC resulting from contracts concluded by the ITC in its own name.[127]

The House of Lords agreed with this view.[128]

In adopting the Draft Articles, the ILC confirmed that member states cannot generally be regarded as responsible for the internationally wrongful acts of the organization. However, it would be contrary to good sense if one or a few states could avoid responsibility by creating an international organization to do something they could not lawfully do themselves.[129] But regard must be had to each set of circumstances. In relation to the use of forces under UN authority in peacekeeping operations, the general practice is that financial responsibility is determined by agreements between contributing governments and the UN,[130] and between the latter and the host state. Draft Article 7 here contributes, providing that:

The conduct of an organ of a State or an organ or agent of an international organization that is placed at the disposal of another international organization shall be considered under international law an act of the latter organization if the organization exercises effective control over that conduct.

Additionally, provision is made at length in Part V for the joint responsibility of states and organizations with respect to internationally wrongful acts. States may be held responsible for aiding and abetting wrongful acts by organizations (Draft Article 58), as well as the exercise of direction or control (Draft Article 59), coercion (Draft Article 60), and the acceptance of responsibility (Draft Article 62). Of special note is Draft Article 61, which provides that a state member may incur international responsibility if it causes an organization to commit an act that would have breached an international obligation if committed by the state, irrespective of whether the organization by so doing commits a breach.

In practice the United Nations has accepted responsibility for the acts of its agents.[131] However, in the case of more specialized organizations with a smaller membership, it may be necessary to fall back on the collective responsibility of members. There is a strong presumption against a delegation of responsibility by a state to an organization

---

[127] Ibid, 307. Ralph Gibson LJ, expressed a similar view: ibid, 341–56. But Nourse LJ proposed a residual liability of the member states for debts not discharged by the ITC itself: ibid, 326–34.

[128] [1989] 3 WLR 969, 983–4 (Lord Templeman); 1010–12 (Lord Oliver). Also: Marston (1991) 40 *ICLQ* 403; Higgins, 2 *Themes and Theories* (2009) 920; Akande, in Evans (3rd edn, 2010) 252, 268–9.

[129] *Waite and Kennedy v Germany* (1999) 118 ILR 121, 135. Also: Draft Article 61 of the Draft Articles on the Responsibility of International Organizations. Further: Brownlie, in Ragazzi (ed), *Essays in Memory of Oscar Schachter* (2005) 355; Yee, ibid, 435.

[130] For the UN's comments on the draft articles: A/CN.4/637/Add, 17 February 2011, 30.

[131] UN *Ybk* 1965, 138; ILC *Ybk* 1967/II, 216–20.

arising simply from membership. But the organization may occasionally be conceived of as creating risks and incurring liabilities in the course of its activities and as a vehicle for the distribution of costs and risks. This can be seen from Article XXII(3) of the Convention on International Liability for Damage Caused by Space Objects, which, subject to certain preliminary conditions, provides that '[i]f an international inter-governmental organization is liable for damage by virtue of the provisions of this Convention, that organization and those of its members which are States Parties to this Convention shall be jointly and severally liable'.[132]

5. INTERPRETATION OF THE CONSTITUENT INSTRUMENT[133]

Unlike states, international organizations do not possess general competence: they may only exercise those powers expressly or impliedly bestowed upon them. The fundamental rule of the law of international organizations is the principle of attributed powers or speciality (*compétences d'attribution*). This was stated by the International Court in the *Nuclear Weapons* opinion:

[I]jnternational organizations…do not, unlike States, possess a general competence. International organizations are governed by the 'principle of speciality', that is to say, they are invested by the States which create them with powers, the limits of which are a function of the common interests whose promotion those States entrust to them.[134]

(A) IDENTITY OF THE INTERPRETER[135]

(i) Self-interpretation within international organizations

Within international organizations, each organ must interpret its own jurisdiction, irrespective of whether a power is expressly conferred.[136] The International Court

---

[132] 29 March 1972, 961 UNTS 187.

[133] Hexner (1959) 53 *AJIL* 341; Lauterpacht, *Development* (1958) 267–81; Amerasinghe (1994) 65 *BY* 175; Schermers & Blokker (4th edn, 2003) 153–83; Alvarez (2005) 65–108; Amerasinghe (2nd edn, 2005) ch 2; Smith & Klein (6th edn, 2009) 448–61; Alvarez (2005) ch 2; Blokker, 'International Organizations or Institutions, Implied Powers' (2009) *MPEPIL*.

[134] *Legality of the Use by a State of Nuclear Weapons in Armed Conflict*, ICJ Reports 1996 p 66, 78. Also: *Competence of the ILO to Regulate Incidentally the Personal Work of the Employer* (1926) PCIJ Ser B No 13, 18; *European Commission of the Danube* (1927) PCIJ Ser B No 14, 64; *Reparation for Injuries*, ICJ Reports 1949 p 174, 182–3; *Effect of Awards of Compensation Made by the United Nations Administrative Tribunal*, ICJ Reports 1954 p 47, 57.

[135] For a useful summary of a wide range of organizations and their approach to interpretation: Sands & Klein (6th edn, 2009) 451–4.

[136] Sands & Klein (6th edn, 2009) 451. Further: Sohn, in Schachter & Joyner (eds), *United Nations Legal Order* (1995) 169.

accepted this reality in *Certain Expenses*, holding that, in the absence of further direction within the Charter, each constituent organ of the United Nations was entitled to
determine its jurisdiction in the first instance. Moreover such determinations, when
accompanied by an assertion of propriety, are presumptively *intra vires*.[137] Full advantage of this has been taken by the General Assembly, which has determined its own
jurisdiction on multiple occasions.[138] The Security Council has also been willing to
engage in such introspection, notably when considering the meaning of 'threat to the
peace' under Article 39 of the Charter.

(ii) Judicial and other third-party interpretation

In the event of dispute as to the interpretation of an organization's constituent instrument, the instrument itself may provide for resolution through a judicial organ. In
the context of the UN, this is the International Court which, through its advisory
jurisdiction, is able to opine on the capacity of the organs[139] and specialized agencies
of the Organization.[140] But advisory opinions are not—absent special agreement[141]—
binding on the organization concerned, although in practice implementation is
normal.

In *Certain Expenses,* the Court faced an issue on which members of the United
Nations were divided, the constitutional basis for the use of armed forces in the United
Nations Emergency Force (UNEF) and the United Nations Mission in the Congo
(ONUC). The Court concluded that 'when the Organization takes action which war-
rants the assertion that it was appropriate for the fulfilment of one of the stated pur-
poses of the United Nations, the presumption is that such action is not *ultra vires*

---

[137] *Certain Expenses of the United Nations (Article 17, paragraph 2, of the Charter)*, ICJ Reports 1962 p
151, 168 ('when the Organization takes action which warrants the assertion that it was appropriate for the
fulfilment of one of the stated purposes of the United Nations, the presumption is that such action is not
ultra vires the Organization').

[138] Though sometimes after considering a legal opinion provided by the Office of the Legal Counsel:
Amerasinghe (2nd edn, 2005) 26.

[139] UN Charter, Art 96(1) (General Assembly, Security Council), (2) (other authorized organs and specialized agencies). On the advisory jurisdiction: chapter 32.

[140] A specialized agency can only request advisory opinions if (a) it is so provided in its constitution, or
(b) it is the subject of separate agreement with the UN: e.g. WHO Constitution, Art 76; Convention on the
International Maritime Organization, 6 March 1948, 289 UNTS 3, Art 66. Further: (c) a specialized agency
'is not empowered to seek an interpretation of its Constitution in relation to matters outside the scope of its
functions': *Nuclear Weapons in Armed Conflict*, ICJ Reports 1996 p 66, 82. Cf Akande (1998) 9 *EJIL* 437, 452–7
(arguing that an agency is always entitled to seek an interpretation of its constituent instrument). In fact of
26 requests for an advisory opinion since 1945, only five were made by specialized agencies: *Judgments of the
Administrative Tribunal of the ILO upon Complaints made against UNESCO*, ICJ Reports 1956 p 77 (UNESCO);
Constitution of the Maritime Safety Committee of the Inter-Governmental Maritime Consultative Organization,
ICJ Reports 1960 p 150 (IMO); *Interpretation of the Agreement of 25 March 1951 between the WHO and Egypt*,
ICJ Reports 1980 p 73 (WHO); *Nuclear Weapons in Armed Conflict*, ICJ Reports 66 (WHO); *Judgment No 2867
of the Administrative Tribunal of the International Labour Organization upon a Complaint Filed against the
International Fund for Agricultural Development* (IFAD), Advisory Opinion of 1 February 2012.

[141] E.g. General Convention, Art VIII, s30.

the Organization'.[142] The majority opinion held that the operations were in pursuance of the stated purposes and that the corresponding expenses were 'expenses of the Organization' under Article 17(2). The Opinion has been cogently criticized on the ground that it permits non-obligatory recommendations to result in binding financial obligations, giving the General Assembly a supranational budgetary power denied to more integrated communities.[143] To speak of 'institutional effectiveness' or 'implied powers' is to beg the question. More generally, this type of judicial control does not reconcile major divisions between member states: indeed, the opinion could have had a disastrous outcome had the issue of arrears attributable to peacekeeping not been settled by negotiation.[144]

Aside from judicial options for the interpretation of a constituent instrument, other *sui generis* options may also exist.[145] A constitution may call for the convening of an arbitral tribunal to hear disputes.[146] Alternatively, an arbitral tribunal established under an agreement between an organization and another party may have to interpret the organization's constituent instrument.[147] Finally, an international tribunal may interpret an organization's constituent instrument incidentally to determining its own jurisdiction. For example in *Tadić*, the International Criminal Tribunal for the Former Yugoslavia held that the Security Council had the capacity to establish an international criminal tribunal under Article 41 of the Charter.[148]

(B) PRINCIPLES OF INTERPRETATION[149]

Whilst acknowledging that 'the constituent instruments of international organizations are multilateral treaties, to which the well-established rules of treaty interpretation apply', the Court has sought to distinguish 'certain special characteristics':

[T]he constituent instruments of international organizations are also treaties of a particular type; their object is to create new subjects of law endowed with a certain autonomy, to which the parties entrust the task of realizing common goals. Such treaties can raise specific problems of interpretation owing, *inter alia*, to their character which is conventional and at the same time institutional; the very nature of the organization created, the objectives

---

[142] ICJ Reports 1962 p 151, 168; 204, 208 (Judge Fitzmaurice); 223 (Judge Morelli); 298 (Judge Bustamante, diss).

[143] Gross (1963) 16 *Int Org* 1; Simmonds (1964) 13 *ICLQ* 854; Verzijl (1963) 10 *NILR* 1.

[144] The US invoked Art 19 of the Charter in consequence of the Opinion and for a whole session no voting took place in the General Assembly: (1965) 4 ILM 1000.

[145] Notably the international financial organizations may refer such questions to the Executive Board, Board of Directors, Board of Governors, etc: e.g. IBRD Articles, Art IX(a); Articles of Agreement of the International Monetary Fund, 22 July 1944, 2 UNTS 35, Art XXIX(a) (IMF Articles); Agreement Establishing the Asian Development Bank, 4 December 1965, 571 UNTS 123, Art 59.

[146] E.g. Constitution of the Universal Postal Union, 10 July 1964, 611 UNTS 7, Art 32. The UPU has not been authorized by the GA to seek an interpretation of its constitution: Sands & Klein (6th edn, 2009) 453.

[147] E.g. *Westland Helicopters v Arab Organization for Industrialization & Others* (1989) 80 ILR 595.

[148] *Prosecutor v Tadić (Jurisdiction)* (1995) 105 ILR 419 (Appeals Chamber).

[149] Schermers & Blokker (4th edn, 2003) 840–6; Amerasinghe (2nd edn, 2005) 33–61; Sands & Klein (6th edn, 2009) 454–6; Akande, in Evans (3rd edn, 2010) 252, 262–4.

which have been assigned to it by its founders, the imperatives associated with the effective performance of its functions, *as well as its own practice*, are all elements which may deserve special attention when the time comes to interpret these constituent treaties.[150]

Thus, when the issue of interpretation relates to an organization's constitution, a flexible and even teleological approach may be evident. However, this does not justify the outright abandonment of the unitary process of interpretation outlined in VCLT Article 31(1), as distinct from the reorganization of priorities within it.

In *Reparation for Injuries* the Court observed that 'the rights and duties of an entity such as the Organization must depend upon its purpose and functions as specified or implied in its constituent documents and developed in practice'.[151] Interpretation is to be accomplished with reference to what will enable the organization to achieve its goals effectively.[152] Thus the Court has held that a capacity to establish a tribunal to do justice between the Organization and staff members, absent an express provision, 'arises by necessary intendment out of the Charter'.[153]

(i) Subsequent practice within the organization

As indicated in the *Nuclear Weapons in Armed Conflict* advisory opinion, 'the imperatives associated with the effective performance of its functions, *as well as its own practice*, are all elements which may deserve special attention when the time comes to interpret...constituent treaties'.[154] The Court thus identified the canon of interpretation in VCLT Article 31(3)(b) ('any subsequent practice in the application of the treaty which establishes the agreement of the parties regarding its interpretation') as particularly pertinent. Article 31(3)(b), is not, however, a perfect analogue, referring impliedly as it does to the practice of states parties to the treaty rather than that of the organization itself.[155]

When interpreting the text of a constituent instrument, regard is to be had to the fact that '[t]he practice of the organization may have altered the application of the text without affecting its actual wording'.[156] In *Namibia*, the Court held, in light of established Security Council practice concerning the use of the term 'concurring vote' in Article 27(3) of the Charter, that abstention on the part of a permanent member amounted to a concurrence and did not involve the exercise of a veto.[157] The words were barely capable of sustaining that interpretation, but the supporting practice was of lengthy duration and universal in its scope.

---

[150] *Nuclear Weapons in Armed Conflict*, ICJ Reports 1996 p 66, 74–5 (emphasis added). Also: *Certain Expenses*, ICJ Reports 1962 p 151, 157.

[151] ICJ Reports 1949 p 174, 180.

[152] Akande, in Evans (3rd edn, 2010) 252, 263.

[153] *Effect of Awards*, ICJ Reports 1954 p 47, 56–7. Also: E Lauterpacht (1976) 52 Hague *Recueil* 377, 420.

[154] ICJ Reports 1996 p 66, 75.

[155] Schermers & Blokker (4th edn, 2003) 842.

[156] Ibid, 841.

[157] *Legal Consequences for States of the Continued Presence of South Africa in Namibia (South West Africa) notwithstanding Security Council Resolution 276 (1970)*, ICJ Reports 1971 p 16, 22.

(ii) Implied powers

This raises the difficult issue of implied powers of international organizations. As was stated in *Reparation for Injuries*:

Under international law, an Organization must be deemed to have those powers which, though not expressly provided in the Charter, are conferred upon it by necessary implication as being essential to the performance of its duties.[158]

The underlying idea is that an international organization is expected to evolve and adapt to changes on the international plane.

Obviously the organization's power of appreciation is wide, but it is not unlimited. Thus in *Nuclear Weapons in Armed Conflict* the Court denied the World Health Organization (WHO) the capacity to address the legality of the use of nuclear weapons:

In the opinion of the Court, to ascribe to the WHO the competence to address the legality of the use of nuclear weapons—even in view of their health and environmental effects—would be tantamount to disregarding the principle of speciality; for such competence could not be deemed a necessary implication of the Constitution of the Organization in the light of the purposes assigned to it by its member States.[159]

The need for balance has led Blokker to identify four limitations on the existence and scope of implied powers.[160] First, the implied power in question must be essential or indispensable to the organization. Secondly, it must not contradict the express provisions of the constituent instrument. Thirdly, it must not violate fundamental rules and principles of international law. Fourthly, it must not change the distribution of power between organs of the organization. Testing the boundaries of interpretive power with respect to constituent instruments may lead to significant disagreements between members.[161]

6. RELATIONS OF INTERNATIONAL ORGANIZATIONS

(A) RELATIONS WITH MEMBERS

A central aspect of any international organization is the relationship between the institution and its membership. International organizations are normally composed

---

[158] ICJ Reports 1949 p 174, 182. A substantial contribution has also been made by the European Court of Justice: Blokker, 'International Organizations or Institutions, Implied Powers' (2009) *MPEPIL*, §C. E.g. Opinion 1/76, *Draft Agreement Establishing a European Laying-up Fund for Inland Waterway Vessels* [1977] ECR 741; Opinion 2/91, *Convention No 170 of the International Labour Organization concerning Safety in the Use of Chemicals at Work* [1993] ECR I-1061; Opinion 1/94, *Competence of the Community to Conclude International Agreements concerning Services and the Protection of Intellectual Property—Article 228(6) of the EC Treaty* [1994] ECR I-5267. Further: Dashwood (1996) 21 *ELR* 113.

[159] ICJ Reports 1993 p 66, 79. For comment: E Lauterpacht, in Boisson de Chazournes & Sands (eds), *International Law, the International Court of Justice and Nuclear Weapons* (1999) 92; Bothe, ibid, 103; Leary, ibid, 112.

[160] Blokker, 'International Organizations or Institutions, Implied Powers' (2009) *MPEPIL*, §D.

[161] E.g., GA Res 377(V), 3 November 1950. Further: Binder, 'Uniting for Peace Resolution (1950)' (2006) *MPEPIL*.

of states, but a number of organizations have operated an effectively functional concept of membership compatible with their special purposes. Thus the Universal Postal Union is a union of postal administrations, the World Meteorological Organization a union of states and territories having their own meteorological service, and the World Trade Organization a union of separate customs territories.

Under this type of membership regime dependent territories have a functional equality with member states. In other organizations dependent territories are given 'associate' membership,[162] although in practice they may have equality with other members.

(i) Decision-making

In the League of Nations decisions could in general only be taken on a basis of unanimity.[163] Today the principle of majority decision is commonly adopted,[164] although voting rules may vary between organizations and even between organs of the same organization.[165] In the International Monetary Fund, weighted voting applies; in the UN Security Council the five permanent members have a veto on matters of substance.

International organizations are constrained by the fact that they are ordinarily poorly situated to carry out substantive decisions directly.[166] For example, the Security Council may identify a threat to international peace or security under Article 39 of the Charter, and attempt to redress it under Articles 41 and 42, but it does not have an economy of its own with which to levy sanctions, nor a military with which to forcibly address the situation (absent troop contribution agreements under Article 43). In effect all it can do is make decisions binding on its Members under Articles 25, 39, and 103.[167]

(ii) Domestic jurisdiction

The type of international co-operation undertaken through an organization and its constituent treaty will normally leave the reserved domain of domestic jurisdiction untouched. When the powers of the organization are extensive, as in the case of the UN, an express reservation may be inserted (Article 2(7) of the Charter).[168] However,

---

[162] E.g. ITU, WHO, IMCO, UNESCO, and FAO.

[163] Covenant, Art 4(6), 5(1), but cf Arts 5(2) (matters of procedure), 15(6), (7) (parties to a dispute unable to prevent adoption of a Council report on the dispute). Also: *Voting Procedure on Questions Relating to Reports and Petitions Concerning the Territory of South West Africa*, ICJ Reports 1955 p 67, 98–103 (Judge Lauterpacht).

[164] Under the Dispute Settlement Body of the WTO (DSU Arts 6.1, 16.4, 17.14, and 22.6) a rule of 'reverse consensus' has been adopted; all WTO Members must agree that a decision of a panel or the Appellate Body *not* be adopted in order to prevent implementation: Matsushita, Schoenbaum & Mavroidis, *The World Trade Organization* (2nd edn, 2008) 107. Further: chapter 32.

[165] Sands & Klein (6th edn, 2009) 268–81.

[166] Schermers & Blokker (4th edn, 2003) 1202–3; Klabbers (2nd edn, 2009) 174–6.

[167] Tzanakopoulos, *Disobeying the Security Council* (2010).

[168] Cf also its progenitor, Art 15(8) of the League Covenant. Further: Charter of the OAS, 30 April 1948, 119 UNTS 3, Art 1; cf Caminos & Lavalle (1989) 83 *AJIL* 395.

the Charter does not allow the reservation to affect the application of enforcement measures against states under Chapter VII.

The classic declaration of precisely what constitutes domestic jurisdiction was made by the Permanent Court in *Nationality Decrees*, where it was said that matter remaining solely within the domestic jurisdiction of states are such 'matters which are not, in principle, regulated by international law' and 'with respect to which States, therefore, [remain] sole judge'. The Court continued:

The question whether a certain matter is or is not solely within the domestic jurisdiction of a State is essentially a relative question; it depends on the development of international relations.[169]

Some elaboration has been provided by Nolte:

[T]he concept of 'domestic jurisdiction' does not denote specific areas which are clearly defined, irreducible or in any way inherently removed from the international sphere. It rather circumscribes areas which, taking into account the situation in issue, are not even *prima facie* affected by rules of international law.[170]

But provisions such as Article 2(7) have not proved a generally effective restraint.[171]

(iii) Agency[172]

By agreement between the states and the organization concerned, the latter may become an agent for member states, and others, in regard to matters outside its ordinary competence. Conversely, a state may become an agent of an organization for a particular purpose, for example, as an administering authority of a trust territory under Article 81 of the UN Charter.[173]

(iv) Applicable law[174]

An organization may enter into legal relations both on the international plane and with persons of private law within particular systems of municipal law. In principle the relations of the organization with other persons of international law will be

---

[169] *Nationality Decrees in Tunis and Morocco* (1923) PCIJ Ser B No 4, 24.

[170] Nolte, in 1 Simma (2nd edn, 2002) 148, 157. Further: McGoldrick, in Lowe & Warbrick (eds), *The United Nations and Principles of International Law* (1994) 85, 86ff; Conforti, *Law and Practice of the United Nations* (3rd edn, 2005) 132–3.

[171] Schermers & Blokker (4th edn, 2003) 159. Also: Nolte, in 1 Simma (2nd edn, 2002) 148, 159; cf Alvarez (2005) 156–83, on the shrinking concept of domestic jurisdiction. Also: chapter 20.

[172] Generally: Hawkins, Lake, Neilson & Tierney (eds), *Delegation and Agency in International Organizations* (2006).

[173] On territorial administration by international organizations: Knoll, *The Legal Status of Territories Subject to Administration by International Organizations* (2008); Wilde, *International Territorial Administration* (2008); Stahn, *The Law and Practice of International Territorial Administration* (2008); chapter 9.

[174] On the law applicable to the relations between international organizations and private persons: Seyersted (1967) 122 Hague *Recueil* 427; Valticos (1977) *Ann de l'Inst* 1; Amerasinghe (2nd edn, 2005) ch 13.

governed by international law, with the norms of the constituent treaty predominating when relations with member states of the organizations are concerned. When an issue arises from relations with persons of private law, the question may be regulated by a choice of law provision in a treaty which refers to a system of municipal law or possibly to 'general principles of law'. Otherwise, everything will depend on the forum before which the issue is brought and on the rules of conflict of laws applicable.[175]

Indeed, for expediency, most international organizations will subject their contracts to one or more systems of municipal law (usually that of the host state); thus, the majority of the Universal Postal Union and WHO contracts are governed by Swiss law, whereas those of the International Civil Aviation Organization (ICAO) are governed by the law of Quebec.

As for personal injury and other forms of tort, the host state agreement may provide a regime of liability for the institution.[176] Where no indication exists, however, it is a generally accepted principle that the organization can be held liable, with the applicable law being that of the place of the injury.[177]

(B) RELATIONS WITH NON-MEMBER STATES

The general rule is that only parties to a treaty are bound by the obligations contained in it, and this rule applies in principle to the constituent instruments of international organizations. An apparent exception appears in UN Charter Article 2(6), which provides: 'The Organization shall ensure that States which are not Members of the United Nations act in accordance with the Principles so far as may be necessary for the maintenance of international peace and security'. The exception, if it is one,[178] rests on the special character of the UN as a quasi-universal organization concerned primarily with the maintenance of global peace and security.

With international legal personality comes the capacity to contract. Certainly, third states enter into agreements with organizations which are valid on the international plane. Non-member states may also enter into relations with an organization via special missions. However, the existence of legal personality in an organization does not connote the spectrum of legal capacities, and the constituent instrument remains the prime determinant of specific powers in the matter of third state relations.

---

[175] Sands & Klein (6th edn, 2009) 466.

[176] E.g. Headquarters Agreement between the Organization of American States and the United States, 14 March 1992, US Treaty Doc 102–40, Art VIII(1).

[177] Sands & Klein (6th edn, 2009) 470.

[178] For the view that the provision does not bind non-members: Bindschedler (1963) 108 Hague *Recueil* 307, 404–6. For the opposite view: Kelsen (1950) 85–6, 106–10; Vitzthum, in 1 Simma (2nd edn, 2002) 146–7.

(C) RELATION TO MUNICIPAL LAW[179]

An organization will necessarily enter into relations within particular systems of municipal law, both in the state in which the headquarters are sited and in the course of its wider activities. The extent to which the particular system recognizes its legal personality will depend on the local law as modified by any relevant agreement. Thus the Treaty on the Functioning of the European Union[180] provides in Article 335 that the Union shall be accorded legal capacity in each member state to the greatest extent accorded to 'legal persons under their laws'. In the case of the ICAO, the Constitution makes no provision as to the precise content of its legal personality, and as a consequence the status of the organization varies according to the unco-ordinated municipal laws of its members.

In the case of the English courts a foreign entity will only be recognized as having legal personality if it has been accorded it under the law of a foreign state recognized by the UK. An international organization will be accorded legal personality (and the capacity to sue) if it has been accorded the legal capacity of a corporation under the law of one or more of the member states or of the law of the state where it has its seat, if that state is not a member state.[181]

7. LAW-MAKING THROUGH ORGANIZATIONS[182]

The activities of international organizations do not feature in the sources of international law enumerated in Article 38 of the Statute of the International Court. But they are well placed to contribute to its development. This is due primarily to the capacity for international organizations to express collectively the practice of member states. As Higgins has noted:

The United Nations is a very appropriate body to look to for indications of developments in international law, for international custom is to be deduced from the practice of States, which includes their international dealings as manifested by their diplomatic actions and public pronouncements. With the development of international organizations, the votes and views of States have come to have legal significance as evidence of customary law...Collective

---

[179] O'Connell (1963) 67 *RGDIP* 6, 26–9, 34; Skubiszewski (1972) 2 *Pol YIL* 80; Schreuer (1978) 27 *ICLQ* 1; Reinisch (2000).

[180] 25 March 1957, *OJEU* C 83/47.

[181] *Arab Monetary Fund v Hashim (No 3)* [1991] 2 AC 114, 161 (Lord Templeman); *Westland Helicopters Ltd v AOI* [1995] 2 WLR 126, 140–1 (Colman J). Also: Marston (1991) 40 *ICLQ* 403.

[182] Skubiszewski (1965–66) 41 *BY* 198; Virally (1956) *AFDI* 66; Johnson (1955–56) 32 *BY* 97; Sørensen (1960) 101 Hague *Recueil* 5, 91–108; Sloan (1987) 58 *BY* 39; Higgins, *Development* (1963); Yemin, *Legislative Powers in the United Nations and Specialized Agencies* (1969); Buergenthal, *Law-Making in the International Civil Aviation Organization* (1969); Vignes, in Macdonald and Johnston (eds), *The Structure and Process of International Law* (1983) 809–53; Schwebel, *The Legal Effect of Resolutions and Codes of Conduct of the United Nations* (1986); Alvarez (2005); Johnstone (2008) 40 *G Wash ILR* 87; Klabbers (2009) 188–93.

acts of States, repeated by and acquiesced in by sufficient numbers with sufficient frequency, eventually attain the status of law. The existence of the United Nations—and especially its accelerated trend towards universality of membership since 1955—now provides a very clear, very concentrated focal point for state practice.[183]

But the United Nations is a special case in this regard. The same may not be said for other international organizations, the relative influence of which will depend on their competence and membership. The varied roles played by organizations may be distinguished as follows:

(A) FORUMS FOR STATE PRACTICE

Statements on legal questions by governments through their representatives in organs and committees of organs can provide evidence of customary law; so also with the voting on resolutions concerned with legal matters, for example the resolution of the General Assembly affirming the principles of the Nuremberg Charter.[184] In this sense there is nothing inherently special about an international organization; whilst it may provide a state with the *opportunity* to make a statement on or consider an issue, any opinion so expressed reflects state practice with respect to that state alone.

(B) PRESCRIPTIVE RESOLUTIONS

A resolution, not in itself binding,[185] may prescribe principles of international law and purport to be merely declaratory. However, the mere formulation of principles may articulate and develop the law.[186] When a resolution of the General Assembly touches on subjects dealt with in the UN Charter, it may be regarded as an authoritative interpretation: examples are the Declaration on the Granting of Independence to Colonial Countries and Peoples[187] and the Friendly Relations Declaration.[188] Resolutions on new legal problems provide a means of corralling and defining the growing practice of states, while remaining formally hortatory.[189] As the International Court said in *Nuclear Weapons*:

General Assembly resolutions, even if they are not binding, may sometimes have normative value. They can, in certain circumstances, provide evidence important for establishing the existence of a rule or the emergence of an *opinio juris*. To establish whether this is true of a given General Assembly resolution, it is necessary to look at its content and the conditions of

---

[183] Higgins (1963) 2. Further: Higgins (1994) 23.

[184] GA Res 95(I), 11 December 1946.

[185] Thus General Assembly resolutions are recommendations creating prima facie no legal obligation. Cf however, *Voting Procedure*, ICJ Reports 1955 p 57, 118–19, 122 (Judge Lauterpacht); and *Digest of US Practice* (1975) 85. Generally: Amerasinghe (2nd edn, 2005) ch 6.

[186] Higgins (1994) 25–8.

[187] GA Res 1514(XV), 14 December 1960.

[188] GA Res 2625(XXV), 24 October 1970.

[189] Cf the declaration of principles governing activities in outer space: GA Res 1962(XVII), 13 December 1963.

its adoption; it is also necessary to see whether an *opinio juris* exists as to its normative character. Or a series of resolutions may show the gradual evolution of the *opinio juris* required for the establishment of a new rule.[190]

(C) CHANNELS FOR EXPERT OPINION

Organizations often establish bodies of legal experts, the most important being the ILC,[191] the central project of which is the codification and progressive development of international law as a whole.[192] Key areas of ILC influence include diplomatic and consular relations, the law of the sea, the law of treaties, and the law of responsibility. Paradoxically perhaps, it has been less successful in influencing the law of international organizations, emphasizing the diversity and particularity of that field and the unwillingness of states to be subject to indirect constraints or potential liabilities in their action through international organizations.

(D) DECISIONS OF ORGANS WITH JUDICIAL FUNCTIONS

Clearly decisions of judicial organs, such as the International Court and the Court of Justice of the European Union, contribute to the development of the law of treaties including principles of interpretation as well as general international law.[193] The specialized function of such bodies may naturally limit their contribution to the latter.

(E) THE PRACTICE OF POLITICAL ORGANS

Political organs, and particularly the General Assembly and the Security Council of the United Nations, make numerous recommendations and decisions relating to specific issues which involve the application of general international law or the provisions of the Charter and other instruments. Such continued practice may have considerable legal significance. However, as with state practice, the content of the particular decision and the extent to which legal matters were considered must be examined before

---

[190] *Nuclear Weapons*, ICJ Reports 1999 p 225, 254–5. Also: *South West Africa*, ICJ Reports 1966 p 248, 291 (Judge Tanaka, diss); *North Sea Continental Shelf (Federal Republic of Germany/Netherlands; Federal Republic of Germany/Denmark)*, ICJ Reports 1969 p 3, 177 (Judge Tanaka, diss).

[191] Statute of the International Law Commission, 21 November 1947, GA Res 174(II), 21 November 1947 (ILC Statute). Generally: United Nations, *The International Law Commission 50 Years After* (2000); Morton, *The International Law Commission of the United Nations* (2000); United Nations, *The Work of the International Law Commission* (6th edn, 2004); Watts, Pronto & Wood, 1–4 *The International Law Commission, 1949–1998* and *1999–2009* (1999, 2010).

[192] Further: UN Charter, Art 13(1)(a); Fleischhauer, in 1 Simma (2nd edn, 2002) 298; Rao, 'International Law Commission (ILC)' (2006) *MPEPIL*; Watts, 'Codification and Progressive Development of International Law' (2006) *MPEPIL*. Other UN expert bodies include UNCTAD, the United Nations Commission on International Trade Law (UNCITRAL), and the International Institute for the Unification of Private Law (UNIDROIT).

[193] Generally: Lauterpacht, *Development* (1958); McMahon (1961) 37 *BY* (1961) 320; Lowe & Fitzmaurice (eds), *Jennings Essays* (1996); Amerasinghe (2nd edn, 2005) ch 8.

legal weight is ascribed. Furthermore, to give legal significance to an omission of an organ is problematic Many jurists seem to treat the decisions of political organs in terms of the arithmetic of voting, the decisions being taken to represent the views of *n* states in the majority and their cogency being roughly on a scale *n* majority divided by *n* minority states. However, states cannot by their control of numbers of international organizations raise the value of their state practice by reference to the 'practice of organizations'.[194]

On occasion a consistent interpretation by members of an organ based upon a persistent practice, for example, in matters of voting, adopted *by that organ* will be opposable to *all* members provided that there is substantial evidence of general acceptance by members of the organization. This was the basis for the decision in *Namibia*[195] as to the meaning of Article 27(3) of the Charter.

It may be that the recent jurisprudence of the International Court has adopted a more liberal view as to the value of the practice of international organizations. In *Nuclear Weapons in Armed Conflict,* the Court indicated that the practice of the organization is one of the 'elements which may deserve special attention' in the interpretation of constituent instruments.[196] The Court went on to consider the practice of the WHO in deciding whether the legality of nuclear weapons fell within its competence as a specialized agency. In the *Kosovo* advisory opinion, the Court suggested that the 'silence of the Special Representative of the Secretary-General in the face of the declaration of independence of 17 February 2008' corroborated the conclusion that the declaration had been made outside of the framework established by the Security Council.[197] This is more problematic: the silence of the Special Representative was more likely a result of the neutrality policy adopted by the Secretariat than of a legal conviction concerning the authorship of the declaration.

(F) EXTERNAL PRACTICE OF ORGANIZATIONS

Organizations may make agreements with member and non-member states and with other organizations, and may present international claims and make official pronouncements on issues affecting them. Subject to what has been said about the need for care in evaluating acts of political organs, the practice of organizations provides evidence of the law. In addition, the behaviour of international organizations 'in the field' may influence the discourse of international law, and thereby indirectly influence the formation of custom.[198]

---

[194] Cf Sørensen (1960) 101 Hague *Recueil 1,* 100–1, 105–6. For views on the reliability of subsequent practice of organs in interpretation of the Charter: *Certain Expenses,* ICJ Reports 1962 p 151, 187 (Judge Spender), 210 (Judge Fitzmaurice).

[195] ICJ Reports 1971 p 16, 22.

[196] *Nuclear Weapons in Armed Conflict,* ICJ Reports 1996 p 66, 75.

[197] *Accordance with International Law of the Unilateral Declaration of Independence in respect of Kosovo,* Opinion of 22 July 2010, §108.

[198] Generally: Johnstone (2008) 40 *G Wash ILR* 87.

(G) INTERNAL LAW-MAKING[199]

Organizations have considerable autonomy in internal matters such as procedure and the relations between the organization and its staff. Resolutions of organs of the United Nations on questions of procedure create internal law for members. The UN has developed a code of staff regulations governing the service of its officials, and in 1949 the General Assembly established the United Nations Administrative Tribunal (UNAT) to adjudicate upon applications alleging non-observance of employment contracts of staff members of the Secretariat.[200] The United Nations Internal Justice System has been reformed, and the UNAT has replaced by a two-tiered system comprising a United Nations Dispute Tribunal and a United Nations Appeals Tribunal.[201] Other international organizations also have staff tribunals which have collectively built up substantial administrative jurisprudence.[202]

8. CONTROL OF ACTS OF ORGANIZATIONS

(A) RESPONSIBILITY UNDER GENERAL INTERNATIONAL LAW

There is no compulsory system for review of the acts of international organizations by external bodies. In this situation limited control is provided by general international law. As noted, the correlative of legal personality and a capacity to present international claims is responsibility.[203] Moreover, when creating institutions states cannot always hide behind the organization when its activities cause damage to third party interests.

(B) INTERNAL POLITICAL AND JUDICIAL CONTROL

The question of practical control turns on the powers of the executive and deliberative organs and the constitutional limitations placed upon them.[204] The division of competence between organs and the limits to the powers of the organization as a whole may be carefully drawn, and, as in the UN Charter, the obligations set out in the relevant instrument may be expressed to apply to the organization itself and

---

[199] Schermers & Blokker (4th edn, 2003) ch 8; Amerasinghe (2nd edn, 2005) ch 9; Sands & Klein (6th edn, 2009) ch 14.

[200] Generally: Amerasinghe, *The Law of the International Civil Service* (1988); *Effect of Awards*, ICJ Reports 1954 p 47.

[201] GA Res 61/261, 4 April 2007; Reinisch (2008) 12 *MPUNYB* 447.

[202] Amerasinghe (2nd edn, 2005) ch 9; Riddell, 'Administrative Boards, Commissions and Tribunals in International Organizations' (2006) *MPEPIL*.

[203] Generally: Klein, *La Responsabilité des Organisations internationales* (1998); Wellens, *Remedies against International Organisations* (2002).

[204] Generally: Bindschedler (1963) 108 Hague *Recueil* 307, 312–418.

its organs.[205] Interpretation of the constituent treaty by the organ entrusted with the power in question is the general rule. Under the Charter, however, reference to the International Court depends on the readiness of political organs to request an advisory opinion and to comply with it once given. Thus in *Namibia* it was remarked that 'undoubtedly, the Court does not possess powers of judicial review or appeal in respect of the decisions taken by the United Nations organs concerned'. However, the Court did in fact consider the validity of acts of organs 'in the exercise of its judicial function and since objections have been advanced'.[206]

Notwithstanding the self-determining jurisdiction of many organizations, there is momentum towards greater accountability, as illustrated by the establishment of an Inspection Panel within the World Bank in 1993 and of an Independent Evaluation Office within the International Monetary Fund in 2001.[207] But these bodies remain the exception rather than the rule.[208]

Judicial organs may produce an impressive and consistent case-law on points of interpretation. However, the political organs may support constitutional developments which are distinctly controversial. An early example was the use of the Uniting for Peace Resolution to create the United Nations Emergency Force following the Suez crisis in 1956.[209] A similar situation arose when the Security Council gave a mandate to the Secretary-General to organize forces for operations in the Congo.[210] The practice of the Security Council in passing overtly 'legislative' resolutions responding to a general phenomenon as a threat to peace under Article 39, rather than a specific, geographically defined, situation is a more recent example.[211]

The fact is that individual states have no right of recourse and minority opinion can be over-ridden.[212] States in a minority may withdraw from the organization, acquiesce in what they regard as unlawful operations, resist military forces acting under putative authority of the organization, or simply disobey what they perceive to be a resolution *ultra vires*. As Judge Morelli said in *Certain Expenses*:

In the case of acts of international organizations... there is nothing comparable to the remedies existing in domestic law in connection with administrative acts. The consequence of this is that there is no possibility of applying the concept of voidability to the acts of the United Nations. If an act of an organ of the United Nations had to be considered as an invalid act, such invalidity could constitute only the *absolute nullity* of the act.[213]

---

[205] UN Charter, Arts 2, 24(2), 55.

[206] ICJ Reports 1971 p 16, 45.

[207] On the prospects of current non-judicial accountability mechanisms: de Wet (2008) 9 *GLJ* 1987. On the World Bank Inspection Panel: Shihata, *The World Bank Inspection Panel* (2nd edn, 2000); Gualtieri (2002) 72 *BY* 213; Orakhelashvili (2005) 2 *Int Org LR* 57.

[208] De Wet (2008) 2010.

[209] GA Res 998(ES-1), 4 November 1956; GA Res 1000(ES-1), 5 November 1956.

[210] SC Res 143 (1960).

[211] SC Res 1373 (2001); SC Res 1540 (2004). Further: Talmon (2005) 99 *AJIL* 175; Bianchi (2007) 17 *EJIL* 881; Hinojosa-Martinez (2009) 57 *ICLQ* 333.

[212] Generally: Akande (1997) 46 *ICLQ* 309; Alvarez (1996) 90 *AJIL* 1; de Wet (2000) 47 *NILR* 181.

[213] ICJ Reports 1962 p 151, 222.

States may also withhold financial contributions. This course was adopted in *Certain Expenses*, and eventually the General Assembly requested an advisory opinion.[214] Even at this juncture political control was prominent. The request was formulated in a manner calculated to narrow the issue artificially to the interpretation of 'expenses of the Organization within the meaning of Article 17, paragraph 2, of the Charter of the United Nations'. Moreover, the Court's opinion was sought retrospectively, long after the actions were authorized and enormous expenditure incurred.[215] As a general matter, the problems arising from the *ultra vires* acts of international organizations are far from being resolved. They are certainly not susceptible to resolution through simplified formulations.[216]

(c) THE RULE OF LAW AND INTERNATIONAL ORGANIZATIONS

So far one organization seems to escape from this pervasive sense of non-accountability. Direct judicial control of the acts of organizations by a specially created organ is rare, but it appears in a developed form in the European Court of Justice.[217] The Court has considerable powers of review in respect of acts of organs of the European Union on grounds of incompetence, violation of the relevant treaty or rules for its application, procedural irregularity, and *détournement de pouvoir*. The Treaty on the Functioning of the European Union also provides for a reference to a judicial organ of the question of compatibility with the basic treaty of an agreement at the stage of negotiation.[218]

Out of this arose the decisions of the Court in the *Kadi* cases,[219] brought in response to Security Council Resolutions 1333 and 1373 of 2001 and successor resolutions[220] compelling Members to freeze the assets of certain suspected terrorists and their listed confederates as part of a targeted sanctions regime. The identity of those whose assets were to be frozen was determined by a Security Council committee.[221] As originally composed, listed individuals were given no facility to contest the decisions made against them or to challenge the measure before a court.[222] The European Court, applying the

---

[214] Ibid, 203–4 (Judge Fitzmaurice), 232 (Judge Winiarski, diss), 304–5 (Judge Bustamante, diss).

[215] Ibid, 237 (Judge Basdevant).

[216] Generally: E Lauterpacht, in *Cambridge Essays in International Law* (1965) 88; Cahier (1972) 76 *RGDIP* 645, 659; Osieke (1983) 77 *AJIL* 239; Furukawa, in *Mélanges Reuter* (1981) 293; Bernhardt, in Makarczyk (ed), *Essays in Honour of Krzysztof Skubiszewski* (1996) 599; Buchowska (2006–08) 28 *Pol YIL* 9.

[217] E.g. Arnull, *The European Union and its Court of Justice* (2nd edn, 2006); Hilpold (2009) 13 *MPUNYB* 141; Reinisch (ed), *Challenging Acts of International Organizations before National Courts* (2010).

[218] TFEU, Art 218(11).

[219] Joined Cases C-402/05P and C-415/05P, *Kadi & Al Barakaat International Foundation v Council & Commission* [2008] ECR I-06351. Further: the Opinion of Advocate-General Poiares Maduro and at first instance Case T-315/01, *Kadi v Council and Commission* [2005] ECR II-3649; Case T-306/01, *Yusef & Al Barakaat International Foundation v Council and Commission* [2005] ECR II-3533. Also: Tzanou (2009) 10 *GLJ* 123; Hilpold, in Reinisch (2010) 18.

[220] SC Res 1390 (2002); SC Res 1344 (1003); SC Res 1526 (2004); SC Res 1617 (2005); SC Res 1735 (2006); SC Res 1822 (2008).

[221] The Al Qaeda/Taliban Sanctions Committee: SC Res 1267 (1999).

[222] Cf SC Res 1822 (2008). Further: Almqvist (2008) 57 *ICLQ* 303.

doctrine of equivalent protection formulated in *Bosphorus v Ireland*,[223] recognized
that implementation of the sanctions required the positive action of the EU, which
was bound to do so in accordance with fundamental rights as provided by the ECHR.
Although the Charter required that the EU comply with Security Council directives, it
did not require transposition of these resolutions in a strict and pre-determined fashion.[224] It was open to the Court to order that the resolutions be implemented in such a
fashion as to respect human rights—and particularly ECHR Article 6(1).[225] This interpretive approach represents a useful mechanism by which international organizations
may be held to account, an area of weakness in current international law. Difficulties
would arise, however, if the Security Council directed Members to permit no flexibility in application.[226] In such a situation, Article 103 requires the resolution to be
implemented by Members to the letter, irrespective of how the EU and ECHR view
the subject, and irrespective of the absence of equivalent protection on the level of the
Security Council. So the ultimate question of compliance with authority at the international level turns out to be a question of the law of international organizations!

---

[223] [2005] ECtHR 45036/98.

[224] [2008] ECR I-6351, §298. More controversially, the Court also built a second line of defence based
on the principle that UN law cannot prevail over EC primary law, of which fundamental rights form a part:
at §§304–8. Art 103 of the Charter is conspicuous by its absence from the Court's reasoning: Hipold, in
Reinisch (2010) 18, 34–5.

[225] [2008] ECR I-6351, §§334, 348ff.

[226] Hipold, in Reinisch (2010) 11, 34. For subsequent proceedings see *Commission v Kadi (No 2)*, pending
before ECJ (GC).

PART III

TERRITORIAL SOVEREIGNTY

8

FORMS OF GOVERNMENTAL
AUTHORITY OVER TERRITORY

1. THE CONCEPT OF TERRITORY

In spatial terms the law knows four types of regime: territorial sovereignty, territory not subject to the sovereignty of any state or states and which possesses a status of its own (e.g. trust territories), *res nullius*, and *res communis*. Territorial sovereignty extends principally over land territory and the territorial sea, its seabed and subsoil. The concept of territory includes islands, islets, rocks, and (in certain circumstances) reefs.[1] Exceptionally an area of territory may be under the sovereignty of several states (a condominium), though in practice these have always been states with other territory subject to their exclusive sovereignty.[2] A *res nullius* consists of an area legally susceptible to acquisition by states but not as yet placed under territorial sovereignty. The *res communis*, consisting of the high seas (which for present purposes include exclusive economic zones) and also outer space, is not capable of being placed under sovereignty. In accordance with customary international law and the dictates of convenience, the airspace above and subsoil beneath state territory, the *res nullius*, and the *res communis* are included in each category.

---

[1] For the dispute over the large Caribbean reef structure Quitasueño Bank: Pratt (2001) *IBRU Boundary and Security Bulletin* 108. Generally: *Argentina/Chile (Beagle Channel)* (1977) 21 RIAA 53, 189; *Eritrea v Yemen (Territorial Sovereignty)* (1998) 114 ILR 1, 138–9; *Maritime Delimitation and Territorial Questions between Qatar and Bahrain*, ICJ Reports 2001 p 40, 200, and on the distinction between low- and high-tide elevations: chapter 11.

[2] Generally: Bantz (1998) *12 Florida JIL* 77; Barberis, *in* Kohen (ed), *Liber Amicorum Lucius Caflisch* (2007) 673; Samuels (2008) 29 *Mich JIL* 732. The best-known example is the former condominium of the New Hebrides (now Vanuatu): O'Connell (1968–69) 43 *BY* 71. The legal regime may be used to deal with problems of neighbourhood relating to boundary rivers and the like: *Dutch-Prussian Condominium* (1816) 6 ILR 50; also: Brown, *The Saudi Arabia Kuwait Neutral Zone* (1963). For the Anglo-Egyptian Sudan: Taha (2005) 76 *BY* 337. In certain cases, e.g. land-locked lakes and bays bounded by two or more states, it has been argued that riparian states have a *condominium* by the operation of law. This is doubtful, but it is possible for such a regime to arise by usage. In relation to the Gulf of Fonseca the Chamber held that its waters, other than the three-mile maritime belts, 'are historic waters and subject to a joint sovereignty of the three coastal states': *Land, Island and Maritime Frontier Dispute (El Salvador/Honduras)*, ICJ Reports 1992 p 351, 601. Also *Gulf of Fonseca* (1917) 11 *AJIL* 674. In each case the particular regime will depend on the facts, and it is unsafe to rely on any general theory of community of property.

2. KEY TERMS AND DISTINCTIONS

(A) SOVEREIGNTY AND JURISDICTION

State territory and its appurtenances (airspace and territorial sea), together with the government and population within its boundaries, constitute the physical and social base for the state. The legal competence of states and the rules for their protection depend on and assume the existence of this stable, physically identified (and normally legally delimited) base.

The competence of states in respect of their territory is usually described in terms of sovereignty and jurisdiction, but the terminology is not employed very consistently even in legal sources. At the same time, some uniformity of usage may be noted. The normal complement of state rights, the typical case of legal competence, is described commonly as 'sovereignty': particular rights, or accumulations of rights quantitatively less than the norm are referred to as 'jurisdiction'. In brief, 'sovereignty' is shorthand for legal personality of a certain kind, that of statehood; 'jurisdiction' refers to particular aspects of the substance, especially rights (or claims), liberties, and powers. Of particular significance is the criterion of consent. State A may have considerable forces stationed within the boundaries of state B. State A may also have exclusive use of a certain area of state B, and exclusive jurisdiction over its own forces. If, however, these rights exist with the consent of the host state then state A has no claim to sovereignty over any part of state B.[3] In such case there has been a derogation from the sovereignty of state B, but state A does not gain sovereignty as a consequence. It would be otherwise if state A had been able to claim that exclusive use of an area hitherto part of state B belonged to state A *as sovereign*, as of right and independently of the consent of any state.

(B) SOVEREIGNTY AND OWNERSHIP

The analogy between sovereignty over territory and ownership of real property appears more useful than it really is. For the moment it is sufficient to establish certain distinctions. The legal competence of a state includes considerable liberties in respect of internal organization and the disposal of territory. This general power of government, administration, and disposition is *imperium*, a capacity recognized and delineated by international law. *Imperium* is distinct from *dominium* in the form of public ownership of property within the state;[4] *a fortiori* in the form of private ownership recognized as such by the law.[5]

---

[3] E.g. British Sovereign Base Areas in Cyprus. Further: Hendry & Dickson, *British Overseas Territories Law* (2011) 339–42.

[4] Or elsewhere: cf the John F Kennedy Memorial Act 1964, s1 which transferred to and vested in the US land at Runnymede, England for an estate in fee simple absolute to be held in perpetuity.

[5] Cf Lauterpacht, 1 *International Law* (1970) 367, 367–70. Generally: Shan et al (eds), *Redefining Sovereignty in International Economic Law* (2008).

(C) SOVEREIGNTY AND ADMINISTRATION

It may happen that the process of government over an area, with the concomitant privileges and duties, falls into the hands of another state. Thus after the defeat of Nazi Germany in the Second World War the four major Allied Powers assumed supreme power in Germany.[6] The German state did not, however, disappear. What occurred is akin to legal representation or agency of necessity. Indeed, the legal basis of the occupation depended on its continued existence. The very considerable derogation of sovereignty involved in the assumption of powers of government by foreign states, without the consent of Germany, did not constitute a transfer of sovereignty. A similar case, long recognized in customary law, is the belligerent occupation of enemy territory in time of war.[7] The important features of 'sovereignty' in such cases are the continued existence of a legal personality and the attribution of territory to that legal person and not to holders of the territory for the time being.[8]

(D) 'SOVEREIGN RIGHTS' BEYOND STATE TERRITORY

A further source of confusion is the fact that sovereignty is not only used as a description of legal personality accompanied by independence but also as a reference to various types of rights, indefeasible except by special grant, in the patrimony of a state, for example the 'sovereign rights' a coastal state has over the resources of the continental shelf,[9] or a prescriptive right of passage between the main territory and

---

[6] It is assumed that the form which the occupation took was lawful. See Jennings (1946) 23 *BY* 112, and on post-1945 Germany, Crawford, *Creation of States* (2nd edn, 2006) 452–66, 523–6; chapter 5.

[7] *L v N* (1947) 14 ILR 242. The basic rule in the modern law of military occupation that the occupation of territory during war does not confer sovereignty upon the occupying power is borne out, *inter alia*, in Arts 43, 45 of the Hague Regulations 1907 which establish the occupying force as a mere *de facto* administrator: Pictet (ed), *Commentary on Geneva Convention IV of 1949* (1958) 273. Further: Fleck (ed), *The Handbook of International Humanitarian Law* (2nd edn, 2008) 273–84. Cf McCarthy (2005) 10 *JCSL* 43, questioning the right of the Coalition forces to implement structural changes in the government of Iraq during its occupation 2003–04. Another instance is provided by the situation in which the ceding state still administers the ceded territory, by agreement with the state taking cession: *Gudder Singh v The State (India)* (1953) 20 ILR 145. Further examples of delegated powers: *Quaglia v Caiselli* (1952) 19 ILR 144; *Nicolo v Creni* (1952) 19 ILR 145. On belligerent occupation generally: Benvenisti, *The International Law of Occupation* (1993); Dinstein, *The Law of Belligerent Occupation* (2009). On the issue of Northern Cyprus, see e.g. *Loizidou v Turkey* (1996) 108 ILR 443, 462: Cyprus, which does not exercise effective control over Northern Cyprus, 'has remained the sole legitimate Government of Cyprus'; also *Tomko v Republic of Cyprus*, ILDC 834 (CY 2007). Further, the lack of effective control over part of a state's territory does not diminish that state's rights over that territory under international law. E.g. the Republic of Cyprus, whilst not having effective control over the occupied northern part of the island, is still entitled to exercise its sovereign rights over the latter's airspace under the Chicago Convention on Civil Aviation: *KTHY v Secretary of Transport* [2009] EWHC 1918 (Admin) §52; [2010] EWCA Civ 1093, §§38, 68–9; also Franklin (2011) 36 *Air & Space L* 109; Franklin & Porter (2010) 35 *Air & Space L* 63.

[8] On recent international administrations: e.g. Knoll, *The Legal Status of Territories Subject to Administration by International Organisations* (2008); Stahn, *The Law and Practice of International Territorial Administration* (2008); Wilde, *International Territorial Administration* (2008).

[9] E.g. GCCS, 28 April 1958, 499 UNTS 311, Art 2, recognized as customary law in *North Sea Continental Shelf (Federal Republic of Germany/Netherlands; Federal Republic of Germany/Denmark)*, ICJ Reports 1969 p 3, 19, reiterated in UNCLOS, 10 December 1982, 1833 UNTS 3, Art 77.

an enclave. Rights which are 'owned' and in this special sense 'sovereign' involve a broader concept, not reducible to *territorial* sovereignty.

3. TERRITORIAL ADMINISTRATION SEPARATED FROM STATE SOVEREIGNTY

While the concept of territorial sovereignty normally applies in relation to states, there is now considerable experience with international organizations not only administering territory in the capacity of agent but also assuming legal responsibility for territory in respect of which no state has title. Such a situation arose in 1966 when the General Assembly terminated the Mandate of South West Africa. The legal relations of an organization to the territory in such a case can only be classified as *sui generis* because terms and concepts like 'sovereignty' and 'title' are historically associated with the patrimony of states.[10]

(A) TERMINABLE AND REVERSIONARY RIGHTS

Territorial sovereignty may be defeasible in certain circumstances by operation of law, for example by fulfilment of a condition subsequent or the failure of a condition under which sovereignty was transferred where there is an express or implied condition that title should revert to the grantor. The first situation is exemplified by the status of Monaco before 2005; its independence was conditional, in that if there was a vacancy in the Crown of Monaco it would have become a protectorate of France.[11] Until such a condition operates the tenant had an interest equal in all respects to that of sovereignty.[12]

The second type of case was represented, on one view, by the system of mandates created after the First World War. The mandatories, or administering states for the various ex-German territories, were nominated by the five principal Allied and Associated Powers, in whose favour Germany had renounced sovereignty. On this basis, and because they took the decision to place the territories under mandate, it was suggested that 'the Principal Powers retained a residual or reversionary interest in the actual territories concerned except where these have attained self-government or independence'.[13] The precise incidents of such a reversion would depend on the circumstances of each

---

[10] *International Status of South West Africa*, ICJ Reports 1950 p 128, 150 (Lord McNair). Also Perritt (2003) 8 *UCLA JILFA* 385.

[11] Treaty of Friendship, 17 July 1918, 981 UNTS 364, Art 3.

[12] Now Treaty of 24 October 2002, 48 *AFDI* 792, 48; Crawford (2nd edn, 2006) 328.

[13] *South West Africa (Ethiopia v South Africa; Liberia v South Africa)*, Preliminary Objections, ICJ Reports 1962 p 319, 482 (Judges Spender & Fitzmaurice, diss).

case.[14] But they did not amount to sovereignty; they took the form of a power of disposition, or of intervention or veto in any process of disposition.

(B) RESIDUAL SOVEREIGNTY

Occupation of foreign territory in time of peace may occur on the basis of a treaty with the territorial sovereign. The grantee under the treaty may receive very considerable powers of administration, amounting to a delegation of the exercise of many of the powers of the territorial sovereign to the possessor for a particular period. Thus, in Article 3 of the Treaty of Peace of 8 September 1951, Japan agreed that, pending any action to place the Ryukyu Islands under the trusteeship system of the UN:

The United States will have the right to exercise all and any powers of administration, legislation and jurisdiction over the territory and inhabitants of these islands, including their territorial waters.[15]

US courts, in holding that inhabitants of the Ryukyus were not nationals of the US and that the islands were a 'foreign country' in connection with the application of various US statutes, referred to the 'de facto sovereignty' of the US and to the Japanese interest in terms of 'residual sovereignty' or 'de iure sovereignty'.[16] Restoration of full Japanese sovereignty was the subject of subsequent bilateral agreements.[17]

This type of interest may have practical consequences. In Lighthouses in Crete and Samos, the Permanent Court held that in 1913 Crete and Samos were under the sovereignty of Turkey, which therefore had the power to grant or renew concessions with regard to the islands. As regards Crete the Court said:

Notwithstanding its autonomy, Crete has not ceased to be a part of the Ottoman Empire. Even though the Sultan had been obliged to accept important restrictions on the exercise of his rights of sovereignty in Crete, that sovereignty had not ceased to belong to him, however it might be qualified from a juridical point of view.[18]

(C) INTERNATIONAL LEASES

There are examples of concessions of territory, including full governmental authority, for a period of years (the New Territories of Hong Kong prior to 1997)[19] or even in

---

[14] Eritrea v Yemen (Territorial Sovereignty) (1998) 114 ILR 1, 40, 115, where the Tribunal held that Yemen had not shown that the doctrine of reversion exists in international law.

[15] 136 UNTS 45.

[16] E.g. Burna v US, 240 F.2d 720 (1957). Also: Oda & Owada (eds), The Practice of Japan in International Law 1961–1970 (1982) 76–96.

[17] (1968) 7 ILM 554; Rousseau (1970) 74 RGDIP 682, 717; Rousseau (1970) 64 AJIL 647.

[18] Lighthouses in Crete and Samos (1937) PCIJ Ser A/B No 71, 126–30. Also: 1 Lauterpacht (1970) 367, 372–3.

[19] Treaty between China and Great Britain, 29 August 1842, 30 BFSP 389. On the expiry of the lease: UKMIL (1985) 56 BY 363, 483–5; UKMIL (1986) 57 BY 487, 513–14, 529–34. Further: Malanczuk, 'Hong Kong' (2010) MPEPIL.

perpetuity (Guantanamo Bay). In such cases the term 'lease' may be applied, but it is no more than a superficial guide to the interest concerned: each case depends on its particular facts and especially on the precise terms of the grant. Certainly there is a presumption that the grantor retains residual sovereignty. Certain types of 'lease' were however, virtual cessions of territory.[20] The return of full control over several leased territories (Hong Kong in 1997, Macao in 1999, the Panama Canal Zone in 2000)[21] may indicate a trend towards confirming the lessor's sovereignty.

The best-known extant international lease is that between Cuba and the US with respect to Guantanamo Bay.[22] The initial lease was concluded in 1903,[23] shortly after Cuba was declared independent. A second lease was concluded in 1934.[24] The revolutionary government in place since 1959 has consistently claimed both to be illegal.[25] Although rarely articulated in legal terms, the basis for the Cuban claim is that the leases are voidable due to their inequitable character and the change in circumstances since the end of the Cold War.[26] Material in this context is Article III of the 1903 Lease, which provides that:

While on the one hand the United States recognizes the continuance of the ultimate sovereignty of the Republic of Cuba over the above described areas of land and water, on the other hand the Republic of Cuba consents that during the period of occupation by the United States of said areas under the terms of this agreement the United States shall exercise complete jurisdiction and control over and within said areas with a right to acquire... for the public purposes of the United States any land over or other property therein by purchase or by exercise of eminent domain with full compensation to the owners thereof.

---

[20] *Secretary of State for India v Sardar Rustam Khan* (1941) 10 ILR 98. Also: *Union of India v Sukumar Sengupta* (1990) 92 ILR 554, for discussion on the difference between a lease and servitude.

[21] Panama-US Convention of 18 November 1903, *USTS* No 431. In *In re Cia de Transportes de Gelabert* (1939) 9 ILR 118, the Panama Supreme Court held that Panama retained 'its jurisdictional rights of sovereignty' in the airspace of the Canal Zone. Cf *Stafford Allen & Sons, Ltd v Pacific Steam Navigation Co* [1956] 2 All ER 716. The Panama Canal Treaty and the Treaty Concerning the Permanent Neutrality and Operation of the Panama Canal, 7 September 1977, 1161 UNTS 177, 1280 UNTS 3, superseded the 1903 Convention: Arcari, 'Panama Canal' (2009) *MPEPIL*.

[22] Lazar (1968) 62 *AJIL* 730; Lazar (1969) 63 *AJIL* 116; Johns (2005) 16 *EJIL* 613; Strauss (2006–07) 10 *NYCLR* 479. Another example is the British Indian Ocean Territory (BIOT). In 1966, the UK made the BIOT available to the US for a period of at least 50 years; it subsequently agreed to the establishment of a military base on Diego Garcia Island and to allow the US to occupy the other islands of the Archipelago if they should wish to do so. Cf *Bancoult v Foreign Secretary* [2008] UKHL 61. On the alleged violations of the indigenous people's rights in BIOT: *Bancoult v McNamara*, 445 F.3d 427 (DC Cir, 2006); 549 US 1166 (2007); and the cases pending before the ECtHR, *Chagos Islanders v UK*, Application 35622/04, and an UNCLOS Annex VII Tribunal (*Mauritius v UK*): see ITLOS/Press 164, 25 March 2011.

[23] Agreement between Cuba and the United States for the Lease of Lands for Coaling and Naval Stations, 16 and 23 February 1903, 192 CTS 429.

[24] Treaty Concerning the Relations between the United States of America and the Republic of Cuba, 29 May 1934, 150 LNTS 97.

[25] Further: de Zayas, 'Guantánamo Naval Base' (2009) *MPEPIL*.

[26] Ronen, 'Territory, Lease' (2008) *MPEPIL*. Further: *Gabčíkovo-Nagymaros Project (Hungary/Slovakia)*, ICJ Reports 1997 p 7, 64–5.

The apparently perpetual character of the rights assigned by this clause has given rise to much commentary, a key issue being whether US constitutional rights protections extend to Guantanamo Bay.[27]

The difficulties concerning the nature of the grantor's interest in this type of case, new examples of which are unlikely to arise, are not present in the amenity-providing 'lease' of railway station or a military, naval, or air base.[28] Here the rights conferred by a treaty, executive agreement or other intergovernmental agreement are of a more limited kind: consequently the grantor has a right to revoke the 'contractual licence' (according to its terms) and, after a reasonable time has elapsed, proportionate steps (even, in the last resort, force) may be employed to evict the trespasser.

(D) DEMILITARIZED AND NEUTRALIZED TERRITORY

Restrictions on use of territory, accepted by treaty, do not affect territorial sovereignty as a title, even when the restriction concerns matters of national security and preparation for defence.[29] The same applies where demilitarized zones have been imposed by the Security Council[30] or even (in the context of provisional measures) by the International Court.[31]

(E) VASSALAGE, SUZERAINTY, AND PROTECTION

As noted, a condominium involves a sovereignty jointly exercised by two (or more) states on a basis of equality. Historically, other types of shared sovereignty have occurred in which the dominant partner, state A, has acquired a significant role in the government of state B, and particularly in the taking of executive decisions relating to the conduct of foreign affairs. The legal aspects of the relationship will vary with the circumstances of each case, and not too much can be deduced from the terminology of the relevant instruments.[32] It may be that the protected community or 'state' is a

---

[27] Particularly in relation to the US use of its naval facility at Guantanamo to house detainees captured as part of the so-called 'war on terror': e.g. Steyn (2004) 53 *ICLQ* 1 (describing the facility as a 'legal black hole'); *Abbasi v Foreign Secretary* [2002] EWCA Civ 1598 (Eng) §64. Also: de Zayas (2003–04) 37 *UBCLR* 277; Neuman (2004) 50 *Loyola LR* 1; Johns (2005) 16 *EJIL* 613. Key US decisions are *Rasul v Bush*, 542 US 466 (2004); *Hamdan v Rumsfeld*, 548 US 557 (2006); *Boumediene v Bush*, 553 US 723 (2008); *Al Maqaleh v Gates*, 605 F.3d 84 (DC Cir, 2010). Also: *Khadr v Canada (No 1)* (2008) 143 ILR 212; *Khadr v Canada (No 2)* (2009) 143 ILR 225.

[28] Another example of a modern lease agreement is the US Manas Airbase in Kyrgyzstan, renewed in 2010: US–Kyrgyzstan Status of Forces Agreement, 4 December 2001.

[29] *A-G of Israel v El-Turani* (1951) 18 ILR 164.

[30] E.g. SC Res 687 (1991) re-confirming the territorial sovereignty of both Iraq and Kuwait while imposing a demilitarized zone in the border region between the states; SC Res 1973 (2011) re-confirming the territorial sovereignty of Libya while imposing a no-fly zone.

[31] *Request for Interpretation of the Judgment of 15 June 1962 in the case concerning the Temple of Preah Vihear (Cambodia v Thailand)*, Order of 18 July 2011, §§39–42, 61.

[32] Verzijl, 2 *International Law in Historical Perspective* (1969) 339–454; Rousseau, 2 *Droit International Public* (1974) 276–300. On the unique co-seigneury of Andorra before the adoption of its constitution in 1993

part of state A and, as a colonial protectorate, has no international legal personality, although for purposes of internal law it may have a special status.[33] The question of the status of colonial protectorates is complex and can only be approached on a case by case basis.[34] The protected state may retain a measure of externally effective legal personality, although the exercise of its legal capacities be delegated to state A. In this latter case treaties by state A will not necessarily apply to state B. However, for certain purposes, including the law of neutrality and war, state B may be regarded as an agent of state A. Thus if state A declares war the protected state may be treated as belligerent also, although much will depend on the precise nature of the relations between states A and B.[35] These questions, though they can still be important for the determination of the legal status of territory, pertain closely to the question of the independence of states, considered in chapter 5.

4. RESTRICTIONS ON DISPOSITION OF TERRITORY

(A) TREATY PROVISIONS

States may by treaty agree not to alienate certain parcels of territory in any circumstances, or they may agree not to transfer to a particular state or states.[36] Moreover, a state may agree not to unite with another state: by the State Treaty of 1955, Austria is obliged not to enter into political or economic union with Germany.[37] Previously, in Article 88 of the Treaty of St Germain of 1919, the obligation was expressed differently: the independence of Austria was 'inalienable otherwise than with the consent of the Council of the League of Nations'.[38] An obligation not to acquire territory may also be undertaken. In case of a breach of a treaty obligation not to alienate, or acquire, territory, the grantee may regard the treaty as *res inter alios acta*, and it is doubtful if the existence of a claim by a third state for breach of a treaty can result in the nullity of the transfer.

---

see *Cruzel v Massip* (1960) 39 ILR 412; *Re Boedecker & Ronski* (1965) 44 ILR 176; Crawford (1977) 55 *RDISDP* 258. Now: Duursma, *Fragmentation and the International Relations of Micro-States* (1996) 316–73.

[33] *Ex parte Mwenya* [1960] 1 QB 241 (sovereignty of the British Crown over the protectorate of Northern Rhodesia indistinguishable in legal effect from that of a British colony; *habeas corpus* thus available). *Mwenya* was cited by the US Supreme Court in *Rasul v Bush*, 542 US 466, 482 (2004).

[34] *Land and Maritime Boundary between Cameroon and Nigeria (Cameroon v Nigeria)*, ICJ Reports 2002 p 303, 402–7 (kings and chiefs of Old Calabar).

[35] Cf *Nationality Decrees Issued in Tunis and Morocco* (1923) PCIJ Ser B No 4, 27.

[36] Rousseau, 3 *Droit International Public* (1977) 197–8; Verzijl (1969) 477–8.

[37] 15 May 1955, 217 UNTS 223, Art 4.

[38] (1920) 14 *AJIL Supp* 30. See *Customs Regime between Germany and Austria* (1931) PCIJ Ser A/B No 41.

(B) THE PRINCIPLE OF APPURTENANCE

The territory of a state by legal implication includes a territorial sea and the airspace above its land territory and territorial sea.[39] Thus if state A merges with state B, state B's territory will include the territorial sea and the airspace formerly of state A.[40] This simple idea is sometimes described as the principle of appurtenance,[41] and high authority supports the view that as a corollary the territorial sea cannot be alienated without the coast itself (no doubt similarly in the case of airspace).[42] But the logical and legal basis for the corollary is not compelling. Another form of appurtenance appears in the dissenting opinion of Judge McNair in the *Anglo-Norwegian Fisheries* case. In his words: '[i]nternational law imposes upon a maritime State certain obligations and confers upon it certain rights arising out of the sovereignty which it exercises over its maritime territory. The possession of this territory is not optional, not dependent upon the will of the State, but compulsory'.[43] Attractive though this view may seem at first sight, it raises many difficulties. How many of the various territorial extensions are possessed by compulsion of law? The desire to invest the coastal state with responsibility for the maintenance of order and navigational facilities is not a sufficient basis for McNair's rule; indeed, this kind of logic would equally support a doctrine of closed seas. States are permitted to abandon territory, leaving it *res nullius*, whereas the presumptive consequence of disclaiming the territorial sea is simply to extend a *res communis*, the high seas.

5. CONCLUSIONS

(A) THE CONCEPT OF TITLE[44]

The content of sovereignty has been examined from various points of view. By and large the term denotes the legal competence which a state enjoys in respect of its territory.

---

[39] E.g. when Great Britain acquired sovereignty over Australia's Northern Territory in 1824 it also acquired sovereignty over the territorial sea 'by operation of international law': *Yarmirr v Northern Territory* (2001) 125 ILR 320, 350. Cf Art 1 of the Convention on International Civil Aviation, 7 December 1944, 15 UNTS 295, reflecting customary law: '[t]he contracting States recognize that every State has complete and exclusive sovereignty over the airspace above its territory'; *KTHY v Secretary of Transport* [2009] EWHC 1918 (Admin), §41; [2010] EWCA Civ 1093, §26.

[40] Claims to territory and treaties of transfer usually refer to territory as specified, or islands, without referring to territorial waters: e.g. the Italian Peace Treaty, 10 February 1947, 49 UNTS 3, Arts 11, 14; Treaty between US and Cuba relating to the Isle of Pines, 2 March 1904, 127 LNTS 143: Wright (1925) 19 *AJIL* 340.

[41] *Grisbadarna (Norway v Sweden)* (1909) 11 RIAA 147, 155. Cf *Procurator General v D* (1948) 15 ILR 70 (status of the maritime belt determined by that of the adjoining land); on the power of the mandatory to legislate for the territorial waters of the mandated territory, *Naim Molvan v A-G for Palestine* [1948] AC 351.

[42] 1 Oppenheim 479–84; also Towey (1983) 32 *ICLQ* 1013.

[43] *Fisheries (UK v Norway)*, ICJ Reports 1951 p 116, 160 (Judge McNair, diss). Also: Fitzmaurice (1954) 31 *BY* 371, 372–3; Fitzmaurice (1957) 92 Hague *Recueil* 1, 129, 137–8.

[44] The following works are helpful, since the problems in the sphere of international law are basically the same: Honoré, in Guest (ed), *Oxford Essays in Jurisprudence* (1961) 107, 134–41; Buckland & McNair,

This competence is a consequence of title and by no means conterminous with it. Thus an important aspect of state competence, the power of disposition, may be limited by treaty, but the restriction, provided it is not total, leaves title unaffected. However, the materials of international law employ the term sovereignty to describe both the concept of title and the legal competence which flows from it. In the former sense the term 'sovereignty' explains (a) why the competence exists and what its fullest possible extent may be; and (b) whether claims may be enforced in respect of interference with the territorial aspects of that competence against a particular state.

The second aspect mentioned is the essence of title: the validity of claims to territorial sovereignty against other states. The equivalent concept in French, *titre*, has been defined as follows: '*[t]erme qui, pris dans le sens de titre juridique, désigne tout fait, acte ou situation qui est la cause et le fondement d'un droit*'.[45] In principle the concept of ownership, opposable to all other states and unititular,[46] does exist. Thus the first and undisputed occupation of land which is *res nullius* may give rise to title which is equivalent to the *dominium* of Roman law. However, in practice the concept of title employed to solve disputes approximates to the notion of the better right to possess familiar in the common law.[47] The operation of the doctrines of acquiescence and recognition makes this type of approach inevitable, but in any case tribunals will favour an approach which reckons with the limitations inherent in a procedure dominated by the presentation of evidence by two claimants, the result of which is not automatically opposable to third states.[48]

(B) TITLE, DELIMITATION, DEMARCATION

In a broad sense many questions of title arise in the context of 'boundary disputes', but as a matter of principle the determination of the location in detail of the boundary line is distinct from the issue of title. Considerable dispositions of territory may take place in which the grantee enjoys the benefit of a title derived from the grant although no determination of the precise boundary line is made.[49] On the other hand precise determination of the boundary may be made a suspensive condition in a treaty of

---

Roman Law and Common Law (2nd edn, 1965) 71–88 (excursus by Lawson). Also: Castellino & Allen, *Title to Territory in International Law* (2003).

[45] Basdevant, *Dictionnaire de la terminologie du droit international* (1960) sv. Cf Salmon (ed), *Dictionnaire de droit international public* (2001) 1084.

[46] Honoré, in Guest (1961) 137, for a definition of a unititular system: '[u]nder it, if the title to a thing is in A, no title to it can be acquired (independently) by B, except by a process which divests A. There is only one "root of title" for each thing, and the present title can ultimately be traced back to that root.'

[47] Jennings, *Acquisition of Territory in International Law* (1963) 5–6. The common law is 'multititular': Honoré, in Guest (1961) 139; so is international law: *Legal Status of Eastern Greenland* (1933) PCIJ Ser A/B No 53, 46; *Island of Palmas (Netherlands v US)* (1928) 2 RIAA 829, 840.

[48] Statute of the International Court of Justice, 26 June 1945, 33 UNTS 993, Art 59.

[49] On the effect of treaties of cession or renunciation relating to territories the boundaries of which are undetermined: *Interpretation of Article 3, Paragraph 2, of the Treaty of Lausanne* (1925) PCIJ Ser B No 12, 21.

cession. The process of determination is carried out in accordance with a special body of rules. For example according to the *thalweg principle* in the case of a navigable river, the middle of the principal channel of navigation is accepted as the boundary. In the case of non-navigable watercourses the boundary is constituted by the median line between the two banks.[50]

The practical aspects of boundaries must be emphasized. Agreement as to the precise details of a boundary is often followed by the separate procedure of demarcation, that is, the marking, literally, of the boundary on the ground by means of posts, stone pillars, and the like. A boundary may be legally definitive and yet remain undemarcated. Boundaries which are *de facto*, either because of the absence of demarcation or because of the presence of an unsettled territorial dispute, may nevertheless be accepted as the legal limit of sovereignty for some purposes, for example those of civil or criminal jurisdiction, nationality law, and the prohibition of unpermitted intrusion with or without the use of arms.

(C) *NEMO DAT QUOD NON HABET*[51]

This maxim, together with some exceptions, is a familiar feature of English law, but the principle is undoubtedly part of international law also. In *Island of Palmas*, Arbitrator Huber stated:

The title alleged by the United States of America as constituting the immediate foundation of its claim is that of cession, brought about by the Treaty of Paris, which cession transferred all rights of sovereignty which Spain may have possessed in the region. ... It is evident that Spain could not transfer more rights than she herself possessed.[52]

The effect of the principle is much reduced by the operation of acquiescence and recognition.

Certain connected principles require consideration. First, in principle the adjudication by a tribunal of a piece of territory as between states A and B is not opposable to state C. The tribunal, insofar as adjudication of itself gives title, only has jurisdiction to decide as between the parties before it.[53] The fact that state C claims a particular parcel of territory does not deprive the tribunal of power to adjudicate and does not prevent states A and B from defining their rights in relation to the parcel mutually.[54] In

---

[50] *Kasikili/Sedudu Island (Botswana v Namibia)*, ICJ Reports 1999 p 1045, 1061–2; *Frontier Dispute (Benin v Niger)*, ICJ Reports 2005 p 90, 149–50. Also: *Guyana/Suriname Arbitration* (2007) 139 ILR 566, §§137, 194, 226, 301. Generally: Cukwurah, *The Settlement of Boundary Disputes in International Law* (1967); 3 Rousseau (1977) 231–72; Brownlie, *African Boundaries* (1979); Shaw, *Title to Territory in Africa* (1986) 221–63; Biger (1989) 25 *MES* 249; McCaffrey, *The Law of International Watercourses* (2nd edn, 2007) 70–2; Islam, *The Law of Non-Navigational Uses of International Watercourses* (2010).

[51] *Cameroon v Nigeria*, ICJ Reports 2002 p 303, 400–7. Also McNair, *Treaties* (1961) 656, 665.

[52] *Island of Palmas (Netherlands v US)* (1928) 2 RIAA 829, 842.

[53] *Guiana Boundary (Brazil v UK)* (1904) 11 RIAA 11, 22.

[54] Boundary Agreement between China and Pakistan, 2 March 1963, (1963) 57 *AJIL* 713, which is expressed as fixing 'the alignment of the boundary between China's Sinkiang and the contiguous areas the

certain cases, the principle operates through particular rules governing special problems. Thus an aggressor, having seized territory by force may purport to transfer the territory to a third state. The validity of the cession will depend on the effect of specific rules relating to the use of force by states. Again, a state may transfer territory which it lacks the capacity to transfer. In this type of situation much turns on the extent to which defects of title may be cured by acquiescence, and recognition.

Under certain conditions it is possible that the law accepts the existence of encumbrances passing with territory ceded. McNair refers to 'treaties creating purely local obligations' and gives as examples territory over which the ceding state has granted to another state a right of transit[55] or a right of navigation on a river,[56] or a right of fishery in territorial or internal waters.[57] This is also the approach of the 1978 Vienna Convention on the Succession of States in Respect of Treaties, Article 21 of which provides that a succession of states shall not affect obligations or rights 'relating to the use of territory' which are 'established by a treaty for the benefit of any territory of a foreign state and considered as attaching to the territories in question'.[58]

---

defence of which is under the actual control of Pakistan'. Thus India's rights in respect of Kashmir are not foreclosed (Art 6 of the Agreement).

[55] 'A right of transit by one country across the territory of another can only arise as a matter of specific agreement': *Iron Rhine (Belgium v Netherlands)* (2005) 27 RIAA 35, 64.

[56] E.g. the rights of Costa Rica over the San Juan River: *Navigational and Related Rights (Nicaragua v Costa Rica)*, ICJ Reports 2009 p 213.

[57] McNair (1961) 656. Others speak of 'international servitudes', a term McNair rejects since it 'would make the category depend upon the recognition by international law of the institution known as a servitude, which is highly controversial'. See however *Eritrea v Yemen (Territorial Sovereignty)* where the Tribunal noted that the traditional open fishing regime in the southern Red Sea together with the common use of the islands in the area by populations of both coasts was capable of creating historic rights accruing to the two states in dispute in the form of 'a *"servitude internationale"* falling short of territorial sovereignty': (1998) 114 ILR 1, 40–1. Evidently the Tribunal could not quite stomach the idea of a servitude in English. In the region this well-meaning dictum has been a further source of conflict. On the question of servitudes see also *Right of Passage over Indian Territory (Portugal v India)*, ICJ Reports 1960 p 6; *Aaland Islands* (1920) *LNOJ Sp Supp* No 3, 18; *SS Wimbledon* (1920) PCIJ Ser A No 1, 24. Traditionally, such rights were to be interpreted restrictively as limitations to sovereignty. However, such a restrictive interpretation has been rejected in more recent cases: e.g. *Iron Rhine* (2005) 27 RIAA 35, 64–7; *Navigational Rights*, ICJ Reports 2009 p 213, 237–8.

[58] 23 August 1978, 1946 UNTS 3. Art 12 does not however say when rights and duties are so considered.

9

ACQUISITION AND TRANSFER OF TERRITORIAL SOVEREIGNTY[1]

1. INTRODUCTION

Disputes concerning title to land territory, including islands, and over the precise determination of boundaries are regularly the subject of international proceedings. Recourse to arbitration may be part of an overall peace settlement.[2] But many such conflicts are dormant and it is only when a dispute flares up that it receives publicity. While the occupation of territory not belonging to any state (*terra nullius*) is no longer a live issue, issues concerning such occupation in the past may still arise. Legally relevant events may have occurred centuries ago.[3] The pressures of national sentiment, the exploitation of areas once thought barren or inaccessible, the strategic significance of areas previously neglected, and the pressure of population on resources suggest that territorial disputes will continue to be significant.

---

[1] Jennings, *The Acquisition of Territory in International Law* (1963); Fitzmaurice (1955–56) 32 *BY* 20; de Visscher, *Les Effectivités du droit international public* (1967) 101; Blum, *Historic Titles in International Law* (1965); Bardonnet (1976) 153 Hague *Recueil* 9; Kaikobad (1983) 54 *BY* 119; Shaw, *Title to Territory in Africa* (1986); Thirlway (1995) 66 *BY* 10; Kohen, *Possession contestée et souveraineté territoriale* (1997); Sharma, *Territorial Acquisition, Disputes and International Law* (1997); Ratner (2006) 100 *AJIL* 808; Prescott & Triggs, *International Frontiers and Boundaries* (2008); Shaw, *The International Law of Territory* (2012). For acquisition of maritime territory and zones see chapter 11; for maritime delimitation, chapter 12.

[2] E.g. *Eritrea-Ethiopia Boundary Delimitation* (2002) 130 ILR 1; Simma & Khan, in Ando, McWhinney & Wolfrum (eds), 2 *Liber Amicorum Judge Shigeru Oda* (2002) 1179; Shaw (2007) 56 *ICLQ* 755; Kohen, in Kohen (ed), *Liber Amicorum Lucius Caflisch* (2007) 767. Also, for Sudan: *Government of Sudan v Sudan People's Liberation Movement/Army (Abyei Arbitration)* (2009) 144 ILR 348; Daly & Schofield, 'Abyei Arbitration' (2010) *MPEPIL*; Bockenforde (2010) 23 *LJIL* 555.

[3] In *Minquiers and Ecrehos (France/UK)*, ICJ Reports 1953 p 47, the parties and, to a lesser extent, the Court considered it necessary to investigate legal transactions of the medieval period.

2. DETERMINING TITLE

(A) THE CENTRALITY OF TITLE[4]

If the basic unit of the international legal system is the state, the space which the state occupies in the world is its territory, traditionally thought of as realty, with the state (a person) its proprietor. Thus there were sales and bequests of state territory, leaseholds and reversions, with little or no regard for the wishes of the inhabitants. Indeed international law developed a notion of entitlement to territory well before the state itself developed as a normative concept. Thereafter title arose not simply by physical occupation (i.e. actual administration, often referred to as *effectivités*) but through acquisition in accordance with law—although until 1928, the law included the rule that coerced treaties were valid.[5] Yet there were areas of uncertainty, with territory (often islands, islets, or rocks but sometimes whole provinces) contested between states.[6] In such cases it was largely a historical question which of the claimant states had the better claim.

The basic principle in the modern law is that stated by the Chamber in *Frontier Dispute (Burkina Faso/Mali)*:

Where the act corresponds exactly to law, where effective administration is additional to the *uti possidetis iuris*, the only role of *effectivité* is to confirm the exercise of the right derived from a legal title. Where the act does not correspond to the law, where the territory which is the subject of the dispute is effectively administered by a State other than the one possessing the legal title, preference should be given to the holder of the title. In the event that the *effectivité* does not co-exist with any legal title, it must invariably be taken into consideration. Finally, there are cases where the legal title is not capable of showing exactly the territorial expanse to which it relates. The *effectivité* can then play an essential role in showing how the title is interpreted in practice.[7]

Thus title prevails over possession, but if title is equivocal, possession under claim of right matters.

Title to territory, like ownership of land, is normally 'objective', but there is no system of registration, no international Torrens title.[8] Unquestioned title is a contingency

---

[4] Fitzmaurice (1955–56) 32 *BY* 20, 64–6; Schwarzenberger (1957) 51 *AJIL* 308, 320–2; Castellino & Allen, *Title to Territory in International Law* (2003); Kohen (2004) 108 *RGDIP* 562; Shaw (ed), *Title to Territory* (2005); Ratner (2006) 100 *AJIL* 808. See also chapter 8. For linguistic confusion over the term: O'Keefe (2011) 13 *Int Comm LR* 147, 153–4.

[5] Thus the objection to British acquisition of the Boer Republics was merely that it was premature, not that it was intrinsically unlawful: *West Rand Central Gold Mining Co v R* [1905] 2 KB 391. For the development of rules relating to the use of force see chapter 33.

[6] On Gibraltar see Waibel, 'Gibraltar' (2009) *MPEPIL*.

[7] ICJ Reports 1986 p 554, 586–7. The term *uti possidetis (iuris)* refers to the presumption that the boundaries of a new state or entity follow those that existed under the previous (usually colonial) regime. Further: Lalonde, *Determining Boundaries in a Conflicted World* (2002); Castellino & Allen (2003) ch 1.

[8] That is, a system of municipal title registration whereby inclusion on the register confers on the holder indefeasible title: see *Black's Law Dictionary* (9th edn, 2010) 1625. The civil law equivalent is a cadastre.

arising from history, general recognition, and the absence of any other claimant. Title may be relative in several quite different contexts.

(1) The principle *nemo dat quod non habet* (no donor can give a greater interest than he or she already has) places a restrictive effect on titles dependent on bilateral agreement: see chapter 8.

(2) A judicial decision on issues of title cannot foreclose the rights of third parties.

(3) In a situation where physical holding is not conclusive of the question of right, recognition becomes important, and this may be forthcoming from some states and not others.

(4) The *compromis* on the basis of which a dispute is submitted to a court or tribunal may assume that title is to go to one of the two claimants. In *Minquiers and Ecrehos* the Court interpreted the *compromis* as excluding a finding that the islets were *res nullius* or subject to a *condominium*.[9] In such a case, in the absence of any other claimant, the result seems to be a title valid against all, but the parties have not had to come up to any minimum requirements of effective control.

(5) In any event, in instances such as *Island of Palmas* and *Minquiers and Ecrehos*,[10] the Court assesses the relative intensity of the competing acts of state authority to determine which party has the better right.

(6) In appropriate circumstances the Court will lean in favour of title in one claimant even though there are grounds for a finding that the territory was at the relevant time *terra nullius*. Thus in *Eastern Greenland*[11] Danish activity in the disputed area had hardly been intensive, but the Court refused to consider the area *terra nullius*.[12]

(7) In some cases the sheer ambiguity of the facts may lead the Court to rely on matters which are less than fundamental,[13] or to seek evidence of acquiescence by one party. In this context it is academic to use the classification 'inchoate'. A title, though resting on very preliminary acts, is sufficient as against those without a better title.[14] In coming to a decision on the question of right, it may be necessary to measure 'titles' against each other.[15]

---

[9] ICJ Reports 1953 p 47, 52. See also the special agreement in *Island of Palmas* (1928) 2 RIAA 831, 869.

[10] Also: *Temple of Preah Vihear (Cambodia v Thailand)*, ICJ Reports 1962 p 6, 72 (Judge Moreno Quintana).

[11] *Legal Status of Eastern Greenland* (1933) PCIJ Ser A/B No 53. Further: Alfredsson, 'Eastern Greenland Case' (2007) *MPEPIL*.

[12] Cf Lauterpacht, *Development* (1958) 241. Also: *Clipperton Island* (1931) 2 RIAA 1105.

[13] *Sovereignty over Certain Frontier Land (Belgium/Netherlands)*, ICJ Reports 1959 p 209, 231 (Judge Lauterpacht), 232 (Judge Spiropoulos), 249–51 (Judge Armand-Ugon), where title resting on an ambiguous treaty conflicted with various acts of administration.

[14] Cf French rights as against Mexico in *Clipperton*; Danish rights as against Norway in *Eastern Greenland*. See Beckett (1934) 50 Hague *Recueil* 189, 230, 254–5.

[15] *Island of Palmas* (1928) 2 RIAA 831, 870.

(B) THE INTERTEMPORAL LAW[16]

In many instances the rights of parties to a dispute derive from a legally significant act done, or treaty concluded, long ago. As Fitzmaurice says, it is 'an established principle of international law that in such cases the situation in question must be appraised, and the treaty interpreted, in the light of the rules of international law as they existed *at the time*, and not as they exist today'.[17] In *Island of Palmas,* Judge Huber stated the principle and continued: 'The effect of discovery by Spain is … to be determined by the rules of international law in force in the first half of the 16th century—or (to take the earliest date) in the first quarter of it …'.[18] The rule has also been applied in the interpretation of treaties concerning territory.[19] It is justified by reference to the need for predictability and stability in the international system of title.[20]

In *Island of Palmas,* Judge Huber had to consider whether Spanish sovereignty over the island subsisted at the critical date in 1898. In doing so he gave a new dimension to the rule:

As regards the question which of different legal systems prevailing at successive periods is to be applied in a particular case (the so-called intertemporal law), a distinction must be made between the creation of rights and the existence of rights. The same principle which subjects the act creative of a right to the law in force at the time the right arises, demands that the existence of the right, in other words its continued manifestation, shall follow the conditions required by the evolution of law.[21]

This extension of the doctrine has been criticized on the grounds that to require title to be actively maintained at every moment of time would threaten many titles and lead to instability.[22] This emphasizes the need for care in applying the rule.[23] In any case the intertemporal principle does not operate in a vacuum: its impact will be reduced

---

[16] Jennings (1963) 28; Fitzmaurice (1953) 30 *BY* 1, 5; Elias (1980) 74 *AJIL* 285; Thirlway (1995) 66 *BY* 128; Higgins, in Makarczyk (ed), *International Law at the Threshold of the 21st Century* (1996) 173; Kotzur, 'Intertemporal Law' (2008) *MPEPIL*.

[17] Fitzmaurice (1953) 30 *BY* 1, 5 (emphasis added). See also Fitzmaurice (1975) 56 *Ann de l'Inst* 536, Art 1 ('Unless otherwise indicated, the temporal sphere of application of any norm of public international law shall be determined in accordance with the general principle of law by which any fact, action or situation must be assessed in light of the rules that are contemporaneous with it').

[18] *Island of Palmas* (1928) 2 RIAA 831, 845. Further: Jessup (1928) 22 *AJIL* 735; also *Banks of Grisbadarna* (1909) 11 RIAA 155, 159.

[19] *Rights of Nationals of the United States of America in Morocco (France v US),* ICJ Reports 1952 p 176, 189; *Right of Passage over Indian Territory (Portugal v India),* ICJ Reports 1960 p 6, 37; also *Legal Consequences for States of the Continued Presence of South Africa in Namibia (South West Africa) notwithstanding Security Council Resolution 276 (1970),* ICJ Reports 1971 p 16, 31; *Aegean Sea Continental Shelf (Greece v Turkey),* ICJ Reports 1978 p 3, 32.

[20] E.g. *Eritrea and Yemen* (1998) 114 ILR 1, 46, 115; *Eritrea-Ethiopia Boundary* (2002) 130 ILR 1, 34; *Land and Maritime Boundary between Cameroon and Nigeria,* ICJ Reports 2002 p 303, 404–7.

[21] *Island of Palmas* (1928) 2 RIAA 831, 845.

[22] Lauterpacht, *Function of Law* (1933, repr 2011) 283–5. See Jessup (1928) 22 *AJIL* 735, 739; Jennings (1963) 28; Jennings (1967) 121 Hague *Recueil* 422.

[23] This form of the doctrine was applied sensibly in *Minquiers and Ecrehos,* ICJ Reports 1953 p 47, 56; see also *Western Sahara,* ICJ Reports 1975 p 12, 38; ibid, 168 (Judge de Castro).

by the effect of recognition, acquiescence, and the rule that abandonment is not to be presumed. Thus in *Pedra Branca*, the historic title of the Sultanate of Johore to the disputed features survived into the modern period, despite little or nothing by way of the exercise of governmental authority over them.[24]

(C) THE CRITICAL DATE[25]

In any dispute a certain date will assume prominence in the process of evaluating the facts. The choice of such a date is within the province of the tribunal and will depend on the logic of the law applicable to the facts as well as on the practical necessity of confining the dossier to the more relevant facts and thus to acts prior to the existence of a dispute. In the latter context the tribunal is simply excluding evidence consisting of self-serving acts of parties after the dispute arose. But evidence of acts and statements occurring after the critical date may be admissible if not self-serving, as in the case of admissions against interest. There are several types of critical date, and it is difficult and probably misleading to formulate general definitions:[26] the facts of the case are dominant (including the terms of the special agreement empowering the tribunal to hear the case) and there may be no necessity for a tribunal to choose any date whatsoever.

In some cases there will be several dates of significance. *Eastern Greenland* arose from a Norwegian proclamation of 10 July 1931 announcing occupation of the area. The Court held that 'as the critical date is July 10th, 1931 ... it is sufficient [for Denmark] to establish a valid title in the period immediately preceding the occupation.'[27] In *Island of Palmas* the US claimed as successor to Spain under a treaty of 10 December 1898, and everything turned on the nature of Spanish rights at that time. The Court did not specifically choose a critical date in *Minquiers and Ecrehos*.[28] In *Argentine-Chile Frontier* the tribunal 'considered the notion of the critical date to be of little value in the present litigation and ... examined all the evidence submitted to it, irrespective of the date of the acts to which such evidence relates'.[29]

---

[24] *Sovereignty over Pedra Branca/Pulau Batu Puteh, Middle Rocks and South Ledge (Malaysia/Singapore)*, ICJ Reports 2008 p 12.

[25] Fitzmaurice (1955–56) 32 BY 20; Blum (1965) 208; Thirlway (1995) 66 BY 31. See also the Chamber in *Land, Island and Maritime Frontier Dispute (El Salvador/Honduras)*, ICJ Reports 1992 p 351, 401. For the problems arising in the context of treaties of cession and the rights of successor states see *Lighthouses (France and Greece)* (1956) 23 ILR 659, 668.

[26] See Jennings (1963) 31; Jennings (1967) 121 Hague *Recueil* 423.

[27] *Eastern Greenland* (1933) PCIJ Ser A/B No 53, 45.

[28] ICJ Reports 1953 p 47. France relied on the date of the Convention between France and Great Britain for Defining the Limits of Exclusive Fishing Rights, 2 August 1839, 89 CTS 221; the UK on the date of the *compromis* (29 December 1950). See Johnson (1954) 3 *ICLQ* 189, 207–11. Critical dates did not feature in *Temple*, ICJ Reports 1962 p 6. However, the Court treated two dates as material: 1904, the date of a frontier treaty between France and Thailand, and 1954, when Thailand sent military or police forces to occupy the area. See also *Rann of Kutch* (1968) 50 ILR 2, 470.

[29] (1966) 38 ILR 10, 79–80. Also: *Eritrea and Yemen* (1998) 114 ILR 1, 32; *Sovereignty over Pulau Ligitan and Pulau Sipidan (Indonesia/Malaysia)*, ICJ Reports 2002 p 625, 682; *Territorial and Maritime Dispute between Nicaragua and Honduras in the Caribbean Sea*, ICJ Reports 2007 p 659, 697–701.

(D) *TERRA NULLIUS*[30]

Terra nullius is land not under the sovereignty or authority of any state; *occupatio* was the mode by which such territory could be acquired.[31] In the modern context, it has fallen into disuse. This is because there remains on the surface of the earth no truly 'vacant' territory,[32] but also because the term gradually assumed imperialist overtones when it was used to justify colonization of large areas of inhabited lands through a theory of European supremacy. That theory underlay the Congress of Berlin of 1885 but now 'stands condemned'.[33] In *Western Sahara*, the Court had to decide whether the Western Sahara was *terra nullius* at the time of Spanish colonization (in the 1890s). It held it was not, because the people of the territory were socially and politically organized under chiefs with a capacity to represent them. In fact the territory was acquired by treaty, not occupation.[34]

3. THE 'MODES' OF ACQUISITION

(A) BASIC PRINCIPLES

Standard textbooks, particularly those in English, classify the modes of acquisition in a stereotyped way reflecting those of Roman law.[35] According to this analysis there are five modes of acquisition—occupation, accretion, cession, conquest, and prescription. But the concept of modes of acquisition is unsound in principle: such labels only make the task of analysis more difficult.[36] The inadequacies of the orthodox approach are more apparent when the relevant questions have been examined, but a few things may be usefully said here.

First, it is common to classify the five orthodox modes of acquisition as 'original' or 'derivative'. Occupation and accretion are usually described as 'original', cession as 'derivative'. There are differences of opinion in regard to conquest and prescription, and again the classification has no practical value.[37] In one sense all titles are original, since much depends on the acts of the grantee in the case of a cession. In any event the

---

[30] Generally: Andrews (1978) 94 *LQR* 408.

[31] E.g. *Eastern Greenland* (1933) PCIJ Ser A/B No 53, 44–51; *Western Sahara*, ICJ Reports 1975 p 12, 38–40, 85–6 (Vice-President Ammoun).

[32] Aside from some very small rocks and a small sector of Antarctica (over which in any case no sovereignty may be claimed by virtue of the Antarctic Treaty, 1 December 1959, 402 UNTS 71, Art IV). Also: Shaw, in Shaw (2005) 3, 24; Ratner (2006) 100 *AJIL* 808, 811.

[33] *Western Sahara*, ICJ Reports 1975 p 12, 86.

[34] Ibid, 39–40. For the classification of Australia as *terra nullius*: *Mabo v Queensland (No 2)* (1992) 112 ILR 457, 491–2. Generally on the 18th–19th century practice: Crawford, *Creation of States* (2nd edn, 2006) 263–74.

[35] Castellino & Allen (2003) ch 2.

[36] For criticism: Johnson (1955) 13 *CLJ* 215; Jennings (1963) 6–7.

[37] Thus an 'original' mode does not necessarily give a title free of encumbrances: *Right of Passage*, ICJ Reports 1960 p 6.

dual classification oversimplifies the situation, and the modes described as 'derivative' are so in rather different ways. Moreover the usual analyses do not explain how title is acquired when a new state comes into existence.[38] Events leading to independence of the new state are mostly within the domestic jurisdiction of another state, yet they are legally relevant to territorial disputes involving the new state. In this type of case there is no 'root of title' *as such*: title is a by-product of the events leading to the creation of a state as a new source of territorial sovereignty.[39]

Secondly, in determining title, a tribunal will concern itself with proof of the exercise of sovereignty via conduct *à titre de souverain* before the critical date or dates, and will not apply the orthodox analysis to describe its process of decision. The issue of territorial sovereignty is often complex and involves the application of various legal principles to the facts, including (as concerns the modern period) principles deriving from the prohibition on the acquisition of territory by force and the invalidity of coerced treaties. The result often cannot be ascribed to any single 'mode of acquisition'. Orthodox analysis does not allow for the interaction of acquiescence and recognition with the other rules. Furthermore, a category like 'cession' or 'prescription' may bring quite distinct situations into unhappy fellowship.[40] Lastly, the importance of showing a better right in contentious cases, that is, of relative title, is obscured if too much credit is given to the five 'modes'. Thus the following headings represent categories of convenience.

(B) ORIGINAL AND HISTORIC TITLE

It may happen that a current dispute involves not only reliance upon the exercise of state authority but the invocation of an ancient, original or historic title. The concept informs the principle of 'immemorial possession' and reliance upon evidence of general repute or opinion as to matters of historical fact. Particularly in Asia, traditional boundaries play a significant role.[41] International tribunals have recognized the concept of ancient or original title,[42] but require appropriate evidence in support.

(C) EFFECTIVE OCCUPATION[43]

The concept of effective occupation in international law represents the type of legal relation which in private law would be described as possession. In *Eastern Greenland*

---

[38] Jennings (1963) 7–11. Also: 1 Hyde 390; 1 Hackworth 444–5.

[39] Crawford (2nd edn, 2006) 664–5; see further chapter 5.

[40] The term 'annexation' is neither a term of art nor a root of title, but describes an official state act signifying an extension of sovereignty. Whether it is legally effective is another matter. See McNair, 1 *Opinions* 285, 289; 1 Hackworth 446–9.

[41] Kaikobad (1983) 54 *BY* 119, 130–4.

[42] *Minquiers and Ecrehos*, ICJ Reports 1953 p 47, 53–7, 74–9 (Judge Basdevant); *Rann of Kutch* (1968) 50 ILR 2, 474; *Western Sahara*, ICJ Reports 1975 p 12, 42–3; *El Salvador/Honduras*, ICJ Reports 1992 p 351, 564–5; *Eritrea and Yemen* (1998) 114 ILR 1, 37–45.

[43] Waldock (1948) 25 *BY* 311; von der Heydte (1935) 29 *AJIL* 448; Fitzmaurice (1955–56) 32 *BY* 20, 49–71; Shaw, in Shaw (2005) xi.

the Permanent Court said 'a claim to sovereignty based not upon some particular act or title such as a treaty of cession but merely upon continued display of authority, involves two elements each of which must be shown to exist: the intention and will to act as sovereign, and some actual exercise or display of such authority'.[44] This statement has not lost its force, and was (in part) reiterated in *Eritrea/Yemen*: '[t]he modern international law of the acquisition (or attribution) of territory generally requires that there be: an intentional display of power and authority over the territory, by the exercise of jurisdiction or State functions, on a continuous and peaceful basis'.[45]

In the absence of a formal basis of title in a treaty or judgment, and in a system without registration of title, possession plays a significant role. It must be borne in mind that 'legal possession' involves a search for an interest worth protection by the law. Legal policy may lead a court to regard as sufficient a tenuous connection with the territory in certain conditions. Moreover, what is important is *state activity* and especially acts of administration: use by local peoples generally lacks this element and is only tangentially relevant.[46] 'Occupation' here derives from *occupatio* in Roman law and does not necessarily signify occupation in the sense of actual settlement and a physical holding.

As in private law, the concept of effective occupation is complex, and many difficulties arise in applying it to the facts. Precisely what acts will be sufficient to found sovereignty is a matter of fact and degree,[47] and may depend on the character of the territory: for example, the bar with respect to remote and sparsely settled areas will be set lower than in the context of more heavily populated territory.

Effective and long-established occupation is key to a claim of acquisitive prescription, although courts and tribunals have rarely applied that doctrine as such.[48] In practice it may not be easy to distinguish effective occupation and prescription, and neither *Island of Palmas* nor *Eastern Greenland* employs the categories. Beckett classified the former as a case of prescription, the latter as resting on occupation.[49] But in both cases the issue was simply which of two competing sovereignties had the better right. Prescription classically involves usurpation, yet these cases involved, for all practical purposes, contemporaneous, competing acts of state sovereignty. In

---

[44] (1933) PCIJ Ser A/B No 53, 45–6, 63; *Western Sahara*, ICJ Reports 1975 p 6, 12, 42–3. These criteria were applied in *Caribbean Sea*, ICJ Reports 2007 p 659, 711–21.

[45] (1998) 114 ILR 1, 69.

[46] *Kasikili/Sedudu Island (Botswana/Namibia)*, ICJ Reports 1999 p 1045, 1105–6.

[47] E.g. *Eastern Greenland* (1933) PCIJ Ser A/B No 53, 45–6; *Maritime Delimitation and Territorial Questions between Qatar and Bahrain*, ICJ Reports 2001 p 40, 100 (and see Kohen (2002) 106 *RGDIP* 295); *Pulau Ligitan/Sipadan*, ICJ Reports 2002 p 625, 682; *Pulau Batu Puteh*, ICJ Reports 2008 p 12, 34–7.

[48] E.g. *Pulau Batu Puteh*, ICJ Reports 2008 p 12.

[49] Beckett (1934) 50 Hague *Recueil* 218, 220. *Eastern Greenland* (1933) PCIJ Ser A/B No 53 is commonly thought to have been decided on the basis that the area concerned was *terra nullius* at the critical date, but this is a misreading: de Visscher (1967) 105. The Belize Supreme Court held that Britain gained sovereignty over Belize 'by a combination of the various treaties with Spain and later with Guatemala, first acquired interests in British Honduras and by effective occupation and administration together with the passage of time': *Cal v Attorney General* (2007) 46 ILM 1022, 1038.

Minquiers and Ecrehos, the Court stated the issue as one of possession,[50] which in the context was equated with sovereignty.[51] Its task was 'to appraise the relative strength of the opposing claims to sovereignty over the Ecrehos'.[52]

(i) Discovery[53]

This category, much employed, is equally unsatisfactory for the purpose of legal analysis. It links the concept of 'discovery' to that of *terra nullius,* and is discredited for the same reasons. At one time it was thought that in the fifteenth and sixteenth centuries discovery conferred a complete title.[54] But it seems that it gave no more than an inchoate title: an effective act of appropriation seems to have been necessary.[55] The modern view, certainly, is that it gave no more than an inchoate title, an option, as against other states, to proceed to effective occupation within a reasonable time.[56] In *Island of Palmas* the US argued that, as successor to Spain, its title derived from Spanish discovery in the sixteenth century. Huber responded that, even if discovery without more gave title at that time, the continued existence of the right must be determined according to the law prevailing in 1898, the critical date. In his opinion the modern law is that 'an inchoate title of discovery must be completed within a reasonable period by the effective occupation of the region claimed to be discovered'.[57] British[58] and Norwegian[59] practice supports this view. The US view now is that mere discovery gives no title, inchoate or otherwise, and this has much to commend it.[60] The notion of discovery only makes sense if it is placed firmly in the context of effective occupation, and it is best to avoid the category altogether. Further, the notion of inchoate title is misleading. Title is never 'inchoate', though it may be weak if it rests on slight evidence of state activity.

---

[50] *Minquiers and Ecrehos,* ICJ Reports 1953 p 47, 55–7.

[51] Ibid, 58–9.

[52] Ibid, 67. Cf *Eastern Greenland* (1933) PCIJ Ser A/B No 53, 22, 46.

[53] See 1 Hyde 312–30; Lindley (1926) ch 8; von der Heydte (1935) 29 *AJIL* 448; Goebel, *The Struggle for the Falkland Islands* (1927) 47–119; Waldock (1948) 25 *BY* 311, 322–5; McDougal, Lasswell, Vlasic & Smith (1963) 111 *U Penn LR* 521, 543–4, 558–60, 598–611; McDougal, Lasswell & Vlasic, *Law and Public Order in Space* (1963) 829–44; Kohen & Hébié, 'Territory, Discovery' (2011) *MPEPIL.*

[54] Hall, *International Law* (1880) 126.

[55] In the 16th century Roman law relating to acquisition by finding was applied, and this emphasized actual taking. Contemporary state practice usually demanded a first taking followed by public and continuous possession evidenced by state activity. See the instructions of Charles V of Spain to his ambassador of 18 December 1523 respecting the Spanish claim to the Moluccas: Goebel (1927) 96–7; 1 Hyde 324. Keller, Lissitzyn & Mann argue that whereas mere discovery could not give a valid title, symbolic acts of taking of possession could do so: *Creation of Rights of Sovereignty through Symbolic Acts, 1400–1800* (1938) 148–9.

[56] Hall (1880) 127; McNair, 1 *Opinions* 285.

[57] See also *Clipperton Island* (1931) 2 RIAA 1105, in which Mexico relied unsuccessfully on alleged discovery by Spain.

[58] McNair, 1 *Opinions* 285, 287, 320; 1 Hackworth 455.

[59] 1 Hackworth 400, 453, 469, 459 (French view on Adélie Land); Orent & Reinsch (1941) 35 *AJIL* 443; cf 1 Hyde 325 (Portuguese view in 1782).

[60] 1 Hackworth 398–400, 457, 460.

(ii) Symbolic annexation[61]

Symbolic annexation[62] may be defined as a declaration or other act of sovereignty or an act of private persons, duly authorized, or subsequently ratified by a state, intended to provide unequivocal evidence of the acquisition of sovereignty over a parcel of territory or an island. The subject must be seen as a part of the general question of effective occupation. There is no magic in the formal declaration of sovereignty by a government, whether or not this is preceded, accompanied or followed by a formal ceremony in the vicinity. In the case of uninhabited, inhospitable and remote regions little is required in the nature of state activity and a first, decisive act of sovereignty may suffice to create a valid title. But in principle the state activity must satisfy the normal requirements of 'effective occupation'. 'Symbolic annexation' does not give title except in special circumstances (as in *Clipperton Island*). However, it is a part of the evidence of state activity. It has been stated that 'a prior State act of formal annexation cannot after a long interval prevail against an actual and continuous display of sovereignty by another State'.[63] But if the initial act was effective to vest title then a latecomer can only succeed, if at all, on the basis of prescription or acquiescence. To require too much in respect of the maintenance of rights may encourage threats to the peace. In the case of remote islands, it is unhelpful to require a determinate minimum of 'effectiveness', once title is actually established.[64]

In *Clipperton Island* a French lieutenant, duly authorized, proclaimed French sovereignty in 1858: this was notified to the government of Hawaii by the French consulate. In 1897, after inactivity in the intervening years, a French vessel called at the island and found three Americans collecting guano for an American company. The US denied any intention of claiming sovereignty. In the same year the island received its first visit from a Mexican gunboat and a diplomatic controversy began. The Mexican case rested on Spanish discovery, but the arbitrator held that even if a historic right existed it was not supported by any manifestation of Mexican sovereignty. The award continues:

if a territory, by virtue of the fact that it was completely uninhabited, is, from the first moment when the occupying State makes its appearance there, at the absolute and undisputed disposition of that State, from that moment the taking of possession must be considered as accomplished, and the occupation is thereby completed.[65]

---

[61] McDougal, Lasswell, Vlasic & Smith (1963) 111 *U Penn LR* 521, 543–4, 558–60, 598–611; McDougal, Lasswell, Vlasic & Smith, *Law and Public Order in Space* (1963) 829–44; 1 Hackworth 398–9; Waldock (1948) 25 *BY* 311, 323–5; McNair, 1 *Opinions* 314ff; Marston (1986) 57 *BY* 337.

[62] The term 'annexation' is neither a term of art nor a root of title. The term commonly describes an official state act signifying an extension of sovereignty. Whether it is legally effective is another matter. See McNair, 1 *Opinions* 285, 289; 1 Hackworth 446–9.

[63] See Waldock (1950) 36 *GST* 325. Cf Fitzmaurice (1955–6) 32 *BY* 20, 65.

[64] On the establishment of British sovereignty over Rockall in 1955: Verzijl, 3 *International Law in Historical Perspective* (1968) 351.

[65] (1931) 2 RIAA 1105, 1110.

The annexation, though symbolic in form, had legal effect.

(iii) Effective and continuous display of state authority

As was noted by Huber in *Island of Palmas* 'the actual continuous and peaceful display of state functions is in the case of dispute the sound and natural criterion of territorial sovereignty'.[66] This is in contrast to older works on international law, stressing a nineteenth-century view of occupation in terms of settlement and close physical possession.[67] Rather the question has become one of administrative character, under which those acts which are reflective of the intention to govern, and not merely to possess in some nominal fashion, are constitutive of title.[68]

Thus, in *Island of Palmas* the Dutch claim to the contested territory was preferred on the basis of evidence 'which tends to show that there were unchallenged acts of peaceful display of Netherlands sovereignty from 1700 to 1906 and which...may be regarded as sufficiently proving the existence of Netherlands sovereignty'.[69] In *Eastern Greenland* the Danish claim, based not on any physical presence in the contested territory but on (a) the long-term presence of colonies in other parts of Greenland, (b) the wording of legislation and treaties so as to render them applicable to Eastern Greenland, and (c) seeking to have the resulting title recognized internationally, was held to be superior to the Norwegian claim, based on the wintering of various expeditions in the territory and the construction of a wireless station there. The Permanent Court held that Denmark, at least in the 10 years prior to Norwegian involvement, had 'displayed and exercised her sovereign rights to an extent sufficient to constitute valid title to sovereignty'.[70]

The emphasis on the display of state activity, and the interpretation of the facts in the light of a legal policy which favours stability and allows for the special characteristics of uninhabited and remote territories, suggest a change in the law.[71] The modern law concentrates on title, on evidence of sovereignty, and the notion of occupation has been refined accordingly.[72] Thus in *Minquiers and Ecrehos* in relation to the Ecrehos group the Court was concerned with acts involving the exercise of jurisdiction, local administration, such as the holding of inquests,[73] and a British Treasury Warrant of 1875 constituting Jersey a Port of the Channel Islands.[74]

---

[66] E.g. *Island of Palmas* (1928) 2 RIAA 831, 839.

[67] See Hall, *International Law* (8th edn, 1924) 125. Also: McNair, 1 *Opinions* 291, 315–16; 1 Hyde 342.

[68] Cf *Eritrea-Ethiopia Boundary* (2002) 130 ILR 1, 42.

[69] *Island of Palmas* (1928) 2 RIAA 829, 870–1.

[70] (1933) PCIJ Ser A/B No 53, 63.

[71] See Shaw, in Shaw (2005) xi, xxiii–xxiv.

[72] See von der Heydte (1935) 29 *AJIL* 448, 462ff; 3 Rousseau, 169.

[73] ICJ Reports 1953 p 47, 65–6. On acts relating to the Minquiers see ibid, 67–70.

[74] *Minquiers and Ecrehos*, ICJ Reports 1953 p 47. Further: *Frontier Dispute (Belgium/Netherlands)*, ICJ Reports 1959 p 209, 228–9, 231–2, 248–50, 251, 255; *Temple*, ICJ Reports 1962 p 6, 12, 29–30, 59–60, 72, 91–6; *Pulau Ligitan/Sipidan*, ICJ Reports 2002 p 625, 678–86.

By contrast acts by private persons purporting to appropriate territory may be ratified by the state and may then constitute evidence of its effective occupation.[75] Otherwise they will have no legal effect.[76]

(iv) The intention to act as sovereign

The requirement of an intention to act as sovereign, otherwise referred to as *animus occupandi*[77] or *animus possidendi*,[78] is generally stressed. However, the notion may create more problems than it solves: Ross described the subjective requirement of the 'will to act as sovereign' as 'an empty phantom'.[79] In truth the subjective criterion is unrealistic in seeking a coherent intention from activity involving numerous individuals often over a considerable period of time. Furthermore, the criterion begs the question in many cases where there are competing acts of sovereignty.[80]

In certain contexts, however, the *animus occupandi* (or something like it) *has* a function. First, the activity must be *à titre de souverain* in the sense that the agency must be that of the state and not of unauthorized persons. Secondly, it has a negative role: if the activity is by the consent of another state recognized as the rightful sovereign then no amount of state activity is capable of maturing into sovereignty. Thirdly, the state activity taken as a whole may be explicable only on the basis that sovereignty is assumed.[81] Thus in *Minquiers and Ecrehos* the fact that both parties had conducted official hydrographic surveys of the area was not necessarily referable to an assertion of sovereignty by either. But certain forms of activity, whilst not necessarily connected with territorial sovereignty, have probative value, for example, the exercise of criminal jurisdiction.

(D) CESSION[82]

A right to territory may be conferred by treaty, provided the transferee takes in accordance with the treaty.[83] An actual transfer is not required.[84] The date on which title

---

[75] McNair, 1 *Opinions* 295, 314, 316–19, 323–5. Also: Orent & Reinsch (1941) 35 *AJIL* 443, 450–4; Shaw, in Shaw (2005) xi, xxiii.

[76] E.g. *Qatar v Bahrain*, ICJ Reports 2001 p 40, 99–100 (digging of artesian wells not reflective of sovereignty); *Pulau Ligitan/Sipadan*, ICJ Reports 2002 p 625, 683 (illegal fishing not evidence of sovereign conduct). See also the Court's treatment of the persistent presence of indigenous peoples in the contested territory in *Kasikili/Sedudu Island*, ICJ Reports 1999 p 1045.

[77] Cf Fitzmaurice (1955–56) 32 *BY* 20, 55–8; *Clipperton Island* (1931) 2 RIAA 1105, 1110.

[78] See *Eastern Greenland* (1933) PCIJ Ser A/B No 53, 83 (Judge Anzilotti, diss). See also *Frontier Dispute (Belgium/Netherlands)*, ICJ Reports 1959 p 209, 255 (Judge Moreno Quintana, diss).

[79] Ross, *International Law* (1947) 147.

[80] Cf *Eastern Greenland* (1933) PCIJ Ser A/B No 53, 45–6.

[81] Fitzmaurice (1955–56) 32 *BY* 20, 56–8.

[82] The term 'cession' is used to cover a variety of transactions: cf *Différends Sociétés Dufay et Gigandet* (1962) 16 RIAA 197, 208–12. Also: *Christian v R* [2006] UKPC 47, §11. See generally Dörr, 'Cession' (2006) *MPEPIL*. On the possibility of cession by the people of a territory (Malta) see *Sammut v Strickland* [1938] AC 678.

[83] *San Lorenzo Title & Improvement Co v City Mortgage Co* (1932) 6 ILR 113, 116; *Franco-Ethiopian Railway Co* (1957) 24 ILR 602, 616, 623; *Christian v R* [2006] UKPC 47, §11. Cf *Certain German Interests in Polish Upper Silesia* (1926) PCIJ Ser A No 7, 30; *Lighthouses in Crete and Samos* (1937) PCIJ Ser A/B No 71, 103.

[84] Some cases of transfer may be better classified as renunciation: *Sorkis v Amed* (1950) 17 ILR 103, although the term cession is sometimes used: *German Reparations* (1924) 1 RIAA 429, 443; *Banin v Laviani*

changes will normally be the date on which the treaty comes into force:[85] an unratified treaty does not confer sovereignty.[86] Naturally the transferee cannot receive any greater rights than those possessed by the transferor: *nemo dat quod non habet*.[87]

Apart from cession and transfer in accordance with a treaty, title may exist on the basis of a treaty alone, the treaty marking a reciprocal recognition of sovereignty in solemn form.[88] In the case of a disputed frontier the boundary treaty which closes the dispute will *create* title, previously unsettled, whereas a treaty of cession merely transfers an extant (though definitive) title.[89] In the case where a territorial regime is established by a treaty, this settlement achieves a permanence which the treaty itself does not necessarily enjoy: the continued existence of that regime is not dependent upon the continuing life of the treaty under which the regime is agreed.[90]

(i) Agreements concluded with indigenous rulers[91]

Treaties between indigenous peoples and the state were a feature of the period of colonization but are of limited relevance, externally, following the partition of the world into independent equal states. The early position was defined primarily in the era of Western European colonial expansion, notably in the so-called 'Scramble for Africa',[92] under which an immense number of treaties were concluded with various African polities.[93] Such arrangements with indigenous rulers were not normally considered as cessions, but gave a form of derivative title distinguishing the act of acquisition from that of mere occupation. This was characterized by Huber in *Island of Palmas* as follows:

In substance, it is not an agreement between equals; it is rather a form of internal organisation of a colonial territory, on the basis of autonomy of the natives ... And thus suzerainty

---

and Ellena (1949) 16 ILR 160; *Différends Sociétés Dufay et Gigandet* (1962) 16 RIAA 197, 208–12. In the Treaty on the Final Settlement with Respect to Germany, 12 September 1990, 1696 UNTS 115, Germany confirmed its border with Poland and other territorial changes.

[85] *Date of Entry into Force of Versailles Treaty* (1961) 32 ILR 339; *N Masthan Sahib v Chief Commissioner* (1976) 49 ILR 484; and see Treaty of Cession relating to the Kuria Muria Islands, 15 November 1967, 617 UNTS 319.

[86] *Territorial Dispute (Libya/Chad)*, ICJ Reports 1994 p 6, 25. Further: VCLT, 22 May 1969, 1155 UNTS 331, Art 14.

[87] E.g. *Island of Palmas* (1928) 2 RIAA 829, 842.

[88] Consequently disputes as to title may involve the interpretation of a treaty and nothing more: e.g. *Beagle Channel* (1977) 52 ILR 93.

[89] See McNair, *Law of Treaties* (1961) 656–7; McNair, 1 *Opinions* 287; *Frontier Dispute (Belgium/Netherlands)*, ICJ Reports 1959 p 209, 226, 231, 256; *Temple*, ICJ Reports 1962 p 6, 16, 52, 67, 73–4, 102–3.

[90] *Territorial and Maritime Dispute (Nicaragua v Colombia)*, Preliminary Objections, ICJ Reports 2007 p 832, 861; *Libya/Chad*, ICJ Reports 1994 p 6, 37.

[91] Generally: Crawford (2nd edn, 2006) ch 6; Alfredsson, 'Indigenous Peoples, Treaties with' (2007) *MPEPIL*. See also UN Declaration on the Rights of Indigenous Peoples, GA Res 61/295, 13 September 2007, Art 37.

[92] Generally: Pakenham, *The Scramble for Africa* (1991); Anghie, *Imperialism, Sovereignty and the Making of International Law* (2005).

[93] The Court estimated that during the later 19th century, some 350 treaties were concluded between Great Britain and the local chieftains of the Niger Delta: *Cameroon v Nigeria*, ICJ Reports 2002 p 303, 404. Also: Castellino & Allen (2003) ch 4.

over the native States becomes the basis of territorial sovereignty as towards other members of the community of nations.[94]

Subsequent decisions of the International Court have qualified Huber's dictum to a degree. In *Western Sahara* the Court stated that in the period beginning in 1884, 'agreements with local rulers, whether or not considered as an actual "cession" of the territory, were regarded as derivative roots of title, and not original titles obtained by occupation of *terra nullius*'.[95]

In *Cameroon v Nigeria*, the Court was called upon to determine the legal effect of an 1884 treaty between the UK and the 'Kings and Chiefs of Old Calabar', an area in the Niger Delta, and its consequent effect on the UK's capacity to deal later with the territory.[96] Nigeria considered the 1884 treaty to have created an international protectorate, which did not therefore result in the transfer of title to the UK; rather it remained vested in Old Calabar as a sovereign entity. The Court disagreed, noting that: (a) at the time, the UK did not regard Old Calabar as a state, a position consistent with its activity in the rest of the region; (b) the region did not possess a central federal authority sufficient to create a protectorate; (c) British activity in the region was reflective of an intention to administer, rather than merely protect; and (d) Nigeria was unable to identify with any degree of precision the source and character of Old Calabar's international personality, either in 1884 or thereafter.[97] The Court concluded that 'under the law at the time, Great Britain was in a position in 1913 to determine its boundaries with Germany in respect of Nigeria, including in the southern section'.[98]

(ii) Renunciation or relinquishment

It is possible for states to renounce title over territory in circumstances in which the subject-matter does not thereby become *terra nullius*. This distinguishes renunciation from abandonment. Furthermore, there is no element of reciprocity, and no commitment to transfer, as in the case of a treaty of cession. Renunciation may be recognition that another state now has title[99] or an agreement to confer a power of disposition to be exercised by another state or a group of states.[100]

---

[94] *Island of Palmas* (1928) 2 RIAA 829, 858.

[95] *Western Sahara*, ICJ Reports 1975 p 12, 39; 123–4 (Judge Dillard). But cf *Cameroon v Nigeria*, ICJ Reports 2002 p 303, 405, referring in passing to 'treaties for cession of land'.

[96] 10 September 1884, 163 CTS 182.

[97] *Cameroon v Nigeria*, ICJ Reports 2002 p 303, 404–7.

[98] Ibid, 407.

[99] E.g. Treaty of St Germain-en-Laye, 10 September 1919, 226 CTS 8, Arts 36, 43, 46–7, 53–4, 59; South Africa-Namibia, Treaty with Respect to Walvis Bay and the Offshore Islands, 28 February 1994, 33 ILM 1256, Art 2. Also: *German Reparations* (1924) 1 RIAA 429, 442.

[100] Treaty of St Germain-en-Laye, Arts 89–91; *Lighthouses (France and Greece)* (1956) 23 ILR 659, 663–6. On Italian renunciation of all right and title to territories in Africa see the Treaty of Peace, 10 February 1947, 49 UNTS 3, Art 23; *Banin v Laviani and Ellena* (1949) 16 ILR 73; *Sorkis v Amed* (1950) 17 ILR 101; *Farrugia v Nuova Comp Gen Autolinee* (1951) 18 ILR 77; *Cernograz and Zudich v INPS* (1978) 77 ILR 627; *Différends Sociétés Dufay et Gigandet* (1962) 16 RIAA 197, 208–12. Also: Treaty of Peace with Japan, 8 September 1951,

A series of unilateral acts may constitute evidence of an implicit relinquishment of rights.[101] Renunciation is to be distinguished from reversion, that is, recognition by an aggressor that territory seized is rightfully under the sovereignty of the victim. Here, there is no title to renounce.[102]

(E) ADJUDICATION

While the subject is generally neglected, some jurists accept adjudication by a judicial organ as a mode of acquisition.[103] The question then, as with a treaty of cession, is whether the award is self-executing, or merely gives an executory right.[104] At least in certain cases the award is dispositive as between the parties: (a) when the character of the territory is such that no physical act is necessary to its effective appropriation (this is true of maritime delimitations); (b) where the two disputants are both exercising acts of administration in respect of the territory concerned and the award merely declares which of the two 'possessors' is a lawful holder; (c) where the loser is to continue in possession with delegated powers of administration and jurisdiction; (d) when the successful claimant is already in possession; and (e) (perhaps) where the award relates only to the detailed fixing of a frontier line.[105]

4. DISPLACEMENT OF TITLE

(A) THE CONCEPT OF 'PRESCRIPTION'[106]

(i) The place of prescription in the law

At its core, prescription refers to the removal of defects in a putative title arising from usurpation of another's sovereignty by the acquiescence of the former sovereign. The standard apology for the principle rests on considerations of good faith and the need

---

136 UNTS 45, Art 2. For the former German eastern territories: Treaty on the Final Settlement with Respect to Germany, 12 September 1990, 1696 UNTS 115, Art 1.

[101] *Rann of Kutch* (1968) 17 RIAA 1, 531–53, 567–70.

[102] *Franco-Ethiopian Railway Co* (1957) 24 ILR 602, 605.

[103] 3 Rousseau 186; 1 Guggenheim 442; Shaw, in Shaw (2005) xi, xvii. Also: *Minquiers and Ecrehos*, ICJ Reports 1953 p 47, 56; *Brazil-British Guiana Boundary* (1904) 11 RIAA 22; further Kaikobad, *Interpretation and Revision of International Boundary Decisions* (2007) 3–14.

[104] At any rate, before execution of the award the successful claimant cannot simply seize the territory: UN Charter, Art 94(2); Mosler & Oellers-Frahm, in Simma (ed), 2 *The Charter of the United Nations* (2nd edn, 2002) 1174.

[105] 3 Rousseau 186.

[106] Generally: 2 Whiteman 1062–84; Fitzmaurice (1953) 30 *BY* 1, 27–43; Fitzmaurice (1955–56) 32 *BY* 20, 31–7; Jennings (1963) 20–3; Blum (1965) 6–37; Thirlway (1995) 66 *BY* 1, 12–14; Lesaffer (2005) 16 *EJIL* 25; O'Keefe (2011) 13 *Int Comm LR* 147; Wouters & Verhoeven, 'Prescription' (2008) *MPEPIL*.

to preserve international order and stability. It is inelegant to describe it as a mode of acquisition: the real source of title is recognition of or acquiescence in the consequences of unchallenged possession and control.

Prescription is distinct from the outright abandonment or relinquishment of territory. Abandonment refers to a situation where a state is held to have surrendered its title, converting the territory to *res nullius*, before another state establishes its own title by way of lawful allocation or effective occupation. In the case of abandonment, there is no usurpation of sovereignty since there are no contemporaneous competing claims.[107] Relinquishment is the giving up of a claim to territory in face of what is thereby acknowledged to be a better claim, or at least a subsisting one.[108]

In particular cases the difference between prescription and effective occupation is not easy to establish. In *Island of Palmas* and cases like it, there is simply contemporaneously competing state activity: in deciding on title the tribunal will apply the criterion of effective control associated with 'effective occupation'.[109] To speak of prescription is unhelpful,[110] and significantly Huber avoided the term, apart from a passing reference to 'so-called prescription', by which he meant merely 'continuous and peaceful display of State sovereignty'.

(ii) The role of private law analogies

In addressing problems of prescription, writers have drawn on analogies from the private law of both civil and common law traditions.[111] From the civilian tradition has been drawn the concept of abandonment or *derelictio*, under which the title-holder makes a conscious decision to relinquish its rights with respect to the contested territory, which may result in its becoming *res nullius* prior to the assertion of the other state's claim. From the common law comes the doctrine of estoppel, under which a representation made by one state that is relied on by another to its detriment may preclude the former state from acting in a contrary fashion. Another, now declining, source of analogy has been the civil law doctrine of acquisitive prescription and the common law 'equivalent' of adverse possession.[112]

---

[107] In particular cases the distinction may wear thin: O'Keefe (2011) 13 *Int Comm LR* 147, 179–80.

[108] See Judges Simma and Abraham (diss) in *Pulau Batu Puteh*, ICJ Reports 2008 p 12, 121: 'In fact, it is not of great importance that … the Court should use this or that legal category or characterization, as those categories, it must be acknowledged, are often not hermetically separated from one another.'

[109] *Island of Palmas* (1928) 2 RIAA 829, 840; *Frontier Dispute (Burkina Faso/Mali)*, ICJ Reports 1986 p 554, 587; *El Salvador/Honduras*, ICJ Reports 1992 p 351, 398, 429; *Kasikili/Sedudu Island*, ICJ Reports 1999 p 1045, 1094–5. Also: the dictum in *Argentine-Chile Frontier* (1966) 16 RIAA 109, 173, emphasizing the relevance of effective administration.

[110] Examples of references to *Island of Palmas* as an instance of prescription: Beckett (1934) 50 Hague *Recueil* 220, 230; Johnson (1950) 27 *BY* 342, 348. Other cases misleadingly classified in this way include the *Brazil-British Guiana Boundary* (1904) 11 RIAA 21; *Grisbadarna* (1909) 11 RIAA 155; *Guatemala-Honduras Boundary* (1933) 2 RIAA 1322.

[111] Lauterpacht, *Private Law Sources and Analogies of International Law* (1927) 91; Lesaffer (2005) 16 *EJIL* 25; Kohen (1997) 10–48.

[112] O'Keefe (2011) 13 *Int Comm LR* 147, 176–88.

Apart from the imperfect nature of these 'sources', there is the distinct issue of the effect of the presumption of legality. Analogies with municipal law reveal the difficulty with any general doctrine of prescription. Although it is sometimes said that the International Court would accept acquisitive prescription as a general principle of law,[113] what is the content of the general principle? Instead of providing guidance, analogies to acquisitive prescription, adverse possession or similar concepts tend to spark confusion and lead to inconsistent terminology.[114]

(B) THE REQUIREMENTS OF PRESCRIPTION

(i) Conduct on the part of the usurping party

To establish such a case for the usurpation of title, certain prerequisites need to be clearly established.[115]

(1) Possession must be exercised *à titre de souverain*. There must be a display of state authority and the absence of recognition of sovereignty in another state, for example under conditions of a protectorate leaving the protected state with a separate personality. Without adverse possession there can be no prescription.

(2) The possession must be public, peaceful, and uninterrupted. As Johnson has remarked: 'Publicity is essential because acquiescence is essential'.[116] By contrast in a situation of competing state activity, as in *Island of Palmas*, publicity will not play an important role because acquiescence may not be relevant except in minor respects.

(3) Finally, possession must persist. In the case of recent possession it is difficult to adduce evidence of tacit acquiescence. A few writers have prescribed fixed periods of years.[117] Such suggestions are due to a yearning after municipal models and to the influence of the view that 'acquiescence' may be 'implied' in certain conditions. The better view is that the length of time required is a matter of fact depending on the particular case.[118]

---

[113] Johnson (1950) 27 *BY* 343.

[114] See Schwarzenberger (1957) 51 *AJIL* 308, 324 ('it appears that the practice of international courts and tribunals fits easily into a pattern which dispenses completely with analogies from private law. It then emerges that titles to territory are governed primarily by the rules underlying the principles of sovereignty, recognition, consent and good faith').

[115] E.g. *Kasikili/Sedudu Island*, ICJ Reports 1999 p 1045, 1103–4; *Pulau Batu Puteh*, ICJ Reports 2008 p 12, 122 (Judges Simma and Abraham, diss).

[116] (1950) 27 *BY* 347.

[117] Field, *Outlines of an International Code* (1872) §52 (50 years). The 50-year period specified in Art IV(a) of the arbitration treaty relative to the British Guiana–Venezuela boundary represents an ad hoc rule of thumb: 2 February 1897, 89 BFSP 57; *British Guiana-Venezuela Boundary* (1899) 28 RIAA 331, 333–7. In *Frontier Dispute (Belgium/Netherlands)*, an important factual aspect was that Belgium had not challenged the Netherlands' exercise of effective administration over the territory in question for at least 50 years: ICJ Reports 1959 p 209, 231 (Judge Lauterpacht).

[118] Johnson (1950) 27 *BY* 347, 354; 1 Hyde 388–9.

Where the necessary *effectivités* on the part of the usurping party have been established, the competing conduct of the title-holder must be assessed to determine
whether title has been relinquished.

(ii) The importance of acquiescence[119]

In *Island of Palmas*, Huber observed that the continuous and peaceful display of *effectivités* by a state 'may prevail even over a prior, definitive title put forward by another
State'.[120] In the face of competing activity and claims by another, a state may by conduct or admission acquiesce in the extension of its competitor's sovereignty.

At its simplest, this may take the form of an express declaration by one state that it
considers another to hold title to the territory, combined with evidence of conduct *à
titre de souverain* by that other. This was a key feature in *Eastern Greenland*: Norway
had, through a declaration by its Foreign Minister, Nils Ihlen, accepted Danish title to
the disputed territory.[121] In *Pulau Buta Puteh* the Court gave great weight to a response
given in 1953 by the Acting Secretary of State of Johor that 'the Johor government [did]
not claim ownership of Pedra Branca':

Johor's reply shows that as of 1953 Johor understood that it did not have sovereignty over
Pedra Branca/Pulau Batu Puteh. In light of Johor's reply, the authorities in Singapore had no
reason to doubt that the United Kingdom had sovereignty over the island.[122]

Even without an express declaration of relinquishment, the absence of state activity,
combined with an absence of protest that might otherwise be expected in response
to the *effectivités* of the opposing party, may be decisive.[123] In the jurisprudence of
the International Court, this has become known as acquiescence, a concept which
is equivalent to tacit recognition manifested by unilateral conduct which the other
party may properly interpret as consent. Although the term originally emerged in the
context of maritime delimitation,[124] it has been adopted by the Court in the context of
territorial disputes as well. In *Pulau Bata Puteh*, it was said that:

Under certain circumstances, sovereignty over territory might pass as a result of the failure of a state which has sovereignty to respond to conduct *à titre de souverain* of the other

---

[119] 1 Hyde 392–4; McNair, 1 *Opinions* 299–305; Moore, 1 *Digest* 300; Beckett (1934) 50 Hague *Recueil* 189,
252–5; 1 Hackworth 442–3; Fitzmaurice (1955–56) 32 *BY* 20, 67; Jennings (1963) 36–40; Kaikobad (1983)
54 *BY* 119; Marston (1986) 57 *BY* 337; Marques Antunes & Bradley, *Estoppel, Acquiescence and Recognition
in Territorial and Boundary Dispute Settlement* (2000); O'Keefe (2011) 13 *Int Comm LR* 147, 147; Kohen,
'Abandonment' (2008) *MPEPIL*.

[120] *Island of Palmas* (1928) 2 RIAA 828, 838–9, 846.

[121] *Eastern Greenland* (1933) PCIL Ser A/B No 53, 73. The better view is that the facts disclosed an agreement rather than a unilateral act, the *quid pro quo* being Danish recognition of Norwegian sovereignty over
Svalbard (Spitzbergen). On unilateral acts generally see chapter 18.

[122] ICJ Reports 2008 p 12, 81. Although there is a distinction between sovereignty and 'ownership', the
Court took them here to be synonymous: ibid, 80.

[123] Thus mere protest will be sufficient to prevent the conclusion that title has been abandoned: e.g.
Chamizal (1911) 11 RIAA 309.

[124] *Delimitation of the Maritime Boundary in the Gulf of Maine Area (Canada/US)*, ICJ Reports 1984 p
246, 305.

State...Such manifestations of the display of sovereignty may call for a response if they are not opposable to the State in question. The absence of a reaction may well amount to acquiescence...That is to say, silence may also speak, but only if the conduct of the other State calls for a response.[125]

But because of the need to maintain stability and to avoid temptations to 'squatting', abandonment is not to be presumed.[126] As the Chamber said in *Burkina Faso/Mali*, where there is a conflict between title and *effectivités*, preference will be given to the former.[127] Accordingly, very little evidence of *effectivités* will be required to prove maintenance of title, particularly in regard to remote and uninhabited areas. In *Clipperton Island* it was stated: 'There is no reason to suppose that France has subsequently lost her right by *derelictio*, since she never had the *animus* of abandoning the island, and the fact that she has not exercised her authority there in a positive manner does not imply the forfeiture of an acquisition already definitively protected'.[128] In *Eastern Greenland* Norway had argued that Greenland became *terra nullius* after the disappearance of the early settlements. The Court, rejecting the argument, observed:

It is impossible to read the records of the decisions in cases as to territorial sovereignty without observing that in many cases the tribunal has been satisfied with very little in the way of the actual exercise of sovereign rights, provided that the other State could not make out a superior claim. This is particularly true in the case of claims to sovereignty over areas in thinly populated or unsettled countries.[129]

Similarly, in *Cameroon v Nigeria* the Court found that Cameroon had not abandoned its title to the Bakassi region, despite having engaged in only occasional acts of administration in the area due to a lack of resources.[130]

Thus it would seem that nothing short of the total (or near-total) absence of conduct *à titre de souverain* in an area by the title-holder will be sufficient to signal movement away from the status quo. An illustration is *Pulau Batu Puteh* where the Court held that 'any passing of sovereignty over territory on the basis of the conduct of the Parties...must be manifested clearly and without any doubt by that conduct and the relevant facts...especially so if what may be involved, in the case of one of the parties, is in effect the abandonment of sovereignty over part of its territory'.[131] This was only

---

[125] *Pulau Batu Puteh*, ICJ Reports 2008 p 12, 50–1.

[126] Tribunals for many years avoided pronouncing on whether *derelictio* was even possible, preferring instead to find the claim was not made out on the facts: e.g. *Chamizal* (1911) 11 RIAA 309, 328 (displacement of extant title 'very controversial'); *Frontier Dispute (Belgium/Netherlands)*, ICJ Reports 1959 p 207, 227–31; *Kasikili/Sedudu Island*, ICJ Reports 1999 p 1045, 1105. See also O'Keefe (2011) 13 *Int Comm LR* 147, 158–62.

[127] ICJ Reports 1986 p 554, 586–7. See also *Island of Palmas* (1928) 2 RIAA 829, 867; *Argentine-Chile Frontier* (1966) 16 RIAA 109, 173; *Eritrea and Yemen* (1998) 114 ILR 1, 51.

[128] (1931) 2 RIAA 1105, 1110–11.

[129] *Eastern Greenland* (1933) PCIJ Ser A/B No 53, 46. The Court then went on to say that 'As regards voluntary abandonment, there is nothing to show any definite renunciation on the part of the Kings of Norway or Denmark' (ibid, 47).

[130] It did, however, collect taxation from the area: *Cameroon v Nigeria*, ICJ Reports 2002 p 303, 415–16.

[131] ICJ Reports 2008 p 12, 50–1.

established with reference to Pulau Batu Puteh (Pedra Branca) itself and then only because of the declaration of the Acting State Secretary.

(iii) Estoppel[132]

Recognition, acquiescence, admissions constituting a part of the evidence of sovereignty,[133] and estoppel form an interrelated subject-matter; everything depends on the precise alchemy of the opposing parties' *effectivités*, combined with the presence of some form of representation by a party that it does not consider itself as sovereign. In *Temple* the Court held that by its conduct Thailand had recognized the frontier line contended for by Cambodia in the area of the temple, as marked on the map drawn up by French members of a Mixed Delimitation Commission. In particular the Court placed reliance on a visit of a 'quasi-official character' by a member of the Siamese royal family to the disputed territory where he was 'officially received' by the local French plenipotentiary 'with the French flag flying'.[134] The Court remarked:

Looking at the incident as a whole, it appears to have amounted to a tacit recognition by Siam of the sovereignty of Cambodia (under French Protectorate) over Preah Vihear, through a failure to react in any way, on an occasion that called for a reaction in order to affirm of preserve title in the face of an obvious rival claim. What seems clear is that either Siam did not in fact believe that she had any title—and this would be wholly consistent with her attitude all along... —or else she decided not to assert it, which again means she accepted the French claim, or accepted the frontier of Preah Vihear as it was drawn on the map.[135]

In many situations acquiescence and express admissions are but part of the evidence of sovereignty. Estoppel differs in that, if the conditions for an estoppel are satisfied, it suffices to settle the issue. Resting on good faith and the principle of consistency in state relations, estoppel may involve holding a government to a declaration which in fact does not correspond to its real intention, if the declaration is unequivocal and the state to which it is made has relied on it to its detriment. Such a principle must be used with caution, more particularly in dealing with territorial issues.[136] Thus the Court held that the declaration of the Acting State Secretary that Johor did not possess sovereignty over Pedra Branca did not give rise to an estoppel. The Court said:

---

[132] See Bowett (1957) 33 *BY* 176; MacGibbon (1958) 7 *ICLQ* 468, 5069; Martin, *L'Estoppel en droit international public* (1979); Thirlway (1989) 60 *BY* 29; Sinclair, in Lowe & Fitzmaurice, *Fifty Years of the International Court of Justice* (1996) 104. Generally see chapter 18.

[133] See Fitzmaurice (1955–56) 32 *BY* 20, 60–2; Bowett (1957) 33 *BY* 176, 196–7.

[134] *Temple*, ICJ Reports 1962 p 6, 30.

[135] Ibid, 30–1.

[136] See Bowett (1957) 33 *BY* 176, 197–201, 202; and *Temple*, ICJ Reports 1962 p 6, 142–6 (Judge Spender, diss). In his view, on the facts, the elements of estoppel were not present in any case. For criticism: Chan (2004) 3 *Chin JIL* 555; Buss (2010) 9 *Chin JIL* 111. The dispute has returned to the Court, under the guise of a request for interpretation under Art 60 of the Statute: *Request for Interpretation of the Judgment of 15 June 1962 in the Case Concerning the* Temple of Preah Vihear (Cambodia v Thailand) *(Cambodia v Thailand)* (2011, pending).

[A] party relying on an estoppel must show, among other things, that it has taken distinct acts in reliance on the other party's statement... The Court observes that Singapore did not point to any such acts. To the contrary, it acknowledges in its Reply that, after receiving the letter, it had no reason to change its behaviour; the actions after 1953 to which it refers were a continuation and development of the actions it had taken over the previous century.[137]

By contrast, in cases such as *Temple*, where much of the evidence is equivocal, acquiescence over a long period may be treated as decisive: here it is not itself a root of title but an aid in the interpretation of the facts and legal instruments.[138] To be decisive acquiescence must rest on very cogent evidence. Express recognition in a treaty of the existence of title in the other party (as opposed to recognition by third states) is of course conclusive.[139]

(C) 'NEGATIVE PRESCRIPTION'

Some writers seem to suggest that prescriptive title arises even without acquiescence, simply by lapse of time and possession not disturbed by measures of forcible self-help.[140] A similar result is reached by formulations which presume acquiescence under certain conditions. Such views are not supported by the jurisprudence,[141] which sets an exacting evidentiary standard for the displacement of confirmed title, a standard which requires at least some evidence (tacit or express) of acquiescence. They commonly antedate the period when forcible self-help and conquest were prohibited. It is probably the case now that prescription cannot create rights out of situations brought about by illegal acts.[142] Finally, it must be remembered that in *Island of Palmas, Minquiers and Ecrehos* and other like cases, the possession upheld by the tribunal is adverse only in a special sense; there is no deliberate usurpation with a sequel of adverse holding, but a more or less contemporaneous competition.

(D) HISTORICAL CONSOLIDATION OF TITLE: AN EPITAPH

Historical consolidation as a concept refers to an acquisition of title on the basis of its use without challenge over a significant period of time. Its origin is generally seen to lie in *Anglo-Norwegian Fisheries*; there, the Court, having established that Norway had delimited the territorial sea by a system of straight baselines since 1869, had to

---

[137] *Pulau Batu Puteh*, ICJ Reports 2008 p 12, 81.

[138] Jennings (1963) 51.

[139] See McNair, *Treaties* (1961) 487, referring to *Eastern Greenland* (1933) PCIJ Ser A/B No 53, 68–9. McNair takes a less strict view of estoppel than Bowett (1957) 33 *BY* 197, 202.

[140] See Moore, 1 *Digest* 293–5 (ambiguous and diverse dicta of publicists collected); 1 Hyde 386, 387 (stressing the element of acquiescence); 1 Guggenheim 442.

[141] *Cameroon v Nigeria*, ICJ Reports 2002 p 303, 346; *Pulau Batu Puteh*, ICJ Reports 2008 p 12, 120 (Judges Simma and Abraham, diss).

[142] Lauterpacht (1950) 27 *BY* 367, 397–8.

decide whether, as against other states, it had title to waters so delimited. The Court said:

[I]t is indeed this system itself [of straight baselines] which would reap the benefit of general toleration, the basis of an historical consolidation which would make it enforceable as against all States...The general toleration of foreign States with regard to the Norwegian practice is an unchallenged fact. The notoriety of the facts, the general toleration of the international community, Great Britain's position in the North Sea, her own interest in the question, and her prolonged abstention would in any case warrant Norway's enforcement of her system against the United Kingdom.[143]

The attitude of other states was taken as evidence of the legality of the system, but there were certain special features. The extension of sovereignty claimed was over a *res communis* and therefore the toleration of foreign states in general was of significance. Moreover, the Court appeared to regard British silence as an independent basis of legality as against the UK.

De Visscher took the decision as an example of the 'fundamental interest of the stability of territorial situations from the point of view of order and peace', which 'explains the place that consolidation by historic titles holds in international law':

This consolidation, which may have practical importance for territories not yet finally organized under a State regime as well as for certain stretches of sea-like bays, is not subject to the conditions specifically required in other modes of acquiring territory. Proven long use, which is its foundation, merely represents a complex of interests and relations which in themselves have the effect of attaching a territory or an expanse of sea to a given State.[144]

Thus, 'consolidation' differs from prescription and occupation in de Visscher's doctrine. It is, moreover, certain that the elements which he calls 'consolidation' are influential; the essence of the matter is peaceful holding and acquiescence or toleration by other states.[145] But the concept of historical consolidation is not much more than a compendium of pre-existing modes of acquisition. Certainly, as late as 1998 a distinguished arbitral tribunal referred to the concept of consolidation of title with approval.[146] Nonetheless, the accepted view is that consolidation does not exist as a concept independent of the established rules governing effective occupation and prescription. In *Cameroon v Nigeria,* the Court stated that 'the theory of historical consolidation is highly controversial and cannot replace the established modes of acquisition of title under international law'.[147]

---

[143] ICJ Reports 1951 p 116, 130, 138–9.
[144] De Visscher, *Theory and Reality in Public International Law* (4th edn, 1970) 226.
[145] Schwarzenberger (1957) 51 *AJIL* 308, 316–24.
[146] *Eritrea and Yemen* (1998) 114 ILR 1, 117.
[147] *Cameroon v Nigeria,* ICJ Reports 2002 p 303, 352.

5. EXTENT OF SOVEREIGNTY: TERRITORIAL DISPUTES[148]

We are here concerned with certain logical and equitable principles which are not roots of title but are important in determining the actual extent of sovereignty derived from some source of title such as a treaty of cession or effective occupation.

(A) THE PRINCIPLE OF CONTIGUITY

Considerations of contiguity and geographical unity come to the fore when the disputed territory is uninhabited, barren or uncharted. In relation to islands contiguity is a relevant concept.[149] Thus, in *Land, Maritime and Frontier Dispute*, the Chamber held that the island of Meanguerita was a dependency of the larger island of Meanguera, due to its small size, its proximity, and the fact that the claimants to the dispute treated the two as a single unit.[150] But this is a presumption only: in *Pulau Batu Puteh* one of three disputed features was held to belong to Singapore, a second (and by inference a third) to Malaysia.[151]

The principles are simply a part of judicial reasoning, but have significance in other respects. State activity as evidence of sovereignty need not press uniformly on every part of territory. Associated with this is the presumption of peripheral possession based on state activity, for example, on the coast of a barren territory.[152] Lastly, in giving effect to principles of geographical unity in *Eastern Greenland*,[153] and thus concluding that somewhat localized Danish activity gave title over the whole of Greenland, the Permanent Court was not swayed the significance of unity isolated from the context of effective occupation. Writing of the decision, Lauterpacht remarked on 'those principles of finality, stability and effectiveness of international relations which have characterized the work of the Court'.[154] Contiguity may be in itself an earnest of effectiveness.

In conclusion the 'principle of contiguity' is little more than a technique in the application of the normal principles of effective occupation.[155] In the case of islands in

---

[148] 1 Hyde 331–6; von der Heydte (1935) 29 *AJIL* 448, 463–71; Waldock (1948) 25 *BY* 311, 339ff; Lauterpacht (1950) 27 *BY* 376, 423–31; Fitzmaurice (1955–56) 32 *BY* 20, 72–5; Kelsen, *Wehberg Festschrift* (1956) 200–11; McNair, 1 *Opinions* 287–8, 292; 3 Rousseau, 193–203; Sharma (1997); Ratner (2006) 100 *AJIL* 808; Prescott & Triggs (2008).

[149] See further Sharma (1997) 51–61.

[150] ICJ Reports 1992 p 351, 570.

[151] ICJ Reports 2008 p 12, 95–6 (Pedra Branca (Pulau Bata Puteh)), 99 (Middle Rocks), 100–1 (South Ledge).

[152] *Brazil-British Guiana Boundary* (1904) 11 RIAA 21. See also *Island of Palmas* (1928) 2 RIAA 855; *Minquiers and Ecrehos*, ICJ Reports 1953 p 47, 99; Jennings (1963) 74–6.

[153] (1933) PCIJ Ser A/B No 53, 45–52; also *Western Sahara*, ICJ Reports 1975 p 12, 42–3.

[154] Lauterpacht, *Development* (1958) 241.

[155] For a different opinion: 1 Guggenheim, 440–1. Also: 2 Whiteman 1104–8.

particular the notion of contiguity may be unhelpful. Huber in *Island of Palmas* said that 'the alleged principle itself is by its very nature so uncertain and contested that even governments of the same State have on different occasions maintained contradictory opinions as to its soundness ...'.[156]

(B) THE *UTI POSSIDETIS* PRINCIPLE

Put simply, the concept of *uti possidetis* provides that states emerging from the dissolution of a larger entity inherit as their borders those administrative boundaries which were in place at the time of independence. In *Burkina Faso/Mali*, the Chamber in applying the principle to Africa said as follows:[157]

The essence of the principle lies in its primary aim of securing respect for territorial boundaries at the moment when independence is achieved. Such territorial boundaries might be no more than delimitations between different administrative divisions or colonies all subject to the same sovereign. In that case, the application of the principle of *uti possidetis* resulted in administrative boundaries being transformed into international frontiers in the full sense of the term.

Though like many concepts in this chapter it has its origins in Roman law,[158] the modern application of the doctrine began in Latin America in the nineteenth century, whereby the elites who had declared independence from Spain adopted the administrative divisions imposed by the Spanish as the borders of the new states that emerged in the region.[159] Thus by their practice the successor states agreed to apply, as between themselves, and later in their disputes with Brazil, a principle for the settlement of frontier disputes in an area in which *terra nullius* (territory belonging to no state) by stipulation did not exist: the independent republics regarded their titles as co-extensive with that of the former Spanish empire. The principle involves implied agreement to base territorial settlement on a rule of presumed possession by the previous Spanish administrative unit in 1821, in Central America, or in 1810, in South America. Its use has persisted throughout the twentieth century, and in a slightly different form it has

---

[156] *Island of Palmas* (1928) 2 RIAA 854. Other disputes involving arguments based on contiguity: *Bulama Island* (1870), Moore, 2 *Int Arb* 1909; *Lobos Islands* (1852), Moore, 1 *Digest* 265–6, 575; *Navassa Island* (1872), Moore, 1 *Digest* 266–7; *Aves Island* (1865), Moore, 5 *Int Arb* 5037 (Spanish report). Further: 1 Hyde 343–6; McNair, 1 *Opinions* 315.

[157] *Burkina Faso/Mali*, ICJ Reports 1986 p 554, 566; see also *El Salvador/Honduras*, ICJ Reports 1992 p 351, 386–8 ('*uti possidetis juris* is essentially a retrospective principle, investing as international boundaries administrative limits intended originally for another purpose'). Further: Shaw (1993) 42 *ICLQ* 929; Lalonde, *Determining Boundaries in a Conflicted World* (2002); Abi-Saab, in Kohen (2007) 657.

[158] In litigation over contested property, the *praetor* would issue an edict granting provisional title to the party already in possession of the land, unless he had come about it through trickery, violence or in some form revocable by the other party, hence the maxim 'as you possess, so you may possess' (*uti possidetis, ita possidetis*): Ratner (1996) 90 *AJIL* 590, 593; Castellino & Allen (2003) 8–11.

[159] Further: Ratner (1996) 90 *AJIL* 590, 593–5; Shaw (1996) 67 *BY* 75, 98–100; Castellino & Allen (2003) ch 3.

been adopted by governments and tribunals concerned with boundaries in Asia[160] and Africa.[161] The principle was also applied in relation to the appearance of new states on the territory of the former Yugoslavia.[162]

The operation of *uti possidetis* does not always give satisfactory solutions.[163] The administrative boundaries are frequently ill-defined or difficult to prove.[164] Furthermore, the colonial boundaries on which the future of contested regions now rely were often not drawn in the first place with any degree of ethnic sensitivity, leading to the inclusion of opposed groups within the same new state.[165] Finally, the doctrine may impede the recognition of new states due to the unwillingness of states to acknowledge a desire for independence contrary to *uti possedetis*. In a worst case scenario, this may result in an otherwise successful polity being shackled to a 'failed state'.[166]

No doubt the principle is not peremptory and the states concerned are free to adopt other principles as the basis of a settlement.[167] But the general principle that pre-independence boundaries of former administrative divisions subject to the same sovereign remain in being is in accordance with good policy. Three arguments are generally posited as justifying this conclusion:[168] (a) the doctrine renders the division of a state susceptible to only one outcome, preventing armed conflict over territory; (b) a division based on administrative boundaries is as valid as any other approach in principle, and far simpler in execution; and (c) *uti possidetis* has achieved the status of a general principle or default rule of international law.[169]

---

[160] See *Temple*, ICJ Reports 1962 p 6; *Rann of Kutch* (1968) 50 ILR 2. Cf *Eritrea and Yemen* (1998) 114 ILR 1, 32–4.

[161] OAU Resolution on Border Disputes, AHG/Res 16(I), 21 July 1964; Touval (1967) 21 *Int Org* 102; *Burkina Faso/Mali*, ICJ Reports 1986 p 554, 565–8, 586–7; *Guinea-Guinea (Bissau) Maritime Delimitation* (1985) 77 ILR 636, 657; *Guinea (Bissau)-Senegal Delimitation* (1989) 83 ILR 1, 22; 56–85 (Bedjaoui, diss). Also: *Libya/Chad*, ICJ Reports 1994 p 6, 83–92 (Judge ad hoc Ajibola).

[162] Badinter Commission, *Opinion No 2* (1992) 92 ILR 167; *Opinion No 3* (1992) 92 ILR 170; Craven (1995) 66 *BY* 333, 385–90.

[163] Ratner identifies two central complaints: (1) its inherent simplicity gives rise to the temptation on the part of ethnic separatists to further divide territory along existing boundaries; (2) application of the principle to modern state collapses may lead to significant populations both unsatisfied with their status in the new state and uncertain of their political participation there; see Ratner (1996) 90 *AJIL* 590.

[164] See *Guatemala-Honduras Boundary* (1933) 2 RIAA 1322. For comment: Fisher (1933) 27 *AJIL* 403. Cf Waldock (1948) 25 *BY* 325. Also: *El Salvador/Honduras*, ICJ Reports 1992 p 351, 386–95; *Frontier Dispute (Benin/Niger)*, ICJ Reports 2005 p 90, 108–10, 133–49; *Caribbean Sea*, ICJ Reports 2007 p 659, 727–9.

[165] Further: Luker (2008) 158–61.

[166] On Somaliland: see Poore (2009) 45 *Stanford JIL* 117; Crawford (2nd edn, 2006) 412–18.

[167] *Opinion No 2* (1992) 92 ILR 167, 168.

[168] Ratner (1996) 90 *AJIL* 590, 591.

[169] Further: *Burkina Faso/Mali*, ICJ Reports 1986 p 554, 565: 'Nevertheless [*uti possidetis*] is not a special rule which pertains solely to one specific system of international law. It is a general principle, which is logically connected with the phenomenon of obtaining independence, wherever it occurs. Its obvious purpose is to prevent the independence and stability of new states being endangered by fratricidal struggles.' Also: Badinter Commission, *Opinion No 3* (1992) 92 ILR 170, 171–2. Some scholars have come to attribute to it the status of customary international law: Ratner (2006) 100 *AJIL* 808, 811.

(C) ACCRETION[170]

Accretion concerns the process of increase of territory through new geological formations. In the simple case, deposits on a sea coast may result in an extension of sovereignty. A more dramatic example is provided with the emergence of an island within the territorial sea of Iwo Jima due to volcanic activity in 1986; this was subject to immediate recognition by the UK government as part of the territory of Japan.[171] In such a case, '[n]o formal acts of appropriation are required'.[172]

(D) HYDRAULIC BOUNDARIES

(i) Boundary rivers[173]

The principle of delimitation apparently established in the law is that of the *thalweg*, presumed to mean the middle of the main navigable channel. However, the term may have another meaning in particular instruments and treaties, viz., the line of deepest soundings. The two definitions will often coincide. But conditions prevailing, even within the same river system, are very variable and the learning in the books tends to be unhelpful in practice. Expertise is called for, particularly in relation to the determination of the main channel among several arms of a river.[174]

Unlike purely terrestrial borders, boundary rivers may change their course. This is not a true case of accretion. Thus, in relation to the southern boundary of New Mexico, the solution of disputes between the US and Mexico depended on principles of acquiescence and the interpretation of agreements as to the outcome of natural changes.[175] In this type of case, even in the absence of applicable agreements, sudden, forcible, and significant changes in river courses (avulsion) will not be considered to have changed the frontier line:[176] in other words, the boundary will be fixed along the route of the former river bed, following not the river but the land underneath. Accretion, the gradual and imperceptible addition of sediments, can give rise to an extension of the sovereignty of the co-riparian to areas already under

---

[170] See 1 Hackworth 409–21; 1 Hyde 355; *Island of Palmas* (1928) 2 RIAA 829, 839; Kanska & Manko (2002–3) 26 *Pol YIL* 135.

[171] UKMIL (1986) 57 *BY* 487, 563.

[172] 1 Hyde 355–6.

[173] See E Lauterpacht (1960) 9 *ICLQ* 208; Bouchez (1963) 12 *ICLQ* 789; McEwen, *International Boundaries of East Africa* (1971) 76–96; Kaikobad, *The Shatt-al-arab Boundary Question* (1988); Bardonnet (1976) 153 Hague *Recueil* 9, 83–95; Schroeter (1992) 38 *AFDI* 948. Also: the dispute related to the boundary river San Juan between Nicaragua and Costa Rica, *Certain Activities carried out by Nicaragua in the Border Area (Costa Rica v Nicaragua)*, Order of 8 March 2011.

[174] See *Argentine-Chile Frontier* (1966) 38 ILR 10, 93; *Kasikili/Sedudu Island*, ICJ Reports 1999 p 1045, 1060–74; *Eritrea-Ethiopia Boundary* (2002) 130 ILR 1, 116; *Benin/Niger*, ICJ Reports 2005 p 90, 149–50.

[175] See *Chamizal* (1911) 11 RIAA 309, 316; *San Lorenzo* (1932) 6 ILR 113. Also: Chamizal Convention, 28 August 1963, 505 UNTS 185.

[176] *Nebraska v Iowa*, 143 US 359 (1892); *Kansas v Missouri*, 322 US 213 (1943); *Georgia v South Carolina*, 497 US 376 (1991); *El Salvador/Honduras*, ICJ Reports 1992 p 351, 546; cf *Chamizal* (1911) 11 RIAA 309.

effective occupation[177] on the basis of principles of contiguity and certainty. The gradual nature of the process leads to a presumption of occupation by the riparian state and one of acquiescence by other states; thus the boundary will be held to move with the river.[178]

(ii) Boundary lakes

As to boundary lakes the principle of the median line applies, but as usual express agreement or acquiescence may produce other modes of division.

(E) THE POLAR REGIONS: THE SECTOR PRINCIPLE[179]

Particularly in the case of the Arctic, the question of rights over frozen sea or 'ice territory' arises,[180] but otherwise normal principles apply to territory situated in polar regions. In the making of claims to ice deserts and remote groups of islands, it is hardly surprising that governments should seek to establish the limits of territorial sovereignty by means of straight lines, and similar systems of delimitation may be found in other regions, for example in North America. In the polar regions use has been made of lines of longitude converging at the Poles to produce a sector of sovereignty. While the 'sector principle' does not give title, it may represent a reasonable application of the principles of effective occupation as they are now understood, and as applied in *Eastern Greenland*.[181] It remains a rough method of delimitation, and has not become a separate rule of law.

Confusion of claims has arisen primarily from the indecisive nature of state activity in the polar regions. However, three reservations may be made: the 'sector principle' has the defects of any doctrine based upon contiguity; its application is a little absurd insofar as there is claim to a narrow sliver of sovereignty stretching to the Pole; and, lastly, it cannot apply so as to include areas of the high seas.

---

[177] See *Island of Palmas* (1928) 2 RIAA 839.

[178] *El Salvador/Honduras*, ICJ Reports 1992 p 351, 546. Also: *Arkansas v Tennessee*, 246 US 158 (1918); *Louisiana v Mississippi*, 282 US 458 (1940); *Georgia v South Carolina*, 497 US 376 (1991).

[179] On the Antarctic: 1 Hackworth 399–400, 449–76; Waldock (1948) 25 *BY* 311; Auburn (1970) 19 *ICLQ* 229; Watts, *International Law and the Antarctic Treaty System* (1992); Kaye, in Oude Elferink & Rothwell (eds), *The Law of the Sea and Polar Maritime Delimitation and Jurisdiction* (2001) 157. On the Arctic: Lakhtine (1930) 24 *AJIL* 703; 1 Hyde 349–50; Head (1963) 9 *McGill LJ* 200. Further: Smedal, *Acquisition of Sovereignty over Polar Areas* (1931); 2 Whiteman 1051–61; 3 Rousseau, 203–30; Scovazzi, in Oude Elferink & Rothwell (2001) 69; Churchill, ibid, 105; Timchencko, ibid, 269; Scott, (2009) 20 *Ybk IEL* 3. Generally: Rothwell, *The Polar Regions and the Development of International Law* (1996).

[180] Some writers take the view that permanently frozen ice shelves are susceptible to effective occupation. See Waldock (1948) 25 *BY* 311, 317–18; Fitzmaurice (1957) 92 Hague *Recueil* 1, 155. The USSR was particularly fond of such claims: for state practice see Lakhtine (1930) 24 *AJIL* 703; 1 Hackworth 449–52; 2 Whiteman 1266–7. On the status of ice in international law, see further Joyner (1991) 31 *NRJ* 213; Joyner (2001) 23. In the Antarctic context, see the New Zealand claim over the Ross Dependency, part of which includes a claim over the Ross ice shelf: Rothwell (1996) 55, Fig 3. Also: Richardson (1957) 33 *NZLJ* 38; Auburn, *The Ross Dependency* (1972).

[181] See Wall (1947) 1 *ILQ* 54.

In the Arctic,[182] Denmark, Finland, Norway, and the US have refrained from sector claims linked to territories peripheral to the polar seas. On the other hand Canada[183] and the Russian Federation[184] have made use of the sector principle. It is probable that it is recognition by treaty or otherwise which creates title in the Arctic rather than the sector principle as such.[185]

Sector claims in Antarctica have been made by the UK,[186] New Zealand, Australia, France, Norway, Argentina, and Chile.[187] The state practice calls for brief comment. First, some claims are made which do not depend on contiguity but on discovery. Secondly, claimants are not confined to peripheral neighbours as in the Arctic. And thirdly, recognition[188] is obviously important in establishing title in an otherwise fluid situation created by overlapping claims, many of which in law may amount to little more than ambit claims or declarations of interest. Overlaying all such claims, however, is the Antarctic Treaty[189] which in Article IV(2) prevents any additional claims to the continent being made and signals non-recognition by third states of claims already made.

6. TERRITORIAL SOVEREIGNTY AND PEREMPTORY NORMS

The complex question of the effect of breaches of peremptory norms on the validity of interstate transactions is considered in chapter 27. The concern here is the effect of certain rules on the power of alienation.

(A) TRANSFER BY AN AGGRESSOR

The modern law forbids conquest and regards a treaty of cession imposed by force as a nullity, a logical extension of the prohibition on the use of force contained in Article 2(4) of the UN Charter.[190] Even if—and this is open to considerable doubt—the

---

[182] Head (1963) 9 *McGill LJ* 200; Rothwell (1996) 4–6, 166–73; also 288–91 (on the 'Arctic lake' theory). See also Scovazzi (2001) 69.

[183] No precise declaration was made, but see 1 Hackworth 463; 2 Whiteman 1267. For the Canadian declaration that the sector principle does not apply to the Arctic: (1970) 9 ILM 607, 613.

[184] Decree of 15 April 1926; 1 Hackworth 461.

[185] 1 Hackworth 463–8; 2 Whiteman 1268. Also: Rothwell (1996) 59–63.

[186] The first sector claim in the area was by Letters Patent in 1917 defining the Falkland Islands Dependencies. Further: Rothwell (1996) 54.

[187] For the various claims: ibid, 51–8.

[188] Thus the Norwegian proclamation of 1939 was accompanied by a minute of the Ministry of Foreign Affairs which recognized the British, New Zealand, Australian, and French claims: ibid, 57–8. Norway does not accept the sector principle as such.

[189] 1 December 1959, 402 UNTS 72.

[190] Also: Arts 3 and 4 of the Helsinki Final Act, 1 August 1975, 14 ILM 1292.

vice in title can be cured by recognition by third states, it is clear that the loser is not precluded from challenging any title based upon a transfer from the aggressor. It is the force of a powerful prohibition, the stamp of illegality, which operates here rather than the principle *nemo dat quod non habet*. In the event, the Charter era has been attended by far less acquisition of territory by force than periods before it.[191] This is reflected in the terms of SC Resolution 242 (1967), which highlighted the inadmissibility of the acquisition of territory by force, and more emphatically, the Friendly Relations Declaration of 1970, which stipulates that:

the territory of a state shall not be the object of acquisition by another state resulting from the threat or use of force. No territorial acquisition resulting from the threat or use of force shall be recognized as legal.[192]

Exceptions could perhaps occur when there is a disposition of territory by the principal powers or some other international procedure valid as against states generally. So far in the modern period such dispositions have not resulted in an aggressor keeping territory seized.

(B) THE PRINCIPLE OF SELF-DETERMINATION AND TERRITORIAL TRANSFERS

Is there a rule of law inhibiting the transfer of territory if certain minimum conditions of local consent are not fulfilled? Dispositions by the principal powers, transfers under procedures prescribed by international organizations, and bilateral cessions in the period since 1919 have been expressed to be in accordance with the principle of self-determination. The machinery of the plebiscite is sometimes applied,[193] or affected individuals may be given an option of nationality and/or repatriation.[194]

Some opinions support the view that transfers must satisfy the principle. However, there is insufficient practice to warrant the view that a transfer is invalid simply because there is no sufficient provision for expression of opinion by the inhabitants.[195] At present most claims are made in terms which do not include a condition as to due consultation of the population concerned. Those jurists who insist on the principle refer to exceptions, in particular the existence of a collective decision of states representing

---

[191] Zacher (2001) 55 *Int Org* 215, 223–4; Ratner (2006) 100 *AJIL* 808, 811.

[192] GA Res 2625(XXV), 24 October 1970. See also SC Res 662 (1990) §1, declaring that the Iraqi annexation of Kuwait 'under any form and whatever pretext has no legal validity and is considered null and void'. Further: VCLT, Art 52 (treaty procured through use or threat of force is void *ab initio*).

[193] 1 Hyde 364–5, 372; 2 Whiteman 1168–72. This most recently occurred in the cases of East Timor and South Sudan.

[194] E.g. India–Bangladesh, Agreement Concerning the Demarcation of the Land Boundary between India and Bangladesh and Related Matters, 16 May 1974, available at www.hcidhaka.org/agreement_india_bd.php, Art 3 as enacted by the Protocol of 6 September 2011, www.mea.gov.in/mystart.php?id=500418206.

[195] Ratner (2006) 100 *AJIL* 808, 811.

the international community to impose measures on an aggressor,[196] and the principle of respect for pre-independence administrative divisions following attainment of independence by former colonies (*uti possidetis*).[197] In any event the application of the principle may be difficult in practice. In relation to the British–Argentine dispute over the Malvinas/Falklands the relevant UN resolutions call for transfer by virtue of a principle of decolonization while the UK regards transfer without local consent as a breach of the principle of self-determination.[198]

---

[196] Cf the debate over the Oder-Neisse frontier established by the Potsdam Declaration (1945) 39 *AJIL* Supp 245; Brownlie, *Use of Force* (1963) 409.

[197] See *Burkina Faso/Mali*, ICJ Reports 1986 p 554, 566–7; ibid, 652–3 (Judge ad hoc Luchaire).

[198] See UKMIL (1985) 56 *BY* 402–6, 473–4. Also: Reisman (1983) 93 *Yale LJ* 287; Crawford (2nd edn, 2006) 637–47. On Kosovo: e.g. Corten, in Cot (ed), *Liber Amicorum Jean-Pierre Cot, le procès international* (2009) 30.

10

STATUS OF TERRITORY: FURTHER PROBLEMS

1. INTERNATIONAL PROCEDURES OF TERRITORIAL DISPOSITION[1]

A basic assumption of the international system is that sovereignty—plenary power over territory—inheres individually in each state which has the better claim to title over that territory, and that it is not shared. But this is an assumption; from a legal point of view it may even be a presumption: it is not a rule, still less a peremptory norm. There is nothing to prevent a state from freely abandoning its sovereignty in favour of merger in another state, and what can be done in whole can be done in part. Groups of states, or an international organization, can come to exercise dispositive authority over a given territory: questions may then arise as to the modalities of the exercise of such powers and their relation to the self-determination of the people of the territory concerned. Some of these situations are grouped for consideration here.

(A) AGREEMENT BETWEEN THE STATES CONCERNED

A cession of territory may depend on the political decision of the states concerned in a dispute. Such a cession may be the result of a political claim, on grounds of history or security, a legal claim, or a combination of these. The conditions under which transfer occurs may be influenced by the recommendations of political organs of international organizations and, latterly, by the principle of self-determination (see chapters 5, 29). On numerous occasions, plebiscites have been organized under the auspices of the United Nations, with the results treated as indicative or binding.[2]

---

[1] See esp Jennings, *Acquisition of Territory* (1963) 69–87; Crawford, *Creation of States* (2nd edn, 2006) 501–647.

[2] Wambaugh, *Plebiscites since the World War* (1933); Beigbeder, *International Monitoring of Plebiscites, Referenda and National Elections* (1994).

(B) JOINT DECISION OF THE PRINCIPAL POWERS

Likewise on a number of occasions a group of leading powers, perhaps in association with a number of other states, have assumed a power of disposition, although the legal bases of such a power were sometimes problematic.[3] It is possible that, as in the case of the creation of a new constitution by rebellion, the political and legal bases are inseparable: certainly the legal consequences of this power of disposition are commonly accepted. The mandates system rested in substantial part at least on such a power of disposition, and the International Court accepted its consequences in its successive advisory opinions on the status of South West Africa.[4]

Disposition of territory alone is not enough for a transfer of sovereignty, however. In the *Eritrea/Yemen* arbitration, the Tribunal considered the status of certain Red Sea islands in light of Article 16 of the Treaty of Lausanne, by which the Ottoman Empire renounced sovereignty over the islands. It held that no doctrine of reversion of historical title applied, so that sovereignty over the islands in question had remained indeterminate after Turkey divested itself of the territory.[5] What was required for acquisition of the territory was 'an intentional display of power and authority over the territory, by the exercise of jurisdiction and state functions, on a continuous and peaceful basis'.[6]

(C) ACTION BY UNITED NATIONS ORGANS

It is doubtful if the UN has a capacity to convey title, in part because it cannot assume the role of territorial sovereign: in spite of the principle of implied powers, the UN is not a state and the General Assembly only has a power of recommendation. On this basis it can be argued that GA Resolution 181(II) of 29 November 1947, approving a partition plan for Palestine, was if not *ultra vires* at any rate not binding on member states.[7]

However this may be, the fact is that states may agree to delegate a power of disposition to a political organ of the UN, at least where the previous sovereign has relinquished title; but there is no transfer of sovereignty and no disposition of a title inhering in the Organization. In such cases the Organization acts primarily as a referee. The General Assembly played this type of role in relation to the creation of the new states of Libya and Somalia and in the case of territory relinquished by Italy under the Peace Treaty of 1947.[8]

---

[3] Cf *International Status of South West Africa*, ICJ Reports 1950 p 128, 146–63 (Lord McNair).

[4] *Status of South West Africa*, ICJ Reports 1950 p 128; *Legal Consequences for States of the Continued Presence of South Africa in Namibia (South West Africa) notwithstanding Security Council Resolution 276 (1970)*, ICJ Reports 1971 p 16; *Western Sahara*, ICJ Reports 1975 p 12.

[5] *Eritrea and Yemen (Territorial Sovereignty)* (1998) 114 ILR 1, 40.

[6] Ibid, 69.

[7] Kelsen, *The Law of the United Nations* (1950) 195–7; Crawford (2nd edn, 2006) 424–36.

[8] See GA Res 289A(IV), 21 November 1949; GA Res 387(V), 17 November 1950; GA Res 1418(XIV), 5 December 1959. Further: GA Res 515(VI), 1 February 1952, on the transfer of Eritrea to Ethiopia.

On similar principles, the General Assembly probably retained a power to terminate trusteeship status for cause.[9] But the termination of mandates was a matter of more difficulty, partly because the power of disposition arguably inhered in the principal Allied Powers participating in the Treaty of Versailles.[10] It may be that, in the historic cases of mandate and trusteeship, and also of the few remaining territories to which Chapter XI of the Charter applies, the UN does not 'confer sovereignty', but rather decides on or approves the manner in which the principle of self-determination is to be implemented. Certainly resolutions of the General Assembly play an important element in the consolidation of title over territory. This is especially the case with the resolutions based on Resolution 1514(XV), the Declaration on the Granting of Independence to Colonial Countries and Peoples.[11]

However that may be, the General Assembly assumed the power to terminate the Mandate for South West Africa in Resolution 2145(XXI) of 27 October 1966.[12] Subsequently the General Assembly established the Council for South West Africa, appointed a UN Commissioner to administer the territory, and renamed the territory 'Namibia'. South Africa failed to respond to these developments and the Security Council adopted resolutions in 1969 and 1970 'recognizing' the decision of the General Assembly to terminate the Mandate and calling upon all states to take measures to implement the finding that South Africa's continued presence in Namibia was illegal. By a further resolution the International Court was asked to give an advisory opinion on the question, 'What are the legal consequences for States of the continued presence of South Africa in Namibia notwithstanding Security Council Resolution 276 (1970)?' As a preliminary to giving its views on the substance of the question, the Court considered the validity of GA Resolution 2145(XXI) in terms of the Charter.[13] The Court held that the power of the League of Nations, and therefore of the United Nations, to revoke the Mandate for reasons recognized by general international law (termination on the ground of material breach of a treaty) was to be implied.[14] The role adopted by the General Assembly, assisted by the Security Council, was to take such action as was necessary to ensure the application of the provisions of Resolution 1514(XV) to the people of Namibia. In formal terms at least, this did not involve a power of disposition as such, but the application of the provisions of the Charter, as interpreted by the practice of the organs, relating to the principle of self-

---

[9] This may be inferred from Arts 76 and 85 of the Charter: Jennings (1963) 81. No express provision appears, but (except with strategic trusteeships) it was the GA that approved the trusteeship agreement in each case. Further: Marston (1969) 18 *ICLQ* 1; Crawford (2nd edn, 2006) 581–6.

[10] Also: *Status of South West Africa*, ICJ Reports 1950 p 128, 150 (Judge McNair), 168 (Judge Read), 180–1 (Judge Alvarez, diss); Crawford (2nd edn, 2006) 574–81.

[11] 14 December 1960. Further: Jennings (1963) 82–7.

[12] For contemporary comment: Dugard (1968) 62 *AJIL* 78; Marston (1969) 18 *ICLQ* 1, 28ff; Rousseau (1967) 71 *RGDIP* 382.

[13] *Namibia*, ICJ Reports 1971 p 16, 45–50.

[14] Ibid, 47–9. Also: Dugard (1968) 62 *AJIL* 78, 84–8.

determination.[15] Namibia eventually achieved independence in 1990 after elections supervised by the UN Transition Assistance Group.[16]

The role of the General Assembly in the decolonization of Western Sahara has involved a complex of issues concerning the principle of self-determination and the legal interests of Morocco (and at one time Mauritania).[17] The situation remains unresolved.[18]

In the aftermath of the Iraqi invasion and occupation of Kuwait the Security Council adopted Resolution 687 (1991). The resolution specified the measures to be taken under Chapter VII of the Charter. In particular, the Security Council demanded respect for the agreed territorial delimitation,[19] and decided 'to guarantee the inviolability of the ... international boundary and to take as appropriate all necessary measures to that end in accordance with the Charter of the United Nations'. In the event, following the eviction of Iraq by a broad-based coalition acting under a Security Council mandate, a Demarcation Commission was created: it submitted a Final Report on the demarcation of the international boundary between Iraq and Kuwait on 20 May 1993.[20] In Resolution 833 (1993) the Security Council adopted the decisions of the Commission as 'final'. The exercise was, at least in form, the demarcation of an already agreed alignment and no 'reallocation' was intended. However, when the Final Report is examined it follows almost inexorably that elements of delimitation *were* involved, especially in relation to the maritime delimitation.[21] The outcome was controversial but it is important to remember that the Security Council expressly disclaimed an intention to use the demarcation process for the purpose of 'reallocating territory between Kuwait and Iraq'. Iraq subsequently recognized the boundary so determined.[22]

In the context of maintaining international peace and security UN organs have also been prepared to assume administrative functions in relation, for example, to the

---

[15] For criticism of the opinion on the basis that neither the GA nor the SC has the power to abrogate or alter territorial rights, see Judge Fitzmaurice (diss), ICJ Reports 1971 p 16, 280–3, 294–5. But in the Friendly Relations Declaration, the GA stated that achieving *any* political status freely determined by plebiscite is tantamount to achieving self-determination: Declaration on Principles of International Law concerning Friendly Relations and Co-operation among States in accordance with the Charter of the United Nations, Annex to GA Res 2625(XXV), 24 October 1970.

[16] GA Res S-18, 23 April 1990, following SC Res 652 (1990).

[17] *Western Sahara*, ICJ Reports 1975 p 12, 69–77 (Judge Gros), 105–15 (Judge Petrén), 116–26 (Judge Dillard), 127–72 (Judge de Castro).

[18] Franck (1976) 70 *AJIL* 694; Shaw (1978) 49 *BY* 118; Crawford (2nd edn, 2006) 637–47; S/2007/210.

[19] Iraq-Kuwait, Agreed Minutes Between the State of Kuwait and the Republic of Iraq Regarding the Restoration of Friendly Relations, Recognition and Related Matters, Baghdad, 4 October 1963, 485 UNTS 321. The Agreed Minutes did not delimit maritime areas.

[20] S/25811, 21 May 1993.

[21] Mendelson & Hulton (1993) 64 *BY* 135.

[22] S/1994/1173, 14 October 1994. Also: SC Res 949 (1994).

City of Jerusalem,[23] the Free City of Trieste,[24] East Timor,[25] and Kosovo.[26] The existence of such administrative powers rests legitimately on the principle of necessary implication and is not incompatible with the view that the UN cannot have territorial sovereignty.

2. SOVEREIGNTY DISPLACED OR IN ABEYANCE

Although an undivided sovereignty is the normal mode of territorial administration, exceptional situations exist which cannot be forced into the sovereignty straightjacket. Thus sovereignty may be held jointly by two states, as in a condominium,[27] or distributed in time, as with a leasehold or other grant of sovereign rights subject to an ultimate right of reversion.[28] Or it may be in abeyance, as with the mandate and trusteeship systems.[29] A brief analysis of some other possibilities follows.

(A) TERRITORY *SUB IUDICE*

When a territorial dispute is referred to adjudication, there is a real sense in which sovereignty is in abeyance *pendente lite*: at any rate the tribunal cannot acknowledge either state as sovereign pending its decision, although the decision once given will be declaratory in form. The analogy here is perhaps with the right of possession which the *sequester* or stakeholder had in Roman law.[30] The existing regime rests on acts in the law which in principle could not create sovereignty in the existing holder but which do not render the region *terra nullius*. For practical purposes the present possessor may be regarded as exercising normal powers of jurisdiction and administration, subject only to external limitations arising from the legal instruments determining the status of the region. Thus the relevant agreement may contain provisions for demilitarization.

Furthermore, there must be an implied obligation not to act in such a way as to render fulfilment of the ultimate objective of the arrangement impossible. Thus if the

[23] See Trusteeship Council, Statute for the City of Jerusalem, T/592, 4 April 1950; Stahn (2001) 5 *MPUNYB* 105, 126–7, 134; Chesterman, *You, The People: The United Nations, Transitional Administration, and State-Building* (2004) 52–4.

[24] See Permanent Statute for the Free Territory of Trieste, Annex VI to the Treaty of Peace with Italy, 10 February 1947, 49 UNTS 3; Stahn (2001) 5 *MPUNYB* 105, 125–6, 135–6, 180; 3 Whiteman 68–109; Chesterman (2004) 50–2.

[25] On the UN Transitional Administration in East Timor (1999–2002) see Crawford (2nd edn, 2006) 560–2; Chesterman (2004) 60–4, 135–43.

[26] Ruffert (2001) 50 *ICLQ* 613; Stahn (2001) 5 *MPUNYB* 105; Wilde (2001) 95 *AJIL* 583; Chesterman (2004) 79–83. Further: chapter 4.

[27] Lauterpacht (1956) 5 *ICLQ* 409; Seyersted (1961) 37 *BY* 351, 45–3. Cf Kelsen (1950) 195–7, 684–7.

[28] E.g. O'Connell (1968–69) 43 *BY* 71 (New Hebrides).

[29] The best-known case is Guantanamo Bay under the Cuba–US Treaty of 23 February 1903, 193 CTS 314.

[30] Holmes, *The Common Law* (1881) 209.

stated objective is to provide for an expression of opinion by certain minority groups it would be *ultra vires* to deport or to harass and blackmail the groups concerned.[31] In this respect, the absence of a textually-prescribed enforcement mechanism is not enough to offset the obligation not to impede fulfilment of the end goal, though the presence of such a mechanism will add yet another arrow to the bow. The status of the inhabitants in terms of nationality and citizenship will depend on the circumstances of the particular case.[32] If one accepts the obligations inherent in the doctrine of the ultimate objective then the conferment and deprivation of nationality would not be a matter of domestic jurisdiction for the administering state.

(B) TERRITORY TITLE TO WHICH IS UNDETERMINED

It may happen that a piece of territory not a *res nullius* has no determinate sovereign. This is not simply a case where two states have conflicting claims to territory. In principle such cases can be assessed according to law, with judgment in the form of a declaration. By contrast there are cases where title is in effect suspended pending some future event.

Existing cases spring chiefly from the renunciation of sovereignty by the former holder and the existence of an interregnum with disposition postponed until a certain condition is fulfilled, or where the states having a power of disposition for whatever reason do not exercise the power or fail to exercise it validly. For example, in the 1951 Peace Treaty Japan renounced all rights to Taiwan.[33] But the better view is that Taiwan was not the subject of any act of disposition; it was not transferred to any state. The former view of the British government was that: 'Formosa and the Pescadores are…territory the *de iure* sovereignty over which is uncertain or undetermined'.[34] Since 1972 the British government has acknowledged the position of the Chinese government that Taiwan is a province of China.[35]

(C) *TERRA NULLIUS*[36]

For practical purposes the cases of *terra nullius* and territory *sub iudice* or title to which is undetermined may, to a certain extent, be assimilated. In both cases activity is limited by principles similar to those protecting a reversioner's interest in municipal law. However, in the case of the *terra nullius* the state which is in the course of

---

[31] Genocide Convention, 9 December 1948, 78 UNTS 277.

[32] Cf *Eritrea/Ethiopia Claims Commission, Partial Award: Loss of Property in Ethiopia owned by Non-Residents (Eritrea's Claim No 24)*, 19 December 2005, §§8–11.

[33] Treaty of Peace with Japan, 8 September 1951, 136 UNTS 45, Art 2(b).

[34] Written answer by the Secretary of State, 4 February 1955, in (1956) 5 *ICLQ* 405, 413; also: (1959) 8 *ICLQ* 146, 166.

[35] See the official statements in (1986) 57 *BY* 509, 512; (1991) 62 *BY* 568; (1995) 66 *BY* 618, 620–1. On the legal status of Taiwan cf Crawford (2nd edn, 2006) 206–21.

[36] *Island of Palmas* (1928) 2 RIAA 829; Fitzmaurice (1957) 92 Hague *Recueil* 129, 140–4. Cf McNair, 1 *Opinions* 314–25; *Jacobsen v Norwegian Government* (1933) 7 ILR 109. Also: chapter 9.

consolidating title[37] is in principle entitled to carry out acts of sovereignty. The important difference is that whereas a *terra nullius* is open to acquisition by any state, the territory *sub iudice* is not susceptible to occupation, since the express conditions for its attribution may have been laid down already. In any case, there already is a possessor whose interim possession may have received some form of recognition.

A *terra nullius* is subject to certain rules of law which depend on two assumptions, first, that such zones are for the time being free for the use and exploitation of all and, second, that persons are not deprived of the protection of the law merely because of the absence of state sovereignty—the law of the sea gives the relevant analogy for this. States may exercise jurisdiction in respect of their individuals and companies carrying on activities in a *terra nullius*, as well as in respect of stateless persons. There is also universal jurisdiction in certain cases: Article 101 of the UN Convention on the Law of the Sea defines piracy to include acts directed 'against a ship, aircraft, persons or property in a place outside the jurisdiction of any State'.[38] Acts in the nature of aggression or breaches of the peace, war crimes, or crimes against peace and humanity, will equally be so in *terra nullius*.[39] Unjustified interference from agencies of another state with lawful activity will create international responsibility in the ordinary way. As far as succession of obligations to the new state goes, it is doubtful whether private interests established prior to the reduction into sovereignty of a *terra nullius* must be respected by the new sovereign.[40]

Several issues remain unsettled. It is not clear that a *terra nullius* has a territorial sea: the logic, such as it is, of the doctrine of appurtenance[41] does not apply here, and it would be reasonable to regard the adjacent waters as high seas.[42]

(D) *RES COMMUNIS*

The high seas are commonly described as *res communis omnium*,[43] and occasionally as *res extra commercium*.[44] The use of these terms is innocent enough, providing not too

---

[37] Since states do not always advertise an *animus possidendi* this is probably to be presumed, except where representations from other states provoke a disclaimer. See Escorihuela (2003) 14 *EJIL* 703, 717 (presenting one view of *animus possidendi* as an 'empty phantom'); *Legal Status of Eastern Greenland* (1933) PCIJ Ser A/B No 53.

[38] UNCLOS, 10 December 1982, 1833 UNTS 3. Also: UNCLOS, Arts 100, 105; ILC *Ybk* 1956/II, 282–3 (Arts 38–9 and 43 and commentary thereon). On piracy: chapter 13.

[39] Fitzmaurice (1957) 92 Hague *Recueil* 129, 142.

[40] Cf *Mabo v Queensland (No 2)* 112 ILR 457.

[41] E.g. *Cohen v Whitcomb* (1919) 142 Minn 20, 23 (Minn SC) defining *appurtenance* as '[t]hat which belongs to something else. Something annexed to another thing more worthy.'

[42] GCTS, 29 April 1958, 516 UNTS 215, Art 10 and UNCLOS Art 2 speak of the extension of the sovereignty of a state, not of the extent of a territory.

[43] Fitzmaurice (1957) 92 Hague *Recueil* 129, 142, 143, 150–1, 156–7, 160–2. In Roman law the concept did not acquire a very definite content and was confused at times with *res publicae*. On the high seas: chapter 13.

[44] Lindley, *The Acquisition and Government of Backward Territory in International Law* (1926) 23 uses the term *territorium nullius*.

much is read into them. They represent only a few basic guideposts and do not provide a viable regime of themselves. The *res communis* may not be subjected to the sovereignty of any state, general acquiescence apart, and states are bound to refrain from any acts which might adversely affect the use of the high seas by other states or their nationals. It is now generally accepted that outer space and celestial bodies have the same general character. Legal regimes that are similar in type may be applied by treaty to other resources, for example an oilfield underlying parts of two or more states.[45]

(E) TERRITORIAL ENTITIES (OTHER THAN STATES) ENJOYING LEGAL PERSONALITY

In *Western Sahara* the International Court considered the legal status of the 'Mauritanian entity' at the time of colonization by Spain in the years 1884 onwards. It was accepted that the entity was not a state. However, in coming to this conclusion the Court accepted as a principle that in certain conditions a legal entity, other than a state, 'enjoying some form of sovereignty', could exist distinct from the several emirates and tribes which composed it.[46] These conditions were not described with any precision by the Court but were related to the existence of 'common institutions or organs' and of an entity which was in 'such a position that it possesses, in regard to its Members, rights which it is entitled to ask them to respect'.[47]

(F) ANTARCTICA[48]

Escaping all classifications—but illustrating well the possibilities and weaknesses of international arrangements for the government of territory—is Antarctica. Virtually the whole continent is claimed by one of the seven claimant states (there is a small unclaimed sector which is the last surviving *terra nullius* on earth). But these claims are not recognized by any other participant in Antarctic activity, and the legal positions of both claimants and non-claimants are protected by a continental 'without prejudice' clause, Article IV of the Antarctic Treaty.[49] It is on this fragile basis of claims and their non-recognition that the entire edifice of Antarctic scientific and (increasingly) touristic activity is based, as well as the regulatory framework of the Antarctic Treaty System.

---

[45] UK-Netherlands, Agreement relating to the Exploitation of Single Geological Structures extending across the Dividing Line on the Continental Shelf under the North Sea, 6 October 1965, 595 UNTS 106.

[46] ICJ Reports 1975 p 12, 57–65, 67–8.

[47] Ibid, 63, referring to *Reparation for Injuries Suffered in the Service of the United Nations*, ICJ Reports 1949 p 174, 178. On legal personality: chapter 4.

[48] See Bush, *Antarctica and International Law* (1988); Rothwell, *The Polar Regions and the Development of International Law* (1996); Stokke & Vidas, *Governing the Antarctic* (1996); Crawford, in French, Saul & White (eds), *International Law and Dispute Settlement* (2010) 271.

[49] Antarctic Treaty, 1 December 1959, 402 UNTS 71, Art IV.

PART IV

LAW OF THE SEA

11

THE TERRITORIAL SEA AND OTHER MARITIME ZONES[1]

1. THE TERRITORIAL SEA

(A) INTRODUCTION

Traditionally states were regarded as exercising sovereignty, subject to a right of innocent passage, over a belt of sea adjacent to their coastlines and bounded by the high seas. The breadth of this 'territorial sea'[2] was never definitively settled despite codification attempts in 1930, 1958, and 1960; claims varied between three and six nautical miles (nm) and even more.[3] It came to be understood that the territorial sea was founded on a baseline, related to the low-water mark, and enclosing internal waters (rivers, bays, gulfs, harbours, etc) lying on its landward side. Both the 1958 Geneva Convention on the Territorial Sea and Contiguous Zone (GCTS)[4] and the UN Convention on the Law of the Sea (UNCLOS)[5] assume that every coastal state has a territorial sea.[6]

---

[1] Generally: Nordquist (ed), *United Nations Convention on the Law of the Sea 1982* (1985); O'Connell, 1–2 *The International Law of the Sea* (ed Shearer, 1982, 1984); Platzöder (ed), 1–17 *Third United Nations Conference on the Law of the Sea* (1982–88); Kittichaisaree, *The Law of the Sea and Maritime Boundary Delimitation in South-East Asia* (1987); Dupuy & Vignes (eds), 1–2 *A Handbook on the New Law of the Sea* (1991); Lucchini & Voelckel, 1–2 *Droit de la Mer* (1990, 1996); Churchill & Lowe, *The Law of the Sea* (3rd edn, 1999); Roach & Smith, *United States Responses to Excessive Maritime Claims* (2nd edn, 1996); UN, *Handbook on the Delimitation of Maritime Boundaries* (2000); Coustère, Daudet, Dupuy, Eisemann & Voelckel (eds), *La Mer et son droit* (2003); Prescott & Schofield, *The Maritime Political Boundaries of the World* (2nd edn, 2005); Rothwell & Stephens, *The International Law of the Sea* (2010).

[2] Other terms in use included the 'marginal sea', and 'territorial waters'. The term 'territorial waters' was used occasionally in national legislation to describe internal waters, or internal waters and the territorial sea combined. Cf *Fisheries (UK v Norway)*, ICJ Reports 1951 p 116, 125.

[3] The marine or nautical mile (nm) is equivalent to 1,852 metres. National definitions have historically varied, however, this value was approved by the International Hydrographic Conference in 1929: see International Hydrographic Organization (IHO), Hydrographic Dictionary, Special Publication No 32 (5th edn, 1994) 116. Although a nautical mile is not an SI unit it has been accepted for use by the General Conference on Weights and Measures as defined by the IHO; www.bipm.org/en/si/si_brochure/chapter4/table8.html.

[4] 29 April 1958, 516 UNTS 205.

[5] 10 December 1982, 1833 UNTS 3, Art 311.

[6] GCTS, Art 21; UNCLOS, Art 2.

Following early debate,[7] it came to be settled that states have sovereignty over the territorial sea. GCTS Article 2 and UNCLOS Article 3 both state that sovereignty is exercised subject to the provisions of the respective conventions and other rules of international law. This was intended to highlight that the limitations upon sovereignty in this area set out in the Convention are non-exhaustive. The sovereignty of the coastal state extends to the seabed and subsoil of the territorial sea and the airspace above it.[8]

An understanding of the modern law depends on an understanding of its history. In the eighteenth century extravagant claims to sovereignty over the seas came to be seen as obsolete or nearly so. In 1702, the Dutch jurist Bynkershoek propounded the doctrine that the power of the territorial sovereign extended to vessels within cannon range of shore.[9] At first this doctrine seemed commensurate with the control of the actual guns of ports and fortresses over adjacent waters: it was not a maritime belt of uniform breadth.[10] However, in the latter half of the eighteenth century, several states laid down limits for belts for purposes of customs or fishery control in legislation and treaties, and Danish practice—after 1745 based on a four-mile belt[11]—had some impact on European thinking.[12]

In the later eighteenth century, two developments occurred. Writers and governments conceived of a hypothetical cannon-shot rule, a *belt* over which cannons could range if they were placed along the whole seaboard. Further, as 'cannon-shot' was a somewhat imprecise criterion, suggestions for a convenient substitute appeared. In 1782, the Italian writer Galiani proposed three nautical miles, or one marine league.[13] The diplomatic birth of the three-mile limit appears to have been the US Note to Britain and France of 8 November 1793, in which the limit was employed for purposes of neutrality.[14] During and after the Napoleonic wars, British and American prize courts translated the cannon-shot rule into the three-mile rule.[15]

A significant legal development was the shift from claims to jurisdiction for particular purposes to the extension of sovereignty over a maritime belt. Some claims, such as those of Denmark and Sweden, though commencing as pronouncements for

---

[7]   Gidel, 3 *Droit international public de la mer* (1934) 181; O'Connell (1971) 45 *BY* 303; 1 O'Connell (1982) 59.

[8]   GCTS, Art 2; UNCLOS, Art 2.

[9]   Bynkershoek, *De Dominio Maris* (1702, tr Magoffin 1923) ch 2.

[10]   This is the view of Walker (1945) 22 *BY* 210. The concept of actual control is probably referable to the diplomatic practice of Holland and France in the 17th and 18th centuries.

[11]   So also Sweden, at least after 1779. Vattel adopted the theory of a maritime belt, but regarding breadth concluded that 'all that can reasonably be said, is, that, in general, the dominion of the state over the neighbouring sea extends as far as her safety renders it necessary and her power is able to assert it': Vattel, *Le Droit des gens* (1758, tr Anon 1797) I.xxiii.§289.

[12]   Kent (1954) 48 *AJIL* 537; O'Connell (1971) 45 *BY* 303, 320–3.

[13]   Similar views were expressed by Azuni in *Sistema universale dei principii del diritto marittimo dell'Europa* (1795, tr Johnson 1806). Also: Kent (1954) 48 *AJIL* 537, 548.

[14]   1 Hyde 455. See also US Proclamation of Neutrality, 22 April 1793, which refers to the range of a cannon-ball, 'usually stated at one sea league'.

[15]   *The Twee Gebroeders* (1800) 3 C Rob 162; (1801) 3 C Rob 336; *The Anna* (1805) 5 C Rob 373; *The Brig Ann* (1815) 1 Gallison's US Cir Ct R 62. Also McNair, 1 *Opinions* 331.

neutrality purposes, quickly developed into assertions of sovereignty,[16] especially when associated with exclusive fishery limits. In other cases it remained unclear whether a claim was only to certain types of jurisdiction or a general limit of sovereignty.[17]

Such claims to jurisdiction have tended to harden into claims to sovereignty, and indeed a few states still claim a territorial sea or other zone of sovereignty beyond 12nm, the limit now laid down by UNCLOS Article 3. This process was, however, arrested to some extent by recognition of a legal distinction between the territorial sea as an extension of sovereignty and special jurisdictional zones.[18] A variety were claimed during the twentieth century, and four were eventually accepted, namely the contiguous zone, the continental shelf and the exclusive economic zone (EEZ), and (in certain cases) archipelagic seas. These are now regulated by UNCLOS, with non-parties showing little disposition to challenge its provisions. UNCLOS characterizes the coastal state's rights over the continental shelf and the EEZ as 'sovereign rights', but they co-exist with high seas rights applicable to other matters, notably maritime transit, the laying of submarine cables, etc (see chapter 13).

(B) THE BASELINE FOR MEASUREMENT OF THE TERRITORIAL SEA

The baseline from which the breadth of the territorial sea is measured is normally the coastal low-water line.[19] There is no standard by which states determine this line, although UNCLOS Article 5 defines the line 'as marked on large scale charts officially recognised by coastal States'.[20]

---

[16] In the case of Denmark and Norway, probably in 1812. Also: Fulton, *The Sovereignty of the Sea* (1911) 566ff; Verzijl, 3 *International Law in Historical Perspective* (1970) 60–5.

[17] Cf the Portuguese six-mile limit for customs and neutrality: Jessup, *The Law of Territorial Waters and Maritime Jurisdiction* (1927) 41. The Spanish six-mile limit for a territorial sea appears to have originated in customs legislation. The 12-mile zone claimed by Imperial Russia related to customs and fisheries legislation.

[18] Such general recognition certainly existed by 1920 and perhaps as early as 1880. Generally: Masterson, *Jurisdiction in Marginal Seas* (1929) 375ff. In 1914, Chile, which already had a territorial sea with a three-mile limit, declared the same limit for purposes of neutrality. British sources often refer to 'territorial jurisdiction'.

[19] GCTS, Art 3; UNCLOS, Art 5; ILC *Ybk* 1956/II, 266; Waldock (1951) 28 *BY* 114, 131–7; McDougal & Burke, *The Public Order of the Oceans* (1962) 305ff; Gihl (1967) 11 *Scan SL* 119.

[20] Art 5 states this as a definition and not as presumptive evidence. See *Li Chia Hsing v Rankin* (1978) 73 ILR 173. The relevant subcommittee of the Hague Codification Conference entered a proviso 'provided the latter line does not appreciably depart from the line of mean low-water spring tides'; however, this was neither discussed nor adopted by the Second Committee given disagreement between states regarding the breadth of the territorial sea: 1 Hackworth 643–4; and the critical comment in McDougal & Burke (1962) 322–6. In its 1989 Baselines Report, the UN Office for Ocean Affairs and the Law of the Sea describes '[t]he low-water mark on a chart' as 'the line depicting the level of chart datum', going on to endorse the IHO reference to 'a plane so low that the tide will not frequently fall below it'. The UN Report identifies four possibilities consistent with this general requirement: the lowest astronomical tide (LAT); mean low-water springs (MLWS); mean lower low-water (MLLS); and mean sea level (MSL). These widely accepted chart data are drawn from the British Admiralty Tables, however, there may be other options open to states: UN Office for Ocean Affairs and the Law of the Sea, *Baselines: An Examination of the Relevant Provisions of the United Nations Convention on the Law of the Sea* (1989) 3, 43.

At one time it was arguable that the baseline was for all purposes the low-water mark. But in the signal case *Anglo–Norwegian Fisheries* the Court decided otherwise.[21]

The Norwegian limit of four nautical miles for territorial waters had been established by royal decree in 1812 and was not at issue in the case. However, later decrees of 1869, 1881, and 1889 continued the measure of 1812 in terms of a system of straight lines drawn from certain outermost points of the *skjaergaard* or rampart of rocks and islands which fringes much of the Norwegian coast. By a decree of 12 July 1935, Norway applied the system in a more detailed way, and the validity of the new limits was challenged by the UK. After a series of incidents, the UK took the case to the Court, seeking damages for interference with British fishing vessels outside the permissible limits.[22] The Court held that the system of straight baselines following the general direction of the coast had been consistently applied by Norway and was unopposed by other states. The UK had not explicitly protested the position of baselines until 1933.[23] Thus the decree of 1935 could have been upheld on the basis of acquiescence; indeed, Judge Hackworth would have upheld Norway's historic title to the areas in question.[24]

But the Court went further, holding that the Norwegian system of baselines was lawful in principle.[25] It stressed the broken and indented character of the Norwegian coastline:[26] to draw the baseline along the outer limit of the *skjaergaard* was a solution 'dictated by geographical realities'.[27] By contrast, a line which was an exact image of the coastline (the *tracé parallèle*), assumed to be the normal method of applying the low-water mark rule,[28] did not apply to a coast where the baseline could only be determined by means of a geometric construction.[29]

The British argument that the length of closing lines must not exceed 10nm was criticized in these terms:

[T]he practice of States does not justify the formulation of any general rule of law… [A]part from any question of limiting the lines to ten miles, it may be that several lines can be envisaged. In such cases the coastal State would seem to be in the best position to appraise the local

---

[21] ICJ Reports 1951 p 116. For contemporary comment: Waldock (1951) 28 *BY* 114; Hudson (1952) 46 *AJIL* 23; Johnson (1952) *ICLQ* 145; Evensen (1952) 46 *AJIL* 609; Wilberforce (1952) 38 *GST* 151; Auby (1953) 80 *JDI* 24; Fitzmaurice (1953) 30 *BY* 8; Fitzmaurice (1954) 31 *BY* 371; Lauterpacht, *Development* (1958) 190–9.

[22] Under the 1935 decree (not strictly enforced until 1948), 48 fixed points were employed: 18 lines exceeded 15nm in length, one was 44nm in length. The decree refers to a fisheries zone, but both parties assumed in argument that it delimited the territorial sea: ICJ Reports 1951 p 116, 125.

[23] Ibid, 138, but see 171–80 (Judge McNair, diss).

[24] Ibid, 206. Also the *Anglo-French Continental Shelf* (1978) 54 ILR 6, 74–83 on acceptance of a basepoint by conduct.

[25] The later references to the attitude of other governments appear to have been partially intended as evidence of legality: ICJ Reports 1951 p 116, 139.

[26] Ibid, 127.

[27] Ibid, 128.

[28] See Waldock (1951) 28 *BY* 114, 132–7.

[29] ICJ Reports 1951 p 116, 129–30.

conditions dictating the selection... [A]ll that the Court can see [in the Norwegian system] is the application of general international law to a specific case.[30]

The Court went on to elaborate criteria for determining the validity of straight baselines. First, because of the dependence of the territorial sea upon the land, 'the drawing of baselines must not depart to any appreciable extent from the general direction of the coast'.[31] Secondly, a close geographical relationship between sea areas and land formations is a 'fundamental consideration' in deciding 'whether certain sea areas lying within [the baselines] are sufficiently closely linked to the land domain to be subject to the regime of internal waters'.[32] Thirdly, it is relevant that there exist 'certain economic interests peculiar to a region, the reality and importance of which are evidenced by long usage'.[33]

Even if one regards *Anglo-Norwegian Fisheries* as an instance of judicial legislation, its significance for the development of the law cannot be underestimated. The Court's pronouncements on the straight lines method were intended to have general application to coasts of that type. They have been codified in GCTS Article 4 and UNCLOS Article 7, which confirm the place of *Anglo-Norwegian Fisheries* in the modern law of the sea. A good number of states employ straight baselines, although not always in conformity with the rules.[34]

UNCLOS Article 14 provides that '[t]he coastal State may determine baselines in turn by any of the methods provided for... to suit different conditions.' Thus straight baselines may be used in conjunction with closing lines across river mouths[35] and bays.[36] Furthermore, under UNCLOS Article 7(2) straight baseline systems may apparently be maintained despite changes in coastal morphology.

(C) BREADTH OF THE TERRITORIAL SEA[37]

In the seventeenth century several forms of limit were known, including the range of vision on a fair day and the range of cannons on shore. By the last quarter of the eighteenth century, the cannon-shot rule obtained in western and southern Europe. It was not dominant, however, and other claims rested simply on a belt with a stated breadth.[38] In 1793, the cannon-shot rule was first given a standard value of one marine league

---

[30] Ibid, 131.

[31] Ibid, 133.

[32] Ibid, 133.

[33] See also the statement that 'in these barren regions the inhabitants of the coastal zone derive their livelihood essentially from fishing': ibid, 128.

[34] Roach & Smith (2000) 31 *ODIL* 47. Generally: US Department of State, *Limits in the Seas* No 36 and revisions; UN Division for Ocean Affairs and the Law of the Sea, Deposit of Charts/Lists of Coordinates, www.un.org/Depts/los/LEGISLATIONANDTREATIES/depositpublicity.htm.

[35] GCTS, Art 13; UNCLOS, Art 9.

[36] GCTS, Art 7; UNCLOS, Art 10.

[37] Gidel (1934) 62ff; McDougal & Burke (1962) 446–564; Fulton (1911) 537ff.

[38] Denmark and Norway, 4nm (1745); Sweden, 4nm (1779); Spain, 6nm (1760).

or three nautical miles in diplomatic practice.[39] By 1862,[40] and probably earlier, the cannon-shot rule and the three-mile limit were generally regarded as synonymous.[41]

The three-mile limit gained currency during the nineteenth century. However, practice was not uniform,[42] and France, Belgium, Portugal, Germany, and Russia did not differentiate clearly in their practice between territorial sea and jurisdictional zones. Many states with a three-mile limit claimed contiguous zones extending beyond three nautical miles.

Thus some jurists doubted whether the three-mile limit had been unequivocally settled.[43] The results of the Hague Codification Conference of 1930 provide a significant balance sheet. Although a majority of states favoured a three-mile limit, some also claimed contiguous zones. In its report to the Conference the second committee explained that, due to differences of opinion, it preferred not to express any conclusion.[44] Likewise the ILC indicated that a majority of members did not regard the three-mile rule as positive law.[45] It proved impossible to agree on a limit at UNCLOS I (1958) and II (1960). But as part of the trade-off which occurred at UNCLOS III, agreement was reached. UNCLOS Article 3 provides that 'every state has the right to establish the breadth of its territorial sea up to a limit not exceeding 12 nautical miles'.

Until 1987 and 1988 respectively, the US and the UK supported the three-mile limit and protested wider claims. British adherence to the three-mile limit was reinforced by the legislative embodiment of the limit, commencing with the Territorial Waters Jurisdiction Act 1878. Now, however, most states have a 12nm limit,[46] including non-parties to UNCLOS such as the US.[47] Claims apparently in excess of 12nm call for careful assessment. Certain of these are fishing conservation zones, wrongly characterized.[48]

---

[39] 1 Hyde 455. Also US Proclamation of Neutrality, 22 April 1793, which refers to the range of a cannon-ball, 'usually stated at one sea league'.

[40] Cf Moore, 1 *Digest* 706–7.

[41] An isolated case of reliance on the rule to justify a limit of 12nm occurred in 1912, when Russia referred to the rule to justify extensions of jurisdiction for customs and fishery purposes: 1 Hackworth 635. Also *Costa Rica Packet* (1902), in Moore, 4 *Int Arb* 4948; *The Alleganean,* in Moore, 4 *Int Arb* 4332.

[42] Spain had a 6-mile limit; Norway, Denmark, and Sweden claimed 4 nm. Cf (1926) 20 *AJIL Sp Supp* 73–4; Gidel (1934) 69ff, on treaty practice.

[43] E.g. Hall, *International Law* (1880) 191–2; Westlake, *International Law* (1904) part I, 184–6. Also Fulton (1911) 664.

[44] For the views expressed: (1930) 24 *AJIL Sp Supp* 253; 1 Hackworth 628.

[45] ILC *Ybk* 1956/II, 265–6.

[46] For information on maritime claims: UN Office of Legal Affairs, *Law of the Sea Bulletin*. The current situation is as follows: Jordan claims 3nm; Greece claims 6nm. Six states claim 200nm: Benin, Ecuador (only in one area), El Salvador, Liberia, Peru, Somalia. The remainder claim 12nm.

[47] Presidential Proclamation No 5928, 27 December 1988, 54 FR 777.

[48] UNCLOS, Art 310, allows states to make 'declarations or statements, however phrased or named, with a view, *inter alia*, to the harmonization of its laws and regulations with the provisions of this Convention'. Such declarations or statements may clarify how zones characterized differently at the national level might correspond with those under UNCLOS. In *Anglo-Norwegian Fisheries*, the Court took the fisheries zone delimited by the Norwegian Royal Decree of 1935 as 'none other than the sea are which Norway considers to be her territorial sea': ICJ Reports 1951 p 116, 125.

(D) BAYS[49]

In certain circumstances, bays may be enclosed by a line which leaves internal waters on its landward side and provides a baseline for delimiting the territorial sea.

(i) Bays the coasts of which belong to a single state

The drawing of a closing line is possible only where the coast of the bay belongs to a single state. GCTS Article 7(2) and UNCLOS Article 10(2) provide a geometrical, semi-circle test for bays.[50] This is a necessary but not sufficient condition for the existence of a bay: there must be 'a well-marked indentation with identifiable headlands'.[51] Gulfs, fjords, and straits, or parts thereof, are not excluded from the legal concept of a bay. On the other hand the provisions concerning bays are not intended to introduce the system of straight lines to coasts whose configuration does not justify this.

It was asserted formerly that the closing line was limited to 10nm. Practice was, however, not uniform,[52] and in *Anglo-Norwegian Fisheries* the International Court concluded that 'the ten-mile rule has not acquired the authority of a general rule of international law'.[53] GCTS Article 7(4) and UNCLOS Article 10(4) prescribe 24nm.

Coastal states may derive title to bays as a consequence of the *Anglo-Norwegian Fisheries* system of straight lines. A considerable number of claims related to 'bays' are based on historic title, often on questionable or equivocal evidence.[54]

(ii) Bays bounded by the territory of two or more states

Although the issue has not been uncontroversial, GCTS Article 12(1) and UNCLOS Article 15 now represent the law. Article 15 provides:

Where the coasts of two States are opposite or adjacent to each other, neither of the two States is entitled, failing agreement between them to the contrary, to extend its territorial

---

[49] In particular: Gidel (1934) 532ff; Waldock (1951) 28 *BY* 114, 137–42; Fitzmaurice (1959) 8 *ICLQ* 73, 79–85; McDougal & Burke (1962) 327–73; 4 Whiteman 207–33; Bouchez, *The Regime of Bays in International Law* (1964); Blum, *Historic Titles in International Law* (1965) 261–81; Gihl (1967) *Scan SL* 119; Edeson (1968–69) 5 *AYIL* 5; 1 O'Connell (1982) 338–416; Westerman, *The Juridical Bay* (1987).

[50] UNCLOS, Art 10(2). On the application of this provision: *Post Office v Estuary Radio* [1967] 1 WLR 1396. Also: *US v California* (1952) 57 ILR 54; *US v California*, 381 US 139 (1965); *US v Louisiana*, 389 US 155 (1967); *US v Louisiana*, 394 US 11 (1969); *Texas v Louisiana*, 426 US 465 (1976). In Australia: *Raptis v South Australia* (1977) 69 ILR 32.

[51] *North Atlantic Fisheries* (1910) 11 RIAA 167, 199; *US v Louisiana*, 394 US 11, 48–55 (1969); *Raptis v South Australia* (1977) 69 ILR 32. Cf 1 O'Connell (1982) 384; Westerman (1987) 79–98.

[52] McNair, 1 *Opinions* 353–6, 360.

[53] ICJ Reports 1951 p 116, 131. Also ibid, 163–4 (Judge McNair). However Judge Read regarded the rule as customary: ibid, 188.

[54] For bays claimed as 'historic bays' (over 30 in all): Jessup (1927) 383–439; Colombos, *International Law of the Sea* (6th edn, 1967) 180–8. Further: Gidel (1934) 621–63; McDougal & Burke (1962) 357–68 (discounting the basis in authority of some claims); Goldie (1984) 11 *Syracuse JILC* 211. The Central American Court of Justice in 1917 declared that the Gulf of Fonseca was 'an historic bay possessed of the characteristics of a closed sea' and further, that without prejudice to the rights of Honduras, El Salvador and Nicaragua had a right of co-ownership in the extra-territorial waters of the Gulf. See the *Land, Island and Maritime Frontier Dispute (El Salvador/Honduras)*, ICJ Reports 1992 p 351, 588–605. On claims to treat the Straits of Tiran and the Gulf of Aqaba as a closed sea: Gross (1959) 53 *AJIL* 564, 566–72; Selak (1958) 52 *AJIL* 660, 689–98.

sea beyond the median line every point of which is equidistant from the nearest points on the baselines from which the breadth of the territorial seas of each of the two States is measured.

The above provision does not apply, however, where it is necessary by reason of historic title or other special circumstances to delimit the territorial seas of the two States in a way which is at variance therewith.

The reference to 'other special circumstances' is vague, but seems to cater for geographical peculiarities and the elimination of practical problems.[55]

(E) ISLANDS, ROCKS, AND LOW-TIDE ELEVATIONS[56]

(i) Definition of 'island'

Whatever its size or population, a formation is legally an island if two conditions are satisfied: (1) the formation must be 'a naturally formed area of land'; (2) it must always be above sea level. Permanently submerged banks and reefs generally do not produce a territorial sea, and formations visible only at low tide (low-tide elevations) will only do so in limited circumstances. Islands are ordinarily entitled to a territorial sea, contiguous zone, EEZ, and continental shelf.[57]

However, UNCLOS Article 121(3) provides that '[r]ocks which cannot sustain human habitation or economic life of their own shall have no exclusive economic zone or continental shelf'. This provision reflects the concern that minor features permanently above sea level but otherwise insignificant should not generate extended maritime zones up to or beyond 200nm. It is unlikely that the term 'rocks' further restricts the application of Article 121(3) to features meeting unspecified geological criteria. A UN study on baselines published in 1989 suggests as a definition, '[a] solid mass of limited extent'.[58] Yet proposals to limit those islands capable of supporting an EEZ by reference to size were not accepted.[59] The term 'rocks' might be considered to refer to islands meeting conditions (1) and (2) which cannot sustain habitation or economic life of their own.

But the qualifying phrase is unclear. Is past, present, or future sustenance of human habitation or economic life sufficient? The conjunction 'or' may suggest that an island may generate an EEZ provided it is capable of sustaining independently *either* human habitation or economic life; or it may operate cumulatively. The concept of 'economic life of their own' is also vague:[60] many small island populations are dependent on

---

[55] See the declaration on Art 12 by Venezuela: McDougal & Burke (1962) 1184.

[56] GCTS, Art 10; UNCLOS, Art 121(1); ILC *Ybk* 1956/II, 270. Also: Gidel (1934) 670ff; McNair, 1 *Opinions*, 363ff; Fitzmaurice (1959) 8 *ICLQ* 73, 85–8; McDougal & Burke (1962) 373, 391–8; Bowett, *The Legal Regime of Islands in International Law* (1979); Symmons, *The Maritime Zones of Islands in International Law* (1979); Jayewardene, *The Regime of Islands in International Law* (1990).

[57] UNCLOS, Art 121(2).

[58] UN Office for Ocean Affairs and the Law of the Sea, *Baselines* (1989) 61.

[59] 3 *Virginia Commentary* (1985) 328–36.

[60] Soons & Kwiatkowska (1990) 21 *NYIL* 139, 160–9.

remittances and metropolitan aid but presumably qualify as having an 'economic life of their own'. It is possible that sovereign rights to exploit living and non-living marine resources in the territorial sea could fulfil the requirement of 'economic life'. By contrast fisheries or sea-bed minerals beyond 12nm could not do so: otherwise every rock would be capable of sustaining economic life of its own and the provision would be entirely circular. State practice is equivocal. While the UK's renunciation of any claim to an EEZ or continental shelf off Rockall upon acceding to UNCLOS is often cited in this context,[61] other states continue to claim extended maritime zones for similar features.[62]

Whatever interpretative difficulties may attach to Article 121(3), it is part of the negotiated text and must be given effect. Moreover the only explicit definition of 'island' in the 1958 Conventions is in the GCTS, and it is not disputed that islands and rocks of any size are entitled to a territorial sea. What is disputed is whether they are entitled to maritime zones beyond 12nm, but the conventions do not contemplate the EEZ, and the Geneva Convention on the Continental Shelf (GCCS) is equivocal.[63]

(ii) Low-tide elevations[64]

In two cases low-tide elevations (by definition not islands) affect the limit of the territorial sea. GCTS Article 4(3) and UNCLOS Article 7(4) provide that straight baselines shall not be drawn to or from low-tide elevations unless lighthouses or similar installations which are permanently above sea level have been built on them.[65] Secondly, and independently, the low-water line on an elevation situated at a distance not exceeding the breadth of the territorial sea from the mainland or an island may serve as the baseline.[66] Low-tide elevations outside the territorial sea have no territorial sea of their own.

---

[61] Hansard, HC Deb 21 July 1997 vol 298 cc397–8W: 'The United Kingdom's fishery limits will need to be redefined based on St Kilda, since Rockall is not a valid base point for such limits under article 121(3) of the convention.' Cf [1997] UKMIL 591, 599–600.

[62] E.g. Japan's claims to an extended continental shelf in respect of Okinotorishima, as indicated in its submission to the Commission on the Limits of the Continental Shelf on 12 November 2008. This claim has been protested by China (Letter of the Permanent Mission to the UN of the People's Republic of China to the UN Secretary-General, 6 February 2009, CML/2/2009 [translation]) and the Republic of Korea (Letter of the Permanent Mission to the UN of the Republic of Korea to the UN Secretary-General, 27 February 2009, MUN/046/2009).

[63] 29 April 1958, 499 UNTS 311. In the context of maritime delimitation, small islands and rocks are frequently ignored or discounted: e.g. *Maritime Delimitation in the Black Sea (Romania v Ukraine)*, ICJ Reports 2008 p 61 (giving nil effect to Serpents' Island beyond 12nm), and further: chapter 12.

[64] *Maritime Delimitation and Territorial Questions between Qatar and Bahrain*, ICJ Reports 2001 p 40, 100–3. Also : Marston (1972–73) 46 *BY* 405; Weil, 1 *Liber Amicorum Judge Shigeru Oda* (2002) 307; Guillaume, *Mélanges offerts à Laurent Lucchini et Jean-Pierre Quéneudec* (2003) 287.

[65] Marston (1972–73) 46 *BY* 405. Also: *Qatar v Bahrain*, ICJ Reports 2001 p 40, 100–3.

[66] GCTS, Art 11; UNCLOS, Art 13. Also *Anglo-Norwegian Fisheries*, ICJ Reports 1951 p 116, 128, and cf *R v Kent Justices, ex p Lye* [1967] 2 QB 153; *US v Louisiana*, 394 US 11 (1969).

(iii) Groups of islands: archipelagos[67]

The ILC failed to produce a draft article on archipelagos for inclusion in GCTS, although in its commentary on Article 10 it noted that the straight baselines system might be applicable.[68] This provides no solution to the problem of extensive island systems unconnected with a mainland. Indonesia and the Philippines[69] have for some time employed straight baselines to enclose such island systems, and it may be that a polygonal system is the only feasible one. It is arguable that this is only a further application, to special facts, of principles of unity and interdependence inherent in *Anglo-Norwegian Fisheries*. The difficulty is to allow for such cases without giving a general prescription which, being unrelated to any clear concept of mainland, will permit abuse.

At UNCLOS III the archipelagic states as a group[70] successfully advanced the cause of straight archipelagic baselines. UNCLOS includes a Part concerning archipelagic states (Articles 46 to 54). These are defined as 'a state constituted wholly by one or more archipelagos and may include other islands'. This definition unaccountably excludes archipelagic baselines for those states, such as Ecuador and Canada, which also consist of continental coasts as well as one or more archipelagos.

Archipelagic straight baselines may be employed subject to conditions: for example, that these baselines 'shall not depart to any appreciable extent from the general configuration of the archipelago'. The archipelagic state has sovereignty over the waters enclosed by the baselines subject to limitations created by the provisions of this Part of the convention. These limitations consist of the right of innocent passage for ships of all states, and, unless the archipelagic state designates sea lanes and air routes, the right of archipelagic sea lanes passage 'through the routes normally used for international navigation'.[71]

(F) LEGAL REGIME OF THE TERRITORIAL SEA

The coastal state has all the practical rights and duties inherent in sovereignty, whereas foreign vessels have privileges, associated particularly with the right of innocent passage, which have no general counterparts in respect of the land domain. The coastal

---

[67] Gidel (1934) 706–27; Waldock (1951) 28 *BY* 114, 142–7; Evensen, UNCLOS, 1 Official Recs (1958) A/CONF.13/18, 289; Fitzmaurice (1959) 8 *ICLQ* 73, 88–90; McDougal & Burke (1962) 373–87; ILC *Ybk* 1953/II, 69, 77; O'Connell (1971) 45 *BY* 1; Hodgson & Alexander, Law of the Sea Institute, Occasional Paper No 13 (1972); Bowett(1979) 73–113; Symmons (1979) 62–81; Anand (1979) 19 *Indian JIL* 228; Lattion, *L'Archipel en droit international* (1984); Herman (1985) 23 *CYIL* 172; Rajan (1986) 29 *GYIL* 137; Jayewardene (1990) 103–72; Churchill & Lowe (3rd edn, 1999) 118–31; Jiménez Piernas, 'Archipelagic Waters' (2009) *MPEPIL*.

[68] ILC *Ybk* 1956/II, 270.

[69] Philippines claim: ILC *Ybk* 1956/II, 69–70. For the Indonesian claim and the UK protest: (1958) 7 *ICLQ* 538.

[70] 22 coastal states parties to UNCLOS claim archipelagic status. In *Qatar v Bahrain*, the Court declined to consider whether Bahrain, which had not formally claimed status as an archipelagic state, was entitled to do so: ICJ Reports 2001 p 40, 97.

[71] UNCLOS, Art 53(12). For archipelagic sea lanes passage: chapter 13.

state may reserve fisheries for national use. It may also exclude foreign vessels from navigation and trade along the coast (*cabotage*). Obviously, there are general police powers in matters of security, customs, fiscal regulation, and sanitary and health controls.

Foreign ships have a right of innocent passage through the territorial sea in customary law.[72] GCTS Article 14 and UNCLOS Article 17 codify this right (see further chapter 13).

2. THE CONTIGUOUS ZONE

The power of the coastal state may be manifested in other ways. The territorial sea is, however, the form which involves a concentration of 'sovereign' legal rights. The general interest in maintaining the freedom of the seas outside the territorial sea has been reconciled with the tendencies of coastal states to extend their power seaward by the development of generally-recognized specialized extensions of jurisdiction and associated rights. The contiguous zone was the first to emerge.

(A) THE CONCEPT OF THE CONTIGUOUS ZONE[73]

There is general recognition that contiguous zones give jurisdiction beyond the territorial sea for special purposes. In 1958, the sole article on the contiguous zone was GCTS Article 24, which referred to control by the coastal state 'in a zone of the high seas contiguous to its territorial sea'. UNCLOS Article 33 describes it simply as a zone contiguous to the territorial sea of the coastal state. Under UNCLOS Article 55 the contiguous zone, if claimed, will be superimposed upon the EEZ. In the absence of a claimed EEZ, the areas concerned form part of the high seas (see Article 86). It follows that the rights of the coastal state in such a zone do not constitute sovereignty,[74] and other states have the rights exercisable over the high seas save as qualified by these jurisdictional zones.

Only recently has a consistent doctrine of contiguous zones appeared.[75] UNCLOS Article 33 provides for the creation of contiguous zones for the same purposes and on the same basis as GCTS Article 24, except that (a) the contiguous zone is no longer

---

[72] GCTS, Art 14; UNCLOS, Art 17.

[73] Jessup (1927) 75–112, 241–352; Gidel (1934) 361–492; François, ILC *Ybk* 1951/II, 91–4; Fitzmaurice (1959) 8 *ICLQ* 73, 108–21; Lowe (1981) 52 *BY* 109; 2 O'Connell (1984) 1034–61; Roach & Smith (2nd edn, 1996) 163–72.

[74] Fitzmaurice (1959) 8 *ICLQ* 73, 111–13; Sørensen (1960) 101 Hague *Recueil* 145, 155–8. Also: *Sørensen and Jensen* (1991) 89 ILR 78.

[75] Gidel (1934) 372ff deserves credit for giving the concept authority and coherence. Cf the materials of the Hague Codification Conference; and Renault (1889–92) 11 *Ann de l'Inst* 133, 150. Colombos (6th edn, 1967) 111–13 gives rather idiosyncratic treatment, as do McDougal & Burke (1962) 565–630.

considered 'a zone of the high seas'; and (b) the maximum limit is expressed to be 24nm from the territorial sea baselines. Most coastal states claim a contiguous zone within and up to this maximum limit;[76] these, when limited to the purposes specified in Article 33, are uncontroversial.

(B) FUNCTIONAL JURISDICTION IN THE CONTIGUOUS ZONE

In considering the purposes for which a contiguous zone may be maintained, UNCLOS Article 33 is now the departure point. It refers to the exercise of control necessary to prevent infringement of 'customs, fiscal, immigration or sanitary regulations within the territory or territorial sea of the coastal State'. Although it does not refer to the exercise of control for *security* purposes, some states have claimed jurisdiction in a zone contiguous to the territorial sea on this basis, both prior to and after the entry into force of the GCTS and UNCLOS.[77] A set of draft articles relating to the territorial sea in times of peace approved by the Institut in 1928 included security measures among the controls exercised in a zone contiguous to the territorial sea.[78] In 1956, however, the ILC stated that it

did not recognize special security rights in the contiguous zone. It considered that the extreme vagueness of the term 'security' would open the way for abuses and that the granting of such rights was not necessary. The enforcement of customs and sanitary regulations will be sufficient in most cases to safeguard the security of the State. In so far as measures of self-defence against an imminent and direct threat to the security of the State are concerned, the Commission refers to the general principles of international law and the Charter of the United Nations.[79]

It may be added that recognition of such rights would go far toward equating rights over the contiguous zone and the territorial sea.

(i) Customs

The exercise of this jurisdiction is frequent and no doubt rests on customary international law. UNCLOS Article 33 refers compendiously to 'customs and fiscal' regulations in the contiguous zone; other sources refer to 'revenue laws'. Modern vessels would find smuggling quite straightforward if a narrow enforcement area were employed, and customs zones of 6 and 12nm were common. The US exercised customs jurisdiction over inward-bound foreign vessels within a four-league zone from 1790. The UK had similar 'hovering acts' operating against foreign vessels from 1736 until

---

[76] UN Division for Ocean Affairs and the Law of the Sea, table of claims to maritime jurisdiction, www.un.org/Depts/los/LEGISLATIONANDTREATIES/claims.htm.

[77] Shearer (2003) 17 *Ocean Ybk* 548.

[78] Institut de droit international, 3 Projet de règlement relatif à la mer territoriale en temps de paix (1928) *Ann de l'Inst* 755; Caminos, 'Contiguous Zone' (2008) *MPEPIL*.

[79] ILC *Ybk* 1956/II, 295. Also: Oda (1962) 11 *ICLQ* 131, 147–8.

1876.[80] Claims for the enforcement of national legislation in areas of the high seas are limited by reasonableness, and regulations designed for revenue enforcement cannot be employed in such a way as to accomplish another purpose, for example the exclusion of foreign vessels.[81] Treaty regimes may be created for the mutual recognition of zones and enforcement procedures, reducing the likelihood of incidents.[82]

(ii) Immigration

In practice customs and fiscal regulations might be applied to deal with immigration, and this jurisdiction shares the same policy basis as that relating to customs. Immigration zones were reconciled partially by inclusion in the GCTS and UNCLOS.[83] The limitation to immigration may be significant, although in its 1955 report the ILC indicated that the term was intended to include emigration.[84]

(iii) Sanitary purposes

Such zones are included in GCTS Article 24 and UNCLOS Article 33. The ILC's commentary notes:

Although the number of States which claim rights over the contiguous zone for the purpose of applying sanitary regulations is fairly small, the Commission considers that, in view of the connection between customs and sanitary regulations, such rights should also be recognized for sanitary regulations.[85]

Doctrine supports this type of claim.[86]

Sanitary purposes might cover measures to prevent pollution, particularly by oil, but the position is unclear. Jurisdiction to police pollution has been advanced by the extension of the territorial sea and the appearance of the EEZ, wherein the coastal state has the right of *conserving and managing* natural resources.[87] UNCLOS Part XII also sets out a general obligation to protect and preserve the marine environment.[88] States are further required to take 'all measures consistent with [the] Convention that are necessary to prevent, reduce and control pollution of the marine environment from any source' and to 'take all measures necessary to ensure that activities under their jurisdiction or control are so conducted as not to cause damage by pollution to other States and their environment, and that pollution arising from incidents or activities under their jurisdiction or control does not spread beyond the areas where

---

[80] On British and American legislation and the diplomatic repercussions: Masterson (1929).

[81] See the opinion excerpted in 1 Hackworth 657–9.

[82] Helsingfors Convention for the Suppression of the Contraband Traffic in Alcoholic Liquors, 19 August 1925, 42 LNTS 75. On the 'liquor treaties' concluded by the US: Masterson (1929) 326ff.

[83] The type had appeared in the ILC draft articles in 1955, but was deleted from the draft in 1956: ILC *Ybk* 1956/II, 295. Cf Fitzmaurice (1959) 8 *ICLQ* 73, 117–18 (critical of inclusion); Oda (1962) 11 *ICLQ* 131, 146.

[84] GAOR, 8th Sess, Supplement No 9, A/2456, §111.

[85] ILC *Ybk* 1956/II, 294–5.

[86] Gidel (1934) 455–7, 476, 486; Fitzmaurice (1959) 8 *ICLQ* 73, 117.

[87] UNCLOS, Arts 56, 61, 73.

[88] UNCLOS, Art 192.

they exercise sovereign rights'.[89] The coastal state may adopt 'laws and regulations for the prevention, reduction and control of pollution from vessels conforming to and giving effect to generally accepted international rules and standards' in their EEZs.[90] UNCLOS Article 220 sets out coastal state rights of enforcement in respect of vessels within its territorial sea and EEZ.

(C) ISSUES OF ENFORCEMENT

Under general international law the coastal state may take steps necessary to enforce compliance with its laws in the prescribed zone. The power is one of police and control, and transgressors cannot be visited with consequences amounting to reprisal or summary punishment. Forcible self-help may not be resorted to as readily as in the case of trespass over a terrestrial frontier.

Thus the conventional law may be more restrictive from the perspective of a coastal state than customary law.[91] Both GCTS Article 24(1) and UNCLOS Article 33 provide for the exercise of control necessary to prevent and punish infringement of customs, fiscal, immigration or sanitary laws or regulations within its territory or territorial waters. Fitzmaurice promoted this text prominently in the ILC. In his view:[92]

It ... is control, not jurisdiction, that is exercised ... [T]aken as a whole, the power is essentially supervisory and preventative. The basic object is anticipatory. No offence against the laws of the coastal State is actually being committed at the time. The intention is to avoid such an offence being committed *subsequently*, when, by entering the territorial sea, the vessel comes within the jurisdiction of the coastal State; or else to punish such an offence already committed when the vessel was within such jurisdiction ... Whatever the eventual designs of the [incoming] vessel, she cannot *ex hypothesi* at this stage have committed an offence 'within [the coastal State's] territory or territorial sea' ... As regards ordering, or conducting, the vessel into port under escort, the case is less clear. Though formally distinct from arrest, enforced direction into port is, in the circumstances, almost tantamount to it, and should therefore in principle be excluded: any necessary inquiries, investigation, examination, search, etc., should take place at sea while the ship is still in the contiguous zone. ... In case this may seem to be unduly restrictive, it must be observed that only by insistence on such limitations is it possible to prevent coastal States from treating the contiguous zone as virtually equivalent to territorial sea.

This interpretation, whilst open, is not inevitable, and the *travaux préparatoires* indicate that most delegations at UNCLOS I did not intend to restrict rights by distinguishing between 'control' and 'jurisdiction'.[93] The language of GCTS Article 24 was retained in UNCLOS Article 33: again the record of negotiations does not indicate an intention to limit coastal state powers in the contiguous zone by using the term

---

[89] UNCLOS, Art 94(1)–(2).
[90] UNCLOS, Art 211.
[91] Oda (1962) 11 *ICLQ* 131; McDougal & Burke (1962) 621–30.
[92] (1959) 8 *ICLQ* 73, 113. Also: Fitzmaurice (1954) 31 *BY* 371, 378–9; 2 O'Connell (1984) 1057–9.
[93] Oda (1962) 11 *ICLQ* 131; 2 O'Connell (1984) 643–4.

'control'.[94] The decision to retain the contiguous zone, however, seems to have been based upon the observation that coastal state jurisdiction in the EEZ related primarily to natural resources and did not cover the functions specified for the exercise of control in the contiguous zone. Although enforcement jurisdiction in the contiguous zone relates to the threatened or actual infringement of laws and regulations within the territory or territorial waters and does not extend jurisdiction to the contiguous zone, a small number of states argue that this limitation was not supported by the majority at UNCLOS I or by state practice.[95] Nevertheless, a Polish amendment removing the reference to infringement within the territory or the territorial sea (and adding security to the list of recognized purposes for the exercise of control) failed in plenary.

3. THE CONTINENTAL SHELF

Submarine areas may be classified as follows: (a) the seabed of the internal waters and territorial seas of coastal states, which are under territorial sovereignty; (b) the seabed and subsoil of the EEZ, which is part of that zone; (c) the continental shelf area, which overlaps with the EEZ within 200nm but may extend further; and (d) the seabed and ocean floor beyond the outer limits of the continental shelf and EEZ, which come within the legal regime of the high seas.

UNCLOS Article 56 purports to solve the problem of overlapping regimes by providing that rights with respect to the seabed and subsoil in the EEZ shall be exercised in accordance with Part VI, that is, the continental shelf regime. But this does not solve the problem entirely, since an area may be within 200nm of state A (and thus part of its EEZ) but beyond 200nm from state B yet claimed by it as outer continental shelf.[96] The legal regime of the international seabed 'Area' and the International Seabed Authority are discussed in chapter 13.

(A) ORIGINS OF THE CONTINENTAL SHELF

Much of the seabed consists of the deep ocean floor, several thousand metres deep. In many parts of the world the 'abyssal plain' is separated from the coast of the land masses by a terrace or shelf. This is geologically part of the continent itself, overlain by

---

[94] 2 *Virginia Commentary* (1985) 267–75.

[95] Caminos, 'Contiguous zone' (2008) *MPEPIL*.

[96] Indeed this will be the case, to a degree, wherever the lateral maritime boundary between A and B departs from equidistance. The tribunal in *Barbados v Trinidad and Tobago* (2006) 45 ILM 798 sought to eliminate it by tapering the EEZ/shelf boundary to a single point 200nm from the nearest (Tobago) coast. By contrast in *Bangladesh/Myanmar*, ITLOS delimited the grey area by allocating water column rights over that area to Myanmar and continental shelf rights to Bangladesh: *Dispute concerning Delimitation of the Maritime Boundary between Bangladesh and Myanmar in the Bay of Bengal*, Judgment of 14 March 2012, ITLOS Case No 16, §§471–6, 506.

the relatively shallow waters of the continental margin. The width of the shelf varies from a mile to some hundreds of miles and the depth ranges from 50 to 550 metres. The configuration of the seabed has certain regularities. The increase in depth is gradual until the shelf edge or break is reached, when there is a steep descent to the ocean floor. The average depth of the edge is between 130 and 200 metres. The relatively steep incline of the continental slope gives way to the often large apron of sediments, which masks the boundary between the deep ocean floor and the pedestal of the continental mass, and is called the continental rise.

The shelf carries oil and gas deposits in many areas and the seabed itself provides sedentary fishery resources. In 1944, an Argentine Decree created zones of mineral reserves in the epicontinental sea.[97] However, the decisive event in state practice was a US proclamation of 28 September 1945 relating to the natural resources of the subsoil and seabed of the continental shelf (the Truman Proclamation).[98] The shelf was regarded as a geological feature extending up to the 100 fathoms line. The resources concerned were described as 'appertaining to the United States, subject to its jurisdiction and control'. Significantly, the claim was limited to the resources themselves and the proclamation declared that 'the character as high seas of the waters of the continental shelf and the right to their free and unimpeded navigation are in no way thus affected'.

The Truman Proclamation was in substance followed by Orders in Council of 1948 relating to the Bahamas and Jamaica, and by proclamations issued by Saudi Arabia in 1948 and nine Gulf sheikhdoms under UK protection in 1949.[99] Practice varied, however. The Truman Proclamation and an Australian proclamation of 10 September 1953 related the claim to the *exploitation of the resources* of the seabed and subsoil of the continental shelf, and stipulated that the legal status of the superjacent waters as high seas was unaffected. Other states claimed sovereignty over the seabed and subsoil of the shelf but reserved consideration of the status of the waters above.[100]

The Truman Proclamation proved attractive to many states. It provided a basis for the exploitation of petroleum and at the same time accommodated freedom of fishing and navigation in the superjacent waters. However, practice was uneven,[101] and the discussions in the ILC from 1951 to 1956 indicated the immaturity of the regime.

---

[97] Decree 1836 of 24 February 1944.

[98] Truman Proclamation (1946) 40 *AJIL Sp Supp* 45; 4 Whiteman 756. For the background: Hollick (1976) 17 *Va JIL* 23; Hollick, *United States Foreign Policy and the Law of the Sea* (1981). On the impact of the Proclamation in terms of custom: Crawford & Viles, in Crawford, *Selected Essays* (2002) 317.

[99] Surveys of state practice: 4 Whiteman 752–814; UN Legis Series, 1 *The Regime of the High Seas* (1951) and Special Supp (1959); UN Secretariat, Survey of National Legislation Concerning the Seabed and the Ocean Floor, and the Subsoil thereof, underlying the High Seas beyond the Limits of Present National Jurisdiction, A/AC.135/11, 4 June 1968; UN Legis Series, *National Legislation and Treaties Relating to the Territorial Sea* (1970) 319–476; US Department of State, *Limits in the Seas* No 36 and revisions.

[100] E.g. Bahamas (1948), Saudi Arabia (1949), Pakistan (1950), India (1955).

[101] See the award in *Abu Dhabi* (1951) 18 ILR 144. The date at which the concept of the shelf matured as part of custom may still matter: *Re Seabed and Subsoil of the Continental Shelf Offshore Newfoundland* (1984) 86 ILR 593.

Inevitably the text of the GCCS represented in part an essay in progressive development.[102] Nevertheless, the first three articles by 1958 reflected the customary law position.[103] Article 1 defined the continental shelf by reference to a general concept of adjacency and a more specific (but still apparently open-ended) depth-plus-exploitability limit; it also extended the shelf regime to islands (undefined). Article 2 defined the rights of the coastal state over the shelf as 'sovereign rights for the purpose of exploring it and exploiting its natural resources': these rights are exclusive and do not require proclamation. Article 3 preserved 'the legal status of the superjacent waters as high seas, or that of the air space above those waters'.

The GCCS may remain relevant where both parties to a dispute are parties to it and not to UNCLOS.[104] However, the present position in general international law depends upon numerous sources, each given appropriate weight. The Chamber in *Gulf of Maine* recognized the relevance of codification conventions, the decisions of the Court and of other international tribunals, and the proceedings of UNCLOS III where they indicated that certain provisions reflected a consensus.[105] In its decision in *Continental Shelf (Libya/Malta)*, the International Court took careful account of certain aspects of UNCLOS as evidence of custom,[106] while emphasizing state practice.[107]

(B) RIGHTS OF THE COASTAL STATE IN THE SHELF

According to GCCS Article 2, repeated in UNCLOS Article 77, the coastal state exercises 'sovereign rights for the purpose of exploring [the shelf] and exploiting its natural resources'. The term 'sovereignty' was deliberately avoided, as it was feared that this term, redolent of territorial sovereignty (which operates in three dimensions), would prejudice the status as high seas of the waters over the shelf. While the area within a claimed 200nm EEZ is not designated 'high seas',[108] UNCLOS Article 78(1) provides that 'the rights of the coastal State over the continental shelf do not affect the legal status of the superjacent waters or of the airspace above those waters'.[109] In the absence of a claimed EEZ, and also when the shelf extends beyond 200nm, the superjacent waters will be legally considered the high seas. When an EEZ exists, the superjacent waters remain subject to most high seas freedoms in accordance with custom and UNCLOS Article 58.

---

[102] For contemporary discussion: Whiteman (1958) 52 *AJIL* 629; Gutteridge (1959) 35 *BY* 102; Young (1961) 55 *AJIL* 359.

[103] *North Sea Continental Shelf (Federal Republic of Germany/Netherlands; Federal Republic of Germany/Denmark)*, ICJ Reports 1969 p 3, 39.

[104] *Anglo-French Continental Shelf* (1977) 54 ILR 6; *Delimitation of the Maritime Boundary in the Gulf of Maine Area (Canada/US)*, ICJ Reports 1984 p 246, 291, 300–3; *Maritime Delimitation in the Area between Greenland and Jan Mayen (Denmark v Norway)*, ICJ Reports 1993 p 38, 57–9.

[105] ICJ Reports 1984 p 246, 288–95.

[106] ICJ Reports 1985 p 13, 29–34.

[107] Ibid, 29–30, 33, 38, 45.

[108] UNCLOS, Arts 55, 86.

[109] Cf GCCS, Art 3.

Several provisions attest to the delicate problem of balancing the rights of the coastal state in exploiting shelf resources and the rights of other states. UNCLOS Article 78(2) provides that 'the exercise of the rights of the coastal State over the continental shelf must not infringe or result in any unjustifiable interference with navigation and other rights and freedoms of other States as provided for in this Convention' (see also GCCS Article 5(1)). UNCLOS Article 79 provides that 'all States are entitled to lay submarine cables and pipelines on the continental shelf' subject to certain conditions. The coastal state 'shall have the exclusive right to authorise and regulate drilling on the continental shelf for all purposes'.[110]

A major objective has been to provide a stable basis for operations on the seabed and to avoid squatting by offshore interests. Thus 'sovereign rights' inhere in the coastal state by law and are not conditioned on occupation or claim. They are indefeasible except by express grant. While coastal states apply various parts of criminal and civil law to activities in the shelf area, it is by no means clear that they do this as an aspect of their territorial or other rights in the shelf area. Legislation of the UK[111] and other states indicates that the shelf regime is not assimilated to state territory.[112]

(C) NATURAL RESOURCES OF THE SHELF[113]

The Truman Proclamation concerned the mineral resources of the shelf, especially hydrocarbons. Subsequently Latin American states pressed for recognition of the interest of coastal states in offshore fisheries (whether or not they had a geophysical shelf). The ILC had decided to include sedentary fisheries in the shelf regime,[114] and GCCS Article 2(4) defines 'natural resources' to include 'sedentary species, that is to say, organisms which, at the harvestable stage, either are immobile on or under the seabed or are unable to move except in constant physical contact with the seabed or the subsoil'.[115] The definition excludes dermersal species which swim close to the seabed; it is reproduced in UNCLOS Article 77(4). Provided an encompassing EEZ has been claimed, definitional issues will not arise, as living resources will be caught by one regime or the other.

---

[110] UNCLOS, Art 81.

[111] Continental Shelf Act 1964; *Clark (Inspector of Taxes) v Oceanic Contractors Inc* [1983] 2 AC 130.

[112] For jurisdiction over shelf resources in federal states: *United States v California*, 332 US 19 (1947); *United States v Texas*, 339 US 707 (1950); *United States v Louisiana*, 339 US 699 (1950); *In re Ownership and Jurisdiction over Offshore Mineral Rights* (1967) 43 ILR 93; *Bonser v La Macchia* (1969) 51 ILR 39; *Queensland v Commonwealth* (1975) 135 CLR 337.

[113] Gutteridge (1959) 35 *BY* 102, 116–19; 1 O'Connell (1982) 498–503; Brown, 1 *Sea-bed Energy and Minerals* (1992).

[114] ILC *Ybk* 1956/II, 297–8.

[115] This distinction presents difficulties in relation to king crabs: Oda (1969) 127 Hague *Recueil* 371, 427–30, and some species of lobster: Azzam (1964) 13 *ICLQ* 1453.

(D) ARTIFICIAL ISLANDS AND INSTALLATIONS ON THE SHELF

The right to authorize and regulate artificial islands, installations and other structures within the EEZ is set out in UNCLOS Article 60, which is applied 'mutatis mutandis to artificial islands, installations and structures on the continental shelf' by Article 80. Such installations do not have their own territorial sea.[116] The coastal state may, where necessary, establish safety zones not exceeding 500 metres around them.[117] Installations must not be established where they will interfere with the use of recognized sea lanes essential to international navigation.[118]

The GCCS and UNCLOS are silent on the subject of defence installations on the shelf. Defence installations may thus be lawful if some other justification exists.[119] To suggest that the coastal state may create defence installations and prohibit comparable activities by other states[120] is to risk justifying a shelf-wide security zone.

(E) REGIME OF THE SUBSOIL

UNCLOS Article 85 provides that Part VI 'does not prejudice the right of the coastal State to exploit the subsoil by means of tunnelling irrespective of the depth of water above the subsoil' (see also GCCS Article 7). In other words, such activity falls outside the scope of the Convention and is governed by custom. There is a notable distinction; if exploitation is by tunnel from the mainland, a different regime applies: if exploitation of the subsoil occurs from above the shelf, the UNCLOS regime applies.[121]

(F) OUTER LIMIT OF THE SHELF

The inner limit is the outer edge of the territorial sea and its seabed. As to the outer limit, the solution proposed by UNCLOS is substantively and procedurally different from the criteria in GCCS Article 1. According to Article 1 the 200-metre depth criterion is subject to the exploitability criterion, but the latter is controlled by the generally geological conception of the shelf, and by the principle of adjacency.[122] Only a handful of states still rely on this formula.[123]

---

[116] GCCS, Art 5(4); UNCLOS, Art 60(8) via Art 80.

[117] GCCS, Art 5(3); UNCLOS, Art 60(5) via Art 80.

[118] GCCS, Art 5(6); UNCLOS, Art 60(7) via Art 80.

[119] Treves (1980) 74 *AJIL* 808; Zedalis (1981) 75 *AJIL* 926; Treves (1981) 75 *AJIL* 933; Brown (1992) 23 *ODIL* 115, 122–6; Hayashi (2005) 29 *Marine Policy* 123, 129–30, 131–2.

[120] 1 O'Connell (1982) 507.

[121] On the Channel tunnel project: van den Mensbrugghe (1967) 71 *RGDIP* 325; Marston (1974–75) 47 *BY* 290.

[122] Further: Jennings (1969) 18 *ICLQ* 819; 1 O'Connell (1982) 488–95, 509–11; Goldie (1968) 8 *NRJ* 434; Weissberg (1969) 18 *ICLQ* 41, 62; Henkin (1969) 63 *AJIL* 504; Finlay (1970) 64 *AJIL* 42; Goldie (1970) 1 *JMLC* 461; Hutchinson (1985) 56 *BY* 111; Vasciannie (1987) 58 *BY* 271.

[123] According to the UN unofficial table of claims to maritime space, 11 states use 200m depth plus exploitability; a further three use an exploitability criterion alone: www.un.org/Depts/los/LEGISLATIONANDTREATIES/claims.htm.

UNCLOS Article 76 adopts a different approach. It recognizes a 200nm *breadth* limit as an independently valid criterion, and provides complex guidelines for locating the 'outer edge of the continental margin', if that feature lies beyond 200nm from the relevant baselines. Article 76(5) sets maximum limits for the outer continental shelf, either 350nm from the relevant baselines or '100 nautical miles from the 2,500 metre isobath'.

So much for substantive difference. The key procedural difference is that Annex II provides for an expert Commission on the Outer Limits of the Continental Shelf. In accordance with Article 76(8):

Information on the limits of the continental shelf beyond 200 nautical miles from the base-lines from which the breadth of the territorial sea is measured shall be submitted by the coastal State to the Commission ... The Commission shall make recommendations to coastal States on matters related to the establishment of the outer limits of their continental shelf. The limits of the shelf established by a coastal State on the basis of these recommendations shall be final and binding.

The relationship between the work of the Annex II Commission and interstate delimitation of shelf areas is discussed in chapter 12.

Despite its complexity and the evident signs of diplomatic compromise in its formulations, Article 76 is generally recognized as representing the new standard of customary law for the shelf. There is always the possibility that states opposing the 200-mile breadth criterion might have adopted the role of persistent objectors, but in practice this has not happened.[124]

4. THE EXCLUSIVE ECONOMIC ZONE/FISHERIES ZONE

(A) INTRODUCTION

Although the EEZ is considered one of the central innovations of UNCLOS, it was foreshadowed by claims to fisheries jurisdiction beyond the territorial sea. While most states now secure their right to fisheries by claiming an EEZ of up to 200nm from the territorial sea baseline, a number of states continue to claim Exclusive Fishery Zones (EFZ) either instead of or as well as an EEZ. The EEZ is not only a fisheries zone: it covers the exploitation and management of non-living as well as living resources. UNCLOS Article 56 further provides for the sovereign rights of the coastal state 'with regard to other activities for the economic exploitation and exploration of the zone'; it also lays down certain duties (though these are not denominated 'sovereign').

---

[124] There are now 81 states with shelf limits based on Article 76. 46 states have made submissions (some more than one) to the Annex II Commission: 27 others have submitted preliminary information: ibid.

(B) FISHERY ZONES

Since 1945, at least, coastal states with particular interests in offshore fisheries have sought means of limiting major operations by extra-regional fishing fleets. Paradoxically it was the US, historically an opponent of fishing zones, which drove initial change. In the first place the US took an important initiative in claiming the mineral resources of the continental shelf in 1945, on the basis of the generous concept of 'adjacency'. Unsurprisingly other states were ready to claim the biological resources of the adjacent waters or 'epicontinental sea' by a general parity of reasoning. Secondly, the US produced a Fisheries Proclamation also of 28 September 1945,[125] which empowered the government to establish 'explicitly bounded' conservation zones in areas of the high seas 'contiguous to the United States'.

Beginning in 1946 a number of Latin American states made claims to the natural resources of the epicontinental sea, in effect a fishery conservation zone of 200nm breadth.[126] Icelandic legislation on these lines was adopted in 1948. The tendency was initially incoherent. Adherents were scattered and the legal quality of some of the claims was uncertain and varied. Some, for example the Peruvian claim, were on one view an extended territorial sea with certain concessions to overflight and free navigation. In 1970 nine out of 20 Latin American states subscribed to the Montevideo Declaration on the Law of the Sea,[127] which asserted a 200nm zone, involving 'sovereignty and jurisdiction to the extent necessary to conserve, develop and exploit the natural resources of the maritime area adjacent to their coasts, its soil and its subsoil', but without prejudice to freedom of navigation and overflight.

Meanwhile the fishery conservation zone was attracting support as customary law. In the *Fisheries Jurisdiction* cases an Icelandic fishing zone 50nm in breadth was held to be not opposable to the UK and Germany as a consequence of a 1961 bilateral agreement.[128] The Court avoided taking a position on the validity of the Icelandic claim in general international law.[129] But the Court went half-way, upholding as customary law 'preferential rights of fishing in adjacent waters in favour of the coastal state in a situation of special dependence on its coastal fisheries, this preference operating in regard to other states concerned in the exploitation of the same fisheries'.[130] The status of fishery zones in custom was also recognized by the Court in *Jan Mayen*.[131] Thus the

---

[125] (1946) 40 *AJIL Sp Supp* 45; 4 Whiteman 954. The Proclamation has never been implemented by Executive Order.

[126] Argentina (1946), Panama (1946), Peru (1947), Chile (1947), Ecuador (1947), Honduras (1950), El Salvador (1950).

[127] Text: (1970) 64 *AJIL* 1021.

[128] *Fisheries Jurisdiction (UK v Iceland)*, ICJ Reports 1974 p 3; *Fisheries Jurisdiction (Germany v Iceland)*, ICJ Reports 1974 p 175.

[129] ICJ Reports 1974 p 3, 35–8 (Judge Ignacio-Pinto); 39 (Judge Nagendra Singh). In a joint separate opinion five judges expressed the firm view that no rule of customary law concerning maximum fishery limits had yet emerged: ibid, 45ff (Judges Forster, Bengzon, Jiménez de Aréchaga, Nagendra Singh & Ruda).

[130] Ibid, 23–31.

[131] *Jan Mayen*, ICJ Reports 1993 p 38, 59, 61–2.

concept of preferential fishing rights seems to have survived in customary law despite its absence from UNCLOS.[132]

But the development of 200nm fishery zones has been made largely redundant by the preponderance of EEZs. By 2010 only 14 states retained fishing zones of up to 200nm.[133] The adherents to such zones included the US,[134] Japan, and certain EU members.[135] The UK claims a 200nm fishing zone, together with a 200nm fishery conservation zone in respect of the Falkland (Malvinas) Islands.[136]

(C) THE EEZ AS AN ESTABLISHED ZONE[137]

The increase in claims to exclusive rights in respect of the fisheries in an adjacent maritime zone, described above, led eventually to claims encompassing all natural resources in and of the seabed and superjacent waters in a zone 200nm in breadth. By 1972 this development was presented, in more or less programmatic form, as a 'patrimonial sea',[138] or 'economic zone'.[139]

At UNCLOS III there was widespread support for the EEZ, and UNCLOS Articles 55 to 75 provide a detailed structure. The zone is to extend no further than 200nm from the baselines of the territorial sea. It is not defined as a part of the high seas (Article 86) and is *sui generis*. But apart from the freedom of fishing, the freedoms of the high seas apply (Article 87). The position of the coastal state is described as follows in Article 56(1):

In the EEZ, the coastal State has:

(a) sovereign rights for the purpose of exploring and exploiting, conserving and managing the natural resources, whether living or non-living, of the waters superjacent to the sea-bed and of the sea-bed its sub-soil, and with regard to other activities for the economic exploitation and exploration of the zone, such as the production of energy from the water, currents and winds;

(b) jurisdiction as provided for in the relevant provisions of the present Convention with regard to:

---

[132] For a more sceptical view: Churchill & Lowe (3rd edn, 1999) 285.

[133] US Department of State, *Limits in the Seas*, No 36 and revisions.

[134] Fishery Conservation and Management Act 1976; 15 ILM 635. This legislation has some controversial features: Statement by the President, ibid, 634.

[135] On EU fisheries jurisdiction: Churchill (1992) 23 *ODIL* 145; Berg, *Implementing and Enforcing European Fisheries Law* (1999); Churchill & Owen, *The EC Common Fisheries Policy* (2010).

[136] Fishery Limits Act 1976 (UK). For the dispute over the Falkland (Malvinas) Islands: chapter 9.

[137] Phillips (1977) 26 *ICLQ* 585; Extavour, *The Exclusive Economic Zone* (1979); Moore (1979) 19 *Va JIL* 401; Orrego Vicuña (ed), *The Exclusive Economic Zone* (1984); Charney (1985) 15 *ODIL* 233; Orrego Vicuña (1986) 199 Hague *Recueil* 11; Smith, *Exclusive Economic Zone Claims* (1986); Attard, *The Exclusive Economic Zone in International Law* (1987); McLean & Sucharitkul (1988) 63 *Notre Dame LR* 492; Orrego Vicuña, *The Exclusive Economic Zone* (1989); Roach & Smith (2nd edn, 1996) 173–92.

[138] Declaration of Santo Domingo, 9 June 1972, 11 ILM 892; Castañeda (1972) 12 *Indian JIL* 535; Nelson (1973) 22 *ICLQ* 668; Gastines (1975) 79 *RGDIP* 447; cf the Declaration of Lima, 8 August 1970, 10 ILM 207.

[139] Lay, Churchill & Nordquist, 1 *New Directions in the Law of the Sea* (1973) 250.

(i) the establishment and use of artificial islands, installations and structures;

(ii) marine scientific research;

(iii) the protection and preservation of the marine environment;

(c) other rights and duties provided for in this Convention.

No less than 137 states claim an EEZ and these claims are recognized by states generally. Thus the EEZ forms part of customary law, as has been recognized by the International Court[140] and by the US.[141] The customary law version of the concept is closely related to the version which emerged within UNCLOS III.

Both under UNCLOS and customary law the zone is optional and its existence depends upon an actual claim. Certain states, such as Canada, Germany, and Japan, are content to maintain 200-mile exclusive fishing zones.

When claimed, an EEZ co-exists with the regime of the continental shelf which governs rights with respect to the seabed and the subsoil (UNCLOS Article 56(3)). It may also co-exist with a contiguous zone out to 24nm.

The US initially took the view that 'highly migratory species', including the commercially important tuna, were excluded from the jurisdiction of the coastal state, and therefore available for foreign distant water fishing fleets.[142] This position became increasingly untenable; it was contradicted by the provisions of UNCLOS Article 64 and is not reflected in state practice.[143]

The legal regime of the EEZ has various facets. UNCLOS Article 60 provides (in part) as follows:

1. In the EEZ, the coastal State shall have the exclusive right to construct and to authorise and regulate the construction, operation and use of:

    (a) artificial islands;

    (b) installations and structures for the purposes provided for in Article 56 and other economic purposes;

    (c) installations and structures which may interfere with the exercise of the rights of the coastal State in the zone.

2. The coastal State shall have exclusive jurisdiction over such artificial islands, installations and structures, including jurisdiction with regard to customs, fiscal, health, safety and immigration laws and regulations.

The same article confirms that artificial islands, installations, and structures have no territorial sea of their own and do not affect the delimitation of the territorial sea, EEZ, or continental shelf (paragraph 8).

---

[140] *Continental Shelf (Tunisia/Libya)*, ICJ Reports 1982 p 18, 38, 47–9, 79; *Gulf of Maine*, ICJ Reports 1984 p 246, 294–5; *Libya/Malta*, ICJ Reports 1985 p 13, 32–4.

[141] US Presidential Proclamation, 10 March 1983, 22 ILM 461.

[142] Ibid. Nevertheless, the US conceded that tuna was included in the EEZ resources of Pacific Island States in the Treaty of Port Moresby, 2 April 1987, 2176 UNTS 173.

[143] Burke (1984–85) 14 *ODIL* 273; Attard (1987) 184–7. The position was eventually abandoned via a 1996 amendment to the Magnuson–Stevens Fisheries Management and Conservation Act of 1976: 16 USC § 1802(21).

Article 61 elaborates upon coastal state responsibility in managing the living resources in the zone via its duty to 'ensure through proper conservation and management measures that the maintenance of the living resources in the EEZ is not endangered by over-exploitation'. Similarly, Article 62 requires the coastal state to promote the optimum utilization of the living resources in the zone. In particular it is provided that:

2. The coastal State shall determine its capacity to harvest the living resources of the exclusive economic zone. Where the coastal State does not have the capacity to harvest the entire allowable catch, it shall, through agreements or other arrangements and pursuant to the terms, conditions, laws and regulations referred to in paragraph 4, give other States access to the surplus of the allowable catch, having particular regard to the provisions of Articles 69 and 70, especially in relation to the developing States mentioned therein.

The allocation of the respective rights and duties of the coastal state and those of other states in the zone involves a delicate balancing process which is articulated in fairly general terms in the provisions of the Convention.[144] Article 58 provides as follows:

1. In the exclusive economic zone, all States, whether coastal or land-locked, enjoy, subject to the relevant provisions of this Convention, the freedoms referred to in Article 87 of navigation and overflight and of the laying of submarine cables and pipelines, and other internationally lawful uses of the sea related to these freedoms, such as those associated with the operation of ships, aircraft and submarine cables and pipelines, and compatible with the other provisions of this Convention.

...

3. In exercising their rights and performing their duties under this Convention in the exclusive economic zone, States shall have due regard to the rights and duties of the coastal State and shall comply with the laws and regulations adopted by the coastal State in accordance with the provisions of this convention and other rules of international law in so far as they are not incompatible with this Part.[145]

Article 59 appears under the rubric 'basis for the resolution of conflicts regarding the attribution of rights and jurisdiction in the EEZ' and provides:

In cases where this Convention does not attribute rights or jurisdiction to the coastal State or to other States within the exclusive economic zone, and a conflict arises between the interests of the coastal State and any other State or States, the conflict should be resolved on

[144] Attard relies on the reference to 'sovereign rights' in Art 56(1)(a) to support a presumption in favour of the coastal state: *Attard* (1987) 48. This may be true of the modalities of the recognized rights of the coastal state, but not when independently constituted rights (like those of land-locked and geographically disadvantaged states) are in question (Arts 69, 70, 71). The general formulations of Art 59 beg the question, but Churchill & Lowe (3rd edn, 1999) 175–6, hold that the article rules out any presumption.

[145] On the interpretation of Art 58 and various related issues see the *M/V Saiga (No 2)* (1999) 120 ILR 145, 188–92.

the basis of equity and in the light of all the relevant circumstances, taking into account the respective importance of the interests involved to the parties as well as to the international community as a whole.

The coastal state has the power to take reasonable measures of enforcement of its rights and jurisdiction within the zone in accordance with the standards of general international law and UNCLOS itself (Article 73).

(D) THE EEZ AND CONTINENTAL SHELF COMPARED

Comparison of the legal concepts of the continental shelf and EEZ is instructive. They co-exist both in the sphere of customary law and under UNCLOS, and contain significant elements of similarity and interpenetration. Both concepts focus upon control of economic resources and are based, in varying degrees, upon adjacency and the distance principle.[146] The EEZ includes the continental shelf interest in the seabed of the 200nm zone.

However, there are significant points of distinction:

(1) The EEZ is optional, whereas rights to explore and exploit the resources of the shelf inhere in the coastal state by operation of law. Thus several states of the Mediterranean have shelf rights unmatched by an EEZ (which is less relevant in semi-enclosed seas in any case).

(2) Shelf rights exist beyond the limit of 200nm from the pertinent coasts when the continental shelf and margin extend beyond that limit. Consequently, within the UNCLOS regime the rights of the International Sea-bed Authority must be reconciled with those of the coastal state.

(3) The EEZ regime involves the water column and consequently its resources (apart from sedentary species of fish) are subject to the rules about sharing the surplus of the living resources of the EEZ with other states and, in particular, with land-locked and geographically disadvantaged states of the same region or subregion (UNCLOS Articles 62, 68, 69, 70, and 71).

(4) The EEZ regime confers upon coastal states a substantial jurisdiction over pollution by ships, and also greater control in respect of marine scientific research.

5. OTHER ZONES FOR SPECIAL PURPOSES

The twentieth century produced a number of national claims to non-contiguous, but adjacent, zones for special purposes.

---

[146] *Libya/Malta*, ICJ Reports 1985 p 13, 33.

(A) SECURITY ZONES

Defence zones[147] in polygonal or similar forms extending beyond the territorial sea, and zones for purposes of air identification[148] have made their appearance in the practice of states. Insofar as those zones represent claims to extra-territorial jurisdiction over nationals they do not necessarily conflict with general international law, and, furthermore, groups of states may co-operate and be mutually obligad to respect such zones by convention. Again, such zones may take the form of a lawful aspect of belligerent rights in time of war. Otherwise such zones would be incompatible with the status of waters beyond the limit of the territorial sea, at least if they involved the application of powers of prevention or punishment in regard to foreign vessels or aircraft.

(B) OTHER MISCELLANEOUS CLAIMS

Evidently the period 1945–82 saw a growth not only in the extent of seaward claims but in new types of maritime zone. To the simple long-established picture of territorial sea and internal waters were added the four newcomers discussed here. The widespread ratification of UNCLOS has done much to stabilize the law, and for the moment it seems unlikely that new exclusive claims to high seas resources will be made. Yet new developments cannot be categorically excluded in a dynamic customary law system. Chile's claim to a so-called 'Presencial Sea' is perhaps a case in point, although it has been authoritatively explained as a non-exclusive zone of interest and not a territorial claim.[149]

---

[147] See legislation of Ethiopia and South Korea in UN Legis Series, *Laws and Regulations on the Regime of the Territorial Sea* (1957) 128, 175; Park (1978) *AJIL* 866. On maritime security generally: Klein, *Maritime Security and the Law of the Sea* (2011).

[148] Murchison, *The Contiguous Air Space Zone in International Law* (1956); 4 Whiteman 495–8; Hailbronner (1983) 77 *AJIL* 490, 500, 515–19; Dutton (2009) 103 *AJIL* 691; Pedrozo (2011) 10 *Chin JIL* 207, 211–13.

[149] Kibel (2000) 12 *JEL* 43.

12

MARITIME DELIMITATION AND ASSOCIATED QUESTIONS

Coram et judice in alto mare sumus in manu Dei.

1. INTRODUCTION[1]

The rules of entitlement to maritime zones are set out in chapter 11. But a coastal state may be so located vis-à-vis its neighbours that its potential zones overlap considerably—what may be termed 'overlapping potential entitlement'. In fact there is no coastal state in the world that does not have an overlapping maritime zone with at least one other state (see Figure 12.1). There is also a question of entitlement vis-à-vis the high seas and its seabed, an effective delimitation between the coastal states severally and the international public domain or 'global commons', a commons until recently in sharp retreat.

Most maritime boundaries are determined by agreement and recorded in a treaty.[2] Many remain undelimited. A significant number are disputed.[3] Resolving such disputes has become an important task for the International Court and, to a lesser extent, other tribunals.[4] A great variety of geographical situations is encompassed, from

---

[1] Generally: O'Connell, 2 *The International Law of the Sea* (1984) 684–732; Jagota, *Maritime Boundary* (1985); Kittichaisaree, *The Law of the Sea and Maritime Delimitation in South-East Asia* (1987) 57–119; Johnston & Saunders (eds), *Ocean Boundary Making* (1988); Weil, *The Law of Maritime Delimitation* (1989); Evans, *Relevant Circumstances and Maritime Delimitation* (1989); Evans (1991) 40 *ICLQ* 1; Churchill & Lowe, *The Law of the Sea* (3rd edn, 1999) ch 10; Antunes, *Towards the Conceptualisation of Maritime Delimitation* (2003); Lagoni & Vignes (eds), *Maritime Delimitation* (2006); Tanaka, *Predictability and Flexibility in the Law of Maritime Delimitation* (2006); Rothwell & Stephens, *The International Law of the Sea* (2010) ch 16; Scovazzi, 'Maritime Delimitation Cases before International Courts and Tribunals' (2008) *MPEPIL*.

[2] For a partial collection: www.un.org/Depts/los/LEGISLATIONANDTREATIES/regionslist.htm.

[3] Including, perhaps surprisingly, the maritime boundaries between Canada and the US: McDorman, *Salt Water Neighbours* (2009).

[4] Since the first decision in 1969, 18 cases out of 87 on the Court's docket (including cases later consolidated) have concerned either maritime delimitation or applications for the reconsideration of earlier

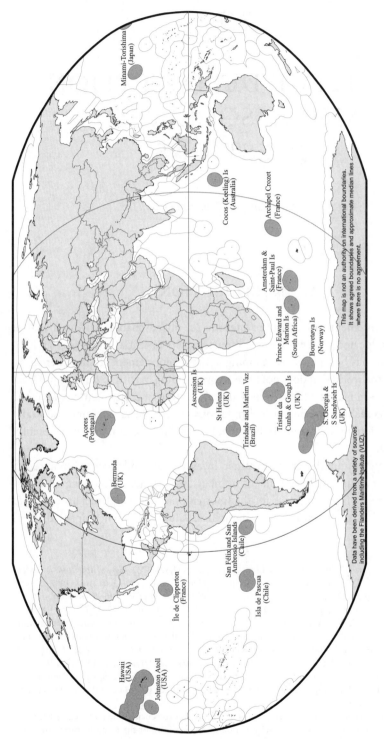

Figure 12.1 Global Maritime Zones

Map showing 200m maritime zones and associated boundaries.
Highlighted areas are those islands without overlapping zones; all of which are dependencies.

Source: Dr Robin Cleverly, Head, Law of the Sea, UK Hydrographic Office, Taunton

long-coastline adjacent states crowded together on a concave coastline[5] to small islands facing out into the open ocean.[6] Yet courts and tribunals are expected to decide on maritime delimitation in a principled way, without recasting geography yet still achieving an equitable result. The consequence has been a considerable test of judicial technique—or according to some, a demonstration of its failure.

2. TERRITORIAL SEA DELIMITATION BETWEEN OPPOSITE OR ADJACENT STATES[7]

Delimitation of territorial seas between states opposite or adjacent to each other is primarily governed by Article 15 of the UN Convention on the Law of the Sea (UNCLOS),[8] which is virtually identical to Article 12(1) of the Geneva Convention on the Territorial Sea (GCTS)[9] and is considered reflective of customary international law.[10] Article 15 provides:

Where the coasts of two States are opposite or adjacent to each other, neither of the two States is entitled, failing agreement between them to the contrary, to extend its territorial sea beyond the median line every point of which is equidistant from the nearest points on the baselines from which the breadth of the territorial seas of each of the two States is measured. The above provision does not apply, however, where it is necessary by reason of historic title or other special circumstances to delimit the territorial seas of the two States in a way which is at variance therewith.

Article 15 stipulates primacy of agreement, and failing that, application of the principle of equidistance. Departure from the equidistance principle is possible only where necessary by reason of historic title or other 'special circumstances'.[11] Thus a presumption of equidistance exists in the case of the territorial sea, justified by the comparatively small distances involved.

---

decisions on maritime delimitation. A further four cases have concerned related questions of sovereignty over islands in overlapping maritime zones or boundaries lying along rivers.

[5] E.g. *North Sea Continental Shelf (Federal Republic of Germany/Netherlands; Federal Republic of Germany/Denmark)* ICJ Reports 1969 p 3; *Guyana v Suriname* (2007) 139 ILR 566.

[6] E.g. *Barbados v Trinidad and Tobago* (2006) 139 ILR 449.

[7] Generally: Arnaut (2002) 8 *OCLJ* 21; Shi (2010) 9 *Chin JIL* 271, 279–81.

[8] 10 December 1982, 1833 UNTS.

[9] 29 April 1958, 516 UNTS 205.

[10] *Maritime Delimitation and Territorial Questions between Qatar and Bahrain (Qatar v Bahrain)*, ICJ Reports 2001 p 40, 93–4.

[11] As to what may be considered 'special circumstances', there is no closed list: *Continental Shelf (Libya/Malta)*, ICJ Reports 1985 p 13, 40; *Guyana v Suriname* (2007) 139 ILR 566, 650–1. On occasion, a tribunal may need to have recourse to the ILC commentary to the 1956 draft articles to determine the meaning of the term: e.g. *Guyana v Suriname* (2007) 139 ILR 566, 650; *Territorial and Maritime Dispute between Nicaragua and Honduras in the Caribbean Sea (Nicaragua v Honduras)*, ICJ Reports 2007 p 659, 744. Also: Rothwell & Stephens (2010) 400.

Given the institutional age of the territorial sea, many of the disputes surrounding its application have been resolved. Major cases have included *Qatar v Bahrain*,[12] *Caribbean Sea*,[13] *Guyana v Suriname*,[14] *Eritrea v Yemen*,[15] and *Bangladesh/Myanmar*[16] but several decisions were handed down pre-UNCLOS, notably the *Banks of Grisbadarna* between Norway and Sweden[17] and the *St Pierre and Miquelon* arbitration between France and Canada.[18] Following the *Qatar v Bahrain* and *Caribbean Sea* maritime delimitations, a methodology[19] has developed; in *Caribbean Sea* the Court considered the application of the following process in the context of an UNCLOS Article 15 territorial sea boundary delimitation:

(1) Consideration should first be given to the drawing of a provisional line of equidistance.[20]

(2) But the provisional equidistance line may be abandoned due to special circumstances.[21]

(3) The tribunal in question may then consider its own means of delimitation, or adopt those proposed by the parties.[22]

(4) At all stages, the tribunal will need to take into account relevant coasts, including the geography of the immediate coastline, the delimitation of the territorial sea of adjacent states and geomorphological features of the area adjacent to the endpoint of a land boundary.[23]

---

[12] ICJ Reports 2001 p 40.

[13] ICJ Reports 2007 p 659.

[14] (2007) 139 ILR 566.

[15] *Eritrea v Yemen (Phase Two)* (1999) 119 ILR 417.

[16] *Dispute concerning Delimitation of the Maritime Boundary between Bangladesh and Myanmar in the Bay of Bengal (Bangladesh/Myanmar)*, Judgment of 14 March 2012, ITLOS Case No 16. Further; Churchill (2012) 1 *CJICL* 137.

[17] (1909) 11 RIAA 147.

[18] *Delimitation of Maritime Areas between Canada and the French Republic (St Pierre and Miquelon)* (1992) 95 ILR 645 (though in that case, the parties continued to update their positions based on developments occurring at UNCLOS III).

[19] In the context of the territorial sea, boundaries are often delimited within the context of a single determination encompassing both the EEZ and related continental shelf areas: e.g. *Guyana v Suriname* (2007) 139 ILR 566, where an UNCLOS Annex VII tribunal first delimited the territorial sea, followed by the continental shelf and the EEZ.

[20] *Caribbean Sea*, ICJ Reports 2007 p 659, 740.

[21] ICJ Reports 2007 p 659, 744–5. Also: *Qatar v Bahrain*, ICJ Reports 2001 p 40, 179 ('The most logical and widely practiced approach is first to draw provisionally an equidistance line and then to consider whether the line must be adjusted in light of the existence of special circumstances.'). Cf *Bangladesh/Myanmar*, ITLOS Case No 16, §§151–2 (holding that St Martin's Island was not considered a special circumstance requiring abandonment of equidistance).

[22] Thus, in *Caribbean Sea*, the Court found that the presumption of an equidistance line was displaced due to the nature of the coastline and the difficulty in identifying suitable baseline points from which a determination of equidistance could be made. The alternative was a 'bisector' line: ICJ Reports 2007 p 659, 741–5.

[23] Ibid, 748. This will be especially important where a river mouth forms part of the land boundary: Rothwell & Stephens (2010) 398.

Whether or not there is a formal presumption of equidistance in territorial sea delimitation may be debated, but it is certainly the norm.

3. CONTINENTAL SHELF DELIMITATION BETWEEN OPPOSITE OR ADJACENT STATES[24]

(A) SOURCES

The continental shelf has its immediate origins in the Truman Proclamation of 28 September 1945. In a remarkable exercise in prescience, the Proclamation addressed delimitation in the following terms:

In cases where the continental shelf extends to the shores of another State, or is shared with an adjacent State, the boundary shall be determined by the United States and the State concerned in accordance with equitable principles.[25]

At this time there was almost no delimitation practice: the 1942 Gulf of Paria Treaty, the first seabed delimitation treaty, represented an attempt by Venezuela and the UK to delimit the Gulf, a shallow inland sea between the British colony of Trinidad and the Venezuelan coast.[26] At its core, the treaty simply described three lines according to longitude and latitude, allocating to the UK those areas east and north of these lines.[27]

Practice was not much further advanced upon consideration by the ILC beginning in 1953.[28] On cartographical advice, the ILC proposed and the Geneva Conference adopted GCCS Article 6.[29] Article 6 applies to those cases where the 'same continental shelf' extends between opposite or adjacent states. In separate provisions, it stipulates that the boundary is determined by agreement but 'in the absence of agreement, and unless another boundary line is justified by special circumstances', the boundary shall be determined by a median line, that is, a line equidistant from the nearest points of the baselines from which the breadth of the territorial sea of each state is measured.

---

[24] Generally: Bowett (1978) 49 BY 1; Pazarci, *La Délimitation du plateau continental et les îles* (1982); Hutchinson (1984) 55 BY 133; Colson (2003) 97 AJIL 91; Kunoy (2006) 53 NILR 247; Rothwell & Stephens (2010) ch 16.

[25] 1945 United States Presidential Proclamation No 2667, reprinted in Lowe & Talmon, *The Legal Order of the Oceans* (2009) 19.

[26] Treaty relating to the Submarine Areas of the Gulf of Paria, 26 February 1942, 205 LNTS 121.

[27] Ibid, Art 3.

[28] In 1952, Chile, Peru, and Ecuador adopted the Santiago Declaration, 18 August 1952, 1006 UNTS 323, establishing an EEZ-type zone; its effect on delimitation is *sub iudice* in *Maritime Dispute (Peru v Chile)* (2008, pending). Further: Colson (2003) 97 AJIL 91.

[29] 29 April 1958, 499 UNTS 311.

In 1969 the International Court rejected the equidistance/special circumstances rule articulated in Article 6 as a matter of custom,[30] and after many vicissitudes in the cases and doctrine and in the negotiations, this position was apparently upheld in 1982.[31] UNCLOS Article 83(1) provides:

The delimitation of the continental shelf between States with opposite or adjacent coasts shall be effected by agreement on the basis of international law, as referred to in Article 38 of the Statute of the International Court of Justice, in order to achieve an equitable solution.

Article 83(1) appears as an elaborated version of the Truman Proclamation provision concerned with delimitation. To that extent UNCLOS Part VI had returned to its customary law origins.[32]

(B) THE ESTABLISHED APPROACH

In the meantime, practice and case-law had moved on. In *Libya/Malta*,[33] the Court was called upon to delimit the continental shelf boundary between the two states. The parties were in agreement that their dispute was governed by customary international law, with the Court discerning its reflection in UNCLOS (notably Article 83(1)).[34] The Court went on to emphasize the preference in Article 83(1) for an 'equitable' solution to delimitation problems concerning the continental shelf, and further noted that:

The Convention sets a goal to be achieved, but is silent as to the method to be followed to achieve it. It restricts itself to setting a standard, and it is left to the States themselves, or the courts, to endow this standard with specific content.[35]

The Court held:

Thus the justice of which equity is an emanation, is not abstract justice but justice according to the rule of law; which is to say that its application should display consistency and a degree of predictability; even though it looks with particularity to the peculiar circumstances of an instant case, it also looks beyond it to principles of more general application.[36]

Taking account of the differences in coastal length, the Court adopted a proportionality test to justify deviation from the median line,[37] while stressing that it was not required to achieve a predetermined ratio between the relevant coasts and the respective continental shelf areas.[38]

---

[30] *North Sea Continental Shelf*, ICJ Reports 1969 p 6, 38 and further chapter 2.
[31] UNCLOS, Art 83(4) preserves existing delimitation agreements, including those based on different principles.
[32] Nordquist (ed), 2 *United Nations Convention on the Law of the Sea* (1993) 953–4.
[33] *Libya/Malta*, ICJ Reports 1985 p 13.
[34] ICJ Reports 1985 p 13, 55.
[35] Ibid, 30.
[36] Ibid, 39.
[37] Ibid, 49–50.
[38] Ibid, 55.

As a result of this and subsequent decisions, a 'received approach' has emerged, though it is not invariable.[39] This is first to draw provisionally an equidistance line.[40] If this proves inappropriate, the court or tribunal may use a different method of delimitation, such as the bisector method, according to which the line is formed by bisecting the angle created by a linear approximation of coastlines.[41] The court may then move to consider whether the line so created must be adjusted in the light of 'relevant circumstances', such as small islands, maritime features or coastal geography. An equidistance line is usually seen as the most equitable starting point for any delimitation. The 'relevant circumstances' that have been produced by custom are similar to the 'special circumstances' seen in GCCS Article 6.[42]

Accordingly, delimitation of the continental shelf is usually done in three stages. First, the relevant tribunal establishes a provisional delimitation line based on 'methods that are geometrically objective and also appropriate for the geography of the area in which the delimitation is to take place'.[43] This provisional delimitation line is an equidistance line in case of two adjacent coasts, and a median line when two opposite coasts are concerned.[44] Secondly, the tribunal considers whether there are 'relevant circumstances' calling for the adjustment or shifting of the provisional equidistance line in order to achieve an equitable result.[45] Thirdly, the tribunal verifies that the delimitation line as it stands does not lead to an inequitable result by reason of any marked disproportion between the ratio of the respective coastal lengths and the ratio between the relevant maritime area of each state.[46]

(C) THE EQUITABLE PRINCIPLES

The notion that an equidistance line is the ordinary starting point for continental shelf delimitation is only one of the equitable principles governing the solution under UNCLOS Article 83(1) and customary international law. The 'equitable principles', as defined judicially since *North Sea Continental Shelf*, have a normative character as a part of general international law, and their application is to be distinguished

---

[39] Further: Scovazzi, 'Maritime Delimitation Cases before International Courts and Tribunals' (2008) *MPEPIL*, §F.

[40] E.g. *Qatar v Bahrain*, ICJ Reports 2001 p 40, 94; *Caribbean Sea*, ICJ Reports 2007 p 659, 742–5; *Bangladesh/Myanmar*, ITLOS Case No 16, §§239–40.

[41] *Caribbean Sea*, ICJ Reports 2007 p 659, 746; *Delimitation of the Maritime Boundary in the Gulf of Maine Area (Canada/US)*, ICJ Reports 1984 p 246, 327.

[42] *Maritime Delimitation in the Area between Greenland and Jan Mayen (Denmark v Norway)*, ICJ Reports 1993 p 38, 62. Also: *Guyana v Suriname* (2007) 139 ILR 566, 650–1.

[43] *Maritime Delimitation in the Black Sea (Romania v Ukraine)*, ICJ Reports 2009 p 61, 101.

[44] *Libya/Malta*, ICJ Reports 1985 p 13, 46–9; *Black Sea*, ICJ Reports 2009 p 61, 101.

[45] *Land and Maritime Boundary between Cameroon and Nigeria (Cameroon v Nigeria; Equatorial Guinea intervening)*, ICJ Reports 2002 p 303, 441; *Black Sea*, ICJ Reports 2009 p 61, 101–3; *Bangladesh/Myanmar*, ITLOS Case No 16, §292.

[46] *Black Sea*, ICJ Reports 2009 p 61, 103, 129–30.

from decision-making *ex aequo et bono*.[47] Nonetheless the 'principles' are general in character. As was noted in *Libya/Malta*, the term 'equitable' in Article 83(1) sets an amorphous standard.[48] Nonetheless, specific criteria or indicia have emerged. These may be formulated as follows:

(1) Delimitation is to be effected by agreement on the basis of international law.[49]

(2) As far as possible neither party should encroach on the natural prolongation of the other (the principle of non-encroachment).[50]

(3) As far as possible, there should be no undue cut-off of the seaward projection of the coast of either of the states concerned.[51]

(4) Delimitation is to be effected by the application of equitable criteria and by the use of practical methods capable of ensuring, with regard to the geographical configuration of the area and other relevant circumstances, an equitable result.[52]

(5) There is a mild presumption that the equitable solution is an equal division of the areas of overlap of the continental shelves of the states in dispute.[53]

(D) RELEVANT CIRCUMSTANCES

The application of equitable principles involves (variously) reference to the 'relevant circumstances', or 'factors to be taken into account', or 'auxiliary criteria'.[54] Relevant circumstances recognized by international tribunals include the following:

(1) the general configuration of the coasts of the parties;[55]

(2) disregarding or giving less than full effect to incidental features (e.g. minor offshore islands) which would otherwise have a disproportionate effect on the delimitation;

---

[47] *North Sea Continental Shelf*, ICJ Reports 1969 p 3, 46–7; *Continental Shelf (Tunisia/Libya)*, ICJ Reports 1982 p 18, 60; *Libya/Malta*, ICJ Reports 1985 p 13, 38–9.

[48] ICJ Reports 1985 p 13, 30.

[49] UNCLOS, Art 83(1); *North Sea Continental Shelf*, ICJ Reports 1969 p 3, 46–8, 53; *Gulf of Maine*, ICJ Reports 1984 p 246, 292–3, 299; *Libya/Malta*, ICJ Reports 1985 p 13, 39.

[50] *North Sea Continental Shelf*, ICJ Reports 1969 p 3, 46–7, 53; *Gulf of Maine*, ICJ Reports 1984 p 246, 312–13; *Libya/Malta*, ICJ Reports 1985 p 13, 39; *Dubai-Sharjah Border* (1981) 91 ILR 543, 659; *Barbados v Trinidad and Tobago* (2006) 139 ILR 449, 521.

[51] *North Sea Continental Shelf*, ICJ Reports 1969 p 3, 17–88; *Gulf of Maine*, ICJ Reports 1984 p 246, 298–9, 312–13, 328, 335; *Guinea–Guinea-Bissau Maritime Delimitation* (1985) 77 ILR 635, 681; *Barbados v Trinidad and Tobago* (2006) 139 ILR 449, 521; *Bangladesh/Myanmar*, ITLOS Case No 16, §331.

[52] *Gulf of Maine*, ICJ Reports 1984 p 246, 299–300; *Libya/Malta*, ICJ Reports 1985, p 13, 38–9, 57; *Barbados v Trinidad and Tobago* (2006) 139 ILR 449, 521.

[53] *North Sea Continental Shelf*, ICJ Reports 1969 p 3, 36, 52–3; *Gulf of Maine*, ICJ Reports 1984 p 246, 300–1, 312–13, 327–32; *Libya/Malta*, ICJ Reports 1985 p 13, 47.

[54] *Libya/Malta*, ICJ Reports 1985 p 13, 40.

[55] *North Sea Continental Shelf*, ICJ Reports 1969 p 3, 49, 53–4; *Tunisia/Libya*, ICJ Reports 1982 p 18, 61–3; *Gulf of Maine*, ICJ Reports 1984 p 246, 327–31; *Libya/Malta*, ICJ Reports 1985 p 13, 50, 52; *Guinea–Guinea-Bissau Maritime Delimitation* (1985) 77 ILR 635, 676–9; *Cameroon v Nigeria*, ICJ Reports 2002 p 303, 445–6.

(3)   disparity of coastal lengths in the relevant area;[56]

(4)   the general geographical framework or context;[57]

(5)   the principle of equitable access to the natural resources of the disputed area.[58]

Factors sometimes referred to, but not as well accepted, include:

(6)   the geological structure of the sea-bed and its geomorphology (or surface features);[59]

(7)   the conduct of the parties, such as the *de facto* line produced by the pattern of grants of petroleum concessions in the disputed area;[60] such concessions need to be, however, premised on express or tacit agreement between the parties;[61]

(8)   the incidence of natural resources in the disputed area;[62]

(9)   defence and security interests of the states in dispute;[63]

(10) navigational interests of the states in dispute;[64]

(11) consistency with the general direction of the land boundary;[65]

(12) maritime delimitations already effected in the region.[66]

Some comment is called for on several of these.

As to the second factor, given a geographical situation of quasi-equality as between coastal states, it is often necessary to abate the effects of an incidental special feature from which an unjustifiable difference of treatment would result. This principle has been employed to avoid, or at least to diminish, the effects of a concave coast,[67] the location of islands of state A near the coast of state B[68] and the eccentric alignment of

---

[56] *Gulf of Maine*, ICJ Reports 1984 p 246, 323; *Libya/Malta*, ICJ Reports 1985 p 13, 48–50; *Jan Mayen*, ICJ Reports 1993 p 38, 65–70; *Cameroon v Nigeria*, ICJ Reports 2002 p 303, 446–7; *Barbados v Trinidad and Tobago* (2006) 139 ILR 449, 523; *Black Sea*, ICJ Reports 2009 p 61, 116–18.

[57] *Anglo-French Continental Shelf* (1977) 54 ILR 6, 95–8; *Libya/Malta*, ICJ Reports 1985 p 13, 42, 50–3; *Guinea–Guinea-Bissau Maritime Delimitation* (1985) 77 ILR 635, 683–5.

[58] *Jan Mayen*, ICJ Reports 1993 p 38, 70–3 (fisheries).

[59] *North Sea Continental Shelf*, ICJ Reports 1969 p 3, 53–4; *Tunisia/Libya*, ICJ Reports 1982 p 18, 58, 64.

[60] *Tunisia/Libya*, ICJ Reports 1982 p 18, 83–4; *Gulf of Maine*, ICJ Reports 1984 p 246, 310–11; *Jan Mayen*, ICJ Reports 1993 p 38, 75–7.

[61] *Cameroon v Nigeria*, ICJ Reports 2002 p 303, 447–8.

[62] *North Sea Continental Shelf*, ICJ Reports 1969 p 3, 54; *Tunisia/Libya*, ICJ Reports p 18, 77–8; *Libya/Malta*, ICJ Reports 1985 p 13, 41.

[63] *Anglo-French Continental Shelf* (1977) 54 ILR 6, 98; *Libya/Malta*, ICJ Reports 1985 p 13, 42; *Guinea–Guinea-Bissau Maritime Delimitation* (1985) 77 ILR 635, 689; *Maritime Delimitation in the Area between Greenland and Jan Mayen*, ICJ Reports 1993 p 38, 74–5; *Black Sea*, ICJ Reports 2009 p 61, 127–8.

[64] *Anglo-French Continental Shelf* (1977) 54 ILR 6, 98.

[65] *Tunisia/Libya*, ICJ Reports 1982 p 18, 64–6; *Guinea–Guinea-Bissau Maritime Delimitation* (1985) 77 ILR 635, 682–3.

[66] *Black Sea*, ICJ Reports 2009 p 61, 118–20.

[67] *North Sea Continental Shelf*, ICJ Reports 1969 p 3, 36, 49–50.

[68] *Anglo-French Continental Shelf* (1977) 54 ILR 6, 100–2 (Channel Islands enclaved).

small islands lying off a peninsula.[69] On occasion, the effect of a group of islands has been reduced by half when the geography was not markedly eccentric.[70]

As to existing or reasonably-suspected incidence of resources, resource-related criteria have been treated much more cautiously by international courts and tribunals, which have not generally applied this factor as a relevant circumstance—at least explicitly.[71] An exception—concerning delimitation within 200nm—was *Jan Mayen,* where a portion of the line was adjusted to a take account of Danish access to an established capelin fishery.[72] Thus in the context of a single maritime boundary, considerations relating to the EEZ determined the location of a shelf boundary.

It is to an extent misleading to talk of a recognized canon of relevant circumstances justifying deviation from the provisional line. As with delimitation in the territorial sea, the list of relevant circumstances is not closed. However an outer limit has been imposed by *Libya/Malta*, where the Court remarked:

[A]lthough there may be no legal limit to the considerations which States may take account of, this can hardly be true for a court applying equitable procedures. For a court, although there is assuredly no closed list of considerations, it is evident that only those that are pertinent to the institution of the continental shelf as it has developed within the law, and to the application of equitable principles to its delimitation, will qualify for inclusion. Otherwise, the legal concept of continental shelf could itself be fundamentally changed by the introduction of considerations strange to its nature.[73]

Irrelevant factors include the population, extent of hinterland or development status of the coastal state.[74]

(E) PROPORTIONALITY[75]

In *North Sea Continental Shelf* the Court stated that one of the factors 'to be taken into account' in delimitation is 'the element of a reasonable degree of proportionality, which a delimitation in accordance with equitable principles ought to bring about between the extent of the continental shelf areas appertaining to the coastal State and the length of the coast measured in the general direction of the coastline, account being taken for this purpose of the effects, actual or prospective, of any other continental

---

[69] Ibid, 123–4 (Scilly Isles given half-effect).

[70] *Tunisia/Libya*, ICJ Reports 1982 p 18, 88–9. For criticism of this approach: ibid, 149–56 (Judge Gros, diss). Also: *Dubai-Sharjah Border* (1981) 91 ILR 543, 673–7.

[71] *Barbados v Trinidad and Tobago* (2006) 139 ILR 449, 523; *Black Sea*, ICJ Reports 2009 p 61, 125–6.

[72] *Maritime Delimitation in the Area between Greenland and Jan Mayen*, ICJ Reports 1993 p 38, 70–2. Cf *Cameroon v Nigeria*, ICJ Reports 2002 p 303, 447–8 (irrelevance of oil practice).

[73] ICJ Reports 1985 p 13, 40. The use of the term 'equitable principles' here is reflective of a mild conflation in the case-law, under which 'relevant circumstances' represent another, more situationally responsive, equitable principle: e.g. *Jan Mayen*, ICJ Reports 1993 p 38, 62. *Also: Guyana v Suriname* (2007) 139 ILR 566, 650–1.

[74] *Tunisia/Libya*, ICJ Reports 1982 p 18, 77–8; *Libya/Malta*, ICJ Reports 1985 p 13, 41; *Guinea–Guinea-Bissau Maritime Delimitation* (1985) 77 ILR 635, 688–9.

[75] Jaenicke, in Bos & Siblesz (eds), *Realism in Law-Making* (1986) 51.

shelf delimitations between adjacent States in the same region'.[76] Proportionality, however, is not an independent principle of delimitation (based on the ratio of the lengths of the respective coasts), but only a test of the equitableness of a result arrived at by other means.[77] This process of *ex post facto* verification of a line arrived at on the basis of other criteria may take two forms. Exceptionally, it may take the form of a ratio loosely based on the lengths of the respective coastlines.[78] More generally, it takes the form of vetting the delimitation for evident disproportionality resulting from particular geographical features.[79] If coasts are not born equal, delimitations are to achieve proportionality—but not to have it thrust upon them.[80]

(F) APPLICATION OF THE EQUITABLE PRINCIPLES AND RELEVANT CIRCUMSTANCES

The International Court has emphasized that there must be a process of balancing up all pertinent considerations wherein the relative weight to be given to the various principles and factors varies with the circumstances.[81] The practical application of the equitable principles normally involves drawing a boundary line and the method chosen will be the method (or combination of methods) which will produce an equitable result. Methods available include a median or equidistance line, a median line subject to a factor of equitable correction, a perpendicular to the general direction of the coast, using a bisector of the angle of the lines expressing the general direction of the relevant coasts[82] and the creation of a zone of joint development or joint access to resources.[83]

(G) THE CONCEPT OF NATURAL PROLONGATION[84]

A further factor is that of natural prolongation, but its precise relevance is problematic. Its initial significance, reflected in *North Sea Continental Shelf*, was that shelf was seen as a physical or geomophological feature appurtenant to the land territory and as a natural prolongation of land territory into and under the sea: states lacking the

---

[76] ICJ Reports 1969 p 3, 52–4. In *Bangladesh/Myanmar*, the test was referred to as the 'disproportionality test': ITLOS Case No 16, §§477–99.

[77] *Libya/Malta*, ICJ Reports 1985 p 13, 45–6.

[78] *Tunisia/Libya*, ICJ Reports 1982 p 18, 75–6, 78, 91, 93.

[79] *Anglo-French Continental Shelf* (1977) 54 ILR 6, 67–8; *Gulf of Maine*, ICJ Reports 1984 p 246, 323; *Libya/Malta*, ICJ Reports 1985 p 13, 53–5.

[80] Shakespeare, *Twelfth Night*, Act II sc 4.

[81] *North Sea Continental Shelf*, ICJ Reports 1969 p 3, 50–1; *Tunisia/Libya*, ICJ Reports 1982 p 18, 59–61; *Libya/Malta*, ICJ Reports 1985 p 13, 40.

[82] Cf the Judgment of the Chamber in *Gulf of Maine*, ICJ Reports 1984 p 246, 313–14; and the Judgment of the Full Court in *Caribbean Sea*, ICJ Reports 2007 p 659, 745–9, 759–60.

[83] *North Sea Continental Shelf*, ICJ Reports 1969 p 3, 53; *Jan Mayen Continental Shelf* (1981) 62 ILR 108.

[84] Generally: Hutchinson (1984) 55 BY 133; Highet, in Dallmeyer & De Vorsey (eds), *Rights to Oceanic Resources* (1989) 87; Colson (2003) 97 AJIL 91, 102–7; Kaye (2008) 14 OCLJ 73, 74–9.

feature had no shelf entitlement.[85] This encouraged the view that geological factors should enjoy qualified pre-eminence in the process of delimitation. In practice, these formulations constitute no more than a simple epitome of the shelf concept and the root of title of the coastal state. Indeed, starting with the *Libya/Malta* the International Court has stressed the principle of distance as a basis of entitlement and concluded that, within the areas at a distance of under 200nm from either of the coasts in question, there is no role for geological or geophysical factors either in terms of verifying title or as factors in delimitation.[86] It has also been established that natural prolongation is not *as such* a test of equitableness.[87] Even when the seabed contains marked discontinuities, these will not play any significant role as an equitable criterion, unless they 'disrupt the essential unity of the continental shelf' (and in practice they rarely do),[88] or occur *outside* areas within 200nm of the coasts in question.[89]

(H) CONTINENTAL SHELF DELIMITATION BEYOND 200NM[90]

Delimitation of the continental shelf beyond the 200nm line is a complex process legally, geographically, and geologically. The criteria for determining the outer limits of the continental shelf are set out in UNCLOS Article 76. In contrast with continental shelf delimitation within 200nm from the baseline, when a coastal state wants to establish the outer limits of its continental shelf beyond 200nm, it has to submit particulars of such limits to the Commission on the Limits of the Continental Shelf.[91] Based on the file, the Commission makes recommendations, and when these are accepted and implemented by the state, the limits of the shelf become final and binding.[92]

The procedure before the Commission is available only for non-contentious delimitation. The Court of Arbitration in *St Pierre and Miquelon* declared itself not competent to comment upon the arguments regarding French rights to continental shelf areas beyond the 200nm limit because any such decision would have constituted a pronouncement involving a delimitation not 'between the parties' but between each one of them and the Commission, representing the international community.[93] Conversely, the Arbitration Tribunal in *Newfoundland and Labrador v Nova Scotia* found itself able to engage in delimitation beyond the 200nm line. It gave two reasons: first, it was a national and not an international tribunal; and second, it was called to specify the offshore areas of the two parties *inter se* for the purposes of the Accord Acts, which it could do by providing that the line did not extend beyond the point of

[85] ICJ Reports 1969 p 3, 22, 32, 37, 46–7, 51, 53; *Jan Mayen Continental Shelf* (1981) 62 ILR 108, 119, 124.
[86] *Libya/Malta*, ICJ Reports 1985 p 13, 32–7, esp 35.
[87] *Tunisia/Libya*, ICJ Reports 1982 p 18, 46–7.
[88] *Anglo-French Continental Shelf* (1977) 54 ILR 6, 68–70. Also: *North Sea Continental Shelf*, ICJ Reports 1969 p 3, 32; *Tunisia/Libya*, ICJ Reports 1982 p 18, 57–8, 64.
[89] *Libya/Malta*, ICJ Reports 1985 p 13, 35–6.
[90] Generally: Kunoy (2006) 53 *NILR* 247; McDorman (2009) 18 *J Trans LP* 155.
[91] UNCLOS, Annex II, esp Art 4.
[92] UNCLOS, Art 76(8).
[93] *St Pierre and Miquelon* (1992) 95 ILR 645, 648, 673–5.

intersection with the outer limit of the continental margin determined in accordance with international law.[94] The second reason is compelling, and the *St Pierre and Miquelon* decision is in this as in other respects eccentric. However, in *Caribbean Sea*, the Court indicated that the delimitation line could not extend more than 200nm because claims to outer continental shelf had to be submitted to the Commission.[95] The situation is slightly different again with respect to the International Tribunal for the Law of the Sea (ITLOS). In *Bangladesh/Myanmar*, the Tribunal confirmed that it possessed jurisdiction to delimit the continental shelf beyond 200nm at least as between adjacent states. More controversial was whether the jurisdiction should be exercised.[96] The Tribunal eventually decided that it was appropriate to engage in delimitation beyond the 200nm limit, as delimitation would not impede the Commission in carrying out its functions;[97] furthermore, it was noted, without ITLOS intervention, the shelf might never been delimited, due to a lack of consent to the Commission's consideration by the two coastal states.[98]

4. EXCLUSIVE ECONOMIC ZONE DELIMITATION BETWEEN ADJACENT OR OPPOSITE STATES[99]

The provisions of UNCLOS Article 74 concerning delimitation of the Exclusive Economic Zone (EEZ) between states with opposite or adjacent coasts are identical with those of Article 83 relating to continental shelf delimitation. Moreover, the basis of entitlement of the coastal state to the EEZ is less differentiated from that of shelf areas since the International Court emphasized the distance principle of 200nm in *Libya/Malta*.[100] The principles of delimitation are strikingly similar, unless the coasts involved are more than 400nm apart. However, some differences may manifest themselves in balancing equitable factors, more especially when the EEZ areas to be delimited are of interest on account of fisheries rather than oil and gas.

In this context, the state practice and decisions of international tribunals relating to single maritime boundaries are significant.[101] Such a boundary divides areas of

---

[94] *Arbitration between Newfoundland and Labrador and Nova Scotia concerning Portions of the Limits of their Offshore Areas* (2002) 128 ILR 425, 537–9.

[95] *Caribbean Sea*, ICJ Reports 2007 p 659, 759.

[96] *Bangladesh/Myanmar*, ITLOS Case No 16, §§360–3.

[97] Ibid, §§378–90, 393.

[98] Ibid, §§390–2.

[99] Generally: Evensen, in Rozakis & Stephanou (eds), *The New Law of the Sea* (1983) 107; 2 O'Connell (1984) 727–32; Attard, *The Exclusive Economic Zone in International Law* (1987) 221–76; Weil (1989); Evans (1989) 39–62; 2 Nordquist (1993) 796–817; Rothwell & Stephens (2010) 401–7.

[100] ICJ Reports 1985 p 35. Cf *Tunisia/Libya*, ICJ Reports 1982 p 18, 48–9, 114–15 (Judge Jiménez de Aréchaga), 222 (Judge Oda).

[101] Generally: Oda, 2 *International Law at the Time of its Codification* (1987) 349; Evans (1993) 64 *BY* 283; Rothwell & Stephens (2010) 407–8.

different status, for example, a continental shelf and a fisheries zone of 200nm, as in *Gulf of Maine*.[102] There, the Chamber applied equitable criteria essentially identical with those applicable to shelf delimitation, while emphasizing the need to use criteria suited to a multi-purpose delimitation involving the shelf and the superjacent water column.[103]

A further issue of interest with respect to delimitation of the continental shelf beyond 200nm is that of the 'grey zone' or 'grey area'. This refers to situations in which the natural prolongation of state A's continental shelf extends into state B's EEZ. In *Bangladesh/Myanmar*, the Tribunal noted that the grey area created in Myanmar's EEZ by reason of the Bangladesh's continental shelf did not 'otherwise limit Myanmar's rights [with respect to the EEZ]',[104] and granted Bangladesh the rights to the continental shelf in the area whilst giving Myanmar the rights to the superjacent water column: each state was required to 'exercise its rights and perform its duties with due regard to the rights and duties of the other'[105] by reference to UNCLOS Articles 56, 58, and 78 to 79.

5. THE EFFECT OF ISLANDS UPON DELIMITATION[106]

Islands may constitute a relevant circumstance for the purpose of delimiting areas of continental shelf or exclusive economic zone between opposite or adjacent states and in this context they may be given full effect[107] or half-effect.[108] Alternatively they may be ignored or enclaved.[109]

---

[102] ICJ Reports 1984 p 246. For comment: Rhee (1981) 75 *AJIL* 590; Legault & McRae (1984) 22 *CYIL* 267; Legault & Hankey (1985) 79 *AJIL* 961; Schneider (1985) 79 *AJIL* 539; Oda (1987) 349; Kaye (2008) 14 *OCLJ* 73.

[103] ICJ Reports 1984 p 246, 326–7. Also: the Court of Arbitration decision in the *Guinea–Guinea-Bissau Maritime Delimitation* (1985) 77 ILR 635, 658–9, 685–7; *Dubai-Sharjah Border* (1981) 91 ILR 543; *St Pierre and Miquelon* (1992) 95 ILR 645, 663–4; *Eritrea v Yemen (Phase Two)* (1999) 119 ILR 417, 457–8; *Qatar v Bahrain*, ICJ Reports 2001 p 40, 91–3; *Cameroon v Nigeria*, ICJ Reports 2002 p 303, 440–2; *Caribbean Sea*, ICJ Reports 2007 p 659, 738–40.

[104] *Bangladesh/Myanmar*, ITLOS Case No 16, §§471, 474.

[105] Ibid, §475.

[106] Generally: Bowett, *The Legal Regime of Islands in International Law* (1979); Dipla, *Le Régime juridique des îles dans le droit international de la mer* (1984); 2 O'Connell (1984) 714–23, 731–2; Symmons (1986) 35 *ICLQ* 344; Jayewardene, *The Regime of Islands in International Law* (1990); Rothwell & Stephens (2010) 404–6; Scovazzi, 'Maritime Delimitation Cases before International Courts and Tribunals' (2008) *MPEPIL*, §D2. On artificial islands: Johnson (1951) 4 *ILQ* 203; Papadakis, *The International Legal Regime of Artificial Islands* (1977); 1 O'Connell (1982) 196–7. On the Rockall issue: Symmons (1986) 35 *ICLQ* 344.

[107] *Anglo-French Continental Shelf* (1977) 54 ILR 6, 123 (Island of Ushant); *Bangladesh/Myanmar*, ITLOS Case No 16, §§151–2 (St Martin's Island given a full 12nm territorial sea).

[108] *Tunisia/Libya*, ICJ Reports 1982 p 18, 88–9 (Kerkennah Islands); *Anglo-French Continental Shelf* (1977) 54 ILR 6, 121–4 (Scilly Isles); *Gulf of Maine*, ICJ Reports 1984 p 246, 336–7 (Seal Island).

[109] *Anglo-French Continental Shelf* (1977) 54 ILR 6, 98–104 (Channel Islands); *Bangladesh/Myanmar*, ITLOS Case No 16, §§318–19 (St Martin's Island given no effect with respect to the EEZ and continental shelf).

Much will depend on the particular geographical relationships of the island rather than its classification, which can be avoided if it is not central to a particular case. UNCLOS Article 121(2) provides that all islands, as defined, count as land territory,[110] but Article 121(3) then formulates an exception. 'Rocks which cannot sustain human habitation or economic life of their own' have no EEZ or continental shelf. Consequently, such features need not be taken into account, as between UNCLOS parties, in delimitations beyond 12nm; whereas as a matter of customary international law the question was whether taking such features into account would have a disproportionate effect on the putative delimitation line. Thus, in *Libya/Malta*, the Court found it equitable to disregard the uninhabited Maltese islet of Filfa when drawing the boundary line.[111]

Whether an island plays a significant role in maritime delimitation is to a large extent dependent on the stage of the delimitation process at which the island is considered. If the island is taken into consideration at the initial stage of drawing the provisional line, its impact will generally be significant. If the island is assessed only at a later stage as a relevant factor for adjustment or shifting of the provisional equidistance line, its impact will be reduced considerably. The latter was the case of Serpents' Island, a maritime feature of $0.17km^2$ located 20nm to the east of the Danube delta, which was not considered as generating base points for drawing the provisional line at the first delimitation stage, and its presence was later not seen as requiring adjustment of the provisional equidistance line.[112] In such a case the potential impact of Article 121(3) may be occluded.

In other cases, an island may be given varying treatment depending on the act of delimitation in question. In *Bangladesh/Myanmar*, St Martin's Island was given a 12nm territorial sea,[113] but no additional continental shelf or EEZ so as to avoid undue distortion of the equidistance line:[114] it was thus largely irrelevant in the drawing of the single maritime boundary of the continental shelf and EEZ.

---

[110] Also: GCTS Art 10.

[111] *Libya/Malta*, ICJ Reports 1985 p 13, 48. Also: *Qatar v Bahrain*, ICJ Reports p 40, 104; *Caribbean Sea*, ICJ Reports 2007 p 659, 751–2; *Black Sea*, ICJ Reports 2009 p 61, 122.

[112] *Black Sea*, ICJ Reports 2009 p 61, 68–70, 110–12, 122–3.

[113] *Bangladesh/Myanmar*, ITLOS Case No 16, §§151–2.

[114] Ibid, §§317–19.

13

MARITIME TRANSIT
AND THE REGIME OF
THE HIGH SEAS

1. INTRODUCTION[1]

The modern law of the high seas is largely set out in two multilateral treaties, one built substantially on and intended to replace the other, both setting out propositions in 'all states' form. The first is the Geneva Convention on the High Seas (GCHS),[2] the preamble of which asserts that its articles 'are generally declaratory of established principles of international law'. Its provisions were substantially co-opted by Part VII (High Seas) of the UN Convention on the Law of the Sea (UNCLOS),[3] which, despite the continued non-participation of some states, can for most purposes be taken to reflect the definitive position on the subject.[4]

The high seas traditionally encompassed all parts of the sea beyond the territorial sea and the internal waters of a state.[5] By contrast UNCLOS specifies that the provisions of Part VII 'apply to all parts of the sea that are not included in the exclusive economic zone, in the territorial sea or in the internal waters of a State, or in the archipelagic waters of an archipelagic State' (Article 86). This invites two observations. First, by

---

[1] Still of considerable authority are the Secretariat Memo of 14 July 1950, ILC *Ybk* 1950/II, 67 (believed to be the work of Gidel), and the reports of Special Rapporteur François: ILC *Ybk* 1950/II, 36; ILC *Ybk* 1951/II, 75; ILC *Ybk* 1952/II, 44; ILC *Ybk* 1954/II, 7. Further McDougal & Burke, *The Public Order of the Oceans* (1962) 730–1007; Bardonnet & Virally (eds), *Le Nouveau droit international de la mer* (1983); O'Connell, 2 *The International Law of the Sea* (1984) 792–830; Dupuy & Vignes (eds), *Traité du nouveau droit de la mer* (1985) 337–74; 3 Nordquist (1995); Churchill & Lowe, *The Law of the Sea* (3rd edn, 1999) 203–432; Klein, *Dispute Settlement in the UN Convention on the Law of the Sea* (2005); Guilfoyle, *Shipping Interdiction and the Law of the Sea* (2009); Rothwell & Stephens, *The International Law of the Sea* (2010) ch 7.

[2] 29 April 1958, 450 UNTS 82.

[3] 10 December 1982, 1833 UNTS 3.

[4] There are currently 162 parties to UNCLOS, including the EU: www.un.org/Depts/los/reference_files/chronological_lists_of_ratifications.htm. The US is conspicuous by its continuing absence; it remains a party to the GCHS. Some US courts have declared UNCLOS to be reflective of customary international law: e.g. *Sarei v Rio Tinto*, 456 F.3d 1069, 1078 (9th Cir, 2006); but cf Mank (2007) *Utah LR* 1085.

[5] GCHS, Art 1.

no means all coastal states claim an Exclusive Economic Zone (EEZ). Secondly, many high seas freedoms are applicable in the EEZ (Articles 58, 86), and this is also the position in customary international law.[6]

The regime of the high seas does not apply to international lakes and land-locked seas, which are not open to free navigation except by special agreement. However, seas which are virtually land-locked may acquire the status of high seas: this is so of the Baltic and Black Seas. In such cases much turns on the maintenance of freedom of transit through the straits communicating with other large bodies of sea.[7] It is doubtful whether, apart from special agreements on access and other issues, the Baltic and Black Seas would have the status of open seas. The Caspian Sea does not.[8]

2. FREEDOM OF THE HIGH SEAS

(A) HISTORICAL AND JURISPRUDENTIAL ORIGINS

The modern law governing the high seas has its foundation in the rule that the high seas were not open to acquisition by occupation on the part of states individually or collectively: it was *res extra commercium* or *res communis*. The emergence of the rule is associated with the rise to dominance of maritime powers and the decline of the influence of states which had favoured closed seas. By the eighteenth century the position had changed completely. Dutch policies had supported freedom of navigation and fishing, and Grotius had written against the Portuguese monopoly of navigation and commerce in the East Indies.[9] After the accession of William of Orange to the English throne in 1689, English disputes with Holland over fisheries ceased. By the

---

[6] Cf the reference to freedom of navigation in the EEZ in *Military and Paramilitary Activities in and Against Nicaragua (Nicaragua v US)*, ICJ Rep 1986 p 14, 111–12.

[7] On access to the Black Sea: the Montreux Convention Regarding the Regime of the Turkish Straits, 20 July 1936, 173 LNTS 214. This agreement in effect gave Turkey full control of the straits whilst guaranteeing the free passage of civilian vessels during peacetime. The International Court considered various questions of the delimitation of maritime boundaries in the Black Sea in *Maritime Delimitation in the Black Sea (Romania v Ukraine)*, ICJ Reports 2009 p 61.

[8] Following the dissolution of the Soviet Union, the political and economic interests of the Caspian states (now Russia, Kazakhstan, Turkmenistan, Iran, and Azerbaijan) resulted in a prolonged and fruitless dispute over its status. Differing interpretations of the pre-existing Soviet–Iranian treaties led to a dispute over the international law applicable to the Caspian: e.g. Persia–Russian Socialist Federal Soviet Republic, Treaty of Friendship, 26 February 1921, 9 LNTS 383, Art 11; Iran–USSR, Treaty of Establishment, Commerce and Navigation, 27 August 1935, 176 LNTS 301, Arts 14, 15; Iran–USSR, Treaty of Commerce and Navigation, 25 March 1940, 144 BFSP 419 (referring to the Caspian as a 'Soviet–Iranian Sea'); Iran–USSR, Treaty concerning the Settlement of Frontier and Financial Questions, 2 December 1954, 451 UNTS 250. At the present time, the littoral states cannot agree on the overall legal status of the Caspian, though they appear to agree on sectoral division of the sea bed: Mehdiyoun (2000) 94 *AJIL* 179.

[9] *Mare Liberum sive de jure quod Batavis competit ad Indicana commercia dissertatio* (1609, tr Hakluyt 2004). *Mare Liberum* was a chapter of *De iure praedae*, which was not published until unearthed in the 19th century: *De iure praedae* (1868, tr Hamaker 2006). On its significance: Blom (ed), *Property, Piracy and*

late eighteenth century the British claim to sovereignty (the King's Chambers) was obsolete; insistence on the flag ceremony ended in 1805. Also by this time, the cannon-shot rule predominated and claims to large areas of sea faded away.[10] In the nineteenth century naval power and commercial interests dictated British, French, and American support for the principle of freedom of the seas. Whatever special interests the principle may have served historically, it commended itself as representing a sensible concept of shared use in circumstances where the level of technology did not threaten the maritime global commons.

Although the freedom of the high seas was described by Gidel as '*multi-forme et fugace*',[11] in truth it is a general principle of international law, a policy or concept from which particular rules may be inferred. But its application to specific problems often fails to give precise results. For example, weapons testing, which involves the temporary closure of large areas of ocean, is regarded by some as a legitimate use and by others as a serious denial of the freedom of the seas.[12] Gidel regards the concept as essentially negative, in the sense that states are prima facie obliged not to impede vessels under the flag of another state from going about their business on the high seas, and vice versa.[13] However, both the substance of the principle and its character as such give rise to certain presumptions which may aid in the resolution of particular problems, and some consideration of its positive content is, therefore, useful. Grotius stated two propositions: first, that the sea could not be the object of private or public appropriation; secondly, that the use of the high seas by one state would leave the medium available for use by another.[14] To these propositions it is necessary to add that the general principle applies in time of war or armed conflict as well as time of peace.[15] On two occasions the International Court has taken the opportunity to invoke 'the principle of the freedom of maritime communication'.[16]

(B) UNCLOS AND THE FREEDOM OF THE HIGH SEAS

UNCLOS Article 87 renders the principle of freedom of the high seas as follows:

Punishment (2009); Feenstra (ed), *Hugo Grotius Mare Liberum 1609–2009* (2009). Generally: Fulton, *The Sovereignty of the Sea* (1911).

[10] The extravagant Portuguese and Spanish pretensions had ended before this. Spain supported a six-mile limit in 1760. On earlier British claims and the general development of the concept of the territorial and high seas: Selden, *Mare Clausum* (1636); Churchill & Lowe (3rd edn, 1999) 71–5.

[11] Gidel, ILC *Ybk* 1950/II, 68.

[12] Churchill & Lowe (3rd edn, 1999) 206, 426; Gidel, in *Festschrift für Jean Spiropolous* (1957) 173; Oda & Owada (eds), *The Practice of Japan in International Law 1961–1970* (1982) 110–21 and the applications of Australia and New Zealand in *Nuclear Tests (Australia v France)*, ICJ Reports 1974 p 253; *Nuclear Tests (New Zealand v France)*, ICJ Reports 1974 p 457.

[13] Gidel, in *Festschrift Spiropolous* (1957) 691. Also: *SS Lotus* (1927) PCIJ Ser A No 10, 25.

[14] Grotius, *Mare Liberum* (1609, tr Hakluyt 2004) ch 5.

[15] On the modern law of maritime blockade: Guilfoyle (2010) 81 *BY* 9. Also: International Committee of the Red Cross, *San Remo Manual on International Law Applicable to Armed Conflicts at Sea* (1994).

[16] *Corfu Channel (UK v Albania)*, ICJ Reports 1949 p 4, 22; *Nicaragua*, ICJ Reports 1986 p 14, 111–12.

1. The high seas are open to all States, whether coastal or land locked. Freedom of the
    high seas is exercised under the conditions laid down by this Convention and by other
    rules of international law. It comprises, *inter alia*, for both coastal and land-locked
    States:

    (a) freedom of navigation;

    (b) freedom of overflight;

    (c) freedom to lay submarine cables and pipelines, subject to Part VI;

    (d) freedom to construct artificial islands and other installations permitted under
         international law, subject to Part VI;

    (e) freedom of fishing, subject to the conditions laid down in section 2;

    (f) freedom of scientific research, subject to Parts VI and XIII.

2. These freedoms shall be exercised by all States with due regard to the interests of other
    States in their exercise of the freedom of the high seas, and also with due regard for the
    rights under this Convention with respect to activities [on the sea bed and ocean floor
    and subsoil thereof].

Of the six freedoms enumerated in Article 87, only freedom of navigation, fishing,
the laying of submarine cables and pipelines, and overflight were included in GCHS
Article 2. These four freedoms are supported by arbitral jurisprudence and are inherent in many particular rules of law. Freedom of fishing is an assumption at the base
of the decision in *Anglo-Norwegian Fisheries*[17] and the awards in the *Behring Sea
Fisheries* arbitrations in 1893[18] and 1902.[19] Both arbitrations arose from attempts
to enforce conservation measures on the high seas. In the former case the US had
arrested Canadian sealers, and in the latter Russian vessels had arrested American
sealers, with the object of preventing the depletion of seal stocks. Both awards rejected
claims to enforce conservation measures against foreign vessels on the high seas. In
the absence of a treaty, a coastal state could only apply such measures to vessels flying
its own flag. Of the questions submitted for decision to the tribunal of 1893 the fifth
concerned an issue of general law: 'Has the United States any right, and if so, what
right of protection or property in the fur-seals frequenting the islands of the United
States in Behring Sea when such seals are found outside the ordinary three-mile limit?'
The arbitrators found, by a majority, that 'the United States has not any right of protection or property in the fur-seals frequenting the islands of the United States in Behring
Sea, when such seals are found outside the ordinary three-mile limit'.[20]

UNCLOS Article 86(1) places additional limitations upon high-seas freedoms as
compared with the earlier law. The existing freedom to lay submarine pipes and cables

---

[17] *Fisheries (UK v Norway)*, ICJ Reports 1951 p 116; cf 187–9 (Judge Read, diss).

[18] (1893) 28 RIAA 263, 1 IELR 43.

[19] (1902) 9 RIAA 51. The seal fishery was later regulated by the Convention between Great Britain, Japan,
Russia and the United States Requesting Measures for the Preservation and Protection of Fur Seals in the
North Pacific Ocean, 7 December 1911, 214 CTS 80.

[20] 28 RIAA 263, 267; 1 IELR 43, 53.

and the 'new' freedoms to construct artificial islands and other structures and to undertake scientific research are limited by UNCLOS Part VI, governing activities on the continental shelf. The freedom to fish is limited by Part VII, section 2, concerning the conservation and management of living resources on the high seas. In particular, Articles 117 and 118 condition the freedom to fish by requiring states parties to co-operate with other states in taking such measures for their respective nationals as may be necessary for the conservation and management of living resources on the high seas, to the extent of establishing subregional or regional fisheries management organizations to this end.[21]

UNCLOS Part XI is also relevant, regulating activities on the sea bed and ocean floor and its subsoil beyond the limits of national jurisdiction. It establishes the International Seabed Authority, an international organization through which the states parties to UNCLOS can organize and control seabed activities, with a particular focus on administering resources beneath the sea floor.[22]

The most significant modification to customary international law arising from by UNCLOS, however, is the emergence of the EEZ as a separate jurisdictional zone claimable by each coastal state as of right.[23] The concept of the EEZ only gained traction in the later part of the twentieth century;[24] it was not recognized in the third Geneva Convention of 1958, which instead endorsed a coastal state right of preference.[25] By 1974, however, when the Third UN Conference on the Law of the Sea (UNCLOS III) opened, it was clear that a majority of especially developing states supported the concept and that all that remained was its full articulation. UNCLOS Part V provides a set of rules which regulate EEZs, and, in Article 57, sets the outer limit of the EEZ at 200nm seaward of the coastal state's baselines: Article 56 provides for the rights, jurisdiction, and duties of the coastal state in its EEZ. As provided in Article 86, an EEZ does not form part of the high seas, though significant aspects of the regime of the high seas apply to the zone. This is seen primarily in the wording of Article 58(1), which sets out the rights and duties of other states in an EEZ, and preserves for them the freedoms of navigation, overflight, the laying of submarine cables and pipelines, and all other internationally lawful uses of the seas relating to these freedoms. Furthermore, Article 58(2) extends the application of Articles 88 to 115 (the bulk of

---

[21] On these organizations: Young, *Trading Fish, Saving Fish* (2011) 38–46.

[22] UNCLOS, Arts 156–7.

[23] On the evolution of the EEZ: Attard, *The Exclusive Economic Zone in International Law* (1985); Orrego Vicuña, *The Exclusive Economic Zone* (1989); Churchill & Lowe (3rd edn, 1999) ch 9; Rothwell & Stephens (2010) ch 4.

[24] The first claim to an exclusive fisheries zone beyond 12nm was made by Chile and Peru in 1947, mutually recognized in the Santiago Declaration on the Maritime Zone, 18 August 1952, 1006 UNTS 325 (Chile, Peru, Ecuador). Currently *sub iudice*: *Maritime Dispute (Peru v Chile)* (2008, pending).

[25] Convention on Fishing and Conservation of the Living Resources of the High Seas, 29 April 1958, 559 UNTS 285. This was the least successful of the four Geneva Conventions, having at its height only 38 parties. For the state of customary international law after 1958: *Fisheries Jurisdiction (UK v Iceland)*, ICJ Reports 1974 p 3, 24, 29; *(Federal Republic of Germany v Iceland)*, ICJ Reports 1974 p 175, 196, where the Court expressed matters in terms of opposability rather than validity of claims.

the general provisions regulating the high seas, with the exception of the additional freedoms of Article 87(1)) to the EEZ to the extent they do not conflict with the provisions of Part V, creating in the process substantial overlap between the two fields.

(C) JURISDICTIONAL ASPECTS OF THE HIGH SEAS REGIME

Although the basal principle of the law of the high seas is that one state cannot interfere with vessels sailing under the flag of another without the consent of the latter, UNCLOS Article 110 provides a number of exceptions, conferring power to stop, search, and even seize foreign vessels as an exercise of a state's jurisdiction to enforce in certain cases.[26] In other cases the parties are obliged only to incorporate the relevant prohibition in their national legislation, and enforcement is left to national courts in respect of the flag vessels and nationals of the forum state. The system of enforcement, whether specified by treaty or custom, rests on co-operation under international law and notably under the national laws of states possessing a maritime flag. Every state is under a duty to fix the conditions for the grant of nationality, for the registration of ships in its territory, and for the right to fly its flag. Ships have the nationality of the state whose flag they are entitled to fly.[27]

Insofar as jurisdiction is concerned, UNCLOS Part VII generally reflects customary international law, providing in Articles 88 and 89 respectively that the high seas are reserved for peaceful purposes[28] and that no state may subject any part of the high seas to its sovereignty. Article 90 grants every state, coastal or land locked, the right to sail ships flying its flag on the high seas. Article 92(1) provides that ships shall sail under the flag of one state only; subject to certain exceptions, ships are subject to the exclusive jurisdiction of the flag state whilst on the high seas. Article 94 fixes the obligations of states with respect to vessels flying its flag. The right to enjoy the protection of the law balances the responsibility of the flag state for the behaviour of its ships.[29]

A ship without nationality[30] loses the protection of the law with respect to boarding (and potentially seizure) on the high seas.[31] However, such ships are not outside the law altogether; their occupants are protected by elementary considerations of humanity.

---

[26] To be distinguished from a state's jurisdiction to prescribe, which is not regulated by UNCLOS but by the general law: Guilfoyle (2009) 7–10; and see chapter 21.

[27] GCHS, Art 5; UNCLOS, Art 91; Churchill & Lowe (3rd edn, 1999) 257–63.

[28] This has by no means demilitarized the oceans: Oxman (1983–84) 24 *Va JIL* 809, 830–1.

[29] On the nationality of ships: generally *Constitution of the Maritime Safety Committee of the Inter-Governmental Maritime Consultative Organization*, ICJ Reports 1960 p 150; *M/V Saiga (No 2) (St Vincent and the Grenadines v Guinea)* (1999) 120 ILR 143. Also: O'Keefe (2000) 59 *CLJ* 428; Simmonds (1963) 12 *ICLQ* 56. Further: chapter 24.

[30] To which will be assimilated a vessel flying a flag without authority of the flag state and a ship sailing under the flags of two or more states, using them according to convenience: GCHS, Art 6.2; UNCLOS, Art 92(2); Churchill & Lowe (3rd edn, 1999) 213–14.

[31] *Naim Molvan v AG for Palestine* [1948] AC 351, 369; François, ILC *Ybk* 1950/II, 36, 38; but cf UNCLOS, Art 110(1)(d), which makes reference only to boarding, not seizure, with reference to ships without nationality: Guilfoyle (2009) 16–18. On the status of derelict vessels: *Costa Rica Packet* (1897), in Moore, 5 *Int Arb* 808.

The seizure of ships by insurgents has created some difficult problems, and the issues have been obscured by a tendency for courts to describe ships under the control of insurgents as pirates. Such ships, it seems, should not be interfered with provided they do not attempt to exercise belligerent rights against foreign vessels and the lives of any 'neutral' aliens on board are not threatened.

(D) PIRACY[32]

Piracy is the principal exception to the freedom of the high seas, and one that has attained a new significance. The dissenting opinion of Judge Moore in the *Lotus* provides a useful starting-point. He said that

in the case of what is known as piracy by law of nations, there has been conceded a universal jurisdiction, under which the person charged with the offence may be tried and punished by any nation into whose jurisdiction he may come. I say 'piracy by law of nations', because the municipal laws of many States denominate and punish as 'piracy' numerous acts which do not constitute piracy by law of nations, and which therefore are not of universal cognizance, so as to be punishable by all nations. Piracy by law of nations, in its jurisdictional aspects, is *sui generis*. Though statutes may provide for its punishment, it is an offence against the law of nations; and as the scene of the pirate's operations is the high seas, which it is not the right or duty of any nation to police, he is denied the protection of the flag which he may carry, and is treated as an outlaw, as the enemy of all mankind—*hostis humani generis*—whom any nation may in the interest of all capture and punish.[33]

The term 'universal jurisdiction' refers to the jurisdiction of a state to prescribe conduct occurring extraterritorially without a territorial, national or other internationally recognized nexus, as well as the capacity to enforce that jurisdiction on the high seas.[34]

(i) The definition of piracy

The definition of piracy was historically a source of controversy,[35] but UNCLOS Article 101 (reflecting almost verbatim GCHS Article 15) represents the existing

---

[32] Guilfoyle (2009) 26–74; Shearer, 'Piracy' (2010) *MPEPIL*. Also: Gidel, 1 *Le Droit international public de la mer* (1932) 303–55; Harvard Research in International Law, Draft Convention on Piracy (1932) 26 *AJIL Supp* 739; Secretariat Memorandum, ILC *Ybk* 1950/II, 70; Johnson (1957) 43 *GST* 63 (a useful mid-20th century signpost); McNair, 1 *Opinions* 265–81; Shubber (1968–69) 43 *BY* 193 (distinguishing aircraft hijacking from piracy; 2 O'Connell (1984) 967–83; Rubin, *The Law of Piracy* (1988).

[33] (1927) PCIJ Ser A No 10, 70.

[34] Further: *Arrest Warrant of 11 April 2000 (Democratic Republic of the Congo v Belgium)*, ICJ Reports 2002 p 3, 36–44 (Judge Guillaume), 53 (Judge Oda, diss), 56–7 (Judge Ranjeva), 62 (Judge Koroma), 75, 79–80 (Judges Higgins, Kooijmans & Buergenthal); O'Keefe (2002) 2 *JICJ* 735.

[35] Note that definitions by municipal courts are often out of date, and may involve an amalgam of municipal rules and international law, or the narrow issue of the meaning of 'piracy' in an insurance policy. The treatment in 2 Oppenheim, 610–14, presents an unusually wide conception of piracy. For judicial essays in definition: *United States v Smith*, 18 US 153, 163–80 (1820); *The Serhassan Pirates* (1845) 2 Wm Rob 354; *The Magellan Pirates* (1853) 1 Sp Ecc & Ad 81; *Republic of Bolivia v Indemnity Mutual Marine Assurance Co* [1909] KB 785; *In re Piracy Jure Gentium* [1934] AC 586; *Athens Maritime Enterprises Corporation v Hellenic*

customary law—or rather, custom has come to reflect it.[36] Article 101 provides:

1. Piracy consists of any of the following acts:

   (a) any illegal acts of violence or detention, or any act of depredation, committed for private ends by the crew or passengers of a private ship or private aircraft, and directed:

      (i) on the high seas, against another ship or aircraft, or against persons or property on board such ship or aircraft;

      (ii) against a ship, aircraft, persons or property in a place outside the jurisdiction or any State;

   (b) any act of voluntary participation in the operation of a ship or of an aircraft with knowledge of facts making it a pirate ship or aircraft;

   (c) any act of inciting or of intentionally facilitating an act described in subparagraph (a) or (b).

The only innovation here as compared with the pre-1958 understanding of piracy is the reference to aircraft, a sensible application of analogy.[37] The essential feature is that the acts must be committed for private ends.[38] Piracy cannot be committed by warships or other government ships, or government aircraft, except where the crew 'has mutinied and taken control of the ship or aircraft' (Article 102). Acts committed on board a ship by the crew and directed against the ship itself or against persons or property on the ship are also not within the definition.[39]

Article 101(1) confines piracy to acts on the high seas or 'in a place outside the territorial jurisdiction of any State'. An illegal act of violence or depredation committed against a ship whilst in the territorial sea of a state is not piracy; it is armed robbery, murder or another crime under the municipal law of the territorial state committed at sea.[40]

Article 105 (replicating GCHS Article 19) provides:

On the high seas, or in any other place outside the jurisdiction of any State, every State may seize a pirate ship or aircraft, or a ship taken by piracy and under the control of pirates, and arrest the persons and seize the property on board. The courts of the State which carried out the seizure may decide upon the penalties to be imposed, and may also determine the action to be taken with regard to the ships, aircraft or property, subject to the rights of third parties acting in good faith.

Mutual War Risks Association (Bermuda) Ltd [1983] QB 647; *Castle John and Nederlandse Stichting Sirius v NV Mabeco & NV Parfin* (1986) 77 ILR 537.

[36] Guilfoyle (2009) 26–79. Also: the ILC draft and comment: ILC *Ybk* 1956/II, 282.

[37] The ILC draft did not refer to attacks by aircraft on aircraft. Further: Tokyo Convention Act 1967 (UK), s4 and Schedule, subsequently repealed and replaced by the Merchant Shipping and Maritime Security Act 1997 (UK), s26(1), (3), Schedule 5, which incorporates the UNCLOS, Art 101 definition of piracy and its associated reference to aircraft.

[38] Guilfoyle (2009) 32–42.

[39] Cf 2 Oppenheim, 751; Hall, *International Law* (8th edn, 1924) 314. Further: 2 O'Connell (1984) 970–3.

[40] Guilfoyle (2009) 42–5.

The second part of this provision reflects the maxim *pirata non mutat dominium*: the rightful owner is not deprived of his title by virtue of acts of piracy relating to his goods.[41] Seizures on account of piracy may only be carried out by warships or military aircraft, or other government ships or aircraft authorized to that effect (Article 107). Capture may occur in other circumstances as a consequence of acts of self-defence by an intended victim of piratical action.[42]

Piracy has often been considered to be something of a historical curiosity.[43] In the early part of the twenty-first century, however, interference by pirates operating from bases in Somalia with commercial shipping in the Gulf of Aden has become a matter of significant international alarm.[44] The human and economic cost of Somali piracy has resulted in a co-ordinated international effort to combat it. Concerns raised before the International Maritime Organisation (IMO) led to a Memorandum of Understanding to combat the problem on an African level.[45] UN Security Council Resolution 1816 utilized the powers of Chapter VII of the UN Charter to authorize foreign military incursions by 'co-operating states' into Somali territorial waters over an initial six-month period.[46] UN Security Council Resolution 1851 went further still, authorizing the use of military force to prosecute land-based operations against pirates.[47] A number of those detained for piracy have been handed over for trial in neighbouring states, notably Kenya.[48]

(ii) Other illegal acts committed on the high seas

The use of force against foreign vessels on the high seas may be unlawful and yet may not fall within the definition of piracy. From time to time, however, tribunals, governments, and writers have assimilated certain categories of acts to piracy,[49] though the definition in UNCLOS Article 101 would now appear to preclude any such extension. The subject as a whole is dominated by the problem of keeping order beyond the territorial jurisdiction of states and, in particular, of maintaining legal controls in respect of those not identifiable with a state on which responsibility may be placed. Thus Hall

---

[41] Wortley (1947) 24 *BY* 258.

[42] Further: ILC *Ybk* 1956/II, 283.

[43] E.g. Dickinson (1924–25) 38 *Harv LR* 334.

[44] Guilfoyle (2009) 61–74. Concern also arose in relation to pirate activity off the coast of South East Asia, South America, and Africa, but did not result in much attention from the SC: Churchill & Lowe (3rd edn, 1999) 209. Further: IMO, Acts of Piracy and Armed Robbery against Ships (MSC/Circ.4 – Series), available at www.imo.org/blast/mainframe.asp?topic_id=334.

[45] Guilfoyle (2009) 72–4; Roach (2010) 104 *AJIL* 397, 409–11.

[46] SC Res 1816 (2008); reenacted in SC Res (2008) and annually since that time. For a useful summary of the efforts of the IMO and Security Council to combat piracy, Guilfoyle (2008) 57 *ICLQ* 690.

[47] SC Res 1851 (2008).

[48] Kenya has concluded Memoranda of Understanding with the US and UK to accept and try piracy suspects apprehended off the Gulf of Aden. Universal prescriptive jurisdiction over non-nationals captured on the high seas is established through the provisions of the Kenyan Merchant Shipping Act, Act No 4 of 2009, Part XVI: generally Gathii (2010) 104 *AJIL* 416. Also: Guilfoyle (2008) 57 *ICLQ* 690; Roach (2010) 104 *AJIL* 397; Kontorovoch & Art (2010) 104 *AJIL* 436; UKMIL (2010) 81 *BY* 453, 675–87.

[49] E.g. the Nyon Agreement, 14 September 1937, 181 LNTS 137.

considered piracy to include acts done 'by persons not acting under the authority of any politically organized community, notwithstanding that the objects of the persons so acting may be professedly political'.[50]

(iii) Actions by insurgents at sea

Ships controlled by insurgents may not, without recognition of belligerency, exercise belligerent rights against the shipping of other states. Forcible interference of this kind is unauthorized by law and may be resisted. It is very doubtful that it is correct to characterize such acts as piracy:[51] UNCLOS Article 101(a) covers only acts committed 'for private ends'.[52] However, it may be lawful to punish acts constituting murder, robbery, and so on—carried out *ultra vires* by insurgents.[53] Opinions which favour the treatment of insurgents as such as 'pirates' are surely incorrect,[54] save perhaps in circumstances where insurgents attack foreign flagged private vessels in international waters, a conclusion reached not only from the plain words of the definition in Article 101, but from the general prohibition in international humanitarian law on attacks upon civilians.[55]

(iv) Acts committed with the authority of a lawful government

Illegal attacks on or seizures of innocent merchant ships by warships or government ships result in the responsibility of the flag state, but the offending ships do not become pirate ships. This was the basis for the older practice of privateering, in which a private ship authorized by a belligerent to act in its service, was not treated as piratical, even if acts of violence were committed against neutral ships. In the latter case the belligerent was responsible as principal.[56]

Guilfoyle's conclusion is persuasive:

The test of piracy lies not in the pirate's subjective motivation, but in the lack of public sanction for his or her acts. This is why vessels on military or government service, absent the revolt of the crew, cannot, by definition, be pirate vessels. To claim that a political motive can exclude an act from the definition of piracy is to mistake the applicable concept of 'public'

---

[50] Hall (8th edn, 1924) 311, 314; Johnson (1957) 43 *GST* 63, 77–80.

[51] For the view doubted: Hall (8th edn, 1924) 314, 318–19; 2 Oppenheim, 751–2; McNair, 1 *Opinions* 274–80; Lauterpacht (1939) 46 *RGDIP* 513; Secretariat Memorandum, ILC *Ybk* 1950/II, 70. Further: van Zwanenberg (1961) 10 *ICLQ* 798; Green (1961) 37 *BY* 496; Halberstam (1988) 82 *AJIL* 269, 282; Garmon (2002) 27 *Tul Mar LJ* 257, 265 (expanding the definition to terrorism).

[52] A limitation which has existed in the law since the preparation of the 1932 Harvard Draft Convention on Piracy (1932) 26 *AJIL Supp* 739. Further: Guilfoyle (2009) 32–42. This question was brought to a head in relation to the events surrounding the *Santa Maria* and the *Achille Lauro*, and the response was to create a new offence, not to extend the definition of piracy.

[53] Convention on the Rights and Duties of States in the Event of Civil Strife, 20 February 1928, 134 LNTS 45, Arts 1–2.

[54] E.g. *Ambrose Light* (1885) 25 F 408.

[55] Guilfoyle (2009) 35.

[56] Privateering was abolished by the Declaration of Paris, 16 April 1856, 61 BFSP 155.

and 'private' acts. The essence of a piratical act is that it neither raises 'the immunity which pertains to state or governmental acts' nor engages state responsibility.[57]

(v) Politically motivated acts by organized groups

Harassing operations by organized groups deploying forces on the high seas may have political objectives,[58] and yet be neither connected with insurgency against a particular government nor performed by agents of a lawful government. Ships threatened by such activities may be protected, and yet the aggressors not be regarded as pirates. However certain municipal courts have demonstrated flexibility in attributing private ends to prima facie political acts.[59]

(vi) Unrestricted submarine warfare

The term 'piracy' has been employed on occasion to describe acts by ships acting on the orders of a recognized government 'which are in gross breach of International Law and which show a criminal disregard of human life'.[60] By the 1937 Nyon Agreement[61] eight states agreed on collective measures 'against piratical acts by submarines' with regard to attacks on merchant ships in the Mediterranean during the Spanish Civil War, in effect creating an early species of naval exclusion zone.[62] The acts were stated to be 'acts contrary to the most elementary dictates of humanity which should be justly treated as acts of piracy'. The word 'piracy', however, was used purely for rhetorical effect and nothing in the Convention dealt with individual criminal liability.

(E) OTHER EXCEPTIONS TO THE PRINCIPLE OF THE FREEDOM OF THE HIGH SEAS

(i) The right of approach in time of peace[63]

To maintain order on the high seas, it is necessary to provide for an approach by warships in order to verify the identity and nationality of ships. Such a right of approach

---

[57] Guilfoyle (2009) 36–7, citing Harvard Research in International Law: Draft Convention on Piracy, (1932) 26 *AJIL Supp* 739, 798.

[58] E.g. the activities of the NGO Greenpeace in relation to French nuclear testing in the South Pacific, and in more recent times, the tactics of the anti-whaling organization Sea Shepherd in relation to Japanese whaling in the Southern Ocean: Roeschke (2009) 20 *Villanova ELJ* 99.

[59] E.g. the Belgian Court of Cassation in *Castle John and Nederlandse Stichting Sirius v NV Mabeco & NV Parfin* (1986) 77 ILR 537, which held that a Greenpeace vessel which attacked an allegedly polluting Dutch ship committed an act of piracy as the act in question was not political in character, 'but in support of a political point of view'. Further: Guilfoyle (2009) 36–7; Geiß & Petrig, *Piracy and Armed Robbery at Sea* (2010) 61; Klein, *Maritime Security and the Law of the Sea* (2011) 119.

[60] 2 Oppenheim, 750.

[61] 14 September 1937, 181 LNTS 137.

[62] Guilfoyle (2009) 37.

[63] 2 Oppenheim, 736–7; 1 Gidel (1932) 299; Colombos, *The International Law of the Sea* (6th edn, 1967) 311; François, First Report, ILC *Ybk* 1950/II, 41; Second Report, ILC *Ybk* 1951/II, 81; 2 O'Connell (1984) 802–3. Further: *United States v Postal*, 589 F.2d 862 (5th Cir, 1979); *United States v Monroy*, 614 F.2d 61 (5th Cir, 1980).

(*droit d'approche; enquéte ou vérification du pavillon; reconnaissance*) is recognized by customary law, though it is not mentioned expressly in UNCLOS Part VII. The right of approach exists in all circumstances, but does not extend to the actual examination of papers or seizure of the vessel.

(ii) Visit, search, and seizure in time of peace[64]

There is no general power of police exercisable over foreign merchant ships on the high seas, and the occasions on which ships can be visited and seized by warships in time of peace are limited.[65] Early British and American jurisprudence refused to admit a right of visit in the case of ships suspected of taking part in the slave-trade,[66] and, apart from piracy, the right could only exist on the basis of treaty or if a ship refused to show its flag.

The legal regime of high-seas freedom has met with a number of threats. Apart from attempts to extend the concept of piracy, claims to a right of self-defence on the high seas constitute another source of instability. A further source of confusion lies in the definition of the right of approach or verification of flag. It was realized that the right of visit could be abused and that there must be reasonable ground for suspicion, for example a refusal by a ship to hoist a flag.[67]

This has been codified in UNCLOS Article 110,[68] which provides as follows:

1. Except where acts of interference derive from powers conferred by treaty, a warship which encounters on the high seas a foreign ship, other than a ship entitled to complete immunity in accordance with articles 95 and 96, is not justified in boarding it unless there is a reasonable ground for suspecting that:

   (a) the ship is engaged in piracy;

   (b) the ship is engaged in the slave trade;

   (c) the ship is engaged in unauthorized broadcasting, and the flag state of the warship has jurisdiction under article 109;

   (d) the ship is without nationality;

   (e) though flying a foreign flag or refusing to show its flag, the ship is, in reality, of the same nationality as the warship.

---

[64] Generally: Guilfoyle (2009); Churchill & Lowe (3rd edn, 1999) 208–20; McNair, 1 *Opinions* 229–45; Colombos (6th edn, 1967) 310–14; 1 Gidel (1932) 288–300; McDougal & Burke (1962) 885–93; 2 O'Connell (1984) 757, 801–8, 1114–15. Also: *United States v Cadena*, 585 F.2d 1252 (5th Cir, 1978).

[65] McNair, 1 *Opinions* 233. For the contemporaneous US position, see 2 Hackworth 659–65; Moore, 2 *Digest* 987–1001.

[66] Cf the decisions of Lord Stowell in *Le Louis* (1817) 2 Dods 210; and the US Supreme Court in *Antelope* (1825) 10 Wheaton 66. Further: Moore, 2 *Digest* 914–18.

[67] E.g Hall (8th edn, 1924) 317–18 ('when weighty reasons exist for suspecting'); 1 Gidel (1932) 299; McNair, 1 *Opinions* 233, 240 ('vehement suspicion of Piracy'); François, ILC *Ybk* 1951/II, 81–3; Colombos (6th edn, 1967) 312–13; Churchill & Lowe (3rd edn, 1999) 210.

[68] Itself a descendent of GCHS, Art 22(1). UNCLOS, Art 110, however, provides for the right of visit in cases of unauthorized broadcast and statelessness, though the latter arguably already existed as a matter of custom: *Molvan v AG for Palestine* [1948] AC 351, 369.

The modalities of the exercise of jurisdiction over foreign ships on the high seas are spelt out in Article 110(2) to (5).

Despite the broad range of circumstances in which a warship may exercise the right of *visit* on the high seas, UNCLOS appears to limit the circumstances in which *seizure* may occur, expressly providing for such a right only with respect to pirate ships under Article 105 and ships engaged in unauthorized broadcasting under Article 109(4). A right of search and seizure with respect to the slave trade operates under a separate *sui generis* set of treaty obligations.[69] In an even more restrictive vein, UNCLOS Article 108(1) provides that states must co-operate in the suppression of the trafficking of narcotics and illicit drugs on the high seas, but does not expressly provide a right of seizure, or even a right of visit.

The matter is most complicated when considering stateless vessels. Article 110(1)(d) provides a right of visit but is silent on seizure. Guilfoyle identifies two schools of practice.[70] The first, adopted by the US and in certain circumstances the UK, is that a stateless vessel enjoys the protection of no state, and as such may be subject to the jurisdiction of any.[71] The second is that some further jurisdictional nexus is required to convert a right of visit into a right of seizure, a position more consistent with existing treaty practice.

The act of boarding, even when 'reasonable ground' for boarding exists, is a privilege, and under UNCLOS Article 107, if no act justifying the suspicions has been committed by the ship boarded, there is strict liability, and the flag state of the warship must compensate for 'any loss or damage'.[72] In its commentary the ILC stated that the severe penalty 'seems justified in order to prevent the right of visit being abused'.[73]

(iii) The right of self-defence

The claim to visit and seize vessels on the high seas may take the form of a 'security zone', a 'defence zone', or a 'neutrality zone'; the legality of these zones has been considered in chapter 11. Quite apart from claims to contiguous and other zones, however, some states have asserted a right to detain vessels on the ground of security or self-defence.[74] Nevertheless the legal basis of such a right, in the absence of an attack on other shipping by the vessel sought to be detained, is lacking. In the present context

---

[69] On maritime aspects of the slave trade: Guilfoyle (2009) 75–7.

[70] Ibid, 17–18. Also: McDougal & Burke (1966) 767, 881ff.

[71] *United States v Cortes*, 588 F.2d 106, 110 (5th Cir, 1979); *United States v Marino-Garcia*, 679 F.2d 1373, 1383 (11th Cir, 1982). Also: *Molvan v AG for Palestine* [1948] AC 351, 369.

[72] Cf *Marianna Flora* (1826) 11 Wheaton 1; Moore, 2 *Digest* 886.

[73] ILC *Ybk* 1956/II, 284.

[74] E.g. Hall (8th edn, 1924) 328; Colombos (6th edn, 1967) 314–15. Also: ILC *Ybk* 1950/II, 61; *United States v F/V Taiyo Maru*, 395 F.Supp 413 (D Me, 1975); *United States v Gonzales*, 776 F.2d 931 (11th Cir, 1985) (purporting to enable the extension of the contiguous zone for security reasons). Further Churchill & Lowe (3rd edn, 1999) 216–18. Generally on the use of force under this title: Brownlie, *Use of Force* (1963) 305–8. Also: chapter 33.

it is significant that the ILC, and the majority of states, do not accept the legality of security zones and that states are unlikely to regard an ambulatory exercise of a right of (anticipatory) self-defence with any favour.[75] Similarly, UNCLOS Part VII contains no express right of self-defence.

(iv) Blockade and contraband

In time of war the exercise of belligerent rights will be justified and may take the form of a blockade of the enemy's ports and coast. Enforcement may take place on the high seas adjoining the coast, and neutral merchant ships may be confiscated if they attempt to break the blockade. The right of visit, search, and capture may be exercised against neutral ships or aircraft carrying contraband or engaged in acts of non-neutral service.[76] Self-evidently, a blockade which is illegal under international law will not support a right of visit, search, and capture. A controversial example of the right of visit, search, and capture in order to preserve the integrity of a blockade occurred in relation to the *Mavi Marmara*,[77] a passenger vessel carrying humanitarian aid and construction materials which attempted to breach the Israeli–Egyptian blockade of the Gaza Strip in May 2010. The matter was complicated in that Hamas, the target of the blockade, was a non-state actor and the blockade was in aid of a non-international armed conflict.[78] Whilst still on the high seas, the flotilla was intercepted by the Israeli Navy, and boarded by Israeli commandos, resulting in the deaths of nine civilians and injury to several dozen more. Several Israeli soldiers were also injured. An investigation by a UN Human Rights Commission fact-finding mission concluded that as the blockade itself was illegal under international law due to the humanitarian crisis that had developed in Gaza, so too was Israel's visit, search, and capture of the *Mavi Marmara*[79] and that, even if the blockade could be considered legal, the disproportionate force exercised by Israeli forces rendered its exercise of the right unlawful.[80] In contrast, the Palmer Report, commissioned by the United Nations Secretary-General, concluded that the blockade was lawful but the use of force excessive.[81]

---

[75] ILC *Ybk* 1956/II, 284. Also the Secretariat Memorandum, ILC *Ybk* 1950/II, 71.

[76] ICRC, *San Remo Manual on International Law Applicable to Armed Conflicts at Sea* (1994) §§67–71 (purporting to codify custom).

[77] Generally: Guilfoyle (2010) 81 *BY* 9.

[78] Limited precedents include the Confederate States of America during the US Civil War: Guilfoyle (2010) 81 *BY* 9, 21.

[79] A/HRC/15/21, 27 September 2010, §261. Also: Guilfoyle (2010) 81 *BY* 9.

[80] A/HRC/15/21, 27 September 2010, §264.

[81] Report of the Secretary-General's Panel of Inquiry on the 31 May 2010 Flotilla Incident, 3 September 2011, available at www.un.org/News/dh/infocus/middle_east/Gaza_Flotilla_Panel_Report.pdf. The Israeli inquiry, The Public Commission to Examine the Maritime Incident of 30 May 2010, 23 January 2011, available at www.turkel-committee.gov.il/files/wordocs/8808report-eng.pdf exonerated Israeli forces entirely.

(v) The right of hot pursuit[82]

Although a state may not, with certain exceptions, enforce its laws on the high seas, it may continue on the high seas a pursuit validly commenced in the territorial sea or contiguous zone (or by extension the EEZ) and if it apprehends the suspect vessel, may arrest it on the high seas. The right of hot pursuit, and its rationale, was expressed by Hall as follows:

The reason for the permission seems to be that pursuit under these circumstances is a continuation of an act of jurisdiction which has been begun, or which but for the accident of immediate escape would have been begun, within the territory itself, and that it is necessary to permit it in order to enable the territorial jurisdiction to be efficiently exercised.[83]

This statement remains a neat encapsulation of the concept, despite its considerable geographical extension beyond the territorial sea.

In its present form hot pursuit had appeared in Anglo-American practice in the first half of the nineteenth century, but it was not until the Hague Codification Conference of 1930 that there was sufficient evidence of general recognition by states. This provided the basis for the draft article adopted by the ILC,[84] which, with some amendment, became GCHS Article 23, now UNCLOS Article 111(1).[85] Hot pursuit may be undertaken when the authorities of the coastal state have good reason to believe that a foreign ship has violated applicable laws and regulations of that state. Such pursuit must be commenced when the ship or one of its boats is within the internal waters, the archipelagic waters, the territorial sea or the contiguous zone of the pursuing state and may only be continued outside that zone if the pursuit has not been interrupted.

Article 111(2) applies the right of hot pursuit *mutatis mutandis* to violations of the laws of the territorial state in the EEZ or the continental shelf, including safety zones around continental shelf installations. Under Article 111(3) the right of hot pursuit is exhausted as soon as the ship pursued enters the territorial waters of another state, whether or not the flag state. Article 111(4) stipulates the conditions under which hot pursuit may commence, requiring the pursuing ship to confirm that the pursued ship—or any craft using the pursued ship as a mother ship—is within its territorial waters, contiguous zone or EEZ before giving chase. It further requires that a visual or auditory signal to stop (the proverbial 'shot across the bow') is given prior to commencing pursuit.[86] Under Article 111(5) only military or clearly identifiable government ships or aircraft are capable of giving hot pursuit. Under Article 111(8), if it turns out

---

[82] McDougal & Burke (1962) 893–923; 2 Hackworth, 700–9; François, First Report, ILC *Ybk* 1950/II, 43–5; Second Report, ILC *Ybk* 1951/II, 89–91; Bowett, *Self-Defence in International Law* (1958) 82–6; McNair, 1 *Opinions* 253–5; 2 O'Connell (1984) 1075–93; Gilmore (1995) 44 *ICLQ* 949. The question of hot pursuit was among the issues raised by *I'm Alone* (1935) 3 RIAA 1609. Also: Fitzmaurice (1936) 17 *BY* 82. Irregularities in hot pursuit do not affect ITLOS's prompt release jurisdiction: *The Volga (Russia v Australia) (Prompt Release)* (2002) 126 ILR 433 (failure to warn within 200nm).

[83] Hall, *International Law* (1st edn, 1880) 309.

[84] ILC *Ybk* 1956/II, 284–5.

[85] Itself derived from GCHS, Art 23.

[86] There is a historical controversy as to whether a signal by radio meets this criterion: Klein (2011) 110; cf ILC *Ybk* 1956/II, 285.

that the right of hot pursuit has been exercised mistakenly, the ship and its owners must be compensated for loss or damage which may have resulted.

(F) RESTRICTIONS BY TREATY

Treaties conferring powers of visit and capture beyond those permitted by customary law relate to a variety of subject-matter. Great Britain was a party to numerous bilateral treaties after 1815 concerning repression of the slave-trade; in 1841 the Treaty of London[87] provided that warships with special warrants could search, detain, or send for trial suspected merchant ships flying the flags of contracting states. The General Act for the Repression of the Slave Trade of 1890 provided for a limited right of search of suspected vessels in a defined zone.[88] The General Act was in major part abrogated as between parties to the Treaty of St Germain-en-Laye,[89] and the Slavery Conventions of 1926[90] and 1956[91] do not provide for visit, search, and seizure: a right of visit is provided for, however, in GCHS Article 23 and UNCLOS Article 110. Mutual powers of visit and search are conferred by bilateral treaties the parties to which are concerned to conserve fish stocks, to control smuggling, or to repress certain aspects of the trade in arms.[92]

The Convention for the Protection of Submarine Cables of 1884, Article 10, confers the right to stop and verify the nationality of merchant ships suspected of breach of the treaty.[93] GCHS Articles 26 to 29 do not refer to such a right, but it was not intended to supersede the Convention of 1884; the same is true of UNCLOS Article 311(2). States have also been willing to agree by treaty on the mutual exercise of hot pursuit.[94]

3. JURISDICTION OVER SHIPS ON THE HIGH SEAS

(A) THE DECISION IN THE *LOTUS*

UNCLOS affirms the general principle enunciated by the Permanent Court in the *Lotus*:

Vessels on the high seas are subject to no authority except that of the State whose flag they fly. In virtue of the principle of the freedom of the seas, that is to say, the absence of any

---

[87] 20 December 1841, 92 CTS 437 (Austria, Great Britain, Prussia, and Russia. Belgium acceded. France signed but did not ratify).

[88] 2 July 1890, 173 CTS 293.

[89] Treaty between the Allied and Associated Powers and the Kingdom of the Serbs, Croats and Slovenes, 10 September 1919, 226 CTS 186.

[90] Convention to Suppress the Slave Trade and Slavery, 25 September 1926, 60 LNTS 254.

[91] Supplementary Convention on the Abolition of Slavery, the Slave Trade, and Institutions and Practices Similar to Slavery, 7 September 1956, 226 UNTS 3.

[92] Guilfoyle (2009) chs 6, 9.

[93] 14 March 1884, 163 CTS 391. Also: McDougal & Burke (1962) 843; 4 Whiteman 727–39.

[94] E.g. Niue Treaty on Cooperation in Fisheries Surveillance and Law Enforcement in the South Pacific Region, 9 July 1992, 32 ILM 136.

territorial sovereignty upon the high seas, no State may exercise any kind of jurisdiction over foreign vessels upon them.[95]

Thus UNCLOS Article 92(1) provides that '[s]hips shall sail under the flag of one State only and, save in exceptional cases expressly provided for in international treaties or in these articles, shall be subject to its exclusive jurisdiction on the high seas'.[96] Article 97(1) provides:

In the event of a collision or of any other incident of navigation concerning a ship on the high seas, involving the penal or disciplinary responsibility of the master or of any other person in the service of the ship, no penal or disciplinary proceedings may be instituted against such persons except before the judicial or administrative authorities either of the flag State or of the State of which such person is a national.

This provision negatives the decision in the Lotus that there could be concurrent penal jurisdiction in respect of collisions on the high seas. In its commentary on the relevant draft article, the ILC commented:

This judgement, which was carried by the President's casting vote after an equal vote of six to six, was very strongly criticized and caused serious disquiet in international maritime circles. A diplomatic conference held at Brussels in 1952 disagreed with the conclusions of the judgement. The Commission concurred ... It did so with the object of protecting ships and their crews from the risk of penal proceedings before foreign courts in the event of collision on the high seas, since such proceedings may constitute an intolerable interference with international navigation.[97]

(B) JURISDICTION OVER OIL POLLUTION CASUALTIES

States may claim special zones of jurisdiction over areas of high seas adjacent to their coasts in order to regulate activities of various kinds: the contiguous zone is an example. But new problems requiring regulation may arise. When the *Torrey Canyon*, registered in Liberia, ran aground off the Cornish coast in 1967 and lost some 60,000 tons of oil, the British government ordered that the wreck be bombed, after salvage attempts had failed. Even so, British and French coasts received serious pollution. Such remedial action may be justified on the ground of necessity (but not of self-defence).[98] This led to the conclusion of an International Convention Relating to Intervention on the High Seas in Cases of Oil Pollution Casualties.[99] The use of protective measures is now recognized by UNCLOS Article 221(1), which preserves the right of states 'to

---

[95] (1927) PCIJ Ser A No 10, 25.

[96] Also: GCHS, Art 6(1).

[97] ILC *Ybk* 1956/II, 281, citing the International Convention for the Unification of Certain Rules relating to Penal Jurisdiction in matters of Collisions and Other Incidents of Navigation, 10 May 1952, 439 UNTS 233.

[98] Brown (1968) 21 *CLP* 113; Queneudec (1968) *AFDI* 701; Caflisch (1972) 8 *RBDI* 7; 2 O'Connell (1984) 997–1012; Churchill & Lowe (3rd edn, 1999) 328–96. On necessity as a defence: chapter 25.

[99] 29 November 1969, 970 UNTS 211.

take and enforce measures beyond the territorial sea proportionate to the actual or threatened damage to protect their coast line or related interests, including fishing, from pollution or threat of pollution following upon a maritime casualty ... which may reasonably be expected to result in major harmful consequences'.[100]

(c) UNAUTHORIZED BROADCASTING[101]

The Council of Europe sponsored the conclusion in 1965 of an Agreement for the Prevention of Broadcasts Transmitted from Stations outside National Territories.[102] The Convention focuses on acts supporting 'pirate' broadcasting committed within the national jurisdiction of states parties and does not authorize interference with foreign ships, aircraft, or nationals. By contrast UNCLOS provides for broad bases of jurisdiction and powers of arrest in respect of 'the transmission of sound radio or television broadcasts from a ship or installation on the high seas intended for reception by the general public contrary to international regulations, but excluding the transmission of distress calls' (Articles 109 to 110).[103]

(d) DRUG INTERDICTION

In respect of certain varieties of transnational crime, sui generis treaty regimes provide states with high-seas boarding rights.[104] One of these is the interdiction of drug traffickers.[105] Whilst UNCLOS Article 27(1)(d) provides a coastal state with jurisdiction over a foreign ship suspected of carrying illicit narcotics within its territorial sea, waiting for drug runners to enter the territorial sea before exercising a right of arrest may not be practicable. Article 108(1) provides a minor exhortation to states to co-operate in suppressing the trafficking of illicit narcotics on the high seas. Article 108(2), however, provides only that any state 'with reasonable grounds for believing' that a vessel sailing under *its own* flag is engaged in the trafficking of illicit narcotics 'may request' the co-operation of other states, leaving unaddressed the (much more likely) situation in which a state suspects a ship sailing under the flag of *another* state to be carrying such substances.[106]

---

[100] Generally: Boyle (1985) 79 *AJIL* 347; Brubacker, *Marine Pollution and International Law* (1993); Churchill & Lowe (3rd edn, 1999) ch 15. In protection of the marine environment: chapter 15.

[101] On 'pirate' radio: François (1965) 12 *NILR* 113; Bos (1965) 12 *NILR* 337; Woodliffe (1965) 12 *NILR* 365; 2 O'Connell (1984) 814–19; Guilfoyle (2009) 170–9.

[102] 2 January 1965, 4 ILM 115.

[103] UNCLOS, Article 109 introduces to the high seas regime the offence of unauthorized broadcasting from the high seas, and grants the capacity to arrest, seize, and prosecute to states affected. Further *Post Office v Estuary Radio Ltd* [1968] 2 QB 740 (CA). With the end of state monopolies on broadcasting the problem of commercial 'pirate' radio stations has not recurred.

[104] Churchill & Lowe (3rd edn, 1999) 218–19.

[105] Generally: Guilfoyle (2009) ch 5.

[106] Gilmore (1991) 15 *Mar Policy* 183, 185.

In this respect UNCLOS is supplemented by the UN Convention Against Illicit Traffic in Narcotic Drugs and Psychotropic Substances (Narcotics Convention).[107] Article 17(1) requires states parties to co-operate to the fullest extent possible to suppress the carriage of drugs by sea, in conformity with the law of the sea.[108] Article 17(2) and (3) provides that a party with 'reasonable grounds' to suspect that a vessel flying the flag of another party and 'exercising freedom of navigation' may request 'confirmation of registry and…authorization to take appropriate measures'.[109] If consent is granted, Article 17(4) provides that the flag state may authorize the inquiring state to board and search the vessel and take appropriate action.[110] The inclusion of the words 'exercising freedom of navigation' in Article 17(3) arguably encompasses all vessels outside territorial waters, including in the EEZ.[111]

(E) MIGRANT SMUGGLING

Migrant smuggling is the unlawful movement of persons with a view to evading immigration control;[112] it frequently involves maritime transport often in hazardous conditions. As defined by the Migrant Smuggling Protocol, it involves the procurement of a person's entry into a state 'of which the person is not a national or permanent resident' for personal gain without complying with municipal migration laws.[113]

The Migrant Smuggling Protocol principally provides for the criminalization of the movement of persons across international borders (Articles 3 and 6), but also includes high seas interdiction provisions based on Article 17 of the Narcotics Convention. Article 7 of the Protocol provides that 'States Parties shall cooperate to the fullest extent possible to prevent and suppress the smuggling of migrants by sea, in accordance with the international law of the sea'. Article 8(2) permits a state party with a reasonable suspicion that a ship flying the flag of another state party is smuggling migrants to request the permission of the flag state to take appropriate measures, in response to which the flag state may authorize boarding, search or seizure as it sees fit.[114] Article 8(5) expressly preserves the jurisdiction of the flag state. Where the

---

[107] 20 December 1988, 1582 UNTS 95. Further Guilfoyle (2009) 83–5.

[108] E.g. Agreement to facilitate the interdiction by the United States of vessels of the United Kingdom suspected of trafficking in drugs, 13 November 1981, 1285 UNTS 197; Treaty between the Kingdom of Spain and the Italian Republic to Combat Illicit Drug Trafficking at Sea, 23 March 1990, 1776 UNTS 229; Agreement on Illicit Traffic by Sea implementing Article 17 of the United Nations Convention against Illicit Traffic in Narcotic Drugs and Psychotropic Substances, 3 January 1995, ETS 156. Further Siddle (1982) 31 *ICLQ* 726; Gilmore (1989) 13 *Mar Policy* 218; Gilmore (1996) 20 *Mar Policy* 3.

[109] UN Narcotics Convention, 28th meeting, E/CONF.82/C.2/SR.28, §7.

[110] The discursive nature of this list implies that the flag state may decide exactly how far the inquiring state may exercise its enforcement jurisdiction. Flag states may therefore reserve their position on seizure until evidence of illicit narcotics is discovered; Gilmore (1991) 15 *Mar Policy* 183, 190; Guilfoyle (2009) 83–5. Also: UN Narcotics Convention, 29th meeting, E/CONF.82/C.2/SR.29, §§8, 108, 123–4.

[111] Guilfoyle (2009) 83–4; cf Gualde (1996) 4 *Sp YIL* 91, 95.

[112] Generally: Guilfoyle (2009) 182–226.

[113] Protocol against the Smuggling of Migrants by Land, Sea and Air, Supplementing the United Nations Convention against Transnational Organized Crime, GA Res 55/25 (Annex III), 15 November 2000, Arts 3, 6.

[114] Narcotics Convention, Art 17(4).

vessel in question appears stateless, Article 8(7) allows the interdicting state to board and search the vessel if there are reasonable grounds to suspect that it is engaged in migrant smuggling. If evidence confirming the suspicion is found, the interdicting state may take appropriate measures in accordance with relevant international and municipal law. This perpetuates the ambiguity regarding the exercise of prescriptive and enforcement jurisdiction over stateless vessels.[115]

Unlike the Narcotics Convention, however, the Protocol does not expressly permit the interdicting state to exercise prescriptive jurisdiction over an intercepted vessel. The jurisdiction of the flag state will prevail unless it permits the interdicting state to prosecute.[116]

(F) HUMAN TRAFFICKING

The modern equivalent of slavery, human trafficking involves the recruitment and transportation of persons by coercive means for the purpose of exploitation, including sexual exploitation, forced labour, and 'slavery or practices similar to slavery'.[117] The Human Trafficking Protocol does not provide for the interdiction of ships engaged in human trafficking on the high seas, due principally to the fact that those trafficked are seldom moved in large groups or by sea.[118] There is, however, an overlap between migrant smuggling and human trafficking in the sense that someone may agree to be smuggled by sea, only to be exploited when they reach their destination. This would arguably provide a nexus for interdiction under the Migrant Trafficking Protocol, Article 8.[119]

(G) SUPPRESSION OF TERRORISM AND THE MARITIME TRANSPORT OF WEAPONS[120]

Another *sui generis* regime relating to the suppression of terrorist activities against ships (and latterly, the suppression of the maritime transport of chemical, biological, and nuclear weapons) is the object of the Convention for the Suppression of Unlawful Acts against the Safety of Maritime Navigation (SUA Convention) adopted on 10 March 1988 at a diplomatic conference convened by IMO[121] and later amended by way of a Protocol concluded in 2005 (SUA Protocol).[122]

---

[115] UNCLOS, Art 110(1)(d); Narcotics Convention, Art 17(2). Further Guilfoyle (2009) 185.

[116] Guilfoyle (2009) 186.

[117] Protocol to Prevent, Suppress and Punish Trafficking in Persons, Especially Women and Children, supplementing the United Nations Convention against Transnational Organized Crime, GA Res 55/25, Annex II, 15 November 2000.

[118] Obokata (2005) 54 *ICLQ* 445, 448; Guilfoyle (2009) 227.

[119] Guilfoyle (2009) 227–8. If a person is being trafficked into outright slavery, a right of visit and search would arise under UNCLOS, Art 110(1)(b).

[120] (2004) 98 *AJIL* 526; Guilfoyle (2007) 12 *JCSL* 1; Guilfoyle (2009) ch 9.

[121] 10 March 1988, 1678 UNTS 221. Further Ronzitti (ed), *Maritime Terrorism and International Law* (1990); Halberstam (1988) 82 *AJIL* 269; Tuerk (2008) 15 *U Miami ICLR* 337.

[122] Protocol to the Convention for the Suppression of Unlawful Acts against the Safety of Maritime Navigation, 14 October 2005, IMO Doc LEG/CONF.15/21.

Drafted in the wake of the *Achille Lauro* affair,[123] the SUA Convention is one of the 13 'sectoral' agreements concluded once it became apparent that agreement on a comprehensive and general definition of terrorism was not in prospect. Article 3 defines an offence of ship hijacking, for example unlawfully 'seizing or exercising control over a ship by force or threat thereof or any other form of intimidation' and cognate acts. The scope of the SUA Convention was altered by the SUA Protocol, which was directed not at maritime terrorism but at enhancing the Treaty on the Non-Proliferation of Nuclear Weapons.[124] On its entry into force in 2010, the SUA Protocol became the first international instrument creating a crime of transporting biological, chemical or nuclear weapons (BCN weapons) by sea: it also provides for high seas interdictions. It had its origins in the 'Proliferation Security Initiative' (PSI), a US project,[125] though its inspiration was arguably UN Security Council Resolution 1540, the second attempt by the Security Council to create 'international legislation' by using Chapter VII of the UN Charter: it obliged states to take measures against trade in such weapons and their precursors.[126] Article 3*bis*(1) creates an offence of intentionally using a ship as part of an action 'likely to cause death or serious injury' when the purpose of that act 'by its nature or context, is to intimidate a population, or compel a government or international organization to do or abstain from doing any act', irrespective of whether that action involves the carriage of a BCN weapon. The high seas interdiction regime of the SUA Convention is contained in Article 8*bis*. It provides for an interdicting state to request from the flag state authorization to board and search the vessel. The flag state is under no obligation to accede to the request (thus replicating the weakness seen in Article 17 of the Narcotics Convention).[127]

4. REGIMES OF TRANSIT TO AND FROM THE HIGH SEAS

A vital aspect of the law of the sea in general, and UNCLOS in particular, is its articulation of the various maritime transit regimes. The scope of transit rights depends on the zones in question.

---

[123] In 1985 the *Achille Lauro* was hijacked by members of the Palestinian Liberation Front (PLF) while still in port: Halberstam (1988) 82 *AJIL* 269; Guilfoyle (2009) 32–42.

[124] Treaty on the Non-Proliferation of Nuclear Weapons, 1 July 1968, 729 UNTS 161.

[125] Murphy (2004) 98 *AJIL* 349, 355–7. A complete list of PSI bilateral treaties can be found at www.state.gov/t/isn/trty/index.htm. Further Guilfoyle (2005) 29 *Melb ULR* 733, Guilfoyle (2009) 246–54.

[126] The first such resolution was SC Res 1373 (2001). Generally: Talmon (2005) 99 *AJIL* 175; Bianchi (2006) 17 *EJIL* 881; Hinojosa-Martinez (2008) 57 *ICLQ* 333.

[127] SUA Convention, Arts 8*bis*(4), 8*bis*(5) reflect UNCLOS, Art 108(2) and Narcotics Convention, Art 17 in relation to the interdiction of drug shipments on the high seas.

(A) INNOCENT PASSAGE[128]

Customary law recognizes the right of innocent passage through the territorial sea, reflected in UNCLOS Article 17. Article 8 preserves the right of innocent passage in internal waters previously considered part of the territorial sea or high seas where enclosed by straight baselines. These provisions were based on GCTS Articles 14 and 15.

Historically the right of innocent passage evolved at a time when special zones of jurisdiction were not clearly distinguished from zones of sovereignty: the maritime belt was considered to be the high seas but with restrictions in favour of the coastal state. As a question of policy innocent passage is a sensible accommodation between the necessities of sea communication and the interests of the coastal state.

The definition of innocent passage was previously a matter of some difficulty. But the basic rule of innocent passage is now clear; it is elaborated upon in UNCLOS Articles 18 and 19. Article 18(1) lists the purposes for which innocent passage may be exercised: these do not include coastal trade (*cabotage*) or fishing. Under Article 18(2), passage must be 'continuous and expeditious'. Article 19(1) provides that passage shall be considered innocent 'so long as it is not prejudicial to the peace, good order or security of the coastal State'. Article 20 provides that '[i]n the territorial sea, submarines and other underwater vehicles are required to navigate on the surface and to show their flag'.

Whilst Article 19 is phrased in terms of the 'peace, good order and security' of the coastal state, the list in Article 19(2) makes mention of several acts which can be considered as causing solely economic prejudice to the coastal state, notably fishing.[129] Indeed, Article 19(2)(l) provides that any activity not having a direct bearing on passage will be considered prejudicial to the coastal state's interests.

Under UNCLOS Article 25(1) the coastal state may take the necessary steps in its territorial sea to prevent passage which is not innocent. Vessels exercising the right of passage are subject to local laws and regulations, providing these conform with international law and treaty obligations (Articles 21, 22, and 25(2)). Article 25(3) confers on the coastal state a right to suspend innocent passage *temporarily* in specified areas of the territorial sea if such suspension 'is essential for the protection of its security'. Article 26 provides that no charge may be levied on foreign vessels by reason only of their passage, but only for specific services rendered to the ship.

UNCLOS Article 30 contains a special regime applicable to warships and other government ships operated for non-commercial purposes. It excludes enforcement

---

[128] 3 Gidel (1934) 193–291; 4 Whiteman 343–417; François, ILC *Ybk* 1952/II(2), 38; Fitzmaurice (1959) 8 *ICLQ* 73, 90–108; McDougal & Burke (1962) 174–269; 1 O'Connell (1982) 260–98; Lucchini & Voelckel, 2 *Droit de la mer* (1996) 202–303.

[129] Fishing vessels are capable of undertaking passage, though any unauthorized act of fishing actually occurring in the territorial waters of the coastal state will render passage prejudicial to the interests of the coastal state and hence not innocent.

against warships, which in case of non-compliance with the regulations of the coastal state can only be required to leave the territorial sea.[130]

(B) CRIMINAL JURISDICTION DURING INNOCENT PASSAGE

Although the coastal state has both prescriptive and enforcement jurisdiction over its territorial sea, this jurisdiction does not extend to foreign ships exercising a right of innocent passage unless certain conditions are met. In relation to criminal matters, UNCLOS Article 27(1) provides that jurisdiction over a foreign ship passing innocently through the coastal state's territorial waters can only be exercised if: (a) the consequences of the crime extend to the host state; (b) the crime is of such a nature as to disturb the peace of the coastal state or the good order of its territorial sea; (c) the assistance of the coastal state has been requested by the master of the foreign ship or a diplomatic or consular official of its flag state; or (d) such measures are necessary for the suppression of illicit traffic in narcotic drugs or other psychotropic substances.[131] Where the foreign ship has entered the territorial sea from the coastal state's internal waters, the coastal state does not lose its right to arrest the foreign ship, provided the flag state is notified.[132]

UNCLOS Article 28(1) provides that the coastal state should not stop or divert a foreign ship passing through the territorial sea for the purpose of exercising its civil jurisdiction in relation to a person on board. Likewise, Article 28(2) provides that the coastal state may not levy execution against or arrest the foreign ship for the pursuit of any civil proceedings,[133] save only in respect of liabilities incurred by the ship during such passage. But if the foreign ship is passing through the territorial sea after leaving internal waters or has dropped anchor in the territorial sea in a manner inconsistent with innocent passage,[134] jurisdiction may be exercised under Article 28(3).

---

[130] Harvard Research (1929) 23 *AJIL Sp Supp* 295–6; 3 Gidel (1934) 227–89; Jessup (1959) 59 *Col LR* 234, 247–9; François, ILC *Ybk* 1952/II, 42–3; UN Legislative Series, *Laws and Regulations on the Regime of the Territorial Sea* (1957) 361–420; McDougal & Burke (1962) 192–4, 216–21; Oxman (1984) 24 *Va JIL* 809; Butler (1987) 81 *AJIL* 331; 1 O'Connell (1982) 274–98; Roach & Smith, *United States Responses to Excessive Maritime Claims* (2nd edn, 1996) 251–78; Hakapää, 'Innocent Passage' (2008) *MPEPIL*; Heintschel von Heinegg, 'Warships' (2009) *MPEPIL*; US–USSR, Uniform Interpretation of Rules of International Law Governing Innocent Passage, 23 September 1989, 28 ILM 1444, 1446. Also: *Corfu Channel*, ICJ Reports 1949 p 4, 28.

[131] The position may not be absolute. UNCLOS, Art 27(1) commences with the words 'should not', which were deliberately chosen to exhort restraint not impose absolute limitations: Shearer (1986) 35 *ICLQ* 320, 327; Churchill & Lowe (3rd edn, 1999) 95–8; Guilfoyle (2009) 11. Nonetheless, there is some state practice suggesting the provision is exhaustive: e.g. the US–USSR, Joint Statement on the Uniform Interpretation of Rules of International Law Governing Innocent Passage, 23 September 1989, 28 ILM 1444.

[132] UNCLOS, Arts 25(5), 27(2).

[133] E.g. by attempting to seize a ship in order to enforce an arbitral award where that ship is merely passing innocently through the enforcing state's territorial sea.

[134] That is, in situations other than where the ship is lying in the territorial sea in a manner incidental to ordinary navigation, by reason of *force majeure* or in order to respond to a distress signal: UNCLOS, Art 18(2).

As to foreign warships or government vessels operating for non-commercial purposes, UNCLOS Article 32 preserves their customary immunity. Such vessels must still comply with the rules applicable to all ships in exercising innocent passage but in the event of violation the most that the coastal state can do is require the offending vessel to depart its territorial sea under Article 30. In the event that the non-compliance of such a vessel results in any loss or damage to the coastal state, the flag state bears responsibility under Article 31.

(C) TRANSIT PASSAGE THROUGH INTERNATIONAL STRAITS[135]

Transit passage refers to the movement of a foreign vessel through international straits in order to access the high seas or the EEZ. UNCLOS Part III governs such movement. Article 37 provides that the section applies to 'straits which are used for international navigation between one part of the high seas or an [EEZ] and another part of the high seas or an [EEZ]'. Article 38(2) defines transit passage as 'the exercise in accordance with this Part of the freedom of navigation and overflight solely for the purpose of continuous and expeditious transit of the strait' and includes passage 'for the purpose of entering, leaving or returning from a State bordering the strait, subject to the conditions of entry to that State'.

The right of transit passage in the territorial sea is subject to fewer constraints than the right of innocent passage. But Articles 36 and 38(1) only apply where there is no 'route through the high seas or through an exclusive economic zone of similar convenience with respect to navigational and hydrographical characteristics'. UNCLOS also provides obligations specific to ships in transit passage in Article 39(2) and aircraft in Article 39(3).

(D) PASSAGE THROUGH THE EEZ

For the purposes of passage through the EEZ, UNCLOS treats the zone much the same as the high seas as a whole, a position consistent with custom.[136] Article 58 reserves the freedoms of navigation, overflight, and the laying of submarine cables in the EEZ, as well as the rights and obligations laid out in Articles 88 to 115. The conditions of passage with respect to the EEZ accordingly have less in common with passage through the territorial sea or international straits, and more in common with the more liberal high seas regime.

(E) ARCHIPELAGIC SEA LANES PASSAGE

UNCLOS Articles 52(1) and 53(2) provide for 'the right of archipelagic sea lanes passage in such sea lanes and air routes'. This type of passage is akin to transit passage

---

[135] Churchill & Lowe (3rd edn, 1999) ch 5; Rothwell & Stephens (2010) ch 11.
[136] *Nicaragua*, ICJ Reports 1986 p 14, 111–12.

in international straits. The right is not entirely uncontrolled, however: under Article 53(1) the archipelagic state may designate sea lanes and air routes suitable for the continuous and expeditious passage for foreign ships and aircraft through or over its archipelagic waters and territorial sea. Moreover, Article 52(2) allows the archipelagic state to suspend temporarily in its archipelagic waters the innocent passage of foreign ships if this is essential for the protection of its security.

(F) COMPULSORY PILOTAGE[137]

In certain situations, a coastal state may insist that a vessel passing through superjacent waters take on an approved pilot to navigate it through particularly treacherous waters or through significant and delicate ecosystems. Pilotage regimes must accord with the terms of UNCLOS, and recommendatory programmes will prima facie comply. Compulsory regimes are more controversial.

Under UNCLOS Article 21(1)(a) and (f), the coastal state may adopt laws and regulations relating to innocent passage through the territorial sea for various protective purposes: this includes, where necessary, the introduction of a compulsory pilotage regime.[138]

The imposition of compulsory pilotage through international straits is more controversial, and states have demonstrated their willingness to challenge compulsory pilotage with respect to transit passage, notably in relation to Australian and Papua New Guinean attempts to introduce a pilotage regime to the Torres Strait.[139] Charging for the cost of pilot services is not in contravention of UNCLOS and will not impair transit.[140]

5. REGULATION OF HIGH SEAS FISHERIES[141]

(A) HISTORICAL OVERVIEW

After freedom of navigation, the freedom to fish is arguably the fundamental historical freedom of the high seas. Fish were historically seen as an inexhaustible

---

[137] Generally: Kachel, *Particularly Sensitive Sea Areas* (2008) 202–4; Mahmoudi, 'Transit Passage' (2008) *MPEPIL*; Kaye, 'Torres Strait' (2009) *MPEPIL*; Hakapää, 'Innocent Passage' (2008) *MPEPIL*; Bateman & White (2009) 40 *ODIL* 184.

[138] E.g. the pilotage regime with regard to navigation through the Great Barrier Reef: Great Barrier Reef Marine Park Act 1975 (Cth) Part VIIA.

[139] The Australian and Papua New Guinean governments succeeded in gaining IMO support for a recommended pilotage regime for certain large vessels and oil and gas tankers: IMO Res A.619/13, 6 November 1991. The IMO further agreed to extend the Great Barrier Reef's PSSA designation to include the Torres Strait, but did not expressly provide for compulsory pilotage: IMO Res MEPC.133/53, 22 July 2005. Further Bateman & White (2009) 40 *ODIL* 184.

[140] 2 Nordquist (1995) 236.

[141] On fisheries: Burke, *The New International Law of Fisheries* (1994); Orrego Vicuña, *The Changing International Law of High Seas Fisheries* (1999); Churchill & Lowe (3rd edn, 1999) ch 14; Guilfoyle (2009) ch

resource,[142] an expectation which has been thoroughly debunked by the refinement of industrial fishing technology since the Second World War.[143]

The modern law of fisheries can be divided into two phases. The first is the period up to the mid-1970s, characterized by generally narrow coastal state maritime zones, with a large number of high seas fisheries regulated by international commissions. The second is the period since the mid-1970s, typified by the emergence of the EEZ. The EEZ embraced most commercially exploitable fish stocks, reducing somewhat the role of the international fisheries commissions. Their exclusion from coastal fisheries led distant water fishing states to focus on often remote and slow-breeding species (e.g. Patagonian toothfish). The result has been a progressive tragedy of the commons, redeemed by a few cases of successful coastal state or regional regulation (e.g. Norwegian spring spawning herring).

(B) FREEDOM OF FISHERIES AND ITS LIMITATIONS

The freedom of fishing on the high seas was well established in customary international law, though it did little more than to state the existence of the principle in a negative sense: states should not interfere with vessels fishing under another flag.[144] But while freedom of navigation has been relatively unabated since its Grotian formulation, the freedom to fish has been constrained in various ways in an attempt to promote the goals of conservation and orderly access.

UNCLOS Article 87(1)(e) establishes the freedom of fishing on the high seas, subject to the conditions laid down in UNCLOS Part VII, Section 2.[145] Article 116 provides that all states have the right for their nationals to engage in fishing on the high seas, subject to treaty obligations, the rights, duties, and interests of the coastal state. Article 63(2) concerns straddling stocks, that is, where the same or associated fish species occur within an EEZ and adjacent high seas areas. In such cases co-operation is mandated, either directly or through an appropriate fisheries organization.

The position under customary international law was at one time less clear. In the *Fisheries Jurisdiction* cases,[146] the Court was asked to determine the validity of Iceland's extension of its fishing limits from 12 to 50nm. It held that according to custom, a coastal state particularly dependent on fishing for its economic livelihood

---

6; Young (2011); Serdy (2011) 60 *ICLQ* 387. On the practice and ecology of fishing as a whole: Jennings, Kaiser & Reynolds, *Marine Fisheries Ecology* (2001).

[142] Grotius, *Mare Liberum* (1609, tr Hakluyt 2004) 25–30; Wolff, *Jus gentium methodo scientifica pertractatum* (1764, tr Drake 1934) 64; cf Vattel, *Le Droit des gens* (1758, tr Anon 1797) I.xxiii.§287.

[143] Roberts & Hawkins (1999) 14 *TEE* 241, 241; Caddy & Garibaldi (2000) 43 *OCM* 615, 649–50; Churchill & Lowe (3rd edn, 1999) 279–83.

[144] Orrego Vicuña (1999) 13.

[145] 29 April 1958, 559 UNTS 285. Art 1(1) contains the freedom to fish. Further Orrego Vicuña (1999) 18–21.

[146] *Fisheries Jurisdiction (FRG v Iceland)*, ICJ Reports 1974 p 175, 195; *(UK v Iceland)*, ICJ Reports 1974 p 4, 26.

enjoyed in certain circumstances preferential rights of access to high seas fisheries adjacent to its territorial sea. The judgment was criticized for the lack of evidence and general imprecision of the rule so identified.[147] No coastal state before or since the Court's judgment has attempted to rely on it to further its share of a high seas fishery, and the decision—transitional in terms—has been superseded by the introduction of the EEZ.

(i) The obligation of conservation and co-operation

The principal obligation of states as to high seas fisheries is that of conservation and co-operation. UNCLOS Article 117 requires parties to 'take, or to cooperate with other States in taking, such measures for their respective nationals as may be necessary for the conservation of the living resources of the high seas'. This is not only an obligation to regulate the behaviour of flag vessels; it arguably extends to *all nationals* irrespective of the flag they sail under.[148] This interpretation has been endorsed by the UN Food and Agriculture Organization (FAO).[149]

UNCLOS Article 118 establishes an obligation on the part of states parties to co-operate for the purpose of conserving and managing living resources on the high seas.[150] Articles 63 to 67 lay down further specific conservation and co-operation obligations in relation to straddling stocks, highly migratory species, marine mammals, and anadromous[151] and catadromous[152] species. Of particular significance are the provisions on straddling stocks and highly migratory species. Article 63(2) provides that any states with an interest in a straddling stock

shall seek, either directly or through appropriate subregional or regional organizations, to agree upon the measures necessary for the conservation of these stocks in the adjacent area.

As to highly migratory species, Article 64 provides that the coastal state and other states whose nationals fish in the region for such species 'shall co-operate directly or

---

[147] Churchill & Lowe (3rd edn, 1999) 285; Orrego Vicuña (1999) 15–17.

[148] Guilfoyle (2009) 101.

[149] FAO International Plan of Action to Prevent, Deter and Eliminate Illegal, Unreported and Unregulated Fishing, 23 June 2001, §18, available at www.fao.org/docrep/003/y1224e/y1224e00.htm.

[150] The Lacey Act, 16 USC §§3371–8, makes it a crime for US nationals to violate any applicable fisheries regulations anywhere, effectively co-opting other states' conservation measures adopted under UNCLOS. For prosecutions: *United States v Cameron*, 888 F.2d 1279 (9th Cir, 1989) (violating International Pacific Halibut Commission regulations); *Wood v Verity*, 729 F.Supp 1324 (SD Fla, 1989) (violating Bahamian EEZ regulations). Also: the forfeiture proceedings in *United States v 594,464 Pounds of Salmon, More or Less*, 687 F.Supp 525 (WD Wash, 1987) (violation of Taiwanese Salmon regulations); *United States v Proceeds from Approximately 15,538 Panulirus Argus Lobster Tails*, 834 F.Supp 385 (SD Fla, 1993) (Turks and Caicos Islands fishing restrictions); *United States v 144,774 Pounds of Blue King Crab*, 410 F.3d 1131 (9th Cir, 2005) (Russian Federation fishing and resource protection laws).

[151] Species of fish which migrate from salt to fresh water to breed, such as the various species of Pacific salmon: UNCLOS, Art 66.

[152] Species of fish which migrate from fresh to salt water to breed, such as the freshwater eels of the genus *Anguilla*: UNCLOS, Art 67.

through appropriate international organisations with a view to ensuring conservation and promoting the objective of optimum utilization of such species throughout the region'.

Obligations of co-operation and conservation are insufficient. High seas fisheries can only be managed appropriately through international cooperation, for example through the creation of regional or species-specific agencies. However, except for highly migratory species (Article 64), states parties are under no obligation in this regard; UNCLOS either presents the creation of regional bodies as an alternative to direct negotiation, as in the case of straddling stocks (Article 63), or qualifies the obligation with considerations of 'appropriateness', as seen more generally in Article 118.

(ii) Regional fisheries management organizations

Despite these somewhat weak obligations of co-operation, numerous regional fisheries management organizations (RFMOs) have been created.[153] As their name implies, RFMOs co-operate in managing high seas fisheries for certain stocks in a defined area, principally through the prescription of management and conservation measures. There are common responsibilities such as the collection and distribution of fisheries statistics,[154] the evaluation and management of fish stocks within their jurisdiction,[155] the determination and allocation of the total allowable catch (TAC),[156] the regulation of equipment,[157] and the oversight of scientific research. RMFO agreements frequently contain dispute resolution provisions or provide for a compliance committee.[158]

(iii) Straddling and highly migratory stocks

The creation of credible RFMOs has been aided by the development of the Straddling Stocks Agreement,[159] which reflects considerable effort to create a comprehensive

---

[153] E.g. Convention on the Conservation and Management of Fishery Resources in the South East Atlantic Ocean, 20 April 2001, 41 ILM 257 (2002) (SEAFOC); Convention on the Conservation of Antarctic Marine Living Resources, 20 May 1980, 19 ILM 841 (1982) (CCAMLR); Convention for the Conservation of Southern Bluefin Tuna, 10 May 1993, 1819 UNTS 360 (CCSBT); Treaty between the Government of Canada and the United States of America concerning Pacific Salmon, 28 January 1985, 1469 UNTS 358 (PST).

[154] SEAFOC, Art 6(3)(k)–(l); CCAMLR, Art IX(1)(c)–(d); CCSBT, Arts 5(2), 8(1); PST, Arts II(17), XIV(c).

[155] SEAFOC, Art 6(3)(a)–(b), (g)–(h); CCAMLR, Art IX(1)(e), (1)(f), (2), XI; CCSBT, Art 8(2); PST, Art II(8).

[156] SEAFOC, Arts 6(3)(c), (8)(a)–(c); CCAMLR, Art IX(1)(f), (2)(a)(g); CCSBT, Art 8(3)(a), (4); PST, Art IV(3), (4), (5).

[157] SEAFOC, Arts 6(3)(c), 8(d)–(e); CCAMLR, Art IX(1)(f), (2)(h); CCSBT, Art 8(3)(b), (4); PST, Art IV(3)–(5).

[158] SEAFOC, Art 9; CCAMLR, Art XXV; CCSBT, Art 16; PST, Art XXI, Annex III. The capacity for these provisions to oust the jurisdiction of an ITLOS tribunal under UNCLOS, Part XV and Annex VII was highlighted in the Annex VII tribunal decision in the *Southern Bluefin Tuna* decision, which concerned CCSBT, Art 16: *Southern Bluefin Tuna (Australia and New Zealand v Japan)* (2000) 119 ILR 508. The decision has been criticized heavily: Boyle (2001) 50 *ICLQ* 447; Boyle, 'Southern Bluefin Tuna' (2008) *MPEPIL*.

[159] Agreement for the Implementation of the Provisions of the United Nations Convention on the Law of the Sea of 10 December 1982 Relating to the Conservation and Management of Straddling Fish Stocks and Highly Migratory Fish Stocks, 4 December 1995, 2167 UNTS 3.

regulatory framework for the management of high seas fisheries, while addressing some of the weaknesses stemming from the generalized terms of UNCLOS.[160]

Articles 8 to 13 of the Agreement assign a central role to RFMOs in the co-operative management of straddling and highly migratory fish stocks. Article 8(1), like UNCLOS,[161] calls for co-operation in relation to straddling and highly migratory fish stocks. But it envisages a regime which attempts to eliminate free riders and a system whereby 'only those who play by the rules can fish'.[162] In particular Article 8(4) provides that only states which are members of or agree with the RFMO shall have access to the fisheries which the RFMO oversees.

These obligations are bolstered by a boarding, inspection, and enforcement regime which exceeds that directed to even more serious international maladies such as drug running, human trafficking, the smuggling of migrants, and the transport of biological, chemical, and nuclear weapons. Members of RFMOs are instructed to establish schemes whereby one member of the RFMO can board and inspect vessels of any state party to the Straddling Stocks Agreement (whether a member of the RFMO or otherwise).[163] Where, following a boarding and inspection, there are clear grounds for believing that a vessel has engaged in activity contrary to an applicable RFMO regime, the interdicting state shall secure evidence and promptly notify the flag state of the alleged violation.[164] The flag state may then investigate itself or authorize the interdicting state to do so.[165] Where the interdicting state or its own investigators uncover sufficiently incriminating evidence, the flag state is bound to take enforcement action, or to authorize the inspecting state to take such enforcement action as the flag state specifies, consistent with the terms of the Agreement.[166] This is subject to the flag state's right to require that the vessel be released to it,[167] in which case the flag state's obligation to take appropriate enforcement action will remain.

(iv) The role of the WTO[168]

The World Trade Organization (WTO) is relevant to the management of high seas fisheries in that WTO Members interested in the preservation of threatened fish stocks are able to introduce discriminatory trade policies which would otherwise

---

[160] Orrego Vicuña (1999) 201; Churchill & Lowe (3rd edn, 1999) 309–10; Guilfoyle (2009) 103.

[161] Notwithstanding the use of the term 'states parties' here, the Straddling Stocks Agreement makes reference throughout to 'states', raising a question whether the Agreement purported to require even non-states parties to comply with its provisions: Guilfoyle (2009) 104. The Chairman of the drafting conference, however, reiterated the parties' understanding that the Agreement was to apply to states parties only: Rayfuse (1999) 20 AYIL 253, 268.

[162] Balton (1996) 27 ODIL 125, 138. Also: Guilfoyle (2009) 104.

[163] Straddling Stocks Agreement, Art 21(1). Further Churchill & Lowe (3rd edn, 1999) 310; Guilfoyle (2009) 106.

[164] Straddling Stocks Agreement, Art 21(5).

[165] Ibid, Art 21(6).

[166] Ibid, Art 21(7).

[167] Ibid, Art 21(12).

[168] Generally: Young (2011) ch 5.

be in violation of various provisions of the General Agreement on Tariffs and Trade (GATT).[169] GATT Article XX(b) provides that nothing in the GATT can be construed to prevent the adoption or enforcement by a WTO Member of a trade policy which is *necessary* to protect human, animal or plant life or health. Likewise, under GATT Article XX(g), a Member may introduce an otherwise GATT-inconsistent measure which *relates to* the conservation of exhaustible natural resources if such measures are made effective in conjunction with restrictions on domestic production or consumption. The measures in question must also comply with the so-called 'chapeau' conditions of GATT Article XX.

In the *Tuna Dolphin* I decision, a GATT panel held that a US embargo on tuna caught using fishing methods which resulted in a high level of dolphin mortality could not be justified under these provisions, as the measure was neither 'necessary' for the preservation of animal health nor sufficiently 'related to' the conservation of an exhaustible natural resource, a conclusion reiterated in the *Tuna Dolphin* II decision.[170] In particular, the unilateral nature of the regime was seen as objectionable. The decisions were never adopted, but were treated as received wisdom. They were overturned when the Appellate Body returned to consider GATT Article XX in the *US—Shrimp* decision, which concerned another US embargo, this time on shrimp caught by trawlers without a device to exclude sea turtles. The Appellate Body considered the measure as one 'related to' the conservation of an exhaustible natural resource,[171] but held that some negotiation with the state or states affected is required to meet the chapeau conditions.

A similar set of circumstances also gave rise to a long-running dispute over swordfish fisheries in the South Pacific between Chile and the EU.[172] Before the International Tribunal for the Law of the Sea (ITLOS), Chile claimed that the EU had failed to cooperate with the coastal state in order to ensure the conservation of highly migratory swordfish stocks in violation of UNCLOS.[173] This proceeding was issued in response to a parallel action before the Dispute Settlement Body, claiming that Chile's denial of port access violated GATT Article V relating to freedom of transit for goods.[174]

---

[169] Marrakesh Agreement Establishing the World Trade Organization (Annex 1A: GATT 1994), 15 April 1994, 1867 UNTS 187.

[170] *US—Restrictions on the Imports of Tuna* (1991) 30 ILM 1594; *US—Restrictions on the Imports of Tuna* (1994) 33 ILM 839. Further Matsushita, Schoenbaum & Mavroidis, *The World Trade Organization* (2nd edn, 2006) 794–6. The decisions prompted vigorous criticism from those who wish to see a stronger link between trade and the environment: e.g. Charnovitz (1994) 27 *Cornell ILJ* 459; Charnovitz (1993) 6 *GIELR* 1; Bhagwati, in Zaelke et al (eds), *Trade and the Environment* (1993) 159; cf Petersmann (1993) 27 *JWT* 43.

[171] WTO Doc WT/DS58/AB/R, 12 October 1998, §§134–42. For commentary: Howse (2002) 27 *Col JEL* 491; Mann (1998) 9 *Ybk IEL* 28; Schoenbaum (1998) 9 *Ybk IEL* 35; Wirth (1998) 9 *Ybk IEL* 40.

[172] Generally: Stoll & Vöneky (2002) 62 *ZaöRV* 21.

[173] *Conservation and Sustainable Exploitation of Swordfish Stocks in the South-Eastern Pacific Ocean*, Order of 20 December 2000 [2000] ITLOS Rep 148.

[174] Request for Consultations: *Chile—Swordfish*, WTO Doc WT/DS193/1, 26 April 2000. Request for Establishment of a Panel: *Chile—Swordfish*, WTO Doc WT/DS193/2, 7 November 2000.

The parties suspended proceedings in 2001 following an agreement for bilateral co-operation.

(C) REGULATION OF WHALING[175]

Whaling is the subject of a separate international agreement, the 1946 International Convention for the Regulation of Whaling (ICRW).[176] It established the International Whaling Commission (IWC), which plays the role of international regulator of whaling and whaling practices. Initially catch limits were set too high and the use of generalized units of capture resulted in the near-extinction of several species. By 1974, a new procedure had been introduced, and the hunting of all but the five most populous species of whale was prohibited.[177] Then in 1986 the IWC adopted a total moratorium on all commercial whaling.[178] The measure was objected to by Japan, Norway, and the USSR, but Japan subsequently withdrew its opposition, though it still undertakes a programme of 'scientific' whaling by reference to ICRW Article VIII(1).[179] Norway returned to commercial whaling in 1994 and Iceland has similarly resumed whaling since 2006, having left the IWC in 1992 and returned in 2002 with a (controversial) reservation to the moratorium.

6. THE SEABED AND OCEAN FLOOR BEYOND THE LIMITS OF NATIONAL JURISDICTION

(A) THE PRE-EXISTING SEABED REGIME[180]

Under classical international law, the seabed of the high seas was not susceptible of appropriation by states, and the regime of the freedom of the high seas applied (GCHS Article 2). Historic title and prescription could play a role, and title to certain seabed (sedentary) fisheries (e.g. pearl, oyster, and sponge fisheries) could be acquired on the basis of prescription, but these were marginal exceptions, in the nature of *profits à prendre* rather than involving a right to the seabed as such.[181] The category of sedentary fisheries was made effectively redundant by the continental shelf and the EEZ.

---

[175] Generally: Gillespie, *Whaling Diplomacy* (2005).

[176] 2 December 1946, 161 UNTS 72; amended by the Protocol to the International Convention for the Regulation of Whaling, 19 November 1956, 338 UNTS 336.

[177] Churchill & Lowe (3rd edn, 1999) 317–18.

[178] Whaling Convention, Schedule, §10(e).

[179] In May 2010, Australia filed a challenge to Japan's whaling programme in the International Court: *Whaling in the Antarctic (Australia v Japan)* (2010, pending).

[180] 1 Gidel (1932) 493–501; François, ILC *Ybk* 1951/II, 94–9; O'Connell (1955) 49 *AJIL* 185; 1 O'Connell (1982) 449–57; Churchill & Lowe (3rd edn, 1999) 223–54; Nandan, in Freestone, Barnes & Ong (eds), *The Law of the Sea* (2006) 75.

[181] McNair, 1 *Opinions* 258–64.

(B) UNCLOS AND THE INTERNATIONAL SEABED AUTHORITY[182]

During the 1960s it was asserted that exploitation of the mineral resources of the deep seabed and ocean floor was technically possible in areas not included in the regime of the continental shelf, and proposals were made which would have permitted either the partition of the ocean floor between coastal states or the development of mining operations by individual enterprises. The prize in view took the form of allegedly vast deposits of polymetallic nodules, principally in the Pacific and Indian Oceans, containing manganese, nickel, copper, and cobalt.

On 1 November 1967, Dr Arvid Pardo (Malta) presented a proposal to the First Committee of the UN General Assembly to the effect that the seabed and its resources beyond the limits of national jurisdiction should be declared to be part of the 'common heritage of mankind'.[183] This proposal became a key issue of UNCLOS III. In the event UNCLOS Part XI contained a regime for the internationalization of the mineral resources of the deep seabed. These 'resources' and the 'Area' were declared to be 'the common heritage of mankind' (Article 136).

This regime applied beyond the 200nm EEZ limit, and thus overlapped with those areas of continental shelf extending beyond that limit (see Articles 82, 134, 142). In general the treaty regime for the mineral resources of the Area co-existed with the legal regime of the high seas. Thus Article 135 provided that the treaty regime would not affect the legal status of the waters superjacent to the Area or that of the airspace above those waters. The institutional underpinning of the regime relating to the resources of the Area was to be the International Seabed Authority, of which all states parties are *ipso facto* members, which is empowered to organize and control activities in the Area (Article 157).[184]

The regime for the development of the resources of the Area had four key elements. First, it purported to establish an *erga omnes* regime: no state could claim sovereignty or sovereign rights over any part of the Area or its resources and no state or natural or juridical person could appropriate any part thereof (Article 137(1)). Secondly and correlatively, activities in the Area were to be organized and controlled exclusively by the Authority and carried out for the benefit of mankind as a whole.[185] Thirdly, exploration and exploitation of the Area would involve parallel activities by the Enterprise (an organ of the Authority) and by operators;[186] such operators had to possess the

---

[182] Anand, *Legal Regime of the Seabed and the Developing Countries* (1976); Bennouna (1980) 84 *RGDIP* 120; Kronmiller, 1–3 *The Lawfulness of Deep Seabed Mining* (1980–81); Paolillo (1984) 188 Hague *Recueil* 135; Dupuy & Vignes (eds), *Traité du nouveau droit de la mer* (1985) 499–686; Brown, 1–3 *Sea-Bed Energy and Mineral Resources and the Law of the Sea* (1986); Joyner (1986) 35 *ICLQ* 190; Churchill & Lowe (3rd edn, 1999) 223–54.

[183] Churchill & Lowe (3rd edn, 1999) 224–9.

[184] UNCLOS, Art 157. For the delimitation of the outer limits of the continental shelf (and therefore of the Area): chapter 12.

[185] UNCLOS, Arts 137(2), 140, 150(i), 153(2), 156, 157. Also: Art 149 ('Archaeological and historical objects').

[186] UNCLOS, Art 153.

nationality of a state party or be effectively controlled by a party. Fourthly, the Authority was required to provide for the equitable sharing of the economic benefits of activities in the Area,[187] but in doing so was entitled to pay special regard to the interests of developing states.[188]

This was an ambitious regime, and a claim by UNCLOS parties to represent the international public domain of the Area. But it was vulnerable in a number of respects. First, from an economic viewpoint it depended on sufficient recoverable resources being discovered and being commercially exploitable (at a time of volatile demand for land-based minerals). Secondly, despite the uncertain economic prospects, a sub-stantial bureaucratic structure was created and had to be funded. Thirdly, the claim of UNCLOS parties not merely to represent the international public domain but to appropriate all its benefits was legally problematic: *nemo dat quod non habet*.[189] The issue of non-parties was made even more acute in that potential seabed miners hav-ing the nationality of and controlled by non-parties to UNCLOS or their nationals were disqualified: they thus had no incentive to organize so as to bring themselves within the regime, and every reason to oppose it. In an attempt to head off such oppos-ition, the Preparatory Commission (Prepcom) undertook the recognition of so-called 'pioneer investors' (Resolution II).[190]

Partly for these reasons and partly out of ideological opposition to schemes of 'inter-national government', a group of states, mostly western but eventually including Japan and Russia, developed a competing regime of reciprocal recognition of claims to deep seabed resources.[191] This produced something of a diplomatic impasse: under neither scheme did any significant seabed exploration, still less exploitation, occur.

The diplomatic impasse was resolved in 1994 when the General Assembly adopted the Agreement relating to the Implementation of Part XI (Deep Seabed Agreement),[192] thereby allowing UNCLOS to enter into force in amended form, with the express or tacit consent of all signatories. Under this dispensation the Deep Seabed Agreement and UNCLOS are to be interpreted and applied together 'as a single instrument'

---

[187] UNCLOS, Arts 140(2), 160(2)(f)(i).

[188] UNCLOS, Arts 140(1), 144(2), 148, 150, 152(2), 160(2)(f)(i). Reference was also made to the 'special need' of the land-locked and geographically disadvantaged states among the developing states: Arts 148, 152(2), 160(2)(k).

[189] Bennouna (1980) 84 *RGDIP* 120; 2 Brown (1986); 1 Kronmiller (1981) 207–521; Malone (1983) 46 *LCP* 29.

[190] Churchill & Lowe (3rd edn, 1999) 230–1. Registrations were lodged of sites for India, France, Japan, and the USSR with respect to eight investors.

[191] Deep Seabed Hard Mineral Resources Act 1980 (US), 19 ILM 1003, and equivalent interim legisla-tion passed by France, Germany, Italy, Japan, Russian Federation, and UK; Agreement concerning Interim Arrangements relating to Polymetallic Nodules of the Deep Seabed, 2 September 1982, 21 ILM 950 (France, Germany, US, UK); Provisional Understanding Regarding Deep Seabed Matters, 3 August 1984, 23 ILM 1354 (Belgium, France, Germany, Italy, Japan, the Netherlands, UK, US). Also: Agreement on the Resolution of Practical Problems with Respect to Deep Seabed Mining Areas, 14 August 1987 (Canada, Belgium, Italy, Netherlands, USSR); Exchange of Notes between the United States and the Parties to the Agreement, 14 August 1987, 26 ILM 1502.

[192] Agreement relating to the Implementation of Part XI, 28 July 1994, 1836 UNTS 3.

(Article 2). The Deep Seabed Agreement modified certain aspects of Part XI in order to meet the objections raised by the US and others.[193]

(C) THE AMENDED SEABED REGIME

(i) The Deep Seabed Agreement and the Mining Code

The Deep Seabed Agreement is relatively brief, consisting of 10 operative provisions, a preamble and a substantive Annex. It is largely procedural, but its Annex includes new rules for the operation of the seabed regime, including an agreed interpretation of certain provisions of Part XI and new provisions regarding the operation of the Authority. Articles 4 and 5 provide a unified and simplified approach to the granting of state consent to be bound by UNCLOS and the Deep Seabed Agreement operating in severalty under Article 2. The Agreement thus modifies UNCLOS, providing alternative rules to secure universal participation.

In 2000 the International Seabed Authority adopted the Regulation on Prospecting and Exploration for Polymetallic Nodules in the Area (RPNM). This is the first instrument to be promulgated by the Authority in what is known as the Mining Code,[194] a set of comprehensive rules, regulations, and procedures to be issued by the Authority to administer the prospecting, exploration, and exploitation of marine minerals in the Area. In 2010 the Authority also adopted the Regulations on Prospecting and Exploration for Polymetallic Sulphides and a third set of Regulations on Prospecting and Exploration for Cobalt-Rich Crusts will eventually be adopted as well. The RPNM enabled the Authority in 2001 to enter into a series of 15-year contracts for the exploration of polymetallic nodules. In this way the Prepcom's regime of Resolution II came to an end.[195]

(ii) State liability for sponsored entities and contractors

In its Advisory Opinion on responsibility and liability for international seabed mining,[196] the Seabed Disputes Chamber of ITLOS made several important clarifications regarding a state's liability for private entities that it sponsors to carry out seabed mining.

First, the basic obligation of a state in such cases is 'to ensure' that 'activities in the Area' conducted by a sponsored entity or contractor are in conformity or compliance with UNCLOS Part XI, relevant Annexes to UNCLOS, the regulations and procedures of the Authority, the terms of its exploration contract with the Authority, and any other

---

[193] Nash (1994) 88 *AJIL* 733; Oxman (1994) 88 *AJIL* 687; Sohn (1994) 88 *AJIL* 696; Charney (1994) 88 *AJIL* 705.

[194] Available at www.isa.org.jm/en/documents/mcode.

[195] Oude Elferink & Rothwell, *Oceans Management* (2004) 341–5.

[196] *Obligations of States Sponsoring Persons and Entities with Respect to Activities in the Area*, ITLOS Case No 17 (Advisory Opinion, 1 February 2011).

obligations under UNCLOS and the Seabed Agreement.[197] Sufficient due diligence on the project must also be done, and undertaken in light of the precautionary principle, best environmental practices, and an environmental impact assessment.[198]

Second, UNCLOS Article 139(2) sets out the limits of state liability in respect of the actions of sponsored entities and contractors, and identifies several 'liability gaps' in respect of which states do not bear residual liability.[199] ITLOS raised the possibility of an addition to the Mining Code that may assign liability within these lacunae, and further hinted that the obligation to preserve the environment of the high seas and the seabed may be *erga omnes* in character.[200]

Finally, states must have in place effective laws and supporting administrative regulations that oversee such operations which exceed mere contractual safeguards. These must be 'no less effective than international rules, regulations and procedures' adopted by the Authority and other international bodies.[201]

---

[197] Ibid, §§103–4.
[198] Ibid, §§110–20, 125–37, 141–50, 148. Further *Southern Bluefin Tuna* (1999) 117 ILR 148.
[199] *Seabed Advisory Opinion*, ITLOS Case No 17, §204.
[200] Ibid, §180 (citing ARSIWA, Art 48).
[201] Ibid, §241; UNCLOS Art 209(2).

PART V

THE ENVIRONMENT AND NATURAL RESOURCES

14

COMMON SPACES AND CO-OPERATION IN THE USE OF NATURAL RESOURCES

1. INTRODUCTION

The world's resources and environment are at the same time shared and partitioned, indivisible and divided. A world of sovereigns creates the greatest collective action problem in history: international law is both the product of this world and one of the few tools at our disposal for addressing the problem. Yet apart from the concepts of *res communis* as applied to the high seas and outer space, and 'the common heritage of mankind' as variously and vaguely applied to the atmosphere and the oceans,[1] international law depends to a great extent on voluntarist devices, in the form of treaties, agreements, international agencies, and organizations, in order to regulate access to resources not located wholly within national territory. Indeed, the use of such devices in the political conditions of the past led to a situation where the law appeared to prevent developing states from having control over their own resources, creating by way of backlash a demand for a 'new international economic order'.[2]

Apart from such questions of economic self-determination, the subject as a whole is concerned with machinery, organization, and also the influence of technical considerations to a degree uncommon in other areas of the law. Customary international law plays a role, at times a dynamic role, but caution is needed to avoid postulating as rules what are in truth local or temporary factors. Moreover the agenda evolves with

---

[1] Baslar, *The Concept of the Common Heritage of Mankind in International Law* (1998) ch 3; Wolfrum, 'Common Heritage of Mankind' (2009) *MPEPIL*. The concept has been explored in the context of the deep seabed: Brown, *Sea-Bed Energy and Minerals* (2001); Antarctica: Bastmeijer, *The Antarctic Environmental Protocol and its Domestic Legal Implementation* (2003); and the moon: Tronchetti, *The Exploitation of Natural Resources of the Moon and Other Celestial Bodies* (2009).

[2] E.g. Declaration on the Establishment of a New International Economic Order, GA Res 3201(S-VI), 1 May 1974; Agarwala, *The New International Economic Order* (1983); Ghosh (ed), *New International Economic Order* (1984).

changes in technology: in the 1960s lawyers were concerned with activities such as atmospheric nuclear testing with potential to seriously affect the environment; more recently the concerns surrounding anthropogenic climate change have prompted the development of an international climate change regime.[3]

The following sections briefly identify some legal issues that can arise in connection with the use of shared resources; the generation and use of energy and other uses of transboundary water resources, and other forms of transboundary co-operation, as well as issues specific to the polar regions and outer space.

2. CO-OPERATION IN THE GENERATION AND USE OF ENERGY

(A) NUCLEAR ENERGY AND THE NON-PROLIFERATION TREATY[4]

The utilization of atomic energy for peaceful purposes has been a major field for co-operation between states, and between organizations and states, for several reasons: its relation to questions of security and disarmament; its (controversial) contribution to dealing with anthropogenic climate change by providing a non-fossil-fuel-based energy source; the immense cost of development, and the risk posed to human health by nuclear accidents. The most important organization, the International Atomic Energy Agency (IAEA), was established in 1957.[5] The IAEA provides assistance of various kinds for the development of atomic energy in particular states under a system of inspection and control to ensure, *inter alia*, that the aid is not used for military purposes. Following the increased concern about nuclear reactors after the Chernobyl accident,[6] the IAEA oversaw the development of two new international agreements: the Convention on Nuclear Safety[7] and the Joint Convention on the Safety of Spent Fuel and Radioactive Waste Management.[8] The disaster at the Fukushima nuclear plant in Japan in 2011 has raised fresh concerns about the risks of nuclear power, and the regime is under scrutiny once again.[9]

---

[3] Stockholm Conference, Declaration on the Human Environment, 16 June 1972, 11 ILM 1416; Yamin & Depledge, *The International Climate Change Regime* (2004); Voigt, *Sustainable Development as a Principle of International Law* (2009) 57–87; Faure & Peeters (eds), *Climate Change Liability* (2011).

[4] Generally: van Leeuwen (ed), *Future of the International Nuclear Non-Proliferation Regime* (1995); Shaker (2006) 321 Hague *Recueil* 9; Falk & Krieger (eds), *At the Nuclear Precipice* (2008); Stoiber et al, *Handbook on Nuclear Law* (2010); International School of Nuclear Law (ISNL) (ed), *International Nuclear Law* (2010); Joyner, *Interpreting the Nuclear Non-Proliferation Treaty* (2011).

[5] Statute of the International Atomic Energy Agency, 26 October 1956, 276 UNTS 3. See Jankowitsch-Prevor, in ISNL (2010) 13; Rockwood, in ISNL (2010) 243.

[6] Smith & Beresford, *Chernobyl* (2005).

[7] 20 September 1994, 1963 UNTS 293.

[8] 5 September 1997, 2153 UNTS 303.

[9] The UN System-Wide Study on the Implications of the Accident at the Fukushima Daiichi Nuclear Power Plant, SG/HLM/2011/1, 16 August 2011, addresses numerous safety issues, including the IAEA's role and the adequacy of nuclear disaster preparedness and response frameworks.

Other relevant agencies include the European Atomic Energy Community (Euratom)[10] and the Nuclear Energy Agency of the Organisation for Economic Co-operation and Development (OECD).[11]

As for the use of nuclear energy for non-peaceful purposes, international law does not contain a comprehensive prohibition of the threat or use of nuclear weapons as such, although it is unlikely that any actual use of nuclear weapons would be consistent with international law.[12] The current nuclear disarmament regime consists primarily of the Treaty on the Non-Proliferation of Nuclear Weapons (NPT),[13] the Partial Test Ban Treaty of 1963,[14] and the Comprehensive Nuclear Test Ban Treaty (CTBT).[15] CTBT bans all nuclear explosions on earth, whether for military or peaceful purposes, and sets up a global verification regime monitored by the CTBT Organization. It was opened for signature in 1996 but is not yet in force, pending ratification by nine of the 44 'Annex 2 states', being those states that possess nuclear technology. Pressure is mounting on those states that are yet to ratify, including the US, Iran, China, and Israel. There is also a strong movement to conclude a multilateral convention banning nuclear weapons, supported by over 130 states at the NPT Review Conference in 2010.[16] However, the regime has faced many challenges, including North Korea's continued testing of weapons and its withdrawal from the NPT,[17] growing concern over Iran's nuclear programme,[18] and an apparently contradictory special deal between the US and India.[19] French nuclear testing in the South Pacific has been the subject of disputes before the International Court.[20] It is unlikely CTBT will come into force in the near future,[21] and the conclusion of a multilateral ban could take decades. Nonetheless, recent steps taken by the US, including negotiating Strategic Arms Reduction treaties

---

[10] 25 March 1957, 298 UNTS 167. See Kilb, in ISNL (2010) 43.

[11] 14 December 1960, 888 UNTS 179. See Wolfe, in Mahon & McBride (eds), *The OECD and Transnational Governance* (2008) 25. On the Nuclear Energy Agency: Shaw, *Europe's Nuclear Power Experiment* (1983); Schwarz, in ISNL (2010) 31.

[12] *Legality of the Threat or Use of Nuclear Weapons*, ICJ Reports 1996 p 226, 266. The Court was divided on whether or not the use of nuclear weapons might be lawful in self-defence against a threat to the life of the nation itself. Further: Boisson de Chazournes & Sands (eds), *International Law, the International Court of Justice and Nuclear Weapons* (1999).

[13] 1 July 1968, 729 UNTS 168. See Moxley, Burroughs & Granoff (2011) 34 *Fordham ILJ* 595; Joyner (2011).

[14] 5 August 1963, 480 UNTS 43.

[15] GA Res 50/245, 10 September 1995.

[16] See the revised Model Nuclear Weapons Convention submitted by Costa Rica and Malaysia in 2007: A/62/605, 18 January 2008. Further: Weiss (2011) 34 *Fordham ILJ* 776.

[17] See SC Res 1718, 14 October 2006; SC Res 1874, 12 June 2009. Further: Falk & Krieger (2008); Joyner (2011).

[18] Bâli, in Falk & Krieger (2008) 97; Ronen, *The Iran Nuclear Issue* (2011).

[19] USA–India, Agreement for Cooperation concerning Peaceful Uses of Nuclear Energy, 10 October 2008, www.state.gov/documents/organization/122068.pdf; India–IAEA, Agreement for the Application of Safeguards to Civilian Nuclear Facilities, 29 May 2009, INFCIRC/754. See Ranganathan (2011) 51 *Indian JIL* 146.

[20] *Nuclear Tests (Australia v France)*, ICJ Reports 1974 p 253; *Nuclear Tests (New Zealand v France)*, ICJ Reports 1974 p 457; *Request for an Examination of the Situation in Accordance with Paragraph 63 of the Court's Judgment of 20 December 1947 in the* Nuclear Tests (New Zealand v France) Case, ICJ Report 1995 p 388.

[21] Mackby (2011) 34 *Fordham JIL* 697.

with Russia[22] and pursuing CTBT ratification in the Senate, suggest that the only nuclear power to have actually used nuclear weapons is once more (and for the time being) ready to take a responsible role in the move towards nuclear disarmament.

(B) THE ENERGY CHARTER TREATY[23]

The Energy Charter Treaty, together with the Protocol on Energy Efficiency and Related Environmental Aspects,[24] establishes an ambitious multilateral regime for energy co-operation, building on the political declaration of the 1991 European Energy Charter[25] following the collapse of the Soviet Union. The Charter was an attempt to accelerate economic recovery in Eastern Europe through co-operation in the energy sector. Its current membership reflects the growing importance of the Asian energy market. There are 52 members including the European Union. Russia signed the Treaty in 1994, but in 2009 announced its intention not to ratify the Treaty; provisional application ended on 18 October 2009 in accordance with Article 45(3)(a).[26]

The Treaty includes provisions on energy-related foreign investment and trade, dispute resolution, and energy efficiency. The investment regime is particularly noteworthy, being the first such regime contained in a widely ratified multilateral agreement. The regime is divided into pre-investment and post-investment provisions. The pre-investment provisions govern market access, and are largely framed as 'best endeavours' undertakings. By contrast, the post-establishment regime provides for binding obligations resting on the principles of most-favoured nation and national treatment. A salient feature is the inclusion of the right for foreign private investors to initiate compulsory arbitration proceedings against non-compliant state parties (Article 26).

(C) OTHER CASES

Further areas of concern in the sharing of energy resources include the creation and maintenance of transnational energy grids and the international transport of energy. Liberalization of energy-related trade has proceeded apace but the corresponding extension and integration between national grids has not kept up. As yet there are no multilateral instruments governing transnational energy grids, but there

---

[22] The latest of these is the New START (Strategic Arms Reduction Treaty): Measures for the Further Reduction and Limitation of Strategic Offensive Arms, 8 April 2010, Senate Treaty Doc 111–15.

[23] 17 December 1994, 2080 UNTS 95. See Doré & de Bauw, *The Energy Charter Treaty* (1995); Wälde, '*Sustainable Development' and the 1994 Energy Charter Treaty* (1997); Ostry, in Kirton, Larionova & Savona (eds), *Making Global Economic Governance Effective* (2010) 131.

[24] 17 December 1994, 2081 UNTS 3.

[25] Concluding Document of the Hague Conference on the European Energy Charter, 17 December 1991, text reproduced in Wälde & Ndi, *International Oil and Gas Investment* (1994) 367–73.

[26] For the putative continuing effects of provisional application: *Yukos Universal Limited v Russia*, 30 November 2009, at www.italaw.com.

are proposals for extensive integrated grids in Northern Europe,[27] and progress has been made with hydropower development and power interconnection in the Greater Mekong Subregion.[28] The Association of South East Asian Nations (ASEAN) signed an Agreement on ASEAN Energy Cooperation in 1986 and is working towards the establishment of an ASEAN power grid, as well as trans-ASEAN gas pipelines.[29] Initiatives such as these present numerous legal and political challenges.

Article 7 of the Energy Charter Treaty provides that parties shall facilitate free transit of energy materials and products on a non-discriminatory basis, and shall 'encourage relevant entities to cooperate' in modernization, development, and operation of the infrastructure required for the transport of energy, such as transmission lines and pipelines. Various European states have declared that Article 7 is subject to general and conventional international law on jurisdiction over submarine cables and pipelines, reflected in Article 7(8). The transport of nuclear energy is governed by IAEA Regulations and the Convention on Physical Protection of Nuclear Material.[30]

3. TRANSBOUNDARY WATER RESOURCES

(A) SHARED FRESHWATER AND CANALS

(i) Shared freshwater resources[31]

The term 'international' with reference to a body of water is merely a general indication of rivers and reservoirs which geographically and economically affect the territory and interests of two or more states. Conceivably a body of water could be 'internationalized', that is, given a status entirely distinct from the territorial sovereignty and jurisdiction of any state, on the basis of treaty or custom, general or regional. Rivers separating or traversing the territories of two or more states are usually subject to the territorial jurisdiction of riparian states up to the *medium filum aquae*, taken to be

---

[27] North Seas Countries' Offshore Grid Initiative, Memorandum of Understanding, 3 December 2010, available at www.ec.europa.eu/energy/renewables/grid/doc/north_sea_countries_offshore_grid_initiative_mou.pdf.

[28] Lei, in de Jong, Snelder & Ishikawa (eds), *Transborder Governance of Forests, Rivers, and Seas* (2010) 163.

[29] Atchatavivan, in Moomaw & Susskind (eds), 15 *Papers on International Environmental Negotiation* (2006); Ansari, *Energy Law in Malaysia* (2011) 78–80.

[30] 3 March 1980, 1456 UNTS 101. Cf Jankowitsch-Prevor, in ISNL (2010) 187.

[31] Generally: Fuentes (1996) 67 *BY* 337; Fuentes (1998) 69 *BY* 119; Upadhye (2000) 8 *Cardozo JICL* 61; Malla (2008) 77 *Nordic JIL* 461; McIntyre, *Environmental Protection of International Watercourses under International Law* (2007); McCaffrey, *The Law of International Watercourses* (2nd edn, 2007); Dinar, *International Water Treaties* (2008); Islam, *The Law of Non-Navigational Uses of International Watercourses* (2010).

the deepest channel of navigable waters or *thalweg*.[32] But there are exceptions where some other boundary is agreed—for example the River San Juan, which forms part of the boundary between Nicaragua and Costa Rica, runs wholly in Nicaragua: the boundary is the right bank of the river on the Costa Rican side. However, the border treaty between the riparians also provides Costa Rica with a right of navigation on the San Juan '*con objetos de comercio*'.[33] This right and its qualifier were considered in *Navigational Rights*, with the International Court determining, *inter alia*, that the phrase meant 'for the purposes of commerce', thereby ascribing to Costa Rica the right to carry goods and passengers on the river,[34] as well as finding that persons so travelling were not required to obtain Nicaraguan visas or make payment to Nicaragua.[35]

The legal regime of rivers, creating rights for other riparians and non-riparian states and limiting the exercise of territorial jurisdiction for individual riparians, consists to a large extent of treaty law, and the International Court has focused on the terms of the particular treaty, making secondary reference to general international law or local custom.[36] Broadly, there are different legal regimes for navigational and non-navigational uses of rivers.[37] The early assumption that navigational uses enjoyed primacy is no longer accurate; irrigation, hydro-electricity generation, and industrial uses are now more prominent in many regions than navigation, fishing, and floating of timber, and domestic use is growing rapidly.

Lac Lanoux concerned the interpretation of a treaty between France and Spain. However, the tribunal made observations on certain Spanish arguments based on customary law. On the one hand, the tribunal seemed to accept the principle that an upstream state is acting unlawfully if it changes the waters of a river in their natural condition in a way that could do serious injury to a downstream state. On the other, the tribunal stated that 'the rule according to which States may utilize the hydraulic force of international watercourses only on condition of a prior agreement between the interested States cannot be established as a custom, or even less as a general principle of law'.[38]

---

[32] On the problems of river boundaries: E Lauterpacht (1960) 9 *ICLQ* 208, 216–22; Biger (1988) 17 *Geo J* 341; Caflisch (1989) 219 Hague *Recueil* 9; Biger (1989) 25 *MES* 249; McCaffrey (2nd edn, 2007) 70–2.

[33] Treaty of Limits, 15 April 1858, 118 CTS 439, Art VI.

[34] Police patrol vessels were excluded, as were vessels resupplying Costa Rican border posts: *Navigational and Related Rights (Costa Rica v Nicaragua)* ICJ Reports 2009 p 213, 232–48.

[35] Ibid, 248–63.

[36] *Diversion of Water from the Meuse* (1937) PCIJ Ser A/B No 70; *Gabčíkovo-Nagymaros Project (Hungary/Slovakia)*, ICJ Reports 1997 p 7; *Dispute regarding Navigational and Related Rights (Costa Rica v Nicaragua)*, ICJ Reports 2009 p 213; *Pulp Mills on the River Uruguay (Argentina v Uruguay)*, ICJ Reports 2010 p 14.

[37] Salman (2007) 23 *WRD* 625.

[38] (1957) 24 ILR 101. Also: Duléry (1958) 62 *RGDIP* 469; Griffin (1959) 53 *AJIL* 50. For the Convention made subsequently by the parties: (1958) 4 *AFDI* 692, 708–11. Further: Treaty Relating to Co-operative Development of the Water Resources of the Columbia River Basin (Canada–USA), 17 January 1961, 542 UNTS 245; Helsinki Convention on the Protection and Use of Transboundary Watercourses and International Lakes, 17 March 1992, 1936 UNTS 269.

The issues of liability for changes in the flow of a river as between riparian states will be determined within the framework of the law of treaties in combination with the principles of state responsibility, as in *Gabčíkovo-Nagymaros*. At the same time the Court referred to the 'basic right' of Hungary 'to an equitable and reasonable sharing of the resources of an international watercourse'.[39] The case was in some respects special since a boundary river was involved.

In the case of navigable rivers it is accepted that customary law does not recognize a right of free navigation.[40] Only a minority of states have accepted the Barcelona Convention and Statute on the Regime of Navigable Waterways of International Concern of 1921,[41] which provides for free navigation as between the parties on navigable waterways of international concern. Several treaty regimes for specific river systems provide for free navigation and equality of treatment for riparian states only.[42] By contrast the treaty regime for the Danube has long conferred rights of navigation on non-riparians. The Belgrade Convention of 1948 maintained free navigation for all states whilst retaining powers of control for riparian states.[43] Navigation by warships of non-riparian states is prohibited. In construing a treaty which creates machinery for supervision of an international regime of navigation, a tribunal may prefer not to employ a restrictive interpretation of the powers of the agency of control as against the territorial sovereigns.[44]

In the *River Oder* case, the Permanent Court, referring to the various conventions since the Act of the Congress of Vienna in 1815, stressed the 'community of interest of riparian States' which in a navigable river 'becomes the basis of a common legal right, the essential features of which are the perfect equality of all riparian States in the use of the whole course of the river and the exclusion of any preferential privilege of any one riparian State in relation to the others'.[45]

In 1966 the International Law Association (ILA) adopted the Helsinki Rules on the Uses of Waters of International Rivers as a statement of existing international law covering both navigational and non-navigational uses.[46] The ILA also adopted the

---

[39] *Gabčíkovo-Nagymaros*, ICJ Reports 1997 p 7, 54.

[40] *Faber* (1903) 10 RIAA 438, 439–41. Also: Baxter & Triska, *The Law of International Waterways* (1964) 133; Uprety, *The Transit Regime for Landlocked States* (2006) 37–44. Cf Caflisch (1989) 219 Hague *Recueil* 9, 104–32 (suggesting that a regional custom of free navigation has developed in Europe, and possibly in South America); McCaffrey (2nd edn, 2007) ch 6.

[41] 20 April 1921, 7 LNTS 35.

[42] E.g. Treaty Relating to Boundary Waters between the US and Canada (US–Great Britain), 11 January 1909, 4 *AJIL Supp* 239.

[43] Convention Regarding the Regime of Navigation on the Danube, 18 August 1948, 33 UNTS 181; see Kunz (1949) 43 *AJIL* 104.

[44] *Territorial Jurisdiction of the International Commission of the River Oder* (1929) PCIJ Ser A No 23, 29; *Jurisdiction of the European Commission of the Danube* (1927) PCIJ Ser B No 14, 61, 63–4.

[45] (1929) PCIJ Ser A No 23, 28; the Court referred also to the interest of non-riparian states in navigation on the waterways in question.

[46] ILA, Report of the 52nd Conference (1966) 477–533. On the status of the Rules: Salman (2007) 23 *WRD* 625, 630.

comprehensive revised Berlin Rules on Water Resources in 2004.[47] The International Law Commission worked on the topic for over 20 years, culminating in the adoption of the Convention on the Law of Non-Navigational Uses of International Watercourses in 1997. Part II of the Convention sets out general principles for watercourses, including factors to be considered for ensuring equitable and reasonable utilization and participation, the avoidance of significant harm and how to remedy it, and general obligations of co-operation including sharing of information. Part III contains detailed provisions on prior notification of planned measures. In the absence of agreement no particular use of the watercourse enjoys inherent priority over others.[48]

A further advance occurred in *Gabčíkovo-Nagymaros*. There, the Court considered a dispute arising from a 1977 agreement between Czechoslovakia and Hungary to dam the Danube River in their respective territories in order to produce hydro-electric power in peaking mode. When Hungary refused to construct its dam due to environmental concerns, Slovakia diverted the river further onto its territory and built a second upstream dam—a contingency known as 'Variant C'. The question was whether Slovakia was entitled to undertake Variant C despite the objections of its co-riparian. The Court noted that not only was the Danube a shared international watercourse, but also an international boundary river to which the principle of perfect equality between riparian states applied. Thus, by unilaterally diverting the Danube, Czechoslovakia assumed control of a shared resource and deprived Hungary of its right to a reasonable and equitable share thereof. In so deciding, the Court extended the principle in the *River Oder* case to non-navigational uses of watercourses.[49]

(ii) International canals

Canals are in principle subject to the territorial sovereignty and jurisdiction of the state or states which they separate or traverse. Where the canal serves more than one state or otherwise affects the interests of more than one state a treaty regime may be created to regulate use and administration. The history of three canals of international concern has provided the basic materials for jurists seeking to establish general rules.

The Suez Canal was built and opened in 1869 under a private law concession for 99 years granted by the Egyptian government to the Universal Suez Maritime Canal Company. For most of its history the latter was a joint Franco-Egyptian company with aspects of its existence and functioning subjected to either French or Egyptian law. The British government was the largest shareholder. Eventually the affairs of the Canal were regulated by the Convention of Constantinople in 1888.[50] Article I provided that the Canal 'shall always be free and open, in time of war as in time of peace, to every

---

[47] ILA, Report of the 71st Conference (2004) 334–421; Salman (2007) 23 *WRD* 625, 635–8.
[48] GA Res 51/229, 21 May 1997 (not yet in force).
[49] ICJ Reports 1997 p 7, 55–7.
[50] Convention Respecting the Free Navigation of the Suez Canal, 29 October 1888, 171 CTS 241. See Matthews (1967) 21 *Int Org* 81.

vessel of commerce or of war, without distinction of flag'. The parties agreed not to interfere with the free use of the Canal and not to subject it to the right of blockade.

In 1954 Britain and Egypt agreed on British withdrawal from the Suez Canal base; the parties recognized that the Canal 'which is an integral part of Egypt, is a waterway economically, commercially and strategically of international importance'.[51] In 1956 the Egyptian government nationalized the Canal Company, under a law providing for compensation,[52] but made no claim to alter the status of the Canal itself. Britain, France, and other states argued for the illegality of this measure, linking the status of the Company and the concession with the status of the Canal, and alleging that the nationalization was incompatible with the 'international status' of the Canal. As a result of the Franco-British invasion later in the same year Egypt abrogated the 1954 Agreement.[53] On 24 April 1957 Egypt made a declaration confirming the rights and obligations arising from the Convention of Constantinople: the Declaration was registered under Charter Article 102, although in law it was a unilateral act.[54]

Until 1978 the Panama Canal Zone was occupied and administered by the US, independently of Panama, under the Hay–Bunau–Varilla Treaty of 1903,[55] which provided that the Canal should be neutral in perpetuity and open to the vessels of all nations. Even before this, the Hay–Pauncefote Treaty had guaranteed free navigation, even in time of war, in terms borrowed from the Convention of Constantinople.[56] But by a Treaty of 1977 (as amended in 1978), Panama was recognized as 'territorial sovereign' with rights of management of the Canal granted to the US for the duration of the Treaty.[57]

The Kiel Canal, though important for international commerce, was controlled by Germany untrammelled by special obligations until, in the Treaty of Versailles, it was provided that, except when Germany was a belligerent, the Canal was to be open to vessels of commerce and of war of all nations on terms of equality (Article 380). In 1936 the relevant provisions of the Treaty of Versailles were denounced by Germany, and other states seem to have acquiesced in this.[58]

It is doubtful if the existing materials justify any general principle of international canals. But there is some authority to the contrary in *The SS Wimbledon*. In 1921 a British vessel chartered by a French company, en route to Danzig with munitions for the Polish government, was refused access to the Kiel Canal. The issue was whether, given that Poland and Russia were at war, Germany was justified in holding that

---

[51] UK–Egypt, Agreement regarding the Suez Canal Base, 19 October 1954, 221 UNTS 227; further: Selak (1955) 49 *AJIL* 487.

[52] Suez Canal Company Nationalisation Law, Decree Law No 285, 1956; for the heads of agreement as to compensation of 29 April 1958, see (1960) 54 *AJIL* 493.

[53] (1957) 51 *AJIL* 672.

[54] 265 UNTS 300. See E Lauterpacht, *The Suez Canal Settlement* (1960) 35; Mensbrugghe (1964) 397.

[55] 18 November 1903, 33 Stat 2234; TS 431.

[56] 18 November 1901, 32 Stat 1903; TS 401.

[57] Panama Canal Treaty, 7 September 1977, 16 ILM 1022. The Protocol to the Treaty Concerning the Permanent Neutrality and Operation of the Panama Canal (ibid, 1042) is open to accession by all states.

[58] Böhmer (1995) 38 *GYIL* 325; Lagoni, 'Kiel Canal' (2009) *MPEPIL*.

Article 380 of the Versailles Treaty did not preclude the observance of neutrality. The judgment, in upholding an expansive interpretation of the right of transit, referred to the Suez and Panama Canals as 'precedents' which were

merely illustrations of the general opinion according to which when an artificial waterway connecting two open seas has been permanently dedicated to the use of the whole world, such waterway is assimilated to natural straits in the sense that even the passage of a belligerent man-of-war does not compromise the neutrality of the sovereign State under whose jurisdiction the waters in question lie.[59]

It will be noted that this proposition was ancillary to an exercise in treaty interpretation and that even the general proposition depends on the incidence of 'permanent dedication'. Moreover, interested states are reluctant to generalize: in 1956 the US regarded the Suez Canal as having an 'international status', while denying this in the case of the Panama Canal.[60]

(B) JOINT BOUNDARY COMMISSIONS

Joint boundary commissions have been used to facilitate trans-border co-operation and the resolution of boundary disputes between neighbouring states for centuries, with the Ottoman commissions in the late 1400s,[61] or the Caro-Ornano commission attempting to negotiate the border between France and Spain in the 1780s.[62] Today there are 72 joint boundary commissions operating in different regions of the world.

Traditionally the primary function of a boundary commission has been to delimit or demarcate and maintain the boundary, frequently as part of a peace settlement or dispute resolution process. Commissions are often also involved in ongoing cross-border water and environmental management.[63] They are usually established by treaty, and can be temporary or permanent. Examples include the Canada/US International Joint Commission,[64] the US/Mexico International Boundary and Water Commission,[65] and the Cameroon/Nigeria Mixed Commission.[66]

---

[59] (1923) PCIJ Ser A No 1, 28.

[60] Baxter & Triska (1964) 182, 308, 343.

[61] Wright, *Bartolomeo Minio: Venetian Administration in 15th-Century Nauplion* (2000) ch 3.

[62] Sahlins, *Boundaries* (1989) 98–102.

[63] E.g. the Joint Rivers Commission (Bangladesh/India); Joint Commission on Protection and Sustainable Use of Transboundary Waters (Estonia/Russia); Chu and Talas Rivers Commission (Kazakhstan/Kyrgyzstan).

[64] Boundary Waters Treaty, 11 January 1909, 36 Stat 2448. See Lemarquand (1993) 33 *NRJ* 59; O'Sullivan (2001) 9 *Boundary & Security Bulletin* 86; Tarlock (2008) 54 *Wayne LR* 1671.

[65] Treaty Relating to the Utilization of Waters of Colorado and Tijuana Rivers and of the Rio Grande, 3 February 1944, 59 Stat 1219; Mumme (2001) 9 *Boundary & Security Bulletin* 117; Handl, 'American-Mexican Boundary Disputes and Cooperation' (2010) *MPEPIL*.

[66] Established by the UN Secretary-General to facilitate implementation of the ruling of the International Court in *Land and Maritime Boundary between Cameroon and Nigeria (Cameroon v Nigeria; Equatorial Guinea intervening)*, ICJ Reports 2002 p 303; further: Bekker (2003) 97 *AJIL* 387, 398; Udogu (2008) 7 *Af & Asian S* 77, 89–96.

In *Pulp Mills*, the Court had occasion to consider the role of the Administrative Commission of the River Uruguay (CARU), as established by the 1975 Statute of the River Uruguay.[67] The Statute established CARU as a co-operative interface between Argentina and Uruguay for management of the river, a position that the Court took seriously. Accordingly, when Uruguay failed to inform Argentina through CARU that it was ready to issue initial environmental approval for two contested pulp mills, the Court held it to be in breach of its international obligations.[68]

(C) JOINT DEVELOPMENT ZONES[69]

Since the Second World War the jurisdiction of coastal states over marine resources (living and non-living) has expanded dramatically.[70] The need for co-operation in the exploitation of such resources in areas that are subject to competing unresolved territorial claims, or where the resources straddle maritime boundaries, has led to the practice among states of establishing joint development zones (JDZs). In other cases the establishment of a JDZ may actually be a permanent alternative to drawing a definitive boundary line.

The practice of establishing JDZs as an interim measure to enable exploitation to proceed for the benefit of two or more states with overlapping claims is reinforced by UNCLOS Articles 74(3) and 83(3), which provide that pending agreement on the delimitation of the EEZ or continental shelf, respectively, the states concerned 'shall make every effort to enter into provisional arrangements of a practical nature'.[71] These arrangements are set down in bilateral treaties, governing matters such as the allocation of rights and obligations arising from exploitation activities, supervision and management of the exploitation, protection of the marine environment, inspection rights, and dispute settlement.[72]

JDZs are important both in the context of non-living resources, such as offshore hydrocarbon deposits,[73] and for the exploitation, conservation, and management of transboundary fish stocks.[74] Examples include zones established between Nigeria and

---

[67] 26 February 1975, 1295 UNTS 339.

[68] *Pulp Mills*, ICJ Reports 2010 p 14, 56–7, 66–7.

[69] Generally: Fox (ed), *Joint Development of Offshore Oil and Gas* (1990); Churchill & Lowe, *The Law of the Sea* (3rd edn, 1999) 198–202, 294–6; Kim, *Maritime Delimitation and Interim Arrangements in North East Asia* (2004); Gao (2008) 23 IJMCL 55.

[70] Churchill, in Fox (1990) 55–8.

[71] 10 December 1982, 1833 UNTS 3. Generally: Nordquist, Rosenne & Nandan, 2 *United Nations Convention on the Law of the Sea, 1982* (1993) 796–816, 948–85.

[72] For a model agreement: Fox (1990) 3–23.

[73] Ong (1999) 93 *AJIL* 771.

[74] Also: Agreement on Straddling Fish Stocks and Highly Migratory Fish Stocks, 4 December 1995, 2167 UNTS 3.

São Tomé and Principe;[75] Indonesia and Australia;[76] and various arrangements in North East Asia.[77]

(D) LAND-LOCKED STATES AND ENCLAVES

There are 43 land-locked states (plus Kosovo) and numerous enclaves detached from the metropolitan territory and lacking access to the sea.[78] Rights of transit, particularly for trade purposes, are normally arranged by treaty, but they may exist by revocable licence or local custom.[79] A right of transit may be posited as a general principle of law in itself or on the basis of a principle of servitudes or other general principles of law.[80] However, a general right of transit is difficult to sustain.

Against this unpromising background must be considered various attempts to improve the legal position of land-locked states. At UNCLOS I the Fifth Committee considered the question of free access to the sea of land-locked states. The result was Article 3 of the Convention on the High Seas,[81] which provides for free transit on a basis of reciprocity, and equal treatment in respect of port access and use. Article 4 recognized the right of every state, whether coastal or not, to sail ships under its flag on the high seas. The UN Convention on the Transit Trade of Landlocked States[82] adopts the principle of free access and sets out the conditions under which freedom of transit will be granted. The Convention provides a framework for the conclusion of bilateral treaties and is not directly dispositive with respect to rights of access.

UNCLOS Part X is devoted to the 'right of access of land-locked states to and from the sea and freedom of transit' (Articles 124 to 132).[83] The key provision is Article 125, which provides for land-locked states to enjoy freedom of transit through the territory of transit states by all means of transport (Article 125(1)), in accordance with bilateral, subregional, or regional agreements between the land-locked states and transit states (Article 125(2)). Article 125(3) provides that transit states have the right to take all measures necessary to ensure their legitimate interests are not thereby infringed. While this article constitutes a clear recognition of the principle involved, the modalities called for in paragraphs (2) and (3) must involve substantial qualifications in practice.

---

[75] Treaty between the Federal Republic of Nigeria and the Democratic Republic of São Tomé and Príncipe on the Joint Development of Petroleum and other Resources, in respect of Areas of the Exclusive Economic Zone of the Two States, 21 February 2001. See Tanga Biang, *The Joint Development Zone between Nigeria and Sao Tome and Principe* (2010).

[76] 11 December 1989, 1654 UNTS 105; see Burmester, in Fox (1990) 128; Marques Antunes (2003) 13 *CEPMLP*, at www.dundee.ac.uk/cepmlp/journal/html/Vol13/vol13–13.html.

[77] Kim (2004).

[78] Generally: Vasciannie, *Land-Locked and Geographically Disadvantaged States in the International Law of the Sea* (1990); Uprety (2006); Mishra & Singh (2008) 64 *India Quarterly* 55.

[79] *Right of Passage over Indian Territory (Portugal v India)*, ICJ Reports 1960 p 6, esp 66 (Judge Wellington Koo), 79–80 (Judge Armand-Ugon).

[80] Uprety (2006) 27–44.

[81] 29 April 1958, 450 UNTS 11.

[82] 8 July 1965, 597 UNTS 3.

[83] Nordquist, Rosenne & Nandan, 3 *Commentary* (1995) Part X.

Thirty-one of the land-locked states are developing states, among them 16 least developed countries.[84] The economic marginalization and special needs of these countries were recognized in the Millennium Declaration and at subsequent international conferences, leading to the convening of an international ministerial conference on the issue in 2003.[85] The conference resulted in the adoption of the Almaty Declaration and Programme of Action, setting as priorities the strengthening of transit transport co-operation, infrastructure, and trade for the benefit of developing land-locked and transit states. The UN Office of the High Representative for the Least Developed Countries, Landlocked Developing Countries and Small Island Developing States, established in 2001, has a primary role in co-ordinating and monitoring implementation.[86]

4. THE POLAR REGIONS[87]

(A) ANTARCTICA

The issues arising from territorial claims in polar regions were outlined in chapter 10. The object of the Antarctic Treaty is to ensure that Antarctica is used for peaceful purposes only, to promote international scientific co-operation within Antarctica and also to put aside disputes about territorial sovereignty.[88] Military personnel and equipment may be used in pursuing peaceful purposes. Nuclear explosions, for whatever purpose, are prohibited. The treaty applies to the area south of 60°S, and includes all the shelves but reserves the rights of states (not only contracting parties) with regard to the high seas in the area (Article VI).

Article IV reserves the rights and claims of contracting parties to territorial sovereignty in the area; also the legal position of the non-recognizing states.[89] Thus states with outstanding claims are protected from new sources of competition, while non-claimants are free to pursue scientific research without seeking permission.[90]

---

[84] See www.unohrlls.org/.

[85] GA Res 56/180, 21 December 2001.

[86] A/CONF.202/3, 29 August 2003, §51.

[87] Generally: Verhoeven, Sands & Bruce (eds), *The Antarctic Environment and International Law* (1992); Watts, *International Law and the Antarctic Treaty System* (1993); Francioni & Scovazzi (eds), *International Law for Antarctica* (1996); Rothwell, *The Polar Regions and the Development of International Law* (1996); Vidas, *Protecting the Polar Marine Environment* (2000); Koivurova, *Environmental Impact Assessment in the Arctic* (2002); Triggs & Riddell (eds), *Antarctica* (2007); Byers, 'Arctic Region' (2010) *MPEPIL*; Loukacheva (ed), *Polar Law Textbook* (2010); Crawford, in French, Saul & White (eds), *International Law and Dispute Settlement* (2010) 2; Joyner, in Berkman et al (eds), *Science Diplomacy* (2011) 97.

[88] 1 December 1959, 402 UNTS 71, Arts I–IV.

[89] On sovereignty and jurisdiction in Antarctica: Scott (2009) 20 *Ybk IEL* 3.

[90] On the question whether the Antarctic regime is an objective regime: Wolfrum, *The Convention on the Regulation of Antarctic Mineral Resource Activities* (1991) 18–20.

Two other matters may be mentioned. First, there is a liberal inspection system involving a right to designate observers unilaterally and provision for complete freedom of access for such observers at any time to all areas of Antarctica. Secondly, jurisdiction cannot in the context rest on the principle of territoriality. From the jurisdictional point of view the area is treated as *res nullius* and the nationality principle governs. However, general principles will have to be resorted to when a national of one party commits an offence or civil wrong against a national of another party or of a non-party.[91]

Three instruments supplement the regime: the Convention on the Conservation of Antarctic Seals (1972),[92] the Convention on the Conservation of Antarctic Marine Living Resources (1980),[93] and the Protocol on Environmental Protection to the Antarctic Treaty (1991).[94] Whaling disputes, continental shelf claims, prospecting for offshore hydrocarbon resources, and the effects of climate change present significant challenges to the Antarctic treaty system.[95]

(B) THE ARCTIC

No overarching regime equivalent to the Antarctic Treaty system operates in the Arctic,[96] which is instead governed largely by the law of the sea,[97] as well as various multilateral and bilateral agreements on specific issues,[98] soft law declarations and understandings, and the domestic legislation of the eight Arctic states.[99] These states work together to implement the Arctic Environmental Protection Strategy, also known as the Rovaniemi Process.[100] In 1996 they created the Arctic Council as a forum for intergovernmental co-operation and co-ordination on issues of sustainability and

---

[91] The nationality principle is applied to observers and scientific personnel exchanged under the Treaty: Art VIII(1).

[92] 1 June 1972, 1080 UNTS 175.

[93] 20 May 1980, 1329 UNTS 47. See Brown, in Triggs & Riddell (2007) 85; Potts, in Loukacheva (2010) 65; Rose & Milligan (2009) 20 *Ybk IEL* 41.

[94] Madrid, 4 October 1991, 30 ILM 1461. Annex II of the Protocol replaced the Agreed Measures for the Protection of Flora and Fauna (1964). See generally Joyner (1987) 81 *AJIL* 888; Blay (1992) 86 *AJIL* 377; Joyner, in Vidas (2000) 104; Bastmeijer (2003). The Madrid Protocol effectively replaces the Convention on the Regulation of Antarctic Mineral Resource Activities, 2 June 1988, 27 ILM 868.

[95] Joyner (2011). Further: Rogan-Finnemore, in Leane & von Tigerstrom (eds), *International Law Issues in the South Pacific* (2005) 199; Triggs & Riddell (2007); Hemmings & Stephens (2009) 20 *Public LR* 9.

[96] Vidas, in Vidas (2000) 78.

[97] Pharand, *The Law of the Sea in the Arctic* (1973); Byers, 'Arctic Region' (2010) *MPEPIL*.

[98] E.g. International Convention for the Prevention of Pollution from Ships, 2 November 1973, 1340 UNTS 184, modified by Protocol of 17 February 1978, 1340 UNTS 61; Agreement on Conservation of Polar Bears, 15 November 1973, 13 ILM 13; Espoo Convention on Environmental Impact Assessment in a Transboundary Context, 25 February 1991, 1989 UNTS 309; Stockholm Convention on Persistent Organic Pollutants, 22 May 2001, 2256 UNTS 119.

[99] Canada, Denmark, Finland, Iceland, Norway, Russia, Sweden, US.

[100] Vukas, in Vidas (2000) 34; Sands, *Principles of International Environmental Law* (2nd edn, 2003) 728–30.

environmental protection in the region. Several indigenous organizations are recognized as permanent participants in the Council.

The presence of a permanent human population in the Arctic (around 4 million people), the fact that there is no land territory underlying the Arctic ice cap, and other fundamental differences mean many of the successful measures of the Antarctic regime could not feasibly be transposed there.[101] Prominent areas of environmental concern in the Arctic include the melting of the sea ice and other effects of global warming, particularly for the indigenous peoples of the region; mineral exploitation; pollution; and the protection of living resources.[102] There are also numerous sources of potential conflict in terms of the law of the sea, including maritime delimitation and regulating navigation as the ice melts.[103]

5. OUTER SPACE[104]

There is no reason for believing that international law is spatially restricted. It may not be required to boldly go in advance of human interaction—but it is applicable to international exchanges and relations wherever they may occur. New arenas of human activity create problems and the law may have to adapt very quickly to cope with them, as it did in the case of exploitation of the continental shelf after 1945 (see chapter 11). The General Assembly has proclaimed that '[i]nternational law, including the Charter of the United Nations, applies to outer space and celestial bodies'.[105] The analogy most applicable is that of the high seas, a *res communis*, but such a category is not a source of precise rules.

Although much remains to be done, particularly in relation to controlling military uses of space, a solid area of agreement on some basic rules has been achieved since space exploration began in 1957 with the launch of Sputnik 1 by the Soviet Union. The basis for agreement has been an early acceptance of the principle that outer space and

---

[101] For comparison: Loukacheva (2010).

[102] Nowlan, *Arctic Legal Regime for Environmental Protection* (2001); Koivurova (2002); Potts, Tavis & Clive Schofield (2008) 23 *IJMCL* 151; Potts, in Loukacheva (2010) 65; Bankes, in Loukacheva (2010) 101; Smith (2011) 41 *G Wash ILR* 651.

[103] Generally: Joyner, in Triggs & Riddell (2007) 61; Byers, 'Arctic Region' (2010) *MPEPIL*; Smith (2011).

[104] Generally: Lachs, *Law of Outer Space* (1972); Christol, *The Modern International Law of Outer Space* (1982); Reynolds (1992) 25 *Vand JTL* 225; Jasentuliyana (ed), *Space Law* (1992); Lafferranderie & Crowther (eds), *Outlook on Space Law Over the Next 30 Years* (1997); Jasentuliyana, *International Space Law and the United Nations* (1999); Sands (2nd edn, 2003) 382–5; Hermida, *Legal Basis for a National Space Legislation* (2004); Wolter, *Common Security in Outer Space and International Law* (2006); Lyall & Larsen, *Space Law* (2009); Jakhu, *International Space Law* (2011).

[105] GA Res 1721(XVI), 20 December 1961. Also: Treaty on Principles Governing the Activities of States in the Exploration and Use of Outer Space, including the Moon and other Celestial Bodies, 27 January 1967, 610 UNTS 205, Art 3.

celestial bodies are not susceptible to appropriation by states.[106] Evidence of generally accepted principles is provided by the General Assembly Resolution of 13 December 1963,[107] adopted unanimously, which contains 'a declaration of legal principles' governing activities of states in the exploration and use of outer space.[108]

Five multilateral treaties on outer space have been concluded since the 1963 resolution:

(1) Outer Space Treaty (1967);

(2) Agreement on the Rescue of Astronauts, the Return of Astronauts and the Return of Objects Launched into Outer Space (1968);[109]

(3) Convention on International Liability for Damage Caused by Space Objects (1972);[110]

(4) Convention on Registration of Objects Launched into Outer Space (1974);[111] and

(5) Agreement Governing the Activities of States on the Moon and Other Celestial Bodies (1979).[112]

The regime created by the Outer Space Treaty, adopted as a sequel to the 1963 resolution, is not dissimilar to that of the Antarctic Treaty of 1959, with the important difference that there are no claimants to sovereignty in outer space. Article 1 provides that exploration and use of outer space 'shall be carried out for the benefit and in the interests of all countries ... and shall be the province of all mankind'; and further, outer space (including the moon and other celestial bodies) 'shall be free for exploration and use by all states without discrimination of any kind, on a basis of equality and in accordance with international law, and there shall be free access to all areas of celestial bodies'. Freedom of scientific investigation is established. Article 2 provides that outer space 'is not subject to national appropriation by claim of sovereignty, by means of use or occupation, or any other means'.

There is no provision on the precise boundary between outer space and airspace, that is, between the regime of *res communis* and the sovereignty of states over national territory. Until there is agreement on the legality of certain types of activity on the fringes of national airspace, states will tend to reserve their positions on a boundary line beyond which the application of sanctions against unlawful activities may be

---

[106] Although existing principles on acquisition of territory would have been applicable, as they are to uninhabited polar regions.

[107] GA Res 1962(XVII), 13 December 1963 (Declaration of Legal Principles Governing the Activities of States in the Exploration and Uses of Outer Space). On the relations of the Outer Space Treaty and the resolution: Fawcett, *International Law and the Uses of Outer Space* (1968) 4–14.

[108] Other statements of principles on outer space adopted by the GA are compiled in ST/SPACE/11, 2002.

[109] 22 April 1968, 672 UNTS.

[110] 29 March 1972; 961 UNTS 187.

[111] GA Res 3235(XXIX), 12 November 1974, 1023 UNTS 15.

[112] 5 December 1979, 1363 UNTS 3.

problematic.[113] The lowest limit above the earth sufficient to permit free orbit of spacecraft would make a sensible criterion: this limit would be of the order of 100 miles, the lowest technically desirable altitude of orbit.[114] There may be a customary rule that satellites in orbit cannot be interfered with unless interference is justified in terms of the law concerning individual or collective self-defence.

The general regime is, like that of the high seas, based upon free use and a prohibition of claims to sovereignty by individual states. However, if and when the moon and other bodies are the objects of regular human activity, bases will be set up which may create some sort of possessory title. At any rate the existing rules need development to cope with the practical problems of peaceful but competing uses and matters of jurisdiction. Article 8 of the Outer Space Treaty provides that 'a State Party to the Treaty on whose registry an object launched into outer space is carried shall retain jurisdiction and control over such object, and over any personnel thereof, while in outer space or on a celestial body'. The UN has maintained registers of launchings, first in accordance with a 1961 General Assembly resolution,[115] then under the Registration Convention of 1974. Article 6 of the Outer Space Treaty provides that states parties shall bear responsibility for national activities in space, whether carried on by governmental or by non-governmental entities. Article 7 provides that states parties that launch objects into outer space, and states parties from whose territory or facility objects are launched, are strictly liable for damage caused by such objects to other states parties or their nationals. Article 9 of the Outer Space Treaty lays down standards of conduct for states engaged in exploration and use of outer space. Thus activities shall be conducted 'with due regard to the corresponding interests of all other States Parties to the Treaty' and study and exploration shall be carried out so as to avoid harmful contamination of outer space and celestial bodies and also 'adverse changes in the environment of the Earth resulting from the introduction of extraterrestrial matter'.

Article 4 of the Outer Space Treaty creates a regime of demilitarization.[116] But the desire to maintain outer space for peaceful uses has led to growing concern that the regime is inadequate to prevent the 'weaponization' of outer space, through the placement in orbit of devices with destructive capacity.[117] In 2008 Russia and China presented to the Conference a draft treaty on the prevention of the placement of weapons in outer space and of the threat or use of force against outer space objects.[118] The draft

---

[113] Fawcett (1968) 23–4; Goedhuis (1982) 174 Hague *Recueil* 367–408; Marston (1984) 55 *BY* 405, 564–6.

[114] Fawcett (1968) 23–4. In Article 1 of the draft treaty presented by Russia and China to the Conference on Disarmament in 2008, outer space is defined as 'space beyond the elevation of approximately 100 *km* above ocean level of the Earth' (emphasis added; CD/1839, 29 February 2008).

[115] GA Res 1721B(XVI), 20 December 1961.

[116] Also Art 3. Earlier developments: Partial Test Ban Treaty; GA Res 1884(XVIII), 17 November 1963. Further: Fawcett (1968) 29–42; Bridge (1979–80) 13 *Akron LR* 649; Wolter (2006).

[117] E.g. 49th session of the Legal Subcommittee on the Peaceful Uses of Outer Space ('Legal Subcommittee'), A/AC.105/942, 16 April 2010, 6, 8; 53rd session of the Committee on the Peaceful Uses of Outer Space, A/65/20, 18 June 2010, 8. See further Jasentuliyana (1999) 67–129; Wolter (2006).

[118] CD/1839 29, February 2008.

has not yet been adopted, not least because of US opposition.[119] The General Assembly has observed that the Conference on Disarmament has prime responsibility for negotiating a multilateral treaty on preventing an arms race.[120]

An important feature of the use of outer space, as opposed to its exploration, has been the employment of satellites in orbit to develop telecommunications and systems of broadcasting. The major developments so far have been based upon the cooperative management of such activities by means of international organizations. The principal organization is INTELSAT, first established as a consortium of interests in 1964, but placed on a permanent basis in 1973. The definitive arrangements consist of an interstate agreement and an Operating Agreement,[121] to which both governments and designated entities, public or private, may be parties. INTELSAT was privatized in 2005.[122]

In addition there are regional systems and a global specialized network, International Maritime Satellite Organization (INMARSAT).[123] Problems created by these developments include the conservation of the radio frequency spectrum and the powers of the International Telecommunications Union (ITU) and UNESCO to take action in the matter, and also the legal responsibility of international organizations for space activities. Article 6 of the Outer Space Treaty provides that 'responsibility for compliance with this Treaty shall be borne both by the international organization [which carries on activities in outer space] and by the States Parties to the Treaty participating in such organization.'[124] The collision of a dead Russian satellite and an active US satellite in 2009 has highlighted the need for improved management of space debris and traffic.[125]

Activities in outer space necessarily involve the type of problem met with in the context of enjoyment of the freedoms of the high seas. Certain activities are considered in certain quarters either to infringe the principle of non-appropriation or to involve breaches of other principles of general international law. The first category is exemplified by the phenomenon of geostationary (or synchronous) satellites, which remain fixed above a given location on the earth's surface. Eight equatorial states have claimed that the individual segments of the unique (and therefore finite) geostationary orbit

---

[119] E.g. CD/1680, 10 July 2002. Some argue that an international code of conduct for outer space activities would be a more feasible alternative, which might cover other matters of concern including space traffic management and the problem of space debris: see revised draft code approved by the Council of the European Union, 14455/10, 11 October 2010; Krepon & Black, in Pelton & Jakhu (eds), *Space Safety Regulations and Standards* (2010) 239.

[120] E.g. GA Res 62/20, 5 December 2007; GA Res 65/44, 8 December 2010.

[121] Operating Agreement relating to the International Telecommunications Satellite Organization (INTELSAT), 20 August 1971, 1220 UNTS 149; see Bender, *Launching and Operating Satellites* (1998) 120.

[122] Katkin (2005) 38 *Vand JTL* 1323.

[123] 3 September 1976, 15 ILM 219, 1051; amendments: 27 ILM 691.

[124] Also Art 13.

[125] Jakhu (2008–9) 3 *Ybk Space P* 254.

are subject to a regime of national sovereignty.[126] Such claims are difficult to reconcile with Articles 1 and 2 of the Outer Space Treaty.

In any case there is a fine line to be drawn between excessive use of the orbit and appropriation. Space satellites can also be used for the collection of data relating to the earth's surface and also subsurface conditions, that is, remote sensing. The legality of remote sensing is to some extent problematic.[127]

The General Assembly continues to promote international co-operation in the peaceful uses of outer space,[128] as well as transparency and confidence-building measures in outer space activities.[129] It has designated 12 April as the annual International Day of Human Space Flight to commemorate the first human space flight by Soviet Yuri Gagarin in 1961.[130]

---

[126] Bogotá Declaration, 1976, Jasentuliyana & Lee (eds), 2 *Manual on Space Law* (1979) 383–7; *Digest of US Practice* (1979) 1187–8.

[127] Draft Principles adopted by the Legal Sub-Committee, 13 June 1986, 25 ILM 1334. Further: Lyall & Larsen (2009) 411–42.

[128] E.g. GA Res 65/97, 10 December 2010.

[129] E.g. GA Res 65/68, 8 December 2010.

[130] GA Res 65/271, 7 April 2011.

15

LEGAL ASPECTS OF THE PROTECTION OF THE ENVIRONMENT

1. THE ROLE OF INTERNATIONAL LAW IN ADDRESSING ENVIRONMENTAL PROBLEMS

Increased appreciation of the many risks to the earth's environment and the potentially irreversible damage which may be caused by human activity has resulted in a conscious effort by governments acting collectively, by international organizations, and by non-governmental organizations, to enhance legal protection of the environment.[1] The resulting agenda is extensive: it includes the depletion of the ozone layer, problems of transboundary air pollution and anthropogenic climate change, the risks created by reliance upon nuclear power, the protection of the polar regions, the conservation of endangered species of flora and fauna, the control of the disposal of ultrahazardous wastes, and a range of procedural obligations from information exchange to environmental assessment. The policy issues generated by such an agenda are often difficult to resolve: inevitably the issues do not concern the 'environment' in isolation, but relate to economic and social priorities, systems of loss distribution and issues of development. Reconciling the protection of the environment with other issues such as these is sometimes referred to as the goal of sustainable development.

---

[1] Kummer, *International Management of Hazardous Wastes* (1995); Okowa, *State Responsibility for Transboundary Air Pollution* (2000); de Sadeleer, *Environmental Principles* (2002); Sands, *Principles of International Environmental Law* (2nd edn, 2003); Yamin & Depledge, *The International Climate Change Regime* (2004); Stephens (2006) 25 *AYIL* 227; Bodansky, Brunnee & Hey, *The Oxford Handbook of International Environmental Law* (2007); Birnie, Boyle & Redgwell, *International Law and the Environment* (3rd edn, 2009); Stephens, *International Courts and Environmental Protection* (2009); Hunter, Salzman & Zaelke, *International Environmental Law and Policy* (2010); Redgwell, in Evans (ed), *International Law* (3rd edn, 2010) 687.

(A) ENVIRONMENTAL ISSUES UNDER GENERAL INTERNATIONAL LAW

Environmental concerns are reflected in many areas of international law: relevant categories include the law of the sea, the legal regime of Antarctica, and the non-navigational uses of international watercourses. Simultaneously, it is evident that general international law does not provide the focused problem-solving which results from carefully prepared standard-setting treaties linked with domestic and international support systems and funding. The development of specialized environmental regimes by treaty serves to address this deficiency.

Nonetheless, the legal underpinnings of the protection of the environment continue to be institutions of general international law. This is apparent from the literature, which typically invokes the principles of state responsibility of the territorial sovereign for sources of danger to other states created or tolerated within its territory, and cites *Trail Smelter*[2] and (less appropriately) *Corfu Channel*.[3] It comes as no surprise that cases concerning environmental issues have also—and centrally—involved issues of general international law. *Nuclear Tests* concerned issues of admissibility and remedial law, as well as the status of unilateral promises.[4] *Certain Phosphate Lands in Nauru* related to issues of admissibility, the regime of a former UN trust territory, and state responsibility.[5] The advisory opinion of the ITLOS Seabed Disputes Chamber, on responsibility and liability for international seabed mining, addressed important questions of treaty interpretation.[6]

In practice, specific transboundary problems will have a background in treaty relations and other dealings between states. *Gabčíkovo-Nagymaros*, relating to a joint hydroelectric project on the Danube, was concerned with the law of treaties and related points of state responsibility (issues of justification for alleged breaches of treaty obligations).[7] *Pulp Mills* dealt with the law of treaties, international organizations, and international watercourses.[8] Environmental concerns may arise in connection with law of the sea issues,[9] and international trade disputes brought before the WTO Dispute Settlement Body,[10] among others.

---

[2] (1938) 3 RIAA 1905; (1941) 3 RIAA 1938.

[3] *(UK v Albania)*, ICJ Reports 1949 p 4.

[4] *(Australia v France)*, ICJ Reports 1974 p 253; *(New Zealand v France)*, ICJ Reports 1974 p 457.

[5] *(Nauru v Australia)*, ICJ Reports 1992 p 240.

[6] *Responsibilities and Obligations of States Sponsoring Persons and Entities with Respect to Activities in the Area*, ITLOS Case No 17 (Advisory Opinion, 1 February 2011) available at www.itlos.org.

[7] *(Hungary/Slovakia)*, ICJ Reports 1997 p 7.

[8] *Pulp Mills on the River Uruguay (Argentina v Uruguay)*, ICJ Reports 2010 p 14.

[9] E.g. *Southern Bluefin Tuna* (1999) 117 ILR 148; *MOX Plant* (2001) 126 ILR 257.

[10] E.g. *US—Gasoline*, WTO Doc WT/DS2/AB/R, 29 April 1996; *US—Shrimp* WTO Doc WT/DS58/AB/R, 12 October 1998; *Brazil—Measures Affecting Imports of Retreaded Tyres*, WTO Doc WT/DS332/AB/R, 3 December 2007.

(B) DEFICIENCIES IN THE ADVERSARIAL SYSTEM OF RESPONSIBILITY

The key problem with focusing on responsibility as a means of ensuring environmental protection is that it addresses issues after damage has already occurred, instead of focusing on the need for prevention of damage in the first place. This deficiency is reflected in the growing support for the principle of preventive action in the area of environmental protection.

A particular difficulty is the selection and deployment of an appropriate basis of claim. Environmental impacts are often, in physical terms, incremental and may involve complex and diffuse causal mechanisms. The requirement of material or significant damage as a necessary condition of claim bears an uneasy relation to the scientific proof of a certain threshold of damage caused by an overall rise in radiation or other forms of pollution, and problems of multiple causation often arise.

In *Nuclear Tests*, the applicants employed the international law equivalent of trespass to deal with this problem: the deposit of radioactive fall-out was classified as a violation of their territorial sovereignty.[11] Likewise, the concept of 'decisional sovereignty' was used, referring to their right to determine what acts should take place within its territory. Implicit in these arguments was the proposition that little or no material harm to the applicants or their nationals would be caused by levels of fall-out which—over the distances involved—were rather less than the natural background radiation. The Court in a somewhat contrived manner avoided the problem, and French atmospheric testing ceased.[12]

It has been said that the decision in *Nuclear Tests* 'suggested that an international tribunal cannot grant injunctions or prohibitory orders restraining violations of international law'.[13] This is unjustified, and declarations are given by the Court which are injunctive in effect, as the joint dissenting opinion pointed out.[14]

But international claims—whether before the Court or a tribunal—can take many years to resolve, during which time the project in question—whether dam,[15] bridge,[16] or

---

[11] ICJ Pleadings, 1 *Nuclear Tests*, 479–90 (Argument of Byers QC).

[12] The Court dismissed the application on the basis that, as France had made a unilateral declaration that it would cease nuclear testing, the claim raised by Australia and New Zealand was rendered moot: *Australia v France*, ICJ Reports 1974 p 253, 271–2; *New Zealand v France*, ICJ Reports 1974 p 457, 477. See Elkind (1974) 8 *Vand JTL* 39; Thierry (1974) 20 *AFDI* 286; Franck (1975) 69 *AJIL* 612; Lellouche (1975) 16 *Harv ILJ* 614; Macdonald & Hough (1977) 20 *GYIL* 337; Stephens (2009) 137–50; Watts, 'Nuclear Tests Cases' (2007) *MPEPIL*. Also: *Request for an Examination of the Situation in Accordance with Paragraph 63 of the Court's Judgment of 20 December 1974 in the Nuclear Tests Case*, ICJ Reports 1995 p 288.

[13] Birnie, Boyle & Redgwell (3rd edn, 2009) 228.

[14] ICJ Reports 1974 p 457, 494–523 (Judges Onyeama, Dillard, Jiménez de Aréchaga & Waldock, joint diss).

[15] In *Gabčíkovo-Nagymaros*, ICJ Reports 1997 p 7, the Special Agreement specifically excluded provisional measures. But for a successful application see *Indus Waters Kishenganga Arbitration (Pakistan v India)*, Order of 23 September 2011, available at www.pca-cpa.org/showpage.asp? pag_id=1392.

[16] *Passage through the Great Belt (Finland v Denmark)*, Order of 10 September 1992, ICJ Reports 1992 p 348.

large-scale land reclamation project[17]—may have been completed with little prospect of reversal. Requests for interim measures of protection addressed to the International Court or other tribunals thus have a crucial role.[18]

(C) THE RIO CONFERENCE 1992 AND THE DEVELOPMENT OF INTERNATIONAL ENVIRONMENTAL LAW

Evidence of international concern for environmental protection may be found in earlier international agreements[19] such as the Convention relative to the Preservation of Fauna and Flora in their Natural Habitat (1936),[20] the Convention between the United States of America and Mexico for the protection of migratory birds and game mammals (1937),[21] and the International Agreement for the Regulation of Whaling (1938).[22] But greater momentum and political impact was afforded by such organizations as World Wildlife Fund (founded 1961) and Greenpeace (founded 1971). The earlier sectoral approach was to a degree subsumed in a broader political and legal agenda culminating in the Rio Conference in 1992. An important step was the Brundtland Report, produced in 1987 by the World Commission on Environment and Development to address the challenge of finding multilateral paths toward sustainable development.[23] It was the first major report to focus on global sustainability, linking environmental and developmental issues; further, it proposed solutions based on international cooperation, and institutional and legal change.

In 1992, more than 100 governments met in Rio de Janeiro for the UN Conference on Environment and Development. The Earth Summit produced Agenda 21, a comprehensive plan of action calling for the 'further development of international law on sustainable development, giving special attention to the delicate balance between environmental and developmental concerns.'[24] It also produced the Rio Declaration on Environment and Development,[25] containing 27 principles linked to the concept of sustainable development, and the non-binding Authoritative Statement of Principles for a

---

[17] *Land Reclamation by Singapore (Malaysia v Singapore)* (2003) 126 ILR 487 (provisional measures).

[18] See *Southern Bluefin Tuna* (1999) 117 ILR 148, the beneficial consequences of which were not entirely eliminated by the Annex VII tribunal's denial of jurisdiction: (2000) 119 ILR 508. Likewise the improved interstate co-operation that resulted from the limited provisional measures orders in *MOX Plant* (2001) 126 ILR 257 assisted in the resolution of that problem, notwithstanding the subsequent decision of the ECJ: Case C–459/03, *Commission v Ireland* [2006] ECR I-4635. Further: *Indus Waters Kishenganga Arbitration*, Order of 23 September 2011. For environmental cases in which provisional measures were refused: *Great Belt*, Provisional Measures, Order of 29 July 1991, ICJ Reports 1991 p 12; *Pulp Mills*, Provisional Measures, Order of 23 January 2007, ICJ Reports 2007 p 3.

[19] For discussion of environmental treaty ratification in the 1900s: Frank (1999) 69 *Sociological Inquiry* 523.

[20] 9 November 1933, 172 LNTS 241.

[21] 7 February 1936, 178 LNTS 310.

[22] 8 June 1937, 190 UNTS 79.

[23] World Commission on Environment and Development (WCED), *Our Common Future* (1987).

[24] A/CONF.151/26/Rev.1, Annex II, 12 August 1992.

[25] A/CONF.151/26 (Vol 1), Annex I, 12 August 1992.

Global Consensus on the Management, Conservation and Sustainable Development of All Types of Forests (the Forest Principles).[26] In addition, the Convention on Biological Diversity (Biodiversity Convention)[27] and the Framework Convention on Climate Change (UNFCCC)[28] were opened for signature.

2. EMERGENT LEGAL PRINCIPLES

A number of candidate legal principles have emerged from this ferment of activity: the more important of these may be briefly reviewed.

(A) THE PREVENTIVE PRINCIPLE[29]

As the International Court has observed, the 'often irreversible' character of environmental damage, and the limitations of reparation after the fact, mean that prevention is of the utmost importance.[30] The preventive principle requires action to be taken at an early stage. It is supported through a wide range of domestic and international measures directed at prohibiting harmful activities and enforcing compliance with standards.

In 2001 the ILC adopted the Draft Articles on the Prevention of Transboundary Harm from Hazardous Activities.[31] This was the result of dividing its work on transboundary harm into two parts,[32] the other pertaining to liability for transboundary harm.[33] The Draft Articles dealing with prevention 'apply to activities not prohibited by international law which involve a risk of causing significant transboundary harm through their physical consequences'. Limiting activities to those 'not prohibited by international law' was ostensibly intended to separate issues of international liability from the topic of responsibility.[34]

The Draft Articles draw on other established principles of international environmental law. For example, the requirement that a state 'shall take all appropriate measures to prevent significant transboundary harm or at any event to minimize the risk thereof' invokes the precautionary principle, though the formulation used has

---

[26] A/CONF.151/26 (Vol 3), Annex III, 14 August 1992.

[27] 5 June 1992, 1760 UNTS 79.

[28] 9 May 1992, 1771 UNTS 107. Further: Yamin & Depledge (2004).

[29] De Sadeleer (2002) ch 2; Sands (2nd edn, 2003) 246–9.

[30] *Gabčíkovo-Nagymaros*, ICJ Reports 1997 p 7, 78.

[31] ILC *Ybk* 2001/II(2), 144–70.

[32] Knox (2002) 96 *AJIL* 292, 308.

[33] In 2006 the ILC adopted a set of eight draft principles on the allocation of loss in case of transboundary harm arising out of hazardous activities; GAOR, 58th Session, Supplement No 10, A/61/10, 106–82. Further: Boyle (2005) 17 *JEL* 3. Unlike the case of prevention of harm, the adoption of a convention is not envisaged in relation to the allocation of loss.

[34] ILC *Ybk* 2001/II(2), 150 (Commentary to Art 1, §6).

been criticized.[35] Draft Article 7 includes environmental impact as a tool to assess the likelihood of transboundary harm. In requiring co-operation between states to prevent transboundary harm the Draft Articles also rely on the dynamics of international politics and supporting structures of international law to implement the provisions of any convention based upon them. Seeking to address circumstances which formed the basis of disputes in cases such as *Trail Smelter*, the ILC also sets out the 'fundamental principle that the prior authorization of a state is required for activities which involve a risk of causing significant transboundary harm undertaken in its territory or otherwise under its jurisdiction or control'.

Despite the uncertainty surrounding their future status, the Draft Articles provide an authoritative statement on the scope of a state's international legal obligation to prevent a risk of transboundary harm.[36]

(B) THE PRECAUTIONARY PRINCIPLE[37]

Probably the best known of the still evolving legal principles of environmental protection is the precautionary principle. This has been described as 'an attempt to codify the concept of precaution in law'[38] where 'precaution' is defined as a strategy for addressing risk.[39] It concerns 'the manner in which policy-makers, for the purposes of protecting the environment, apply science, technology and economics'.[40] Although well known, it is difficult to define. Sands observes that there is 'no uniform understanding of the meaning of the precautionary principle among states and other members of the international community'.[41] It has been noted that the consequences of applying a precautionary approach differ widely, depending on the context.[42]

On the other hand, from the 1970s a precautionary approach has been used in some national systems (e.g., Germany and the US),[43] and it is part of European law.[44] Extending the logic of precaution to the international level, the 'precautionary approach' receives clear support in the Rio Declaration (Principle 15):

In order to protect the environment, the precautionary approach shall be widely applied by states according to their capabilities. Where there are threats of serious or irreversible

---

[35] Ibid, 153–5 (Art 3): Handl, in Bodansky, Brunnee & Hey (2007) 540.

[36] Handl, in Bodansky, Brunnee & Hey (2007) 540.

[37] De Sadeleer (2002) ch 3; Freestone & Hey (eds), *The Precautionary Principle and International Law* (1996); Sands (2nd edn, 2003) 266–79; Birnie, Boyle & Redgwell (3rd edn, 2009) 159–64; Zander, *The Application of the Precautionary Principle in Practice* (2010); Foster, *Science and the Precautionary Principle in International Courts and Tribunals* (2011); Schröder, 'Precautionary Approach/Principle' (2009) *MPEPIL*.

[38] Bodansky, Brunnee & Hey (2007) 599.

[39] Ibid, 598.

[40] Hey (1991–92) 4 *GIELR* 307.

[41] *Sands* (2nd edn, 2003) 212. For a critical perspective: Sunstein (2002–3) 151 *U Penn LR* 1003.

[42] Birnie, Boyle & Redgwell (3rd edn, 2009) 161.

[43] For an exploration of how the precautionary approach developed in different national jurisdictions: Cameron & Abouchar (1991) 14 *Boston Col ICLR* 4.

[44] Bodansky, Brunnee & Hey (2007) 599–600.

damage, lack of full scientific certainty shall not be used as a reason for postponing cost-effective measures to prevent environmental degradation.

Different permutations of the precautionary principle are found in numerous multilateral instruments, such as the UNFCCC and the Biodiversity Convention. The precautionary principle can be interpreted to imply that precautionary regulation is justified when there is no clear evidence about a particular risk scenario, when the risk itself is uncertain, or until the risk is disproved.[45] The precautionary approach was affirmed as an obligation of sponsoring states in the advisory opinion of the ITLOS Seabed Disputes Chamber.[46]

(C) THE CONCEPT OF SUSTAINABLE DEVELOPMENT[47]

Although emerging as a distinct field of scholarship, the existence of sustainable development as a distinct legal concept, that is, one which gives rise to or defines actionable rights, is controversial. Given the breadth of the concept, which includes trade, investment, and social concerns, it can be argued that sustainable development is better understood as a collection, or collocation, of different legal categories, and as a 'general guideline'.[48]

The most commonly cited definition, from the Brundtland Report, is 'development that meets the needs of the present without compromising the ability of future generations to meet their own needs'.[49] Development, a process of change toward improving quality of life for human beings and their communities, is said to be sustainable when it is achieved by the integration of social, economic, and environmental considerations in a way that provides for and protects the long-term well-being of populations. The field of sustainable development law refers to the emerging body of legal instruments, norms, and treaties directed at implementing this balance, as well as to the distinctive procedural elements (often based upon human rights law) underpinning them. The objective of sustainable development is increasingly included in general economic treaties and regional integration treaties.[50]

---

[45] Birnie, Boyle & Redgwell (3rd edn, 2009) 604–7.

[46] ITLOS Advisory Opinion, §§125–35.

[47] Boyle & Freestone (eds), *International Law and Sustainable Development* (1999); EC Commission, *The Law of Sustainable Development* (2000); Sands (2nd edn, 2003) 252–66; Cordonier Segger & Khlalfan (eds), *Sustainable Development Law* (2004); Beyerlin, 'Sustainable Development' (2009) *MPEPIL*; Cordonier Segger, Gehring & Newcombe (eds), *Sustainable Development in World Investment Law* (2011). Further: ILA, Report of the 70th Conference (2002) 380; ILA New Delhi Declaration of Principles of International Law relating to Sustainable Development, A/57/329, 31 August 2002.

[48] Cassese, *International Law* (2nd edn, 2005) 492–3.

[49] WCED (1987) 43.

[50] E.g. Agreement Establishing the World Trade Organization, 15 April 1994, 1867 UNTS 410, preamble; TFEU (2008) *OJEU* C 115/47, Art 11.

(D) THE POLLUTER-PAYS PRINCIPLE

The polluter-pays principle[51] is again not so much a rule as a 'general guideline'.[52] Article 16 of the Rio Declaration expresses the idea in these terms:

National authorities should endeavour to promote the internalisation of environmental costs and the use of economic instruments, taking into account the approach that the polluter should, in principle, bear the cost of pollution, with due regard to the public interest and without distorting international trade and investment.

Birnie, Boyle, and Redgwell describe the principle as 'an economic policy for allocating the costs of pollution or environmental damage borne by public authorities' with 'implications for the development of international and national law on liability for damage'.[53] It is clear from the language of Article 16 of the Rio Declaration that the principle is essentially programmatic and hortatory: 'it is doubtful whether it has achieved the status of a generally applicable rule of customary international law...'.[54] Its content is vague; it is unclear for example whether it entails strict liability. If so, it goes beyond normal principles of state responsibility for damage affecting the legal interest of another state.

(E) THE *SIC UTERE TUO* PRINCIPLE

The general obligation of states to ensure that activities within their jurisdiction and control respect the environment of other states (and of areas beyond national control) was affirmed by the International Court in *Legality of the Threat or Use of Nuclear Weapons*.[55]

(F) THE OBLIGATION OF ENVIRONMENTAL IMPACT ASSESSMENT[56]

Environmental impact assessment is a technique for integrating environmental considerations into decision-making processes.[57] In international law, the duty to undertake an environmental impact assessment is expressed in Principle 17 of the Rio Declaration:

[E]nvironmental impact assessment, as a national instrument, shall be undertaken for proposed activities that are likely to have a significant adverse impact on the environment and are subject to a decision of a competent national authority.

---

[51] De Sadeleer (2002) ch 1.

[52] Cassese (2nd edn, 2005) 492–3.

[53] Birnie, Boyle & Redgwell (3rd edn, 2009) 322.

[54] *Sands* (2nd edn, 2003) 280.

[55] ICJ Reports 1996 p 226, 241–2. Also: Rio Declaration, Principle 2; Institute of International Law, Resolution on Responsibility and Liability under International Law for Environmental Damage (1998) 67 *Ann de l'Inst* 487; *Gabčíkovo-Nagymaros*, ICJ Reports 1997 p 7, 41.

[56] Generally: Knox (2002) 96 *AJIL* 291; Sands (2nd edn, 2003) ch 16; Craick, *The International Law of Environmental Impact Assessment* (2008); Epiney, 'Environmental Impact Assessment' (2009) *MPEPIL*.

[57] Sands (2nd edn, 2003) 799–800.

EC Directive 85/337/EEC[58] was the first international instrument to adopt environmental impact assessment, although implicit recognition can also be found in Principle
21 of the Stockholm Declaration of 1972.[59] The most prominent international convention in the field is the Espoo Convention on Environmental Impact Assessment in a
Transboundary Context of 1991,[60] which 'requires its parties to assess the transboundary environmental effects of certain actions within their jurisdiction and to notify
and consult with potentially affected states about those effects.'[61] The latest periodic
review of the Convention notes the inconsistent levels of application and communication issues between states.[62] Nonetheless, the requirement to conduct environmental
impact assessments is an important element of preventing transboundary harm from
hazardous activities. This was recognized by the International Court in *Pulp Mills*,
where it was said that the practice of undertaking environmental impact assessments

has gained so much acceptance among States that it may now be considered a requirement
under general international law to undertake an environmental impact assessment where
there is a risk that the proposed industrial activity may have a significant adverse impact in
a transboundary context, in particular, on a shared resource.[63]

On the other hand, the Court held, the *content* of any such assessment is a matter to
be defined by the relevant national law.[64] This 'hybrid' obligation raises problems, in
particular, for the evaluation of transboundary harm.

3. DEVELOPMENT OF MULTILATERAL STANDARD-SETTING CONVENTIONS

A significant development in international law, and one that characterizes international environmental law, is the evolution of multilateral standard-setting conventions. These conventions, drafted and agreed in response to international collective
action problems pertaining to the environment, establish international environmental regimes which provide both the structure and resources for addressing the issue at
their core. Both the development and the effectiveness of international environmental
regimes have been the subject of interdisciplinary scholarship.[65]

---

[58] Directive 85/337/EEC, Council Directive of 27 June 1985 on the assessment of the effects of certain
public and private projects on the environment, 85/337/EEC OJ L175, 05/07/1985 0040–0048.

[59] Further: Knox (2002) 96 *AJIL* 292.

[60] 25 February 1991, 1989 UNTS 309.

[61] Knox (2002) 96 *AJIL* 292, 302.

[62] Economic Commission for Europe, *Review of Implementation of the Espoo Convention*, ECE/
MP.EIA/11 (2008), Section 1.4: Findings of the Review.

[63] ICJ Reports 2010 p 14, 82q–3.

[64] Ibid, 83.

[65] For the effectiveness of international environmental regimes: Raustiala & Slaughter, in Carlsnales,
Risse & Simmons (eds), *Handbook of International Relations* (2002); Young (ed), *The Effectiveness of*

(A) TRAFFIC IN ENDANGERED SPECIES

The Convention on International Trade in Endangered Species of Wild Fauna and Flora (CITES) was agreed in 1973 and now has 175 parties.[66] An earlier meeting of the World Conservation Union (IUCN) in Nairobi (1963) was a catalyst for CITES;[67] IUCN continues to support CITES through scientific advice and advocacy. The CITES Secretariat is located in Geneva and is administered by the UN Environment Program (UNEP). CITES seeks to regulate trade in species threatened with extinction by providing that the trade in such species 'must be subject to particularly strict regulation in order not to endanger further their survival and must only be authorized in exceptional circumstances.'[68] Parties are obliged to penalize trade in listed species and confiscate specimens when found; they are also required to make periodic reports to the Secretariat regarding their implementation of the Convention. CITES is an example of an environmental convention which targets the economic activity (trade) supporting the environmental harm (loss of species) as a means to address the problem; however, it does not directly address the demand-side drivers (such as consumer preference) or the supply-side drivers (such as poverty) of the trade in endangered species.[69]

(B) PROTECTION OF THE OZONE LAYER

The Vienna Convention on the Protection of the Ozone Layer of 1985 is largely a framework requiring further action by the parties.[70] However, it did serve as an important step towards further control measures, notably the Montreal Protocol of 1987 which established substantive controls on substances linked to ozone depletion (Article 2), a mechanism for reporting progress (Article 7), and a multilateral fund 'for the purposes of providing financial and technical co-operation, including the transfer of technologies' to support implementation (Article 10).[71] The Montreal Protocol incorporated a significant amount of the law concerning transboundary pollution (procedural and substantive) which attained customary status prior to its negotiation.[72] This regime has been described as 'dynamic and flexible' in its operation,[73] and the high participation (191 parties) in combination with some evidence supporting a reduction in ozone depletion suggests a measure of success.[74]

International Environmental Regimes (1999); Young, Rosenau & Czempiel (eds), *Governance Without Government* (1992).

[66] 3 March 1973, 993 UNTS 243.

[67] For the history: Sand (1997) 8 *EJIL* 29; Bowman, Davies & Redgwell (eds), *Lyster's International Wildlife Law* (2nd edn, 2011) 483–6.

[68] CITES, Art 2(1)—Fundamental Principles.

[69] Favre (1993) 33 *NRJ* 875; Wijnstekers, *The Evolution of CITES* (1995); Hutton & Dickson (eds), *Endangered Species Threatened Convention* (2000); Young (2003) 14 *CJIELP* 167.

[70] 22 March 1985, 1513 UNTS 293.

[71] Montreal Protocol on Substances That Deplete the Ozone Layer, 16 September 1987, 1522 UNTS 3.

[72] Blegen (1987–88) 16 *DJILP* 413, 424.

[73] Birnie, Boyle & Redgwell (3rd edn, 2009) 354.

[74] Ibid, 355. Also: Christie, *The Ozone Layer* (2001); Yoshida, *The International Legal Régime for the Protection of the Stratospheric Ozone Layer* (2001).

(C) TRANSBOUNDARY MOVEMENT OF HAZARDOUS WASTES

The Basel Convention of 1989[75] was negotiated in response to concerns that the transport of hazardous wastes between countries could pose an environmental hazard to both transit and recipient countries. It does not ban the transport of hazardous wastes, but places limits on their movement: it is permissible to export waste if the exporting country does not have sufficient disposal capacity or disposal sites capable of disposal in an environmentally sound manner, and if the wastes are required as raw material for recycling or recovery industries in the importing country. In addition, the exporting state must obtain the consent of the importing state and transit states before allowing a shipment of hazardous wastes. There is an obligation on parties to reduce hazardous waste and manage it in a manner consistent with environmental protection. Export of hazardous waste to Antarctica is explicitly banned (Article 6). The Basel Convention has been criticized for not adequately regulating the production of hazardous waste within states and, by allowing its trade, endorsing the export of an environmental problem from the developed to the developing world.[76] However, given the political realities underpinning what can be an expensive problem for exporting countries and a cost-effective solution offered by importers who develop an industry around transboundary shipments of such waste, the progress made in regulating some aspects of this issue through the Basel Convention could also be seen as a step forward.

(D) CLIMATE CHANGE[77]

The Fourth Assessment Report of the Intergovernmental Panel on Climate Change confirmed that the release of greenhouse gases into the atmosphere constitutes a major anthropogenic contribution to climate change.[78] The international climate change regime includes the UNFCCC and its Kyoto Protocol,[79] which is designed to facilitate climate protection through market-based initiatives. The Kyoto Protocol established a carbon market until 2012, with rules pertaining to emissions trading and 'flexible mechanisms' to be used by member states to help them meet their emissions reduction targets. The concept of carbon trading is controversial, and the nature of a successor

---

[75] Convention on the Control of Transboundary Movements of Hazardous Wastes and their Disposal, 22 March 1989, 1673 UNTS 57. Generally: Kummer (1992) 41 *ICLQ* 530; Kummer (1995); Sanders & Bowal (2001) 11 *JEL & P* 143; Sands (2nd edn, 2003) 691–5; Moen (2008) 32 *Marine Policy* 1053.

[76] Sands (2nd edn, 2003) 692; Sonak, Sonak & Guriyan (2008) 8 *Int Environ Agreements* 143; Quadri (2010) 22 *Florida JIL* 467.

[77] Generally: Yamin & Depledge (2004); Freestone & Streck (eds), *Legal Aspects of the Kyoto Protocol Mechanisms* (2005); Asselt, Sindico & Mehling (2008) 30 *Law & Policy* 423; Birnie, Boyle & Redgwell (3rd edn, 2009) 356–77; Held, Hervey & Theros (eds), *The Governance of Climate Change* (2011).

[78] Intergovernmental Panel on Climate Change (IPCC), *Climate Change 2007: A Synthesis Report* (2007): www.ipcc.ch/publications_and_data/ar4/syr/en/contents.html. The IPCC's Fifth Assessment Report is currently underway, with completion expected in 2014.

[79] Kyoto Protocol to the United Nations Framework Convention on Climate Change, FCCC/CP/1997/L.7/Add.1, 10 December 1997. Also: UN Convention to Combat Desertification in those Countries Experiencing Serious Drought and/or Desertification, Particularly in Africa, 12 September 1994, 1954 UNTS 3.

agreement to the Kyoto Protocol is the subject of heated debate. The success of emissions trading as a strategy depends not only on binding targets, but on robust reporting and a strong national and international infrastructure to track, verify, and compel compliance, features largely still lacking.[80]

(E) PROTECTION OF THE MARINE ENVIRONMENT[81]

Controlling marine pollution is an increasingly important matter of environmental concern, which features in a large number of international treaties and instruments. UNCLOS Article 192 provides generally that states have the obligation to protect and preserve the marine environment, and the rest of Part XII is dedicated to that objective, with further relevant provisions found throughout.[82] In addition to UNCLOS, numerous regional agreements address aspects of the protection of the marine environment, including the 1992 Convention for the Protection of the Marine Environment of the North-East Atlantic (OSPAR Convention),[83] and the framework conventions developed under the UNEP Regional Seas programme.[84]

Specific sources of marine pollution are also covered by separate instruments. The early focus was on oil spills,[85] but over time international rules have developed to address pollution from a range of sources including land-based activities, dumping at sea, other effects of maritime transport, and seabed activities.[86] Particularly prominent among the specific instruments are MARPOL 73/78,[87] regulating pollution from vessels, and the London Convention regulating dumping of waste.[88] Instruments such as these have had some impact; however, the biggest difficulties lie in effectively regulating pollution from land-based activities, by far the largest source of marine pollution. Chapter 17 of Agenda 21, the plan of action adopted at the Earth Summit in 1992, establishes a programme on marine environmental protection and urges states to adhere to the 1985 Montreal Guidelines for the Protection of the Marine Environment from Land-Based Sources.[89]

---

[80] Peterson,'Mointoring, Accounting and enforcement in Emissisons Trading Regimes', OECD Doc CCNM/GF/SD/ENV(2003)5/Final Yamin & Depledge (2004) 156 ;Tietenberg *Emissions Trading Principles and Practice* (2nd edn, 2006 170).

[81] Sands (2nd edn, 2003) 391–458. Generally chapter 12.

[82] 10 December 1982, 1833 UNTS 3. For discussion: Charney (1994) 28 *Int Lawyer* 879.

[83] 22 September 1992, 2354 UNTS 67.

[84] Generally: Sands (2nd edn, 2003) 399–408.

[85] Ibid, 393–5.

[86] Ibid, 415–48.

[87] International Convention for the Prevention of Pollution from Ships, as modified by the Protocol of 1978, 17 February 1978, 1340 UNTS 61.

[88] Convention for the Prevention of Marine Pollution by Dumping of Wastes and Other Matter, 29 December 1972, 1046 UNTS 138.

[89] A/CONF.151/26/Rev.1 (Vol I), 238.

(F) OTHER CONVENTIONS AND INSTITUTIONS

Numerous other environmental regimes, established by international conventions, exist to regulate different types of environmental risks and impacts. Examples include the Convention on Early Notification of a Nuclear Accident,[90] the Convention on the Protection and Use of Transboundary Watercourses and Lakes,[91] the Convention on the Transboundary Effect of Industrial Accidents,[92] the Biodiversity Convention, the Protocol on Further Reduction of Sulphur Emissions,[93] and the Convention on the Law of the Non-Navigational Uses of International Watercourses.[94]

There is a clear trend towards the development of issue-specific legal mechanisms as a preferred means of dealing with environmental problems; the articulation of international legal principles through dispute resolution processes is gradual and cannot address issues of prevention and collective action in the fine-grained way that law-making via treaty can. Nonetheless, political compromises in negotiation and a reliance on national implementation of texts once adopted both raise their own difficulties, and there can be striking differences between the text of an international environmental agreement and how it operates in practice.

4. EVALUATION

Since the 1970s, general principles of international law have been adapted to reflect concerns as to the protection of the environment, including the prevention of transboundary environmental harm, with some new approaches to collective action emerging: an emphasis on preventing foreseeable harm (the precautionary principle), on assigning responsibility (the polluter-pays principle), and emphasizing the importance of integrating environmental protection within economic activity (sustainable development). In addition, numerous treaty-based regimes have responded to particular environmental issues.

The instruments of international environmental law are found in multilateral, regional, and bilateral agreements. States increasingly have duties not just in respect of transboundary environmental harm or the global environment, but also in respect of conserving their own domestic environment.[95] Although implementation in national law and practice remains uneven, the authoritative statement of principles in international environmental agreements, and the dispute resolution and law-making institutions attached to them, provide a reference point for future development in the field.

---

[90] 28 September 1986, 1439 UNTS 275.
[91] 17 March 1992, 1936 UNTS 269.
[92] 17 March 1992, 2105 UNTS 457.
[93] 14 June 1994, 2030 UNTS 122.
[94] GA Res 51/229, 21 May 1997 (not yet in force).
[95] E.g. Biodiversity Convention, preamble, Arts 6, 8.

PART VI

INTERNATIONAL
TRANSACTIONS

16

THE LAW OF TREATIES

1. INTRODUCTION[1]

Many international disputes are concerned with the interpretation and effects of international agreements, that is, treaties, and much of the practical content of state relations is embodied in and structured by treaties. International organizations, including the United Nations, have their legal basis in multilateral treaties. So too do arrangements on matters ranging from geostationary orbit to the regulation of intellectual property to the governance of Antarctica. Networks of bilateral treaties regulate such matters as aviation, boundaries, extradition, investment protection, and shared natural resources.

Since 1949 the ILC has concerned itself with the law of treaties.[2] In 1966 it adopted a set of 75 draft articles:[3] these formed the basis for the 1969 Vienna Convention on the Law of Treaties (VCLT), which entered into force on 27 January 1980.[4]

At the time of its adoption, it could not have been said that the VCLT was, taken as a whole, declaratory of general international law. Various provisions clearly involved progressive development. Nonetheless it has had a very strong influence, and a good number of articles are now essentially declaratory of existing law; those which are not

[1] Harvard Research (1935) 29 *AJIL Supp*; McNair, *The Law of Treaties* (1961); Jennings (1967) 121 Hague *Recueil* 527; Elias, *The Modern Law of Treaties* (1974); Sinclair, *The Vienna Convention on the Law of Treaties* (2nd edn, 1984); Rosenne, *Developments in the Law of Treaties, 1945–1986* (1989); Thirlway (1991) 62 *BY* 2; Thirlway (1992) 63 *BY* 1; Reuter, *Introduction to the Law of Treaties* (2nd edn, 1995); Aust, *Modern Treaty Law and Practice* (2nd edn, 2007); Villiger, *Commentary on the 1969 Vienna Convention on the Law of Treaties* (2009); Villiger (2009) 344 Hague *Recueil* 9; Corten & Klein (eds), *The Vienna Conventions on the Law of Treaties* (2011).

[2] In addition to its work on interstate treaties, the ILC produced draft articles on treaties of international organizations, which became VCLT II, 21 March 1986, 25 ILM 543 (not yet in force). In 2011 it completed an enormous Guide to Practice on Reservations to Treaties: A/CN.4/L.779, 19 May 2011. It is working on temporal aspects of treaties: www.untreaty.un.org/ilc/summaries/1_11.htm.

[3] The principal items are: Reports by Brierly, ILC *Ybk* 1950/II, 222; ILC *Ybk* 1951/II, 1; ILC *Ybk* 1952/II, 50; Lauterpacht, ILC *Ybk* 1953/II, 90; ILC *Ybk* 1954/II, 123; Fitzmaurice, ILC *Ybk* 1956/II, 104; ILC *Ybk* 1957/II, 16; ILC *Ybk* 1958/II, 20; ILC *Ybk* 1960/II, 69; Waldock, ILC *Ybk* 1962/II, 27; ILC *Ybk* 1963/II, 36; ILC *Ybk* 1964/II, 4; ILC *Ybk* 1965/II, 3; ILC *Ybk* 1966/II, 1; ILC Final Report and Draft Articles, ILC *Ybk* 1966/II, 172.

[4] 22 May 1969, 1155 UNTS 331. See Kearney & Dalton (1970) 64 *AJIL* 495.

constitute presumptive evidence of emergent rules.[5] Indeed its provisions are regarded as the primary source of the law, irrespective of whether the VCLT applies *qua* treaty in the given case.[6] In *Namibia* the Court observed that:

The rules laid down by the Vienna Convention ... concerning termination of a treaty relationship on account of breach (adopted without a dissenting vote) may in many respects be considered as a codification of existing customary law on the subject.[7]

The European Court of Justice has observed that the customary international law of treaties forms part of the European legal order, and it generally follows the VCLT (implicitly or explicitly);[8] the WTO dispute settlement body has also emphasized the customary status of the VCLT rules of treaty interpretation.[9]

The Convention was adopted by a very substantial majority at the Vienna Conference[10] and covers the main areas of the law of treaties. It does not deal with (a) treaties between states and organizations, or between two or more organizations;[11] (b) state succession to treaties;[12] or (c) the effect of armed conflict on treaties,[13] each of which has been the subject of separate ILC projects.

---

[5] Villiger (2009) 24–7.

[6] Under Art 4, VCLT only applies to treaties concluded between states all of which at that time were *already* parties to VCLT. Since only 111 states are parties, this means in effect that VCLT does not apply to major multilateral treaties. In practice it is applied as customary international law in any event.

[7] *Legal Consequences for States of the Continued Presence of South Africa in Namibia (South West Africa) notwithstanding Security Council Resolution 276 (1970)*, ICJ Reports 1971 p 16, 47. Also: *Appeal relating to the Jurisdiction of the ICAO Council (India v Pakistan)*, ICJ Reports 1972 p 46, 67; *Fisheries Jurisdiction (UK v Iceland)*, ICJ Reports 1973 p 3, 18; *Sovereignty over Pulau Ligitan and Pulau Sipidan (Indonesia/ Malaysia)*, ICJ Reports 2002 p 625, 645–6; *Iran–US, Case No A/18* (1984) 75 ILR 175, 187–8; *Lithgow and Others (Shipbuilding Nationalization)* (1986) 75 ILR 438, 483–4; *Restrictions to the Death Penalty* (1983) 70 ILR 449, 465–71; *Asian Agricultural Products Ltd v Republic of Sri Lanka* (1990) 106 ILR 416, 437–46; *Ethyl Corporation v Government of Canada* (1998) 122 ILR 250, 278–80; *Pope and Talbot v Canada* (2001) 122 ILR 293, 328.

[8] E.g. *R v Minister of Agriculture, ex parte SP Anastasiou (Pissouri) Ltd* (1994) 100 ILR 257, 298–9; *Opel Austria v Council of the EU* (1997) 113 ILR 295, 323–4; *Racke v Hauptzollamt Mainz* (1998) 117 ILR 399, 437–43; Case C-268/99 *Jany v Staatssecretaris van Justitie* [2001] ECR I-8615, para 35; Joined Cases C-402/05 P and C-415/05 P *Kadi & Al Barakaat International Foundation v Council & Commission* [2008] ECR I-06351, §291. Further: Kuijper (1998) 25 *Legal Issues of Economic Integration* 1; Klabbers (1999) 30 *NYIL* 45; Verwey, *The European Community and the European Union and the International Law of Treaties* (2004).

[9] E.g. *US—Gasoline*, WTO Doc WT/DS2/AB/R, 29 April 1996, 16–17; *US—Gambling*, WTO Doc WT/ DS285/AB/R, 7 April 2005, 51. Further: van Damme, *Treaty Interpretation by the WTO Appellate Body* (2009).

[10] 79–1 (France): 19.

[11] VCLT II; Gaja (1987) 58 *BY* 253; Zemanek, in Hafner et al (eds), *Liber Amicorum Ignaz Seidl-Hohenveldern* (1998) 843; Menon, *Law of Treaties between States and International Organizations* (1992); Brölmann, in Klabbers & Lefeber (eds), *Essays on the Law of Treaties* (1998) 121; Footer, in Orakhelashvili & Williams (eds), *40 Years of the Vienna Convention on the Law of Treaties* (2010) 183; Tomuschat, in Cannizzaro (ed), *The Law of Treaties Beyond the Vienna Convention* (2011) 206.

[12] Vienna Convention on Succession of States in Respect of Treaties, 22 August 1978, 1946 UNTS 3; also chapter 19.

[13] See ILC website, www.untreaty.un.org/ilc/summaries/1_10.htm.

(A) DEFINITION OF 'TREATY'

A provisional ILC draft defined a 'treaty' as:

any international agreement in written form, whether embodied in a single instrument or in two or more related instruments and whatever its particular designation (treaty, convention, protocol, covenant, charter, statute, act, declaration, concordat, exchange of notes, agreed minute, memorandum of agreement, *modus vivendi* or any other appellation), concluded between two or more States or other subjects of international law and governed by international law.[14]

The reference to 'other subjects' of the law was designed to provide for treaties concluded by international organizations, the Holy See, and other international entities. But the ILC's Final Draft, and the VCLT itself, are confined to treaties between states (Article 1).[15] Article 3 provides that the fact that the Convention is thus limited shall not affect the legal force of agreements between states and other subjects of international law or between such other subjects.

Article 2(1)(a) defines a treaty as 'an international agreement concluded between States in written form and governed by international law, whether embodied in a single instrument or in two or more related instruments and whatever its particular designation'. The distinction between a transaction which is a definitive legal commitment between two states, and one which involves something less than that is difficult to draw. But the form or title of the instrument, for example, a joint communiqué, is not decisive.[16]

Article 2(1)(a) also stipulates that the agreements to which the Convention extends must be 'governed by international law'; this excludes commercial arrangements made between governments under one or more national laws.[17]

(B) THE FUNCTIONS OF TREATIES

McNair long ago pointed to the variety of functions which treaties perform.[18] Some treaties, dispositive of territory and rights in relation to territory, are like conveyances.

---

[14] ILC *Ybk* 1962/II, 161.

[15] On the concept of a treaty: Widdows (1979) 50 *BY* 117; Virally, in Diez et al (eds), *Festschrift für Rudolf Bindschedler* (1980) 159; Thirlway (1991) 62 *BY* 1, 4–15; Klabbers, *The Concept of Treaty in International Law* (1996); Fitzmaurice (2002) 73 *BY* 141.

[16] The conclusion of treaties in simplified form is increasingly common. Many treaties are made by an exchange of notes, the adoption of agreed minutes, etc. See *ILC Ybk* 1966/II, 188; Aust (2nd edn, 2007) 102; Corten & Klein, *Les Conventions de Vienne Sur le Droit des Traités* (2006) 343; Villiger, *Commentary* (2009) 181. Also: *Aegean Sea Continental Shelf (Greece v Turkey)*, ICJ Reports 1978 p 3, 38–44; *Military and Paramilitary Activities in and against Nicaragua (Nicaragua v US)*, ICJ Reports 1986 p 14, 130–2; *Maritime Delimitation and Territorial Questions between Qatar and Bahrain (Qatar v Bahrain)*, Jurisdiction and Admissibility, ICJ Reports 1994 p 112, 120–2.

[17] See Mann (1957) 33 *BY* 20; Mann (1959) 35 *BY* 34; Fitzmaurice (2002) 73 *BY* 141, 168; cf *Diverted Cargoes* (1955) 12 RIAA 53, 70.

[18] McNair (1961) 739–54. On the special role of multilateral treaties: Lachs (1957) 92 Hague *Recueil* 229, 233–41; Crawford (2006) 319 Hague *Recueil* 325, 349–420.

Treaties involving bargains between a few states are like contracts; whereas the multilateral treaty creating either a set of rules, such as the Hague Conventions on the Law of War, or an institution, such as the Copyright Union, is 'law-making'. The treaty constituting an institution is akin to a charter of incorporation. It is certainly fruitful to contemplate the different features of different kinds of treaties and even to expect the development of specialized rules. Thus the effect of war between parties varies according to the type of treaty involved. However, McNair and others have tended to support the position that the genus of treaty produces fairly *general* effects on the applicable rules. Thus the law-making character of a treaty is said (a) to rule out recourse to preparatory work as an aid to interpretation; (b) to avoid recognition by one party of other parties as states or governments; and (c) to render the doctrine of *rebus sic stantibus* inapplicable.[19]

By contrast the ILC deliberately avoided any classification of treaties along broad lines and rejected the concept of the 'objective regime' in relation to the effects of treaties on non-parties. It accepted specialized rules in a few instances,[20] but did not consider it necessary to make a distinction between 'law-making' and other treaties.[21] The ILC and in turn the Vienna Conference saw the law of treaties as essentially a unity.[22] Moreover jurists are now less willing to accept categorical distinctions between treaty-contract (*vertrag*) and treaty-law (*vereinbarung*).[23] The contrast intended between the bilateral political bargain and the 'legislative act' produced by a broad international conference does not correspond to reality. Political issues and bargaining lie behind law-making efforts like UNCLOS III. Further, the distinction obscures the real differences between treaty-making and legislation in a municipal system. Nonetheless, it should be acknowledged that some of the VCLT rules, for example Article 18 and the rules relating to reservations, may work better with contractual-type agreements than with law-making ones.

(C) PARTICIPATION IN TREATIES

In an early draft the ILC defined a 'general multilateral treaty' as 'a multilateral treaty which concerns general norms of international law and deals with matters of general interest to States as a whole'.[24] But which states and other entities are permitted to participate in drawing up such a treaty is a matter for the proponents, or in the case of a treaty concluded under the auspices of an international organization, the organization. In the ILC it was proposed that states should have a right to become parties to this type of treaty, a solution adopted in the insubstantial form that the right existed except where the treaty or the rules of an international organization

---

[19] McNair (1961) 743–9.

[20] VCLT, Art 62(2) (fundamental change of circumstances rule inapplicable to boundary treaties).

[21] ILC *Ybk* 1966/II, 219.

[22] Dehaussy, in *Recueil d'études en hommage à Guggenheim* (1968) 305; Gardiner, *Treaty Interpretation* (2008) 142.

[23] For the history: Lauterpacht, *Private Law Sources and Analogies of International Law* (1927) 156–9, §70.

[24] ILC *Ybk* 1962/II, 161.

provided otherwise.[25] The ILC's Final Draft contained no provision on the subject and amendments intended to give 'all States a right to participate in multilateral treaties' were defeated at the Vienna Conference.[26]

2. CONCLUSION OF TREATIES

(A) FORM AND INTENTION[27]

How treaties are negotiated and brought into force depends on the intention of the parties. There are no overriding requirements of form:[28] for example, an agreement recorded in an exchange of letters or even the minutes of a conference may have the same legal effect as a formally drafted treaty contained in a single instrument.[29] In practice form is governed partly by usage, and will vary according to whether the agreement is expressed to be between states, heads of states, governments, or particular ministers or departments. The VCLT applies only to agreements 'in written form' but Article 3 stipulates that this limitation is without prejudice to the legal force of agreements 'not in written form'.[30]

Where the parties wish to record mutual understandings for the conduct of their business or other relationships, but do not intend to create legally binding obligations, they often conclude non-binding instruments commonly referred to as memoranda of understanding (MOUs).[31] The name of the instrument is not conclusive as to its legal status, however; what matters is the intention of the parties as reflected in the terms of the instrument.[32]

(B) FULL POWERS AND SIGNATURE[33]

The era of absolute monarchs and slow communications produced a practice whereby a state agent would be given full powers to negotiate and to bind his principal. In modern practice, full powers give the bearer authority to negotiate and to sign and seal

---

[25] Draft Articles, I, ILC *Ybk* 1962/II, 167–9 (Art 8); Waldock (1962) 106 Hague *Recueil* 1, 53–8.

[26] ILC *Ybk* 1966/II, 200; UN Secretariat Working Paper, A/CN.4/245, 23 April 1971, 131–4. Also: Lukashuk (1972) 135 Hague *Recueil* 231.

[27] Generally: Aust (1986) 35 *ICLQ* 787.

[28] *Temple of Preah Vihear (Cambodia v Thailand)*, Preliminary Objections, ICJ Reports 1961 p 17, 31–2.

[29] *Qatar v Bahrain*, Jurisdiction and Admissibility, ICJ Reports 1994 p 112, 120–2; Aust (2nd edn, 2007) 16–31.

[30] *ILC Ybk* 1966/II, 190–1 (Art 3).

[31] Aust (2nd edn, 2007) 32–57; E Lauterpacht, in Flume (ed), *Festschrift für FA Mann* (1977) 38; Thirlway (1991) 63 *BY* 1, 18–19.

[32] Aust (2nd edn, 2007) 16–31, esp 23–7.

[33] VCLT, Arts 7–11; Waldock, ILC *Ybk* 1962/II, 38ff; *ILC Ybk* 1966/II, 189, 193–7; Watts (1994) 247 *Hague Recueil* 10, 19; Sabel, *Procedure at International Conferences* (2nd edn, 2006) 58–67. Further: *Armed Activities on the Territory of the Congo (New Application: 2002) (DRC v Rwanda)*, Jurisdiction and Admissibility, ICJ Reports 2006 p 6, 27–9.

a treaty but not to commit the state. In the case of less formal agreements full powers are often dispensed with.[34] Thus the definition in VCLT Article 2(c):

... a document emanating from the competent authority of a State designating a person or persons to represent the State for negotiating, adopting or authenticating the text of a treaty, for expressing the consent of a State to be bound by a treaty, or for accomplishing any other act with respect to a treaty.

One example of full powers arose in *Land and Maritime Boundary between Cameroon and Nigeria*, with the Court confirming that the full powers afforded to a head of state derive from his or her position at the top of a state's hierarchy.[35] This position was expanded upon—beyond the law of treaties—in *Genocide*, with VCLT cited for the proposition that 'every Head of State is presumed to be able to act on behalf of the State in its international relations'.[36]

The successful outcome of negotiation is the adoption and authentication of an agreed text. Signature has, as one of its functions, authentication, but a text may be authenticated in other ways, for example by incorporation in the final act of a conference or by initialling.[37]

Where the signature is subject to ratification, acceptance, or approval, signature does not establish consent to be bound nor does it create an obligation to ratify.[38] What it does is to qualify the signatory to proceed to ratification, acceptance, or approval; it also creates an interim obligation of good faith to refrain from acts calculated to frustrate the objects of the treaty.[39]

Where the treaty is not subject to ratification, acceptance, or approval, signature establishes consent to be bound. Sometimes signature may be dispensed with: the text may be adopted or approved by resolution of the UN General Assembly and submitted to member states for accession.

(C) RATIFICATION

Ratification involves two distinct procedural acts: the first an internal act of approval (e.g. by the parliament, or the Crown in the UK); the second the international procedure

---

[34] Heads of state, heads of government, and foreign ministers are also not required to furnish evidence of their authority: VCLT, Art 7(2). Further: Aust (2nd edn, 2007) 75–83.

[35] ICJ Reports 2002 p 303, 430.

[36] *Application of the Convention on the Prevention and Punishment of the Crime of Genocide (Bosnia and Herzegovina v Yugoslavia)*, Preliminary Objections, ICJ Reports 1996 p 595, 661–2.

[37] VCLT, Art 10.

[38] ILC *Ybk* 1962/II, 171. But cf Lauterpacht, ILC *Ybk* 1953/II, 108–12; Fitzmaurice, ILC *Ybk* 1956/II, 112–13, 121–2. Also: Rosenne (2000) 4 *EPIL* 932; Kolb (2004) 51 *NILR* 185; Corten & Klein (2006) 343–538; Aust (2nd edn, 2007) 94–102; Villiger, *Commentary* (2009) 181–228.

[39] VCLT, Art 18; *Certain German Interests in Polish Upper Silesia* (1926) PCIJ Ser A No 7, 30; Aust (2nd edn, 2007) 116–21; Palchetti, in Cannizzaro (2011) 25. Note Art 18(a): if a state that has signed a treaty makes it clear that it does not intend to ratify it, it is released from any obligations under Art 18 and its signature has no legal effect. The US relied on this to 'unsign' the ICC Statute (17 July 1998, 2187 UNTS 3) in May 2002, by lodging a note with the UN to the effect that it did not intend to become a party: Swaine (2003) 55 *Stanford LR* 2061.

which brings a treaty into force by a formal exchange or deposit of instruments of ratification. Ratification in the latter sense is an important act involving consent to be bound.[40] But everything depends on the intention of the parties, and modern practice contains many examples of less formal agreements intended to be binding on signature.[41] As to the small number of treaties containing no express provision on ratification, the ILC initially considered that ratification should be required.[42] However, it changed its view, partly because of the difficulty of applying the presumption to treaties in simplified form. VCLT Article 14 regulates the matter by reference to the parties' intention without any presumption.

(D) ACCESSION, ACCEPTANCE, AND APPROVAL

'Accession' occurs when a state which did not sign a treaty formally accepts its provisions: this may be before or after the treaty has entered into force. The conditions for accession and the procedure involved depend on the provisions of the treaty. Accession may be the only means of becoming a party, as in the case of a convention approved by the General Assembly and proposed for accession by member states.[43] Recent practice has introduced the terms 'acceptance' and 'approval' to describe the substance of accession. Terminology is not fixed, however, and where a treaty is expressed to be open to signature 'subject to acceptance', this is equivalent to 'subject to ratification'.

(E) OTHER EXPRESSIONS OF CONSENT TO BE BOUND

These are not the only means by which consent to be bound may be expressed. Other means may be agreed, for example an exchange of instruments constituting a treaty.[44]

(F) ENTRY INTO FORCE, DEPOSIT, AND REGISTRATION

The provisions of the treaty determine how and when the treaty enters into force. Where the treaty does not specify a date, there is a presumption that the treaty comes into force as soon as all the negotiating states have consented to be bound.[45]

After a treaty is concluded, the written instruments of ratification, accession, etc and also reservations and other declarations are placed in the custody of a depositary,

---

[40] VCLT, Art 14; for other means of expressing consent to be bound: VCLT, Arts 11–17.

[41] *Cameroon v Nigeria*, ICJ Reports 2002 p 303, 429–30.

[42] Draft Articles, I, ILC *Ybk* 1962/II, 161, 171–3 (Arts 1(1)(d), 12); Waldock, ILC *Ybk* 1962/II, 48–53. Also: ILC Final Report and Draft Articles, ILC *Ybk* 1966/II, 187–9, 195–9, 201 (Arts 2(1)(b), 10–11, 13).

[43] McNair (1961) 153–5.

[44] VCLT, Arts 11, 13; Fitzmaurice, in Klabbers & Lefeber (1998) 59; Fitzmaurice & Hollis (2005) 23 *Berkeley JIL* 137.

[45] VCLT, Art 24(2). The International Court has described Art 24 as declaratory of the general rule: *Cameroon v Nigeria*, Preliminary Objections, ICJ Reports 1998 p 275, 293–4; *Right of Passage over Indian Territory (Portugal v India)*, Preliminary Objections, ICJ Reports 1957 p 125, 145–7.

which may be one or more states or an international organization.[46] The UN Secretariat plays a significant role as depositary of multilateral treaties.

Article 102 of the UN Charter provides as follows:

1. Every treaty and every international agreement entered into by any Member of the United Nations after the present Charter comes into force shall as soon as possible be registered with the Secretariat and published by it.

2. No party to any such treaty or international agreement which has not been registered in accordance with the provisions of paragraph 1 of this Article may invoke that treaty or agreement before any organ of the United Nations.

This provision (which goes back to President Woodrow Wilson)[47] is intended to discourage secret diplomacy and to promote the availability of treaty texts. The Secretariat accepts agreements for registration without conferring any status on them or the parties which they would not have otherwise. However, this is not the case where the regulations provide for *ex officio* registration. This involves initiative by the Secretariat and extends to agreements to which the UN is a party, trusteeship agreements, and multilateral agreements with the UN as depositary. The phrase 'every international agreement' has a wide scope. Technical intergovernmental agreements, declarations accepting the optional clause in the Statute of the International Court, agreements between organizations and states, agreements between organizations, and unilateral engagements of an international character are included.[48]

Non-registration does not affect the validity of agreements, but these may not be relied upon in proceedings before UN organs. In relation to the similar provision in the Covenant of the League the view was expressed that an unregistered agreement could be invoked if otherwise appropriately publicized.[49]

3. RESERVATIONS[50]

VCLT Article 2(d) defines a reservation as 'a unilateral statement, however phrased or named, made by a State, when signing, ratifying, accepting, approving or acceding to

---

[46] VCLT, Arts 76–7; Rosenne (1967) 61 *AJIL* 923; Rosenne (1970) 64 *AJIL* 838.

[47] The first of Wilson's Fourteen Points Address, delivered at a joint session of Congress on 8 January 1918, called for 'open covenants of peace, openly arrived at': US Department of State, *Papers Relating to the Foreign Relations of the United States 1918—Supplement 1, The World War* (1933) 12, 15; Schwietzke, 'Fourteen Points of Wilson (1918)' (2007) *MPEPIL*.

[48] If an agreement is between international legal persons it is registrable even if governed by a particular municipal law; cf Higgins (1963) 329.

[49] *South West Africa (Ethiopia v South Africa; Liberia v South Africa)*, Preliminary Objections, ICJ Reports 1962 p 319, 359–60 (Judge Bustamante), 420–2 (Judge Jessup); cf 503 (Judges Spender & Fitzmaurice, joint diss).

[50] VCLT, Arts 19–23; further: Lauterpacht, ILC *Ybk* 1953/II, 123–36; Fitzmaurice (1953) 2 *ICLQ* 1; McNair (1961) ch 4; Bishop (1961) 103 Hague *Recueil* 249; Draft Articles, I, ILC *Ybk* 1962/II, 161, 163, 175–82 (Arts 1(1)(f), 18–22); Anderson (1964) 13 *ICLQ* 450; Waldock, ILC *Ybk* 1966/II, 27, 60–8; ILC Final Report and

a treaty, whereby it purports to exclude or to modify the legal effect of certain provisions of the treaty in their application to that State'. It is to be distinguished from an interpretative declaration, which is an expression of view by a declarant state as to the meaning of a treaty which is not put forward as a condition of being bound.[51]

Considerable uncertainty has surrounded the law and practice with regard to reservations.

(A) HISTORICAL BACKGROUND

League of Nations practice in regard to multilateral conventions lacked consistency. The League Secretariat, and later the UN Secretary-General, as depositary of conventions concluded under the auspices of the League, followed the principle of absolute integrity: a reservation would only be valid if the treaty permitted it or all contracting parties accepted it; otherwise the reserving state would not be considered a party.[52] In contrast the Pan-American Union, later the Organization of American States, adopted a flexible system which permitted a reserving state to become a party vis-à-vis non-objecting states. This system, dating from 1932, promotes universality at the expense of consistency of obligation.

Following the adoption of the Genocide Convention in 1948, a divergence of opinion arose on the admissibility of reservations to the Convention, which contained no provision on the subject; an advisory opinion was sought. The International Court stressed the divergence of practice and the special characteristics of the Convention, including the intention of the drafters that it be universal in scope. The Court's principal finding was that 'a State which has made ... a reservation which has been objected to by one or more of the parties to the Convention but not by others, can be regarded as being a party to the Convention if the reservation is compatible with the object and purpose of the Convention'.[53]

In 1951 the ILC rejected the 'compatibility' criterion as too subjective, preferring a rule of unanimous consent.[54] However, in 1952 the General Assembly requested the Secretary-General to conform practice to the opinion of the Court and, in respect of

---

Draft Articles, ILC *Ybk* 1966/II, 189–90, 202–9 (Arts 2(1)(d), 16–20); Jennings (1967) 121 Hague *Recueil* 534; Bowett (1976–77) 48 *BY* 67; Sinclair (2nd edn, 1984) 51–82; Greig (1995) 16 *AYIL* 21; Villiger (2009) 344 Hague *Recueil* 9, 77–112; Pellet & Müller, in Cannizzaro (2011) 37; Corten & Klein (2011) 405–627. Further: reports of the Special Rapporteur on Reservations to Treaties (Pellet), available at www.untreaty.un.org/ilc/summaries/1_8.htm and ILC Report 2011, GAOR, 66th Session, Supp No 10, A/66/10, 12–49.

[51] E.g. the Swiss declaration regarding ECHR, 4 November 1950, ETS 5, Art 6(1): *Belilos v Switzerland* (1988) 88 ILR 635, 636. On the difficulty in some cases of distinguishing interpretative declarations from reservations: ibid, 663–6.

[52] On this contractual conception of treaties, a reservation would constitute a counter-offer requiring a new acceptance, failing which the state making the counter-offer would not become a party to the treaty. See *Reservations to the Convention on the Prevention and Punishment of the Crime of Genocide*, ICJ Reports 1951 p 15, 21, 24.

[53] Ibid, 29.

[54] ILC *Ybk* 1951/II, 128–31.

future conventions of which the Secretary-General was depositary, to leave it to each state to draw its own conclusions from reservations communicated to it.[55] In 1959 the General Assembly extended this to cover all UN conventions, unless they contained contrary provisions.[56] In 1962 the ILC decided in favour of the 'compatibility' rule.[57]

(B) IMPERMISSIBLE RESERVATIONS

VCLT Article 20 provides for acceptance of and objection to reservations other than those expressly authorized by a treaty.[58] The 'compatibility' test is by no means ideal;[59] in particular its application is a matter of appreciation, left to individual states. How is the test to apply to provisions for dispute settlement, for example? In practical terms the 'compatibility' test may not sufficiently maintain the balance between the integrity and the effectiveness of multilateral conventions in terms of a firm level of obligation. It is very doubtful whether there can be any place for the 'compatibility' test in relation to unlawful reservations.[60]

The issue of severability in relation to human rights treaties has been particularly controversial.[61] In *Belilos*[62] and *Loizidou*[63] the European Court of Human Rights treated the objectionable reservation as severable. So did the Human Rights Committee: a state could not, for example, reserve the right to subject persons to torture, or to presume a person guilty unless proven innocent;[64] rather than the state's participation in the treaty being negated, it was held to be a party to the treaty without benefit of its reservation, whatever its underlying intention may have been.

(C) THE ILC GUIDE (2011)

Some of the difficulties in respect of permissibility of reservations are addressed in the comprehensive Guide to Practice on Reservations to Treaties adopted by the

[55] GA Res 598(VI), 12 January 1952.

[56] GA Res 1452A(XIV), 7 December 1959.

[57] Draft Articles, I, ILC *Ybk* 1962/II, 175–81 (Arts 18(1)(d) and 20(2)). The Commission rejected a 'collegiate' system which would require acceptance of the reservation by a given proportion of the other parties: cf Anderson (1964) 13 *ICLQ* 450.

[58] Special provisions concerning the making of reservations may present difficult problems of interpretation. See *UK-French Continental Shelf* (1977) 54 ILR 6, 41–57; Bowett (1976–77) 48 *BY* 67.

[59] Waldock, ILC *Ybk* 1962/II, 65–6; ILC *Ybk* 1966/II, 205; Sinclair (1970) 19 *ICLQ* 53.

[60] E.g. Bowett (1976–77) 48 *BY* 67, 70–5; Redgwell (1993) 64 *BY* 245.

[61] See Chinkin et al (Gardner ed), *Human Rights as General Norms and a State's Right to Opt Out* (1997).

[62] *Belilos v Switzerland* (1988) 88 ILR 635. Further: Cameron & Horn (1990) 33 *GYIL* 69; Marks (1990) 39 *ICLQ* 300.

[63] *Loizidou v Turkey*, Preliminary Objections (1995) 103 ILR 622. For a similar approach under the Inter-American system: *Radilla-Pacheco v Mexico*, IACtHR C/209, 23 November 2009, §§299–312.

[64] CCPR, General Comment 24 (1994) CCPR/C/21/Rev.1/Add.6. The UK government was critical: (1995) 66 *BY* 655. Also: Hampson, E/CN.4/Sub.2/1999/28, 28 June 1999; Simma, in Hafner et al (1998) 659; Helfer (2002) 102 *Col LR* 1832. Further: *Armed Activities (2002 Application) (DRC v Rwanda)*, Jurisdiction and Admissibility, ICJ Reports 2006 p 6, 69–70 (Judges Higgins, Kooijmans, El Araby, Owada & Simma).

ILC in 2011, the culmination of 15 years of work.[65] The Guide is intended as a 'tool-box' for practitioners in dealing with the permissibility and effects of reservations, pointing them towards solutions consistent with existing rules. The Guide is not a binding instrument and is not intended to form the basis of a convention[66] but it is likely to make a significant contribution to clarification of law and practice in this area.

On the question of severability the Guide adopts an ingenious intermediate solution. Under Guideline 4.5.1, an invalid or impermissible reservation is null and void, and has no legal effect. Practice has varied on whether the author of an invalid reservation remains bound by the treaty without the benefit of the reservation, or whether the nullity of the reservation vitiates that party's consent to be bound altogether.[67] The Guide provides a presumption that the former applies, unless the contrary intention of that party is expressed or otherwise established.[68] In this way the Guide affirms that the key to the status of the reserving party in relation to the treaty is that party's intention,[69] and offers 'a reasonable compromise between the underlying principle of treaty law—mutual consent—and the principle that reservations prohibited by the treaty or incompatible with the object and purpose of the treaty are null and void'.[70]

4. OBSERVANCE, APPLICATION, AND INTERPRETATION OF TREATIES

(A) *PACTA SUNT SERVANDA*

The VCLT entails a certain presumption as to the validity and continuance in force of a treaty.[71] This may be based upon *pacta sunt servanda* as a general principle of international law: a treaty in force is binding upon the parties and must be performed by them in good faith.[72] Legally, treaties are enduring instruments, not easily disposed of.[73] Internal law may not be invoked to justify a failure to perform a treaty.[74]

---

[65] ILC Report 2011, GAOR, 66th Session, Supp No 10, A/66/10, 12–51 and Add.1.

[66] A/CN.4/647/Add.1, 6 June 2011, 15–20.

[67] A/66/10/Add.1, commentary to Guideline 4.5.2.

[68] Ibid, Guideline 4.5.3, §2.

[69] Ibid, Guideline 4.5.3, §1.

[70] Ibid, commentary to Guideline 4.5.3.

[71] VCLT, Art 42. Also: Draft Articles, II, ILC *Ybk* 1963/II, 189–90 (Art 30); ILC Final Report and Draft Articles, ILC *Ybk* 1966/II, 236–7 (Art 39).

[72] VCLT, Art 26; ILC Final Report and Draft Articles, ILC *Ybk* 1966/II, 210–11 (Art 23); Villiger, *Commentary* (2009) 361–8; Corten & Klein (2011) 659–87.

[73] And this despite General de Gaulle's maxim, 'Treaties are like roses and young girls. They last while they last': *Time*, 12 July 1963.

[74] VLCT, Art 27; Villiger, *Commentary* (2009) 369–75; Corten & Klein (2011) 688–717.

(B) APPLICATION OF TREATIES

Treaties are not retroactive; that is, unless a contrary intention is established, parties are only bound in respect of acts or facts taking place after the treaty has entered into force for the party in question.[75] Unless otherwise stated, they apply within the whole territory of the states parties.[76]

VCLT Article 30 covers the application of successive treaties to the same subject-matter.[77] The relation of treaties between the same parties and with overlapping provisions is primarily a matter of interpretation, aided by presumptions. Thus it is to be presumed that a later treaty prevails over an earlier treaty concerning the same subject-matter. A treaty may provide expressly that it is to prevail over subsequent incompatible treaties; Article 103 of the UN Charter goes further by providing that in the case of conflict, obligations under the Charter prevail over obligations arising under any other international agreement. Article 351 of the Treaty on the Functioning of the European Union (TFEU) provides that pre-existing rights and obligations shall not be affected by its provisions or those of the Treaty on European Union (TEU), but that where incompatibilities exist, parties shall take appropriate steps to eliminate them.[78] Whether or not there is a conflict in a given case is of course a matter of interpretation: thus a resolution which is capable of being performed in a manner consistent with the International Covenant on Civil and Political Rights, for example, may be construed as not intending to override the relevant rights.[79] VCLT Article 59 provides for the termination or suspension of a treaty in certain circumstances where all parties have concluded a later treaty relating to the same subject-matter.

(C) INTERPRETATION OF TREATIES[80]

(i) Competence to interpret

Obviously the parties have competence to interpret a treaty, but this is subject to the operation of other legal rules. The treaty itself may confer competence on an ad hoc

---

[75] VCLT, Art 28; Villiger, *Commentary* (2009) 379–86; Corten & Klein (2011) 718–30.

[76] VCLT, Art 29; Villiger, *Commentary* (2009) 387–94; Corten & Klein (2011) 731–63.

[77] Generally: Draft Articles, III, ILC *Ybk* 1964/II, 185–92 (Art 63); ILC Final Report and Draft Articles, ILC *Ybk* 1966/II, 214–17 (Art 26); Jenks (1953) 30 *BY* 401; Sciso (1987) 38 *ÖZföR* 161; Binder, *Treaty Conflict and Political Contradiction* (1988); Kohen (2000) 106 *RGDIP* 577; Sadat-Akhavi, *Methods of Resolving Conflicts between Treaties* (2003); Villiger, *Commentary* (2009) 395–411; Klabbers, in Cannizzaro (2011) 192.

[78] TFEU (2008) *OJEU* C 115/47.

[79] *Al Jedda v UK* [2011] ECtHR 27021/08, §§105–9.

[80] McNair (1961) chs 20–9; Fitzmaurice (1971) 65 *AJIL* 358; Yasseen (1976) 151 Hague *Recueil* 1; Thirlway (1991) 62 *BY* 1, 16–75; Thirlway (2007) 77 *BY* 1; Torres Bernárdez, in Hafner et al (1998) 721; Berman (2004) 29 *Yale JIL* 315; Kolb, *Interprétation et creation du droit international* (2006); French (2006) 55 *ICLQ* 281; Linderfalk, *On the Interpretation of Treaties* (2007); Gardiner (2008); Orakhelashvili, *The Interpretation of Acts and Rules in Public International Law* (2008); Villiger (2009) 344 Hague *Recueil* 9, 113–34; van Damme (2009); Villiger, in Cannizzaro (2011) 105; Corten & Klein (2011) 804–86.

tribunal or the International Court. The UN Charter is interpreted by its organs, which may seek advisory opinions from the Court.[81]

(ii) The 'rules of interpretation'

Various 'rules' for interpreting treaties have been put forward over the years.[82] These include the textual approach, the restrictive approach, the teleological approach, and the effectiveness principle. Of these only the textual approach is recognized in VCLT: Article 31 emphasizes the intention of the parties as expressed in the text, as the best guide to their common intention.[83] The jurisprudence of the International Court likewise supports the textual approach.[84]

In a number of cases the Permanent Court committed itself to the principle that provisions implying a limitation of state sovereignty should receive a restrictive interpretation.[85] As a general principle of interpretation this is question-begging, and later decisions have given less scope to it.[86] However, the principle may operate in cases concerning regulation of core territorial privileges. In these instances it is not an 'aid to interpretation' but an independent principle.

According to the teleological approach, any ambiguity in a treaty text should be resolved by preferring the interpretation which gives effect to the object and purpose of the treaty.[87] This may involve a judicial implementation of purposes in a fashion not contemplated by the parties. The teleological approach has many pitfalls, not least its overt 'legislative' character.

A version of the teleological approach is often referred to under the rubric of 'evolutive' (or 'progressive') interpretation. It was apparently applied in *Navigational Rights*. There the question was whether the phrase 'for the purposes of commerce' in a boundary treaty of 1858 extended to cover commercial tourism, that is, the carriage

---

[81]   *Certain Expenses of the United Nations (Article 17, paragraph 2, of the Charter)*, ICJ Reports 1962 p 151, 163. Also: *Navigational and Related Rights (Costa Rica v Nicaragua)*, ICJ Reports 2009 p 213, 237.

[82]   For interpretation in the World Court pre-VCLT: Fitzmaurice (1951) 28 *BY* 1.

[83]   On interpretation of treaties authenticated in two or more languages: Art 33; *James Buchanan and Co Ltd v Babco (UK) Ltd* [1977] AC 141; *Young Loan* (1980) 59 ILR 494; *Nicaragua*, Jurisdiction and Admissibility, ICJ Reports 1984 p 392, 522–3 (Judge Ago), 537–9 (Judge Jennings), 575–6 (Judge Schwebel, diss); *LaGrand (Germany v US)*, ICJ Reports 2001 p 466, 502.

[84]   As the International Court put it in 1950, '[i]f the relevant words in their natural and ordinary meaning make sense in their context, that is an end of the matter': *Competence of the General Assembly for the Admission of a State to the United Nations*, ICJ Reports 1950 p 4, 8. Also: *Territorial Dispute (Libya/Chad)*, ICJ Reports 1994 p 6, 21–2; *Qatar v Bahrain*, Jurisdiction and Admissibility, ICJ Reports 1995 p 6, 18; *Pulau Ligitan/Sipadan*, ICJ Reports 2002 p 625, 645; *Genocide (Bosnia and Herzegovina v Serbia and Montenegro)*, ICJ Reports 2007 p 43, 109–10. Further: Fitzmaurice (1951) 28 *BY* 1, 1–28; Fitzmaurice (1957) 33 *BY* 203, 203–38; Thirlway (1991) 62 *BY* 1, 18–37; Gardiner (2008) 13–17.

[85]   E.g. *Territorial Jurisdiction of the International Commission of the River Oder* (1929) PCIJ Ser A No 23, 261. On restrictive interpretation generally: Lauterpacht (1949) 26 *BY* 48; Crook (1989) 83 *AJIL* 278, 304–7; Orakhelashvili (2003) 14 *EJIL* 529; Crema (2010) 21 *EJIL* 681.

[86]   E.g. *Navigational Rights*, ICJ Reports 2009 p 213, 237–8.

[87]   Generally: Waldock, in *Mélanges Reuter*, 535; Klabbers (2001) 34 *Vand JTL* 283; Jonas & Saunders (2010) 43 *Vand JTL* 565, 581.

of passengers for hire. The Court held that the term in the 1858 treaty should be interpreted so as to cover all modern forms of commerce, of which tourism is one:

[W]here the parties have used generic terms in a treaty, the parties necessarily having been aware that the meaning of the terms was likely to evolve over time, and where the treaty has been entered into for a very long period or is 'of continuing duration', the parties must be presumed, as a general rule, to have intended those terms to have an evolving meaning.[88]

The result was evidently correct; it was relevant that the right of transit was permanent in character, being part of the regime of the boundary. But the Court may have assumed that the term 'commerce' in the mid-nineteenth century had a stereotyped meaning; in fact, persons were carried for hire on the river at the time of the treaty.

As to the effectiveness principle, in opinions concerning powers of UN organs, the Court has often adopted a principle of institutional effectiveness and has implied the existence of powers which in its view were necessary or conducive to the purposes of the Charter.[89] The European Court of Human Rights has preferred an effective and 'evolutionary' approach in applying the European Convention on Human Rights.[90] However, this approach suffers from the same defects as the principle of restrictive interpretation. The ILC did not adopt the principle, considering that, as a matter of existing law it was reflected sufficiently in the doctrine of interpretation in good faith in accordance with the ordinary meaning of the text.[91]

Care must be taken to ensure that such 'rules' do not become rigid and unwieldy instruments that might force a preliminary choice of meaning rather than acting as a flexible guide. The ILC avoided taking a doctrinaire position and instead confined itself to isolating 'the comparatively few general principles which appear to constitute general rules for the interpretation of treaties'.[92] Those principles appear as an economical code in VCLT Articles 31 and 32, following exactly the ILC's Final Draft.

(iii) The general rule: VCLT Article 31

VCLT Article 31, entitled 'General rule of interpretation', has been recognized by the International Court as reflecting customary international law.[93] It provides as follows:

1. A treaty shall be interpreted in good faith in accordance with the ordinary meaning to be given to the terms of the treaty in their context and in the light of its object and purpose.

---

[88]   ICJ Reports 2009 p 213, 343.

[89]   *International Status of South West Africa*, ICJ Reports 1950 p 128; *South West Africa,* Preliminary Objections, ICJ Reports 1962 p 319; *Namibia*, ICJ Reports 1971 p 16, 47–50. Also: *Certain Expenses*, ICJ Reports 1962 p 151, 198–215 (Judge Fitzmaurice).

[90]   See *Golder v UK* (1975) 57 ILR 200, 245–6. Also: Letsas, *A Theory of Interpretation of the European Convention on Human Rights* (2008); Gros-Espiell, in Nieto Navia, *La Corte y el Sistema Interamericanos de Derechos Humanos* (1994) 223.

[91]   ILC *Ybk* 1966/II, 219.

[92]   ILC *Ybk* 1966/II, 218–19.

[93]   E.g. *Arbitral Award of 31 July 1989 (Guinea-Bissau v Senegal)*, ICJ Reports 1991 p 53, 70; *Pulau Ligitan/ Sipadan*, ICJ Reports 2002 p 625, 645; *Avena and Other Mexican Nationals (Mexico v US)*, ICJ Reports 2004 p 12, 48; *Genocide (Bosnia and Herzegovina v Serbia and Montenegro)*, ICJ Reports 2007 p 43, 109–10.

2. The context for the purpose of the interpretation of a treaty shall comprise, in addition to the text, including its preamble and annexes:

    (a) any agreement relating to the treaty which was made between all the parties in connection with the conclusion of the treaty;

    (b) any instrument which was made by one or more parties in connection with the conclusion of the treaty and accepted by the other parties as an instrument related to the treaty.

3. There shall be taken into account, together with the context:

    (a) any subsequent agreement between the parties regarding the interpretation of the treaty or the application of its provisions;

    (b) any subsequent practice in the application of the treaty which establishes the agreement of the parties regarding its interpretation;

    (c) any relevant rules of international law applicable in the relations between the parties.

4. A special meaning shall be given to a term if it is established that the parties so intended.

In its Commentary the ILC emphasized that applying this 'general rule' would be a single combined operation: hence the use of the singular. The various elements present in any given case would interact.

    The first principle stated in VCLT Article 31 is that 'a treaty shall be interpreted in good faith in accordance with the ordinary meaning to be given to the terms of the treaty'. In *Polish Postal Service in Danzig* the Permanent Court observed that the postal service which Poland was entitled to establish in Danzig by treaty was not confined to working inside the postal building: 'postal service' must be interpreted 'in its ordinary sense so as to include the normal functions of a postal service'.[94] Since then the principle of ordinary meaning has become well established as a fundamental guide to interpreting treaties.

    A corollary of the principle of ordinary meaning is the principle of integration: the meaning must emerge in the context of the treaty as a whole (including the text, its preamble and annexes, and any agreement or instrument related to the treaty and drawn up in connection with its conclusion)[95] and in the light of its object and purpose.[96] Another corollary is the principle of contemporaneity: the language of

---

[94] (1925) PCIJ Ser B No 11, 37.

[95] VCLT, Art 31(2); further: *Competence of the ILO to Regulate the Conditions of the Labour of Persons Employed in Agriculture* (1922) PCIJ Ser B Nos 2 and 3, 23; *Free Zones of Upper Savoy and the District of Gex* (1932) Ser A/B No 46, 140; *South West Africa*, Preliminary Objections, ICJ Reports 1962 p 319, 335; *Young Loan* (1980) 59 ILR 494, 534–40, 556–8; *Arbitral Award of 31 July 1989*, ICJ Reports 1991 p 53. Also: Bernhardt (1967) 27 ZaöRV 491, 498; Gardiner (2008) 165–6.

[96] *Rights of Nationals of the United States of America in Morocco (France v US)*, ICJ Reports 1952 p 176, 183–4, 197–8; *Pulau Ligitan/Sipadan*, ICJ Reports 2002 p 625, 645–6, 651–3. See also Sur, *L'Interpretation en droit international public* (1974) 227–31; Reuter, in Dinstein & Tabory (eds), *International Law at a Time of Perplexity* (1989) 623, 628; Jennings, in Bedjaoui (ed), *International Law Achievements and Prospects* (1991) 135, 145; Buffard & Zemanek (1998) 3 *Austrian RIEL* 311, 319; Linderfalk (2007) 205.

the treaty must be interpreted in the light of the rules of general international law in force at the time of its conclusion,[97] and also in the light of the contemporaneous meaning of terms.[98] The doctrine of ordinary meaning involves only a presumption: a meaning other than the ordinary meaning may be established, but the proponent of the special meaning has a burden of proof.[99] In complex cases the tribunal will be prepared to make a careful inquiry into the precise object and purpose of a treaty.[100]

Article 31(3) lists further factors to be taken into account along with the context (as defined in Article 31(2)). The parties may make an agreement regarding the interpretation of the treaty, or the application of its provisions. Such agreements can take various forms; they need not be formal amendments to the treaty.[101]

Reference may be made to 'subsequent practice in the application of the treaty which clearly establishes the understanding of all the parties regarding its interpretation'.[102] Subsequent practice by individual parties also has some probative value. In a series of important advisory opinions the Court has made considerable use of the subsequent practice of organizations in deciding controversial issues of interpretation.[103] Two points arise. The first is that members who were outvoted in the organs concerned may not be bound by the practice. Secondly, the practice of political organs involves elements of discretion and opportunism: what is significant is the reasoning *behind* the practice which can indicate its legal relevance, if any.[104]

The rule contained in Article 31(3)(c), requiring interpreters to take into account 'any relevant rules of international law applicable in the relations between the parties', places treaties within the wider context of general international law.[105] In *Oil Platforms* the Court described the application of relevant rules of international law as an 'integral part of the task of interpretation',[106] although the majority judgment has been criticized for the manner in which it then applied substantive customary and Charter

---

[97] *Grisbadarna* (1909) 11 RIAA 159; *Namibia*, ICJ Reports 1971 p 16, 31.

[98] *US Nationals in Morocco*, ICJ Reports 1952 p 176, 189.

[99] For critical comment on the concept of natural or plain meaning: Lauterpacht, *Development* (1958) 52–60.

[100] *Gabčíkovo-Nagymaros Project (Hungary/Slovakia)*, ICJ Reports 1997 p 7, 35–46.

[101] Aust (2nd edn, 2007) 238–41.

[102] ILC *Ybk* 1966/II, 221; *Air Transport Services Agreement (US v France)* (1964) 38 ILR 182, 245–8, 256–8; *Young Loan* (1980) 59 ILR 494, 541–3; ibid, 573–4 (Robinson, Bathurst & Monguilan, diss). Also: Fitzmaurice (1951) 28 *BY* 1, 20–1; Fitzmaurice (1957) 33 *BY* 203, 223–5 (commending subsequent practice for its 'superior reliability' as an indication of meaning); Aust (2nd edn, 2007) 241–3; Villiger, *Commentary* (2009) 431–2.

[103] *Admissions*, ICJ Reports 1950 p 4, 9; *Constitution of the Maritime Safety Committee of the Inter-Governmental Maritime Consultative Organization*, ICJ Reports 1960 p 150, 167–71; *Certain Expenses*, ICJ Reports 1962 p 151. Further: Engel (1967) 16 *ICLQ* 865; Amerasinghe (1994) 65 *BY* 175.

[104] *Certain Expenses*, ICJ Reports 1962 p 151, 187 (Judge Spender); 201–3 (Judge Fitzmaurice); *Namibia*, ICJ Reports 1971 p 16, 52–3.

[105] Aust (2nd edn, 2007) 243–4.

[106] *Oil Platforms (Iran v US)*, ICJ Reports 2003 p 161, 182–3.

rules on the use of force to interpret a treaty provision about freedom of commerce.[107] Article 31(3)(c) has been central to the debate around the so-called 'fragmentation' of international law,[108] forming the basis for arguments promoting systemic integration between different, more or less specialized areas of the law.[109] In a world of multiplying institutions with overlapping jurisdiction and choices to make between various sources of applicable law, it is seen as increasingly important to maintain coherence between what may seem self-contained subsystems of law.[110] Treaties cannot be interpreted in isolation of the wider context, but at the same time, tribunals should be cautious about using Article 31(3)(c) as a guise for incorporating extraneous rules in a manner that oversteps the boundaries of the judicial function.[111]

(iv) Supplementary means of interpretation: VCLT Article 32

The VCLT cautiously qualifies the textual approach by permitting recourse to further means of interpretation in certain circumstances. VCLT Article 32 provides:

Recourse may be had to supplementary means of interpretation, including the preparatory work of the treaty and the circumstances of its conclusion, in order to confirm the meaning resulting from the application of Article 31, or to determine the meaning when the interpretation according to Article 31:

(a) leaves the meaning ambiguous or obscure; or

(b) leads to a result which is manifestly absurd or unreasonable.[112]

In general the Court has refused to resort to preparatory work if the text is sufficiently clear in itself.[113] But on a number of occasions the Court has used preparatory work to confirm a conclusion reached by other means.[114] Preparatory work is an aid to be employed with care, since its use may detract from the textual approach: moreover, particularly in the case of multilateral agreements, the records of conference

---

[107] In her separate opinion Judge Higgins accused the majority of invoking the concept of treaty interpretation to displace the applicable law, with the result that the text of the treaty itself was ignored: ibid, 237–8 (Judge Higgins).

[108] On fragmentation: e.g. Simma (2004) 25 *Mich JIL* 845; Pauwelyn (2004) 25 *Mich JIL* 903; Fragmentation of International Law: Difficulties Arising From The Diversification and Expansion of International Law, Report of the Study Group of the ILC, 58th Session, A/CN.4/L.682, 13 April 2006; Buffard, in Buffard et al (eds), *International Law between Universalism and Fragmentation* (2008) 13.

[109] McLachlan (2005) 54 *ICLQ* 279.

[110] E.g. Dupuy (2002) 297 Hague *Recueil* 9; Higgins (2003) 52 *ICLQ* 1; Pauwelyn, *Conflict of Norms in Public International Law* (2003); Simma & Pulkoswki (2006) 17 *EJIL* 483; Higgins (2006) 55 *ICLQ* 791; Vanneste, *General International Law before Human Rights Courts* (2010).

[111] French (2006) 55 *ICLQ* 281.

[112] ILC *Ybk* 1966/II, 222–3; Schwebel, in Makarczyk (ed), *Theory of International Law at the Threshold of the 21st Century* (1996) 541; Gardiner (1997) 46 *ICLQ* 643; Klabbers (2003) 50 *NILR* 267; Sbolci, in Cannizzaro (2011) 145. See also *Genocide (Bosnia and Herzegovina v Serbia)*, ICJ Reports 2007 p 43, 109–10.

[113] *Conditions of Admission of a State to Membership in the United Nations (Article 4 of the Charter)*, ICJ Reports 1948 p 57, 63; *(Second) Admissions*, ICJ Reports 1950 p 4, 8; Fitzmaurice (1951) 28 *BY* 1, 10–13; (1957) 33 *BY* 203, 215–20.

[114] See *Convention of 1919 concerning the Work of Women at Night* (1932) PCIJ Ser A/B No 50, 380; *Libya/Chad*, ICJ Reports 1994 p 6, 27–8. See also *Banković v Belgium* (2001) 123 ILR 94, 110–11.

proceedings, treaty drafts, etc may be confused or inconclusive.[115] The ILC has taken the view that states acceding to a treaty and not taking part in its drafting cannot claim for themselves the inadmissibility of the preparatory work, which could have been examined before accession.[116]

Resorting to consideration of the preparatory work in cases referred to in Article 32(b) is not the same as the teleological approach. The textual approach in practice often leaves the decision-maker with a choice of possible meanings, and in exercising that choice it is impossible to keep considerations of policy out of account. Many issues of interpretation are by no means narrow technical inquiries.

At the Vienna Conference the US proposed an amendment to combine Articles 31 and 32, thus giving more scope to preparatory work and the circumstances in which the treaty was concluded. This proposal received little support. In its Commentary the ILC pointed out that the two articles should operate in conjunction, and would not have the effect of drawing a rigid line between 'supplementary' and other means of interpretation. At the same time the distinction itself was justified since the elements of interpretation in the first article all relate to the agreement between the parties 'at the time when or after it received authentic expression in the text'. Preparatory work did not have the same authentic character 'however valuable it may sometimes be in throwing light on the expression of agreement in the text'.[117]

(D) OBLIGATIONS AND RIGHTS FOR THIRD STATES[118]

The maxim *pacta tertiis nec nocent nec prosunt* expresses the fundamental principle that a treaty applies only between the parties to it. The VCLT refers to this as the 'general rule'; it is a corollary of the principle of consent and of the sovereignty and independence of states. Article 34 provides that 'a treaty does not create either obligations or rights for a third State without its consent'. This falls slightly short of expressing the customary rule, however: besides not *creating* obligations or rights, treaties cannot *infringe* the rights of third states without their consent.[119] This argument has been central to US objections to the possibility of its nationals becoming subject to the jurisdiction of the International Criminal Court without its consent, through the operation of

---

[115] For an interpretation that constituted a manifest inconsistency between the text of the treaty and its preparatory work: *González ('Cotton Field') v Mexico*, IACtHR, C/205, 16 November 2009, §73: 'inasmuch as it relates to a subsidiary method of interpretation, the preparatory works are completely insufficient to provide solid grounds to reject the interpretation made of Article 12 of the Convention of Belém do Pará.'

[116] Differing thus from *River Oder* (1929) PCIJ Ser A No 23. Further: Sinclair (1963) 12 *ICLQ* 512; *Arbitral Commission on Property, etc, in Germany* (1966) 29 ILR 442, 460.

[117] ILC *Ybk* 1966/II, 219–20.

[118] VCLT, Arts 34–8; Draft Articles, III, ILC *Ybk* 1964/II, 180–5 (Arts 58–62); ILC Final Report and Draft Articles, ILC *Ybk* 1966/II, 226–31 (Arts 30–4); Lauterpacht, *Development* (1958) 306–13; Sinclair (2nd edn, 1984) 98–106; Chinkin, *Third Parties in International Law* (1993) 25–114; Tomuschat (1993) 241 Hague *Recueil* 195; Villiger, *Commentary* (2009) 465–504; Corten & Klein (2011) 887–960.

[119] See O'Keefe (2010) *Cam RIA* 1, 9.

Article 12(2)(a) of the Rome Statute,[120] although the equation of nationals (not being state officials) with the state makes this argument problematic.

The existence and extent of exceptions to the general rule have been controversial. The ILC did not accept the view that treaties creating 'objective regimes' (e.g. the demilitarization of a territory by treaty or a legal regime for a major waterway) had a specific place in the law of treaties.[121] VCLT Article 35 provides that 'an obligation arises for a third State from a provision of a treaty if the parties to the treaty intend the provision to be the means of establishing the obligation and the third State expressly accepts that obligation in writing'.

However, two apparent exceptions to the principle exist. First, a rule in a treaty may become binding on non-parties if it becomes a part of international custom.[122] Secondly, a treaty may provide for lawful sanctions for violations of the law which are to be imposed on an aggressor state.[123] The VCLT contains a reservation in regard to any obligation in relation to a treaty which arises for an aggressor state 'in consequence of measures taken in conformity with the Charter of the United Nations with reference to the aggression' (Article 75).

Article 2(6) of the Charter provides that:

The Organization shall ensure that states which are not Members of the United Nations act in accordance with these Principles so far as may be necessary for the maintenance of international peace and security.

Kelsen held the view that the provision created duties, and liabilities to sanctions under the enforcement provisions of the Charter, for non-members.[124] Assuming that this was the intention of the draftsmen, the provision could only be reconciled with general principles by reference to the status of the principles in Article 2 as general or customary international law. By now the question is largely academic, given that virtually all states are members of the UN and the Charter is binding on them directly as parties.

More controversial is the conferral of rights on third parties, the *stipulation pour autrui*. Not infrequently treaties make provisions in favour of specified third states or for other states generally, for example the treaties concerning certain of the major international waterways, including, on one view, the Panama Canal.[125] The problem has been to discover when, if at all, the right conferred becomes perfect and enforceable by the third state: is the third state required to give express or implicit assent to the

---

[120] ICC Statute, 17 July 1998, 2187 UNTS 3 (currently 119 parties). For analysis of US arguments about the 'third-party effect' of the ICC Statute, see O'Keefe (2010) *Cam RIA* 1.

[121] See McNair (1961) 310. Cf Vienna Convention on the Succession of States in Respect of Treaties, Arts 11, 12; *Gabčíkovo-Nagymaros*, ICJ Reports 1997 p 7, 70–3; Klabbers (1998) 11 *LJIL* 345, 352–5.

[122] VCLT, Art 38; ILC Final Report and Draft Articles, ILC *Ybk* 1966/II, 230–1 (Art 34).

[123] ILC *Ybk* 1966/II, 227.

[124] *The Law of the United Nations* (1951) 106–10; cf Bindschedler (1963) 108 Hague *Recueil* 307, 403–7. Also: McNair (1961) 216–18.

[125] Ibid, 265–8.

creation of the right before it will benefit, or is it unconditional? Views were divided, but the ILC took the view that the two opposing views did not differ substantially in their practical effects. VCLT Article 36 creates a presumption as to the assent of the third state.

The third state may, of course, disclaim any already inhering right expressly or tacitly through failure to exercise the right. The right of a third state may not be revoked or modified by the parties if it is established that it was intended that this could only occur with the consent of the third state: Article 37(2).

5. AMENDMENT AND MODIFICATION OF TREATIES[126]

The amendment of treaties depends on the consent of the parties, and the issue is primarily political. However, the lawyer may be concerned with procedures for amendment, as a facet of the large problem of peaceful change in international relations. Many treaties, including the Charter (Articles 108 and 109), provide a procedure for amendment. International organizations have amendment procedures which in some cases show considerable sophistication. In the League Covenant (Article 19) and, less explicitly, in the Charter (Article 14), provision for peaceful change was made as part of a scheme to avoid threats to the peace.

Apart from amendment, a treaty may undergo 'modification' when some of the parties conclude an *inter se* agreement altering the application of the treaty between themselves alone: VCLT Article 41 restricts this capacity in certain cases.

Modification may also result from the conclusion of a subsequent treaty or even the emergence of a new peremptory norm of general international law. The ILC's Final Draft provided that 'a treaty may be modified by subsequent practice in the application of the treaty establishing the agreement of the parties to modify its provisions'.[127] This was rejected at the Vienna Conference on the ground that such a rule would create instability.[128] This result is unsatisfactory. First, Article 39 provides that a treaty may be amended by agreement without requiring any formality for the expression of agreement. Secondly, a consistent practice may provide cogent evidence of *common* consent to a change. Thirdly, modification of this type occurs in practice. The process of interpretation through subsequent practice is legally distinct from modification, although the distinction is often rather fine.

---

[126] VCLT, Arts 39–41; Draft Articles, III, ILC *Ybk* 1964/II, 193–9 (Arts 65–8); ILC Final Report and Draft Articles, ILC *Ybk* 1966/II, 231–6 (Arts 35–8); Handbook of Final Clauses, ST/LEG/6, 130–52; Hoyt, *The Unanimity Rule in the Revision of Treaties* (1959); Zacklin, *The Amendment of the Constitutive Instruments of the United Nations and Specialized Agencies* (1968, repr 2005); Kontou, *The Termination and Revision of Treaties in Light of New Customary International Law* (1994); Bowman (1995) 44 *ICLQ* 540; Frowein, in Hafner et al (1998) 201; Villiger, *Commentary* (2009) 507–38; Corten & Klein (2011) 961–1011.

[127] ILC *Ybk* 1966/II, 236 (Art 38).

[128] GAOR, 1st Session, 207–15. Also: Kearney & Dalton (1970) 64 *AJIL* 495, 525.

6. INVALIDITY, TERMINATION, AND SUSPENSION OF TREATIES[129]

VCLT Part V governs invalidity, termination, and suspension of the operation of treaties. It sets out an exhaustive list of grounds (see Article 42(2)). However, the grounds for termination and the requirements of essential validity do not exhaust the matters relevant to justification for non-performance of obligations. That issue can arise irrespective of validity or termination of the *source* of obligation, the treaty. The topic of justification belongs to the law of state responsibility,[130] expressly reserved by VCLT Article 73.

(A) INVALIDITY[131]

Generally speaking, the validity and continuance in force of a treaty and of consent to be bound is presumed (Article 42), but various matters may give rise to issues of invalidity. Invalidity may be relative (where a treaty is voidable if a party establishes certain grounds) or absolute (where the treaty is void *per se*). Issues of invalidity tend to arise rarely in practice.

(i) Violations of internal law[132]

The extent to which constitutional limitations on the treaty-making power can be invoked on the international plane is a matter of controversy. Historically, three main views have received support. According to the first, constitutional limitations determine validity on the international plane.[133] Criticism of this view emphasizes the insecurity in treaty-making it would entail. The second view varies from the first in that only 'notorious' constitutional limitations are effective on the international plane. The third view is that a state is bound irrespective of internal limitations by consent given by an agent properly authorized according to international law. Some advocates of this view qualify the rule in cases where the other state is aware of the failure to comply

---

[129] McNair (1961) chs 30–5; Elias (1971) 134 Hague *Recueil* 333; Haraszti, *Some Fundamental Problems of the Law of Treaties* (1973) 229–425; Rozakis (1974) 16 *AdV* 150; Jiménez de Aréchaga (1978) 159 Hague *Recueil* 1, 59–85; Ruda, in Dinstein & Tabory (1989) 61; Conforti & Labella (1990) 44 *EJIL* 44; Thirlway (1992) 63 *BY* 63; Corten & Klein (2006) 1593–2587; Villiger, *Commentary* (2009) 541–798; Corten & Klein (2011) 1015–642.

[130] On the relationship between the law of treaties and the law of state responsibility generally: Dupuy (1997) 43 *AFDI* 7; Lefeber (1998) 11 *LJIL* 609; Crawford & Olleson (2000) 21 *AYIL* 55; Simma & Pulkowski (2006) 17 *EJIL* 483; Verhoeven, in Crawford, Pellet & Olleson (eds), *The Law of International Responsibility* (2010) 105.

[131] McNair (1961) 206–36; Aust (2nd edn, 2007) 312–23; Corten & Klein (2011) 1090–235.

[132] See de Visscher, *De la Conclusion des traités internationaux* (1943) 219–87; Lauterpacht, ILC *Ybk* 1953/II, 141–6; McNair (1961) ch 3; Waldock, ILC *Ybk* 1963/II, 41–6; ILC *Ybk* 1963/II, 190–3; ILC Final Report and Draft Articles, ILC *Ybk* 1966/II, 240–2; de Visscher (1972) 136 Hague *Recueil* 1, 94–8; Meron (1978) 49 *BY* 175; Villiger, *Commentary* (2009) 583–94.

[133] This was the position of the ILC in 1951: ILC *Ybk* 1951/II, 73.

with internal law or where the irregularity is manifest. This position, which involves a presumption of competence and excepts manifest irregularity, was approved by the ILC in 1966.[134] At the Vienna Conference the draft provision was strengthened, and the result appears in VCLT Article 46.[135]

(ii) Defects of authority[136]

The VCLT provides that if the authority of a representative to express the consent of his state to be bound by a particular treaty has been made subject to a specific restriction, omission to observe the restriction may not be invoked as a ground of invalidity unless the restriction was previously notified to the other negotiating states.

(iii) Error[137]

Under VCLT Article 48,[138] a state may invoke an error as invalidating its consent to a treaty if the error relates to 'a fact or situation which was assumed by that State to exist at the time when the treaty was concluded and formed an essential basis of its consent to be bound by the treaty'. However, consistent with the previous law, Article 48(2) provides that this does not apply 'if the State in question contributed by its own conduct to the error or if the circumstances were such as to put that State on notice of a possible error'.[139]

(iv) Fraud[140]

There are few helpful precedents. The VCLT provides[141] that a state which has been induced to enter into a treaty by the fraud of another negotiating state may invoke the fraud as invalidating its consent to be bound by the treaty. Fraudulent misrepresentation of a material fact inducing an essential error is dealt with by the provision relating to error.

The ILC decided that corruption of representatives was not adequately dealt with as a case of fraud[142] and an appropriate provision appears as VCLT Article 50.[143]

---

[134] ILC *Ybk* 1966/II, 240–2.

[135] *Cameroon v Nigeria*, ICJ Reports 2002 p 303, 430.

[136] VCLT, Art 47. See Draft Articles, II, ILC *Ybk* 1963/II, 193; Waldock, ILC *Ybk* 1963/II, 46–7; ILC Final Report and Draft Articles, ILC *Ybk* 1966/II, 242–3 (Art 44); Villiger, *Commentary* (2009) 595–602. Further: *Phillips Petroleum Co, Iran v Iran, National Iranian Oil Co* (1982) 70 ILR 483, 486; *Amoco Iran Oil Co v Iran* (1982) 70 ILR 490, 492.

[137] Lauterpacht, ILC *Ybk* 1953/II, 153; Fitzmaurice (1953) 2 *ICLQ* 25, 35–7; Waldock, ILC *Ybk* 1963/II, 48–50; Oraison, *L'Erreur dans les traités* (1972); Thirlway (1992) 63 *BY* 1, 22–8; Villiger, *Commentary* (2009) 603–12.

[138] Also: ILC *Ybk* 1966/II, 243–4.

[139] *Temple*, ICJ Reports 1962 p 6, 26–7; ibid, 57–9 (Judge Fitzmaurice).

[140] Lauterpacht, ILC *Ybk* 1953/II, 152; Fitzmaurice, ILC *Ybk* 1958/II, 25, 37; Waldock, ILC *Ybk* 1963/II, 47–8; Oraison (1975) 75 *RGDIP* 617; Villiger, *Commentary* (2009) 613–22.

[141] VCLT, Art 49. See ILC Final Report and Draft Articles, ILC *Ybk* 1966/II, 244–5.

[142] ILC *Ybk* 1966/II, 245.

[143] Villiger, *Commentary* (2009) 621–8; Corten & Klein (2011) 1169–78.

(v) Coercion

Coercion includes coercion of state representatives[144] and of states themselves.[145] VCLT Article 51 provides that 'the expression of a State's consent to be bound by a treaty which has been procured by the coercion of its representative through acts or threats directed against him shall be without legal effect'. The concept of coercion extends to blackmailing threats and threats against the representative's family.

As for coercion of a state, the ILC considered that Article 2(4) of the UN Charter, together with other developments, justified the conclusion that a treaty procured by the threat or use of force in violation of the Charter shall be void. VCLT Article 52 so provides.[146] An amendment with the object of defining force to include any 'economic or political pressure' was withdrawn: instead a declaration condemning such pressure appears in the Final Act of the Conference.[147]

(vi) Conflict with a peremptory norm[148]

VCLT Article 53 provides that a treaty is void if at the time of its conclusion it conflicts with a peremptory norm of general international law (*ius cogens*).[149] Further, a treaty *becomes* void if it conflicts with a peremptory norm of general international law established *after* the treaty comes into force.[150] This does not have retroactive effects on the validity of a treaty. The discussion on the issue of *ius cogens* proved to be one of the 'longest, most heated and disorganized debates' at the Vienna Conference.[151] Views differ on whether the VCLT provisions correspond to the existing law on the relationship between treaties and peremptory norms;[152] but the answer seems clear enough. A peremptory norm is one from which no derogation is permitted on the part of one or

---

[144] Fitzmaurice, ILC *Ybk* 1958/II, 26, 38; Waldock, ILC *Ybk* 1963/II, 36, 50; ILC Final Report and Draft Articles, ILC *Ybk* 1966/II, 245–6 (Art 48); de Jong (1984) 15 *NYIL* 209; Villiger, *Commentary* (2009) 629–37.

[145] Draft Articles, II, ILC *Ybk* 1963/II, 197–8 (Art 36); Waldock, ILC *Ybk* 1963/II, 51–2; Lauterpacht, ILC *Ybk* 1953/II, 147–52; McNair (1961) 206–11; Brownlie, *Use of Force* (1963) 404–6; Fitzmaurice, ILC *Ybk* 1957/II, 32, 56–7; Fitzmaurice, ILC *Ybk* 1958/II, 26, 38–9; de Jong (1984) 15 *NYIL* 209; Caflisch (1992) 35 *GYIL* 52. Also: *Fisheries Jurisdiction (UK v Iceland)*, Jurisdiction, ICJ Reports 1973 p 3, 14; Thirlway (1992) 63 *BY* 1, 28–31.

[146] Also: ILC Final Report and Draft Articles, ILC *Ybk* 1966/II, 246–7 (Art 49); Kearney & Dalton (1970) 64 *AJIL* 495, 532; de Jong (1984) 15 *NYIL* 209; Villiger, *Commentary* (2009) 638–50; Corten & Klein (2011) 1201–23.

[147] A/CONF.39/26, 23 May 1969, 285.

[148] De Visscher (1971) 75 *RGDIP* 5; Gaja (1981) 172 Hague *Recueil* 271; D'Amato (1990) 6 *Conn JIL* 1; Charney (1993) 87 *AJIL* 529; Kolb, *Théorie du* Jus Cogens *International* (2001); Kolb (2005) 109 *RGDIP* 305; Tomuschat & Thouvenin (eds), *The Fundamental Rules of the International Legal Order* (2006) 83; Orakhelashvili, *Peremptory Norms in International Law* (2006).

[149] ILC Final Report and Draft Articles, ILC *Ybk* 1966/II, 247–9 (Art 50); Gaja (1981) 172 Hague *Recueil* 271, 279–89; Villiger, *Commentary* (2009) 661–78; Corten & Klein (2011) 1224–35.

[150] VCLT, Art 64. See Fitzmaurice, ILC *Ybk* 1957/II, 29–30, 51; Draft Articles, II, ILC *Ybk* 1963/II, 211 (Art 45); Waldock, ILC *Ybk* 1963/II, 77, 79; ILC Final Report and Draft Articles, ILC *Ybk* 1966/II, 261 (Art 61); Villiger (2009) 344 Hague *Recueil* 9, 135–41.

[151] Villiger (2009) 344 Hague *Recueil* 9, 137.

[152] E.g. Gaja (1981) 172 Hague *Recueil* 271, 279; cf Villiger (2009) 344 Hague *Recueil* 9, 140–1.

a few states: the *form* the attempted derogation takes must be irrelevant. Issues raised by peremptory norms are dealt with in more detail in chapter 27.

(B) TERMINATION AND SUSPENSION[153]

VCLT Part V Section 3 deals with termination and suspension of the operation of treaties. A treaty may of course specify the conditions of its termination, and may provide for denunciation by the parties.[154] Where a treaty contains no provisions regarding its termination, the existence of a right of denunciation depends on the intention of the parties, which can be inferred from the terms of the treaty and its subject-matter, but, according to the VCLT, the presumption is that the treaty is not subject to denunciation or withdrawal.[155] At least in certain circumstances denunciation is conditional upon a reasonable period of notice. Some important law-making treaties contain no denunciation clause. Treaties of peace are not open to unilateral denunciation.

(i) War and armed conflict[156]

Hostile relations do not automatically terminate treaties between the parties to a conflict.[157] Many treaties, including the UN Charter, are intended to be no less binding in case of war, and multipartite law-making agreements such as the Geneva Conventions of 1949 survive war or armed conflict.[158] However, in state practice many types of treaty are regarded as at least suspended in time of war, and war conditions may lead to termination of treaties on grounds of impossibility or fundamental change of circumstances. In many respects the law on the subject is uncertain. Thus it is not clear to what extent the illegality of the use or threat of force has had effects on the right (where it may be said to exist) to regard a treaty as suspended or terminated.[159]

---

[153] E.g Aust (2nd edn, 2007) 277–311; Corten & Klein (2011) 1236–454.

[154] If it is a bilateral treaty, denunciation by one party will terminate it; if it is multilateral, the withdrawal of the denouncing party will usually not terminate the whole treaty. Treaties may also be terminated at any time by the consent of all the parties, after consultation. See VCLT, Art 54; ILC Final Report and Draft Articles, ILC *Ybk* 1966/II, 249 (Art 51); Briggs (1974) 68 *AJIL* 51; Helfer (2005) 91 *Va LR* 1579; Aust (2nd edn, 2007) 277.

[155] VCLT, Art 56; Fitzmaurice, ILC *Ybk* 1957/II, 22; Draft Articles, II, ILC *Ybk* 1963/II, 200–1 (Art 39); Waldock, ILC *Ybk* 1963/II, 63–70; ILC Final Report and Draft Articles, ILC *Ybk* 1966/II, 250–1 (Art 53); Jiménez de Aréchaga (1978) 159 Hague *Recueil* 1, 70–1; Widdows (1982) 53 *BY* 83; Sinclair (2nd edn, 1984) 186–8; Plender (1986) 57 *BY* 133, 143; Villiger, *Commentary* (2009) 695–706. See also *Interpretation of the Agreement of 25 March 1951 between the WHO and Egypt*, ICJ Reports 1980 p 73, 94–6, 128–9 (Judge Mosler), 159–62 (Judge Ago), 176–7 (Judge El-Erian), 184–9 (Judge Sette-Camara); *Nicaragua*, Jurisdiction and Admissibility, ICJ Reports 1984 p 392, 419–20.

[156] McNair (1961) ch 43; Broms (1981/I) 59 *Ann de l'Inst* 201; Chinkin (1981) 7 *Yale JWPO* 177; Delbrück (2000) 4 *EPIL* 1367.

[157] IDI Res, Helsinki/III (1985); Greenwood (1987) 36 *ICLQ* 283, 296–7.

[158] *Masinimport v Scottish Mechanical Light Industries* (1976) 74 ILR 559, 564.

[159] ILC *Ybk* 1963/II, 187, 189.

The ILC decided to include the topic 'effects of armed conflicts on treaties' in its long-term programme of work in 2000.[160] A set of draft articles with commentaries was adopted at second reading in 2011.[161]

(ii) Denunciation and termination by agreement

Termination or withdrawal may take place by consent of all the parties.[162] Such consent may be implied. In particular, a treaty may be considered as terminated if all the parties conclude a later treaty which is intended to supplant the earlier treaty or if the later treaty is incompatible with its provisions.[163] The topic of 'desuetude', which is probably not a term of art, is essentially concerned with discontinuance of use of a treaty and its implied termination by consent.[164] However, it could extend to the distinct situation of a unilateral renunciation of rights under a treaty. Moreover, irrespective of the agreement of the parties, an ancient treaty may become meaningless and incapable of practical application.

(iii) Material breach[165]

It is widely recognized that material breach by one party entitles the other party or parties to a treaty to invoke the breach as the ground of termination or suspension. This option by the wronged party is accepted as a sanction for securing the observance of treaties. However, considerable uncertainty has surrounded the precise circumstances in which such right of unilateral abrogation may be exercised, particularly in respect of multilateral treaties. In practice material breach has rarely been invoked, an exception being *Gabčíkovo-Nagymaros Project (Hungary/Slovakia).*[166]

---

[160] See www.untreaty.un.org/ilc/summaries/1_10.htm. Brownlie was appointed Special Rapporteur; he was succeeded by Caflisch in 2009.

[161] ILC Report 2011, GAOR, 66th Session, Supp No 10, A/66/10, 173–217. Further: Bannelier, in Angelet, Corten & Klein (eds), *Droit du Pouvoir, Pouvoir du Droit* (2007) 125.

[162] VCLT, Art 54; Draft Articles, II, ILC *Ybk* 1963/II, 203–4 (Art 40); ILC Final Report and Draft Articles, ILC *Ybk* 1966/II, 251–2 (Art 54). Also: Kontou (1994).

[163] VCLT, Art 59; Draft Articles, II, ILC *Ybk* 1963/II, 203–4 (Art 41); ILC Final Report and Draft Articles, ILC *Ybk* 1966/II, 252–3 (Art 56); Plender (1986) 57 *BY* 133, 153–7. Also: *Electricity Company of Sofia and Bulgaria* (1939) PCIJ Ser A/B No 77, 92 (Judge Anzilotti).

[164] Fitzmaurice, ILC *Ybk* 1957/II, 28, 47–8, 52; ILC Final Report and Draft Articles, ILC *Ybk* 1966/II, 237; Thirlway (1992) 63 *BY* 1, 94–6; Kohen, in Cannizzaro (2011) 350. Also: *Widjatmiko v Gebroeders Zomer en Keunig's Drukkerij Vada, Uitgeversmij* (1971) 70 ILR 439; *Nuclear Tests (Australia v France)*, ICJ Reports 1974 p 253, 337–8 (Judges Onyeama, Dillard, Jiménez de Aréchaga & Sir Humphrey Waldock, diss), 381 (Judge de Castro, diss), 404, 415–16 (Judge Barwick, diss).

[165] McNair (1961) ch 36; Simma, (1970) 20 *ÖZföR* 5; Rosenne, *Breach of Treaty* (1985); Hutchinson (1988) 58 *BY* 151; Kirgis (1989) 22 *Cornell ILJ* 549; Kontou (1994); Gomaa, *Suspension and Termination of Treaties on Grounds of Breach* (1996); Fitzmaurice (2001) 6 *Austrian RIEL* 3; Laly-Chevalier, *La Violation du traité* (2005); Villiger (2009) 344 Hague *Recueil* 9, 144–59; Corten & Klein (2011) 1350–81.

[166] The Court rejected Hungary's argument: ICJ Reports 1997 p 7, 60–2, 65–7. Of course it makes a difference under Art 60 which party is trying to get rid of the treaty. In *Rainbow Warrior* the tribunal held that France had committed a material breach of the agreement in question but ultimately this finding was of little practical consequence: see (1990) 82 ILR 499.

VCLT Article 60[167] deals with the matter with as much precision as can be reasonably expected, although its formulation has attracted some criticism.[168] Paragraphs 1 and 2 set out what parties to bilateral and multilateral treaties are entitled to do in response to a material breach by another party. Paragraph 3 defines a material breach as a repudiation of the treaty not sanctioned by the VCLT, or the violation of a provision essential to the accomplishment of the object or purpose of the treaty.[169] It should be observed that the focus here is on the importance of the provision violated, not the magnitude of the breach.[170] Paragraph 4 stipulates that the first three paragraphs are without prejudice to any provision in the treaty applicable in the event of a breach, and paragraph 5 excludes the application of the first three paragraphs to 'provisions relating to the protection of the human person contained in treaties of a humanitarian character'.

A state may by its own conduct prejudice its right to terminate a treaty on the ground of material breach.[171]

(iv) Supervening impossibility of performance[172]

The VCLT provides that a party 'may invoke the impossibility of performing a treaty as a ground for terminating it if the impossibility results from the permanent disappearance or destruction of an object indispensable for the execution of the treaty'.[173] Situations envisaged include the submergence of an island, the drying up of a river, or destruction of a railway, by an earthquake, or other disaster. The effect of impossibility is not automatic, and a party must invoke the ground for termination. Impossibility of performance may not be invoked by a party to the relevant treaty when it results from that party's own breach of an obligation flowing from the treaty.[174]

(v) Fundamental change of circumstances[175]

The principles by which fundamental change of circumstances may be invoked as a ground for terminating or withdrawing from a treaty are expressed in VCLT Article 62.

---

[167] Also: Draft Articles, II, ILC *Ybk* 1963/II, 204–6 (Art 42); Waldock, ILC *Ybk* 1963/II, 72–7; ILC Final Report and Draft Articles, ILC *Ybk* 1966/II, 253–5 (Art 57).

[168] E.g. Simma (1970) 20 *ÖZföR* 5; Klabbers, in Tupamäki (ed), *Essays on International Law* (1998) 20; Fitzmaurice (2001) 6 *Austrian RIEL* 3.

[169] This definition was applied by analogy in *Namibia*, ICJ Reports 1971 p 16, 46–7, in respect of South African violations of the Mandate for South West Africa (Namibia) and the consequent revocation of the Mandate by the UN General Assembly.

[170] For comment: Simma (1970) 20 *ÖZföR* 5, 61.

[171] *Gabčíkovo-Nagymaros*, ICJ Reports 1997 p 7, 65–7.

[172] Sinclair (2nd edn, 1984) 190–2; Aust (2nd edn, 2007) 296; Villiger, *Commentary* (2009) 752–61.

[173] VCLT, Art 61(1); Draft Articles, II, ILC *Ybk* 1963/II, 206 (Art 43); ILC Final Report and Draft Articles, ILC *Ybk* 1966/II, 255–6 (Art 58). Another example of impossibility arises from the extinction of one of the parties to a bilateral treaty, apart from any rule of state succession which might allow devolution: Waldock, ILC *Ybk* 1963/II, 77–9. For succession see chapter 18.

[174] *Gabčíkovo-Nagymaros*, ICJ Reports 1997 p 7, 63–4.

[175] Draft Articles, II, ILC *Ybk* 1963/II, 207–11 (Art 44); Waldock, ILC *Ybk* 1963/II, 79–85; ILC Final Report and Draft Articles, ILC *Ybk* 1966/II, 256–60 (Art 59); van Bogaert (1966) 70 *RGDIP* 49; Lissitzyn

An example of a fundamental change would be the case where a party to a military and political alliance, involving exchange of military intelligence and information, has a change of government incompatible with the basis of alliance. The provision reflects the doctrine of *rebus sic stantibus,* which involves the implication of a term that the obligations of an agreement would end if there had been a change of circumstances. As in municipal systems, so in international law it is recognized that changes frustrating the object of an agreement, even if not amounting to actual impossibility, may justify its termination. Some jurists dislike the doctrine, regarding it as a source of insecurity of obligations, more especially in the absence of a system of compulsory jurisdiction. But it has generally been applied very conservatively, as it was in *Free Zones*.[176] Further the VCLT excludes boundary treaties from the operation of the principle in order to avoid an obvious source of threats to the peace.

In *Fisheries Jurisdiction (UK v Iceland)* the International Court accepted VCLT Article 62 as a statement of customary law but decided that the dangers to Icelandic interests resulting from new fishing techniques 'cannot constitute a fundamental change with respect to the lapse or subsistence' of the jurisdictional clause in a bilateral agreement.[177] In *Gabčíkovo-Nagymaros*, Hungary specified profound changes of a political character, the Project's diminishing economic viability, the progress of environmental knowledge, and the development of new norms and prescriptions of international environmental law, as grounds entitling it to invoke the fundamental change of circumstances principle. The Court recalled its findings in *Fisheries Jurisdiction* and rejected the Hungarian argument, holding that:

The changed circumstances advanced by Hungary are, in the Court's view, not of such a nature, either individually or collectively, that their effect would radically transform the extent of the obligations still to be performed in order to accomplish the Project. A fundamental change of circumstances must have been unforeseen; the existence of the circumstances at the time of the Treaty's conclusion must have constituted an essential basis of the consent of the parties to be bound by the Treaty.[178]

Referring to the language of VCLT Article 62, the Court concluded that 'the stability of treaty relations requires that the plea of fundamental change of circumstances be applied only in exceptional cases'.[179] In contrast to this generally accepted position, the Court of Justice of the European Communities applied a relaxed interpretation of the *rebus* doctrine to uphold the suspension of the EC–Yugoslavia Cooperation Agreement in the case of *Racke v Hauptzollamt Mainz*.[180] It conceded that the

---

(1967) 61 *AJIL* 895; Schwelb (1969) 29 *ZaöRV* 39; Haraszti (1975) 146 Hague *Recueil* 1; Cahier, in Lamberti Zanardi et al (eds), *Essays in Honour of Roberto Ago* (1987) 163; Thirlway (1992) 63 *BY* 1, 75–82.

[176] (1932) *PCIJ* Ser A/B No 46, 156–8; the Court observed that the facts did not justify the application of the doctrine, which had been invoked by France.

[177] Jurisdiction, ICJ Reports 1973 p 3, 20–1. Also: *Fisheries Jurisdiction (Germany v Iceland)*, Jurisdiction, ICJ Reports 1973 p 49; and Briggs (1974) 68 *AJIL* 51.

[178] *Gabčíkovo-Nagymaros*, ICJ Reports 1997 p 7, 65.

[179] Ibid.

[180] (1998) 117 ILR 399.

Commission could have continued to grant tariff concessions after the outbreak of hostilities, but noted that impossibility of performance was not required and that there was 'no point' in continuing to grant preferences in circumstances where Yugoslavia was breaking up.[181]

Treaties may also be affected when one state succeeds wholly or in part to the legal personality and territory of another. The conditions under which the treaties of the latter survive depend on many factors, including the precise form and origin of the 'succession' and the type of treaty concerned.[182]

(C) PROCEDURE AND CONSEQUENCES[183]

The consequences of invalidity, termination, and suspension will depend on the grounds relied upon. Certain grounds of invalidity must be invoked by a party[184] and so the treaties concerned are not void but voidable. These grounds are: incompetence under internal law, restrictions on authority of representative, error, fraud, and corruption of a representative. The same is true of certain grounds of termination—material breach, impossibility, and fundamental change of circumstances. On the other hand a treaty is *void* in case of coercion of a state (invalidity), and conflict with an existing or emergent peremptory norm (invalidity or termination). Consent to be bound by a treaty procured by coercion of the representative of a state 'shall be without any legal effect' (Article 51, invalidity). The rules governing separability of treaty provisions (Article 44), that is, the severance of particular clauses affected by grounds for invalidating or terminating a treaty, do not apply to the cases of coercion of a representative, coercion of a state, or conflict with an *existing* peremptory norm.[185] Articles 69 to 72 deal with the consequences of invalidity, termination, or suspension.

---

[181] Ibid, 442. The issue was not addressed in much depth, however, as the Court approached it as a matter of judicial review: see Aust (2nd edn, 2007) 299. For criticism of *Racke*: Klabbers (1999) 36 *CMLR* 179.

[182] VCLT, Art 73. In its work on the law of treaties the ILC put this question aside: ILC Final Report and Draft Articles, ILC *Ybk* 1966/II, 267–8 (Art 69). See also chapter 19.

[183] See VCLT, Part V, Sections 3–4. Further: Cahier (1972) 76 *RGDIP* 645, 672–89; Villiger, *Commentary* (2009) 799–891; Corten & Klein (2011) 1455–62.

[184] Procedure: Arts 65–8. Further: Briggs (1967) 61 *AJIL* 976; Morelli (1974) 57 *RDI* 5; David, *The Strategy of Termination* (1976); Thirlway (1992) 63 *BY* 1, 85; Villiger (2009) 344 Hague *Recueil* 9, 160–82.

[185] ILC *Ybk* 1966/II, 238–9, 261. For comment: Sinclair (1970) 19 *ICLQ* 67.

17

DIPLOMATIC AND CONSULAR RELATIONS

1. MODALITIES OF INTERSTATE RELATIONS[1]

In its simplest sense diplomacy comprises any means by which states establish or maintain mutual relations, communicate with each other, or carry out political or legal transactions, in each case through their authorized agents. Diplomacy may thus exist between states in a state of war or armed conflict with each other, but the concept relates to communication friendly or hostile,[2] rather than the material forms of economic or military conflict.

Normally, diplomacy involves the exchange of permanent diplomatic missions, and similar permanent, or at least regular, representation is necessary for states to give substance to their membership of the United Nations and other major intergovernmental organizations. Then there are the categories of special missions or ad hoc diplomacy, and the representation of states at ad hoc conferences.

The rules of international law governing diplomatic relations are at the most formal end of the spectrum of international communication. They are the product of long-established state practice reflected in treaties, national legislation, and judicial decisions. The law has now been codified substantially in the Vienna Convention on Diplomatic Relations (VCDR).[3] Although parts of the VCDR were progressive, its widespread acceptance and implementation means that it now is mostly reflective

---

[1] ILC *Ybk* 1956/II, 129; ILC *Ybk* 1957/I, 2; ILC *Ybk* 1958/I, 84; ILC *Ybk* 1958/II, 16, 89; 7 *BD* ch 19; Cahier, *Le Droit diplomatique contemporain* (1962); 4 Rousseau 139–210; Salmon, *Manuel de Droit diplomatique* (1994); *Satow's Diplomatic Practice* (ed, Roberts, 6th edn, 2009); Lee & Quigley, *Consular Law and Practice* (3rd edn, 2008); Denza, *Diplomatic Law* (3rd edn, 2008); Fox, *The Law of State Immunity* (2nd edn, 2008) 700–36; van Alebeek, 'Immunity, Diplomatic' (2009) *MPEPIL*; Hestermeyer, 'Vienna Convention on Diplomatic Relations (1961)' (2009) *MPEPIL*. Also Frey & Frey, *The History of Diplomatic Immunity* (1999); Barston, *Modern Diplomacy* (2006).

[2] Cf Sir Henry Wooton's definition of an ambassador: 'an honest man sent to lie abroad for the good of his country' (1604). According to Satow, the joke is in the translation, not in the original Latin: Satow (6th edn, 2009) 82.

[3] 18 April 1961, 500 UNTS 95. Further: Optional Protocol concerning the Acquisition of Nationality, 18 April 1961, 500 UNTS 223; Optional Protocol concerning the Compulsory Settlement of Disputes, 18 April 1961, 500 UNTS 241. The VCDR has 186 parties; the Optional Protocol concerning Acquisition

of custom.[4] The importance of the principles embodied in the VCDR was stressed in *Tehran Hostages*, where the Court observed that 'the obligations of the Iranian Government here in question are not merely contractual … but also obligations under general international law'.[5] For English courts the Diplomatic Privileges Act of 1708 was expressed to be declaratory of the common law. The Act of 1708 was not replaced until the Diplomatic Privileges Act 1964, which gives effect to the VCDR in UK law.[6] The VCDR does not affect customary rules governing 'questions not expressly regulated' by its provisions[7] and states may vary the position by agreement.

2. GENERAL LEGAL ASPECTS OF DIPLOMATIC RELATIONS

(A) INCIDENCE

VCDR Article 2 provides that 'the establishment of diplomatic relations between States, and of permanent diplomatic missions, takes place by mutual consent'. There is no right of legation in general international law, though all states have the capacity to establish diplomatic relations. The mutual consent involved may be expressed quite informally.

(B) RELATION TO RECOGNITION

While recognition is a condition for the establishment and maintenance of diplomatic relations, these are not necessary consequences of recognition. The non-establishment or withdrawal or reduction of diplomatic representation may follow purely practical considerations or constitute a form of non-military sanction. In recent history, this has taken the form of co-ordinated international action against states suspected of shielding or sponsoring terrorism. One example occurred following Libya's refusal to surrender those individuals thought responsible for the bombing of Pan Am Flight 103 over Lockerbie, Scotland and UTA Flight 772 over Chad and Niger. Security Council Resolution 748 provided that:

---

of Nationality, 51 parties; the Optional Protocol concerning the Compulsory Settlement of Disputes, 66 parties.

[4] Fox (2nd edn, 2008) 703; Denza (3rd edn, 2008) 1–12; Hestermeyer, 'Vienna Convention on Diplomatic Relations (1961)' (2009) *MPEPIL*.

[5] *United States Diplomatic and Consular Staff in Tehran (US v Iran)*, ICJ Reports 1980 p 3, 31, 33, 41.

[6] *Empson v Smith* [1966] 1 QB 426; *Shaw v Shaw* [1979] FLR 62. The schedule to the 1964 Act sets out those provisions of the VCDR which are incorporated into UK law. Cf Buckley (1965–66) 41 *BY* 321.

[7] *Philippine Embassy* (1984) 65 ILR 146, 161–2, 186–7; *Republic of 'A', Embassy Bank Account* (1988) 77 ILR 489; *Abbott v Republic of South Africa* (1999) 113 ILR 411.

all States shall ... [s]ignificantly reduce the number and the level of the staff at Libyan diplomatic missions and consular posts and restrict or control the movement within their territory of all such staff who remain; in the case of Libyan missions to international organizations, the host State may, as it deems necessary, consult the organization concerned on the measures required to implement this subparagraph.[8]

When Libya failed to comply with this resolution, Security Council Resolution 883 directed all countries to continue to reduce staff at Libyan diplomatic missions and consular posts.[9]

(C) RATIONALE OF PRIVILEGES AND IMMUNITIES[10]

Diplomatic relations entail the exercise by the sending government of state functions on the territory of the receiving state by licence of the latter. Having agreed to the establishment of diplomatic relations, the receiving state must enable the sending state to benefit from the content of the licence. Doing so results in a body of privileges and immunities. One explanation, now discredited, for this situation was that the diplomatic agent and the mission premises were 'exterritorial', legally assimilated to the territorial jurisdiction of the sending state.[11] The consequences of this theory were never worked out and the law does not rest on any such premise. Indeed it rests on no particular theory or combination of theories, though the system is generally compatible with both the representative theory, which emphasizes the diplomat's role as agent of a state, and the functional theory,[12] resting on practical necessity.[13] Under the functional model, the immunity is first a statement recognizing the sovereign and independent status of the sending state, as well as the public nature of a diplomat's acts and his or her consequent immunity from the receiving state's jurisdiction. Secondly, the immunity exists to protect the diplomatic mission and staff and to ensure the

---

[8] SC Res 748 (1992), operative §6.

[9] SC Res 883 (1993), operative §7.

[10] Salmon (1994) §§271–3; Denza (3rd edn, 2008) 13–15; Fox (2nd edn, 2008) 700–1; Lee & Quigley (3rd edn, 2008) 341–2.

[11] E.g. Grotius, *De Iure Belli ac Pacis* (1695, ed Tuck 2005) II.xviii.§IV.5: 'yet that an Exception should be made in Favour of Embassadors, who, as they are, by a Sort of Fiction, taken for the very Persons whom they represent ... so may they be by the same kind of Fiction be imagined to be out of the Territories of the *Potentate*, to whom they are sent'.

[12] Based on the maxim *ne impediatur legatio*: Fox (2nd edn, 2008) 701. The functional theory is not a latecomer, having been well articulated by Vattel, *Le Droit des gens* (1758, tr Anon 1797) IV.vii.§92: 'Now, embassadors and other public ministers are necessary instruments for the maintenance of that general society, of that mutual correspondence between nations. But their ministry cannot effect the intended purpose unless it be invested with all the prerogatives which are capable of ensuring its legitimate success, and of enabling the minister freely and faithfully to discharge his duty in perfect security.'

[13] ILC *Ybk* 1958/II, 94; *Tietz v People's Republic of Bulgaria* (1959) 28 ILR 369; *Yugoslav Military Mission* (1969) 65 ILR 108; *Parking Privileges* (1971) 70 ILR 396; *Smith v Office National de l'Emploi* (1971) 69 ILR 276; *Private Servant* (1971) 71 ILR 546; *Dorf* (1973) 71 ILR 552; *767 Third Avenue Associates v Permanent Mission of Zaire to the UN*, 988 F.2d 295 (2nd Cir, 1993); *Aziz v Aziz; HM The Sultan of Brunei intervening* [2008] 2 All ER 501. The preamble to the VCDR refers to both considerations.

efficient performance of functions designed to preserve international order and maintain communication between states.[14]

In the final analysis, the question must be related to the dual aspect of diplomatic representation: the state immunity (immunity *ratione materiae*) attaching to official acts of foreign states, and the overlying, yet more conditional, elements of 'functional' privileges and immunities of the diplomatic staff and the premises.[15]

(D) FULFILMENT OF DUTIES BY THE RECEIVING STATE

The observance of legal duties by the receiving state requires the taking of various steps, legislative and administrative, in the municipal sphere. Appropriate care must be shown in providing police protection for personnel and premises and the state will incur responsibility if the judiciary fails to maintain the necessary privileges and immunities.

An obvious example is again *Tehran Hostages*. There, Iran was held responsible for failing to prevent and for subsequently adopting the actions of militants who invaded the US mission in Tehran and holding the diplomatic and consular personnel as hostages. The International Court held:

The approval given to these facts by the Ayatollah Khomeini and other organs of the Iranian State, and the decision to perpetuate them, translated continuing occupation of the Embassy and detention of the hostages into acts of that State. The militants, authors of the invasion and jailers of the hostages, had now become agents of the Iranian State for whose acts the State itself was internationally responsible.[16]

(E) FUNCTIONS OF MISSIONS

VCDR Article 3 sets out succinctly the functions of a diplomatic mission, primarily those of representing the sending state in the receiving state and 'protecting in the receiving State the interests of the sending State and of its nationals, within the limits permitted by international law'.[17] The mission may negotiate with the receiving state's authorities, ascertain and report on local events, promote friendly relations between the two states, etc.

---

[14] Satow (6th edn, 2009) 98; Fox (2nd edn, 2008) 701.

[15] Courts seeking to develop a restrictive doctrine of state immunity are tempted to emphasize the distinction between state immunity and the more extensive immunity of diplomatic agents: e.g. *Foreign Press Attaché* (1962) 38 ILR 160, 162.

[16] ICJ Reports 1980 p 3, 35. In respect of state responsibility for the acts of agents and the co-option of acts: chapter 25. Further: Buffard & Wittich, 'United States Diplomatic and Consular Staff in Tehran Case (US v Iran)' (2007) *MPEPIL*.

[17] Also: VCDR, Art 41 which provides, *inter alia*, that persons enjoying privileges and immunities have a duty not to interfere in the internal affairs of the receiving state. Further: Denza (3rd edn, 2008) 464–8.

(F) ABUSE OF DIPLOMATIC IMMUNITIES

Serious breaches of diplomatic immunity are rare,[18] due principally to the recipro-cal benefits that accrue through mutual observance of diplomatic law.[19] This position might be thought remarkable, given the stringent limitations on jurisdictional compe-tence placed on states by the VCDR and the points of historical, ideological, political, or other friction often existing between states maintaining diplomatic relations with each other.

But there have been serious abuses. A Nigerian former minister was found drugged in a 'diplomatic bag' (a container) at Stansted Airport.[20] Police Constable Yvonne Fletcher, on guard outside the Libyan People's Bureau in London, was killed by a weapon fired from the premises.[21] When, a week later, the embassy was finally evacuated and searched in the presence of a Saudi representative, weapons and relevant forensic evi-dence were uncovered. The House of Commons Foreign Affairs Committee prepared a detailed review of the VCDR,[22] but concluded that any attempt to alter the balance of rights and duties so as to further require protected individuals to respect the laws of the receiving state was undesirable.[23] It recommended more rigorous application of safeguards in the VCDR, notably Articles 9 (*persona non grata*) and 11 (limitation of mission size), a recommendation adopted in full by the government.[24]

3. STAFF, PREMISES, AND FACILITIES OF MISSIONS

(A) CLASSIFICATION OF PERSONNEL

VCDR Article 1 divides mission staff into three categories, the diplomatic staff (those members of the mission having diplomatic rank as counsellors, diplomatic secretaries, or attachés), the administrative and technical staff, and those persons in the domes-tic service of the mission. Two other terms are important. A 'diplomatic agent' is the head of the mission or a member of the diplomatic staff of the mission; the 'head of

---

[18] Cf *Tehran Hostages*, ICJ Reports 1980 p 3. At the height of the Cold War, espionage operations of con-siderable scale were based in both Western and Soviet Embassies: Roberts (6th edn, 2009) 115. Generally: Richelson, *American Espionage and the Soviet Target* (1987); Gaddis (2007) 13 *Diplomatic History* 191.

[19] Higgins (1985) 78 *AJIL* 641, 641.

[20] *R v Lambeth Justices, ex parte Yusufu* (1985) 88 ILR 323.

[21] Further: Satow (6th edn, 2009) 86, 102, 107–8. On the accreditation problem: Denza (3rd edn, 2008) 68.

[22] Generally: Cameron (1985) 34 *ICLQ* 610; Higgins (1985) 79 *AJIL* 641; Higgins (1986) 80 *AJIL* 135; Davidson, Freestone, Lowe & Warbrick (1986) 35 *ICLQ* 425; Herdegen (1986) 46 *ZaöRV* 734; Orrego Vicuña (1991) 40 *ICLQ* 34. Also: UKMIL (1985) 56 *BY* 363, 437–62. Generally: Barker, *The Abuse of Diplomatic Privileges and Immunities* (1996).

[23] Cf VCDR, Art 41(1), which contains this obligation (but without prejudice to the inviolability of pro-tected individuals).

[24] Diplomatic and Consular Premises Act 1987 (UK); UKMIL (1985) 65 *BY* 363, 439–40; UKMIL (1987) 58 *BY* 540.

the mission' is 'the person charged by the sending State with the duty of acting in that capacity'.

(B) HEADS OF MISSION

(i) Accreditation and *agrément*[25]

VCDR Article 4(1) provides that the sending state must secure the *agrément* or 'consent' of the receiving state prior to a proposed head of mission assuming the post. The receiving state holds a unilateral right of rejection in this respect, and is not obliged to provide reasons in the event that *agrément* is refused (Article 4(2)).[26]

(ii) Classes and precedence[27]

Under VCDR Article 14(1) heads of mission fall into three classes: (a) ambassadors or nuncios[28] accredited to heads of state, or other heads of mission of equivalent rank;[29] (b) envoys, ministers and internuncios likewise accredited; and (c) *chargés d'affaires* accredited to Ministers of Foreign Affairs. With the doctrine of sovereign equality now formally embedded, there is no class-based differentiation between heads of mission save as concerns precedence and etiquette (Article 14(2)). VCDR Article 16(1) provides that heads of mission take precedence in their respective classes in the order of taking up their functions in accordance with Article 13, a provision that goes back to 1815.[30]

(C) APPOINTMENT OF MEMBERS OTHER THAN THE HEAD OF MISSION[31]

VCDR Article 7 provides that the sending state may freely appoint the mission staff. In the case of military, naval or air attachés, the receiving state may require their names to be submitted for approval beforehand.

In the ILC there was considerable difference of opinion as to the extent to which the consent of the receiving state conditioned the appointment of members other than the

---

[25] Satow (6th edn, 2009) 84–5.

[26] In case of the appointment of a chargé d'affaires *ad interim* to act provisionally as head of the mission, owing to the vacancy of the post of head or his inability, no *agrément* is required: VCDR, Art 19(1).

[27] Generally: Hardy, *Modern Diplomatic Law* (1968) 21–4; Satow (6th edn, 2009) 90–3. The practice was regulated previously by the Congress of Vienna, 1815, and the Conference of Aix-la-Chapelle, 1818, which established four classes. Further: 7 *BD* 655.

[28] Representatives of the Holy See. On their precedence: VCDR, Art 16(3). Further: Satow (6th edn, 2009) 91.

[29] High Commissioners between Commonwealth countries are considered the equivalent of ambassadors. On occasion, a distinctly lower rank of diplomat may be sent as head of mission, a situation usually reflecting a historical anomaly or coolness in diplomatic relations: Satow (6th edn, 2009) 92.

[30] Règlement on the Precedence of Diplomatic Agents, Vienna, 19 March 1815, 64 CTS 1.

[31] Generally: Satow (6th edn, 2009) 85–90.

head of mission. The text of Article 7 may seem sufficiently clear[32] but at the Vienna Conference several delegations adopted the position that the article was to be interpreted in accordance with prevailing custom,[33] namely that the consent of the receiving state was always required. Practice has now apparently crystallized in favour of an unrestricted right of appointment on the part of the sending state, save as provided for in Article 7.[34]

In a controversial English decision[35] it was held that Article 7 was qualified by Article 10 and that a failure to notify the receiving state precluded an appointee's immunity. In any case the receiving state has special powers of control in case of appointments to more than one state (Article 5(1)), appointment of non-nationals (Article 8), and excessive appointments (Article 11). In addition, Article 9(1) permits the receiving state to declare a proposed appointee *persona non grata* prior to arrival. There is no requirement to give reasons for such a rejection.[36]

(D) TERMINATION OF FUNCTIONS

Diplomatic relations are consensual and may be terminated by withdrawal of the mission by either the sending or receiving state.[37]

The sending state may for its own reasons, practical or political, terminate the functions of individual staff members on notification to the receiving state. Under VCDR Article 9(1), the receiving state may also, at any time and without explanation, declare any member of a diplomatic mission *persona non grata* or not acceptable. In such a case, the sending state must either recall the individual in question or terminate his or her functions within the mission. Under Article 9(2), a refusal by the sending state to comply with such a declaration gives the receiving state the right to refuse recognition of the individual as a member of the mission.

Following its codification in the VCDR, the *persona non grata* rule has been used to respond to conduct which was not considered by the ILC, a sign of versatility rather than misuse.[38] It was used extensively during the Cold War to remove suspected spies. In the modern era, it is most frequently invoked for espionage, involvement in terrorist or subversive activities, and other criminal behaviour. For example, in 1976 the entire diplomatic staff of the North Korean missions to Denmark, Finland, Norway, and Sweden were declared *persona non grata* following the revelation that the embassies

---

[32] 4 Rousseau 158–9; Brown (1988) 37 *ICLQ* 53, 54.

[33] Harvard Research (1932) 26 *AJIL Supp* 15, 67 (Art 8).

[34] Denza (3rd edn, 2008) 60–8; Satow (6th edn, 2009) 85–6.

[35] *R v Lambeth Justices, ex parte Yusufu* (1985) 88 ILR 323; Crawford (1985) 56 *BY* 311, 328–31.

[36] VCDR, Art 4(2) so provides with respect to heads of mission, but this is no basis for an *expressio unius* interpretation in the case of other appointees, e.g. defence attachés: Denza (3rd edn, 2008) 61.

[37] VCDR, Arts 44, 45(a). On the effect of death: Art 39(3) and (4). Further: 7 Whiteman 83–108; Denza (3rd edn, 2008) 449–50; Satow (6th edn, 2009) 206–15. Also: *Gustavo JL* (1987) 86 ILR 517.

[38] Denza (3rd edn, 2008) 76–7.

were a front for the illegal import and sale of drugs, cigarettes, and alcohol.[39] From the mid-1980s the UK has declared various embassy staff members *persona non grata* for the consistent violation of parking regulations in London; when the outstanding fines were paid, the declarations were withdrawn.[40]

(E) PREMISES AND FACILITIES

VCDR Article 25 provides that the receiving state 'shall accord full facilities for the performance of the functions of the mission'. Other provisions refer to freedom of movement for members of the mission, subject to legal restrictions established to ensure national security,[41] and 'free communication on the part of the mission for all official purposes'.[42] A particular problem is the acquisition of premises as some domestic legal systems may exclude a market in land or restrict the acquisition of land by aliens or foreign states. The ILC draft[43] had required the receiving state either to permit acquisition by the sending state or to 'ensure adequate accommodation in some other way'. The VCDR contains less decisive provisions in Article 21.

4. INVIOLABILITY OF MISSIONS

(A) PREMISES[44]

A consequence of the establishment and functioning of a mission is the protection of the premises from external interference. The mission premises, including ancillary land, are the headquarters of the mission and benefit from the immunity of the sending state.[45] The principle flows from the concept of diplomatic immunity, and is pre-Grotian in origin.[46] VCDR Article 22 recapitulates the customary position, providing expressly for the inviolability of the mission from intrusion by agents of the receiving state (Article 22(1)), and setting out the receiving state's duty to take all appropriate

---

[39] Satow (6th edn, 2009) 213.

[40] Denza (3rd edn, 2008) 78–86. It remains the practice of the UK government to ask for the removal of any foreign diplomat who incurs more than a set number of unpaid parking tickets, whilst the US contents itself with the revocation of driving privileges: Satow (6th edn, 2009) 129.

[41] VCDR, Art 26. Also: Denza (3rd edn, 2008) 205–10.

[42] VCDR, Art 27(1). Also: Kerley (1962) 56 *AJIL* 88, 110–18; Denza (3rd edn, 2008) 211–24.

[43] VCDR, Art 19. Also: Hardy (1968) 33–4; Denza (3rd edn, 2008) 128–30.

[44] Denza (3rd edn, 2008) 135–79; Satow (6th edn, 2009) 101–8; *Embassy Eviction* (1965) 65 ILR 248.

[45] It further includes the *droit de chapelle*, the right to maintain within the mission a chapel and to practise the faith of the head of the mission, which, e.g., exempted foreign priests in the service of foreign missions from anti-Catholic laws during the 1745 rebellion in England: Martens, 2 *Causes célèbres de droit des gens* (1827) 22–5. Cf Denza (3rd edn, 2008) 143–4.

[46] Grotius states that diplomatic immunity encompassed the immunity of diplomatic persons and possessions or the levying of execution on embassy premises: Grotius, *De Iure Belli ac Pacis* (1695, ed Tuck 2005) II.xviii.§§8–9.

steps to protect the premises of the mission against intrusion or damage and to prevent any disturbance of the mission's peace or impairment of its dignity (Article 22(2)).[47]

Article 22(1) contains no proviso relating either to cases of emergency, for example, the situation in which the premises present a pressing danger to the surrounding district by reason of fire, or to countermeasures in case of a use of the premises by the staff themselves for unlawful purposes. It is a nice question whether, if remedial steps were taken by the host state, a defence of necessity or *force majeure* could be sustained,[48] and in any event countermeasures infringing on inviolability are excluded.[49] The practice to date has generally been that missions will avoid at all costs calling on external assistance in the event of an emergency.[50]

It follows from Article 22 that writs cannot be served, even by post, within the premises of a mission but only through the local Ministry for Foreign Affairs.[51] Article 22(2) creates a special standard of care over and above the normal obligation to show due diligence in protecting aliens within the state. The International Court found that breaches of Article 22 had occurred in *Armed Activities on the Territory of the Congo (Democratic Republic of the Congo v Uganda)* in respect of attacks against the Ugandan embassy in Kinshasa by Congolese troops.[52]

Embassy bank accounts are protected by VCDR Article 24, as are archives or documents of the mission, which are 'inviolable at any time and wherever they may be'.[53]

(B) DIPLOMATIC ASYLUM[54]

The VCDR contains no provision on diplomatic asylum, although in Article 41 the reference to 'special agreements' allows for bilateral recognition of the right to give asylum to political refugees within the mission. The issue was deliberately excluded from the agenda during the ILC's preparatory work. It is doubtful if a right of asylum for either political or other offenders is recognized by general international law.[55] There is

---

[47] VCDR, Art 1(i) defines 'the premises of the mission' as 'the buildings...and the land ancillary thereto...used for the purposes of the mission'; premises not so 'used' are outside the terms of VCDR, Art 22; *Westminster City Council v Government of the Islamic Republic of Iran* [1986] 3 All ER 284.

[48] E.g. the case of Sun Yat Sen, detained in the Chinese Legation in London in 1896: McNair, 1 *Opinions* 85; and the shooting episode at the Libyan embassy in London in April 1984: UKMIL (1984) 55 *BY* 459, 582–4. Also: Higgins (1985) 79 *AJIL* 641, 646–7; Denza (3rd edn, 2008) 144–5; *Fatemi v United States*, 192 A.2d 535 (1963); *R v Turnbull, ex parte Petroff* (1979) 52 ILR 303.

[49] See ARSIWA, Art 50(2)(b): 'A State taking countermeasures is not relieved from fulfilling its obligations ... (b) to respect the inviolability of diplomatic or consular agents, premises, archives and documents'. See the commentary, paras (14)–(15).

[50] The rationale for this was demonstrated by an incident in which 'firefighters' called to the US embassy in Moscow proved to be KGB agents: Denza (3rd edn, 2008) 145.

[51] *Hellenic Lines Ltd v Moore*, 345 F.2d 978 (DC Cir, 1965). Denza (3rd edn, 2008) 151–3.

[52] ICJ Reports 2005 p 168, 277–9. Also: *Kenyan Diplomatic Residence* (2003) 128 ILR 632.

[53] *Iraq v Vinci Constructions* (2002) 127 ILR 101.

[54] Morgenstern (1948) 25 *BY* 236; 7 *BD*, 905–23; Ronning, *Diplomatic Asylum* (1965); Satow (6th edn, 2009) 108–12.

[55] Harvard Research Draft (1932) 26 *AJIL Supp* 15, 62–6 (Art 6); *Asylum (Columbia/Peru)*, ICJ Reports 1950 p 266, 282–6. Cf Morgenstern (1948) 25 *BY* 236. Denza (3rd edn, 2008) 142 suggests that a limited and temporary

a qualified right under the Havana Convention on Asylum of 1928[56] and it may be that a Latin-American regional custom exists.[57]

The question of diplomatic asylum under the VCDR is dependent on the joint application of Article 41(1)—on respect for law and non-interference in the affairs of the receiving state—and Article 22, which allows no exception to the inviolability of a diplomatic mission. Thus while there is no right to grant asylum, once one or more refugees have been accepted onto embassy property the receiving state cannot retrieve them, a situation which will ordinarily force the sending and receiving state to the negotiating table. In 2002, for example, various groups from North Korea sought refuge in sympathetic Western embassies in Beijing. Twenty-five North Korean defectors took refuge in the Spanish embassy; following negotiations between China, South Korea, Spain, and the Philippines, they were returned to Seoul via Manila.[58]

(C) ARCHIVES, DOCUMENTS, AND OFFICIAL CORRESPONDENCE[59]

The VCDR establishes the inviolability of the archives and documents of the mission 'at any time and wherever they may be',[60] as well as official correspondence.[61] It is provided simply that 'the diplomatic bag shall not be opened or detained'.[62] A significant breach of this obligation was the subject of *Tehran Hostages* before the International Court. The US embassy was ransacked and documents purporting to come from the diplomatic archive of the mission disseminated by the militants and media outlets controlled by the Iranian government.[63]

The evidence of abuse of the diplomatic bag in the form of drug trafficking or involvement in terrorist activities has led the UK government to resort to the scanning of bags where there are strong grounds of suspicion: a member of the relevant mission is invited to be present.[64] In 1989 the ILC adopted a set of more precise rules concerning diplomatic bags and diplomatic couriers, but no agreement could be reached in the General Assembly.[65]

---

right to grant asylum exists in custom where there is immediate danger to the life or safety of a refugee. Satow is more circumspect, suggesting that the question remains an open one: Satow (6th edn, 2009) 108–9.

[56] 20 February 1928, 132 LNTS 323, Art 2(1); also the Montevideo Convention on Political Asylum, 26 December 1933, 165 LNTS 19.

[57] *Asylum*, ICJ Reports 1950 p 266, 395; *Haya de la Torre (Columbia v Peru)*, ICJ Reports 1951 p 71. Cf the Organization of American States Convention on Diplomatic Asylum, 28 March 1954, 1438 UNTS 104; 6 Whiteman, 436; *Almeida de Quinteros and Quinteros Almeida v Uruguay* (1983) 79 ILR 168.

[58] A similar event occurred in 1989 with respect to East German refugees seeking asylum in West German embassies in Czechoslovakia and Poland: Denza (3rd edn, 2008) 142–3; Satow (6th edn, 2009) 111–12.

[59] 7 Whiteman 389–92; Cohen (1948) 25 BY 404; Hardy (1968) 49; Satow (6th edn, 2009) 113–19. Cf *In re Estate of King Faisal* II, 199 NYS.2d 595 (Surr Ct, 1966). Also: *Fayed v Al-Tajir* [1988] 1 QB 712.

[60] VCDR, Art 24.

[61] VCDR, Art 27(2). Denza (3rd edn, 2008) 189–99, 225–6. On the issue of waiver (by way of analogy): *Shearson Lehman Bros v Maclaine Watson & Co Ltd (No 2)* [1988] 1 All ER 116.

[62] VCDR, Art 27(3); also Art 27(4). Also: Denza (3rd edn, 2008) 227–48.

[63] ICJ Reports 1980 p 3, 14, 36.

[64] E.g. UKMIL (1985) 56 BY 446, 459; UKMIL (1987) 58 BY 548, 566, 570.

[65] ILC *Ybk* 1989/II, 8.

A diplomatic bag is given its character by its express label, though its contents may attract *de facto* protection under other provisions of the VCDR. For example, the Eritrea-Ethiopia Claims Commission held that the interception of an Ethiopian diplomatic bag in 1999 by Eritrean officials at Asmara airport violated Article 24. Although the package was incorrectly labelled and shipped by private courier and was thus not a 'diplomatic bag' for the purposes of Article 27, the character of the blank passports, invoices, and receipts found within was apparent.[66]

As the mission does not have separate legal personality, archives and other documents remain the property of the sending state. Where there is a change of government, ownership of these materials will be transferred to the new government by the receiving state. The new government may then enforce any rights accruing to it through ownership of the materials, though in so doing it will also assume responsibility for any related liabilities.[67]

(D) OTHER PROPERTY

VCDR Article 22(3) expands protection to other embassy property: the premises of the mission, their furnishings, and other property, as well as the means of transport of the mission are immune from search, requisition, attachment, or execution.

5. DIPLOMATIC AGENTS

(A) INVIOLABILITY

VCDR Article 29 provides:

The person of a diplomatic agent shall be inviolable. He shall not be liable to any form of arrest or detention. The receiving state shall treat him with due respect and shall take all appropriate steps to prevent any attack on his person, freedom or dignity.

This inviolability is distinct from immunity from criminal jurisdiction. As with inviolability of the mission premises, there is no express reservation for action in cases of emergency, for example a drunken diplomat with a loaded gun in a public place.[68]

VCDR Article 30 provides that the private residence (including a temporary residence) of a diplomatic agent is likewise inviolable, as are the agent's papers, correspondence, and property, subject to Article 31(3). However, there is no jurisdictional immunity in case of a real action concerning immovable property and, whilst no measures of execution may be taken against property, courts may be unwilling to

---

[66] *Partial Award: Diplomatic Claim—Ethiopia's Claim 8* (2005) 26 RIAA 407, 423–4.

[67] Denza (3rd edn, 2008) 197.

[68] 7 *BD* 785; Giuliano (1960) 100 Hague *Recueil* 81, 111, 120–2; Denza (3rd edn, 2008) 162–5; Satow (6th edn, 2009) 122–6. Also: *Fatemi v United States*, 192 A.2d 535 (1963).

support measures of self-help undertaken by the diplomatic agent to recover premises from a person in possession under a claim of right made in good faith.[69]

It has recently been suggested that the scope of the duty in Article 29 should include indirect attacks on the dignity of a diplomat, or even events in general which may embarrass or offend a diplomat. In *Aziz*[70] a former wife of the Sultan of Brunei brought proceedings against a fortune teller for the return of property given under a false understanding. The Sultan intervened, arguing that as a foreign head of state he was entitled to the same protections as offered to a foreign head of mission under section 20 of the State Immunity Act 1978 (enacting VCDR Article 29) and that there was a duty to prevent any attack on his dignity. The Court disagreed, finding that no outrage on the Sultan's dignity would be committed if the judgments in question were published. Collins LJ concluded:

I am far from convinced by the material before us that there is a rule of customary international law which imposes an obligation on a State to take appropriate steps to prevent conduct by individuals which is simply offensive or insulting to a foreign head of state abroad.[71]

This position is consistent with the functional framework of modern diplomatic law.

(B) THE CONCEPT OF IMMUNITY[72]

Diplomatic agents enjoy immunity from local curial jurisdiction, not an exemption from the substantive law.[73] The immunity can be waived and the local law may then be applied. VCDR Article 41(1) stipulates that 'it is the duty of all persons enjoying such privileges and immunities to respect the laws and regulations of the receiving State',[74] though without prejudice to those privileges or immunities.

(C) IMMUNITY OF SERVING AGENTS FROM CRIMINAL JURISDICTION[75]

VCDR Article 31(1) provides without qualification that 'a diplomatic agent shall enjoy immunity from the criminal jurisdiction of the receiving State'.[76] This has long been

---

[69] *Agbor v Metropolitan Police Commissioner* [1969] 2 All ER 707.

[70] *Aziz v Aziz; HM The Sultan of Brunei intervening* [2008] 2 All ER 501. Further: Denza (3rd edn, 2008) 263–4; Satow (6th edn, 2009) 125.

[71] [2008] 2 All ER 501, 522. A protest outside an embassy does not prima facie constitute an attack on the dignity of the mission, provided it does not obstruct the ordinary business of the embassy: *Boos v Barry*, 798 F.2d 1450 (DC Cir, 1986).

[72] The jurisdiction of the sending state applies in principle: Hardy (1968) 55; Denza (3rd edn, 2008) 321–3; VCDR, Art 31(4).

[73] *Dickinson v Del Solar* [1930] 1 KB 376; *Regele v Federal Ministry* (1958) 26 ILR 544; *Fatemi v United States*, 192 A.2d 535 (1963); *Empson v Smith* [1966] 1 QB 426; *Bonne & Company X v Company Y* (1970) 69 ILR 280; *Armon v Katz* (1976) 60 ILR 374. Also: Satow (6th edn, 2009) 128–33.

[74] Further: UKMIL (1981) 52 BY 431.

[75] Generally: 4 Hackworth 515; 7 BD 756; Giuliano (1960) 100 Hague *Recueil* 81, 91–2; 4 Rousseau 200–2; Satow (6th edn, 2009) 129–30.

[76] Further: *Tehran Hostages*, ICJ Reports 1980 p 3, 37.

the position in custom. A diplomatic agent guilty of serious or persistent breaches of the law may be declared *persona non grata* but is immune from prosecution while in post, irrespective of the character of the crime or its relation to the functions or work of the mission.[77]

(D) IMMUNITY FROM CIVIL AND ADMINISTRATIVE JURISDICTION[78]

Article 31(1) also confers immunity on the diplomatic agent from the local civil and administrative jurisdiction, except in the case of: (a) a real action relating to private immovable property in the territory of the receiving state (unless held on behalf of the sending state for the purposes of the mission);[79] (b) an action relating to succession in which the agent is involved as executor, administrator, heir or legatee in his or her capacity as a private individual; and (c) any professional or commercial activity by the diplomatic agent outside his or her official duties.[80]

The exceptions to this form of immunity represent a modern development in the law and reflect the principle that the personal immunities of diplomatic agents should not be unqualified. The exception relating to immovable property applies to the situation in which the property is the residence of the diplomatic agent. However, in that case such measures of execution as affect the inviolability of his person or of his residence are ruled out.[81]

The jurisdictions referred to in VCDR Article 31(1) 'comprise any special courts in the categories concerned, e.g. commercial courts, courts set up to apply social legislation, and administrative authorities exercising judicial functions'.[82] Immunity covers not only direct claims against a diplomat and his or her property, but also family law claims, including proceedings to protect children and other family members.[83] An unsettled point is whether the immunity covers coronial inquests. Article 31 provides no neat answer, but the UK practice is that such an inquest should not take place without the mission's approval.[84]

---

[77] UKMIL (1985) 56 *BY* 363, 451; Denza (3rd edn, 2008) 83–6; Satow (6th edn, 2009) 129–30.

[78] Generally: Giuliano (1960) 100 Hague *Recueil* 81, 92–104; 4 Rousseau, 197–200, 206–9; Denza (3rd edn, 2008) 280–313; Satow (6th edn, 2009) 130–3. On proceedings begun before immunity applied: *Ghosh v D'Rozario* [1963] 1 QB 106.

[79] *Intpro Properties (UK) Ltd v Sauvel* [1983] 2 All ER 495.

[80] VCDR, Art 42 provides that 'a diplomatic agent shall not in the receiving state practise for personal profit any professional or commercial activity'. The exception in VCDR, Art 31(1) applies (a) to cases in which the receiving state allows exceptions to the operation of VCDR, Art 42; and (b) to activities of members of the staff not of diplomatic rank.

[81] VCDR, Art 31(3).

[82] ILC *Ybk* 1958/II, 98. Cf 7 *BD* 798.

[83] E.g. *De Andrade v De Andrade* (1984) 118 ILR 299; *Re P (No 2)* [1998] 1 FLR 1027, 1035; *In re B (a child)* [2003] 2 WLR 168. Further: Satow (6th edn, 2009) 133.

[84] Denza (3rd edn, 2008) 241.

(E) IMMUNITY FROM JURISDICTION FOR ACTS DONE RATIONE PERSONAE[85]

In the case of official acts undertaken by a protected person the immunity is permanent, since it is that of the sending state.[86] In respect of private acts the immunity is contingent and supplementary, terminating when the individual concerned leaves his post.[87] VCDR Article 39(2) refers to the termination of diplomatic functions and the concomitant immunities, and provides: 'However, with respect to acts performed by such a person in the exercise of his functions as a member of the mission, immunity shall continue to subsist'.[88] The definition of official acts is by no means self-evident, though in case of doubt weight should be given to the assertion of the sending state.[89] It appears to extend to acts undertaken by a diplomat which were ordered by the sending state. For example, in a German case,[90] the Syrian Ambassador to the German Democratic Republic was instructed to 'do everything possible' to assist a terrorist organization. He accepted for safekeeping a bag of explosives which were then used in a bombing in West Berlin. The court took the view that the ambassador's acts were subject to immunity *ratione materiae* and any liability consequentially accruing was attributed to Syria.[91]

The principle extends to matters which are essentially 'in the course of' official duties, for example a road accident involving a car on official business.[92] The difficulty this may cause was seen in *Knab v Republic of Georgia*, which concerned the death of a girl caused by a Georgian diplomat, driving intoxicated following a diplomatic reception. The parties agreed he was entitled to personal immunity, leaving the victim's family to proceed against the Georgian state alone.[93]

(F) APPLICATION OF CERTAIN LOCAL LAWS[94]

Certain immunities from the application of the local law are ancillary to the main body of privileges and immunities. Perhaps the most decisive is that from measures

---

[85] Hardy (1968) 64–7; van Panhuys (1964) 13 *ICLQ* 1193; Dinstein (1966) 15 *ICLQ* 76; Harvard Research (1932) 26 *AJIL Supp* 15, 97–9, 104–6, 136–7; Niboyet (1950) 39 *Rev crit DIPriv* 139; Giuliano (1960) 100 Hague *Recueil* 81, 166–80; ILC *Ybk* 1956/II, 145; Parry, *Cambridge Essays* (1965) 122, 127–32; Denza (3rd edn, 2008) 438–43; Satow (6th edn, 2009) 139–40. Also: *Zoernsch v Waldock* [1964] 2 All ER 256; *Foreign Press Attaché* (1962) 38 ILR 160; *Tabatabai* (1983) 80 ILR 388; *Propend Finance Pty Ltd v Sing* [1997] EWCA Civ 1433.

[86] *Zoernsch v Waldock* [1964] 2 All ER 256.

[87] This is similar to the situation with respect to state immunity *ratione materiae* and *ratione personae*: further chapter 22. On the interaction between state and diplomatic immunity: Denza (2008) 102 *PAS* 111.

[88] Also: VCDR, Arts 37(2), (3), 38(1).

[89] Denza (3rd edn, 2008) 439–43.

[90] *Former Syrian Ambassador to the German Democratic Republic* (1997) 115 ILR 595.

[91] The court regarded it as immaterial that the acts in question may have fallen outside the scope of VCDR, Art 3: ibid, 605–7.

[92] Kerley (1962) 56 *AJIL* 88, 120–1. Cf *Re Cummings* (1958) 26 ILR 549; *Caisse Industrielle d'Assurance Mutuelle v Consul Général de la République Argentine* (1972) 45 ILR 381.

[93] *Knab v Republic of Georgia et al* (1998) 1998 US Dist LEXIS 8820.

[94] Generally: Satow (6th edn, 2009) 141–50.

of execution.[95] There is exemption from all dues and taxes with a number of exceptions (notably indirect taxes incorporated in the price of goods or services).[96] Further privileges concern customs duties,[97] personal services, public service (i.e. jury service), military obligations,[98] social security provisions,[99] and the giving of evidence as a witness.[100] The exemption from customs duties of articles for the personal use of the diplomatic agent or members of his or her family belonging to the household is a rendering of a long current practice into a legal rule. The exemption from dues and taxes probably existed in the previous customary law, though practice was inconsistent.[101]

(G) BENEFICIARIES OF IMMUNITIES[102]

Diplomatic agents who are not nationals of or permanently resident in the receiving state are beneficiaries of the privileges and immunities set out in VCDR Articles 29 to 36.[103] The extent to which administrative and technical staff (as non-diplomatic staff members) should have these privileges and immunities was a matter on which state practice was not uniform[104] and on which there was considerable debate at the Vienna Conference. The position for this group and also for members of service staff is regulated by Article 37.[105] Under Article 37(2), members of a mission's administrative and technical staff, as well as members of a diplomatic household enjoy those immunities specified in VCDR Articles 29 to 35. However, the Article 31(1) immunity from civil and administrative jurisdiction is limited in respect of these individuals to acts performed in the course of their official duties (if any). Insofar as the service staff of the mission are concerned, provided they are not nationals of the receiving state, Article 31(2) provides for immunity in respect of acts performed in the course of their duties and exemption from dues and taxes on the emoluments they receive through their employment and from social security provisions.

In the case of diplomatic agents and the administrative and technical staff of the mission the respective immunities extend to 'members of the family' 'forming part

---

[95] VCDR, Arts 31(3) and 32(4).

[96] VCDR, Arts 23 and 34. Cf Art 37 concerning the family of the agent and administrative, technical, and service staff.

[97] VCDR, Art 36. Cf Art 37.

[98] VCDR, Art 35. Cf Art 37.

[99] VCDR, Art 33. Cf Art 37.

[100] VCDR, Art 31(2). Cf Giuliano (1960) 100 Hague *Recueil* 81, 118–19; VCDR, Art 37.

[101] On VCLT Art 34(e) and the dispute over road user charges (e.g. the London congestion charge): Denza (3rd edn, 2008) 370–3; Satow (6th edn, 2009) 144–5.

[102] Hardy (1968) 74–80; Giuliano (1960) 100 Hague *Recueil* 81, 141–65; 7 Whiteman 260–70; Wilson (1965) 14 *ICLQ* 1265; Denza (3rd edn, 2008) 390–425; Satow (6th edn, 2009) 155–67.

[103] VCDR, Art 37(1). There had been some inconsistent practice in relation to diplomatic agents apart from heads of mission: Gutteridge (1947) 24 *BY* 148; cf Giuliano (1960) 100 Hague *Recueil* 81, 142.

[104] Gutteridge (1947) 24 *BY* 148; Giuliano (1960) 100 Hague *Recueil* 81, 153–8.

[105] On the previous position: Giuliano (1960) 100 Hague *Recueil* 81, 159–62.

of' their households. In view of variations in family law and social custom a precise definition was thought inappropriate.[106]

(H) DURATION OF PRIVILEGES AND IMMUNITIES[107]

The duration of privileges and immunities is governed by VCDR Article 39. This provides, first, that privileges and immunities apply from the moment a protected person enters the receiving state, or if already there, the moment that the receiving state is appropriately notified of his or her appointment. Secondly, where the functions of a protected person terminate, the attached privileges and immunities normally cease at the moment when the protected person leaves the country, or on the expiry of a reasonable period in which to do so.[108] Immunity with respect to acts done *ratione materiae* will outlast the termination or expiration of the protected office.

There is no precise definition of a 'reasonable period' under VCDR Article 39(2).[109] Absent a legislative statement on the subject this will vary circumstantially, with those declared *persona non grata* given considerably less leeway. For example, following the shooting of PC Fletcher, the persons expelled were given seven days to leave the UK.[110] In contrast, Swiss law lays down a default 'reasonable period' of six months until the immunity terminates, and Venezuela allows a minimum of a month.[111]

(I) WAIVER[112]

It has always been accepted that immunity may be waived by the sending state.[113] Previous practice had been in part tolerant of implied waiver based on conduct but VCDR Article 32(2) states that 'waiver must always be express'.[114] Under Article 32(3)

---

[106] *In re C (an infant)* [1958] 2 All ER 656; *Dutch Diplomat Taxation* (1980) 87 ILR 76; *Re P (No 1)* [1998] 1 FLR 625. Generally: UKMIL (1978) 49 *BY* 368; UKMIL (1985) 56 *BY* 441; 4 Rousseau 196–7; O'Keefe (1976) 25 *ICLQ* 329; Brown (1988) 37 *ICLQ* 53.

[107] Generally: 7 Whiteman, 436–45; Lauterpacht, 3 *International Law* (1970) 433–57; Denza (3rd edn, 2008) 426–50; Satow (6th edn, 2009) 137–40.

[108] E.g. *Magdalena Steam Navigation Co v Martin* [1859] 2 El & El 94; *Musurus Bey v Gadban* [1894] 2 QB 352; *Re Suarez* (1944) 12 ILR 412; *Shaffer v Singh*, 343 F.3d 324 (DC Cir, 1965); *Propend Finance Pty v Sing* [1997] EWCA Civ 1433.

[109] Denza (3rd edn, 2008) 437–8; Satow (6th edn, 2009) 138–9.

[110] UKMIL (1984) 55 *BY* 405, 458–9.

[111] LeGault (1983) 21 *CYIL* 307; Denza (3rd edn, 2008) 437.

[112] Denza (3rd edn, 2008) 330–48; Satow (6th edn, 2009) 153–7.

[113] The Resolution on Consideration of Civil Claims adopted by the Vienna Conference on 14 April 1961 recommended that the sending state should waive immunity 'in respect of civil claims of persons in the receiving State when this can be done without impeding the performance of the functions of the mission'. It recommended, further, 'that in the absence of waiver the sending state should use its best endeavours to bring about a just settlement of claims'.

[114] For the position in English law: *Engelke v Musmann* [1928] AC 433; *R v Madan* [1961] 2 QB 1; Diplomatic Privileges Act 1964 s2(3); 7 *BD* 867–75. Also: *Armon v Katz* (1976) 60 ILR 374; *Nzie v Vessah* (1978) 74 ILR 519; *Public Prosecutor v Orhan Olmez* (1987) 87 ILR 212.

the initiation of proceedings excludes immunity from jurisdiction in respect of any counterclaim directly connected with the principal claim.[115]

Article 32(4) provides that waiver of immunity from civil or administrative jurisdiction does not imply waiver in respect of the execution of the judgment, for which separate waiver is necessary. But a waiver once given is irrevocable.[116]

Article 32 makes no reference to criminal jurisdiction, but this is a simple oversight: a waiver will be just as valid if invoked in relation to a criminal matter as with respect to civil jurisdiction.[117] But the *scope* of a waiver may be limited to civil or criminal jurisdiction. In *United States v Makharadze* the prequel to *Knab v State of Georgia*, the Georgian state waived the diplomat's immunity in respect of criminal prosecution, but maintained civil immunity in respect of a suit brought by the victim's family.[118]

Self-evidently, the waiver is only valid if given by somebody with the necessary authority to do so. Given that the immunity belongs to the state,[119] only the state can grant the authority to waive it.[120] This applies even when considering a protected person's attempt to waive their *own* immunity; for example, in *Nzie v Vassah*,[121] a letter written by a diplomat from the Cameroon embassy in Paris saying that he agreed to divorce his wife under French law did not constitute a valid waiver of immunity.

6. OTHER MATTERS

(A) CONSULAR RELATIONS[122]

Consuls are in principle distinct in function and legal status from diplomatic agents. Though agents of the sending state for particular purposes, they are not accorded the type of immunity from the laws and enforcement jurisdiction of the receiving state enjoyed by diplomatic agents. Consular functions vary and include the protection of the interests of the sending state and its nationals, development of economic and cultural relations, the issuing of passports and visas, administration of the property of nationals of the sending state, registration of births, deaths, and marriages, and supervision of vessels and aircraft attributed to the sending state.

---

[115] *High Commissioner for India v Ghosh* [1960] 1 QB 134.

[116] Denza (3rd edn, 2008) 337.

[117] Ibid, 343.

[118] No F-1446–97 (DC Sup Ct). Further: Murphy (1999) 93 *AJIL* 485.

[119] VCDR, Art 32(1).

[120] Cf Satow (6th edn, 2009) 135–6.

[121] (1978) 74 ILR 519. Further: *Gustavo JL* (1987) 86 ILR 517; *Public Prosecutor v JBC* (1984) 94 ILR 339.

[122] 8 *BD*; Harvard Research (1932) 26 *AJIL Supp* 189, 189–449; 4 Hackworth 655–949; 7 Whiteman 505–870; 1 Guggenheim 512–15; ILC *Ybk* 1961/II, 55, 89, 129; Zourek (1962) 106 Hague *Recueil*, 357; 3 *Répertoire suisse* 1552–93; *Digest of US Practice* (1979) 654–75; 4 Rousseau 211–63; Angelet, 'Consular Treaties' (2010) *MPEPIL*; Lee & Quigley (3rd edn, 2008); Satow (6th edn, 2009) chs 18–20.

Since the eighteenth century the status of consuls has been based upon general usage rather than law, together with special treaty provisions. The customary law as it has evolved is as follows.[123] The consul must have the authority of the sending state (his commission) and the authorization of the receiving state (termed an exequatur). The receiving state must give consular officials and premises special protection, that is, a higher standard of diligence than that appropriate to protection of aliens generally. The consular premises are not inviolable from entry by agents of the receiving state.[124] Consular archives and documents are inviolable and members of the consulate are immune from the jurisdiction of the judicial and administrative authorities of the receiving state in respect of acts performed in the exercise of consular functions.[125] This immunity for official acts is generally regarded as deriving from state immunity.[126] Articles intended for the use of the consulate are exempt from customs duties, and members of the consulate, other than the service staff, are exempt from all public services, including military obligations. The authorities reveal differences of opinion concerning the personal inviolability of consular officials and in principle they are liable to arrest or detention.[127] In addition they are amenable to criminal and civil jurisdiction in respect of non-official acts, to local taxation, and to customs duties. In a general way it could be said that the jurisdiction of the host state is presumed applicable.

The existence of fairly uniform *practices* (whatever the customary law might be), evidenced by a large number of bilateral treaties,[128] encouraged the ILC to produce draft articles on consular relations, and led to the 1963 Vienna Convention on Consular Relations (VCCR).[129] It is provided that the Convention 'shall not affect other international agreements in force as between parties to them'. The VCCR has a strong element of development and reconstruction of the existing law and brings the status of career consuls, as opposed to honorary consuls, nearer to that of diplomatic agents. Career consuls are exempted from taxation and customs duties in the same way as diplomats. Consular premises are given substantial inviolability (Article 31) and are exempted from taxation (Article 32). Immunities and the duty of protection already recognized

---

[123] ILC *Ybk* 1961/II, 110ff. There are differing views on the ambit of the customary law: compare Zourek (1962) 106 Hague *Recueil* 357, 451; Beckett (1944) 21 *BY* 34; 8 *BD* 146, 151, 158, 164; Lee & Quigley (3rd edn, 2008).

[124] 8 *BD* 125; Beckett (1944) 21 *BY* 34; ILC *Ybk* 1961/II, 109. Cf 7 Whiteman, 744. Lee & Quigley dispute this, and identify the emergence of three schools of thought prior to 1963 (no inviolability, conditional inviolability, and absolute inviolability): Lee & Quigley (3rd edn, 2008) 353–6.

[125] *Princess Zizianoff v Kahn and Bigelow* (1927) 4 ILR 384, 386–7; 8 *BD* 146; Beckett (1944) 21 *BY* 34; 7 Whiteman 770; ILC *Ybk* 1961/II, 117; Parry, *Cambridge Essays* (1965) 122, 127–32, 154; Lee & Quigley (3rd edn, 2008) 388–93.

[126] Also: *Hallberg v Pombo Argaez* (1963) 44 ILR 190; Lee & Quigley (3rd edn, 2008) 440–5.

[127] 8 *BD* 103–22, 214; 7 Whiteman 739; ILC *Ybk* 1961/II, 115; Lee & Quigley (3rd edn, 2008) 433–6.

[128] For a substantial bibliography of consular treaties: Lee & Quigley (3rd edn, 2008) Appendix I.

[129] 24 April 1963, 596 UNTS 261 (187 parties). For comment: do Nascimento e Silva (1964) 13 *ICLQ* 1214; Torres Bernardez (1963) 9 *AFDI* 78; and generally Lee & Quigley (3rd edn, 2008). Substantial parts of the VCCR are incorporated into UK law: Consular Relations Act 1968 (UK) s1. Further: *R (B and Others) v Secretary of State* [2005] QB 643.

by customary law are maintained.[130] A significant extension of protection and immunity occurs in Article 41[131] regarding the personal inviolability of consular officials. Under Article 41(1) such officials shall not be liable to arrest or detention prior to trial, save in the case of a serious criminal offence and a decision to this effect by a competent judicial authority.[132] Likewise, consular officials shall not be liable to any form of restriction on their personal freedom, save in execution of a judicial decision of final effect or the circumstances referred to in Article 41(1) (Article 41(2)). Finally, whilst a consular official may be compelled to appear before a criminal court of the receiving state, they must be treated in a manner commensurate to their station and unless the circumstances referred to in Article 41(1) subside, any penalty imposed must hamper the exercise of consular functions as little as possible (Article 41(3)).

Although the VCCR has attracted no less than 187 parties, it is not yet conclusive evidence on the present state of international law.[133] Nevertheless, states and municipal courts[134] may use its provisions as the best evidence of the *lex lata*, quite apart from its effect for the actual parties.[135] In *Tehran Hostages* the International Court emphasized that the consular obligations disregarded by Iran were part of general international law and not merely contractual obligations established by the VCCR.[136]

In a series of cases involving foreign nationals sentenced to death in various component states of the US, requests for provisional measures have been addressed to the International Court. The requests have been based upon allegations of breaches of the provisions of the VCCR; particularly the requirement that arresting authorities must inform foreign nationals of their right to contact the appropriate consulate (Article 36(1)(b)).[137]

(B) SPECIAL MISSIONS[138]

Beyond the sphere of permanent relations by means of diplomatic missions or consular posts, states make frequent use of ad hoc diplomacy or special missions. These

---

[130] VCCR, Arts 40 (Protection of consular officers), 33 (Inviolability of consular archives and documents), 43 (Immunity from jurisdiction in respect of acts performed in the exercise of consular functions), and 52 (Exemption from personal services and contributions). Also: *L v R* (1977) 68 ILR 175; *United States v Lo Gatto* (1995) 114 ILR 555; *Canada v Cargnello* (1998) 114 ILR 559.

[131] Generally: Lee & Quigley (3rd edn, 2008) chs 28–34.

[132] Moreover, when pre-trial detention is necessary under VCCR, Art 41(1), proceedings against the consular official must be instituted with minimal delay: VCCR, Art 41(3).

[133] Satow (6th edn, 2009) 251.

[134] Cf *Republic of Argentina v City of New York*, 25 NY.2d 252 (1969); *Heaney v Government of Spain*, 445 F.2d 501 (2nd Cir, 1971); 7 Whiteman 825–8; *Digest of US Practice* (1974) 183; *Digest of US Practice* (1975) 249–50, 259–60. Also: *Honorary Consul of X v Austria* (1986) 86 ILR 553.

[135] Cf generally the conclusions drawn as to benefits of the VCCR by Lee & Quigley (3rd edn, 2008) 585–9.

[136] ICJ Reports 1979 p 3, 31, 33, 41.

[137] *Vienna Convention on Consular Relations (Paraguay v US)*, Provisional Measures, ICJ Reports 1998 p 248; *LaGrand (Germany v US)*, ICJ Reports 2001 p 466; *Avena and Other Mexican Nationals (Mexico v US)*, ICJ Reports 2004 p 12; *Request for Interpretation of the Judgment of 31 March 2004 in the Case Concerning Avena and Other Mexican Nationals (Mexico v US) (Mexico v US)*, ICJ Reports 2009 p 3.

[138] 7 Whiteman 33–47; ILC *Ybk* 1964/II, 67; ILC *Ybk* 1965/II, 109; ILC *Ybk* 1966/II, 125; ILC *Ybk* 1967/II, 1; Bartos (1963) 108 Hague *Recueil* 425; Waters, *The Ad Hoc Diplomat* (1963); Kalb, 'Immunities, Special Missions' (2011) *MPEPIL*.

vary considerably in functions: examples include a head of government attending a funeral abroad in his official capacity, a foreign minister visiting his opposite number in another state for negotiations, and the visit of a government trade delegation to conduct official business. The UN General Assembly adopted and opened for signature the Convention on Special Missions 1969, which entered into force in 1985.[139] This provides a fairly flexible code of conduct based on the VCDR with appropriate divergences. The Convention has influenced the customary rules concerning persons on official visits (special missions), which have developed largely though domestic case-law.[140] The Convention confers a higher scale of privileges and immunities upon a narrower range of missions than the extant customary law, which focuses on the immunities necessary for the proper conduct of the mission, principally inviolability and immunity from criminal jurisdiction.[141]

(C) CRIMES AGAINST INTERNATIONALLY PROTECTED PERSONS

Inviolability of diplomatic personnel is one of the oldest principles of international law, but the kidnapping, murder, and assault of diplomatic agents increased markedly after 1961.[142] The International Court found that breaches of VCDR Article 29 had occurred in *Armed Activities (DRC v Uganda)*.[143] In 2005 al-Qaeda abducted and killed the prospective Egyptian Ambassador to Iraq, Ihab al-Sherif, apparently to deter Arab governments from strengthening diplomatic relations with the elected government in Baghdad.[144]

Due to the high incidence of political acts of violence directed against diplomats and other officials, the General Assembly adopted the 1973 Convention on the Prevention and Punishment of Crimes against Internationally Protected Persons, including Diplomatic Agents.[145] The offences envisaged are primarily the 'murder, kidnapping or other attack upon the person or liberty of an internationally protected person', the latter category including heads of state, foreign ministers, etc. Contracting parties undertake to make these crimes punishable by 'appropriate penalties which shall take into account their grave nature', and either to extradite the alleged offender or submit the case to the domestic prosecuting authorities.

---

[139]   8 December 1969, 1400 UNTS 231. Also: GA Res 2531(XXIV), 8 December 1969. On the substance of the Convention: Paszkowski (1974) 6 *Pol YIL* 267; Donnarumma (1972) 8 *RBDI* 34.

[140]   *Khurts Bat v Investigating Judge of the German Federal Court* [2011] EWHC 2029 (Admin).

[141]   Wood (2012) 16 *MPUNYB*.

[142]   Denza (3rd edn, 2008) 256–63.

[143]   ICJ Reports 2005 p 168, 277–9.

[144]   Denza (3rd edn, 2008) 259. If this was the strategy, it appeared to work; Egypt did not appoint another ambassador to Iraq until 2009.

[145]   14 December 1973, 1035 UNTS 167. Further: Internationally Protected Persons Act 1978 (UK); *Duff v R* (1979) 73 ILR 678. Also: Organization of American States Convention to Prevent and Punish the Acts of Terrorism Taking the Form of Crimes Against Persons and Related Extortion That Are Of International Significance, 2 February 1971, 10 ILM 255.

18

UNILATERAL ACTS; ESTOPPEL

1. INTRODUCTION

States are corporate entities that necessarily operate under a regime of representation. In order to hold them bound by consensual obligations, the normal rules of authorization under treaty law apply; in order to attribute conduct to them for the purposes of determining their compliance with such obligations, the normal rules of attribution for the purposes of state responsibility apply. In addition to these normal rules, there are other cases where states' consent is given, assumed or implied.

With respect to the rules of representation in treaty law, the organs authorized to represent the state include the head of state, head of government, and minister of foreign affairs, but may also include heads of executive departments and diplomatic representatives, depending on the circumstances.[1] But the legal boundaries of the state are not to be defined in simple terms. Specific authority may be given to individuals constituting delegations to conferences or special missions to foreign governments. The existence of authority in a particular instance may be a matter regulated in part by international law. Thus, in treaty-making and in the making of unilateral declarations a foreign minister is presumed to have authority to bind the state.[2] Moreover, the quality of 'the state' varies on a functional basis: thus 'sovereign immunity' from other state jurisdictions extends to the agents of the state, including its armed forces and warships, and state property in public use.

---

[1] (1965) 7 BD; Sørensen (1960) 101 Hague *Recueil* 1, 58–68; ILC *Ybk* 1962/II, 164–6. In *Armed Activities on the Territory of the Congo (New Application: 2002) (Democratic Republic of the Congo v Rwanda)*, the ICJ noted, 'that with increasing frequency in modern international relations other persons representing a State in specific fields may be authorized by that State to bind it by their statements in respect of matters falling within their purview. This may be true, for example, of holders of technical ministerial portfolios exercising powers in their field of competence in the area of foreign relations, and even of certain officials': Jurisdiction and Admissibility, ICJ Reports 2006 p 6, 27.

[2] Cf *Legal Status of Eastern Greenland* (1933) PCIJ Ser A/B No 53, 71; McNair, *The Law of Treaties* (1961) 73–5; VCLT, 23 May 1969, 1155 UNTS 331, Art 7(2)(a). Also *Land and Maritime Boundary between Cameroon and Nigeria*, ICJ Reports 2002 p 303, 430–1 (Maroua Declaration).

2. UNILATERAL ACTS

(A) IN GENERAL

The conduct of governments may not be directed towards the formation of agreements but still be capable of creating legal effects. The formation of customary rules and the law of recognition are two of the more prominent (though very different) categories concerned with the 'unilateral' acts of states. Some authors have been prepared to bring unilateral acts (including protest, promise, renunciation, and recognition) within a general concept of 'legal acts', either contractual or unilateral, based upon the manifestation of will by a legal person.[3] This approach may provide a framework for the discussion, but it may also obscure the variety of legal relations involved.[4] Analysis in terms of categories of 'promise', 'protest', and the like tends to confuse conditioning facts and legal consequences. Much will depend on the context in which a 'promise' or 'protest' occurs, including the surrounding circumstances and the effect of relevant rules of law.[5]

It is true that treaties can be very different one from another yet the category 'law of treaties' makes practical as well as analytical sense. It is possible that the same is true of unilateral acts, understood not just as any act of a single state but in some narrower (still to be determined) sense of 'acts implicating the good faith of the state', or more simply as 'commitments and representations implying commitment'. Yet while at some level the principle of good faith undoubtedly applies to unilateral acts as well as to bilateral or multilateral ones, the question which commitments or which representations engage the good faith of the state can only be decided situationally. It has never been the case that they all did, still less can this be true in the age of the twice-daily press conference and the internet.

(B) FORMAL UNILATERAL DECLARATIONS

A state may evidence a clear intention to accept obligations vis-à-vis certain other states by a public declaration which is not an offer or otherwise dependent on reciprocal

---

[3] Especially Suy, *Les Actes juridiques unilatéraux en droit international public* (1962); Jacqué, *Éléments pour une théorie de l'acte juridique en droit international public*, (1972). Further: Martin, *L'Estoppel en droit international public* (1979); Sicault (1979) 83 *RGDIP* 633; Skubiszewski, in Bedjaoui (ed), *International Law* (1991) 221; Reisman & Arsanjani (2004) 19 *ICSID Rev-FILJ* 328; D'Aspremont Lynden (2005) 109 *RGDIP* 163; Rodríguez-Cedeño & Torres Cazorla, 'Unilateral Acts of State in International Law' (2007) *MPEPIL*; Suy, *Mélanges Salmon* (2007) 631.

[4] The ILC's work on unilateral acts was in part vitiated by unfounded assumptions as to the uniform character of unilateral acts as promises: Rodríguez-Cedeño, First Report on Unilateral Acts of States, ILC *Ybk* 1998/II(1), 319–39; Second Report, ILC *Ybk* 1999/II(1), 195–213; Third Report, ILC *Ybk* 2000/II(1), 247–82; Fourth Report, ILC *Ybk* 2001/II(1), 115–136; Fifth Report, ILC *Ybk* 2002/II(1), 91–116; Sixth Report, A/CN.4/534; Seventh Report, A/CN.4/542; Eighth Report, A/CN.4/557; Ninth Report, A/CN.4/569 & Add.1. The ILC work nevertheless ended with a series of Guiding Principles Applicable to Unilateral Declarations of States Capable of Creating Legal Obligations with Commentaries, ILC *Ybk* 2006/II(2), 369.

[5] Reuter (1961) 103 Hague *Recueil* 425, 547–82; Charney (1985) 56 *BY* 1; Breutz, *Der Protest Im Völkerrecht* (1997); Eick, 'Protest' (2006) *MPEPIL*; Suy & Angelet, 'Promise' (2007) *MPEPIL*.

undertakings from its addressees.[6] Apparently the terms of such a declaration will determine the conditions under which it can be revoked.[7] In 1957 the Egyptian government made a Declaration on the Suez Canal and the Arrangements for its Operation in which certain obligations were accepted. The Declaration was communicated to the UN Secretary-General together with a letter which explained that the Declaration was to be considered as an 'international instrument' and it was registered as such by the Secretariat.[8] Such a declaration may implicitly or otherwise require acceptance by other states as a condition of its validity or at least of its effectiveness.[9] In short, it seems that while a bare (unaccepted) declaration may be valid, it can produce its intended effects only if accepted (expressly or implicitly).

In the *Nuclear Tests* cases the International Court held that France was legally bound by publicly given undertakings, made at the highest level of government, to cease carrying out atmospheric nuclear tests.[10] The criteria of obligation were: the intention of the state making the declaration that it should be bound according to its terms; and that the undertaking be given publicly. There was no requirement of a *quid pro quo* or of any subsequent acceptance or response.[11] As a result of the French

---

[6] See McNair (1961) 11; Brierly, ILC *Ybk* 1950/II, 227; Lauterpacht, ILC *Ybk* 1953/II, 101–2; *South West Africa*, Preliminary Objections, ICJ Reports 1962 p 319, 402–4, 417–18; (Judge Jessup); Fitzmaurice (1957) 33 *BY* 229; Lachs (1980) 169 Hague *Recueil* 9, 198; Virally, in Bedjaoui (1991) 241; Charpentier, in Makarczyk (ed), *Theory of International Law at the Threshold of the 21st Century* (1996) 367; Torres, *Los actos unilaterales de los estados* (2010).

[7] Cf Fitzmaurice, ILC *Ybk* 1960/III, 79 (Art 12), 81 (Art 22), 91, 105; ILC Guiding Principles applicable to unilateral declarations of States capable of creating legal obligations, with commentaries thereto, ILC *Ybk* 2006/II(2), Principle 10 and commentary, 380–1. See further *Military and Paramilitary Activities in and Against Nicaragua*, Jurisdiction and Admissibility, ICJ Reports 1984 p 392, 415; *Fisheries Jurisdiction (Germany v Iceland)*, Jurisdiction, ICJ Reports 1973 p 49, 63; *Gabčíkovo-Nagymaros Project*, ICJ Reports 1997 p 7, 64.

[8] Declaration of the Government of the Republic of Egypt on the Suez Canal and the arrangements for its operation, 24 April 1957, 265 UNTS 299. See also the Declaration of 18 July 1957 recognizing the ICJ's jurisdiction 'over all legal disputes that may arise under ... paragraph 9 (b)' of the substantive Declaration: 272 UNTS 299.

[9] Cf the Austrian Declaration of 1955, contained in the Constitutional Federal Statute on Austria's permanent neutrality, 26 October 1955, *Bundesverfassungsgesetz*, BGBl 1955, 4 November 1955, No 211; Kunz (1956) 50 *AJIL* 418.

[10] *Nuclear Tests (Australia v France)*, ICJ Reports 1974 p 253, 267–71; *Nuclear Tests (New Zealand v France)*, ICJ Reports 1974 p 457, 472–5. For comment: Bollecker-Stern (1974) 20 *AFDI* 299; Thierry (1974) 20 *AFDI* 286; Franck (1975) 59 *AJIL* 612; Sur (1975) 79 *RGDIP* 972; Dupuy (1977) 20 *GYIL* 375; Hough & Macdonald (1977) 20 *GYIL* 337; Ruiz (1977) 20 *GYIL* 358; Scobbie (1992) 41 *ICLQ* 808; Carbone (1975) 1 *It YIL* 166; Rubin (1977) 71 *AJIL* 1; de Visscher, in Makarczyk (ed), *Essays in Honour of Manfred Lachs* (1984) 459; Thirlway (1989) 60 *BY* 1, 8–17.

[11] But cf *Nuclear Tests (Australia v France)*, ICJ Reports 1974 p 253, 373–4 (Judge de Castro, diss), accepting the principle, but deciding on the facts that the French statements lay within 'the political domain'. The Court's own unease at its solution can be detected in the unprecedented provision (ibid, 272) for either claimant to ask for an 'examination of the situation' if France did not comply with the Court's *soi-disant* commitment. In response to later French underground tests, New Zealand did so, but failed on the basis that the 1974 commitment concerned atmospheric tests only: *Request for an Examination of the Situation in Accordance with Paragraph 63 of the Court's Judgment of 20 December 1974 in* Nuclear Tests (New Zealand v France), ICJ Reports 1995 p 288.

undertaking, so interpreted by the Court, the dispute, it held, had disappeared and 'the claim advanced...no longer has any object'. While the principle applied—that a unilateral declaration may have certain legal effects—is not new, when the declaration is not directed to a specific state or states but is expressed *erga omnes*, as here, the detection of an intention to be legally bound, and of the structure of such intention, involves very careful appreciation of the facts. In any event the principle recognized in the *Nuclear Tests* cases was applied by the Court in *Nicaragua*[12] and also by the Chamber in *Frontier Dispute (Burkina Faso/Mali)*.[13]

(C) WITHDRAWAL OF UNILATERAL COMMITMENTS

Principle 10 of the ILC Guiding Principles applicable to unilateral declarations of states provides:

A unilateral declaration that has created legal obligations for the State making the declaration cannot be revoked arbitrarily. In assessing whether a revocation would be arbitrary, consideration should be given to: ...

  (b) The extent to which those to whom the obligations are owed have relied on such
       obligations...[14]

Unilateral declarations may reflect commitments but they are not treaties, and are not subject to the relatively strict VCLT regime for termination or withdrawal.

(D) EVIDENCE OF INCONSISTENT RIGHTS

Unilateral declarations involve, in principle at least, concessions which are intentional, public, coherent, and conclusive of the issues. However, acts of acquiescence and official statements may have probative value as admissions of rights inconsistent with the claims of the declarant, such acts individually not being conclusive. In *Eastern Greenland* the Court, as a subsidiary matter, attached significance to the fact that Norway had become a party to several treaties which referred to Danish sovereignty over Greenland as a whole, Norway having contended that Danish sovereignty had not been extended over the whole of Greenland.[15]

(E) OPPOSABLE SITUATIONS

Once a dispute is already known to exist, the other party may damage its case seriously by recognition or acquiescence. Consent by way of acquiescence, recognition, or implied consent may have the result of conceding as lawful the rights claimed.

---

[12] *Nicaragua,* ICJ Reports 1986 p 14, 132. Also ibid, 384–5 (Judge Schwebel, diss).
[13] ICJ Reports 1986 p 554, 573–4. Also *Filleting within the Gulf of St Lawrence (Canada v France)* (1986) 19 RIAA 225, 265.
[14] ILC *Ybk* 2006/II(2), Principle 10, 380.
[15] PCIJ Ser A/B No 53, 70–1. Also *Minquiers and Ecrehos (France/UK)*, ICJ Reports 1953 p 47, 66–7, 71–2.

A similar role appears when a state is claiming rights on a basis which is plausible to some extent, and yet rests either on ambiguous facts, or on a contention that the law has changed or provides an exception in its favour. Here acquiescence involves an acceptance of the legal basis of the opponent's claim, which can perhaps be more readily proved than in the case of a state faced by an undoubted usurper.[16]

(F) ACQUIESCENCE[17]

As a substantive legal concept, acquiescence has its origins in the common law, although the civil law has a similar procedural notion. It crystallized in the system of international law through international adjudication.[18]

In 1910, an arbitral tribunal constituted to delimit the maritime boundary between Norway and Sweden upheld Swedish sovereignty based on its uncontested extensive practice in the disputed region, including the fishing of lobsters, the conduct of measurements, and the stationing of a light boat, concluding that:

It is a settled principle of the law of nations that a state of things which actually exists and has existed for a long time should be changed as little as possible.[19]

The International Court upheld the legality of the straight baselines established by Norway, reasoning in similar vein that:

The notoriety of the facts, the general toleration of the international community, Great Britain's position in the North Sea, her own interest in the question, and her prolonged abstention would in any case warrant Norway's enforcement of her system against the United Kingdom.[20]

The requirements for acquiescence include: the notoriety of the facts and claims, their prolonged tolerance by the state(s) whose interests are specially affected, and general toleration by the international community. As to the burden of proof, it has been said that the inference from the conduct amounting to acquiescence may be 'so probable as to almost certain'.[21] Acquiescence has so far been applied mostly to claims over

---

[16] *Fisheries (UK v Norway)*, ICJ Reports 1951 p 116, 138–9.

[17] MacGibbon (1957) 33 *BY* 115; Bowett (1957) 33 *BY* 176, 197; Thirlway (1989) 60 *BY* 1, 29–49; Sinclair, in Lowe & Fitzmaurice (eds), *Jennings Essays* (1996) 104; Antunes, *Estoppel, Acquiescence and Recognition in Territorial and Boundary Dispute Settlement* (2000); Chan (2004) 3 *Chin JIL* 421; Tams, in Crawford, Pellet & Olleson (eds), *The Law of International Responsibility* (2010) 1035.

[18] E.g. *Maritime Boundary Dispute between Norway and Sweden* (1910) 4 *AJIL* 226, 233–5; *Anglo-Norwegian Fisheries*, ICJ Reports 1951 p 116, 138–9; *Right of Passage over Indian Territory (Portugal v India)*, ICJ Reports 1960 p 6, 39–44; *Temple of Preah Vihear (Cambodia v Thailand)*, ICJ Reports 1962 p 6, 23–33; *Continental Shelf (France v UK)* (1977) 18 RIAA 3, 68–74; *Land, Island and Maritime Frontier Dispute (El Salvador v Honduras)*, ICJ Reports 1992 p 351, 401–9, 566–70; *Sovereignty over Pedra Branca/Pulau Batu Puteh, Middle Rocks and South Ledge (Malaysia/Singapore)*, ICJ Reports 2008 p 12, 50–1, 120–1.

[19] *Maritime Boundary Dispute between Norway and Sweden* (1910) 4 *AJIL* 226, 233.

[20] *Anglo-Norwegian Fisheries*, ICJ Reports 1951 p 116, 139.

[21] *Maritime Boundary Dispute between Norway and Sweden* (1910) 4 *AJIL* 226, 234.

territory. As tacit acceptance justifying an assumption of consent over time, however, it falls within the broader category of unilateral acts.

In the *North Sea Continental Shelf* cases the International Court stated that uni-lateral assumption of the obligations of a convention by conduct was 'not lightly to be presumed', and that 'a very consistent course of conduct' was required in such a situation.[22] But in the Jurisdiction Phase of *Nicaragua* the Court held that Nicaragua's 'constant acquiescence' in the publication of its purported optional clause declara-tion in the Court's *Yearbook* 'constitutes a valid mode of manifestation of its intent to recognize the compulsory jurisdiction of the Court'.[23] Apparently this amounted to 'a very consistent course of conduct'.

3. ESTOPPEL

(A) THE PLACE OF ESTOPPEL IN INTERNATIONAL LAW

There is a tendency to refer to any representation or conduct having legal significance as creating an estoppel, precluding the author from denying the 'truth' of the representa-tion, express or implied. By analogy with principles of municipal law, and by reference to decisions of international tribunals, Bowett has stated the essentials of estoppel to be: (a) an unambiguous statement of fact; (b) which is voluntary, unconditional, and authorized; and (c) which is relied on in good faith to the detriment of the other party or to the advantage of the party making the statement.[24] A considerable weight of authority supports the view that estoppel is a general principle of international law, resting on principles of good faith and consistency.[25] The essence of estoppel is the element of conduct which causes the other party, in reliance on such conduct, detri-mentally to change its position or to suffer some prejudice.[26] But it is necessary to

---

[22] *North Sea Continental Shelf (Federal Republic of Germany/Netherlands; Federal Republic of Germany/ Denmark)*, ICJ Reports 1969 p 3, 25.

[23] *Nicaragua*, ICJ Reports 1984 p 392, 411–13; also ibid, 413–15, on issues of estoppel. Further: ibid, 458–60 (Judge Ruda); 463–5 (Judge Mosler); 483–9 (Judge Oda); 527–31 (Judge Ago); 595–600 (Judge Schwebel, diss).

[24] Bowett (1957) 33 *BY* 176, 202. This author takes some pains to isolate estoppel from other things. Further: Dominicé, in Battelli (ed), *Recueil d'études en hommage à Paul Guggenheim* (1968) 327, 364–5; Vallée (1973) 77 *RGDIP* 949; Martin (1979); Thirlway (1989) 60 *BY* 1, 29–49; Youakim, *Estoppel in International Law* (1994); Sinclair, in Lowe & Fitzmaurice (1996) 104; Cottier & Müller, 'Estoppel' (2007) *MPEPIL*.

[25] *Temple*, ICJ Reports 1962 p 6, 61–5 (Judge Fitzmaurice); *Delimitation of the Maritime Boundary in the Gulf of Maine Area (Canada/US)*, ICJ Reports 1984 p 246, 305. Also: Bowett (1957) 33 *BY* 176, 202; MacGibbon (1958) 7 *ICLQ* 468; Lauterpacht, *Development* (1958) 168–72; ILC *Ybk* 1963/II, 212–13; Waldock, ibid, 39–40; ILC *Ybk* 1966/II, 239. Cf Fauvarque-Cosson, *La Confiance légitime et l'Estoppel* (2007).

[26] *Gulf of Maine*, ICJ Reports 1984 p 246, 309. Also *El Salvador v Honduras, Application to Intervene by Nicaragua*, ICJ Reports 1990 p 92, 118; *Cameroon v Nigeria*, Preliminary Objections, ICJ Reports 1998 p 275, 303–4. Also: *Golshani v Islamic Republic of Iran* (1993) 29 Iran–US CTR 78; *Chevron-Texaco v Ecuador*, 30 March 2010, 161–2, available at www.italaw.com.

point out that estoppel in municipal law is regarded with great caution, and that the 'principle' has no particular coherence in international law, its incidence and effects not being uniform.[27] Thus before a tribunal, the principle largely defined may operate to resolve ambiguities and as a principle of equity and justice:[28] here it becomes a part of the reasoning. Elsewhere, its content is taken up by the principles noted in the last section, which are interrelated.[29]

A good example of judicial application of the broader version of the principle is *Arbitral Award by the King of Spain*. Nicaragua challenged the validity of the award: the Court held the award valid and added that it was no longer open to Nicaragua, which, by express declaration and by conduct had recognized the award as valid, to challenge it.[30] This and similar cases support a particular type of estoppel, but the rule concerned could operate independently of any general doctrine.

4. RELATION BETWEEN UNILATERAL ACTS AND ESTOPPEL

The relation between unilateral acts and estoppel needs clarification. The two institutions were imported in international law from the systems of civil and common law respectively, and grew up separately, shading into each other. Even though they are both rooted in the principle of good faith, unilateral acts are in their essence statements or representations intended to be binding and publicly manifested as such, whereas estoppel is a more general category, consisting of statements or representations not intended as binding nor amounting to a promise, whose binding force crystallizes depending on the circumstances.

The issue of rescinding unilateral acts is also distinct from estoppel. A binding unilateral act may be revoked with a good justification when it has not been relied upon or when the circumstances have materially changed. Given that the essential circumstance for creating the legal obligation in the first place is the publicity of the unilateral act, publicity is also a condition for the notice of its withdrawal, subject to the particular circumstances. There is no such requirement of publicity for an estoppel to arise. A common feature of both is that there is no reason to assume that either is subject to the rules of terminating obligations under the law of treaties.

---

[27] *Temple*, ICJ Reports 1962 p 6, 39 (Judge Alfaro), 143 (Judge Spender, diss).

[28] Cf Cheng, *General Principles* (4th edn, 1987) 141–58. Also: Schwarzenberger (1955) 87 Hague *Recueil* 191, 312–14; Bowett (1957) 33 *BY* 176, 195; Lauterpacht (1958) 168–72.

[29] Comments of Venturini (1964) 112 Hague *Recueil* 363, 370–4. Bowett uses the principle of reliance to isolate 'simple' or 'true' estoppel from the other principles. In some contexts, such as renunciation, reliance is not active in determining legal consequences: see *Pulau Batu Puteh*, ICJ Reports 2008 p 12. Nor does his distinction as to statements of fact have much viability. Further: Vallée (1973) 77 *RGDIP* 949.

[30] *Arbitral Award Made by the King of Spain on 23 December 1906 (Honduras v Nicaragua)*, ICJ Reports 1960 p 192, 213. Cf Johnson (1961) 10 *ICLQ* 328.

Estoppel should be distinguished from acquiescence too: the latter involves allowing an existing legal or factual situation to continue in circumstances where objection could and should have been made, leading, in the course of time, to the assumption of consent. Acquiescence is not subject to the requirement of detrimental reliance but is a promise implied in the context of lapse of time. In the words of the Chamber in *Gulf of Maine*:

[T]he concepts of acquiescence and estoppel, irrespective of the status accorded to them by international law, both follow from the fundamental principles of good faith and equity ... [They] are, however, based on different legal reasoning, since acquiescence is equivalent to tacit recognition manifested by unilateral conduct which the other party may interpret as consent, while estoppel is linked to the idea of preclusion.[31]

To summarise:

(1) There is a principle of estoppel recognized in international law.

(2) An estoppel is precisely *not* a unilateral act; it is a representation the truth of which the entity on whose behalf it is made is precluded from denying in certain circumstances, notably reliance and detriment.

(3) By contrast a unilateral act in the sense of international law is a commitment intended to be binding and accepted as such.

(4) The principle of good faith in international law is not exhausted by these two doctrines; what further role it may play, however, depends on the facts and circumstances.

---

[31] *Gulf of Maine*, ICJ Reports 1984 p 246, 305.

19

SUCCESSION TO RIGHTS AND DUTIES

1. INTRODUCTION AND OVERVIEW

(A) STATE SUCCESSION AS A CATEGORY[1]

State succession occurs when there is a definitive replacement of one state by another in respect of sovereignty over a given territory, that is, a replacement in conformity with international law.[2] The political events concerned include dismemberment of an existing state, secession or separation of part of a state, decolonization, merger of existing states into a new state, and cession or annexation of state territory. Succession is predicated upon the permanent displacement of sovereign power, and thus temporary changes resulting from belligerent occupation, agency, or grants of exclusive possession of territory by treaty are excluded.

When the sovereignty of one state replaces that of another, a number of legal problems arise. Is the successor state bound by all or any of the treaties of the predecessor? Do the inhabitants of the territory concerned automatically become nationals of the successor? Is the successor state affected by international claims involving the predecessor, by the predecessor's national debt and its other obligations under the legal system now supplanted? It is important to note that the phrase 'state succession' is employed to *describe* an area, a source of problems: it does not connote any overriding principle, or even a presumption, that a transmission or succession of legal rights and duties occurs in a given case. The phrase 'state succession' is well established,

---

[1] Principal items of literature include: Zemanek (1965) 116 Hague *Recueil* 187; O'Connell, *State Succession in Municipal Law and International Law* (1967); O'Connell (1970) 130 Hague *Recueil* 95; Bedjaoui (1970) 130 Hague *Recueil* 455; Verzijl, *7 International Law in Historical Perspective* (1974); Crawford (1980) 51 *BY* 1; Makonnen, *International Law and the New States of Africa* (1983); Makonnen (1986) 200 Hague *Recueil* 93; Hafner & Kornfeind (1996) 1 *Austrian RIEL* 1; Stern (1996) 262 Hague *Recueil* 164; Eisemann & Koskenniemi (eds), *State Succession* (2000); Craven, *The Decolonisation of International Law* (2007).

[2] Where territory is occupied by a state in circumstances not in accordance with international law (or at least with a peremptory norm), there is no succession and the regime is one of occupation pending resolution of the problem: Ronen, *Legal Aspects of Transition from Illegal Territorial Regimes in International Law* (2010), and further: chapter 27.

despite the misleading municipal law analogy of continuity of legal personality in an individual's general property, passing as an inheritance, involving a complete or 'universal succession'. Generally speaking the only event of 'universal succession' in international law is state continuity—life rather than death.

State succession is an area of uncertainty and controversy. Much of the practice is equivocal and could be explained on the basis of special agreement or of rules distinct from the concept of legal succession. Indeed, it is possible to take the view that not many settled rules have yet emerged.

Nonetheless, the ILC has sought to codify the law on state succession leading to two separate conventions; the 1978 Vienna Convention on the Succession of States in Respect of Treaties[3] and the 1983 Vienna Convention on the Succession of States in Respect of Property Archives and Debts.[4] Both were criticized for departing from established international law,[5] they have attracted a limited number of ratifications (the 1978 Convention only entered into force in 1996 and has 22 parties; the 1983 Convention is not yet in force).[6] The territorial transformations of the last two decades however, revealed a tendency to rely on them or at least some of their provisions to resolve controversial questions, for want of any better articulation of the legal principles involved.[7]

(B) THE PRE-EMPTION OF ISSUES BY AGREEMENT

When multilateral peace treaties constituted new states or reallocated territory (e.g. in 1815, 1919–23, or 1947) they would often regulate succession problems as part of the territorial rearrangement. The Treaty of St Germain provided for the responsibility of the successor states of the Austro-Hungarian monarchy for its public debts.[8] Provisions of the Italian Peace Treaty of 1947 determined questions concerning the relations of Italy and its former colony of Libya.[9] On other occasions the conduct of states might produce informal novation by means of unilateral declarations, legislation, or other expressions of position.[10] In 1958 when the United Arab Republic was created by the union

---

[3] 23 August 1978, 1946 UNTS 3.

[4] 7 April 1983, 22 ILM 306. The Convention was adopted by 54–11:11.

[5] O'Connell (1979) 39 *ZaöRV* 730; Vagts (1992–93) 3 *Va JIL* 275, 295; Stern (ed), *Dissolution, Continuation and Succession in Eastern Europe* (1998).

[6] See also ILC draft articles on nationality of natural persons in relation to the succession of states, ILC *Ybk* 1999/II(2), 23–47; in Pronto & Wood, *The International Law Commission 1999–2009* (2010) IV, 75–126. The draft articles were brought to the attention of governments by GA Res 55/153, 12 December 2000, and finalized as a non-treaty text by GA Res 66/469, 9 December 2011.

[7] *Gabčíkovo-Nagymaros Project (Hungary/Slovakia)*, ICJ Reports 1997 p 7, 70–2; Badinter Commission, *Opinion No 9* (1992) 92 ILR 203, *Opinion No 12* (1993) 96 ILR 729, *Opinion No 14* (1993) 96 ILR 723, *Opinion No 15* (1993) 96 ILR 733; *Partial Award: Prisoners of War—Eritrea's Claim 17* (2003) 26 RIAA 23, 38.

[8] Principal Allied & Associated Powers-Austria, Treaty of St Germain-en-Laye, 10 September 1919, 226 CTS 8, Art 203. Also: *Administrative Decision no 1* (1927) 6 RIAA 203; *Ottoman Debt* (1925) 1 RIAA 529.

[9] Treaty of Peace with Italy, 10 February 1947, 49 UNTS 124; and e.g. *Italy v United Kingdom* (1953) 25 ILR 2.

[10] Waldock, ILC *Ybk* 1971/II(1), 149–53; ILC *Ybk* 1972/II, 272–7; ILC *Ybk* 1974/II(1), 236–41. Also e.g. *DC v Public Prosecutor* (1972) 73 ILR 38 (continuity of post-1992 FRY); *R v Director of Public Prosecutions, ex*

of Egypt with Syria, the Minister of Foreign Affairs of the Union said in a Note to the Secretary-General: '… all international treaties and agreements concluded by Egypt or Syria with other countries will remain valid within the regional limits prescribed on their conclusion and in accordance with the principles of international law'.[11] Such a declaration of itself could not bind third states parties to treaties with Egypt and Syria. However, third states acquiesced in the position adopted by the United Arab Republic and the US expressly took note of the assurance given.[12] New states may become parties to treaties by notification of succession the validity of which is accepted by other states, by international organizations and, if necessary, by the Court.[13]

The devolution of treaty rights and obligations has often been the subject of agreements between the predecessor and successor states.[14] Such agreements promote certainty and stability of relations.[15] They also create certain problems. First, the agreement may appear to be a part of the bargain exacted by the outgoing colonial power at independence and the new state may seek legal means of disputing its validity and application. Secondly, third states cannot be bound by inheritance agreements unless by express declaration or conduct they agree to be bound.[16]

2. THE FORMS OF TERRITORIAL CHANGE

There is clearly some relation between the form of territorial change and the transmissibility of rights and duties. Thus the 'moving treaty boundaries' principle holds that a transfer of territory from state A to state B is presumed not to affect existing treaties: state B's treaties cover the transferred territory whereas state A's cease to apply. However, there seems to be little value in establishing, as major categories, concepts of cession, dismemberment, merger, decolonization, and the like.[17] It may be

parte *Schwartz* (1976) 73 ILR 44 (reliance on Jamaican constitutional provision); *M v Federal Department of Justice and Police* (1979) 75 ILR 107 9 (continuity of 1880 Anglo-Swiss Extradition Treaty based on the tacit acceptance of Switzerland and South Africa).

[11] ILC *Ybk* 1958/II, 77.

[12] 2 Whiteman 959–62, 1014. The UAR dissolved in 1964 with similar consequences in terms of treaty continuity: 2 O'Connell (1967) 71–4, 169–70.

[13] Cf SC Res 757 (1992); SC Res 777 (1992); *Application of the Convention on the Prevention and Punishment of Genocide (Bosnia and Herzegovina v Yugoslavia)*, Preliminary Objections, ICJ Reports 1996 p 595, 612. There the ICJ did not consider it necessary to decide whether Bosnia and Herzegovina became a party to the Genocide Convention through succession or accession after independence: ibid. It relied on the 'object and purpose' of the Genocide Convention to establish its jurisdiction *ratione tempore* rather than an acceptance of Yugoslavia's notification of succession (indeed, it implicitly discounted the notification of succession by applying the Convention retroactively: ibid, 617).

[14] Lauterpacht (1958) 7 *ICLQ* 514, 524–30; 2 O'Connell (1967) 352–73.

[15] ILA, *The Effect of Independence on Treaties* (1965) 191; 2 O'Connell (1967) 154; Craven (2007) 122.

[16] UK–Venezuela Agreement, 17 February 1966, 561 UNTS 321, Art VIII; Waldock, Second Report, ILC *Ybk* 1969/II, 54–62; ILC *Ybk* 1972/II, 236–41; ILC *Ybk* 1974/II(1), 183–7; Craven (2007) 120–31.

[17] But see Bedjaoui, ILC *Ybk* 1968/II, 100–1. Other ILC members adopted a similar point of view: ILC *Ybk* 1969/I, 53ff.

that decolonization attracts special principles but there is no *general* significance in the distinction between decolonization, dismemberment, secession, and annexation. Too ready a reliance on such distinctions is deceptive. Particular factual situations are presented as though they are legal categories. Distinctions are made in the legal rules adduced which may seem anomalous or invidious. Thus O'Connell employs the category of 'annexation' and accepts the view that annexation terminates 'personal' treaties.[18] But he adopts a different approach to survival of treaties in the case of 'grants of independence' without explaining why there should be such a different outcome.

The events producing a change of sovereignty may nevertheless have legal relevance in particular circumstances. Thus if the successor repudiates or acknowledges continuity with the predecessor this may produce the effect of preclusion in respect of consequential legal matters. There may well be a presumption against continuity in cases where the political and legal machinery of change has involved relinquishment of sovereignty followed by reallocation in the form of a multilateral territorial settlement, as in the case of the peace treaties in Europe in 1919–20.[19] Similarly, there will be a presumption against continuity in the case of a forcible secession or its equivalent, as with the creation of Israel.[20] The reference to either acknowledged or repudiated continuity with a predecessor state raises problems for third states, which are not bound to accept the determination of the putative successor.[21] The recognition of continuity by third states must be an important element since continuity is very much a matter of election and appreciation.[22] This is also true where complex political change produces a double succession within a short space of time, as with India and Pakistan, Senegal and Mali. Normally, these matters will be regulated by treaty: thus Turkey as a new political entity was treated as continuous with the Ottoman Empire by the Treaty of Lausanne.[23]

(A) THE DISTINCTION BETWEEN CONTINUITY AND SUCCESSION

In short, there is a 'fundamental distinction' between state continuity and state succession; 'continuity' denoting cases where the same state continues to exist, succession

---

[18] 2 O'Connell (1967) chs 2, 8. Luke O'Connell, Jennings (1967) 121 Hague *Recueil* 323, 447–8 regards 'evolution towards independence' within the British Commonwealth as creating a continuity in personality with the pre-independence colonial government. This view is not reflected in the relevant materials except in the rather different case where a protectorate is held to have had international personality before the subordinate status was removed: Zemanek (1965) 116 Hague *Recueil* 195, 228; Crawford, *Creation of States* (2nd edn, 2006) 307–10. Cf Rosenne (1950) 27 BY 267.

[19] Cf *Affaires des réparations allemande selon l'article 260 du Traité de Versailles* (1924) 1 RIAA 429, 441–4. Special provision was made in the treaties for the maintenance of public debts.

[20] UN Legis Series, *Materials on Succession of States* (1967) 38; *Shimshon Palestine Portland Cement Factory Ltd v A-G* (1950) 17 ILR 72.

[21] 2 Whiteman 758–9; 3 *Répertoire suisse* 1337–57.

[22] *DC v Public Prosecutor* (1972) 73 ILR 38.

[23] *Ottoman Debt* (1925) 1 RIAA 529, 571–4, 590–4, 599.

referring to the replacement of one state by another with respect to a particular territory.[24] The question of continuity precedes that of succession: state continuity presupposes stability in legal relations. In other words, where the 'same' state continues to exist, the question of succession to rights and obligations does not arise for that state.[25]

Nonetheless, distinguishing cases of identity from succession can present difficulties, particularly where drastic changes have occurred to a state's territory, government, or population.[26] This question can be particularly problematic as concerns membership of international organizations.[27] Because there are no well-defined criteria for state extinction, subjective factors may be pertinent, including the state's own claim to continuity, as well as recognition by other states.[28] Despite the precarious character of determinations of identity and continuity, a number of criteria have been advanced to resolve questions of state continuity. Marek relies on the criterion of formal 'independence' (or the preservation of the concerned state's legal order) as the touchstone.[29] Another possibility is to refer to the basic criteria for statehood (such as continuity of territory and population), applied in the context of claim, recognition, and acquiescence by third states.[30]

(B) DISMEMBERMENT OF FEDERAL STATES[31]

Much has been written about the dissolution, or partial dissolution, of the USSR and the SFRY. In the case of the Russian Federation, the principal surviving component of the USSR, the international community accepted the Russian assertion made in communications to the UN and a circular note to all states with diplomatic missions in Moscow that Russia was the continuator of the former Soviet Union. Russia was also accepted by the members of the Security Council as the continuator of the USSR. Russia assumed all treaty obligations and consolidated the debts and property abroad of the USSR (although Soviet property and indebtedness might have been apportioned among all the former republics).

---

[24] Cf Stern (1996) 262 Hague *Receuil* 9, 39; Crawford (2nd edn, 2006) 667–8.

[25] Marek, *Identity and Continuity of States in International Law* (1968) 10; Mälksoo, *Illegal Annexation and State Continuity* (2003). But see Craven (2007) 78–80.

[26] The general rule is that internal changes of government do not affect a state's identity: Crawford (2nd edn, 2006) 678–80. Claims by the USSR of discontinuity with Tsarist Russia were rejected.

[27] Russia assumed the USSR's place as a permanent member of the SC: Müllerson (1993) 42 *ICLQ* 473, 475–8; Shaw (1994) 5 *Fin YIL* 34, 49–50; Craven (2007) 218–19. By contrast Serbia-Montenegro was denied automatic UN membership as a continuator of Yugoslavia. The Czech Republic and Slovakia agreed to re-apply to UN membership as new states; their attempt to divide between themselves Czechoslovakia's seats in the specialized agencies was rejected: Scharf (1995) 28 *Cornell ILJ* 29, 30–1.

[28] Bühler, in Eismann & Koskenniemi (2000) 187–201; Caflisch (1963) 10 *NILR* 337, 338. But see Crawford (2nd edn, 2006) 668.

[29] Marek (1968) 188, 216.

[30] Crawford (2nd edn, 2006) 670–1.

[31] Schachter (1948) 25 *BY* 91, 101–9; Zemanek (1965) 116 Hague *Recueil* 181, 254; 2 O'Connell (1967) 183–211; 2 Whiteman 1016–27; Bühler, in Eisemann & Koskenniemi (2000) 187.

In the wake of the disintegration of Yugoslavia, Serbia and Montenegro, then denominated the Federal Republic of Yugoslavia, declared that it was the sole successor of the former Yugoslavia. This position was unacceptable to the European Community and its member states.[32] Apparently as a consequence of this difference, Yugoslavia was prevented from exercising many of its rights as a member of the UN, but without affecting for the time being its status as a party to the Statute of the International Court of Justice. Yet after 2001 a completely different view was taken of the situation; the Court for its part oscillated.[33] It is difficult to give legal articulation to these episodes.

(C) THE DOCTRINE OF REVERSION[34]

It is possible that continuity by virtue of general recognition by third states can arise in the form of reversion. The successor state may be regarded as recovering a political and legal identity displaced by an intervening period of dismemberment or colonization.[35] Such cases will be rare and the consequences of a doctrine of reversion may create a threat to the security of legal relations: thus the successor may not consider itself bound by territorial grants or recognition of territorial or even demographic changes imposed by the predecessor.[36] The suggestion has been made that, quite apart from recognition by third states, in a case of post-colonial reversion, the principle of self-determination may create a presumption in favour of the successor state.[37] This raises large issues of the relation between peremptory norms (including self-determination) and the law relating to state succession.

3. STATE SUCCESSSION AND MUNICIPAL LEGAL RELATIONS

After a change of sovereignty various issues may be raised in the context of municipal law, viz., the destiny of the property of the ceding or former state, the continuity of

---

[32] Badinter Commission, *Opinion No 9* (1992) 92 ILR 203. For other Opinions: *Opinion No 11* (1992) 96 ILR 718; *Opinion No 12* (1993) 96 ILR 723; *Opinion No 13* (1993) 96 ILR 726; *Opinion No 14* (1993) 96 ILR 729. Also *Federal Republic and National Bank of Yugoslavia v Republics of Croatia, Slovenia, Macedonia and Bosnia-Herzegovina* (1999) 128 ILR 627.

[33] Further: *Legality of the Use of Force (Serbia and Montenegro v Belgium)*, ICJ Reports 2004 p 279; *Application of the Convention on the Prevention and Punishment of the Crime of Genocide (Bosnia and Herzegovina v Serbia and Montenegro)*, ICJ Reports 2007 p 43; *Croatia v Serbia*, ICJ Reports 2008 p 412.

[34] Alexandrowicz (1969) 45 *International Affairs* 465; Jain (1969) 9 *Indian JIL* 525; Långström, in Eisemann & Koskenniemi (2000) 723, 730–3.

[35] Cf the history of Poland and India: Crawford (2006) 697–9.

[36] The major modern example is the Baltic States: Ziemele, *State Continuity and Nationality* (2005); Crawford (2006) 689–90. Only limited consequences flowed from recognition of pre-1940 continuity.

[37] *Right of Passage over Indian Territory (Portugal v India)*, ICJ Reports 1960 p 6, 93–6 (Judge Quintana, diss). Cf Bedjaoui, ILC *Ybk* 1968/II, 128. In the *Red Sea Islands,* the Yemeni argument based on reversion was rejected on the facts: (1998) 114 ILR 1, 115–17. It is not clear that the Court of Arbitration appreciated the precise historical sequence of events.

the legal system, the status of private property rights, including rights deriving from contracts and concessions concluded under the former law, and issues of nationality. Hyde and others have maintained that the municipal law of the predecessor remains in force until the new sovereign takes steps to change it.[38] O'Connell and others support a principle of vested or acquired rights, that is, that a change of sovereignty has no effect on the acquired rights of foreign nationals.[39] The principle has received support from tribunals,[40] but it is a source of confusion since it is question-begging and is used as the basis for a variety of propositions. For some, it means simply that private rights are not affected by the change of sovereignty as such. For others it appears to mean that the successor state faces restrictions on its powers in relation to private rights of aliens additional to the ordinary rules of international law governing treatment of aliens in cases not involving a succession. Moreover, writers often fail to relate the concept of acquired rights to other principles affecting a change of sovereignty. The new sovereign receives the same sort of sovereignty as the transferor had, and this involves normal powers of legislation and jurisdiction. Survival of the old law depends on the consent of the new sovereign, not in the sense that there is a legal vacuum pending such consent, but in the sense (a) that the constitutional or public law of the territory will necessarily change to accommodate the new situation, and (b) that the new sovereign has, prima facie, the same freedom to change the law as the old sovereign had.[41] Indeed some proponents of acquired rights formulate the principle in a qualified form. Thus O'Connell states that 'the principle of respect for acquired rights in international law is no more than a principle that change of sovereignty should not touch the interests of individuals more than is necessary', and goes on to say that the successor state which alters or terminates acquired rights must comply with the minimum standards of international law.[42] In the case of decolonization, the continuation of the pre-independence economic structure, which commonly involves extensive foreign ownership of major resources, would produce a situation in which political independence and formal sovereignty were not matched by a normal competence to regulate the national economy. The declaration of the UN

[38] 1 Hyde 397ff.

[39] 2 O'Connell (1967) chs 6–18; O'Connell (1970) 130 Hague *Recueil* 95, 134–46. Zemanek (1965) 116 Hague *Recueil* 181, 279, points out that only when one assumes that the chain of continuity is broken does it become necessary to have recourse to a special rule on vested rights.

[40] *Forests of Central Rhodopia* (1933) 3 RIAA 1405, 1431–6; *Lighthouses* (1956) 23 ILR 79, 79–80.

[41] Kaeckenbeeck (1936) 17 *BY* 1, 13; Rosenne (1950) 27 *BY* 267, 273, 281–2; 1 Guggenheim 136; Zemanek (1965) 116 Hague *Recueil* 181, 281; Bedjaoui, ILC *Ybk* 1968/II, 115; Bedjaoui, ILC *Ybk* 1969/II, 69. For the debate: ILC *Ybk* 1969/I, 53ff; Bedjaoui (1970) 130 Hague *Recueil* 455, 531–61. The often-quoted passage in *German Settlers in Poland* (1923) PCIJ Ser B No 6, 36, that, in the instance of German territory transferred to Poland after 1918, German law had continued to operate in the territory in question, is a factual statement. Further *L and JJ v Polish State Railways* (1957) 24 ILR 77.

[42] 1 O'Connell (1967) 266. O'Connell points out that the principle of continuity of law is only a presumption: ibid, 170. Also O'Connell (1970) 130 Hague *Recueil* 95, 141.

General Assembly on 'Permanent Sovereignty over Natural Resources'[43] contains a proviso thus:

Considering that nothing in paragraph 4 below in any way prejudices the position of any Member State on any aspect of the question of the rights and obligations of successor States and Governments in respect of property acquired before the accession to sovereignty of countries formerly under colonial rule....

This is a reservation of competence; it does not give the new sovereign *carte blanche*.

(A) STATE PROPERTY[44]

It is generally accepted that succession to the public property of the predecessor state located on the territory in question is a principle of customary international law and the jurisprudence of the Permanent Court of International Justice supports this position.[45] Another approach would be to say that the 'principle' is really a presumption that acquisition of state property is inherent in the grant of territorial sovereignty and is a normal consequence of the acquisition of sovereignty in situations apart from a grant or cession. The position is in general confirmed by the Vienna Convention on Succession of States in respect of State Property, Archives and Debts of 1983,[46] although the Convention propounds a rather different legal regime for the case where the successor is a 'newly independent state'.

In practice, the partition of state property among successor states may raise difficulties, which are usually resolved by negotiations and bilateral agreements based on the principle of 'equity'. Differences of opinion regarding the form of change in sovereignty for the purposes of regulating succession to property (particularly the distinction between dissolution and secession) may lead to conflict,[47] and in some cases, the very definition of 'state property' may be disputed: the competing claims of the SFRY's successors relating to 'social property' is a case in point.[48]

---

[43] GA Res 1803, 18 December 1972.

[44] For ILC proceedings: ILC *Ybk* 1970/II, 131; ILC *Ybk* 1971/II(1), 157; ILC *Ybk* 1973/II, 3; ILC *Ybk* 1974/II(1), 91; ILC *Ybk* 1975/II, 110; ILC *Ybk* 1976/II(1), 55; ILC *Ybk* 1976/II(2), 122; ILC *Ybk* 1981/II(2), 24–47; *Union of Burma v Kotaro Toda* (1965) 53 ILR 149. Also: Dronova, in Eisemann & Koskenniemi (2000) 782, 798–810; Terol, ibid, 889, 916–24; Staničč (2001) 12 *EJIL* 751; Resolution, Institut de Droit International (2001) 69 *Ann de l'Inst* 713.

[45] *Peter Pázmány University* (1933) PCIJ Ser A/B No 61, 237. Also *Haile Selassie v Cable and Wireless, Ltd (No 2)* [1939] Ch 182, 195.

[46] 22 ILM 298, 306. For comment: Streinz (1983) 26 *GYIL* 198; Monnier (1984) 30 *AFDI* 221. Further: Badinter Commission, *Opinion No 9* (1992) 92 ILR 203, *Opinion No 12* (1993) 96 ILR 729, *Opinion No 14* (1993) 96 ILR 723, *Opinion No 15* (1993) 96 ILR 733.

[47] *Republic of Croatia v GiroCredit Bank AG der Sparkassen* (1996) 36 ILM 1520; *Re AY Bank Ltd (in liquidation)* [2006] EWHC 830; *Republic of Croatia v Republic of Serbia* [2009] EWHC 1559; Bosnia and Herzegovina-Croatia-Macedonia-Slovenia-FRY, Agreement on Succession Issues, 29 June 2001, 2262 UNTS 253.

[48] Badinter Commission, *Opinion No 14* (1993) 96 ILR 723.

In the aftermath of the USSR's break-up, special solutions were required to address the partition of nuclear forces and other military property, deviating significantly from both the principles of territoriality and equitable apportionment. Despite initial protest, it was eventually agreed that Russia would maintain control of all nuclear weapons, while other members of the Commonwealth of Independent States in whose territories nuclear weapons had been located (Belarus, Kazakhstan, and Ukraine) would commit to total nuclear disarmament. Agreement was reached through negotiations and guarantees of compensation.[49] The Black Sea fleet, located in the Crimean peninsula (which had been transferred to Ukraine in 1954) was partitioned between Russia (81.7%) and Ukraine (18.3%), with Russia maintaining the right to use the Ukrainian port of Sevastopol for 20 years.[50]

(B) PUBLIC LAW CLAIMS AND PUBLIC DEBTS[51]

It follows from what has already been said that the successor state has a right to take up fiscal claims belonging to the former state which relate to the territory in question, including the right to collect taxes due. Much more a matter of controversy is the fate of the public debts of the replaced state. It may be that there is no rule of succession established,[52] but some writers have concluded that in cases of annexation or dismemberment (as opposed to cession, i.e. where the ceding state remains in existence), the successor is obliged to assume the public debts of the extinct state.[53] Zemanek confines succession to the situation where before independence an autonomous political dependency has, through the agency of the metropolitan power, contracted a 'localized debt' which is automatically attributed to the new state after separation.[54] In practice, however, municipal courts will enforce obligations of the predecessor state against the successor only when the latter has recognized them,[55] although recognition could take

---

[49] Långström, in Eisemann & Koskenniemi (2000) 742, 743–5; Dronova, ibid, 800–2.

[50] Agreement Between the Russian Federation and Ukraine on the Status and Conditions of the Russian Federation Black Sea Fleet's Stay on Ukrainian Territory, 28 May 1997, *RG* (7 June 1997) analysed in Sherr (1997) 39 *Survival* 33, extended for 25 years by the Russian-Ukrainian Naval Base for Natural Gas Treaty, 21 April 2010, *RG* (28 April 2010): Anatoly Medetsky, 'Deal Struck on Gas, Black Sea Fleet' (*The Moscow Times*, 22 April 2010). Cf Dronova, in Eisemann & Koskenniemi (2000) 805–10.

[51] ILA, Report of the 53rd Conference (1968) 598, 603; Lauterpacht, 3 *International Law* (1977) 121; Cazorla, in Eisemann & Koskenniemi (2000) 663–71, 696–706; Stanič (2001) 12 *EJIL* 751. For ILC proceedings: Bedjaoui, ILC *Ybk* 1971/II(1), 185; ILC *Ybk* 1977/II(1), 45; ILC *Ybk* 1977/II(2), 59; ILC *Ybk* 1978/II(1), 229; ILC *Ybk* 1978/II(2), 113; ILC *Ybk* 1979/II(2), 40; ILC *Ybk* 1981/II(2), 72–113. As to state archives see ILC *Ybk* 1979/II(1), 67; 1 ILC *Ybk* 1979/II(2), 77; ILC *Ybk* 1980/II(1), 1; ILC *Ybk* 1980/II(2), 11; ILC *Ybk* 1981/II(2), 47–71.

[52] *Ottoman Debt* (1925) 1 RIAA 531, 573; *Franco-Ethiopian Railway Company* (1957) 24 ILR 602, 629.

[53] Feilchenfeld, *Public Debts and State Succession* (1931); Sack (1931–32) 80 *U Penn LR* 608; 1 O'Connell (1967) 369ff. Also *Lighthouses* (1956) 23 ILR 659.

[54] (1965) 116 Hague Recueil 181, 255–70. Also: 1 Guggenheim 472; Bedjaoui, ILC *Ybk* 1968/II, 109–10. Cf *Pittacos v État Belge* (1964) 45 ILR 24, 31–2.

[55] E.g. *West Rand Central Gold Mining Company v R* [1905] 2 KB 391; *Shimshon Palestine Portland Cement Company Ltd v AG* (1950) 17 ILR 72; *Dalmia Dadri Cement Company Ltd v Commissioner of Income Tax* (1958) 26 ILR 79.

the form of unqualified continuation of the legal system under which the debts arise. The 1983 Vienna Convention provides for the passing of the state debt to the successor state (as a general principle) with a reduction according to an equitable proportion in the cases of transfer of part of a state, secession, or dissolution of a state (Articles 36 to 37, 39 to 41). However, when the successor state is a 'newly independent State', no state debt shall pass, except by agreement (and then only if certain other conditions are satisfied) (Article 38). According to Article 2(1)(e) a 'newly independent State' means a successor state the territory of which had been 'a dependent territory for the international relations of which the predecessor State was responsible'. This distinction between 'newly independent states' and other successor states is problematic, especially when it has such categorical effects.

(C) STATE CONTRACTS AND CONCESSIONS

As in the case of all rights acquired under the municipal law of the predecessor state, rights deriving from state contracts and concessions are susceptible to change by the new sovereign. Limitations on such interference derive from relevant international standards concerning treatment of aliens or human rights in general.[56] However, a number of writers[57] state the principle that the acquired rights of a concessionaire must be respected by a successor state.[58] There is a certain anomaly in the selection of concessions as beneficiaries of the principle, which could be related to other matters, including contracts of employment and pension rights. It will be appreciated that judicial pronouncements to the effect that the mere change of sovereignty does not cancel concession rights[59] do not give support to the acquired rights doctrine in the form that *after* the change of sovereignty the new sovereign must maintain the property rights of aliens acquired before the change of sovereignty.

In the *Lighthouses Arbitration* between France and Greece certain claims were concerned with an alleged Greek responsibility for breaches of concessions occurring prior to extension of Greek sovereignty over the autonomous state of Crete.[60] The tribunal also approached the matter on the basis of recognition and adoption by Greece of the breach of the concession contract occurring before and even after the change of sovereignty over the island in question. The tribunal said:

Greece, having adopted the illegal conduct of Crete in its recent past as autonomous state, is bound, as successor state, to take upon its charge the financial consequences of the breach of the concession contract. Otherwise, the avowed violation of a contract committed by one

---

[56] 1 Guggenheim 474; Castrén, ILC *Ybk* 1969/I, 63; Ruda, ILC *Ybk* 1969/II, 82; Ago, ILC *Ybk* 1969/II, 88.

[57] E.g. 3 Rousseau 393–425; 1 Guggenheim 476–7; 1 O'Connell (1967) 266, 304ff.

[58] Also: Bedjaoui, ILC *Ybk* 1968/II, 115–17; 3 *Répertoire suisse* 1394–403; Cazorla, in Eisemann & Koskenniemi (2000) 707–12.

[59] *Sopron-Köszeg Railway* (1929) 2 RIAA 961, 967.

[60] (1956) 23 ILR 79. Of some interest, though depending on treaty provisions, is *Mavrommatis Jerusalem Concessions* (1925) PCIJ Ser A No 5, 21, 27.

of the two States...with the assent of the other, would, in the event of their merger, have the thoroughly unjust consequence of cancelling a definite financial responsibility and of sacrificing the undoubted rights of a private firm holding a concession to a so-called principle of non-transmission of debts in cases of territorial succession, which in reality does not exist as a general and absolute principle. In this case the Greek Government with good reason commenced by recognising its own responsibility.[61]

The short point remains that territorial change of itself neither cancels nor confers a special status on private rights: they gain no regulatory or other immunity post-succession but they continue subject to the international minimum standard of protection (as to which see chapter 29). Where the private rights involve a substantial foreign control of the economy, some modern exponents of the principle of vested or acquired rights are moved to formulate qualifications concerning 'odious concessions' or 'concessions contrary to the public policy of the successor state',[62] for example a major concession granted on the eve of independence and involving vital resources. Qualified to this degree, the principle would seem to lose its viability.

(D) NATIONALITY[63]

The problem involved is that of the nationality of inhabitants of the transferred territory. In resolving that problem little or no help is to be derived from the categories of the law of state succession.[64]

(i) Nationality as a consequence of territorial transfer

In fact the evidence is overwhelmingly in support of the view that the population follows the change of sovereignty in matters of nationality. At the end of the First World War the peace treaties contained a number of provisions, more or less uniform in content, relating to changes of sovereignty which exhibited all the variations of state succession.[65] Thus Article 4 of the Minorities Treaty signed at Versailles provided as follows:

Poland admits and declares to be Polish nationals *ipso facto* and without the requirements of any formality persons of German, Austrian, Hungarian or Russian nationality who were born in the said territory of parents habitually resident there, even if at the date of the coming into force of the present Treaty they are not themselves habitually resident there.

---

[61] (1956) 23 ILR 79, 92.

[62] Zemanek (1965) 116 Hague *Recueil* 181, 282–9. Also Craven (2007) 43–5, 84–7.

[63] ILC Draft Articles on Nationality of Natural Persons in Relation to the Succession of States, ILC *Ybk* 1999/II(2), 21–3. Also Memorandum by the Secretariat, Nationality in Relation to the Succession of States, A/CN.4/497, 8 March 1999.

[64] Cf Weis, *Nationality and Statelessness in International Law* (2nd edn, 1979) 136, 144; Zimmermann, in Eisemann & Koskenniemi (2000) 611.

[65] UN, *Laws Concerning Nationality* (1954) 586ff. Also: Treaty of Neuilly-sur-Seine, 27 November 1919, 112 BFSP 781, Arts 51–2; Treaty of Lausanne, 24 July 1923, 28 LNTS 11, Arts 30–6.

Nevertheless, within two years after coming into force of the present Treaty, these persons may make a declaration before the competent Polish authorities in the country in which they are resident stating that they abandon Polish nationality, and they will then cease to be considered as Polish nationals. In this connexion a declaration by a husband will cover his wife and a declaration by parents will cover their children under 18 years of age.[66]

The Treaties of St Germain,[67] Trianon,[68] and Paris[69] had similar provisions, except that the Treaties of St Germain and Trianon refer to persons born of parents 'habitually resident or possessing rights of citizenship [*pertinenza–heimatrecht*] as the case may be there'. The precedent value of such provisions is considerable in view of their uniformity and the international character of the deliberations preceding the signature of these treaties. The objection that they give a right of option does not go far, since the option is a later and additional procedure. Only when the option is exercised does the nationality of the successor state terminate: there is no statelessness. The Italian Peace Treaty of 1947 provided that Italian citizens domiciled in territory transferred would become citizens of the transferee; and a right of option was given.[70]

State practice evidenced by the provisions of internal law is to the same effect. The law of the UK has been expressed as follows by McNair:

The normal effect of the annexation of territory by the British Crown, whatever may be the source or cause of the annexation, for instance, a treaty of cession, or subjugation by war, is that the nationals of the State whose territory is annexed, if resident thereon, become British subjects; in practice, however, it is becoming increasingly common to give such nationals an option, either by the treaty of cession or by an Act of Parliament, to leave the territory and retain their nationality.[71]

In view of the state practice it is hardly surprising to find works of authority stating that persons attached to territory change their nationality when sovereignty changes hands.[72] Somewhat surprising is the caution of Weis. In his view:

there is no rule of international law under which the nationals of the predecessor State acquire the nationality of the successor State. International law cannot have such a direct effect, and the practice of States does not bear out the contention that this is inevitably the result of the change of sovereignty. As a rule, however, States have conferred their national-ity on the former nationals of the predecessor State, and in this regard one may say that there

---

[66] Principal Allied and Associated Powers-Poland, Minorities Treaty, 28 June 1919, 225 CTS 412.

[67] Principal Allied & Associated Powers-Austria, Treaty of St Germain-en-Laye, 10 September 1919, 226 CTS 8.

[68] Allied and Associated Powers-Hungary, Treaty of Peace and Protocol and Declaration, 4 June 1920, 6 LNTS 188.

[69] Allied Powers-Roumania, Treaty of Peace, 10 February 1947, 42 UNTS 3, Art 4. Also: *Markt v Prefect of Trent* (1945) 10 ILR 281; Caggiano (1976) 2 *It YIL* 248, 264–71.

[70] Allied Powers-Italy, Treaty of Peace, 10 February 1947, 49 UNTS 4, Art 19.

[71] McNair, 2 *Opinions* 24. Also Parry, *Nationality and Citizenship Laws of the Commonwealth* (1957) 274–5. Cf British Nationality Act 1948 (repealed by the British Nationality Act 1981).

[72] 3 Rousseau 343; 2 Hyde 1090; Harvard Draft, Art 18 (1929) 23 *AJIL Sp Supp* 61.

is, in the absence of statutory provisions of municipal law, a *presumption* of international law that municipal law has this effect.[73]

But if international law can create a presumption it can create a rule: whether it is complied with is not the question, but in fact practice bears out the rule. Variations of practice, and areas of doubt, certainly exist, but they are hardly inimical to the general rule. Some difficulties merely concern modalities of the general rule itself. Thus, the position of nationals of the predecessor state who at the time of the transfer are resident outside the territory the sovereignty of which changes is unsettled. The rule probably is that, unless they have or forthwith acquire a domicile in the transferred territory, they do not acquire the nationality of the successor state.[74] This, it seems, is the British doctrine.[75]

The general principle is that of a substantial connection with the territory concerned by citizenship, residence or family relation to a qualified person. This principle may be a special aspect of the general principle of the effective link.[76] However, it could be argued that for the individuals concerned, at the moment of transfer, the connection with the successor state is fortuitous. Whatever the merits of this, the link, in cases of territorial transfer, has special characteristics. Territory, both socially and legally, is not to be regarded as an empty plot: with obvious geographical exceptions, it connotes population, ethnic groupings, loyalty patterns, national aspirations, a part of humanity, or, if one is tolerant of the metaphor, an organism. To regard a population, in the normal case, as related to particular areas of territory, is not to revert to forms of feudalism but to recognize a human and political reality which underlies modern territorial settlements. Sovereignty denotes responsibility, and a change of sovereignty does not give the new sovereign the right to dispose of the population concerned at

---

[73] Weis (2nd edn, 1979) 143–4. Under the rubric 'Partial succession' he concludes: 'the predecessor state is under an obligation *vis-à-vis* the successor state to withdraw its nationality from the inhabitants of the transferred territory if they acquire the nationality of the successor state. In the absence of explicit provisions of municipal law there exists a presumption of international law that the municipal law of the predecessor state has this effect': ibid, 147–8. A formula involving a presumption as to the effect of municipal law is infelicitous: *inter alia* one cannot be criticized for failure to comply with a presumption. But other authors offer similarly cautious opinions: Graupner (1946) 32 *GST* 87, 92; Jones, *British Nationality Law* (1956) 206; Crawford (1986) 27 *Seoul LJ* 34.

[74] *Slouzak Minority in Teschen (Nationality)* (1940) 11 ILR 179; *Ministry of Home Affairs v Kemali* (1962) 40 ILR 191; *North Transylvania Nationality* (1970) 40 ILR 43, 191. Cf *In re Andries* (1950) 17 ILR 109 (dual nationality); Weis (2nd edn, 1979) 140–4, 149–53; Draft Articles on Nationality of Natural Persons in relation to Succession of States, Arts 20–4, ILC *Ybk* 1997/II(2), 13, 20, 36–42; Blackman (1997–98) 19 *Mich JIL* 1141, 1155–71

[75] McNair, 2 *Opinions* 21–6; Weis (2nd edn, 1979) 140; Fransman, *British Nationality Law* (3rd edn, 2011) 601–2. Parry (1957) 163–4, 275, believes the rule is uncertain. Also *Murray v Parkes* [1942] 2 KB 123.

[76] Cf Secretariat Survey, 14 May 1954, ILC *Ybk* 1954/II, 61: '[t]he opinion is widely held that, in case of change of sovereignty over a territory by annexation, or its voluntary cession by one State to another, the annexing State is obliged to grant its nationality to the inhabitants of the territory concerned who were citizens of the ceding State, at least if they have, at the time of annexation, their permanent residence in the ceded territory. In most instances these questions are settled by treaty'. Also the UN Convention on the Reduction of Statelessness, 30 August 1961, 989 UNTS 175, Art 10.

discretion. The population goes with the territory: on the one hand, it would be unlawful, and a derogation from the grant, for the transferor to try to retain the population as its own nationals (though a right of option is another matter). On the other hand, it would be unlawful for the successor to take any steps which involved attempts to avoid responsibility for conditions on the territory, for example by treating the population as *de facto* stateless. The position is that the population has a 'territorial' or local status, and this is unaffected whether there is a universal or partial successor or whether there is a cession, that is, a 'transfer' of sovereignty, or a relinquishment by one state followed by a disposition by international authority.

In certain cases other considerations arise. Where one of the states concerned claims continuity, retention of the former nationality may be more common, but in the event the result may not be very different than in cases of succession.[77] The question of the legality of population transfer (apart from voluntary exercise of rights of option) may also arise.[78]

(ii) Diplomatic claims and the principle of continuous nationality

In principle the requirement of continuity of nationality between the time of injury and the presentation of the claim (or, in cases of resort to judicial settlement, the making of the award) is not satisfied if the individual concerned suffers a change of nationality as a result of a change of territorial sovereignty.[79] At least one of the arguments used to support the continuity principle, namely that it prevents the injured citizen choosing a protector by a shift of nationality, has no application in such a case. The rule of continuous nationality would have adversely affected the whole citizen population of Tanzania after the voluntary union of Tanganyika and Zanzibar. In some cases of transfer the predecessor and successor states may act jointly in espousing claims on behalf of persons of their nationality successively, but this solution is inapplicable in case of mergers and dismemberment of states. The correct solution in principle

---

[77] *Costa v Military Service Commission of Genoa* (1939) 9 ILR 26; *United States, ex rel Reichel v Carusi*, 157 F.2d 732 (3rd Cir, 1946) 13 ILR 119; *Re Tancredi* (1950) 17 ILR 203; *Secession of Austria* (1954) 21 ILR 175; *Austrian Nationality* (1955) 22 ILR 430; *In re Feiner* (1956) 23 ILR 367; *Austro-German Extradition* (1956) 23 ILR 364 *Koh-i-noor L&C v Koh-i-noor Tužkárna L&C Hardtmuth* (1958) 26 ILR 40, 42. Cf *Austrian Nationality* (1953) 20 ILR 250; *Loss of Nationality (Germany)* (1965) 45 ILR 353. After the breakup of Yugoslavia, the Badinter Commission stated that the consequences of the principle of self-determination might include for 'the members of the Serbian population in Bosnia-Hercegovina and Croatia to be recognised under agreements between the Republics as having the nationality of their choice': *Opinion No 2* (1991) 92 ILR 167, 169.

[78] There is no rule that prevents transfer of populations (such as the 2011 agreement concluded between India and Bangladesh to swap 162 territorial enclaves between the two states: Protocol to the Agreement Concerning the Demarcation of the Land Boundary between India and Bangladesh and Related Matters, Dhaka, 6 September 2011, www.mofa.gov.bd/bd_in/Boundary_Demarcation.pdf). But Ethiopia's forced expulsion of dual Ethiopian–Eritrean nationals in 1992–93 was held to breach international law: Eritrea-Ethiopia Claims Commission, *Civilian Claims* (2004) 26 RIAA 195, 224–30. Cf Henckaerts, *Mass Expulsion in Modern International Law* (1995); Bruce, *Twice a Stranger* (2006).

[79] Wyler, *La règle dite de la continuité de la nationalité dans le contentieux international* (1990) 111–17, and further: chapter 23.

is surely a rule of substitution, putting the successor in charge of claims belonging to the predecessor. This would be consonant with the idea of an effective change of sovereignty.

In *Panevezys–Saldutiskis Railway* the Permanent Court was concerned with an Estonian claim and a Lithuanian counterclaim relating to the property of a company established under the law of the Russian Empire and operating in the territory which in 1918 constituted the new states of Estonia and Lithuania.[80] In 1923 the company became an Estonian company with registered offices in Estonia. Estonia subsequently claimed compensation for assets of the company which Lithuania had seized in 1919; the Court upheld Lithuania's preliminary objection of non-exhaustion of local remedies. Judge van Eysinga (dissenting) referred to the 'inequitable results' of a rule requiring continuity and concluded that it had not been established that the rule could not resist the normal operation of the law of state succession.[81]

The continuous nationality rule was considered by the ILC in its work on diplomatic protection. Article 5 of the ILC Articles of 2006 provides:

1. A State is entitled to exercise diplomatic protection in respect of a person who was a national of that State continuously from the date of injury to the date of the official presentation of the claim. Continuity is presumed if that nationality existed at both these dates.

2. Notwithstanding paragraph 1, a State may exercise diplomatic protection in respect of a person who is its national at the date of the official presentation of the claim but was not a national at the date of injury, provided that the person had the nationality of a predecessor State or lost his or her previous nationality and acquired, for a reason unrelated to the bringing of the claim, the nationality of the former State in a manner not inconsistent with international law.

3. Diplomatic protection shall not be exercised by the present State of nationality in respect of a person against a former State of nationality of that person for an injury caused when that person was a national of the former State of nationality and not of the present State of nationality.[82]

According to this formulation, a change of nationality by reason of state succession would not preclude espousal by the successor state against a third state, but would do so against the predecessor state.

---

[80] (1939) PCIJ Ser A/B No 76.

[81] Ibid, 32–5. Also: Monnier (1962) 8 *AFDI* 65, 68–72; 1 O'Connell (1967) 537–41; Jennings (1967) 121 Hague *Recueil* 323, 476.

[82] ILC *Ybk* 2006/II(2), 35. According to the commentary to Art 5, §(10), the condition to Art 5(2) 'is designed to limit exceptions to the continuous nationality rule mainly to cases involving compulsory imposition of nationality, such as those in which the person has acquired a new nationality as a necessary consequence of factors such as marriage, adoption or the succession of States': ibid, 39. The matter is not dealt with in the 1999 Articles on nationality of persons in relation to succession of states.

4. STATE SUCCESSION: FIELDS OF OPERATION

A common fault of writers is to classify issues primarily as 'succession' and consequently to consider particular issues in isolation from the matrix of rules governing the subject-matter, which might involve, for example, the law of treaties, state responsibility, or the constitution of an international organization. The need to consider problems precipitated by a change of sovereignty in relation to the particular body of legal principles is well illustrated by the law of treaties.

(A) SUCCESSION TO TREATIES: IN GENERAL[83]

It seems to be generally accepted that in cases of 'partial succession', that is, annexation or cession, where the predecessor state is not extinguished, no succession to treaties can occur. Existing treaties of the successor state will apply prima facie to the territories concerned. Other problems should be approached on the basis that the law of treaties is the prime reference and the fact of succession fitted into that context.

When a new state emerges it is not bound by the treaties of the predecessor by virtue of a mandatory rule of state succession. In many instances the termination of a treaty affecting a state involved in territorial changes will be achieved by the normal operation of provisions for denunciation. However, as a matter of general principle a new state, *ex hypothesi* a non-party, is not bound by a treaty, and other parties to a treaty are not bound to accept a new party, as it were, by operation of law.[84]

The rule of non-transmissibility applies both to secession of 'newly independent states' (i.e. to cases of decolonization) and to other appearances of new states by the union or dissolution of states. The distinctions drawn by the ILC and, subsequently, the Vienna Convention on Succession of States in respect of Treaties[85] are not reflected in the practice of states.[86] This is not to deny that considerations of principle and

---

[83] ILC *Ybk* 1950/II, 206–18. For ILA proceedings: ILA, The Effect of Independence on Treaties (1965); ILA, Report of the 53rd Conference (1968) 596; ILA, Report of the 54th Conference (1970); O'Connell, in ILA, The Present State of International Law (1973) 331. Generally: Onory, *La Succession d'états aux traités* (1968); Udokang, *Succession of New States to International Treaties* (1972). Caggiano (1975) 1 It YIL 69; Mériboute, *La Codification de la succession d'états aux traités* (1984); Vagts (1992–93) 3 *Va JIL* 275; Eisemann & Koskenniemi (2000); Craven (2007).

[84] McNair, *Law of Treaties* (1961) 592, 600–1, 629, 655; Sørensen (1968) 294–5, 298–9; Jennings (1967) 121 Hague *Recueil* 323, 442–6; 1 Guggenheim 463; ILC *Ybk* 1970/II, 31–7; ILC *Ybk* 1972/II, 227, 250–4; ILC *Ybk* 1974/II(1), 7–9, 168–9, 211–14. But see Craven (2007) 120–31, 138–9.

[85] 23 August 1978, 1946 UNTS 3. The Swiss Federal Tribunal has recognized the ILC final draft as 'authoritative': *M v Federal Department of Justice and Police* (1979) 75 ILR, 107. Further: Sinclair, *Essays in Honour of Erik Castrén* (1979) 149. Also Badinter Commission, *Opinion No 1* (1991) 92 ILR 162, *Opinion No 9* (1992) 92 ILR 203.

[86] Reports to GA; ILC *Ybk* 1972/II, 250, 286; ILC *Ybk* 1974/II(1), 211, 252. The evidence set forth in the reports does not satisfy the criteria of a rule of customary law. Also *R v Commissioner of Correctional Services, ex parte Fitz Henry* (1976) 72 ILR 63.

policy may call for a different outcome in the case of a union of states (see the Vienna Convention, Articles 31 to 33). However, the distinction between secession and the dissolution of federations and unions is unacceptable, both as a proposition of law and as a matter of principle.

To the general rule of non-transmissibility (the 'clean slate' doctrine) certain important exceptions are said to exist.

(i) Boundary treaties

Many jurists regard boundary treaties as a special case depending on clear considerations of stability in territorial matters. It would seem that the question depends on normal principles governing territorial transfers: certainly the change of sovereignty does not as such affect boundaries.[87] This principle is expressed in the Vienna Convention of 1978 (Article 11). A Chamber of the International Court has referred to the obligation to respect pre-existing boundaries in the event of a state succession.[88]

(ii) 'Objective regimes' and localized treaties in general

A number of writers, including O'Connell[89] and McNair,[90] have taken the view that there is a category of dispositive or localized treaties concerning the incidents of enjoyment of a particular piece of territory in the matter of demilitarized zones, rights of transit, navigation, port facilities, and fishing rights. This category of treaties in their view is transmissible. The subject-matter overlaps considerably with the topic of international servitudes considered elsewhere. Others consider that there is insufficient evidence in either principle or practice for the existence of this exception to the general rule.[91] First, much of the practice is equivocal and may rest on acquiescence. Secondly, the category is difficult to define[92] and it is not clear why the treaties apparently included should be treated in a special way. Supporters of the alleged exception lean on materials which are commonly cited as evidence of an independent concept of state servitudes.[93] However, the Vienna Convention of 1978 provides that a succession of states shall not affect obligations, or rights, 'relating to the use of territory', and 'established by a treaty for the benefit of any territory of a foreign state and considered as attaching to the territories in question' (Article 12). In *Gabčíkovo-Nagymaros* the International Court had to determine whether the relevant Treaty of 1977 between

---

[87] 2 O'Connell (1967) 273; Waldock, ILC *Ybk* 1968/II, 92–3; Bedjaoui, ILC *Ybk* 1968/II, 112–14; Waldock, ILC *Ybk* 1972/II, 44–59; ILC *Ybk* 1972/II, 298–308; ILC *Ybk* 1974/II(1), 196–208.

[88] *Frontier Dispute (Burkina Faso/Mali)*, ICJ Reports 1986 p 554, 566; cf *Guinea-Guinea (Bissau) Maritime Delimitation* (1985) 77 ILR 635, 657. Also: Kaikobad (1983) 54 *BY* 119; Kaikobad (1985) 56 *BY* 49.

[89] 2 O'Connell (1967) 12–23, 231ff.

[90] McNair (1961) 655–64. Also: Zemanek (1965) 161 Hague *Recueil* 181, 239–44; 3 Rousseau 491–4; Sørensen (1968) 297–8; 1 Guggenheim 465. Further: 3 *Répertoire suisse* 1333–4, 1339–40, 1358–92.

[91] E.g. Castrén (1951) 78 Hague *Recueil* 379, 448–9; Jennings (1967) 121 Hague *Recueil* 323, 442.

[92] See the miscellany in McNair (1961) 656–64, 705, 740–2.

[93] *Free Zones of Upper Savoy and the District of Gex* (1932) PCIJ Ser A/B, No 46; *SS Wimbledon* (1923) PCIJ Ser A No 1.

Hungary and Czechoslovakia had survived the dissolution of Czechoslovakia.[94] The Court held that Article 12 'reflects a rule of customary international law' and, further, that the content of the 1977 Treaty indicated that it must be regarded as establishing a territorial regime within the meaning of Article 12.[95]

In fact the 1977 Treaty at stake in that case, although subsequent to the treaty establishing the boundary,[96] could have been regarded as a treaty 'relating to the regime of a boundary' in the sense of Article 11(b) of the 1978 Vienna Convention, if only because it modified the boundary in a minor respect contingent on the functioning of the upstream barrage. If the boundary survives the succession, it is reasonable that provisions which form part of the boundary regime should equally survive. But it was unnecessary for the Court to express a view as to such wider and less certain categories as 'servitudes', and *a fortiori* 'localized treaties', especially where the localization takes the form merely of prior application to the transferred territory.

(iii) Other categories

Most writers deny that other exceptions exist. But some consider that in the case of general multilateral or 'law-making' treaties there is a transmission. O'Connell's view is that in such cases the successor state is obliged by operation of law.[97] However, practice rather indicates that the successor has an *option* to participate in such a treaty in its own right even if this is not expressly envisaged in the final clauses of that treaty.[98] It is probable that the regular acquiescence of states parties to such conventions and of depositaries in such informal participation indicates an *opinio juris*. However, there is some difficulty in producing a definition of general multilateral treaties for this purpose.[99] Common characteristics are the generality of participation allowed for in the conventions themselves, and the primary object of providing a comprehensive code of rules or standards for the particular subject-matter.[100] Recent state practice indicates that successor states will often accept human rights[101] and arms control agreements[102] of their predecessors, although this is arguably contingent on the successor state's consent rather than a rule of automatic succession.[103]

---

[94] Hungary–Czechoslovakia, Treaty concerning the Gabčíkovo-Nagymaros Barrage System, 16 September 1977, 1109 UNTS 211.

[95] ICJ Reports 1997 p 7, 69–72.

[96] Treaty of Peace with Hungary, 15 September 1947, 41 UNTS 135.

[97] 1 O'Connell (1967) 212–29.

[98] Waldock, ILC *Ybk* 1968/II, 130–1, 145–6; Castañeda, ibid, 137; Waldock, ILC *Ybk* 1970/II, 37–60; ILC *Ybk* 1972/II, 254–72; ILC *Ybk* 1974/II(1), 214–36; Indonesian Note in UN Legis Series (1967) 37. Further: the Secretariat studies in ILC *Ybk* 1968/II, 1; ILC *Ybk* 1969/II, 23; ILC *Ybk* 1970/II, 61.

[99] UN Secretariat Memo, A/CN4/150, ILC *Ybk* 1962/II, 106, ch 11.

[100] Jennings (1967) 121 Hague *Recueil* 323, 444.

[101] *Genocide (Bosnia and Herzegovina v Yugoslavia)*, ICJ Reports 1996, 595 (Judge Weeramantry); *Genocide (Bosnia and Herzegovina v Serbia and Montenegro)*, ICJ Reports 2007 p 43; *Croatia v Serbia*, ICJ Reports 2008 p 412. Also: Schachter (1992–93) 33 *Va JIL* 253; Müllerson (1993) 42 *ICLQ* 473; Kamminga (1996) 7 *EJIL* 469. But see Rasulov (2003) 14 *EJIL* 141.

[102] Långström, in Eismann & Koskenniemi (2000) 742, 745.

[103] Ibid, 742, 749–56, 775.

The Vienna Convention of 1978 adopts a fairly restrictive view of participation in multilateral treaties but allows an informal regime of participation for 'newly independent States' on the basis of 'a notification of succession' (see Articles 10, 17 to 23, 31).

In practice problems of succession are usually dealt with by devolution agreements, or by original accession to conventions by new states or unilateral declarations. In 1961 the government of Tanganyika made a declaration containing the following elements: (a) valid bilateral treaties would continue to apply for two years unless abrogated or modified earlier by mutual consent; (b) at this point they would prima facie be regarded as having terminated unless they would have been succeeded to under international law; (c) multilateral treaties would be reviewed individually and decisions taken; (d) during the review period any party to a multilateral treaty which has prior to independence been applied or extended to Tanganyika could, on the basis of reciprocity, rely against Tanganyika on its terms.[104] This approach has been adopted, with variations, by a considerable number of states.[105] Such declarations combine a general recognition that unspecified treaties do survive as a result of the application of rules of customary law with an offer of a grace period in which treaties remain in force on an interim basis without prejudice to the declarant's legal position but subject to reciprocity.[106] Practice based on such declarations suggests that what eventually occurs is either termination or novation as the case may be in respect of the particular treaty.

The practice concerning optional continuance of treaties is not confined to multilateral treaties.[107] The question arises whether the practice in relation to multilateral conventions is to be interpreted on the basis that the new state has the option to participate as of right. The answer is, probably, yes, but this can only be tentative; the practice of continuity of treaties of all types may be explicable simply as a novation of the original treaty by the new state and the other pre-existing contracting party or parties.[108]

(iv) Succession to signature, ratification, and reservations

Within the existing possibilities of inheritance of treaties, there is considerable practice to the effect that a new state can inherit the legal consequences of a ratification by a predecessor of a treaty which is not yet in force. But it is doubtful if a new state can

---

[104] UN Legis Series (1967) 177. Also: Seaton & Maliti, *Tanzania Treaty Practice* (1973); Waldock, ILC *Ybk* 1969/II, 62–8; ILC *Ybk* 1972/II, 241–6; ILC *Ybk* 1974/II(1), 187–93.

[105] E.g. UN Legis Series (1967) 233 (Malagasy); Waldock, Second Report, ILC *Ybk* 1969/II, 62–8; UKMIL (1981) 52 *BY* 384 (Kiribati); UKMIL (1981) 52 *BY* 443 (Suriname).

[106] But see *Molefi v Principal Legal Adviser* (1969) 39 ILR 415, where the Privy Council treated a declaration of this type as an accession to the 1951 Convention Relating to the Status of Refugees.

[107] For the unilateral declarations noted above: Zemanek (1965) 116 Hague *Recueil* 181, 243; ILA, *The Effect of Independence on Treaties* (1965) 99–100, 109, 144ff; UN Legis Series (1967) 37, 42, 218.

[108] UK view on a bilateral treaty with France as affecting Laos: UN Legis Series (1967) 188–9; ILC *Ybk* 1969/II, 60.

inherit the consequences of signature of a treaty which is subject to ratification.[109] A further issue, as yet unsettled, is whether a state continuing the treaties of a predecessor inherits the latter's reservations or is entitled to make reservations and objections of its own.[110] The Vienna Convention of 1978 contains a number of provisions creating privileges in matters of this kind in favour of 'newly independent States' (Articles 18 to 20).

(B) SUCCESSION TO RESPONSIBILITY

The preponderance of authority is in favour of a rule that responsibility for an international delict is extinguished when the responsible state ceases to exist either by annexation or voluntary cession.[111] Such liability is considered 'personal' to the responsible state and remains with that state if it continues to exist after the succession. This reasoning is, however, less cogent in relation to voluntary merger or dissolution. Nor does it apply when a successor state accepts the existence of succession. In the *Lighthouses Arbitration* it was held in connection with one claim that Greece had by conduct adopted an unlawful act by the predecessor state and recognized responsibility.[112]

A related problem is the status of the local remedies rule when, for example, a taking of property has occurred under the law of the previous sovereign. If continuity of the legal system is accepted, does it follow that the successor by providing 'local remedies' is precluded from contesting succession to responsibility after such remedies have been exhausted? The answer is presumably in the negative as a matter of international law, though if the responsible unit or entity is continuous before or after succession as a matter of national law, the remedy will survive, and with it the possibility of a denial of justice claim if the remedy is subsequently denied on discriminatory or other unreasonable grounds.

(C) MEMBERSHIP OF INTERNATIONAL ORGANIZATIONS[113]

The prevailing view is that principles of succession to treaties have no application to membership of international organizations. The position is determined by the

---

[109] ILC *Ybk* 1962/II, 124.

[110] Waldock, ILC *Ybk* 1970/II, 46–52; Gaja (1975) 1 *It YIL* 52.

[111] *Brown* (1923) 6 RIAA 120; *Hawaiian Claims* (1925) 6 RIAA 157, and Hurst (1924) 5 *BY* 163; 1 Guggenheim 474; Monnier (1962) 8 *AFDI* 65; Czaplinski (1990) 28 *Can YIL* 339; Dumberry (2006) 49 *GYIL* 413; Dumberry, *State Succession to International Responsibility* (2007).

[112] *Lighthouses* (1956) 23 ILR 81. The decision rests on the adoption of the wrongful act by Greece. The tribunal referred to 'the vagaries of international practice and the chaotic state of authoritative writings': ibid, 91–2. Further: 7 Verzijl (1974) 219–28; *Minister of Defence, Namibia v Mwandinghi* (1991) 91 ILR 341; ARSIWA, Art 11 & commentary.

[113] Schachter (1948) 25 *BY* 91, 101–9; ILC *Ybk* 1962/II, 101, 106 (§§144–9); 2 Whiteman, 1016–27; Zemanek (1965) 116 Hague *Recueil* 181, 254; Green, in Schwarzenberger (ed), *Law, Justice and Equity* (1967) 152; 2 O'Connell (1967) 183–211; ILC *Ybk* 1968/II, 1; ILC *Ybk* 1969/II, 23; Bühler, in Eisemann & Koskenniemi (2000) 187.

provisions of the constitution of the particular organization. In the case of the United Nations all new states are required to apply for membership. However, the member states by general tacit agreement or acquiescence may treat particular cases in a special way. When an original member of the UN, India, was partitioned in 1947 the General Assembly treated the surviving India as the 'successor' to pre-1947 India and admitted Pakistan as a new member of the UN. The union of Egypt and Syria in 1958 as the United Arab Republic and the dissolution of the union in 1961 resulted in informal consequential changes in membership of the UN rather than formal admission, in the first instance of the United Republic, and in the second instance of the restored Egypt (still called the United Arab Republic) and Syria.[114]

Because a state's membership of an international organization is personal in character, the only way it can be retained is in the case of legal continuity. The form of territorial change is therefore central to the question of succession to membership in an international organization, as evidenced by the contrasting cases of Russia and Serbia-Montenegro.[115] Where, despite one or more secessions, the 'rump' state continues to exist (such as the former USSR) it may assert continued membership of the organization; on the other hand, dissolution presupposes the complete extinction of the predecessor state and all successors must apply for membership as new states.[116] This was the position taken in relation to the former Yugoslavia, and eventually acquiesced in by Serbia.

5. CONCLUSIONS

The territorial transformation of Europe in the aftermath of the collapse of communism (the unification of Germany, dissolution of the USSR, Yugoslavia, and Czechoslovakia) prompted scholars to revisit the question of state succession, largely overlooked since the ILC's attempted codification coinciding with the end of decolonization. The significant number of recent state successions has resulted in an attempted re-engagement with the law of state succession in a different historical and political context, based on the accumulation of relatively consistent state practice over the past two decades.

Although the law of state succession remains politicized and is strongly influenced by interactions with other areas of law, it is possible to discern certain legal rules. In

---

[114] Crawford (2nd edn, 2006) 489, 690, 706.

[115] The UN's general practice is to consider the 'parent' state's membership unaffected by the loss of territory, whereas the new state must apply for membership: Blum (1992) 3 *EJIL* 354, 355–7. Therefore, Eritrea was admitted to the UN as a new member after it seceded from Ethiopia, while the latter continued its prior membership. SC Res 828 (1993); GA Res 47/230, 28 May 1993. Similarly, South Sudan was admitted as a new state, while Sudan's membership was unaffected. SC Res 1999 (2011); GA Res 65/308, 14 July 2011.

[116] Blum (1992) 3 *EJIL* 354, 359; Scharf (1995) 28 *Cornell ILJ* 29, 34–6, 67–8.

the area of state succession with respect to treaties, there has been a slow move towards greater continuity of treaty relations,[117] or at least less by way of unilateral repudiation of the predecessor's treaties. Alongside this has been the consolidation of an obligation to enter into negotiations in good faith where readjustments of legal relations are necessary.[118] Various principles can also be identified in the areas of state succession to public property (with exceptions for special categories of property) and membership in international organizations. Nonetheless, traditional critiques of the law of state succession, which posit it as an area dominated by politically-motivated bilateral agreements rather than generalizable rules, predicated upon the will of 'new' states rather than general principles of automaticity, and dependent on recognition by other states parties, retain their salience.

[117] Schachter (1992–93) 33 *Va JIL* 253, 258.
[118] Müllerson (1993) 42 *ICLQ* 473, 473.

PART VII

STATE JURISDICTION

20

SOVEREIGNTY AND
EQUALITY OF STATES

1. THE CONCEPT OF SOVEREIGNTY[1]

The sovereignty of states represents the basic constitutional doctrine of the law of nations, which governs a community consisting primarily of states having, in principle, a uniform legal personality.[2] If international law exists, then the dynamics of state sovereignty can be expressed in terms of law. If states (and only states) are conceived of as sovereign, then in this respect at least they are equal, and their sovereignty is in a major aspect a relation to other states (and to organizations of states) defined by law.

The corollaries of the sovereignty and equality of states are: (a) a jurisdiction, prima facie exclusive, over a territory and the permanent population living there; (b) a duty of non-intervention in the area of exclusive jurisdiction of other states; and (c) the ultimate dependence upon consent of obligations arising whether from customary law or from treaties. The last of these has certain special applications: in principle the jurisdiction of international tribunals depends on the consent of the parties; membership of international organizations is not obligatory; and the powers of the organs of such organizations to determine their own competence, to take decisions by majority vote, and to enforce decisions depend ultimately on the consent of member states.[3]

The manner in which the law expresses the content of sovereignty varies, and much of the law could be expressed in terms of the co-existence and conflict of sovereignties. Yet another perspective is provided by the notion of sovereignty as discretionary

---

[1] Kelsen (1944) 53 *Yale LJ* 207; Rousseau (1948) 73 Hague *Recueil* 167, 171–253; van Kleffens (1953) 82 Hague *Recueil* 1, 5–130; Fitzmaurice (1957) 92 Hague *Recueil* 1, 48–59; Lauterpacht, *Development* (1958) 297–400; Verzijl, 1 *International Law in Historical Perspective* (1968) 256–92; Lachs (1980) 169 Hague *Recueil* 9, 77–84; Virally (1983) 183 Hague *Recueil* 9, 76–88; Anand (1986) 197 Hague *Recueil* 9; Koskenniemi (1991) 32 *Harv ILJ* 397; Schreuer (1993) 4 *EJIL* 447; Koskenniemi, *From Apology to Utopia* (2005) ch 4; Crawford, in Crawford & Koskenniemi (eds), *Cambridge Companion to International Law* (2012) 117.

[2] *Reparation for Injuries Suffered in the Service of the United Nations*, ICJ Reports 1949 p 174, 177–8.

[3] The qualifier 'ultimately' bears some considerable weight. In practice the sovereignty of most states is sullied by consent—e.g. the consent of UN member states that are not permanent members of the Security Council to be bound by the Council's resolutions. The principle of consent has retained practical content more in some fields than others, and more in certain formal settings—e.g. the jurisdiction of the ICJ (see chapter 32).

power within areas delimited by the law. Thus states alone can confer nationality for purposes of municipal law, delimit the territorial sea, and decide on the necessity for action in self-defence. Yet in all these cases the exercise of the power is conditioned by international law, and compliance with those conditions is not a matter for the acting state alone.

2. SOME USES OF 'SOVEREIGNTY'

(A) THE COMPETENCE OF STATES

The term 'sovereignty' is variously used to describe the legal competence which states have in general, to refer to a particular function of this competence, or to provide a rationale for a particular exercise of this competence. The word itself has a lengthy and troubled history, and is susceptible to multiple meanings and justifications.[4] In its most common modern usage, however, the term is rather descriptive in character, referring in a 'catch-all' sense to the collection of rights held by a state, first in its capacity as the entity entitled to exercise control over its territory and second in its capacity to act on the international plane, representing that territory and its people.[5] Sovereignty is not to be equated with any specific substantive right, still less is it a precondition to state-hood.[6] Thus jurisdiction, including legislative competence over national territory, may be referred to by the terms 'sovereignty' or 'sovereign rights'. Sovereignty may refer to the title to territory or to the rights accruing from the exercise of title. The correlative duty of respect for territorial sovereignty,[7] and the privileges in respect of territorial jurisdiction referred to as sovereign (or state) immunity, are described after the same fashion. In general 'sovereignty' characterizes powers and privileges resting on customary law which are independent of the particular consent of another state.

(B) SOVEREIGNTY AS EQUALITY

A corollary of their independence is the equality of states,[8] historically expressed by the maxim *par in parem non habet imperium*.[9] In international law, the maxim is

---

[4] Koskenniemi (2005) 228–33, 240–5. Many consider the term to be outdated: Charney recommends its eradication as evoking 'the total independence and autonomy of the state … a fundamentalist view that is difficult to debate in light of its emotive baggage': Charney (1997) 91 *AJIL* 394, 395.

[5] Although states are not the only entities with international legal personality, there is certainly a perception that they are paramount: Schreuer (1993) 4 *EJIL* 447, 455. This perception is reaffirmed by scholars of international relations: Abbott (1989) 14 *Yale JIL* 335; Jackson, *Sovereignty* (2007).

[6] Crawford, *Creation of States* (2nd edn, 2005) 32–3.

[7] *Corfu Channel (UK v Albania)*, ICJ Reports 1949 p 4, 35; UN Charter, Art 2(4).

[8] Draft Declaration on the Rights and Duties of States, ILC *Ybk* 1949, 287, Art 3. Cf *SS Lotus* (1927) PCIJ Ser A No 10, 25.

[9] The maxim may be traced back to the 14th-century jurist Bartolus, who wrote '*Non enim una civitas potest facere legem super alteram, quia par in parem non habet imperium*' ('For it is not for one city to make

frequently invoked as a basis for state immunity, at the core of which (in its restricted modern application) is the concept of equality between sovereigns.[10] But equality has further implications: it refers to the juridical conceptualization of the division of power between states. Obviously, the allocation of power and the capacity to project it in reality are different things, which suggests that while all states are equal, some are more equal than others.[11]

But nonetheless formal equality remains and has meaning. When, by legislation or executive decree, a state delimits a fishing zone or the territorial sea, the manner and provenance of the exercise of such power is in the first place a matter for the state. But when it is comes to enforcing the limit vis-à-vis other states, the issue is placed on the international plane. Similarly, the conferral or withdrawal of nationality may lead to a collision of interest between two states as to the right to exercise diplomatic protection. One might conclude that the criterion depends on a distinction between internal competence—no outside authority can annul or prevent the internally valid act of state power—and international responsibility for the consequences of the wrongful exercise of that competence. This distinction certainly has wide application, but it is not absolute in character. Thus, in particular contexts, international law may place restrictions on the 'internal' territorial competence of states as a consequence of treaty obligations, for example, forbidding legislation which discriminates against certain groups among the population. In the case of various territorial privileges, created either by general or local custom or by treaty, other states are permitted to exercise governmental functions, that is, perform sovereign acts, within the territorial domain.

3. THE INTERACTION OF STATES WITH INTERNATIONAL LAW

At this point it may be useful to review some of the ways states interact with international law.

(A) SOVEREIGNTY AND THE APPLICATION OF RULES[12]

(i) The performance of obligations arising from treaties

One of the central canons of the customary international law of treaties is the rule *pacta sunt servanda*, that is, the notion that states must comply with their obligations

---

the law upon another, for an equal has no power over an equal'): Badr, *State Immunity* (1984) 89, citing Bartolus, *Tractatus Repressalium* (1394) Quaestio 1/3, §10.

[10] Kokott, 'States, Sovereign Equality' (2007) *MPEPIL*.

[11] Cf Orwell, *Animal Farm* (1945) 90; and see Simpson, *Great Powers and Outlaw States* (2004).

[12] Fitzmaurice (1953) 30 *BY* 1, 8–18; Fitzmaurice (1957) 92 Hague *Recueil* 1, 49–59; Lauterpacht (1958) 359–67; McNair, *Law of Treaties* (1961) 754–66; Waldock (1962) 106 Hague *Recueil* 1, 159–69; Crawford (1995) 38 *American Behavioural Scientist* 867.

in good faith.[13] No case has yet arisen in which an international court or tribunal repudiated the rule or challenged its validity. From a certain point of view, the rule is axiomatic and self-evident.[14] From another, it is in tension with the concept of sovereignty, in that the obligation to perform (and to be held to account for non-performance) appears to restrain a state's ability to exercise its sovereignty.

In the *Wimbledon* the Permanent Court firmly rejected the argument that a treaty provision could not deprive a state of the sovereign right to apply the law of neutrality to vessels passing through the Kiel Canal. The *SS Wimbledon* was a British-owned steamship time-chartered to a French company. On board was a cargo of Italian munitions destined for the Polish naval base at Danzig. Poland was at war with Russia, a conflict in respect of which Germany had pledged neutrality. For fear that German neutrality would be breached if the ship were allowed passage, the *Wimbledon* was detained and eventually forced to find its way to Danzig through the Denmark Strait, with consequent delays. Britain, France, Italy, and Japan (but not Poland) claimed reparation, asserting that Germany's refusal to grant passage to the *Wimbledon* was contrary to Article 308 of the Treaty of Versailles,[15] requiring Germany to allow passage through the Kiel Canal to all vessels of nations with which it was not at war.

The Court held that the idea that the treaty restrained Germany's sovereign right to impose the law of neutrality on the Kiel Canal was fallacious. The treaty itself was an expression of conduct to which the state consented to be bound. Rather than removing the right to apply the law of neutrality to the Kiel Canal, it created an obligation to exercise that right in a certain way, with the capacity to enter into an agreement giving rise to an internationally binding obligation being itself an attribute of sovereignty.[16]

(ii) Interpretation of treaties

On occasion the International Court has referred to sovereign rights as a basis for a restrictive interpretation of treaty obligations.[17] But under the unitary theory of

---

[13] VCLT, 23 May 1969, 1155 UNTS 331, Art 26. Also: Aust, *Modern Treaty Law and Practice* (2nd edn, 2007) 179–81; Villiger, *Commentary on the 1969 Vienna Convention on the Law of Treaties* (2009) 363–8.

[14] It was one of Kelsen's two candidates for the *grundnorm* of international law: Kelsen, *Reine Rechtslehre* (1934) 129–30; Kelsen (1936) 10 *RITD* 253, 254–6. Also: Rigaux (1998) 9 *EJIL* 325; von Bernstorff, *The Public International Law Theory of Hans Kelsen* (2010) and further: chapter 3.

[15] Treaty of Peace between the Allied and Associated Powers and Germany, 28 June 1919, 225 CTS 188.

[16] (1923) PCIJ Ser A No 1, 25. Further: Feinäugle, 'The *Wimbledon*' (2008) *MPEPIL*. But the principle operates equally in favour of freedom as constraint: cf the view of the International Court on reservations by states to multilateral treaties: *Reservations to the Convention on the Prevention and Punishment of the Crime of Genocide*, ICJ Reports 1951 p 15, 24.

[17] *Wimbledon* (1923) PCIJ Ser A No 1, 24; *Free Zone of Upper Savoy and the District of Gex* (1930) PCIJ Ser A No 24, 12; (1932) PCIJ Ser A/B No 46, 96, 167; *Rights of Access to Danzig Harbour* (1931) PCIJ Ser A/B No 43, 142; *Interpretation of the Statute of Memel* (1932) PCIJ Ser A/B No 49, 294, 313–14; *Interpretation of Peace Treaties with Bulgaria, Hungary and Romania*, ICJ Reports 1950 p 221, 227; *Fisheries (UK v Norway)*, ICJ Reports 1951 p 116, 143; *Anglo-Iranian Oil Company (UK v Iran)*, ICJ Reports 1952 p 93, 105, cf 143 (Judge Read, diss); *Continental Shelf (Libya v Malta)*, ICJ Reports 1985 p 13, 22; *Nuclear Tests (Australia v France)*, ICJ Reports 1974 p 253, 267; ibid, 286 (Judge Gros); 306 (Judge Petrén); 365–6 (Judges Oneyana, Dillard, Jiménez de Aréchaga & Waldock, diss) (on unilateral declarations). Also: Lauterpacht (1949) 26 *BY*

interpretation set out in VCLT Article 31 and customary international law, everything depends on the context, the intention of the parties, and the relevance of other, countervailing, principles such as that of effectiveness. In certain contexts, this application of other canons of interpretation has led to a complete reversal of the restrictive approach, particularly in circumstances where a dispute concerns a state and a private party.[18] Investor-state arbitration tribunals are particularly forward in this respect, often holding that international investment agreements be interpreted either neutrally[19] or for the benefit of the private investor.[20]

(iii) Presumptions and burdens

Many areas of international law are uncertain or contain principles which do not admit of easy application to concrete issues. Thus much could turn on the answer to the question whether there is a presumption in favour of sovereignty. In another form the issue is whether, in case of doubt as to the mode of application of rules or in case of an absence of rules, the presumption is that states have legal competence or not. In the *Lotus* the Court decided the issue of jurisdiction on the basis that 'restrictions upon the independence of States cannot be presumed'.[21] But yet again there is no general rule, and in judicial practice issues are approached empirically. Indeed, a general presumption of either kind would lead to inconvenience or abuse. The context of a problem will determine the incidence of the burdens of proof of a given issue: whether that produces a burden of proving a restriction on sovereignty will vary. The 'jurisdictional geography' of the problem may provide useful indications: more than one sovereignty may be involved. Thus in *Asylum* the Court stressed the fact that diplomatic asylum involves a derogation from sovereignty as represented by the normally exclusive jurisdiction of the territorial state.[22]

(B) SOVEREIGNTY AND INTERNATIONAL ORGANIZATIONS[23]

The institutional aspects of organizations of states result in an actual, as opposed to a formal, qualification of the principle of sovereign equality. In an organization subject

---

48; Koskenniemi (2005) 253–4; Linderfalk, *On the Interpretation of Treaties* (2007) 280–4; Gardiner, *Treaty Interpretation* (2008) 60–2.

[18] Crema (2010) 21 *EJIL* 681, 691.

[19] E.g. *Mondev International Ltd v United States of America* (2002) 125 ILR 98, 123. Further: Dolzer & Schreuer, *Principles of International Investment Law* (2008) 62; Amerasinghe, *Jurisdiction of Specific International Tribunals* (2009) 438.

[20] *Tradax Hellas SA v Albania* (1996) 5 ICSID Reports 43, 68–9; *Fraport AG Frankfurt Airport Services Worldwide v Republic of the Philippines*, 16 August 2007, §80, available at www.italaw.com.

[21] Cf *Lake Lanoux (France v Spain)* (1957) 12 RIAA 281, 306. Further: *De Pascale* (1970) 40 ILR 250, 256.

[22] *Asylum (Columbia/Peru)*, ICJ Reports 1950 p 266, 274–5.

[23] Van Kleffens (1953) 82 Hague *Recueil* 1, 107–26; Bourquin, *L'Etat souverain et l'organisation internationale* (1959); Broms, *The Doctrine of Equality of States as Applied in International Organizations* (1959); Korowicz, *Organisations internationales et souveraineté des états membres* (1961); Waldock (1962) 106 Hague *Recueil* 1, 20–38, 171–2; Lachs (1980) 169 Hague *Recueil* 9, 141–2; Morgenstern, *Legal Problems of*

to majority or weighted voting, organs may be permitted to take decisions, and even to make binding rules, without the express consent of all member states. But on joining the organization each member consented in advance to the institutional aspects, and thus in a formal way the principle that obligations can only arise from the consent of states and the principle of sovereign equality are satisfied.

On the other hand, international organizations can evolve and may assume roles very different to that initially contemplated. In the case of the UN the organs have interpreted the Charter in accordance with the principles of effectiveness and implied powers at the expense, it may seem, of Article 2(1) and (7).[24] In *Certain Expenses*, the Court held that in the absence of any particular procedure to determine the validity of the acts of the UN's institutions, each of them must determine its own jurisdiction.[25] Some 40 years later, this position arguably enabled the Security Council to pass several 'legislative' resolutions, using its Chapter VII powers.[26] These resolutions require states to enact particular domestic laws, thereby supplanting the recommendatory role of the General Assembly, the treaty-making process and the principle of consent.[27] True, the Security Council has always had the power to bind UN members to the point of overriding other treaty obligations,[28] but legislative resolutions require members to respond to a general phenomenon (the financing of terrorism, the transport of nuclear weapons) rather than a specific situation involving a particular country or region. That is at odds with the original conception of the Security Council as a force for the maintenance of world peace, not the alteration of world order.[29]

If an organization encroaches on the domestic jurisdiction of members to a substantial degree the structure may approximate to a federation. Given the modern conception of the relationship between states and international organizations, such a position seems inherently unlikely, and in any event, the consent-based conception of this relationship precludes the argument that state sovereignty is under threat from some form of overarching 'world government'. Pending an (unlikely) revolution, 'world government' is an essentially decentralized enterprise, something international law provides because states have accepted it: it is the government we have when we are not having *a* government.

International Organizations (1986) 46–68; Amerasinghe, *Principles of the Institutional Law of International Organizations* (2nd edn, 2005) 48; Duxbury, *The Participation of States in International Organisations* (2011) 166–7.

[24] Simma (ed), *The Charter of the United Nations* (2nd edn, 2002) 149–76; and further: chapter 7.

[25] *Certain Expenses of the United Nations (Article 17, paragraph 2, of the Charter)*, ICJ Reports 1962 p 151, 162. Also *Reparation for Injuries*, ICJ Reports 1962 p 174, 185.

[26] SC Res 1373 (2001) and 1540 (2004).

[27] On the scope and potential limitations of these resolutions: Talmon (2005) 99 *AJIL* 175; Bianchi (2006) 17 *EJIL* 881; Hinojosa-Martinez (2008) 57 *ICLQ* 333. Also Koskenniemi (1995) 6 *EJIL* 325.

[28] UN Charter, Arts 25, 39, 41–2, 103.

[29] E.g. *Legal Consequences for States of the Continued Presence of South Africa in Namibia (South West Africa) notwithstanding Security Council Resolution 276 (1970)*, ICJ Reports 1971 p 16, 294 (Judge Fitzmaurice, diss).

(C) ARTICLE 2(7) OF THE UN CHARTER: DOMESTIC JURISDICTION[30]

Matters within the competence of states under general international law are said to be within the reserved domain, the domestic jurisdiction, of states. But this is tautologous, and in practice the category of domestic jurisdiction is not very fruitful. As a source of confusion, however, it deserves some consideration.

(i) Original intent

The advent of international organizations with powers to settle disputes on a political basis caused some states to favour express reference to the reserved domain in order to reinforce state sovereignty. Article 15(8) of the League of Nations Covenant provided, in relation to disputes submitted to the Council as distinct from arbitration or judicial settlement:

If the dispute between the parties is claimed by one of them, and is found by the Council, to arise out of a matter which by international law is solely within the domestic jurisdiction of that party, the Council shall so report, and shall make no recommendation as to its settlement.

In making a political settlement the Council might well touch on the reserved domain, since this contains matters frequently the cause of disputes, and the need to write in the legal limit of action was apparent. During the drafting of the UN Charter similar issues arose, and the result was Article 2(7):

Nothing contained in the present Charter shall authorize the United Nations to intervene in matters which are essentially within the domestic jurisdiction of any State or shall require the Members to submit such matters to settlement under the present Charter; but this principle shall not prejudice the application of enforcement measures under Chapter VII.

Certain contrasts with Article 15(8) of the Covenant will be apparent. There is no reference to international law, the reference is to matters 'essentially' within the domestic jurisdiction, and there is no designation of the authority which is to have the power to qualify particular matters. Article 2(7) of the Charter was intended to be flexible and non-technical. At the same time the restriction was meant to be comprehensive, the use of the formula 'essentially within' stemming from the wide implications of the economic and social provisions of the Charter (Chapter IX).

(ii) The practice of the political organs

But these intentions have in practice worked against each other. The flexibility of the provision, and the assumption in practice that it does not override other, potentially conflicting, provisions have resulted in the erosion of the domain of domestic

---

[30] Kelsen, *The Law of the United Nations* (1950) 769–91; Verdross, *Mélanges offerts à Charles Rousseau* (1974) 267. For the practice of UN organs: Rajan, *The United Nations and Domestic Jurisdiction* (2nd edn, 1961); Higgins, *Development* (1963) 58–130; Nolte, in 1 Simma (2nd edn, 2002) 148; Oxman, 'Jurisdiction of States' (2007) *MPEPIL*.

jurisdiction, although the drafters intended its reinforcement. Moreover, the word 'intervene' has been approached empirically. Discussion, recommendations in general terms, and even resolutions addressed to particular states have not been inhibited by the formulation of Article 2(7).[31]

Ultimately, the early debates about the meaning of the term 'to intervene' in the context of Article 2(7) have lost their importance. Over time, it has been proved that the provision does not serve as an effective restraint on the activities of the UN.[32] This is not due to a narrow interpretation of the term 'intervention'[33] but to a narrowing of those things which are seen as solely within the domestic jurisdiction of states. As the Permanent Court already said in *Nationality Decrees*:

The question whether a certain matter is or is not solely within the jurisdiction of a State is an essentially relative question; it depends on the development of international relations.[34]

The implications are far-reaching:

This means that the concept of 'domestic jurisdiction' does not denote specific areas which are clearly defined, irreducible or in any way inherently removed from the international sphere. It rather circumscribes areas which, taking into account the situation at issue, are not even prima facie affected by rules of international law...In order to remove an area from the sphere of domestic jurisdiction, it is sufficient that this area be regulated by international law only in certain respects.[35]

UN organs have taken action on a wide range of topics dealing with the relations of governments to their own people. Resolutions on breaches of human rights, the right of self-determination, and democratic governance have been adopted regularly. If the organ concerned felt that the acts complained of were contrary to the purposes and principles of the Charter and also that the issue was 'endangering international peace and security', a resolution was passed. Certain issues are regarded as inherently matters of international concern, without the need for express reference to any threat to international peace and security.[36] The Security Council initially adopted a resolution concerning apartheid only partly on the basis that the situation 'constitutes a potential threat to international peace and security'.[37] But over time the potential has become actual. In 1992, the President of the Security Council stated that those economic, social, humanitarian, and ecological factors that could *lead* to a threat to peace

---

[31] *Nationality Decrees in Tunis and Morocco* (1923) PCIJ Ser B No 4, 7; *Peace Treaties*, ICJ Reports 1950 p 65, 70–1; Lauterpacht (1958) 270–2.

[32] Goodrich, Hambro & Simons, *Charter of the United Nations* (3rd edn, 1969) 68.

[33] Which has been interpreted broadly: *Military and Paramilitary Activities in and Against Nicaragua (Nicaragua v US)*, ICJ Reports 1986 p 14, 107; Abi-Saab, in Wellens (ed), *International Law* (1998) 230–3; Conforti, *The Law and Practice of the United Nations* (3rd edn, 2005) 143–5.

[34] (1923) PCIJ Ser B No 4, 24.

[35] Nolte, in 1 Simma (2nd edn, 2002) 157.

[36] On the concept of international concern: Higgins (1963) 77–81.

[37] SC Res 282 (1970). Note that this and other SC resolutions on the same subject were adopted under Chapter VI.

and security were *themselves* threats that could justify Security Council action under Chapter VII.[38]

As a separate notion in general international law, the reserved domain is mysterious only because many have failed to see that it stands for a tautology. However, if a matter is prima facie within the reserved domain because of its character and the issue presented in the normal case, then certain presumptions against any restriction on that domain may be created. Thus the imposition of customs tariffs is prima facie unrestricted by international law, whilst the introduction of forces into another state is not prima facie an internal matter for the sending state.[39] As with other issues associated with sovereignty, domestic jurisdiction has content as presumption rather than rule.[40]

---

[38] S/23500 (1992) §3; Talmon (2005) 99 *AJIL* 175, 180.

[39] See, however, the opinion of Judge Lauterpacht in *Certain Norwegian Loans (France v Norway)*, ICJ Reports 1957 p 9, 51–2.

[40] For the decline of the plea of domestic jurisdiction as a preliminary plea before international courts and tribunals: *Interhandel (Switzerland v US)*, Preliminary Objections, ICJ Reports 1959 p 6; *Peace Treaties*, ICJ Reports 1950 p 65, 70–1. Also: Nolte, in 1 Simma (2nd edn, 2002) 159; Tams, 'Interhandel Case' (2007) *MPEPIL*.

21

JURISDICTIONAL COMPETENCE

1. OVERVIEW[1]

Jurisdiction is an aspect of sovereignty: it refers to a state's competence under international law to regulate the conduct of natural and juridical persons. The notion of regulation includes the activity of all branches of government: legislative, executive, and judicial. Although the state is conceived in international law as a single unit, nonetheless for the purposes of analysing jurisdiction and its limits some distinctions are usually made. On the one hand is the power to make laws, decisions or rules (*prescriptive* jurisdiction); on the other is the power to take executive or judicial action in pursuance of or consequent on the making of decisions or rules (respectively *enforcement* or *adjudicative* jurisdiction).[2]

The starting-point in this part of the law is the presumption that jurisdiction (in all its forms) is territorial, and may not be exercised extra-territorially without some specific basis in international law. However, the territorial theory has been refined in

---

[1] Generally: Mann (1964) 111 Hague *Recueil* 1; Jennings (1967) 121 Hague *Recueil* 323, 515–26; Akehurst (1972–73) 46 *BY* 145; Mann, *Studies in International Law* (1973) 1; Bowett (1982) 53 *BY* 1; Schachter (1982) 178 Hague *Recueil* 240; Rosenthal & Knighton, *National Laws and International Commerce* (1982); Lowe, *Extraterritorial Jurisdiction* (1983); Mann (1984) 186 Hague *Recueil* 11; Meessen (1984) 78 *AJIL* 783; Lange & Born (eds), *The Extraterritorial Application of National Laws* (1987); 1 *Restatement Third* §§401–33; Neale & Stephens, *International Business and National Jurisdiction* (1988); Stern (1992) 38 *AFDI* 239; Gilbert (1992) 63 *BY* 415; Meessen (ed), *Extra-territorial Jurisdiction in Theory and Practice* (1996); O'Keefe (2004) 2 *JICJ* 735; Oxman, 'Jurisdiction of States' (2007) *MPEPIL*; Ryngaert, *Jurisdiction in International Law* (2008); Simma & Müller, in Crawford & Koskenniemi (eds), *Cambridge Companion to International Law* (2012) 134. On the developing area of jurisdiction over the Internet: Wilske & Schiller (1997) 50 *Fed Comm LJ* 117; Reidenberg (2004–5) 153 *U Penn LR* 1951; Kohl, *Jurisdiction and the Internet* (2007); Schultz (2008) 19 *EJIL* 799.

[2] On adjudicative jurisdiction (also referred to as *judicial* or *curial* jurisdiction): Akehurst (1972–73) 46 *BY* 145, 152–78; Schachter (1982) 178 Hague *Recueil* 9, 244–9; 1 *Restatement Third* §§401, 421–33; Cassese (2002) 13 *EJIL* 853, 858; Oxman, 'Jurisdiction of States' (2007) *MPEPIL*. This refers to the competence of a municipal court to sit in judgment over a foreign national and may be better seen as a manifestation of prescriptive jurisdiction: the application of municipal law by the court is, in effect, the actualization of prescription, though the carrying out of any judgment or sentence is an expression of enforcement jurisdiction: O'Keefe (2004) 2 *JICJ* 735, 737. But the different elements may be difficult to separate out in this way.

the light of experience and what amounts to extra-territorial jurisdiction is to some extent a matter of appreciation. If there is a cardinal principle emerging, it is that of genuine connection between the subject-matter of jurisdiction and the territorial base or reasonable interests of the state in question.[3]

It should be stressed that this sufficiency of grounds for jurisdiction is normally considered relative to the rights of other states.[4] There is no assumption (even in criminal cases) that individuals or corporations will be regulated only once, and situations of multiple jurisdictional competence occur frequently. In such situations there is no 'natural' regulator and the consequences of multiple laws applying to the same transaction are managed rather than avoided—double taxation being a case in point.[5]

2. PRESCRIPTIVE JURISDICTION OVER CRIMES[6]

(A) GENERAL BASES OF JURISDICTION

The discussion which follows concerns the general principles for determining whether a state may prescribe acts as criminal under municipal law. The question emerged as a distinct one only after about 1870,[7] and the appearance of clear principles has been retarded by the prominence in the sources of municipal decisions, which exhibit empiricism and adherence to national policies. The early structure of prescriptive criminal jurisdiction was provided by the Permanent Court in the *SS Lotus*. That case concerned a collision on the high seas between a French steamer and a Turkish collier in which the latter sank and Turkish crew members and passengers lost their lives. The French steamer having put into port in Turkey for repairs, the officers of the watch were tried and convicted of involuntary manslaughter. On the question of jurisdiction in general the Permanent Court said:

---

[3] Cf the doctrine stated in *Nottebohm (Liechtenstein v Guatemala)*, ICJ Reports 1955 p 4 (further: chapter 23); *Kingdom of Greece v Julius Bär and Co* (1956) 23 ILR 195; and the statements in *Application of the Convention of 1902 Governing the Guardianship of Infants (Netherlands v Sweden)*, ICJ Reports 1958 p 55, 109 (Judge Moreno Quintana), 135–6 (Judge Winiarski, diss), 145 (Judge Córdova, diss), 155 (Judge ad hoc Offerhaus, diss).

[4] Thus jurisdiction may be exercised over stateless persons or over non-nationals by agreement with their state of nationality. Cf European Agreement for the Prevention of Broadcasts Transmitted from Stations outside National Territories, 22 January 1965, 634 UNTS 239.

[5] E.g. OECD Model Tax Convention on Income and Capital (8th edn, 2010); UN Model Double Taxation Convention between Developed and Developing Countries, ST/ESA/PAD/SER.E/21 (2001).

[6] Fitzmaurice (1957) 92 *Hague Recueil* 2, 212–17; Mann (1964) 111 Hague *Recueil* 1, 82ff; Jennings (1957) 33 *BY* 146; Fawcett, (1962) 38 *BY* 181; Harvard Research (1935) 29 *AJIL Supp* 439; Higgins, *Problems and Process* (1994) ch 4; Ryngaert (2008); Oxman, 'Jurisdiction of States' (2007) *MPEPIL*.

[7] An early *cause célèbre* was *R v Keyn (The Franconia)* (1878) 2 Ex D 63, which concerned criminal jurisdiction over the German captain of a German merchant ship which collided with a British vessel in the UK territorial sea. The Court denied jurisdiction (on a vote of 8–7), a decision quickly reversed by statute: Territorial Waters Jurisdiction Act 1878. Further: Crawford (1980) 51 *BY* 1, 48–61.

Far from laying down a general prohibition to the effect that States may not extend the application of their laws and the jurisdiction of their courts to persons, property or acts outside their territory, [international law] leaves them in this respect a wide measure of discretion which is only limited in certain cases by prohibitive rules; as regards other cases, every State remains free to adopt the principles which it regards as best and most suitable.[8]

This passage has been much criticized.[9] Its emphasis on plenary state discretion is contradicted by the approach of the Court in *Anglo-Norwegian Fisheries*[10] and *Nottebohm*,[11] which concerned comparable competences of states, respectively, to delimit the territorial sea and to confer nationality on individuals: we may call them regulatory competences. Following *Arrest Warrant*,[12] there are hints that it has been reversed: if a state wishes to project its prescriptive jurisdiction extra-territorially, it must find a recognized basis in international law for doing so. This shift in focus is, however, largely cosmetic, and in general the Permanent Court's statement that 'all that can be required of a State is that it should not overstep the limits which international law places upon its jurisdiction; within these limits, its title to exercise jurisdiction rests in its sovereignty' remains correct.[13]

(i) The territorial principle

The principle that the courts of the place where the crime is committed may exercise jurisdiction is universally recognized. It is an application of the essential territoriality of sovereignty, the sum of legal competences which a state has. In the case of crime, the principle has a number of practical advantages, including the convenience of the forum and the presumed involvement of the interests of the state where the crime was committed. The territorial principle has been given an extensive application. In the first place, there is *subjective* territoriality, which creates jurisdiction over crimes commenced within the state even if completed or consummated abroad.[14] Generally accepted and often applied is the *objective* territorial principle, according to which jurisdiction is founded when any essential constituent element of a crime is consummated on the forum state's territory. The classic illustration is the firing of a gun across a border causing death on the territory of the forum, but the principle can be employed

---

[8] (1927) PCIJ Ser A No 10, 19.

[9] E.g. Brierly (1936) 58 Hague *Recueil* 1, 146–8, 183–4; Basdevant (1936) 58 Hague *Recueil* 471, 594–7; Fitzmaurice (1957) 92 Hague *Recueil* 1, 56–7; Lauterpacht, 1 *International Law* (1970) 488–9; Higgins, *Problems and Process* (1994) 76–7; Cameron, *The Protective Principle of International Criminal Jurisdiction* (1994) 319; Ryngaert (2008) 22–6. Further: Opinion of the Inter-American Juridical Committee, 23 August 1996, 35 ILM 1329.

[10] *Fisheries (UK v Norway)*, ICJ Reports 1951 p 116, 131–4.

[11] ICJ Reports 1955 p 4, 20. Also chapter 23.

[12] *Arrest Warrant of 11 April 2000 (Democratic Republic of the Congo v Belgium)*, ICJ Reports 2002 p 3, 78 (Judges Higgins, Kooijmans & Buergenthal), 169 (Judge ad hoc van den Wyngaert).

[13] *Lotus* (1927) PCIJ Ser A No 10, 19.

[14] Harvard Research (1935) 29 *AJIL Supp* 439, 480, 484–7; *The Tennyson* (1918) 45 *JDI* 739; *Public Prosecutor v DS* (1958) 26 ILR 209; *State of Arizona v Willoughby*, 862 P.2d 1319 (Az Sup Ct, 1995).

to found jurisdiction in cases of conspiracy,[15] violation of antitrust[16] and immigration laws[17] by activity abroad, and in many other fields of policy.[18] The effect of the two principles combined is that whenever the constituent elements of a crime occur across an interstate boundary both states have jurisdiction.

The objective principle received general support in the *Lotus*; what was controversial was its application to collisions in international waters. France contended that the flag state alone had jurisdiction over acts performed on board on the high seas. Turkey argued, *inter alia*, that vessels on the high seas were to be considered part of the territory of the flag state. By the casting vote of the President, the Court decided that Turkey had not acted in conflict with the principles of international law by exercising criminal jurisdiction. The basis of the majority view (with which Judge Moore concurred) was the principle of objective territorial jurisdiction. The principle was familiar but to apply it the Court had to assimilate the Turkish vessel to Turkish national territory.[19] This crucial step did not attract a majority, and is out of line with subsequent developments.

(ii) The nationality principle

Nationality, as a mark of allegiance and an aspect of sovereignty, is also generally recognized as a basis for jurisdiction over extra-territorial acts.[20] The application of the principle may be extended by reliance on residence[21] and other connections as

---

[15] *Board of Trade v Owen* [1957] AC 602, 634 (Lord Tucker); *R v Cox* [1968] 1 All ER 410, 413; *DPP v Doot* [1973] AC 807, esp 817 (Lord Wilberforce); *DPP v Stonehouse* [1977] 2 All ER 909, 916 (Lord Diplock); *Liangsiripraset v United States* [1991] 1 AC 225. Under US law, conspiracy can be seen as either an inchoate or independent crime, allowing the protective principle and effects doctrine to found jurisdiction independently: *Ford v United States*, 273 US 593 (1927); *Iannelli v United States*, 420 US 770 (1975); *United States v Winter*, 509 F.2d 975 (5th Cir, 1975); *United States v Baker*, 609 F.2d 134 (5th Cir, 1980); *United States v Ricardo*, 619 F.2d 1124 (5th Cir, 1980); *United States v Mann*, 615 F.2d 669 (5th Cir, 1980); *United States v DeWeese*, 352 F.2d 1267 (5th Cir, 1980); *United States v Wright Barker*, 784 F.2d 161 (3rd Cir, 1986); *United States v Mendez-Casarez*, 624 F.3d 233 (5th Cir, 2010). Further: 18 USC §371. Generally: Blackmore (2006) 17 *CLF* 71; Ryngaert (2009) 9 *Int Crim LR* 187, 194–7.

[16] *United States v Aluminium Company of America*, 148 F.2d 416 (2nd Cir, 1945). In US antitrust cases wide extension of the territorial principle might be explained by, though it is not expressed in terms of, a principle of protection. It can also be described in terms of the effects doctrine: Ryngaert (2008) 76–7. At length: Ryngaert, *Jurisdiction over Antitrust Violations in International Law* (2008).

[17] Cf *Naim Molvan v AG for Palestine* [1948] AC 351.

[18] The European approach is notable; as soon as one of the constituent elements of an offence is committed in a state's territory, the state will ordinarily have jurisdiction: Ryngaert (2009) 9 *Int Crim LR* 187, 197–202 (review of France, Germany, the Netherlands, and Belgium).

[19] (1927) PCIJ Ser A No 10, 23.

[20] Ibid, 92 (Judge Moore); Harvard Research (1935) 29 *AJIL Supp* 519; Jennings (1957) 33 *BY* 146, 153; Sarkar (1962) 11 *ICLQ* 446, 456–61. See also *United States v Baker*, 136 F.Supp 546 (SDNY, 1955); *Re Gutierrez* (1957) 24 ILR 265; *Weiss v Inspector-General* (1958) 26 ILR 210; *Public Prosecutor v Günther B and Manfred E* (1970) 71 ILR 247; *Passport Seizure* (1972) 73 ILR 372; *Greek National Military Service* (1973) 73 ILR 606; UKMIL (1986) 57 *BY* 487, 561; *Al-Skeini v Secretary of State for Defence* [2008] 1 AC 153. Also Ergec, *La Compétence extraterritoriale à la lumiére du contentieux sur le gazoduc Euro-Sibérien* (1984) 53–68; Ryngaert (2008) 88–92.

[21] E.g. Terrorism Act 2000 (UK), ss63B, 63C.

evidence of allegiance owed by aliens,[22] and also by ignoring changes of nationality.[23] For example the UK legislature has conferred jurisdiction on its courts in respect of, *inter alia*, treason,[24] murder,[25] bigamy,[26] soccer hooliganism,[27] child sexual abuse,[28] and breaches of the Official Secrets Acts[29] wherever committed by British nationals or residents.

The territorial and nationality principles (as well as the increasing incidence of dual nationality) create parallel jurisdictions and possible double jeopardy, and many states place limitations on the nationality principle,[30] for example, by confining it to serious offences.[31] But such limitations are not required by international law.[32] Nationality provides the primary criterion for criminal acts in locations such as Antarctica, where the 'territorial' criterion is not generally recognized.[33]

For nationality jurisdiction, it is often asserted that the person over whom the state purports to exercise its prescriptive jurisdiction must have been a national at the time of the offence. Otherwise, it is argued, a violation of the principle of *nullum crimen sine lege* could occur.[34] However, state practice is varied, with some states providing for nationality jurisdiction over persons who subsequently acquire their nationality.[35]

---

[22] *Public Prosecutor v Drechsler* (1946) 13 ILR 73; *Re Penati* (1946) 13 ILR 74; *In re Bittner* (1949) 16 ILR 95; cf *DPP v Joyce* [1946] AC 347; *Re P (GE) (an infant)* [1964] 3 All ER 977.

[23] *In re Mittermaier* (1946) 13 ILR 69; *In re SS Member Ahlbrecht* (1947) 14 ILR 196, 200–1; *Ram Narain v Central Bank of India* (1951) 18 ILR 207.

[24] Treason Act 1351, sII; further: *R v Lynch* [1903] 1 KB 444; *R v Casement* [1917] 1 KB 98; Lew (1978) 27 *ICLQ* 168.

[25] Offences Against the Person Act 1861, s9.

[26] Ibid, s57.

[27] Football Spectators Act 1989, s22.

[28] Sexual Offences Act 2003, s72, Schedule 2.

[29] Official Secrets Act 1989, s15.

[30] Harvard Research (1935) 29 *AJIL Supp 439*, 519; Ryngaert (2008) 88–91.

[31] E.g. UKMIL (2006) 77 *BY* 597, 756. See also Ryngaert (2008) 89. Naturally, this will depend on the definition of 'serious': cf Misuse of Drugs Act (Singapore) ss8A, 33, 33A, Schedules 2 and 4.

[32] Ryngaert (2008) 89. The practice of limiting the use of nationality jurisdiction to serious offences is largely common law in origin, with civil law countries applying a more expansive approach: e.g. Bosnia/Herzegovina Criminal Code, Art 12(2) ('The criminal legislation of Bosnia and Herzegovina shall be applied to a citizen of Bosnia and Herzegovina who, outside the territory of Bosnia and Herzegovina, perpetrates a criminal offence').

[33] Antarctic Treaty, 1 December 1959, 402 UNTS 71, Art VIII(1) and e.g. Antarctic Act 1994 (UK), s21. The same situation subsists with respect to criminal jurisdiction on the International Space Station, though the governing instrument also provides for subsidiary territorial and passive personality jurisdiction in certain cases: Agreement Concerning Cooperation on the Civil International Space Station, 29 January 1998, TAIS 12927, Art 22. Further: Sinha (2004) 30 *J Space L* 85. The position is not replicated with respect to the earlier Treaty on Principles Governing the Activities of States in the Exploration and Use of Outer Space, Including the Moon and Other Celestial Bodies, 27 January 1967, 610 UNTS 205: Art 8 provides that when a state party launches an object into outer space, it retains jurisdiction over that object and over any personnel—a species of flag state jurisdiction.

[34] O'Keefe (2004) 2 *JICJ* 735, 742–3.

[35] E.g. Swedish Penal Code, ch 2, s2. Further: Harvard Research (1935) 29 *AJIL* 439, 535; Ryngaert (2008) 88–9.

(iii) The passive personality principle[36]

If the nationality head of jurisdiction may be characterized as one of 'active personality', the reverse of the coin is 'passive personality'. According to this principle aliens may be punished for acts abroad harmful to nationals of the forum. This is considerably more controversial, as a general principle, than the territorial and nationality principles. In *Cutting* a Mexican court exercised jurisdiction in respect of the publication by a US citizen in a Texas newspaper of matter defamatory of a Mexican citizen. The court applied the passive nationality principle among others. This led to diplomatic protests from the US, although the outcome was inconclusive.[37]

In the *Lotus*, the Turkish penal code provided for punishment of acts abroad by foreigners against Turkish nationals; in effect it was a comprehensive exercise of passive personality jurisdiction. The Court declined to assess the law as such. The question was whether the specific factual situation fell within Turkish jurisdiction or not;[38] it held that it did, invoking the protective principle.[39] Judge Moore, in a separate opinion, agreed with the majority as to the outcome but expressly rejected the protective principle.[40]

The passive personality principle has been much criticized. One early complaint was that it served no wider goal of criminal justice: it did not correspond to a domestic conceptualization of jurisdiction, would not close an enforcement gap and lacked any social aim of repression.[41] There is also concern that it could expose individuals to a large number of jurisdictions.[42] Such objections have not, however, prevented the development of something approaching a consensus on the use of passive personality in certain cases, often linked to international terrorism.[43] Moreover, *aut dedere aut iudicare* provisions in most criminal law treaties authorize the use of passive personality jurisdiction as between states parties.[44]

---

[36] Jennings (1957) 33 *BY* 146, 154; Sarkar (1962) 11 *ICLQ* 446, 461; Harvard Research (1953) 29 *AJIL Supp* 439, 443, 445, 573, 579; Mann (1964) 111 Hague *Recueil* 1, 40–1; Akehurst (1972–73) 46 *BY* 145, 162–6; Watson (1993) 28 *Texas ILJ* 1; Higgins (1994) 65–9; Ryngaert (2008) 92–6. Also *United States v Yunis (No 2)*, 681 F.Supp 896, 901–3 (DDC, 1990).

[37] Moore, 2 *Digest* 228–42; *FRUS* (1887) 751–867.

[38] (1927) PCIJ Ser A No 10, 15.

[39] Lauterpacht has stated that in the *Lotus* the Court 'declared the exercise of such protective jurisdiction to be consistent with international law': (1947) 9 *CLJ* 330, 343. Cf Verzijl, 1 *The Jurisprudence of the World Court* (1965) 78–80.

[40] (1927) PCIJ Ser A No 10, 89–94 (Judge Moore, diss). Also *Flatow v Islamic Republic of Iran*, 999 F.Supp 1, 15–16 (DDC, 1998). For comment on the extension of US jurisdiction with respect to terrorism: Higgins (1994) 66–7.

[41] Donnedieu de Vabres, *Les Principes modernes du droit penal international* (1928) 170. Also Ryngaert (2008) 92–3.

[42] Brierly (1928) 44 *LQR* 154, 161; Ryngaert (2008) 93–4.

[43] E.g. *Arrest Warrant*, ICJ Report 2002 p 3, 76–7 (Judges Higgins, Kooijmans & Buergenthal): 'Passive personality jurisdiction, for so long regarded as controversial, is reflected not only in the legislation of various countries…and today meets with relatively little opposition, at least so far as a particular category of offences is concerned'. Also Higgins (1994) 66; Ryngaert (2004) 94.

[44] E.g. Convention on Offences Committed on Board Aircraft, 14 September 1963, 704 UNTS 219, Art 4(b); Convention for the Suppression of Unlawful Acts Against the Safety of Maritime Navigation, 10 March 1988, 1678 UNTS 221; Convention Against Torture, 10 December 1984, 1485 UNTS 85, Art 5(1)(c).

(iv) The protective or security principle[45]

Nearly all states assume jurisdiction over aliens for acts done abroad which affect the internal or external security or other key interests of the state, a concept which takes in a variety of offences not necessarily confined to political acts.[46] Currency, immigration, and economic offences are frequently punished. The UK and the US allow significant exceptions to the doctrine of territoriality, though without express reliance upon the protective principle. Thus, courts of the former have punished aliens for acts on the high seas concerning illegal immigration,[47] and perhaps considerations of security helped the House of Lords in *Joyce v Director of Public Prosecutions*[48] to the view that an alien who left the country in possession of a British passport owed allegiance and was accordingly guilty of treason when he subsequently broadcast propaganda for Germany in wartime. Insofar as the protective principle rests on the protection of concrete interests, it is sensible enough, but the interpretation of the concept of 'protection' may vary widely. For example, the protective principle was invoked in the *Eichmann* case in relation to the Jewish victims of the accused,[49] despite the fact that Israel was not a state when the offences in question occurred.[50]

The categories of what may be considered a vital interest for the purposes of protective jurisdiction are not closed,[51] and no criteria exist for determining such interests beyond a vague sense of gravity. Ultimately, the identification of exorbitant jurisdiction may be a matter of knowing it when one sees it.[52]

(v) The effects doctrine

In addition, it has been suggested that there exists a further head of prescriptive jurisdiction, the so-called 'effects doctrine'.[53] This may gain traction where an

---

[45] Bourquin (1927) 16 Hague *Recueil* 117, 121–89; Harvard Research (1935) 29 *AJIL Supp* 439, 543; Sarkar (1962) 11 *ILCQ* 446, 462–6; Garcia-Mora (1957–58) 19 *U Pitt LR* 567; van Hecke (1962) 106 Hague *Recueil* 253, 317–18; Ryngaert (2008) 96–100.

[46] *Nusselein v Belgian State* (1950) 17 ILR 136; *Public Prosecutor v L* (1951) 18 ILR 206; *Re van den Plas* (1955) 22 ILR 205; *Rocha v United States*, 288 F.2d 545 (9th Cir, 1961); *Italian South Tyrol Terrorism Case (2)* (1970) 71 ILR 242; *Arrest Warrant*, ICJ Reports 2002 p 3, 37 (President Guillaume), 92 (Judge Rezek).

[47] *Naim Molvan v AG for Palestine* [1948] AC 531; *Giles v Tumminello* (1969) 38 ILR 120.

[48] [1946] AC 347 (on which see Lauterpacht, 3 *International Law* (1977), 221). Also *Board of Trade v Owen* [1957] AC 602, 634 (Lord Tucker). Further: the US Anti-Smuggling Act of 1935 (19 USC §§1701–11); Preuss (1944) 30 *GST* 184; Sarkar (1962) 11 *ICLQ* 446, 453–6.

[49] (1962) 36 ILR 5, 18, 54–7 (Dist Ct), 304 (Sup Ct).

[50] Lasok (1962) 11 *ICLQ* 355, 364. Notwithstanding this, the District Court of Jerusalem felt able to say that the law under which Eichmann was prosecuted 'conforms to the best traditions of the law of nations': (1962) 36 ILR 5, 18, 25. Also the statement of the Supreme Court, ibid, 287.

[51] E.g. the US asserts jurisdiction over foreigners on the high seas on the basis of the protective principle, arguing that the illegal trade in narcotics is sufficiently prejudicial to its national interest: *United States v Gonzalez*, 776 F.2d 931 (11th Cir, 1985); *United States v Davis*, 905 F.2d 245 (1st Cir, 1990); Maritime Drug Law Enforcement Act 1986; Murphy (2003) 97 *AJIL* 183.

[52] *Jacobellis v Ohio*, 378 US 184, 197 (1964) (Justice Stewart).

[53] O'Keefe (2004) 2 *JICJ* 735, 739. The doctrine focuses on the deleterious effects of extra-territorial acts *to the state*. It is therefore primarily manifested in the criminal and regulatory spheres. Although civil manifestations are possible, it is presented here for the sake of convenience.

extra-territorial offence causes some harmful effect in the prescribing state, without actually meeting the criteria of territorial jurisdiction or representing an interest sufficiently vital to the internal or external security of the state in question to justify invoking the protective principle.

While controversial, the doctrine is not objectionable in all cases.[54] It was at least acknowledged by the majority in the *Lotus*[55] and by certain members of the International Court in *Arrest Warrant*.[56] Today, 'effects' or 'impact' jurisdiction is practised largely by the US and, with greater qualifications, by the EU.[57] In *Alcoa*, for example, Judge Learned Hand stated that it was 'settled law' that 'any state may impose liabilities, even upon persons not within its allegiance, for conduct outside its borders which has consequences within its borders which the state reprehends',[58] a position since followed extensively in US antitrust jurisprudence.[59]

Since *Alcoa*, the effects doctrine and its expansion have, in many cases, been driven by the US approach to jurisdiction. Whereas previously this resembled closely the conception of various heads of prescriptive jurisdiction, it has now changed its perspective; it is possible to speak of antitrust jurisdiction, tort jurisdiction, and taxation jurisdiction, with some of these having a broader extra-territorial reach than others. This has the potential to muddy the waters, resulting in the uncertain position of the effects doctrine within international law as either a head of prescription in its own right, or a subject-driven application of the territorial or protective principles with unusual reach.[60] These policies have provoked a strong reaction from a number of foreign governments. The UK[61] and other states have enacted legislation to provide defensive measures against American policy. Similar episodes have arisen as a result of the application of the US Export Administration Act in particular, in the face of US measures directed against non-American corporations involved in contracts relating to the construction of the West Siberian pipeline.[62] Both the European Community[63] and the UK[64] protested and asserted the illegality of the actions of US authorities

---

[54] E.g. in respect of inchoate conspiracies to murder or import illegal narcotics, where these offences are almost certainly illegal in those countries in which the plotting took place. In other areas, notably the fields of antitrust/competition law, such illegality cannot be assumed, and the validity of the doctrine remains uncertain: ibid, 739.

[55] (1927) PCIJ Ser A No 10, 23.

[56] ICJ Reports 2002 p 3, 77 (Judges Higgins, Kooijmans & Buergenthal).

[57] E.g. Case T-102/96, *Gencor Ltd v Commission* [1999] ECR II-753. Further: Agreement between the European Communities and the Government of the United States on the Application of Positive Comity Principles in the Enforcement of their Competition Laws, 4 June 1998 [1998] *OJEU* L 173/28.

[58] *United States v Aluminium Co of America*, 149 F.2d 416, 443 (2nd Cir, 1945).

[59] Generally: Raymond (1967) 61 *AJIL* 558; Metzger (1967) 61 *AJIL* 1015; Norton (1979) 28 *ICLQ* 575; Kelley (1991) 23 *U Miami IA LR* 195. Further Basedow, 'Antitrust or Competition Law, International' (2009) *MPEPIL*.

[60] Lowe & Staker, in Evans (ed), *International Law* (3rd edn, 2010) 322–3.

[61] Shipping Contracts and Commercial Documents Act 1964 (UK).

[62] Lowe (1984) 27 *GYIL* 54; Kuyper, ibid, 72; Meessen, ibid, 97.

[63] Cf the Note dated 12 August 1982 and comments, Lowe (1983) 197.

[64] Note dated 18 October 1982, UKMIL (1982) 53 *BY* 337, 453; Lowe (1983) 212.

intended to prevent the re-export of machinery of American origin and the supply of products derived from American data. But it must be noted that competition legislation in several European states is based on principles similar to those adopted in the US.[65] Moreover, the European Court of Justice has applied a principle similar to the American 'effects doctrine' in respect of company subsidiaries[66] and the Advocate-General espoused this view in his Opinion in the *Woodpulp Cases*.[67] In any event US legislation has continued to provoke protests from the EU and from individual states.[68] This legislation includes the Cuban Democracy Act (1992),[69] the D'Amato-Kennedy Act (1996),[70] and the Helms-Burton Act (1996).[71]

(B) JURISDICTION OVER SHIPS AND AIRCRAFT

Jurisdiction over ships on the high seas or exercising the right of innocent passage through the territorial sea or EEZ is discussed in chapters 11 and 13. The question here is the relation between the territorial sovereign and the flag state in the matter of jurisdiction over private vessels in ports or other internal waters.[72] The view that a ship is a floating part of state territory has long fallen into disrepute, but the special character of the 'internal economy' of ships is still recognized, the rule being that the law of the flag depends on the nationality of the ship[73] and that the flag state has regulatory responsibility for and jurisdiction over the ship.[74] But when a foreign ship enters a port, except perhaps as a consequence of distress,[75] temporary allegiance is owed to the territorial sovereign and concurrent jurisdiction arises.[76]

---

[65] On the German position: Gerber (1983) 77 *AJIL* 756; Steinberger, in Olmstead (ed), *Extra-territorial Application of Laws and Responses Thereto* (1984) 77.

[66] *ICI v EEC Commission* (1972) 48 ILR 106, 121–3.

[67] (1988) 96 ILR 174. However, the Court based its decision on 'the territoriality principle as universally recognized in public international law': (1988) 96 ILR 193, 196–7. Further: Waelbroeck, in Olmstead (ed), *Extra-territorial application of laws and responses thereto* (1984) 74; Akehurst (1988) 59 *BY* 408, 415–19.

[68] E.g. UKMIL (1992) 63 *BY* 615, 724–9; UKMIL (1993) 64 *BY* 579, 643–5; UKMIL (1995) 66 *BY* 583, 669–71; UKMIL (1996) 67 *BY* 683, 763–5; UKMIL (1998) 69 *BY* 433, 534; UKMIL (2001) 72 *BY* 551, 627, 631.

[69] 22 USC §6001.

[70] Iran and Libya Sanctions Act, 110 Stat 1541.

[71] Cuban Liberty and Democratic Solidarity (Libertad) Act, 22 USC §6021.

[72] Gidel, 2 *Le Droit international public de la mer* (1932) 39–252; Jessup, *The Law of Territorial Waters and Maritime Jurisdiction* (1927) 144–208; Harvard Research (1929) 23 *AJIL Supp* 241, 307–28; Harvard Research (1935) 29 *AJIL Supp* 508; McDougal & Burke, *The Public Order of the Oceans* (1962) 161–73; Churchill & Lowe, *The Law of the Sea* (3rd edn, 1999) 65–9; Molenaar, 'Port State Jurisdiction' (2009) *MPEPIL*; Rothwell & Stephens, *The International Law of the Sea* (2010) 56–7. For analogous cases of concurrence: Beale (1922–23) 36 *Harv LR* 241, 247–51; Lauterpacht (1960) 9 *ICLQ* 208, 231–2.

[73] Also *Lauritzen v Larsen*, 345 US 571, 584–6 (1953); Churchill & Lowe (3rd edn, 1999) 66–7.

[74] Further: UNCLOS, 10 December 1982, 1833 UNTS 3, Arts 91–4; UN Convention on the Conditions of Registration of Ships, 7 February 1986, 26 ILM 1229; *M/V Saiga (No 2)* (1999) 120 ILR 143.

[75] Molenaar, *Coastal State Jurisdiction over Vessel Source Pollution* (1998) 187; Churchill & Lowe (3rd edn, 1999) 68; Rothwell & Stephens (2010) 56.

[76] *United States v Flores*, 289 US 137 (1933); *Re Bianchi* (1957) 24 ILR 173.

There has been debate on the limits of the local criminal jurisdiction. In principle, there are no limits provided action is taken with regard only to breaches of local law and not to breaches of rules set by the law of the flag state.[77] During the preparatory work of the Hague Codification Conference of 1930, the UK stated its opinion on the issues as follows:

[T]he State is entitled to exercise jurisdiction over a foreign merchant vessel lying in its ports and over persons and goods on board...In criminal matters it is not usual for the authorities to intervene and enforce the local jurisdiction, unless their assistance is invoked by, or on behalf of the local representative of the flag State, or those in control of the ship, or a person directly concerned, or unless the peace or good order of the port is likely to be affected. In every case it is for the authorities of the State to judge whether or not to intervene.[78]

On this view derogation from the exercise of local criminal jurisdiction is a matter of comity and discretion, but may be invoked in practice where: (a) the act in question disturbs the peace and good order of the port; (b) assistance is requested by the captain or a representative of the flag state of the ship; or (c) a non-crew member is involved.[79]

Quite aside from matters relating to the internal economy of ships, port state jurisdiction is increasingly recognized as a remedy for the failure of flag states to exercise effective jurisdiction and control of their ships. The jurisdiction is no longer used solely to enforce local questions of civil and criminal law, but is actively playing a role in the international regulatory sphere. This is especially notable in the context of maritime pollution, with Article 218 of the UN Convention on the Law of the Sea (UNCLOS) granting port states the right to institute proceedings or impose monetary penalties for illegal discharges that occur outside of their territorial sea and EEZ. Port state jurisdiction is also used as a response to illegal and unregulated fishing on the high seas. Under Article 23 of the Straddling Stocks Agreement,[80] a port state has the right (and indeed duty) to take certain steps to combat illegal fishing, revolving centrally around the inspection of documents, fishing gear, and the catch itself. This provision is not the equivalent of UNCLOS Article 218 optimized for use in relation to fishing, but it does underwrite the use of existing port state jurisdiction in a certain fashion. The same may be said of Article 15 of the UNESCO Convention on the Protection of Underwater Cultural Heritage,[81] which requires states parties to prohibit the use of their ports in support

[77] 2 Gidel (1932) 204, 246; Churchill & Lowe (3rd edn, 1999) 65–6.

[78] McNair, 2 *Opinions* 194.

[79] Churchill & Lowe (3rd edn, 1999) 66–7.

[80] Agreement for the Implementation of the Provisions of the United Nations Convention on the Law of the Sea of 10 December 1982 relating to the Conservation and Management of Straddling Fish Stocks and Highly Migratory Fish Stocks, 4 August 1995, 2167 UNTS 3.

[81] 2 November 2001, 41 ILM 40. Further: Rau (2006) 6 *MPUNYB* 387.

of any activity directed at underwater cultural heritage which is not in conformity with the Convention.

Aircraft initially posed some problems for the jurisdictional rules of domestic and international law, and crimes on board civil aircraft over the high seas or in the airspace of foreign states were the subject of considerable variations of opinion.[82] In the UK, for example, the extra-territorial commission of common law offences such as murder and theft is punishable,[83] but many provisions, apart from aeronautical regulations made under the Civil Aviation Act 1949, have no application to crimes on aircraft abroad or over the high seas.[84] The practice of states on the relation between the national law of the aircraft and the law of any foreign territory overflown was not very coherent; however, work sponsored by the International Civil Aviation Organization produced the Convention on Offences and Certain Other Acts Committed on Board Aircraft (Tokyo Convention),[85] which in Article 3(1) provides that the state of registration of the aircraft is competent to exercise jurisdiction over offences and acts committed on board and further requires the state to take necessary measures to claim jurisdiction over such acts (Article 3(2)). Article 3(3) provides that criminal jurisdiction exercised in accordance with national law is not excluded.

In addition, Article 4 of the Tokyo Convention prohibits states other than the state of registration interfering with an aircraft in flight, save where an offence committed on board: (a) has effect in the territory of the intercepting state; (b) has been committed by or against a national or permanent resident of such state; (c) is against the security of the state; or (d) consists of a breach of any rules or regulations relating to the flight of aircraft.

Aircraft hijacking has prompted multilateral conventions creating duties for states to punish the seizure of aircraft in flight and to exercise jurisdiction in specified conditions, for example, when the offence is committed on board an aircraft registered in the contracting state.[86]

---

[82] E.g. Shubber, *Jurisdiction over Crimes on Board Aircraft* (1973).

[83] *R v Martin* [1956] 2 QB 272, 285–6 (Devlin J); *R v Naylor* [1962] 2 QB 527.

[84] In *R v Martin* [1956] 2 QB 272 it was decided that s62 of the Civil Aviation Act 1949 (UK) has procedural effect and confers jurisdiction only if a substantive rule makes the act concerned criminal when committed on board a British aircraft; that case involved the Dangerous Drugs Regulations 1953 (UK). Generally: Cheng (1959) 12 *CLP* 177.

[85] 14 September 1963, 704 UNTS 219. Further: Mendelsohn (1967) 53 *Va LR* 509; and, for the UK, the Tokyo Convention Act 1967; comment by Samuels (1967) 42 *BY* 271.

[86] Convention for the Suppression of Unlawful Seizure of Aircraft, 16 December 1970, 860 UNTS 105; Convention for the Suppression of Unlawful Acts Against the Safety of Civil Aviation, 23 September 1971, 974 UNTS 178; Convention on the Suppression of Unlawful Acts Relating to International Civil Aviation, 10 September 2010, available at www.icao.int/DCAS2010/restr/docs/beijing_convention_multi.pdf; the Aviation Security Act 1982 (UK).

(C) UNIVERSAL JURISDICTION[87]

(i) Defining universal jurisdiction

Defined simply, universal jurisdiction amounts to the assertion of criminal jurisdiction by a state in the absence of any other generally recognized head of prescriptive jurisdiction.[88] In O'Keefe's words:

universal jurisdiction can be defined as prescriptive jurisdiction over offences committed abroad by persons who, at the time of the commission, are non-resident aliens, where such offences are not deemed to constitute threats to the fundamental interests of the prescribing state or, in appropriate cases, to give rise to effects within its territory.[89]

A considerable number of states have adopted, usually with limitations, a principle allowing jurisdiction over acts of non-nationals where the circumstances, including the nature of the crime, justify repression as a matter of international public policy. In this sense, universal jurisdiction is defined by the character of the crime concerned, rather than by the presence of some kind of nexus to the prescribing state. The prosecution of crimes under customary international law is often expressed as an acceptance of the principle of universality,[90] but this is not strictly correct, since what is punished is the breach of international law. The case is thus different from the punishment, under national law, of acts which international law permits and even requires all states to punish, but does not itself declare criminal.

(ii) The content of universal jurisdiction

How then to define the content of universal jurisdiction? As alluded, some commentators have argued for its extension on moral or public policy grounds, and that universal jurisdiction accordingly applies to certain crimes under customary international law the commission of which is generally accepted 'as an attack upon the international order'.[91] As the District Court of Jerusalem in the *Eichmann* case remarked:

The abhorrent crimes defined in [the Israeli Law] are not crimes under Israeli law alone. These crimes, which struck at the whole of mankind and shocked the conscience of nations, are grave offences against the law of nations itself (*delicta juris gentium*). Therefore, so far from international law negating or limiting the jurisdiction of countries with respect to such

---

[87] Harvard Research (1935) 29 *AJIL Supp* 439, 563; Jennings (1957) 33 *BY* 146, 156; Bishop (1965) 115 Hague *Recueil* 147, 323–4; Bowett (1982) 53 *BY* 1, 11–14; Brown (2001) 35 *NELR* 383; Higgins (1994) 56–65; *The Princeton Principles on Universal Jurisdiction* (2001); Reydams, *Universal Jurisdiction* (2003); Ryngaert (2008) ch 5; and esp O'Keefe (2004) 2 *JICJ* 735.

[88] O'Keefe (2004) 2 *JICJ* 735, 745. Cf Reydams (2003) 5. Also la Pradelle, in Ascensio, Decaux & Pellet (eds), *Droit International Pénal* (2005) 905.

[89] O'Keefe (2004) 2 *JICJ* 735, 745.

[90] Brand (1949) 26 *BY* 414; Baxter (1951) 28 *BY* 382. Cf Röling (1960) 100 Hague *Recueil* 323, 357–62. Also *Re Sharon and Yaron* (2003) 127 ILR 110; *Javor and Others* (1996) 127 ILR 126; *Munyeshyaka* (1998) 127 ILR 134.

[91] Higgins (1994) 58. See also *Arrest Warrant*, ICJ Reports 2002 p 3, 81 (Judges Higgins, Kooijmans & Buergenthal).

crimes, international law is, in the absence of an International Court, in need of the judicial and legislative organs of every country to give effect to its criminal interdictions and bring the criminals to trial. The jurisdiction to try crimes under international law is *universal*.[92]

The original crime to which universal jurisdiction attached was that of piracy *iure gentium*,[93] which was in turn followed by slavery.[94] In modern times, it has been extended to the so-called 'core crimes' of customary international law,[95] being genocide,[96] crimes against humanity and breaches of the laws of war, and especially of the Hague Convention of 1907 and grave breaches of the Geneva Conventions of 1949.[97] Torture within the meaning of the Torture Convention 1984 is also likely to be subject to universal jurisdiction.[98]

Beyond such clear cases, public policy is less useful as a criterion. There are no examples of prosecutions for the crime of aggression under universal jurisdiction, but given the relatively recent formulation of an agreed definition of the crime in international law[99] this is not surprising.[100] At the same time, however, the intense political implications of the charge of aggression may also explain the unwillingness of states to attempt prosecutions on the basis of universal jurisdiction. For now, therefore, it is questionable as to whether aggression can be considered a crime of universal jurisdiction. The better view may be that it is not.

Thus, notwithstanding the fact that the 'moral' justification for universal jurisdiction has dominated discussion of this subject,[101] it does not explain the reality of universal jurisdiction, which is often influenced—sometimes decisively—by political considerations. It seems that attempting to derive a coherent theory for the extension of universal jurisdiction with respect to some crimes but not others may be to

[92] (1968) 36 ILR 18, 26.

[93] This can be explained by the fact that no state could exercise territorial jurisdiction: e.g *Lotus* (1927) PCIJ Ser A No 10, 51 (Judge Finlay, diss), 70–1 (Judge Moore, diss), 95 (Judge Altamira, diss); *Arrest Warrant*, ICJ Reports 2002 p 3, 37–8, 42 (President Guillaume), 55–6 (Judge Ranjeva), 78–9, 81 (Judges Higgins, Kooijmans & Buergenthal). On piracy: UNCLOS, Art 105, and chapter 13.

[94] E.g. *Lotus* (1927) PCIJ Ser A No 10, 95 (Judge Altamira, diss); *Arrest Warrant*, ICJ Reports 2002 p 3, 61–2 (Judge Koroma).

[95] Ryngaert (2008) 110–15.

[96] *Jorgic v Germany* [1997] ECtHR 74614/01, §69. Institut de Droit International, Seventeenth Commission, *Universal Jurisdiction Over Genocide, Crimes Against Humanity and War Crimes* (2005) 2. Generally: Kreß (2006) 4 *JICJ* 561; Reydams (2003) 1 *JICJ* 428; cf Reydams (2003) 1 *JICJ* 679. This has become the position despite the fact that the Genocide Convention, 9 December 1948, 78 UNTS 277, Art VI reserves universal jurisdiction in case of genocide for an international court: cf *In re Koch* (1966) 30 ILR 496; *Jorgic v Germany* [1997] ECtHR 74614/01 (alternate interpretation of Genocide Convention, Art VI, which permits universal jurisdiction for states); Schabas (2003) 1 *JICJ* 39.

[97] Higgins (1994) 61.

[98] *R v Bow Street Metropolitan Stipendiary Magistrate, ex parte Pinochet Ugarte (No 3)* [2000] 1 AC 147, 275 (Lord Millett); *Furundžija* (2002) 121 ILR 213, 262; Cassese, *International Criminal Law* (2nd edn, 2008) 338.

[99] ICC Doc RC/Res.6, 16 June 2010; ICC Statute, 17 July 1998, 2187 UNTS 3, Arts 8*bis*, 15*bis*, 15*ter*.

[100] An attempt to persuade German authorities to prosecute for aggression with respect to the US invasion of Iraq failed: Kreß (2004) 2 *JICJ* 245; Kreß (2004) 2 *JICJ* 347.

[101] Ryngaert (2008) 113–15.

overstate the situation: rather, it may simply be that such jurisdiction is extended on a case-by-case basis in customary international law, with the notion of an attack upon the international order being a necessary but not sufficient condition.

(iii) Universal jurisdiction *in absentia*?

The most substantial consideration of universal jurisdiction by an international court or tribunal occurred in *Arrest Warrant,* even though the discussion was obiter (the Court felt it could address immunity without deciding upon jurisdiction).[102] The opinions of those judges who did consider universal jurisdiction reveal a deeply divided court. Four judges (President Guillaume, Judges Ranjeva, Rezek, and Judge ad hoc Bula-Bula) were opposed to the use of the jurisdiction, whereas six (Judge Koroma, Judges Higgins, Kooijmans, Buergenthal in their joint separate opinion, Judge al-Khasawneh (impliedly), and Judge ad hoc van den Wyngaert) supported its application by Belgium.[103]

On examination, however, of those judges who opposed the use of universal jurisdiction by Belgium, only President Guillaume[104] and Judge Rezek[105] disagreed with a concept of universal jurisdiction in general. Judge Ranjeva and Judge ad hoc Bula-Bula criticized only its use *in absentia*, that is, where the prescribing state did not have custody of the accused.[106]

Although the notion of universal jurisdiction *in absentia* is not unknown in academic literature prior to the *Arrest Warrant* case,[107] it is not compelling. Universal jurisdiction is a manifestation of a state's jurisdiction to prescribe. The question whether jurisdiction is exercised *in personam* or *in absentia* is a manifestation of a state's jurisdiction to enforce.[108] In the context of *Arrest Warrant*, the Belgian law on war crimes and the issue of an arrest warrant in support of that law were separate acts. To speak of universal jurisdiction *in absentia* is to conflate prescriptive and enforcement jurisdiction.[109]

(iv) Treaty-based quasi-universal jurisdiction[110]

Another, more restricted, form of quasi-universal jurisdiction arises from *sui generis* treaty regimes incorporating penal characteristics. These regimes have for the most

---

[102] Generally: Winants (2003) 16 *LJIL* 491; O'Keefe (2004) 2 *JICJ* 735; Goldmann, 'Arrest Warrant Case (Democratic Republic of Congo v Belgium)' (2009) *MPEPIL*.

[103] Cf also the dissenting opinion of Judge Oda: ICJ Reports 2002 p 3, 51.

[104] President Guillaume took an extremely conservative stance on universal jurisdiction holding that under customary international law it only applied with respect to piracy and within the confines of certain *sui generis* treaty regimes: ibid, 37–8.

[105] Ibid, 94.

[106] Ibid, 55–7 (Judge Ranjeva), 121–6 (Judge ad hoc Bula-Bula).

[107] Reydams (2003) 55, 74, 88–9, 156, 177, 222, 224, 226–7; Cassese (2nd edn, 2008) 338.

[108] O'Keefe (2004) 2 *JICJ* 735, 750.

[109] Ibid, 751.

[110] Generally: Reydams (2003) ch 3; Ryngaert (2008) 100–27; Scharf, '*Aut dedere aut iudicare*' (2008) *MPEPIL*.

part been developed in order to respond to particular behaviours viewed as undesirable; they require states parties to exercise mandatory prescriptive jurisdiction over certain individuals within their territories, independent of any ordinary nexus. They are frequently characterized by the obligation of *aut dedere aut iudicare*, which will compel a state party to either try the accused or extradite to a state that is willing to do so.[111]

An example[112] arises in the context of the Convention for the Suppression of Unlawful Seizure of Aircraft (Hague Convention).[113] This provides in Article 4(2) that:

Each Contracting State shall likewise take such measures as may be necessary to establish its jurisdiction over the offence in the case where the alleged offender is present in its territory and it does not extradite him pursuant to Article 8 to any of the States mentioned in paragraph 1 of this Article.

This formula has been applied, more or less identically, in a considerable number of international conventions.[114] Early examples include the *aut dedere aut iudicare* obligations also appeared in the Geneva Conventions in 1949.[115] Chief amongst the more recent treaties are the 12 'sectoral' anti-terrorism agreements which were developed

---

[111] The concept again comes from Grotius, who found the notion of a fugitive arriving on the territory of a state and there remaining to enjoy the fruits of his iniquity offensive: Grotius, *De Iure Belli ac Pacis* (1625, Tuck 2005) II.xxi.§4.1. The position was later reversed by Enlightenment philosophers who sought to restrict the prescriptive jurisdiction of states to territorial concerns alone: e.g, Beccaria, *Traité des délits et des peines* (1764) §21. Further: *Arrest Warrant*, ICJ Reports 2002 p 3, 36–40 (President Guillaume).

[112] In the modern era, the concept first appeared in the International Convention for the Suppression of Counterfeiting Currency, 20 April 1929, 112 LNTS 371, Art 9.

[113] 16 December 1970, 860 UNTS 105, Art 4(1).

[114] E.g Convention for the Suppression of Unlawful Acts Against the Safety of Civilian Aviation, 23 September 1971, 974 UNTS 117, Art 5(1)(c), (2) and (2*bis*); Convention on the Prevention and Punishment of Crimes against Internationally Protected Persons, including Diplomatic Agents, 14 December 1973, 1035 UNTS 167, Art 3(2); International Convention Against the Taking of Hostages, 17 December 1979, 1316 UNTS 205, Art 5(2); Convention on the Physical Protection of Nuclear Material, 3 March 1980, 1456 UNTS 124, Art 8(2); Convention Against Torture, 10 December 1984, 1465 UNTS 85, Art 5(2); Convention for the Suppression of Unlawful Acts against the Safety of Maritime Navigation, 20 March 1988, 1678 UNTS 221, Art 6(4); Protocol for the Suppression of Unlawful Acts against the Safety of Fixed Platforms Located on the Continental Shelf, 10 March 1988, 1678 UNTS 304, Art 3(2), Convention against the Recruitment, Use, Financing and Training of Mercenaries, 4 December 1989, 2163 UNTS 96, 9(2); Convention on the Safety of United Nations and Associated Personnel, 9 December 1994, 2051 UNTS 363, Art 10(4); International Convention for the Suppression of Terrorist Bombings, 15 December 1997, 2149 UNTS 256, Art 6(4); International Convention for the Suppression of the Financing of Terrorism, 9 December 1999, A/RES/54/109, Art 7(4); Convention against Transnational Organized Crime, 15 November 2000, 2225 UNTS 209, Art 15(4); International Convention for the Suppression of Acts of Nuclear Terrorism, 13 April 2005, 2445 UNTS 89, Art 9(4); Convention for the Protection of All Persons from Enforced Disappearance, 20 December 2006, A/RES/61/177, Art 9(2); Convention on the Suppression of Unlawful Acts relating to International Civil Aviation, 10 September 2010, Art 8(3), available at www.icao.int/DCAS2010/.

[115] Geneva Convention for the Amelioration of the Condition of the Wounded and Sick in Armed Forces in the Field, 12 August 1949, 75 UNTS 31, Art 49; Geneva Convention for the Amelioration of the Condition of Wounded, Sick and Shipwrecked Members of Armed Forces at Sea, 12 August 1949, 75 UNTS 85, Art 50; Geneva Convention Relative to the Treatment of Prisoners of War, 75 UNTS 135, Art 129; Geneva Convention Relative to the Protection of Civilian Persons in Time of War, 12 August 1949, 85 UNTS 287, Art 146.

when it became clear that meaningful agreement on a generic definition of 'terrorism' was unreachable.[116]

To describe the jurisdictional regime established by these treaties as 'universal' is a misnomer.[117] As Ryngaert notes:

The operation of the *aut dedere* requirement is indeed limited to States Parties, which pool their sovereignty and explicitly authorize each other to exercise jurisdiction over crimes committed by their nationals or on their territory.[118]

That, however, has not prevented certain states from insisting on the application of *sui generis* bases of jurisdiction to nationals of non-states parties to the treaties in question. The US is notable in this regard, often exercising jurisdiction over suspected terrorists who are nationals of states not party to the relevant sectoral agreements.[119] In *Yunis*, for example, a Lebanese national was prosecuted with respect to the hijacking of Royal Jordanian Airlines Flight 402 from Beirut to Amman. The plane carried several American nationals, but was registered in Jordan, flew the Jordanian flag and never landed on American soil or flew over American airspace. The Court found that it had universal jurisdiction to prosecute with respect to the act of hijacking *and* the taking of hostages by the accused. Although jurisdiction was grounded on the fact that Lebanon was a state party to the Hague and Montreal Conventions, the Court further held that jurisdiction was also furnished by the provisions of the Hostage Taking Convention. This was despite the fact that Lebanon and Jordan were not parties to that treaty.[120]

3. CIVIL PRESCRIPTIVE JURISDICTION

There are different views as to the law concerning civil jurisdiction. On one view, exorbitant assertions of civil jurisdiction could lead to international responsibility. Further, as civil jurisdiction is ultimately reinforced by criminal sanctions through contempt of court, there is in principle no great difference between the problems created by assertion of civil and criminal jurisdiction over aliens.[121] In particular, antitrust

---

[116] Generally: Saul (2005) 52 *NILJ* 57; Saul, *Defining Terrorism in International Law* (2006); cf Cassese (2nd edn, 2008) ch 8.

[117] Higgins (1994) 64 ('Although these treaties seek to provide wide alternative bases of jurisdiction, they are not examples of universal jurisdiction. Universal jurisdiction, properly called, allows *any* state to assert jurisdiction over an offence').

[118] Ryngaert (2008) 105. Also Lowe & Staker, in Evans (3rd edn, 2010) 313, 318–35.

[119] E.g. *United States v Rezaq*, 899 F.Supp 697 (DDC, 1995); *United States v Rezaq*, 134 F.3d 1121 (DC Cir, 1998); *United States v Wang Kun Lue*, 134 F.3d 79 (2nd Cir, 1997); *United States v Lin*, 101 F.3d 760 (DC Cir, 1996); *United States v Ni Fa Yi*, 951 F.Supp 42 (SDNY, 1997); *United States v Chen De Yian*, 905 F.Supp 160 (SDNY, 1995).

[120] *United States v Yunis (No 2)*, 681 F.Supp 896, 901 (DDC, 1988).

[121] There are many specialized areas, e.g. those relating to conscription and taxation. On the former: Parry (1954) 31 *BY* 437; 8 Whiteman 540–72. On the latter: Mann (1964) 111 Hague *Recueil* 1, 109–19; Martha, *The Jurisdiction to Tax in International Law* (1989).

legislation (the source of many of the difficulties in practice) involves a process which, though formally 'civil', is in substance coercive and penal, as is the field of securities regulation.[122] On another view, there is little by way of limitation on a state's exercise of civil jurisdiction in what are effectively private law matters; different states assert jurisdiction on different grounds, but deference to foreign law through conflicts rules mitigates any exorbitant elements.

(A) THE BASIS OF CIVIL JURISDICTION IN DIFFERENT LEGAL TRADITIONS

Notwithstanding broad similarities, the different legal traditions conceive of the civil jurisdiction to prescribe in different ways. This division is particularly apparent when considering the willingness of municipal courts to exercise jurisdiction over a foreign party as an actualization of prescriptive jurisdiction.

In order to satisfy international law standards in regard to the treatment of aliens a state must in normal circumstances maintain a system of courts empowered to decide civil cases and, in doing so, be prepared to apply private international law where appropriate in cases containing a foreign element.[123] Municipal courts may be reluctant to assume jurisdiction in cases concerning a foreign element, adhering to the territorial principle conditioned by the *situs* of the facts in issue, and supplemented by criteria relating to the concepts of allegiance or domicile and doctrines of submission to the jurisdiction (including tacit submission on the basis of ownership of property in the forum state).[124]

As a general rule, the common law systems will assert jurisdiction over a foreign defendant who can be served with originating process.[125] Under the most basic formulation, a writ may be served whenever the defendant sets foot[126] or establishes a commercial presence[127] in the jurisdiction, no matter how temporarily. Where the defendant has no such presence, a writ may nonetheless be served outside of the jurisdiction in certain cases.[128] Though civil lawyers complain of the perceived exorbitance

---

[122] Ryngaert (2008) 76–8. Also Ryngaert, *Jurisdiction over Antitrust Violations in International Law* (2008).

[123] On the relations of public and private international law: Mann (1964) 111 Hague *Recueil* 9, 10–22, 54–62; Akehurst (1972–73) 46 *BY* 145, 216–31, Mills, *The Confluence of Public and Private International Law* (2009).

[124] Beale (1922–23) 36 *Harv LR* 241. For a different view see Akehurst (1972–73) 46 *BY* 145, 170–7; and see *Derby & Co Ltd v Larsson* [1976] 1 WLR 202; Crawford (1976–77) 48 *BY* 333, 352. Also *Thai-Europe Tapioca Service v Government of Pakistan* [1975] 1 WLR 1485, 1491–2 (Lord Denning).

[125] *Russell & Co v Cayzer, Irvine Ltd* [1916] 2 AC 298, 302.

[126] E.g. *Maharanee of Baroda v Wildenstein* [1972] 2 QB 283.

[127] E.g. *Dunlop Ltd v Cudell & Co* [1902] 1 KB 342; *Cleveland Museum of Art v Capricorn International SA* [1990] 2 Lloyd's Rep 166.

[128] E.g. *Spiliada Maritime Corp v Cansulex Ltd* [1987] AC 460; *Airbus Industrie GIE v Patel* [1999] 1 AC 119; *Lubbe v Cape plc* [2000] 1 WLR 1545. Where the defendant has a territorial connection with England sufficient to allow the writ to be served directly, the court may decline jurisdiction on the basis that England is *forum non conveniens*. Generally: Fentiman, *International Commercial Litigation* (2010) chs 8–9, 12.

of the service rule,[129] common lawyers point out that the defendant may challenge the exercise of the jurisdiction on the basis that the appropriate forum for the hearing of the dispute is elsewhere.[130]

Some common law jurisdictions have extended the concept of jurisdiction by service further still. In the US, 'minimum [territorial] contacts'[131] will suffice for the purpose of finding jurisdiction over the defendant, a term which has been subject to liberal interpretation by the courts.[132] For example, the mere presence of a subsidiary of a foreign corporation in the US may provide the necessary minimum contact for the parent corporation.[133]

In contrast, the civil law approach to the exercise of jurisdiction is predicated on the principle that, where possible, the defendant ought to be sued in its domicile. This may be seen in EC Regulation 44/2001 on jurisdiction and the recognition and enforcement of judgments in civil and commercial matters (the Brussels 1 Regulation),[134] Article 2 of which provides that '[s]ubject to this Regulation, persons domiciled in a Member State [of the EU] shall, whatever their nationality, be sued in the courts of that Member State'.[135] The Regulation, however, provides alternative bases of jurisdiction that are not so rigorously territorial where the defendant is already domiciled in the EU, including, *inter alia*, the *locus delicti* in cases of tort (Article 5(3)), in cases of contract, the place of performance of the obligation which has been breached (Article 5(1)(a)), the place of delivery of goods or performance of services (Article 5(1)(b)) or, as regards commercial disputes arising out of the operations of a branch, agency or other establishment, the place in which the branch, agency or other establishment is situated (Article 5(5)).[136]

---

[129] E.g. Ehrenzweig (1956) 65 *Yale LJ* 289. Relations between common law and civil law countries on the service of process have been a source of difficulty: e.g. *Decision of 7 December 1994 concerning Service of Punitive Damage Claims* (1995) 34 ILM 975.

[130] The unfortunate corollary of which is that the onus is then on the defendant to disprove jurisdiction: Fentiman (2010) 230.

[131] *International Shoe Co v Washington*, 326 US 310, 316 (1945). Also *World-Wide Volkswagen Corp v Woodson*, 444 US 286, 297 (1980); *Helicopteros Nacionales de Columbia v Hall*, 466 US 408, 415–16 (1984); *Burger King v Rudzewicz*, 471 US 462, 473 (1985); *In the Matter of an Application to Enforce Admin Subpoenas Deces Tecum of the SEC v Knowles*, 87 F.3d 413, 417 (10th Cir, 1996); *Goodyear Dunlop Tyres Operations SA v Brown*, 131 SC 2846 (2011).

[132] Ryngaert (2008) 12.

[133] E.g. *Boryk v de Havilland Aircraft Co*, 341 F.2d 666 (2nd Cir, 1965); cf also *Lakah Group v Al Jazeera Satellite Channel* [2002] EWHC 1297 (QB); aff'd [2003] EWCA Civ 1781.

[134] [2001] *OJEU* L 12/1, an elaboration on the Convention on Jurisdiction and the Enforcement of Judgments in Civil and Commercial Matters, Brussels, 27 September 1968, 1262 UNTS 153 As an EU member, the UK is bound by the terms of the Brussels 1 Regulation. To the extent that the Regulation does not apply, however, the common law rules of jurisdiction will have residual effect: Brussels 1 Regulation, Art 4. Also of note is EC Regulation 593/2008 on the law applicable to contractual relations: [2008] *OJEU* L 177/6 (Rome 1 Regulation).

[135] The Brussels 1 Regulation permits certain exceptions to this principle based on questions of subject-matter and the relationship between the parties: e.g. Arts 5(1) (matters relating to a contract), 5(3) (matters relating to a tort or delict), 5(5) (matters relating to a dispute arising from the activities of a branch, agent or other establishment); 22 (exclusive jurisdiction), 23 (jurisdiction agreements), and 27 and 28 (*lis pendens* and related actions).

[136] Further: Fentiman (2010) 384–96.

In a further significant difference with the common law, the notion of discretionary refusal of jurisdiction is anathema to the civil law. As a general rule, if properly seised, a court will be unable to decline jurisdiction unless expressly authorized to do so by the terms of the Regulation.[137] For example, under Article 27, in the event of *lis pendens*, the court second seised must stay the proceedings before it in favour of the court first seised unless the latter determines that it lacks jurisdiction.[138]

Whilst this approach has the virtue of certainty and consistency, its rigidity may lead to unfortunate practical consequences. In *Owusu*,[139] for example, a single English defendant and five Jamaican defendants were sued in the English courts with respect to an alleged tort taking place in Jamaica. Although the *forum conveniens* was clearly Jamaica, the mandatory wording of Article 2 and the English domicile of one of the defendants prevented the court from declining jurisdiction.

(B) JURISDICTION AND THE CONFLICT OF LAWS[140]

Conflict of laws, also known as private international law, is concerned with issues of the jurisdiction of national courts, the municipal law applicable to disputes with foreign elements, and the cross-border enforcement of judgments. It is usually considered to be merely municipal law, and a bright line is drawn between its study and the study of public international law. If it must be considered international law, the argument runs, then it is international only in the sense that it involves competing and horizontal 'inter-national' claims.

According to Mills, the adoption of an international systemic perspective on the conflict of laws reveals an 'essential confluence' of public and private international law, sharing as they do similar intellectual progenitors.[141] Nationality, for example, is the defining jurisdictional principle for civil legal systems. Article 15 of the French Civil Code provides that 'French persons may be called before a court of France for obligations contracted by them in a foreign country, even with an alien'. Passive personality is also the focus of Article 14 of the French Civil Code, which permits a foreign person to be called before the French courts with respect to obligations entered into with a French national.

The influence of the territoriality principle in private international law is likewise pervasive, notably in common law systems where the presence of the defendant within the jurisdiction is sufficient to ground the court's adjudicative power. This is rightly

---

[137] Cf Brussels 1 Regulation, Art 28.

[138] E.g. because the court second seised is the beneficiary of an exclusive jurisdiction agreement between the parties (Art 23) or the subject-matter of the dispute is something within the exclusive jurisdiction of the court second seised (Art 22).

[139] Case C-281/02, *Owusu v Jackson* [2005] ECR I-1383 (ECJ). Also Case C-159/02, *Turner v Grovit* [2005] ECR I-3565 (ECJ); Case C-116/02, *Erich Gasser GmbH v MISAT srl* [2003] ECR I-14693 (ECJ); Case C-185/07, *Allianz SpA v West Tankers Inc* [2009] ECR I-663.

[140] Ryngaert (2008) ch 1; Mills (2009).

[141] Mills (2009) 298 and generally: chs 1–3.

controversial, for under the public international law conception of territoriality, the act or thing which is the subject of adjudicative power must be done within the jurisdiction; the subsequent presence of the defendant will be insufficient. That said, this perceived overreach is reduced by the use of *forum non conveniens* to decline jurisdiction where another forum is better suited to hear the matter; in the US, consideration of 'reasonableness' may also come into play.[142] Territoriality is also (less controversially) present in Article 22(1) of the Brussels 1 Regulation, which provides for the exclusive jurisdiction for certain courts, regardless of the defendant's domicile, where the proceedings in question have as their object rights *in rem* in immovable property or tenancies in immovable property.

(C) THE ALIEN TORT STATUTE AND COGNATE LEGISLATION[143]

The universality principle, as expressed in the *Eichmann* case, is most often associated with the prosecution of particularly heinous crimes. Only a few states assert universal *civil* jurisdiction, that is, prescriptive jurisdiction absent any minimal territorial or national nexus to the delict in question.[144] The example *par excellence* is the United States' Alien Tort Claims Act 1789, now codified as the Alien Tort Statute (ATS).[145]

The ATS provides in its relevant part that '[t]he district courts shall have original jurisdiction of any civil action by an alien for a tort only, committed in violation of the law of nations or a treaty of the United States'. Apparently enacted for the purpose of providing a recourse in tort for acts of piracy or the violation of safe conduct or of the rights of ambassadors,[146] the statute fell dormant for almost two centuries before gaining modern importance in *Filartiga v Peña-Irala*,[147] where the Second Circuit Court of Appeals held that it was to be read as *incorporating* current customary international law protective of individual rights.

An actionable ATS violation will occur only where (a) the plaintiff is an alien, (b) the defendant[148] is responsible for a tort, and (c) the tort in question violates international

---

[142] E.g. *Timberland Lumber Co v Bank of America*, 549 F.2d 597 (9th Cir, 1976).

[143] Dodge (1996) 19 *Hastings ICLR* 221; Steinhardt & D'Amato (eds), *The Alien Tort Claims Act* (1999); Paust (2004) 16 *Fla JIL* 249; Ryngaert (2007) 38 *NYIL* 3; Ryngaert (2008) 126–7; Seibert-Fohr, 'United States Alien Tort Statute' (2008) *MPEPIL*.

[144] Reydams (2008) 126–7.

[145] 28 USC §1350. After the 'rediscovery' of the Alien Tort Claims Act, the Torture Victims Protection Act of 1991 was passed: it provides a cause of action for any victim of torture or extrajudicial killing wherever committed: 106 Stat 73.

[146] These are the offences against the law of nations described by Blackstone as addressed by the criminal law of England: *Sosa v Alvarez-Machain*, 542 US 692, 725 (2004). The origins of the original statute are obscure: Paust (2004) 16 *Fla JIL* 249; Seibert-Fohr, 'United States Alien Tort Statute' (2008) *MPEPIL*.

[147] 630 F.2d 876 (2nd Cir, 1980).

[148] There is no nationality requirement imposed on the defendant by the ATS; accordingly, US companies are named as defendants in most ATS cases, converting the statute into a corporate social responsibility tool: e.g. *Doe v Unocal*, 249 F.3d 915 (9th Cir, 2001). That said, a determination by the Supreme Court as to whether corporations can be held liable under the ATS has not yet been made: cf *Presbyterian Church of Sudan v Talisman Energy Inc*, 582 F.3d 244 (2nd Cir, 2009); *Kiobel v Royal Dutch Petroleum*, 621 F.3d 111 (9th

law.[149] Not every violation of international law will, however, be considered actionable: the Supreme Court in *Sosa v Alvarez-Machain*, while falling short of articulating a coherent category, limited the scope of the statute to 'norm[s] of an international character accepted by the civilized world'.[150] In this sense, the ATS draws its legitimacy at least to some extent from the same well-spring as universal criminal jurisdiction over genocide, war crimes, and crimes against humanity.[151]

Perhaps because of its prescriptive and procedural limitations, the ATS has been the subject of surprisingly little opposition.[152] Whilst European states may prefer criminal or administrative remedies for gross human rights violations, they do not seem resistant in principle to 'universal' tort jurisdiction of this kind, though they remain opposed to the perceived exorbitance of the US regime of civil jurisdiction *in personam*.[153]

(D) CONCLUSION

Notwithstanding the prevailing understanding of a conceptual rift between public and private international law, the two share a certain theoretical underpinning. Although perhaps not recognized by practitioners, states are certainly taking action to unify their approaches to conflict of laws, and moreover, doing it through the conclusion of treaties, the tool of public international law. Aside from those regimes concluded on a regional basis,[154] global international conventions have also emerged, notably the Hague Conventions on Private International Law and on International Civil Procedure.[155]

4. THE SEPARATENESS OF THE GROUNDS OF JURISDICTION

(A) THE RELATIONSHIP BETWEEN THE SEPARATE GROUNDS

The status of treaty-based crimes under international law involves special considerations and can be left on one side. The various principles held to justify jurisdiction over

---

Cir, 2010); and Crook (2010) 104 *AJIL* 119. The Supreme Court has ordered a rehearing of the *Kiobel* appeal on grounds related to the scope of jurisdiction under the ATS.

[149] Ryngaert (2008) 126.

[150] 542 US 692, 749 (2004).

[151] Ryngaert (2003) 38 *NYIL* 3, 35–8.

[152] E.g. *Arrest Warrant*, ICJ Reports 2002 p 3, 77 (Judges Higgins, Kooijmans & Buergenthal) ('[w]hile this unilateral exercise of the function of guardian of international values has been much commented on, it has not attracted the approbation of States generally'). Cf Ramsay (2009) 50 *Harv ILJ* 271.

[153] Ryngaert (2008) 126.

[154] The Brussels 1 Regulation and the Rome I Regulation are the characteristic examples of this, but cf also the results of the Organization of American States Specialized Conferences on Private International Law: www.oas.org/dil/privateintlaw_interamericanconferences.htm.

[155] Cf the list of conventions at www.hcch.net/index_en.php.

aliens are commonly listed as independent and cumulative,[156] although some may be labelled 'subsidiary' to some others.[157] However, it must be remembered that the 'principles' are in substance generalizations of a mass of national provisions which by and large do not reflect categories of jurisdiction specifically recognized by international law. It may be that each individual principle is only evidence of the reasonableness of the exercise of jurisdiction.[158] The various principles often interweave in practice. Thus, the objective applications of the territorial principle and also the passive personality principle have strong similarities to the protective or security principle. Nationality and security may go together, or, in the case of the alien, factors such as residence may support an ad hoc notion of allegiance. These features of the practice have led some jurists to formulate a broad principle resting on some genuine or effective link between the crime and the state of the forum.[159]

(B) CONSEQUENCES OF EXCESS OF PRESCRIPTIVE JURISDICTION[160]

(i) The legal position

If enforcement action is taken in a case of exorbitant jurisdiction with consequent injury, an international wrong will presumably have been committed. The consequences of the mere *passage* of legislation asserting exorbitant jurisdiction remain an open question. The situation is clouded by the uncertain status of the statement in the *Lotus* that, in the absence of a rule in international law to the contrary, a state may do whatever it pleases;[161] although the various separate opinions in the *Arrest Warrant* case may have signalled the reversal of this position,[162] the reversal itself is inchoate, and it remains to be seen whether it represents merely a cosmetic shift in emphasis or something more substantive.[163] In part, this is due to the fact that although vigorously

---

[156] E.g. *Janković*, Decision on Art 11*bis* referral (ICTY Appeals Chamber, Case No IT-96–23/2-AR11*bis*.2, 15 November 2005), §34 ('In this context, the Appeals Chamber notes that attempts among States to establish a hierarchy of criteria for determining the most appropriate jurisdiction for a criminal case, where there are concurrent jurisdictions on a horizontal level (i.e. among States), have failed thus far'). Available at www.icty.org/x/cases/stankovic/acdec/en/051115.htm.

[157] E.g. *Eichmann* (1962) 36 ILR 277, 302; *Arrest Warrant*, ICJ Reports 2002 p 3, 80 (Judges Higgins, Kooijmans & Buergenthal) (arguing that universal jurisdiction can only be exercised once the territorial state has declined to take action).

[158] Further: Ryngaert (2008) ch 5.

[159] Mann (1964) 111 Hague *Recueil* 9, 43–51, 82–126; Sarkar (1962) 11 *ICLQ* 446, 466–70; Fawcett (1962) 38 *BY* 181, 188–90; Steinberger, in Olmstead (1984) 77, 91–3. Cf Fitzmaurice (1957) 92 Hague *Recueil* 1, 215–17.

[160] Ryngaert (2008) ch 2; Kamminga, 'Extraterritoriality' (2008) *MPEPIL*.

[161] (1927) PCIJ Ser A No 10, 19.

[162] ICJ Reports 2002 p 3, 78 (Judges Higgins, Kooijmans & Buergenthal), 169 (Judge ad hoc van den Wyngaert). Further: *Barcelona Traction, Light and Power Co Ltd (Belgium v Spain)*, Second Phase, ICJ Reports 1970 p 3, 105 (Judge Fitzmaurice).

[163] Ryngaert (2008) 22–6; cf Higgins (1994) 162–3.

criticized and perceived widely to be obsolete,[164] the *Lotus* remains the only judgment of an international court to tackle directly this particular aspect of jurisdiction.[165]

(ii) Practical consequences

As a practical matter, whilst states may protest the use of exorbitant prescriptive jurisdiction by others, unless the prescribing state attempts to enforce the jurisdiction claimed, it is unlikely that any substantive legal action will be taken. As O'Keefe notes, although the concepts of jurisdiction to prescribe and jurisdiction to enforce are logically independent, they are practically intertwined.[166] At the same time, a prescriptive statement—even absent immediate enforcement action—is fundamentally a threat, which may compel foreign nationals to alter their behaviour.[167] This may cause the other state to take its own action in the form of a 'blocking statute', being a law enacted in one jurisdiction to obstruct the local (extra-jurisdictional) application of a law enacted in another jurisdiction.[168]

5. ENFORCEMENT JURISDICTION

(A) THE BASIC PRINCIPLE[169]

As with prescriptive jurisdiction, a state's use of enforcement jurisdiction within its own territory is uncontroversial. By contrast, the unilateral and extra-territorial use of enforcement jurisdiction is impermissible. As the Permanent Court said in the *Lotus*:

[T]he first and foremost restriction imposed by international law upon a state is that—failing the exercise of a permissive rule to the contrary—it may not exercise its power in any form in the territory of another State. In this sense jurisdiction is certainly territorial; it cannot be exercised by a State outside its territory except by virtue of a permissive rule derived from international custom or a convention.[170]

---

[164] E.g. Mann (1964) 111 Hague *Recueil* 1, Higgins (1994) 77; Ryngaert (2008) 21–6; *Arrest Warrant*, ICJ Reports 2002 p 3, 140–1 (Judge ad hoc van den Wyngaert).

[165] Cf Ryngaert (2008) 26–41.

[166] O'Keefe (2004) 2 *JICJ* 735, 741.

[167] Ryngaert (2008) 24–5.

[168] E.g. Protection of Trading Interests Act 1980 (UK) (which has however been little used). Also EC Regulation 2271/96, enacted in response to the Helms-Burton and D'Amato-Kennedy Acts. Further: the 1982 comments of the European Community regarding the so-called 'pipeline dispute': Lowe (1984) 33 *ICLQ* 515.

[169] Mann (1964) 111 Hague *Recueil* 9, 126–58; Mann (1964) 13 *ICLQ* 1460; Jennings (1957) 33 *BY* 146; 6 Whiteman 118–83; Verzijl (1961) 8 *NILR* 3; van Hecke (1962) 106 Hague *Recueil* 253, 257–356; Akehurst (1972–73) 46 *BY* 145, 179–212; Rosenthal & Knighton, *National Laws and International Commerce* (1982); Meessen (ed), *Extra-territorial Jurisdiction in Theory and Practice* (1996).

[170] (1927) PCIJ Ser A No 10, 18.

The governing principle of enforcement jurisdiction is that a state cannot take measures on the territory of another state by way of enforcement of its laws without the consent of the latter.[171] Persons may not be arrested, a summons may not be served, police or tax investigations may not be mounted, orders for production of documents may not be executed, on the territory of another state, except under the terms of a treaty or other consent given.[172] One key example of such consent is a Status of Mission or Status of Forces Agreement (SOMA or SOFA), whereby one state consents to the presence of another's troops on its territory and to related military jurisdiction.[173]

(B) ENFORCEMENT WITH RESPECT TO EXTRA-TERRITORIAL ACTIVITIES

The principle of territoriality is not infringed just because a state takes action within its own borders with respect to acts done in another state. But the correctness of this position has not prevented controversy from arising. This is especially the case when considering the use by US courts of the 'effects doctrine' to promote certain prescriptive objectives in the field of economic regulation, especially antitrust law. US courts in, for example, *Alcoa*[174] and *Watchmakers of Switzerland*,[175] have taken the view that whenever activity abroad has consequences or effects within the US which are contrary to local legislation then the American courts may make orders requiring the disposition of patent rights and other property of foreign corporations, the reorganization of industry in another country, the production of documents, and so on. The American doctrine appears to be restricted to agreements abroad intended to have material effects within the US and actually having such effects.[176] Such orders may be enforced by action within the US against individuals or property present within the territorial jurisdiction, and the policy adopted goes beyond the normal application of the objective territorial principle. US courts have, in the past, adopted a principle of the balancing of the various national interests involved, which, though unhelpfully vague, could result in some mitigation of the cruder aspects of the 'effects doctrine'.[177]

---

[171] E.g. *Armed Activities on the Territory of the Congo (Democratic Republic of the Congo v Uganda)*, ICJ Reports 2005 p 168, 196–9.

[172] *Lotus* (1927) PCIJ Ser A No 10, 18; *Service of Summons* (1961) 38 ILR 133; 2 *Répertoire suisse de droit international public*, 986–1017.

[173] E.g. Agreement between the Parties to the North Atlantic Treaty regarding the Status of their Forces, 19 June 1951, 199 UNTS 67, Art VII; Agreement between the Democratic Republic of East Timor and the United Nations concerning the Status of the United Nations Mission of Support in East Timor, 20 May 2002, 2185 UNTS 368, Arts 43–4. Further: chapter 22.

[174] *United States v Aluminium Co of America*, 148 F.2d 416 (1945).

[175] *United States v Watchmakers of Switzerland Information Center Inc*, 133 F.Supp 40 (SDNY, 1955); 134 F.Supp 710 (SDNY, 1955).

[176] Intention was not a prominent requirement in *United States v ICI*, 100 F.Supp 504 (SDNY, 1951); 105 F.Supp 215 (SDNY, 1952), and in many circumstances it can be inferred.

[177] *Timberlane Lumber Company v Bank of America*, 549 F.2d 597 (9th Cir, 1976); *Mannington Mills Inc v Congoleum Corporation*, 595 F.2d 1287 (3rd Cir, 1979). The 'balancing' approach was criticized in *Laker Airways Ltd v Sabena*, 731 F.2d 909 (DC Cir, 1984). Also Meessen (1984) 78 *AJIL* 783. *Hartford Fire Insurance*

The courts, the US government,[178] and foreign governments in reacting to US meas-ures assume that there are *some* limits to enforcement jurisdiction but there is no con-sensus on what those limits are.[179] The UK view appears to be that a state 'acts in excess of its own jurisdiction when its measures purport to regulate acts which are done out-side its territorial jurisdiction by persons who are not its own nationals and which have no, or no substantial, effect within its territorial jurisdiction'.[180] Jennings has stated the principle 'that extra-territorial jurisdiction may not be exercised in such a way as to contradict the local law at the place where the alleged offence was committed'.[181] In the case of corporations with complex structures and foreign-based subsidiaries, a principle of substantial or effective connection could be applied as a basis for jurisdic-tion.[182] This approach would accord with the relevant notions of the conflict of laws, in particular, the 'proper law' of a transaction. The present position is probably this: a state has enforcement jurisdiction abroad only to the extent necessary to enforce its legislative jurisdiction. This latter rests upon the existing principles of jurisdiction and these, it has been suggested, are close to the principle of substantial connection.

(C) RECOGNITION AND ENFORCEMENT ABROAD

(i) Criminal jurisdiction

In a criminal context, enforcement jurisdiction will ordinarily entail the pursuit and arrest of the accused, detention and trial, and the carrying out of any sentence.[183]

With respect to extra-territorial enforcement action leading to the capture of the accused, state consent can be given on ad hoc basis,[184] but in circumstances where movement between two states is relatively regular and straightforward, bi- or multi-lateral agreements may be entered into in order to provide standing orders for enforcement jurisdiction between states. The most notable of these is the Schengen

---

v California, 509 US 764 (1993) ignored almost all the balancing factors and held that US courts should exer-cise jurisdiction where there is a substantial effect within the US and there is no conflict, i.e. no foreign law requires that a party act or not act in a certain manner contrary to US laws.

[178] 6 Whiteman 133, 159, 164.

[179] *Barcelona Traction*, Second Phase, ICJ Reports 1970 p 3, 103–6 (Judge Fitzmaurice); ICJ Pleadings, *Barcelona Traction*, Belgian Memorial, 114; ICJ Pleadings, 1 *Barcelona Traction (New Application: 1962)*, Belgian Memorial, 165, 167–8.

[180] The Attorney-General, Sir John Hobson, 15 July 1964; *British Practice* (1964) 146, 153.

[181] (1957) 33 BY 146, 151. Also *British Nylon Spinners Ltd v ICI Ltd* [1952] 2 All ER 780; [1954] 3 All ER 88; Kahn-Freund (1955) 18 *MLR* 65.

[182] *Carron Iron Co v Maclaren* (1855) 5 HLC 416, 442 (Lord Cranworth); *The Tropaioforos* (1962) 1 Lloyd's List LR 410; Mann (1964) 111 Hague *Recueil* 1, 149–50.

[183] Generally: McClean, *International Co-operation in Civil and Criminal Matters* (2002).

[184] E.g. police officials of various nationalities were permitted to enter Indonesia in the wake of the Bali bombings (2002), UK police were permitted to operate in Germany during the soccer World Cup in order to regulate football hooliganism (2006), and French forces were permitted to enter Somali territory in order to capture the pirates responsible for the seizure of the French yacht *Le Ponant* (2008).

Convention[185] between some members of the EU. Article 40(1) provides that where the officials of one contracting party are keeping under surveillance a person suspected of an extraditable offence, they may request that surveillance be continued in the territory of another contracting party by officials of that party. Article 40(2) further provides that in circumstances where, for particularly urgent reasons, authorization cannot be requested from the other contracting party, the officials carrying out the surveillance may be authorized to continue the surveillance in the territory of the other contracting party. On similar lines, Article 41 of the Convention permits the officials to engage in hot pursuit of a subject across state borders, where due to the urgency of the situation, the permission of the other contracting state cannot be obtained.

More generally, Article 39(1) provides that, subject to the requirements of municipal law, the police authorities of each contracting party undertake to assist each other for the purpose of detecting and preventing criminal offences, though this does not expressly mandate extra-territorial enforcement. Article 39 is supplemented in this respect by the Convention on Mutual Assistance in Criminal Matters between the Member States of the European Union.[186] Treaties of mutual criminal assistance, like enforcement agreements, can also be concluded on a bilateral or multilateral basis.[187]

Unlike activities connected to the surveillance of the accused and his or her arrest, trial and incarceration is rarely carried out in an extra-territorial capacity, particularly in circumstances not linked to a SOMA or SOFA. But when the Libyan government refused to extradite those thought to be responsible for the 1988 bombing of Pan Am Flight 103 over Lockerbie, Scotland, unless they were tried in a neutral country, the UK and the Netherlands entered into an agreement to permit a Scots court applying Scots criminal law to sit in a former US Air Force base in Zeist in order to try the accused.[188]

---

[185] Convention implementing the Schengen Agreement of 14 June 1985 between the Governments of the States of the Benelux Economic Union, the Federal Republic of Germany and the French Republic on the gradual abolition of checks at their common borders [2000] *OJEU* L 239/19.

[186] [2001] *OJEU* C 197/1. Also: Convention on the Establishment of a European Police Office [1995] *OJEU* C 316/2. Further: McClean (2002) 167–8, 224–37.

[187] The UN has concluded a series of model and actual treaties designed to secure greater co-operation in criminal matters: UN Model Treaty on Mutual Assistance in Criminal Matters, 14 December 1990, A/RES/45/117, amended by A/RES/53/112, 20 January 1999; Model Treaty on the Transfer of Proceedings in Criminal Matters, 14 December 1990, A/RES/45/118; UN Convention Against Transnational Organized Crime, 15 November 2000, A/RES/55/25 (Annex I). Further: McClean (2002) 213–20; *Certain Questions of Mutual Assistance in Criminal Matters (Djibouti v France)*, ICJ Reports 2008 p 117.

[188] Agreement between the Government of the United Kingdom of Great Britain and Northern Ireland and the Government of the Kingdom of the Netherlands concerning a Scottish trial in the Netherlands, 18 September 1998, 2062 UNTS 81. This approach was approved in SC Res 1192 (1998). Further: Scharf (1999–2000) 6 *ILSA JICL* 355; Elegab (2000) 34 *Int Lawyer* 289; Aust (2000) 49 *ICLQ* 278; Plachta (2001) 12 *EJIL* 125. Also: Agreement between the Government of the United Kingdom of Great Britain and Northern Ireland and the Government of New Zealand concerning trials under Pitcairn law in New Zealand and related matters, 11 October 2002, 2219 UNTS 57; Pitcairn Trials Act 2002 (NZ); *R v Seven Named Accused* (2004) 127 ILR 232; *Christian & Ors v R* [2007] 2 WLR 120.

Provision is also made by treaty for the enforcement of foreign criminal judgments. Here, there is generally a divide between the civil and common law approaches to the subject, with the latter rejecting in principle the enforcement of the penal law of another state.[189] Civil law systems are less averse to the concept, as witness the European Convention on the International Validity of Criminal Judgments.[190]

Apart from trial *in absentia*, an unsatisfactory procedure, states have to depend on the co-operation of the other states in order to obtain surrender of suspected criminals or convicted criminals who are, or have fled, abroad. Where this co-operation rests on a procedure of request and consent, regulated by certain general principles, the form of international judicial assistance is called extradition.[191] Due to the profusion of extradition treaties, it is possible to speak of an international law of extradition, a term which does not imply the existence of custom, but of a significant corpus of conventional law exhibiting certain common elements. Such treaties are usually bilateral,[192] but the European Convention on Extradition (ECE)[193] is in effect between EU Member States (though it has been largely replaced by the European arrest warrant (EAW), which combines elements of arrest and extradition).[194] The UN has also issued a Model Treaty on Extradition (UNMTE).[195] Common conditions include double criminality (the act in question must be criminal under the laws of both the requesting and requested states),[196] non-extradition for 'political offences',[197] and the rule of speciality which prevents prosecution founded on a treaty-based extradition

---

[189] E.g. *Wisconsin v Pelican Insurance Co*, 127 US 265 (1887); *Huntington v Attrill* [1893] AC 150; *United States v Inkley* [1989] QB 255 (CA).

[190] 28 May 1970, ETS No 70. Further: McClean (2002), 367–78.

[191] Generally: Shearer, *Extradition in International Law* (1971); Stanbrook & Stanbrook, *Extradition Law and Practice* (2nd edn, 2000); Sambei & Jones, *Extradition Law Handbook* (2005); Nicholls & Montgomery, *The Law of Extradition and Mutual Assistance* (2nd edn, 2007); Stein, 'Extradition' (2006) *MPEPIL*. On reciprocity as a basis for extradition: Rezek (1981) 52 *BY* 171.

[192] E.g. Extradition Treaty between the Government of the United Kingdom of Great Britain and Northern Ireland and the Government of the United States of America, 31 March 2003, Cm 5821.

[193] 13 December 1957, 359 UNTS 273. Also: Additional Protocol to the European Convention on Extradition, 15 October 1975, CETS No 86; Second Additional Protocol to the European Convention on Extradition, 17 March 1978, CETS No 98.

[194] Cf EC Framework Decision of 13 June 2002 on the European arrest warrant and surrender procedures between Member States [2002] *OJEU* L 190/1; and see *Assange v Swedish Prosecution Authority* [2012] UKSC 22. A similar though voluntary scheme persists between Commonwealth nations: London Scheme for Extradition within the Commonwealth (incorporated agreed amendments at Kingstown, November 2002), in Commonwealth Secretariat, *2002 Meeting of Commonwealth Law Ministers and Senior Officials* (2003) Annex B.

[195] 14 December 1990, A/RES/45/116. The Model Treaty has been supplemented by a UN Model Law on Extradition, issued by the UN Office on Drugs and Crime: 10 May 2004, E/EN.15/2004/CRP.10.

[196] E.g. UNMTE, Art 2. Older treaties phrased this requirement in terms of an exhaustive list of offences for which extradition could be requested: ECE, Art 2, but cf Art 2(4). The EAW does away with this entirely with respect to certain serious offences, including those deemed to be crimes under the ICC Statute: EAW, Art 2(2).

[197] E.g. UNMTE, Art 3(a), ECE, Art 3. Also the European Convention on Extradition, 13 December 1957, 359 UNTS 273, Art 3, supplemented by Additional Protocol, 15 October 1975, 1161 UNTS 450, Art 1.

from proceeding on any basis other than that upon which the request was founded.[198] Another significant limitation is the rule *ne bis in idem*, which precludes extradition of persons already tried for the same offence.[199] Finally, many states reserve the right to refuse extradition owing to human rights concerns, for example, where extradition may mean that the accused is liable to torture,[200] or the death penalty.[201]

Since the attacks by al-Qaeda on the US in 2001, there has been an increase in 'informal' extradition or rendition, though the practice is not new.[202] If it takes place with the consent of the 'sending' state, there is no transgression of international law standards.[203] If, however, there is no extradition of any kind—informal or otherwise—but the suspect is simply seized by the agents of the receiving state in the absence of any legal process, then there is clearly a breach of international law.[204] This described generally as 'extraordinary rendition', has been practised by the US since 2001. Depending on the legal system in question, the attendant illegality may not prevent the trial of the suspect, an application of the maxim *male captus bene detentus*.[205]

(ii) Civil and administrative jurisdiction

With respect to civil and administrative jurisdiction, extra-territorial enforcement revolves largely around the recognition and enforcement of judgments and orders abroad. This is one of the central preoccupations of private international law. In general, the field is parochial, with each state developing its own process and criteria for recognition and enforcement. The Brussels 1 Regulation seeks to unify the proce-

---

[198] E.g. UNMTE, Art 14, ECE, Art 14.

[199] E.g. UNMTE, Art 3(d), ECE, Arts 8–9. EAW, Art 4(5), extends the principle to situations where third states have given judgment against the accused, subject to the treaty in question.

[200] E.g. UNMTE, Art 3(f). Additionally, the European Court of Human Rights held that all parties to the ECHR could not knowingly extradite an individual where that individual would be in danger of torture: *Soering v United Kingdom* (1989) 98 ILR 270. Cf *Netherlands v Short* (1990) 29 ILM 1375; *Ng v Canada* (1993) 98 ILR 497; *Aylor* (1993) 100 ILR 664; *US v Burns and Rafay* (2001) 124 ILR 298; *Mamatkulov and Askarov v Turkey* (2005) 134 ILR 230.

[201] E.g. UNMTE, Art 3(d), ECE, Art 11.

[202] Cf notoriously, *Eichmann* (1962) 36 ILR 5. There, the accused was abducted from Argentina, drugged, and dressed as a flight attendant for rendition to Israel. Further: Fawcett (1962) 38 *BY* 181.

[203] Including human rights standards: *Öcalan v Turkey* [2005] ECtHR 46221/99 (irregular rendition not automatically contrary to ECHR Art 5(1)).

[204] E.g. *Opinion of the Inter-American Jurisdiction Committee on the International Legality of SCOTUS Case 91–712* (1993) 4 *CLF* 119; *Stocké v Germany* (1991) 95 ILR 327. Further: Parry (2005) 6 *Melb JIL* 516; Sadat (2005) 37 *Case WRJIL* 309; Weissbrodt & Bergquist (2006) 19 *Harv HRJ* 123; Sands, in *Mélanges Salmon* (2007) 1074; Satterthwaite (2007) 75 *G Wash LR* 1333; Winkler (2008) 30 *Loyola LA ICLR* 33; Messineo (2009) 7 *JICJ* 1023; Jensen & Jenks (2010) 1 *Harv NSJ* 171. Cf also the reports of the Council of Europe on rendition: EC Docs 10957, 12 June 2006, 11302 rev, 11 June 2007.

[205] This is so in the US: *United States v Alvarez-Machain*, 504 US 655 (1992). But cf *R v Horseferry Road Magistrates' Court, ex parte Bennett* [1994] 1 AC 42; *S v Ebrahim* (1991) 95 ILR 417. Traditionally European jurisdictions would ordinarily accept jurisdiction in exorbitant circumstances, but this has changed with the ECtHR: *Re Argoud* (1964) 45 ILR 90; cf *Stocké v Germany* (1991) 95 ILR 350. Further: *El-Masri v Macedonia*, *al Nasheri v Poland* & *Abu Zubaydaf v Lithuania*, pending before the ECtHR.

dures for the recognition of judgments between EU member states.[206] The judgment of a court of a member state is subject to automatic recognition (Article 33) and enforcement (Article 38) by the courts of other member states, with the onus on the defendant to contest enforcement according to a limited number of clearly defined exceptions.[207]

However, the need to approach the court of the jurisdiction where enforcement is sought is circumvented—in form if not in substance—when considering certain orders issued by common law courts (notably in England but also the US) which act *in personam* on the conscience of a party properly before the court to restrain its dealings with assets or processes outside the jurisdiction. The first of these, the so-called 'freezing injunction',[208] acts *in personam* to prevent a defendant from moving, hiding or otherwise dissipating its assets so as to render itself judgment-proof.[209] The injunction neither creates, transfers nor revokes property rights; it merely affects the capacity of the defendant to exercise them freely.[210] But what the freezing injunction lacks in extra-territorial form, it makes up for in extra-territorial effect. The scope of the order has been expanded considerably. First, by virtue of its *in personam* operation, the injunction can be granted with respect to assets which are not within the jurisdiction of the court granting the order.[211] Further, it can be given effect against foreign third parties, normally multinational banks with a branch within the jurisdiction granting the order.[212] Finally, it can be granted in aid of foreign proceedings even where no proceedings are on foot before the court granting the order.[213]

The second example is the anti-suit injunction, which acts to restrain a party subject to the jurisdiction of the court from launching or continuing proceedings in a foreign court injurious to the defendant in those proceedings.[214] Ordinarily, the claimant in the foreign proceedings must be already before the court,[215] though the relief may be

---

[206] Generally: Brussels 1 Regulation, Ch III; Kennett, *The Enforcement of Judgments in Europe* (2000); Fentiman (2010) ch 18.

[207] Brussels 1 Regulation, Arts 34, 35.

[208] *Mareva Compania Naviera SA v International Bulkcarriers SA* [1975] 2 Lloyd's Rep 509; and cf generally: Fentiman (2010) 642–90. Also: Senior Courts Act 1981 (UK) s37(1) and (3); Civil Jurisdiction and Judgments Act 1982 (UK) s25.

[209] *Ashtiani v Kashi* [1987] QB 888.

[210] *Babanaft International Co v Bassatne* [1990] Ch 13, 37–9 (Kerr LJ), 41–2 (Nicholls LJ).

[211] E.g. *Babanaft International Co v Bassatne* [1990] Ch 13; *Derby & Co Ltd v Weldon* [1990] Ch 48 (CA).

[212] Where compliance with the freezing injunction would prevent the third party complying with what it reasonably believes to be its obligations under the law of the jurisdiction in which the assets are located, it need not comply with the order: *Babanaft International Co v Bassatne* [1990] Ch 13; *Baltic Shipping v Translink* [1995] 1 Lloyd's Rep 673; *Bank of China v NMB LLC* [2002] 1 WLR 844.

[213] E.g. *Credit Suisse Fides Trust SA v Coughi* [1998] QB 818; *Republic of Haiti v Duvalier* [1990] 1 QB 202; *Refco v Eastern Trading Co* [1999] 1 Lloyd's Rep 159 (CA); *Ryan v Friction Dynamics* [2001] CP Rep 75; *Motorola Credit Corporation v Uzan* [2004] 1 WLR 113.

[214] *Castanho v Brown & Root* [1981] AC 557, 573; *Airbus Industrie GIE v Patel* [1999] 1 AC 119, 133; *Amchem Products Inc v British Columbia Workers Compensation Board* (1993) 102 DLR (4th) 96, 119; *Turner v Grovit* [2002] 1 WLR 107. Generally: Fentiman (2010) ch 15; Senior Courts Act 1981 (UK) s27.

[215] *Masri v Consolidated Contractors International (UK) Ltd (No 3)* [2009] QB 503, 533. This also includes cases where the foreign claimant is prevented from re-litigating previous proceedings: e.g. *Royal Bank of Scotland plc v Hicks & Gillette* [2010] EWHC 2579 (Ch).

granted autonomously of any domestic proceedings where the subject-matter of the proceedings[216] or the relationship between the parties[217] is such as to give the granting court exclusive jurisdiction. Although the order is usually granted where the claimant in the foreign proceedings has commenced them in a manner which is somehow objectionable, it may also be granted where the foreign claimant has apparently acted without blame.[218]

The perceived exorbitance of the common law jurisdictions in respect of these orders is often criticized on the basis of 'comity'.[219] Comity arises from the horizontal arrangement of state jurisdictions in private international law and the field's lack of a hierarchical system of norms. It plays the role of a somewhat uncertain umpire: as a concept, it is far from a binding norm, but it is more than mere courtesy exercised between state courts. The Supreme Court of Canada said in *Morguard v De Savoye*,[220] citing the decision of the US Supreme Court in *Hilton v Cuyot*,[221] that:

Comity is the recognition which one nation allows within its territory to the legislative, executive or judicial acts of another nation, having due regard both to international duty and convenience, and to the rights of its own citizens or of other persons who are under the protection of its law.

Common lawyers have been anxious to justify the development of the freezing and anti-suit injunctions on the basis of comity.[222] For this reason, as with the doctrine of *forum non conveniens*, whilst the jurisdiction to grant the remedy may be easily established, the claimant must nonetheless persuade the court to exercise its discretion. A substantial body of jurisprudence has built up around these remedies to guide the court in its use of discretion. But so far these efforts at justification have fallen on deaf European ears: the European Court of Justice has repeatedly disqualified such injunctive measures as inconsistent with full faith and credit as between EU member state courts, however dilatory or parochial the latter may be.[223]

---

[216] E.g. *Midland Bank plc v Laker Airways Ltd* [1986] QB 689; cf *Siskina (Owners of cargo lately laden on board) v Distos Compania Naviera SA* [1979] AC 210.

[217] Notably where the parties have concluded an exclusive jurisdiction agreement in favour of the injuncting court: e.g. *Donohue v Armco Ltd* [2002] 1 Lloyd's Rep 425.

[218] As was the case in *Société Nationale Industrielle Aérospatiale v Lee Kui Jak* [1987] AC 871 (PC).

[219] Generally: Maier (1982) 76 *AJIL* 280; Paul (1991) 32 *Harv JIL* 1; Collins, in Fawcett (ed), *Reform and Development of Private International Law* (2002) 89.

[220] [1990] 3 SCR 1077, 1096.

[221] 159 US 113, 164 (1895).

[222] E.g. in relation to anti-suit injunctions, *Turner v Grovit* [2002] 1 WLR 107, §28 (Lord Hobhouse). Further: Hartley (1987) 35 *AJCL* 487; Peel (1998) 114 LQR 543; Fentiman (1998) 57 *CLJ* 467; Fentiman (2010) 579–85. In relation to freezing injunctions: *Credit Suisse Fides Trust SA v Cuoghi* [1998] QB 818; *Refco v Eastern Trading Co* [1999] 1 Lloyd's Rep 159.

[223] E.g. Case C-150/02, *Turner v Grovit* [2005] ECR I-3565; Case C-116/02, *Erich Gasser GmbH v MISAT srl* [2003] ECR I-14693 (ECJ); Case C-185/08, *Allianz SpA v West Tankers Inc* [2009] ECR I-663.

6. A GENERAL VIEW OF THE LAW

To conclude, based on this review the following propositions may be suggested:

First, the exercise of civil jurisdiction in respect of aliens presents essentially the same problems as the exercise of criminal jurisdiction over them, though in practical terms there are differences, both procedurally and in the reactions that can be expected.

Secondly, the two generally recognized bases for prescriptive jurisdiction of all types are the territorial and nationality principles, but their application is complemented by the operation of other principles especially in certain fields. The use of the passive personality principle in cases of international terrorism appears to be accepted and, over time, opposition to the use of the effects doctrine by the US and EU in the pursuit of certain competition law objectives is diminishing. As a general rule, however, it remains true that if a state wishes to avoid international criticism over its exercise of extra-territorial jurisdiction, it is better to base the prescriptive elements on territoriality or nationality.

Thirdly, extra-territorial acts can lawfully be the object of prescriptive jurisdiction only if certain general principles are observed:

(1) There should be a real and not colourable connection between the subject-matter and the source of the jurisdiction (leaving aside cases of universal jurisdiction).[224]

(2) The principle of non-intervention in the territorial jurisdiction of other states should be observed, notably in an enforcement context.[225]

(3) Elements of accommodation, mutuality, and proportionality should be duly taken into account. Thus nationals resident abroad should not be constrained to violate the law of their place of residence.

(4) These basic principles do not apply or do not apply very helpfully to (a) certain cases of concurrent jurisdiction, and (b) crimes against international law within the ambit of universal jurisdiction. In these areas special rules have evolved. Special regimes also apply to the high seas, continental shelf, EEZ, outer space, and Antarctica.

(5) Jurisdiction is often concurrent and there is no hierarchy of bases for jurisdiction. However, an area of exclusivity may be established by treaty, as in the case of offences committed on board aircraft in flight.

---

[224] The various principles of criminal jurisdiction overlap and could be synthesized in this way. Further: Mann (1964) 111 Hague *Recueil* 1, 44–51, 126; *Survey of International Law*, 23 April 1971, A/CN.4/245, §§80–90; *Barcelona Traction*, Second Phase, ICJ Reports 1970 p 3, 248–50, 262–3 (Judge Padilla Nervo). Cf ibid, 103–6 (Judge Fitzmaurice).

[225] E.g. *Buck v Attorney-General* [1965] Ch 745, 770–2 (Diplock LJ); *Lauritzen v Larsen*, 345 US 571, 584–6 (1953); *Rio Tinto Zinc Corporation v Westinghouse* [1978] AC 547, 607ff (Lord Wilberforce), 618ff (Lord Dilhorne). For the view of the Federal Cartel Office, German Federal Republic, and the Constitutional Court: Gelber (1983) 77 *AJIL* 756, 776–7. Further: UKMIL (1978) 49 *BY* 329, 388–90; (1984) 55 *BY* 405, 540; (1985) 56 *BY* 363, 385–6. Cf *Aérospatiale v District Court*, 482 US 522, 554–61 (1987) (Justice Blackmun, diss).

22

PRIVILEGES AND IMMUNITIES OF FOREIGN STATES

1. EVOLUTION OF THE INTERNATIONAL LAW OF IMMUNITY[1]

(A) THE LAW IN CONTEXT

State immunity is a rule of international law that facilitates the performance of public functions by the state and its representatives by preventing them from being sued or prosecuted in foreign courts. Essentially, it precludes the courts of the forum state from exercising adjudicative and enforcement jurisdiction in certain classes of case in which a foreign state is a party. It is a procedural bar (not a substantive defence) based on the status and functions of the state or official in question.[2] Previously described as a privilege conferred at the behest of the executive,[3] the grant of immunity is now understood as an obligation under customary international law.[4] But although the

---

[1] Harvard Research (1932) 26 *AJIL Supp* 451; Fitzmaurice (1933) 14 *BY* 101; Allen, *The Position of Foreign States before National Courts* (1933); Mann (1938) 2 *MLR* 57; Lauterpacht (1951) 28 *BY* 220; Lalive (1953) 84 Hague *Recueil* 205; Mann (1955) 18 *MLR* 184; Sucharitkul, *State Immunities and Trading Activities* (1959); Sucharitkul (1976) 149 Hague *Recueil* 87; Sinclair (1980) 167 Hague *Recueil* 113; UN Legislative Series, *Materials on Jurisdictional Immunities of States and Their Property* (1982); Higgins (1982) 29 *NILR* 265; ILA, Report of the 60th Conference (1982) 325; Badr, *State Immunity: An Analytical and Prognostic View* (1984); Trooboff (1986) 200 Hague *Recueil* 235; Schreuer, *State Immunity* (1988); ILA, Report of the 64th Conference (1990) 393; IDI (1991) 64/II *Ann de l'Inst* 388; ILA, Report of the 66th Conference (1994) 452; Cosnard, *La Soumission des États aux tribunaux internes* (1996); Pingel-Lenuzza, *Les Immunités des États en droit international* (1997); IDI (2001) 69 *Ann de l'Inst* 742; Dickinson, Lindsay & Loonam, *State Immunity* (2004); Pingel, *Droit des immunités et exigencies du procès equitable* (2004); Bankas, *The State Immunity Controversy in International Law* (2005); Hafner, Kohen & Breau (eds), *State Practice Regarding State Immunities* (2006); Fox, *The Law of State Immunity* (2nd edn, 2008); IDI (2009) 73 *Ann de l'Inst* 3; Franey, *Immunity, Individuals and International Law* (2011); Yang, *State Immunity in International Law* (2012).

[2] On the personal character of the plea of state immunity: Fox (2nd edn, 2008) 102–3.

[3] Caplan (2003) 97 *AJIL* 741. This notion persists in the US: *Republic of Austria v Altmann*, 541 US 677, 689 (2004).

[4] E.g. *Holland v Lampen-Wolfe* [2000] 1 WLR 1573, 1583; *Distomo Massacre* (2000) 129 ILR 513, 516; *Al-Adsani v UK* (2001) 123 ILR 24, §54; *Arrest Warrant of 11 April 2000 (DRC v Belgium)*, ICJ Reports 2002 p 3, 20–1; *Schreiber v Germany* (2002) 216 DLR (4th) 513, 518; *Iraq v Vinci* (2002) 127 ILR 101, 109; *X v Israel* (2002) 127 ILR 310, 310–11; *X v Saudi School in Paris* (2003) 127 ILR 163, 166; *Kenyan Diplomatic Residence* (2003) 128 ILR 632, 635–6; *Ferrini v Federal Republic of Germany* (2004) 128 ILR 658, 663–4; *Jones v Saudi*

existence of this obligation is supported by ample authority, no general statement of principle appeared at the international level until 2004: the law developed primarily through domestic case-law and limited treaty practice, supplemented more recently by comprehensive legislation in certain states. Immunity exists as a rule of international law, but its application depends substantially on the law and procedural rules of the forum. Increasingly, however, these issues are being elevated to an international level, including through international litigation.[5] This development may tend to the consolidation of the law of immunity at more or less its present phase of development.

(B) RATIONALES FOR STATE IMMUNITY

Derived from the immunity historically attaching to the person of a visiting sovereign, reflected in the Latin maxim *par in parem non habet imperium* (an equal has no authority over an equal), state immunity operates on twin bases. First, as an immunity *ratione materiae*, it is a direct inference from the equality and independence of states.[6] If organs of the forum state could decide on core questions pertaining to the functioning of a respondent state without its consent, the respondent state's sovereignty would be to that extent impugned. But this rationale goes only so far; it does not cover matters remote from sovereign authority, notably transactions within the host state, especially those of a commercial or private law character. This provoked the development of the so-called restrictive theory of immunity, which holds that immunity is only required with respect to transactions involving the exercise of governmental authority (*acta iure imperii*) as distinct from commercial or other transactions which are not unique to the state (*acta iure gestionis*). But the distinction raises difficulties of application and definition having regard to the range of functions in which states engage.[7]

The second rationale for immunity (immunity *ratione personae*) operates on the personal or functional level: foreign state officials should not be impeded in the performance of their functions by a host state's exercise of adjudicative or enforcement jurisdiction over them. (Immunity does not bar prescriptive jurisdiction, however; foreign officials are not exempt from compliance with the laws of the host state.) This rationale for immunity is pragmatic in nature, analogous to immunities granted to diplomats. Immunity *ratione personae* covers all acts by the agent during the period of office, whether performed in a private or official capacity, given that the rationale

---

Arabia [2007] 1 AC 270, 291, 306; *Jurisdictional Immunities of the State (Germany v Italy)*, Judgment of 3 February 2012, §§53–61. Cf Finke (2010) 21 *EJIL* 853.

[5] *Arrest Warrant*, ICJ Reports 2002 p 3; *Certain Criminal Proceedings in France (Republic of the Congo v France)*, Provisional Measure, Order of 17 June 2003, ICJ Reports 2003 p 102; *Certain Questions of Mutual Assistance in Criminal Matters (Djibouti v France)*, ICJ Reports 2008 p 177. Also: *Germany v Italy*, ICJ, Judgment of 3 February 2012; Gattini (2011) 24 *LJIL* 173.

[6] *Arrest Warrant*, ICJ Reports 2002 p 3, 84 (Higgins, Kooijmans & Buergenthal), 98 (Al-Khasawneh, diss), 151 (van den Wyngaert, diss); *Al-Adsani v UK* (2001) 123 ILR 24, §54; *Fogarty v UK* (2001) 123 ILR 53, §34; *McElhinney v Ireland* (2001) 123 ILR 73, §35; Council of Europe, *Explanatory Reports on the European Convention on State Immunity and the Additional Protocol* (1972) §1. See also chapter 20.

[7] Further: Crawford (1983) 54 *BY* 75.

is to prevent interference with the performance of the official's role (and by extension with the sovereignty of the sending state). Historically, immunity *ratione personae* was exemplified in the head of state, who was seen as personifying the state itself.[8] However, the law has developed to recognize personal immunities for other high-ranking state officials, including heads of government, foreign ministers, and others.[9] There are no settled criteria for determining which types of official enjoy personal immunity,[10] but it is clear that the immunity belongs to the state and not the individual.[11] Once the period of office ends, immunity *ratione personae* will expire; however, immunity *ratione materiae* continues if the acts concerned are such that state immunity attaches. In all cases the immunity can be waived by the state.

(C) CURRENT STATE OF THE LAW

In 1978 the ILC took on the task of reconciling the forum state's territorial jurisdiction with the foreign state's sovereign authority,[12] culminating in Draft Articles of 1991.[13] The Sixth Committee, however, had difficulty adopting a consensus text. Upon resuming consideration of the topic in 1999, the General Assembly sought the ILC's views on five outstanding issues.[14] The formation of an Ad Hoc Committee in 2000[15] finally provided the impetus for agreeing a text. Following the Committee's final report,[16] the General Assembly adopted the UN Convention on Jurisdictional Immunities of States and Their Property on 2 December 2004.[17]

The Convention closely follows the ILC Draft Articles.[18] Like the Draft Articles, it conclusively adopts the restrictive theory of immunity. Like the 1972 European Convention on State Immunity[19] and domestic legislation, it does so by asserting a general rule that states and their property benefit from immunity from adjudicative jurisdiction,[20] and then enumerating proceedings in which state immunity cannot be invoked[21]

---

[8] E.g. Fox (2nd edn, 2008) 203; *Pinochet (No 3)* [2000] 1 AC 147, 269 (Lord Millett).

[9] E.g. *Arrest Warrant*, ICJ Reports 2002 p 3; *Mofaz* (2004) 128 ILR 709; *Bo Xilai* (2005) 128 ILR 713. Cf *Mutual Assistance in Criminal Matters*, ICJ Reports 2008 p 177; *Bat v Investigating Judge of the German Federal Court* [2011] EWHC 2029 (Admin).

[10] In the criminal context see UN Secretariat memorandum, A/CN.4/596, 31 March 2008, §§93–136.

[11] E.g. *Marcos and Marcos v Federal Department of Police* (1989) 102 ILR 198, 203; *Arrest Warrant*, ICJ Reports 2002 p 3, 21.

[12] GA Res 32/151, 19 December 1977.

[13] With commentaries; ILC *Ybk* 1991/II(2), 12.

[14] GA Res 53/98, 8 December 1998, §2. See ILC *Ybk* 1999/II(2), 149.

[15] GA Res 55/150, 12 December 2000, §3.

[16] Report of the Ad Hoc Committee on Jurisdictional Immunities of States and Their Property, A/59/22, 5 March 2004.

[17] GA Res 59/38, Annex, 2 December 2004.

[18] It should be read together with the ILC commentary: GAOR, Summary Record of the 13th Meeting, Sixth Committee, A/C.6/59/SR.13, 22 March 2005, §35.

[19] 16 May 1972, ETS 74.

[20] UN Convention, Art 5. See FSIA, 28 USC §1604; State Immunity Act 1978, s1; European Convention, Art 15.

[21] Ibid, Arts 10–17.

or is considered to have been waived.[22] The Convention treats immunity from adjudicative jurisdiction and immunity from execution as distinct, in accordance with general state practice. It is not applicable to criminal proceedings[23] nor to the immunities of a head of state *ratione personae*.[24]

Although not yet in force, the UN Convention has been understood by several courts to reflect an international consensus on state immunity.[25] It was cited by the Supreme Court of Japan to support its adoption of the restrictive theory of immunity,[26] and it has been signed, though not yet ratified, by several states historically opposed to restrictive immunity, such as China and Russia.[27]

Independently of the UN Convention, the restrictive theory of immunity is now very widely, although not unanimously, accepted.[28] But at a certain point, the respondent state's adherence to 'absolute' immunity is not the issue: the question is whether a forum state is free to adopt a regime of restrictive immunity, despite the dissenting views of a few states. Of that there seems no doubt. Though adoption of the restrictive theory does not avoid the problem of determining its precise boundaries, a broad consensus exists as to the type of exceptions. These are reflected in the legislation, the European Convention, and the UN Convention.[29]

The position in the UK evidences the approach described. Despite its earlier adherence to absolute immunity, English courts applied the restrictive theory of immunity at common law in the 1970s[30] and cemented the distinction between acts *iure imperii* and acts *iure gestionis*, notably in *I Congreso del Partido*.[31] The State Immunity

---

[22] Ibid, Arts 7–8. Note also Art 20.

[23] GA Res 59/38, 2 December 2004, §2.

[24] UN Convention, Art 3(2).

[25] *AIG Capital Partners Inc v Republic of Kazakhstan* [2006] 1 WLR 1420, 1446; *Fang v Jiang Zemin* (2006) 141 ILR 702, 717; *Jones v Saudi Arabia* [2007] 1 AC 270, 280, 289, 293; *Svenska Petroleum Exploration AB v Government of the Republic of Lithuania (No 2)* [2007] QB 886, 929.

[26] *Case No 1231 (Ju) [2003]*, 21 July 2006 (Japan), discussed in Jones (2006) 100 *AJIL* 908. For further civil law practice: *Case 00–02837 K/04* (2001) (Norway), discussed in Fife & Jervell (2001) 70 *Nordic JIL* 531, 551.

[27] But note China's recent position on the UN Convention: 'the Convention has no binding force on China, and moreover it cannot be the basis of assessing China's principled position on relevant issues. After signature of the Convention, the position of China in maintaining absolute immunity has not been changed, and has never applied or recognized the so-called principle or theory of "restrictive immunity"', cited in *DRC v FG Hemisphere Associates LLC*, Hong Kong Court of Final Appeal, Judgment of 8 June 2011, §202.

[28] E.g. the early practice of Poland adopting absolute immunity, based on reciprocity, and the lack of contrary recent practice: *Czechoslovak Republic* (1926) 3 ILR 180; *Trade Delegation at Warsaw of USSR v Maurycy Fajans* (1928) 4 ILR 170; *German Immunities in Poland* (1937) 8 ILR 239; *French Consulate in Cracow* (1958) 26 ILR 178; *Maria B v Austrian Cultural Institute* (1987) 82 ILR 1; UN Legislative Series, *Materials on Jurisdictional Immunities of States and Their Property* (1982) 90–1; Wyrozumska (2000) 24 *Pol Ybk* 77. Note, however, the Polish delegation's support of the ILC Draft Articles: GAOR, Summary Record of the 22nd Meeting, Sixth Committee, A/C.6/46/SR.22, 28 October 1991, §§66, 68. Poland has neither signed nor ratified the European or the UN Convention.

[29] See the review of earlier approaches in ALRC 24, *Foreign State Immunity* (1984) on which the 1985 Australian Act was based.

[30] *The Philippine Admiral* [1977] AC 373, 401–2 (actions *in rem*); *Trendtex Trading Corporation v The Central Bank of Nigeria* [1977] QB 529 (actions *in personam*); *I Congreso del Partido* [1983] 1 AC 244.

[31] See Lord Wilberforce's much-cited test at [1983] 1 AC 244, 267, though there is no 'bright line': *Littrell v US (No 2)* [1995] 1 WLR 82, 95.

Act 1978,[32] enacted to 'bring [the UK's] law on the immunity of foreign States more into line with current international practice' and to implement the European Convention, interrupted this process.[33] It is broadly consistent with the UN Convention, which the UK signed on 30 September 2005.

The Act does not apply to criminal matters, nor does it affect diplomatic and consular immunities,[34] but it extends state immunity to heads of state and separate entities.[35] In certain respects (notably visiting forces) it contemplates the parallel operation of the common law.[36] The Act also deals with immunity from execution, allowing execution against property used for 'commercial purposes', though this exception has a narrow scope.[37] It provides for waiver in the same manner as the common law, with separate waiver required for adjudication and enforcement.[38]

State immunity is treated as a public claim in open court.[39] There is a presumption that a state possesses immunity, with the plaintiff bearing the burden of proof to the contrary.[40] In the absence of the respondent state, the court has a duty to determine immunity *proprio motu*.[41]

2. THE MODALITIES OF GRANTING IMMUNITY

(A) DEFINITIONAL ISSUES

(i) The sovereign act

Though a US court made an early attempt to deal with the issue by delineating particular categories of exclusively sovereign activity,[42] the domestic legislation has primarily

---

[32] Bowett (1978) 37 *CLJ* 193; Delaume (1979) 73 *AJIL* 185; Mann (1979) 50 *BY* 43; White (1979) 42 *MLR* 72. For the US counterpart: Foreign Sovereign Immunities Act 1976 (FSIA), 28 USC §1602ff. For comment: Delaume (1977) 71 *AJIL* 399; von Mehren (1978) 17 *Col JTL* 33; Brower, Bistline, Loomis (1979) 73 *AJIL* 200.

[33] Hansard, House of Lords, vol 388, c59, 17 January 1978 (Second Reading).

[34] State Immunity Act 1978, s16. Criminal matters are still dealt with by the common law: see *R (on the application of Alamieyeseigha) v Crown Prosecution Service* [2005] EWHC 2704 (Admin).

[35] State Immunity Act 1978, s14(1), (2). On s14(1): *Kuwait Airways Corporation v Iraqi Airways Co* [1995] 1 WLR 1147.

[36] *Holland v Lampen-Wolfe* [2000] 1 WLR 1573, 1575–6. The US FSIA, by contrast, was intended to cover the field formerly governed by the common law: *Samantar v Yousuf* 130 S.Ct 2278, 2289 (2010).

[37] State Immunity Act 1978, s13(4). See *Alcom Ltd v Republic of Colombia* [1984] AC 580; Crawford (1981) 75 *AJIL* 820.

[38] State Immunity Act 1978, s13(3). See the broad interpretation of waiver in *A Company v Republic of X* [1990] 2 Lloyd's Rep 570; *Sabah Shipyard (Pakistan) Ltd v Islamic Republic of Pakistan* [2002] EWCA Civ 1643. Cf s9 and the narrower approach in *Svenska Petroleum Exploration AB v Republic of Lithuania (No 2)* [2007] QB 886.

[39] *Aziz v Aziz* [2008] 2 All ER 501.

[40] *Re International Tin Council (No 2)* [1988] 3 All ER 257, 358.

[41] State Immunity Act 1978, s1(2).

[42] *Victory Transport Incorporation v Comisaria General de Abastecimientos y Transportes*, 336 F.2d 354 (2nd Cir, 1964). Also: Lauterpacht (1951) 28 *BY* 220, 237–9.

regulated the scope of state immunity through a catalogue of detailed exceptions. This approach does not eliminate the distinction between acts *iure imperii* and acts *iure gestionis*, although it reduces its operational significance. In the State Immunity Act 1978, several sections demand factual inquiries into acts done 'in the exercise of sovereign authority' and for 'commercial purposes';[43] others simply call for literal interpretation (e.g. sections 4 (contracts of employment), 5 (local personal injuries and damage to property)).

(ii) Constituent units and political subdivisions

State practice has diverged on whether immunity extends to political subdivisions, for example, the component units of federal states. One school of thought considers the ability of a state to act *iure imperii* on its own behalf to be decisive.[44] The point is that political subdivisions are generally unable to satisfy this requirement. Another view (held by most federal states themselves) is that constituent units exercise governmental authority, even if subordinated to the federal unit, and that immunity is not lost because such authority is exercised locally. The divergence in state practice is reflected in the texts. Under the European Convention, immunity is not accorded to 'constituent states of a federal state', unless a contracting state issues a declaration to the opposite effect.[45] No reference is made to political subdivisions. In the State Immunity Act 1978, 'constituent territories of a federal state' are considered to be 'separate entities', only enjoying immunity if the requirements of section 14(2) are satisfied (unless an Order in Council is made according immunity to a specific territory).[46] The UN Convention takes a different approach, equating constituent units with political subdivisions and extending immunity to those entities 'which are entitled to perform acts in the exercise of sovereign authority, and are acting in that capacity'.[47] By applying the criterion of sovereign authority to both kinds of entity, it is perhaps more reflective of state practice.

(iii) Separate entities

There are also diverse approaches to the question of separate entities like state corporations. In the UK, the legislation enacts a presumption against immunity for 'separate

---

[43] State Immunity Act 1978, ss 4(3), 10–11, 13(4), (5), 14(4) ('commercial purposes'); (3)(c), 14(2)(a) ('in the exercise of sovereign authority').

[44] E.g. *Neger v Hesse* (1969) 52 ILR 329, 330; *R (on the application of Alamieyeseigha) v Crown Prosecution Service* [2005] EWHC 2704 (Admin); cf *Mellenger v New Brunswick Development Corporation* [1971] 1 WLR 604.

[45] European Convention, Art 28(1), (2). See Declaration of Republic of Austria, 10 July 1974; Declaration from the Permanent Representative of the Federal Republic of Germany, 5 June 1992; Declaration from the Minister of Foreign Affairs of Belgium, 4 September 2003.

[46] State Immunity Act 1978, s14(5), (6). Also: *Bank of Credit and Commerce International (Overseas) Ltd v Price Waterhouse* [1997] 4 All ER 108 (immunity denied the head of a constituent territory for which an Order in Council had not been issued). Cf the broader common law position in *Mellenger v New Brunswick Development Corporation* [1971] 1 WLR 604.

[47] UN Convention, Art 2(1)(b)(ii); cf ILC *Ybk* 1990/II(1), 7; ILC *Ybk* 1991/II/(2), 13.

entities', only according immunity where two further criteria are satisfied. First, the entity must be separate from the state, that is, 'distinct from the executive organs of the government of the State and capable of suing or being sued': these are hardly words of limitation.[48] Secondly, the act in question must have been carried out 'in the exercise of sovereign authority'.[49] The focus here is on whether 'the act in question is of its own character a governmental act, as opposed to an act which any private citizen can perform'.[50]

An entirely different approach is taken by the US Act. Any 'agency or instrumentality of a foreign state' enjoys a presumption of immunity[51] and its terms encompass, for example, state-owned corporations.[52] Whilst the US courts have also adopted a multi-faceted test to determine an entity's status,[53] the analysis of function that occupies the English courts is not called for by the inclusive definition in USC §1603. On the other hand §1603 requires an entity to have some connection to the state, unlike in the UK, where a wholly private corporation could (in theory) be accorded immunity.

The UN Convention attempts to reconcile these competing positions by including both status and functions. It establishes a presumption that 'agencies and instrumentalities of the state or other entities' will have immunity 'to the extent that they are entitled to perform and are actually performing acts in the exercise of the sovereign authority of the state'.[54] By including separate entities within the definition of the state, it adheres to the US formulation; by requiring that they exercise sovereign authority, it reflects the UK approach.

(iv) Individuals

In addition to organs and entities of the state, it is important to specify exactly which individuals are entitled to immunity whether *ratione personae* or *ratione materiae*. Despite some recent contrary US practice, it seems to be generally settled that state officials acting in their official capacity enjoy the same immunity as the state they represent.[55] This position is reflected in UK practice: the common law long considered

---

[48] State Immunity Act 1978, s14(1). See also the treatment of 'legal entities' in European Convention, Art 27. Cf the combination of US, European, and UK approaches in Foreign States Immunities Act 1985, s3 (Australia). Also: *Ministry of Trade of the Republic of Iraq v Tsavliris Salvage (International) Ltd* [2008] 2 All ER (Comm) 805, 825–6; *Wilhelm Finance Inc v Ente Administrador Del Astillero Rio Santiago* [2009] EWHC 1074 (Comm), §§12, 52. For the position pre-1978: *Trendtex Trading Corporation v Central Bank of Nigeria* [1977] QB 529, 573–5.

[49] State Immunity Act 1978, s14(2). See *Kuwait Airways Corporation v Iraqi Airways Co* [1995] 1 WLR 1147, 1158, 1174.

[50] *Kuwait Airways Corporation v Iraqi Airways Co* [1995] 1 WLR 1147, 1160.

[51] *Saudi Arabia v Nelson*, 507 US 349, 355 (1993).

[52] FSIA, 28 USC §1603(a), (b).

[53] *First National City Bank v Banco Para el Comercio Exterior de Cuba*, 462 US 611, 624 (1983).

[54] UN Convention, Art 2(1)(b)(iii). Also: comments in the Annex to the Convention on the interpretation of 'entity' in Art 19(c).

[55] *Church of Scientology* (1978) 65 ILR 193, 198; *Indian Foreign Minister* (1988) 90 ILR 408, 410; *Schmidt v Home Secretary* (1997) 2 IR 121; *Prosecutor v Blaškić* (1997) 110 ILR 607, 707; *USA v Friedland* (1999) 120 ILR 417, 450; *Pinochet (No 3)* [2000] 1 AC 147, 269, 285–6; *Holland v Lampen-Wolfe* [2000] 1 WLR 1573, 1583;

state agents to share the immunity of the state and sought (through the concept of indirect impleading) to ensure that state immunity was not circumvented by suing an individual defendant rather than the Crown or a government department.[56] No distinction is made between a state official acting as an organ of the state or as an agent.[57] Even though it does not expressly refer to officials,[58] the definition of 'state' has been interpreted expansively by English courts: '[s]ection 14(1) must be read as affording to individual employees or officers of a foreign State protection under the same cloak as protects the State itself.'[59] The House of Lords endorsed this position in *Jones v Saudi Arabia*.[60] The UN Convention takes a similar approach by extending immunity to state officials, and takes the further step of including 'representatives of the state acting in that capacity' within the definition of 'state'.[61]

The US Supreme Court recently expressed a contrary position. It had long been understood that the US Act covered individuals,[62] but the Supreme Court held that individuals (in that case the former Prime Minister of Somalia) were not included in the definition of 'foreign state' or as 'agencies or instrumentalities'.[63] The Court also firmly rejected the petitioner's argument that the Act covered his claim to immunity due to its purpose and intent to codify the law on the immunity of individual officials.[64] Nor was the Court concerned that its interpretation would 'make the statute optional'.[65] The viability of this position is yet to be determined; presumably individuals may be covered to some extent at least at common law. But a dual regime is untidy and undesirable: as observed by the Ontario Court of Appeal, '[w]hat is the point of the state having immunity if its personnel have none when carrying out their official duties in the host country?'[66]

The State Immunity Act 1978 specifically extends privileges and immunities *ratione materiae* to 'the sovereign or other head of that state in his public capacity'.[67] While

---

AXA c Asecna (2005) 94 *Rev crit DIPriv* 470; *Fang v Jiang Zemin* (2006) 141 ILR 702, 706–7; cf *Samantar v Yousuf* 130 S.Ct 2278 (2010).

[56] Whomersley (1992) 41 *ICLQ* 848, 850. See *Twycross v Drefus* [1877] 5 Ch 605; *Rahimtoola v Nizam of Hyderabad* [1958] AC 379.

[57] Ibid, 406.

[58] As noted by Mance LJ in *Jones v Saudi Arabia* [2005] QB 699, 721.

[59] *Propend Finance Pty Ltd v Sing* (1997) 111 ILR 611, 669.

[60] [2007] 1 AC 270, 281, 299; followed in *Fang v Jiang Zemin* (2006) 141 ILR 702, 706–7. On *Jones*: O'Keefe (2006) 77 *BY* 500. Also: *Grovit v De Nederlandsche* [2006] 1 WLR 3323, 3338–9 (aff'd [2008] 1 WLR 51, 56–7).

[61] UN Convention, Art 2(1)(b)(iv). Further: Fox (2nd edn, 2008) 460.

[62] *Chuidian v Philippines*, 912 F.2d 1095 (9th Cir, 1990); *Keller v Central Bank*, 277 F.3d 811 (6th Cir, 2002); *In re Terrorist Attacks*, 538 F.3d 71 (2nd Cir, 2008).

[63] *Samantar v Yousuf*, 130 S.Ct 2278, 2286–7, 2289 (2010).

[64] Ibid, 2289–91.

[65] Ibid, 2292.

[66] *Jaffe v Miller* (1993) 95 ILR 446, 458–9.

[67] State Immunity Act 1978, s14(1). See the comparable position under the Australian Foreign States Immunities Act 1985, s3(3)(b).

in office, such officials will also enjoy immunity *ratione personae*.[68] Although the UN Convention does not (along with the European Convention and the US legislation) specify the immunity of heads of state, such individuals are included through article 2(1)(b)(i) and (iv). It must be emphasized, however, that *former* heads of state occupy a distinct category and enjoy only immunity *ratione materiae*; absolute personal immunity ceases on termination of office.[69]

(B) FOREIGN STATES AS CLAIMANTS

Foreign states generally have the capacity to appear in foreign courts as claimants, and quite frequently do so.[70] Having submitted to the jurisdiction of the foreign court by instituting proceedings, the state has no immunity from jurisdiction in respect of those proceedings.[71] This extends to counterclaims relating to the legal relationship or facts arising from the state's principal claim,[72] but does not entail a waiver of immunity from enforcement jurisdiction.[73] In the US, a state may be subject to a counterclaim unrelated to its original claim provided that the counterclaim 'does not seek relief exceeding in amount or differing in kind from that sought by the foreign state'.[74] This principle is said to prevent a foreign state 'invoking [United States] law but resisting a claim against it which fairly would curtail its recovery'.[75]

(C) FOREIGN STATES AS RESPONDENTS

(i) Commercial transactions

The 'most significant'[76] exception to the rule of immunity from jurisdiction concerns 'commercial transactions'[77] or 'commercial activity'.[78] Section 3 of the State Immunity

---

[68] State Immunity Act 1978, s20(1) by reference to the Diplomatic Privileges Act 1964.

[69] If a state claims immunity on behalf of one of its organs, it assumes responsibility for any internationally wrongful acts committed by its agent or organ: *Mutual Assistance in Criminal Matters*, ICJ Reports 2008 p 177, 244.

[70] E.g. *Republic of Haiti v Duvalier* [1990] 1 QB 202.

[71] European Convention, Art 1(1); FSIA, 28 USC §1605; State Immunity Act 1978, s2(1), (3)(a); UN Convention, Art 8(1)(a); ILC *Ybk* 1991/II(2), 29.

[72] European Convention, Art 1(2); State Immunity Act 1978, s2(6); UN Convention, Art 9. Also: *High Commissioner for India v Ghosh* [1960] 1 QB 134, 140.

[73] European Convention, Arts 1(2), 20(1)(a); State Immunity Act 1978, s13(3); UN Convention, Art 20. See the common law rule as articulated in *Duff Development Co Ltd v Government of Kelantan* [1924] AC 797.

[74] FSIA, 28 USC §1607; *National City Bank of New York v Republic of China*, 348 US 356 (1955).

[75] Ibid, 361.

[76] *Republic of Argentina v Weltover*, 504 US 607, 611 (1992).

[77] State Immunity Act 1978, s 3(1)(a); State Immunity Act 1979, s5 (Singapore); State Immunity Ordinance 1981, s5 (Pakistan); Foreign States Immunities Act 1981, s4 (South Africa); Foreign States Immunities Act 1985, s11(1) (Australia); UN Convention, Arts 2(1)(c), 10(1). See Fox (1994) 43 *ICLQ* 193.

[78] European Convention, Art 7(1); FSIA, 28 USC §1605(a)(2); State Immunity Act 1982, s5 (Canada); Immunity of Foreign States from the Jurisdiction of Argentinean Courts 1995, Art 2(c) (Argentina).

Act 1978, on which Article 2(1) of the UN Convention is based,[79] typifies the list approach adopted for the former category. As well as providing an exception for contracts to be performed in the UK,[80] it includes three categories of exceptions under the 'commercial transactions' umbrella: contracts for the supply of goods or services; financial transactions; and a residual category covering other acts *iure gestionis*.[81] This residual category has been interpreted as expressing the distinction between acts *iure imperii* and *iure gestionis* in respect of transactions generally. It is only for this latter category that the court will have to consider the sovereign character of the act, since section 3(3) extends to *all* transactions and contracts.[82] Further, the relationship between the proceedings and the commercial transaction must also be firmly established. Indeed, it has been held by the majority of the Supreme Court that an enforcement judgment is insufficiently related to the transaction with which the original judgment was concerned.[83]

A second group of domestic laws relies on a broad reference to 'commercial activity' as the basis of the exception, but a precise definition of this term is not provided.[84] In the US, the commercial activity must have a sufficient nexus to the US;[85] no such territorial link is required under the 'commercial transaction' exception in section 3(1)(a) of the UK Act. The US Supreme Court has also placed strict emphasis on the nature of the act as the determinative criterion.[86]

(ii) Local employment

The exception for 'contracts of employment' is likewise subject to diverse approaches.[87] Though the trend towards limiting state immunity in respect of local employment disputes is clear,[88] different jurisdictions treat the same subject-matter differently.[89] The more significant problem arising from contracts of employment is the inadequacy

---

[79] On the similarity between the two sections: *Svenska Petroleum Exploration AB v Republic of Lithuania (No 2)* [2007] QB 886, 929.

[80] State Immunity Act 1978, s3(1)(b). Also: European Convention, Art 4.

[81] State Immunity Act 1978, s3(3).

[82] Cf *Koo Golden East Mongolia v Bank of Nova Scotia* [2008] QB 717. See O'Keefe (2007) 78 *BY* 582.

[83] *NML Capital Ltd v Republic of Argentina* [2011] 3 WLR 273, 306–10, 313, approving the narrow construction of 'relating to' in *AIC Ltd v Federal Government of Nigeria* [2003] EWHC 1357 and *Svenska Petroleum Exploration AB v Republic of Lithuania (No 2)* [2007] QB 886. Cf the dissentients' disapproval of these cases: [2011] 3 WLR 273, 288 (Lord Phillips of Worth Matravers PSC), 318 (Lord Clarke JSC).

[84] FSIA, 28 USC §1603(d), 1605(a)(2); *Republic of Argentina v Weltover*, 504 US 607, 612 (1992): 'This definition … leaves the critical term "commercial" largely undefined.' Also: Immunity of Foreign States from the Jurisdiction of Argentinean Courts 1995, Art 2(c).

[85] FSIA, 28 USC §1605(a)(2).

[86] *Republic of Argentina v Weltover*, 504 US 607, 614 (1992). Also: *Saudi Arabia v Nelson*, 507 US 349 (1993), a controversial decision.

[87] Garnett (1997) 46 *ICLQ* 81. Also: Fox (1995) 66 *BY* 97.

[88] *Fogarty v UK* (2001) 123 ILR 53, §37.

[89] E.g. *Barrandon v USA* (1992) 113 ILR 464, 466; *Barrandon v USA* (1995) 113 ILR 464, 469; *Barrandon v USA* (1998) 116 ILR 622, 624; *Canada v Employment Appeals Tribunal & Burke* (1991) 95 ILR 467, 470; (1992) 95 ILR 470, 473, 481. In the case of interpreters: *Conrades v UK* (1981) 65 ILR 205; *Special Representative of State of the City of the Vatican v Pieciukiewicz* (1982) 78 ILR 120; *UAE v Abdelghafar* (1995) 107 ILR 626;

of the private law criterion in this context.[90] Neither this criterion, nor an examination of the 'nature of the act', provides any scope for the recognition of sovereign activity. States have also taken different approaches in evaluating which duties of an employee amount to participation in sovereign activity.[91]

States have essentially resorted to two distinct models, with the differences represented again by the UK and US legislation. The State Immunity Act 1978 excludes employment contracts from the definition of 'commercial transaction', with the exclusion of immunity in respect of those contracts depending on a 'minimum contacts' approach, rather than requiring a characterization of the breach.[92] The commerciality of the arrangement is not a relevant factor; the focus is on meeting the statutory thresholds of connection between the defendant and the forum.[93] By contrast, the US Act treats employment contracts under the rubric of 'commercial activity'.[94] The operation of the exception from immunity under this model depends on the characterization of the claim as one arising from a commercial contract between the foreign state and the individual.[95] Nationality or residence is not relevant.[96] Across the jurisdictions, factors including the employment relationship,[97] the duties of the employee,[98] and the status of the employer[99] have been considered to militate against immunity.[100]

(iii) Other local private law claims

There are several exceptions from state immunity within the realm of private law. They extend, *inter alia*, to claims concerning personal injury and damage to property locally occurring,[101] ownership, possession, and use of property,[102] intellectual property

---

Saudi Arabia v Nasser [2000] EWCA Civ J 1114; cf the denial of immunity in *Embassy Interpreter Dismissal* (1985) 77 ILR 485; *Zambian Embassy v Sendanayake* (1992) 114 ILR 532; *R v Iraq* (1994) 116 ILR 664.

[90] *Sengupta v India* (1982) 64 ILR 352, 360–1. Also: Re *Canada Labour Code* (1989) 86 ILR 626, 630; *X v Argentina* (1996) 114 ILR 502, 504–6.

[91] *R v Iraq* (1994) 116 ILR 664, 667; cf *X c Saudi School in Paris* (2003) 127 ILR 163, 166.

[92] State Immunity Act 1978, s3(3), 4. Also: European Convention, Art 5; State Immunity Act 1979, s6 (Singapore); State Immunity Ordinance 1981, s6 (Pakistan); Foreign States Immunities Act 1981, s5 (South Africa); States Immunities Act 1985, s12 (Australia); Immunity of Foreign States from the Jurisdiction of Argentinean Courts 1995, Art 2(d) (Argentina); UN Convention, Arts 2(1)(c), 11.

[93] On the notion of 'minimum contacts' generally: Trooboff (1986) 200 Hague *Recueil* 235, 331–2.

[94] FSIA, 28 USC §1605(a)(2); State Immunity Act 1982, s5 (Canada). For jurisdictions without legislation: e.g. *USA v Guinto* (1990) 102 ILR 132, 145.

[95] *Saudi Arabia v Nelson*, 507 US 349 (1993). US courts have recently employed a multi-factor inquiry in analysing these issues: *El-Hadad v UAE*, 496 F.3d 658, 665 (2007).

[96] Indeed, §1605(a)(2) makes no reference to nationality. Also: *Verlinden v Central Bank*, 461 US 480, 490–1 (1983).

[97] E.g. *De Queiroz v Portugal* (1992) 115 ILR 430, 434.

[98] E.g. *X v Israel* (2002) 127 ILR 310, 313.

[99] E.g. *USA v Guinto* (1990) 102 ILR 132, 145.

[100] *Fogarty v UK* (2001) 123 ILR 53, §38. This term is not defined in any of the domestic or international instruments. The State Immunity Act 1978 appears to encompass statutory claims where the claimant was an independent contractor: see s4(6).

[101] European Convention, Art 11; State Immunity Act 1978, s5; UN Convention, Art 12. Also: FSIA, 28 USC §1605(a)(5).

[102] European Convention, Arts 9, 10; State Immunity Act 1978, s6; UN Convention, Art 13.

rights,[103] and membership of bodies corporate.[104] Of particular interest is the exception for (*ex hypothesi*) non-commercial torts. Given that jurisdiction for tort claims is founded on the fact of injury locally caused, the traditional *acta iure gestionis/acta iure imperii* dichotomy has no place:[105] thus torture on embassy premises would be covered, but not defamation. In other words, the exception applies irrespective of the sovereign character of the delictual act.[106] However, despite the irrelevance of this distinction in each of the statutes and conventions, common law courts have maintained it,[107] in a manner similar to civil law jurisdictions.[108]

The key criterion is the occurrence of a tortious act or omission within the territory; the fact of damage occurring in the territory is insufficient under UK law. Thus personal injuries inflicted by agents of a foreign state in another jurisdiction have been held to be excluded from the exception.[109] This can be contrasted with the position in Canada, where the key criterion is the occasioning of physical *injury* in Canada,[110] and the US, where it appears that both the act and the injury must occur locally.[111] Under the UK Act the author need not be present locally, in contrast to the position under the European and UN Conventions. Though the equivalent exception in the Foreign Sovereign Immunities Act 1976 requires that the tortious act or omission have been committed in the US, discretionary decisions, as well as certain claims (such as libel, slander, deceit, and misrepresentation) remain protected by immunity.[112] Further, the UK Act concerns physical, rather than mental injury,[113] and loss of or damage to tangible property, rather than pure economic loss.[114]

While exceptions for non-commercial torts were originally directed towards 'insurable' personal risks, such as traffic accidents, there has been some controversy over the extent of their application. In particular, there have been contrary findings in cases of war damage.[115] Generally, states appear to retain their immunity in the

---

[103] European Convention, Art 8; State Immunity Act 1978, s7; UN Convention, Art 14.

[104] European Convention, Art 6; State Immunity Act 1978, s8; UN Convention, Art 15.

[105] *Letelier v Chile*, 488 F.Supp 665, 671 (1980); Crawford (1983) 54 *BY* 75, 111.

[106] See e.g. *Schreiber v Germany* (2002) 216 DLR (4th) 513, 528–30.

[107] *Littrell v US (No 2)* [1995] 1 WLR 82; *Holland v Lampen-Wolfe* [2000] 1 WLR 1573; Mizushimi (2001) 64 *MLR* 472.

[108] See the review of state practice undertaken in *McElhinney v Ireland* (2000) 121 ILR 198.

[109] *Al-Adsani v UK* (2001) 123 ILR 24; *Jones v Saudi Arabia* [2007] 1 AC 270. Cf the reference to 'national jurisdiction' in IDI Res, Basel/III (1991), Art 2(e).

[110] State Immunity Act 1982, s6 (Canada); *Bouzari v Islamic Republic of Iran* (2004) 128 ILR 586.

[111] *Argentine Republic v Amerada Hess Shipping Corp*, 488 US 428 (1989).

[112] The Act allows the exercise of extra-territorial jurisdiction in the case of specific terrorist acts committed by state: FSIA, 28 USC §1605A. E.g. *In re Iran* (2009) 659 F.Supp 2d 31.

[113] *Caramba-Coker v Military Affairs Office of the Embassy of the State of Kuwait* [2003] All ER (D) 186. Also: *Bouzari v Islamic Republic of Iran* (2004) 128 ILR 586.

[114] State Immunity Act 1978, s5(b).

[115] *Distomo Massacre* (2000) 129 ILR 513, (2003) 129 ILR 556; *Margellos v Federal Republic of Germany* (2002) 129 ILR 525; *Ferrini v Federal Republic of Germany* (2004) 128 ILR 658 (confirmed by the Court of Cassation in *Germany v Mantelli*, No 14201/2008, 29 May 2008; *Milde v Italy*, No 1027/2008, 21 October 2008). Also: *Germany v Italy*, ICJ, Judgment of 3 February 2012.

case of tortious acts occasioned by their armed forces.[116] For example, in *Germany v Italy* the International Court concluded that customary international law continues to require that a state be accorded immunity in proceedings for torts allegedly committed on the territory of another state by its armed forces and other organs of state in the course of conducting an armed conflict. The Court held that practice in the form of judicial decisions, *opinio iuris*, and an almost complete absence of contrary authority supported this position.[117] This limitation on the exception to immunity has been subject to criticism, particularly in the context of human rights violations causing personal injuries.[118]

(D) CRIMINAL JURISDICTION

Whether and when state immunity will apply in domestic criminal proceedings is a complex question. In theory it should not matter for the purposes of immunity under international law if the conduct is classified by the forum state as civil or criminal. The European Convention impliedly endorses the absolute immunity of the state from foreign criminal jurisdiction.[119] The UN Convention and the domestic statutes arguably implicitly allow a distinction on the basis of the domestic characterization of the act by excluding criminal proceedings from their scope.[120]

The scope of immunity from foreign criminal jurisdiction is yet to be conclusively determined.[121] Customary international law in principle extends immunity *ratione materiae* to acts of state officials undertaken in their official capacity; but there is practice supporting an exception if the act was committed in the territory of the forum state.[122]

The situation is even more complex if the conduct in question amounts to an international crime.[123] It is well established that serving heads of state enjoy immunity

---

[116] *Littrell v US (No 2)* [1995] 1 WLR 82; *Holland v Lampen-Wolfe* [2000] 1 WLR 1573; *McElhinney v Ireland* (2001) 123 ILR 73; *Margellos v Federal Republic of Germany* (2002) 129 ILR 525.

[117] *Germany v Italy*, Judgment of 3 February 2012, §§77–8.

[118] *Al-Adsani v UK* (2001) 123 ILR 24; Hall (2006) 55 *ICLQ* 411.

[119] European Convention, Art 15 (Arts 1–14 relate only to civil matters).

[120] GA Res 59/38, 2 December 2004, §2; FSIA, 28 USC §1603(a); State Immunity Act 1978, s16(4); State Immunity Act 1979, s19(2)(b) (Singapore); State Immunity Ordinance 1981, s17(2)(b) (Pakistan); State Immunity Act 1982, s18 (Canada); Foreign States Immunities Act 1981, s2(3) (South Africa); States Immunities Act 1985, s3(1) (Australia). Note the human rights-related provision in Immunity of Foreign States from the Jurisdiction of Argentinean Courts 1995, Art 3 (not yet in force), also Art 2(e). On immunity from criminal jurisdiction for diplomatic agents: e.g. Diplomatic Privileges Act 1964, c81, Schedule 1, art 31(1).

[121] The scope of state immunity from foreign criminal jurisdiction is presently before the ILC: ILC Report 2008, GAOR, 63rd Session, Supp No 10, A/63/10, Ch X; Second Report of Special Rapporteur Kolodkin, A/CN.4/631, 10 June 2010. For the related UN Secretariat memorandum: A/CN.4/596, 31 March 2008.

[122] E.g. *Bat v Investigating Judge of the German Federal Court* [2011] EWHC 2029 (Admin) and practice referred to therein.

[123] Zappala (2001) 12 *EJIL* 595; Cassese (2002) 13 *EJIL* 853; Wirth (2003) 13 *EJIL* 877; Akande (2004) 98 *AJIL* 407; van Alebeek, *The Immunity of States and their Officials in International Criminal Law and International Human Rights Law* (2008); Akande & Shah (2010) 21 *EJIL* 815.

ratione personae from foreign criminal jurisdiction for international crimes as they do for domestic crimes.[124] Other 'holders of high-ranking office in a State' are also now recognized as enjoying this same immunity,[125] although given the functional basis for recognition of immunity *ratione personae* the category of officials enjoying immunity on these grounds has no obvious limit. It appears that this privileged group extends to heads of government,[126] defence ministers,[127] and ministers for commerce and international trade.[128] The International Court was not prepared to extend personal immunities to the Djiboutian Procureur de la République and Head of National Security, though the lack of clarity in Djibouti's submissions on this point may have affected the Court's position.[129]

It is less clear whether international crimes committed by *former* officials before or during their period of office will be covered by immunity *ratione materiae*, given that immunity *ratione personae* will have ceased to apply. There are increasing examples of state practice denying immunity in such circumstances,[130] and some jurists go so far as to suggest that there is an emerging norm of customary international law denying immunity *ratione materiae* for international crimes.[131] The starting point for such arguments is normally the decision of the House of Lords in *Pinochet (No 3)*, refusing to uphold the immunity *ratione materiae* of a former head of state in a prosecution for torture at international law.[132] However, despite the common assumption that immunity was denied because torture was considered not to be an official function subject to immunity *ratione materiae*, most of the Law Lords put forward other rationales for not allowing immunity; the case ultimately turned on the specific circumstances of Chile's treaty obligations.[133] There is a striking contrast between what the case narrowly decided and the far-reaching influence it has had. However, practice is not yet sufficiently widespread or consistent, whatever the position may be *de lege ferenda*, to assert that a customary norm has crystallized denying immunity *ratione materiae* in prosecutions of international crimes in domestic courts.

This is not necessarily inconsistent with the practice of international criminal tribunals denying immunity to those accused of having committed international crimes.

---

[124] *Pinochet (No 3)* [2000] 1 AC 147, 244, 261, 265, 268–9, 277; *Gaddafi* (2001) 125 ILR 490; *Re Sharon & Yaron* (2003) 127 ILR 110; *Tatchell v Mugabe* (2004) 136 ILR 572. Cf *Bouterse* (2000) 3 *Ybk IHL* 677. Note the omission of any exception for international crimes in *Arrest Warrant*, ICJ Reports 2002 p 3, 25.

[125] Ibid, 20–1, 24 (noted in Yang (2002) 61 *CLJ* 242).

[126] *Arrest Warrant*, ICJ Reports 2002 p 3, 21.

[127] *Re Mofaz* (2004) 128 ILR 709.

[128] *Re Bo Xilai* (2005) 128 ILR 713.

[129] *Mutual Assistance in Criminal Matters*, ICJ Reports 2008 p 177, 243–4. Also: *Bat v Investigating Judge of the German Federal Court* [2011] EWHC 2029 (Admin), §§61–2.

[130] E.g. *Bouterse* (2000) 3 *Ybk IHL* 677; *Lozano v Italy* (2008) Case No 31171/2008, ILDC 1085 (IT 2008); IDI Res, Naples/I (2009), Art 3(1); IDI (2009) 73 *Ann de l'Inst* 3.

[131] E.g. Zappalà (2001) 12 *EJIL* 595; Cassese (2002) 13 *EJIL* 853; Wirth (2003) 13 *EJIL* 877.

[132] For commentary on *Pinochet (No 3)*: Denza (1999) 48 *ICLQ* 949; Chinkin (1999) 93 *AJIL* 703; Fox (1999) 48 *ICLQ* 687; van Alebeek (2000) 71 *BY* 29; McLachlan (2002) 51 *ICLQ* 959. See also *Bat v Investigating Judge of the German Federal Court* [2011] EWHC 2029 (Admin), in which immunity was denied.

[133] *Pinochet (No 3)* [2000] 1 AC 147, 266–7, 277–8; *Jones v Saudi Arabia* [2007] 1 AC 270, 286.

Individual state agents can commit crimes *intuitu personae*, and their status as agents generally will not be a defence against individual responsibility for international crimes in an otherwise competent international forum.[134] But the matter is heavily dependent on the structure and legal foundation of the relevant tribunal, including whether or not the UN Security Council is involved.[135] In the case of the International Criminal Court, for example, states parties have consented to the waiver of immunity for their nationals.[136] The entitlement of nationals of non-parties to personal immunity is not obviously eroded, particularly in the light of Article 98(1) of the ICC Statute.[137] However, the Pre-Trial Chamber holds a firm opinion to the contrary.[138]

(E) WAIVER OF IMMUNITY

Subject to the doctrine of non-justiciability, no fundamental principle prohibits the exercise of jurisdiction, and immunity may be waived by the state concerned either expressly or by conduct. Whether express or implied, consent must be granted by an authorized state agent.[139] Under the State Immunity Act 1978 (in this respect broadly reflective of the European and UN Conventions),[140] a foreign state will be deemed to have waived its immunity from jurisdiction in one of four ways: (a) by submission to the jurisdiction after the dispute has arisen; (b) by prior written agreement; (c) by the institution of proceedings; and (d) by intervening or taking a step in the proceedings (other than to assert immunity).[141] The Act's inclusion of waiver by prior written agreement is a change from the common law, which required a genuine and unequivocal submission in the face of the court.[142] In terms of prior agreements specifying recourse to arbitration, the state cannot avoid proceedings related to the arbitration, which

---

[134] E.g. *International Military Tribunal (Nuremberg), Judgment and Sentences* (1947) 41 *AJIL* 172, 221; *Prosecutor v Blaškić* (1997) 110 ILR 607, 710; *Arrest Warrant*, ICJ Reports 2002 p 3, 25; *Prosecutor v Taylor* (2004) 128 ILR 239, 264. Further: e.g. ICTY Statute, SC Res 827 (1993), Art 7(2); ICC Statute, Art 27.

[135] Akande (2004) 98 *AJIL* 407, 417; O'Keefe (2011) 24 *Cam RIA* 334, 345–50.

[136] ICC Statute, Art 27.

[137] Note the AU's public opposition to the denial of immunities in the case of Omar Al-Bashir: AU Assembly Decision 245 (XIII), 3 July 2009; AU Assembly Decision 296 (XV), 27 July 2010; AU Assembly Decision 334 (XVI), 31 January 2011; AU Assembly Decision 366 (XVII), 1 July 2011. Further: O'Keefe (2011) 24 *Cam RIA* 334, 340.

[138] *Prosecutor v Omar Al Bashir*, ICC-02/05–01/09, Pre-Trial Chamber, Decision on the Prosecution's Application for a Warrant of Arrest against Omar Hassan Ahmad Al Bashir, 4 March 2009, §§41–5 (noted by Ssenyonjo (2010) 59 *ICLQ* 205). Also: *Warrant of Arrest for Muammar Mohammed Abu Minyar Gaddafi*, ICC-01/11, Pre-Trial Chamber I, 27 June 2011. On international criminal jurisdiction see chapter 30.

[139] State Immunity Act 1978, s2(7); *Aziz v Republic of Yemen* [2005] EWCA Civ 745, §48. Also: *Donegal International Ltd v Republic of Zambia* [2007] EWHC 197.

[140] State Immunity Act 1978, s2(1)–(3); European Convention, Arts 2–3; UN Convention, Arts 7–8. Also: FSIA, 28 USC §§1605(a)(1), 1610(a)(1).

[141] Pleading non-justiciability or *forum non conveniens* will not constitute such a step: *Kuwait Airways Corporation v Iraqi Airways Co* [1995] 1 Lloyd's Rep 25 (aff'd in *Kuwait Airways Corporation v Iraqi Airways Co* [1995] 1 WLR 1147). See further chapter 3.

[142] *Mighell v Sultan of Johore* [1894] 1 QB 149; *Duff Development Co Ltd v Government of Kelantan* [1924] AC 797; *Kahan v Pakistan Federation* [1951] 2 KB 1003.

extends to enforcement proceedings.[143] However, an arbitration agreement specifying the application of the law of the UK is not regarded as a waiver.[144] Although a foreign state may be deemed to have consented to the enforcement stage of an arbitration, a waiver to the jurisdiction of the court does not, as a rule, entail a waiver of immunity from enforcement.[145]

3. ATTACHMENT AND SEIZURE IN EXECUTION[146]

The issue of immunity from adjudicative jurisdiction is distinct from the question of immunity from measures of constraint consequent upon the exercise of enforcement jurisdiction, that is, immunity from execution.[147] The terms 'measures of constraint' and 'execution' in this context encompass the full variety of pre- and post-judgment measures available in national legal systems, from injunctions preventing a respondent state from disposing of certain assets pending resolution of a dispute to attachment or seizure orders against a foreign state's property for enforcing a final judgment.[148]

There is no absolute rule prohibiting execution against property of a foreign state within the forum, but there are significant restrictions on such execution.[149] One important restriction is that measures of constraint cannot be enforced *in personam* against state officials acting in their official capacity.[150] Most attempts at enforcement against foreign states focus instead on state property.[151]

The exceptions to immunity from execution against state property are covered in Articles 18 (pre-judgment) and 19 (post-judgment) of the UN Convention, generally

---

[143] State Immunity Act 1978, s9; *Svenska Petroleum Exploration AB v Republic of Lithuania (No 2)* [2007] QB 886. Cf *DRC v FG Hemisphere Associates LLC*, Hong Kong Court of Final Appeal, Judgment of 8 June 2011.

[144] State Immunity Act 1978, s2(2). Note the limitations in UN Convention, Art 17.

[145] State Immunity Act 1978, s13(3); UN Convention, Art 20. Cf the broad clauses in *A Company v Republic of X* [1990] 2 Lloyd's Rep 570; *Sabah Shipyard (Pakistan) Ltd v Islamic Republic of Pakistan* [2002] EWCA Civ 1643.

[146] Generally: Crawford (1981) 75 *AJIL* 820; ILC *Ybk* 1991/II(2), 13, 55–9; Ostrander (2004) 22 *Berkeley JIL* 541; Stewart (2005) 99 *AJIL* 194, 206–7; Reinisch (2006) 17 *EJIL* 803; Fox (2nd edn, 2008) 599–662; Fox (2009) 125 *LQR* 544; Yang (2012) ch 9.

[147] E.g. in *Germany v Italy* (Judgment of 3 February 2012, §113) the Court held that the 'rules of customary international law governing immunity from enforcement and those governing jurisdictional immunity (understood *strictosensu* as the right of a State not to be the subject of judicial proceedings in the courts of another State) are distinct, and must be applied separately'.

[148] Yang (2012) 398–400.

[149] *Philippine Embassy Bank Account* (1977) 65 ILR 146; *NML Capital Ltd v Republic of Argentina* [2011] 3 WLR 273, §29. Further: Crawford (1981) 75 *AJIL* 820, esp 838–9, 860–6.

[150] See the decision of the ICTY Appeals Chamber in *Prosecutor v Blaškić* (1997) 110 ILR 607, 707–13 (Objection to the Issue of *Subpoenae Duces Tecum*).

[151] An example of such an attempt is the registration of a legal charge on Villa Vigoni, German state property, by Italian authorities, which was considered in *Germany v Italy* and held to constitute a violation by Italy of its obligation to respect the immunity owed to Germany (§§109–20).

reflecting the position developed by national courts.[152] As a starting point, immunity from execution of foreign judgments and orders against the property of a state can be waived by the express consent of that state.[153] Such consent is not to be inferred from a waiver of immunity from foreign jurisdiction;[154] it is well established that the regimes governing immunity from adjudicative jurisdiction and immunity from execution are separate.[155] The Convention sets out two further exceptions to immunity from execution: first, state property will not be immune if it has been specifically earmarked for satisfaction of the claim in question.[156] Secondly, in the case of post-judgment measures only, property will not be immune if it is used or intended to be used for 'other than government non-commercial purposes' and it is in the territory of the forum state.[157] Article 21 specifies five categories of state property that are presumed to be excluded from this exception.[158] The purpose exception in the UN Convention also comes with a proviso that post-judgment measures of constraint may be taken only against property that has a connection with the entity against which the proceeding was directed.[159] The purpose exception is the most commonly invoked, as it is rare for states to waive their immunity from execution or to earmark property.

The transition from absolute immunity towards a restrictive doctrine has been slower to take hold in the case of immunity from execution against state property than for immunity from adjudicative jurisdiction.[160] The exceptions to immunity from execution are narrow in scope, and courts tend to respect the discretion of states in claiming that the property at issue is used for public purposes. This is understandable, given that measures of constraint are much more intrusive on state sovereignty than the mere exercise of declaratory jurisdiction by a foreign court. State property

---

[152] Reinisch (2006) 17 *EJIL* 803, 835. See also the European Convention, Arts 23 and 26. For domestic provisions see e.g. UK: State Immunity Act 1978, s13 and Civil Jurisdiction and Judgments Act 1982, s31; US: FSIA, 28 USC §§1609–11.

[153] Arts 18(a), 19(a); Fox (2nd edn, 2008) 630. Domestic regimes differ over whether waiver must be express or can be implied: Ostrander (2004) 22 *Berkeley JIL* 541, 548–52.

[154] Art 20; further: Crawford (1981) 75 *AJIL* 820, 860–1.

[155] E.g. Fox (2nd edn, 2008) 600–4.

[156] Arts 18(b), 19(b); see Reinisch (2006) 17 *EJIL* 803, 820–1.

[157] Art 19(c). Cf UK State Immunity Act 1978, s13(4): 'property which is for the time being or is intended for use for commercial purposes'; US: FSIA, 28 USC §1610(a): 'property in the United States of a foreign state,... used for a commercial activity in the United States'.

[158] These are: (a) property, including any bank account, which is used or intended for use in the performance of the functions of the diplomatic activities of the state (including consular activities, special missions, and so forth); (b) property of a military character; (c) property of the central bank or other monetary authority of the state; (d) property forming part of the cultural heritage of the state or part of its archives and not placed or intended to be placed on sale; and (e) property forming part of an exhibition of objects of scientific, cultural, or historical interest and not placed or intended to be placed on sale. For comment: Reinisch (2006) 17 *EJIL* 803, 823–34; Fox (2nd edn, 2008) 634–51.

[159] Art 19(c); further: Fox (2nd edn, 2008) 631–4. The ILC Draft Articles were more closely based on the controversial version of the 'nexus requirement' articulated in the US legislation, requiring a link between the property and the underlying claim in the proceeding. For comparative analysis: Ostrander (2004) 22 *Berkeley JIL* 541, 557–61; Reinisch (2006) 17 *EJIL* 803, 822–3; Sun (2010) 9 *Chin JIL* 699.

[160] Generally: Reinisch (2006) 17 *EJIL* 803; Fox (2nd edn, 2008) 600–1.

used for public purposes is not the same as property of private persons.[161] On the other hand, there should be no justification for refusing to enforce a judgment if the use to which the asset is put does not involve a foreign state's sovereignty.[162] The purpose test is a means of balancing respect for state sovereignty and the judgment debtor's right to be paid amounts judged due and owing.

4. FURTHER CONCERNS AND ISSUES

(A) THIRD WORLD CONCERNS

The transition from absolute immunity *ratione materiae* has not been straightforward or unproblematic for states whose primary exposure is as defendants in foreign courts. Although the Asian-African Legal Consultative Committee published a report adopting restrictive immunity as early as 1960[163] and certain Asian and African states actually introduced legislation to this effect,[164] many states, including China and Japan, stuck steadfastly to the doctrine of absolute immunity.[165] Japan now embraces restrictive immunity, and is a signatory to the UN Convention.[166] China, too, has signed the Convention, having actively participated in its drafting, and has demonstrated a willingness to waive immunity through bilateral arrangements.[167] However, China's commitment to restrictive immunity has been called into question by its confirmation of its practice of absolute immunity, in connection with a recent case before the Hong Kong Court of Final Appeal. A majority of the Court considered that, although Hong Kong embraced restrictive immunity before handover, the doctrine of state immunity adopted in the Hong Kong Special Administrative Region must, as a matter of legal and constitutional principle, mirror that espoused by the Central People's Government in China.[168] In finding that China adopted the absolute theory of immunity, the Court relied on statements issued by the Office of the Commissioner of the

---

[161] Yang (2012) 401–2.

[162] *Abbott v South Africa* (1992) 113 ILR 411, 422.

[163] Asian-African Legal Consultative Committee Report, *The Immunity of States in Respect of Commercial Transactions*, Third Session, Colombo, 1960.

[164] State Immunity Act 1979 (as revised in 1985) (Singapore); State Immunity Ordinance 1981 (Pakistan); Foreign Sovereign Immunity Act 1981 (South Africa). Note also Law of the People's Republic of China on the Immunity of the Property of Foreign Central Banks from Judicial Compulsory Measures 2005 (PRC).

[165] *Rizaeff Frères v Soviet Mercantile Fleet* (1927) 40 ILR 84; *Matsuyama v Republic of China* (1928) 4 ILR 168; *Jackson v People's Republic of China*, 794 F.2d 1490 (1986). See further Qi (2008) 7 *Chin JIL* 307.

[166] *Tokyo Sanyo Boeki Co Ltd v Pakistan*, 21 July 2006, 60(6) *Minshu* 2542. Translated: (2006) 49 *JAIL* 144. Noted: Jones (2006) 100 *AJIL* 908; Yokomizo (2008) 51 *JYIL* 485.

[167] E.g. Treaty of Trade and Navigation between the Union of Soviet Socialist Republics and the People's Republic of China, 25 July 1958, 152 UNTS 1958, Annex, Art 4.

[168] *DRC v FG Hemisphere Associates LLC*, Hong Kong Court of Final Appeal, Judgment of 8 June 2011 (provisional judgment finalized 8 September 2011).

Ministry of Foreign Affairs to this effect.[169] China's (and thus Hong Kong's) proclaimed acceptance of absolute immunity in connection with this judgment and its anomalous position on its signature of the UN Convention create an obstacle to the consolidation of the customary rule of restrictive immunity.

(B) STATE IMMUNITY AND HUMAN RIGHTS

There is a persistent tension in the case-law between the profile of state immunity and the principles of human rights. A large body of academic opinion has developed on this issue, particularly on the subject of immunity for civil claims relating to torture.[170] An exception for civil claims for serious violations for human rights was considered but not adopted in the UN Convention due to a lack of consensus.[171] Despite the calls for progressive development of the law to encompass an exception, recent case-law has confirmed that state immunity provides a procedural bar to civil claims for damages arising from human rights violations.[172] Moreover, the European Court of Human Rights has held that the grant of state immunity in this context does not infringe Article 6 of the 1950 European Convention on Human Rights.[173] In *Jones v Saudi Arabia*, *Pinochet (No 3)* was firmly distinguished from civil proceedings under the State Immunity Act 1978.[174] The House of Lords held that no exception to the rule of immunity existed in the case of torture committed abroad. Not only was there no statutory exception to the rule of immunity, but the peremptory character of the prohibition had no bearing on the grant of immunity. Consistent with other state practice, the House of Lords rejected the argument that a peremptory norm is hierarchically superior to and thus abrogates the operation of state immunity.[175] As Fox has observed, 'there is no substantive content in a procedural plea of state immunity upon which a *ius cogens* mandate can bite'.[176] This was confirmed in *Germany v Italy*, where the Court drew a fundamental distinction between questions of substance and procedure, holding that the peremptory status of the rule (as a substantive matter) could

[169] Ibid, §§202, 211, 222–6. See further China's position in *Morris v People's Republic of China*, 478 F.Supp 2d 561 (2007).

[170] Brohmer, *State Immunity and the Violation of Human Rights* (1997); Bianchi (1999) 10 *EJIL* 237; Fox (2005) 121 *LQR* 353; McGregor (2006) 55 *ICLQ* 437; Parlett [2006] *EHRLR* 49; Fox [2006] *EHRLR* 142; McGregor (2007) 18 *EJIL* 903; van Alebeek (2008); Wright (2010) 30 *OJLS* 143.

[171] ILC *Ybk* 1999/II(2), 172.

[172] *Al-Adsani v UK* (2001) 123 ILR 24; *Kalogeropoulou v Greece* (2002) 129 ILR 537; *Bouzari v Islamic Republic of Iran* (2004) 128 ILR 586; *Fang v Jiang Zemin* (2006) 141 ILR 702; *Jones v Saudi Arabia* [2007] 1 AC 270; *Zhang v Zemin* (2010) 141 ILR 542. Also: *Saudi Arabia v Nelson*, 507 US 349 (1993); *Samantar v Yousuf*, 130 S.Ct 2278 (2010); *Germany v Italy*, Judgment of 3 February 2012.

[173] 4 November 1950, ETS 5. See *Al-Adsani v UK* (2001) 123 ILR 24; *Kalogeropoulou v Greece* (2002) 129 ILR 537.

[174] *Jones v Saudi Arabia* [2007] 1 AC 270, 286, 290, 293, 300, 303–4.

[175] Ibid, 288–9, 293. Also: *Al-Adsani v UK* (2001) 123 ILR 24, §§61, 66; *Kalogeropoulou v Greece* (2002) 129 ILR 537, 546–7; *Bouzari v Islamic Republic of Iran* (2004) 128 ILR 586, 604–6; *Fang v Jiang Zemin* (2006) 141 ILR 702; *Zhang v Zemin* (2010) 141 ILR 542, 551–3.

[176] Fox (2nd edn, 2008) 151 (cited in *Jones v Saudi Arabia* [2007] 1 AC 270, 288–9, 293).

have no impact on the question of state immunity (as a procedural matter).[177] Unless the relevant prohibition develops to include an ancillary procedural rule requiring the assumption of civil jurisdiction, state immunity remains unaffected.[178] Despite the emphasis in *Distomo* and *Ferrini* on the peremptory character of the relevant prohibitions, the fact that the impugned conduct was committed in the territory of the forum state suggests that these cases may not be irreconcilable with the *Al-Adsani/Jones* line of authority, at least insofar as concerns acts not performed *iure belli*.[179]

---

[177] *Germany v Italy*, Judgment of 3 February 2012, §93.

[178] *Jones v Saudi Arabia* [2007] 1 AC 270, 293.

[179] *Distomo Massacre* (2000) 129 ILR 513, 516; *Ferrini v Federal Republic of Germany* (2004) 128 ILR 658. Further: Gattini (2005) 3 *JICJ* 224; Yang (2006) 3 *NZYIL* 131; O'Keefe (2011) 44 *Vand JTL* 999.

PART VIII

NATIONALITY AND RELATED CONCEPTS

23

THE RELATIONS OF NATIONALITY

1. INTRODUCTION

(A) THE DOCTRINE OF THE FREEDOM OF STATES IN MATTERS OF NATIONALITY[1]

It is widely thought that states have general freedom of action in matters of nationality. For example in *Nationality Decrees Issued in Tunis and Morocco* the Permanent Court said:

The question whether a certain matter is or is not solely within the jurisdiction of a State is an essentially relative question; it depends upon the development of international relations. Thus, in the present state of international law, questions of nationality are, in the opinion of this Court, in principle within this reserved domain.[2]

Or as ILC Special Rapporteur Manley Hudson put it, '[i]n principle, questions of nationality fall within the domestic jurisdiction of each state'.[3]

There are compelling objections of principle to the doctrine of the complete freedom of states in the present context. Before these are considered it is necessary to recall the significance of nationality in the law. First a state whose national has suffered an injury caused by an internationally wrongful act of another state may exercise diplomatic protection.[4] Secondly, numerous duties of states in relation to war and neutrality, resting for the most part on customary law, are framed in terms of the acts or

---

[1] Generally on nationality: Fitzmaurice (1957) 92 Hague *Recueil* 191; van Panhuys, *The Role of Nationality in International Law* (1959); Brownlie (1963) 39 *BY* 284; Weis, *Nationality and Statelessness in International Law* (2nd edn, 1979); Rezek (1986) 198 Hague *Recueil* 333; Bederman (1993) 42 *ICLQ* 119; Donner, *The Regulation of Nationality in International Law* (2nd edn, 1994); Rubenstein & Adler (2000) 7 *Indiana JGLS* 519; Muchmore (2005) 26 *Imm & Nat LR* 327; Bosniak, *The Citizen and the Alien* (2006); van Waas, *Nationality Matters* (2008); Sloane (2009) 50 *Harv ILJ* 1; Trevisanut, 'Nationality Cases before International Courts and Tribunals' (2011) *MPEPIL*.

[2] (1923) PCIJ Ser B No 4, 24.

[3] ILC *Ybk* 1952/II, 3, 7.

[4] ILC Articles on Diplomatic Protection, GAOR, 61st Sess, Supp No 10, A/61/10; Amerasinghe, *Diplomatic Protection* (2008). For the nationality of claims rule in the law of diplomatic protection: chapter 31.

omissions by nationals which states should prevent and, in some cases, punish. Thirdly, aliens on the territory of a state produce a complex of legal relations consequent on their status of non-nationals. Governmental acts may give rise to questions of international responsibility when they affect aliens or their property. Aliens may be expelled for sufficient cause and their home state is bound to receive them. Many states will not extradite their nationals. Fourthly, nationality provides a regular basis for the exercise of civil and criminal jurisdiction and this even in respect of acts committed abroad (see chapter 21).

(B) THE STRUCTURAL PROBLEM

Nationality involves the assignment of persons to states, and regarded in this way resembles the law relating to territorial sovereignty.[5] National law prescribes the extent of the territory of a state, but this prescription does not preclude an international forum from deciding questions of title in its own way, using criteria of international law. A sovereignty in principle unlimited by the existence of other states is ridiculous. For instance, as regards the delimitation of the territorial sea, the Court in *Anglo-Norwegian Fisheries* allowed that in regard to rugged coasts the coastal state is in the best position to appraise the local conditions dictating the selection of baselines, but the Court did not support complete autonomy.[6] The conferral of nationality as a status is in this respect akin to a process of delimitation.

It is important to avoid relying on abstract statements purporting to establish the boundaries of the reserved domain.[7] Everything depends on how a particular issue arises. Nationality is not confined either to the reserved domain or the realm of state relations: in principle it has two aspects, either of which may be dominant depending on the facts and type of dispute. The approach of the International Court in *Nottebohm* would seem to be perfectly logical in this respect. The Court said:

It is for Liechtenstein, as it is for every sovereign State, to settle by its own legislation the rules relating to the acquisition of its nationality, and to confer that nationality by naturalization granted by its own organs in accordance with that legislation. It is not necessary to determine whether international law imposes any limitations on its freedom of decision in this domain ... Nationality serves above all to determine that the person upon whom it is conferred enjoys the rights and is bound by the obligations which the law of the State in question grants to or imposes on its nationals. This is implied in the wider concept that nationality is within the domestic jurisdiction of the State. But the issue which the Court must decide is not one which pertains to the legal system of Liechtenstein. It does not depend on the law

---

[5] Parry, 1 *Nationality and Citizenship Laws of the Commonwealth and the Republic of Ireland* (1957) 17, regards the analogy of territory as 'very attractive', but remarks that it should not be pushed too far: ibid, 21. However, for the purpose of comment on the possible *results* of a certain type of doctrine the analogy would seem to be valid.

[6] *Fisheries (UK v Norway)*, ICJ Reports 1951 p 116, 132. Further: Fitzmaurice (1953) 30 *BY* 1, 11. Cf *Asylum (Colombia/Peru)*, ICJ Reports 1950 p 274, 278.

[7] De Visscher, *Theory and Reality in Public International Law* (4th edn, 1968) 229–31.

or on the decision of Liechtenstein whether that State is entitled to exercise its protection ... To exercise protection, to apply to the Court, is to place oneself on the plane of international law. It is international law which determines whether a State is entitled to exercise protection and to seise the Court.[8]

Similarly, Article 3 of the European Convention on Nationality of 1997 provides:

Each State shall determine under its own law who are its nationals. This law shall be accepted by other States in so far as it is consistent with applicable international conventions, customary international law and principles of law generally recognised with regard to nationality.[9]

(C) COMMON CRITERIA FOR NATIONALITY[10]

The two main principles on which nationality has traditionally been based are descent from a national (*ius sanguinis*) and birth within state territory (*ius soli*). More recent developments have included giving equal status to men and women in the determination of nationality, and providing reinforced guarantees against statelessness, both trends underwritten by multilateral treaties.[11] Except for the presumption against statelessness (where the *ius soli* applies in case of doubt), it is incorrect to regard the two principles as mutually exclusive: in varying degrees the law of a large number of states rests on both.[12] A common special stipulation is that children born to non-nationals who are members of diplomatic and consular missions do not thereby acquire the nationality of the receiving state.[13]

The Harvard Research draft refers to 'territory or a place assimilated thereto', and states have generally applied the principle of the *ius soli* to birth on ships and aircraft registered under the flag.[14] Where apparent conflict may arise, as in the case of birth on a foreign ship in territorial waters, it seems clear that the child does not in principle acquire *ipso facto* the nationality of the littoral state.[15]

---

[8] *Nottebohm (Liechtenstein v Guatemala)*, ICJ Reports 1955 p 4, 20.

[9] 6 November 1997, ETS No 166. There are 20 states parties. Also Convention Concerning Certain Questions Relating to the Conflict of Nationality Laws, 12 April 1930, 179 LNTS 89, Art 1.

[10] For earlier studies: Sandifer (1935) 29 *AJIL* 248; Survey of the problem of multiple nationality prepared by the Secretariat, ILC *Ybk* 1954/II, 52, 63. Also Kemp (2002) 4 *JEMIE* i; Bosniak (2002) 42 *Va JIL* 979.

[11] For the equality of men and women in nationality matters: e.g. Convention on the Nationality of Married Women, 20 February 1957, 309 UNTS 65; CEDAW, 18 December 1979, 1249 UNTS 13, Art 9(2); CEDAW Committee, General Recommendation No 21 (13th session, 1994) §6. For protection against statelessness: UN Convention on the Reduction of Statelessness, 30 August 1961, 989 UNTS 175. Also van Waas (2008) 31.

[12] The Harvard draft provided that states must choose between the two principles: (1929) 23 *AJIL Supp* 1, 27 (Art 3). But there is no legal basis for such a stipulation (cf Weis (2nd edn, 1979) 95); hybrid sets of nationality laws have not attracted criticism as such, provided they address the question of statelessness.

[13] VCDR, Optional Protocol concerning Acquisition of Nationality, 18 April 1961, 500 UNTS 223, Art II; Johnson (1961) 10 *ICLQ* 597; ILC *Ybk* 1958/II, 89, 101; VCCR, Optional Protocol concerning Acquisition of Nationality, 24 April 1963, 596 UNTS 469, Art II; ILC *Ybk* 1961/II, 92, 122.

[14] (1932) 26 *AJIL Supp* 1. Generally: Córdova, ILC *Ybk* 1953/II 167, 177 (Art IV).

[15] UN Convention on the Reduction of Statelessness, Art 3 (test of flag of registration); van Waas (2008) 31.

The position as regards naturalization is stated as follows by Weis:

Naturalisation in the narrower sense may be defined as the grant of nationality to an alien by a formal act, on an application made for the specific purpose by the alien … It is generally recognised as a mode of acquiring nationality. The conditions to be complied with for the grant of naturalisation vary from country to country, but residence for a certain period of time would seem to be a fairly universal requisite.[16]

Hudson remarks: '[n]aturalization must be based on an explicit voluntary act of the individual or of a person acting on his behalf'.[17] Some jurists have concluded that prolonged residence is a precondition for naturalization. But in regard to *voluntary* naturalization two points must be borne in mind. First, the voluntary nature of the act supplements other social and residential links. Not only is the act voluntary but it is specific: it has that very objective. The element of deliberate association of individual and state is important and should rank with birth and descent, not to mention marriage, legitimation, and adoption. Secondly, while it is true that a considerable number of states allow naturalization on easy terms, the legislation often presents such relaxed conditions as available exceptionally.

Nationality *ex necessitate iuris* is a convenient notion to analyse a further situation. It is not in all respects satisfactory, since acquisition by marriage, legitimation, and adoption might also be so described. However, the cases to be mentioned are sufficiently clear to justify the concept. For example, there is in the legislation of many countries a provision that a child of parents unknown is presumed to have the nationality of the state where the child is found. In a great many instances it is provided that the rule applies to children born to parents of unknown nationality or who are stateless. The rule as to foundlings appears in the Convention on Certain Questions relating to the Conflict of Nationality Laws, Article 14,[18] and in the 1961 Convention on the Reduction of Statelesness, Article 2.[19]

(D) LEGAL STATUS OF THE 'GENERAL PRINCIPLES'

Some at least of the principles considered above are generally recognized as far as the laws of the various states are concerned. But Weis is very cautious in assessing this material in terms of state practice:

Concordance of municipal law does not yet create customary international law; a universal consensus of opinion of States is equally necessary. It is erroneous to attempt to establish rules of international law by methods of comparative law, or even to declare that rules of municipal law of different States which show a certain degree of uniformity are rules of international law.[20]

---

[16] Weis (2nd edn, 1979) 99.
[17] *ILC Ybk* 1952/II, 3, 8. His rubric is: '[n]aturalization in the narrower sense. Option'. In his terminology naturalization means every nationality acquired subsequent to birth.
[18] 12 April 1930, 179 LNTS 89.
[19] 30 August 1961, 989 UNTS 175.
[20] Weis (2nd edn, 1979) 96, 99.

This is unexceptionable insofar as the reversal of the statement would result in a proposition much too dogmatic. But Weis underestimates the significance of legislation as evidence of the *opinio* of states. In the case of the territorial sea, the evidence of state practice available to the ILC was chiefly in the form of legislation, and the comments of governments concentrated on their own legislation.

It might be said that, particularly in the field of nationality, the necessary *opinio iuris* is lacking; but insistence on clear evidence of this may produce capricious results. The fact is that municipal law overwhelmingly rests on significant links between the individual and the state. Such lack of uniformity as there is in nationality laws is explicable not in terms of a lack of *opinio iuris*, but by reference to the fact that inevitably municipal law allocates natonality in the first place, and also to the occurrence of numerous permutations and hence possible points of conflict in legislation on a subject-matter so mobile and complex. But in spheres where conflict on the international plane is easily foreseeable, the rules are there to meet the case.

Thus the conclusions of the Court in *Nottebohm* are not particularly novel. After considering the evidence for the doctrine of the real or effective link,[21] the judgment proceeds:

According to the practice of States, to arbitral and judicial decisions and to the opinions of writers, nationality is a legal bond having as its basis a social fact of attachment, a genuine connection of existence, interests and sentiments, together with the existence of reciprocal rights and duties. It may be said to constitute the juridical expression of the fact that the individual upon whom it is conferred, either directly by the law or as the result of an act of the authorities, is in fact more closely connected with the population of the State conferring nationality than with that of any other State. Conferred by a State, it only entitles that State to exercise protection *vis-à-vis* another State, if it constitutes a translation into juridical terms of the individual's connection with the State which has made him its national.[22]

2. THE EFFECTIVE LINK PRINCIPLE AND *NOTTEBOHM*

(A) PRECURSORS OF *NOTTEBOHM*

Seen in its proper perspective, the decision in *Nottebohm* is a reflection of a fundamental concept long present in the materials concerning nationality on the international plane. The doctrine of the effective link had already been recognized for some time in continental literature[23] and the decisions of some national courts.[24] That was

---

[21] ICJ Reports 1955 p 4, 22, and for the Liechtenstein law: ibid, 13–14.
[22] ICJ Reports 1955 p 4, 23.
[23] Basdevant (1909) 5 *Rev crit DIPriv* 41, 59.
[24] *Magalhais v Fernandes* (1936) 10 ILR 290. Also *German Nationality* (1952) 19 ILR 319.

commonly in connection with dual nationality, but the particular context does not obscure its role as a general principle with a variety of applications.

In its reply to the Preparatory Committee of the Hague Codification Conference the German government declared that 'a State has no power ... to confer its nationality on all the inhabitants of another State or on all foreigners entering its territory ... if the State confers its nationality on the subjects of other States without their request, when the persons concerned are not attached to it by any particular bond, as, for instance, origin, domicile or birth, the States concerned will not be bound to recognize such naturalization'.[25] The legislation of states makes general use of residence, domicile, immigration with an intent to remain permanently, and membership of ethnic groups associated with the state territory, as connecting factors. International law has rested on the same principles in dealing with the situations where a state has no national-ity legislation or where certain parts of the population fall outside the scope of such legislation. The principle of effective link may be seen to underlie much of the practice on state succession and to support the concept of *ressortissant* found frequently in treaties.[26]

(B) THE DECISION AND ITS CRITICS

In *Nottebohm* Liechtenstein claimed damages in respect of the acts of the government of Guatemala in arresting, detaining, expelling, and refusing to readmit Nottebohm, and in seizing and retaining his property without compensation.[27] Guatemala asked the Court to declare the claim inadmissible, in part 'because Liechtenstein had failed to prove that Nottebohm ... properly acquired Liechtenstein nationality in accord-ance with the law of that Principality'; because anyway that law could not be regarded as 'in conformity with international law'; and because he appeared 'in any event not to have lost, or not validly to have lost, his German nationality'. In the final submis-sions, inadmissibility was also based on 'the ground that M. Nottebohm appears to have solicited Liechtenstein nationality fraudulently, that is to say, with the sole object of acquiring the status of a neutral national before returning to Guatemala, and with-out any genuine intention to establish a durable link, excluding German nationality, between the Principality and himself'.

In its judgment the Court regarded the plea relating to Nottebohm's nationality as fundamental. The issue was one of admissibility and the Court observed:

In order to decide upon the admissibility of the Application, the Court must ascer-tain whether the nationality conferred on Nottebohm by Liechtenstein by means of a

---

[25] League of Nations, Conference for the Codification of International Law, 1 *Bases for Discussion Drawn up for the Conference by the Preparatory Committee* (1929) 13.

[26] Weis (2nd edn, 1979) 7; *Kahane (Successor) v Parisi and Austrian State* (1929) 5 ILR 213.

[27] ICJ Reports 1955 p 4. For contemporary comment: Mervyn Jones (1956) 5 *ICLQ* 230; Loewenfeld (1956) 42 *GST* 5; de Visscher (1956) 60 *RGDIP* 238; Bastid (1956) 45 *Rev crit DIPriv* 607; Maury (1958) 23 *ZaöRV* 515; Kunz (1960) 54 *AJIL* 536; Lauterpacht, 4 *International Law* (1978) 5.

naturalization which took place in the circumstances which have been described, can be validly invoked as against Guatemala, whether it bestows upon Liechtenstein a sufficient title to the exercise of protection in respect of Nottebohm as against Guatemala ... what is involved is not recognition [of acquisition of Liechtenstein nationality] for all purposes but merely for the purposes of the admissibility of the Application, and, ... secondly, that what is involved is not recognition by all States but only by Guatemala.[28]

In the event, having applied the doctrine of the effective link to the facts, the Court held the claim inadmissible. Dissenting judges[29] and critics[30] have pointed out that Guatemala had not argued the case on the basis that there was no effective link, and also that the precise *ratio* of the decision was the question of opposability as against Guatemala. This is true, but the effect of such formal arguments in limiting the significance of the judgment is negligible. The tendency to look for precise grounds for decision is a standard judicial technique, and few jurists seriously believe that, apart from cases of treaty interpretation, the pronouncements of the Court can be placed in quarantine by formal devices.[31] In any case, the fact that admissibility was the issue does not affect the general significance of the decision. As the Court said: '[t]o exercise protection, to apply to the Court, is to place oneself on the plane of international law. It is international law which determines whether a State is entitled to exercise protection and to seise the Court'.[32] The Court did not base its decision on estoppel as against Liechtenstein, but focused on the existence or not of a right of protection, an issue which necessarily affects states in general and not just the parties.[33]

To those who regard the Court's approach as a novelty,[34] the inadequacy of its review of state practice is a source of disquiet. But, first, the Court is usually somewhat oracular in its announcement of rules of customary law; this does not mean the relevant materials were not duly assessed. Secondly, the Court's somewhat varied collection of propositions and references to previous practice reads not as a survey but rather as an attempt at further and better particulars as to the logical necessity of the general principle for which the Court was contending. The relevant section of the judgment commences well before the 'survey of materials', and the burden of the section as a whole is that, to settle issues on the plane of international law, principles have to be applied apart from the rules of national law.[35] The major point is made on the basis of a 'general principle of international law' and not on the basis of a customary rule of the usual sort. Thirdly, critics of the judgment seek materials which support the 'link' theory explicitly as a specific rule. Not all the materials support such a rule, but there

---

[28] ICJ Reports 1955 p 4, 16. Also ibid, 20.

[29] ICJ Reports 1955 p 4, 30 (Judge Klaestad, diss), 35 (Judge Read, diss), 53 (Judge ad hoc Guggenheim, diss).

[30] E.g. Mervyn Jones (1956) 5 *ICLQ* 230, 238; Kunz (1960) 54 *AJ* 536, 541, 552; Weis (2nd edn, 1979) 176.

[31] Cf the effect of *Anglo-Norwegian Fisheries*, ICJ Reports 1951 p 116.

[32] ICJ Reports 1955 p 4, 20.

[33] Cf Kunz (1960) 54 *AJIL* 536, 564.

[34] Jones (1956) 5 *ICLQ* 230, 240; Kunz (1960) 54 *AJIL* 536, 552, 555.

[35] ICJ Reports 1955 p 4, 20.

is much material which supports the general principle. Moreover there was very little on the international plane which expressly *denied* the effective link doctrine, and the incidental rejection of it in *Salem*[36] was regarded by contemporaries as a novelty.[37]

Judge Read[38] and others[39] have also contended that the Court relied irrelevantly on the principles adopted by arbitral tribunals in dealing with cases of double nationality,[40] since the facts of *Nottebohm* did not present this problem: Nottebohm either had Liechtenstein nationality or none. But the principle of effectiveness is not restricted to cases of dual nationality. If the principle exists it applies to the *Nottebohm* permutation also.

In terms of the application of the principle to the facts, Nottebohm was German by birth and was still a German national when he applied for naturalization in Liechtenstein in October 1939. He had left Germany in 1905, although he maintained business connections there. As a consequence of naturalization he lost his German nationality.[41] The Court decided that the effective nationality was not that of Liechtenstein (but without characterizing the links with Guatemala in terms of effective nationality): it found 'the absence of any bond of attachment between Nottebohm and Liechtenstein and, on the other hand, the existence of a long-standing and close connection between him and Guatemala, a link which his naturalization in no way weakened'.[42]

The Court did not consider whether an absence of connection when the nationality was originally acquired can be cured by later events. However, while in 1955 Nottebohn's effective nationality was that of Liechtenstein, when the main acts complained of occurred it was not: it is doubtful, to say the least, if after suffering a wrong a national can then take on another nationality and, after a lapse of time, call on the new state to espouse the claim against the state of former nationality.[43]

As to the implications of the *Nottebohm* judgment in the realm of policy, critics have concentrated on the severance of diplomatic protection and nationality.[44] The practical result of the decision is seen to be a narrowing of the ambit of diplomatic protection. In fact in the vast number of cases effective nationality matches formal nationality.[45] Long-resident refugees are an important source of problems, and it would seem likely that the link doctrine is more helpful here than reference to national laws. The latter method leaves the refugee stateless or links him or her to a community which has proved repugnant or been abandonded.

---

[36] (1932) 6 ILR 188.

[37] Ibid, 192, note by Lauterpacht; Jones (1956) 5 *ICLQ* 230, 242.

[38] ICJ Reports 1955 p 4, 41.

[39] Ibid, 59 (Judge ad hoc Guggenheim, diss). Also Kunz (1960) 54 *AJIL* 536, 556.

[40] E.g. *Mergé* (1955) 22 ILR 443, 450.

[41] ICJ Reports 1955 p 4, 55 (Judge ad hoc Guggenheim, diss).

[42] Ibid, 25.

[43] For the continuous nationality rule as eventually formulated: ILC Articles on Diplomatic Protection 2006, Art 5, and further: chapter 31.

[44] ICJ Reports 1955 p 4, 46 (Judge Read, diss).

[45] Cf ILC Articles on Diplomatic Protection, commentary to Art 4, §5.

The UN Convention on the Reduction of Statelessness of 1961[46] contains detailed provisions relying on various criteria of factual connection and evidence of allegiance. The 1961 Conference also adopted a resolution recommending 'that persons who are stateless *de facto* should as far as possible be treated as stateless *de jure* to enable them to acquire an effective nationality'.[47] Weis remarks that the convention and recommendation 'clearly reflect the importance which is attached to an increasing degree to effectiveness of nationality'.[48]

(C) THE ILC'S WORK ON DIPLOMATIC PROTECTION

In its work on diplomatic protection the ILC took a narrow view of *Nottebohm*'s implications. Article 4 of the ILC Articles on Diplomatic Protection of 2006 reads as follows:

State of nationality of a natural person

For the purposes of the diplomatic protection of a natural person, a State of nationality means a State whose nationality that person has acquired, in accordance with the law of that State, by birth, descent, naturalization, succession of States, or in any other manner, not inconsistent with international law.

The commentary elaborates:

Draft article 4 does not require a State to prove an effective or genuine link between itself and its national, along the lines suggested in the *Nottebohm* case, as an additional factor for the exercise of diplomatic protection, even where the national possesses only one nationality. Despite divergent views as to the interpretation of the case, the Commission took the view that there were certain factors that served to limit *Nottebohm* to the facts of the case in question, particularly the fact that the ties between Mr. Nottebohm and Liechtenstein ... were 'extremely tenuous' compared with the close ties between Mr. Nottebohm and Guatemala ... for a period of over 34 years, which led the International Court of Justice to repeatedly assert that Liechtenstein was 'not entitled to extend its protection to Nottebohm vis-à-vis Guatemala'. This suggests that the Court did not intend to expound a general rule applicable to all States but only a relative rule according to which a State in Liechtenstein's position was required to show a genuine link between itself and Mr. Nottebohm in order to permit it to claim on his behalf against Guatemala with whom he had extremely close ties. Moreover, it is necessary to be mindful of the fact that if the genuine link requirement proposed by *Nottebohm* was strictly applied it would exclude millions of persons from the benefit of diplomatic protection ...[49]

---

[46]   30 August 1961, 989 UNTS 175.

[47]   UN Conference on the Elimination or Reduction of Future Statelessness, Resolutions, 29 August 1961, A/CONF.9/14/Add.1, Res I.

[48]   Weis (1962) 11 *ICLQ* 1073, 1087. For diplomatic protection of refugees: chapter 31.

[49]   Commentary to Art 4, §5: ILC Report 2006, GAOR, 61st Session, Supp No 10, A/61/10, 32–3. Also Dugard's First Report on Diplomatic Protection, ILC, 52nd Session: ILC *Ybk* 2000/II(1), 228.

The use of the double negative in draft Article 4 ('not inconsistent') is intended to show that the burden of proving that nationality was acquired in violation of international law rests upon the state which disputes the nationality of the injured person.[50] This is said to follow from the proposition that the state conferring nationality must be given a 'margin of appreciation';[51] correspondingly there is a presumption in favour of the validity of the conferral of nationality.[52] It would follow in any event on the basis of the maxim *actori incumbit probatio*.

A factor not to be overlooked in discussions of *Nottebohm* was that the case involved a putative enemy alien. Nottebohm acquired the nationality of Liechtenstein, a neutral state, with a view to avoiding the risk of becoming an enemy alien if Guatemala entered the Second World War.[53]

3. THE APPLICATION OF RULES OF INTERNATIONAL LAW

(A) THE LIMITS OF STATE AUTHORITY IN THE MATTER OF NATIONALITY

If rules of international law are to work effectively or at all, there must be limitations on the powers of individual states to treat persons as their nationals. Some of these limitations must now be considered.

It may happen that a state has not adopted any nationality laws on the modern pattern. Although such cases are rare,[54] examples of the absence of nationality legislation arise from the creation of new states. By definition they must possess a population which is their own. In a decision on the status of former Palestine citizens[55] prior to the enactment of the Israeli Nationality Law of 1952, a judge of the District Court of Tel-Aviv observed:

So long as no law has been enacted providing otherwise, my view is that every individual who, on the date of the establishment of the State of Israel was resident in the territory which today constitutes the State of Israel, is also a national of Israel. Any other view must lead to

---

[50] Commentary to draft Art 4, §7.

[51] Ibid, citing the advisory opinion of the IACtHR in *Proposed Amendments to the Naturalization Provisions of the Political Constitution of Costa Rica*, IACtHR OC-4/84, 19 January 1984, §§58–63.

[52] Commentary to draft Art 4, §7.

[53] In *Nottebohm* Rolin for Guatemala argued that, because Nottebohm's aim was to acquire neutral status by naturalization, there was no genuine link. This point was taken by the Court at the end of its judgment, ICJ Reports 1955 p 4, 26. The dissenting judges regarded the question as a part of the issues concerning abuse of rights and fraud: ICJ Reports 1955 p 4, 32 (Judge Klaestad, diss), 48 (Judge Read, diss), 64 (Judge ad hoc Guggenheim, diss).

[54] Cf Parry (1957) 355.

[55] Palestine citizenship had ceased to exist: *Hussein v Governor of Acre Prison* (1950) 17 ILR 112.

the absurd result of a State without nationals—a phenomenon the existence of which has not yet been observed.[56]

If a new state, relying on the absence of a municipal law, tried to deport a part of its permanent population, it would be acting in clear breach of its obligations and would be internationally responsible.

Another situation concerns persons outside the scope of national legislation. The legislation of a number of states has categorized the population into those with a higher status, usually designated 'citizens', and others. In the case of the UK, the position is that the inhabitants of dependencies, whatever their internal status under the British Nationality Act 1981, are considered to have the status of national for purposes of international law.[57] US law has the category '"non-citizen" nationals'.[58] The necessity for assignment of nationality where a deliberate denial of citizenship occurs is apparent. In an arbitral award the status of the Cayuga Indians, who had migrated from the US to Canada, was established on the basis of factual connection.[59] They were held to have become British nationals, and the assumption was that, for purposes of international law, they had previously been attached to the US.[60] In *Kahane (Successor) v Parisi and Austrian State* the tribunal in substance regarded Romanian Jews as Romanian nationals, since Romania, while withholding citizenship, did not consider them to be stateless.[61] However, the main point of the decision was to establish the meaning of the term *ressortissant* in the Treaty of St Germain.[62]

(B) STATE RESPONSIBILITY AND THE DOCTRINE OF THE GENUINE LINK

States cannot plead their internal law in justification of international wrongs,[63] and they may be held responsible for conditions on their territory which constitute a breach of their international obligations.[64] However, many important duties of a specific character are prescribed by reference to nationals of a state. For example there is a duty to admit nationals expelled from other states and, by way of corollary, a duty not to expel

---

[56] *AB v MB* (1951) 17 ILR 110. However, the same court in another case assumed the absence of nationality until the Nationality Law: *Oseri v Oseri* (1952) 17 ILR 111 (and cf *Shifris* (1950) ibid, 110). Also Rosenne (1954) 81 *JDI* 4, 6.

[57] Generally: Fransman, *British Nationality Law* (3rd edn, 2011).

[58] 8 USC §1542.

[59] *Cayuga Indians (Great Britain) v United States* (1926) 6 RIAA 173, 177.

[60] Also *Rothmann v Austria and Hungary* (1928) 4 ILR 254; *Margulies v Austria and Hungary* (1929) 6 RIAA 279. Both cases turn on the interpretation of a US statute. Further: *Mathison* (1903) 9 RIAA 485, 490; *Valeriani v Amuna Bekri Sichera* (1934) 8 ILR 283; *Logan v Styres* (1959) 27 ILR 239 (as to the Six Nations Indians of Ontario).

[61] (1929) 5 ILR 213.

[62] Principal Allied & Associated Powers–Austria, Treaty of St Germain-en-Laye, 10 September 1919, 226 CTS 8, Arts 249, 256.

[63] ARSIWA, Arts 3, 32.

[64] *Kahane (Successor) v Parisi and Austrian State* (1929) 5 ILR 213.

nationals. Yet obviously ad hoc denationalization would provide a ready means of evading these duties. In appropriate circumstances responsibility would be established for the breach of duty if it were shown that the withdrawal of nationality was itself a part of the wrongful conduct, facilitating the result.[65] Again, states could avoid rules governing the treatment of aliens if they could at their discretion impose nationality on aliens resident in or passing through state territory, however brief their stay. Similar considerations apply to the law of belligerent occupation[66] and the law of neutrality.

The principles needed to solve this type of problem are simple enough if, on the facts of the case, the manipulation of the law of nationality is part and parcel of the wrongful conduct. However, it is possible to postulate a general principle of genuine link relating to the *causa* for conferment of nationality (and the converse for deprivation), a principle distinguishable from that of effective link. Significantly enough, authors,[67] with support from state practice and the jurisprudence of international tribunals,[68] have often stated the rule that a diplomatic claim cannot be validly presented if it is based on a nationality which has been fraudulently acquired. Admittedly the rule is often formulated with the acts of the individual in mind, but in principle it is applicable to fraud on the part of a state. In *Nottebohm* Guatemala contended that Liechtenstein had acted fraudulently in granting nationality to Nottebohm, and further, that Nottebohm himself acted fraudulently in applying for and obtaining the certificate of naturalization.[69] The Court did not address these arguments explicitly, but, in adverting to Nottebohm's motive of acquiring neutral status,[70] the Court accepted the substance of the argument: in this context the doctrine of genuine link, in the narrow sense, and the broad concept of effective link were brought into close relation.

In applying the principle of genuine link, two considerations are relevant. In the first place, there is a presumption of the validity of an act of naturalization, since acts of governments are presumed to have been performed in good faith.[71] Secondly, this is reinforced by the concept of nationality as a status, since an act of conferment is not to be invalidated except in very clear cases.[72]

(C) NATIONALITY BY ESTOPPEL

In many cases where the basic facts concerning the individual are ambiguous, the conduct of governments may provide the answer. Express declarations and admissions by

---

[65] Weis (2nd edn, 1979) 123; also Williams (1927) 8 *BY* 45, 59; Jennings (1939) 20 *BY* 98, 112.

[66] Thus the German ordinance of 1942, which authorized the grant of nationality to certain classes of the population in territories occupied by Germany was not opposable to third states as it was contrary to international law: ICJ Reports 1955 p 4, 54 (Judge ad hoc Guggenheim, diss).

[67] E.g. Weis (2nd edn, 1979) 218.

[68] E.g. *Salem* (1932) 6 ILR 188; *Flegenheimer* (1958) 25 ILR 91, 98.

[69] ICJ Reports 1955 p 4, 26.

[70] Ibid, 26.

[71] On proof of nationality *ex lege* in the face of declarations by the executive that legal requirements have been fulfilled see *Soufraki v United Arab Emirates*, Decision on Annulment, 5 June 2007, §§60–78,

[72] Jennings (1967) 121 Hague *Recueil* 323, 459.

diplomatic representatives may create an estoppel. However, acts of administration of an incidental or routine nature, especially in the absence of any actual or apprehended dispute, may not have this effect. In *Nottebohm* Liechtenstein argued that Guatemala had recognized his naturalization on the basis of the entry of a visa in his Liechtenstein passport and official acts relating to the control of aliens. The Court observed:

All of these acts have reference to the control of aliens in Guatemala and not to the exercise of diplomatic protection. When Nottebohm thus presented himself before the Guatemalan authorities, the latter had before them a private individual: there did not thus come into being any relationship between governments. There was nothing in all this to show that Guatemala then recognized that the naturalization conferred upon Nottebohm gave Liechtenstein any title to the exercise of protection.[73]

Admissions by the parties in the face of a court will normally be relied upon in matters of nationality.[74] In some cases the tribunal has been prepared to rely on the conduct of governments in the absence of any declaration. In *Hendry* the Mexican–US General Claims Commission held that Mexico was estopped from denying Hendry's American nationality by reason of its having discharged him from employment because he was an American.[75] However, in *Flegenheimer* the Italian–US Conciliation Commission rejected an Italian argument that the claim was inadmissible because at the date of the acts complained of Flegenheimer's apparent nationality was German, since he had used a German passport in dealings with the Italian authorities. This argument failed on the facts, but the Commission noted 'that the doctrine of apparent nationality cannot be considered as accepted by the Law of Nations'.[76]

The issue was confronted in an important decision of the Eritrea Ethiopia Claims Commission (EECC) in 2004.[77] The case concerned expulsion and deprivation of property of a large number of persons of Eritrean origin who continued to live in Ethiopia after the separation of Eritrea in 1993 and who were still resident there when war broke out in 1998. Numbers of them had voted in the April 1993 Referendum on Eritrean independence (voting in which was limited by law to 'Eritrean citizens'). But they continued to exercise civil and political rights as Ethiopian nationals, until their denationalization and expulsion. The EECC held that in the special circumstances they were dual nationals by estoppel—and this despite the fact that the law of neither state allowed dual nationality.

[T]he Commission is not...persuaded by Eritrea's argument that registration as an Eritrean national in order to participate in the 1993 Referendum was without important legal consequences. The governing entity issuing those cards was not yet formally recognized as independent or as a member of the United Nations, but it exercised effective and independent control over a defined territory and a permanent population and carried on effective and

---

[73] ICJ Reports 1955 p 4, 18. Cf ibid, 48 (Judge Read, diss).
[74] *Expropriated Religious Properties* (1920) 1 RIAA 7, 46.
[75] (1930) 4 RIAA 616, 616.
[76] (1958) 25 ILR 91, 151.
[77] *Civilians Claims, Eritrea's Claims 15, 16, 23 & 27–32* (2004) 135 ILR 374.

substantial relations with the external world, particularly in economic matters. In all these respects, it reflected the characteristics of a State in international law. On the other hand, neither is the Commission persuaded by Ethiopia's argument that the continued issuance of Ethiopian passports and other official documents was not evidence of continued Ethiopian nationality. Passports in particular contain the issuing State's formal representation to other States that the bearer is its national. The decision to issue such a document, intended to be presented to and relied upon by friendly foreign States, is an internationally significant act, not a casual courtesy...

... nationality is ultimately a legal status. Taking into account the unusual transitional circumstances associated with the creation of the new State of Eritrea and both Parties' conduct before and after the 1993 Referendum, the Commission concludes that those who qualified to participate in the Referendum in fact acquired dual nationality. They became citizens of the new State of Eritrea pursuant to Eritrea's Proclamation No. 21/1992, but at the same time, Ethiopia continued to regard them as its own nationals.[78]

In so holding the EECC was influenced by an Agreed Minute of 1996 which, whether or not it was a treaty, postponed a process by which 'Eritreans who have so far been enjoying Ethiopian citizenship' should be made to elect one or other nationality.[79]

(D) COMPULSORY CHANGE OF NATIONALITY

Existing practice and jurisprudence do not support a general rule that deprivation of nationality is unlawful.[80] On the other hand, Article 15(2) of the Universal Declaration of Human Rights of 1948 stipulates that persons may not be 'arbitrarily deprived' of their nationality, and although this has no equivalent in the International Covenant,[81] there is some basis for holding it to be a rule of customary international law.

The EECC's Civilian Claims decision of 2004 is relevant here. As to the applicable law it said:

[T]he Commission also recognizes that international law limits States' power to deprive persons of their nationality. In this regard, the Commission attaches particular importance to the principle expressed in Article 15, paragraph 2, of the Universal Declaration of Human Rights, that 'no one shall be arbitrarily deprived of his nationality.' In assessing whether deprivation of nationality was arbitrary, the Commission considered several factors, including whether the action had a basis in law; whether it resulted in persons being rendered stateless; and whether there were legitimate reasons for it to be taken given the totality of the circumstances.[82]

---

[78] Ibid, 394–5.

[79] Ibid, 395–6, and on the status of the 1996 Agreed Minute: ibid, 396 (§53).

[80] Conclusions of Hudson, ILC *Ybk* 1952/II, 3, 10; Weis (2nd edn, 1979) 125. Also Convention on the Reduction of Statelessness, Art 8; ICERD, 21 December 1965, 660 UNTS 195, Art 5(d)(iii). Nationality of adults is not addressed in the ICCPR.

[81] ICCPR, 23 March 1976, 999 UNTS 171. A discriminatory denationalization would infringe Art 26. Further: chapter 29.

[82] *Civilians Claims, Eritrea's Claims 15, 16, 23 & 27–32* (2004) 135 ILR 374, 397–8.

In applying these criteria the EECC distinguished between differently situated groups. On the one hand, as to persons considered a security risk, it held:

Deprivation of nationality is a serious matter with important and lasting consequences for those affected. In principle, it should follow procedures in which affected persons are adequately informed regarding the proceedings, can present their cases to an objective decision maker, and can seek objective outside review. Ethiopia's process often fell short of this … Notwithstanding the limitations of the process, the record also shows that Ethiopia faced an exceptional situation. It was at war with Eritrea. Thousands of Ethiopians with personal and ethnic ties to Eritrea had taken steps to acquire Eritrean nationality. Some of these participated in groups that supported the Eritrean Government and often acted on its behalf. In response, Ethiopia devised and implemented a system applying reasonable criteria to identify individual dual nationals thought to pose threats to its wartime security. Given the exceptional wartime circumstances, the Commission finds that the loss of Ethiopian nationality after being identified through this process was not arbitrary and contrary to international law.[83]

But as to a group of registered dual nationals the Commission held:

Whatever the numbers affected, there was no evidence indicating that the dual nationals in this group threatened Ethiopian security or suggesting other reasons for taking away their Ethiopian nationality. There was no process to identify individuals warranting special consideration and no apparent possibility of review or appeal. Considering that rights to such benefits as land ownership and business licenses, as well as passports and other travel documents were at stake, the Commission finds that this wide-scale deprivation of Ethiopian nationality of persons remaining in Ethiopia was, under the circumstances, arbitrary and contrary to international law.[84]

Similar analyses were applied to other affected sub-groups.[85]

The analogue of deprivation of nationality is provided by the cases described as compulsory change of nationality and 'collective naturalization'. The whole pattern of rules and the practice of states is based on the circumstance that states set the conditions under which nationality is acquired and lost. The law concerned may call for expressions of will on the part of individuals directly, or indirectly, by their establishing residence or service in the armed forces, but the conditions are set by the law. Nevertheless tribunals have occasionally stated in terms that international law does not permit compulsory change of nationality.[86]

The US, the UK, France, and other states have often protested against 'forced naturalization provisions', as they are sometimes called, in the laws of various Latin American states.[87] This practice is bound up with the rule that international law does

---

[83] Ibid, 400.
[84] Ibid, 401.
[85] Ibid, 401–2.
[86] *In re Rau* (1930) 6 ILR 251, 251.
[87] Hudson, ILC *Ybk* 1952/II, 3, 8; Weis (2nd edn, 1979) 102. It is important to determine the exact bases of such protests. The US was concerned with the principle of voluntary expatriation. Other states were in

not permit states to impose their nationality on aliens resident abroad.[88] But the practice is again better seen as yet another aspect of the effective link principle,[89] according to which nationality is not to be conferred on nationals of other states unless the new nationality is based upon adequate links. Even an unlawful deprivation of nationality may become irreversible if the individual voluntarily becomes permanently resident elsewhere at a stage when resumption of the original citizenship would have been possible.[90]

(E) NATIONALITY OF THE EUROPEAN UNION[91]

The 1992 Treaty on European Union created the concept of European citizenship with Article 8(1):

Citizenship of the Union is hereby established. Every person holding the nationality of a Member State shall be a citizen of the Union.[92]

This marked the first time in the history of the Westphalian political order that a citizenship design beyond the nation state emerged, challenging the exclusivity of national citizenship.[93] Most commentators initially saw European citizenship as a purely symbolic concept with limited content, premised on the pre-existing Community law rights of free movement and non-discrimination on grounds of nationality.[94] The concept experienced a subsequent transformation in the hands of the European Court of

---

substance reserving their rights and at the same time intimating that these matters were not within the discretion of the territorial sovereign. The British view seems to have been that conferment of nationality on the basis of a number of years' residence, provided that due notice is given and a declaration of a contrary intention may be made, was lawful: indeed in such circumstances it is probably not involuntary. See ibid, 104; 5 *BDIL* 28, 250.

[88] Morgenstern, note in (1948) 15 ILR 211.

[89] Cf Makarov (1949) 74 Hague *Recueil* 269, 299.

[90] *Oppenheimer v Cattermole* [1976] AC 249; Mann (1973) 89 *LQR* 194; Mann (1976–77) 48 *BY* 1, 43, 50. Cf *Loss of Nationality (Germany)* (1965) 45 ILR 353. Further: Lauterpacht, 3 *International Law* (1977) 383.

[91] Generally on EU nationality: Kostakopoulou, *Citizenship, Identity and Immigration in the European Union* (2001); Barber (2002) 27 *ELR* 241; Cygan & Szyszczak (2006) 55 *ICLQ* 977; Jacobs (2007) 13 *ELJ* 591; Kostakopoulou (2007) 13 *ELJ* 623; Shaw, *The Transformation of Citizenship in the European Union* (2007); Somek (2007) 32 *ELR* 787; Spaventa (2008) 45 *CMLR* 13; Kochenov (2009) 15 *Col J Eur L* 169;

[92] 29 July 1992, *OJEU* C 191.

[93] Kostakopoulou (2007) 13 *ELJ* 623, 624–5.

[94] EU citizenship confers rights: (a) to move and reside freely within the territory of the member states; (b) to vote and to stand as candidates in elections to the European Parliament and in municipal election in their state of residence; (c) to enjoy the protection of the diplomatic and consular authorities of any member state on the same conditions as the nationals of that state (if the state of which the person is a national does not have representation in that country); (d) to petition the institutions and advisory bodies of the Union in any of the Treaty languages and to obtain a reply in the same language: TFEU (former Treaty of Rome, as renamed by the Treaty of Lisbon), 25 March 1957, *OJEU* C 83/47, Art 20. For the initial scholarly response to EU citizenship: e.g. Everson, in Shaw & More (eds), *The New Dynamics of European Union* (1995); d'Oliveira, in Rosas & Antola (eds), *A Citizens' Europe* (1995); Lehning, in Lehning & Weale (eds), *Citizenship, Democracy and Justice in the New Europe* (1997) 175; Downes, in Bellamy & Warleigh (eds), *Citizenship and Governance in the European Union* (2001) 93.

Justice. Union citizenship has been used by the Court as a means to expand the material and personal scope of the Treaty to encompass situations where the reliance on free movement might seem artificial.[95]

EU citizenship is a derivative or dependent citizenship. A person is a citizen of the Union only if he or she is a citizen of a member state. EU member states attached Declaration No 2 to the Maastricht Treaty stating that 'the question whether an individual possesses the nationality of the Member State shall be settled solely by reference to the national law of the Member State concerned'.[96] In *Micheletti* the European Court of Justice confirmed that determination of nationality falls within the exclusive competence of the member states, but added that member states have to have 'due regard to Community law'.[97]

Micheletti has been interpreted as a first hint at the development of a new approach. In *Rottman v Freistaat Bayern*, the Court held that nationality laws of the member states are within the scope of EU law and that EU law has to be taken into account when member states exercise their powers in the sphere of nationality. The European Court of Justice further asserted that it is the final arbiter in disputes arising in this context.[98] This decision has been described as a 'serious blow to one of the last bastions of state sovereignty'.[99]

4. A FUNCTIONAL APPROACH TO NATIONALITY

Despite the continued reiteration of the proposition that nationality depends exclusively on municipal law, it is common for legislation and judicial decisions to create functional nationality[100] whereby aspects of national law are applied on the basis of allegiance, residence or other connections. There seems to be general acquiescence in this splitting up of the legal content of nationality for particular purposes. Thus legislation in many countries has defined enemy alien status in functional terms without depending on the technical nationality of the country in question. The control test has

---

[95] E.g. Case C-148/02, *Garcia Avello* [2003] ECR I-11613; Case C-224/98, *D'Hoop* [2002] ECR I-6191; C-209/03, *Bidar* [2005] ECR I- 2119; Case C-403/03, *Schempp* [2005] ECR I-6421; Case C-192/05, *Tas-Hagen and Tas* [2006] ECR I-10541.

[96] 1992 *OJEU* C 191, 98.

[97] Case C-369/90, *Micheletti and Others v Delegacion del Gobierno en Catanbria* [1992] ECR I-4329.

[98] Case C-135/08, *Rottman v Freistaat Bayern*, Judgment of 2 March 2010, available at www.curia.europa. eu/, §§42, 45–6. For commentary: e.g. Mantu (2010) 24 *JIANL* 182; D'Oliveira (2011) 7 *ECLR* 138; De Groot & Seling (2011) 7 *ECLR* 150.

[99] Mantu (2010) 24 *JIANL* 182, 191.

[100] A different type of functionalism may occur when a forum is prepared to disregard dual nationality where policy demands a choice. Note also the provision in the staff regulations and rules of the UN which make it mandatory for the Secretary-General to select a single nationality for the purpose of the staff rules: *Julhiard v Secretary-General of the United Nations* (1955) 22 ILR 809.

been widely applied to corporations and goods in determining enemy character.[101] The use of factual tests occurs equally widely when the issue is one of the law of war and neutrality.[102]

Moreover, in the context of treaties, rules are often functional rather than declaratory as to general status. Thus in *IMCO* the issue was the interpretation of the phrase 'the largest ship-owning nations' in Article 28 of the Convention for the Establishment of the Inter-Governmental Maritime Consultative Organization, and the Advisory Opinion delivered rested on an inquiry into the legislative history of the provision and usage under other maritime conventions.[103] The Geneva Convention on the Status of Refugees of 1951 provides that a refugee must be treated, for the purpose of access to the courts and related matters, as if a national of the country where the refugee is habitually resident.[104] The Vienna Convention on Diplomatic Relations restricts the conferment of privileges and immunities in the case of members of the mission if they are nationals of the receiving state or 'permanently resident' there.[105] There is thus an interplay between nationality as a core concept of international and national law and elements associated with the effective link which provide a functional overlay. Taken together these ingredients avoid the extremity of solipsism implied in the mantra that nationality of individuals falls within the domestic jurisdiction of each state.

---

[101] *Daimler v Continental Tyre Co* [1916] 2 AC 307; *Contomichalos v Drossos* (1937) 8 ILR 314. Further: Watts (1957) 33 *BY* 52, 78.

[102] For early examples: *The Athinai* (1942) 12 ILR 386; *The Nordmeer* (1946) 13 ILR 401; *The Arsia* (1949) 16 ILR 577; *The Inginer N Vlassopol* (1951) 18 ILR 725; *The Nyugat* (1956) 24 ILR 916; *The SS Lea Lott* (1959) 28 ILR 652. Cf *The Unitas* [1950] 2 All ER 219 on the conclusiveness of a vessel's flag and limitations thereon. On the evolution of the law of neutrality: Schindler, in Delissen & Tanja (eds), *Humanitarian Law of Armed Conflict* (1991) 367.

[103] *Constitution of the Maritime Safety Committee of the Inter-Governmental Maritime Consultative Organization*, ICJ Reports 1960 p 149, 171; and Simmonds (1963) 12 *ICLQ* 56.

[104] Geneva Convention Relating to the Status of Refugees, 28 July 1951, 189 UNTS 150, Art 16(3); *Grundul v Bryner* (1957) 24 ILR 483. The same provision occurs in the Convention Relating to the Status of Stateless Persons, 28 September 1954, 360 UNTS 117, Art 16(3).

[105] 18 April 1961, 500 UNTS 95, Arts 8, 33(2)(a), 38.

24

NATIONALITY OF CORPORATIONS AND ASSETS

1. GENERAL ASPECTS

The assignment of persons (including corporations) and property to states, in particular for the purposes of diplomatic protection, is normally approached through the concept of nationality. Yet the problem must be solved in a variety of contexts, including jurisdiction. It is suggested that problems of jurisdiction can be solved on a satisfactory basis by the use of the principle of genuine connection affirmed in *Nottebohm*.[1] The need for international law to have its own rules of nationality rather than simply leaving nationality to be defined entirely by municipal law is apparent when issues of nationality on the plane of international law are related to corporations, ships, aircraft, and other assets, not to mention the assets of international organizations.[2]

2. NATIONALITY OF CORPORATIONS[3]

The borrowing of a concept developed in relation to individuals is awkward in some respects but is now well established. A major point of distinction is the absence of domestic legislative provisions which assign nationality to corporations: domestic nationality laws do not concern themselves with corporations, and corporations laws

---

[1] *Nottebohm (Liechtenstein v Guatemala)*, ICJ Reports 1955 p 4, 23; and see chapter 23.
[2] On issues of diplomatic protection and admissibility of claims: Amerasinghe, *Diplomatic Protection* (2008) ch 10; also chapter 31.
[3] Generally: Jenks, in Friedmann (ed), *Transnational Law in a Changing Society* (1972); Ijalave, *The Extension of Corporate Personality in International Law* (1978); Lipson, *Standing Guard: Protecting Foreign Capital in the 19th and 20th Century* (1985); Seidl-Hohenveldern, *Corporations in and under International Law* (1987); Rahman (1988) 28 *Indian JIL* 222; Proceedings Fourth Annual International Business Law Symposium: Multinational Corporations and Cross Border Conflicts, Nationality, Veil Piercing and Successor Liability (1995) 10 *Florida JIL* 221; Zerk, *Multinational Corporations and Corporate Social Responsibility* (2006); Pannier, in Ortino (ed), *Nationality and Investment Treaty Claims* (2007) 1; Muchlinski, *Regulating Multinationals* (2008); Juratowitch (2010) 81 *BY* 281.

rarely deal with nationality. Nationality must be derived either from the fact of incorporation, that is, creation as a legal person, within a given system of domestic law, or from links to a particular state such as the centre of administration (*siège social*) or the nationality of the natural or legal persons that own or control the company.

Rules of municipal law may make use of the concept of nationality of legal persons even without explicit treatment of the subject. Areas of domestic law referring to the nationality of corporations include private international law (conflict of laws), the law relating to trading with the enemy, sanctions, and (in some jurisdictions) taxation.

In international law, many treaty provisions define 'nationals' to include corporations for specified purposes. Treaty provisions may explicitly or implicitly adopt the conflict of laws rule that the law of the place of creation determines whether an association has legal personality. For the purposes of a particular treaty, unincorporated associations—including partnerships—may be assimilated to corporations. Public corporations may also be included.[4]

In *Barcelona Traction* the Court affirmed that:

> In allocating corporate entities to States for the purposes of diplomatic protection, international law is based, but only to a limited extent, on an analogy with the rules governing the nationality of individuals. The traditional rule attributes the right of diplomatic protection of a corporate entity to the State under the laws of which it is incorporated and in whose territory it has its registered office. These two criteria have been confirmed by long practice and by numerous international instruments.[5]

Thus the Canadian nationality of the corporation was confirmed notwithstanding its 75 per cent Belgian shareholding.[6] In *Diallo*, the Court relied on *Barcelona Traction* to conclude that despite the Guinean nationality of Diallo as the sole shareholder in the two companies in question, 'the normal rule of nationality' applied and that having regard to their place of incorporation, '[t]he companies in question have Congolese nationality'.[7] Thus under customary international law the nationality of a corporation will normally be determined by its place of incorporation. In *Diallo* the Court acknowledged that,

> in contemporary international law, the protection of the rights of companies and the rights of their shareholders, and the settlement of the associated disputes, are essentially governed by bilateral or multilateral agreements for the protection of foreign investments, such as the

---

[4] *Certain German Interests in Polish Upper Silesia* (1926) PCIJ Ser A No 6; *Peter Pázmány University* (1933) PCIJ Ser A/B No 61.

[5] *Barcelona Traction, Light and Power Company, Limited (Belgium v Spain)*, Second Phase, ICJ Reports 1970 p 3, 42.

[6] Ibid, 25.

[7] *Ahmadou Sadio Diallo (Guinea v Democratic Republic of the Congo)*, Preliminary Objections, Judgment of 24 May 2007, §31. Cf *Elettronica Sicula SpA (ELSI) (US v Italy)*, ICJ Reports 1989 p 15, where a Chamber of the Court upheld the admissibility of the claim of the national state of the sole shareholder of a company registered in the respondent state on the basis of the applicable 1948 Treaty of Friendship, Commerce and Navigation between Italy and the US.

treaties for the promotion and protection of foreign investments…and also by contracts between States and foreign investors.[8]

Free trade agreements also create standards of treatment in relation to 'nationals', 'companies' or 'enterprises' of the contracting parties. The North American Free Trade Agreement (NAFTA) contains the following definitions:

enterprise means any entity constituted or organized under applicable law, whether or not for profit, and whether privately-owned or governmentally-owned, including any corporation, trust, partnership, sole proprietorship, joint venture or other association;

enterprise of a Party means an enterprise constituted or organized under the law of a Party;…

person means a natural person or an enterprise;

person of a Party means a national, or an enterprise of a Party …[9]

NAFTA allows investors to bring claims 'on behalf of an enterprise of another Party that is a juridical person that the investor owns or controls directly or indirectly'.[10] This permits derivative claims without deeming corporations to have a nationality that they do not have.

Certain treaties concerned with the protection of investments employ more complex formulations.[11] Pursuant to Article 25(2)(b) of the Convention on the Settlement of Investment Disputes, 'national of another Contracting State' means:

any juridical person which had the nationality of a Contracting State other than the State party to the dispute…and *any juridical person which had the nationality of the Contracting State party to the dispute* on that date and which, because of foreign control, the parties have agreed should be *treated as a national of another Contracting State* for the purposes of this Convention.[12]

The Treaty on the Functioning of the European Union provides in Article 54 that corporations under the law of a member state and having their 'registered office', 'central administration', or 'principal place of business' within the Union are assimilated, for the purposes of the chapter on the right of establishment, to 'natural persons who are nationals of Member States'.[13] For this purpose corporations include all legal persons whether of public or private law other than non-profit-making bodies.

Bilateral treaties concerned with double taxation contain rules of assignment which may invoke the concepts of nationality, residence or fiscal domicile, while defining the

---

[8] *Diallo*, Preliminary Objections, Judgment of 24 May 2007, §88.

[9] 17 December 1992, 32 ILM 289, Art 201.

[10] NAFTA, Art 1117(1). In such cases restitution or damages shall be made or paid to the enterprise: Art 1135(2).

[11] Mann (1981) 52 *BY* 241, 242.

[12] Washington Convention on the Settlement of Investment Disputes between States and Nationals of Other States, 18 March 1965, 575 UNTS 160, Art 25(2)(b) (emphasis added). Also Energy Charter Treaty, 17 December 1994, 2080 UNTS 95, Art 1(7).

[13] TFEU, 30 March 2010, *OJEU* C 83/47.

crucial points of contact. These are commonly management and control.[14] Air transport agreements may require that airlines acquiring a foreign carrier permit satisfy a condition of substantial ownership and effective control by nationals of the other contracting party.[15] Important provisions ascribing a national character to corporations and other associations appear in peace treaties, agreements on reparation for war losses, SC resolutions imposing sanctions,[16] treaties of cession, and agreements for compensation in case of nationalization and other events causing loss to foreign interests on state territory. In *Peter Pázmány University* the Permanent Court found that the University, as a legal person under Hungarian law, was a Hungarian national for the purpose of submitting a claim to restitution of property under Article 250 of the Treaty of Trianon.[17] Treaty provisions employ a variety of criteria including place of creation, sometimes accompanied by a requirement to have substantial business activities in that place, *siège social*,[18] the national source of actual control or effective management,[19] and immediate or ultimate ownership.

3. NATIONALITY OF SHIPS[20]

In maintaining a viable regime for common use of the high seas, the law of the flag and the necessity for a ship to have a flag are paramount. Historical opinion was strongly in favour of the unqualified freedom of each state to determine for itself the conditions under which its nationality could be conferred on vessels.[21] This view of state competence suffers from the faults considered in a wider setting in chapter 23. The act of conferment of nationality (registration) is within the competence of states, but

[14] US Model Income Tax Convention, 20 September 1996, Art 3.
[15] *Aerolíneas Peruanas SA, Foreign Permit* (1960) 31 ILR 416.
[16] E.g. SC Res 1929 (2010) (Iran).
[17] (1933) PCIJ Ser A/B No 61, 232. Also: *German Interests* (1926) PCIJ Ser A No 7, 69–71; *Flexi-Van Leasing, Inc v Iran* (1986) 70 ILR 496; *RayGo Wagner Equipment Company v Iran Express Terminal Corporation* (1983) 71 ILR 688, 690–3.
[18] This concept of French law overlaps with residence and domicile. Normally the *siège social* is the place where the administrative organs operate and where general meetings are held. However, tribunals may insist that the *siège social* should not be nominal and thus relate the test to that of effective control. See *Bakalian & Hadjithomas v Banque Ottomane* (1965) 47 ILR 216.
[19] E.g. *Yaung Chi Oo Trading v Myanmar* (2003) 8 ICSID Reports 463, 473–8.
[20] Especially: Watts (1957) 33 BY 52, 84; Meyers, *The Nationality of Ships* (1967); Jennings (1967) 121 Hague *Recueil* 327, 460–5; Singh (1962) 107 Hague *Recueil* 1, 38–64; Dupuy & Vignes, *Traité du nouveau droit de la mer* (1985) 354–9; McConnell (1985) 16 *JMLC* 365; Churchill (1991) 26 *ETL* 591; Anderson (1996) 21 *Tul Mar LJ* 139; Ready, *Ship Registration* (3rd edn 1998); Jacobsson, in Nordquist & Mahmoudi (eds), *The Stockholm Declaration and Law on the Marine Environment* (2003); Kamto, in Coussirat-Coustère et al (eds), *La mer et son droit* (2003); Witt, *Obligations and Control of Flag States* (2007); König, 'Flag of Ships' (2009) *MPEPIL*.
[21] Gidel, 1 *Le droit international public de la mer* (1932) 80; Harvard Research (1935) 29 *AJIL Supp* 435, 518–19; Rienow, *The Test of the Nationality of a Merchant Vessel* (1937) 218–19.

registration is only evidence of nationality, and valid registration under the law of the flag state does not preclude an assessment of nationality under international law. The *Nottebohm* principle applies equally here. The UN Convention on the Law of the Sea of 1982 provides in Article 91(1):

Every State shall fix the conditions for the grant of its nationality to ships, for the registration of ships in its territory, and for the right to fly its flag. Ships have the nationality of the State whose flag they are entitled to fly. There must exist a genuine link between the State and the ship.[22]

Jennings has remarked that 'the assumption that the "genuine link" formula, invented for dealing with people, is capable of immediate application to ships and aircraft, smacks of a disappointing naiveté' and, further, that 'a provision which might seem to encourage governments to make subjective decisions whether or not to recognize the nationality of this aircraft or that vessel is clearly open to abuse and for that reason to grave criticism'.[23]

Article 91(1) has met with criticism from partisans of the exclusive competence of states to ascribe national character to vessels.[24] The US Department of State has argued that the requirement of a genuine link is not a condition for recognition of the nationality of the ship but an independent obligation to exercise effective jurisdiction and control over ships once registered.[25]

Article 91(1) repeats most of Article 5 of the High Seas Convention of 1958.[26] However, the duties of the flag state are enumerated separately in Article 94. The general opinion is that the position remains the same, with the opponents of the 'genuine link' un-appeased. The UN Convention on Conditions for Registration of Ships adopted by a diplomatic conference in 1986 seeks to impose precise modalities for the effective exercise of jurisdiction and control by the flag state.[27] The convention has not yet entered into force as it lacks the requisite 40 ratifications.

In relation to ships' crews, the ILC has affirmed the right of the state of nationality of a ship's crew to exercise diplomatic protection on their behalf, while at the same time

[22] 10 December 1982, 1833 UNTS 3, Art 91. Further: 9 Whiteman 7–17; UNCLOS I, 1 *Off Recs* 78, 83, 85, 91, 108, 111–12; 4 *Off Recs* 61ff; *IMCO* Pleadings (1960) 357–58 (Riphagen), 364–8 (Seyersted), 383 (Vallat); Jessup (1959) 59 *Col LR* 234, 256; *Barcelona Traction,* Second Phase, ICJ Reports 1970 p 184, 186–9 (Judge Jessup).

[23] Jennings (1967) 121 Hague *Recueil* 327, 463.

[24] McDougal, Burke & Vlasic (1960) 54 *AJIL* 25; McDougal & Burke, *The Public Order of the Oceans* (1962) 1008–140; Boczek, *Flags of Convenience* (1962). The debate relates to the use of flags of convenience by American interests in competition with European shipping. Further on flags of convenience: OECD Study on Flags of Convenience (1973) 4 *JMLC* 231; Sieke (1979) 73 *AJIL* 604; Metaxas, *Flags of Convenience* (1985); Marti (1991) 15 *Mar Policy* 193; FAO Code of Conduct for Responsible Fisheries 1995, available at: www.ftp.fao.org/docrep/fao/005/v9878e/v9878e00.pdf; OECD, *Ownership and Control of Ships* (2003); Treves (2004) 6 *San Diego ILJ* 179; Ademuni-Odeke (2005) 36 *ODIL* 339; König, 'Flags of Convenience' (2008) *MPEPIL*.

[25] 9 Whiteman 27, 29. For the contrary view: Recommendation 108, General Conference of the ILO, 1958 (144:0–3); Meyers (1967) 225.

[26] 29 April 1958, 450 UNTS 82

[27] 7 February 1986, 26 ILM 1229. Wefers Bettink (1987) 18 *NYIL* 69.

acknowledging that the state of nationality of the ship also has a right to seek redress on behalf of its crew.[28]

In *M/V Saiga (No 2)* the International Tribunal for the Law of the Sea rejected an objection to admissibility based upon the absence of a genuine link:

83. The conclusion of the Tribunal is that the purpose of the provisions of the Convention on the need for a genuine link between a ship and its flag State is to secure more effective implementation of the duties of the flag State, and not to establish criteria by reference to which the validity of the registration of ships in a flag State may be challenged by other States.

84. This conclusion is not put into question by the United Nations Convention on Conditions for Registration of Ships of 7 February 1986 invoked by Guinea. This Convention … sets out as one of its principal objectives the strengthening of 'the genuine link between a State and ships flying its flag'. In any case, the Tribunal observes that Guinea has not cited any provision in that Convention which lends support to its contention that 'a basic condition for the registration of a ship is that also the owner or operator of the ship is under the jurisdiction of the flag State'.[29]

In *The Juno Trader*[30] the Tribunal found on the facts that there had been no change in the flag state and that accordingly it had jurisdiction. However, in a Joint Separate Opinion, Judges Mensah and Wolfrum rejected the view that a change in the ownership of a ship resulted in the automatic change of the flag of a ship:

The term 'nationality', when used in connection with ships, is merely shorthand for the jurisdictional connection between a ship and a State. The State of nationality of the ship is the flag State or the State whose flag the ship is entitled to fly; and the law of the flag State is the law that governs the ship. The jurisdictional connection between a State and a ship that is entitled to fly its flag results in a network of mutual rights and obligations, as indicated in part in article 94 of the Convention. For example, granting the right to a ship to fly its flag imposes on the flag State the obligation to effectively exercise its jurisdiction and control in administrative, technical and social matters. In turn, the ship is obliged to fully implement the relevant national laws of the State whose flag it is entitled to fly. All States which have established ships' registers provide for specific procedural and factual requirements to be met before a ship is entered on their registers or is granted the right to fly the flag of the particular State. Ships receive respective documents to prove that they are entitled to fly a particular flag. Similarly, the laws of these States establish clear procedures to be followed for ships to leave the register, including the conditions under which a ship may lose the right to remain on the register.[31]

Treaties may contain specialized rules determining nationality.[32] The *IMCO* case concerned the constitution of the Maritime Safety Committee of the IMCO (now the

---

[28] ILC Draft Articles on Diplomatic Protection with Commentaries, ILC *Ybk* 2006/II, 22, Art 18 with commentary, ibid, 90–4.

[29] (1999) 120 ILR 179. The Tribunal also held that the evidence was not sufficient to establish a genuine link.

[30] (2004) 128 ILR 267.

[31] Ibid, 307.

[32] E.g. Treaty of Peace with Italy, 10 February 1947, 49 UNTS 3, Art 78(9)(c), Annex VI, Art 33.

IMO). The convention provided that '[t]he Maritime Safety Committee shall consist of fourteen Members elected by the Assembly from the Members, governments of those nations having an important interest in maritime safety, of which not less than eight shall be the largest ship-owning nations'.[33] Panama and Liberia had not been elected and they and other states contended that the proper test was registered tonnage, not beneficial ownership. The Court found that the reference in the convention was solely to registered tonnage. This conclusion depended on the construction of the text and was assumed to be consistent with the general purpose of the Convention. The Court thus found it unnecessary to examine the argument that registration was qualified by the requirement of a genuine link.[34]

US courts have refused to apply US law to the internal management of vessels in American ports flying Honduran or Liberian flags despite their close contacts with the US.[35] This refusal to go behind the law of the flag and the fact of registration was based in part upon the construction of the relevant treaty and in part upon the general principle governing jurisdiction over ships in port.

4. OTHER RULES OF ALLOCATION

(A) NATIONALITY OF AIRCRAFT[36]

The Convention for the Regulation of Aerial Navigation of 1919,[37] and later the Chicago Convention of 1944,[38] provided that the nationality of aircraft is governed by the state of registration. The former stipulated that registration could only take place in the state of which the owners were nationals; the latter merely forbids dual registration. Neither convention applies in time of war, and the Chicago Convention does not apply to state aircraft, that is, 'aircraft used in military, customs and police services'. The Tokyo Convention on Offences Committed on Board Aircraft provides that the state of registration has jurisdiction over offences and acts committed on board.[39] These

---

[33] Convention for Establishment of Inter-Governmental Maritime Consultative Organization, 6 March 1948, 289 UNTS 3, Art 28(a).

[34] *Constitution of the Maritime Safety Committee of the Inter-Governmental Maritime Consultative Organization*, ICJ Reports 1960 p 150, 171.

[35] *McCulloch v Sociedad Nacional* (1963) 34 ILR 51; *Incres v International Maritime Workers Union* (1963) 34 ILR 66; *United States v Anchor Line Ltd*, 232 F.Supp 379 (SDNY, 1964). Generally on the US position: *Greenpeace USA v Stone*, 924 F.2d 175 (9th Cir, 1991); *Equal Employment Opportunity Commission v Arabian American Oil Co*, 499 US 244 (1991).

[36] Generally: Lambie, *Universality versus Nationality of Aircraft* (1934); Fitzgerald (1964) 5 *CYIL* 191; Milde (1985) 10 *Ann ASL* 133; Naveau, Godfroid & Frühling, *Précis de droit aérien* (2nd edn, 2006) ch 2; Wouters & Verhoeven, 'State Aircraft' (2008) *MPEPIL*.

[37] 13 October 1919, 11 LNTS 173, Arts 5–10.

[38] Convention on International Civil Aviation, 7 December 1944, 15 UNTS 296, Arts 17–21.

[39] 14 September 1963, 704 UNTS 220.

provisions may be thought to support a doctrine of freedom in conferring national status by registration, in contrast to UNCLOS Article 91.[40] However, in the absence of flags of convenience in air traffic, it may be that the issue was left on one side by the authors, the assumption being that registration in practice depended on the existence of substantial connections. In the absence of substantial connections the state of registry will not be in a position to ensure that an aircraft is operated in accordance with the Chicago Convention. However, the application of a genuine link test is by no means straightforward and, as in the case of naturalization of individuals, registration is itself a presumptively valid and genuine connection of some importance.[41] Obviously the *Nottebohm* principle ought to apply to aircraft as it does to ships. It must surely apply at the least to discover to which state non-civil aircraft belong, but even where the Chicago Convention applies, registration by one state may not preclude another state from exercising diplomatic protection. In bilateral treaties the US has reserved the right to refuse a carrier permit to an airline designated by the other contracting party 'in the event substantial ownership and effective control of such airlines are not vested in nationals of the other contracting party'.[42]

In principle, aircraft of joint operating agencies, for example, the Scandinavian Airlines System, must be registered in one of the states involved. However, in 1967 the ICAO Council adopted a resolution requiring the constitution of a joint register in such cases for the purposes of Article 77 of the Chicago Convention and the designation of a state as recipient of representations from third states.[43]

(B) NATIONALITY OF SPACE OBJECTS[44]

The Outer Space Treaty of 1967 does not employ the concept of nationality in relation to objects launched into outer space.[45] Article VIII provides in part that the state of registration 'shall retain jurisdiction and control over such object, and over any

---

[40] Makarov (1959) 48 *Ann de l'Inst* 359. Cf *Affaire F OABV* (1958) 4 *AFDI* 282. UNCLOS, Art 91 states that '[e]very State shall fix the conditions for the grant of its nationality to ships, for the registration of ships in its territory, and for the right to fly its flag. Ships have the nationality of the State whose flag they are entitled to fly. There must exist a genuine link between the State and the ship': 10 December 1982, 1833 UNTS 3.

[41] Jennings (1967) 121 Hague *Recueil* 327, 460–6. Parties to the Chicago Convention may be precluded from contesting nationality based on registration: Cheng, *The Law of International Air Transport* (1962) 128–31.

[42] *Aerolíneas Peruanas SA, Foreign Permit* (1960) 31 ILR 416.

[43] 9 Whiteman 383–90; Cheng (1966) 5 *Ybk Air & Space Law* 31; ILA, Report of the 52nd Conference (1966) 228–86; ILA, Report of the 53rd Conference (1968) 147–56.

[44] McDougal, Lasswell & Vlasic, *Law and Public Order in Space* (1963) 513–87; Goedhuis (1963) 109 Hague *Recueil*, 257, 301–8; Lachs, *The Law of Outer Space* (1972) 68–78; Fawcett, *Outer Space* (1984) 27–8; Cheng, *Studies in International Space Law* (1997); Kayser, *Launching Space Objects* (2001); Hole, Schmidt-Tedd & Schrogl (eds), *Current Issues in the Registration of Space Objects* (2005); Lee (2006) 1 *Space Policy* 42; Hobe, 'Spacecraft, Satellites and Space Objects' (2007) *MPEPIL*; Tronchetti, *The Exploitation of Natural Resources of the Moon and Other Celestial Bodies* (2008). Also Outer Space Act 1986 (UK), ss1, 7, 13(1).

[45] Treaty on Principles Governing the Activities of States in the Exploration and Use of Outer Space, including the Moon and Other Celestial Bodies, 27 January 1967, 610 UNTS 205.

personnel thereof, while in outer space or on a celestial body'. The Convention on Registration of Objects Launched into Outer Space provides that the launching state shall maintain a register of space objects.[46] Each state of registry has a duty to furnish certain information to the UN Secretary-General.

(C) STATE PROPERTY IN GENERAL

Ownership in international law is normally seen either in terms of private rights under national law, which may become the subject of diplomatic protection and state responsibility, or in terms of territorial sovereignty.[47] However, situations arise which call for a counterpart of ownership on the international plane. This is the case for state ships, aircraft, space vehicles, and national treasures.[48] Many treaties confer or refer to 'property' or 'title' without referring to the national law of the *situs* or to any other local law.[49] Thus the US agreed to lend a vessel to the Philippines for five years, title to remain with the US and the transferee having the right to place the vessel under its flag.[50] In *Monetary Gold* (1953),[51] Sauser-Hall (sole arbitrator) referred in his award to a concept of 'patrimoine nationale' which could extend to gold functioning as a monetary reserve, although the gold did not belong to the state concerned under its national law but to a private bank under foreign control.

Issues of title under international law can also arise, even if sometimes incidentally, in connection with the disposition of vessels taken in prize, title to booty of war, the taking of reparation in kind, the effect of territorial cession on public property in the territory concerned,[52] and claims by the victors of 1945 to German assets in neutral countries.[53]

---

[46] GA Res 3235(XXIX), 12 November 1974, 1023 UNTS 15.

[47] Generally: Staker (1987) 58 *BY* 151, 252.

[48] Cambodian claim in *Temple of Preah Vihear (Cambodia v Thailand)*, ICJ Reports 1962 p 6. Further: Williams (1977) 15 *CYIL* 146, 172. Note also the case of a sunken Soviet submarine (Rubin (1975) 69 *AJIL* 855) and a Confederate warship (Roach (1991) 85 *AJIL* 381). Cf Wright (2008–9) 33 *Tul Mar LJ* 285; Aznar-Gómez (2010) 25 *IJMCL* 209.

[49] Soviet–Swedish Agreement on Construction of Embassy Buildings, 27 March 1958, 428 UNTS 322. Also the contract between the International Atomic Energy Agency, the US, and Pakistan for the transfer of enriched uranium for a reactor, 19 October 1967, 425 UNTS 69.

[50] Exchange of Notes constituting an Agreement relating to the Loan of a Vessel to the Philippines, 4 October 1961, 433 UNTS 83.

[51] (1953) 20 ILR 441, 469. Further: Lalive (1954) 58 *RGDIP* 438; Fawcett (1968) 123 Hague *Recueil* 215, 248–51. Cf *Monetary Gold Removed from Rome in 1943 (Italy v France, UK and US)*, ICJ Reports 1954 p 19. Also *Deutsche Amerikanische Petroleum Gesellschaft Oil Tankers* (1926) 2 RIAA 777, 795.

[52] *German Interests* (1926) PCIJ Ser A No 7, 41; *Peter Pázmány University* (1933) PCIJ Ser A/B No 61, 237; also chapter 19.

[53] Mann (1957) 24 *BY* 239; Simpson (1958) 34 *BY* 374.

PART IX

THE LAW OF RESPONSIBILITY

25

THE CONDITIONS FOR INTERNATIONAL RESPONSIBILITY

1. CONFIGURING THE LAW OF RESPONSIBILITY[1]

In international relations as in other social relations, the invasion of the legal interest of one subject of the law by another creates responsibility in a form and to an extent determined by the applicable legal system. International responsibility is traditionally attributed to states as the major subjects of international law, but it is a broader question inseparable from legal personality in all its forms. As with the law of treaties, historically the issue of responsibility of states was treated first, and the potential for international organizations and individuals to make claims and to bear responsibility on the international plane (to the extent it exists at all) has been developed later and by analogy.

As also with the law of treaties, the law of responsibility has been largely articulated through the work of the ILC, here in three texts, the ILC Articles on Responsibility of States for Internationally Wrongful Acts of 2001 (ARSIWA),[2] the ILC Articles on Diplomatic Protection of 2006,[3] and the ILC Draft Articles on Responsibility of International Organizations of 2011.[4] In this chapter, the focus will be on state responsibility and on ARSIWA.[5]

---

[1] Anzilotti, *Teoria Generale della Responsabilità dello Stato nel Diritto Internazionale* (1902); de Visscher, 2 *Bibliotheca Visseriana* (1924) 89; Eagleton, *The Responsibility of States in International Law* (1928); Reuter (1961) 103 Hague *Recueil* 583; Brownlie, *System of the Law of Nations* (1983); Riphagen, in Macdonald & Johnston (eds), *The Structure and Process of International Law* (1983) 581; Dupuy (1984) 188 Hague *Recueil* 9; Spinedi & Simma (eds), *United Nations Codification of State Responsibility* (1987); Fitzmaurice & Sarooshi (eds), *Issues of State Responsibility before International Judicial Institutions* (2004); Ragazzi (ed), *International Responsibility Today* (2005); Crawford, Pellet & Olleson (eds), *The Law of International Responsibility* (2010).

[2] Appended to GA Res 56/83, 12 December 2001.

[3] Available with commentary in A/61/10.

[4] A/CN.4/L.778.

[5] ARSIWA and its accompanying commentary are reproduced with apparatus in Crawford, *The International Law Commission's Articles on State Responsibility* (2002). Of continuing value are the reports

Following an intuition of Roberto Ago,[6] in all three projects the ILC focused on what he termed 'secondary rules', that is, the framework rules of attribution, breach, excuses, reparation, and response to breach (i.e. invocation)—as distinct from the primary obligations whose disregard gives rise to responsibility. The distinction is no doubt somewhat artificial—but any other course would have entailed a spelling out of the rights and duties of states generally, and these vary indefinitely between states depending on their treaty lists and general commitments.

Unlike the two Vienna Conventions of 1969 and 1986 on the law of treaties, the ILC Articles have not (or not yet) been reduced to treaty form. But even before 2001 and more especially since, they have been much cited and have acquired increasing authority as an expression of the customary law of state responsibility.[7] This has led some authors and governments to conclude that a convention is not needed, and that a diplomatic conference could rupture the delicate equilibrium achieved by ARSIWA.[8] Others, however, would like to see certain articles, especially those expressive of the idea of 'multilateral responsibility', reopened, a process likely to be interminable (or terminal).

2. THE BASIS AND CHARACTER OF STATE RESPONSIBILITY

It is a general principle of international law that a breach of an international obligation entails the responsibility of the state concerned. Shortly, the law of responsibility is concerned with the incidence and consequences of unlawful acts, and particularly the forms of reparation for loss caused. However, the law may incidentally prescribe compensation for the consequences of legal or 'excusable' acts, and it is proper to consider this aspect in connection with responsibility in general.

(A) ORIGINS

In the early modern period treaties laid down particular duties and sometimes specified the liabilities and procedures to be followed in case of breach. But the inconvenience of

---

of successive Special Rapporteurs published in ILC *Ybk* II: García-Amador (1956–61), Ago (1969–80), Riphagen (1980–6), Arangio-Ruiz (1988–96), and Crawford (1998–2001).

[6] ILC *Ybk* 1970/II, 177, 179. Ago distinguished 'rules of international law which, in one sector of inter-State relations or another, impose particular obligations on States, and which may, in a certain sense, be termed "primary", as opposed to the other rules—precisely those covering the field of responsibility—which may be termed "secondary", inasmuch as they are concerned with determining the consequences of failure to fulfil obligations established by the primary rules'.

[7] A/62/62, 1 February 2007 & Add.1; A/65/76, 30 April 2010, identifying 154 cases referring to ARSIWA.

[8] Caron (2002) 96 *AJIL* 857; Crawford & Olleson (2005) 54 *ICLQ* 959. For the conflicting views of governments: A/65/96 & Add.1 (2010).

private reprisals,[9] the development of rules restricting forcible self-help, and the work of international tribunals have contributed towards a concept of responsibility more akin to that of national law. Of course the notions of reparation and restitution in the train of unlawful acts had long been part of the available stock of legal concepts in Europe, and the classical writers referred to reparation and restitution in connection with unjust war.[10]

(B) THE CLASSIFICATION OF INTERNATIONAL WRONGS

State responsibility is not based upon delict in the municipal sense, and 'international responsibility' relates both to breaches of treaty and to other breaches of obligation. There is no harm in using the term 'delict' to describe a breach of duty actionable by another legal person, but the term must be understood broadly; the term 'tort', also sometimes used,[11] could mislead. The compendious term 'international responsibility' is widely used and is least confusing.

In *Spanish Zone of Morocco* Judge Huber said: '[r]esponsibility is the necessary corollary of a right. All rights of an international character involve international responsibility. If the obligation in question is not met, responsibility entails the duty to make reparation'.[12] In *Factory at Chorzów (Jurisdiction)*, the Permanent Court stated that: '[i]t is a principle of international law that the breach of an engagement involves an obligation to make reparation in an adequate form. Reparation therefore is the indispensable complement of a failure to apply a convention and there is no necessity for this to be stated in the convention itself'.[13] This was repeated with emphasis in *Chorzów Factory (Indemnity)*:

It is a principle of international law, and even a general conception of law, that any breach of an engagement involves an obligation to make reparation. ... The Court has already said that reparation is the indispensable complement of a failure to apply a convention, and there is no necessity for this to be stated in the convention itself.[14]

Corfu Channel involved a finding that Albania was, by reason of its failure to warn of the danger, liable for the consequences of mine-laying in its territorial waters even though it had not laid the mines. The International Court said: '[t]hese grave, omissions involve

---

[9] Formerly sovereigns authorized private citizens to perform acts of reprisal (special reprisals) against the citizens of other states: Wheaton, *Elements of International Law* (1866) 309–11.

[10] Gentili, *De Iure Belli Libri Tres* (1612) II.iii; Grotius, *De Iure Belli ac Pacis* (1625, ed Tuck 2005) III.x.§4, and generally Crawford, Grant & Messineo, in Boisson de Chazournes & Kohen (eds), *International Law and the Quest for its Implementation* (2010) 377.

[11] *Union Bridge Company* (1924) 6 RIAA 138, 142; cf Jenks, *The Prospects of International Adjudication* (1964) 514–33.

[12] Translation; French text, 2 RIAA 615, 641. Also *Coenca Bros v Germany* (1924) 4 ILR 570.

[13] (1927) PCIJ Ser A No 9, 21. See, however, *Land and Maritime Boundary between Cameroon and Nigeria (Cameroon v Nigeria)*, ICJ Reports 2002 p 303, 452–3; *Guyana v Suriname* (2008) 47 ILM 166, 232.

[14] (1928) PCIJ Ser A No 17, 29. *Interpretation of Peace Treaties with Bulgaria, Hungary and Romania*, Second Phase, ICJ Reports 1950 p 221, 228; *Phosphates in Morocco*, Preliminary Objections, (1938) PCIJ Ser A/B No 74, 28.

the international responsibility of Albania [which] is responsible under international law for the explosions which occurred... and for the damage and loss of human life which resulted from them'.[15]

In *Genocide (Bosnia and Herzegovina v Serbia and Montenegro)*, the Court considered whether a violation of the Genocide Convention entailed particular consequences for the breaching state:

The Court observes that the obligations in question in this case, arising from the terms of the Convention, and the responsibilities of States that would arise from breach of such obligations, are obligations and responsibilities under international law. They are not of a criminal nature.[16]

These pronouncements show that there is no acceptance of a contract/delict (tort) dichotomy, still less one between delicts and international crimes of states.[17] Rather there is a single undifferentiated concept of responsibility, the key elements of which are the breach of an obligation of the state by a person or body whose conduct is, in the circumstances, attributable to the state.[18] When requested to establish the responsibility of Iran in *US Diplomatic and Consular Staff in Tehran (US v Iran)*, the Court formulated its task as follows:

First, it must determine how far, legally, the acts in question may be regarded as imputable to the Iranian State. Secondly, it must consider their compatibility or incompatibility with the obligations of Iran under treaties in force or under any other rules of international law that may be applicable.[19]

In listing attribution and breach as the two elements of the internationally wrongful act, ARSIWA Article 2 reflects a long-standing jurisprudence.[20]

3. ATTRIBUTION TO THE STATE

(A) GENERAL ASPECTS

Every breach of duty on the part of states must arise by reason of the act or omission of one or more organs or agents (although the 2001 Articles eschew the

---

[15] *Corfu Channel (UK v Albania)*, ICJ Reports 1949 p 4, 23.

[16] *Application of the Convention for the Prevention and Punishment of the Crime of Genocide (Bosnia and Herzegovina v Serbia and Montenegro)*, ICJ Reports 2007 p 43, 115.

[17] For the absence of a contract/delict distinction: ARSIWA, Art 12. For the rejection of a category of 'international crimes': ARSIWA, commentary to Art 12, §§5–7. Doctrinal attempts have been made to define different regimes for responsibility depending on the gravity of the breach. E.g. Jørgensen, *The Responsibility of States for International Crimes* (2000); Crawford, in Crawford, Pellet & Ollesen (2010) 405; Ollivier, ibid, 703.

[18] ARSIWA, Art 2 & commentary.

[19] ICJ Reports 1980 p 3, 29. Also *Dickson Car Wheel Company (USA) v United Mexican States* (1931) 4 RIAA 669, 678; *Phosphates in Morocco*, Preliminary Objections (1938) PCIJ Ser A/B No 74, 28.

[20] Christenson, in Lillich (ed), *International Law of State Responsibility for Injuries to Aliens* (1983) 321–60.

terminology of agency). The status of the individual actor is only one factor in establishing attribution—in effect, a causal connection between the corporate entity of the state and the harm done.

There is no need for state agents to be the direct perpetrators of the unlawful act. In *Corfu Channel* Albania was held responsible for the consequences of mine-laying in her territorial waters by reason of the Albanian authorities' knowledge and failure to warn of the presence of the mines. In fact (though the Court did not say this), the mines were laid by Yugoslavia. Similarly, a neutral state may be responsible for allowing armed expeditions to be fitted out within its jurisdiction which subsequently carry out belligerent operations against another state.[21] Depending on the obligation in question, failure to ensure compliance may be attributed to the state even when the conduct was that of private entities. In *Canada—Dairy (21.5 II)*, the WTO Appellate body observed that 'irrespective of the role of private parties...the obligations...remain obligations imposed on Canada... The question is not whether one or more individual milk producers, efficient or not, are selling CEM at a price above or below their individual costs of production. The issue is whether Canada, on a national basis, has respected its WTO obligations'.[22] With these extensive reservations, attention may be directed to the problems associated with particular categories of organs and persons.

(B) STATE ORGANS

Pursuant to ARSIWA Article 4, 'the conduct of any State organ shall be considered an act of that State under international law', regardless of the character of that organ and whatever functions it exercises. This is in line with established jurisprudence.[23]

(i) Executive and administration

Early arbitrations established the principle that governmental action or omission by the executive gives rise to international responsibility. This was most visible in the failure by states to provide security to foreigners and their property. In *Massey*[24] the US recovered $15,000 by reason of the failure of the Mexican authorities to take adequate measures to punish the killer of a US citizen working in Mexico. Commissioner Nielsen stated:[25]

It is undoubtedly a sound general principle that, whenever misconduct on the part of [persons in state service], whatever may be their particular status or rank under domestic law,

---

[21] *Alabama* (1872) in Moore, 1 *Int Arb*, 653.

[22] *Canada—Dairy (21.5 II)*, WTO Doc WT/DS103/AB/RW2, 20 December 2002, §§95–6.

[23] *Salvador Commercial Company* (1902) 15 RIAA 455, 477; *Chattin* (1927) 4 RIAA 282, 285–6; *Difference Relating to Immunity from Legal Process of a Special Rapporteur of the Commission on Human Rights*, ICJ Reports 1999 p 62, 87. Also *Genocide (Bosnia and Herzegovina v Serbia and Montenegro)*, ICJ Reports 2007 p 43, 202.

[24] (1927) 4 RIAA 155. Also *Way* (1928) 4 RIAA 391.

[25] *Massey* (1927) 4 RIAA 155, 159.

results in the failure of a nation to perform its obligations under international law, the nation must bear the responsibility for the wrongful acts of its servants.

Unreasonable acts of violence by police officers and a failure to take the appropriate steps to punish the culprits will also give rise to responsibility.[26] In principle the distinction between higher and lower officials has no significance in terms of responsibility.[27]

More recently, the situation has grown more complex with the assumption by governments of functions of an economic and social character. On occasions, governments act not by agents of the state but by delegating governmental functions to para-statal entities. Companies with varying degrees of governmental participation, as well as regulatory agencies with varying degrees of independence, blur the usual public-private distinction and demand a detailed examination of their function in order to determine when their conduct is attributable to the state. ARSIWA tackles the issue by providing an open formulation: under Article 5, entities not formally state organs may still engage the responsibility of the latter when 'empowered by the law of that State to exercise elements of the governmental authority' and so long as they are 'acting in that capacity in the particular instance'.

This formulation has been influential directly but also by analogy. In *US—Anti-Dumping and Countervailing Duties (China)*, a WTO Panel had decided that a 'public body' for the purposes of the Agreement on Subsidies and Countervailing Measures was 'any entity controlled by a government', including a private corporation with more than 50 per cent government ownership, irrespective of its functions.[28] On appeal, the Appellate Body recalled its earlier finding that 'the essence of government is that it enjoys the effective power to regulate, control, or supervise individuals, or otherwise restrain their conduct, through the exercise of lawful authority'; 'this meaning is derived, in part, from the functions performed by a government and, in part, from the government having the powers and authority to perform those functions'.[29] It went on to reverse the finding of the Panel, providing a set of guidelines to determine whether an entity is a public body which draw in part on ARSIWA Article 5.[30]

Another topic of growing importance is the question of attribution for the acts of entities not belonging to the state or acting under official governmental authority but which hold enough links with the state that a degree of control by the state can be envisaged. This is a difficult matter, in particular regarding the assessment of evidence.

---

[26] *Roper* (1927) 4 RIAA 145; *Pugh* (1933) 3 RIAA 1439.

[27] *Massey* (1927) 4 RIAA 155; *Way* (1928) 4 RIAA 391. For another opinion: Borchard, *Diplomatic Protection of Citizens Abroad* (1928) 185–90.

[28] WTO Doc WT/DS/379/R, 22 October 2010, §8.94.

[29] *US—Anti-Dumping and Countervailing Duties (China)*, WTO Doc WT/DS379/AB/R, 11 March 2011, §290. The finding paraphrased concerned the issue whether Canada's provincial milk marketing boards were 'government agencies' for the purposes of the Agreement on Agriculture. See *Canada—Dairy*, WTO Doc WT/DS103/AB/R, 13 October 1999, §§97, 101.

[30] *US—Anti-Dumping and Countervailing Duties (China)*, WTO Doc WT/DS379/AB/R, 11 March 2011, §318. For a thorough treatment of the subject: ibid, §§282–356.

The International Court discussed the relevant jurisprudence in *Genocide (Bosnia and Herzegovina v Serbia and Montenegro)*. After determining that the massacre at Srebrenica in July 1995 constituted the crime of genocide within the meaning of the convention, the Court dealt with the question whether this conduct was attributable to the respondent. The Court said:

This question has in fact two aspects, which the Court must consider separately. First, it should be ascertained whether the acts committed at Srebrenica were perpetrated by organs of the Respondent, i.e., by persons or entities whose conduct is necessarily attributable to it, because they are in fact the instruments of its action. Next, if the preceding question is answered in the negative, it should be ascertained whether the acts in question were committed by persons who, while not organs of the Respondent, did nevertheless act on the instruments of, or under the direction or control of, the Respondent.[31]

The Court decided that the Bosnian Serb militia did not have the status of organs, *de iure* or *de facto*, at the material time.[32] The Court then moved to the further alternative argument of the Applicant, namely, that the actions at Srebrenica were committed by persons who, although not having the status of organs of the respondent, acted on its instructions or under its direction or control, applying ARSIWA Article 8. The Court concluded that there was no sufficient factual basis for finding the Respondent responsible on the basis of direction or control.[33]

(ii) Armed forces

The same principles applicable for the executive apply to members of the armed forces, but a higher standard of prudence in their discipline and control is required.[34] In *Kling*, Commissioner Nielsen said: '[i]n cases of this kind it is mistaken action, error in judgment, or reckless conduct of soldiers for which a government in a given case has been held responsible. The international precedents reveal the application of principles as to the very strict accountability for mistaken action'.[35] Another example of responsibility arising from mistaken but culpable action by units of the armed forces is the shooting down of a South Korean commercial aircraft by Soviet forces in 1983.[36]

In *Armed Activities on the Territory of the Congo (Democratic Republic of the Congo v Uganda)* the International Court addressed the question whether Uganda was responsible for the acts and omissions of its armed forces on the territory of the DRC as follows:

The conduct of the UPDF as a whole is clearly attributable to Uganda, being the conduct of a State organ. According to a well-established rule of international law, which is of customary

---

[31] ICJ Reports 2007 p 43, 201.

[32] Ibid, 202–5.

[33] Ibid, 211–15. For criticism: Cassese (2007) 18 *EJIL* 649.

[34] *Spanish Zone of Morocco* (1925) 2 RIAA 615, 645; *García & Garza* (1926) 4 RIAA 119; *Naulilaa* (1928) 2 RIAA 1011; *Caire* (1929) 5 RIAA 516, 528–9; *Chevreau* (1931) 2 RIAA 1113; *Eis* (1959) 30 ILR 116.

[35] *Kling* (1930) 4 RIAA 575, 579.

[36] (1983) 22 ILM 1190–8, 1419 (requests from affected states and third states that the USSR provide compensation); (1983) 54 *BY* 513 (request from the UK).

character, 'the conduct of any organ of a State must be regarded as an act of that State' ...
In the Court's view, by virtue of the military status and function of Ugandan soldiers in the
DRC, their conduct is attributable to Uganda. The contention that the persons concerned
did not act in the capacity of persons exercising governmental authority in the particular
circumstances, is therefore without merit. It is furthermore irrelevant for the attribution
of their conduct to Uganda whether the UPDF personnel acted contrary to the instructions given or exceeded their authority. According to a well-established rule of a customary
nature, as reflected in Article 3 of the Fourth Hague Convention respecting the Laws and
Customs of War on Land of 1907 as well as in Article 91 of Protocol 1 additional to the
Geneva Conventions of 1949, a party to an armed conflict shall be responsible for all acts by
persons forming part of its armed forces.[37]

A related issue is whether the conduct of state military forces acting under the command and control of a different entity may be attributed to the state of nationality
of the military forces. In *Behrami*, the European Court of Human Rights refused
to attribute to states the conduct of their forces participating in the deployment of
forces to Kosovo in 1999, on the grounds that the deployment had been authorized
by an SC resolution and 'the UNSC retained ultimate authority and control and that
effective command of the relevant operational matters was retained by NATO'.[38] But
the Court of Appeal in The Hague explicitly refuted this reasoning in *Mustafic* and
Nuhanovic, two cases concerning the responsibility of the Dutch state for the omissions of the Dutch battalion of the Airborne Brigade (Dutchbat) during the massacre
of Srebrenica:

[T]he Court adopts as a starting point that the possibility that more than one party has
'effective control' is generally accepted, which means that it cannot be ruled out that the
application of this criterion results in the possibility of attribution to more than one party.
For this reason the Court will only examine if the State exercised 'effective control' over
the alleged conduct and will not answer the question whether the UN also had 'effective
control'...

An important part of Dutchbat's remaining task after 11 July 1995 consisted of the aid
to and the evacuation of the refugees. During this transition period, besides the UN, the
Dutch Government in The Hague had control over Dutchbat as well, because this concerned
the preparations for a total withdrawal of Dutchbat from Bosnia and Herzegovina. In this
respect [the commanding officer] fulfilled a double role because he acted on behalf of the
UN and also on behalf of the Dutch Government. The fact that The Netherlands had control
over Dutchbat was not only theoretical, this control was also exercised in practice... The
Court concludes therefore that the State possessed 'effective control' over the alleged conduct of Dutchbat that is the subject of Nuhanovic's claim and that this conduct can be attributed to the State.[39]

---

[37] ICJ Reports 2005 p 168, 242.

[38] *Behrami & Saramati v France, Germany & Norway* [2007] ECtHR (GC) 71412/01 & 78166/01, §140. The
matter will be discussed in chapter 29.

[39] *Mustafic & Nuhanovic v Netherlands; Nuhanovic v Netherlands*, 5 July 2011, LJN: BR5386 & BR5388,
§§5.9, 5.18, 5.20. See further: Nollkaemper (2011) 9 *JICJ* 1143; Boutin (2012) 25 *LJIL* 521.

In *Al-Jedda*, the European Court of Human Rights issued a decision recognizing attribution, but under different circumstances. The case concerned the detention of an Iraqi citizen, held for three years in Basra by UK forces. The Court considered that:

the United Nations' role as regards security in Iraq in 2004 was quite different from its role as regards security in Kosovo in 1999...the United Nations Security Council had neither effective control nor ultimate authority and control over the acts and omissions of troops within the Multi-National Force and that the applicant's detention was not, therefore, attributable to the United Nations...The internment took place within a detention facility in Basrah City, controlled exclusively by British forces, and the applicant was therefore within the authority and control of the United Kingdom throughout...[40]

In holding that the internment of Al-Jedda was attributable to the UK, the Court attached great weight to the lack of an SC resolution such as that for the deployment of forces to Kosovo in 1999. In making this formal distinction, it stopped short of considering, as the Dutch court did, that multiple entities may have 'effective control' over forces, and that effective control by a state makes the conduct of these forces attributable to the state regardless of the legal form taken by the operation. But both propositions are true.

(iii) Federal units, provinces, and other internal divisions[41]

A state cannot plead its own law, including its constitution, in answer to an international claim. ARSIWA Article 4 makes explicit reference to this, specifying that acts of a state organ are attributable to a state 'whatever its character as an organ of the central government or of a territorial unit of the state'. Arbitral jurisprudence contains examples of the responsibility of federal states for acts of authorities of units of the federations.[42] This was confirmed in *LaGrand (Provisional Measures)*, where the Court observed that the governor of Arizona was legally empowered to take the action necessary to comply with the provisional measure, and stressed that, from the viewpoint of international law, the domestic distribution of functions between federated entities is irrelevant: 'the international responsibility of a State is engaged by the action of the competent organs and authorities acting in that State, whatever they may be...the Governor of Arizona is under the obligation to act in conformity with the international undertakings of the United States'.[43]

---

[40] *Al-Jedda v UK* [2011] ECtHR (GC) 27021/08, §§83–5. For an account of the earlier cases: Messineo (2009) 61 *NILR* 35; Milanovic, *Extraterritorial Application of Human Rights Treaties* (2011).

[41] Accioly (1959) 96 Hague *Recueil* 349, 388–91; McNair, 1 *Opinions* 36–7; Bernier, *International Legal Aspects of Federalism* (1973) 83–120.

[42] *Youmans* (1926) 4 RIAA 110; *Mallén* (1927) 4 RIAA 173; *Pellat* (1929) 5 RIAA 534; *Heirs of the Duc de Guise* (1951) 13 RIAA 150, 161; *Metalclad Corporation v United Mexican States* (2000) 119 ILR 615; *SD Myers Inc v Canada* (2000) 121 ILR 72.

[43] *LaGrand (Germany v US)*, Provisional Measures, ICJ Reports 1999 p 9, 16. Also *Request for Interpretation of the Judgment of 31 March 2004 in the Case concerning* Avena and Other Mexican Nationals (Mexico v US), Provisional Measures, ICJ Reports 2008 p 311, 329.

In *Australia—Salmon*, regarding a ban on imports of salmon imposed by Tasmania, the WTO Panel observed that 'the Tasmanian ban is to be regarded as a measure taken by Australia, in the sense that it is a measure for which Australia, under both general international law and relevant WTO provisions, is responsible'.[44] More controversially, the Inter-American Court of Human Rights has construed the 'federal clause' in the American Convention to imply state responsibility for the actions of federated units.[45]

(iv) The legislature

The legislature is in normal circumstances a vital part of state organization and gives expression to official policies by its enactments. The problem specific to this category is to determine when the breach of duty entails responsibility. Commonly, in the case of injury to aliens, a claimant must establish damage consequent on the implementation of legislation or the omission to legislate.[46] However, it may happen that, particularly in the case of treaty obligations,[47] the acts and omissions of the legislature are, without more, creative of responsibility.[48] For example, if a treaty creates a categorical obligation to incorporate certain rules in domestic law (as with uniform law treaties), failure to do so entails responsibility without proof of actual damage.

(v) The judicature

The activity of judicial organs relates substantially to the rubric 'denial of justice', which will be considered in chapter 29. However, the doings of courts may affect the responsibility of the forum state in other ways. Thus in respect of the application of treaties McNair states: 'a State has a right to delegate to its judicial department the application and interpretation of treaties. If, however, the courts commit errors in that task or decline to give effect to the treaty or are unable to do so because the necessary change in, or addition to, the national law has not been made, their judgments involve the State in a breach of treaty'.[49] In *US—Shrimp*, in response to the argument that discriminatory treatment had been a consequence of the government's obligation to follow judicial decisions, the WTO Appellate Body affirmed that '[t]he United States, like all other members of the WTO and of the general community of states, bears responsibility for acts of all its departments of government, including its judiciary'.[50]

---

[44] *Australia—Salmon (21.5)*, WTO Doc WT/DS18/RW, 18 February 2000, §7.12.

[45] *Garrido & Baigorria v Argentina*, IACtHR, C/39, 27 August 1998, §38.

[46] *Mariposa* (1933) 6 RIAA 338, 340–1.

[47] Where, on a reasonable construction of the treaty, a breach creates a claim without special damage. In any case, representations may be made and steps to obtain redress may be taken on a *quia timet* basis. On the Panama Canal Tolls controversy between the UK and the US: McNair, *Law of Treaties* (1961) 547–50; 6 Hackworth 59.

[48] *International Responsibility for the Promulgation and Enforcement of Laws in Violation of the Convention*, IACtHR A/14, 9 December 1994, §50.

[49] McNair (1961) 346.

[50] WTO Doc WT/DS58/AB/R, 12 October 1998, §173.

In *LaGrand*[51] and *Avena*,[52] foreigners in the US had been condemned to capital punishment without regard for their consular rights under the Vienna Convention.[53] In *LaGrand (Provisional Measures)*, the Court ordered the stay of the executions, reminding the parties that 'the international responsibility of a State is engaged by the action of the competent organs and authorities acting in that State, whatever they may be'.[54] Following the rejection of the order by the US courts, the ICJ adjudged 'that the United States, by applying rules of its domestic law...violated its international obligations'.[55] Similarly, in *Avena*, the Court considered that 'the rights guaranteed under the Vienna Convention are treaty rights which the United States has undertaken to comply with...the legal consequences of [a] breach have to be examined and taken into account in the course of review and reconsideration...the process of review and reconsideration should occur within the overall judicial proceedings relating to the individual defendant concerned'.[56]

(C) *ULTRA VIRES* OR UNAUTHORIZED ACTS[57]

It has long been apparent in the sphere of domestic law that acts of public authorities which are *ultra vires* should not by that token create immunity from legal consequences for the state. In international law there is a clear reason for disregarding a plea of unlawfulness under domestic law: the lack of express authority cannot be decisive as to the responsibility of the state.

It is thus well established that states may be responsible for *ultra vires* acts of their officials committed within their apparent authority or general scope of authority. In *Union Bridge Company*, a British official of the Cape Government Railways appropriated neutral (American) property during the Second Boer War, mistakenly believing it was not neutral: the tribunal considered that responsibility was not affected by the official's mistake or the lack of intention on the part of the British authorities to appropriate the material, stating that the conduct was within the general scope of duty of the official.[58] In *Caire* a captain and a major in the Conventionist forces in control of Mexico had demanded money from Caire under threat of death, and had then ordered the shooting of their victim when the money was not forthcoming. In holding Mexico responsible, the Commission said:

The State also bears an international responsibility for all acts committed by its officials or its organs which are delictual according to international law, regardless of whether

---

[51] ICJ Reports 2001 p 466, 508.

[52] ICJ Reports 2004 p 12, 66.

[53] Also *Vienna Convention on Consular Relations (Paraguay v US)*, Provisional Measures, ICJ Reports 1998 p 248.

[54] ICJ Reports 1999 p 9, 16.

[55] ICJ Reports 2001 p 466, 472–3. Also *Avena Interpretation*, ICJ Reports 2009 p 3, 15.

[56] ICJ Reports 2004 p 12, 65–6.

[57] Meron (1957) 33 *BY* 85; García-Amador, ILC *Ybk* 1957/II 107, 109–10; Accioly (1959) 96 Hague *Recueil* 349, 360–3; Anzilotti, 1 *Cours* (1929) 470–4; Freeman (1955) 88 Hague *Recueil* 263, 290–2; Quadri (1964) 113 Hague *Recueil* 237, 465–8; ILC *Ybk* 1975/II 47, 61–70. Now ARSIWA, Art 7 & commentary.

[58] (1924) 2 ILR 170, 171.

the official or organ has acted within the limits of his competency or has exceeded those limits ... However, in order to justify the admission of this objective responsibility of the State for acts committed by its officials or organs outside their competence, it is necessary that they should have acted, at least apparently, as authorized officials or organs, or that, in acting, they should have used powers or measures appropriate to their official character ...[59]

In *Youmans,* the Commission stated: '[s]oldiers inflicting personal injuries or committing wanton destruction or looting always act in disobedience of some rules laid down by superior authority. There could be no responsibility whatever for such misdeeds if the view were taken that any acts committed by soldiers in contravention of instructions must always be considered as personal acts'.[60]

It is not always easy to distinguish personal acts and acts within the scope of (apparent) authority. In the case of higher organs and officials the presumption will be that there was an act within the scope of authority.[61] Where the standard of conduct required is very high, as in the case of military leaders and cabinet ministers in relation to control of armed forces, it may be quite inappropriate to use the dichotomy of official and personal acts: here, as elsewhere, much depends on the type of activity and the related consequences *in the particular case.*[62]

It is not difficult to find cases in which the acts of state agents were clearly *ultra vires* and yet responsibility has been affirmed. In the *Zafiro* the US was held responsible for looting by the civilian crew of a merchant vessel employed as a supply vessel by American naval forces, under the command of a merchant captain who in turn was under the orders of an American naval officer.[63] The tribunal emphasized the failure to exercise proper control in the circumstances.[64] What really matters, however, is the amount of control *which ought to have been exercised* in the particular circumstances, not the amount of actual control.[65]

This principle is of particular importance in relation to administrative practices involving violations of human rights, as well as for the conduct of armed forces during conflict. In *Armed Activities (DRC v Uganda),* the International Court observed that

[59] (1929) 5 ILR 146, 147–8.

[60] (1926) 3 ILR 223.

[61] But see *Bensley* (1850), in Moore, 3 *Int Arb* 3018 (responsibility denied for the personal act of the governor of a Mexican state).

[62] Cf the finding of the International Military Tribunal for the Far East on the operations by the Japanese Kwantung Army at Nomonhan in 1939, reproduced in Brownlie, *International Law and the Use of Force by States* (1963) 210–11.

[63] (1925) 3 ILR 221. Also *Metzger* (1903) 10 RIAA 417; *Roberts* (1905) 9 RIAA 204; *Crossman* (1903) 9 RIAA 356.

[64] Viz, the absence of civil or military government in Manila during the Spanish–American war. The tribunal might seem to overemphasize the need for failure to control, but the case is different from those in which unauthorized acts of armed forces occur within the area of established sovereignty of the state to which the armed forces belong: cf *Caire* (1929) 5 ILR 146.

[65] *Henriquez* (1903) 10 RIAA 727; *Mallén* (1927) 4 RIAA 173; *Morton* (1929) 4 RIAA 428 (murder in a *cantina* by a drunken officer off duty); *Gordon* (1930) 4 ILR 586 (army doctors at target practice with privately acquired pistol); *Ireland v UK* [1978] ECtHR 5310/71.

customary international law provides that, in the case of armed conflict, all the acts of a state's armed forces are attributable to that state, regardless of which instructions were given or whether personnel acted *ultra vires*:

The conduct of individual soldiers and officers of the UPDF [Uganda People's Defence Force] is to be considered as the conduct of a State organ. In the Court's view, by virtue of the military status and function of Ugandan soldiers in the DRC, their conduct is attributable to Uganda. The contention that the persons concerned did not act in the capacity of persons exercising governmental authority in the particular circumstances, is therefore without merit.[66]

In *Velásquez Rodríguez*, the Inter-American Court of Human Rights observed that unlawful conduct may arise from acts of any state organs, officials or public entities and that:

[t]his conclusion is independent of whether the organ or official has contravened provisions of internal law or overstepped the limits of his authority: under international law a State is responsible for the acts of its agents undertaken in their official capacity and for their omissions, even when those agents act outside the sphere of their authority or violate internal law.[67]

(D) MOB VIOLENCE, INSURRECTION, REVOLUTION, AND CIVIL WAR[68]

The general principles considered below apply to a variety of situations involving acts of violence either by persons not acting as agents of the lawful government of a state, or by persons acting on behalf of a rival or candidate government set up by insurgents. The latter may be described as a '*de facto* government'. In the case of localized riots and mob violence, substantial neglect to take reasonable precautionary and preventive action and inattention amounting to outright indifference or connivance on the part of responsible officials may create responsibility for damage to foreign public and private property in the area.[69] In the proceedings arising from the seizure of US diplomatic and consular staff as hostages in Tehran, the International Court based responsibility for breaches of the law of diplomatic relations upon the failure of the Iranian authorities to control the militants (in the early phase) and also upon the adoption and approval of the acts of the militants (at the later stage).[70]

---

[66] ICJ Reports 2005 p 168, 242.

[67] *Velásquez Rodríquez v Honduras*, IACtHR C/4, 29 July 1988, §170. Also *Blake v Guatemala*, IACtHR C/36, 24 January 1998.

[68] Ago, ILC *Ybk* 1972/II, 126–52; McNair, 2 *Opinions* 238–73, 277; Harvard Research Draft (1929) 23 *AJIL Sp Supp* 133, 188–96.

[69] *Ziat, Ben Kiran* (1924) 2 RIAA 729, 730; *Youmans* (1926) 4 RIAA 110; *Noyes* (1933) 6 RIAA 308; *Pinson* (1928) 5 RIAA 327; *Sarropoulos v Bulgaria* (1927) 4 ILR 245.

[70] *Tehran Hostages*, ICJ Reports 1980 p 3, 29–30, 33–6. *Short v Iran* (1987) 82 ILR 148. Also *Yeager v Iran* (1987) 82 ILR 178; *Rankin v Iran* (1987) 82 ILR 204.

McNair extracts five principles from the reports of the legal advisers of the British Crown on the responsibility for the consequences of insurrection or rebellion. The first three principles are as follows:

(i)   A State on whose territory an insurrection occurs is not responsible for loss or damage sustained by a foreigner unless it can be shown that the Government of that State was negligent in the use of, or in the failure to use, the forces at its disposal for the prevention or suppression of the insurrection;

(ii)   this is a variable test, dependent on the circumstances of the insurrection;

(iii) such a State is not responsible for the damage resulting from military operations directed by its lawful government unless the damage was wanton or unnecessary, which appears to be substantially the same as the position of belligerent States in an international war.[71]

The general rule of non-responsibility rests on the premise that even objective responsibility requires a normal capacity to act, and a major internal upheaval is tantamount to *force majeure*. But uncertainty arises when the qualifications put upon the general rule are examined. There is general agreement among writers that the rule of non-responsibility cannot apply where the government concerned has failed to show due diligence.[72] However, the decisions of tribunals and the other sources offer no definition of 'due diligence'. No doubt the application of this standard will vary according to the circumstances,[73] yet, if 'due diligence' be taken to denote a fairly high standard of conduct the exception will overwhelm the rule. In a comment on the Harvard Research Draft it is stated that: '[i]nasmuch as negligence on the part of the government in suppressing an insurrection against itself is improbable, the claimant should be deemed to have the burden of showing negligence.'[74]

In fact there is no modern example of a state being held responsible for negligent failure to suppress insurgents. The ILC made the point in its commentary to ARSIWA Article 10, referring to '[t]he general principle that the conduct of an insurrectional or other movement is not attributable to the State...on the assumption that the structures and organization of the movement are and remain independent of those of the State...Exceptional cases may occur where the State was in a position to adopt measures of vigilance, prevention or punishment in respect of the movement's conduct but improperly failed to do so'.[75] There is older authority for the view that the granting of an amnesty to rebels constitutes a failure of duty and an acceptance of responsibility for their acts, but again this is doubtful absent conduct of the state amounting to complicity or adoption.[76]

---

[71]   McNair, 2 *Opinions* 245.

[72]   Brierly (1928) 9 *BY* 42; de Frouville, in Crawford, Pellet & Olleson (2010) 257, 261–4.

[73]   This may be particularly strict in the case of alleged breach of human rights: *A v UK* [1998] ECtHR 25599/94, §22; *Velásquez Rodríquez v Honduras*, IACtHR C/4, 29 July 1988, §148.

[74]   Harvard Research Draft (1929) 23 *AJIL Sp Supp* 133, 194.

[75]   ARSIWA, Art 10 & commentary, §§4, 15. Also García-Amador, ILC *Ybk* 1957/II, 121–3.

[76]   Accioly (1959) 96 Hague *Recueil* 349, 402–3.

The other two principles propounded by McNair are generally accepted:

(iv) such a State is not responsible for loss or damage caused by the insurgents to a foreigner after that foreigner's State has recognized the belligerency of the insurgents;

(v) such a State can usually defeat a claim in respect of loss or damage sustained by resident foreigners by showing that they have received the same treatment in the matter of protection or compensation, if any, as its own nationals (the plea of *diligentia quam in suis*).[77]

Victorious rebel movements are responsible—*qua* new government of the state—for unlawful acts or omissions by their forces occurring during the course of the conflict.[78] The state also remains responsible for the unlawful conduct of the previous government.

(E) JOINT RESPONSIBILITY

Two issues affecting responsibility in the context of the 'joint' action of states demand attention. The first concerns the official acting in different capacities. In *Chevreau*, part of the French claim against the UK related to loss flowing from the negligence of the British consul in Persia, acting at the material time as agent for the French consul: the tribunal rejected this part of the claim.[79] The second problem concerns the dependent state. In the case where the putative dependent state cannot be regarded as having any degree of international personality because of the extent of outside control, then the incidence of responsibility is no longer in question. In other cases a state may by treaty or otherwise assume international responsibility for another government.[80] In *Spanish Zone of Morocco*, Huber said:

[I]t would be extraordinary if, as a result of the establishment of the Protectorates, the responsibility incumbent upon Morocco in accordance with international law were to be diminished. If the responsibility has not been assumed by the protecting Power, it remains the burden of the protected State; in any case, it cannot have disappeared. Since the protected State is unable to act without an intermediary on the international level, and since every measure by which a third State sought to obtain respect for its rights from the Cherif, would inevitably have an equal effect upon the interests of the protecting Power, it is the latter who must bear the responsibility of the protected State, at least by way of vicarious liability ... the responsibility of the protecting State ... is based on the fact that it is that State alone which represents the protected State in international affairs ...[81]

---

[77] McNair, 2 *Opinions* 245. Also García-Amador, ILC *Ybk* 1957/II, 122.

[78] *Bolivar Railway Company* (1903) 9 RIAA 445; *Pinson* (1928) 5 RIAA 327.

[79] (1931) 2 RIAA 1113, 1141. Also *Prince Sliman Bey v Minister for Foreign Affairs* (1959) 28 ILR 79.

[80] The basis of responsibility may then rest either on the actual extinction of the personality of the protected state or on estoppel. *Studer (US) v Great Britain* (1925) 6 RIAA 149. Cf agreements for indemnification of the agent: *Zadeh v US* (1955) 22 ILR 336; *Oakland Truck Sales Inc v US* (1957) 24 ILR 952.

[81] (1925) 2 RIAA 615, 648–9. Also *Trochel v State of Tunisia* (1953) 20 ILR 47.

However, in cases where the dependent state retains sufficient legal powers to maintain a separate personality and the right to conduct its own foreign relations, the incidence of responsibility will depend on the circumstances.[82]

The principles relating to joint responsibility of states are as yet indistinct, and municipal analogies are unhelpful. A rule of joint and several responsibility in delict should certainly exist as a matter of principle, but practice is scarce.[83] Practice in the matter of reparation payments for unlawful invasion and occupation in the immediate post-war period rested on the assumption that Axis countries were liable on the basis of individual causal contribution to damage and loss, unaffected by the existence of co-belligerency.[84] However, if there is joint participation in specific actions, for example where state A supplies planes and other material to state B for unlawful dropping of guerrillas and state B operates the aircraft, what is to be the position?

In *Certain Phosphate Lands in Nauru (Nauru v Australia)* the International Court held that the possibility of the existence of a joint and several responsibility of three states responsible for the administration of the Trust Territory at the material time did not render inadmissible a claim brought against only one of them.[85] The question of substance was reserved for the merits. In fact, a negotiated settlement was reached[86] and, subsequently, the UK and New Zealand, the other states involved, agreed to pay contributions to Australia on an *ex gratia* basis.[87]

ARSIWA Article 47 incorporates this reasoning, providing that the responsibility of each state may be invoked in the case of plurality of responsible states, as long as total compensation does not exceed the damage suffered by the injured state. In other words, each state is separately responsible and that responsibility is not reduced by the fact that one or more other states are also responsible for the same act.

(F) COMPLICITY

In *Genocide (Bosnia and Herzegovina v Serbia and Montenegro)*, an issue arose concerning Serbia's alleged complicity for genocide within the meaning of Article III(e) of the Genocide Convention. The Court said:

[A]lthough 'complicity', as such, is not a notion which exists in the current terminology of the law of international responsibility, it is similar to a category found among the customary rules constituting the law of State responsibility, that of the 'aid or assistance' furnished by one State for the commission of a wrongful act by another State...to ascertain whether the Respondent is responsible for 'complicity in genocide' within the meaning of Article III, paragraph (e), which is what the Court now has to do, it must examine whether organs of

---

[82] *Brown* (1923) 6 RIAA 120, 130–1.

[83] Brownlie, *State Responsibility Part I* (1983) 189–92. On the question of complicity Ago, ILC *Ybk* 1978/II(1), 52–60; ILC *Ybk* 1978/II(2), 98–105; ILC *Ybk* 1979/II(2), 94–106; Quigley (1986) 57 *BY* 77; Aust, *Complicity and the Law of State Responsibility* (2011).

[84] But see *Anglo-Chinese Shipping Co Ltd v US* (1955) 22 ILR 982, 986.

[85] ICJ Reports 1992 p 240, 258–9; ibid, 301 (President Jennings, diss).

[86] Australia–Nauru Settlement, 10 August 1993, 32 ILM 1471.

[87] UK Agreement, 24 March 1994, in UKMIL (1994) 65 *BY* 625.

the respondent State, or persons acting on its instructions or under its direction or effective control, furnished 'aid or assistance' in the commission of the genocide in Srebrenica, in a sense not significantly different from that of those concepts in the general law of international responsibility.[88]

The Court thereby endorsed ARSIWA Article 14, which provides:

Aid or assistance in the commission of an internationally wrongful act

A State which aids or assists another State in the commission of an internationally wrongful act by the latter is internationally responsible for doing so if:

(a) That State does so with knowledge of the circumstances of the internationally wrongful act; and

(b) The act would be internationally wrongful if committed by that State.

This is a potentially wide-ranging principle of ancillary responsibility (although valuable clarifications are offered in the commentary).[89]

(G) APPROVAL OR ADOPTION BY A STATE OF WRONGFUL ACTS[90]

Responsibility accrues, quite apart from the operation of other factors, if a state accepts or otherwise adopts the conduct of private persons or entities as its own. The International Court applied this principle to the actions of the militants in *Tehran Hostages*.[91] It is expressed in ARSIWA Article 11, which specifies that the state only becomes responsible 'if and to the extent that the State acknowledges and adopts the conduct in question as its own'. The commentary adds:

The phrase…is intended to distinguish cases of acknowledgement and adoption from cases of mere support or endorsement…In international controversies States often take positions which amount to 'approval' or 'endorsement' of conduct in some general sense but do not involve any assumption of responsibility. The language of 'adoption', on the other hand, carries with it the idea that the conduct is acknowledged by the State as, in effect, its own conduct.[92]

4. BREACH OF AN INTERNATIONAL OBLIGATION

(A) 'VICARIOUS RESPONSIBILITY'

In general, broad formulas on state responsibility are unhelpful and, when they suggest municipal analogies, even a source of confusion. Unhappily Oppenheim draws a

---

[88] ICJ Reports 2007 p 43, 217.
[89] ARSIWA, commentary to Art 16, §§3–6.
[90] Brownlie (1983) 157–8; ARSIWA, Art 11 & commentary.
[91] ICJ Reports 1980 p 3, 29–30, 33–6.
[92] ARSIWA, commentary to Art 6, §6.

distinction between original and vicarious state responsibility. Original responsibility flows from acts committed by, or with authorization of, the government of a state; vicarious responsibility flows from unauthorized acts of the agents of the state.[93] It is true that the legal consequences of the two categories of acts may not be the same; but there is no fundamental difference between the two categories, and, in any case, the use of 'vicarious responsibility' here is surely erroneous.

(B) 'OBJECTIVE RESPONSIBILITY'

Technically, objective responsibility rests on the doctrine of the voluntary act: provided that agency and causal connection are established, there is a breach of duty by result alone. Defences, such as act of third party, are available, but the defendant has to exculpate itself.[94] In the conditions of international life, which involve relations between complex communities acting through a variety of institutions and agencies, the public law analogy of the *ultra vires* act is more realistic than a seeking for subjective *culpa* in specific natural persons who may, or may not, 'represent' the legal person (the state) in terms of wrongdoing. Where, for example, an officer in charge of a cruiser on the high seas orders the boarding of a fishing vessel flying the flag of another state, there being no legal justification for the operation, and the act being in excess of authority, a tribunal will not regard pleas that the acts were done in good faith, or under a mistake of law, with any favour.[95]

The practice of states and the jurisprudence both of arbitral tribunals and the International Court have followed the theory of objective responsibility as a general principle (which may be modified or excluded in certain cases).[96] Objective tests of responsibility were employed by the US–Mexico General Claims Commission in *Neer*[97] and *Roberts*.[98] In *Caire*,[99] Verzijl, President of the Franco-Mexican Claims Commission, applied

the doctrine of the objective responsibility of the State, that is to say, a responsibility for those acts committed by its officials or its organs, and which they are bound to perform, despite the absence of *faute* on their part ... The State also bears an international responsibility for all acts committed by its officials or its organs which are delictual according to international law, regardless of whether the official organ has acted within the limits of his competency or has exceeded those limits. ... However, in order to justify the admission of this objective responsibility of the State for acts committed by its officials or organs outside

---

[93] Oppenheim 501. Further: Kelsen, *Principles of International Law* (2nd edn, 1952) 199–201.

[94] *Corfu Channel*, ICJ Reports 1949 p 4, 85–6 (Judge Azevedo).

[95] *The Jessie* (1921) 6 RIAA 57; *The Wanderer* (1921) 6 RIAA 177; *The Kate* (1921) 6 RIAA 188; *The Favourite* (1921) 6 RIAA 82.

[96] Borchard (1929) 1 *ZaöRV* 223, 225; Schachter (1982) 178 Hague *Recueil* 1, 189; Gattini (1992) 3 *EJIL* 253; Cheng, *General Principles of Law as Applied by International Courts and Tribunals* (1994) 218–32.

[97] *Neer* (1926) 6 RIAA 60, 61.

[98] *Roberts* (1926) 6 RIAA 77, 80.

[99] *Caire* (1929) 5 RIAA 516.

their competence, it is necessary that they should have acted, at least apparently, as authorised officials or organs, or that, in acting, they should have used powers or measures appropriate to their official character ... [100]

This view has general support in the literature.[101] At the same time certain authorities
have supported the Grotian view that *culpa* provides the basis of state responsibility
in all cases.[102] A small number of arbitral awards also support the *culpa* doctrine.[103] In
Home Missionary Society, the tribunal referred to a 'well-established principle of international law that no government can be held responsible for the act of rebellious bodies of men committed in violation of its authority, where it is itself guilty of no breach
of good faith, or of no negligence in suppressing insurrection'.[104] However, many of the
awards cited in this connection are concerned with the standard of conduct required
by the law *in a particular context*, for example claims for losses caused by acts of rebellion, of private individuals, of the judiciary, and so on. Thus in *Chattin* the General
Claims Commission described the judicial proceedings in Mexico against Chattin as
'being highly insufficient' and referred, *inter alia*, to 'an insufficiency of governmental
action recognizable by every unbiased man'.[105] Chattin had been convicted on a charge
of embezzlement and sentenced by the Mexican court to two years' imprisonment.
The Commission referred to various defects in the conduct of the trial and remarked
that 'the whole of the proceedings discloses a most astonishing lack of seriousness on
the part of the Court'. Furthermore, both writers[106] and tribunals[107] may use the words
faute or fault to mean a breach of legal duty, an unlawful act. *Culpa*, in the sense of
culpable negligence, will be relevant when its presence is demanded by a particular
rule of law. Objective responsibility would seem to come nearer to being a *general*
principle, and provides a better basis for maintaining acceptable standards in international relations and for effectively upholding the principle of reparation.

The proposition that the type of advertence required varies with the legal context can be illustrated by *Corfu Channel*. In fact the Court was concerned with the
particular question of responsibility for the creation of danger in the North Corfu
Channel by the laying of mines, warning of which was not given. The necessary
predicate for responsibility was Albania's knowledge of the presence of the mines.
The Court considered 'whether it has been established by means of indirect evidence

---

[100] Ibid, 529.
[101] Reports by García-Amador, ILC *Ybk* 1956/II, 186; ILC *Ybk* 1957/II, 106. This was the approach ultimately adopted in ARSIWA, commentary to Art 2, §§1–4. But see Gattini (1999) 10 *EJIL* 397.
[102] Eagleton (1928) 209; Lauterpacht (1937) 62 Hague *Recueil* 95, 359; Ago (1939) 68 Hague *Recueil* 415,
498; Accioly (1959) 96 Hague *Recueil* 349, 364.
[103] *Casablanca* (1909) 11 RIAA 119; *Cadenhead* (1914) 6 RIAA 40; *Iloilo* (1925) 6 RIAA 158, 160; *Pugh*
(1933) 3 RIAA 1439; *Wal-Wal Incident* (1935) 3 RIAA 1657. Also: *Davis* (1903) 9 RIAA 460, 463; *Salas* (1903)
10 RIAA 720.
[104] *Home Missionary Society* (1920) 6 RIAA 42, 44.
[105] *Chattin* (1927) 4 ILR 248, 250. Also *Spanish Zone of Morocco* (1925) 2 RIAA 615, 644.
[106] Accioly (1959) 96 Hague *Recueil* 349, 369.
[107] *Prats* (1868), in Moore, 3 *Int Arb* 2886, 2895; *Russian Indemnity* (1912) 11 RIAA 421, 440. Further:
Cheng (1994) 218–32.

that Albania has knowledge of mine-laying in her territorial waters independently of any connivance on her part in this operation'.[108] Later on it concluded that the laying of the minefield 'could not have been accomplished without the knowledge of the Albanian Government' and referred to 'every State's obligation not to allow knowingly its territory to be used for acts contrary to the rights of other States'.[109] Responsibility thus rested upon violation of a particular legal duty. The Court was not concerned with *culpa* as such, and it fell to the dissentients to affirm the doctrine of *culpa*.[110]

In *Genocide (Bosnia and Herzegovina v Serbia and Montenegro)*, the International Court excluded the *culpa* doctrine, reaffirming what it termed 'the well-established rule, one of the cornerstones of the law of State responsibility, that the conduct of any State organ is to be considered an act of the State under international law, and therefore gives rise to the responsibility of the State if it constitutes a breach of an international obligation of the State. This rule, which is one of customary international law, is reflected in Article 4 of the ILC Articles on State Responsibility'.[111]

Although *culpa* is not a general condition of responsibility, it may play an important role in certain contexts. Thus where the loss complained of results from acts of individuals not employed by the state, or from activities of licensees or trespassers on the territory of the state, responsibility will depend on an unlawful omission. In this type of case questions of knowledge may be relevant in establishing responsibility for failure to act.[112] However, tribunals may set standards of 'due diligence' and the like, in respect of the activities, or failures to act, of particular organs. In effect, since looking for specific evidence of a lack of proper care on the part of state organs is often a fruitless task, the issue becomes one of causation.[113] In the *Lighthouses* arbitration between France and Greece one of the claims arose from the eviction of a French firm from their offices in Salonika and the subsequent loss of their stores in a fire which destroyed the temporary premises. The Permanent Court of Arbitration said:

> Even if one were inclined … to hold that Greece is in principle responsible for the consequences of that evacuation, one could not … admit a causal relationship between the damage caused by the fire, on the one part, and that following on the evacuation, on the other, so as to justify holding Greece liable for the disastrous effects of the fire … The damage was neither a foreseeable nor a normal consequence of the evacuation, nor attributable to any want of care on the part of Greece. All causal connection is lacking, and in those circumstances Claim No 19 must be rejected.[114]

---

[108]   *Corfu Channel*, ICJ Reports 1949 p 4, 18. But see ibid, 65 (Judge Badawi, diss) supporting a doctrine of fault which was in fact based on the notion of the unlawful, voluntary act.

[109]   Ibid, 22.

[110]   ICJ Reports 1949 p 4, 71 (Judge Krylov, diss), 127 (Judge ad hoc Ečer, diss).

[111]   ICJ Reports 2007 p 43, 202.

[112]   Cf *Corfu Channel*, ICJ Reports 1949 p 4, 18, 22. Also Lévy (1961) 65 *RGDIP* 744.

[113]   García-Amador, ILC *Ybk* 1960/II 41, 63.

[114]   (1956) 23 ILR 352.

In any case, as Judge Azevedo pointed out in his dissenting opinion in *Corfu Channel*,[115] the relations of objective responsibility and the *culpa* principle are very close: the effect of the judgment was to place Albania under a duty to take reasonable care to discover hazardous activities of third parties.

When a state engages in lawful activities, responsibility may be generated by *culpa* in the execution of the lawful measures. In *In re Rizzo*, concerning the sequestration of Italian property in Tunisia by the French government after the defeat of Italy, the Conciliation Commission said: 'the act contrary to international law is not the measure of sequestration, but an alleged lack of diligence on the part of the French State—or, more precisely, of him who was acting on its behalf—in the execution of the said measure …'.[116] The existence and extent of *culpa* may affect the extent of damages,[117] and, of course, a requirement to exercise due diligence may be stipulated for in treaty provisions.

(c) THE PROBLEM OF STATE MOTIVE OR INTENT

Motive and intention are frequently a specific element in the definition of permitted conduct. Once it is established that conduct is unlawful, however, the fact that an *ultra vires* act of an official is accompanied by malice, that is, an intention to cause harm, without regard to whether or not the law permits the act, does not affect the responsibility of the state (although it may be relevant to quantum). Indeed, the principle of objective responsibility dictates the irrelevance of intention to harm as a condition of responsibility. Yet general propositions of this sort should not lead to the conclusion that intention plays no role. For example the existence of a deliberate intent to injure may have an effect on remoteness of damage as well as helping to establish the breach of duty.[118]

(d) THE INDIVIDUALITY OF ISSUES

At this stage it is perhaps unnecessary to repeat that over-simplification of the problems, and too much reliance on general propositions about objective responsibility and the like, can result in lack of finesse in approaching particular issues. Legal issues, particularly in disputes between states, have an individuality which resists a facile application of general rules. Much depends on the assignment of the burden of proof, the operation of the law of evidence, acquiescence and estoppel, the terms of the *compromis*, and the content of the relevant substantive rules or treaty provisions.

---

[115] ICJ Reports 1949 p 4, 85 (Judge Azevedo, diss).
[116] *In re Rizzo* (1955) 22 ILR 317, 322. Also: *Philadelphia-Girard National Bank* (1929) 8 RIAA 67, 69; *Ousset* (1954) 22 ILR 312, 314.
[117] *Baldwin* (1842), in Moore, 4 *Int Arb* 3235; *Janes* (1926) 4 RIAA 81; *Rau* (1930), in 1 Whiteman 26.
[118] *Dix* (1903) 9 RIAA 119, 121; cf *Monnot* (1903) 9 RIAA 232, 233.

Thus in *Corfu Channel*, the approach adopted by the majority fails to correspond neatly with either the *culpa* doctrine or the test of objective responsibility. 'Intention' is a question-begging category and appears in the case only in specialist roles. Thus, in the case of the British passage 'designed to affirm a right which had been unjustly denied' by Albania, much turned on the nature of the passage.[119] Taking all the circumstances into account, the Court held that the passage of two cruisers and two destroyers through a part of the North Corfu Channel constituting Albanian territorial waters, was an innocent passage. As to the laying of the mines which damaged the destroyers, Saumarez and Volage, the Court looked for evidence of knowledge on the part of Albania. The case also illustrates the interaction of the principles of proof and responsibility. The Court said:

[I]t cannot be concluded from the mere fact of the control exercised by a State over its territory and waters that that State necessarily knew, or ought to have known, of any unlawful act perpetrated therein, nor yet that it necessarily knew, or should have known, the authors. This fact, by itself and apart from other circumstances, neither involves *prima facie* responsibility nor shifts the burden of proof.

On the other hand, the fact of this exclusive territorial control exercised by a State within its frontiers has a bearing upon the methods of proof available to establish the knowledge of that State as to such events. By reason of this exclusive control, the other State, the victim of a breach of international law, is often unable to furnish direct proof of facts giving rise to responsibility. Such a State should be allowed a more liberal recourse to inferences of fact and circumstantial evidence. The Court must examine therefore whether it has been established by means of indirect evidence that Albania has knowledge of mine-laying in her territorial waters independently of any connivance on her part in this operation. The proof may be drawn from inferences of fact, provided they leave *no room* for reasonable doubt. The elements of fact on which these inferences can be based may differ from those which are relevant to the question of connivance.[120]

(E) LIABILITY FOR LAWFUL ACTS

It may happen that a rule provides for compensation for the consequences of acts which are not unlawful in the sense of being prohibited.[121] Thus UNCLOS Article 110 provides for the boarding of foreign merchant ships by warships where there is reasonable ground for suspecting piracy or certain other activities. Paragraph 3 then provides: '[i]f the suspicions prove to be unfounded, and provided that the ship boarded has not committed any act justifying them, it shall be compensated for any loss or damage that may have been sustained'.[122]

---

[119] ICJ Reports 1949 p 4, 30.

[120] Ibid, 18.

[121] Sørensen (1960) 101 Hague *Recueil* 1, 221; Quadri (1964) 113 Hague *Recueil* 237, 461; Boyle (1990) 39 *ICLQ* 1.

[122] 10 December 1982, 1833 UNTS 396. Further: chapter 13.

Liability for acts not prohibited by international law has acquired great relevance in the field of international environmental law, as lawful economic activity may produce pollution and other externalities that transcend the borders of a single state.[123] Yet there is little authority supporting the category as such, apart from express stipulations such as Article 110(3). In *Trail Smelter*, a smelter located in Canada was producing air pollution which affected the US. The Arbitral Tribunal considered that Canada was responsible under international law for the damage, regardless of the legality of the activity itself. Drawing analogies essentially from domestic law cases, the Tribunal concluded 'that, under the principles of international law, as well as of the law of the United States, no State has the right to use or permit the use of its territory in such a manner as to cause injury by fumes in or to the territory of another or the properties or persons therein, when the case is of serious consequence and the injury is established by clear and convincing evidence'.[124]

The topic was examined at length by the ILC, which eventually concluded in 2006 its Draft Principles on the Allocation of Loss in the Case of Transboundary Harm Arising out of Hazardous Activities.[125] Principle 4(1) provides that states must 'ensure that prompt and adequate compensation is available for victims of transboundary damage'. While it is doubtful whether courts will be willing to impose responsibility for transboundary damage on states in the absence of an express obligation,[126] specific regimes have advanced in establishing different means of legal redress in the case of environmental harm.[127]

In all of these cases, one can always refer back to the duty of due diligence. The fact that an activity is itself not prohibited by international law does not exclude that damage caused by poor judgement or poor management in carrying out the activity cannot entail responsibility.[128] In that sense, the sole example unanimously accepted as creating liability for an act that is completely lawful under international law is contained in the 1972 Convention on International Liability for Damage Caused by Space Objects. Article II provides that '[a] launching State shall be absolutely liable to pay compensation for damage caused by its space object on the surface of the Earth or to aircraft in flight'; Article III contains the usual provision of liability for fault in the case of damage caused by a space object outside the surface of the earth.[129]

---

[123] Akerhurst (1985) 16 *NYIL* 3; Barboza (1994) 247 Hague *Recueil* 295; Brans, *Liability for Damage to Public Natural Resources* (2001); Xue, *Transboundary Damage in International Law* (2003); Voigt (2008) 77 *Nordic JIL* 1.

[124] (1949) 3 RIAA 1905, 1965. See Read (1963) 1 *CYIL* 213. Also *Lac Lanoux* (1957) 12 RIAA 281 (potential harm only not actionable in a transboundary context).

[125] A/61/10, 101. Cf Boyle, in Crawford, Pellet & Olleson (2010) 95.

[126] *Pulp Mills on The River Uruguay (Argentina v Uruguay)*, Judgment of 20 April 2010, §§271–6.

[127] Koskenniemi (1992) 3 *Ybk IEL* 123; Treves, Tanzi, Pineschi, Pitea, Ragni & Jacur, *Non-Compliance Procedures and the Effectiveness of International Environmental Agreements* (2009).

[128] Caubet (1983) *AFDI* 99, 107; Dupuy, *La Responsabilité internationale des États pour les dommages d'origine technologique et industrielle* (1976) 189.

[129] 961 UNTS 187. See Christol (1980) 74 *AJIL* 346. Damage caused in Canadian territory by the fall in 1977 of a Soviet satellite, *Cosmos 954*, was settled by diplomatic means, including the payment of C$3 million compensation: 20 ILM 689; Burke (1984) 8 *Fordham ILJ* 255.

(F) 'ABUSE OF RIGHTS'

Several systems of law recognize the doctrine of abuse of rights.[130] Thus Article 1912 of the Mexican Civil Code: 'If in the exercise of a right damage is caused to another, there is an obligation to indemnify the injured party if it is shown that the right was exercised only to cause injury, without any benefit to the holder of the right'.[131] This doctrine has had only limited support from international tribunals.[132] In *Certain German Interests in Polish Upper Silesia,* the Permanent Court held that, after the peace treaty came into force and until the transfer of sovereignty over Upper Silesia, the right to dispose of state property in the territory remained with Germany. Alienation would constitute a breach of her obligations if there was a 'misuse' of this right.[133] But in the view of the Court, German policy in alienating land in that case amounted to no more than the normal administration of public property.

In *Free Zones of Upper Savoy and the District of Gex* the Court held that French fiscal legislation applied in the free zones (which were French territory), but that 'a reservation must be made as regards the case of abuse of a right, an abuse which, however, cannot be presumed by the Court'.[134]

It is not unreasonable to regard the principle of abuse of rights as a general principle of law. However, its application is a matter of some delicacy. After considering the work of the International Court, Lauterpacht observed:

> These are but modest beginnings of a doctrine which is full of potentialities and which places a considerable power, not devoid of a legislative character, in the hands of a judicial tribunal. There is no legal right, however well established, which could not, in some circumstances, be refused recognition on the ground that it has been abused. The doctrine of abuse of rights is therefore an instrument which ... must be wielded with studied restraint.[135]

In some cases the doctrine may help explain the genesis of a rule of law, for example the principle that no state has a right to use or permit the use of its territory in such a manner as to cause injury by fumes to the territory of another.[136] Often it represents a plea for legislation or the modification of rules to suit special circumstances. In gen-

---

[130] Kiss, *L'Abus de droit en droit international* (1953); Schwarzenberger (1956) 42 *GST* 147; Taylor (1972) 46 *BY* 323; Iluyomade (1975) 16 *Harv ILJ* 47; Byers (2002) 47 *McGill LJ* 389.

[131] Vargas, *Mexican Civil Code Annotated* (2009) 653.

[132] Citations often involve *ex post facto* recruitment of arbitral awards, e.g. *Portendick* (1843), in 1 Lapradelle & Politis (1905) 512.

[133] (1926) PCIJ Ser A No 7, 30. The Court added: '[s]uch misuse cannot be presumed, and it rests with the party who states that there has been such misuse to prove its statement'.

[134] (1930) PCIJ Ser A No 24, 12. Also *Free Zones of Upper Savoy and the District of Gex* (1932) PCIJ Ser A/B No 46, 94, 167; *Electricity Company of Sofia and Bulgaria* (1939) PCIJ Ser A/B No 77, 98 (Judge Anzilotti); *Conditions of Admission of a State to Membership in the United Nations (Article 4 of Charter),* ICJ Reports 1948 p 57, 79 (Judge Azevedo, diss); *Admissibility of Hearings of Petitioners by the Committee on South West Africa,* ICJ Reports 1955 p 65, 120 (Judge Lauterpacht).

[135] Lauterpacht, *Development* (1958) 164. Also Verzijl, 1 *International Law in Historical Perspective* (1968) 316–20.

[136] *Trail Smelter* (1941) 9 ILR 315.

eral the question is whether the exercise of a state power or privilege is dependent on the presence of certain objectives. The presumption in the case of acts prima facie lawful is that motive is irrelevant, but the law may provide otherwise. When the criteria of good faith, reasonableness, normal administration, and so on are provided by an existing legal rule, reference to 'abuse of rights' adds nothing. Similarly, in the case of international organizations, responsibility for excess of authority, *détournement de pouvoir*, exists independently of any general principle of abuse of rights. In conclusion while the doctrine is a useful agent in the progressive development of the law as a general principle, it is not part of positive international law. Indeed it is doubtful if it could be safely recognized as an ambulatory doctrine, since it would encourage doctrines as to the relativity of rights and would result, outside the judicial forum, in instability.

5. CIRCUMSTANCES PRECLUDING WRONGFULNESS[137]

Circumstances precluding wrongfulness are 'excuses', 'defences', and 'exceptions', that is, justifications available to states which exclude responsibility when it would otherwise be engaged. After much refinement and debate, the ILC included in ARSIWA five types of circumstances precluding wrongfulness: these are consent (Article 20), self-defence (Article 21), countermeasures (Article 22), *force majeure* (Article 23), distress (Article 24), and necessity (Article 25). These classifications however, are conventional and not entirely logical; the very presence of this section has been criticized as being outside the scope of the Articles, since some of the circumstances—notably consent and self-defence—seem more akin to 'primary' rules, which define the content of obligations than to 'secondary' ones.[138]

The existence of a separate category for 'defences' should imply a legal burden of proof on the proponents of defences, and some adjudicating organs, such as the WTO Appellate Body, have instituted complex procedural rules. In *EC—Tariff Preferences*, it said:

In cases where one provision permits, in certain circumstances, behaviour that would otherwise be inconsistent with an obligation in another provision, and one of the two provisions refers to the other provision, the Appellate Body has found that the complaining party bears the burden of establishing that a challenged measure is inconsistent with the provision permitting particular behaviour only where one of the provisions suggests that the obligation is not applicable to the said measure. Otherwise, the permissive provision has been

---

[137] ARSIWA, Arts 20–5 & commentary. Szurek, in Crawford, Pellet & Olleson (2010) 427, 475, 481; Ben Mansour, ibid, 439; Ménard, ibid, 449; Thouvenin, ibid, 455; Lesaffre, ibid, 469; Heathcote, 491. Also: Alland, in Spinedi & Simma (1987) 143; Malanczuk, ibid, 197; Salmon, ibid, 235; Elagab, *The Legality of Non-forcible Counter-Measures in International Law* (1988); Thirlway (1995) 66 *BY* 1, 70–80.

[138] Christakis, in *Droit du pouvoir, pouvoir du droit* (2007) 223.

characterized as an exception, or defence, and the onus of invoking it and proving the consistency of the measure with its requirements has been placed on the responding party.[139]

But this is not always the case. In international law the incidence of the burden of proof is not simply dependent on a claimant-respondent relation as assumed in systems of municipal law.[140] When cases are submitted to courts through a *compromis*, neither of the parties can be considered respondent—and often both make affirmative claims. Moreover, defences such as extinctive prescription and consent (acquiescence or waiver) may be considered as issues of admissibility or may be reserved to the merits. In general the rule is *actori incumbit probatio* (he who asserts a proposition must prove it).

Tribunals accept defences of voluntary assumption of risk[141] and contributory fault.[142] *Force majeure*[143] will apply to acts of war[144] and, under certain conditions, to harm caused by insurrection and civil war.[145] It has been doubted whether necessity exists as an omnibus category, and in any event its availability as a defence is circumscribed by rigorous conditions. While necessity has been argued before a number of tribunals in a diversity of situations, its recognition as a possibility is usually followed by a denial of its applicability. This was so both before arbitral tribunals, in the *Neptune*[146] and *Russian Indemnity*,[147] and before courts, in *Gabčíkovo-Nagymaros Project*[148] and in *M/V Saiga (No 2)*.[149] In *LG&E Energy Corp. v Argentina*, the tribunal affirmed that necessity 'should be only strictly exceptional and should be applied exclusively when faced with extraordinary circumstances'.[150]

In particular contexts in the law of armed conflict, military necessity may be pleaded, and the right of angary allows requisition of ships belonging to aliens lying within the jurisdiction in time of war or other public danger.[151] The use of force in self-defence, collective self-defence, and defence of third states now involves a specific legal regime, though it related in the past to the ambulatory principle of self-preservation. Armed

---

[139] *EC—Tariff Preferences*, WTO Doc WT/DS246/AB/R, 7 April 2004, §88. Also: *EC—Hormones*, WTO Doc WT/DS26/AB/R & WT/DS48/AB/R, 16 January 1998, §104; *Brazil—Aircraft*, WTO Doc WT/DS46/AB/R, 2 August 1999, §§139–41; *EC—Sardines*, WTO Doc WT/DS231/AB/R, 26 September 2002, §275.

[140] Lauterpacht (1958) 363–7.

[141] *Home Missionary Society* (1920) 6 RIAA 42. Cf *Yukon Lumber* (1913) 6 RIAA 17, 20. Also Brownlie, in *Festschrift für FA Mann* (1977) 309.

[142] *Davis* (1903) 9 RIAA 460; Salmon, in 3 *International Law at the Time of Its Codification* (1987) 371; Bederman (1989) 30 *Va JIL* 335.

[143] UN Secretariat Study, ST/LEG/13, 27 June 1977; *Rainbow Warrior (New Zealand v France)* (1990) 82 ILR 499, 551–5.

[144] *American Electric and Manufacturing Co* (1905) 9 RIAA 145; *Russian Indemnity* (1912) 11 RIAA 421, 443; *Lighthouses* (1956) 23 ILR 354. Cf *Kelley* (1930) 4 RIAA 608; *Chevreau* (1931) 2 RIAA 1113, 1123.

[145] *Spanish Zone of Morocco* (1925) 2 RIAA 615, 642.

[146] Moore, 4 *Int Arb* 3843.

[147] (1912) 12 RIAA 44.

[148] ICJ Reports 1997 p 7, 46.

[149] (1999) 120 ILR 143.

[150] (2007) 46 ILM 40, 228. Also *CMS Gas Transmission Company v Argentina* (2005) 44 ILM 1205, 1243.

[151] McNair, 3 *Opinions* 398.

reprisals are clearly excluded by the law of the UN Charter, but the propriety of economic reprisals and the plea of economic necessity is still a matter of controversy.[152]

Finally, the increase in the number of multilateral treaties and the emergence of a diversity of treaty regimes in past decades means that specialized courts may consider themselves unable to examine an argument based on a rule outside their domain of competence. This is particularly the case when the circumstance argued is the application of general countermeasures before a specialized tribunal. In *Mexico—Soft Drinks*, Mexico claimed that its WTO-inconsistent measures were in fact countermeasures necessary to secure compliance by the US with its NAFTA obligations. The WTO Appellate Body rejected this argument, affirming the impossibility for WTO adjudicative organs 'to assess whether the relevant international agreement has been violated'.[153] Even a tribunal considering an argument based on its own treaty regime may consider that a circumstance precluding wrongfulness in not applicable with regard to a third party. In *Cargill, Inc v Mexico*, the tribunal affirmed that '[c]ountermeasures may not preclude the wrongfulness of an act in breach of obligations owed to third States [and] would not necessarily have any such effect with regard to *nationals* of the offending State, rather than to the offending State itself'.[154]

---

[152] Zoller, *Peacetime Unilateral Remedies* (1984); Elagab (1988).

[153] *Mexico—Soft Drinks*, WTO Doc WT/DS308/AB/R, 6 March 2006, §78.

[154] *Cargill v Mexico* (2009) 146 ILR 643, 764. Also: *Archer Daniels Midland Co and Tate & Lyle v Mexico* (2007) 146 ILR 440, 498–500; *Corn Products International v Mexico* (2008) 146 ILR 581, 627–9.

26

CONSEQUENCES OF AN INTERNATIONALLY WRONGFUL ACT

1. INTRODUCTION

In the event of an internationally wrongful act by a state or other subject of international law, other states or subjects may be entitled to respond. This may be done by invoking the responsibility of the wrongdoer, seeking cessation and/or reparation, or (if no other remedy is available) possibly by taking countermeasures. Cessation and reparation are dealt with in Part Two of the ILC's 2001 Articles on Responsibility of States for Internationally Wrongful Acts (ARSIWA),[1] whereas countermeasures are dealt with in Part Three. There are important differences between them: cessation and reparation are obligations which arise by operation of law on the commission of an internationally wrongful act, whereas countermeasures (if available at all) are an ultimate remedy which an injured state may take after efforts to obtain cessation and reparation have failed. They are responsive not just to the breach as such but to the responsible state's failure to fulfil its secondary obligations, which is why they are dealt with in Part Three on invocation.

Not all states are entitled to respond to all breaches. For example in bilateral relations (e.g. as between the parties to a bilateral treaty) only the parties are presumed to have rights, including standing to object. But not all legal relations are bilateral and that holds also for responsibility relations. This too is the subject-matter of Part Three on invocation.[2]

---

[1] Appended to GA Res 56/83, 12 December 2001.
[2] For analysis of ARSIWA on this point see Crawford, in Fastenrath et al (eds), *From Bilateralism to Community Interest: Essays in Honour of Judge Bruno Simma* (2011) 224.

2. CESSATION, REPARATION, INVOCATION

The consequences of international responsibility must be treated with care. They raise substantial issues as to the character of responsibility and are far from being a mere appendix. While the systems of responsibility developed within municipal legal systems may be helpful by way of analogy, in the sphere of international relations there are important elements, including the rules as to satisfaction, which might seem out of place in the law of tort and contract in common law systems, or in the law of obligations in civil law jurisdictions.

The terminology adopted here largely follows that of the ILC Articles of 2001, with some additions. The term 'breach of an international obligation' denotes an unlawful act or omission. 'Damage' denotes loss, *damnum*, usually a financial quantification of physical or economic injury or damage or of other consequences of such a breach. 'Cessation' refers to the basic obligation of compliance with international law, which in principle remains due in spite of any breaches. Cessation is required, not as a means of reparation but as an independent obligation, whenever the obligation in question continues to exist. 'Reparation' will be used to refer to all measures which may be expected from the responsible state, over and above cessation: it includes restitution, compensation, and satisfaction. 'Restitution' refers to restitution in kind, a withdrawal of the wrongful measure or the return of persons or assets seized illegally. While restitution and cessation may sometimes overlap—for example, in the case of release of an individual detained unlawfully—they remain conceptually distinct. 'Compensation' will be used to describe reparation in the narrow sense of the payment of money in the measure of the wrong done. The award of compensation sometimes described as 'moral' or 'political' reparation, terms connected with concepts of 'moral' and 'political' injury, creates confusion. 'Injury' arises from a breach of a *legal* duty and in such cases the only special feature is the absence of a neat method of quantifying loss. 'Satisfaction' refers to means of redressing a wrong other than by restitution or compensation. It may take a variety of forms, including an apology, trial and punishment of the individuals responsible, taking steps to prevent a recurrence of the breach, etc.

Underlying this way of looking at the problem are certain basic propositions about international responsibility (and about states as the primary subjects of responsibility). First, international responsibility is undifferentiated: just as custom and treaty are alternative (and even complementary) ways of generating obligation, so there is no difference in principle between responsibility arising, so to speak, *ex contractu* or *ex delicto*.[3] For a state party to the UN Convention on the Law of the Sea (UNCLOS), the obligation to allow innocent passage through the territorial sea arises by treaty; for the US as a non-party, it arises under general international law. Materially the obligations

---

[3] The distinction, associated with the topic of 'crimes of state', was debated by the ILC since the 1976 draft, but excluded from the final version. Crawford, ILC *Ybk* 1998/II(1), 9–23; Crawford, in Crawford, Pellet & Olleson (eds), *The Law of International Responsibility* (2010) 17. For earlier literature see also Weiler, Cassese & Spinedi, *International Crimes of State* (1989). Further: chapter 27.

are indistinguishable and it would be odd if a wholly different regime of responsibility applied to one as compared with the other.[4] Secondly, the regime of responsibility is undifferentiated also in the sense that it applies to the whole array of obligations under international law. There is no *a priori* limit to the content of international obligations, which can range from rules about navigation of submarines to the protection of the ozone layer.[5] In both cases, the primary point of having the rule is to ensure perform-ance; the responsible state is not simply given an option to perform or pay (perhaps unquantifiable) damages. International law fulfils the function both of a public law system regulating shared resources (such as the oceans or the atmosphere) and a pri-vate law system covering bilateral (e.g. diplomatic) relations.[6]

Thirdly, and as a corollary, the function of reparation is, as far as possible, the resto-ration of relations reflected in the *status quo ante*. In *Factory at Chorzów (Merits)*, the Permanent Court declared that:

The essential principle contained in the actual notion of an illegal act...is that reparation must, as far as possible, wipe out all the consequences of the illegal act and re-establish the situation which would, in all probability, have existed if that act had not been committed. Restitution in kind, or, if this is not possible, payment of a sum corresponding to the value which a restitution in kind would bear; the award, if need be, of damages for loss sustained which would not be covered by restitution in kind or payment in place of it—such are the principles which should serve to determine the amount of compensation due for an act con-trary to international law.[7]

That was a claim for breach of a bilateral treaty having as its aim the protection of the interests of the claimant state. It is to be distinguished from the type of case in which the individual state is seeking to establish *locus standi* in order to protect legal interests not identifiable with itself alone or possibly with any state in particular. In stand-ard cases, a state protects its own legal interests in seeking reparation for damage—material or otherwise—suffered by itself or its citizens. As put by ITLOS in *M/V Saiga (No 2)*:

It is a well-established rule of international law that a State which suffers damage as a result of an internationally wrongful act by another State is entitled to obtain reparation for the damage suffered from the State which committed the wrongful act and that 'reparation must, as far as possible, wipe out all the consequences of the illegal act and reestablish the situation which would, in all probability, have existed if that act had not been committed'.[8]

This is complemented, in the case of injury suffered by nationals, by the rule, enunci-ated by the Permanent Court in *Mavrommatis*, that '[b]y taking up the case of one of its subjects and by resorting to diplomatic action or international judicial proceedings

---

[4] ARSIWA, Art 12 & commentary. This does not, of course, prevent states from designing particular regimes of responsibility by treaty: ARSIWA, Art 55 & commentary.

[5] *SS Wimbledon* (1923) PCIJ Ser A No 1, 25.

[6] See Simma (1994) 250 Hague *Recueil* 217, 229–55.

[7] (1928) PCIJ Ser A No 17, 47.

[8] (1999) 120 ILR 143, 199, citing *Factory at Chorzów (Merits)* (1928) PCIJ Ser A No 17, 47.

on his behalf, a State is in reality asserting its own rights—its right to ensure, in the person of its subjects, respect for the rules of international law'.[9] But there are also cases where states seek to vindicate collective or innominate interests, for example, in the field of human rights or the environment. A different rule, expressed by the International Court in its famous dictum in *Barcelona Traction*, applies to these cases: '[i]n view of the importance of the rights involved, all States can be held to have a legal interest in their protection'.[10] In practice, it may be difficult to apply reparation to interstate cases in which the obligations violated protect a community interest. The principle of full reparation applies generally, but the law has to take account of the entire range of possibilities.[11] In many cases claimants will focus on cessation and redress to the individuals affected, or on remediation of environmental harm, without seeking reparation for themselves.[12]

3. THE FORMS OF REPARATION[13]

(A) RESTITUTION IN KIND AND *RESTITUTIO IN INTEGRUM*[14]

To achieve the object of reparation tribunals may give 'legal restitution', in the form of a declaration that an offending act of the executive, legislature or judicature is unlawful and without international effect.[15] Such action can be classified either as a genuine application of the principle of *restitutio in integrum* or as an aspect of satisfaction. Restitution in kind is a logical means of repairing an injury. Customary law or treaty may create obligations to which is annexed a power to demand specific restitution. Thus in *Chorzów Factory* the Permanent Court took the view that, the purpose of

---

[9] *Mavrommatis Palestine Concessions* (1924) PCIJ Ser A No 2, 12.

[10] *Barcelona Traction, Light and Power Company, Limited (Belgium v Spain)*, ICJ Reports 1970 p 3, 32.

[11] Further: Tomuschat (1993) 241 Hague *Recueil* 209, 353–68; Crawford (2006) 319 Hague *Recueil* 325, 421–51.

[12] Tams, *Enforcing Obligations* Erga Omnes *in International Law* (2005); Gaja, in Crawford, Pellet & Olleson (2010) 941; Vaurs-Chaumette, ibid, 1023.

[13] Generally: Eagleton (1929) 39 *Yale LJ* 52; Whiteman, *Damages in International Law* (1937–43); García Amador, ILC *Ybk* 1961/II, 2–45; Bollecker-Stern, *Le Préjudice dans la théorie de la responsabilité internationale* (1973); Gray, *Judicial Remedies in International Law* (1987); Shelton (2002) 96 *AJIL* 833; ARSIWA, Art 34 & commentary; and the essays in Crawford, Pellet & Olleson (2010) part IV, section 1.

[14] Baade (1960) 54 *AJIL* 801, 814–30; García Amador, ILC *Ybk* 1961/II, 17–18; Wortley (1961) 55 *AJIL* 680; Jiménez de Aréchaga (1978) 159 Hague *Recueil* 1, 285–6; Schachter (1982) 178 Hague *Recueil* 9, 190–1; Gray (1987) 95–6. Also ARSIWA, Art 35 & commentary; Gray, in Crawford, Pellet & Olleson (2010) 599.

[15] Such action has become important in the jurisprudence of the IACtHR. E.g. *Barrios Altos v Peru* IACtHR C/75, 14 March 2001, §51. Also: *Almonacid Arellano v Chile*, IACtHR C/154, 26 September 2006; *Gomes Lund v Brazil*, IACtHR C/219, 24 November 2010. On a similar trend in the ECtHR: Nifosi-Sutton (2010) 23 *Harv HRJ* 52. Outside human rights law this is unusual, but see *Martini* (1930) 2 RIAA 975, 1002. Also: McNair, 1 *Opinions* 78; *Barcelona Traction*, Preliminary Objections, ICJ Reports 1964 p 6; *Barcelona Traction*, Second Phase, ICJ Reports 1970 p 4; *South West Africa (Ethiopia v South Africa; Liberia v South Africa)*, Second Phase, ICJ Reports 1966 p 3, 32 (with particular reference to the apartheid laws).

the Geneva Convention of 1922 being to maintain the economic status quo in Polish Upper Silesia, restitution was the 'natural redress' for violation of or failure to observe the treaty provisions.[16] In imposing obligations on aggressor states to make reparation for the results of illegal occupation, the victims may be justified in requiring restitution of 'objects of artistic, historical or archaeological value belonging to the cultural heritage of the [retro]ceded territory'.[17] It would seem that territorial disputes may also be settled by specific restitution, although the declaratory form of judgments of the International Court often masks the element of restitution.[18]

Apart from express treaty provisions, restitution in kind, that is, specific restitution, is exceptional; the vast majority of claims conventions and agreements to submit to arbitration provide for the adjudication of pecuniary claims only.[19] Writers[20] and, from time to time, governments and tribunals[21] assert a right to specific restitution, sometimes quoting the *Chorzów Factory* dictum. The International Court reaffirmed in *Pulp Mills* that 'customary international law provides for restitution as one form of reparation for injury, restitution being the re-establishment of the situation which existed before occurrence of the wrongful act'.[22] But, while this form of redress has a place in the law, it is difficult to state with any certainty the conditions of its application, outside of cases in which it is provided for explicitly.

In *Rainbow Warrior*, New Zealand demanded the return to custody of two individuals released from detention by the French government in violation of a previous settlement. The tribunal understood that this was a case of cessation, and not of restitution, and went on to find that cessation could not be granted on the implausible ground that the unfulfilled obligation to detain had expired in the meantime.[23]

Tribunals should avoid encouraging the purchase of impunity by the payment of damages; specific restitution will be appropriate in certain cases. At the same time,

---

[16] (1927) PCIJ Ser A No 8, 28. Cf *Italy v FRG* (1959) 29 ILR 442, 474–6; *Amoco International Finance v Iran* (1987) 83 ILR 500.

[17] Italian Peace Treaty, 10 February 1947, 49 UNTS 3, Arts 12, 37, 78, Annex XIV, §4; cf *Franco-Ethiopian Railway Co* (1957) 24 ILR 602. Further: part III of the Agreement on Reparation from Germany, on the Establishment of an Inter-Allied Reparation Agency and on the Restitution of Monetary Gold, 14 January 1945, 555 UNTS 70, §A.

[18] *Legal Status of Eastern Greenland* (1933) PCIJ Ser A/B No 53; *Temple of Preah Vihear (Cambodia v Thailand)*, ICJ Reports 1961 p 17. In the latter the Court found *inter alia* that Thailand was obliged to restore to Cambodia any sculpture, stelae, fragments of monuments, and pottery which might have been removed by the Thai authorities. In fact nothing was shown to have been removed and Cambodia did not press the point at the time.

[19] Also General Act for the Pacific Settlement of International Disputes, 26 September 1928, 93 LNTS 342, Art 32; Revised General Act, 28 April 1949, 71 UNTS 101, Arts 1, 17.

[20] Especially: Mann (1977) 48 *BY* 1, 2–5; Verzijl, 6 *International Law in Historical Perspective* (1973) 742.

[21] *Walter Fletcher Smith* (1927) 2 RIAA 913, 918; *Greece v Bulgaria (Treaty of Neuilly)* (1933) 7 ILR 91, 99. In these two awards restitution was not considered appropriate for practical reasons. Cf *Interhandel (Switzerland v US)*, ICJ Reports 1959 p 6. Also: *BP Exploration Company (Libya) Ltd v Libyan Arab Republic* (1973) 53 ILR 297 (*restitutio in integrum* not favoured); *Texaco v Libyan Arab Republic* (1977) 53 ILR 389 (*restitutio* affirmed as a principle); *LIAMCO v Libyan Arab Republic* (1982) 62 ILR 140 (*restitutio* not favoured).

[22] *Pulp Mills on the River Uruguay (Argentina v Uruguay)*, 20 April 2010, §273.

[23] (1990) 20 RIAA 215, 268–71.

in many situations it may be clear that a remedy which accommodates the internal competence of governments while giving redress to those adversely affected is to be preferred: restitution is too inflexible. ARSIWA Article 35 includes a proviso whereby restitution is only due if it 'does not involve a burden out of proportion to the benefit deriving from restitution instead of compensation'. Two examples from the jurisprudence of the International Court illustrate the difficulty. In *Arrest Warrant of 11 April 2000 (Democratic Republic of the Congo v Belgium)*, the Court recognized that a mere declaration of unlawfulness under international law would be insufficient, and considered that Belgium was under an obligation to cancel the arrest warrant issued illegally.[24] In *Avena and Other Mexican Nationals (Mexico v US)*, however, the Court rejected a request to order the cancellation of the death sentences passed without consular notification or assistance. It merely established that the US was under an obligation to provide means for review and reconsideration of sentences issued in violation of the Vienna Convention on Consular Relations.[25] In the latter case, the difficulties faced by the federal executive in the American political system had already generated non-compliance with the provisional measures ordered by the Court.[26] These difficulties would only be confirmed in the US Supreme Court decision in *Medellín v Texas*.[27]

(B) COMPENSATION, DAMAGES[28]

Pecuniary compensation is usually an appropriate and often the only remedy for injury caused by an unlawful act. Under ARSIWA Article 36 whenever restitution is not possible compensation becomes the standard consequence for injury, covering 'any financially assessable damage including loss of profits'. This is consistent with the long-standing jurisprudence of international courts, tribunals, and claims commissions. In its judgment in *Gabčíkovo-Nagymaros Project*, the Court reaffirmed the 'well-established rule of international law that an injured State is entitled to obtain compensation from the State which has committed an internationally wrongful act for the damage caused by it'.[29]

Applying compensation is straightforward enough in the case of material damages, whether to a state or to its nationals. Starting with the commissions under the 1794 Jay Treaty, claims commissions and arbitral tribunals have been established by treaty to

---

[24] ICJ Reports 2002 p 3, 32.

[25] ICJ Reports 2004 p 12, 60, 72.

[26] ICJ Reports 2003 p 77.

[27] (2008) 552 US 491, 525: '[t]he President has an array of political and diplomatic means available to enforce international obligations, but unilaterally converting a non-self-executing treaty into a self-executing one is not among them. The responsibility for transforming an international obligation arising from a non-self-executing treaty into domestic law falls to Congress'. See Charnovitz (2008) 102 *AJIL* 551.

[28] Further: Salvioli (1929) 28 Hague *Recueil* 231, 235–86; Yntema (1924) 24 *Col LR* 134. Gattini (2002) 13 *EJIL* 161; Shelton, *Remedies in International Human Rights Law* (2005); Marboe, *Calculation of Compensation and Damages in International Investment Law* (2009); Barker, in Crawford, Pellet & Olleson (2010) 599.

[29] ICJ Reports 1997 p 7, 81. Also *M/V Saiga (No 2)* (1999) 120 ILR 143, 199. *Chorzów Factory* (1928) PCIJ Ser A No 17, 47.

rule on claims and determine the extent of damages following situations of conflict.[30] Although the International Court has seldom awarded damages,[31] their jurisprudence has served as a basis both for lump sum agreements[32] and for awards by other international bodies, such as the Iran–US Claims Tribunal,[33] the UN Compensation Commission,[34] and the Eritrea–Ethiopia Claims Commission.[35] The burgeoning jurisprudence of investment tribunals deals almost exclusively with claims for pecuniary compensation.[36]

When it comes to quantifying damages, international tribunals face the same problems as other tribunals as regards indirect damage and deal with the issues in much the same way.[37] The particular context of and the mode of breach, may determine the approach to damages.[38] While problems of causation may present particular theoretical difficulties,[39] ARSIWA pragmatically avoids the issue, leaving specific determinations to the particularities of each case. This is consistent with the practice, for, even if tribunals are often obscure in this respect, there is a close connection between 'remoteness' and 'measure of damages', on the one hand, and substantive rules on the other.

One nonetheless finds important similarities in the reasoning of adjudicators. In *LG&E v Argentina*, an ICSID Tribunal considered that the appropriate amount of damages, given the 'economic collapse that affected all assets in the country', was that of which Argentina's conduct was the 'proximate cause'.[40] The same standard was used by the Eritrea–Ethiopia Claims Commission when deciding which damages to consider as connected with the violation of *ius ad bellum* by Eritrea. While observing that other criteria ('any direct injury' and damage 'reasonably foreseeable') had been used in the past,[41] the Commission noted that if:

a State initiating a conflict through a breach of the *jus ad bellum* is liable under international law for a wide range of ensuing consequences, the initiating State will bear extensive liability

---

[30] For a summary of their work: Gray (1987) 5–58.

[31] Ibid, 77 (*Wimbledon*), 83 (*Corfu Channel*); *Ahmadou Sadio Diallo (Guinea v Democratic Republic of the Congo)*, Compensation, Judgment of 19 June 2012, §56 (where the Court took account of post-judgment interest). Damages are reserved in *Armed Activities on the Territory of the Congo (Democratic Republic of the Congo v Uganda)*, ICJ Reports 2005 p 168, 257, were refused in *Fisheries Jurisdiction (Federal Republic of Germany v Iceland)*, ICJ Reports 1974 p 175, 204, and *Land and Maritime Boundary between Cameroon and Nigeria*, ICJ Reports 2002 p 303, 450–3, and were netted off in *Gabčíkovo-Nagymaros Project (Hungary/Slovakia)*, ICJ Reports 1997 p 7, 81 (where the Court usefully distinguished debt from damages).

[32] Lillich & Weston (1988) 82 *AJIL* 69.

[33] Drahozal & Gibson (eds), *The Iran–US Claims Tribunal at 25* (2007).

[34] Heiskanen (2002) 296 Hague *Recueil* 255.

[35] Gray (2006) 17 *EJIL* 699; Matheson (2010) 9 *LPICT* 1.

[36] Crawford (2010) 25 *ICSID Rev-FILJ* 127.

[37] Cheng, *General Principles of Law as Applied by International Courts and Tribunals* (1994) 233–40.

[38] Dix (1903) 9 RIAA 119, 121, and cf Jennings (1961) 37 *BY* 156; Salvioli (1929) 28 Hague *Recueil* 231, 268. On causation see also Cheng (1994) 241–53.

[39] Bollecker-Stern (1973) 177–359.

[40] 25 July 2007, §50, available at www.italaw.com.

[41] *Decision No 7: Guidance Regarding Jus Ad Bellum Liability* (2007) 26 RIAA 1, 12–15.

whether or not its actions respect the *jus in bello*... Imposing extensive liability for conduct that does not violate the *jus in bello* risks eroding the weight and authority of that law and the incentive to comply with it, to the injury of those it aims to protect.[42]

Both tribunals seem to have had in mind the need to adjust the amount of compensation in such a way that it fits the wrongful conduct. Outside of the few cases of objective liability,[43] it may be that the rule is simply that if harm is caused by wrongful or negligent conduct, whether or not in the course of lawful activity, then compensation is payable. The scale of compensation in cases of lawful activity may be less ambitious than that applicable to activity unlawful at birth, such as unprovoked attacks or unlawful expropriations. In *SD Myers, Inc v Canada*, the tribunal went to great pains to identify the proportion of the losses suffered by the claimant which were in fact connected with the period in which Canada was in breach of its NAFTA obligations.[44]

There is some debate as to the possibility of 'punitive' or 'penal' damages in international law.[45] The problem concerns in part the granting of compensation for breach of legal duties without actual damage, for example by unlawful but temporary intrusion into the territory or airspace of another state. The award of compensation in such cases is sometimes described as 'penal damages',[46] but this is incorrect: their characterization by the ILC as 'moral damages' is more accurate.[47] Fitzmaurice expressed the view that any breach of treaty entails the payment of 'some damages... irrespective of whether the breach has caused any actual material damage or pecuniary loss'.[48] However, tribunals are cautious in approaching cases of non-material loss, and there is no simple solution to the problem of valuation of such losses.

In *Janes* the US presented a claim based on a failure by Mexico to take adequate steps to apprehend the murderer of an American citizen.[49] The award approached compensation in terms of the damage caused to the individuals concerned rather than to the US,[50] and gave compensation to the relatives of Janes for the 'indignity' caused by the non-punishment of the criminal.[51] However, the US was only claiming 'on behalf of' Janes' dependants, and the only concern of the Claims Commission was one of valuation rather than ascription. Although the practice of awarding 'nominal' or 'token' damages was once common,[52] violations of national honour or dignity will nowadays

---

[42] *Final Award—Eritrea's Damages* (2009) 26 RIAA 505, 600–1.

[43] E.g. damage caused by space objects: chapter 25.

[44] (2002) 8 ICSID Reports 3.

[45] Eagleton (1929) 39 *Yale LJ* 52; García Amador, ILC *Ybk* 1956/II, 211–12; Jorgensen (1998) 68 *BY* 247; Wittich, in Crawford, Pellet & Olleson (2010) 667.

[46] *Lusitania* (1924) 18 *AJIL* 361, 368; *Moke* (1868), in Moore, 4 *Int Arb* 3411. Also: Cheng (1994) 235–8; Gray (1987) 26–8.

[47] ARSIWA, Arts 31, 36, with commentary.

[48] (1936) 17 *BY* 82, 109.

[49] (1925) 4 RIAA 82.

[50] General Claims Convention (US–Mexico), 8 September 1923, 6 RIAA 7, Art 1.

[51] *Janes* (1925) 4 RIAA 82, 89.

[52] Gray (1987) 28–9.

often be dealt with by satisfaction, agreed with the responsible state or awarded by a tribunal in the form of a declaratory judgment.[53]

(C) SATISFACTION[54]

(i) The role of satisfaction

Satisfaction may be defined as any measure which the responsible state is bound to take under customary law or under an agreement by the parties to a dispute, apart from restitution or compensation. Satisfaction is an aspect of reparation in the broad sense. However, it is not easy to distinguish between pecuniary satisfaction and compensation in the case of breaches of duty not resulting in death, personal injuries, or damage to or loss of property. Claims of this sort are commonly expressed as a claim for an 'indemnity', which may create confusion. If there is a distinction between this and a claim for compensation, it would seem to be in the intention behind the demand. If it is predominantly that of seeking a token of regret and acknowledgement of wrongdoing then it is a matter of satisfaction.

Satisfaction may take many forms, which may be cumulative: apologies or other acknowledgement of wrongdoing by means of a payment of an indemnity or a (somewhat outmoded) salute to the flag; the trial and punishment of the individuals concerned, or the taking of measures to prevent a recurrence of the harm. In the *I'm Alone* the Canadian government complained of the sinking on the high seas of a liquor-smuggling vessel of Canadian registration by a US coastguard vessel, as the climax to a hot pursuit which commenced outside US territorial waters but within the inspection zone provided for in the 'Liquor Treaty' between Great Britain and the US.[55] The Canadian claim was referred to Commissioners who reported that the ship 'although a British ship of Canadian registry, was *de facto* owned, controlled, and at the critical times, managed... by a group of persons acting in concert who were entirely, or nearly so, citizens of the United States, and who employed her for the purposes mentioned [i.e. smuggling alcohol] ... [I]n view of the facts, no compensation ought to be paid in respect of the loss of the ship or the cargo'.[56] However the sinking having been unlawful, the Commissioners recommended

---

[53] See also the ruling of the Secretary-General in *Rainbow Warrior* (1986) 74 ILR 241, 271, determining US$7 million in compensation as a middle-ground solution between the amounts proposed by France and New Zealand. In the subsequent arbitration, New Zealand did not claim damages, and the tribunal did not award any sum by way of compensation. However, the tribunal did recommend the setting up of a joint fund to promote friendly relations and the making of an initial monetary payment by France: *Rainbow Warrior (New Zealand v France)* (1990) 20 RIAA 215, 272, 274–5. This was paid.

[54] Wyler & Papaux, in Crawford, Pellet & Olleson (2010) 623; ARSIWA, Art 37 & commentary. Further: Bissonnette, *La Satisfaction comme mode de réparation en droit international* (1952); Przetacznik (1974) 78 *RGDIP* 919, 944–74.

[55] (1933) 7 ILR 203.

[56] Ibid, 206.

that the United States ought formally to acknowledge its illegality, and to apologize to His Majesty's Canadian Government therefor; and, further, that as a material amend in respect of the wrong the United States should pay the sum of $25,000 to His Majesty's Canadian Government...[57]

This approach was taken up by the Secretary-General in his ruling on the *Rainbow Warrior* affair. The vessel destroyed belonged to Greenpeace, a Dutch NGO, but its destruction by French agents in the port of Auckland was a violation of New Zealand's sovereignty. Besides ordering compensation, the Secretary-General ruled 'that the Prime Minister of France should convey to the Prime Minister of New Zealand a formal and unqualified apology for the attack, contrary to international law, on the Rainbow Warrior by French service agents'.[58] New Zealand also demanded that the two agents responsible, who had been imprisoned after trial in New Zealand, be kept in custody if returned to France. The Secretary-General ruled that these agents 'should be transferred to a French military facility on an isolated island outside of Europe for a period of three years ... [and] prohibited from leaving the island for any reason, except with the mutual consent of the two Governments'.[59]

Thus various modalities of satisfaction continue to be used in modern state practice, and this is reflected in ARSIWA Article 37 and its commentary.

A number of ancillary questions remain. It is sometimes suggested that an affront to the honour of a state or intention to harm are preconditions for a demand for satisfaction, but this is very doubtful. Such elements may enter into the assessment of compensation, as also may the failure to undertake measures to prevent a recurrence of the harm or to punish those responsible. Measures demanded by way of apology should today take forms which are not humiliating and excessive.[60] There is no evidence of a rule that satisfaction is alternative to and, on being given, exclusive of a right to compensation for the breach (parties to a dispute may, of course, agree otherwise).

(ii) Declaratory judgments[61]

In some cases a declaration by a court as to the illegality of the act of the defendant state constitutes a measure of satisfaction (or reparation in the broad sense). However, international tribunals may give a declaratory judgment in cases where this is the appropriate and constructive method of dealing with a dispute and the object is not

---

[57] Ibid. Also *Manouba* (1913) 11 RIAA 471, 475; Hyde (1935) 29 *AJIL* 296; Fitzmaurice (1936) 17 *BY* 82; and for the *Panay* incident (1937): 5 Hackworth 687.

[58] (1986) 19 RIAA 199, 213.

[59] Ibid, 214.

[60] Cf Stowell, *Intervention in International Law* (1921) 21–35, on measures of 'expiation' demanded in the past. On the *Tellini* incident: Eagleton (1925) 19 *AJIL* 293, 304. ARSIWA, Art 47(3): '[s]atisfaction shall not be out of proportion to the injury and may not take a form humiliating to the responsible State'.

[61] Lauterpacht, *Development* (1958) 206, 250; de Visscher, *Aspects récents du droit procédural de la Cour internationale de justice* (1966) 187–94; Ritter (1975) 21 *AFDI* 278; Gray (1987) 96–107; Brownlie, *Essays in Honour of Sir Robert Jennings* (1996) 557.

primarily to give 'satisfaction' for a wrong received.[62] While the International Court is unwilling to deal with hypothetical issues and questions formulated in the abstract, the Permanent Court already established the practice of giving declaratory judgments,[63] and in some cases, for example those concerning title to territory, it found it appropriate to give a declaratory rather than an executory form to the judgment.[64] The applicant states in *South West Africa* were seeking a declaration that certain legislation affecting the territory was contrary to the obligations of South Africa under the Mandate.[65] In the *US Diplomatic and Consular Staff in Tehran,* the Court's judgment included several declaratory prescriptions concerning the termination of the unlawful detention of the persons concerned.[66] In *Nicaragua* the judgment contained an injunctive declaration 'that the United States is under a duty immediately to cease and refrain from all such acts as may constitute breaches of the foregoing legal obligations'.[67]

Sometimes it is difficult to separate neatly satisfaction through declaratory judgments from the Court's regular adjudicative function. In *Corfu Channel*, the International Court declared that the mine-sweeping operation by the Royal Navy in Albania's territorial waters was a violation of sovereignty, and then stated: '[t]his declaration is in accordance with the request made by Albania through her Counsel, and is in itself appropriate satisfaction'.[68] In spite of the terminology, this is not an instance of satisfaction in the usual meaning of the word: the declaration is that of a court and not a party, and is *alternative* to compensation.

In *Corfu Channel*, no pecuniary compensation had been asked for by Albania, and a judicial declaration was therefore the only means of giving an effective decision on this aspect of the matter.[69] But in *M/V Saiga (No 2)*, compensation was effectively sought. Saint Vincent and the Grenadines claimed damages not only for injury to the vessel flying its flag and its crew, but also for breach of its rights as the flag state. The tribunal, however, preferred to award damages for the former injuries, while considering that for the latter the declaration of illegality constituted adequate reparation.[70]

This was also the approach taken by the *Rainbow Warrior* tribunal. New Zealand argued that the appropriate reparation for the release of the two agents responsible for the bombing of the Rainbow Warrior—a breach by France of the 1986 Ruling of the

---

[62] *Arabian-American Oil Co v Saudi Arabia* (1963) 27 ILR 117, 144–6.

[63] *Mavrommatis* (1925) PCIJ Ser A No 5, 51; *Certain German Interests in Polish Upper Silesia* (1926) PCIJ Ser A No 7, 18; *Interpretation of Judgments Nos 7 and 8* (1927) PCIJ Ser A No 13, 20–1.

[64] *Eastern Greenland* (1933) PCIJ Ser A/B No 53, 23–4, 75.

[65] ICJ Reports 1962 p 319; ICJ Reports 1966 p 6.

[66] ICJ Reports 1980 p 3, 44–5.

[67] *Military and Paramilitary Activities in and against Nicaragua (Nicaragua v US)*, ICJ Reports 1986 p 14, 146–9. Also *Nuclear Tests (Australia v France)*, ICJ Reports 1974 p 253, 312–19 (Judges Onyeama, Dillard, Jiménez de Aréchaga & Sir Humphrey Waldock, joint diss).

[68] ICJ Reports 1949 p 4, 35. Also *Carthage* (1913) 11 RIAA 457, 460; *Manouba* (1913) 11 RIAA 471, 476; *Rainbow Warrior (New Zealand v France)* (1990) 82 ILR 499, 574–7.

[69] ICJ Reports 1949 p 4, 113–14 (Judge Azevedo, diss); *Aerial Incident of 27 July 1955 (Israel v Bulgaria)*, Preliminary Objections, ICJ Reports 1959 p 127, 129–31.

[70] *M/V Saiga (No 2)* (1999) 120 ILR 143, 200.

Secretary-General—was to return the two agents to custody. While considering that France had indeed violated its commitments, the tribunal merely

declare[d] that the condemnation of the French Republic for its breaches of its treaty obligations to New Zealand, made public by the decision of the Tribunal, constitutes in the circumstances appropriate satisfaction for the legal and moral damage caused to New Zealand ...[71]

In *Genocide (Bosnia and Herzegovina v Serbia and Montenegro)*, three findings of violations were considered to 'constitute appropriate satisfaction' to Bosnia and Herzegovina, since 'the case [was] not one in which an order for payment of compensation, or ... a direction to provide assurances and guarantees of non-repetition, would be appropriate'.[72] In these cases, the declaratory judgment would seem to be a way for the Court to provide to the injured party a form of satisfaction which does not depend on any action by the violator, when another type of reparation could risk re-igniting or aggravating a conflict.

(D) INTEREST[73]

Whenever compensation for a violation is due, the question arises whether interest should be paid, at what rate, and from which date. This is particularly relevant in cases where compensation is determined by adjudication, since exhausting local remedies, going through the adjudication process and obtaining the compensation may take considerable time. The right to award interest as part of compensation has been assumed by international tribunals in early decisions,[74] although in many cases interest was refused in the circumstances of the case.[75] More recent tribunals have been more willing to award interest including compound interest.[76]

Rates vary widely: sometimes a rate is agreed upon by contract or treaty; at other times tribunals will apply private international law rules and select a national rate; other options include applying general principles of international law or simply principles of fairness and reasonableness.[77] As for the date from which interest starts running, tribunals are not consistent either: it may be the date when the obligation became due and owing, the date of the violation or the date damages are awarded. Again, much depends on the circumstances: tribunals will often try to find a formula that is

---

[71] (1990) 20 RIAA 215, 275.

[72] *Application of the Convention on the Prevention and Punishment of the Crime of Genocide (Bosnia and Herzegovina v Serbia and Montenegro)*, ICJ Reports 2007 p 43, 239.

[73] ARSIWA, Art 37 & commentary. Further: Nevill (2007) 78 *BY* 255; Lauterpacht & Nevill, in Crawford, Pellet & Olleson (2010) 613–22.

[74] *Delagoa Bay Railway Company* (1900), in 3 Whiteman (1943) 1694, 1703; *Dix* (1903) 9 RIAA 119, 121; *Lindisfarne* (1913) 6 RIAA 21, 24; *Illinois Central Railroad Co* (1926) 4 RIAA 134, 136.

[75] *Montijo* (1875), in Moore, 2 *Int Arb* 1427; *Canadienne* (1914) 6 RIAA 29; *Pinson* (1928) 5 RIAA 327, 329.

[76] On compound interest: Nevill (2007) 78 *BY* 255, 307–29; *Ahmadou Sadio Diallo (Guinea v Democratic Republic of the Congo)*, Compensation, Judgment of 19 June 2012, §56.

[77] Gotanda (1996) 90 *AJIL* 40, 50–5.

not excessively punitive—although thereby running the risk of under-compensation and of rewarding delay in payment.[78]

(E) SERIOUS BREACHES OF PEREMPTORY NORMS: ARSIWA ARTICLES 40 AND 41

Although international rules may cover any topic, not all rules have the same salience. The debate on a hierarchy of norms is vast,[79] but few today would question the notion of obligations *erga omnes*. The International Court has noted that the obligations relating to the prevention and punishment of genocide,[80] requiring respect for the right to self-determination,[81] as well as relevant obligations determined by international humanitarian law,[82] constitute obligations of this kind. Likewise, peremptory norms have been a component of the international legal system since the 1969 Vienna Convention on the Law of Treaties (VCLT)[83] (although the International Court only dared to speak their name for the first time in 2006).[84] The existence of this superior normative rank entails the question of whether violations of these rules, and especially 'gross' violations of particularly important rules, warrant a different regime of responsibility than that which corresponds to other internationally wrongful acts. This was answered in the affirmative in the 1976 version of the Draft Articles on State Responsibility, adopted by the ILC following the proposals of Special Rapporteur Roberto Ago. Its Article 19(2) provided that 'the breach of an obligation so essential for the protection of fundamental interests of the international community' should be considered to constitute 'an international crime'.[85]

Ago never proposed any consequences to the aggravated responsibility regime, and it is not even clear that all 'crimes of state' would in his view have entailed a single, uniform set of consequences.[86] His initial statement on the issue of the aggravated regime was as follows: 'the responsibility flowing from the breach of those [*erga omnes*] obligations is entailed not only with regard to the State that has been the direct victim of the breach... it is also entailed with regard to all other members of the international community'.[87] This is certainly relevant to assess entitlement to invoke responsibility

---

[78] Fellmeth (2010) 13 *JIEL* 423.

[79] Weiler & Paulus (1997) 8 *EJIL* 545; Koskenniemi, ibid, 566; Salcedo, ibid, 583; Pauwelyn, *Conflict of Norms in Public International Law* (2003); Shelton (2006) 100 *AJIL* 291.

[80] *Genocide (Bosnia and Herzegovina v Serbia and Montenegro)*, Preliminary Objections, ICJ Reports 1996 p 595, 616.

[81] *East Timor (Portugal v Australia)*, ICJ Reports 1995 p 90, 102.

[82] *Legal Consequences of the Construction of a Wall in the Occupied Palestinian Territory*, ICJ Reports 2004 p 136, 199.

[83] 22 May 1969, 1155 UNTS 331.

[84] *Armed Activities (DRC v Rwanda)*, ICJ Reports 2006 p 6, 31–2, and see chapters 16, 27.

[85] ILC *Ybk* 1976/II(2), 95–6.

[86] Spinedi, in Weiler, Cassese & Spinedi (1989) 7, 30–2.

[87] Ago, ILC *Ybk* 1976/II(1), 3, 129.

(see below), and has been retained in ARSIWA in the form of Article 48; but problems appear regarding the precise object of this responsibility.

The notion that violations of these obligations would constitute 'crimes of state' for a long time generated heated debate, both within the ILC[88] and in the literature[89] before being pragmatically abandoned by the Special Rapporteur in favour of the notion of 'serious breaches of obligations under peremptory norms of general international law'.[90] The commentary quotes the 1946 International Military Tribunal, which affirmed that 'crimes against international law are committed by men, not by abstract entities'.[91] For all the symbolic overtones lost in this change of terminology, it has settled the issue to which norms the special regime applies: they are the same as those accorded peremptory status under VCLT Articles 53 and 64.[92]

On closer examination, ARSIWA Articles 40 and 41 provide not so much a regime of *aggravated* consequences as one of *additional* consequences. These affect in particular the legal status of situations deriving from the wrongfulness. ARSIWA Article 41 provides three such consequences. First, all states are to co-operate through lawful means to bring an end to the violation. Second, all states must refrain from recognizing as lawful the situation created thereby. Third, no state may aid or assist the wrongdoer in maintaining the unlawful situation. No punishment of the state responsible for the grave breaches is envisaged by the Articles.

Other consequences remain *de lege ferenda*, and have seen only sparse practice. A proposed reaction to particularly grave breaches, following the lead of Special Rapporteur Arangio-Ruiz, is the possibility of the award of punitive damages.[93] But it is far from clear that the concept has any place in international law, and the case-law certainly does not warrant a general conclusion that it does.[94] In the face of grave breaches in the fields of human rights and armed conflict, courts and tribunals have refused to award penal damages. The Inter-American Court has held that 'although some domestic courts... award damages in amounts meant to deter or to serve as an example, this principle is not applicable in international law at this time'.[95] The European Court of Human Rights often observes that it 'does not award aggravated or punitive damages'.[96] The Eritrea–Ethiopia Claims Commission reduced the potential

---

[88] Reports by Special Rapporteurs Ago, Arangio-Ruiz, and Riphagen and the respective reports of the ILC to the General Assembly.

[89] Weiler, Cassese & Spinedi (1989); Abi-Saab (1999) 10 *EJIL* 339; Gaja, ibid, 365; Pellet, ibid, 425; Crawford, ibid, 435. Also Jørgensen, *The Responsibility of States for International Crimes* (2000); Rao, in Ragazzi (ed), *International Responsibility Today* (2005).

[90] Crawford, ILC *Ybk* 1998/II(1), 9–23. That the responsibility arising from violations of these norms is 'not of a criminal nature' has been confirmed by the ICJ: *Genocide (Bosnia and Herzegovina v Serbia and Montenegro)*, Judgment of 26 February 2007, §170.

[91] ARSIWA commentary, part 2, ch III, §5.

[92] But cf Cassese, in Crawford, Pellet & Olleson (2010) 415.

[93] Arangio-Ruiz, ILC *Ybk* 1989/II(1), 41. Cf Jørgensen (1997) 68 *BY* 247; Wittich (2004) 14 *Fin YIL* 321.

[94] Wittich, in Crawford, Pellet & Olleson (2010) 667; Ollivier, ibid, 713.

[95] *Velásquez Rodríguez v Honduras*, IACtHR C/4, 21 July 1989, §38.

[96] *BB v UK* [2004] ECtHR 53760/00, §36.

damages it could have awarded for the violation of *ius ad bellum* by Eritrea, arguing that '[t]he Parties' limited economic capacity is relevant in determining damages
claims', and explaining that '[c]ompensation has a limited role which is remedial, not
punitive'.[97] The consequences that flow from particularly grave violations are thus not
qualitatively different from those that flow from a breach of any customary or conventional rule. The distinctive regime of responsibility that exists for grave violations does
not affect reparation, but finds its main effects in the possibilities open to non-injured
states of demanding cessation and responding to illegality.

4. INVOCATION OF RESPONSIBILITY[98]

(A) EVOLUTION OF THE LAW

The question who can invoke the responsibility of a state for a breach of international
law is a disputed one. Early writers, for whom judicial intervention was truly exceptional, dealt with this matter under the heading of entitlement to punish a wrong committed against a third state. Grotius, who saw natural law as standing over the mutual
relations of political entities, asserted a right of sovereigns to punish violations of that
law, even if they have not been especially affected:

[K]ings, and those who possess equal rights to those kings, have the right of demanding
punishments not only on account of injuries committed against themselves or their subjects, but also on account of injuries which do not directly affect them but excessively violate
the law of nature or of nations in regard to any persons whatsoever.[99]

Vattel argued that for a sovereign 'to grant reprisals against a nation in favor of foreigners, is to set himself up as a judge between that nation and those foreigners; which
no sovereign has a right to do ... reprisals can only be granted to maintain the rights
of the state'.[100] Likewise, the only states justified in going to war against a violator were
those who have suffered an injury.[101] The only exception admitted was in relation to
nations that 'openly despise justice', trampling the rights of others whenever possible.
In Vattel's words: '[t]o form and support an unjust pretension, is only doing an injury
to the party whose interests are affected by that pretension; but, to despise justice in
general, is doing an injury to all nations'.[102]

---

[97] *Final Award—Ethiopia's Damages Claims* (2009) 26 RIAA 631, 633–4.
[98] Mbaye (1988) 209 Hague *Recueil* 223; Simma (1994) 250 Hague *Recueil* 217, 229–55; Queneudec
(1995) 255 Hague *Recueil* 339; Weiss (2002) 96 *AJIL* 798; Alland (2002) 13 *EJIL* 1221; Tams (2005); Brunnée
(2005) 36 *NYIL* 21; Noellkamper (2009) 16 *Indiana JGLS* 535; Proukaki, *The Problem of Enforcement in
International Law* (2010).
[99] Grotius, *De Iure Belli ac Pacis* (1625, ed Tuck 2005) II.xx.§40(1).
[100] Vattel, *Le Droit des gens* (1758, tr Anon 1797) II.viii.§348.
[101] Ibid, III.iii.§27.
[102] Ibid, II.v.§70.

With the consolidation of international law in the nineteenth century, the dominant view among positivist international lawyers became that only states may invoke the responsibility of other states, and only when specially affected by the breach—that is, the state invoking the responsibility, or one of its nationals, must have suffered material or moral injury relating to the wrongful act. This view, reflected in the *Mavrommatis* dictum,[103] had Anzilotti as one of its early champions and is still sometimes found among French writers.[104] Its classical formulation is expressed by Anzilotti in 1906:

The law of nations does not award rights to individuals...A State may indeed be obliged to treat certain individuals in a certain way; but the State's obligation does not exist vis-à-vis individuals, it exists vis-à-vis another State, which holds the right to demand that the former treat the relevant individuals as desired, and not otherwise.[105]

This is complemented by the view that the violation of a rule requires some sort of injury, 'a disturbance of the interest it protects',[106] and that only the injured state is entitled to invoke the responsibility of the wrongdoer. Although the specific theoretical grounds for this have often been disputed,[107] international claims which involve direct harm to the legal rights of the claimant state are relatively uncontroversial, and the rules discussed above apply. In *Reparation for Injuries*, the International Court affirmed that, at least for breaches of obligations owed to individual states, 'only the party to whom an international obligation is due can bring a claim in respect of its breach'.[108] These rules are reflected in ARSIWA Article 42(a) and (b)(i).

But it may happen that individual states ground a claim either in a broad concept of legal interest or in special conditions which give the individual state *locus standi* in respect of legal interests of other entities. In the *South West Africa* cases[109] Ethiopia and Liberia asked the Court to affirm the status of South West Africa as a territory under mandate and to declare that South Africa had violated various articles of the Mandate Agreement and Article 22 of the Covenant of the League of Nations in consequence of aspects of its administration of South West Africa, in particular, the introduction of apartheid. South Africa submitted that Ethiopia and Liberia had no *locus standi* in the proceedings.

In 1962, the Court accepted jurisdiction over the dispute, skimming over the issue of *locus standi* and concentrating on the fact that the claim corresponded to what had been provided for in Article 7 of the Mandate Agreement. It fell to the dissenting

---

[103] (1924) PCIJ Ser A No 2, 12.
[104] Combacau (1986) 31 *Archives de Philosophie du Droit* 85; Weil (1992) 237 Hague *Recueil* 11, 313–69.
[105] Anzilotti (1906) 13 *RGDIP* 5, 6.
[106] Ibid, 13.
[107] E.g. García Amador, ILC *Ybk* 1956/II, 192–3.
[108] *Reparation for Injuries Suffered in the Service of the United Nations*, ICJ Reports 1949 p 174, 181–2.
[109] Preliminary Objections, ICJ Reports 1962 p 319. Cf Verzijl (1964) 11 *NILR* 1.

judges to call attention to the issue of the legal interest of the claimants.[110] In 1966, however, the view of the previously dissenting judges was to prevail.[111] In considering the argument that interpretation of the Mandate should proceed in the light of the necessity for effectiveness in the system of supervision, the Court said:

[T]he argument amounts to a plea that the Court should allow the equivalent of an 'actio popularis', or right resident in any member of a community to take legal action in vindication of a public interest. But, although a right of this kind may be known to certain municipal systems of law, it is not known to international law as it stands at present.[112]

The Court said that it did not decide on whether there could be claims for non-material or non-tangible interests, making specific reference to 'agreements of a humanitarian character'.[113] It affirmed that '[s]tates may have a legal interest in vindicating a principle of international law, even though they have, in the given case, suffered no material prejudice, or ask only for token damages...[but] such rights or interests, in order to exist, must be clearly vested in those who claim them, by some text or instrument, or rule of law'.[114] As this was not the case, the claims were rejected.

A similar issue could have arisen in *Northern Cameroons (Cameroon v UK)*, but the Court rejected Cameroon's request for a declaratory judgment based on the absence of practical effect of any such declaration.[115] The major shift in the Court's position came in the form of an *obiter dictum* in *Barcelona Traction*, a dispute concerning wrongful treatment of an investment made in Spain by a company incorporated in Canada. Belgium claimed standing to exercise diplomatic protection of its nationals, who comprised a vast majority of the shareholders of the Canadian company, and demanded reparation for the damage. The Court said:

When a State admits into its territory foreign investments or foreign nationals, whether natural or juristic persons, it is bound to extend to them the protection of the law and assumes obligations concerning the treatment to be afforded them. These obligations, however, are neither absolute nor unqualified. In particular, an essential distinction should be drawn between the obligations of a State towards the international community as a whole, and those arising vis-à-vis another State in the field of diplomatic protection. By their very nature the former are the concern of all States. In view of the importance of the rights involved,

---

[110] *South West Africa*, Preliminary Objections, ICJ Reports 1962 p 319, 455–7 (Judge Winiarski, diss). Also ibid, 547–9 (Judges Spender & Fitzmaurice, joint diss); ibid, 569–71 (Judge Morelli, diss).

[111] ICJ Reports 1966 p 6. Changes in the composition of the Court meant that the minority of 1962 now appeared as a majority (the case was decided 7 to 7, with the casting vote of President Spender). For comment: Higgins (1966) 42 *International Affairs* 573; Jennings (1967) 121 Hague *Recueil* 323, 507–11; de la Rasilla (2008) 2 *Int Comm LR* 171. Also on the concept of *actio popularis*: Scobbie (2002) 13 *EJIL* 1201.

[112] *South West Africa*, Second Phase, ICJ Reports 1966 p 6, 47.

[113] Ibid, 32. Also Preliminary Objections, ICJ Reports 1962 p 319, 424–33 (Judge Jessup, sep).

[114] *South West Africa*, Second Phase, ICJ Reports 1966 p 6, 32.

[115] ICJ Reports 1963 p 15, 27. This is hard to reconcile with *Corfu Channel*, ICJ Reports 1949 p 4, 36. Also: *Right of Passage over Indian Territory (Portugal v India)*, ICJ Reports 1960 p 6; Gross (1964) 58 *AJIL* 415, 427–8.

all States can be held to have a legal interest in their protection; they are obligations *erga omnes*.[116]

The Court went on to explain that *erga omnes* obligations derive 'in contemporary international law, from the outlawing of acts of aggression, and of genocide, as also from the principles and rules concerning the basic rights of the human person, including protection from slavery and racial discrimination'.[117]

Simma refers to the *Barcelona Traction* judgment as 'a great leap forward':[118] it was certainly a leap, but since it evaded the (then-controversial) issue of peremptory norms, it might equally be described as a great leap sideways. A number of requests for declaratory judgments have since been made in cases brought by states that were not specially injured. But, as the International Court has so far applied the usual, fairly restrictive rules regarding jurisdiction and admissibility of claims, its effects have been limited. In *Nuclear Tests (Australia v France)*[119] Australia asked the Court to declare that the carrying out of nuclear tests in the South Pacific was 'not consistent with applicable rules of international law'.[120] Four judges were of the opinion that the purpose of the claim was to obtain a declaratory judgment.[121] The majority of the judges thought otherwise and, in the light of a French undertaking not to continue tests, held that the dispute had disappeared and that, since damages had not been requested, there was no need for a judgment.[122] In *East Timor*, Portugal claimed its rights as an administering power but also invoked the right of the people of East Timor to self-determination. The Court recognized the *erga omnes* nature of the obligation to respect self-determination, only to dismiss the application, made against Australia, on the grounds that it could not decide on the matter without determining the lawfulness of the conduct of Indonesia. The latter had not accepted the compulsory jurisdiction of the International Court of Justice, and, in the Court's view, 'the *erga omnes* character of a norm and the rule of consent to jurisdiction are two different things'.[123]

In these cases much turns on the interpretations of the relevant adjudication clause, the definition of a dispute, and notions of judicial propriety. However, assuming that the hurdles of jurisdiction, admissibility, and propriety are surmounted, there is no inherent limitation of the concept of legal interest to 'material' interests. Thus states acting in collective self-defence, or a war of sanction against an aggressor, would seem

---

[116] ICJ Reports 1970 p 3, 32.

[117] Ibid.

[118] Simma (1994) 250 Hague *Recueil* 217, 293.

[119] ICJ Reports 1974 p 253. Ritter (1975) 21 *AFDI* 471.

[120] ICJ Reports 1974 p 253, 256. By contrast, New Zealand had requested a declaration that the tests constituted 'a violation of New Zealand's rights under international law': *Nuclear Tests (New Zealand v France)*, ICJ Reports 1974 p 457, 460.

[121] ICJ Reports 1974 p 253, 312–21 (Judges Onyeama, Dillard, Jiménez de Aréchaga & Sir Humphrey Waldock, joint diss).

[122] Ibid, 270.

[123] ICJ Reports 1995 p 90, 102.

to have a claim for costs and losses.[124] 'Protective' claims in respect of 'dependent' peoples may have special features; for example, a tribunal should be reluctant to reject a claim on account of prescription or laches of the protecting sovereign.

Other possibilities are open, in particular in the field of environmental law. Australia's application against Japan for whaling activities in the Antarctic Ocean presents a clear case of a state filing an application without being either injured or specially affected. The remedies sought by Australia are in consequence not focused on reparation for any damage, but go beyond a mere declaration, and demand specific orders for cessation of the allegedly unlawful conduct and assurances of non-repetition.[125]

(B) ARSIWA ARTICLES 42 AND 48

In the cases examined above one can observe a marked difference between the remedies that are requested and granted in cases of claims made by non-injured states, when compared to those usually requested by injured states. In the latter case, the claimant state may demand, for injury done to itself or to its nationals, reparation in the form of restitution, compensation, and satisfaction. This holds true even when the injury in question is not material—the problem then is one of valuation of the injury; reparation is equally a possibility in cases in which the substantive rules invoked are geared primarily to protecting a 'collective interest', so long as the state invoking responsibility can be identified as specifically injured.[126]

Cases in which the state invoking the responsibility of the violator is not individually injured may present more difficulties. On the one hand, the claimant cannot be 'made whole', since it has not suffered damage in the first place; even if 'punitive damages' for violations of particular rules could be contemplated, it would be hard for tribunals to calibrate these in order not to overburden the responsible state. On the other hand, empowering all states that feel aggrieved by the violation of a multilateral treaty to react by means of countermeasures could generate pernicious effects for political stability and undermine the function of international law as a system that regulates interstate relations.

The ILC did not adopt in its codification work the vocabulary proposed by the last Special Rapporteur, distinguishing between states holding a 'right' and those having merely a 'legal interest'.[127] But it still agreed with the establishment of two different regimes of invocation, one for injured states, in Article 42, and the second for other ('non-injured states') in Article 48. An injured state, as explained by the

---

[124] Koliopoulos, *La Commission d'indemnisation des Nations Unies et le droit de la responsabilité international* (2001); Gattini, *The UN Compensation Commission* (2002). Also McNair (1936) 17 *BY* 150, 157; Brownlie, *Use of Force by States* (1963) 148.

[125] *Whaling in the Antarctic (Australia v Japan)*, Application instituting procedures (2010) 18.

[126] E.g. *Genocide (Bosnia and Herzegovina v Serbia and Montenegro)*, ICJ Reports 2007 p 43, 65–6, *Application of the International Convention on the Elimination of All Forms of Racial Discrimination (Georgia v Russia)*, Preliminary Objections, 1 April 2011, §§16–17.

[127] Crawford, ILC *Ybk* 2000/II(1), 33; Gaja, in Crawford, Pellet & Olleson (2010) 941–2.

commentary, 'is entitled to resort to all means of redress contemplated in the articles'.[128] It may demand reparation of the injury and cessation of the conduct, and it may resort to countermeasures in order to demand the fulfilment by the violator of its legal obligations.

'Injured state', here, refers both to states to which the obligation is owed individually, for example, for violations of the law of diplomatic relations or of a commercial treaty, and to states which are 'specially affected' by an obligation owed to a group of states or to the international community as a whole.[129] A state may also be injured if the obligation breached is of the so-called 'interdependent' type—an obligation the violation of which by any state 'radically changes the position of all the other States to which the obligation is owed with respect to the further performance of the obligation'.[130]

For other states, Article 48 envisages a much more limited scope of action. First, responsibility may only be invoked by a state to which the obligation is owed and which has some sort of interest in its fulfilment—either because the obligation in question, owed to a group of states, protects a collective interest of the group, or because it is an *erga omnes* obligation, which is due not to any state in particular but to the international community as a whole. What may be demanded from the violator by a non-injured state is, in accordance with Article 48(2), merely:

(a) cessation of the internationally wrongful act, and assurances and guarantees of non-repetition in accordance with the preceding articles, in the interest of the injured State or of the beneficiaries of the obligation breached; and

(b) performance of the obligation of reparation in accordance with the preceding articles, in the interest of the injured State or of the beneficiaries of the obligation breached.

This is coherent with the practice, noted above, of invocation by states of the responsibility of other states for breaches of humanitarian and environmental obligations. But perhaps the most relevant impact of the distinct responsibility regimes for injured and non-injured states relates not to what the latter may request from a court, but to the options open to each group to take measures in reaction to illegality.

(C) COUNTERMEASURES[131]

Countermeasures constitute one of the most distinctive aspects of international law when compared to domestic legal systems. In essence, the term refers to the possibility for a state to resort to 'private justice' when its demands for cessation of an illegal conduct and/or adequate reparation are not met by the wrongdoer. The wronged state may

---

[128] ARSIWA, commentary to Art 42, §3.

[129] *Teheran Hostages*, ICJ Reports 1980 p 3, 43; *LaGrand (Germany v US)*, ICJ Reports 2001 p 466; *Avena*, ICJ Reports 2004 p 12.

[130] Art 42(b)(ii). This reproduces the language of VCLT, Art 60(2)(c).

[131] Zoller, *Peacetime Unilateral Remedies* (1984); Alland, *Justice privée et ordre juridique international* (1994); Bederman (2002) 96 *AJIL* 817; Franck (2008) 102 *AJIL* 715; Proukaki (2010).

then respond by taking measures which would in principle violate its duties to the latter state, but which are regarded as lawful due to their character as countermeasures.

While the terminology of countermeasures is relatively recent, early international lawyers already considered that, in the absence of compulsory jurisdiction, sovereigns could take justice into their own hands. Thus Grotius considered that a state which does not receive reparation for injury done to itself or its nationals may justly seize goods of the wrongdoing state and its nationals to recover the loss. Additionally, both Grotius and Vattel accepted reprisals as an 'enforcement of right',[132] the right of nations 'to do themselves justice'.[133] The use of armed force by a state to enforce its rights was accepted until the beginning of the twentieth century, and it was only in the 1907 Hague Conference that contracting states agreed not to have recourse to armed force for the recovery of contract debts.[134] For other cases, however, reprisals were still permitted. In the *Naulilaa* arbitration, the tribunal explained that '[a] reprisal is an act of self-help (*Selbsthilfhandlung*) of the injured State, which responds to…an act contrary to the law of nations commited by the wrongdoing State. Its effect is to suspend momentarily, in the relations between the two States, the observation of this or that rule of the law of nations'.[135]

With the growing restrictions on the use of force as an instrument of foreign policy in the twentieth century, the vocabulary of 'reprisals', comprising both the use of force and other measures short of such use, was replaced by two different concepts: self-defence, now dealt with in ARSIWA Article 21, and countermeasures, contained in Article 22. Whereas most responses will fall under countermeasures, self-defence, authorizing the use of force, applies only to an incoming armed attack. This was confirmed by the International Court in *Nicaragua*. The Court affirmed:

While an armed attack would give rise to an entitlement to collective self-defence, a use of force of a lesser degree of gravity … could not justify counter-measures taken by a third State, the United States, and particularly could not justify intervention involving the use of force.[136]

Countermeasures thus do not admit of the use of force, even in response to a 'use of force of a lesser gravity'. They nonetheless retain the essence of the idea expressed by the *Naulilaa* tribunal: permitting a state to resort to what would otherwise be internationally wrongful conduct in order to enforce its rights vis-à-vis another state. The concept has been well explained by the arbitral tribunal in the *Air Service Agreement*:

Under the rules of present-day international law, and unless the contrary results from special obligations arising under particular treaties, notably from mechanisms created within the framework of international organisations, each State establishes for itself its legal situation

---

[132] Grotius (1646) III.ii.§4.
[133] Vattel (1758) II.xviii.§342.
[134] International Convention respecting the Limitation of the Employment of Force for the Recovery of Contract Debts (1907) TS 007/1910 (Cd 5028), Art 1.
[135] *Naulilaa* (1928) 2 RIAA 1011, 1026.
[136] ICJ Reports 1986 p 14, 127.

vis-à-vis other States. If a situation arises which, in one State's view, results in the violation of an international obligation by another State, the first State is entitled, within the limits set by the general rules of international law pertaining to the use of armed force, to affirm its rights through 'counter-measures'.[137]

Countermeasures are of course not unconditionally lawful. A series of requirements exist to prevent the unrestrained use of countermeasures and to avoid the danger of escalation of the conflict. Thus, before resorting to countermeasures a state that finds itself injured must call upon the wrongdoing state to cease the wrongful conduct, if it is continuing, and to make reparation for any injury.[138] ARSIWA Article 52(1) adds the requirement to formally notify the responsible state of the decision to take countermeasures, as well as the need to offer to negotiate.

Additionally, given that countermeasures are an instrument to exert pressure on the responsible state precisely in the absence of an impartial adjudicator they must not be taken while a dispute is pending before an international adjudicative organ. As the tribunal in *Air Services Agreement* noted, '[t]o the extent that the tribunal has the necessary means to achieve the objectives justifying the counter-measures, it must be admitted that the right of the Parties to initiate such measures disappears'.[139] The tribunal must be capable of exercising, for example by way of interim measures, the function that would otherwise be that of a countermeasure. Thus in the *High-Fructose Corn Syrup* dispute Mexico took countermeasures against the US for the breach of a NAFTA obligation, after having had its access to a NAFTA panel blocked by US inaction. The effective blocking of the NAFTA panel by the US, which refused to appoint its panel member, arguably entitled Mexico to take countermeasures under general international law—although the tribunal rejected the actual measures taken on various grounds.[140]

A central requirement of countermeasures is that they must be *proportional* to the wrongful conduct. Many measures which are claimed to be countermeasures are found by tribunals to be out of proportion with the initial offence. Thus, in the *Naulilaa* arbitration, the tribunal found an 'evident disproportion' between the killing of two German officials in the Portuguese fort of Naulilaa and the subsequent attack and destruction of six other forts by German forces.[141] In *Gabčíkovo-Nagymaros*, the International Court found that the unilateral assumption of control over a large percentage of the waters of the Danube was not 'commensurate with the injury suffered,

---

[137] (1978) 18 RIAA 417, 443.

[138] *Naulilaa* (1928) 2 RIAA 1011, 1026; *Gabčíkovo-Nagymaros*, ICJ Reports 1997 p 7, 56.

[139] (1978) 18 RIAA 417, 445.

[140] *Mexico—Soft Drinks*, WTO Doc WT/DS308/AB/R, 6 March 2006. Also: *Archer Daniels Midland Co and Tate & Lyle Ingredients v Mexico* (2007) 146 ILR 440, 484–505; *Corn Products International v Mexico* (2008) 146 ILR 581, 624–38; *Cargill Inc v Mexico* (2009) 146 ILR 642, 752–66. Further: Pauwelyn (2006) 9 *JIEL* 197; Henckels (2008) 19 *EJIL* 571. On the articulation of different responsibility regimes: Simma (1985) 16 *NYIL* 111; Simma & Pulkowski (2006) 17 *EJIL* 483; Gradoni, *Regime Failure nel Diritto Internazionale* (2009).

[141] (1928) 2 RIAA 1011, 1026.

taking account of the rights in question'.[142] Conversely, in the *Air Service Agreement* arbitration, the tribunal, taking into account the rights violated and the positions of the parties, found that there was no compelling evidence that the measures taken by the US had been 'clearly disproportionate when compared to those taken by France'.[143] It thus accepted the legality of the countermeasures taken by the US.

In all of these cases, it must be noted, countermeasures were employed in response to an injury done to the state that adopted them. ARSIWA Article 49, following the opinion expressed by the International Court in *Nicaragua*, provides that (except for an armed attack giving rise to collective self-defence) only a state injured by the violation may resort to countermeasures against the wrongdoer.[144] ARSIWA Article 54, which regulates the response of non-injured states, limits their legitimate reaction to 'lawful measures ... to ensure cessation of the breach and reparation'. These lawful if unfriendly measures, such as suspending aid and expelling an ambassador, are known as retorsion. Being lawful, retorsion is available to any state at any time to express disapproval towards the conduct—whether or not unlawful—of another state.

One may ask, however, whether some illegalities, and in particular 'serious breaches of peremptory norms', do not entail a right to take countermeasures in the collective interest. The strong emphasis on bilateralism that accompanied the consolidation of international law until the Second World War, however, led to their marginalization, and the developments in international law after the creation of the UN were not sufficient to endow the notion of crimes of state with a concrete content in terms of responsibility. While the notion of international crimes was finally dropped, the need for 'a different regime of responsibility'[145] was taken into account by the last Special Rapporteur, who accordingly maintained a proposal for third-party countermeasures in his Fourth Report.[146]

But strong reactions from many states, concerned in particular with the potential for arbitrariness in imposition of third-party countermeasures, led the ILC to adopt a mere saving clause, leaving the issue open.[147] The commentary lists a number of occasions when states did take countermeasures in response to injuries done to third states or to grave breaches. Its conclusion, however, is that the law on the matter is 'uncertain' and that there is 'no clearly recognized entitlement of [non-injured states] to take countermeasures in the collective interest'.[148] The final text falls short of legitimizing third-party countermeasures in response to grave violations, and has been criticized for that.[149]

---

[142] ICJ Reports 1997 p 7, 56.
[143] (1978) 18 RIAA 417, 444.
[144] ICJ Reports 1986 p 14, 127.
[145] Ago, ILC *Ybk* 1976/II(1), 3
[146] Crawford, ILC *Ybk* 2000/II(1) 3, 106–9.
[147] ILC *Ybk* 2001/I, 112–13.
[148] ARSIWA, Art 54 & commentary, §§3–7.
[149] Proukaki (2010).

It is perhaps an exaggeration to claim, as Alland does, that the choice was 'between the subjectivism of a decentralized response in defence of general interests and the absence of any consequences for the most serious wrongful acts'.[150] There is broad agreement that mechanisms and institutions for collective reaction to grave violations must be put in place and those that exist improved. But it is far less certain that a helpful way to protect the collective interest is by entrusting the protection of collective interests to individual states, acting based on their own understanding of international legality. Simma's conclusion appears appropriate:

It is precisely in these instances that the neuralgic points of the development from bilateralism to community interest will become visible: the grafting upon traditional international law of innovative, and entirely positive, conceptions, and, at the same time, the surrender of these concepts to the mercy of individual auto-determination and auto-enforcement.[151]

---

[150] Alland (2002) 13 *EJIL* 1221, 1239.
[151] Simma (1994) 250 Hague *Recueil* 217, 331.

27

MULTILATERAL PUBLIC ORDER AND ISSUES OF RESPONSIBILITY[1]

1. THE VARYING CONTENT OF ILLEGALITY

The law of responsibility has had a precarious existence in a decentralized system of international relations lacking compulsory jurisdiction and generally applicable enforcement procedures. Much of international law consists of rules concerning competence and functional co-operation, and the most common mechanism for airing and maybe resolving disputes is not a court or tribunal but diplomatic exchanges and negotiated settlement. Thus acceptance of the delictual character of breaches of treaty and of other rules, and the appearance of developed principles of responsibility focusing on performance or damages rather than political 'indemnity' or 'satisfaction', are relatively recent. Customary international law historically developed through the form of liberties and prohibitions, and has remained imprecise with respect to the scope and consequences especially of serious, systemic illegality.

True, the contrast between old and new should not be overdrawn, nor the capacity of the classical system for innovation completely discounted. In addition to responsibility for one state's causing material harm to another, there were always situations in which illegality was formulated in more general, *per se* terms, even within the normal framework of international responsibility. Acts of trespass, for example temporary intrusion into the airspace or territorial sea of another state, are delictual without proof of special damage.[2] Indeed the principle *pacta sunt servanda* implies as much; in international law a breach of treaty is actionable without proof of special damage,

---

[1] Rozakis, *The Concept of Jus Cogens in the Law of Treaties* (1976); Dugard, *Recognition and the United Nations* (1987); Hannikainen, *Peremptory Norms (Jus Cogens) in International Law* (1988); Kadelbach, *Zwingendes Völkerrecht* (1992); Kolb, *Théorie du jus cogens international* (2001); Tams, *Enforcing Obligations Erga Omnes in International Law* (2005); Orakhelashvili, *Peremptory Norms in International Law* (2006); Crawford, *Creation of States* (2nd edn, 2006) 99–105; Dawidowicz, in Crawford, Pellet & Olleson (eds), *The Law of International Responsibility* (2010) 677; Jørgensen, ibid, 687; Ollivier, ibid, 703; Vaurs-Chaumette, ibid, 1023.

[2] Cf *Corfu Channel (UK v Albania)*, ICJ Reports 1949 p 4.

unless the treaty otherwise provides. There are many cases where the performance interests of states as promisees greatly outweigh any material loss they might individually suffer from a breach—this is true of most environmental treaties and all human rights treaties. The collective action problem at the international level is serious enough as things stand, without disabling rules about special damage based on inappropriate domestic analogies.[3]

Moreover classical international law accepted that state conduct could not only be unlawful but invalid, even invalid *erga omnes*. Any other position would have amounted to a form of multilateral disarmament in the face of unilateral action, no matter how outrageous. But beyond those scenarios, open under the bilateral, 'billiard-ball' international law of the period from Vattel to *Mavrommatis*,[4] there can now be envisaged broader possibilities of collective action under law. The process by which these have emerged has not been based on logic but on some mixture of hope and experience.[5] Both the ILC and the Court have played significant roles. The trajectory may be marked as follows:

1919: League of Nations Covenant (embodying responses to breaches of the Covenant, co-ordinated by the Council);[6]

1928: Kellogg–Briand Pact (outlawing use of force in international relations, closing 'gap' in the Covenant);[7]

1932: Stimson doctrine of non-recognition (propounding collective non-recognition of Japanese aggression in Manchuria and puppet state of Manchukuo);[8]

1936: Ineffective sanctions against Italy for invasion of Ethiopia (involving failure and subsequent collapse of League's collective security system leading to Second World War);[9]

1945: UN Charter (reinstituting a collective security system acceptable to the US, USSR, and others, reaffirming general prohibition on use of force in international relations);[10]

1966: *South West Africa* cases (rejecting public interest standing of Ethiopia and Liberia to determine legality of apartheid in South West Africa);[11]

---

[3] See especially Parry (1956) 90 Hague *Recueil* 657, 674ff.

[4] *Mavrommatis Palestine Concessions* (1924) PCIJ Ser B No 3, and for the epochs of international law: chapter 1.

[5] Crawford (2006) 319 Hague *Recueil* 325; further: Daillier in Crawford, Pellet & Olleson (2010) 37; Koskenniemi, ibid, 45.

[6] Covenant of the League of Nations, 28 June 1919, 225 CTS 195.

[7] 27 August 1928, 94 LNTS 57.

[8] *LNOJ*, Sp Supp No 101 (1932) 87–8 ('it is incumbent upon the members of the League of Nations not to recognize any situation, treaty or agreement which may be brought about by means contrary to the Covenant of the League of Nations or the Pact of Paris').

[9] Talmon, *Recognition of Governments in International Law* (1996) 102–3.

[10] 26 June 1945, 892 UNTS 119.

[11] *South West Africa (Ethiopia v South Africa; Liberia v South Africa)*, ICJ Reports 1966 p 6.

1969: Inclusion of peremptory norms in VCLT Articles 53, 64 (recognizing category of norms of general international law from which no derogation is permissible);[12]

1970: *Barcelona Traction* dictum (recognizing analogous (or identical) category of obligations *erga omnes*);[13]

1971: *Namibia* Advisory Opinion (confirming validity of General Assembly's revocation of mandate; specifying collective non-recognition of South Africa's authority over territory);[14]

1976: ILC adopts draft Article 19 (recognizing collective interest in certain fundamental norms, although under the questionable rubric 'international crimes of states');[15]

1990: Collective action consequential upon Iraqi invasion and purported annexation of Kuwait (providing for collective non-recognition; restoration of Kuwaiti sovereignty; machinery for substantial compensation of affected interests under Security Council auspices);[16]

1998: Rome Statute for an International Criminal Court (creating institutional machinery for the prosecution of certain crimes under international law, including of state officials);[17]

1999: Independence of Timor Leste (achieved despite earlier Indonesian 'annexation'; collective non-recognition helped keep issue alive);[18]

2001: ILC Articles on State Responsibility, Articles 40, 41, 48, 54 (endorsing consequences for third parties of serious breach of peremptory norms; implementing *Barcelona Traction* dictum; reserves possibility of collective countermeasures);[19]

2004: *Wall* Advisory Opinion (pronouncing *erga omnes* illegality of Wall, indicating consequences for third states, borrowing language from ILC Article 41);[20]

---

[12] VCLT, 22 May 1969, 1155 UNTS 331.

[13] *Barcelona Traction, Light and Power Company, Limited (Belgium v Spain)*, Second Phase, ICJ Reports 1970 p 3, 32.

[14] *Legal Consequences for States of the Continued Presence of South Africa in Namibia (South West Africa) notwithstanding Security Council Resolution 276 (1970)*, ICJ Reports 1971 p 16.

[15] ILC *Ybk* 1976/I, 239.

[16] E.g. SC Res 660 (1990); SC Res 661 (1990); SC Res 662 (1990); SC Res 664 (1990), SC Res 665 (1990); SC Res 678 (1990); SC Res 686 (1991).

[17] 17 July 1998, 2187 UNTS 3.

[18] The details of the referendum were agreed in the Agreement between the Republic of Indonesia and the Portuguese Republic on the Question of East Timor, 5 May 1999, available at www.un.org/peace/etimor99/agreement/agreeFrame_Eng01.html.

[19] ARSIWA, appended to GA Res 56/83, 12 December 2001.

[20] *Legal Consequences of the Construction of a Wall in the Occupied Palestinian Territory*, ICJ Reports 2004 p 136.

2006: *Congo/Rwanda* (Court for the first time explicitly endorsing category of peremptory norms);[21]

2010: Kampala Conference (agreeing definition of crime of aggression in ICC Statute).[22]

These developments have not been unalloyed or unequivocal. Following the rather swift and effective response to the Iraq invasion of Kuwait, the Security Council did nothing to avert the Rwanda genocide (1994). It stood back during the Iran–Iraq (1980–88) and Eritrea–Ethiopia (1998–2000) wars, to mention only two examples of catastrophic human conflicts that could have been stopped. The Security Council's authority is both large and at large: it has broad discretion as to the appreciation of a situation and how to respond to it, with no explicit limitation on its authority in case of a Chapter VII situation.[23] The Charter enjoins it to have regard to international law,[24] but there is no sanction for not doing so and virtually no recourse if it does not. Perhaps the individual components of the system—the states, the EU, other actors— may insist on compliance with fundamental rights as a condition of giving effect to Security Council sanctions affecting individuals, but even that is controversial.[25] There is a price to be paid for the equivocal relation of the Security Council to the law and so far there is, it seems, no way of avoiding paying it.

Furthermore there have been retreats as well as advances. Among the developments listed above, it was proposed, in draft article 19 of the ILC Articles on State Responsibility as adopted on first reading in 1996, to recognize a category of international crimes of state.[26] But no penal consequences could be allowed to flow from this, nor any requirements of due process: the exercise would have been little more than name-calling and amidst some controversy the category was abandoned.[27] Of course, irrespective of the putative criminality of an act *qua* act of state, individual criminal responsibility of those participating (including state officials) may arise under

---

[21] *Armed Activities on the Territory of the Congo (New Application: 2002) (Democratic Republic of the Congo v Rwanda)*, Jurisdiction and Admissibility, ICJ Reports 2006 p 6, 32, 52.

[22] ICC Statute, Art 8*bis*.

[23] But see *Application of the Convention on the Prevention and Punishment of the Crime of Genocide (Bosnia and Herzegovina v Serbia and Montenegro)*, Provisional Measures, Order of 13 September 1993, ICJ Reports 1993 p 325, 400 (Judge ad hoc Lauterpacht): '[t]he relief which Article 103 of the Charter may give the Security Council in case of conflict between one of its decisions and an operative treaty obligation cannot—as a matter of simple hierarchy of norms—extend to a conflict between a Security Council resolution and *jus cogens*.'

[24] UN Charter, Arts 1(1), 24(2), 36(3).

[25] See Joined Cases C-402/05 P and C-415/05 P, *Kadi & al Barakaat International Foundation v Council & Commission* [2008] ECR I-06351; *Kadi v European Commission*, Judgment of the General Court (Seventh Chamber) of 30 September 2010 (appeal pending); and further: Tzanakopoulos, *Disobeying the Security Council* (2011).

[26] ILC *Ybk* 1996/II(2), 60.

[27] ARSIWA, commentary to Art 12, §§5–7. Further: chapter 25.

international law.[28] But if sometimes the appropriate maxim might be *reculer pour mieux sauter*, sometimes the opposite seems to fit better![29]

2. OBJECTIVE CONSEQUENCES OF ILLEGAL ACTS

In the literature the principle of effectiveness (*ex factis ius oritur*) is often set against the principle of legality (*ex iniuria ius non oritur*).[30] A decentralized custom-based system in which sovereignty is a cardinal value must necessarily have regard to considerations of effectiveness—but not at any price. The notion of *delicta iuris gentium*, as opposed to the idea of torts as obligations of reparation between tortfeasor and claimant, has thus developed. A number of elements are now engaged.

(A) PEREMPTORY NORMS (*IUS COGENS*)

Jurists have from time to time attempted to classify rules, or rights and duties, on the international plane by using terms like 'fundamental' or, with respect to rights, 'inalienable' or 'inherent'. Such classifications have not had much success, but have intermittently affected the tribunals' interpretation of treaties. But during the 1960s scholarly opinion came to support the view that there can exist overriding norms of international law, referred to as peremptory norms (*ius cogens*).[31] Their key distinguishing feature is their relative indelibility. According to VCLT Article 53, they are rules of customary law that cannot be set aside by treaty or by acquiescence but only through the formation of a subsequent customary rule of the same character.

The concept of peremptory norms (*ius cogens*) was accepted by the ILC[32] and incorporated in the final draft on the law of treaties in 1966. Draft Article 50 provided that: 'a treaty is void if it conflicts with a peremptory norm of general international law from which no derogation is permitted and which can be modified only by a subsequent norm of general international law having the same character'.[33] This was inelegant

---

[28] Maison, in Crawford, Pellet & Olleson (2010) 717; and further: chapter 30.

[29] Viz., *sauter pour mieux reculer*. The original maxim translates as '[t]o run back in order to give a better jump forwards; to give way a little in order to take up a stronger position': Brewer, *Dictionary of Phrase and Fable* (1898) *sv*.

[30] E.g. Lauterpacht, *Recognition in International Law* (1947) 427; Wright (1953) 47 *AJIL* 365, 368; Cheng, *General Principles of Law as Applied by International Courts and Tribunals* (1987, repr 1994) 186–7.

[31] Lauterpacht, ILC *Ybk* 1953/II 90, 154–5, esp §4; Fitzmaurice (1957) 92 Hague *Recueil* 5, 120, 122, 125; Fitzmaurice (1959) 35 *BY* 183, 224–5. Also *In re Flesche* (1949) 16 ILR 266, 269. For an early source: Anzilotti, 1 *Opere* (3rd Italian edn, 1927) 289. Further: *North Sea Continental Shelf (Federal Republic of Germany/ Netherlands; Federal Republic of Germany/Denmark)*, ICJ Reports 1969 p 3, 97–8 (Judge Padilla Nervo), 182 (Judge Tanaka, diss), 248 (Judge Sørensen, diss).

[32] ILC *Ybk* 1963/II, 187, 198 (Art 37), 211 (Art 45), 216 (Art 53). Also: Lauterpacht ILC *Ybk* 1953/II, 90, 154–5; Fitzmaurice ILC *Ybk* 1958/II, 20, 27 (Art 17), 40; McNair, *Treaties* (1961) 213–18.

[33] ILC *Ybk* 1966/II, 172, 247–9, 261 (Art 61), 266 (Art 67).

in that it appeared to leave open the possibility of a peremptory norm not having a non-derogable character: the final text of Article 53 (cited below) in this respect is preferable.

The ILC's commentary makes it clear that 'derogation' refers to an agreement to contract out of rules of general international law.[34] Thus an agreement by a state to allow another state to stop and search its ships on the high seas would be valid,[35] but an agreement with a neighbouring state to carry out a joint operation against a racial group straddling the frontier in a manner that would constitute genocide is void, since the prohibition with which the treaty conflicts is peremptory in character. After some controversy, the Vienna Conference on the Law of Treaties reached agreement on a provision, Article 53.[36] The principal difference is that for the purposes of the VCLT a peremptory norm of general international law is defined as 'a norm accepted and recognized by the international community of States as a whole as a norm from which no derogation is permitted and which can be modified only by a subsequent norm of general international law having the same character'.

The least controversial members of this class are the prohibition of the use of force in Article 2(4) of the Charter,[37] of genocide,[38] of crimes against humanity (including systematic forms of racial discrimination),[39] and the rules prohibiting trade in slaves.[40] In *Barcelona Traction* the International Court drew a distinction between an obligation of a state arising vis-à-vis another state and an obligation 'towards the international community as a whole'—but the list it then gave is indistinguishable from contemporary catalogues of peremptory norms. The Court said:

Such obligations derive, for example, in contemporary international law, from the outlawing of acts of aggression, and of genocide, as also from the principles and rules concerning

---

[34] Commentary to Art 50 of the Draft Articles on the Law of Treaties, ILC *Ybk* 1966/II, 187, 247–9.

[35] Certain peremptory norms—notably the prohibition of the use of force in international relations—are defeasible by consent, which could presumably be given by treaty. The interaction between such norms and the general principle of indefeasibility has not been well articulated. For the controversy over Art IV of the Treaty of Guarantee, 16 August 1960, 382 UNTS 3. Further: Ehrlich, *Cyprus 1958–67* (1974) 37–8, 140, 148–9; Jacovides (1995) 10 *AUJIL & Pol* 1221, 1226–7; Hoffmeister, 'Cyprus' (2009) *MPEPIL*; Dinstein, *War, Aggression and Self-Defence* (5th edn, 2011) 292.

[36] UN Conference on the Law of Treaties, 1st Sess, Official Records, A/CONF.39/11, 26 March–24 May 1968, 293–328. Also Arts 64 (effect on treaties of a subsequent peremptory norm), 71 (consequences of the invalidity of a treaty which conflicts with a peremptory norm).

[37] McNair (1961) 214–15; Nash (1980) 74 *AJIL* 418 (discussing US Department of State Memorandum of December 29, 1979); *Military and Paramilitary Activities in and against Nicaragua (Nicaragua v US)*, ICJ Reports 1986 p 14, 100–1. Also Marston (1983) 54 *BY* 361, 379.

[38] *Armed Activities (DRC v Rwanda)*, Jurisdiction and Admissibility, ICJ Reports 2006 p 6, 32; *Genocide (Bosnia and Herzegovina v Serbia and Montenegro)*, ICJ Reports 2007 p 43, 111.

[39] *South West Africa*, Second Phase, ICJ Reports 1966 p 6, 298 (Judge Tanaka, diss), *Barcelona Traction*, Second Phase, ICJ Reports 1970 p 3, 304 (Judge Ammoun); *Namibia*, ICJ Reports 1971 p 16, 78–81 (Vice-President Ammoun).

[40] *Roach and Pinkerton (Case 9647)*, IACHR 3/87, 22 September 1987, §54. Also *Michael Domingues*, IACHR 62/02, 22 October 2002.

the basic rights of the human person, including protection from slavery and racial discrimination.[41]

Other rules that have this special status include the principle of self-determination, at least in its application to colonial countries and peoples or peoples under alien domination.[42]

The ILC provided its own authoritative synopsis in 2006:

(33) *The content of jus cogens.* The most frequently cited examples of *jus cogens* norms are the prohibition of aggression, slavery and the slave trade, genocide, racial discrimination apartheid and torture, as well as basic rules of international humanitarian law applicable in armed conflict, and the right to self-determination. Also other rules may have a *jus cogens* character inasmuch as they are accepted and recognized by the international community of States as a whole as norms from which no derogation is permitted.[43]

More authority exists for the concept of peremptory norms than for its particular consequences.[44] But certain suggestions may be made. For example, if outright state consent cannot derogate from a peremptory norm, the same must be true for congeners of consent such as acquiescence. This would imply that protest or recognition are irrelevant where the breach of a peremptory norm is at issue. Nor, presumably, can prescription remove the illegality—although at some level it must be possible for the states concerned to regulate the consequences of such a breach, provided this is done in a way which does not amount to mere ratification of the breach.

Moreover, consequences must flow from a breach of a peremptory norm, beyond the confines of the law of treaties. An aggressor should not benefit from the rule that belligerents are not responsible for damage caused to subjects of neutral states in military operations.[45] Yet many problems of application remain, for example with regard to the effect of self-determination on the transfer of territory. If a state uses force to implement the principle of self-determination, is it possible to assume that one peremptory norm is more peremptory than another? Particular corollaries of the concept are still being explored.[46]

---

[41] Second Phase, ICJ Reports 1970 p 3, 32. Also *East Timor (Portugal v Australia)*, ICJ Reports 1995 p 90, 102.

[42] *Barcelona Traction,* Second Phase, ICJ Reports 1970 p 3, 304 (Judge Ammoun).

[43] ILC, Fragmentation of International Law: Difficulties arising from the Diversification and Expansion of International Law, A/CN.4/L.702, 18 July 2006, §33.

[44] See the trenchant comment by Schwarzenberger (1965) 43 *Texas LR* 455, who regards the principle as a source of instability in treaty relations, and the reply by Verdross (1966) 60 *AJIL* 55. For further sceptical opinion: Weil (1983) 77 *AJIL* 413; Virally (1983) 183 Hague *Recueil* 25, 175–8.

[45] McNair, 2 *Opinions,* 277. Authority also exists for the view that an aggressor does not acquire title to property acquired even if the confiscation and requisition were within the Hague Regulations. See Brownlie, *Use of Force* (1963) 406.

[46] E.g. Gaja (1981) 172 Hague *Recueil* 271, 290–301 (issues of state responsibility); Schachter (1982) 178 Hague *Recueil* 21, 182–4 (rights of third states to take countermeasures). On self-determination and the use of force: Crawford (2nd edn, 2006) 134–48.

An area where the influence of peremptory norms has so far not been felt is that of curial jurisdiction. The International Court has gone out of its way to emphasize that the basic requirements for jurisdiction must be met, irrespective of the status of the norm relied on. Thus in *Armed Activities (DRC v Rwanda)* it said:

The Court observes...that 'the *erga omnes* character of a norm and the rule of consent to jurisdiction are two different things' (*East Timor (Portugal* v. *Australia), Judgment, I.C.J. Reports 1995*, p. 102, para. 29), and that the mere fact that rights and obligations *erga omnes* may be at issue in a dispute would not give the Court jurisdiction to entertain that dispute.

The same applies to the relationship between peremptory norms of general international law (*jus cogens*) and the establishment of the Court's jurisdiction: the fact that a dispute relates to compliance with a norm having such a character, which is assuredly the case with regard to the prohibition of genocide, cannot of itself provide a basis for the jurisdiction of the Court to entertain that dispute. Under the Court's Statute that jurisdiction is always based on the consent of the parties ...[47]

And it said it not once but twice:

Finally, the Court deems it necessary to recall that the mere fact that rights and obligations *erga omnes* or peremptory norms of general international law (*jus cogens*) are at issue in a dispute cannot in itself constitute an exception to the principle that its jurisdiction always depends on the consent of the parties.[48]

A similar distinction has been maintained, on the whole, with respect to state immunity, in particular the immunity of serving senior officials from arrest in third states. In *Arrest Warrant* the Court was categorical:

The Court has carefully examined State practice, including national legislation and those few decisions of national higher courts, such as the House of Lords or the French Court of Cassation. It has been unable to deduce from this practice that there exists under customary international law any form of exception to the rule according immunity from criminal jurisdiction and inviolability to incumbent Ministers for Foreign Affairs, where they are suspected of having committed war crimes or crimes against humanity.[49]

Such decisions confirm that the mere invocation of a peremptory norm is not an automatic answer to the question at hand: it injects a new element into the inquiry which may be expected to be influential but not necessarily decisive.[50]

---

[47] Jurisdiction and Admissibility, ICJ Reports 2006 p 6, 32.

[48] Ibid, 50–1.

[49] *Arrest Warrant of 11 April 2000 (Democratic Republic of the Congo v Belgium)*, ICJ Reports 2002 p 3, 24.

[50] Similarly, that certain international crimes or human rights are peremptory does not mean that any concomitant obligation to prosecute violations of these norms is equally peremptory, even less that on that account amnesties for these crimes are by definition prohibited. See Scharf (1996) 59 *LCP* 41; O'Brien (2005) 74 *Nordic JIL* 261; Sterio (2006) 34 *DJILP* 373; Freeman, *Necessary Evils: Amnesties and the Search for Justice* (2009).

(B) THE OBLIGATION NOT TO RECOGNIZE A SITUATION AS LAWFUL

Employing the category of 'serious breach by a State of an obligation arising under a peremptory norm of general international law',[51] the ILC Articles of 2001 articulated the following specific consequences:

Article 41

Particular consequences of a serious breach of an obligation under this Chapter

1. States shall cooperate to bring to an end through lawful means any serious breach within the meaning of article 40.

2. No State shall recognize as lawful a situation created by a serious breach within the meaning of article 40, nor render aid or assistance in maintaining that situation.

3. This article is without prejudice to the other consequences referred to in this Part and to such further consequences that a breach to which this Chapter applies may entail under international law.

This is very much a residual set of obligations, involving no very strenuous individual obligation to act on the part of third states. Despite this, Article 41 is probably as much progressive development as codification. If there is an element of customary international law here, it is the element of collective non-recognition, which goes back to the Stimson doctrine announced at the time of the Manchurian crisis in 1934—and significantly involving not just League members but also the US, a non-member.[52] This precedent was relied on in the ILC's commentary to Article 41:

The Declaration on Principles of International Law Concerning Friendly Relations and Co-operation Among States in Accordance with the Charter of the United Nations affirms this principle by stating unequivocally that States shall not recognize as legal any acquisition of territory brought about by the use of force. As the International Court of Justice held in *Military and Paramilitary Activities*, the unanimous consent of States to this declaration 'may be understood as an acceptance of the validity of the rule or set of rules declared by the resolution by themselves.'[53]

The principle of non-recognition was confirmed by the Court in *Namibia*, but it was qualified in the following significant way:

[T]he non-recognition of South Africa's administration of the Territory should not result in depriving the people of Namibia of any advantages derived from international co-operation. In particular, while official acts performed by the Government of South Africa on behalf of or concerning Namibia after the termination of the Mandate are illegal and invalid, this invalidity cannot be extended to those acts, such as, for instance, the registration of births,

---

[51] ARSIWA, Art 40(1): 'serious breach' is defined in Art 40(2) as one which 'involves a gross or systematic failure by the responsible State to fulfil the obligation'.

[52] See Crawford (2nd edn, 2006) 75–6, 78, 132–3, with references to relevant resolutions and declarations.

[53] Commentary to Art 41, §(6), citing *Nicaragua*, ICJ Reports 1986 p 14, 100.

deaths and marriages, the effects of which can be ignored only to the detriment of the inhabitants of the Territory.[54]

The 'Namibia exception' has been applied by the European Court of Human Rights,[55]
latterly in ways which have tended to make it the rule rather than the exception.[56]

The first occasion after 2001 on which some of these issues were judicially tested
before the International Court was the *Wall* advisory opinion.[57] There the Court discussed the existence of consequences for third states as a result of the breaches by Israel
of its obligations 'to respect the right of the Palestinian people to self-determination
and…obligations under international humanitarian law and international human
rights law.'[58] The 'Separation Barrier' erected by Israel in the West Bank encompassed
(or when completed, would encompass) most of the Israeli settlements there, together
with most water sources and much vacant land. The settlements themselves, the
Court indicated, were in violation of Article 49, paragraph 6 of the Fourth Geneva
Convention, which prohibits an occupying power from 'organiz[ing] or encourag[ing]
transfers of parts of its own population into the occupied territory.'[59] The Wall also
raised the risk of 'creat[ing] a "*fait accompli*" on the ground that could well become
permanent,' including, in addition to forced demographic changes, prejudicing a
future frontier between Israel and Palestine. It would give 'expression *in loco* to the
illegal measures taken by Israel with regard to Jerusalem.'[60] The Court noted evidence
(in the form of UN and other reports) that the Wall had disrupted economic life as
well as hindering access to medical services.[61] Above all, the Wall prejudiced the right
to self-determination of the Palestinian people, which the Court indicated was recognized in UN practice and by the agreements and exchanges of letters between Israel
and the PLO in the early 1990s.[62] On the evidence before it the Court concluded that
the Wall was not necessary to attain Israel's security objectives, and thus that security
exceptions under the relevant instruments were not a justification.[63]

Turning to the consequences of these findings, the Court noted that the norms in
question constituted rights and obligations *erga omnes* and then held that '[g]iven
the character and the importance of the rights and obligations involved', other states
were under an obligation not to recognize the unlawful situation resulting from the
construction of the Wall. Furthermore they were under an obligation not to render aid
and assistance in maintaining the situation thereby created, as well as to see to it that

[54] *Namibia*, ICJ Reports 1971 p 16, 56, §125.
[55] *Loizidou v Turkey* (1996) 108 ILR 443; *Cyprus v Turkey* (2001) 120 ILR 10, 42–5.
[56] *Demopoulos v Turkey* [2010] ECtHR (GC) 46113/99, 3843/02, 13751/02, 13466/03, 14163/04, 10200/04,
19993/04 & 21819/04, §94. And Ronen, *Transition from Illegal Regimes under International Law* (2011).
[57] ICJ Reports 2004 p 136.
[58] Ibid, 197.
[59] Ibid, 183.
[60] Ibid, 184.
[61] Ibid, 189–92.
[62] Ibid, 183.
[63] Ibid, 192–4.

'while respecting the United Nations Charter and international law...any impedi-
ment, resulting from the construction of the wall, to the exercise by the Palestinian
people of its right to self-determination is brought to an end.'[64] In addition, the Court
was of the view that the 'United Nations, and especially the General Assembly and the
Security Council, should consider what further action is required to bring to an end
the illegal situation resulting from the construction of the wall'.[65] Although the Court
made no express reference to Articles 40 and 41 it did use, unacknowledged, formulations drawn from Article 41.

The Court's approach should be contrasted with the partially dissenting opinion of
Judge Kooijmans. Agreeing on the illegality of the Wall and on the consequences for
Israel as the responsible state, he did not agree on the consequences for third states.
He said:

I must admit that I have considerable difficulty in understanding why a violation of an obligation *erga omnes* by one State should necessarily lead to an obligation for third States. The
nearest I can come to such an explanation is the text of Article 41 of the International Law
Commission's Articles on State Responsibility...

Article 41, paragraph 2, however, explicitly mentions the duty not to recognize as lawful a
situation created by a serious breach...In its commentary the ILC refers to unlawful situations which—virtually without exception—take the form of a legal claim, usually to territory...In other words, all examples mentioned refer to situations arising from formal or
quasi-formal promulgations intended to have an *erga omnes* effect. I have no problem with
accepting a duty of non-recognition in such cases.

I have great difficulty, however, in understanding what the duty not to recognize an illegal
fact involves. What are the individual addressees of this part of [the judgment] supposed to
do in order to comply with this obligation?...The duty not to recognize amounts, therefore,
in my view to an obligation without real substance.[66]

One can sympathize with the view that an obligation not to recognize a fact is illusory
and insubstantial. But that was not what was at stake with regard to the Separation
Barrier. Article 41, or rather the customary law obligation it seeks to embody, is not
concerned with the recognition of facts but with their legitimation. States are obliged
not to recognize *as lawful* a situation created by a serious breach of a peremptory
norm. The recognition as lawful of a regime—whether of apartheid in South Africa or
of other forms of separation or alienation elsewhere—is not just the recognition of a
fact. It legitimates the regime and tends to its consolidation. The widespread recognition of a regime as unlawful has the reverse effect—as events have shown. There are,
after all, few enough weapons in the armoury of international law.

---

[64] Ibid, 300.
[65] Ibid.
[66] Ibid, 231–2.

(C) THE OBLIGATION OF PUTTING AN END TO AN UNLAWFUL SITUATION

When competent organs of the UN make a binding determination that a situation is unlawful, the states that are addressees of the relevant resolution or resolutions are under an obligation to bring that situation to an end.[67] Much depends on the precise manner in which such resolutions spell out the consequences of non-compliance. At the least, this should involve a 'duty of non-recognition', which must be observed irrespective of or in the absence of any directives from a competent organ of the UN if, in the careful judgement of the individual state, a situation has arisen the illegality of which is opposable to states in general.

In 1970 the Security Council adopted Resolution 276 in which it recognized the decision of the General Assembly to terminate the mandate of South West Africa and to assume direct responsibility for the territory until its independence. The General Assembly had also declared that the South African presence in South West Africa (Namibia), as well as all later acts by the South African government concerning Namibia, were illegal and invalid.[68] In Resolution 283 (1970) the Security Council called upon all states to take specific steps in response to the illegality of the South African presence, including the termination of diplomatic and consular representation as far as such relations extended to Namibia, the ending of dealings relating to the territory by state enterprises, and the withdrawal of financial support from nationals and private corporations that would be used to facilitate trade or commerce with Namibia.

In Resolution 284 (1970) the Security Council asked the International Court for an advisory opinion on the following question: '[w]hat are the legal consequences for States of the continued presence of South Africa in Namibia, notwithstanding Security Council Resolution 276 (1970)'? In its Opinion the Court considered a variety of issues including the legal status of the GA resolution by which the Mandate was terminated. The Court held that as a consequence of SC Resolution 276, which under the UN Charter generated legal obligations, member states were under an obligation to recognize the illegality and invalidity of South Africa's continued presence in Namibia.[69] The Court recognized that the precise determination of appropriate measures was a matter for the political organs. Thus the Court would 'confine itself to giving advice on those dealings with the Government of South Africa which, under the Charter of the United Nations and general international law, should be considered as inconsistent

---

[67] *Namibia*, ICJ Reports 1971 p 16, 54; and Decree No 1 for the Protection of the Natural Resources of Namibia, UN Council for Namibia, approved by GA Res 3295(XXIX), 13 December 1974. Also *Loizidou v Turkey* (1996) 108 ILR 443.

[68] GA Res 2145(XXI), 27 October 1966. On Namibia see also Crawford (2nd edn, 2006) 591–6.

[69] ICJ Reports 1971 p 16, 54–6, 58 (supported by 11 votes to 4). By 13 votes to 2 it was held that, because the continued presence of South Africa in Namibia was unlawful, South Africa was under an obligation to withdraw its administration immediately. Judges Fitzmaurice and Gros dissented and considered the Mandate not validly terminated. Further: ibid, 89–100 (Vice-President Ammoun), 119–20 (Judge Padilla Nervo), 133–7 (Judge Petrén), 147–9 (Judge Onyeama), 165–7 (Judge Dillard), 217–19 (Judge de Castro), 295–8 (Judge Fitzmaurice, diss). See Dugard (1971) 88 *S Af LJ* 460.

with the declaration of illegality and invalidity made in paragraph 2 of Resolution 276 (1970), because they may imply a recognition that South Africa's presence in Namibia is legal'.[70] Matters touched upon in connection with this included treaty relations in cases in which South Africa purported to act on behalf of or concerning Namibia, diplomatic relations, and economic dealings. The Opinion excluded acts such as registration of births, deaths, and marriages from the taint of legal invalidity. Finally, the Court expressed the view that the illegality of the situation was opposable to all states and not merely to members of the United Nations.[71]

In legal terms the consequences of illegality, including 'the duty of non-recognition', are distinct from the application of economic and military sanctions, voluntary or mandatory, in compliance with a UN resolution. Such sanctions were, for example, imposed against Rhodesia following the Smith regime's unilateral declaration of independence.[72] Politically speaking the practical consequences of non-recognition are similar to non-military sanctions.[73] It may be true, as Judge Petrén suggests in his separate opinion, that the resolutions concerning Namibia impose certain duties going beyond the requirements of mere non-recognition in general international law.[74]

This was explicitly recognized by Judge Kooijmans in his separate opinion in the *Wall*, referring to

the second obligation mentioned in Article 41, paragraph 2, namely the obligation not to render aid or assistance in maintaining the situation created by the serious breach. I...fully support that part of operative subparagraph (3) (D). Moreover, I would have been in favour of adding in the reasoning or even in the operative part a sentence reminding States of the importance of rendering humanitarian assistance to the victims of the construction of the wall...[75]

3. AN EMERGING SYSTEM OF MULTILATERAL PUBLIC ORDER?[76]

It was obvious—not least to the dissenters—that the notion of peremptory norms, once accepted in 1969, could not be confined to the law of treaties.[77] So fundamental

[70] *Namibia*, ICJ Reports 1971 p 16, 55.

[71] Ibid, 56.

[72] An early instance of collective action under General Assembly and Security Council auspices was that taken against Southern Rhodesia: Gowlland-Debbas, *Collective Responses to Illegal Acts in International Law* (1990) 179–486.

[73] See *Namibia*, ICJ Reports 1971 p 16, 134–7 (Judge Petrén).

[74] Ibid, 148 (Judge Onyeama), 165 (Judge Dillard), 297 (Judge Fitzmaurice, diss).

[75] ICJ Reports 2004 p 133, 231–2.

[76] On the cognate debate over constitutionalization see generally: Orakhelashvili, in Muller & Frishman (eds), *The Dynamics of Constitutionalism in the Age of Globalization* (2009) 153; Klabbers, Peters & Ulfstein, *The Constitutionalization of International Law* (2009).

[77] See the position of France, voting against the VCLT because of Art 53: UN Conference on the Law of Treaties, 2nd Sess, *Official Records* A/CONF.39/11/Add.1, 203–4. On 'relative normativity': Weil (1983) 77 *AJIL* 413.

a notion as a norm from which states cannot (individually or even multilaterally) derogate was bound to have consequences beyond the law of treaties, and so it has proved.[78]

The developments listed above constitute modest measures in the direction of objective illegality and its consequences. But it should be stressed that international law has other functions than the pursuit of illegality, functions that may well have to be performed concurrently. Thus unlawful conduct may entail a legal regime that arises by virtue of that very conduct. For example, an 'armed conflict', the initiation of which may have been a breach of the UN Charter and of customary international law, will bring into operation most, if not all, of the rules governing the conduct of war. Similarly, states have in some instances at least operated according to a principle of effectiveness in circumstances of questionable legality.[79]

But with whatever qualifications, the developments which form the subject of the present chapter are based upon the premise that there are certain peremptory norms and an acceptance of the corollary that there is a duty not to recognize as lawful a situation created by a breach of a peremptory norm. It was thus that the ILC, after considerable debate, included Chapter III (of Part Two) in the Articles on State Responsibility adopted on second reading in 2001: that Part was eventually entitled 'Serious Breaches of Obligations under Peremptory Norms of General International Law'. These normative structures look progressive on paper but, in certain political circumstances, the result may be to give an appearance of legitimacy to questionable policies based on objectives which are (to say the least) collateral to the enforcement of the law. Great caution is accordingly called for in their implementation.[80]

---

[78] The point was noted in the first edition of this book, even before the adoption of the VCLT: see Brownlie, *Principles of Public International Law* (1st edn, 1966) 417–18.

[79] Generally: Touscoz, *Le Principe d'effectivité dans l'ordre international* (1964); Lauterpacht, *Development* (1958) 227ff.

[80] Koskenniemi (2001) 72 *BY* 337; and cf Crawford, in Crawford, Pellet & Olleson (2010) 931.

PART X

THE PROTECTION OF INDIVIDUALS AND GROUPS

28

THE INTERNATIONAL
MINIMUM STANDARD:
PERSONS AND PROPERTY

1. STATE AND INDIVIDUAL: THE SEARCH
FOR STANDARDS

The legal consequences of belonging to a political community with a territorial base have not changed a great deal since the seventeenth century, despite changes in the various theories used to describe or explain the relation. Ties of allegiance, citizenship, and nationality have provided the basis for the community of the state, whether regarded primarily as an organic unity expressed in terms of 'personal' sovereignty or as a territorial domain. Modern practice tends toward the latter view, but has not wholly abandoned the doctrine of Vattel who, in a much-quoted passage, wrote: '[w]hoever uses a citizen ill, indirectly offends the state, which is bound to protect this citizen'.[1] This is often described as a fiction, but the legal relation between a 'corporate' legal person and its members cannot be simply dismissed in this way. Vattel was not contending that any harm to an alien was as such an injury to the alien's state: the link was indirect. In effect the relation of nationality provided a basis for principles of responsibility and protection.[2] In particular, the state has a legal interest represented by its citizens, and anyone harming its citizens may have to account to that state in its protective capacity. If nationals are subjected to injury or loss by another state, then, whether the harm occurs in the territory of a state, or on the high seas or in outer space, the state of nationality may present a claim on the international plane. The conditions on which it may do so were set out in the ILC's Articles on Diplomatic Protection (2006), some aspects of which reflect general international law:[3] the ILC did not however deal with the substantive standards of protection.[4]

---

[1] Vattel, *Le Droit des gens* (1758, tr Anon 1797) II.vi.§71.

[2] But see *Barcelona Traction, Light & Power Company, Limited (Belgium v Spain)*, Second Phase, ICJ Reports 1970 p 3, 290–4, 300–1 (Judge Ammoun).

[3] 19 May 2006, ILC *Ybk* 2006/II, 2, 71–6; and Crawford (2006) 31 *S Af YIL* 19.

[4] But see ILC, Expulsion of Aliens, A/CN.4/617, 21 July 2009; Secretariat Memorandum, Expulsion of Aliens, A/CN.4/565, 10 July 2006; Special Rapporteur Kamto, Seventh Report, A/CN.4/462, 4 May 2011.

The law which has developed under the rubric of diplomatic protection is now being affected by the jurisprudence of tribunals sitting under bilateral and multilateral investment treaties. To a considerable extent the standards involved are those of the particular treaty: the International Court refused to draw any more general inferences from the large number of similarly-worded treaties in *Barcelona Traction*[5] and again, four decades later, in *Diallo*.[6] Nonetheless, some investment treaties articulate a standard of general international law, notably the international minimum standard of treatment. This is embodied, for example, in North American Free Trade Agreement (NAFTA) Article 1105[7] as interpreted by the member states.[8]

Thus there are now two discrete streams of authority—one based on the practice and jurisprudence of diplomatic protection, the other based on the generic standards in over 2,500 BITs, as applied in some 300 reported or unreported tribunal decisions.[9] For the purposes of exposition the two streams will be presented together, but this is without prejudice to the need for analysis of the specific context and the basis of claim in every case.

2. ADMISSION, EXPULSION, AND LIABILITIES OF ALIENS

Problems of responsibility arise most frequently when aliens and their assets are stationed on host state territory, and by way of preliminary, something must be said of the entry of aliens within the state. In principle this is a matter of domestic jurisdiction: a state may choose not to admit aliens or may impose conditions on their admission.[10]

---

[5] *Barcelona Traction*, Second Phase, ICJ Reports 1970 p 3, 32–4. The Court noted that 'whenever legal issues arise concerning the rights of States with regard to the treatment of companies and shareholders, as to which rights international law has not established its own rules, it has to refer to the relevant rules of municipal law'. This passage was quoted with approval in *Ahmadou Sadio Diallo (Guinea v Democratic Republic of the Congo)*, Judgment of 30 November 2010, §34.

[6] Judgment of 24 May 2007, §§30–1, holding that BIT practice 'is not sufficient to show that there has been a change in the customary rules of diplomatic protection; it could equally show the contrary'.

[7] 17 December 1992, 32 ILM 289, Art 1105.

[8] NAFTA Free Trade Commission, Notes of Interpretation of Certain Chapter 11 Provisions, 31 July 2001, 13 *WTAM* 139, stating that 'the concepts of "fair and equitable treatment" and "full protection and security" do not require treatment in addition to or beyond that which is required by the customary international law minimum standard of treatment of aliens'.

[9] The texts of BITs and awards cited in this chapter can be found at www.unctadxi.org and/or www.italaw.com. There are some 269 reported BIT cases at www.italaw.com of which 224 involve ICSID. The first reported BIT decision was *Asian Agricultural Products Ltd v Sri Lanka* (1990) 4 ICSID Reports 245.

[10] For British practice: McNair, 2 *Opinions* 105–8; *Musgrove v Toy* [1891] AC 272; 6 *BD* 9–77. Generally on admission and exclusion of aliens: McDougal, Lasswell & Chen (1976) 70 *AJIL* 432; Goodwin-Gill, *International Law and the Movement of Persons between States* (1978) chs 1–2, 6–10; Nafziger (1983) 77 *AJIL* 804; Madureira, *Aliens' Admission to and Departure from National Territory* (1989); Aleinikoff (ed), *From Migrants to Citizens* (2000); Guild (ed), *International Migration and Security* (2005). Also the International Convention on the Protection of the Rights of All Migrant Workers and Members of their Families, 18 December 1990, 2220 UNTS 3; European Convention on Establishment, 13 December 1955, 529 UNTS

Internal economic policies and aspects of foreign policy may result in restrictions on the economic activity of aliens. National policy may require prohibition or regulation of the purchase of immovables, ships, aircraft and the like, and the practice of certain professions by aliens. Provisions for the admission of aliens in treaties of friendship, commerce, and navigation are qualified by references to 'public order, morals, health or safety'.[11] BITs normally provide expressly that the question of admission is one for the law of the host state.[12]

In principle expulsion of aliens is also within the discretion of the state,[13] but this discretion is not unlimited.[14] In particular, the power of expulsion must be exercised in good faith and not for an ulterior motive.[15] While the expelling state has a margin of appreciation in applying the concept of 'ordre public', this concept is to be measured against human rights standards.[16] The latter are applicable also to the *manner* of expulsion.[17] In certain conditions expulsion may infringe the principle of non-discrimination (racial or religious) which is part of customary international law.[18] Expulsion which causes specific loss to the national state forced to receive large groups without adequate notice could ground a claim for indemnity. Finally, the expulsion of persons who by long residence and exercise of civil rights have acquired prima facie the effective nationality of the host state is not a matter of discretion, since the issue of nationality places the right to expel in question.

The International Court considered the issue of expulsion in *Diallo*. It concluded that under the ICCPR and the relevant regional human rights treaty (the African Charter):

the expulsion of an alien lawfully in the territory of a State which is a party to these instruments can only be compatible with the international obligations of that State if it is decided

---

142. Further: *Kleindienst v Mandel*, 408 US 753 (1972); *R (Ullah) v Special Adjudicator* [2004] UKHL 26; *Aderhold v Dalwigk, Knüppel*, 2 BvR 1908/03, 24.10.2006.

[11] E.g. USA–Italy, Treaty of Friendship, Commerce and Navigation, 2 February 1948, 326 UNTS 71.

[12] E.g. Germany–Guyana BIT (1989) 1909 UNTS 3, Art 2 (1); Sweden–Argentina BIT (1991), Art 1(1); Switzerland–Croatia BIT (1996), Art 2; Germany Model BIT (2008), Art 2.

[13] 6 *BD* 83–241; 8 Whiteman 850–63; Kälin, 'Aliens, Expulsion and Deportation' (2010) *MPEPIL*. E.g. People's Initiative 'Expulsion of Foreign Criminals', Switzerland, adopted by referendum on 28 November 2010, providing for automatic expulsion and ban on re-entry of aliens convicted of certain crimes.

[14] *Yeager v Islamic Republic of Iran* (1987) 82 ILR 178; *Short v Islamic Republic of Iran* (1987) 82 ILR 148; *Libyan Arab Foreign Investment Co v Republic of Burundi* (1991) 96 ILR 279. Generally: Goodwin-Gill (1978) 201–310. Further: Henckaerts, *Mass Expulsion in Modern International Law and Practice* (1995); Alleweldt, *Protection against Expulsion in the Case of Threat of Torture or Inhuman or Degrading Treatment or Punishment* (1996); Guild & Minderhoud (eds), *Security of Residence and Expulsion* (2001); Edwards & Ferstman (eds), *Human Security and Non-Citizens* (2010).

[15] For expulsion as disguised extradition: e.g. *Muller v Superintendent, Presidency Jail, Calcutta* (1955) 22 ILR 497; *R v Governor of Brixton Prison, ex parte Soblen* [1963] 2 QB 283; *R v Horseferry Road Magistrates' Court, ex parte Bennett* [1993] 3 WLR 90; *Conka v Belgium* [2002] ECtHR 51564/99.

[16] CCPR, General Comment 15: The Position of Aliens under the Covenant (1986); *Maroufidou v Sweden* (1981) 62 ILR 278, 284.

[17] The view is sometimes expressed that the expelling state must have complied with its own law: 6 *BD* 151–2; Goodwin-Gill (1978) 263–81.

[18] *R (European Roma Rights Centre) v Immigration Officer at Prague Airport* [2004] UKHL 55, and on non-discrimination: chapter 29.

in accordance with 'the law', in other words the domestic law applicable in that respect. Compliance with international law is to some extent dependent here on compliance with internal law. However ... [this] is not a sufficient condition. First, the applicable domestic law must itself be compatible with the other requirements of the Covenant and the African Charter; second, an expulsion must not be arbitrary in nature, since protection against arbitrary treatment lies at the heart of the rights guaranteed.[19]

The Court further underlined the obligation to provide grounds for expulsion, the prohibition of mistreatment of aliens subject to expulsion, the obligation to inform without delay the consular authorities of the state of origin of the aliens pending expulsion, and the obligation to respect the property rights of those being expelled.[20]

The liabilities of alien visitors under their own and under the local law can lead to overlapping and conflicting claims of the state of origin and the host state in various areas of jurisdiction, including antitrust, labour, and welfare standards, monetary regulation, and taxation. The principles on which conflicts of jurisdiction may be approached have been considered in chapter 21. The point here is to examine the limits of the competence of the host state in placing liabilities on aliens of a special kind, for example, duties to serve in the armed forces, militia, or police and to submit to requisitions in time of emergency.[21] The legal position is not in all respects clear. Thus there is authority to support the rule that an alien cannot be required to serve in the regular armed forces of the host state.[22] However, in American and Australian practice an alien admitted with a view to permanent residence or who has participated in the local political franchise may be conscripted to serve in local militia and also in forces for external defence.[23] The basis for obligations of this kind is the reciprocity between residence and local protection, on the one hand, and the responsibilities of a 'functional' citizenship. In some cases long residence and local connections may create a new, effective nationality opposable to the state of origin (see chapter 23).

3. REQUIREMENTS FOR AND STANDARDS OF DIPLOMATIC PROTECTION

(A) OVERVIEW

The exercise of diplomatic protection of nationals visiting or resident in foreign countries has subsisted, with changes of terminology and concept, since the Middle Ages.

---

[19] *Diallo*, Judgment of 30 November 2010, §24.

[20] Ibid, §§29, 31, 35–7. Also: *Diallo*, Compensation, Judgment, of 19 June 2012, §§ 11–17.

[21] For British practice: 6 *BD* 368–405; McNair, 2 *Opinions* 113–37. Also: Parry (1954) 31 *BY* 437; Goodwin-Gill (1978) ch 3; Pérez Vera (1996) 261 Hague *Recueil* 243; Hailbronner & Gogolin, 'Aliens' (2009) *MPEPIL*.

[22] Verdross (1931) 37 Hague *Recueil* 327, 379. The law of war and neutrality may reinforce the position when the host state is involved in civil or foreign war. See 1 *Répertoire suisse* 348; *Polites v Commonwealth of Australia* (1945) 12 ILR 208.

[23] (1967) 3 *AYIL* 249; 8 Whiteman 540–73.

Modern practice emerged in the late eighteenth century, when the grant of letters of reprisal, an indiscriminate right of private war, to citizens harmed by aliens disappeared.[24] It was the nineteenth century which produced political and economic conditions in which the status of aliens abroad became a problem of wide dimensions. The history has been primarily concerned with the conflicts of interest between foreign investors (represented by their national state) and the more-or-less exploited hosts to foreign capital. In the century after 1840 some 60 mixed claims commissions were set up to deal with such disputes.[25] Literature on protection of aliens from the point of view of investor states grew particularly after 1890; influential contributions were made by Anzilotti and the Americans, Moore, Borchard, and Eagleton.[26]

This area of law has always been controversial. In the period 1945–80, concepts of economic independence and political and economic principles favouring nationalization and the public sector made headway. The legal reasoning offered on precise issues stems from a small number of general principles and the relations between them. Presumptively the ordering of persons and assets is an aspect of the domestic jurisdiction of a state and an incident of its territorial sovereignty.[27] Exceptions may be created by treaty, and in the past immunity for aliens was sometimes coupled with the privilege of the sending state to maintain a special system of courts for nationals on the territory of the receiving state (capitulations).[28]

In principle, however, the territorial competence of the state subsists, and the alien is admitted, at discretion, as a visitor with a duty to submit to local law and jurisdiction. However, residence abroad does not deprive an individual of the protection of the state of nationality. Diplomatic protection is best seen as a function of the relation of nationality in the absence of any better means of security. Where the state authorities cause injury to the alien visitor, for example in the form of brutality by police officials, the legal position is clear. The host state is responsible, but, as a condition for

---

[24] Saxoferrato, *Tractatus represaliarum* (1354), in *Consiliorum Bartoli Libri Duo* (1555); Legnano *Tractatus de bello, de represaliis et de duello* (1360; repr 1917); Vattel (1758) II.xvi; Onuf, *Reprisals* (1974); Kalshoven, *Belligerent Reprisals* (2nd edn, 2005); Ruffert, *The Public–Private Law Divide* (2009). At sea, letters of marque survived into the 19th century: Cooperstein (2009) 40 *JMLC* 221.

[25] These included claims settlement conventions between Mexico and the US of 1839, 1848, 1868, and 1923; the Venezuelan arbitrations of 1903 involving claims of 10 states against Venezuela; and conventions between Great Britain and the US of 1853, 1871, and 1908. See Borchard (1927) 21 *AJIL* 472; Feller, *The Mexican Claims Commissions 1923–1934* (1935); Stuyt, *Survey of International Arbitrations 1794–1989* (3rd edn, 1990); Dolzer, 'Mixed Claims Commissions' (2006) *MPEPIL*.

[26] Anzilotti (1906) 13 *RGDIP* 5, 285; Anzilotti *The Diplomatic Protection of Citizens Abroad* (2nd edn, 1927); Eagleton, *The Responsibility of States in International Law* (1928); Dunn, *The Protection of Nationals* (1932); Freeman, *The International Responsibility of States for Denial of Justice* (1938); Brownlie, *System of the Law of Nations; State Responsibility* (1983) 1–9; Lillich (ed), *International Law of State Responsibility for Injuries to Aliens* (1983). Also: Lillich (1978) 161 Hague *Recueil* 329; Lillich, *The Human Rights of Aliens in Contemporary International Law* (1984); Dugard, in Crawford, Pellet & Olleson (eds), *The Law of International Responsibility* (2010) 1051.

[27] For a misguided attempt to exclude host state law: *Kardassopoulos v Georgia*, 6 July 2007, §§142–6. The decision was right on the facts as Georgia was plainly estopped from denying the legality of the investment.

[28] On the abolition of capitulations: Bentwich (1933) 13 *BY* 89. In general: Bell, 'Capitulations' (2009) *MPEPIL*.

the presentation of the claim by the national state, the alien must exhaust any remedies available in the local courts.[29] The reasons for this condition of admissibility are practical: claims by individuals are handled better in municipal courts, governments dislike the multiplication of claims for diplomatic intervention, and it is reasonable for the resident alien to submit to the local system of justice. The ILC's Articles on Diplomatic Protection reaffirm that 'diplomatic protection ... is the procedure employed by the State of nationality of the injured person to secure protection of that person and to obtain reparation for the internationally wrongful act inflicted.'[30] Article 14 purports to codify the customary rule of exhaustion of local remedies 'as a prerequisite for the exercise of diplomatic protection'.[31] Article 15 sets out exceptions to the rule, including where local courts offer no prospect of redress, where circumstances make it unfair or unreasonable to exhaust the local remedies and where the respondent state has waived the requirement.[32]

More difficult are the cases where the alien is harmed by acts or omissions which are on their face a normal exercise of the competence of organs of the host state. These situations include the malfunction of judicial organs dealing with acts which are breaches of the local law affecting the interests of the alien ('denial of justice'), and also general legislative measures, not directed at aliens as such, affecting the ownership or enjoyment of foreign-owned assets. There has always been a current of opinion to the effect that the alien, having submitted to the local law, can only expect treatment on a basis of equality with nationals of the host state. It is also said that the status of the alien is not the subject of a privilege, but is simply that of an individual within the territorial sovereignty and jurisdiction of the host state.[33]

(B) THE NATIONAL TREATMENT STANDARD[34]

An initial point of agreement is that certain forms of inequality are admissible. Thus aliens are not entitled to political rights in the host state. Moreover, the alien must accept local law in regard to regulation of the economy, including restrictions on employment

---

[29] Generally: Amerasinghe, *Local Remedies in International Law* (2nd edn, 2004), and see chapter 31.

[30] Ibid, 23–4.

[31] Ibid, 71.

[32] Conspicuous among examples of waiver are almost all BITs, which dispense with the procedural requirement of exhaustion. See Douglas, *The International Law of Investment Claims* (2009) §§610–15; and for the local remedies rule as a ground of inadmissibility: chapter 31.

[33] The debate: ILC *Ybk* 1957/I, 154–62; cf Sornarajah, *The International Law on Foreign Investment* (3rd edn, 2010).

[34] Harvard Draft Convention on Responsibility of States for Damage Done in Their Territory to the Person or Property of Foreigners (1929) 23 *AJIL Sp Supp* 131; Jessup (1946) 46 *Col LR* 903; Roth, *The Minimum Standard of International Law Applied to Aliens* (1949); Sohn & Baxter (1961) 55 *AJIL* 545; 6 *BD* 247–440; 8 Whiteman 704–6; García Amador, Sohn & Baxter, *Recent Codification of the Law of State Responsibility for Injuries to Aliens* (1974). Further: Melloni, *The Principle of National Treatment in the GATT* (2005); Kurtz, in Kahn & Wälde, *Les aspects nouveaux du droit des investissements internationaux* (2007) 311; Bjorklund, in Yannaca-Small (ed), *Arbitration under International Investment Agreements* (2010) 411; Gerhart & Baron, in Qureshi & Gao (eds), 3 *International Economic Law* (2011) 77.

of aliens in particular types of employment. Access to the courts must be maintained, but rules in ancillary matters may be modified: thus an alien need not have access to legal aid and may have to give security for costs.[35] Exceptions may of course be created by treaty, most notably BITs. Standards of treatment commonly employed in treaties include national, most-favoured-nation, and fair and equitable treatment.

The national treatment standard was supported by jurists both in Europe and Latin America prior to 1940,[36] by a small number of arbitral awards,[37] and by 17 states at the Hague Codification Conference in 1930.[38] At the conference 21 states opposed the standard, although some had relied on it in presenting claims to international tribunals.[39]

(C) THE INTERNATIONAL MINIMUM STANDARD[40]

Since the beginning of the twentieth century the preponderant doctrine has supported an 'international minimum standard'.[41] A majority of the states represented at the Hague Codification Conference endorsed that standard, and it was affirmed in the Declaration on Permanent Sovereignty over Natural Resources in 1962.[42] The standard is articulated in BITs, and has been applied by many tribunals and claims commissions. Thus in the *Neer Claim* the General Claims Commission set up by the US and Mexico expressed the position as follows:

[T]he propriety of governmental acts should be put to the test of international standards...the treatment of an alien, in order to constitute an international delinquency should amount to an outrage, to bad faith, to wilful neglect of duty, or to an insufficiency of governmental action so far short of international standards that every reasonable and impartial man would readily recognize its insufficiency.[43]

---

[35] The *cautio iudicatum solvi* of civil law systems.

[36] Also the citations by Herz (1941) 35 *AJIL* 243, 259. The equality principle was advocated as early as 1868 by the Argentinian jurist Calvo, *Derecho Internacional teórico y práctico de Europa y América* (1868).

[37] *Canevaro* (1912) 9 RIAA 397; *Cadenhead* (1914) 11 ILR 177; *Standard-Vacuum Oil Company* (1959) 30 ILR 168.

[38] Roth (1949) 72–4. Also Guerrero, Rapporteur, League of Nations, Responsibility of States for Damage Done in their Territory to the Person or Property of Aliens (1926) 20 *AJIL Sp Supp* 176.

[39] E.g. the US in *Norwegian Shipowners* (1922) 1 ILR 189. Also Havana Convention on Status of Aliens, 20 February 1928, 132 LNTS 301, Art 5; draft Convention on the Treatment of Aliens proposed by the Paris Conference, 1929, Art 17, in Bustamante, *La Comisión de Jurisconsultos de Rio de Janeiro y el Derecho Internacional* (1927) 206; Montevideo Convention on Rights and Duties of States, 26 December 1933, 165 LNTS 19, Art 9.

[40] Harvard Draft Convention (1929) 23 *AJIL Sp Supp* 131; Jessup (1946) 46 *Col LR* 903; Roth (1949); Sohn & Baxter (1961) 55 *AJIL* 545; 6 *BD* 247–440; García Amador, Sohn & Baxter (1974). For current literature: Kurtz, in Kahn & Wälde (2007) 311; Paparinskis, *The International Minimum Standard and Fair and Equitable Treatment* (2012).

[41] Leading proponents include Anzilotti, Verdross, Borchard, Oppenheim, Guggenheim, de Visscher, Scelle, and Jessup. Also 2 *Restatement Third*, §722; Schachter (1982) 178 Hague *Recueil* 1, 314–21; Dolzer & Schreuer, in 4 Qureshi & Gao (2011) 3.

[42] GA Res 1803(XVII), 14 December 1962 (87–2:12).

[43] (1926) 3 ILR 213. Also *Roberts* (1926) 3 ILR 227; *Hopkins* (1926) 3 ILR 229; *British Claims in the Spanish Zone of Morocco* (1925) 2 RIAA 615, 644.

This passage has become a focus for debate. On the one hand the NAFTA Tribunal in *Mondev* said:

A reasonable evolutionary interpretation of Article 1105(1) is consistent both with the *travaux*, with normal principles of interpretation and with the fact that, as the Respondent accepted in argument, the terms 'fair and equitable treatment' and 'full protection and security' had their origin in bilateral treaties in the post-war period. In these circumstances the content of the minimum standard today cannot be limited to the content of customary international law as recognised in arbitral decisions in the 1920s.[44]

On the other hand, another NAFTA Tribunal in *Glamis Gold* said:

Although situations may be more varied and complicated today than in the 1920s, the level of scrutiny is the same. The fundamentals of the *Neer* standard thus still apply today: to violate the customary international law minimum standard of treatment codified in Article 1105 of the NAFTA, an act must be sufficiently egregious and shocking—a gross denial of justice, manifest arbitrariness, blatant unfairness, a complete lack of due process, evident discrimination, or a manifest lack of reasons—so as to fall below accepted international standards and constitute a breach of Article 1105(1).[45]

(D) THE TWO STANDARDS IN PERSPECTIVE

The controversy concerning the national and international standards has not been finally resolved, and this is not surprising as the two viewpoints reflect conflicting economic and political interests. Those supporting the national treatment standard are not committed to the view that municipal law has supremacy over international law: their position is that, as a matter of *international* law, the standard of treatment is to be defined in terms of equality under the local law. Protagonists of national treatment point to the role the law associated with the international standard has played in maintaining a privileged status for aliens and supporting alien control of large areas of the national economy. The experience of the Latin American states and others suggests caution in handling the international standard, but it is necessary to distinguish between, on the one hand, the content of the standard and its application in particular cases and, on the other hand, the core principle, which is simply that the territorial sovereign cannot avoid responsibility by pleading that aliens and nationals had received equally bad treatment. Conversely, the rules of international law authorize at least a measure of discrimination, for example in matters of taxation.

A source of difficulty has been the tendency of some writers and tribunals to give the international standard too ambitious a content. For example in *Tecmed* the tribunal said:

The foreign investor expects the host State to act in a consistent manner, free from ambiguity and totally transparently in its relations with the foreign investor ... The foreign investor also

---

[44] *Mondev v US* (2002) 6 ICSID Reports 192, 224.
[45] *Glamis Gold v US*, 8 June 2009, §§614–16. Also *Cargill Inc v Mexico* (2009) 146 ILR 642, 724.

expects the host state to act consistently, i.e. without arbitrarily revoking any pre-existing decisions or permits issued by the state that were relied upon by the investor to assume its commitments as well as to plan and launch its commercial and business activities.[46]

This is an attempt to rewrite the fair and equitable treatment standard by reference to the hypothetical expectations of one class of participant, as distinct from using the specific expectations generated through the parties' actual course of dealings as relevant to the *application* of the standard. Indeed many governments would fail to meet this utopian standard much of the time.[47]

Another cause of difficulty has been the extension of delictual responsibility to the malfunction of administrative and judicial organs, as in the field of denial of justice. This aspect involves the imposition of the law of delict where a better analogy would be the use of administrative law remedies to ensure the proper exercise of legal powers. In regard to non-exercise or malfunction of legal powers national treatment has some significance, at least as creating a presumption of absence of malice.[48]

In short there is no universally applicable standard. Circumstances, for example, the outbreak of war, may create exceptions to the international treatment standard, even where this applies in principle. Where a reasonable care or due diligence standard is applicable,[49] it would represent a more sophisticated version of national treatment. It would allow for variations in wealth and educational standards between the various states of the world and yet would not be a mechanical matter, tied to equality.

Successive attempts have been made to synthesize the concept of human rights and the principles governing the treatment of aliens. Early on, García Amador, first ILC Special Rapporteur on state responsibility, proposed the following formulation:

1. The State is under a duty to ensure to aliens the enjoyment of the same civil rights, and to make available to them the same individual guarantees as are enjoyed by its own nationals. These rights and guarantees shall not however, in any case be less than the 'fundamental human rights' recognized and defined in contemporary international instruments.

2. In consequence, in case of violation of civil rights, or disregard of individual guarantees, with respect to aliens, international responsibility will be involved only if internationally recognized 'fundamental human rights' are affected.[50]

This particular synthesis involves codifying the 'international minimum standard', raising that standard, extending it to new subject-matter, and relating internal affairs and local law to international responsibility to a degree which most states would find

---

[46] *TECMED v Mexico* (2003) 10 ICSID Reports 130, 192.

[47] Cf the more balanced articulations in *Waste Management Inc (No 2) v United Mexican States* (2004) 11 ICSID Reports 361, 386; *MTD v Chile* (2007) 13 ICSID Reports 500, 521–2.

[48] Paulsson, *Denial of Justice in International Law* (2005) 88–90; McLachlan, Shore & Weiniger, *International Investment Arbitration* (2007) 243.

[49] For references to such a standard: *British Claims in the Spanish Zone of Morocco* (1925) 2 RIAA 615, 644 (Huber).

[50] ILC *Ybk* 1957/II, 112. Generally on human rights: chapter 29.

intolerable.[51] It is true that since 1945 a new content for the international standard based upon those human rights principles which have become a part of customary international law has arguably emerged. Yet the world is not governed by tribunals and a careful synthesis of human rights standards and the modern 'treatment of aliens' standards is required.[52] Notably, the concept of discrimination calls for more sophisticated treatment in order to identify unreasonable discrimination as distinct from the different treatment of non-comparable situations.[53]

It was precisely such difficulties that led to Ago's reformulation of state responsibility as concerned with 'secondary rules': the ILC Articles of 2001 are without prejudice to the substantive content of the international obligations of states.[54]

(E) FORMS OF DELICTUAL RESPONSIBILITY

The general principles of state responsibility were examined in chapter 25. They apply to cases where aliens are injured, whether within or outside the territory of the respondent state. Thus one might expect to rely upon a rule that a state is liable for failure to show due diligence in matters of administration, for example by failing to take steps to apprehend the murderer of an alien. However, the position is more complex. International law is not a system replete with nominate torts or delicts, but the rules are specialized in certain respects.

(i) Breach of the fair and equitable treatment standard[55]

The fair and equitable treatment standard (FET) is an autonomous standard of investment protection set out in the vast majority of BITs,[56] though in varying formulations.

---

[51] For criticisms see ILC *Ybk* 1957/I, 154–62, and for the Special Rapporteur's response: ibid, 1957/II, 104–31.

[52] Further: McDougal, Lasswell & Chen (1976) 70 *AJIL* 432; Lillich (1984). Cf UN Draft Norms on the Responsibilities of Transnational Corporations and other Business Enterprises with regard to Human Rights, E/CN.4/Sub.2/2003/12, 30 May 2003, 2 (which failed to gain endorsement by the UN Human Rights Commission). Further: Simma & Kill, in Binder et al (eds), *International Investment Law for the 21st Century* (2009) 678; Pisillo-Mazzeschi, in Fastenrath et al (eds), *From Bilateralism to Community Interest* (2011) 552; Paparinskis (2012) chs 7–8.

[53] McDougal, Lasswell & Chen (1976) 70 *AJIL* 432, 450–1; Schachter (1982) 178 Hague *Recueil* 1, 314–21; Weiler, *International Investment Law and Arbitration* (2005) 557; Lowenfeld, *International Economic Law* (2nd edn, 2008) 22–36. Generally: Vierdag, *The Concept of Discrimination in International Law* (1973); Schiek, *Cases, Materials and Text on National, Supranational and International Non-Discrimination Law* (2007); Baetens, in Schill (ed), *International Investment Law and Comparative Public Law* (2010) 279; Baetens, *Nationality Discrimination in International Law* (2012). In relation to discriminatory conduct see also *Saluka Investments BV v Czech Republic* (2006) 15 ICSID Reports 274, 340–2.

[54] Commentary, §1, in Crawford, *The International Law Commission's Articles on State Responsibility* (2002) 74; Crawford, in Crawford, Pellet & Olleson (2010) 20.

[55] OECD Working Paper 2004/3, *Fair and Equitable Treatment Standard in International Investment Law* (2004). Further: Tudor, *The Fair and Equitable Treatment Standard in the International Law of Foreign Investment* (2008); Kläger, *Fair and Equitable Treatment in International Investment Law* (2011); Alvarez (2011) 344 Hague *Recueil* 197; UNCTAD, *Fair and Equitable Treatment* (2011); Paparinskis (2012).

[56] Dolzer & Stevens, *Bilateral Investment Treaties* (1995) 60. Instances of BITs not containing a FET clause include the Croatia–Ukraine BIT (1997), a number of BITs concluded by Turkey and some FTAs

There are four main approaches: (a) a self-standing standard without additional reference to international law or other criteria;[57] (b) FET defined in 'accordance with international law';[58] (c) FET linked to the customary standard of minimum treatment of aliens;[59] and (d) FET with express reference to substantive obligations, for example prohibiting denial of justice or unreasonable or discriminatory measures.[60] Thus the application of the standard depends on the particular treaty invoked, although there are common generic questions.

The FET standard has become a focus of interpretation in investment treaty arbitration, invoked in most of the cases brought. Host state measures challenged for breach of FET vary widely, including revocation or non-renewal of licences,[61] imposition of new regulatory requirements by the legislative and executive organs affecting the economic operation of the investment,[62] tax and tariff measures,[63] termination, modification and breach of investment contracts,[64] abusive treatment of investors,[65] and denial of justice by both the executive and the judiciary.[66] In ascertaining the meaning and scope of the FET standard, tribunals have often considered it in its relation to the international minimum standard of treatment, particularly in the context of NAFTA arbitration.[67] In the substantive protections afforded by the FET standard,

---

adopting a national treatment standard instead (e.g. the 2003 Australia–Singapore and the 2001 India–Singapore FTAs).

[57] Belgium–Luxembourg Economic Union–Tajikistan BIT (2009); China–Switzerland BIT (2009); OECD Draft Convention on the Protection of Foreign Property (1967).

[58] El Salvador–US BIT (1999); Croatia–Oman BIT (2004).

[59] NAFTA, Article 1105 (1) Notes of Interpretation, 31 July 2001, NAFTA Free Trade Commission; Rwanda–US BIT (2008); Agreement Establishing the ASEAN-Australia–New Zealand Free Trade Area 2009, Ch 11, Art 6.

[60] Romania–United States BIT (1994); ASEAN Comprehensive Investment Agreement (2009), Art 11; Netherlands–Oman BIT (2009).

[61] *Wena Hotels Ltd v Egypt* (2000) 6 ICSID Reports 89; *Genin v Estonia* (2001) 6 ICSID Reports 236; *Tecmed v Mexico* (2003) 10 ICSID Reports 130.

[62] *Pope & Talbot v Canada* (2001) 7 ICSID Reports 102; *ADF v US* (2003) 6 ICSID Reports 470; *Eastern Sugar BV v Czech Republic*, 12 April 2007; *Glamis Gold v US*, 8 June 2009.

[63] *Occidental Exploration v Ecuador* (2004) 12 ICSID Reports 54; *CMS v Argentina* (2005) 14 ICSID Reports 158; *Biwater Gauff v Tanzania*, 24 July 2008.

[64] *Azinian v Mexico* (1999) 5 ICSID Reports 269; *Mondev v USA* (2002) 6 ICSID Reports 181; *Waste Management Inc v Mexico* (2004) 11 ICSID Reports 361; *Siemens AG v Argentina* (2007) 14 ICSID Reports 518; *Vivendi v Argentina*, 20 August 2007; *Rumeli Telecom v Kazakhstan*, 29 July 2008; *Duke Energy v Ecuador*, 18 August 2008; *Bayindir v Pakistan*, 27 August 2009.

[65] *Tokios Tokelés v Ukraine*, 26 July 2007; *Vivendi v Argentina*, 20 August 2007; *Desert Line Projects LLC v Yemen*, 6 February 2008.

[66] *Azininan v Mexico* (1999) 5 ICSID Reports 269; *Petrobart v Kyrgiz Republic* (2003) 13 ICSID Reports 335; *Loewen v USA* (2003) 7 ICSID Reports 442; *Amto v Ukraine*, 26 March 2008; *Jan de Nul v Egypt* (2008) 15 ICSID Reports 437.

[67] *Mondev v US* (2002) 6 ICSID Reports 192, 221–3; *ADF v US* (2003) 6 ICSID Reports 470, 527–8; *Waste Management v Mexico* (2004) 11 ICSID Reports 361, 386, and *International Thunderbird Gaming Corp v Mexico*, 26 January 2006, §194, all interpreting the *Neer* standard as an evolving one. But see the narrow interpretation of minimum standard in *Glamis Gold v US*, 8 June 2009, §§614–16.

tribunals have included protection of investors' legitimate expectations,[68] non-abusive treatment,[69] non-arbitrary and non-discriminatory exercise of public powers,[70] and its adherence to due process requirements.[71]

One influential formulation of the FET standard in the context of NAFTA, that is, with reference to the minimum standard of treatment under customary international law, was given by the tribunal in *Waste Management (No 2) v Mexico*:

The minimum standard of fair and equitable treatment is infringed by conduct attributable to the State and harmful to the claimant if the conduct is arbitrary, grossly unfair, unjust or idiosyncratic, is discriminatory and exposes the claimant to sectional or racial prejudice, or involves a lack of due process leading to an outcome which offends judicial propriety—as might be the case with a manifest failure of natural justice in judicial proceedings or a complete lack of transparency and candour in an administrative process.[72]

In a BIT context, the tribunal in *Saluka v Czech Republic* was called upon to assess what constituted permissible regulatory action by the Czech National Bank in the course of the reorganization of the banking sector. It observed that:

The 'fair and equitable treatment' standard in Article 3.1 of the Treaty is an autonomous Treaty standard and must be interpreted, in light of the object and purpose of the Treaty, so as to avoid conduct of the Czech Republic that clearly provides disincentives to foreign investors. The Czech Republic, without undermining its legitimate right to take measures for the protection of the public interest, has therefore assumed an obligation to treat a foreign investor's investment in a way that does not frustrate the investor's underlying legitimate and reasonable expectations. A foreign investor whose interests are protected under the Treaty is entitled to expect that the Czech Republic will not act in a way that is manifestly

---

[68] *TECMED v Mexico* (2003) 10 ICSID Reports 130, 192–3, on the expectation that the host state 'acts in a consistent manner, free from ambiguity and totally transparently'; *Duke Energy v Ecuador*, 18 August 2008, §340 stating that '[t]he stability of the legal and business environment is directly linked to the investor's justified expectations'. On the balancing of investors' legitimate expectations against the 'host State's legitimate right subsequently to regulate domestic matters in the public interest': *Saluka v Czech Republic* (2006) 15 ICSID Reports 274, 338–9; *Continental Casualty v Argentina*, 22 Februay 2008, §258; *EDF v Romania*, 8 October 2009, §217 stating that '[e]xcept where specific promises or representations are made by the State to the investor, the latter may not rely on a bilateral investment treaty as a kind of insurance policy against the risk of any changes in the host State's legal and economic framework. Such expectation would be neither legitimate nor reasonable.' On the relevance of legitimate expectations at the quantification of damages stage: *CME v Czech Republic* (2003), 9 ICSID Reports 265, Separate Opinion of Sir Ian Brownlie, 419–21.

[69] *Pope & Talbot v Canada* (2002) 7 ICSID Reports 148, 163–4; *Desert Line Projects LLC v Yemen*, 6 February 2008, §§179–93.

[70] On the due process standard in administrative proceedings: *Waste Management v Mexico (No 2)* (2004) 11 ICSID Reports 361, 386; *Thunderbird v Mexico*, 26 January 2006, §200; *ADC Affiliate Ltd v Hungary* (2006) 15 ICSID Reports 534, 608.

[71] *Elettronica Sicula SpA (ELSI) (US v Italy)*, ICJ Reports 1989 p 15, 74–6 on the meaning of arbitrary and discriminatory measures under a FCN treaty: '[a]rbitrariness is not so much something opposed to a rule of law as something opposed to the rule of law'. Further: *Genin v Estonia* (2001) 6 ICSID Reports 236, 238; *Loewen v USA* (2003) 7 ICSID Reports 442, 467; *LG&E v Argentina*, 3 October 2006, §162.

[72] (2004) 11 ICSID Reports 361, 386.

inconsistent, non-transparent, unreasonable (i.e. unrelated to some rational policy), or discriminatory (i.e. based on unjustifiable distinctions).[73]

Irregularities in the investor's conduct have sometimes influenced the determination of whether a breach of FET has occurred.[74] The standard required for a breach of FET to be found varies depending on the circumstances (and the decisions are notably inconsistent), but the holding in *SD Myers v Canada* is indicative in underlying that 'determination must be made in light of the high measure of deference that international law generally extends to the right of domestic authorities to regulate matters within their own borders'.[75]

(ii) Denial of justice[76]

The term 'denial of justice' has sometimes been used to cover the general notion of state responsibility for harm to aliens,[77] but it is better confined to a particular category of deficiencies on the part of the host state, principally concerning the administration of justice.[78] A helpful definition was offered by the NAFTA Tribunal in *Azinian v United Mexican States*:

A denial of justice could be pleaded if the relevant courts refuse to entertain a suit, if they subject it to undue delay, or if they administer justice in a seriously inadequate way... There is a fourth type of denial of justice, namely the clear and malicious misapplication of the law. This type of wrong doubtless overlaps with the notion of 'pretence of form' to mask a violation of international law. In the present case ... the evidence [is] sufficient to dispel any shadow over the bona fides of the Mexican judgments. Their findings cannot possibly be said to have been arbitrary, let alone malicious.[79]

This approach was approved in *Mondev v US*.[80]

The most controverted issue is the extent to which erroneous decisions may constitute a denial of justice. There is authority for the view that an error of law accompanied

---

[73] (2006) 15 ICSID Reports 250, 339.

[74] *Azinian v United Mexican States* (1999) 5 ICSID Reports 269, 291–2; *Noble Ventures Inc v Romania* (2005) 16 ICSID Reports 210, 274.

[75] (2000) 8 ICSID Reports 18, 56. Also: *Eastern Sugar BV v Czech Republic*, 12 April 2007, §272; *AES v Hungary*, 23 September 2010, §9.3.40.

[76] Eagleton (1928) 22 *AJIL* 538; Harvard Draft Convention (1929) 23 *AJIL Sp Supp* 131, 173–87; Fitzmaurice (1932) 13 *BY* 93; Lissitzyn (1936) 30 *AJIL* 632; Freeman (1938); García Amador, ILC *Ybk* 1957/II, 110–12; Jiménez de Aréchaga (1978) 159 Hague *Recueil* 1, 278–82; Paulsson (2005); Focarelli, 'Denial of Justice' (2009) *MPEPIL*. Also *ELSI*, ICJ Reports 1989 p 15, 66–7, for an influential articulation, and for representative BIT jurisprudence: *Amco Asia Corporation v Indonesia* (1990) 1 ICSID Reports 569, 604–5; *Azinian v United Mexican States* (1999) 5 ICSID Reports 272, 290–1; *Mondev v US* (2002) 6 ICSID Reports 192, 225–6; *Waste Management v Mexico No 2* (2004) 11 ICSID Reports 361, 384–6; *Petrobart Limited v Kyrgyz Republic No 2* (2005) 13 ICSID Reports 387, 415–16; *Saipem SpA v Bangladesh*, 30 June 2009, §§176–84; *Chevron Corporation and Texaco Petroleum v Ecuador*, 30 March 2010, §§241–51.

[77] *Robert E Brown* (1923) 6 RIAA 120, 128–9.

[78] (1929) 23 *AJIL Sp Supp* 133, 173.

[79] (1999) 5 ICSID Reports 269, 290.

[80] (2002) 6 ICSID Reports 192, 225.

by a discriminatory intention is a breach of the international standard.[81] However, it is well established that the decision of a lower court open to challenge does not constitute a denial of justice and that the claimant must pursue remedies available higher in the judicial system as a matter of substance.[82]

As in other contexts the international standard has been applied ambitiously by tribunals and writers and difficulties have arisen. First, the application of the standard may involve decisions upon fine points of national law and the quality of national remedial machinery.[83] In regard to the work of the courts a distinction is sought to be made between error and 'manifest injustice'.[84] Secondly, the application of the standard in this field seems to contradict the principle that the alien, within some limits at least, accepts the local law and jurisdiction. Thirdly, the concept of denial of justice embraces many instances where the harm to the alien is a breach of local law only and the 'denial' is a failure to reach a non-local standard of competence in dealing with the wrong. Thus the concept of the foreign state wronged in the person of its nationals is extended to cases where the primary wrong is a breach of municipal law alone. This is an eccentric application of the principles of responsibility;[85] and it would be better if such claims were regarded as resting on an equitable basis only. The existence of the rule of admissibility that the alien should first exhaust local remedies is a reflection of the special character of denial of justice claims.[86]

(iii) Expropriation of foreign property[87]

A state may place conditions on the entry of an alien on its territory and may restrict acquisition of certain kinds of property by aliens. Apart from such restrictions, an alien individual, or a corporation controlled by aliens, may acquire title to property within a state under local law. The subject-matter may be shares in enterprises, items such as

---

[81] Jiménez de Aréchaga, in Friedmann, Henkin & Lissitzyn (eds), *Transnational Law in a Changing Society* (1972) 171, 179, referring to the submissions of both parties in *Barcelona Traction*, ICJ Reports 1970 p 3; 8 Whiteman 727–31. Further: Greenwood, in Fitzmaurice et al (eds), *Issues of State Responsibility before International Judicial Institutions* (2004) 55.

[82] *Loewen Group Inc v US* (2003) 7 ICSID Reports 442, 469–72.

[83] Cf Mann (1967) 42 *BY* 1, 26–9.

[84] McNair, 2 *Opinions* 205; 6 *BD* 287–95.

[85] Cf Parry (1956) 90 Hague *Recueil* 653, 695–6. Further: *Janes* (1926) 3 ILR 218. The application of principles of responsibility is eccentric in the context of international relations: there is no objection of legal principle to extension of responsibility to cases of maladministration.

[86] Further: Ténékidès (1933) 14 *RDILC* 514; de Visscher (1935) 52 Hague *Recueil* 365, 421–32. But see *Saipem SpA v Bangladesh*, 30 June 2009, §§181–2.

[87] Friedman, *Expropriation in International Law* (1953); Bindschedler (1956) 90 Hague *Recueil* 173, 179–306; Wortley, *Expropriation in Public International Law* (1959); García Amador, ILC *Ybk* 1959/II, 2–24; Foighel, *Nationalization and Compensation* (1961); Sohn & Baxter (1961) 55 *AJIL* 545; White, *Nationalisation of Foreign Property* (1961); Domke (1961) 55 *AJIL* 585; Fouilloux, *La Nationalisation et le droit international public* (1962); Petrén (1963) 109 Hague *Recueil* 487, 492–575; 2 *Restatement Third*, §712; 8 Whiteman 1020–185; Amerasinghe, *State Responsibility for Injuries to Aliens* (1967) 121–68; Akinsanya, *The Expropriation of Multinational Property in the Third World* (1980); Dolzer (1981) 75 *AJIL* 553; Higgins (1982) 176 Hague *Recueil* 259; Asante (1988) 37 *ICLQ* 588; Norton (1991) 85 *AJIL* 474; Wälde & Kolo (2001) 50 *ICLQ* 811; Newcombe, in Kahn & Wälde (2007) 391; Sornarajah (3rd edn, 2010) ch 10.

estates or factories, or, on a monopoly basis, major areas of activities such as railways and mining. In a number of countries foreign ownership has extended to proportions of between 50 per cent and 100 per cent of all major industries, resources and services such as insurance and banking.[88] Even in *laissez-faire* economies, the taking of private property for certain public purposes and the establishment of state monopolies have long been familiar. After the Soviet revolution and the extension of the public sector in many economies, socialist and non-socialist, the conflict of interest between foreign investors and their governments and the hosts to foreign capital, seeking to regain control over their economies, became more acute. The terminology of the subject is by no means settled, and in any case form should not take precedence over substance. The essence of the matter is the deprivation by state organs of a right of property either as such, or by permanent transfer of the power of management and control.[89] The deprivation may be followed by transfer to the territorial state or to third parties, as in systems of land distribution as a means of agrarian reform. The process is commonly described as expropriation. If compensation is not provided, or the taking is regarded as unlawful, the taking is sometimes described as confiscation. Expropriation of one or more major national resources as part of a general programme of social and economic reform is generally referred to as nationalization.

State measures, prima facie lawful, may affect foreign interests considerably without amounting to expropriation. Thus foreign assets and their use may be subjected to taxation, trade restrictions such as quotas,[90] revocation of licences for breach of regulations, or measures of devaluation.[91] While special facts may alter cases, in principle such measures are not unlawful and do not constitute expropriation. If the state gives a public enterprise special advantages, for example by directing that it charge nominal rates of freight, the resulting *de facto* or quasi-monopoly is not an expropriation of the competitors driven out of business:[92] but it might be otherwise if this were the object of a monopoly regime. Taxation which has the precise object and effect of confiscation is unlawful but high rates of tax, levied on a non-discriminatory basis, are not.[93] In general there is no expectation that tax rates will not change: a foreign investor must obtain a clear commitment to that effect, for example, in a stabilization agreement.

---

[88] UNCTAD Handbook of Statistics (2009) part 7, available at: www.unctad.org/en/docs/tdstat34_enfr.pdf.

[89] On the various procedures of taking: Sohn & Baxter (1961) 55 *AJIL* 545; Christie (1962) 38 *BY* 307; 8 Whiteman 1006–20; Reisman & Sloane (2003) 74 *BY* 115; Hobér, *Investment Arbitration in Eastern Europe* (2007). Also: *ELSI*, ICJ Reports 1989 p 15, 67–71; *Starrett Housing Corporation v Iran* (1983) 85 ILR 349, 380–93.

[90] Treaties may make such restrictions unlawful: e.g. Energy Charter Treaty, 17 December 1994, 2080 UNTS 95, Art 21.

[91] Currency depreciation is lawful unless it is discriminatory: *Tabar* (1954) 20 ILR 211, 212–13; *Zuk* (1956) 26 ILR 284, 285–6; *Furst* (1960) 42 ILR 153, 154–5; cf *CMS Gas Transmission v Argentina* (2005) 14 ICSID Reports 158, 180; *Suez, Sociedad General de Aguas de Barcelona SA v Argentina*, 30 July 2010, §§125–5.

[92] *Oscar Chinn* (1934) PCIJ Ser A/B No 63, 65. Further: Christie (1962) 38 *BY* 307, 334–6.

[93] *Application to Aliens of the Tax on Mortgagors' Gains* (1963) 44 ILR 149, 153–4.

A constant difficulty is to establish the line between lawful regulatory measures and forms of indirect or creeping expropriation.[94] In *Pope and Talbot v Canada*, the investor argued that a statutory regime of export control involved a form of expropriation.[95] The tribunal held:

The ... question is whether the Export Control Regime has caused an expropriation of the Investor's investment, creeping or otherwise. Using the ordinary meaning of those terms under international law, the answer must be negative. ... The sole 'taking' that the Investor has identified is interference with the Investment's ability to carry on its business of exporting softwood lumber to the US. While this interference has ... resulted in reduced profits for the Investment, it continues to export substantial quantities of softwood lumber to the US and to earn substantial profits ... [T]he degree of interference with the Investment's operations due to the Export Control Regime does not rise to an expropriation (creeping or otherwise) within the meaning of Article 1110.[96]

In *Metalclad*, another NAFTA case concerning a refusal to grant a construction permit and a change of the regime of land to a national area of protection, the tribunal found that indirect expropriation had taken place, stating in a much quoted paragraph:

Thus, expropriation under NAFTA includes not only open, deliberate and acknowledged takings of property, such as outright seizure or formal or obligatory transfer of title in favour of the host State, but also covert or incidental interference with the use of property which has the effect of depriving the owner, in whole or in significant part, of the use or reasonably-to-be-expected economic benefit of property even if not necessarily to the obvious benefit of the host State.[97]

This language has been criticized for its breadth and lack of correspondence to the facts of the case.[98]

(iv) The compensation rule

The rule supported by all leading 'Western' governments and many jurists in Europe and North America is as follows: the expropriation of alien property is only lawful if 'prompt, adequate, and effective compensation'[99] is provided for. In principle, therefore,

---

[94] Waelde & Kolo (2001) 50 *ICLQ* 811. Further: *Saluka v Czech Republic* (2006) 15 ICSID Reports 250, 326–31.

[95] (2000) 122 ILR 293.

[96] Ibid, 335–7.

[97] *Metalclad Corporation v Mexico* (2000) 5 ICSID Reports 209, 260; also *CME v Czech Republic* (2001) 9 ICSID Reports 121, 236 and for overview of the case-law and definitions: *Generation Ukraine v Ukraine* (2003) 10 ICSID Reports 236, 300–6. But see *Telenor v Hungary*, 13 September 2006, §§65–70, for a narrow definition. For the Energy Charter Treaty: *Nykomb Synergetics AB v Latvia* (2003) 11 ICSID Reports 153, 194. Also US Model BIT 2004, Art 6 (1) & Annex B, available at www.unctadxi.org; OECD Working Paper 4/2004, *Indirect Expropriation and the Right to Regulate in International Investment Law* (2004).

[98] *Mexico v Metalclad* (2001) 125 ILR 468.

[99] The formula appears in a Note from US Secretary of State Cordell Hull to the Mexican government dated 22 August 1938: 3 Hackworth 658–9. The formula appears in most BITs. On the criteria of adequacy, effectiveness, and promptness: García Amador, ILC *Ybk* 1959/II, 16–24; White (1961) 235–43; Jiménez de Aréchaga, ILC *Ybk* 1963/II, 237–44; Cole (1965–66) 41 *BY* 368, 374–9; Schachter (1984) 78 *AJIL*

expropriation, as an exercise of territorial competence, is lawful, but the compensation rule (in this version) makes the legality conditional. The justifications for the rule are based on the assumptions prevalent in a liberal regime of private property and in the principle that foreign owners are to be given the protection accorded to private rights of nationals, provided that this protection involves the provision of compensation for any taking. These assumptions are used to support the compensation principle as yet another aspect of the international minimum standard governing the treatment of aliens. The emphasis is on respect for property rights both as 'acquired rights'[100] and as an aspect of human rights.[101] The principle of acquired rights is unfortunately vague, and the difficulty is to relate it to other principles of law: in short this and other general principles beg too many questions.

Whatever the justifications offered for the compensation rule, it has received considerable support from state practice and international tribunals.[102] Agreements involving provision for some sort of compensation in the form of the 'lump sum settlement' are numerous, but jurists disagree as to their evidential value: many agreements rest on a bargain and on special circumstances.[103] Although some awards were in substance diplomatic compromises,[104] a good number of international tribunals have supported the compensation rule and the principle of acquired rights.[105] Dicta in a number of decisions of the Permanent Court involving treaty interpretation and the effects of state succession on various categories of property, may be regarded as supporting the compensation principle.[106]

121; McLachlan, Shore & Weiniger (2007) ch 9; Marboe, *Calculation of Compensation and Damages in International Law* (2009). See discussion in *Wena Hotels v Egypt* (2000) 6 ICSID Reports 89, 117–30; *AIG v Kazakhstan* (2003) 11 ICSID Reports 7, 83–93; *Kardassopoulos v Georgia*, 3 March 2010, §§501–17.

[100] The statements of the Permanent Court on vested or acquired rights occur in the context of state succession. Also *Lighthouses* (1956) 23 ILR 341.

[101] Cf First Protocol to the ECHR, 20 March 1952, ETS 9, Art 1; also *Lithgow and others v UK* (1986) 75 ILR 438.

[102] The pre-1914 practice included the following cases: *Charlton* (1841) 31 BFSP 1025; *Finlay* (1846) 39 BFSP 40; *King* (1853), in Moore, 6 *Digest* 262; *Savage* (1852), in Moore, 2 *Digest* 1855; *Delagoa Bay Railway* (1900), in La Fontaine, *Pasicrisie international*, 398; *Expropriated Religious Properties* (1920) 1 RIAA 7.

[103] Friedman (1953) 86–101; White (1961) 193–243; Lillich, *The Protection of Foreign Investment* (1965) 167–88; Lillich & Weston (1988) 82 *AJIL* 69; Sacerdoti (1997) 269 Hague *Recueil* 251, 379–411; Lillich, Weston & Bederman, *International Claims* (1999); McLachlan, Shore & Weiniger (2007) 332; Bank & Foltz, 'Lump Sum Agreements' (2009) *MPEPIL*.

[104] *Delagoa Bay Railway Arbitration*, in Moore, 2 *Digest* 1865; *Expropriated Religious Properties* (1920) 1 RIAA 7; Martens, 30 *NRG* 2nd Ser 329.

[105] *Norwegian Ships* (1921) 1 ILR 189; *French Claims against Peru* (1921) 1 ILR 182; *Landreau* (1921) 1 ILR 185; *British Claims in the Spanish Zone of Morocco* (1925) 2 RIAA 615; *Hopkins* (1927) 3 ILR 229; *Goldenberg* (1928) 4 ILR 542; *Hungarian Optants* (1927) 8 *LNOJ* No 10, 1379 ; *Portugal v Germany* (1930) 5 ILR 150, 151; *Shufeldt* (1930) 5 ILR 179; *Mariposa* (1933) 7 ILR 255; *de Sabla* (1933) 7 ILR 241, 243; *Saudi Arabia v Arabian American Oil Company (Aramco)* (1958) 27 ILR 117, 144, 168, 205; *Amoco International Finance Corporation v Government of the Islamic Republic of Iran* (1987) 83 ILR 500, 541–3. Also: *El Triunfo* (1901) 15 RIAA 467; *Upton* (1903) 63 ILR 211; *Selwyn* (1903) 9 RIAA 380.

[106] *German Interests in Polish Upper Silesia* (1926) PCIJ Ser A No 7, 21–2, 33, 42; *Factory at Chorzów*, Jurisdiction (1927) PCIJ Ser A No 927, 31; *Interpretation of Judgments Nos 7 and 8*, PCIJ Ser A No 13, 19;

There are a number of exceptions to the compensation rule.[107] The most widely accepted are as follows: under treaty provisions; as a legitimate exercise of police power, including measures of defence against external threats; confiscation as a penalty for crimes;[108] seizure by way of enforcement of unpaid taxation or other fiscal measures; loss caused indirectly by health and planning legislation and concomitant restrictions on the use of property; the destruction of property of neutrals as a consequence of military operations; and the taking of enemy property as agreed war reparation.[109]

(v) Expropriation unlawful *per se*

The position may be summarized as follows:

(1) Expropriation for certain public purposes, for example, exercise of police power and defence measures in wartime, is lawful even if no compensation is payable.

(2) Expropriation of property is otherwise unlawful unless there is provision for the payment of effective compensation.

(3) Nationalization, that is, expropriation of a major industry or resource, is unlawful if there is no provision for compensation payable on a basis compatible with the economic objectives of the nationalization, and the viability of the economy as a whole.

Thus expropriation under (2) and (3) is unlawful only *sub modo*, that is, if appropriate compensation is not provided for. The controversial difference between (2) and (3) is the basis on which compensation is assessed. Whatever may be the relation of these two categories, there is evidence of a category of types of expropriation which are illegal apart from a failure to provide for compensation, in which cases lack of compensation is an additional element in, and not a condition of, the illegality. It has been suggested that this category includes interference with the assets of international organizations[110] and taking contrary to binding promises or (perhaps) legitimate expectations.[111] Certainly it includes seizures which are a part of crimes against

---

Factory at Chorzów, Indemnity (1928) PCIJ Ser A No 17, 46–7; *German Settlers in Poland* (1923) PCIJ Ser B No 6, 23–4, 38; *Peter Pázmány University* (1933) PCIJ Ser A/B No 61, 243.

[107] Herz (1941) 35 *AJIL* 243, 251–2; Friedman (1953) 1–3; Wortley (1959) 40–57; García Amador, ILC *Ybk* 1959/II, 11–12; Sohn & Baxter (1961) 55 *AJIL* 545, 553, 561–2; Bishop, Crawford & Reisman, *Foreign Investment Disputes* (2005) ch 8(I–J); Newcombe, in Kahn & Wälde (2007); Sornarajah (3rd edn, 2010) ch 10(2); Wittich, 'Compensation' (2008) *MPEPIL*.

[108] *Allgemeine Gold- und Silberscheideanstalt v Customs and Excise Commissioners* [1980] 2 WLR 555; Crawford (1980) 51 *BY* 305. Generally: Brower & Brueschke, *The Iran–United States Claims Tribunal* (1998) 463; Meyler (2007) 56 *DePaul LR* 539; Henry (2010) 31 *U Penn JIL* 935.

[109] *AKU* (1956) 23 ILR 21; *Prince Salm-Salm v Netherlands* (1957) 24 ILR 893. This view is controversial, however. Further: *Assets of Hungarian Company in Germany* (1961) 32 ILR 565; *Re Dohnert, Muller, Schmidt & Co* (1961) 32 ILR 570.

[110] Delson (1957) 57 *Col LR* 771.

[111] Friedmann (1956) 50 *AJIL* 475, 505. On estoppel: chapter 18.

humanity or genocide, involve breaches of international agreements,[112] are measures of unlawful retaliation or reprisal against another state,[113] are discriminatory, that is, aimed at particular racial groups or nationals of particular states,[114] or concern property owned by a foreign state and dedicated to public purposes.[115]

The practical distinctions between expropriation unlawful *sub modo* and expropriation unlawful *per se* would seem to be these: the former involves a duty to pay compensation only for direct losses, that is, the value of the property, the latter involves liability for consequential loss (*lucrum cessans*);[116] the former confers a title which is recognized in foreign courts (and international tribunals), the latter produces no valid title.[117] The case-law of the Iran–US Claims Tribunal includes examination of the relevance of the distinction between lawful and unlawful expropriation in the remedial sphere.[118]

(vi) Conclusions on expropriation

The Declaration of 1962 places emphasis on the rights of host states and in a general way contradicts the acquired rights thesis. Its actual formulations tend to cover up the real differences of opinion by the use of such terms as 'appropriate compensation'. But it is significant that the right to compensation, on whatever basis, is recognized in principle.[119] Since 1962, the climate of opinion has shifted, from the Charter of

---

[112] Cf *German Interests* (1926) PCIJ Ser A No 7; *Factory at Chorzów*, Indemnity (1928) Ser A No 17, 46–7.

[113] Netherlands Note to Indonesia, 18 December 1959 (1960) 54 *AJIL* 484; US Notes to Libya, 8 July 1973, *US Digest* 1973, 334–5; 20 June 1974, *US Digest* 1975, 490–1. Also *Banco Nacional de Cuba v First National City Bank* (1961) 35 ILR 2, 42, 45; *Banco Nacional de Cuba v Sabbatino* (1962) 35 ILR 2. An obvious difficulty is to determine when a countermeasure is lawful: in principle it should be a reaction to a prior breach of legal duty, proportionate, and reversible. These conditions will rarely if ever be met in BIT (as distinct from interstate) cases: *Archer Daniels Midland Co and Tate & Lyle v Mexico* (2007) 146 ILR 439, 484–505; *Corn Products International v Mexico* (2008) 146 ILR 581, 624–38; *Cargill Ltd v Mexico* (2009) 146 ILR 642, 752–66; *Mexico—Soft Drinks*, WT/DS308/AB/R, 6 March 2006, §§66–80. Commentary in Paparinskis (2008) 79 *BY* 264.

[114] There is much authority for this: *Banco Nacional de Cuba v Sabbatino* (1962) 35 ILR 2; *In re by Helbert Wagg & Co Ltd* (1955) 22 ILR 480; *Bank Indonesia v Senembah Maatschappij & Twentsche Bank* (1959) 30 ILR 28. The test of discrimination is the intention of the government: the fact that only aliens are affected may be incidental, and, if the taking is based on economic and social policies, it is not directed against particular groups simply because they own the property involved. ICJ Pleadings 1951, *Anglo-Iranian Oil Co*, Memorial of the UK, 97; *Anglo-Iranian Oil Co Ltd v SUPOR Company* (1954) 22 ILR 23, 39–40; 8 Whiteman 1041–57. Also *ELSI*, ICJ Reports 1989 p 15, 71–3.

[115] White (1961) 151–3.

[116] *Amoco International Finance Corporation v Islamic Republic of Iran* (1987) 83 ILR 500, 507–8. Also Ripinsky, in Ripinsky (ed), *Investment Arbitration* (2009) 47.

[117] Municipal courts often recognize measures lawful under the *lex situs*: *Luther v Sagor* [1921] 3 KB 532; *In re Helbert Wagg & Co Ltd* [1956] 1 Ch 323; *NV Verenigde Deli-Maatschappijen v Deutsch-Indonesische Tabak-Handelsgesellschaft mbH* (1959) 28 ILR 16. Cf Staker (1987) 58 *BY* 151.

[118] *Amoco International Finance v Iran* (1987) 83 ILR 500. Generally: Mouri, *The International Law of Expropriation as Reflected in the Work of the Iran–US Claims Tribunal* (1994); Aldrich, *The Jurisprudence of the Iran–United States Claims Tribunal* (1996); Brower & Brueschke (1998).

[119] Further: Mann (1981) 52 *BY* 241; Dolzer & Stevens (2005) ch 4; Wittich, 'Compensation' (2008) *MPEPIL*. Cf Energy Charter Treaty, 17 December 1994, 2080 UNTS 95, Art 13 (1)(d); NAFTA, 17

Economic Rights and Duties of States,[120] via the collapse of the USSR, to the BIT 'revolution', still in spate. The position was summarized by the tribunal in *CME v Czech Republic*:

The requirement of compensation to be 'just' and representative of the 'genuine value of the investment affected' evokes the famous Hull Formula ... That formula was controversial. ... The controversy came to a head with the adoption by the General Assembly of the United Nations of the 'Charter of Economic Rights and Duties of States.' ... But in the end, the international community put aside this controversy, surmounting it by the conclusion of more than 2200 bilateral (and a few multilateral) investment treaties. These treaties ... concordantly provide for payment of 'just compensation', representing the 'genuine' or 'fair market' value of the property taken. ... These concordant provisions are variations on an agreed, essential theme, namely, that when a State takes foreign property, full compensation must be paid ... The determination of the compensation on the basis of the 'fair market value'—to eliminate the consequences of the wrongful act for which the State is responsible—is acknowledged in international arbitration.[121]

In his Separate Opinion, Sir Ian Brownlie concluded with respect to the Declaration on Permanent Sovereignty over Natural Resources and the Charter of Economic Rights and Duties that:

Whilst caution must be exercised in evaluating these resolutions, there can be no doubt that the Cordell Hull formula no longer reflects the generally accepted international standard ... The standard of appropriate or just compensation carries the strong implication that, in the case of a going concern and more generally, the compensation should be subject to legitimate expectations and actual conditions.[122]

According to Brownlie, three considerations are particularly pertinent to the assessment of compensation in investment law context:

First: the nature of an investment as a form of expenditure or transfer of funds for the precise purpose of obtaining a return.

Secondly: the element of reasonableness, which rules out the compensation of returns which go beyond the legitimate expectations of the investor.

Thirdly: the element which derives from the general principle that merely speculative benefits, based upon unproven economic projections, do not count as investment or as returns.[123]

December 1992 (1993) 32 ILM 289, Art 1110; US Model BIT (2004) Art 6; France Model BIT (2006) Art 6; Germany Model BIT (2008) Art 4; UK Model BIT (2005 as amended 2006) Art 4; cf China Model BIT (1997) Art 4.

[120] GA Res 3281(XXIX), 12 December 1974 (120–6:10). For contemporary comment: Lillich (1975) 69 AJIL 359; Jiménez de Aréchaga (1978) Hague *Recueil* 1, 297–310; Brownlie (1979) 162 Hague *Recueil* 245.

[121] *CME v Czech Republic* (2003) 9 ICSID Reports 264, 369–71 referring to the *Compañía del Desarrollo de Santa Elena SA v Costa Rica* (2000) 5 ICSID Reports 157.

[122] *CME v Czech Republic* (2003) 9 ICSID Reports 264, Separate Opinion by Ian Brownlie, 418–19, citations omitted.

[123] Ibid, 419.

4. BREACH AND ANNULMENT OF STATE CONTRACTS

(A) GENERAL PRINCIPLES[124]

Governments make contracts of various kinds with aliens or foreign-owned corporations: loan agreements (including the issue of state bonds), contracts for supplies and services, contracts of employment, agreements for operation of industrial and other patent rights under licence, agreements for the construction and operation of transport or telephone systems, agreements conferring the sole right, or some defined right, to exploit natural resources on payment of royalties, and exploration and production-sharing agreements. Agreements involving resource exploitation are sometimes described as 'concession agreements', but this is not a term of art and these are not significantly different from other state contracts. The contracting government may act in breach of contract, legislate in such a way as to make the contract worthless (e.g., by export or currency restrictions), use its powers under domestic law to annul the contract, or repudiate the contract by means contrary to its own law. What, then, is the position in terms of international law?

In principle, the position is regulated by the general principles governing the treatment of aliens. Thus, the act of the contracting government will entail state responsibility if, by itself or in combination with other circumstances, it constitutes a denial of justice or an expropriation contrary to international law. The general view is that a breach of contract (as opposed to its confiscatory annulment) does not create state responsibility on the international plane.[125] On this view the situation in which the state exercises its executive or legislative authority to destroy the contractual rights as an asset comes within the ambit of expropriation.[126] Thus, it is often stated that

---

[124] Generally: Jennings (1961) 37 BY 156; Greenwood (1982) 53 BY 27; Bowett (1988) 59 BY 49; Schwebel, *Justice in International Law* (1994) 425; Leben (2003) 302 Hague *Recueil* 197; Douglas (2003) 74 BY 151; Crawford (2008) 24 *Arb Int* 351.

[125] Borchard, *The Diplomatic Protection of Citizens Abroad or the Law of International Claims* (1927) ch 7; Eagleton (1928) 157–68 ; Dunn (1932) 165–7, 171; Feller (1935) 174 ; Foighel (1961) 178–93; Amerasinghe (1967) 66–120; Mann, *Studies in International Law* (1973) 302–26; Jiménez de Aréchaga (1978) 159 Hague *Recueil* 1, 305–6 ; Schachter (1982) 178 Hague *Recueil* 1, 309–12; Lalive (1983) 181 Hague *Recueil* 9, 21–284; Bowett (1988) 59 BY 49; Paasivirta, *Participation of States in International Contracts and Arbitral Settlement of Disputes* (1990); Westberg, *International Transactions and Claims Involving Government Parties* (1991); Kischel, *State Contracts* (1992); Shihata & Parra (1995) 10 *ICSID Rev-FILJ* 183; Delaume (1997) 12 *ICSID Rev-FILJ* 1; Nassar (1997) 4 *JIA* 185; Kamto (2003) 3 *Rev Arb* 719; Alexandrov (2004) 5 *JWIT* 556. Further: Crawford (2002) 96; Marboe & Reinisch, 'Contracts between States and Foreign Private Law Persons' (2007) *MPEPIL*.

[126] *Shufeldt* (1930) 5 ILR 179; *Feierabend* (1960) 42 ILR 157; *Hexner* (1962) 42 ILR 169; *Valentine Petroleum & Chemical Corporation v Agency for International Development* (1967) 44 ILR 79, 85–91; *BP Exploration Company (Libya) Ltd v Government of Libyan Arab Republic* (1974) 53 ILR 297; *Texaco v Libyan Government* (1977) 53 ILR 389; *LIAMCO v Libya* (1977) 62 ILR 140; *Revere Copper & Brass v Overseas Private Investment Corporation* (1978) 56 ILR 258. Cf *Mobil Oil Iran Inc v Government of the Islamic Republic of Iran* (1987) 86 ILR 230, 274–6; *Liberian Eastern Timber Corporation (LETCO) v Government of the Republic of Liberia* (1986) 89 ILR 313, 337–8; *Amco Asia Corporation v Republic of Indonesia* (1990) 89 ILR 366, 466–8. On the expropriation of contractual rights as expropriation of investment: *Consortium RFCC v Kingdom of*

the annulment is illegal if it is arbitrary or discriminatory.[127] These terms cover two situations. First, action directed against persons of a particular nationality or race is discriminatory. Secondly, action which lacks a normal public purpose is 'arbitrary'. A government acting in good faith may impose trade restrictions which incidentally (and without discrimination) lead to the unenforceability of contractual rights. It is difficult to treat such action as unlawful on the international plane.

There is a school of thought which supports the view that the breach of a state contract by the contracting government of itself creates international responsibility.[128] Jennings has argued (though with some caution) that there are no basic objections to the existence of an international law of contract.[129] He points out that in the field of nationality, for example, rights created in municipal law may be evaluated according to international law standards. Exponents of the international law character of state contracts also use arguments based upon the doctrine of acquired rights[130] and the principle of *pacta sunt servanda*, and refer to certain decisions of international tribunals.[131]

However there is little evidence that the 'internationalized contract' idea corresponds to the existing law. Rather, some element is required, beyond the mere breach of contract, to constitute a confiscatory taking or denial of justice *stricto sensu*.[132] Most of the arbitral decisions cited for the 'internationalized contract' thesis are not in point, either because the tribunal was not applying international law or because the decision rested on some element apart from the breach of contract.[133] There is no evidence that the principles of acquired rights and *pacta sunt servanda* have the particular consequences contended for.[134] The arguments based upon acquired rights could be applied to a number of reliance situations created by the host state by the grant of public rights such as citizenship or permission to reside or to work. The distinction

---

Morocco, 22 December 2003, 85–9; *Tokios Tokelés v Ukraine* (2004) 11 ICSID Reports 313, 336; *Siemens v Argentina* (2007) 14 ICSID Reports 518, 571–2.

[127] *Waste Management v Mexico* (2004) 11 ICSID Reports 361, 382–6.

[128] Harvard Draft Convention (1929) 23 *AJIL Sp Supp* 131, Art 8, 167–73 (but the comment considerably modifies the text). Also 2 *Restatement Third* §712; Schwebel, 3 *Essays in Honour of Roberto Ago* (1987) 401–13.

[129] Jennings (1961) 37 *BY* 156.

[130] Ibid, 173–5, 177. The award in *Saudi Arabia v Aramco* (1958) 27 ILR 117 referred to acquired rights as a 'fundamental principle'. Also McNair (1957) 33 *BY* 1, 16–18.

[131] E.g. *Delagoa Bay Railway* (1900) 30 Martens, *NRG*, 2nd Ser 329; *El Triunfo* (1901) 15 RIAA 467; *Rudloff* (1905) 9 RIAA 244; *Landreau* (1922) 1 ILR 185; *Shufeldt* (1930) 5 ILR 179; *Saudi Arabia v Aramco* (1958) 27 ILR 117. Also: *Sapphire International Petroleum Ltd v National Iranian Oil Company (NIOC)* (1963) 35 ILR 136; *Texaco v Libya* (1977) 53 ILR 389.

[132] *Azinian v Mexico* (1999) 5 ICSID Reports 272, 289; *Consortium RFCC v Kingdom of Morocco*, 22 December 2003, §§85–9; *Waste Management v Mexico* (2004) 11 ICSID Reports 361, 390; *Impregilo SpA v Islamic Republic of Pakistan* (2005) 12 ICSID Reports 245, 296–8; *Glamis Gold v US*, 8 June 2009, §620.

[133] Mann (1960) 54 *AJIL* 572, 575–88. The award in *Saudi Arabia v Aramco* (1958) 27 ILR 117 had a declaratory character as the principle of acquired rights had been recognized by both parties.

[134] English courts have upheld legislative abrogation of gold clauses: *R v International Trustee for the Protection of Bondholders AG* [1937] AC 500; *Kahler v Midland Bank* [1950] AC 24. Cf Mann, *The Legal Aspect of Money* (6th edn, 2005).

drawn by partisans of responsibility in contract situations between loan agreements, concessions, and other contracts is unsatisfactory.

In the proceedings arising from the Iranian cancellation of the 1933 Concession Agreement between the Iranian government and the Anglo-Iranian Oil Company, the UK contended that violation of an explicit undertaking in a concession by the government party not to annul was unlawful *per se*.[135] This view almost certainly does not represent the law but it is not without merit.[136]

The issue of breaches and annulment of state contracts is even more pertinent in the era of investment treaty arbitration. Under BITs, investment contracts are invoked by reference to the treaty standards of investment protection.[137] It should be underlined however that the distinction between treaty and contract remains valid in investor-state arbitration, even with the 'umbrella clause'. As the tribunal in *Waste Management* concluded, the

mere non-performance of a contractual obligation [by the host State] is not to be equated with a taking of property, nor (unless accompanied by other elements) is it tantamount to expropriation... [I]t is one thing to expropriate a right under a contract and another to fail to comply with the contract.[138]

Special standards are prescribed in NAFTA and virtually all BITs. Article 1105 of NAFTA provides that: '[e]ach Party shall accord to investments of investors of another Party treatment in accordance with international law, including fair and equitable treatment and full protection and security'.[139]

(B) STABILIZATION CLAUSES[140]

The term 'stabilization clause' relates to any clause contained in an agreement between a government and a foreign legal entity by which the government party undertakes not to annul the agreement nor to modify its terms, either by legislation or by administrative measures. The legal significance of such clauses is controversial, since the clause involves a tension between the legislative sovereignty and public interest of

---

[135] UK Memorial, *Anglo-Iranian Oil Co*, ICJ Pleadings 1951, 86–93. Comment by Mann (1960) 54 *AJIL* 572, 587; cf *US Digest* (1975) 489–90.

[136] Also *Radio Corporation of America v National Government of China* (1935) 8 ILR 26.

[137] Alexandrov (2006) 5 *TDM*; Crawford (2008) 24 *Arb Int* 351.

[138] *Waste Management v Mexico* (2004) 11 ICSID Reports 361, 403–8. Further: ARSIWA, ILC *Ybk* 2001/II, 31, Art 4 §6 with commentary.

[139] *SD Myers, Inc v Canada* (2000) 8 ICISD Reports 18; *Pope & Talbot, Inc v Government of Canada* (2000–1) 7 ICSID Reports 69; *Mondev v US* (2002) 6 ICSID Reports 192, 215–26. On the standard of full protection and security in investment law: Cordero Moss, in Reinisch (ed), *Standards of Investment Protection* (2008) 131; Schreuer (2010) 1 *JIDS* 353; Zeitler, in Schill (2010) 183.

[140] Generally: Weil (1969) 128 Hague *Recueil* 95, 229–34; Higgins (1982) 176 Hague *Recueil* 259, 298–314; Greenwood (1982) 53 *BY* 27, 60–4; Lalive (1983) 181 Hague *Recueil* 9, 56–61, 147–62; Redfern (1984) 55 *BY* 65, 98–105; Paasivirta (1989) 60 *BY* 315; Toope, *Mixed International Arbitration* (1990); García-Amador (1993) 2 *J Trans LP* 23; Coale (2001) 30 *DJILP* 217; Faruque (2006) 23 *JIA* 317; Duruigbo, in Nweze (ed), *Contemporary Issues of Public International and Comparative Law* (2009) 631.

the state party and the long-term viability of the contractual relationship. If the position is taken that state contracts are valid on the plane of public international law then it follows that a breach of such a clause is unlawful under international law.[141] Another view is that stabilization clauses as such are invalid in terms of public international law as a consequence of the principle of permanent sovereignty over natural resources.[142]

The problem calls for careful classification. If a state party to a contract purports to annul it this may, depending on the circumstances, constitute an expropriation: and the consequences will depend on the general principles relating to expropriation. The legal position will not, on this view, depend upon the existence of a stabilization clause. If there is a provision for arbitration, the issue will be governed either by the express choice of law (if there is one) or by the choice of law derived by a process of interpretation. If the choice of law involves elements of public international law, the arbitral tribunal will then approach the stabilization clause in the light of all the relevant circumstances, including the history of the relationship, the conduct of the parties, and the reasonable expectations of the parties.[143] It is to be noted that the tribunal in *Aminoil* adopted the view that stabilization clauses were not prohibited by international law, but gave a cautious interpretation to the particular undertaking in question. Thus, such a clause could operate but only in respect of 'nationalisation during a limited period of time'. In the instant case, the clause could not be presumed to exclude nationalization for a period of 60 years.[144]

(C) THE 'UMBRELLA CLAUSE'[145]

Umbrella clauses, whose origins can be traced back to the aftermath of *Anglo-Iranian Oil Company (UK v Iran)* of 1952,[146] are now contained in some 40 per cent of modern BITs. A standard formulation would be a promise by the host state to comply with obligations assumed. For instance, the Switzerland–Philippines BIT provides in Article X(2) '[e]ach Contracting Party shall observe any obligation it has assumed with

---

[141] *Texaco v Libya* (1977) 53 ILR 389, 494–5. In *Libyan American Oil Company (LIAMCO) v Government of the Libyan Arab Republic* (1977) 62 ILR 140, 196–7, the sole arbitrator held that breach of a stabilization clause was lawful but gave rise to a right to receive an equitable indemnity. The issue was not considered in *BP v Libya* (1973) 53 ILR 297. Also: *Revere v OPIC* (1978) 56 ILR 258, 278–94; Weil, *Mélanges offerts à Charles Rousseau* (1974) 301–28.

[142] Jiménez de Aréchaga (1978) 159 Hague *Recueil* 1, 308; Rosenberg, *Le Principe de souveraineté des états sur leurs ressources naturelles* (1983) 297–332.

[143] Majority Award in *Aminoil* (1982) 66 ILR 518, 587–91. In his Opinion, Sir Gerald Fitzmaurice stated that the stabilization clauses rendered the expropriation (in effect) unlawful; ibid, 621–2. Further: Mann (1983) 54 *BY* 213; Redfern (1984) 55 *BY* 65, 98–105.

[144] (1982) 66 ILR 518, 587–92.

[145] Sinclair (2004) 20 *Arb Int* 411; Schreuer (2004) 5 *JWIT* 231; Wälde (2005) 6 *JWIT* 183; OECD, *Interpretation of the Umbrella Clause in Investment Agreements* (2006); Halonen, in Weiler (ed), 1 *Investment Treaty Arbitration and International Law* (2008) 27; Crawford (2008) 24 *Arb Int* 351; Gallus (2008) 24 *Arb Int* 157; McLachlan (2008) 336 Hague *Recueil* 199, 398; Schill, in Schill (2010) 317.

[146] Jurisdiction, ICJ Reports 1952 p 93.

regard to specific investments in its territory by investors of the other Contracting Party'.[147]

The meaning and function of umbrella clauses is subject to an ongoing debate with at least four discernable schools of thought: (a) the first adopts a very narrow interpretation of umbrella clauses as being operative only and to the extent that there is an identifiable shared intent of the parties that any breach of contract is a breach of the BIT;[148] (b) the second purports to limit the application of umbrella clauses to breaches of contract committed by the host state in the exercise of sovereign authority;[149] (c) according to the third view, umbrella clauses internationalize investment contracts by automatically transforming contractual claims into treaty ones;[150] (d) the fourth approach stipulates that umbrella clauses are operative and may serve as the basis for a substantive treaty claim, but do not *ipso iure* transform a contractual claim into a treaty one.[151]

This fourth view is preferable as it allows for integration between the treaty terms and the contract, while respecting the construction of the treaty clause at hand as well as the proper law and dispute settlement provisions of the contract. In short, umbrella clauses do not erase the distinction between treaty and contract, but create a shortcut to the enforcement of contractual claims without internationalizing or transforming the basis of the underlying obligation. As concluded by the ad hoc Committee in *CMS v Argentina*:

> The effect of the umbrella clause is not to transform the obligation which is relied on into something else; the content of the obligation is unaffected, as is its proper law.[152]

(D) THE RELEVANCE OF FORUM CLAUSES[153]

A claim for breach of a contract between an alien and a government will be decided in accordance with the applicable system of municipal law designated by the rules of private international law of the forum. Questions are however raised if the parties to a state contract expressly choose an applicable law other than a particular system of local law, either 'general principles of law' or public international law.[154] A choice by

---

[147] Switzerland–Philippines BIT (1997) Art X(2), available at www.unctadxi.org.

[148] *SGS v Pakistan* (2003) 8 ICSID Reports 406; *Joy Mining v Egypt* (2004) 13 ICSID Reports 123.

[149] *Pan American Energy v Argentina*, 27 July 2006; *El Paso Energy v Argentina*, 27 April 2006.

[150] *Fedax v Venezuela* (1997) 5 ICSID Reports 183; *Eureko v Poland* (2005) 12 ICSID Reports 331; *Noble Ventures Inc v Romania* (2005) 16 ICSID Reports 210.

[151] *SGS v Philippines* (2004) 8 ICSID Reports 515; *CMS v Argentina* (2007) 14 ICSID Reports 251.

[152] (2007) 14 ICSID Reports 251, 268.

[153] Generally: Born, *International Arbitration and Forum Selection Agreements* (1999); Bishop, Crawford & Reisman (2005) ch 3(III), 225; Douglas (2009) rules 20–1.

[154] *Abu Dhabi (Petroleum Development Ltd v Sheikh of Abu Dhabi)* (1951) 18 ILR 144; McNair (1957) 33 BY 1, 4–10; Sereni (1959) 96 Hague *Recueil* 129, 133–232; Mann (1959) 35 BY 33, 34–7; Mann (1967) 42 BY 1; O'Connell, 2 *International Law* (1965) 977–84, 990–1; Weil (1969) 128 Hague *Recueil* 95, 120–88; Mann et al (1975) 11 *RBDI* 562; (1977) 57 Ann de l'Inst 192–265; (1979) 58 Ann de l'Inst 192 (Res); Weil, *Mélanges Reuter* (1981) 549–82; Greenwood (1982) 53 BY 27; Alexandrov (2004) 5 *JWIT* 556.

the parties of public international law is assumed by some writers to place the contract on the international plane, but this cannot be right; a state contract is not a treaty and cannot involve state responsibility as an international obligation.[155] In practice choice of law clauses in state contracts often specify the local law 'and such principles and rules of public international law as may be relevant', and in face of such clauses arbitrators have a certain discretion in selecting the precise role of public international law.[156] The tribunal in the case of *Aminoil v Kuwait*[157] decided that by implication the choice of law was that of Kuwait, that public international law was a part of the law of Kuwait, and that in any event considerable significance was to be accorded to the 'legitimate expectations of the parties'.[158]

In the context of investment treaty arbitration, *Vivendi v Argentina* illustrates the relevance of forum selection clauses. The dispute arose under a contract between the claimants and a province of Argentina for the operation of water and sewerage systems. All claims brought concerned the performance of the contract, which itself conferred exclusive jurisdiction to the courts of the province. While the BIT Tribunal upheld its jurisdiction to hear these claims, the ad hoc Committee partially annulled the award, reasoning:

In a case where the essential basis of a claim brought before an international tribunal is a breach of contract, the tribunal will give effect to any valid choice of forum clause in the contract.[159]

On the other hand, where the 'fundamental basis of the claim' is a treaty laying down an independent standard by which the conduct of the parties is to be judged, the existence of an exclusive jurisdiction clause in a contract between the claimant and the respondent state or one of its subdivisions cannot operate as a bar to the application of the treaty standard... It is one thing to exercise contractual jurisdiction... and another to take into account the terms of the contract in determining whether there has been a breach of a distinct standard of international law.[160]

---

[155] (1977) 57 *Ann de l'Inst* 246–53 (Report of van Hecke); Schachter (1982) 178 Hague *Recueil* 1, 301–9. For a different view: *Texaco Overseas Petroleum Company & California Asiatic Oil Company v Government of the Libyan Arab Republic* (1977) 53 ILR 389. Also: von Mehren & Kourides (1981) 75 *AJIL* 476; Leben (2003) 302 Hague *Recueil* 197; Marboe & Reinisch, 'Contracts between States and Foreign Private Law Persons' (2007) *MPEPIL*. Further: *Waste Management Inc v Mexico* (2004) 11 ICSID Reports 361, 404; *Impregilo SpA v Islamic Republic of Pakistan* (2005) 12 ICSID Reports 245, 297–8.

[156] *BP Exploration Company v Libya* (1974) 53 ILR 297; *Texaco v Libya* (1977) 53 ILR 389; *LIAMCO v Libya* (1977) 62 ILR 140; *AGIP v Government of the Popular Republic of Congo* (1979) 67 ILR 318; *Benvenuti & Bonfant Srl v Government of the Popular Republic of the Congo* (1980) 67 ILR 345.

[157] *Government of Kuwait v American Independent Oil Company (Aminoil)* (1982) 66 ILR 518. For comment: Mann (1983) 54 *BY* 213; Redfern (1984) 55 *BY* 65.

[158] Further: *Eurotunnel* (2007) 132 ILR 1, 120–5; *Ecuador v Occidental* [2007] EWCA Civ 656, §21.

[159] *Vivendi v Argentina* (2002) 6 ICSID Reports 340, 366.

[160] Ibid, 367–8.

This may be contrasted with *SGS v Philippines* where the tribunal held:

Article X(2) makes it a breach of the BIT for the host State to fail to observe binding commitments, including contractual commitments, which it has assumed with regard to specific investments.[161]

According to this view, contractual claims under a BIT ought not to be pursued in breach of an applicable forum selection clause set out in the contract in question, as by choosing to include this clause in the investment contract the investor in effect has renounced the right to arbitrate contract claims in a treaty forum.

---

[161] *SGS v Philippines* (2004) 8 ICSID Reports 515, 553.

29

INTERNATIONAL HUMAN RIGHTS

1. INTRODUCTION

The events of the Second World War, and concern to prevent a recurrence of catastrophes associated with the policies of the Axis Powers, led to a programme of increased protection of human rights and fundamental freedoms at the international level. A notable pioneer in the field was Hersch Lauterpacht, who stressed the need for an International Bill of the Rights of Man.[1] No such instrument was included in the UN Charter of 1945, but the Charter's heuristic references to human rights provided a basis for development of the law.[2] The more important results of the drive to protect human rights are recorded here, but first some comment may be made on the forms it has assumed. Inevitably it has carried to the international forum the differing concepts of freedom asserted by various leading states, and ideological differences have influenced the debates.

Human rights are a broad area of concern. Their potential subject-matter ranges from questions of torture and fair trial to social, cultural, and economic rights, for example, the right to housing or to water. While 'human rights' is a convenient category of reference, it is also a potential source of confusion. Human rights problems arise in specific factual and legal contexts. They must be decided by reference to the applicable law, whether it is the law of a particular state, the provisions of a convention, *or* principles of general international law. Human rights treaties are not a distinct species, still less a phylum. They are, first of all, treaties negotiated and entered into by states which oblige states parties as to their treatment of people, including their own

---

[1] Lauterpacht, *An International Bill of the Rights of Man* (1945); Lauterpacht, *International Law and Human Rights* (1950). Further: McDougal, Lasswell & Chen, *Human Rights and World Public Order* (1980); Henkin (ed), *The International Bill of Rights* (1981); Alston, *The United Nations and Human Rights* (1992); Jayawickrama, *The Judicial Application of Human Rights Law* (2002); Steiner, Alston & Goodman (eds), *International Human Rights in Context* (3rd edn, 2008); Moeckli, Shah & Sivakumaran (eds), *International Human Rights Law* (2010); Rehman, *International Human Rights Law* (2nd edn, 2010); Parlett, *The Individual in the International Legal System* (2011); Tyagi, *The UN Human Rights Committee* (2011).

[2] Preamble, Arts 1, 55(c), 56. Also: Arts 62, 68, 76.

nationals. While in this and other ways expanding the scope of international law, they are also and as such part of the system of international law.

2. HISTORICAL PERSPECTIVES

(A) THE EQUIVOCAL EXPERIENCE OF THE LEAGUE OF NATIONS

The appearance of human rights in the sphere of international law and organizations is often traced to the era of the League Covenant of 1919[3] and associated minorities treaties and mandates.[4] The minorities treaties, in particular, constituted an important stage in the recognition of human rights standards.

But neither the mandates system nor the minorities regimes were representative: both only applied by way of exception and only to designated territories or groups. The Covenant did not contain a minorities clause, let alone any general statement of rights. Amongst the proposals discarded was this Japanese amendment:

The equality of nations being a basic principle of the League of Nations, the High Contracting Parties agree to accord as soon as possible to all aliens [who are] nationals of states members of the League equal and just treatment in every respect making no distinction either in law or fact on account of their race or nationality.[5]

The idea of universal human rights had to await the Allied wartime planners: a draft bill of rights was prepared as early as December 1942.[6] But the idea of universal human rights was at the same time a reaction against special rights for particular groups, and it was agreed after 1945 that the inter-war minorities treaties had lapsed.[7]

---

[3] An important precursor was the anti-slavery movement: Davis, *The Problem of Slavery in the Age of Revolution, 1770–1823* (1999); Miers, *Slavery in the Twentieth Century* (2003) 1–46; Weissbrodt, 'Slavery' (2007) *MPEPIL*; Martinez, *The Slave Trade and the Origins of International Human Rights Law* (2012). Key steps towards a comprehensive international legal prohibition of slavery included the Slavery Convention, 25 September 1926, 60 LNTS 254, the Convention for the Suppression of the Traffic in Persons and of the Exploitation of the Prostitution of Others, 21 March 1950, 96 UNTS 271, and the Supplementary Convention on the Abolition of Slavery, the Slave Trade, and Institutions and Practices Similar to Slavery, 7 September 1956, 266 UNTS 3. The struggle against 'modern' forms of servitude continues: e.g. Rassam (1999) 39 *Va JIL* 303; Miers (2003). See also chapter 13.

[4] On the minorities system: McKean, *Equality and Discrimination under International Law* (1983) 14–26; Thornberry, *International Law and the Rights of Minorities* (1991) 38–52. On mandates: Wright, *Mandates under the League* (1930); Knop, *Diversity and Self-Determination in International Law* (2002) 198–200; Parlett (2011) 287–91.

[5] Miller, 2 *The Drafting of the League Covenant* (1928) 229, 323–5.

[6] Russell & Muther, *A History of the United Nations Charter* (1958) 323–9, 777–89.

[7] Commission of Human Rights, Study of the Legal Validity of the Undertakings Concerning Minorities, E/CN.4/367, 7 April 1950, 70–1. This is the only occasion a whole group of treaties was held to have lapsed on grounds of *rebus sic stantibus*. For criticism of the study: Parlett (2011) 286–7. But the Court refused to hold that the mandates had lapsed: *International Status of South West Africa*, ICJ Reports 1950 p 128, 132–6.

(B) THE INTERNATIONAL LABOUR ORGANIZATION (ILO)

Although its work is rather specialized, the ILO, created in 1919, has done a great deal towards giving practical expression to some important human rights and towards establishing standards of treatment. Its agenda has included forced labour, freedom of association, discrimination in employment, equal pay, social security, and the right to work.[8] The ILO's Constitution has a tripartite structure, with separate representation of employers and workers, as well as governments, in the Governing Body and the General Conference. In addition, there are provisions for union and employer organizations to make representations and complaints. This procedure was augmented in 1951 when the ILO Governing Body established a fact-finding and conciliation commission on freedom of association.[9]

(C) THE UNIVERSAL DECLARATION OF HUMAN RIGHTS, 1948[10]

In 1948, the General Assembly adopted a Universal Declaration of Human Rights which has been notably influential.[11] The Declaration is not a treaty, but many of its provisions reflect general principles of law or elementary considerations of humanity, and the Declaration identified the catalogue of rights whose protection would come to be the aim of later instruments. Overall the indirect legal effect of the Declaration should not be underestimated. It has been invoked, for example, by the European Court of Human Rights as an aid to interpretation of the European Convention on

---

[8] See Jenks, *Social Justice in the Law of Nations* (1970); McNair, *The Expansion of International Law* (1962) 29–52; Wolf, in Meron (ed), 2 *Human Rights in International Law* (1984) 273; Swepston, in Symonides (ed), *Human Rights* (2003) 91–109; Rodgers, Swepston, Lee & van Daele (eds), *The International Labour Organization and the Quest for Social Justice, 1919–2009* (2009); Servais, *International Labour Law* (2nd edn, 2009); van Daele (ed), *ILO Histories* (2010).

[9] Other key developments included the creation of the International Institute for Labour Studies in 1960, an amendment to the Constitution in June 1986 affecting core aspects of the ILO's function and structure (not yet in force), the adoption of the Active Partnership Policy in 1993 to strengthen the ILO's field structure, and the establishment of the independent World Commission on the Social Dimension of Globalization in 2002. See www.ilo.org/public/english/support/lib/resource/subject/history.htm. On the impact of the 1998 ILO Declaration on Fundamental Principles and Rights at Work: Alston (2004) 15 *EJIL* 457.

[10] GA Res 217(III), 10 December 1948; Alfredsson & Eide (eds), *The Universal Declaration of Human Rights* (1999); Jaichand & Suksi (eds), *Sixty Years of the Universal Declaration of Human Rights in Europe* (2009); Baderin & Ssenyonjo (eds), *International Human Rights Law* (2010).

[11] For domestic recourse to the UDHR: e.g. *In re Flesche* (1949) 16 ILR 266, 269; *Duggan v Tapley* (1951) 18 ILR 336, 342; *Robinson v Secretary-General of the UN* (1952) 19 ILR 494, 496; *Extradition of Greek National (Germany)* (1955) 22 ILR 520, 524; *American European Beth-El Mission v Minister of Social Welfare* (1967) 47 ILR 205, 207–8; *Iranian Naturalization* (1968) 60 ILR 204, 207; *Waddington v Miah* [1974] 1 WLR 683, 694; *M v UN and Belgium* (1969) 69 ILR 139, 142–3; *Police v Labat* (1970) 70 ILR 191, 203; *Basic Right to Marry* (1971) 72 ILR 295, 298; *Charan Lal Sahu v Union of India* (1989) 118 ILR 451. Further: Hannum (1995–96) 25 *Ga JICL* 287.

Human Rights (ECHR),[12] and by the International Court in relation to the detention of hostages 'in conditions of hardship'.[13]

The Declaration is a good example of an informal prescription given legal significance by actions of authoritative decision-makers, and thus it has been used as an agreed point of reference in the Helsinki Final Act, the second of the 'non-binding' instruments which have been of considerable importance in practice.[14]

(D) THE HELSINKI FINAL ACT, 1975

On 1 August 1975 the Final Act of the Conference on Security and Co-operation in Europe was adopted in Helsinki.[15] It contains a declaration of principles under the heading 'Questions Relating to Security in Europe'. The Final Act was signed by the representatives of 35 states, including the US and the USSR.

The Declaration is not in treaty form and was not intended to be legally binding.[16] At the same time it signified the acceptance by participating states of certain principles, including human rights standards. This significance was recognized by the International Court in *Nicaragua v US*.[17] That was a special context, but the Helsinki process was a significant element in the gradual move to acceptance, on the one hand, of the political status quo in Europe and, on the other hand, of the salience of human rights standards for Eastern Europe. As such it was a precursor to the changes of 1989.[18]

(E) SUBSEQUENT DECLARATIONS

Subsequent important declarations on human rights include the Vienna Declaration and Programme of Action adopted by the World Conference on Human Rights on 25 June 1993, which led to the establishment of the Office of the High Commissioner for Human Rights,[19] the Beijing Declaration and Programme for Action adopted by the Fourth World Conference on Women on 15 September 1995,[20] and the UN Millennium Summit Declaration adopted on 8 September 2000,[21] among many others.

---

[12] 4 November 1950, ETS 5: e.g. *Golder* (1975) 57 ILR 200, 216–17.

[13] *United States Diplomatic and Consular Staff in Tehran (US v Iran)*, ICJ Reports 1980 p 3, 42.

[14] Some US writers have laid emphasis on the Universal Declaration as custom, given the weaknesses and lacunae in subsequent US human rights treaty practice: e.g. Sohn (1977) 12 *Texas ILJ* 129, 133; Lillich (1995–96) 25 *Ga JICL* 1; Hannum (1995–96) 25 *Ga JICL* 287.

[15] 1 August 1975, 14 ILM 1292.

[16] *US Digest* (1975) 325–7.

[17] *Military and Paramilitary Activities in and against Nicaragua (Nicaragua v US)*, ICJ Reports 1986 p 14, 100; also 133.

[18] E.g. van der Stoel (1995) 6 *Helsinki Monitor* 23; Brett (1996) 18 *HRQ* 668.

[19] GA Res 48/141, 20 December 1993.

[20] Endorsed by GA Res 50/203, 23 February 1996.

[21] GA Res 55/2, 8 September 2000.

3. SOURCES OF HUMAN RIGHTS STANDARDS

(A) MULTILATERAL CONVENTIONS

The corpus of human rights standards derives from an accumulation of multilateral standard-setting conventions. These fall into four general categories: first, the two comprehensive International Covenants adopted in 1966;[22] secondly, regional conventions; thirdly, conventions dealing with specific wrongs: for example, genocide, racial discrimination, torture, and disappearances; and fourthly, conventions related to the protection of particular categories of people: for example, refugees, women, children, migrant workers, and people with disabilities. These conventions form a dense, overlapping pattern of prescriptions, the more so as most states are parties to most of the general treaties; likewise the regional treaties are widely ratified within their regions. To a great degree, human rights law involves the interpretation and application of these and other treaty texts; only subsidiarily does it involve questions of substantive customary international law.

(i) The International Covenants of 1966

The Universal Declaration of Human Rights was widely regarded as a first step toward the preparation of a Covenant in treaty form. After extensive work in the Commission on Human Rights and the Third Committee of the General Assembly, the latter in 1966 adopted two Covenants and a Protocol: the International Covenant on Economic, Social, and Cultural Rights (ICESCR; 160 parties to date); the International Covenant on Civil and Political Rights (ICCPR; 167 parties to date);[23] and an Optional Protocol to the latter (114 parties to date) relating to the processing of individual communications. In 1989 a Second Protocol to the ICCPR was adopted, aiming at the abolition of the death penalty (73 parties to date),[24] and in 2008 an Optional Protocol to the ICESCR relating to the processing of individual communications (five parties to date; not yet in force).[25]

The Covenants, which came into force in 1976, have legal effect as treaties for the parties to them and constitute a detailed juridification of human rights. The ICESCR contains various articles in which the parties 'recognize' such rights as the right to work, to social security, and to an adequate standard of living.[26] This type of obligation

---

[22] GA Res 2200A(XXI), 16 December 1966; respectively 993 UNTS 3 and 999 UNTS 171.

[23] Ibid. See Schwelb, in Eide & Schou (eds), *International Protection of Human Rights* (1968) 103; Meron, *Human Rights Law-Making in the United Nations* (1986) 83–127; Craven, *The International Covenant on Economic, Social and Cultural Rights* (1995); Joseph, Schultz & Castan, *International Covenant on Civil and Political Rights* (2nd edn, 2004); Nowak, *UN Covenant on Civil and Political Rights* (2nd edn, 2005).

[24] GA Res 44/128, 15 December 1989; 1642 UNTS 414.

[25] GA Res 63/117, 10 December 2008.

[26] See Eide, Krause & Rosas (eds) *Economic, Social and Cultural Rights* (2nd edn, 2001); Ssenyonjo (ed), *Economic, Social and Cultural Rights* (2011). On the basis of Arts 11–12 of the Covenant, CESCR has held that there is a human right to water: General Comment 15 (2002) E/C.12/2002/11; for a critique see Tully (2005) 23 *NQHR* 43.

is programmatic and promotional, except in the case of the provisions relating to trade unions (Article 8). Each party 'undertakes to take steps...to the maximum of its available resources, with a view to achieving progressively the full realization of the rights recognized in the present Covenant by all appropriate means, including particularly the adoption of legislative measures' (Article 2(1)). The rights recognized are to be exercised under a guarantee of non-discrimination, but there is a qualification in the case of the economic rights 'recognized' in that 'developing countries...may determine to what extent they would guarantee' such rights to non-nationals. The machinery for supervision consists of an obligation to submit reports on measures adopted, for transmission to the Economic and Social Council. Since 1986 an expert Committee on Economic, Social and Cultural Rights (CESCR) has assisted in supervising compliance.[27]

The ICCPR is more specific in its delineation of rights, stronger in its statement of the obligation to respect those rights, and better provided with means of review and supervision.[28] Its provisions clearly owe much to the ECHR and the experience based upon it. Article 2(1) contains a firm general stipulation: 'Each State Party to the present Covenant undertakes to respect and to ensure to all individuals within its territory and subject to its jurisdiction the rights recognized in the present Covenant, without distinction of any kind, such as race, colour, sex, language, religion, political or other opinion, national or social origin, property, birth, or other status'.[29] The rights are reasonably well defined and relate to classical issues including liberty and security of the person, equality before the law, fair trial, etc. Parties must submit to the Human Rights Committee (HRC) reports on measures adopted to give effect to the Covenant.[30] There is also a procedure for parties to the Covenant to complain of non-compliance, subject to a bilateral attempt at adjustment and prior exhaustion of domestic remedies, provided that such complaints are only admissible if both states have recognized the Committee's competence to receive complaints (Article 41).[31]

In addition, the Optional Protocol to this Covenant provides for applications to the HRC from individuals subject to its jurisdiction who claim to have suffered violations of the Covenant, and who have exhausted all available domestic remedies.[32] The respondent state submits to the HRC 'written explanations or statements clarifying the matter and the remedy, if any, that may have been taken by that state'. The HRC forwards what are referred to as 'views' to the state party concerned and to the

---

[27] See Alston, in Alston (1992) 473; Craven (1995) 30–105; Craven, in Eide, Krause & Rosas (2nd edn, 2001) 455.

[28] Generally: Rodley, in Krause & Scheinin (eds), *International Protection of Human Rights* (2009) ch 6.

[29] The firmness of the stipulation is placed in question by para 2, which makes it apparent that states may become parties on the basis of a *promise* to bring their legislation into line with the obligations of the Covenant: see Robertson (1968–69) 43 BY 21, 25. But see the clear view of the HRC in General Comment 31 (2004) HRI/GEN/1/Rev.7, 192, §5, according to which the obligation to respect and to ensure has 'immediate effect'.

[30] Generally: Tyagi (2011); also Cohn (1991) 13 HRQ 295.

[31] The interstate complaint procedure has never been used: Tyagi (2011) 325–85.

[32] De Zayas, Möller & Opsahl (1985) 28 GYIL 9; Ghandhi, *The Human Rights Committee and the Right of Individual Communication* (1998); Tyagi (2011) 386–630.

individual. The HRC's 'views' are not per se binding,[33] but they are published and are often influential in bringing about internal legislative or administrative changes.[34] By December 2011 the HRC had registered 2,115 communications, 826 of which had been concluded by adopting 'views' under Article 5(4) of the Protocol.[35]

The work of the CESCR and HRC has been supplemented by interpretive statements known as 'General Comments', for example the HRC's General Comment 12 on the right to self-determination.[36] These comments serve to clarify the application of specific provisions and issues relating to the Covenants, and as such are of significant normative value within the human rights system.[37] Other human rights treaty bodies also follow this practice.

(ii) Regional conventions

In addition to the multilateral human rights conventions, various regional conventions recognize a range of civil, political, social, economic, and cultural rights, and establish regional frameworks for their protection.[38] The first of the comprehensive regional human rights conventions was the ECHR of 1950.[39] It was followed by the American Convention on Human Rights of 1969,[40] and the African Charter on Human and Peoples' Rights of 1981.[41]

Another regional human rights convention is the Arab Charter on Human Rights adopted by the League of Arab States on 22 May 2004.[42] The Arab Charter is a revision of a 1994 Charter which never came into force.[43] There is no binding human rights convention covering the Asia-Pacific region, and there is debate over whether the notion of 'universal human rights' conflicts with 'Asian values', said to focus more on the collective good and civic order than on individual rights.[44]

[33] See CCPR, General Comment 33 (2008) CCPR/C/GC/33, §§11–15; cf *Tangiora v Wellington District Legal Services Committee* (1999) 24 ILR 570, 575.

[34] E.g. *Lovelace v Canada* (1981) 68 ILR 17; *Toonen v Australia* (1994) 112 ILR 328. Further: Tyagi (2011) 626–9.

[35] Information provided by the Petitions and Inquiries Section of the Office of the High Commissioner for Human Rights, 1 December 2011 (email correspondence on file with the editor).

[36] CCPR, General Comment 12: Article 1 (1984) HRI/GEN/1/Rev.7, 134.

[37] Further: Tyagi (2011) 7.

[38] Generally: Shelton (ed), *Regional Protection of Human Rights* (2008).

[39] 4 November 1950, ETS 5. All Council of Europe member states are parties to the ECHR (47 in total), and new members are expected to ratify the convention as soon as possible: Parliamentary Assembly Resolution 1031 (1994).

[40] 22 November 1969, OAS Treaty Series 36 (currently 25 parties).

[41] 17 June 1981, 1520 UNTS 323 (currently 53 ratifications). There is also a Commonwealth of Independent States Convention on Human Rights and Fundamental Freedoms, 26 May 1995 (1996) 3 IHRR 212. Only Belarus, Kyrgyzstan, Tajikistan, and the Russian Federation have ratified it. The envisaged Human Rights Commission has not been created.

[42] (2005) 12 IHRR 893.

[43] El Din Hassan, in Symonides (2003) 239; Rishmawi (2005) 5 *HRLR* 661; Rishmawi (2010) 10 *HRLR* 169.

[44] See Smith, *Textbook on International Human Rights* (4th edn, 2010) 90–2. On the Asian values debate: e.g. Davis (1998) 11 *Harv HRJ* 111; Donnelly, in Bauer & Bell (eds), *The East Asian Challenge for Human Rights* (1999) 60; Avonius & Kingsbury (eds), *Human Rights in Asia* (2008).

(iii) Conventions dealing with specific rights

Besides the treaties of general application, the international human rights framework also includes treaties that address specific wrongs. The first of these was arguably the 1948 Genocide Convention, which defines genocide and confirms it as a crime under international law which states parties undertake to prevent and punish, whether committed in peacetime or in time of war. It is distinguishable from other human rights instruments in that it does not set out specific rights for individuals but operates primarily through criminalizing involvement in genocide.[45]

Other examples in the category of specific conventions include the treaties against racial discrimination and apartheid,[46] the Convention against Torture and Other Cruel, Inhuman or Degrading Treatment or Punishment,[47] and the International Convention for the Protection of All Persons from Enforced Disappearance.[48] The implementation of each treaty is monitored by committees specifically established for that purpose.

(iv) Conventions protecting particular categories or groups

The fourth category of multilateral human rights treaties is directed at protecting certain specific groups. The 1951 Convention Relating to the Status of Refugees sets out a detailed regime for treatment of refugees, as defined in Article 1 of the Convention.[49] A 1967 Protocol extended its coverage, removing geographical and temporal limitations in the definition.[50] Refugee law is generally seen as separate from (although related to) general human rights law, and the system is administered by the UN High Commissioner for Refugees.[51]

---

[45] Genocide Convention, 9 December 1948, 78 UNTS 277; Parlett (2011) 313.

[46] ICERD, GA Res 2106(XX), 21 December 1965, 660 UNTS 195 (currently 175 parties); International Convention on the Suppression and Punishment of the Crime of Apartheid, GA Res 3068(XXVIII), 1015 UNTS 243 (currently 107 parties); International Convention Against Apartheid in Sports, GA Res 40/64, 10 December 1985, 1500 UNTS 161 (currently 60 parties). Generally: Lerner, *The UN Convention on the Elimination of All Forms of Racial Discrimination* (2nd edn, 1980); McKean (1983); Banton, *International Action against Racial Discrimination* (1996); Moeckli, in Moeckli, Shah & Sivakumaran (2010) 189.

[47] GA Res 39/46, 10 December 1984, 1465 UNTS 85 (currently 149 parties). An Optional Protocol has also been adopted, establishing a preventive system of regular visits to places of detention: GA Res 57/199, 18 December 2002 (61 parties). Further: Burgers & Danelius, *The UN Convention against Torture—A Handbook* (1988); Nowak & McArthur, *The United Nations Convention Against Torture* (2008); Rodley, *The Treatment of Prisoners under International Law* (3rd edn, 2009).

[48] GA Res 61/177, 20 December 2006 (currently 30 parties). See Anderson (2006) 7 *Melb JIL* 245; Rodley (3rd edn, 2009) 329–78.

[49] 28 July 1951, 189 UNTS 137 (currently 144 parties).

[50] GA Res 2198(XXI), 16 December 1966; 660 UNTS 267 (currently 146 parties).

[51] Further: Hathaway, *The Rights of Refugees under International Law* (2005); Goodwin-Gill & McAdam, *The Refugee in International Law* (3rd edn, 2007).

Other groups protected under specific treaties include children,[52] women,[53] migrant workers and their families,[54] and people with disabilities.[55] As above, the implementation of each of these treaties is monitored by committees specifically established for that purpose.

(B) CUSTOMARY INTERNATIONAL LAW

It is now generally accepted that the fundamental principles of human rights form part of customary international law, although not everyone would agree on the identity or content of the fundamental principles. In 1970 the International Court in the *Barcelona Traction* case saw as included in the category of 'obligations *erga omnes*' the following: 'the principles and rules concerning the basic rights of the human person, including protection from slavery and racial discrimination'.[56] This relative indeterminacy is echoed in later declarations, some of them influential in promoting the 'cause' of human rights.[57]

The role of the 'customary international law of human rights' is recognized in the *Third Restatement* in the following terms:

A State violates international law if, as a matter of State policy, it practices, encourages, or condones

   (1) genocide

   (2) slavery or slave trade,

   (3) the murder or causing the disappearance of individuals,

   (4) torture or other cruel, inhuman or degrading treatment or punishment,

   (5) prolonged arbitrary detention,

---

[52] UN Convention on the Rights of the Child, 20 November 1989, 1577 UNTS 3 (currently 193 parties). Further: Detrick, *A Commentary on the United Nations Convention on the Rights of the Child* (1999); Fottrell (ed), *Revisiting Children's Rights* (2000); Price Cohen, *Jurisprudence on the Rights of the Child* (2005); Invernizzi & Williams (eds), *The Human Rights of Children* (2011).

[53] Convention on the Elimination of All Forms of Discrimination against Women, 18 December 1979, 1249 UNTS 13 (currently 187 parties); Convention on the Political Rights of Women, 31 March 1953, 193 UNTS 135 (currently 122 parties). Generally: Cook (ed), *Human Rights of Women* (1994); Chinkin & Charlesworth, *Boundaries of International Law* (2000); Brems, in Lyons & Mayall (eds), *International Human Rights in the 21st Century* (2003) 100; Knop (ed), *Gender and Human Rights* (2004); Lockwood (ed), *Women's Rights* (2006).

[54] International Convention on the Protection of the Rights of All Migrant Workers and Members of their Families, 18 December 1990, 2220 UNTS 3 (currently 45 parties). Further: Cholewinski, *Migrant Workers in International Human Rights Law* (1997); de Guchteneire, Pécoud & Cholewinski (eds), *Migration and Human Rights* (2009).

[55] Convention on the Rights of Persons with Disabilities, 13 December 2006, 2515 UNTS 3 (currently 106 parties), with Optional Protocol. Further: Kanter (2007) 34 *Syracuse JILC* 287; Kayess & French (2008) 8 *HRLR* 1; Arnardóttir & Quinn (eds), *The UN Convention on the Rights of Persons with Disabilities* (2009).

[56] *Barcelona Traction, Light and Power Company Ltd (Belgium v Spain)*, ICJ Reports 1970 p 3, 32.

[57] E.g. Helsinki Final Act, Declaration of Principles Guiding Relations between Participating States, 1 August 1975, 14 ILM 1292.

(6) systematic racial discrimination, or

(7) a consistent pattern of gross violations of internationally recognized human rights.[58]

In the *Wall* opinion, the International Court found that the construction of the wall by Israel, the occupying power, in the Occupied Palestinian Territory, and the associated regime, were 'contrary to international law'.[59] In resolving certain questions raised by Israel, the Court had recourse to aspects of customary international law concerning the substance of international humanitarian law.[60] It also relied upon considerations of general international law in determining that the 1966 Covenants apply both to individuals present within a state's territory and to individuals outside that territory but subject to that state's jurisdiction.[61]

(C) SUMMARY

As to the substance of human rights themselves, a wide range of rights is recognized in the core instruments, along with an ever-expanding group of emerging or claimed 'rights' with unclear or contested legal status.[62] Key human rights protected in two or more major instruments are tabled below (see Table 28.1 on p. 644). The groupings are indicative only, as the language and specific formulation of each right differs between texts.

This table suggests that there may be something approaching a 'common core' of human rights at the universal and regional levels. But it also suggests that any such common core is partial and imperfect—and it hides altogether the many differences in the articulation of the various rights in the various treaties. The fact remains that governments have chosen to develop and articulate human rights principles at the international level largely by means of multilateral treaties, individually negotiated. It is those treaties which for most practical purposes constitute the international law of human rights.[63]

---

[58] 2 *Restatement Third* §702. Also: Meron, *Human Rights and Humanitarian Norms as Customary International Law* (1989).

[59] *Legal Consequences of the Construction of a Wall in the Occupied Palestinian Territory*, ICJ Reports 2004 p 136, 200.

[60] Ibid, 172–7.

[61] Ibid, 177–81.

[62] There is concern about the rapid proliferation of interests claimed as human rights, e.g. the assertion of a 'right' to tourism, or disarmament. The international legal system lacks any clear process or criteria for qualifying claims as deserving of legal recognition, and there is a trend for new rights to be 'conjured up' simply by virtue of their being framed in the language of rights: Alston (1984) 78 *AJIL* 607, 607. Further: Kennedy (2002) 15 *Harv HRJ* 101; Kennedy, *The Dark Side of Virtue* (2004) 3–35.

[63] See Raz, in Besson & Tasioulas (eds), *The Philosophy of International Law* (2010) 321–37; Griffin, ibid, 339–55; Skorupski, ibid, 357–73.

Table 29.1 Key human rights protected

	ICCPR	ICESCR	ECHR*	ACHR	African Charter
Self-determination	Art 1	Art 1	-	-	Art 20
Equality & non-discrimination	Arts 2(1), 3, 14(1), 26	Arts 2(2), 3	Art 14	Arts 1, 24	Arts 2, 3, 19
Right to life	Art 6	-	Art 2	Art 4	Art 4
Freedom from torture & other inhuman treatment	Art 7	-	Art 3	Art 5	Art 5
Freedom from slavery	Art 8	-	Art 4	Art 6	Art 5
Liberty & security of person	Art 9	-	Art 5	Art 7	Art 6
Freedom of assembly & association	Arts 21, 22	-	Art 11	Arts 15, 16	Arts 10, 11
Freedom of movement	Art 12	-	OP4, Art 2	Art 22	Art 12
Due process	Arts 9–11, 14–16	-	Arts 6, 7; OP4, Art 1	Arts 3, 8, 9, 24	Arts 3, 7
Freedom of expression	Art 19	-	Art 10	Art 13	Art 9
Freedom of thought, conscience, & religion	Art 18	-	Art 9	Arts 12, 13	Art 8
Free elections/participation in government	Art 25	-	OP1, Art 3	Art 23	Art 13
Rights of the family	Art 23	Art 10	Arts 8, 12	Art 17	Art 18
Right to work	-	Arts 6, 7	-	-	Art 15
Right to education	-	Art 13	OP1, Art 2	-	Art 17
Right to health	-	Art 12	-	-	Art 16
Cultural rights	Art 27	Art 15	-	-	Art 17(2)

* OP1, OP4: First and Fourth Optional Protocols to ECHR.

4. NON-DISCRIMINATION AND COLLECTIVE RIGHTS

The UN Charter contains various references to 'human rights and fundamental freedoms for all without distinction as to race, sex, language or religion'. These general and to some extent promotional provisions have constituted the background to the appearance of a substantial body of multilateral conventions and practice by UN organs. By 1966, at the latest, it was possible to conclude that in terms of the Charter the principle of respect for and protection of human rights on a non-discriminatory basis had become recognized as a legal standard.[64]

---

[64] *South West Africa (Ethiopia v South Africa; Liberia v South Africa)*, Second Phase, ICJ Reports 1966 p 6, 300 (Judge Tanaka, diss); *Legal Consequences for States of the Continued Presence of South Africa in*

There is no great gulf between the legal and human rights of groups, on the one hand, and individuals, on the other. Guarantees and standards governing treatment of individuals tend, by emphasizing equality, to protect groups as well, for example, in regard to racial discrimination. In turn, protection of groups naturally encompasses protection of individual members of those groups; some rights attaching to individuals *qua* group members are only exercisable in community with other members of the group.[65]

(A) NON-DISCRIMINATION

International law contains a legal principle of non-discrimination on grounds of race, articulated in the International Convention on the Elimination of All Forms of Racial Discrimination (ICERD).[66] This principle is based, in part, upon the UN Charter, especially Articles 55 and 56; the practice of organs of the UN (e.g. General Assembly resolutions condemning apartheid); the Universal Declaration of Human Rights; the International Covenants on Human Rights; and the regional human rights conventions.[67] In 1970 the International Court in *Barcelona Traction* referred to obligations *erga omnes* as specifically including 'protection from slavery and racial discrimination'.[68] There is also a legal principle of non-discrimination in matters of sex, based upon the same set of multilateral instruments,[69] together with the widely ratified Convention on the Elimination of All Forms of Discrimination against Women (CEDAW) adopted in 1979.[70]

The principle of equality before the law allows for factual differences, such as age, and is not based on mechanical conceptions of equality.[71] But any distinction drawn must have an objective justification; the means adopted to establish different treatment must be proportionate to the justification for differentiation; and there is a

---

Namibia (South West Africa) notwithstanding Security Council Resolution 276 (1970), ICJ Reports 1971 p 16, 57.

[65] ICCPR, Art 27. On collective rights generally: Dinstein (1976) 25 *ICLQ* 102; Crawford (ed), *The Rights of Peoples* (1988); Lerner, *Group Rights and Discrimination in International Law* (1991); Rodley (1995) 47 *HRQ* 48; Lyons & Mayall (2003); Weller (ed), *Universal Minority Rights* (2007).

[66] GA Res 2106(XX), 21 December 1965, 660 UNTS 195 (175 parties to date). See Lerner (2nd edn, 1980).

[67] E.g. *South West Africa*, Second Phase, ICJ Reports 1966 p 6, 286–301 (Judge Tanaka, diss); *European Roma Rights v Immigration Officer* [2005] 2 AC 1. Further: McKean (1983); Banton (1996); Moeckli, *Human Rights and Non-Discrimination in the 'War on Terror'* (2008); Moeckli, in Moeckli, Shah & Sivakumaran (2010) 189.

[68] ICJ Reports 1970 p 3, 32.

[69] On sexual equality: McDougal, Lasswell & Chen (1975) 69 *AJIL* 497; McKean (1983) 166–93; Meron (1986) 53–82; CCPR, General Comment 28: Article 3 (2000) HRI/GEN/1/Rev.7, 178; Landau & Beigbeder, *From ILO Standards to EU Law* (2008).

[70] GA Res 34/180, 18 December 1979, 1249 UNTS 13 (currently 187 parties).

[71] See *Minority Schools in Albania* (1935) PCIJ Ser A/B No 64; *Association Protestante* (1966) 47 ILR 198; *American European Beth-El Mission v Minister of Social Welfare* (1967) 47 ILR 205; *Gerhardy v Brown* [1985] HCA 11, §§25–6 (Brennan J); CCPR, General Comment 18: Non-discrimination (1989) HRI/GEN/1/Rev.7, 146, §§8–10; *Maya Indigenous Communities of the Toledo District v Belize* (2004) 135 ILR 1, 67.

burden of proof on the party seeking to invoke an exception to the equality principle.[72] ICERD Article 1(4) is of particular interest, making it clear that differential treatment in the form of special measures necessary to secure the advancement of certain disadvantaged groups is not racial discrimination in the sense of the Convention.[73] The Committee on the Elimination of Racial Discrimination clarified the meaning of 'special measures' in its General Recommendation XXXII.[74]

The Declaration on the Elimination of All Forms of Intolerance and Discrimination Based on Religion or Belief, adopted by the UN General Assembly on 25 November 1981, completes the picture.[75]

In a significant determination in 2001 the European Court of Human Rights held that discriminatory treatment as such could be categorized as degrading treatment within the terms of Article 3 ECHR.[76]

(B) SELF-DETERMINATION[77]

The idea of collective or group rights became prominent in connection with the principle of self-determination, progenitor of the category of so-called 'peoples' rights'.[78] Self-determination is articulated variously as political principle, legal principle, and legal right.[79] It has been understood as the right of peoples under colonial, foreign, or alien domination to self-government,[80] whether through formation of a new state, association in a federal state, or autonomy or assimilation in a unitary (non-federal) state.[81] In different contexts, however, self-determination can mean different things,

---

[72] *Belgian Linguistics* (1968) 45 ILR 114; *National Union of Belgian Police* (1975) 57 ILR 262, 265, 281, 287; *Abdulaziz, Cabales and Balkandali* (1985) 81 ILR 139, 171; *Juridical Condition and Rights of Undocumented Migrants*, IACtHR OC-18/03, 17 September 2003, §§82–96; *Burden v UK* [2008] ECtHR 13378/05, §60; *Kiyutin v Russia* [2011] ECtHR 2700/10, §62. Further: CCPR, General Comment 18, §13; CERD, General Recommendation XIV: Article 1(1) (1993) HRI/GEN/1/Rev.7, 206, §2.

[73] In some cases, the provision of special measures is obligatory: see Art 2(2). Cf *South West Africa*, Second Phase, ICJ Reports 1966 p 6, 306–10 (Judge Tanaka, diss).

[74] (2009) CERD/C/GC/32. Further: Brownlie, in Crawford (1988) 1, 6–11; Alfredsson, in Weller (ed), *The Rights of Minorities* (2005) 141, 148–50 (in the context of Art 4 of the European Framework Convention for the Protection of National Minorities, 10 November 1994, CETS 157).

[75] GA Res 36/55, 25 November 1981. For comment: Sullivan (1988) 82 *AJIL* 487.

[76] *Cyprus v Turkey* (2001) 120 ILR 10, 91–3. Also: *East African Asians* (1973) 3 EHRR 76.

[77] See Cristescu, *The Right to Self-Determination* (1981); Higgins, *Problems and Process* (1994) 111–28; Cassese, *Self-Determination of Peoples* (1995); Franck, *Fairness in International Law and Institutions* (1995) 140–69; Quane (1998) 47 *ICLQ* 537; McCorquodale (ed), *Self-Determination in International Law* (2000); Ghanea & Xanthaki (eds), *Minorities, Peoples and Self-Determination* (2005); Crawford, *Creation of States* (2nd edn, 2006) 108–28.

[78] Generally: Alston (ed), *Peoples' Rights* (2001). Also: Knop (2002) 29–49; Xanthaki, *Indigenous Rights and United Nations Standards* (2007) 143, 155–7.

[79] The shift from 'principle' to 'right' first appeared in the Declaration on the Granting of Independence to Colonial Countries and Peoples, GA Res 1514(XV), 14 December 1960: see Higgins (1994) 114.

[80] E.g. GA Res 1514(XV), 14 December 1960; GA Res 1541(XV), 15 December 1960; GA Res 2625(XXV), 24 October 1970. Also: *Namibia*, ICJ Reports 1971 p 16, 31; *Western Sahara*, ICJ Reports 1975 p 12, 68; *East Timor (Portugal v Australia)*, ICJ Reports 1995 p 90, 102; *Wall*, ICJ Reports 2004 p 136, 171–2.

[81] See GA Res 1541(XV), 15 December 1960; GA Res 2625(XXV), 24 October 1970. See further chapter 5.

and there is no universally accepted definition.[82] On a general level, it can be defined as 'the right of a community which has a distinct character to have this character reflected in the institutions of government in which it lives'.[83] The International Court has described self-determination as the 'need to pay regard to the freely expressed will of peoples',[84] but there has been wide disagreement over the meaning of 'peoples', not least in the context of indigenous and minority claims to self-determination.

Common Article 1(1) of the ICCPR and ICESCR upholds the right of 'all peoples' to self-determination, and Article 2 of the Arab Charter contains similar wording. The African Charter on Human and Peoples' Rights recognizes the 'unquestionable and inalienable right to self-determination' of all peoples (Article 20(1)). The advisory opinion of the Court in *Western Sahara* confirms 'the validity of the principle of self-determination' in the context of that dispute.[85] In the *Wall* opinion the Court recognized the principle of self-determination as one of the rules and principles relevant to the legality of the measure taken by Israel: the effect of the wall, in conjunction with the settlement policy, was to impair if not to preclude the exercise of the right of self-determination of the people of Palestine in relation to the territory of Palestine as a whole.[86]

The development of the principle of self-determination in practice has led to a pronounced distinction between the colonial and non-colonial context, reflecting a distinction between full ('external') self-determination and qualified ('internal') self-determination.[87] The question of internal self-determination, and the possibility of remedial secession, remain controversial.[88]

(C) RIGHTS OF MINORITIES[89]

The need to protect the rights of racial, linguistic, and religious minority groups within states has been recognized in a general way since the minorities treaties of the inter-war period,[90] but there is still no agreed definition of what constitutes a 'minority' in international law,[91] and the question of legal personality for minority groups as such

---

[82] E.g. Kirgis (1994) 88 *AJIL* 304.

[83] Brownlie, in Crawford (1988) 1, 5.

[84] *Western Sahara*, ICJ Reports 1975 p 12, 33.

[85] Ibid, 31–3.

[86] *Wall*, ICJ Reports 2004 p 136, 171–2. Also: *East Timor*, ICJ Reports 1995 p 90, 102.

[87] *Reference re Secession of Quebec* (1998) 115 ILR 536, 594–5. See Crawford (1998) 69 *BY* 115; Bayefsky (ed), *Self-Determination in International Law: Quebec and Lessons Learned* (2000); further chapter 5.

[88] Several governments before the Court in *Kosovo* invoked remedial self-determination: the Court did not reach the issue. See *Accordance with International Law of the Unilateral Declaration of Independence in Respect of Kosovo*, Opinion of 22 July 2010, §82; further chapter 5.

[89] Generally: Capotorti, Study of the Rights of Persons Belonging to Ethnic, Religious and Linguistic Minorities, E/CN.4/Sub.2/384/Rev.1; Thornberry (1991); Skurbaty, *As If Peoples Mattered: Critical Appraisal of 'Peoples' and 'Minorities' from the International Human Rights Perspective and Beyond* (2000); Weller (2005); Weller (2007).

[90] Parlett (2011) 282–7; Eide, in Weller (2005) 25, 33–6.

[91] Packer, in Packer & Myntti (eds), *The Protection of Ethnic and Linguistic Minorities in Europe* (1993) 23; Hannum, in Weller (2007) 49.

is fraught.[92] States have traditionally been wary of recognizing rights and status of minority groups within their territory, for fear of claims to secession. The HRC has affirmed that minority rights are different from the right to self-determination, and their enjoyment should not prejudice states' sovereignty and territorial integrity.[93]

The only multilateral treaty dealing specifically with minority rights is the European Framework Convention for the Protection of National Minorities, adopted by the Council of Europe in 1994.[94] The Convention articulates a comprehensive set of principles for the protection of national minorities and persons belonging to those minorities. It covers individual rights as well as provisions directed specifically at protecting the existence and identity of minority groups as such.[95] The decision to adopt the Convention, rather than a proposed additional protocol to the ECHR,[96] attracted criticism. The task of monitoring implementation of the treaty was thus assigned to an Advisory Committee of the Council of Europe, not the Strasbourg Court. In practice, however, the Advisory Committee has made a contribution to the development and enforcement of Convention rights, and states clearly treat the Convention as a legal commitment, despite the general, framework character of some of its provisions.[97]

The position under general international law is rather different. The key text is ICCPR Article 27 which protects the right of members of ethnic, religious, and linguistic minorities, in community with other members, to enjoy their own culture, profess and practise their own religion, and use their own language; this is poised between an individual and a collective rights guarantee, but emphasizes the individual.[98] The interpretative potential in Article 27 has been tested to an extent in individual complaints before the HRC.[99]

In 1992 the General Assembly adopted the Declaration on the Rights of Persons Belonging to National or Ethnic, Religious or Linguistic Minorities. The Declaration was intended to strengthen the implementation of human rights relating to minorities, based on the principles of non-exclusion, non-assimilation, and non-discrimination.[100]

---

[92] Meijknecht, *Towards International Personality* (2001).

[93] CCPR, General Comment 23: Article 27 (1994) HRI/GEN/1/Rev.7, 158. The distinction between minority rights and self-determination is also clear in the European Framework Convention, 10 November 1994, CETS 157, Art 21: see Hofmann, in Weller (2005) 1, 4.

[94] 10 November 1994, CETS 157 (currently 39 parties). There are also bilateral treaties addressing minority rights: see Bloed & van Dijk (eds), *Protection of Minority Rights Through Bilateral Treaties* (1999); and other relevant Council of Europe instruments, including the European Charter for Regional or Minority Languages, 5 November 1992, CETS 148 (currently 25 parties).

[95] E.g. certain linguistic rights (Arts 9–11), state obligations in respect of education (Arts 12–14), the prohibition of forced assimilation (Arts 5(2) and 16), and rights to cross-border contacts and co-operation (Art 17).

[96] See Res 1201 (1993) of the Parliamentary Assembly of the Council of Europe.

[97] Weller, in Weller (2005) 609.

[98] See Nowak (2nd edn, 2005) 635–67; CCPR, General Comment 23.

[99] E.g. *Lovelace v Canada* (1981) 68 ILR 17; *Kitok v Sweden* (1988) 96 ILR 637; *Ominayak and the Lubicon Lake Band v Canada* (1990) 96 ILR 667; *Länsman v Finland* (1996) 115 ILR 300.

[100] GA Res 47/135, 8 December 1992. See Phillips & Rosas (eds), *The UN Minority Rights Declaration* (1993); Eide, Commentary to the Declaration on the Rights of Persons Belonging to National or Ethnic, Religious or Linguistic Minorities (1998) E/CN.4/Sub.2/AC.5/1998/WP.1.

It elaborates on the principle of protection of identity under ICCPR Article 27, and moves towards promotion of identity.

(D) RIGHTS OF INDIGENOUS PEOPLES[101]

The UN Declaration on the Rights of Indigenous Peoples was adopted in 2007 by a large majority of the General Assembly.[102] The Declaration resulted from a drafting process that lasted more than 20 years, and was noteworthy for the level of participation of indigenous groups and their NGOs.[103] This also produced changes within the UN structure, with the creation of the UN Permanent Forum on Indigenous Issues as an advisory body to the Economic and Social Council;[104] the extension of the mandate of the Special Rapporteur on the Situation of Human Rights and Fundamental Freedoms of Indigenous Peoples;[105] and the creation of the Expert Mechanism on the Rights of Indigenous Peoples, subsidiary to the Human Rights Council.[106]

Previously the only international instruments addressing indigenous rights as such[107] were two ILO Conventions with limited participation, characterized by markedly state-driven perspectives.[108] The Declaration represents a shift away from that approach, promoting a more inclusive and consultative relationship with indigenous peoples. Perhaps its most significant feature is the proclamation in Article 3 that indigenous peoples have the right to self-determination. Despite the wording of ICCPR/ICESCR Article 1, recognizing the right of *all peoples* to self-determination, for a long time states resisted recognizing indigenous claims.[109] The HRC refuses to entertain claims for violations of Article 1, taking the view that inherently collective

---

[101] Generally: Tennant (1994) 16 *HRQ* 1; Wiessner (1999) 12 *Harv HRJ* 57; Aikio & Scheinin (eds), *Operationalizing the Right of Indigenous Peoples to Self-Determination* (2000); Thornberry, *Indigenous Peoples and Human Rights* (2002); Anaya, *Indigenous Peoples in International Law* (2nd edn, 2004); Eide (2006) 37 *NYIL* 155; Xanthaki (2007); Daes (2008) 21 *Cam RIA* 7; Allen & Xanthaki (eds), *Reflections on the UN Declaration on the Rights of Indigenous Peoples* (2011).

[102] GA Res 6/1295, 13 September 2007 (143–4 (Australia, Canada, New Zealand, US): 11 (Azerbaijan, Bangladesh, Bhutan, Burundi, Colombia, Georgia, Kenya, Nigeria, Russian Federation, Samoa, Ukraine)). A number of these states have since endorsed the Declaration.

[103] Barsh (1996) 18 *HRQ* 782, 783–6; Eide (2006) 161–2.

[104] Economic and Social Council Res 2000/22, 28 July 2000. See Lindroth (2006) 42(222) *Polar Record* 239.

[105] Human Rights Council Res 6/12, 28 September 2007.

[106] Human Rights Council Res 6/36, 14 December 2007.

[107] Although in many cases indigenous groups constitute minorities within states, indigenous people have consistently differentiated themselves as 'peoples' rather than minorities. See *AD v Canada* (1984) 76 ILR 261, 264–5; see also Falk, in Crawford (1988) 17, 32; Thornberry (1989) 38 *ICLQ* 867, 868–9; Cassidy (2003) 51 *AJCL* 409. Analytically, however, one could be both.

[108] ILO Convention 107 Concerning the Protection and Integration of Indigenous and other Tribal and Semi-Tribal Populations in Independent Countries, 26 June 1957, 328 UNTS 247 is no longer open for ratification, and has effectively been replaced by ILO Convention 169 Concerning Indigenous and Tribal Peoples in Independent Countries, 27 June 1989, 28 ILM 1382. See Xanthaki (2007) 49–101; Erueti, in Allen & Xanthaki (2011) 93–120.

[109] E.g. Barsh (1996) 796–800.

claims cannot be brought under the individual complaints procedure of the First Optional Protocol. The Committee has generally treated indigenous claims as coming within the minority rights protections of Article 27 instead.[110] The explicit recognition of indigenous peoples' right to self-determination in the Declaration is a significant change—though achieved on the 'understanding' that self-determination for this purpose does not equate to a right to secede, as distinct from negotiating the terms of indigenous engagement with the state.[111]

Besides self-determination, the Declaration also affirms a range of individual and group rights of importance to indigenous peoples, including equality and freedom from discrimination,[112] cultural identity and integrity,[113] participation in decision-making,[114] autonomy and self-government,[115] and traditional lands and natural resources.[116] The term 'indigenous peoples' is, however, left undefined.[117] As a General Assembly resolution, the Declaration does not impose obligations on states, but its symbolic weight should not be underestimated.[118]

(E) OTHER COLLECTIVE RIGHTS

The notion of rights being enjoyed by groups of persons collectively, rather than as individuals, remains controversial. A distinction should be made between rights attaching to individuals because of their status as members of a group, and rights attaching to the group as such, which individuals can in practice only enjoy in

---

[110] E.g. *Ominayak and the Lubicon Lake Band v Canada* (1990) 96 ILR 667; *Marshall v Canada* (1991) 96 ILR 707. For criticism: Tyagi (2011) 598–9.

[111] Eide (2006) 196–9, 211–12; Daes (2008) 15–18, 23–4; Quane, in Allen & Xanthaki (2011) 259, 264–9; cf ILA, Report of the 74th Conference (2010) 846–8.

[112] E.g. Arts 1–2. Also: CERD, General Recommendation XXIII: Indigenous Peoples (1997) A/52/18, Annex V (confirming that racial discrimination against indigenous peoples falls within the scope of ICERD).

[113] E.g. Arts 11–16, 24–5, 31. See ILA, Report of the 74th Conference (2010) 857–60; Stamatopoulou, in Allen & Xanthaki (2011) 387. On recognition of traditional laws: ALRC, Report 31, *Recognition of Aboriginal Customary Laws* (1986).

[114] Over 20 provisions in the Declaration articulate different facets of the right to participate in decision-making, setting a high standard beyond mere consultation: see UN Expert Mechanism on the Rights of Indigenous Peoples, Progress Report on the Study on Indigenous Peoples and the Right to Participate in Decision-Making (2010) A/HRC/EMRIP/2010/2. It is notable that the right of political participation is expressed as a collective right, cf the views of the HRC in respect of ICCPR, Art 25: *Marshall v Canada* (1991) 96 ILR 707; *Diergaardt v Namibia* (2000) CCPR/C/69/D/760/1997, §10.8 (but see sep op Scheinin).

[115] Art 4. See ILA, Report of the 74th Conference (2010) 850–7.

[116] E.g. Arts 26–30, 32. Rights over land and natural resources are fundamental to indigenous claims to self-determination: e.g. ILA, Report of the 74th Conference (2010) 863–70; Gilbert & Doyle, in Allen & Xanthaki (2011) 289; Errico, in Allen & Xanthaki (2011), 329.

[117] On the definitional problem and its evasion: e.g. Thornberry (2002) 33–60; Special Rapporteur of the Sub-Commission on the Prevention of Discrimination and Protection of Minorities, José Martínez-Cobo, *Study on the Problem of Discrimination Against Indigenous Populations* (1987); Daes (2008) 8–10.

[118] Barelli (2009) 58 *ICLQ* 957; Coulter (2008) 45 *Idaho LR* 539. Note also Art 46, requiring indigenous rights to be interpreted consistently with respect for the rights of others.

community with others. The instruments on minority and indigenous rights contain examples of both.

Beyond the specific rights of minorities and indigenous peoples, international law recognizes some other collective rights, in particular, a people's right to freely dispose of its natural wealth and resources and not to be deprived of its own means of subsistence (ICCPR/ICESCR Article 1(2)). Examples of other putative collective rights include the right to development,[119] and the right to culture;[120] by now, however, we are approaching the useful limits of law if not of language.

5. SCOPE OF HUMAN RIGHTS STANDARDS: SOME GENERAL ISSUES

(A) TERRITORIAL AND PERSONAL SCOPE OF HUMAN RIGHTS TREATIES

International human rights instruments typically do not define the precise territorial and personal scope of the human rights protections they contain. ECHR Article 1 provides that the parties shall secure the rights and freedoms defined in Section 1 of the Convention 'to everyone within their jurisdiction'. A similar reference to 'jurisdiction' appears in Article 1 of the American Convention on Human Rights. The African Charter is silent on the issue. Other instruments refer to territorial jurisdiction but with no mention of the personal scope of the rights they protect. The question is whether states parties to human rights treaties are bound to apply their protections extra-territorially, including to non-nationals. This arises particularly in the context of armed conflict and belligerent occupation.[121]

The European Court of Human Rights has had to consider the scope of ECHR Article 1 on a number of occasions. Before 2001, it was reasonably settled that 'jurisdiction' in Article 1 is primarily territorial,[122] but that in some cases, acts of states parties performed or producing effects outside their territories might also constitute an exercise of jurisdiction.[123] In particular, a line of cases involving the Turkish occupation of northern Cyprus had established that where a state party exercises effective

---

[119] Declaration on the Right to Development, GA Res 41/128, 4 December 1986; further: Rosas, in Eide, Krause & Rosas (2nd edn, 2001) 119–30; Andreassen & Marks (eds), *Development as a Human Right* (2nd edn, 2010).

[120] Art 15 ICESCR; see O'Keefe (1998) 47 *ICLQ* 904, esp 917–18; Stavenhagen, in Eide, Krause & Rosas (2nd edn, 2001) 86; cf Eide, in Eide, Krause & Rosas (2nd edn, 2001) 289.

[121] Generally: Coomans & Kamminga (eds), *Extraterritorial Application of Human Rights Treaties* (2004); Dennis (2005) 99 *AJIL* 119; Wilde (2007) 40 *Is LR* 503; Milanović (2008) 8 *HRLR* 411; Gondek, *The Reach of Human Rights in a Globalising World* (2009); Milanović, *Extraterritorial Application of Human Rights Treaties* (2011).

[122] *Soering v UK* (1989) 98 ILR 270, 300.

[123] See the review of the case-law in *Al-Skeini v UK* [2011] ECtHR 55721/07, §§130–42.

control of an area outside its national territory as a consequence of military action, the fact of that control triggers the Article 1 obligation to secure Convention rights and freedoms there.[124] Another recognized exception to territoriality is the personal model of extraterritorial jurisdiction, arising when state agents exercise authority and control over individuals outside the national territory.[125]

Banković v Belgium[126] arose out of the airstrike under NATO auspices on the Radio Televizija Srbije building in Belgrade during the Kosovo crisis in 1999. The victims or their representatives brought claims against 17 respondent states, members of NATO, and parties to the ECHR. The Court found that the case fell beyond the scope of Article 1 and was inadmissible.[127] The victims and the applicants were located in the territory of the Federal Republic of Yugoslavia (FRY), outside the territorial jurisdiction of any of the respondent states.[128] In this way the Court appeared to limit the Convention's extraterritorial application to those areas within the regional legal space (*espace juridique*) of the Convention, the territories of the members of the Council of Europe.[129]

Banković has been a source of some confusion in the case-law,[130] notably in the context of the invasion and occupation of Iraq in 2003. In *Al-Skeini v UK* relatives of six Iraqi civilians killed in incidents involving British soldiers in south-east Iraq alleged that the British authorities had failed adequately to investigate the deaths, which occurred during the period in which the UK was an occupying power in that region.[131] The House of Lords held there was 'jurisdiction' only in the case of one person, held in a detention facility,[132] but the ECtHR found that there was a sufficient jurisdictional link for Article 1 purposes in all six cases.[133] It ultimately found a violation of the procedural duty to investigate the deaths, pursuant to Article 2, in five cases.[134]

The Court emphasized that determining whether or not Article 1 is satisfied was a matter of considering the circumstances of each case.[135] It did not make a finding as to

---

[124] See *Loizidou v Turkey* (1995) 103 ILR 622 (preliminary objections); *Loizidou v Turkey* (1996) 108 ILR 443; *Cyprus v Turkey* (2001) 120 ILR 10.

[125] On the different models of extraterritorial jurisdiction generally: Milanović (2011) 118–228.

[126] (2001) 123 ILR 94.

[127] Ibid, 109–10.

[128] Ibid, 113–14.

[129] Ibid, 115–16. On the concept of *espace juridique*: Wilde [2005] *EHRLR* 115; Wilde (2007) 40 *Is LR* 503; Thienel (2008) 6 *JICJ* 115.

[130] For analysis: e.g. Roxstrom, Gibney & Einarsen (2005) 23 *Boston UILJ* 55; Milanović (2008) 8 *HRLR* 411; Altiparmak (2004) 9 *JCSL* 213. For criticism of the UK courts' interpretation of *Banković*: e.g. Williams (2005) 23 *Wisconsin ILJ* 687; Thienel (2008).

[131] *Al-Skeini v UK* [2011] ECtHR 55721/07.

[132] See *Al-Skeini v Secretary of State for Defence* [2007] 3 WLR 33.

[133] *Al-Skeini v UK* [2011] ECtHR 55721/07, §§149–50.

[134] Ibid, §§168–77.

[135] E.g. ibid, concurring opinion of Judge Bonello (advocating a functional test of jurisdiction under Art 1, rather than territorial); *Al-Skeini v Secretary of State for Defence* [2007] 3 WLR 33, §§67–84 (Lord Rodger, on the difficulty in reconciling *Banković* with *Issa v Turkey* (2005) 41 EHRR 567, 588, where the Court

whether or not the UK had 'effective control' of the area in question. Instead, it based its decision on a fresh articulation of the 'state agent authority' exception to territoriality recognized in previous cases: the exercise by state agents of physical power and control over the person in question.[136] It was relevant that the applicants' relatives were killed in the course of security operations while the UK was responsible for the exercise of some of the public powers in that region;[137] this distinguishes *Al-Skeini* from *Banković*. But if *Al-Skeini* cannot be said to overrule *Banković*, it qualifies it in certain respects. First, jurisdiction under Article 1 is not necessarily restricted to the regional *espace juridique* of the Convention.[138] Second, the state exercising jurisdiction has an obligation to secure the rights and freedoms that are relevant to that individual's particular situation; in that sense, the rights and obligations in the Convention *can* be 'divided and tailored'.[139]

The HRC has observed that ICCPR Article 2(1) requires states parties to ensure and respect the Covenant rights of 'anyone within their power or effective control, even if not situated within the territory of the state party', and that this requirement is not limited to citizens; it also includes situations where the state is acting outside its own territory and situations of armed conflict.[140]

The International Court has also considered the issue. It concluded in the *Wall* opinion that Israel was bound to apply the provisions of human rights instruments to which it was a party in the Occupied Palestinian Territory, observing that its position was consistent with that of the HRC.[141] The Court reiterated its finding that international human rights instruments are applicable 'in respect of acts done by a State in the exercise of its jurisdiction outside its own territory, particularly in occupied territories' in respect of Uganda's occupation of the Congolese province of Ituri.[142]

(B) HUMAN RIGHTS AND HUMANITARIAN LAW

This jurisdictional finding adds importance to the relationship between international human rights and humanitarian law.[143] The conventional view saw the two regimes

---

held that 'the Convention cannot be interpreted so as to allow a State party to perpetrate violations of the Convention on the territory of another State, which it could not perpetrate on its own territory').

[136] *Al-Skeini v UK* [2011] ECtHR 55721/07, §§133–7, 149.

[137] Ibid, §§143–9.

[138] Ibid, §142; cf *Banković v Belgium* (2001) 123 ILR 94, 115–16.

[139] *Al-Skeini v UK* [2011] ECtHR 55721/07, §137; cf *Banković v Belgium* (2001) 123 ILR 94, 114. Also: *Al-Jedda v UK* [2011] ECtHR 27021/08; *Al-Saadoon & Mufdhi v UK* [2009] ECtHR 61498/08.

[140] CCPR, General Comment 31 (2004) HRI/GEN/1/Rev.7, 192, §§10–11. Also: *López Burgos v Uruguay* (1981) 68 ILR 29; *Celiberti de Casariego v Uruguay* (1981) 68 ILR 41; and compare Dennis & Surena [2008] EHRLR 714 with Rodley [2009] EHRLR 628.

[141] *Wall*, ICJ Reports 2004 p 136, 177–81.

[142] *Armed Activities on the Territory of the Congo (DRC v Uganda)*, ICJ Reports 2005 p 168, 242–3.

[143] Generally: Provost, *International Human Rights and Humanitarian Law* (2002); Arnold & Quénivet (eds), *International Humanitarian Law and Human Rights Law* (2008); Ben-Naftali (ed), *International Humanitarian Law and International Human Rights Law* (2011); Escorihuela (2011) 19 *MSU JIL* 299.

as mutually exclusive, the former applicable in peacetime, the latter in time of armed conflict. This strict dualism is no longer observed: the two fields are now generally understood to be complementary, not alternative.[144] In short, human rights standards may also be applicable during armed conflict.[145]

The International Court has described the basic standards of humanitarian law as 'elementary considerations of humanity, even more exacting in peace than in war',[146] and has held the rules of Common Article 3 of the four Geneva Conventions of 12 August 1949 to be a 'minimum yardstick' of treatment in all international and non-international armed conflicts.[147] In *Nuclear Weapons*, the Court stated that in principle human rights obligations do not cease in times of armed conflict (unless derogations are permitted by the relevant treaty), but that international humanitarian law may operate as a *lex specialis* excluding more general human rights standards.[148] In other contexts, for example belligerent occupation, it may even be that international human rights law constitutes the more specialized standard.[149]

Despite the shift towards a more nuanced understanding of the relationship, uncertainty remains in respect of various issues including norm conflicts,[150] fragmentation,[151] and whether humanitarian law provides a lower level of protection than human rights law.[152] The classification of the so-called 'war on terror' as an armed conflict[153] also raised human rights concerns. Critics have questioned whether the campaign against al-Qaeda meets the threshold humanitarian law test for the existence of a state of armed conflict, particularly those aspects which have been carried out beyond the active combat zones of Iraq and Afghanistan. Designating the campaign as an armed conflict subject to international humanitarian law, instead of ordinary human rights and criminal law, has facilitated certain operations that would violate international law in the absence of an armed conflict.[154]

---

[144] Ben-Naftali, in Ben-Naftali (2011) 3, 4–5.

[145] See Parlett (2011) 193–6. International human rights law and the law of armed conflict have been described as 'inextricably entangled': Stigall, Blakesley & Jenks (2009) 30 *U Penn JIL* 1367, 1369.

[146] *Corfu Channel*, ICJ Reports 1949 p 4, 22.

[147] *Nicaragua*, ICJ Reports 1986 p 14, 114.

[148] *Legality of the Threat or Use of Nuclear Weapons*, ICJ Reports 1996 p 226, 239–40; reiterated in *Wall*, ICJ Reports 2004 p 136, 178; *DRC v Uganda*, ICJ Reports 2005 p 168, 242–5. For a critical view on the use of the *lex specialis* principle to define the relationship between human rights and humanitarian law: Milanović, in Ben-Naftali (2011) 95; Prud'homme (2007) 40 *Is LR* 356.

[149] Parlett (2011) 195.

[150] E.g. ibid, 195–6; Milanović, in Ben-Naftali (2011) 95.

[151] ILC Study Group, Fragmentation of International Law: Difficulties Arising From the Diversification and Expansion of International Law, ILC *Ybk* 2006/II(2); Escorihuela (2011) 19 *MSU JIL* 299.

[152] Orakhelashvili (2008) 19 *EJIL* 168.

[153] Initially, the Bush administration took the position that its campaign against terrorism was beyond the reach of the Geneva Conventions, as it was not an armed conflict with another state, but that it was international in scope and therefore escaped domestic disciplines. Since *Hamdan v Rumsfeld*, 548 US 557 (2006), the official position has been that it is an armed conflict not of an international character, to which the minimum requirements of Common Art 3 of the Geneva Conventions apply.

[154] E.g. targeted killings of suspected terrorists. See Alston, Report of the Special Rapporteur on Extrajudicial, Summary or Arbitrary Executions: Study on Targeted Killings (2010) A/HRC/13/24/Add.6;

(C) HUMAN RIGHTS IN THE PRIVATE DOMAIN: ISSUES OF 'HORIZONTAL APPLICATION'[155]

To what extent do human rights obligations extend to provide protection against private conduct? Where states are under a positive obligation to protect individuals within their jurisdiction, human rights will indirectly apply to private conduct, with the state acting in a measure as guarantor.[156] However, there is ongoing debate over whether international human rights law can also produce a 'horizontal' effect, or whether states have a monopoly of human rights responsibility. On one view the implications of a guarantee of human rights must extend to private action, and the absence of any institutional expression of that idea is a merely temporary defect. According to another view, it is national not international law which (leaving international crimes to one side) necessarily creates individual responsibility: the focus of the international human rights system remains on states as obligors. In recent years there has been something of an 'end-run' around this theoretical impasse through the development of practices of corporate social responsibility.[157] Steps were taken to develop a draft Declaration on Human Social Responsibilities,[158] and Norms on the Responsibilities of Transnational Corporations and Other Business Enterprises with Regard to Human Rights.[159] In 2005 John Ruggie was appointed Special Representative of the Secretary-General on the Issue of Human Rights and Transnational Corporations and Other Business Enterprises, and he reported to the Human Rights Council in 2008.[160]

Supporters of these developments see them as filling a gap in global standards, serving to balance the power wielded by transnational corporations and other private entities.[161] Critics warn that expanding responsibility for human rights violations may help states evade their own responsibility,[162] and (more subtly) that holding transnational

---

Melzer, *Targeted Killing in International Law* (2008) 37–43, 262–8, 394–419; Duffy, *The War on Terror and the Framework of International Law* (2005) 339–44; O'Connell (2008) 13 *JCSL* 393; Shany, in Ben-Naftali (2011) 13; Sassòli, in Ben-Naftali (2011) 34. Similar problems have arisen in the Occupied Palestinian Territory, where tensions arising from the continued Israeli occupation are treated by the Israeli government and Supreme Court as an international armed conflict: *Public Committee Against Torture in Israel v State of Israel* (1999) 133 ILR 283; Ben-Naftali & Michaeli (2003) 36 *Cornell ILJ* 233; Kretzmer (2005) 16 *EJIL* 171; Milanović (2007) 89 *IRRC* 373; Melzer (2008) 27–36.

[155] Generally: Charney [1983] *Duke LJ* 748; Ratner (2001) 111 *Yale LJ* 443; Alston (ed), *Non-State Actors and Human Rights* (2005); Clapham, *Human Rights Obligations of Non-State Actors* (2006); Zerk, *Multinationals and Corporate Social Responsibility* (2006); Knox (2008) 102 *AJIL* 1.

[156] E.g. CESCR, General Comments 15 (2002) E/C.12/2002/11, §§23–4 and 18 (2005) E/C.12/GC/18, §35.

[157] E.g. Charney [1983] *Duke LJ* 748; Watts (2005) 30 *Ann Rev Env Res* 9.1.

[158] Report of the Special Rapporteur, UN Commission on Human Rights, Promotion and Protection of Human Rights: Human Rights and Human Responsibilities, Annex I (2003) E/CN.4/2003/105.

[159] (2003) E/CN.4/Sub.2/2003/12/Rev.2. See Weissbrodt & Kruger (2003) 97 *AJIL* 901; Kinley, Nolan & Zerial (2007) 25 *C&SLJ* 30; Knox (2008) 102 *AJIL* 1.

[160] See Protect, Respect and Remedy: A Framework for Business and Human Rights (2008) A/HRC/8/5 (including Add.1 and Add.2) and A/HRC/8/16.

[161] E.g. Weissbrodt & Kruger (2003) 97 *AJIL* 901.

[162] Knox (2008) 102 *AJIL* 1.

corporations accountable may imply regulatory prerogatives which corporations do not and should not have.[163] Codes of conduct are all very well, but they influence only the willing and are no substitute for enforcement *by* the state and (at the international level) *against* the state, using existing channels of accountability.

At present, no international processes exist that bind private businesses to protect human rights.[164] Decisions of international tribunals focus on states' responsibility for preventing human rights abuses by those within their jurisdiction.[165] Nor is corporate liability for human rights violations yet recognized under customary international law.[166]

6. PROTECTION AND ENFORCEMENT OF HUMAN RIGHTS

(A) PROTECTION AND ENFORCEMENT UNDER THE UNITED NATIONS SYSTEM

(i) Action under the Charter

UN political organs have sometimes been prepared to exercise a general power of investigation and supervision in this field, but they have difficulty in dealing with particular cases; discussion normally centres on political implications and is often partisan. Nevertheless publicity, fact-finding machinery, and other 'measures' under Article 14 of the Charter can be useful.

For a long time the nearest approach to permanent machinery was the Commission on Human Rights, set up by the Economic and Social Council in 1946. Its principal function has been the preparation of various declarations (starting with the Universal Declaration) and other texts. Since 1967 the Commission has established investigatory procedures (the 1235 Procedure) in respect of country-specific complaints of gross violations.[167]

In 2006 growing unease with the way in which the Commission was functioning led to its replacement by the Human Rights Council, consisting of 47 member states.[168] So far the substitution seems to have made little difference.

---

[163] Charney [1983] *Duke LJ* 748.

[164] See Report of the Special Representative of the Secretary-General on the Issues of Human Rights and Transnational Corporations and Other Business Enterprises (2007) A/HRC/4/035, §44.

[165] E.g. *X and Y v Netherlands* [1985] ECtHR 8978/80; *Velásquez Rodríguez v Honduras* (1989) 95 ILR 232; *Hopu and Bessert v France* (1997) 118 ILR 262; *Social and Economic Rights Action Centre and Anor v Nigeria* (2001) AHRLR 60; *Mayagna (Sumo) Awas Tingni Community v Nicaragua* (2008) 136 ILR 73.

[166] See the disagreement over expert opinions of Crawford and Greenwood (given in *Presbyterian Church of Sudan v Talisman Energy, Inc*, 582 F.3d 244 (2nd Cir, 2009)) in *Kiobel v Royal Dutch Petroleum Co*, 621 F.3d 111 (2nd Cir, 2010), not followed in *Flomo v Firestone Natural Rubber Co*, 643 F.3d 1013 (7th Cir, 2011). The Supreme Court has granted certiorari in *Kiobel*. For the Alien Tort Claims Act see chapter 21.

[167] See Alston, in Alston (1992) 126 (an excellent account).

[168] GA Res 60/251, 15 March 2006; UKMIL (2006) 77 *BY* 726; Ghanea (2006) 55 *ICLQ* 695; Crook (2006) 100 *AJIL* 697.

The General Assembly lacks enforcement powers under the Charter. But it has frequently expressed concern about human rights violations occurring in different parts of the world. The Security Council was unable to act effectively, prior to the end of the Cold War, because of the veto, but did use its powers of investigation under Chapter VI from time to time, as in relation to the situation arising in South Africa (1960). In the period after 1990 the Council began to use its powers in respect of peacekeeping and, on the basis of Chapter VII, to ensure the provision of humanitarian assistance, as in the case of Somalia in 1992.[169] Extensive operations were undertaken in Bosnia in 1993 with the stated purpose of delivering humanitarian assistance. The mandate also included the creation of safe areas and the power to use force to protect UN-established safe areas. These various operations were based upon powers delegated to member States by the Security Council. In 1994 the Council authorized certain member states, on a short-term basis, to establish a safe haven in Rwanda for the protection of displaced persons, refugees, and civilians at risk, but the failure to act earlier to prevent the humanitarian catastrophe in Rwanda has been strongly criticized.[170]

Since that time the Council has authorized several peacekeeping operations;[171] it has also authorized forcible intervention in the Libyan Arab Jamahiriya for the protection of civilians, without the consent of the territorial state.[172] In other cases, however, such as Darfur in Sudan, the consensus recorded at the 2005 World Summit on the existence of a 'responsibility to protect' has failed to translate into collective action. Verbally the 'responsibility to protect' gains broad acceptance; in truth it states the problem without resolving it; and current articulations fall well short of holding that states have a right to forcibly intervene, without Security Council authorization, to alleviate humanitarian crises.[173]

The Security Council can also use its Chapter VII powers to refer situations to the International Criminal Court when crimes within the Court's jurisdiction appear to have been committed.[174] The Council has exercised this power in respect of Sudan[175] and Libya.[176]

---

[169] See Sarooshi, *The United Nations and the Development of Collective Security* (1999) 210–29; Chesterman, *Just War or Just Peace?* (2001) 127–218; Ramcharan, *The Security Council and the Protection of Human Rights* (2002); Gray, *International Law and the Use of Force* (3rd edn, 2008) 264–306.

[170] See Report of the Independent Inquiry into the Actions of the United Nations during the 1994 Genocide in Rwanda (1999) S/1999/1257; Gray (3rd edn, 2008) 292–4.

[171] Ibid, 272–326.

[172] SC Res 1973 (2011). See Hansard, HC Deb, 21 March 2011, cols 700–801 (esp 716–22); Bellamy & Williams, (2011) 87 *International Affairs* 825.

[173] World Summit Outcome Document (2005) A/60/L.70, §139; Gray (3rd edn, 2008) 53–5. On the 'responsibility to protect': Report of the International Commission on Intervention and State Sovereignty, The Responsibility to Protect (2001); Pattison, *Humanitarian Intervention and the Responsibility to Protect* (2010); Badescu, *Humanitarian Intervention and the Responsibility to Protect* (2011).

[174] ICC Statute, 17 July 1998, 2187 UNTS 3, Art 13(b) (currently 117 parties).

[175] SC Res 1593 (2005).

[176] SC Res 1970 (2011).

(ii) Treaty bodies

It is impossible in a general work to provide a detailed picture of the multiform institutions involved in the protection of human rights.[177] However, even in a small compass, attention must be drawn to certain other organs. There are now nine bodies responsible for monitoring implementation of the core international human rights treaties, including the CESCR and HRC. In temporal sequence they are as set out in Table 29.2.

Table 29.2 Implementation of international human rights treaties

Committee	Convention	Commenced	Comment
Committee on the Elimination of Racial Discrimination (CERD)	International Convention on the Elimination of All Forms of Racial Discrimination[179]	1970	
Human Rights Committee (HRC)	ICCPR[180]	1976	Optional Protocol (1966)
Committee on the Elimination of Discrimination against Women (CEDAW)	Convention on the Elimination of All Forms of Discrimination against Women[181]	1981	
Committee against Torture (CAT)	Convention against Torture and other Cruel, Inhuman or Degrading Treatment or Punishment[182]		Optional Protocol (2002) created system of regular visits to prisons and other places of detention[183]
Committee on Economic, Social and Cultural Rights (CESCR)	ICESCR[184]	1986	Optional Protocol (2008)

[177] Further: Alston & Crawford (eds), *The Future of UN Human Rights Treaty Monitoring* (2000); Bayefsky (ed), *The UN Human Rights Treaty System in the 21st Century* (2000); Bayefsky, *How to Complain to the UN Human Rights Treaty System* (2003).

[178] GA Res 2106(XX), 21 December 1965, 660 UNTS 195. Further: Partsch, in Alston (1992) 339; Banton, in Alston & Crawford (2000) 55; Vandenhole, *Non-Discrimination and Equality in the View of the UN Human Rights Treaty Bodies* (2005).

[179] Generally: Tyagi (2011); further: de Zayas, Möller & Opsahl (1985) 28 *GYIL* 9; Cohn (1991) 13 *HRQ* 295; Ghandhi (1998).

[180] GA Res 34/180, 18 December 1979, 1249 UNTS 13. Further: Jacobson, in Alston (1992) 444; Bustelo, in Alston & Crawford (2000) 79; Schöpp-Schilling & Flinterman (eds), *The Circle of Empowerment: Twenty-Five Years of the UN Committee on the Elimination of Discrimination against Women* (2007).

[181] GA Res 39/46, 10 December 1984, 1465 UNTS 85. Further: Byrnes, in Alston (1992) 509; Bank, in Alston & Crawford (2000) 145; Ingelse, *The UN Committee Against Torture* (2001); Nowak & McArthur, *The United Nations Convention Against Torture* (2008) 579–813.

[182] GA Res 57/199, 18 December 2002 (currently 61 parties). See Nowak & McArthur (2008) 937–1192.

[183] See Alston, in Alston (1992) 473; Craven (1995) 30–105; Craven, in Eide, Krause & Rosas (2nd edn, 2001) 455.

Committee on the Rights of the Child (CRC)	Convention on the Rights of the Child[185]	1991	
Committee on the Protection of the Rights of All Migrant Workers and Members of their Families (Committee on Migrant Workers, CMW)	International Convention for the Protection of the Rights of All Migrant Workers and Members of their Families[186]	2004	
Committee on the Rights of Persons with Disabilities (CRPD)	Convention on the Rights of Persons with Disabilities[187]	2009	Optional Protocol (2006)
Committee on Enforced Disappearances (CED)	International Convention for the Protection of All Persons from Enforced Disappearance[188]	2011	

The International Court has indicated that when considering issues arising in relation to the human rights treaties, it will ascribe 'great weight' to the interpretation of the treaty adopted by the relevant court or committee.[188]

The treaty body system has faced major challenges with respect to resources and coherence, amongst other things, and there have been many proposals for its reform. The Dublin Statement on the Process of Strengthening of the UN Human Rights Treaty Body System of 19 November 2009 represents an attempt by 35 serving or former members of UN treaty bodies to create a roadmap for reform and galvanize the debate.[189]

(iii) The High Commissioner for Human Rights

In 1993, the General Assembly created the office of UN High Commissioner for Human Rights,[190] whose principal task is to provide leadership in the human rights field.[191]

---

[184] GA Res 44/25, 20 November 1989, 1577 UNTS 3. Further: Lansdown, in Alston & Crawford (2000) 113–28; Doek, in Invernizzi & Williams (2011) 90.

[185] GA Res 45/158, 18 December 1990, 2220 UNTS 3 (currently 45 parties). Further: Cholewinski (1997); Edelenbos, in de Guchteneire, Pécoud & Cholewinski (2009) 100.

[186] GA Res 61/106, 13 December 2006. Further: Kanter (2007) 34 *Syracuse JILC* 287; Kayess & French (2008) 8 *HRLR* 1.

[187] GA Res 61/177, 20 December 2006. On enforced disappearance: Anderson (2006) 7 *Melb JIL* 245; Rodley (3rd edn, 2009) 329–78.

[188] *Ahmadou Sadio Diallo (Guinea v DRC)*, Judgment of 30 November 2010, §§66–8.

[189] See O'Flaherty (2010) 10 *HRLR* 319.

[190] GA Res 48/141, 20 December 1993. Further: Clapham (1994) 5 *EJIL* 556; Ramcharan, *The United Nations High Commissioner for Human Rights* (2002); Steiner, Alston & Goodman (3rd edn, 2008) 824–35.

[191] Robertson & Merrills, *Human Rights in the World* (4th edn, 1996) 112–14.

(B) REGIONAL MACHINERY

There is machinery for the judicial protection of human rights on a regional basis in Europe, the Americas, and Africa and the Arab world.[192] The emphasis here will be on judicial protection.

(i) Europe

The ECHR[193] is a comprehensive bill of rights on the Western liberal model, born of the Council of Europe. The contracting parties undertake to secure to 'everyone within their jurisdiction' the rights and freedoms defined in Section I of the Convention. The precise definition therein has enabled some of the parties to incorporate the rights in their national law as self-executing provisions. In order to make the draft acceptable to governments, certain qualifications on its field of application had to be incorporated. Article 17 provides: 'Nothing in this Convention may be interpreted as implying for any State, group or person any right to engage in any activity or perform any act aimed at the destruction of any of the rights and freedoms set forth herein'. Article 15 permits measures derogating from the obligations under the Convention 'in time of war or other public emergency threatening the life of the nation'. However, no derogation is permitted under this provision from Articles 2 (right to life) (except in respect of deaths resulting from lawful acts of war), 3 (torture and inhuman punishment), 4(1) (slavery or servitude), and 7 (no retrospective punishment).

The human rights protected by the treaty were originally implemented by three organs: the European Commission of Human Rights, the European Court of Human Rights, and the Committee of Ministers of the Council of Europe. Of those, the principal organ was the European Commission which received every complaint: individual complainants had standing if the government concerned had recognized the competence of the Commission to receive petitions from individuals. In November 1998 this structure was replaced by a new system.[194] Now the European Court of Human Rights deals with both individual applications and interstate cases, and the Commission has been abolished.

The Court has been a major influence in the development of European human rights law, in matters major and minor. It has produced many changes in national legislation and practice.[195] Cases of non-compliance have been relatively few. However, the Court

---

[192] Generally: Shelton (ed), *Regional Protection of Human Rights* (2008).

[193] 4 November 1950, ETS 5. Further: European Social Charter, 18 October 1961, ETS 35. Generally: Higgins, in 2 Meron (1984) 495; Harris & Darcy, *The European Social Charter* (2nd edn, 2001); van Dijk, van Hoof, van Rijn & Zwaak (eds), *Theory and Practice of the European Convention on Human Rights* (4th edn, 2006); Pettiti, Decaux & Imbert, *La Convention Européenne des Droits de l'Homme* (2nd edn, 1999); Harris, O'Boyle & Warbrick, *Law of the European Convention on Human Rights* (2nd edn, 2009); Jacobs, White & Ovey, *The European Convention on Human Rights* (5th edn, 2010).

[194] See Protocol 11, 11 May 1994, CETS 155.

[195] See Drzemczewski, *European Human Rights Convention in Domestic Law* (1997); Keller & Stone Sweet (eds), *A Europe of Rights* (2008).

has been to an extent a victim of its own success; it is inundated with cases and has a substantial backlog.[196] Various reforms involving greater selectivity in caseload are being implemented or are under consideration.[197]

(ii) The Americas[198]

The Inter-American system for the protection of human rights is complex, mainly because it consists of two overlapping mechanisms with different diplomatic starting points. In the first place the Inter-American Commission on Human Rights was created in 1960 as an organ of the Organization of American States (OAS) with the function of promoting respect for human rights. As amended by the Protocol of Buenos Aires,[199] the OAS Charter contains a substantial list of economic, social, and cultural standards, and the Commission, as reordered in accordance with the American Convention on Human Rights[200] of 1969, has an extensive competence in these matters in relation to OAS members. On the basis of this Convention an additional system for the promotion of human rights was created. The Inter-American Commission of Human Rights was re-established and retains its broad powers within the context of the OAS (Articles 41 to 43). At the same time the Commission has responsibilities arising from the provisions of the American Convention. Thus it has jurisdiction *ipso facto* to hear complaints against the parties from individual petitioners (Article 44). In addition, the Commission may deal with interstate disputes provided that both parties have made a declaration recognizing its competence in this respect (Article 45).

In accordance with the American Convention (Articles 52 to 69) an Inter-American Court of Human Rights began to function in 1979. The Court has an adjudicatory jurisdiction according to which the Commission and, if they expressly accept this form of jurisdiction, the states parties may submit cases concerning the interpretation and application of the Convention (Articles 61 to 63). Article 64 creates an advisory jurisdiction according to which OAS member states (and the organs listed in Chapter X of the Charter of the OAS) may consult the Court regarding 'interpretation of this Convention or of other treaties concerning the protection of human rights in the

---

[196] Protocol 14, 13 May 2004, CETS 194 (in force from 1 June 2010) aims to improve the Court's efficiency.

[197] E.g. Helfer (2008) 19 *EJIL* 125; Keller, Fischer & Kühne (2010) 21 *EJIL* 1025.

[198] Gros Espiell (1975) 145 Hague *Recueil* 1; Buergenthal, in 2 Meron (1984) 439; Medina Quiroga, *The Battle of Human Rights* (1988); Davidson, *The Inter-American Court of Human Rights* (1992); Pasqualucci, *The Practice and Procedure of the Inter-American Court of Human Rights* (2003).

[199] Protocol of Amendment to the Charter of the Organization of American States, 27 February 1967, 721 UNTS 324.

[200] 22 November 1969, 1144 UNTS 123. Also: Additional Protocol to the American Convention on Human Rights in the Area of Economic, Social and Cultural Rights, 14 November 1988, OAS Treaty Series 69 (Protocol of San Salvador); 28 ILM 156.

American States'.[201] In general the Court has been an innovator, notably with respect to remedies.[202]

In general the American Convention draws upon the ECHR, the American Declaration of the Rights and Duties of Man (1948),[203] and the ICCPR, and the result is a very extensive set of provisions. Only OAS members have the right to become parties; to date 25 of the 35 OAS members have done so.

In practice the Inter-American Commission has exercised its OAS competence in respect of petitions (concerning the execution of juveniles) on behalf of individuals, against the US, which is not a party to the American Convention, but was held to be bound by the American Declaration of the Rights and Duties of Man.[204]

(iii) Africa

On 17 June 1981 the Organization of African Unity (OAU) adopted the African Charter on Human and Peoples' Rights.[205] While the Charter has much in common with its European and American predecessors, it has features of its own.[206] Not only are rights of 'every individual' specified, but also duties (Chapter II). Several provisions (Articles 19 to 24) define the rights of 'peoples', for example, to 'freely dispose of their wealth and resources' (Article 21). Some of these provisions are framed in vague language, for example Article 24, which provides that 'all peoples shall have the right to a general satisfactory environment favourable to their development'. There are no derogation clauses comparable to Article 15 ECHR (war or other public emergency).

In the sphere of institutional safeguards, the main organ has been the African Commission on Human and Peoples' Rights. The Commission's mandate is in very general terms, and includes the interpretation of the Charter at the request of a state party, an institution of the OAU, or an African organization recognized by the OAU (Article 45). The emphasis is on conciliation. The Commission may investigate complaints by states (Articles 47 to 54) and endeavour to reach an amicable solution (Articles 52 to 53). The Commission may also consider complaints ('communications') from individuals (Articles 55 to 56). Only where a complaint reveals 'a series of serious or massive

---

[201] See *Costa Rica Journalists Association* (1985) 75 ILR 30. Also: *American Declaration of the Rights and Duties of Man within the Framework of Article 64 of the American Convention on Human Rights* (1989) 96 ILR 416; Pasqualucci (2002) 38 *Stanford JIL* 241.

[202] The foundation for this was laid in *Velásquez Rodríguez v Honduras* (1989) 95 ILR 232. Further: Pasqualucci (2003) 230–90; papers compiled in (2007) 56 *AULR* 1675.

[203] American Declaration of the Rights and Duties of Man, OAS Res XXX (1948), reprinted in Basic Documents Pertaining to Human Rights in the Inter-American System (1992) OEA/Ser.L.V/II.82 doc.6 rev.1, 17.

[204] See *Roach and Pinkerton (Case 9647)*, IACHR 3/87, 27 March 1987, §§44–9; *Michael Domingues*, IACHR 62/02, 22 October 2002.

[205] (1981) 1520 UNTS 363 (53 ratifications). See Umozurike (1983) 77 *AJIL* 902; Bello (1985) 194 Hague *Recueil* 13; Murray, *The African Commission on Human and Peoples' Rights in International Law* (2000); Nmehielle, *The African Human Rights System* (2001); Ouguergouz, *The African Charter on Human and Peoples' Rights* (2003); Evans & Murray (eds), *The African Charter on Human and Peoples' Rights: the System in Practice 1986–2006* (2nd edn, 2008).

[206] E.g. Padilla (2002); Naldi, in Evans & Murray (2nd edn, 2008) 20, 24–34.

violations' is the Commission bound to involve the OAU Assembly, which 'may then request the Commission to undertake an in-depth study of these cases, and make a factual report, accompanied by its findings and recommendations' (Article 58). The Commission developed an increasingly judicialized procedure and jurisprudence, despite the lack of an explicit mandate to consider individual communications.[207]

For some time the Commission was the only implementation agency. Since 1998, however, there have been various institutional changes. In 1998, the OAU adopted a Protocol on the Establishment of the African Court on Human and Peoples' Rights ('the African Court Protocol').[208] Two years later, the OAU was replaced by the African Union, with its Constitutive Act of 11 July 2000.[209] Article 5(1)(d) of the Constitutive Act established a Court of Justice. The Assembly of the AU adopted a Protocol of the Court of Justice of the African Union on 11 July 2003.[210] In 2004, however, the Assembly decided to merge the two institutions to form a single Court of Justice and Human Rights.[211] A Protocol on the Statute of the African Court of Justice and Human Rights was adopted on 1 July 2008; it will come into force 30 days after the fifteenth ratification, not yet in sight.[212]

(C) SUPERVISION: KEY LEGAL ISSUES

The work of the European Commission and the European Court of Human Rights over a long period has produced a set of legal concepts. These concepts, or variations of them, are also to be found in decisions under the other regional conventions. They rest in part upon the political premises that the respondent state is itself democratic and that there must be a fair balance between the general interest and the interests of the individual.

(i) Exhaustion of local remedies[213]

Article 35(1) ECHR provides that 'the Court may only deal with the matter after all domestic remedies have been exhausted, according to the generally recognized rules of international law and within a period of six months from the date when the final decision was taken'. This reflects the role of the Court, which is supervisory and not

---

[207] Viljoen, in Evans & Murray (2nd edn, 2008) 76, 77; Naldi, in Evans & Murray (2nd edn, 2008), 20, 34–40; Killander (2006) 10 *LDD* 101.

[208] OAU/LEG/MIN/AFCHPR/PROT.1/rev/2/1997. The African Court Protocol came into force on 25 January 2004; 26 states have ratified the Protocol and the Court was ready to receive cases from June 2008. See Kane & Motala, in Evans & Murray (2nd edn, 2008) 406, 406. On the relationship between the Court and the Commission: Elsheikh (2002) 2 *Af HRLJ* 252; Naldi, in Evans & Murray (2nd edn, 2008) 20, 40–3.

[209] OAU Doc. CAB/LEG23.15 (currently 53 parties).

[210] (2005) 13 *Af JICL* 115 (currently 16 parties).

[211] See Udombana (2003) 28 *Brooklyn JIL* 811; Kane & Motala, in Evans & Murray (2nd edn, 2008) 406, 408–17.

[212] (2009) 48 ILM 334.

[213] See Jacobs, White & Ovey, *The European Convention on Human Rights* (5th edn, 2010) 34–7.

appellate.[214] But the Court will not require recourse to local remedies if the violation originates in an administrative practice of the respondent state.[215] Provisions on the exhaustion of local remedies are similarly found in Article 46(1)(a) of the American Convention[216] and Articles 50 and 56(5) of the African Charter.[217]

(ii) Restrictions upon freedoms 'necessary in a democratic society'[218]

Key provisions in ECHR are expressed to be subject to restrictions which are 'necessary in a democratic society'. In *Silver v UK*, the Court explained the general principles:

(a) the adjective 'necessary' is not synonymous with 'indispensable', neither has it the flexibility of such expressions as 'admissible', 'ordinary', 'useful', 'reasonable' or 'desirable'...;

(b) the Contracting States enjoy a certain but not unlimited margin of appreciation in the matter of the imposition of restrictions, but it is for the Court to give the final ruling on whether they are compatible with the Convention ...;

(c) the phrase 'necessary in a democratic society' means that, to be compatible with the Convention, the interference must, *inter alia*, correspond to a 'pressing social need' and be 'proportionate to the legitimate aim pursued' ...;

(d) those paragraphs of ... the Convention which provide for an exception to a right guaranteed are to be narrowly interpreted ...[219]

The issue arises regularly in cases concerning the right to respect for private and family life;[220] freedom of thought, conscience, and religion;[221] freedom of expression;[222] and freedom of assembly.[223]

The American Convention mirrors the wording of the ECHR with its reference to restrictions 'necessary in a democratic society' (e.g. Articles 15, 16(2), 22(3)).[224] By

---

[214] E.g. *López Ostra v Spain* (1994) 111 ILR 210.

[215] *Ireland v UK* (1978) 58 ILR 188, 2613.

[216] E.g. *Velásquez Rodríguez v Honduras* (1989) 95 ILR 232, 254–8; *Gangaram Panday v Suriname*, IACtHR C/12, 4 December 1991, §§38–40; *Castillo Páez v Peru*, IACtHR C/24, 30 January 1996, §§40–3.

[217] See *Article 19 v Eritrea* (2007) AHRLR 73, §§43–82. Cf Udombana (2003) 97 *AJIL* 1.

[218] See Marks (1995) 66 *BY* 209; Jacobs, White & Ovey (5th edn, 2010) 325–32.

[219] (1983) 72 ILR 334, 369.

[220] *Klass v Germany* (1978) 58 ILR 423, 448–54; *Silver v UK* (1983) 72 ILR 334, 369; *Messina v Italy (No 2)* [2000] ECtHR 25498/94, §§59–74; *Uzun v Germany* [2010] ECtHR 35623/05, §§75–81.

[221] *Young, James and Webster* (1981) 62 ILR 359; *Kokkinakis v Greece* [1993] ECtHR 14307/88, §§28–50; *Jakóbski v Poland* [2010] ECtHR 18429/06, §§42–55.

[222] *Handyside* (1976) 58 ILR 150, 174–80; *Sunday Times* (1979) 58 ILR 490, 529–37; *Lingens* (1986) 88 ILR 513, 527–30; *Müller* (1988) 88 ILR 570, 588–9; *Jersild v Denmark* (1994) 107 ILR 23, 39–45; *MGN Ltd v UK* [2011] ECtHR 39401/04, §§136–56.

[223] *United Communist Party of Turkey v Turkey* (1998) 122 ILR 404, 421–4; *Chassagnou v France* [1999] ECtHR 25088/94, §§109–17; *Hyde Park v Moldova (No 4)* [2009] ECtHR 18491/07, §§45–55; *Republican Party of Russia v Russia* [2011] ECtHR 12976/07.

[224] E.g. *Baena-Ricardo v Panama*, IACtHR C/72, 2 February 2001, §§151–73; cf Art 13 (freedom of thought and expression) which contains no such reference, although it has effectively been incorporated by interpretation in the jurisprudence: e.g. *Costa Rica Journalists Association* (1985) 75 ILR 30, 40–57; *Herrera Ulloa v Costa Rica*, IACtHR C/107, 2 July 2004, §§104–36.

contrast, the text of the African Charter makes no mention of democratic society in its provisions for limitations of rights: for example Article 11 refers to 'necessary restrictions provided for by law in particular those enacted in the interest of national security, the safety, health, ethics and rights and freedoms of others' and Article 12 permits 'restrictions, provided for by law, for the protection of national security, law and order, public health or morality'. Article 27(2), cited in the jurisprudence as containing 'the only legitimate reasons for restricting the rights and freedoms contained in the Charter',[225] provides that 'the rights and freedoms of each individual shall be exercised with due regard to the rights of others, collective security, morality and common interest'.

(iii) Proportionality: the balance between the general interest and the interests of the individual

The ECHR seeks to maintain a balance between the general interest (a pressing social need) and the rights and interests of the individual. To this end the Court applies a principle of proportionality. In *Dudgeon*, the Court said:

[I]n Article 8 ... the notion of 'necessity' is linked to that of a 'democratic society'. According to the Court's case-law, a restriction on a Convention right cannot be regarded as 'necessary in a democratic society'—two hallmarks of which are tolerance and broadmindedness—unless, amongst other things, it is proportionate to the legitimate aim pursued ...[226]

Notwithstanding the margin of appreciation left to the national authorities, the question of proportionality is ultimately one for the Court.

Proportionality has played a major role in the jurisprudence.[227] Whilst it is on its face a logical principle, it inevitably entails significant policy choices. In *Fogarty v UK*[228] the Court held that, as an aspect of proportionality, it was appropriate to interpret the Convention as far as possible in harmony with other rules of international law, including those relating to state immunity. The proportionality principle has also been a significant feature of the American[229] and African jurisprudence.[230]

(iv) Derogation 'in time of national emergency'

As noted above, Article 15 ECHR permits derogation from the obligation to comply with its provisions 'in time of war or other public emergency threatening the life

---

[225] E.g. *Constitutional Rights Project v Nigeria* (2000) AHRLR 227, §41; *Interights v Mauritania* (2004) AHRLR 87, §78.

[226] *Dudgeon (Article 50)* (1981) 67 ILR 395, 414, 416–17.

[227] E.g. *Lithgow (Shipbuilding Nationalization)* (1986) 75 ILR 438, 527–8; *Gillow* (1986) 75 ILR 561, 580–1; *Pine Valley Developments Ltd v Ireland* [1991] ECtHR 12742/87; *Open Door v Ireland* [1992] ECtHR 14234/88, §§67–80; *Steel v UK* [1998] ECtHR 24838/94, §§98–111; *Fayed v UK* [1994] ECtHR 17101/90, §§71–82; *Antonekov v Ukraine* [2005] ECtHR 14183/02, §§59–67; *Ryabikina v Russia* [2011] ECtHR 44150/04, §26.

[228] (2001) 123 ILR 53, 65.

[229] E.g. *Castañeda Gutman v Mexico*, IACtHR C/184, 6 August 2008, §§185–205; *Usón Ramírez v Venezuela*, IACtHR C/207, 20 November 2009, §§76–88.

[230] E.g. *Media Rights Agenda v Nigeria* (2000) AHRLR 200, §§64–71; *Amnesty International v Sudan* (2000) AHRLR 297, §82; *Interights v Mauritania* (2004) AHRLR 87, §§76–85.

of the nation', although certain provisions are specified as non-derogable: Articles 2 (right to life, except insofar as death is caused by lawful acts of war), 3 (prohibition of torture), 4(1) (prohibition of slavery), and 7 (prohibition of punishment without law). Similarly, allowance for 'suspension of guarantees' in time of 'war, public danger, or other emergency that threatens the independence or security of a State Party' is provided in Article 27 of the American Convention, with Article 27(2) excluding a wider range of provisions from derogation than the ECHR.[231]

No such derogation provision appears in the African Charter. The African Commission has emphasized that 'the lack of a derogation clause means that limitations on the rights and freedoms in the Charter cannot be justified by emergencies or special circumstances. The only legitimate reasons for limitations of the rights and freedoms of the African Charter are found in article 27(2)'.[232]

(v) The margin of appreciation[233]

This takes the form of a legal discretion which recognizes that the respondent state can be presumed to be best qualified to appreciate the necessities of a particular situation affecting its jurisdiction. The margin of appreciation is also applied in practice under the American and African frameworks,[234] although the term has been avoided by the Inter-American Court and the Human Rights Committee and raises its own problems of appreciation.

Nonetheless something like it is inevitable if we are not to have government by judiciary or—in the international context—by quasi-judiciary. In *James*, the European Court of Human Rights, rejecting a complaint against British leasehold reform legislation, observed that national authorities are best placed to determine what is in the public interest, and enjoy a wide discretion in implementing social and economic policies. The Court will respect that discretion, but only as long as it is not manifestly without reasonable foundation: 'although the Court cannot substitute its own assessment for that of the national authorities, it is bound to review the contested measures under Article 1 of Protocol No 1 and, in so doing, to make an inquiry into the facts with reference to which the national authorities acted'.[235]

---

[231] Under the American Convention, non-derogable rights include Arts 3 (right to juridical personality), 4 (right to life), 5 (right to human treatment), 6 (freedom from slavery), 9 (freedom from *ex post facto* laws), 12 (freedom of conscience and religion), 17 (rights of the family), 18 (right to a name), 19 (rights of the child), 20 (right to nationality), and 23 (right to participate in government), along with the judicial guarantees essential for the protection of such rights. See IACtHR Advisory Opinions OC-8/87, 30 January 1987; OC-9/87, 6 October 1987.

[232] *Constitutional Rights Project v Nigeria* (2000) AHRLR 227, §41; *Commission Nationale des Droits de l'Homme et des Libertés v Chad* (2000) AHRLR 66, §21; *Article 19 v Eritrea* (2007) AHRLR 73, §§87–108. Art 27(2) provides that individual rights and freedoms shall be exercised with due regard to the rights of others, collective security, morality, and common interest.

[233] See Merrills (2nd edn, 1993) 151–76; Shany (2006) 16 *EJIL* 907; *Mosley v UK* [2011] ECtHR 48009/08, §§106–11.

[234] In the American context: e.g. *Proposed Amendments to the Naturalization Provisions of the Political Constitution of Costa Rica* (1984) 79 ILR 282, 301–3; in the African context: e.g. *Prince v South Africa* (2004) AHRLR 105, §§50–3.

[235] *James* (1986) 75 ILR 396, 417.

(vi) Complaints and proceedings at national level

The classical and still general method of enforcement is by means of the duty of performance of treaty undertakings imposed on the states parties. It is the domestic legal systems of the states parties to the given treaty which are the primary vehicles of implementation. Thus the ICCPR contains express provisions setting forth the duty to ensure that domestic law provides sufficient means of maintenance of treaty standards.[236] It is also a characteristic of such treaties that the means of implementing the treaty provisions are a matter of domestic jurisdiction. In this context it is helpful to recall Robert Jennings' remonstrance that it is a mistake to think of domestic jurisdiction 'in "either/or" terms'.[237]

In some cases, the absence of an official investigation may constitute evidence of a breach. In a series of decisions the European Court has responded to the extraordinary circumstances prevailing in certain regions of Turkey. In order to deal effectively with cases involving ill-treatment,[238] disappearances,[239] the destruction of a village,[240] the death of the applicant's sister,[241] and shooting by unidentified persons,[242] the Court has relied upon the evidence of a lack of effective investigation, or of any investigation, by the authorities, as evidence of violations of Article 2 (right to life),[243] Article 3 (prohibition of torture), Article 5 (right to liberty and security of person), and Article 8 (right to home and family life). In addition, such lack of an effective investigation has been held to constitute a violation of Article 13 (right to an effective remedy).[244] Similar principles have been applied by the Inter-American Court of Human Rights,[245] the Human Rights Committee,[246] and the African Commission.[247]

7. AN EVALUATION

This account of human rights is, it should be emphasized, an analysis from the perspective of public international law. This approach is appropriate for several reasons,

---

[236] See CCPR, General Comment 31.

[237] Jennings (1967) 121 Hague *Recueil* 495, 502.

[238] *Aksoy v Turkey* [1996] ECtHR 21987/93, §§98–100; *Timurtas v Turkey* [2000] ECtHR 23431/94.

[239] *Kurt v Turkey* [1998] ECtHR 24276/94; *Çakici v Turkey* [1999] ECtHR 23657/94, §§81–7.

[240] *Mentes v Turkey* [1997] ECtHR 23186/94.

[241] *Ergi v Turkey [1998]* ECtHR 23818/94, §§78–86.

[242] *Kaya v Turkey* [1998] ECtHR 22729/93, §§84–92; *Ergi v Turkey* [1998] ECtHR 23818/94, §§79–86.

[243] Further: *Al-Skeini v UK* [2011] ECtHR 55721/07, §§161–7.

[244] *Aksoy v Turkey* [1996] ECtHR 21987/93, §§98–100; *Yasa v Turkey* [1998] ECtHR 22495/93, §§109–15; *Kaya v Turkey* [1998] ECtHR 22729/93, §§106–8; *Çakici v Turkey* [1999] ECtHR 23657/94, §§108–14; *Tepe v Turkey* [2003] ECtHR 27244/95, §§192–8.

[245] E.g. *Case of the 'White Van' (Paniagua Morales v Guatemala)*, IACtHR C/23, 25 January 1996. See also *Extrajudicial Executions and Forced Disappearances v Peru*, IACHR 101/01, 11 October 2001.

[246] E.g. *Amirov v Russian Federation* (2009) CCPR/C/95/D/1447/2006.

[247] E.g. *Sudan Human Rights Organisation & Centre on Housing Rights and Eviction v Sudan*, Comm 279/03, 296/05, 28th ACHPR AAR Annex (2009–10).

including the fact that human rights as legal standards were primarily the work of international lawyers; so too the normative development of such standards through the various institutions.

An evaluation of the existing human rights system must begin by placing emphasis on three elements. In the first place, the 'system' depends for its efficacy upon the domestic legal systems of states. The decisions and recommendations of the supervisory and monitoring bodies can only be implemented by means of the legislatures and administrations of the states parties to the various standard-setting conventions. Secondly, the application of human rights forms part of a larger aim, belief in, and maintenance of, the rule of law, including the existence of an independent judiciary: overall the human rights bodies have been a very positive influence in this regard. The third element is related to the second. Adherence to human rights instruments presupposes that the states adhering will apply the standards. In practice, such a system fails when it has to face the worst case scenarios and a recalcitrant respondent state. Practitioners within the Strasbourg system (and governments) are well aware of the failure of Turkey to implement decisions of the European Court of Human Rights, including the case of *Loizidou v Turkey*,[248] and the judgments in the series of applications brought by the Republic of Cyprus against Turkey. These cases concern the rights of large groups, and long-lasting, intractable situations.

The question of the efficacy of the system of human rights leads to a wider problem. On occasion the Security Council may decide to take coercive action under Chapter VII of the Charter, avowedly to deal with the worst cases. This may appear to be the solution. But, in practice, such action has been taken on a selective basis and has been shadowed by ad hoc geopolitical reasons unconnected with human rights. This element of discrimination can best be illustrated by instances of failure to act, in particular, the failure of the Security Council to take any action in face of the gross and persistent measures of discrimination and breaches of humanitarian law on the part of Israel against the Palestinian people and their institutions.[249] The issue of selectivity can lead to claims of human rights violations being used as nothing more than a powerful political weapon.

Perhaps the most egregious example is provided by the case of Iraq. The Iraq–Iran War raged for eight years (1980–88). Iran was not the aggressor. There were several hundred thousand military and civilian casualties. During the conflict leading Western powers gave assistance to the Iraqi government in the form of matrices for chemical weapons (which were used against Iran) and satellite intelligence. The Security Council took no action under Chapter VII or otherwise. In contrast, in the period from 1991 up to the US-led attack on Iraq in March 2003, the same states took a strong line on the human rights record of the Iraqi regime and the attack was justified in part by reference to the human rights factor. Here is revealed a purely cyclical, if not

---

[248]   (1996) 108 ILR 443.
[249]   UN Commission on Human Rights, Res 2003/7, 15 April 2003 (50–1 (US): 2 (Australia, Costa Rica)).

cynical, version of human rights, contingent upon collateral political considerations. Similar criticisms of selectivity could be applied to the Human Rights Commission, now the Council.

Problems of consistency and efficacy affect all systems of law, not only public international law and human rights. The often appalling realities of power politics must be balanced against the 50 years of successful formulation of legal standards of human rights and the development of mechanisms of supervision and monitoring. These at least put the question of enforcement on the agenda.

Three further criticisms of the international human rights system deserve attention. The first is the Marxian critique that the system replicates liberal values and operates through liberal institutions which tend to reinforce class divisions within society, keeping power in the hands of the powerful and leaving those belonging to subordinated sectors to fall through the gaps.[250] This is certainly true to some degree—although it is significant that those criticizing the system on such grounds rarely advocate its destruction.[251]

The second is that the system is 'Eurocentric'.[252] While this too may be true, certainly historically, it is less true than it was, and again the critics do not advocate return to some (unachievable) *status quo ante*. The Inter-American system has gone its own way, as compared to Strasbourg, and the African system will likewise develop according to the region's own characteristics and priorities. The human rights treaties have been widely ratified by countries outside Europe and the West. Although the Universal Declaration was Western in its origin and focus, the human rights system has evolved considerably since 1948. More recent instruments are based on a broader consensus following negotiation between the representatives of states and, to a lesser extent, cultures.[253]

A third criticism is that the system operates under a democratic deficit; in other words, unelected judges and experts sitting in international tribunals and committees are making important decisions of public policy that should be left to elected officials within states.[254] A short answer is that these tribunals and committees are mandated to act by treaties that have been ratified by states; their authority derives from state consent. A longer answer is that international human rights are part of an international law in which state rights and prerogatives (reflecting, in normal circumstances, the autonomy of the community of the state) are set alongside and judged by reference

---

[250] See Marks (ed), *International Law on the Left* (2008), esp Koskenniemi (34–8), Roth (220–51), Chimni (82–4).

[251] A (non-Marxist) exception is Allott, who inveighs memorably against the international system (including the human rights system), while being careful not to prescribe material alternatives: cf 2 Cor 3:6. See Allott, *Eunomia* (1992); Allott, *The Health of Nations* (2002).

[252] E.g. Otto (1997) 29 *Col HRLR* 1; Falk, *Human Rights Horizons* (2000) 89–93; Mutua (2001) 42 *Harv ILJ* 201; Mutua, *Human Rights* (2002); Anghie, *Imperialism, Sovereignty and the Making of International Law* (2004); Mutua (2007) 29 *HRQ* 547; Dembour, in Moeckli, Shah & Sivakumaran (2010) 64, 75–8, 81–4.

[253] E.g. Onuma, in Bauer & Bell (1999) 103–23.

[254] Crawford & Marks, in Archibugi, Held & Köhler (eds), *Re-imagining Political Community* (1998) 72.

to the products of state consent. *Each* system retains a margin of appreciation (explicitly or implicitly); none is immune from judgement in terms of the other. There is no *imperium*, rather a dialectic of consent.

There is a close analogy in the system of closer union which is the EU, and its relation to fundamental rights at the level of the ECHR as well as of national law. Thus the German Federal Constitutional Court declined to rule that laws derived from the Treaty of Maastricht which allegedly took away rights protected by the Federal Constitution were invalid. The Court noted that Community law and domestic law were independent systems, operating side by side; the organs of one system were not competent to assess the interpretation and observance of the laws of the other.[255] The allegation of a violation had to be assessed against the fundamental guarantees inherent in Community law.[256] In normal circumstances, Community law could not be subject to constitutional review by municipal courts without calling into question the legal basis of the Community itself. At the same time, Community law cannot release member states from their obligations under the ECHR.[257] Each system retains competence to inspect the other system and to intervene if there is a sufficiently serious interference with rights. The principle of equivalent protection holds that as long as equivalent rights are protected by the regional human rights system, the state does not breach its obligations to the individual; otherwise there could never be interstate cooperation as envisaged by states when entering the Community. By contrast, an arbitrary refusal to comply with rights is not excused, for example on the grounds that the state is complying with a Security Council resolution.[258] There must be a presumption that the Security Council does not intend to impose obligations on states to violate fundamental human rights.[259] But it is, in the last resort, only a presumption. National systems are judged, or at least appraised, in terms they have formally accepted. They are not silenced.

---

[255] *Internationale Handelsgesellschaft v Einfuhr- und-Vorratsstelle für Getreide und Futtermittel (Solange I)* (1970) 93 ILR 362; *Wünsche Handelsgesellschaft (Solange II)* (1986) 93 ILR 403.

[256] *Re Accession of the European Community to the Convention for the Protection of Human Rights and Fundamental Freedoms (Opinion 2/94)* (1996) 108 ILR 225, 255.

[257] *Bosphorus v Minister for Transport* (1996) 117 ILR 267, 286–7.

[258] Joined Cases C-402/05 P and C-415/05 P, *Kadi & Al Barakaat International Foundation v Council & Commission* [2008] ECR I-06351.

[259] *Al-Jedda v UK* [2011] ECtHR 27021/08, §102.

30

INTERNATIONAL CRIMINAL JUSTICE

1. INTRODUCTION

It is not too much of an exaggeration to say that the United Nations era began with a trial and a promise. The trial was that of the major German war criminals at Nuremberg. The promise was that the principles underlying the Nuremberg Charter would be treated as international law: only thus would the apparent selectivity and retrospectivity of Nuremberg be redeemed. But despite the Tokyo trials and some further trials in Germany, mostly under the auspices of the occupying powers, the arena of international criminal law became populated by conventions largely without implementation, and state practice turned to emphasize national trials for specified treaty-defined offences such as aircraft hijacking and drug trafficking.

Then, in the early 1990s, the arena came to life: ad hoc criminal courts were created by Security Council decree, a permanent International Criminal Court (ICC) was established at great speed, and there was much other activity. More than half a dozen international or 'internationalized' tribunals now exist, and they are generating a more robust body of jurisprudence on war crimes, crimes against humanity and genocide, as well as a more developed set of understandings concerning procedure. Developments at the international level have also sparked changes in domestic jurisdictions, including an increasing—though still small—number of domestic prosecutions of international crimes, including on the basis of universal jurisdiction.

The rapid development of the international criminal law field has not been without pitfalls. The operation of the international criminal tribunals has been far more expensive and time-consuming than anticipated, and the conduct of proceedings has generated controversy, particularly in cases involving high-profile figures. Most importantly, questions remain about the broad goals of this field. Although the prosecution of individuals responsible for the commission of international crimes may be justified on the basis of retribution and deterrence, a balance between national and international processes, and between peacemaking or post-conflict reconciliation and the reduction of impunity, has proved elusive.[1] If there was any jury in this field (which there is not),[2] it would still be out.

2. DEVELOPMENT OF INTERNATIONAL CRIMINAL LAW AND INSTITUTIONS

(A) PRE-1945 ASPIRATIONS

The modern history of international criminal law sputtered into half-life in 1919, when the Allies established a Commission on the Responsibility of the Authors of the War and on the Enforcement of Penalties, which proposed the creation of an Allied High Tribunal to try violations of the laws and customs of war and the law of humanity.[3] The Tribunal never came into being: a few Germans were instead prosecuted domestically at the 'Leipzig trials', suffering token penalties.[4] There were discussions in the League of Nations about an international criminal court, but a statute concluded in 1937 obtained only a single ratification (British India).[5]

(B) THE NUREMBERG AND TOKYO TRIBUNALS

On 8 August 1945, the four Allied Powers concluded the London Agreement, establishing the International Military Tribunal (the Nuremberg Tribunal).[6] The Charter, annexed to the Agreement, provided for the prosecution of individuals for war crimes, crimes against humanity, and crimes against peace.[7] Each of the Tribunal's four principal judges represented one of the major Allied Powers, and the prosecution of the various counts of the indictment was divided among prosecutors from the four powers.[8] After a 10-month trial, three defendants were acquitted; the remaining 19 were convicted and sentenced to death or imprisonment. Three organizations were found to be

---

[1] Nouwen, in Crawford & Koskenniemi, *The Cambridge Companion to International Law* (2012) 327, and further: Akhavan (2001) 95 *AJIL* 7; Tallgren (2002) 13 *EJIL* 561; Drumbl, *Atrocity, Punishment and International Law* (2007).

[2] Even the 'Scottish court' which tried the Lockerbie bombers had no jury: *Her Majesty's Advocate v Abdelbaset Ali Mohmed Al Megrahi and Al Amin Khalifa Fhimah*, Scottish Court in the Netherlands, Judgment of 31 January 2001, Case No 1475/99.

[3] *Report Presented to the Preliminary Peace Conference* (1920) 14 *AJIL* 95.

[4] Mullins, *The Leipzig Trials* (1921); Willis, *Prologue to Nuremberg* (1982) 126–47.

[5] Convention for the Creation of an International Criminal Court, LN Doc C.547(I).M.384(I).1937.V (1938).

[6] Agreement for the Prosecution and Punishment of Major War Criminals of the European Axis, and Establishing the Charter of the International Military Tribunal, 8 August 1945, 82 UNTS 279. For contemporary accounts: Wright (1947) 41 *AJIL* 38; Kelsen (1947) 1 *ILQ* 153; Ehard (1949) 43 *AJIL* 223.

[7] IMT Charter, Art 6.

[8] Ibid, Arts 2, 14.

criminal, three were cleared.[9] The Nuremberg judgment was notable for its rejection of the argument that the Charter breached the principle of legality, as well as its holding that individuals may be held directly responsible under international law.[10]

The International Military Tribunal for the Far East was established not by a multilateral treaty but by a Special Proclamation issued by MacArthur, the Supreme Commander for the Allied Powers in Japan.[11] The Tokyo Tribunal consisted of 11 judges, from the nine signatories to the Japanese Instrument of Surrender as well as India and the Philippines.[12] A lengthy trial concluded in November 1948 with convictions for all surviving 25 defendants, who were sentenced to death or imprisonment.[13] The judgment generated substantial controversy among the judges,[14] and it has attracted criticism to a greater extent than the Nuremberg judgment, procedurally as well as substantively.[15] According to Judith Shklar:

Natural law thinking played no part at Nuremberg, where every effort was made to build on the fiction of a positive international law envisaged as analogous in its formal structure to the legalistic image of municipal law in matured systems. At Tokyo natural law was, indeed, introduced, with very unfortunate results.[16]

In addition, prosecutions for war crimes, crimes against humanity, and crimes against peace were conducted in Germany by the Allied Powers in their respective zones of occupation under Control Council Law 10, as well as in the Pacific theatre.[17]

(C) NORMATIVE DEVELOPMENTS FOLLOWING THE SECOND WORLD WAR

The Nuremberg judgment had an immediate impact. The General Assembly unanimously affirmed 'the principles of international law recognized by the Charter of the Nuremberg Tribunal and the Judgment of the Tribunal'.[18] The ILC was directed to formulate the principles of international law recognized in the Tribunal's judgment, and to prepare a draft code of offences against the peace and security of mankind. The ILC listed the following 'crimes under international law': crimes against peace, war crimes,

---

[9] Taylor, *The Anatomy of the Nuremberg Trials* (1993).

[10] *International Military Tribunal (Nuremberg), Judgment and Sentences* (1947) 41 *AJIL* 172, 216–21. See Metraux (ed), *Perspectives on the Nuremberg Trial* (2008); Heller, *The Nuremberg Military Tribunals and the Origins of International Criminal Law* (2011).

[11] International Military Tribunal for the Far East, Special Proclamation by the Supreme Commander for the Allied Powers at Tokyo, 19 January 1946, 4 Bevans 20.

[12] International Military Tribunal for the Far East, Charter, Art 2.

[13] Boister & Cryer, *Documents on the Tokyo International Military Tribunal* (2008).

[14] Opinions of Justices Röling (diss), Pal (diss), and Jaranilla (sep). Cf Röling & Cassese, *The Tokyo Trial and Beyond* (1992).

[15] Further: Futamura, *War Crimes Tribunals and Transitional Justice* (2007); Boister & Cryer (eds), *The Tokyo International Military Tribunal* (2008). The standard study is still Minear, *Victors' Justice* (1971).

[16] Shklar, *Legalism* (1964) 156; also ibid, 128, 179.

[17] Cryer, *Prosecuting International Crimes* (2005) 119–20.

[18] GA Res 95(I), 21 November 1947.

and crimes against humanity.[19] It also identified as punishable the participation in a common plan or conspiracy for the accomplishment of any such acts, as well as complicity in their commission. But it did not go much beyond the Nuremberg formulations. For example, the category of 'crimes against humanity' was not freestanding:

Murder, extermination, enslavement, deportation and other inhuman acts done against any civilian population, or persecutions on political, racial or religious grounds, when such acts are done or such persecutions are carried on *in execution of or in connexion with any crime against peace or any war crime.*[20]

The ILC's work on a 'code of crimes' proceeded slowly. After two separate phases of drafting between 1947–54 and 1982–96, the ILC in 1996 adopted 20 draft articles constituting a Code of Crimes against the Peace and Security of Mankind.[21] The Code was never implemented as such, being superseded by the Rome Statute.[22]

More important than the early ILC work was the conclusion of the Genocide Convention in 1948,[23] and the 'grave breaches' provisions of the 1949 Geneva Conventions.[24] Both envisaged prosecutions in national courts, but in fact little or nothing was done by way of enforcement, despite the Cambodian 'genocide'[25] and war crimes in a variety of theatres, including Vietnam.[26]

3. INTERNATIONAL CRIMINAL COURTS AND TRIBUNALS

(A) THE AD HOC TRIBUNALS

(i) The Yugoslav Tribunal

The end of the Cold War coincided with the dissolution of Yugoslavia, and increased opportunities for the Security Council to respond to ensuing armed conflicts.[27] In

---

[19] ILC *Ybk* 1950/II, 374–8, Principle VI.

[20] Principle VI(c) (emphasis added).

[21] ILC *Ybk* 1996/II(2), 15–56. Allain & Jones (1997) 8 *EJIL* 100.

[22] GA Res 51/160, 16 December 1996.

[23] Convention on the Prevention and Punishment of the Crime of Genocide, 9 December 1948, 78 UNTS 277; Schabas, *Genocide in International Law* (2nd edn, 2009) 59–116.

[24] Geneva Convention I, 12 August 1949, 75 UNTS 31, Arts 49–50; Geneva Convention II, 12 August 1949, 75 UNTS 85, Arts 50–1; Geneva Convention III, 12 August 1949, 75 UNTS 135, Arts 129–30; Geneva Convention IV, 12 August 1949, 75 UNTS 287, Arts 146–7. Also ICRC commentary on these provisions: Pictet (ed), 1–4 *Geneva Conventions of 1949: Commentary* (1952–60) 362–72 (vol 1), 263–70 (vol 2), 620–9 (vol 3), 589–602 (vol 4). Cf Fischer, in McDonald & Swaak-Goldman (eds), *Substantive and Procedural Aspects of International Criminal Law* (2000) 63.

[25] Kiernan, *Genocide and Democracy and Cambodia* (1993). On the classification of crimes in Cambodia: Schabas (2001) 35 *NELR* 287; Abrams (2001) 35 *NELR* 303; Williams (2005) 5 *Int Crim LR* 447.

[26] Wolfrum, in Dinstein & Tabory (eds), *War Crimes in International Law* (1996) 233.

[27] O'Brien (1993) 87 *AJIL* 639; Cassese, *International Criminal Law* (2nd edn, 2008) 324–5.

May 1993, the Security Council acted under Chapter VII to establish an international tribunal in The Hague for the 'purpose of prosecuting persons responsible for serious violations of international humanitarian law' committed in the former Yugoslavia after 1 January 1991.[28] Because of the tribunal's open-ended temporal jurisdiction, it was able to prosecute crimes committed not only between 1991 and December 1995, when the Dayton Agreement was signed, but also in the late 1990s, when further violence ensued in Kosovo. There was controversy about whether the Security Council could create a criminal tribunal, but the International Criminal Tribunal for the former Yugoslavia (ICTY) upheld its own constitutionality, relying in part on the parallel support of the General Assembly (responsible for the ICTY budget, which exceeded US$100 million per annum).[29]

The ICTY slowly began functioning according to the relatively skeletal statute annexed to SC Resolution 827, and with detailed Rules of Procedure and Evidence made by the judges and frequently amended.[30] The Statute grants the ICTY the power to prosecute persons for violations of the laws or customs of war, genocide, and crimes against humanity (more broadly defined than at Nuremberg).[31] Although the ICTY and national courts have concurrent jurisdiction, the ICTY has primacy, and in its early years the Tribunal requested that national courts defer to its competence in situations where both were seeking to exercise jurisdiction.[32]

The ICTY proceeded slowly, in part because of a lack of accused persons in its custody.[33] It came under early criticism for prosecuting relatively minor figures, 'small fish' such as Duško Tadić, a local leader of the Serb Democratic Party in Bosnia who had no involvement in policy-making or planning and who was already being prosecuted in Germany.[34] This began to change in the late 1990s, when NATO became involved in effecting arrests, pro-EU parties were elected into government in the countries concerned and some accused voluntarily surrendered to the Tribunal.[35] There followed the arrest and transfer in 2001 of Slobodan Milosević, former president of the SFRY. The Prosecution initially charged Milosević with respect to the conflict in Kosovo, but then joined the Kosovo indictment with two separate indictments regarding Croatia

---

[28] SC Res 808 (1993); Report of the Secretary-General pursuant to paragraph 2 of Security Council Resolution 808 (1993), S/25704, 3 May 1993; SC Res 827 (1993), §2. Art 8 of the Statute simply provides that the Tribunal's temporal jurisdiction 'shall extend to a period beginning on 1 January 1991'.

[29] *Prosecutor v Tadić* (1995) 105 ILR 419 (jurisdiction) 430–42; O'Brien (1993) 87 *AJIL* 639, 643; Sarooshi, *The United Nations and the Development of Collective Security* (1999) 92–8.

[30] ICTY Statute, as amended 7 July 2009 by SC Res 1877 (2009); Rules of Procedure and Evidence of the International Criminal Tribunal for the former Yugoslavia, Rev 45, 8 December 2010; Zacklin (2004) 2 *JICJ* 361.

[31] Arts 3–5; Shraga & Zacklin (1994) 5 *EJIL* 360.

[32] ICTY Statute, Art 8; RPE Rule 11.

[33] Cryer, *An Introduction to International Criminal Law and Procedure* (2010) 125–33.

[34] *Prosecutor v Tadić*, ICTY, IT-94-1-A, Appeals Chamber, Judgment, 15 July 1999; Sassoli & Olson (2000) 94 *AJIL* 371.

[35] Schabas (2nd edn, 2009) 380–1.

and Bosnia.[36] The result was an unmanageably large indictment of over 60 counts, and an unwieldy, lengthy trial, during which the judges struggled to deal with Milosević's astute and highly disruptive conduct.[37] His sudden death in 2005, before the end of the trial, was a significant blow. Subsequently the ICTY has gained custody over two other high-profile accused who had eluded capture for many years: Karadzić, the President of Republika Srpska,[38] and Mladić, the Commander of the Main Staff of the Bosnian Serb Army.[39] Remarkably, none of the ICTY's 161 indictees remains at large.

By 2000, the unanticipated length and cost of the Tribunal's operations led the Security Council to press the ICTY to develop a completion strategy.[40] Although the ICTY was already focusing on the prosecution of 'the most senior leaders suspected of being most responsible for crimes', this became an explicit requirement.[41] In addition, the Rules of Procedure and Evidence were amended to allow the ICTY to transfer cases back to national courts, reversing the earlier trend of deferrals to the ICTY. So far the ICTY has indicted 161 persons; proceedings have concluded for 126 accused (with 64 convictions on some or all charges and 13 complete acquittals).[42]

(ii) The Rwanda Tribunal

In April 1994, the assassination of Rwandan President Habyarimana ignited the slaughter of Tutsi and moderate Hutus, resulting in the deaths of approximately 800,000 persons over the course of several months.[43] Given the recent creation of the ICTY in response to an armed conflict in Europe, it was considered necessary to create an analogous tribunal following genocide in Africa.[44] In November 1994, after an ineffectual response to the genocide itself, the Security Council created the International Criminal Tribunal for Rwanda (ICTR), located in Arusha, Tanzania.[45] The Appeals Chamber is shared with the ICTY.[46] The ICTR and the ICTY also shared a prosecutor until 2003, when the Security Council considered it necessary for a prosecutor to be dedicated solely to the ICTR in order for it to fulfil its completion strategy.[47]

The ICTY Statute provided a model for the Statute of the ICTR, which similarly endows the ICTR with 'the power to prosecute persons responsible for serious violations of international humanitarian law.' There are, however, differences between

---

[36] *Prosecutor v Milosević*, Second Amended Indictment 'Kosovo', IT-99–37-PT, 16 October 2001; *Prosecutor v Milosević*, Second Amended Indictment 'Croatia', IT-02–54-T; 23 October 2002; *Prosecutor v Milosević*, Amended Indictment 'Bosnia', IT-02–54-T, 22 November 2002.

[37] Boas, *The Milosević Trial* (2007).

[38] *Prosecutor v Karadzić*, Prosecution's Marked-Up Indictment, IT-95–5/18, 19 October 2009.

[39] *Prosecutor v Mladić*, Second Amended Indictment, IT-09–92, 1 June 2011.

[40] SC Res 1329 (2000); SC Res 1503 (2003)

[41] SC Res 1534 (2003); Rule of Procedure and Evidence 28(A).

[42] ICTY, Key Figures, available at www.icty.org/sections/TheCases/KeyFigures. Proceedings for 13 individuals were transferred to a national jurisdiction and 36 individuals had their indictments withdrawn or they died before or after their transfer to the ICTY.

[43] Schabas (2nd edn, 2009) 24–31.

[44] Akhavan (1996) 90 *AJIL* 501; Cassese (2008) 327; Cryer (2010) 135–6.

[45] SC Res 955 (1994); also SC Res 935 (1994), SC Res 918 (1994); SC Res 977 (1995).

[46] ICTR Statute, 8 November 1994, SC Res 955 (1994), 33 ILM 1598 (1994), Art 12(2).

[47] Ibid, Art 15(3) (original); Art 15(4) (as amended); SC Res 1503 (2003), §8 & Annex I.

the Statutes, such as the omission of an article in the ICTR Statute for prosecution for grave breaches of the Geneva Conventions of 1949, on account of the non-international character of the armed conflict in Rwanda. The Statute instead provides for jurisdiction over violations of Article 3 common to the 1949 Geneva Conventions and of Additional Protocol II, which apply in non-international armed conflicts. In addition, the ICTR Statute requires a discriminatory motive as an element of crimes against humanity, although it has been held that this is not a requirement under customary international law.[48] The scope of the ICTR's jurisdiction is also narrower than that of the ICTY; its temporal jurisdiction runs from 1 January to 31 December 1994. The ICTR issued indictments for only 110 accused[49] and its budget has been smaller than that of the ICTY, although still substantial.[50]

The ICTR also began operations quite slowly, but it initially gained custody of indictees more successfully than did the ICTY.[51] In its early years, it experienced serious mismanagement, leading to the resignations of the Registrar and the deputy Prosecutor.[52] Already strained relations between the ICTR and Rwanda deteriorated following the Appeals Chamber's decision to decline jurisdiction over Barayagwiza, one of the media advocates of the genocide, on the grounds that his pre-trial detention violated his human rights.[53] Rwanda suspended co-operation with the ICTR, thereby impeding the progress of trials at the Tribunal. The next year, the Appeals Chamber controversially reversed its decision[54] and the relationship between Rwanda and the ICTR improved. Trials have nevertheless proceeded slowly, and the Security Council required it to develop a completion strategy which has involved, in part, the referral of cases to third countries such as France,[55] and eventually to Rwanda itself.[56]

Like the *Tadić* case at the ICTY, the *Akayesu* case was the first to go to trial at the ICTR, and has been seminal, representing the first conviction by an international tribunal for genocide, as well as the first time that rape in war was held to constitute genocide.[57] The ICTR's *'Media'* judgment is significant for its conviction of three radio and newspaper executives for public incitement to genocide.[58]

---

[48] Ibid, Art 3.

[49] ICTY, Status of Cases, available at www.unictr.org/Cases/StatusofCases/tabid/204/Default.aspx.

[50] Wippman (2006) 100 *AJIL* 861; Cryer (2010) 142.

[51] Schabas (2nd edn, 2009) 30; Cryer (2010) 137.

[52] A/51/789.

[53] *Prosecutor v Barayagwiza*, ICTR-97–19-AR72, Appeals Chamber, Decision, 3 November 1999.

[54] *Prosecutor v Barayagwiza*, ICTR-97–19-AR72, Appeals Chamber, Decision on Review and/or Reconsideration, 14 September 2000.

[55] SC Res 1503 (2003); Mose, in Bellelli (ed), *International Criminal Justice* (2010) 79.

[56] It was only in June 2011 that the first case was referred to Rwanda: *Prosecutor v Jean Uwinkindi*, ICTR-2001–75-R11bis, Decision on Prosecutor's Request for Referral to the Republic of Rwanda, 28 June 2011. This contrasts with the ICTY, where most of the Art 11bis referrals were to the countries where the crimes were committed.

[57] *Prosecutor v Akayesu*, ICTR-96–4-T, Trial Chamber, Judgment, 2 September 1998; de Bouwer, *Supranational Criminal Prosecution of Sexual Violence* (2005) 41–84.

[58] *Prosecutor v Nahimana*, ICTR-99–52-T, Trial Chamber, Judgment, 3 December 2003; *Prosecutor v Nahimana*, ICTR-99–52-A, Appeals Chamber, Judgment, 28 November 2007. Cf MacKinnon (2004) 98 *AJIL* 325; Zahar (2005) 16 *CLF* 33; MacKinnon (2009) 103 *AJIL* 97.

In 2010, the Security Council decided to establish the International Residual Mechanism for Criminal Tribunals to finish the remaining tasks of the ICTY and ICTR. The Security Council requested both tribunals to take all possible measures to complete all their remaining work no later than the end of 2014. The Mechanism's ICTR branch will commence its operations on 1 July 2012 and the ICTY branch on 1 July 2013. The Mechanism will have the same jurisdiction, rights, obligations and essential functions, subject to provisions of Resolution 1966 and the Statute of the Mechanism.[59]

(iii) The ad hoc tribunals: an evaluation

Between them, the two tribunals have produced a substantial body of jurisprudence. The ICTR has made a significant contribution, for example, regarding gender crimes. Among the developments led by the ICTY, joint criminal enterprise (JCE) has been perhaps the most prominent. Under this doctrine, individuals may be held liable for crimes committed as part of a common plan carried out either jointly or by some members of the group.[60] The Appeals Chamber in *Tadić* explained that JCE constitutes a form of commission, even though Article 7(1) of the Statute does not explicitly provide for it. JCE may take three different forms. Under the 'basic' form, all co-perpetrators carry out a common purpose with the same criminal intention.[61] Under the 'systemic' form, a group of persons acts according to a common plan at a concentration camp or detention facility.[62] Finally, under the particularly controversial 'extended' form, the perpetrator commits a crime which was outside of the common plan, but was a 'natural and foreseeable consequence' of carrying out the common purpose.[63] JCE has generated scholarly criticism as a form of guilt by association (it is colloquially referred to as 'just convict everyone').[64] It is not included in the Rome Statute.

(B) THE INTERNATIONAL CRIMINAL COURT

Proposals for the establishment of a permanent international criminal tribunal date as far back as 1872, when Gustav Moynier, one of the founders of the ICRC, discussed the idea.[65] Although the Genocide Convention contemplated an 'international penal tribunal',[66] no such institution was established: indeed until 1989 such a proposal seemed hopelessly utopian.

---

[59] SC Res 1966 (2010).
[60] *Prosecutor v Tadić*, ICTY, IT-94-1, Appeal Judgment, 15 July 1999, §190. Generally: Cassese (2008) 189–213; Shahabuddeen, in Darcy & Powderly (eds), *Judicial Creativity at the International Criminal Tribunals* (2010) 184; Zahar & Sluiter, *International Criminal Law* (2008) 221–57.
[61] *Prosecutor v Tadić*, ICTY, IT-94-1, Appeal Judgment, 15 July 1999, §196.
[62] Ibid, §202.
[63] Ibid, §204.
[64] E.g. Ohlin (2007) 5 *JICJ* 69; Cassese (2007) 5 *JICJ* 109.
[65] Hall (1998) 322 *IRRC* 57.
[66] Art VI.

(i) The work of the ILC

At the request of the UN General Assembly the ILC produced a draft statute for a permanent court (1953), but the General Assembly never proceeded with the matter due to difficulties concerning the definition of aggression and to underlying Cold War politics.[67] In 1989, Trinidad and Tobago proposed that the issue be put back on the General Assembly's agenda because of its wish to see international prosecutions of drug-related offences.[68] The matter was referred to the ILC which in two years produced a draft statute.[69] The 1994 draft was in most respects a more modest proposal than the statute that was ultimately adopted in 1998, but it paved the way to Rome.

(ii) The Rome Statute (1998)

Following detailed work by the Prepcom, the ICC's Statute was finalized at a five-week conference in 1998: it entered into force on 1 July 2002, after 60 ratifications.[70] The ICC, located in The Hague, began its work in 2003. Its jurisdiction is limited to 'the most serious crimes of concern to the international community as a whole', namely, genocide, crimes against humanity, war crimes, and the crime of aggression. The Assembly of States Parties also adopted the Elements of Crimes, intended to assist the Court in the interpretation and application of these crimes. The ICC's temporal jurisdiction does not extend to offences committed prior to the entry into force of the Statute.[71] Its territorial jurisdiction extends to the territory of states parties; its personal jurisdiction covers nationals of those states. The ICC may also exercise its jurisdiction with respect to the territory and nationals of a state not party to the Rome Statute if that state has accepted the ICC's jurisdiction in accordance with Article 12(3), which provides that a state not a party to the Statute may accept the ICC's jurisdiction by a declaration lodged with the Registrar. This was done, for example, by Côte d'Ivoire.[72] It is also possible for the ICC to exercise jurisdiction over nationals of third states if the conduct in question occurred on the territory of a state party,[73] a possibility which has given rise to major objections on the part of the US. But none of these restrictions with respect to personal or territorial jurisdiction apply in case of a Security Council referral.

---

[67] GA Res 260(III)B, 9 December 1948; Revised Draft Statute for an International Criminal Court; GAOR, 9th Sess, Supp No 12, A/2645, 23; GA Res 898(IX), 14 December 1954.

[68] A/44/195 (1989); GA Res 44/39, 4 December 1989.

[69] ILC *Ybk* 1994/II(1), 18–67; and Crawford (1995) 48 *CLP* 303.

[70] Crawford, in Sands (ed), *From Nuremberg to The Hague* (2003) 109; Lee, *The International Criminal Court* (1999).

[71] Temporal jurisdiction is further limited in the case of a state which becomes a party at a later date and does not explicitly extend the jurisdiction back to 2002: Art 11(2).

[72] In the event it took years for the jurisdiction in Côte d'Ivoire to be triggered, and this was done on the basis of the Prosecutor's *proprio motu* powers rather than a self-referral.

[73] Rome Statute, Art 12(2); and Scharf (2001) 64 *LCP* 98; Morris (2001) 64 *LCP* 131; Akande (2003) 1 *JICJ* 618.

The ICC's exercise of jurisdiction may be triggered in three different ways, all of which have been utilized in its first decade.[74] First, a state party may refer to the ICC a situation where one or more crimes within the Court's jurisdiction appear to have been committed.[75] Uganda, the Democratic Republic of Congo, and the Central African Republic have referred such situations to the ICC, and the Prosecutor initiated investigations in all of them. Secondly, the Security Council, acting under Chapter VII, may refer a situation to the Prosecutor. The Security Council did so in 2005 with respect to the situation in Darfur, Sudan, and in 2011 with respect to the situation in Libya.[76] Finally, the Prosecutor may initiate an investigation independently. In March 2010, Pre-Trial Chamber II granted the Prosecution's request to open an investigation into the post-election violence that took place in Kenya in late 2007 and early 2008, and in October 2011, the Prosecutor's application to proceed in Côte d'Ivoire was also accepted by Pre-Trial Chamber III.[77] Even though three out of these seven situations came before the court by virtue of self-referrals, the fact that all the ICC's situations concern Africa has generated criticism and contributed to strained relations between the ICC and the African Union.[78]

Whereas the ICTY and ICTR had primacy of jurisdiction, the ICC's jurisdiction is 'complementary'. This means that if in a specific case there are, or have been, genuine domestic proceedings, the case is inadmissible before the ICC.[79] It should be stressed that it is cases which are inadmissible, not situations. This is one of the weaknesses of the complementarity regime: in situations of mass crime, the Prosecutor will almost always be able to find a case that has not been prosecuted domestically.[80]

In the spirit of the principle of complementarity, some states parties have enacted legislation allowing national courts to exercise jurisdiction over ICC crimes whether committed by their nationals or on their territory or more broadly (although the Rome Statute does not require this). Neither a national amnesty law nor a promise of immunity conceded in a fragile peace process can halt ICC proceedings on grounds of complementarity since in the absence of domestic proceedings cases are admissible before the ICC. Commentators have suggested that the Prosecutor nevertheless has

---

[74] Art 13; Schabas, *The International Criminal Court: A Commentary on the Rome Statute* (2010); Schabas, *An Introduction to the International Criminal Court* (4th edn, 2011) 157–86.

[75] It had not been expected that states parties would refer situations in their own countries (so-called 'self-referrals'), but there is nothing in the Statute that prevents it. Nouwen & Werner, in Smeulers (ed), *Collective Violence and International Criminal Justice* (2010) 255.

[76] SC Res 1593 (2005); SC Res 1970 (2011).

[77] *Prosecutor v Ruto, Kosgey & Sang*, ICC-01/09–01/11; *Prosecutor v Muthaura, Kenyatta & Ali*, ICC-01/09–02/11; Decision Pursuant to Article 15 of the Rome Statute on the Authorisation of an Investigation into the Situation in the Republic of Côte d'Ivoire, 3 October 2011, ICC-02/11.

[78] Jalloh, Akande & du Plessis (2011) 4 *Af JLS* 5.

[79] Preamble, §10; Arts 1, 17.

[80] *Prosecutor v Germain Katanga and Mathieu Ngudjolo Chui*, Motion Challenging the Admissibility of the Case by the Defence of Germain Katanda, Pursuant to Article 19(2)(a), ICC-01/04–01/07–949, Defence, 11 March 2009, §§39–43.

the discretion to decline to investigate such situations, for example, where an investigation would 'not serve the interests of justice'.[81]

The ICC's process is somewhat more civil-law-oriented than that of the ad hoc tribunals. It includes a Pre-Trial Chamber whose functions include authorizing investigations, issuing arrest warrants and summonses to appear, and deciding on the confirmation of charges. In addition, the Statute provides for the participation of victims in proceedings and for reparations for victims.[82]

(iii) The United States and the ICC

The position of the US towards the ICC has evolved considerably since 1998.[83] The US delegation to the Rome Conference lobbied for significant changes to make the Statute more acceptable.[84] Even though it failed to achieve its goals, President Clinton signed the Rome Statute on 31 December 2000, the last available day for doing so. The position of the US towards the court changed dramatically under President Bush: the US 'unsigned' the Statute[85] and concluded a series of bilateral agreements with states parties under Article 98(2) of the Statute, designed to prevent the latter from surrendering its citizens to the ICC.[86] The US stance softened somewhat during the Bush administration's second term: for example, it refrained from vetoing the Security Council's referral of the Darfur situation to the ICC.[87] While the Obama administration has engaged in a positive manner with the ICC and voted with the majority of the Security Council to refer the situation in Libya, ratification of the Rome Statute remains highly unlikely.

(iv) The crime of aggression

An important development occurred at a Review Conference in Kampala, Uganda in June 2010, when the Assembly of States Parties defied expectations by agreeing upon a definition of the crime of aggression.[88] The definition now included in the Statute requires that an act of aggression constitute a 'manifest violation' of the UN Charter, a term with uncertain meaning. In addition, the states parties resolved a long-standing debate about the trigger mechanisms for prosecutions of aggression by deciding that, in addition to the Security Council, states parties can refer a situation to the ICC, and that the Prosecutor, with the authorization of the Pre-Trial Chamber, can initiate an

---

[81] Art 53(1)(c); Stahn (2005) 3 *JICJ* 695. It is not clear that the Prosecutor agrees. And Nouwen, in Curtis & Dzinesa (eds), *Peacebuilding, Power and Politics in Africa* (2012).

[82] Generally: McCarthy, *Reparations and Victim Support in the International Criminal Court* (2012).

[83] Schabas (4th edn, 2011) 25–34.

[84] Scheffer (1999) 93 *AJIL* 12; Leigh (2001) 95 *AJIL* 124.

[85] Letter from US Under-Secretary of State for Arms Control to Secretary-General (2002) 41 ILM 1014.

[86] Murphy (2002) 96 *AJIL* 725; O'Keefe (2010) 24 *Cam RIA* 335.

[87] Cerone (2007) 18 *EJIL* 227.

[88] Art 5(2); Gaja, in Cassese, Gaeta & Jones (eds), *The Rome Statute of the International Criminal Court* (2002) 427, and for the new definition: 'The Crime of Aggression', Resolution RC/Res.4, adopted at the 13th Plenary Meeting on 11 June 2010 by consensus. Further: Blokker & Kress (2010) 23 *LJIL* 889; Scheffer (2010) 23 *LJIL* 897; Barriga & Kreβ (eds), *The Travaux Préparatoires of the Crime of Aggression* (2012).

investigation *proprio motu*. The Security Council does not have the monopoly on the determination whether an act of aggression has taken place. The amendments regarding aggression will not come into force until 2017 at the earliest; even then, parties may opt out under certain conditions.

(v) Interim evaluation

It is far too soon to offer an evaluation of the ICC, but the legal and practical challenges faced by the court merit some mention.

At the legal level, the ICC has shown a measure of adaptability, even to a fault. For example, unlike the ICTY and ICTR there is no doctrine of joint criminal enterprise, but instead reliance on notions of direct and indirect perpetration.[89] Other features include the early erosion of complementarity; issues with victim participation,[90] and the disregard for President Bashir's immunity. The Rome Statute provides that immunities do not bar the Court from exercising jurisdiction once an accused is present before it, but it is far from clear that a foreign head of state could be surrendered to the Court without violating state immunity.

At the practical level, the fact is that unlike Nuremberg and Tokyo, the ICC does not deal with those already defeated in conflicts but becomes an instrument in conflict. The greatest obstacle so far has been obtaining custody of the accused, particularly of figures such as Omar Al-Bashir, the President of Sudan and Joseph Kony, head of the Lord's Resistance Army. President al-Bashir's visits to other African states parties to the Statute have highlighted the practical difficulties the ICC faces in enforcing arrest warrants. Where it has secured the accused, however, the ICC has proved capable of delivering a verdict.[91]

(C) INTERNATIONALIZED OR HYBRID TRIBUNALS

More recent tribunals have not taken the same shape as the ICTY and the ICTR. Instead 'hybrid' tribunals have been created (East Timor, Kosovo, Sierra Leone, Cambodia, Bosnia and Herzegovina, Lebanon).

The terms 'internationalized', 'hybrid', and 'mixed' have no fixed meaning, but they generally refer to a range of tribunals with a mixed composition which apply both domestic and international law. They operate more or less in relation to or even as part of national institutions, arguably filling national voids, not international ones.[92]

---

[89] Art 27; Akande (2004) 98 *AJIL* 407; Akande (2009) 7 *JICJ* 333.

[90] Trumbull (2007–8) 29 *Mich JIL* 777; Chung (2007–8) 6 *Nw JIHR* 459; Cohen (2008–9) 37 *DJILP* 351. For a positive account: McCarthy (2012).

[91] *Prosecutor v Lubanga*, Judgment pursuant to Article 74 of the Statute, 14 March 2012, ICC-01/04–01/06.

[92] Romano, Nollkaemper & Kleffner (eds), *Internationalized Criminal Courts and Tribunals* (2004); Nouwen (2006) 2 *Utrecht LR* 190; Williams, *Hybrid and Internationalised Criminal Tribunals* (2009).

(i) The Special Court for Sierra Leone

In June 2000, Sierra Leone requested UN assistance in establishing a court to try members of the Revolutionary United Front (RUF) for crimes against Sierra Leoneans and the hostage-taking of UN peacekeepers.[93] At the time the armed conflict in Sierra Leone had been continuing since 1991, and the RUF had recently violated the 1999 Lomé Peace Accord.[94] When the conflict finally ended in 2002, both the Special Court for Sierra Leone (SCSL) and the Truth and Reconciliation Commission came into being; they co-existed until the latter concluded its work in October 2004.[95] The SCSL was established by a treaty between the United Nations and Sierra Leone,[96] combined with detailed implementing legislation.[97]

The SCSL is a 'hybrid' tribunal as it is a court of mixed jurisdiction and composition. The Statute provides for the application of Sierra Leone as well as international law. The Secretary-General is responsible for appointing the majority of the judges in the Trial and Appeals Chambers; the government appoints the others, who have been Sierra Leonean as well as foreign nationals; the prosecutor's office is mixed also. The Statute allows for the prosecution of persons for a limited number of crimes under local law. The Chief Prosecutor decided early on, however, that the indictments would include only charges under international law, so the SCSL has not been hybrid in practice with respect to its applicable law. The SCSL may also be distinguished from the ad hoc tribunals on the basis of its location. With the exception of the Charles Taylor trial, it has operated in Freetown.

The Prosecution indicted 13 individuals, but has convicted only nine because of the deaths of three and the unknown status of a fourth. The relatively small number of trials reflects the narrowness of its personal jurisdiction. The SCSL Statute calls for the prosecution of those 'persons who bear the greatest responsibility for serious violations of international humanitarian law' (as well as Sierra Leone law). Although Sierra Leone originally requested UN help in prosecuting only the RUF, the Prosecution tried the top leaders of the RUF as well as the Armed Forces Revolutionary Council, the Civil Defence Forces—which was controversial in Sierra Leone as it had come to Kabbah's assistance—and Charles Taylor, former president of Liberia. While the SCSL's personal jurisdiction is relatively narrow, its subject-matter jurisdiction is, in some respects, notably more extensive than that of the ICTY and ICTR. Its Statute includes provisions on the recruitment of child soldiers as well as sex-based crimes, such as sexual slavery, enforced prostitution, and forced pregnancy—none of which appear in the Statutes of the ICTY and the ICTR.

---

[93] S/2000/786, 10 August 2000.

[94] Peace Agreement between the Government of Sierra Leone and the Revolutionary United Front of Sierra Leone, 2 June 1999, S/1999/777.

[95] Tejan-Cole (2002) 5 *Ybk IHL* 313; Schabas (2004) 4 *JICJ* 1082; Nesbitt (2007) 8 *GLJ* 977.

[96] UN–Sierra Leone, Agreement on the Establishment of a Special Court for Sierra Leone, 16 January 2002, 2178 UNTS 138.

[97] Special Court Agreement, 2002 (Ratification) Act.

The SCSL is best known for the trial of Charles Taylor, held in The Hague due to concerns about security.[98] Other cases have concluded with the defendants sentenced to prison. The *Taylor* case has generated controversy, in part, because of the Appeals Chamber's May 2004 decision to deny personal immunity to Taylor, President of Liberia at the time the indictment was issued.[99] The Court's interpretation and application of joint criminal enterprise has also been controversial, due in part to departures from the jurisprudence of the ICTY.[100]

(ii) Extraordinary Chambers in the Courts of Cambodia

In 1997, Cambodia's co-prime ministers requested UN assistance in bringing to justice those responsible for the genocide and crimes against humanity during the Khmer Rouge period (1975–79).[101] Difficult and lengthy negotiations were concluded in 2003 with an agreement to establish the Extraordinary Chambers in the Courts of Cambodia (ECCC).[102] In 2004 the Cambodian National Assembly ratified this agreement and amended a 2001 law on the ECCC.[103] The ECCC commenced operations in the summer of 2006, and began trying accused in 2007 after the adoption of Internal Rules.[104] Its structure, composition, and jurisdiction reflect compromises struck due to Cambodian concerns about 'national ownership' over the tribunal and, to a lesser extent, UN concern about judicial independence given the weak state of the Cambodian judicial system.[105]

As a result, the ECCC are located in Cambodia, near Pnom Penh, and form part of Cambodia's judicial system, as the name suggests.[106] In keeping with Cambodia's legal tradition, the ECCC's procedures have a much greater civil law orientation than do the SCSL and the ad hoc tribunals.[107] The ECCC have co-investigating judges (one Cambodian and one foreign), as well as a scheme for 'civil party' or victim participation.[108] In addition, the negotiations resulted in a relatively complex compromise regarding the composition of the Trial Chamber and Supreme Court Chamber. A majority of Cambodian judges serves in each Chamber, but a 'supermajority' is required for decision-making, such that one international judge must cast a vote with

---

[98] Bigi (2007) 6 *LPICT* 303; MacAuliff (2008) 55 *NILR* 365.

[99] Klingberg (2003) 46 *GYIL* 537; Frulli (2004) 2 *JICJ* 1008; Nouwen (2005) 18 *LJIL* 283; Deen-Racsmany (2005) 18 *LJIL* 299.

[100] Rose (2009) 7 *JICJ* 353; Jordash & Van Tuyl (2010) 8 *JICJ* 591.

[101] A/51/930 (Annex), Prince Norodom Ranariddh & Hun Sen to UN Secretary-General, 21 June 1997.

[102] UN–Royal Government of Cambodia, Agreement concerning the Prosecution under Cambodian Law of Crimes Committed during the Period of Democratic Kampuchea, 6 June 2003, 2329 UNTS 41723.

[103] Law Approving the Agreement, NS/RKM/1004/004, 19 October 2004; Law on the amendment of the Extraordinary Chambers in the Courts of Cambodia, NS/RKM/1004/006, 27 October 2004.

[104] Kodama (2010) 9 *LPICT* 37.

[105] Bertelman (2010) 79 *Nordic JIL* 341, 343–4, 346–50.

[106] Unlike the SCSL, the agreement with the UN does not *establish* the ECCC but merely regulates co-operation.

[107] Art 12(1); Internal Rules, as revised 3 August 2011.

[108] Internal Rules, Rules 14, 23. And McGonigle (2009) 22 *LJIL* 127.

the Cambodian judges. The ECCC have jurisdiction over 'crimes and serious violations of Cambodian penal law, international humanitarian law and custom, and international conventions recognized by Cambodia'.[109]

As to personal jurisdiction, the ECCC may prosecute 'senior leaders of Democratic
Kampuchea and those who were most responsible' for violations of Cambodian and
international law committed during the period from 17 April 1975 to 6 January 1979.
Although some 1.7 million persons died during the Khmer Rouge regime, the ECCC
has brought only two cases against five accused. Kain Guek Eav (alias Duch), chairman of the Khmer Rouge S-21 Security Center, was convicted in July 2010 for crimes
against humanity and grave breaches of the Geneva Conventions of 1949. In June
2011, the trial began of four other accused who held senior leadership positions in the
Khmer Rouge. While the International Co-Prosecutor has sought to prosecute other
individuals beyond these five, the Cambodian Co-Prosecutor has publicly opposed
this, on the ground that further prosecutions could destabilize Cambodia.[110]

The most significant jurisprudential development thus far has been the Pre-Trial
Chamber's lengthy ruling on the extended form of joint criminal enterprise (JCE III).
The Trial Chamber determined that while the basic and systemic forms of JCE have
a basis in customary international law, the extended form of JCE did not exist in customary international law between 1975 and 1979.[111] This represents a notable departure from the ICTY's *Tadić* judgment.[112] The ECCC have pioneered extensive victim
participation.

(iii) The Special Tribunal for Lebanon

In late 2005, Lebanon asked the Security Council to establish 'a tribunal of an international character' to try those responsible for a massive car bomb in Beirut on 14
February 2005, which killed Lebanese Prime Minister Rafiq Hariri and 22 others.[113]
The Special Tribunal for Lebanon (STL) is a resolution-based rather than treaty-based
tribunal, established by SC Resolution 1757 (2007) under Chapter VII.[114] It was so
established after the speaker of the Lebanese Parliament refused to call a meeting to
ratify an agreement which had been negotiated, although a majority of members of
Parliament supported the Tribunal's establishment.[115]

---

[109] Law on ECCC, Art 1.
[110] Information available at the ECCC website: www.eccc.gov.kh/en/case/topic/286. On 7 September
2009, the International Co-Prosecutor requested the Co-Investigating Judges to initiate investigations of
five additional persons: ibid.
[111] *Decision on the Appeals against the Co-Investigative Judges Order on Joint Criminal Enterprise (JCE)*,
ECCC Pre-Trial Chamber, 20 May 2010, Case No 002–19–09–2007-ECCC/OCIJ; Karnavas (2010) 21 *CLF*
445; Gustafson (2010) 8 *JICJ* 1323; Marsh & Ramsden (2011) 11 *ICLR* 137.
[112] *Prosecutor v Tadić*, ICTY, IT-94–1, Appeal Judgment, 15 July 1999.
[113] S/2005/783, 13 December 2005.
[114] Cf Wetzel & Mitri (2008) 7 *LPICT* 81, 94–5.
[115] S/2007/281, 16 May 2007; Fassbender (2007) 5 *JICJ* 1091.

By comparison to the ad hoc and other hybrid tribunals, the STL operates under an unusually narrow mandate, which reflects the fact that it was created in the aftermath of a political assassination and connected terrorist attacks. The STL's temporal jurisdiction extends beyond the attack of 14 February 2005, but it is still quite restricted. The STL may exercise jurisdiction over other attacks that occurred in Lebanon between 1 October 2004 and 12 December 2005 only if they are 'connected in accordance with the principles of criminal justice and are of a nature and gravity similar' to the 14 February 2005 attack.[116] While the STL and the national courts of Lebanon have concurrent jurisdiction over crimes committed within this time period, the STL has primacy. So far the STL has brought only two cases, about which little information is publicly available.[117]

The most distinctive feature of the STL may be its application of municipal criminal law, to the exclusion of international criminal law.[118] The applicable criminal law consists of the provisions of the Lebanese Criminal Code that relate to acts of terrorism, crimes and offences against life and personal integrity, illicit associations, failure to report crimes and offences, criminal participation, and conspiracy.[119] A February 2011 decision by the Appeals Chamber, however, suggests that even though the Statute calls for the application of the Lebanese Criminal Code's provision on terrorism, the STL will take every opportunity to develop the crime of terrorism under international law, as domestic Lebanese law must be interpreted in accordance with international law.[120] In addition, the Statute calls for the application of international modes of liability—namely, joint criminal enterprise and superior responsibility. This could breach the principle of legality (*nullum crimen sine lege*) because the Statute allows for the punishment of crimes under the Lebanese Code pursuant to international theories of liability unrecognized by the Code.[121] The STL may have found a way to resolve this problem, however, as the Appeals Chamber indicated in its February 2011 decision that the STL will generally apply Lebanese law regarding forms of responsibility.[122]

Another controversial feature of the STL is the requirement of trials *in absentia*.[123] The Statute provides that the STL *shall* conduct trial proceedings *in absentia* where the

---

[116] Statute of the Special Tribunal for Lebanon, Art 1. The Tribunal may also have jurisdiction over attacks at 'any later time decided by the Parties and with the consent of the Security Council'.

[117] *Prosecutor v Ayyash*, STL-11–01/I/PTJ, Indictment, 10 June 2011. A connected case concerns attacks against Marwan Hamadeh, George Hawi, and Elias El-Murr (STL-11–02).

[118] Jurdi (2007) 5 *JICJ* 1125. Technically speaking, the Bosnian War Crimes Court, for instance, does the same, when it exercises jurisdiction over 'international crimes' *as incorporated in* Bosnian law.

[119] Statute, Art 2(a). The applicable law also includes provisions on 'increasing the penalties for sedition, civil war and interfaith struggle': Art 2(b).

[120] STL, Appeals Chamber, STL-11–01/I, Interlocutory Decision on the Applicable Law: Terrorism, Conspiracy, Homicide, Perpetration, Cumulative Charging, 16 February 2011, §§42–148.

[121] Milanović (2007) 5 *JICJ* 1139, 1142.

[122] Interlocutory Decision on the Applicable Law: Terrorism, Conspiracy, Homicide, Perpetration, Cumulative Charging, §§210–11.

[123] Statute, Art 22; Gaeta (2007) 5 *JICJ* 1165; Jordash & Parker (2010) 8 *JICJ* 487; Riachy (2010) 8 *JICJ* 1295; Pons (2010) 8 *JICJ* 1307.

accused has waived his right to be present, has not been handed over to the STL by state authorities, or cannot be found and all reasonable steps have been taken to secure and inform the accused of the charges against him. An accused convicted *in absentia*, however, has the right to be retried.[124] Such retrials could prove problematic given that the STL has a finite existence as a tribunal.[125] Other procedural aspects include the role of the pre-trial judge, the degree to which judges may conduct proceedings, and the participation of victims in proceedings.[126] These were designed to create more efficient international criminal procedures, but the STL's functioning may nevertheless be inhibited in that the Statute makes no provision for removing the personal or functional immunities of state officials, or for obliging other states to co-operate with the STL.[127]

4. INTERNATIONAL CRIMINAL JUSTICE IN NATIONAL COURTS

(A) HISTORICAL BACKGROUND

Following the Second World War, domestic prosecutions of crimes pursuant to international law took place in a number of European countries, including France, which notably prosecuted Klaus Barbie, the head of the Gestapo in Lyon.[128] Israel prosecuted Adolf Eichmann, one of the organizers of the Holocaust, after abducting him from Argentina.[129] National prosecutions have also been pursued more recently outside the context of the Second World War, most famously in the case of Augusto Pinochet, the former Chilean head of state whose extradition Spain requested from the UK in 1998. In its third hearing in this case, the House of Lords decided that immunity did not prevent Pinochet's extradition for torture, although the judges did not reach agreement on the rationale for this decision.[130] In the event Pinochet was not extradited, ostensibly on health grounds.

(B) UNIVERSAL JURISDICTION

The principle of universal jurisdiction involves jurisdiction to prescribe without a nexus or link between the forum and the relevant conduct at the time of its

---

[124] Statute, Art 22(1,3).
[125] Jenks (2009) 33 *Fordham ILJ* 57.
[126] Aptel (2007) 5 *JICJ* 1107.
[127] Swart (2007) 5 *JICJ* 1153.
[128] *Barbie* (1988) 78 ILR 136.
[129] *Attorney-General v Eichmann* (1968) 36 ILR 277.
[130] *R v Bow Street Metropolitan Stipendiary Magistrate, ex parte Pinochet Ugarte (No 3)* [1999] 2 All ER 97. Further: Davis (ed), *The Pinochet Case* (2003). This holding was later, implicitly, overturned by the ICJ in *Arrest Warrant of 11 April 2000 (Democratic Republic of the Congo v Belgium)*: ICJ Reports 2002 p 3, 29–30.

commission.[131] In circumstances where there is no link of territory, nationality, or otherwise, the principle of universal jurisdiction nevertheless permits the assertion of jurisdiction because the crimes at issue have been prescribed by international law. Universal jurisdiction may now be exercised over a somewhat expanded list of crimes under customary international law.[132] The actual enforcement of universal jurisdiction, however, may be thwarted by a range of practical and legal obstacles.[133] In practice, some states limit their exercise of universal jurisdiction to cases in which the accused is present on its territory. In general, the enforcement of universal jurisdiction has been controversial, as in Belgium, where a series of cases prompted a backlash from the US that led to a substantial revision of its law.[134]

(C) DOMESTIC TRIALS AND THE PRINCIPLE OF COMPLEMENTARITY

The rise of international criminal tribunals since the early to mid 1990s has served as a catalyst for domestic prosecutions of individuals for war crimes, crimes against humanity, and genocide. This is due in part to the fact that the ICC is premised on the principle of complementarity: it operates under the presumption that the vast majority of prosecutions for international crimes will take place at the domestic level, as it lacks the capacity to prosecute large numbers of accused, nor would this be appropriate in any event.

(D) IMMUNITY FROM CRIMINAL JURISDICTION

When state officials face criminal proceedings not in foreign courts, immunities may constitute a significant barrier to prosecution, even for serious international crimes. Under international law, two different forms of immunity may apply: functional or state immunity (immunity *ratione materiae*), and personal immunity (immunity *ratione personae*).[135] Functional immunity is premised on the principle of sovereign equality and applies only to the official acts of a large range of state officials, even after they have left office. Whether functional immunity still applies in cases where state officials have been accused of violations of international criminal law is controversial.[136] While some have argued that customary international law lifts immunity for international crimes, the weight of national practice does not currently support this

---

[131] Reydams, *Universal Jurisdiction* (2003); O'Keefe (2004) 2 *JICJ* 735, 745; Zahar & Sluiter (2008) 496–503; Lowe, in Evans (ed), *International Law* (3rd edn, 2010) 326–7. Generally: chapter 21.

[132] Cryer (2005) 84–95.

[133] Cryer (2010) 55–62.

[134] In particular Belgian law did not respect immunities and allowed for private prosecutions. See now Act Concerning the Punishment of Grave Breaches of International Humanitarian Law, 10 February 1999, 28 ILM 921; Ratner (2003) 97 *AJIL* 888; Vandermeersch (2005) 3 *JICJ* 400.

[135] Van Alebeek, *The Immunity of States and Their Officials in International Criminal Law and International Human Rights Law* (2008); Fox, *The Law of State Immunity* (2008) 667–700. Generally: chapter 22.

[136] *R v Bow Street Metropolitan Stipendiary Magistrate, ex parte Pinochet Ugarte (No 3)* [1999] 2 All ER 97; *Wijngaarde v Bouterse* (2000) *Netherlands Juristenblad* 2001, 51; reprinted in 32 *NYIL* 276, 278–9; *Sharon &*

conclusion.[137] Personal immunity, on the other hand, is premised on a pragmatic need to keep channels open between states: it applies to any conduct of a much smaller range of state officials, but ceases when they leave office.[138] In *Arrest Warrant* the International Court clarified that personal immunities apply to a serving Minister of Foreign Affairs, but the extent to which personal immunities apply to other high-level state officials remains unclear.[139] Personal immunity is relatively uncontroversial, unlike functional immunity, and national courts have upheld it in a range of cases involving torture, war crimes, and genocide.[140]

(E) SUBSTANTIVE CRIMINAL LAW AND PROCEDURE

The field of international criminal law extends far beyond the crimes over which international criminal tribunals exercise jurisdiction. The field also includes drug trafficking, torture, piracy, slavery, terrorism, transnational organized crime and corruption, apartheid, and enforced disappearances (even if not amounting to crimes against humanity).[141] Multilateral treaties generally serve as the source of law for many such international criminal prohibitions, though debates continue about whether customary international law exists, for example, with respect to certain conduct such as terrorism.[142]

These treaties generally do not impose criminal responsibility directly upon individuals, but rather require states parties to prevent and punish certain conduct. Thus, the criminalization of conduct occurs at the domestic not the international level. The Convention against Torture and Other Cruel, Inhuman or Degrading Punishment requires states parties to ensure that all acts of torture are offences under their domestic criminal law. Since the 1970s, an extensive body of multilateral treaties has developed in response to terrorism.[143] These treaties oblige states parties to criminalize the unlawful seizure of aircraft, the taking of hostages, terrorist bombings, and the

Yaron (2003) 127 ILR 110; *Jones v Saudi Arabia* [2007] 1 AC 270; *Lozano v Italy* (2008), Case No 31171/2008, ILDC 1085 (IT 2008).

[137] Cassese (2008) 302–14; Immunity of State officials from foreign criminal jurisdiction, Memorandum by the Secretariat, 31 March 2008, A/CN.4/596, 116–36; Wirth (2002) 13 *EJIL* 877; Institut de Droit International, Resolution: Immunities from Jurisdiction and Execution of Heads of State and of Government in International Law (2001).

[138] Van Alebeek (2008) 158–99.

[139] *Arrest Warrant*, ICJ Reports 2002 p 3, 21–2 (indicating the characteristics of a Foreign Minister which necessitate immunity on a functional basis).

[140] *Gaddafi* (2001) 125 ILR 490; *Tatchell v Mugabe* (2004) 136 ILR 572; *Re Mofaz* (2004) 128 ILR 709; *Re Bo Xilai* (2005) 128 ILR 713.

[141] E.g. International Convention against Transnational Organized Crime, A/RES/55/25, 15 November 2000. For more comprehensive discussions: Bantekas, *International Criminal Law* (2010) chs 11–12, 14.

[142] E.g. Cassese (2008) 162–83.

[143] There are nearly 20 treaties concerning various aspects of terrorism: e.g. Convention for the Suppression of Unlawful Acts against the Safety of Civil Aviation, 23 September 1971, 974 UNTS 177. For a comprehensive list: Bassiouni (2008) 699. Also Bassiouni, *International Terrorism: Multilateral Conventions (1937–2001)* (2001).

financing of terrorism, among other things. In recent years, multilateral treaties have also targeted transnational organized crime and corruption.[144] The 2005 Convention against Corruption, for example, requires states parties to criminalize a range of conduct, including bribery, embezzlement, and money-laundering.

The enforcement of such norms occurs at the domestic rather than the international level, as the treaties envisage punishment only by domestic courts. In addition to obliging states parties to criminalize certain conduct, such treaties generally require them to prosecute or extradite accused persons to other states parties that are willing to prosecute them (*aut dedere aut iudicare*).[145] Mutual legal assistance agreements often govern the extradition of suspects from one state to another. States may also make arrangements on an ad hoc basis. While the enforcement of these norms is dependent on domestic legal systems either prosecuting or extraditing accused persons, various treaty bodies—such as the Committee against Torture—often play an important role in monitoring the implementation of the treaty norms at the domestic level.

5. CONCLUSIONS

The rapid developments in the field of international criminal law leave lawyers with much to study. Yet these developments are no cause for celebration: they reflect repeated failures to prevent serious violations of human rights and international humanitarian law. The deterrent effect of international prosecutions is unclear, and probably always will be. Moreover, international criminal justice represents only one possible response to atrocities. Truth and reconciliation commissions, for example, may be more effective in certain respects—the perpetuation of testimony, the correction of the historical record, solace to victims. While international criminal justice constitutes an increasingly important area, its continued prominence raises questions about how the international legal system can *effectively* respond to atrocities, not limiting itself to the pursuit of the obvious and already ostracized 'enemies of mankind'.

---

[144] Convention against Transnational Organized Crime; Convention against Corruption.

[145] Bassiouni & Wise, *Aut Dedere Aut Judicare* (1995); Bantekas (2010) 373–83; Cryer (2010) 69–73, 85–106.

PART XI

DISPUTES

31

THE CLAIMS PROCESS

1. JURISDICTION AND ADMISSIBILITY DISTINGUISHED

A state presenting an international claim, either in diplomatic exchanges or before an international tribunal, has to establish its entitlement to do so, and the continuing viability of the claim itself, before the merits of the claim can be decided. The same is true for any other claimant in international litigation, whether an individual before the European Court of Human Rights or a putative investor before an ICSID tribunal.

In the case where the claim is presented before an international tribunal, preliminary objections may be classified as follows.[1] Objections to jurisdiction relate to conditions affecting the parties' consent to have the tribunal decide the case at all. If successful, jurisdictional objections stop all proceedings in the case, since they deprive the tribunal of the authority to give rulings as to the admissibility or substance of the claim. An objection to the admissibility of a claim invites the tribunal to dismiss (or perhaps postpone) the claim on a ground which, while it does not exclude its authority in principle, affects the possibility or propriety of its deciding the particular case at the particular time. Examples include undue delay in presenting the claim, failure to exhaust local remedies, mootness,[2] or failure to join a necessary third party. In normal cases the question of admissibility can only be decided once jurisdiction has been affirmed, and issues of admissibility may be so closely connected with the merits of the case so as to justify joining them to the merits.[3]

This chapter will deal with the array of preliminary issues, going both to jurisdiction and admissibility, before an international court or tribunal can decide the substance of the claim. The array of available courts and tribunals is discussed in chapter 32.

---

[1] Fitzmaurice (1958) 34 BY 12; Rosenne, 2 *The Law and Practice of the International Court* (4th edn, 2006) 505–85; Paulsson, in Aksen (ed), *Global Reflections on International Law, Commerce and Dispute Resolution* (2005) 601; Douglas, *The International Law of Investment Claims* (2009) 134–50.

[2] E.g. *Northern Cameroons (Cameroon v UK)*, ICJ Reports 1963 p 15, 28 (where the Court did not find it necessary to explore the meaning of admissibility). Also Gross (1964) 58 *AJIL* 415, 423–9.

[3] Such questions do not 'possess, in the circumstances of the case, an exclusively preliminary character': ICJ Rules of the Court, 1 July 1978, ICJ Acts & Docs No 5 (1990), Art 79(7); 2 Rosenne (4th edn, 2006) 868–70. Since states are normally free to attach conditions of any kind to their consent to jurisdiction, the distinction between jurisdiction and admissibility is a relative one.

2. INTERSTATE CLAIMS: PRIOR NEGOTIATIONS AND THE REQUIREMENT OF A DISPUTE

In *Right of Passage over Indian Territory* India objected that Portugal had failed 'to undertake diplomatic negotiations and continue them to the point where it was no longer profitable to pursue them'.[4] The Court said that negotiations had been pursued 'to the extent permitted by the circumstances of the case'.[5] The jurisprudence of the Court establishes that active negotiations between the parties are not, in general, a prerequisite to the Court's exercise of jurisdiction.[6] However, the Court's decision in *Georgia v Russia*[7] has unsettled the position, and further analysis is required.

(A) THE EXISTENCE OF A DISPUTE

Whether or not a dispute exists is a matter for objective determination.[8] In *South West Africa*[9] the Republic of South Africa objected that the conflict or disagreement alleged by Ethiopia and Liberia was not a 'dispute' in terms of Article 7 of the Mandate for South West Africa, as it did not involve or affect any material interests of those governments or their nationals.[10] The Court held that there was a dispute within the meaning of Article 7.[11] Yet irrespective of the existence of a dispute within the meaning of the adjudication clause relevant to the proceedings, there was a prior question—was there a legal dispute in existence at all? The Court held that there was a dispute as defined in *Mavrommatis*,[12] 'a disagreement on a point of law or fact, a conflict of legal views or of interests between two persons'. The Court also indicated that for a dispute to exist 'it must be shown that the claim of one party is positively opposed by the other'.[13]

---

[4] Preliminary Objections, ICJ Reports 1957 p 125, 130, 132–3.

[5] Ibid, 148–9.

[6] *Aegean Sea Continental Shelf (Greece v Turkey)*, ICJ Reports 1978 p 3, 12; *Military and Paramilitary Activities in and Against Nicaragua (Nicaragua v USA)*, Jurisdiction and Admissibility, ICJ Reports 1984 p 392, 440; *Land and Maritime Boundary between Cameroon and Nigeria*, Preliminary Objections, ICJ Reports 1998 p 275, 302–4.

[7] *Application of the International Convention on the Elimination of All Forms of Racial Discrimination (Georgia v Russia)*, Preliminary Objections, Judgment of 1 April 2011. Cf *Mavrommatis Palestine Concessions* (1923) PCIJ Ser A No 2, 13; *South West Africa (Ethiopia v South Africa; Liberia v South Africa)*, ICJ Reports 1962 p 319; *Northern Cameroons*, ICJ Reports 1963 p 15. Also *Border and Transborder Armed Actions (Nicaragua v Honduras)*, ICJ Reports 1988 p 69, 92–9.

[8] *Interpretation of Peace Treaties with Bulgaria, Hungary and Romania*, ICJ Reports 1950 p 74.

[9] Preliminary Objections, ICJ Reports 1962 p 319.

[10] Ibid, 327.

[11] Ibid, 342–4. Also: ibid, 379–84 (Judge Bustamante); 422–33 (Judge Jessup); 658–62 (Judge van Wyk, diss).

[12] (1923) PCIJ Ser A No 2, 11. The same issue arose in *Northern Cameroons*, ICJ Reports 1963 p 15, 20, 27. Also *East Timor (Portugal v Australia)*, ICJ Reports 1995 p 90, 99–100.

[13] *South West Africa*, ICJ Reports 1962 p 319, 328.

(B) 'CONCERNING THE INTERPRETATION OR APPLICATION OF A TREATY'

Conventions frequently include compromissory clauses conferring jurisdiction over disputes concerning the 'interpretation or application' of the treaty.[14] The inclusion of this language serves to define the scope of the Court's jurisdiction *ratione materiae*.[15] Given that the function of the Court is to decide 'such disputes as are submitted to it',[16] the qualifying words in such clauses should be treated as requiring a connection between the subject-matter of the treaty and the subject-matter of the claim, rather than as a means of unduly restricting access to the Court.

In *Georgia v Russia*, Georgia invoked Article 22 of the International Convention on the Elimination of All Forms of Racial Discrimination (CERD)[17] as the basis for the Court's jurisdiction. Alleging multiple violations of CERD, Georgia requested the Court to order, *inter alia*, that Russia take measures to ensure the safe return of internally displaced persons and pay compensation 'for its role in supporting and failing to bring to an end the consequences of the ethnic cleansing that occurred in the 1991–1994 conflicts'.[18] The Court rejected Russia's argument that the term 'dispute' in Article 22 had a special, narrower meaning than the general meaning of dispute established in previous jurisprudence.[19] In the event, however, its analysis of the evidence reflected a considerably more formalistic approach than the Court had previously taken. Georgia had raised concerns about Russia's role in the deteriorating situation in South Ossetia and Abkhazia during a period of over 10 years, but it did not expressly refer to CERD in its dealings with Russia until 9 August 2008, three days before submitting its application to the Court. Applying an atomistic analysis of the diplomatic correspondence, the Court held that there was no dispute 'concerning the interpretation or application' of CERD until that date.[20] Despite the Court's protestations to the contrary, this arguably marks a departure from previous practice by requiring formal notice and rejection of a claim, with express reference to the relevant treaty, before the claimant can seize the Court.[21]

---

[14] E.g. Convention on the Prevention and Punishment of the Crime of Genocide, 9 December 1948, 78 UNTS 277, Art IX; Montreal Convention for the Suppression of Unlawful Acts against the Safety of Civil Aviation, 23 September 1971, 974 UNTS 177, Art 14(1); further examples in *Georgia v Russia*, Preliminary Objections, Judgment of 1 April 2011, §29.

[15] *Oil Platforms (Iran v US)*, Preliminary Objections, ICJ Reports 1996 p 803, 810.

[16] Statute of the International Court of Justice, 26 June 1945, 15 UNCIO 355, Art 38(1).

[17] 21 December 1965, 660 UNTS 195.

[18] Judgment of 1 April 2011, §16.

[19] Ibid, §§26–30.

[20] Ibid, §§31–114.

[21] Ibid, President Owada, Judges Simma, Abraham, Donoghue & Judge ad hoc Gaja (joint diss) §3; Judge Cançado Trindade (diss). Further: the separate opinions of President Owada and Judges Simma, Abraham & Donoghue.

(C) NOT SETTLED BY NEGOTIATION

Other terminology commonly included in compromissory clauses is that the dispute in question 'is not', 'has not been' or 'cannot be' settled by negotiations. The Court has observed that 'while the existence of a dispute and the undertaking of negotiations are distinct as a matter of principle, the negotiations may help demonstrate the existence of the dispute and delineate its subject-matter'.[22] In *Georgia v Russia*, Russia argued that the words 'which is not settled by negotiation or by the procedures expressly provided for in this Convention' in CERD Article 22 constituted twin preconditions that Georgia must satisfy before resorting to the International Court. The Court noted that the resort to negotiations fulfils three functions: 'it gives notice to the respondent State that a dispute exists and delimits the scope of the dispute and its subject-matter'; 'it encourages the Parties to attempt to settle their dispute by mutual agreement, thus avoiding recourse to binding third-party adjudication'; and it 'performs an important function in indicating the limit of consent given by States'.[23]

At the provisional measures stage, the Court (by a vote of 8–7) had provisionally concluded that on the plain meaning of the compromissory clause, there was no requirement of formal negotiations or recourse to CERD dispute resolution procedures as preconditions to the jurisdiction of the Court, but that Article 22 did suggest that 'some attempt should have been made by the claimant party to initiate, with the Respondent Party, discussions on issues that would fall under CERD'.[24] At the jurisdiction stage, it reversed course, holding (by a vote of 10–6) that the 'express choice of two modes of dispute settlement [in Article 22 CERD] … suggests an affirmative duty to resort to them prior to the seisin of the Court'.[25] Where negotiations are commenced or attempted, the precondition is only satisfied if they have led to an impasse or otherwise failed.[26] Although express reference to the treaty was not required,[27] the negotiations must reflect the subject-matter of the dispute, which must concern the substantive obligations contained in the treaty in question.[28] Negotiations prior to the existence of a dispute were of no legal relevance.[29] The Court was not satisfied there had been genuine negotiations about matters falling under CERD during the relevant period.

Several of the judges criticized the methods of interpretation and resulting inflexibility of the majority's position.[30] The dissenting judges would have given greater weight to the ordinary meaning of the words 'is not settled by negotiations', as distinct from the common alternative 'cannot be settled by negotiations'.

---

[22] Judgment of 1 April 2011, §30.

[23] Ibid, §131. Also on consent: *Armed Activities on the Territory of the Congo (New Application: 2002) (Democratic Republic of the Congo v Rwanda)*, ICJ Reports 2006 p 6, 39.

[24] *Georgia v Russia*, Provisional Measures, ICJ Reports 2008 p 353, 388.

[25] Judgment of 1 April 2011, §134.

[26] Ibid, §159.

[27] *Nicaragua*, Jurisdiction and Admissibility, ICJ Reports 1984 p 392, 428.

[28] *Georgia v Russia*, Judgment of 1 April 2011, §161.

[29] Ibid, §§167–8.

[30] President Owada, Judges Simma, Abraham, Donoghue & Judge ad hoc Gaja (joint diss); Judge Cançado Trindade (diss), §§88–118.

(D) GENERAL JURISDICTION CLAUSES: ARTICLE 36(2)

Article 36(2) of the Court's Statute, referred to as the 'optional clause', provides for advance acceptance of the Court's compulsory jurisdiction by way of unilateral declarations.[31] These operate on a reciprocal basis in relation to any other state accepting the same obligation: 'jurisdiction is conferred on the Court ... to the extent to which the [declarations made] coincide in conferring it'.[32] Other treaties may contain general jurisdiction clauses: for example UNCLOS Article 287(1)[33] provides for states parties to declare their choice of procedure for dispute settlement from among four options. The earlier practice of adding a general jurisdiction clause in an optional additional protocol to a treaty is no longer in use.[34]

Reliance on the optional clause has been limited,[35] with an increasing number of cases brought before the International Court on the basis of compromissory clauses and special agreements instead.[36] Of the five permanent members of the Security Council only the UK still recognizes the Court's jurisdiction under Article 36(2).[37]

3. INTERSTATE CLAIMS: GROUNDS OF INADMISSIBILITY

(A) LEGAL INTEREST

The existence of a legal interest on the part of a claimant is a question distinct from the existence of a *dispute*. In *Northern Cameroons* the Court treated the issue of legal interest as a matter of judicial propriety,[38] but legally this is best treated as a species of admissibility, as some judges pointed out.[39] Judge Wellington Koo even referred to the existence of a legal interest as 'the indispensable basis of a justiciable dispute'.[40]

---

[31] Generally: Waldock (1955–56) 32 *BY* 244; Jennings (1995) 89 *AJIL* 493, 494–6; Tomuschat, in Zimmermann, Tomuschat & Oellers-Frahm (eds), *The Statute of the International Court of Justice* (2006) 589–657; 2 Rosenne (4th edn, 2006) ch 12; Brownlie (2009) 8 *Chin JIL* 267, 277–81.

[32] *Legality of Use of Force (Yugoslavia v Spain)*, ICJ Reports 1999 p 761, 771. On reciprocity generally: 2 Rosenne (4th edn, 2006) 731–7.

[33] 10 December 1982, 1833 UNTS 3.

[34] E.g. Optional Protocol to the VCDR concerning the Compulsory Settlement of Disputes, 18 April 1961, 500 UNTS 241, Art I.

[35] E.g. Waldock (1955–56) 32 *BY* 244.

[36] Jennings (1995) 89 *AJIL* 493, 494–6.

[37] Tomuschat (2006) 626.

[38] *Northern Cameroons*, ICJ Reports 1963 p 15, 37–8.

[39] Ibid, 101, 105 (Judge Fitzmaurice); 132 (Judge Morelli); 150–3 (Judge Badawi, diss); 170–2, 181 (Judge Bustamante). Cf *South West Africa*, ICJ Reports 1962 p 319, 449–57 (President Winiarski).

[40] *Northern Cameroons*, ICJ Reports 1963 p 15, 44–6.

A legal interest in the outcome of the case is also central to a third state request for permission to intervene pursuant to Article 62 of the Statute.[41] It is for the state seeking to intervene to identify its interest, and show that it 'may' be affected by the decision in the case.[42] Permission is at the Court's discretion and has only been granted in three cases: to Nicaragua in *Land, Island and Maritime Frontier Dispute (El Salvador/ Honduras)*;[43] to Equatorial Guinea in *Cameroon v Nigeria*;[44] and most recently to Greece in *Jurisdictional Immunities*.[45] In the latter case, the Court found Greece had a legal interest in the case because it might need to consider decisions of Greek courts arising from the Distomo massacre in 1944, in light of principles of state immunity, in order to decide aspects of the case between Germany and Italy. The permission for Greece to intervene, as a non-party, was limited to those questions.[46]

(B) NECESSARY THIRD PARTIES: THE *MONETARY GOLD* RULE

In some cases, it is not merely that a third state has a legal interest of a tangential kind, but that its legal interest is the very subject-matter of the claim or at least a necessary element in its determination. In such cases the claim is inadmissible unless the necessary third state is joined as a full party to the proceedings. Thus in *Monetary Gold*, Italy asserted a right to the Albanian gold which was in the hands of the three western allies, basing itself on an unliquidated claim for damages against Albania. The Court could have rejected the Italian argument on the ground that Albania's proprietary rights in the gold prevailed, for the purposes of return of war booty, over subsequent *in personam* claims, and it is a pity that the case was not decided on that basis. Instead the Court held that the claim (brought by Italy) could not be decided in the absence of Albania, a necessary third party, and was inadmissible.[47] The result was that the gold stayed on deposit until the various issues between Albania, Italy and the western allies were settled.

More recently, *Monetary Gold* has been both applied and distinguished. It was distinguished in *Phosphate Lands in Nauru* on the basis that the concurrent responsibility of the UK and New Zealand as (with Australia) the administering authority of the trust territory of Nauru did not prevent Nauru bringing an action for maladministration against Australia alone. Australia's responsibility for breach of the trusteeship did not depend on any finding against the other two states which were at most *in*

---

[41] Generally: Rosenne, *Intervention in the International Court of Justice* (1993); Chinkin, in Zimmermann, Tomuschat & Oellers-Frahm (2006) 1331.

[42] *Jurisdictional Immunities of the State (Germany v Italy)*, Application by the Hellenic Republic for Permission to Intervene, Order of 4 July 2011, §22.

[43] ICJ Reports 1990 p 3.

[44] Order of 21 October 1999, ICJ Reports 1999 p 1029.

[45] Application by the Hellenic Republic for Permission to Intervene, Order of 4 July 2011.

[46] Ibid, §§25–6, 32; *Jurisdictional Immunities*, Judgment of 3 February 2012, §§6–12.

[47] *Monetary Gold Removed from Rome in 1943 (Italy v France, UK and US)*, ICJ Reports 1954 p 19, 32–3.

pari delicto.[48] It was applied in *East Timor*, where it was held that the lawfulness or otherwise of Australia's recognition of Indonesia's sovereignty over East Timor could not be determined without first deciding that Indonesia's purported annexation of East Timor was unlawful.[49] It is a measure of the uncertainty surrounding the principle that the successful parties (respectively Italy and Australia) in *Monetary Gold* and *East Timor* were merely fortuitous beneficiaries.[50]

(C) MOOTNESS

The Court may decline to hear the merits of a case if it determines that the application has been rendered without object as a result of events arising after it was filed. For example, in *Nuclear Tests* the Court held that there was no practical purpose to be served by proceeding with the claims because France had declared it would stop atmospheric testing in the Pacific, a declaration the Court guilefully converted into a commitment.[51] In *Lockerbie* the US objected that Libya's claims were moot, as they had been rendered without object by SC Resolutions 748 (1992) and 883 (1993), and a judgment would serve no practical purpose.[52] The Court found the argument in the nature of a defence on the merits, rather than an objection of 'an exclusively preliminary character'. A decision of inadmissibility would pre-determine the Court's findings on whether Libya's obligations under the Montreal Convention were incompatible with its obligations under the SC resolutions, and if so, on whether the resolutions prevailed.[53]

(D) EXTINCTIVE PRESCRIPTION[54]

An unreasonable lapse of time in presentation may bar an international claim, but international law lays down no time limit. Special agreements may exclude categories of claim on a temporal basis; otherwise the question is one for the tribunal.[55] In *Phosphate Lands* the International Court rejected a preliminary objection based on delay in submission of the claim. The Court nevertheless recognized that delay might,

---

[48] *Certain Phosphate Lands in Nauru (Nauru v Australia)*, ICJ Reports 1992 p 240, 259–62, 267.

[49] *East Timor*, ICJ Reports 1995 p 90, 100–5.

[50] Rosenne (2003) 160–76; Chinkin, in Zimmermann, Tomuschat & Oellers-Frahm (2006) 1331, 1337–8.

[51] *Nuclear Tests (Australia v France)*, ICJ Reports 1974 p 253; *Nuclear Tests (New Zealand v France)*, ICJ Reports 1974 p 457.

[52] *Questions of Interpretation and Application of the 1971 Montreal Convention arising from the Aerial Incident at Lockerbie (Libya v US)*, Preliminary Objections, ICJ Reports 1998 p 115, 131.

[53] Ibid, 131–4.

[54] Generally: Borchard, *Diplomatic Protection* (1915) 825–32; King (1934) 15 *BY* 82; de Visscher, in *Hommage d'une génération de juristes au Président Basdevant* (1960) 525; Cheng, *General Principles of Law* (1953, repr 2006) 373–86; 5 Rousseau 178–82; Hondius (ed), *Extinctive Prescription on the Limitation of Actions* (1994); Hober, *Extinctive Prescription and Applicable Law in Interstate Arbitration* (2001); Wouters & Verhoeven, 'Prescription' (2008) *MPEPIL*.

[55] *Ambatielos* (1956) 23 ILR 306, 314–15; *Lighthouses* (1956) 23 ILR 659, 671–2.

in particular circumstances, render a claim inadmissible.[56] Conceivably a claim by a state could be denied because of the difficulty the respondent has in establishing the facts, but where there is no irreparable disadvantage to the respondent, tribunals will be reluctant to allow mere lapse of time to bar claims, given the conditions under which interstate relations are conducted. Thus in the *Cayuga Indians Claim* the respondent was held not to be prejudiced by significant delay on the part of the UK, which claimed on behalf of a protected minority.[57]

Indeed Article 45 of the ILC Articles on State Responsibility, which refers only to waiver or acquiescence in the loss of a claim, may be read as denying the preclusive effect as delay as such. According to the commentary, Article 45

emphasizes *conduct* of the State, which could include, where applicable, unreasonable delay, as the determining criterion for the lapse of the claim. Mere lapse of time without a claim being resolved is not, as such, enough to amount to acquiescence, in particular where the injured State does everything it can reasonably do to maintain its claim.[58]

A number of cases which are cited as instances of prescription are actually based on lapse of time as evidence of acquiescence or waiver.[59]

(E) WAIVER[60]

Abandonment of claims may occur by unilateral acts of waiver or acquiescence implied from conduct, or by agreement. Given that in cases of diplomatic protection the state is asserting its own rights, it may compromise or release the claim, leaving the individual or corporation concerned without an international remedy.[61] Conversely the waiver of a claim by a national does not bind the government. Hence the Calvo clause, by which aliens are called on to waive diplomatic protection at the time of entry, is legally ineffective.[62] The application of these principles to the field of investment arbitration is an open question.[63]

---

[56] ICJ Reports 1992 p 240, 247–50. Certain aspects of the question were reserved to the Merits phase: ibid, 255. Also *LaGrand (Germany v US)*, ICJ Reports 2001 p 466, 486–7.

[57] (1926) 6 RIAA 173; (1926) 20 *AJIL* 574.

[58] Witenberg (1932) 41 Hague *Recueil* 1, 31–3; García-Amador, ILC *Ybk* 1958/II, 57; Suy, *Les Actes juridiques unilatéraux en droit international public* (1962) 154–7; 5 Rousseau 182–6. Also *Wollemborg* (1956) 24 ILR 654; *Haas v Humphrey*, 246 F.2d 682 (DC Cir, 1957).

[59] E.g. *Sarropoulos v Bulgarian State* (1927) 4 ILR 246. Cf Tams, in Crawford, Pellet & Olleson (eds), *The Law of International Responsibility* (2010) 1035.

[60] On the Calvo clause: Manning-Cabrol (1995) 26 *LPIB* 1169; Dalrymple (1996) 29 *Cornell ILJ* 161; Paulsson, *Denial of Justice in International Law* (2005) 20–4.

[61] Cf *Inao Horimoto v The State* (1954) 32 ILR 161; *Public Trustee v Chartered Bank of India, Australia and China* (1956) 23 ILR 687, 698–9; *Austrian Citizen's Compensation* (1960) 32 ILR 153; *Togen Akiyama v The State* (1963) 32 ILR 233; *Restitution of Household Effects Belonging to Jews Deported from Hungary* (1965) 44 ILR 301; *Rudolf Hess* (1980) 90 ILR 386; *Kaunda v President of the Republic of South Africa* (2004) 136 ILR 452; *Regina (Al Rawi) v Foreign Secretary* [2006] EWCA Civ 1279.

[62] Cf *First National City Bank of New York* (1957) 26 ILR 323, 325.

[63] Cf *Loewen v US* (2004) 128 ILR 334; *Eureko BV v Republic of Poland* (2005) 12 ICSID Reports 331; and see chapter 28.

(F) OTHER GROUNDS OF INADMISSIBILITY

Other grounds exist which deserve brief notice:

(1) Conceivably a failure to comply with the rules of court of the tribunal in making an application may provide a ground for an objection as to admissibility, although tribunals are reluctant to give much significance to matters of form.[64]

(2) Analogously to the local remedies rule, it may happen that a respondent can establish that adequate remedies have been or ought to be obtained in another tribunal, whether national or international. Whether there is any international equivalent to the national law doctrines of *lis alibi pendens* and *forum non conveniens* is controversial.[65]

(3) There may be a residue of instances in which questions of inadmissibility and 'substantive' issues are difficult to distinguish. This is the case with the so-called 'clean hands' doctrine, according to which a claimant's involvement in activity unlawful under either municipal or international law may bar the claim.[66]

4. DIPLOMATIC PROTECTION

The heads of inadmissibility dealt with above are generally applicable to international claims, whatever their character. By contrast the nationality of claims and exhaustion of local remedies rules were specifically developed in the context of diplomatic protection. In 2006 they were restated by the ILC in a text aspects of which reflect elements of progressive development.[67]

---

[64] Witenberg (1932) 41 Hague *Recueil* 1, 90–4; *Northern Cameroons*, ICJ Reports 1963 p 15, 27–8, 42–3 (Judge Wellington Koo), 173–4 (Judge Bustamante). Also on procedural inadmissibility: ibid, 172–3 (Judge Bustamante).

[65] Shany, *The Competing Jurisdictions of International Courts and Tribunals* (2003) esp chs 4–6; Shany, *Regulating Jurisdictional Relations between National and International Courts* (2007). For a review of national law rules for declining or restraining the exercise of jurisdiction: Fentiman, *International Commercial Litigation* (2010) part V.

[66] The clean hands doctrine is to the effect that an action may not be maintained by someone who has misbehaved in relation to the subject-matter of the claim: Cheng (1953, repr 2006) 155–8. The International Court has never applied the doctrine, even in cases where it might have done so: see *Oil Platforms*, ICJ Reports 2003 p 161; *Legal Consequences of the Construction of a Wall in the Occupied Palestinian Territory*, ICJ Reports 2004, p 136, 149–50, 163. Cf *Nicaragua*, ICJ Reports 1986 p 14, 392 (Judge Schwebel, diss). The only investment tribunal award to apply the clean hands doctrine did so on the basis of applicable national law: *Inceysa Vallisoletana v Republic of El Salvador*, 2 August 2006, §§231–42, available at www.italaw.com. Generic claims of wrongdoing have not succeeded: e.g. *Gustaf FW Hamester GmbH & Co KG v Republic of Ghana*, 18 June 2010, §§127–8, available at www.italaw.com. For ILC consideration see also Crawford, Second Report on State Responsibility, ILC *Ybk* 1999/II(1), 3, 82–3 (§§332–6); Dugard, Sixth Report on Diplomatic Protection, 11 August 2004, A/CN.4/546, 3–5 (§§5–7) (concluding that 'the evidence in favour of the clean hands doctrine is inconclusive'). Also Salmon (1964) 10 *AFDI* 225; Schwebel, 'Clean Hands, Principle' (2005) *MPEPIL*.

[67] ILC Draft Articles on Diplomatic Protection, A/61/10 (2006).

(A) NATIONALITY OF CLAIMS[68]

An important function of nationality is to establish the legal interest of a state when nationals, including corporations, suffer injury or loss at the hands of another state. In principle if the claimant state cannot establish the nationality of the claim, the claim is inadmissible because of the absence of any legal interest on its part.[69] However, the variety of problems involved necessitates separate treatment.

At the outset certain important exceptions to the principle must be noted.[70] A right to protection of non-nationals may arise from treaty or an ad hoc arrangement establishing an agency. The other generally accepted exceptions are alien seamen on ships flying the flag of the protecting state[71] and members of the armed forces of a state. If the injured party was in the service of the claimant state the latter may be said to have suffered harm to a legal interest although the victim was an alien.[72]

(i) Formulation of the nationality rule

As regards individuals, the rule has been stated by the ILC as follows in Article 5 of the Draft Articles on Diplomatic Protection:

1. A State is entitled to exercise diplomatic protection in respect of a person who was a national of that State continuously from the date of injury to the date of the official presentation of the claim. Continuity is presumed if that nationality existed at both these dates.

2. Notwithstanding paragraph 1, a State may exercise diplomatic protection in respect of a person who is its national at the date of the official presentation of the claim but was not a national at the time of the injury, provided that the person had the nationality of a predecessor State or lost his or her previous nationality and acquired, for a reason unrelated to the bringing of the claim, the nationality of the former State in a manner not inconsistent with international law.

3. Diplomatic protection shall not be exercised by the present State of nationality in respect of a person against a former State of nationality of that person for an injury caused when that person was a national of the former State of nationality and not of the present State of nationality.

---

[68] On diplomatic protection and the operation of the nationality rule generally: Borchard (1934) 43 *Yale LJ* 359; Sinclair (1950) 27 *BY* 125; García-Amador (1958) 94 Hague *Recueil* 365, 426ff; Lillich (1964) 13 *ICLQ* 899; Duchesne (2004) 36 *G Wash ILR* 783; ILA, Report of the 72nd Conference (2006) 353–405; Amerasinghe, *Diplomatic Protection* (2008) ch 10; Dugard, 'Diplomatic Protection' (2009) *MPEPIL*. On the work of the ILC see Dugard's Reports (2000–06); ILC Report 2006, 13–100; *Crawford*, (2006) 31 *S Af YIL* 1.

[69] *Panevezys–Saldutiskis Railway* (1939) PCIJ Ser A/B No 76; further: *Nottebohm (Liechtenstein v Guatemala)*, Second Phase, ICJ Reports 1955 p 4. But legal interest may exist on some other basis: Fitzmaurice (1950) 27 *BY* 1, 24–5.

[70] Parry (1953) 30 *BY* 257. On the position of aliens employed in diplomatic and consular services: Fitzmaurice (1950) 27 *BY* 1, 25; Roberts (ed), *Satow's Diplomatic Practice* (2009) 165–7.

[71] Watts (1958) 7 *ICLQ* 691. Further: ILC Draft Article 18 and commentary. Cf *M/V Saiga (No 2)* (1999) 120 ILR 143.

[72] Fitzmaurice (1950) 27 *BY* 1, 25.

4. A State is no longer entitled to exercise diplomatic protection in respect of a person who acquires the nationality of the State against which the claim is brought after the date of the official presentation of the claim.[73]

The commentary notes that this provision preserves the traditional rule in that it requires that the injured individual have the nationality of the claimant state at the time of the injury and at the date of the official presentation of the claim, but leaves open the question whether nationality has to be retained between injury and presentation of the claim.[74] Draft Article 5 also clarifies the relevant end point as the date of presentation of the claim; this is the date most frequently used in treaties, judicial decisions, and doctrine as the *dies ad quem*. The term 'official' was added to indicate a formal demand as opposed to informal enquiries and contacts on the subject.[75]

The principle of continuity has been criticized because it permits incidental matters, for example, change of nationality by operation of law, to affect reasonable claims, and also because, if the legal wrong is to the state of origin, then the wrong must have matured at the time of injury and should be unaffected by subsequent changes in the status of the individual. The essence of the rule is probably a desire to prevent the individual choosing a powerful protecting state by a shift of nationality.[76] This view does not support the application of the principle in cases of involuntary changes brought about by death or state succession.[77] Draft Articles 5 and 10 justifiably except cases of succession; draft Article 5 also excepts other cases where the change in nationality occurs 'for a reason unrelated to the bringing of the claim', that is, otherwise than as a result of forum shopping by the individual concerned.[78]

(ii) Succession on death[79]

The nationality of an heir must be the same as that of the decedent on whose behalf the claim would have been made: in other words the principle of continuous nationality is applied to the beneficial interest in the property.[80] Since the beneficial interest is crucial a claim will be denied if the residuary legatee does not have the requisite

[73] Similarly, Art 10 of the ILC Draft Articles deals with continuous nationality of corporations and allows for continuity despite succession of states (§1), and despite the corporation ceasing to exist (§3).

[74] Commentary to Art 5, §2.

[75] Commentary to Art 5, §§4–5.

[76] Borchard (1934) 43 *Yale LJ* 359, esp 377–80.

[77] *Barcelona Traction*, Second Phase, ICJ Reports 1970 p 3, 99–103 (Judge Fitzmaurice), 202 (Judge Jessup). On nationality in state succession generally see further: O'Connell, 2 *State Succession* (2nd edn, 1967) 1033–9; Jennings (1967) 121 Hague *Recueil* 323, 474–7; Zimmermann, in Eisemann & Koskenniemi (eds), *State Succession* (2000) 611.

[78] Duchesne (2004) 36 *G Wash ILR* 783.

[79] Hurst (1926) 7 *BY* 163, 166; Diena (1934) 15 *RDILC* 173; Blaser, *La Nationalité et la protection juridique internationale de l'individu* (1962) 39–44. The ILC, in the commentary to the Draft Articles on Diplomatic Protection, whilst accepting that a claim could not be made if the heirs had the nationality of the responsible state, refrained from attempting to lay down any rules in relation to the situation in which the heir held the nationality of a third state: Commentary to draft Article 5, §14.

[80] *Stevenson* (1903) 9 RIAA 385; *Flack* (1929) 5 RIAA 61; *Gleadell* (1929) 5 RIAA 44; *Eschauzier* (1931) 5 RIAA 207; *Kren* (1955) 20 ILR 233; *Bogovic* (1955) 21 ILR 156. Cf *Hanover Bank* (1957) 26 ILR 334.

nationality although the executrix has.[81] But a claims commission may presume continuity of nationality in the heirs of the deceased creditor.[82]

(iii) Assignment of claims

If during the critical period a claim is assigned to or by a non-national of the claimant state, the claim must be denied.[83] This was the situation in the *Loewen* case, where a Canadian company, after a flawed trial leading to a jury award of $500 million damages (including $400 million punitive damages), was reorganized as a US company pursuant to Chapter 11 of the United States Bankruptcy Code. Before going out of business the company assigned its right, title, and interest in the NAFTA claim to a newly created Canadian corporation. An unblinking tribunal composed of three domestic appellate judges dismissed the claim: there had been a manifest denial of justice at trial, but the continuity of nationality rule had not been observed; in substance the national character of the claimant had changed, and the Canadian assignee of the NAFTA claim was a 'naked entity' which could not 'qualify as a continuous national for the purposes of the proceeding'.[84] Although it is said that assignment does not affect the claim if the principle of continuity is observed, great care is required: BIT claims are essentially claims *intuitu personae* under international law, and this imposes limits on their assignability.

(iv) Beneficial owners[85]

The relevant principle is set forth in the decision of the US Foreign Claims Settlement Commission in *American Security and Trust Company*:

It is clear that the national character of a claim must be tested by the nationality of the individual holding a beneficial interest therein rather than by the nationality of the nominal or record holder of the claim. Precedents for the foregoing well-settled proposition are so numerous that it is not deemed necessary to document it with a long list of authorities ...[86]

In that case the claim was denied as the beneficiaries were not nationals of the US although the trustee presenting the claim was. Treaties, and internal legislation

---

[81] *Gleadell* (1929) 5 RIAA 44.

[82] *Straub* (1953) 20 ILR 228.

[83] *Perle* (1954) 21 ILR 161; *First National City Bank of New York* (1957) 26 ILR 323; *Dobozy* (1958) 26 ILR 345; *Einhorn-Fielstein v Netherlands Claims Commission (Czechoslovakia)* (1971) 73 ILR 378. Also *Batavian National Bank* (1957) 26 ILR 346 (on assignment after filing of claim).

[84] *Loewen v US* (2004) 128 ILR 334, 412–18. The decision has attracted much criticism, focused more on denial of justice than continuity of nationality. But it is more vulnerable in the latter respect than the former.

[85] Lillich (1964) 13 *ICLQ* 899; 8 Whiteman 1261–3; Bederman (1989) 38 *ICLQ* 935; Douglas (2009) ch 12.

[86] (1957) 26 ILR 322, 322. Also *Binder-Haas* (1953) 20 ILR 236; *Knesevich* (1954) 21 ILR 154; *First National City Bank of New York* (1957) 26 ILR 323; *Methodist Church* (1957) 26 ILR 279; *Hanover Bank* (1957) 26 ILR 334; *Chase National Bank* (1957) 26 ILR 463; *Barcelona Traction*, ICJ Reports 1970 p 3, 218–19 (Judge Jessup).

regulating the consequences of international settlements for lump sums, may however allow trustees to claim irrespective of the nationality of the beneficiaries.

(v) Insurers and subrogation[87]

Insurers may claim on the basis of subrogation provided the principle of continuity of nationality is satisfied. Subrogation may be regarded as a form of assignment or a form of representation: in any case it could be supported as a general principle of law.[88] There are cogent arguments against allowing the nationality of the insurer to affect the nationality of the claim. In particular, because of the practice of reinsurance, the ultimate bearer of loss is not readily ascertainable. However, if the insurer's interest is established and the principle of continuity is satisfied there would seem to be no very good reason for denial of a claim. In cases where the state of the insured does not pursue a claim, Meron has argued *de lege ferenda* that the state of the insurer should have standing with respect to the interests of the insurer, on the basis that the responsible state should not be able to escape liability because the injured party and the insurer do not have the same nationality.[89]

(vi) Partnership claims

In principle, as a firm is not a legal person in English law, partners would receive protection as individuals to the extent of their interest in the partnership. However, British claims practice, reflected in settlement agreements and Orders in Council, has in general permitted claims by firms constituted under English law, as such, irrespective of the nationality of the partners.[90]

(vii) Corporations[91]

In principle it would appear normal for a corporation to be considered as having the nationality of the state under whose law it is constituted, unless a particular treaty

---

[87] Ritter (1961) 65 *RGDIP* 765; Blaser (1962) 47–50; McNair, 2 *Opinions* 290–2; 2 O'Connell (2nd edn, 1967) 1050–2; Meron (1974) 68 *AJIL* 628; van Niekerk (2007) 19 *S Af Mercantile LJ* 502; Sornarajah, *The International Law on Foreign Investment* (3rd edn 2010) 222.

[88] *Federal Insurance Company* (1958) 26 ILR 316, in which the US Foreign Claims Settlement Commission said: '[b]y virtue of [a] ... principle, recognized and applied alike by courts of law and equity ... an insurer who indemnifies the person who has suffered loss through another's wrongdoing, thereby acquires, to the extent of such indemnification, the assured's rights against the wrong-doer'. Also: *Continental Insurance Company* (1958) 26 ILR 318.

[89] Meron (1974) 68 *AJIL* 628.

[90] Lillich (1964) 13 *ICLQ* 899, 907–8; Lillich & Weston (1982) 3, 31–2, 148–50; 8 Whiteman 1270 (quoting Jiménez de Aréchaga). Cf Amerasinghe (2008) 138–41.

[91] Generally: de Hochepied, *La Protection diplomatique des societés et des actionnaires* (1965); Harris (1969) 18 *ICLQ* 275; Caflisch, *La Protection des sociétés commerciales et des intérêts indirects en droit international public* (1969); Seidl-Hohenveldern, *Corporations in and under International Law* (1987) 7–12; Dugard, Fourth Report on Diplomatic Protection, A/CN.4/530, 13 March 2003, 20–44; Lowe, in Crawford, Pellet & Olleson (2010) 1005. Further: chapter 24.

imposes a different rule.[92] It is after all the state of incorporation which is responsible for ensuring that the requirements of corporate accountability (auditing, reporting, shareholders meetings, etc) are fulfilled.

British and American practice requires the existence of a substantial beneficial interest owned by nationals in the corporation.[93] In many instances the beneficial interest exists in connection with a corporation incorporated under the law of the claimant state, but the crucial question is whether, on the basis of the beneficial interest, protection may be exercised in respect of a corporation incorporated in another state, and even in the respondent state.[94]

Barcelona Traction is still the leading authority on the question of diplomatic protection for corporations and their shareholders.[95] The Barcelona Traction Company was incorporated under Canadian law and had its registered office in Canada. In reaching the conclusion that Belgium had no capacity to espouse the claims of the Belgian shareholders in the company, the International Court took the view that Canada was the national state, finding that a 'close and permanent connection ha[d] been established, fortified by the passage of over half a century' and that the company had 'manifold' connections to Canada.[96] But the Court rejected the analogy of the *Nottebohm* case[97] and the 'genuine connection' principle as applied to the naturalization of individuals. It held that in the context of corporate entities the analogy could only apply in a limited manner and 'no absolute test of "the genuine connection" has found general acceptance'.[98]

This may be true: however, the *Nottebohm* principle is essentially the assertion that in referring to institutions of municipal law, international law has a reserve power to guard against giving effect to ephemeral, abusive, and simulated creations.[99] Moreover, there is at least a presumption of validity in favour of the nationality created

---

[92] Under the Convention on the Settlement of Investment Disputes between States and Nationals of Other States, 18 March 1965, 575 UNTS 159, Art 25(2)(b), a corporation incorporated in the respondent state may claim if the parties have agreed that because of foreign control it should be treated as a national of another contracting state for the purposes of the Convention: Schreuer, Malintoppi, Reinisch & Sinclair, *The ICSID Convention* (2nd edn, 2009) 760–902.

[93] The jurisprudence of arbitral tribunals is inconclusive. Further: *I'm Alone* (1935) 3 RIAA 1609; *Interoceanic Railway of Mexico* (1931) 5 RIAA 178, 184; *Westhold Corporation* (1953) 20 ILR 266; *Cisatlantic* (1954) 21 ILR 293. On the practice of the Iran–US Claims Tribunal: *Alcan Aluminium Ltd v Ircable Corporation* (1983) 72 ILR 725; *Sola Tiles Inc v Iran* (1987) 83 ILR 460; *Sedco Inc v NIOC* (1987) 84 ILR 483; *Starrett Housing v Iran* (1987) 85 ILR 349. Cf *Aguas del Tunari SA v Republic of Bolivia* (2005) 16 ICSID Reports 297; *Camuzzi International SA v the Argentine Republic* (2005) 16 ICSID Reports 3.

[94] *Barcelona Traction*, Second Phase, ICJ Reports 1970 p 3, 183 (Judge Jessup). Earlier decisions include *Canevaro* (1912) 11 RIAA 397, 406; *SS Wimbledon* (1923) PCIJ Ser A No 1, 182; *Flack* (1929) 5 RIAA 61; *Madera Company* (1931) 5 RIAA 156.

[95] ICJ Reports 1970 p 3. For analysis: Dugard, Fourth Report on Diplomatic Protection, A/CN.4/53013, March 2003, 2–12.

[96] ICJ Reports 1970 p 3, 42. Also: ibid, 295–6, 300 (Judge Ammoun); and the very qualified expressions of Judge Fitzmaurice: ibid, 83.

[97] ICJ Reports 1955 p 4.

[98] ICJ Reports 1970 p 3, 42.

[99] 8 Whiteman 1270–2, for examples.

by incorporation and, in the case of multinational corporate bodies, no very exacting test of substantial connection should be applied.

Article 9 of the ILC Articles on Diplomatic Protection provides for place of incorporation as the first criterion for nationality of corporations, but with the state of the seat of management and financial control as a secondary option if there is no sufficient connection with the state of incorporation.[100] It may be pointed out that, if a doctrine of substantial connection is employed, some but not all of the difficulties of classification of an entity as a legal person are avoided. If the place of incorporation is not a sufficient criterion, one still has to choose a system which decides whether separate legal personality exists or not, for example in the case of a partnership. Tribunals seem to rely on municipal law in this respect, but by demanding the existence of *siège social*, control, domicile, and so on, they would seem to require a guarantee that the grant of personality is reasonable and not a device for limiting the proper sphere of protection of other governments.

(viii) Shareholder claims[101]

There is considerable authority for the view that shareholders must rely upon the diplomatic protection available in favour of the corporation in which they have invested. The shareholders may receive diplomatic protection from the state of their nationality in certain situations, namely, when the act of the respondent state affects the shareholder's legal rights (e.g. the right to receive dividends) as such, and also when the company has ceased to exist in law in the place of incorporation. Other exceptions may exist but they are controversial.

The admissibility of claims on behalf of shareholders was at issue in *Barcelona Traction*.[102] The Court held that Belgium lacked a legal interest in the subject-matter of the claim and hence did not proceed to the merits. The Court accepted the mechanism of the limited liability company (*société anonyme*) as a general feature of national legal systems which had become a fact of international economic life.[103] Shareholders take advantage of the device of incorporation: if the company is harmed, what is affected is a simple interest and not the *rights* of the shareholders. The Court was unimpressed by the argument that, in the absence of protection by Canada (which had ceased substantial diplomatic activity in 1952), the shareholders should have alternative protection.

---

[100] ILC Articles on Diplomatic Protection, A/61/10 (2006), 52–5.

[101] Jones (1949) 26 *BY* 225; Bagge (1958) 34 *BY* 162; Lillich (1964) 13 *ICLQ* 899; Stern (1990) 116 *JDI* 897; Dugard, Fourth Report on Diplomatic Protection, A/CN.4/530, 13 March 2003, 1–44; Lowe, in Crawford, Pellet & Olleson (2010) 1012–17; Juratowicz (2010) 81 *BY* 281.

[102] ICJ Reports 1970 p 3; for contemporaneous comment: de Visscher (1970) 6 *RBDI* 1; de Visscher (4th edn, 1970) 303–5; Briggs (1971) 65 *AJIL* 327; Lillich (1971) 65 *AJIL* 522–32; Metzger (1971) 65 *AJIL* 532–41; Caflisch (1971) 31 *ZaöRV* 162; de Visscher (1971) 7 *RBDI* 1; Higgins (1971) 11 *Va JIL* 327; various items (1971) 23 *Revista española*; Seidl-Hohenveldern (1971–72) 22 *OZföR* 255; Grisel (1971) 17 *Ann Suisse* 31; Mann (1973) 67 *AJIL* 259.

[103] ICJ Reports 1970 p 3, esp 34–8. Also: ibid, 231–42 (Judge Morelli); 244–64 (Judge Padilla Nervo); 296–333 (Judge Ammoun).

The Court simply pointed out that Canada had the power to exercise protection but that power was discretionary.[104]

The Court recognized that the shareholder has an independent basis for protection if the act complained of was aimed at the direct rights of the shareholder as such, rather than the rights of the corporation, for example, the right to a dividend.[105] This proposition is recognized in Article 12 of the ILC Draft Articles on Diplomatic Protection. Apart from that case, the question remained whether there were special circumstances in which the corporate veil could be lifted in the interest of the shareholders. Treaties and decisions concerned with the treatment of enemy and allied property in the two world wars and the treatment of foreign property in cases of nationalization were *lex specialis* not of general application. In the view of the Court the only special circumstance was the case of the company having ceased to exist as a corporate entity capable in law of defending its rights in the relevant municipal courts.[106]

The carefully argued separate opinions of Judges Tanaka,[107] Jessup,[108] and Gros[109] supported the diplomatic protection of shareholders as a principle. Judge Fitzmaurice had serious misgivings concerning 'an unsatisfactory state of the law that obliges the Court to refrain from pronouncing on the substantive merits of the Belgian claim, on the basis of what is really—at least in the actual circumstances of this case—somewhat of a technicality'.[110]

The Court rejected two propositions for which there had been some support in the sources. The first was that protection for shareholders may be justified when the corporation is 'completely paralysed' or 'practically defunct': the Court held that shareholders could only receive protection as such when the corporation had ceased to exist in law. This was not true of Barcelona Traction since, in spite of its economic paralysis in Spain and receivership in Canada, the company still existed and was capable of legal action. The Court remarked that the description 'practically defunct' 'lacks all legal precision'.[111]

The second proposition was that protection may be exercised where the corporation has the nationality of the very state responsible for the acts complained of. The Court remarked that 'whatever the validity of this theory may be, it is certainly not applicable to the present case, since Spain is not the national State of Barcelona Traction'.[112] The authorities were historically much divided on the issue. Some argued that such an exception was anomalous 'since it ignores the traditional rule that a State is not guilty

---

[104] Ibid, 41–5. Also: ibid, 37.

[105] Ibid, 36.

[106] Ibid, 40–1.

[107] Ibid, 121, 130–5.

[108] Ibid, 168–201.

[109] Ibid, 268–79, on condition that the investments in question are 'connected with the national economy' of the protecting state.

[110] ICJ Reports 1970 p 3, 64.

[111] Ibid, 41. Also: 193–4 (Judge Jessup); 256–7 (Judge Padilla Nervo); 318–20 (Judge Ammoun).

[112] Ibid, 48; see, however, 257 (Judge Padilla Nervo).

of a breach of international law for injuring one of its own nationals'.[113] It was seen as arbitrary to allow the shareholders to emerge from the carapace of the corporation in this situation but not in others. If one accepts the general considerations of policy advanced by the Court then this alleged exception to the rule is disqualified. However, the law has moved on. It is no longer the case that states do not bear international responsibility for injuries caused to their own nationals. Article 11 of the ILC Draft Articles on Diplomatic Protection supports protection in cases where the corporation has ceased to exist, or where the corporation had the nationality of the alleged wrongdoing state and incorporation in that state was a precondition for doing business there.[114]

In *Diallo*, the Court touched upon the issue whether there is indeed an exception to the general rule (that the right of diplomatic protection of a company belongs to its national state), which allows for protection of the shareholders by their own national state by substitution.[115] The admissibility of Guinea's application partly related to the exercise of diplomatic protection with respect to Diallo by substitution for Africom-Zaire and Africontainers-Zaire and in defence of their rights. The Court found that state practice and decisions of international courts and tribunals did not reveal an exception in customary international law allowing for protection by substitution.[116] The Court also considered draft Article 11(b) of the Articles on Diplomatic Protection and reserved the question whether an exception existed as a matter of customary international law in the limited circumstances in which a company's incorporation in the state that committed the alleged violation of international law 'was required as a precondition for doing business there': the facts were such that the companies in any case would not fall within any such exception.[117]

(ix) Dual or multiple nationality

In many cases the individual has the nationality of both the applicant and respondent state. Discussions of this problem generally assign the available evidence to two propositions, which are assumed to be incompatible. The first is to be found in Article 4 of the Convention on Certain Questions relating to the Conflict of Nationality Laws of 1930: '[a] State may not afford diplomatic protection to one of its nationals against a State whose nationality such person also possesses'. British practice appears to reflect this principle.[118] The second is that the effective nationality governs the question: this has been applied by the Permanent Court of Arbitration in *Canevaro*,[119] by the

---

[113] Ibid, 192 (Judge Jessup).
[114] ILC Articles on Diplomatic Protection, A/61/10 (2006), 58–65.
[115] *Ahmadou Sadio Diallo (Guinea v Democratic Republic of the Congo)*, Preliminary Objections, ICJ Reports 2007 p 582, 614.
[116] Ibid, 615.
[117] Ibid, 616.
[118] (1981) 52 *BY* 499; (1982) 53 *BY* 492; (1983) 54 *BY*, 521, 524; (1987) 58 *BY* 622.
[119] 11 RIAA 405.

Italian–US Conciliation Commission in *Mergé*,[120] by the Iran–US Claims Tribunal,[121] by the UN Compensation Commission in category A claims against Iraq,[122] and by other tribunals.[123]

A different case of dual nationality is presented when one of two states of a dual national claims against a third state and the latter pleads that the other nationality is the effective or dominant nationality. A substantial jurisprudence supports the principle of the inopposability of the nationality of a third state in an international claim. In *Salem* the tribunal found that Salem was a Persian national at the time of his American naturalization, and held that it was not open to Egypt to invoke the Persian nationality against the claimant state, the US.[124] The same rule was affirmed by the Italian–US Conciliation Commission in *Flegenheimer*.[125]

The traditional practice was that a state would not exercise diplomatic protection against another state which considered the injured person to be its own national, out of respect for sovereignty.[126] That is no longer the case. The ILC has clarified the principle in its Draft Articles on Diplomatic Protection: Article 6 provides that any state of which the claimant is a national may exercise diplomatic protection against any state of which the claimant is not a national; Article 7 provides that a state of nationality of the claimant may only exercise protection against another state of nationality if the nationality of the former was 'predominant' at the date of injury and of the claim. No criteria for establishing predominance are specified but the commentary suggests the term more accurately captured the balancing exercise to be undertaken by a tribunal assessing the strengths of competing nationalities.[127]

(B) EXHAUSTION OF LOCAL REMEDIES[128]

An important rule of admissibility applies to cases of diplomatic protection as opposed to instances of direct injury to the state. A claim will not be admissible on

---

[120] (1955) 22 ILR 443, 449. Also *Spaulding* (1957) 24 ILR 452; *Flegenheimer* (1958) 25 ILR 91, 147; *Turri* (1960) 30 ILR 371.

[121] Decision of the Iran–US Claims Tribunal, Case 18A (1984) 75 ILR 176, 188 (for the dissenting opinion of the Iranian arbitrators upholding the principle in Art 4 of the Hague Convention, see ibid, 204); and decisions of Chamber Two in *Esphahanian v Bank Tejarat* (1983) 72 ILR 478; *Golpira v Iran* (1983) 72 ILR 493; *Saghi v Iran* (1987) 84 ILR 609. Generally: Charney (1998) 271 Hague *Recueil* 101, 303–14.

[122] (1994–96) 109 ILR 1, 106.

[123] *Mathison* (1903) 9 RIAA 485; *Schmeichler-Pagh* (1965) 92 JDI 689 (Danish Supreme Court); *Proposed Amendments to the Naturalization Provisions of the Political Constitution of Costa Rica*, IACtHR OC-4/84, 19 January 1984, 79 ILR 283, §§36, 63.

[124] (1932) 6 ILR 188.

[125] (1958) 25 ILR 91, 149. Also *Mergé* (1955) 22 ILR 443, 456; *Vereano* (1957) 24 ILR 464.

[126] *Reparation for Injuries Suffered in the Service of the United Nations*, ICJ Reports 1949 p 174, 186.

[127] ILC Articles on Diplomatic Protection, A/61/10 (2006), 41–7.

[128] Generally: Law, *The Local Remedies Rule in International Law* (1961); Chappez, *La règle de l'épuisement des voies de recours internes* (1972); Cançado Trindade, *The Application of the Rule of Exhaustion of Local Remedies in International Law* (1983); Amerasinghe, *Local Remedies in International Law* (2nd edn, 2004); Crawford & Grant, 'Exhaustion of local remedies' (2008) *MPEPIL*. For the work of the ILC: Dugard, Second

the international plane unless the individual alien or corporation concerned has exhausted the legal remedies available in the state which is alleged to be the author of injury.

(i) Function of the local remedies rule

The local remedies rule is justified by practical and political considerations and not by any logical necessity. The more persuasive practical considerations advanced are the greater suitability and convenience of national courts as fora for the claims of private parties, the need to avoid the multiplication of small claims on the level of diplomatic protection, the manner in which aliens by residence and business activity have associated themselves with the local jurisdiction, and the utility of a procedure which may lead to classification of the facts and liquidation of the damages,[129] including apportionment of damages amongst the various participants (which will normally not be possible at the international level, where only the state can be a respondent).[130]

The rule is often described rather loosely in terms of the possibility of 'obtaining redress' in the local courts. As an issue of admissibility the local proceedings are regarded retrospectively, but when proceedings are begun in the local courts various issues of law and fact may be at large. It may not be clear whether there is a breach of international law, or local law, or of either. The alien claimant in the local courts may be able to seek a remedy for a breach of international law *as such*, or may employ a remedy of local law which involves no reference to matters of international law but gives substantial reparation for the harm suffered.

Even in the case of direct injury to the interests of a foreign state (to which the exhaustion rule does not apply)—for example, damage to warships caused by agents of the respondent state—one should not *assume* that no remedy exists in national law. However, it is surely incorrect to state that resort to local remedies is 'required ... in order to determine ... whether or not [such] an act or omission is incompatible with international law'.[131] Further, the local proceedings may simply establish that a particular rule of local law stands in the way of redress and leave aside both the issue of compatibility of that rule with international law, and the whole question of whether the dispute has an international character.[132] Thus in general the exhaustion of local remedies will involve using such local procedures as are available to protect interests which correspond as closely as may be and in practical terms with the interests involved in a subsequent international claim.[133]

Report, ILC *Ybk* 2001/II(1), 97; Third Report, ILC *Ybk* 2002/II(1), 49; ILC Articles, 70–85 (Arts 14–15 & commentary).

[129] Amerasinghe (2nd edn, 2004) 56–64.

[130] In *CME (Czech Republic) BV v Czech Republic* (2001) 9 ICSID Reports 113, the principal wrongdoer was a private sector joint venturer whose liability was assessed at less than 10% of the valuation assigned by the ICSID Tribunal to the respondent state, whose role, though real, was secondary.

[131] Briggs (1956) 50 *AJIL* 921.

[132] *Certain Norwegian Loans (France v Norway)*, ICJ Reports 1957 p 9, 38 (Judge Lauterpacht).

[133] *Finnish Ships* (1934) 3 RIAA 1479; *Interhandel (Switzerland v US)*, ICJ Reports 1959 p 27.

(ii) Distinction between direct and indirect claims

The assumption in the literature and jurisprudence of the subject is that the rule applies only in connection with state responsibility for an unlawful act and in the absence of direct injury to the claimant state. The Arbitral Tribunal for the Agreement on German External Debts decided that the rule, in consequence, cannot apply where the applicant state makes no claim for damages but merely requests a decision on the interpretation and application of a treaty.[134] However, the general character of the claim will determine the issue, as the Chamber held in *Elettronica Sicula SpA (ELSI) (US v Italy)*.[135]

A distinction which is commonly drawn is between cases of direct injury to a state, for example by inflicting damage on its warships[136] or detaining its ambassador, and cases of diplomatic protection, in which the interest of an individual or corporation is affected and the state's interest depends on their nationality. It is only in the latter case that the exhaustion of local remedies is a condition of admissibility. However, in drawing the distinction one is perhaps only stating the problem rather than providing the basis for a solution.

In *Avena*, Mexico argued that the US, in breaching VCCR Article 36(1), had 'violated its international legal obligations to Mexico, in its own right and in the exercise of its right of diplomatic protection of its nationals'. The Court responded by observing that the individual rights of Mexican nationals under the Convention 'are rights which are to be asserted, at any rate in the first place, within the domestic legal system of the United States', and that the exhaustion rule therefore applied. However, Mexico also argued that 'it has itself suffered, directly and through its nationals, as a result of the violation'. The Court accepted this position, and described the relation between state and individual claims as closely connected:

Violations of the rights of the individual under [the Convention] may entail a violation of the rights of the sending State, and ... violations of the rights of the latter may entail a violation of the rights of the individual. In these special circumstances of interdependence of the rights of the State and of individual rights, Mexico may, in submitting a claim in its own name, request the Court to rule on the violation of rights which it claims to have suffered both directly and through the violation of individual rights conferred on Mexican nationals under [the Convention] ... The duty to exhaust local remedies does not apply to such a request.[137]

---

[134] *Swiss Confederation v German Federal Republic (No 1)* (1958) 25 ILR 33, 42–50; and Johnson (1958) 34 *BY* 363.

[135] ICJ Reports 1989 p 15, 42–3. Also *Air Services Agreement of 27 March 1946 (US v France)* (1978) 54 ILR 303, 322–5; *Heathrow Airport User Charges Arbitration* (1993) 102 ILR 215, 277–9.

[136] Cf *Corfu Channel*, ICJ Reports 1949 p 4. Also *Air Services Agreement of 27 March 1946* (1978) 54 ILR 304, 323–5.

[137] *Avena and other Mexican Nationals (Mexico v US)*, ICJ Reports 2004 p 12, 35–6. Cf *Armed Activities on the Territory of the Congo (Democratic Republic of the Congo v Uganda)*, ICJ Reports 2005 p 168.

Cases on the other side of the line include *Interhandel* and *ELSI*: in both the International Court held that the state claims could not be segregated from claims of the individuals injured, which were predominant.[138]

Article 14(3) of the ILC Draft Articles on Diplomatic Protection articulates the test of preponderance as follows:

Local remedies shall be exhausted where an international claim, or request for a declaratory judgement related to the claim, is brought preponderantly on the basis of an injury to a national or other person referred to in draft article 8.

By implication, a claim brought preponderantly on the basis of a direct injury to the state is not subject to the requirement of exhaustion.

(iii) Remedies required to be exhausted

Draft Article 14(2) defines local remedies as 'legal remedies which are open to the injured person before the judicial or administrative courts or bodies, whether ordinary or special, of the State alleged to be responsible for causing the injury'.[139] The remedies to be exhausted comprise all forms of recourse as of right, including administrative remedies of a legal character, but not extra-legal remedies such as *ex gratia* payments.[140] While 'procedural facilities which municipal law makes available to litigants' are included within the remedies to be exhausted, a failure to use them will only fall foul of the local remedies rule if the use of these means of procedure is essential to establish the claimant's case before the municipal courts.[141]

The test appears to be that an effective remedy must be available 'as a matter of reasonable possibility'.[142] No effective remedy is available if a point of law which could have been taken on appeal has previously been decided by the highest court,[143] or if the only issue on appeal would be one of fact and the higher courts lack the power to review findings of fact.[144] However, the local law may be uncertain and an international tribunal should show caution in drawing conclusions on the non-availability of a local remedy.[145] It must be noted, however, that a number of writers[146] and arbitral awards[147] have been willing to presume ineffectiveness of remedies from the circumstances, for

---

[138] *Interhandel*, ICJ Reports 1959 p 28; *ELSI*, ICJ Reports 1989 p 15, 43.

[139] ILC Articles, 70.

[140] *Finnish Ships* (1934) 3 RIAA 1479; *Diallo*, Preliminary Objections, ICJ Reports 2007 p 582, 601.

[141] *Ambatielos (Greece v UK)* (1956) 23 ILR 306, 336.

[142] *Norwegian Loans*, ICJ Reports 1957 p 9, 39 (Judge Lauterpacht); *Barcelona Traction*, Second Phase, ICJ Reports 1970 p 3, 144–5 (Judge Tanaka), 284 (Judge Gros). Further: ILC Draft Art 15(a) & commentary.

[143] *Panevezys–Saldutiskis Railway* (1939) PCIJ Ser A/B No 76; *X v Austria* (1960) 30 ILR 268.

[144] *Finnish Ships* (1934) 3 RIAA 1479, 1484, 1535.

[145] *Norwegian Loans*, ICJ Reports 1957 p 9, 39–40 (Judge Lauterpacht). Also Cançado Trindade (1983) 138–43.

[146] Sørensen (ed), *Manual of Public International Law* (1968) 589–90; 1 Oppenheim 525; Amerasinghe (2nd edn, 2004) 204–10.

[147] E.g. *Forests in Central Rhodopia* (1933) 3 RIAA 1405, 1420; (1934) 28 AJIL 773, 789; *Ambatielos* (1956) 23 ILR 306, 334–5. Also: *Loewen Group v United States* (2003) 1 ICSID Reports 421, 481–4.

example on the basis of evidence that the courts were subservient to the executive.[148] The European Court of Human Rights has found there is no effective remedy, contrary to ECHR Article 13, on many occasions, notably in cases alleging state failure adequately to investigate disappearances and killings.[149]

It may be assumed that no effective remedy is available if the local courts do not have jurisdiction in relation to the matter under their own law.[150] A different issue is whether the local remedies rule can apply when, according to international law, the local courts *could not* have jurisdiction over the matter. Judge Fitzmaurice expressed the opinion that no question of local remedies could arise in respect of proceedings which were exorbitant under international law.[151] The ILC Articles state as an exception the case where 'there was no relevant connection between the injured person and the State alleged to be responsible at the date of injury'.[152] As a matter of principle the outcome depends upon one's view of the policy underlying the local remedies rule. If the rule is related to assumption of risk by the alien and the existence of a proper basis for exercise of national jurisdiction, the requirement of a voluntary link, such as residence, makes good sense.

It is sometimes said to be the law that the rule does not apply when the issue arises from measures taken by 'the constitutional or legislative power or the highest executive organs'.[153] This view is too dogmatic since remedies may be available whatever the constitutional status of the agency concerned. The test remains that of the reasonable possibility of an effective remedy.[154] As to the burden of proof, the Court has observed that in matters of diplomatic protection 'it is incumbent on the applicant to prove that local remedies were indeed exhausted or to establish that exceptional circumstances relieved the allegedly injured person whom the applicant seeks to protect of the obligation to exhaust available local remedies … It is for the respondent to convince the Court that there were effective remedies in its domestic legal system that were not exhausted'.[155]

(iv) What constitutes exhaustion

Central to the question of what constitutes exhaustion is the effectiveness principle: parties are not required to exhaust every last avenue if to do so would be futile in

---

[148] *Brown* (1923) 6 RIAA 120; *Velásquez Rodríguez v Honduras*, IACtHR C/4, 21 July 1989. Also: *Barcelona Traction*, Second Phase, ICJ Reports 1970 p 3, 145–7 (Judge Tanaka); *ELSI*, ICJ Reports 1989 p 15, 47–8.

[149] E.g. *Aksoy v Turkey* [1996] ECtHR 21987/93; *Kaya v Turkey* [1998] ECtHR 22729/93, §§106–8; *Tepe v Turkey* [2003] ECtHR 27244/95, §192.

[150] See the Estonian argument and the Court's acceptance of the principle in the *Panevezys–Saldutiskis Railway* (1939) PCIJ Ser A/B No 76, 18.

[151] *Barcelona Traction*, Second Phase, ICJ Reports 1970 p 3, 103–10, 35–-6 (Judge ad hoc Riphagen, diss).

[152] ILC Articles, Art 15; Dugard, Third Report, ILC *Ybk* 2002/II(1), §§65–89.

[153] E.g. Verzijl (1954) 45 *Ann de l'Inst* 5, 112.

[154] *Interhandel*, ICJ Reports 1959 p 27. The reasonable possibility principle is reflected in ILC Art 15(a). Further: *Diallo*, Preliminary Objections, ICJ Reports 2007 p 582, 601.

[155] *Diallo*, Preliminary Objections, ICJ Reports 2007 p 582, 600, citing *ELSI*, ICJ Reports 1989 p 15, 43–4, 46.

terms of achieving the remedy sought. For example, in the *Finnish Ships* arbitration, a Finnish claim against the British government for use and loss by the Allies of some Finnish ships during the First World War, the arbitrator found that the Finnish ship-owners' failure to appeal certain points of law in the British courts did not amount to a failure to exhaust local remedies. The decision of the domestic Arbitration Board had rested on a factual finding that the ships had been requisitioned by Russia, not Britain, and the appealable points of law 'obviously would have been insufficient to reverse the decision of the Arbitration Board' on that point: the objection that remedies had not been exhausted was rejected.[156]

(v) Waiver and exclusion of local remedies

The local remedies rule is not mandatory. States may consent to waive the requirement, and it is common practice for bilateral investment treaties (BITs) to do so, expressly or by implication. Article 26 of the International Convention for the Settlement of Investment Disputes between States and Nationals of Other States[157] provides that states may make consent to arbitration conditional on exhaustion, but the option is rarely used.[158] Given the importance of the rule, courts have been hesitant to infer a tacit or automatic waiver,[159] but the ILA has concluded that if there is clear demonstration of intent then waiver does not need to be express.[160] Waiver has been inferred when the requirement of exhaustion would be incompatible with the letter and spirit of the agreement.[161]

In *Loewen* the claimant argued that NAFTA Article 1121(1)(b) implicitly eliminated the exhaustion requirement because it stipulated that any claimant wishing to commence international arbitration proceedings thereby waived the right to initiate or continue proceedings relating to the grievance before any administrative tribunal or court. The tribunal distinguished between claims of denial of justice, in which the rule is substantive in character, and other claims in which it is merely a procedural step going to admissibility.[162]

5. MIXED CLAIMS: PRIVATE PERSONS VERSUS STATES

(A) THE AVAILABILITY OF MIXED CLAIMS JURISDICTION

Diplomatic protection developed as a mechanism for transposing grievances from the national to the international level: by positing that the injured party was the state

---

[156] *Finnish Ships* (1934) 3 RIAA 1479.
[157] 18 March 1965, 575 UNTS 159.
[158] Generally: Paulsson (2005) 102–7; Dolzer & Schreuer (2008) 215.
[159] E.g. *ELSI*, ICJ Reports 1989 p 15, 42.
[160] Conclusions of the ILA, Report of the 72nd Conference (2006) 397.
[161] *Applicability of the Obligation to Arbitrate under Section 21 of the United Nations Headquarters Agreement of 26 June 1947*, ICJ Reports 1988 p 12, 29.
[162] *Loewen v US* (2004) 128 ILR 334, 158–71, 207–17; and Paulsson (2005) 102–12.

itself, rather than a national of that state, it was possible thereby to circumvent the constraint that only states had standing on the 'international plane'. Under modern international law, however, it may be possible for individual claimants (individuals or corporations) to bring claims in their own right against states or international organizations, relying either on contractual commitments or on rules of international law, or on some combination of the two, and avoiding constraints of diplomatic protection.

(i) Human rights litigation[163]

Some international human rights instruments provide mechanisms for individuals to take action against their own and other states for alleged violations.[164] Numbers of claims under these mechanisms have exploded, particularly in Europe, with the European Court of Human Rights receiving over 60,000 applications per year. Claimants must still exhaust domestic remedies, which is stipulated (for example) in ECHR Article 35(1) as a criterion of admissibility, but they have standing to claim in their own right without couching their grievance as an injury to the state of nationality. A certain margin of appreciation is generally afforded to respondent states, as being better placed than the international court or tribunal hearing the claim to resolve matters of domestic public policy, but the fact remains that individuals have direct rights of action against states in a way that was not possible under the pre-Charter model of international law.[165]

(ii) Investor-state arbitration

A different form of mixed litigation where private persons (natural or juridical) have standing to sue states directly arises under BITs. In such treaties the standard of treatment is not expressed as a right of the private person as such but rather as a set of bilateral obligations between the states parties: it is consequential upon such obligations that if investors of one state have a grievance against the other, the host state consents to international arbitration. BITs almost always waive the exhaustion of local remedies rule, allowing aggrieved investors to take their claim straight to arbitration. As regards nationality, the traditional nationality rule developed in the context of diplomatic protection is of diminished relevance in investor-state claims.[166] For example the local investment vehicle may be given standing 'because of foreign control', a possibility not open in diplomatic protection.[167] Nonetheless the nationality of the investor will be an important factor in determining which treaties will apply, and the practice

---

[163] Generally: Jayawickrama, *The Judicial Application of Human Rights Law* (2002) ch 29.

[164] E.g. ECHR, 4 November 1950, ETS 5, Art 34; First Optional Protocol to ICCPR, 16 December 1966, 999 UNTS 171, Art 2.

[165] Generally: Parlett, *The Individual in the International Legal System* (2011).

[166] E.g. Duchesne (2004) 36 *G Wash ILR* 783; 807–15. Further: Douglas (2009) ch 1, Rule 2: 'rules of admissibility of diplomatic protection in general international law are not generally applicable to the regime for the settlement of disputes between an investor and the host state created by an investment treaty'.

[167] See e.g. ICSID Convention, Art 25(2)(b); Schreuer et al (2nd edn, 2009) 279–83.

of 'nationality shopping' is a recognized strategy in foreign investment planning.[168] The Draft Articles on Diplomatic Protection are expressly stipulated not to apply to the extent they are inconsistent with 'special rules of international law, such as treaty provisions for the protection of investments'.[169]

(B) ISSUES OF JURISDICTION AND ADMISSIBILITY IN MIXED CLAIMS

Investment treaty claims are usually, to a greater or lesser extent, 'hybrid' claims, with both national and international law potentially relevant. Because jurisdiction is dependent on consent and the forum will be in some sense international, international law requirements for jurisdiction and admissibility of claims prima facie apply. But they may be excluded expressly or by necessary implication. For example the nationality of claims rule may be modified to allow claims by local corporations owned and controlled by a foreign investor, or even derivative claims by minority shareholders.[170] The exhaustion of local remedies rule is typically waived entirely, with implications for the merits of treaty claims that are still being worked out.[171]

The limited capacity of individuals to waive diplomatic protection (e.g. in the context of the Calvo clause) has already been referred to. How this translates to direct claims brought by investors under BITs is uncertain: on the one hand the obligations arising under a BIT are owed on an interstate basis; on the other hand, the allocation of risk is a principal function of investment agreements entered into between investors and states, and large investors can arguably look after themselves. At any rate it must be open to an investor to compromise a pending or apprehended claim. There is thus something to be said for the solution put forward in the *Restatement Third*, viz., that a BIT claim which has arisen can be waived or settled by the investor.[172] But this must be without prejudice to any interest of the other state party to obtain declaratory or other relief in respect of its own rights under the treaty.

In the context of human rights—conceived of as inherent, not granted—it cannot be possible to waive these in advance, although consent freely given may affect the incidence or application of rights. As to settlement of claims, again this must be possible, but even interstate settlements of human rights claims may be subject to a measure of supervision.[173]

---

[168] Generally: Dolzer & Schreuer (2008) 46–56.

[169] ILC Draft Art 17 & commentary, 89–90.

[170] E.g. *Aguas del Tunari SA v Republic of Bolivia* (2005) 16 ICSID Reports 297, 363; *Camuzzi International SA v Argentine Republic* (2005) 16 ICSID Reports 3, 12.

[171] E.g. Douglas (2009) 29–30, 98. Cf *Vivendi v Argentina (No 1)* (2000) 5 ICSID Reports 296, 322; *CME v Czech Republic* (2003) 9 ICSID Reports 121, 195–6; *Waste Management v Mexico (No 2)* (2004) 6 ICSID Reports 538, 557; *Mytilineos v Serbia and Montenegro* (2006) 16 ICSID Reports 567, 611.

[172] 2 *Restatement Third*, §902(i); *Eureko BV v Republic of Poland* (2005) 12 ICSID Reports 331, 370–3.

[173] ECHR, Arts 38(1)(b), 39, and see e.g. *Denmark v Turkey (Friendly Settlement)* [2000] ECtHR 34382/97, 149.

32

THIRD-PARTY SETTLEMENT OF INTERNATIONAL DISPUTES

1. PEACEFUL SETTLEMENT IN GENERAL

The judicial settlement of international disputes is only one facet of the enormous problem of the maintenance of international peace and security. In the period of the UN Charter the use of force by individual states to address international disputes is impermissible,[1] and in fact few disputes are finally resolved by force. However, there is no obligation in general international law *to settle* disputes, and procedures for settlement by formal and legal procedures are consensual in character.

The context of judicial settlement in international relations is thus different to that of municipal courts, and this type of settlement is relatively exceptional in state relations (though less so than previously).[2] This chapter considers the problems of international legal process; that is, the process between states or otherwise at the international level and involving states.[3] Settlement by political means, including through organs of international organizations, must be set aside.[4] However, the two approaches to settlement are not completely divorced. Political organs, like the General Assembly and Security Council, may concern themselves with factual disputes and legal issues,

[1] E.g. UN Charter, Arts 2(3)–(4), 33.

[2] For an excellent overview: Kingsbury, in Crawford & Koskenniemi (eds), *Cambridge Companion to International Law* (2012) 203.

[3] The qualification is necessary because some international courts and tribunals now have jurisdiction in 'mixed' cases, i.e. cases involving states and non-states including individuals and corporations. The PCIJ, created at a time when only states were considered international persons, was not one of these, nor is the ICJ which was modelled on it: ICJ Statute, Art 34. Not even the EU has standing before the ICJ, despite its exercising statal functions within the ICJ's area of subject-matter competence. For international human rights courts and committees: chapter 29.

[4] UN Charter, Chs VI–VII; Goodrich, Hambro & Simons, *Charter of the United Nations* (3rd edn, 1969); Simma (ed), 1–2 *The Charter of the United Nations* (2nd edn, 2002); Conforti, *The Law and Practice of the United Nations* (3rd edn, 2005).

although the basis for action remains political.[5] So also governments conducting nego-tiations with a view to settling disputes commonly take legal advice, and confidential legal advice may be weighty and reasonably objective.

2. DEVELOPMENT OF INTERNATIONAL DISPUTE SETTLEMENT

(A) ARBITRATION AND THE ORIGINS OF INTERNATIONAL DISPUTE SETTLEMENT

In both national and international legal history, the judicial process develops out of less formal administrative and political procedures. International practice has long included negotiation, good offices, and mediation as informal methods of settling dis-putes.[6] Treaties establishing machinery for peaceful settlement frequently provide for these, as well as conciliation. Conciliation is distinct from mediation and emerged from the commissions of inquiry provided for in the Hague Conventions for the Pacific Settlement of International Disputes of 1899[7] and 1907[8] and the commissions which figured in the series of arbitration treaties concluded by the US in 1913 and 1914 (the Bryan treaties).[9] Conciliation has a semi-judicial aspect, since the commission of persons empowered has to elucidate the facts, may hear the parties and must make proposals for a settlement, which is normally non-binding.

Before conciliation was established, interstate arbitration had long been a part of the scene, having the same political provenance. However, arbitration evolved as a sophis-ticated procedure similar to judicial settlement. The salience of arbitration increased considerably after the successful *Alabama Claims* arbitration of 1872 between the US and Great Britain.[10] At this stage, arbitral tribunals were often invited by the parties to resort to 'principles of justice and equity' and to propose extra-legal compromises.

---

[5] Higgins, *Development* (1963); Peck, *The United Nations as a Dispute Settlement System* (1996); Merrills, *International Dispute Settlement* (5th edn, 2011) ch 10. On judicial aspects of the SC: White & Saul, in French, Saul & White (eds), *International Law and Dispute Settlement* (2010) 191.

[6] UN, *Handbook on the Peaceful Settlement of Disputes between States* (1992); Merrills (5th edn, 2011) 1–115. On conciliation: Cot, *International Conciliation* (1972); Bowett (1983) 180 Hague *Recueil* 169, 185–90; Koopmans, *Diplomatic Dispute Settlement* (2008). On commission of inquiry: Bar-Yaacov, *The Handling of International Disputes by Means of Inquiry* (1974) 85; For hybrid forms: *Re Letelier and Moffitt* (1992) 88 ILR 727; *Rainbow Warrior* (1986) 74 ILR 241: *Beagle Channel* (1977) 52 ILR 93.

[7] 29 July 1899, 187 CTS 410.

[8] 18 October 1907, 205 CTS 233.

[9] E.g. France–United States, Treaty for the Advancement of Peace, 15 September 1914, 10 *AJIL Supp* 278. Further: Finch (1916) 10 *AJIL* 882; Scott, *Treaties for the Advancement of Peace between the United States and Other Powers* (1920); Schlochauer, 'Bryan Treaties (1913–14)' (undated) *MPEPIL*.

[10] Moore, 1 *Digest* 653. Further: Cook, *The 'Alabama' Claims* (1975); Bingham (2005) 54 *ICLQ* 1.

However, by the end of the nineteenth century, arbitration was primarily if not exclusively associated with a process of decision according to law, supported by appropriate procedural standards. The contrasts with judicial settlement (as it developed post-1922) are principally these: the agency of decision in arbitration would be designated 'arbitral tribunal' or 'umpire';[11] the tribunal consists of an odd number, usually with national representatives; the tribunal is usually created to deal with a particular dispute or class of disputes; and there is more flexibility than in a system of compulsory jurisdiction with a standing court.[12] Due to this distinction, states see arbitration as a suitable mechanism for settling a certain class of dispute and indeed, of the cases referred to interstate arbitration, the majority have concerned territorial or quasi-territorial disputes.[13]

(B) THE IDEA OF JUDICIAL SETTLEMENT OF INTERNATIONAL DISPUTES

In the modern period there is no sharp line between arbitration and judicial settlement: the latter category is applicable to any international tribunal settling disputes involving states in accordance with international law. Moreover, the permanent institutions developed historically from arbitral experience. It is now common to see the development of integrated systems of dispute resolution which include international 'courts' of relatively formal jurisdiction and process, whilst reserving certain *sui generis* questions for arbitral tribunals convened under the procedures of the same system, for example, in the procedures of UN Convention on the Law of the Sea (UNCLOS)[14] and the WTO. But independent systems exist as expressed through the actions of many ad hoc arbitral tribunals,[15] mixed commissions and semi-permanent specialized tribunals.[16]

The international character of the tribunal derives from organization and jurisdiction. A national tribunal may apply international law: when it does so it is no longer simply an organ of the national legal system, but it does not act independently of the

---

[11] There is no fixed terminology; judicial functions are carried out by agencies labelled 'mixed claims commissions', or even 'conciliation commissions' (as in the case of the Conciliation Commissions set up to hear claims arising under Art 83 of the Treaty of Peace with Italy, 15 September 1947, 42 UNTS 3).

[12] Collier & Lowe, *The Settlement of Disputes in International Law* (1999) 31–5; Merrills (5th edn, 2011) ch 5.

[13] E.g. *Argentina-Chile Frontier (La Palena)* (1966) 38 ILR 10; *Rann of Kutch* (1968) 50 ILR 2; *Beagle Channel* (1977) 52 ILR 93; *Delimitation of the Continental Shelf (UK v France)* (1977) 54 ILR 6; *Delimitation of the Continental Shelf (UK v France)* (1978) 54 ILR 139; *Guinea–Guinea-Bissau* (1985) 77 ILR 635; *Taba* (1988) 80 ILR 224; *St Pierre and Miquelon* (1992) 95 ILR 645; *Red Sea Islands (Eritrea v Yemen)* (1998) 114 ILR 1; *Barbados v Trinidad and Tobago* (2006) 139 ILR 449.

[14] 10 December 1982, 1833 UNTS 3.

[15] For modern arbitrations not involving boundary delimitation: *Lake Lanoux* (1957) 24 ILR 101; *Air Services Agreement of 27 March 1946* (1978) 54 ILR 304; *Belgium, France, Switzerland, UK & USA v Germany (Young Loan Arbitration)* (1980) 59 ILR 494.

[16] Generally: Charney (1998) 271 Hague *Recueil* 101, 104–382.

national system, it is not settling issues between legal persons on the international plane, and its jurisdiction does not rest on international agreement.

3. THE INTERNATIONAL COURT OF JUSTICE[17]

(A) HISTORICAL OVERVIEW: THE PERMANENT COURT OF INTERNATIONAL JUSTICE

The 'World Court' is the label commonly applied to the Permanent Court of International Justice and the International Court of Justice, the latter a new creation in 1945 but substantially a continuation of the earlier body. The Permanent Court began to function in 1922 but as a new standing tribunal it developed from previous experience. Arbitral practice contributed to the development in two ways. Its positive influence shows in certain similarities between the Court and arbitral practice: the institution of national judges, the use of special jurisdictional agreements, the power to decide *ex aequo et bono*, and the application of some basic principles; for example, that, absent contrary agreement, an international tribunal may determine its own jurisdiction.[18] The negative influence was more decisive, since criticism of the Permanent Court of Arbitration, that it was not a standing court and could not develop a jurisprudence, led to a draft Convention Relative to the Creation of a Permanent Court of Arbitral Justice at the Second Hague Peace Conference in 1907.[19] The Convention remained unadopted because of disagreement on the number of judges, some representatives demanding as many judges as there were states members of the Court.[20]

In 1920 the Council of the League of Nations appointed an advisory committee of jurists to prepare a draft Statute for a Permanent Court of International Justice.[21] The draft Statute sprang from three sources: the draft Convention of 1907, a proposal of neutral states for compulsory jurisdiction, and the Root–Phillimore plan for the election of judges. The draft Statute provided for compulsory jurisdiction, but in the Council and the Assembly of the League the great powers and their supporters resisted this successfully. In the Assembly, however, a weak compromise was agreed

---

[17] Generally: Lowe & Fitzmaurice (eds), *Jennings Essays* (1996); Eyffinger, *The International Court of Justice 1946–1996* (1996); Collier & Lowe (1999) ch 7; Rosenne, 1–4 *The Law and Procedure of the International Court 1920–2005* (4th edn, 2006); Zimmermann, Tomuschat & Oellers-Frahm (eds), *The Statute of the International Court of Justice* (2006); Merrills (5th edn, 2011) chs 6–7.

[18] *Nottebohm (Liechtenstein v Guatemala)*, Preliminary Objection, ICJ Reports 1953 p 111, 119.

[19] Scott, *The Project Relative to a Court of Arbitral Justice (No 34)* (1920) 89–98.

[20] Scott (1908) 2 *AJIL* 772; Hudson, *The Permanent Court of International Justice 1920–1942* (1943) 80–4. Further on the PCIJ: Spiermann, *International Legal Argument in the Permanent Court of International Justice* (2005).

[21] Covenant of the League of Nations, Art 14.

in the form of the 'optional clause'. As amended, the Statute came into force in 1921.[22] However, the Statute contained no provision for its own amendment and all changes required unanimous approval, a slow procedure. After the Second World War the Permanent Court could have been revived, but the San Francisco conference decided to create a new court, two important considerations being the dislike of bodies related to the League of Nations felt by the US and USSR, and the problem of amending the Statute if the old Court were to be related to the United Nations.[23]

The new court has a much closer relationship with the UN. The UN Charter provides (Article 92) that the International Court is 'the principal judicial organ of the United Nations'; all UN members are *ipso facto* parties to the Statute of the Court (Article 93). But in other respects the new Court is a continuation of the old: the Statute is virtually the same; jurisdiction under instruments referring to the old Court has been transferred to the new; and there is continuity of jurisprudence.

(B) ORGANIZATION OF THE COURT

A crucial issue for the creation of a standing international tribunal in which states may have confidence is judicial appointment.[24] The Statute emphasizes the independence of judges once appointed. No judge may exercise any political or administrative function, engage in any other professional occupation (Article 16(1)), act as agent or counsel in any case, or participate in the decision of a case with which he or she has previously been connected in another capacity (Article 17; see also Article 24). Dismissal requires the unanimous opinion of the other judges (Article 18(1)). When engaged on Court business members have diplomatic privileges and immunities (Article 19). Salaries are fixed by the General Assembly, may not be decreased during the term of office, and are free of all taxation (Article 32).

The present Court has 15 judges. Five judges are elected every three years. Article 2 of the Statute provides that 'the Court shall be composed of a body of independent judges, elected regardless of their nationality from among persons of high moral character, who possess the qualifications required in their respective countries for appointment to the highest judicial offices, or are jurisconsults of recognized competence in international law'. This formula takes in professors, professional lawyers, and civil service appointees: many judges have been advisers to national foreign ministries. In other provisions of the Statute the question of nationality acquires significance. No two members may be nationals of the same state (Article 3(1)), and Article 9 requires electors to bear in mind 'that in the body as a whole the representation of the main forms of civilization and of the principal legal systems of the world should be

---

[22] Protocol of Signature to the Statute of the Permanent Court of International Justice, 16 December 1920, 6 LNTS 379.

[23] Hudson (1957) 51 *AJIL* 569; 1 Rosenne (4th edn, 2006) 182–8.

[24] Generally: Lauterpacht, *Function of Law* (1933, repr 2011) 219–49; 1 Rosenne (4th edn, 2006) 358–97.

assured'.[25] The principle stated is unimpeachable but practical application is difficult; the system of election ensures the composition of the Court reflects voting strength and political alliances in the Security Council and General Assembly. The permanent members of the Security Council normally have judges on the Court. But judges are elected as individuals and do not represent their states of origin.

The electoral system is based on the Root–Phillimore plan of 1920 and involves independent, simultaneous voting by the Security Council and the General Assembly. States which are parties to the Statute of the Court but not UN members are permitted to nominate and elect, specially augmenting the General Assembly.[26] Candidates must obtain an absolute majority in both organs to be elected (Statute Article 10).[27] In practice political calculations feature prominently, and the attitude of judges in particular cases has occasionally affected the voting when they are considered for re-election. But it is difficult to see a way out: the Court's existence is apparently conditioned on a political basis for elections.

Article 31 of the Statute provides that a party to a case has an effective right to representation by a national judge, and, if there is no judge of its nationality, by a judge ad hoc (who may be of some other nationality). The judge ad hoc is appointed by the party concerned and commonly (though not invariably) supports its view of the case when on the bench.[28]

(C) JURISDICTION IN CONTENTIOUS CASES[29]

The Court has jurisdiction in contentious cases only between states and only on the basis of consent.[30] The Court has often referred to the fact that its jurisdiction depends on the will of the parties.[31] This principle, reflected in Article 36 of the Statute, rests on international practice in dispute settlement and is a corollary of the sovereign equality

---

[25] Also: *Rules of the Court*, 1 July 1978, ICJ Acts & Docs No 5 (1990) (ICJ Rules), Art 7(2).

[26] GA Res 264(III), 8 October 1948.

[27] For procedures to deal with deadlock: ICJ Statute, Arts 11–12. Informal consultation is used to obviate resort to a joint conference.

[28] On the role of a judge ad hoc: *Application of the Convention on the Prevention and Punishment of the Crime of Genocide (Bosnia and Herzegovina v Yugoslavia)*, Provisional Measures, ICJ Reports 1993 p 325, 408–9 (Judge ad hoc Lauterpacht). Also: Schwebel (1999) 48 *ICLQ* 889; Collier & Lowe (1999) 130–1; 3 Rosenne (4th edn, 2006) 1079–109.

[29] Generally: Fitzmaurice (1958) 34 *BY* 1, 8–138; 2 Rosenne (4th edn, 2006) 505–948; Thirlway (1998) 69 *BY* 1; Thirlway (1999) 70 *BY* 1, 3–63; Thirlway (2000) 71 *BY* 71, 73–90; Thirlway (2001) 72 *BY* 37; Thirlway (2003) 74 *BY* 7; Thirlway (2005) 76 *BY* 1; Thirlway (2006) 77 *BY* 1; Thirlway (2007) 78 *BY* 17; Thirlway (2009) 80 *BY* 10.

[30] ICJ Statute, Art 34(1) provides: 'Only states may be parties in cases before the Court.'

[31] E.g. *Anglo-Iranian Oil Co (UK v Iran)*, Jurisdiction, ICJ Reports 1952 p 93, 102–3; *Monetary Gold removed from Rome in 1943 (Italy v France, UK and US)*, Preliminary Question, ICJ Reports 1954 p 19, 32; *Military and Paramilitary Activities in and against Nicaragua (US v Nicaragua)*, Jurisdiction and Admissibility, ICJ Reports 1984 p 392, 431; *Certain Phosphate Lands in Nauru (Nauru v Australia)*, Preliminary Objections, ICJ Reports 1992 p 240, 259–62; *East Timor (Portugal v Australia)*, ICJ Reports 1995 p 90, 101; *Fisheries Jurisdiction (Spain v Canada)*, Jurisdiction, ICJ Reports 1998 p 432, 453, 456. Further: Fitzmaurice (1958) 34 *BY* 1, 66–97; 2 Rosenne (4th edn, 2006) 549–62.

of states, in the absence of contrary provision. The competence of a tribunal vis-à-vis the merits of a claim may be challenged in various ways. Objections to jurisdiction strike at the competence of the tribunal to give rulings as to the admissibility of the claim or the merits. An objection to the admissibility of a claim, for example for non-exhaustion of local remedies, challenges the validity of a claim in a manner which is distinct from issues as to jurisdiction or merits. In practice, the Court may join certain preliminary objections to the merits provided that 'the objection does not possess, in the circumstances of the case, an exclusively preliminary character' (Rules Article 79(9)).[32] It may also decline jurisdiction on grounds of judicial propriety.[33]

States not parties to the Statute are not barred from the Court.[34] Article 35(2) provides that:

The conditions under which the Court shall be open to other states shall, subject to the special provisions contained in treaties in force, be laid down by the Security Council, but in no case shall such conditions place the parties in a position of inequality before the Court.

In the *Legality of the Use of Force* cases, the reference to 'special provisions contained in treaties in force' was read down to refer only to those treaties in force at the time the Statute was concluded.[35] Unlike the situation in 1921, there were in 1945 no such treaties.[36]

Thus access to the Court by non-members is controlled under Article 35(2) by the Security Council. In Security Council Resolution 9, it was provided that the Court would be open to a state which deposits with the Registrar of the Court a declaration by which it accepts the jurisdiction of the Court, undertakes to comply in good faith with any decision it may render and accepts all the obligations of a UN member under Charter Article 94.[37] That said, neither Article 35(2) nor Security Council Resolution 9 exclude the possibility that the Security Council may authorize a state to appear ad hoc before the Court without lodging the required declaration.[38]

Parties to the Statute do not thereby submit to the jurisdiction of the Court: further consent is required. But they are bound to accept the jurisdiction of the Court to

---

[32] *Right of Passage over Indian Territory (Portugal v India)*, Preliminary Objections, ICJ Reports 1957 p 125, 149–52; *Barcelona Traction, Light and Power Company Limited (Belgium v Spain)*, Preliminary Objections, ICJ Reports 1964 p 6, 41–7 (Judge Morelli, diss) 97–115; *Barcelona Traction*, Second Phase, ICJ Reports 1970 p 51, 57 (Judge Bustamante y Rivero); 110–13 (Judge Fitzmaurice); 115 (Judge Tanaka); 286–7 (Judge Ammoun); 356–7 (Judge Riphagen, diss). Also: Fitzmaurice (1958) 34 *BY* 1, 23–5.

[33] *Northern Cameroons (Cameroon v UK)*, Preliminary Objections, ICJ Reports 1963 p 15.

[34] Further: 2 Rosenne (4th edn, 2006) 609–14.

[35] *Legality of Use of Force (Serbia and Montenegro v Belgium)*, Preliminary Objections, ICJ Reports 2004 p 279, 322–4.

[36] *Case Concerning Application of the Convention on the Prevention and Punishment of the Crime of Genocide (Croatia v Serbia) Preliminary Objections*, pleadings, www.icj-cij.org/docket/files/118/14526.pdf, paras 26, 44–5, 68–9. The Court took another route: ICJ Reports 2008 p 412.

[37] SC Res 9 (1946) §§1–2. These requirements have been incorporated into ICJ Rules, Art 41. Further: 2 Rosenne (4th edn, 2006) 614–20.

[38] E.g. *Corfu Channel (UK v Albania)*, Preliminary Objection, ICJ Reports 1947 p 15, 53.

determine its own jurisdiction (Article 36(6)).[39] Further, they are subject to the Court's jurisdiction to indicate interim measures of protection (or 'provisional measures') to preserve the respective rights of the parties (Article 41).[40] Unless it is apparent that there is no consent to the jurisdiction, the Court will assume the power to indicate such measures, without prejudice to the question of its jurisdiction to deal with the merits of the case.[41] In *LaGrand*, the Court established that such interim measures are binding.[42] Lastly, under Article 62 the Court may permit third-party intervention in cases in which a state has a legal interest which may be affected by the decision in the case.[43]

(i) Matters specially provided for in the Charter

Article 36(1) of the Statute includes within the jurisdiction 'all matters specially provided for in the Charter of the United Nations'. This was inserted in the (ultimately frustrated) expectation that the Charter would provide for compulsory jurisdiction. In *Corfu Channel* the UK argued that Article 36(1) of the Statute could be referred to Article 36(1) and (3) of the Charter, which provide for reference of legal disputes to the Court on the recommendation of the Security Council, and that a recommendation involved a decision which was binding in accordance with Article 25 of the Charter. The Court did consider the point, but in a joint separate opinion seven judges rejected the argument, *inter alia* on the ground that the term 'recommendation' was non-compulsory.[44]

(ii) Transferred jurisdiction: Articles 36(5), 37

The Statute of the Permanent Court provided for jurisdiction on the basis of compromissory clauses in treaties or conventions. With respect to these Article 37 of the ICJ Statute provides:

Whenever a treaty or convention in force provides for reference of a matter to a tribunal to have been instituted by the League of Nations, or to the Permanent Court of International

---

[39] *Nottebohm*, Preliminary Objection, ICJ Reports 1953 p 111, 119–20, where the Court regarded this power as grounded in international law apart from any explicit provision in the Statute. Further: Fitzmaurice (1958) 34 *BY* 1, 25–31; Berlia (1955) 88 Hague *Recueil* 105, 109–54; Crawford (2009) 1 *JIDS* 1, 15–20. On the power of the Court to determine the jurisdiction of another international tribunal: *Ambatielos (Greece v UK)*, ICJ Reports 1953 p 10; Fitzmaurice (1958) 34 *BY* 1, 31–66.

[40] Generally: Rosenne, *Provisional Measures in International Law* (2005).

[41] *Anglo-Iranian Oil Co*, Order of 5 July 1951, ICJ Reports 1951 p 89, 92–3, 96 (Judges Winarski & Badawi, diss); *Nicaragua*, Order of 10 May 1984, ICJ Reports 1984 p 169, 179–80; *Interhandel (Switzerland v UK)*, ICJ Reports 1959 p 6, 117 (Judge Lauterpacht, diss). Further: Fitzmaurice (1958) 34 *BY* 1, 107–19; Lauterpacht, *Development* (1958) 110–13; Rosenne, *Provisional Measures in International Law* (2005) 91–4; 3 Rosenne (4th edn, 2006) 1382.

[42] *LaGrand (US v Germany)* ICJ Reports 2001 p 466, 501–6. Thirlway (2001) 72 *BY* 37, 111–26; Jennings, in Valencia-Ospina (ed), 1 *The Law and Practice of International Tribunals* (2002) 13; Rosenne (2005) 34–40; 3 Rosenne (4th edn, 2006) 1375–8.

[43] On intervention under the ICJ Statute, Arts 62 and 63: Fitzmaurice (1958) 34 *BY* 1, 124–9; Chinkin (1986) 80 *AJIL* 495; Chinkin, *Third Parties in International Law* (1993) 147–217; 3 Rosenne (4th edn, 2006) 1439–506.

[44] Preliminary Objection, ICJ Reports 1948 p 15, 31–2. Jurists generally agree with the joint separate opinion: Fitzmaurice (1952) 29 *BY* 1, 31–2, 44; cf Rosenne (4th edn, 2006) 670–1.

Justice, the matter shall, as between the parties to the present Statute, be referred to the International Court of Justice.

Two limitations are prominent: the treaty or convention must be 'in force' between the litigating states, and all parties to the dispute must be parties to the new Statute. In *Nicaragua*, the Court held that the Nicaraguan Declaration of 1929 constituted a valid acceptance of jurisdiction by virtue of Nicaragua's ratification of the Charter in 1945, despite the fact that the Declaration of 1929 had not previously acquired binding force.[45]

(iii) Consent ad hoc: jurisdiction by special agreement

The consent of the parties may be given ad hoc to the Court's jurisdiction over a specific dispute. Normally, consent will take the form of a special agreement (*compromis*). But consent ad hoc may also arise where the plaintiff state has accepted the jurisdiction by a unilateral application followed by a separate act of consent by the other party.[46] Voluntary jurisdiction is thus not restricted by formal requirements: Article 36(1) says simply that 'the jurisdiction of the Court comprises all cases which the parties refer to it'. Special agreement is an attractive method of consenting to the Court's jurisdiction and has been regularly used.

(iv) Advance consent: treaties and conventions

Article 36(1) refers also to 'all matters specially provided for ... in treaties and conventions in force'.[47] A great many multilateral and bilateral treaties contain clauses granting jurisdiction in advance over disputes involving their interpretation or application.[48] Although the jurisdiction is likewise by consent of the parties, it can be described as 'compulsory' in the sense that binding agreement is given in advance of any dispute. However, the label 'compulsory jurisdiction' is often used to describe jurisdiction arising under Article 36(2) of the Statute.

(v) Advance consent: declarations under the optional clause[49]

Article 36(2) of the Statute, commonly referred to as the optional clause, provides as follows:

---

[45] Jurisdiction and Admissibility, ICJ Reports 1984 p 392, 397–411. For criticism: Crawford, 'Military and Paramilitary Activities in and against Nicaragua Case (Nicaragua v United States of America)' (2006) *MPEPIL*; Crawford (2012) 25 *LJIL* 471.

[46] *Corfu Channel*, Preliminary Objection, ICJ Reports 1947 p 15, 27–8.

[47] Unilateral suspension of a treaty does not render jurisdictional clauses inoperative: *Appeal relating to the Jurisdiction of the ICAO Council (India v Pakistan)*, ICJ Reports 1972 p 46, 53–4.

[48] For a list of treaties providing the Court with jurisdiction: www.icj-cij.org/jurisdiction/index.php?p1=5&p2=1&p3=4.

[49] Merrills (1979) 50 *BY* 87; Merrills (1993) 64 *BY* 197; Szafarz, *The Compulsory Jurisdiction of the International Court of Justice* (1994); Merrills, in Ando, McWhinney & Wolfrum (eds), 1 *Liber Amicorum Judge Shigeru Oda* (2002) 435; 2 Rosenne (4th edn, 2006) ch 12.

The States parties to the present Statute may at any time declare that they recognize as compulsory *ipso facto* and without special agreement, in relation to any other state accepting the same obligation, the jurisdiction of the Court in all legal disputes concerning:

(a) the interpretation of a treaty;

(b) any question of international law;

(c) the existence of any fact which, if established, would constitute a breach of an international obligation;

(d) the nature or extent of the reparation to be made for the breach of an international obligation.

Jurisdiction is accepted via unilateral declarations deposited with the Secretary-General, the declarant being bound to accept jurisdiction vis-à-vis any other declarant insofar as the acceptances coincide. On the principle of reciprocity, the lowest common factor in the two declarations is the basis for jurisdiction, and thus a respondent state can take advantage of a reservation or condition in the declaration of the applicant state.[50] The independent declarations are binding in that withdrawal is possible only in accordance with principles analogous to the law of treaties,[51] and they operate contractually with a suspensive condition, viz., the filing of an application by a state with a coincident declaration.[52] This involves acceptance of jurisdiction in advance for categories of disputes which are usually mere contingencies. The commitment in relation to any other state fulfilling the conditions of the Statute is usually described as compulsory jurisdiction, although, as with jurisdiction by treaty or convention, the basis is ultimately consensual.

The origin of the optional clause lay in a compromise, achieved in 1920 and maintained in 1945, between a system of true compulsory jurisdiction based on unilateral applications by claimants, and independent, treaty-based jurisdiction. The expectation was that a general system of compulsory jurisdiction would be generated as declarations multiplied. The conception was sound enough, but the conditions in which the system has functioned have reduced its effectiveness. In 1934 there were 42 declarations in force, reducing to 32 by 1955 but increasing since then to 67 as of 2012. This figure represents only a third of all independent states (193 are parties to the Statute).[53] The negative factors are principally the lack of governmental confidence in

---

[50] *Electricity Company of Sofia and Bulgaria* (1939) PCIJ Ser A/B No 77, 80–2; *Anglo-Iranian Oil Co,* Jurisdiction, ICJ Reports 1952 p 93, 103; *Certain Norwegian Loans (France v Norway)*, ICJ Reports 1957 p 9, 23–4; *Aegean Sea Continental Shelf (Greece v Turkey)*, ICJ Reports 1978 p 3, 37; *Fisheries Jurisdiction (Spain v Canada)*, Jurisdiction, ICJ Reports 1998 p 432, 454. Further: 2 Rosenne (4th edn, 2006) 731–7.

[51] *Nicaragua,* Jurisdiction, ICJ Reports 1984 p 392, 415–21, 466–7 (Judge Mosler); 547 (Judge Jennings); 620–8 (Judge Schwebel, diss). On the denunciation of declarations in general: 2 Rosenne (4th edn, 2006) 785–9.

[52] The declarations are valid without ratification, but may be made subject to ratification. They are registered as 'international agreements' under Art 102 of the Charter. On their interpretation: *Anglo-Iranian Oil Co,* Jurisdiction, ICJ Reports 1952 p 93, 103ff. On the question whether two optional clause declarations are a form of treaty *inter se*: *Nuclear Tests (Australia v France)*, ICJ Reports 1974 p 253, 352–6 (Judges Onyeama, Dillard, Jiménez de Aréchaga & Waldock, diss).

[53] Generally: Merrills (1993) 64 *BY* 197; Merrills, in Kaikobad & Bohlander (eds), *International Law and Power* (2009) 431.

international adjudication, the practice of making declarations subject to various reservations and conditions, frequently arbitrary and ambiguous, and the tactical advantages of staying out of the system.

(vi) Consent *post hoc: forum prorogatum*

Lauterpacht wrote that 'exercise of jurisdiction by virtue of the principle of *forum prorogatum* takes place whenever, after the initiation of proceedings by joint or unilateral application, jurisdiction is exercised with regard either to the entire dispute or to some aspects of it as the result of an agreement, express or implied'.[54] The principle operates because the Statute and rules of court as interpreted contain no mandatory rules as to the formal basis on which the applicant founds jurisdiction, nor as to the form of consent. Consent may take the form of an agreement on the basis of successive acts of the parties, and the institution of proceedings by unilateral application is not confined to cases of compulsory jurisdiction.[55] Thus, in *Corfu Channel*,[56] Albania accepted jurisdiction in a communication to the Court. Informal agreement, agreement inferred from conduct, or formal agreement, in each case *after* the initiation of proceedings, may result in prorogated jurisdiction. More recent examples include two cases where France informed the Court that it consented to jurisdiction.[57] However, the Court will not accept jurisdiction unless there is real, not merely apparent, consent.[58] Resort to technical constructions in order to promote jurisdiction in particular cases may discourage appearances before the Court.

(vii) Jurisdiction to decide *ex aequo et bono*[59]

Article 38(2) of the Statute gives the Court power to decide a case *ex aequo et bono* if the parties agree. This provision qualifies Article 38(1), which refers to the function of the Court as being to decide 'in accordance with international law' such disputes as are submitted to it. The power to decide *ex aequo et bono* has not yet been exercised, and is not easily reconciled with the judicial character of the Court.

(D) JURISDICTIONAL EXCEPTIONS AND RESERVATIONS

(i) Matters of domestic jurisdiction

A plea that the issue concerned is a matter of domestic jurisdiction may appear as a preliminary objection or as a plea on the merits: strictly speaking the plea is available,

---

[54] Lauterpacht (1958) 103.

[55] Generally: 2 Rosenne (4th edn, 2006) 672–6.

[56] Preliminary Objection, ICJ Reports 1948 p 15, 27. But the institution of proceedings was based on a special agreement.

[57] *Certain Criminal Proceedings in France (Republic of the Congo v France)*, Provisional Measure, ICJ Reports 2003 p 102, 103–4; *Certain Questions of Mutual Assistance in Criminal Matters (Djibouti v France)*, ICJ Reports 2008 p 177, 181.

[58] *Ambatielos*, Preliminary Objection, ICJ Reports 1952 p 28, 39; *Anglo-Iranian Oil Co*, Jurisdiction, ICJ Reports 1952 p 93, 114.

[59] Lauterpacht (1958) 213–23; Fitzmaurice (1958) 34 *BY* 1, 132–7; 1 Rosenne (4th edn, 2006) 570–6.

apart from any reservation on the subject, in accordance with general principles of international law.

One form of this reservation has created particular controversy. In 1946 the US deposited a declaration with a reservation of 'disputes with regard to matters which are essentially within the domestic jurisdiction of the United States of America as determined by the United States of America'. Seven other states have used this 'automatic' reservation,[60] which seems incompatible with the Statute, contradicting the Court's power to determine its own jurisdiction and not accepting genuinely jurisdiction *ante hoc*.[61]

(ii) Time limits and reservations *ratione temporis*

Declarations may be expressed to be for a term of years.[62] Some are expressed to be terminable after a period of notice; some immediately. While a power of termination immediately on notice weakens the system of compulsory jurisdiction, it is not incompatible with the Statute.[63] The Court has held that, absent express provision, reasonable notice of termination may be given.[64] Once the Court is seized of a case on the basis of declarations in force at the date of application, however, subsequent expiry of a declaration or other basis of jurisdiction does not affect its jurisdiction in that case.[65]

(iii) Reservation of past disputes

Reservation of past disputes is common, and the reservation may be extended, as in the 'Belgian formula', which refers to all disputes arising after a certain date 'with regard to situations or facts subsequent to the said date'. Disputes often have a long history, and this formula is ambitious. The Court has taken the view that the limitation takes in only situations or facts that are the source, the real cause, of the dispute.[66]

---

[60] Generally: Briggs (1958) 93 Hague *Recueil* 223, 328–63; Gross (1962) 56 *AJIL* 357; Collier & Lowe (1999) 143–6.

[61] The Court has avoided the issue, as in *Norwegian Loans,* ICJ Reports 1957 p 9, and *Interhandel,* ICJ Reports 1959 p 6. A number of judges have held the reservation invalid: ICJ Reports 1957 p 9, 42ff (Judge Lauterpacht), 68–70 (Judge Guerrero); ICJ Reports 1959 p 6, 55–9 (Judge Spender), 76–8 (Judge Klaestad), 92–4 (Judge Armand-Ugon). But cf Crawford (1979) 50 *BY* 63, arguing for the validity of the reservation.

[62] 2 Rosenne (4th edn, 2006) 748–51.

[63] Cf the view of the Court on an analogous reservation in *Right of Passage*, Preliminary Objections, ICJ Reports 1957 p 125, 143–4. Further: Briggs (1958) 93 Hague *Recueil* 223, 273–7; 2 Rosenne (4th edn, 2006) 753–66.

[64] *Nicaragua*, Jurisdiction and Admissibility, ICJ Reports 1984 p 392, 418–20, 466–7 (Judge Mosler), 550 (Judge Jennings), 620–8 (Judge Schwebel, diss).

[65] *Nottebohm*, Preliminary Objection, ICJ Reports 1953 p 111, 122–3. Also: 2 Rosenne (4th edn, 2006) 939–45.

[66] *Right of Passage*, ICJ Reports 1960 p 6, 33–6; *Electricity Company of Sofia and Bulgaria* (1939) PCIJ Ser A/B No 77, 82; *Phosphates in Morocco* (1938) PCIJ Ser A/B No 74, 23–4.

(E) THE ADVISORY JURISDICTION[67]

Article 65(1) of the Statute provides that the Court 'may give an advisory opinion on any legal question at the request of whatever body may be authorized by or in accordance with the Charter ... to make such a request.' Charter Article 96 empowers the General Assembly and Security Council so to request, and provides that the General Assembly may authorize other organs and specialized agencies to do so.[68] The advisory jurisdiction aims to assist the political organs in settling disputes and provides authoritative guidance on points of law arising from the function of organs and specialized agencies. Thus some requests for opinions relate to specific disputes or situations, for example, the various opinions relating to South West Africa (Namibia). Some relate to inter-state disputes referred to the Court without the consent of all parties;[69] such requests utilize political organs as an indirect means of seizing the Court of precise disputes. Others, as in the *Reservations* case,[70] have involved general and abstract questions. The origin of many requests in actual disputes has given a contentious aspect to advisory proceedings. Thus Article 68 of the Statute provides that the provisions applicable in contentious cases shall guide the Court 'to the extent to which it recognizes them to be applicable'.[71] In *Status of Eastern Carelia*[72] the Council of the League of Nations asked for an opinion on a dispute between Finland and the USSR. The USSR objected and the Court refused jurisdiction on the ground that the requesting organ was not competent to seek an opinion in the circumstances: no state can be compelled to submit disputes to a tribunal without its consent, and the USSR was not bound by the Covenant. In the *Namibia*,[73] *Western Sahara*,[74] and *Wall*[75] opinions, *Eastern Carelia* was distinguished on the basis that the situations involved did not constitute an interstate dispute, and the political organ making the request was concerned in the exercise of *its own* functions under the Charter, and not the settlement of a particular dispute.[76]

---

[67] Higgins, in Lowe & Fitzmaurice (1996) 567; 2 Rosenne (4th edn, 2006) 949–1020. Earlier: Lauterpacht, (1958) 107–10, 248–50, 352–8.

[68] For a list of organisations and agencies authorised to request advisory opinions: www.icj-cij.org/jurisdiction/index.php?p1=5&p2=2&p3=1.

[69] *Legal Consequences for States of the Continued Presence of South Africa in Namibia (South West Africa) notwithstanding Security Council Resolution 276 (1970)*, ICJ Reports 1971 p 16, 24; *Western Sahara*, ICJ Reports 1975 p 12, 24–5; *Legal Consequences of the Construction of a Wall in the Occupied Palestinian Territory*, ICJ Reports 2004 p 136, 157–9. Also: *Interpretation of Peace Treaties with Bulgaria, Hungary and Romania*, ICJ Reports 1950 p 65.

[70] *Reservations to the Convention on the Prevention and Punishment of the Crime of Genocide*, ICJ Reports 1951 p 15. Here the issue was the conditions under which reservations to multilateral conventions could be made.

[71] Art 83 of the ICJ Rules provides for appointment of judges ad hoc if the request concerns 'a legal question actually pending between two or more States'.

[72] (1923) PCIJ Ser B No 5. In *Peace Treaties*, ICJ Reports 1950 p 65, the Court distinguished *Eastern Carelia*, *inter alia* by emphasizing its duty to comply with the request of another organ of the United Nations.

[73] ICJ Reports 1971 p 16, 23–4.

[74] ICJ Reports 1975 p 12, 24–6.

[75] ICJ Reports 2004 p 136, 157–9.

[76] Further: Waldock, *Aspects of the Advisory Jurisdiction of the International Court of Justice* (1976) 3–10.

There is no separate proceeding to deal with preliminary objections to advisory opinions, as there is in contentious proceedings, but objections arise frequently and relate both to jurisdiction as such and to questions of propriety. Objections might involve the incapacity of the requesting body[77] or concern the subject-matter of the request, as where a plea of domestic jurisdiction is made.[78] The Court refused a request by the World Health Organization (WHO) for an opinion on the legality of nuclear weapons on the basis that the question was not 'within the scope of the activities' of the WHO;[79] although it did provide an opinion addressing effectively the same issue when asked by the General Assembly.[80]

In practice objections have often challenged the Court's capacity to deal with political questions. Article 65 of the Statute refers to 'any legal question', and the Court has taken the view that, however controversial and far reaching in their implications, issues of treaty interpretation, arising in the context of the Charter, are legal questions.[81] As was said in the *Kosovo* Opinion:

[T]he Court has repeatedly stated that the fact that a question has political aspects does not suffice to deprive it of its character as a legal question…Whatever its political aspects, the Court cannot refuse to respond to the legal elements of a question which invites it to discharge an essentially judicial task, namely, in the present case, an assessment of an act by reference to international law. The Court has also made clear that, in determining the jurisdictional issue of whether it is confronted with a legal question, it is not concerned with the political nature of the motives which may have inspired the request or the political implications which its opinion might have…[82]

As the Court is unwilling to decline jurisdiction by adverting to the political implications of opinions, the issue becomes one of propriety. In the *Admissions*[83] and the *Expenses*[84] opinions, the Court dealt with issues of interpretation which had considerable political ramifications. Significantly, the organs concerned were unable to act on these two opinions. In refusing to decline requests by virtue of its discretion over advisory jurisdiction, the Court has reiterated that as it is an organ of the UN a request for an advisory opinion should not, in principle, be refused.[85] Furthermore, the *Eastern*

---

[77] As in *Eastern Carelia* (1923) PCIJ Ser B No 5; *Peace Treaties*, ICJ Reports 1950 p 65.

[78] *Peace Treaties*, ICJ Reports 1950 p 65, 70.

[79] *Legality of the Use by a State of Nuclear Weapons in Armed Conflict*, ICJ Reports 1996 p 66, 81.

[80] *Legality of the Threat or Use of Nuclear Weapons*, ICJ Reports 1996 p 226.

[81] *Conditions of Admission of a State to the United Nations (Article 4 of the Charter)*, ICJ Reports 1948 p 57, 61; *Competence of the General Assembly for the Admission of a State to the United Nations*, ICJ Reports 1950 p 4, 6–7; *Certain Expenses of the United Nations (Article 7, paragraph 2 of the Charter)*, ICJ Reports 1962 p 151, 155. At the San Francisco conference it was decided not to grant a power to settle disputes on interpretation of the Charter: 13 UNCIO, 668–9, 709–10. Also: *Reservations*, ICJ Reports 1951 p 15, 20.

[82] *Accordance with International Law of the Unilateral Declaration of Independence in respect of Kosovo*, Advisory Opinion of 22 July 2010, §27.

[83] *(First) Admissions*, ICJ Reports 1948 p 57. Also: *(Second) Admissions*, ICJ Reports 1950 p 4.

[84] *Certain Expenses*, ICJ Reports 1962 p 151.

[85] *Peace Treaties*, ICJ Reports 1950 p 65, 71–2; *Reservations*, ICJ Reports 1951 p 15, 19; *Judgments of the Administrative Tribunal of the ILO upon Complaints Made against UNESCO*, ICJ Reports 1956 p 77, 86; *Certain Expenses*, ICJ Reports 1962 p 151, 155; *Kosovo*, Advisory Opinion of 22 July 2010, §30.

Carelia principle, that the matter concerned a dispute between two states and jurisdiction could not be exercised without their consent, can be advanced as an issue both of jurisdiction and of propriety.[86]

(F) AN EVALUATION OF THE COURT[87]

In the period 1922–46 the Permanent Court dealt with 33 contentious cases and 28 advisory opinions; from 1946 to June 2012 the International Court has dealt with approximately 58 judgments on the merits, 23 preliminary objections, eight judgments on jurisdiction and admissibility, and 30 requests for provisional measures, as well as 26 requests for advisory opinions. As of June 2012, there are 13 contentious cases pending. The tempo of the Court has fluctuated since 1945, and acceptance of compulsory jurisdiction under the optional clause has been slow to develop. Several factors explain state reluctance to resort to the Court: the political fact that hauling another state before the Court is often regarded as unfriendly; the greater suitability of other tribunals and other methods of review for regional and technical matters; the general conditions of international relations; and a preference for the flexibility of arbitration versus compulsory jurisdiction. Given the conditions of its existence, the Court has made a reasonable contribution to the maintenance of civilized methods of settling disputes, but it has not been prominent in the business of keeping the peace; indeed, the provisions of the Charter do not place emphasis on the role of the Court. In certain respects, however, the Court has been influential—in the development of international law as a whole and in the giving of advisory opinions on the interpretation of the Charter[88] and other aspects of the law of international organizations. When, in its advisory opinions, the Court has pronounced on the interpretation of the Charter, it has pronounced boldly on political issues (which did not surrender such character because they were also legal issues), including most recently in the *Kosovo* advisory opinion.[89] Its decisions on land and maritime boundary disputes have mostly found acceptance.

The work of the Court in the last quarter century has been characterized by a variety of elements. In the first place, the number of contentious cases before the Court has significantly increased, despite a number of disputes being referred to ad hoc arbitral tribunals. Many of the new cases have been based upon special agreements. There have also been cases initiated by unilateral application and a number of applications

---

[86] *Peace Treaties*, ICJ Reports 1950 p 65, 70–1. Further: Gross (1967) 121 Hague *Recueil* 313, 355–70.

[87] Generally: Gross (ed), *The Future of the International Court of Justice* (1976); Damrosch (ed), *The International Court of Justice at a Crossroads* (1987); Lowe & Fitzmaurice (1996); Bowett et al (eds), *The International Court of Justice* (1997); Muller, Raic & Thuránsky (eds), *The International Court of Justice* (1997); Peck & Lee (eds), *Increasing the Effectiveness of the International Court of Justice* (1997); Jennings (1997) 68 *BY* 1; Higgins (2001) 50 *ICLQ* 121; Higgins (2003) 52 *ICLQ* 1; Schulte, *Compliance with Decisions of the International Court of Justice* (2004); Kooijmans (2007) *ICLQ* 741.

[88] *Reparation for Injuries Suffered in the Service of the United Nations*, ICJ Reports 1949 p 174; *(First) Admissions*, ICJ Reports 1948 p 57; *(Second) Admissions*, ICJ Reports 1950 p 4; *Voting Procedure on Questions relating to Reports and Petitions concerning the Territory of South West Africa*, ICJ Reports 1955 p 67; *Certain Expenses*, ICJ Reports 1962 p 151; *Namibia*, ICJ Reports 1971 p 16.

[89] Advisory Opinion of 22 July 2010, §27.

for permission to intervene in existing proceedings. In recent years the Court has had a full calendar of cases, a pattern likely to continue.

4. OTHER INTERNATIONAL COURTS AND TRIBUNALS

(A) INTERSTATE ARBITRATION

(i) The Permanent Court of Arbitration[90]

The precursor of 'modern' international tribunals is an institution, the Permanent Court of Arbitration (PCA), which is not a court and does not, itself, arbitrate, but which has endured and adapted. Until 1920 the PCA was the major organization for arbitration, but was then largely replaced by the Permanent Court of International Justice. It was established under the Hague Convention for the Pacific Settlement of International Disputes of 1899[91] as an arbitration secretariat and mechanism. The basis of the 'Court' is an arbitral panel to which parties may nominate four persons. When parties to the Convention agree to submit a dispute to the PCA, each appoints two arbitrators from the panel, and the four arbitrators select an umpire. Thus a tribunal is constituted only to hear a particular case.

Between 1900 and 1932, 20 cases were heard, but then occurred almost seven decades of hibernation. Recently, however, the PCA has reinvented itself, adopting a series of new arbitral rules and hosting a significant number of arbitrations, interstate and other.[92] Under the UNCITRAL Arbitration Rules, the Secretary-General of the PCA may, absent agreement by the parties, designate an appointing authority for the purposes of a private arbitration.[93]

(ii) International claims and compensation bodies[94]

Periodically ad hoc dispute resolution bodies have been created to assess claims and compensation between states.[95] Such bodies first became common with the 'mixed commissions' of the late eighteenth to early nineteenth centuries. Although typically

---

[90] Permanent Court of Arbitration, *Basic Documents: Conventions, Rules, Model Clauses and Guidelines* (1998); Ando, 'Permanent Court of Arbitration (PCA)' (2006) *MPEPIL*.

[91] 29 July 1899, 187 CTS 410. Most states supporting the PCA became parties to the 1899 Convention. The 1907 Convention, which has received few ratifications, is not very different: 18 October 1907, 205 CTS 233.

[92] PCA Optional Rules for Arbitrating Disputes between Two States, *PCA Basic Documents* (1998) 43; PCA Optional Rules for Arbitrating Disputes between Two Parties of Which Only One Is a State, *PCA Basic Documents* (1998) 69; PCA Optional Rules for Arbitration between International Organizations and States, *PCA Basic Documents* (1998) 97; PCA Optional Rules for Arbitration between International Organizations and Private Parties, *PCA Basic Documents* (1998) 125. Also: Macmahon & Smith (eds), *Permanent Court of Arbitration* (2010).

[93] UNCITRAL Arbitration Rules (2010), 49 ILM 1644, Arts 6, 41.

[94] Generally: Holtzmann & Kristjánsdóttir, *International Mass Claims* (2007).

[95] Generally: de Chazournes & Campanelli, 'Mixed Commissions' (2005) *MPEPIL*; Dolzer, 'Mixed Claims Commissions' (2006) *MPEPIL*.

composed of four commissioners, it became practice to have such disputes adjudicated by an umpire from a neutral state. The first such body was established between the US and UK under the Jay Treaty of 1794 to resolve certain boundary disputes.[96]

Unlike those tribunals convened to address a specific question,[97] claim and compensation bodies are usually convened to address a specific situation and claims arising therefrom. Consequently, their existence can be prolonged. They may be founded for the purpose of settling a dispute between states, or between a state and nationals of another state.[98]

An example of a modern claims and compensation commission is the Iran–United States Claims Tribunal,[99] created following the Iranian Revolution of 1979. The majority of claims before it concerned nationalization of US-owned assets in Iran during the Revolution. Over the life of the Tribunal some 3,800 claims were filed. All but a few interstate cases have been concluded.

A different form of compensation commission is the United Nations Compensation Commission (UNCC).[100] It was created as a subsidiary organ of the Security Council[101] to deal with claims arising out of Iraq's illegal invasion and occupation of Kuwait in 1990–91. The claims were resolved by panels made up of three independent Security Council-appointed commissioners who were experts in different fields including law, accountancy, loss adjustment, insurance, and engineering. The UNCC was a fact-finding body charged with verifying a claim and then assessing compensation. All of the 2.7 million claims submitted have been determined, with the Commission itself only continuing to exist in order to pay out the final claims and complete outstanding tasks.

(B) DISPUTE SETTLEMENT UNDER UNCLOS

(i) The International Tribunal for the Law of the Sea[102]

The International Tribunal for the Law of the Sea (ITLOS) is a permanent international tribunal established by UNCLOS Article 287, Part XV and Annex VI (ITLOS

---

[96] Great Britain–United States, Treaty of Amity, Commerce and Navigation, 19 November 1794, 52 CTS 243. Generally: Ziegler, 'Jay Treaty (1794)' (2007) *MPEPIL*. Another significant forum for such claims were the Mexican Claims Commissions: Feller, *The Mexican Claims Commissions 1923–34* (1935).

[97] E.g. *Iron Rhine* (2005) 27 RIAA 127.

[98] E.g. Declaration of the Government of Algeria: Claims Settlement Declaration, 19 January 1981, 20 *ILM* 230.

[99] Generally: Aldrich, *The Jurisprudence of the Iran–United States Claims Tribunal* (1996); Lillich & Magraw (eds), *The Iran–United States Claims Tribunal* (1998); Brower & Brueschke, *The Iran–United States Claims Tribunal* (1998); Mohebi, *The International Law Character of the Iran–United States Claims Tribunal* (1999); Brower (2000) 94 *AJIL* 813; Pinto, 'Iran–United States Claims Tribunal' (2005) *MPEPIL*.

[100] Generally: di Rattalma & Treves (eds), *The United Nations Compensation Commission* (1999); Wühler, in Randelzhofer & Tomuschat (eds), *State Responsibility and the Individual* (1999) 213.

[101] SC Res 687 (1991). The resolution was issued under Ch VII of the UN Charter, obviating the need for Iraqi consent.

[102] Collier & Lowe (1999) ch 5; Churchill & Lowe, *The Law of the Sea* (3rd edn, 1999) 19; Klein, *Dispute Settlement in the UN Convention on the Law of the Sea* (2005); Rao, 'International Tribunal for the Law of the Sea' (2005) *MPEPIL*; Rothwell & Stephens, *The International Law of the Sea* (2010) ch 18.

Statute). Article 287(1) provides that a state becoming party to UNCLOS may choose by written declaration to have one of four tribunals determine disputes concerning the interpretation or application of UNCLOS,[103] of which ITLOS is one. ITLOS dealt with its first case in 1997,[104] and since then has heard some 19 cases.

ITLOS is comprised of 21 judges elected by the states parties to UNCLOS from among persons 'enjoying the highest reputation of fairness and integrity and with recognized competence in the field of the law of the sea'.[105] Like their counterparts on the International Court, ITLOS judges are elected for a term of nine years, with one third retiring every three years.[106] Unlike them, they are currently part-time.

(ii) UNCLOS Annex VII arbitration

UNCLOS Annex VII provides for the creation of ad hoc arbitral tribunals to hear interstate disputes, and also for disputes involving international organizations.[107] Annex VII Article 1 provides that any party to a dispute may submit it to Annex VII arbitration by written notification.

Annex VII arbitration may be preferable to ITLOS for the usual reasons that arbitration is preferred to litigation; efficiency, flexibility, confidentiality, and greater influence over the composition of the tribunal.[108] Under Article 5, absent agreement by the parties, a tribunal may develop its own procedure.[109]

In addition, UNCLOS Annex VIII provides for the composition of special arbitral tribunals with respect to certain technical areas.[110] Its inclusion was a concession to Soviet states during the negotiation of UNCLOS in the 1970s, which wanted more control over tribunal composition through the selection of expert members.[111] Annex VIII is structurally similar to Annex VII. One significant difference, however, is the capacity of an Annex VIII tribunal to carry out binding fact-finding between the parties.[112] Annex VIII has never been used.

(iii) Referral jurisdiction and compulsory dispute settlement

ITLOS has jurisdiction over any dispute submitted to it in accordance with UNCLOS Part XV. This requires that the parties first attempt peaceful settlement under

---

[103] Namely (a) ITLOS, (b) the ICJ, (c) an Annex VII arbitral tribunal, or (d) an Annex VIII special arbitral tribunal with respect to disputes falling within its ambit. A state party which has made no declaration will be deemed to have accepted Annex VII arbitration: UNCLOS, Art 297(3).

[104] M/V 'Saiga' (No 1) (1997) 110 ILR 736.

[105] ITLOS Statute, Art 2(1); a representative geographic distribution is also required: Art 2(2).

[106] ITLOS Statute, Arts 4–5.

[107] UNCLOS, Art 305, Annex VII Art 13; Annex IX.

[108] Klein (2005) 56.

[109] Collier & Lowe (1999) 91.

[110] These are fisheries, protection and preservation of the marine environment, marine scientific research, and navigation, including pollution from vessels and by dumping: see UNCLOS, Annex VIII Art 1.

[111] Mestral, in Buergenthal (ed), Contemporary Issues in International Law (1984) 169, 185; Noyes (1989) 4 Conn JIL 675, 679–85; Klein (2005) 56.

[112] UNCLOS, Annex VIII Art 5.

UNCLOS Part XV, Section 1.[113] If this fails, a dispute may be submitted to a nominated tribunal under Article 287. Where both parties select ITLOS by way of Article 287(1) declaration,[114] then ITLOS will have carriage of the dispute.[115] If the parties have made different selections, however, then the dispute will be submitted to Annex VII arbitration unless the parties otherwise agree.[116]

The effectiveness of the compulsory procedure, however, is diluted by UNCLOS Articles 281 and 282.[117] These may create a procedural barrier to Part XV dispute settlement, as seen in the *Southern Bluefin Tuna*[118] and *MOX Plant*[119] cases. Such a situation could also have arisen in the *Swordfish Stocks* case, though the matter was settled before it could materialize.[120]

(iv) Subject-matter jurisdiction

ITLOS jurisdiction is constrained by subject-matter. UNCLOS Article 288(1) gives the tribunal jurisdiction (pending referral) over disputes concerning the application or interpretation of UNCLOS. Article 297 and declarations made under Article 298 (excluding the applicability of compulsory dispute resolution with respect to certain subjects) do not prevent parties from agreeing to submit to ITLOS a dispute otherwise excluded from the tribunal's jurisdiction.

Additionally, Article 288(2) provides ITLOS (or any other Article 287(1) tribunal) with jurisdiction over disputes concerning the interpretation or application of an international agreement related to the purposes of UNCLOS and referred to the tribunal in accordance with Part XV. At least nine such agreements have been concluded, most notably the Straddling Stocks Agreement.[121] Given that there are now

---

[113] UNCLOS, Art 286. Further: Klein (2005) ch 2.

[114] At least 45 of the states parties to UNCLOS have made a declaration of preference, with 30 of these selecting ITLOS as their preferred or equally preferred forum for the settlement of law of the sea disputes. Three further states selected it as a preferred forum in cases involving the prompt release of detained ships and crews: www.un.org/depts/los/settlement_of_disputes/choice_procedure. Further: Rothwell & Stephens (2010) 450–1.

[115] UNCLOS, Arts 287(4), 288.

[116] UNCLOS, Art 287(5). For a case of subsequent agreement to accept ITLOS jurisdiction see *Dispute concerning Delimitation of the Maritime Boundary between Bangladesh and Myanmar in the Bay of Bengal (Bangladesh/Myanmar)*, Judgment of 14 March 2012, ITLOS Case No 16.

[117] Rothwell & Stephens (2010) 446–8.

[118] (2000) 119 ILR 508. Further: Boyle (2001) 50 *ICLQ* 447; Colson & Hoyle (2003) 34 *ODIL* 59.

[119] (2003) 126 ILR 310. Further: Shany (2004) 17 *LJIL* 815; Scott (2007) 22 *IJMCL* 303; Cardwell & French (2007) 19 *JEL* 121.

[120] *Conservation and Sustainable Exploitation of Swordfish Stocks in the South-Eastern Pacific Ocean*, Order of 20 December 2000 [2000] ITLOS Rep 148; Boyle, in Nordquist, Moore & Mahmoudi (eds), *The Stockholm Declaration and the Law of the Marine Environment* (2003) 109; Orellana (2002) 71 *Nordic JIL* 55.

[121] Agreement for the Implementation of the Provisions of the United Nations Convention on the Law of the Sea of 10 December 1982 Relating to the Conservation and Management of Straddling Fish Stocks and Highly Migratory Fish Stocks, 4 August 1995, 2167 UNTS 3, Arts 30–2. Also: Agreement to Promote Compliance with International Conservation and Management Measures by Fishing Vessels on the High Seas, 24 November 1993, 2222 UNTS 91, Art IX; Protocol to the Convention on the

over 20 agreements to which the Straddling Stocks Agreement applies, this expands considerably the reach of Part XV and ITLOS. Significantly, Article 30(2) applies even where the parties to the dispute are not state parties to UNCLOS, extending the jurisdiction of Part XV tribunals on a *sui generis* basis,[122] including to the US, which is a party to the Straddling Stocks Agreement and many regional fisheries agreements.

ITLOS also has compulsory residual jurisdiction under UNCLOS Article 292 over matters involving the prompt release of detained vessels and crews. It possesses similar jurisdiction with respect to provisional measures under Article 290(5). Thirteen of the 19 cases so far brought before the Tribunal have involved prompt release or provisional measures. ITLOS may also give an advisory opinion on a legal question if so provided by 'an international agreement related to the purposes' of UNCLOS, though it has yet to be exercised.[123] Notably, UNCLOS contains no such power of referral.

(v) The Seabed Disputes Chamber

The Seabed Disputes Chamber is a specialized division of ITLOS, established by UNCLOS Part XI, Section 5 and ITLOS Statute Article 14. It comprises 11 of the sitting judges of ITLOS.[124] It has exclusive jurisdiction[125] over disputes arising out of the exploration and exploitation of the Area,[126] including disputes between UNCLOS states parties and the Seabed Authority. It also has advisory jurisdiction at the request of the Seabed Authority Assembly or Council with respect to legal questions arising from the scope of their activities.[127]

Prevention of Marine Pollution by Dumping of Wastes and Other Matter, 7 November 1996, 36 ILM 7, Art 16; Framework Agreement for the Conservation of the Living Marine Resources on the High Seas of the South-Eastern Pacific, 14 August 2000, 45 *Law of the Sea Bulletin* 70, Art 14; Convention on the Conservation and Management of Highly Migratory Fish Stocks in the Western and Central Pacific Ocean, 5 September 2000, 41 ILM 257, Art 24; Convention on the Conservation and Management of Fishery Resources in the South-East Atlantic Ocean, 20 April 2001, 2221 UNTS 189, Art 24; Convention on the Protection of the Underwater Cultural Heritage, 2 November 2001, 41 ILM 40, Art 25; Convention on Future Multilateral Cooperation in North-East Atlantic Fisheries, 18 November 1980, 1285 UNTS 129 (amended 2004), Art 18*bis*; Southern Indian Ocean Fisheries Agreement, 7 July 2006, *OJEU* L 196, 18.7.2006, 14, Art 20; Nairobi International Convention on the Removal of Wrecks, 23 May 2007, 46 ILM 697, Art 15. Further: Örebach, Sigurjonsson & McDorman (1998) 13 *IJMCL* 119; Rothwell & Stephens (2010) 451.

[122] Generally: Treves, in Freestone, Barnes & Ong (eds), *The Law of the Sea* (2006) 417.

[123] ITLOS Rules, Art 138.

[124] ITLOS Statute, Art 35; ITLOS Rules, Art 23.

[125] UNCLOS, Arts 187, 287(2).

[126] UNCLOS, Arts 1(1), 187.

[127] UNCLOS, Arts 159(1), 191. Further: *Obligations of States Sponsoring Persons and Entities with Respect to Activities in the Area*, ITLOS Case No 17 (Advisory Opinion, 1 February 2011).

(C) THE WTO DISPUTE SETTLEMENT BODY[128]

(i) The origins of WTO dispute settlement: the GATT

In the 1994 Agreement Establishing the World Trade Organization,[129] significant changes were made in the dispute settlement procedure for world trade disputes, with the inclusion of the Dispute Settlement Understanding (DSU).[130] The DSU replaced and largely reinforced the system of the GATT.[131]

Notwithstanding its trade–diplomatic origins, the GATT system developed to provide structured adjudication. Disputes were referred to 'panels'; ad hoc groupings of experts to make recommendations to the GATT Council.[132] The GATT system was relatively successful, with the results of an adverse panel report accepted by the losing party in over 90 per cent of cases.[133] But it was procedurally deficient. Crucially, GATT Article XXIII required consensus between the contracting parties for panels to be established and their recommendations adopted. A recalcitrant party could avoid the adverse consequences arising from a panel report by simply withholding consent, a practice which appeared to increase during the 1980s. The emerging impasse led the contracting parties to develop the so-called Montreal Rules,[134] the eventual basis for the DSU.

(ii) Dispute settlement under the DSU

The DSU emerged from the Uruguay Round of trade negotiations, and is annexed to the WTO Agreement. It establishes the Dispute Settlement Body (DSB),[135] now one of the most important international tribunals.[136] The purpose of the DSB is the prompt settlement of disputes between WTO Members[137] arising out of their obligations under the WTO covered agreements. DSU Article 3.2 states that:

The dispute settlement system of the WTO is a central element in providing security and predictability to the multilateral trading system. The Members recognize that it serves to

---

[128] Petersmann, *The GATT/WTO Dispute Settlement System* (1997); Waincymer, *WTO Litigation* (2002); Palmeter & Mavroidis, *Dispute Settlement in the World Trade Organization* (2nd edn, 2004); Matsushita, Schoenbaum & Mavroidis, *The World Trade Organization* (2nd edn, 2006) ch 4; van den Bossche, *The Law and Policy of the World Trade Organization* (2nd edn, 2008) chs 3–6; Bethlehem, McRae, Neufeld & van Damme, *The Oxford Handbook of International Trade Law* (2009).

[129] 15 April 1994, 1867 UNTS 410.

[130] WTO Agreement, Annex 2.

[131] Generally: Petersmann (1997) ch 5; Palmeter & Mavroidis (2nd edn, 2004) 6–11; Matsushita et al (2nd edn, 2006) 105–7.

[132] Matsushita et al (2nd edn, 2008) 107.

[133] Hudec, *Enforcing International Trade Law* (1993) 278.

[134] Improvements to the GATT Dispute Settlement Rules and Procedures, GATT Doc No BISD 36S/61, 12 April 1989.

[135] WTO Agreement, Art IV.3.

[136] Matsushita et al (2nd edn, 2008) 104. Also: Leitner & Lester (2011) 14 *JIEL* 191.

[137] Access to the WTO disputes resolution system is limited to WTO Members, though panels may accept *amicus curiae* briefs: *US—Shrimp*, WTO Doc WT/DS58/AB/R, 12 October 1998, §§101, 104–6.

preserve the rights and obligations of Members under the covered agreements, and to clarify the existing provisions of those agreements in accordance with the customary rules of public international law.[138]

The DSB's jurisdiction is compulsory and exclusive with respect to the covered agreements.[139] Consisting of the WTO Members, it oversees the adjudication of trade disputes and the implementation of any recommendations.[140] It operates via reverse consensus, with the blocking of a recommendation only possible if *every* member of the DSB objects.[141]

A panel is a quasi-judicial body responsible for initially hearing a dispute and assessing the conformity of a Member's challenged measure or policy with the covered agreements.[142] Panels are ordinarily composed of three experts selected ad hoc by the DSB.[143]

A party dissatisfied with a panel decision may resort to the Appellate Body,[144] which will rule after 60 to 90 days.[145] The Appellate Body comprises seven members appointed for a four-year term, renewable once,[146] of which any three will convoke to hear an appeal.[147] It has the power to uphold, modify or reverse any of the legal conclusions reached by the panel, though not determinations of fact.[148] So far almost 70 per cent of panel reports have been appealed.[149]

(iii) Remedies and implementation

The sole final remedy under the DSB is the withdrawal of the violating policy, or those WTO-inconsistent elements thereof.[150] Under DSU Article 21.1, withdrawal or modification must be effected promptly, though parties may be given a 'reasonable' period of time to comply (Article 21.3). Where a Member fails to comply with a recommendation within a reasonable period of time, the complaining Member may access the temporary remedies of compensation (the extension by the implementing

---

[138] Also: *US—Section 301 Trade Act*, WTO Doc WT/DS152/R, 22 December 1999, §7.75.

[139] Ibid, §7.43; *EC—Commercial Vessels*, WTO Doc WT/DS301/R, 22 April 2005, §7.193.

[140] Palmeter & Mavroidis (2nd edn, 2004) 15–16; WTO Secretariat, *A Handbook on the WTO Dispute Settlement System* (2004) 17–21.

[141] DSU, Arts 6.1, 16.4, 17.14, 22.6.

[142] DSU, Art 11; *EC—Hormones*, WTO Doc WT/DS26/AB/R, 16 January 1998, §§116, 133; *Brazil—Retreaded Tyres*, WTO Doc WT/DS332/AB/R, 3 December 2007, §185; *EC—Poultry*, WTO Doc WT/DS69/AB/R, 13 July 1998, §133. Further: van den Bossche (2nd edn, 2008) 248–51.

[143] A list of WTO panellists to date may be found at www.worldtradelaw.net/dsc/database/panelistcases.asp.

[144] Generally: Ehlermann (2002) 36 *JWT* 605.

[145] DSU, Art 17.5.

[146] DSU, Arts 2.4, 17.2.

[147] DSU, Art 17.3.

[148] DSU Art 17.6. Further: *EC—Hormones*, WTO Doc No WT/DS26/AB/R, 16 January 1998, §132; *EC—Bananas III*, WTO Doc No WT/DS27/AB/R, 9 September 1997, §239.

[149] www.worldtradelaw.net/dsc/database/appealcount.asp. Further: van den Bossche (2nd edn, 2008) 262.

[150] DSU, Art 19.2.

party of additional market access privileges to the complaining party),[151] or introduce retaliatory measures. The latter remedy comprises drastically increased tariffs on products of export interest to the implementing party,[152] ordinarily in the same sector, but exceptionally in different trade sectors ('cross-retaliation'), thereby providing the maximum incentive for compliance.[153] When considering retaliation, the complaining party must apply to the DSB within 30 days of the expiry of the reasonable period, which will approve the request by reverse consensus. If the implementing party seeks to challenge the retaliation, an arbitral tribunal will be convened to hear the dispute under DSU Article 22.6.

(iv) International law and the DSB

The extent to which the DSB interacts with other elements of international law is uncertain, a situation complicated by the fact that the DSU contains no express applicable law provision such as Article 38(1) of the ICJ Statute. The covered agreements are not the only source of applicable law for panels; in theory, they may also draw on other DSB reports (especially those of the Appellate Body),[154] acts of the WTO bodies, agreements within the WTO context, customary international law,[155] general principles of international law,[156] other international agreements, the subsequent practice of WTO Members, academic writings, and the negotiating history of the GATT and WTO.[157] All these, to varying degrees, clarify or define the law applicable between WTO Members; as noted by the Appellate Body in *US—Gasoline*, the covered agreements cannot be interpreted 'in clinical isolation' from public international law.[158] Similarly, the panel in *Korea—Procurement* noted that '[c]ustomary international law applies generally to the economic relations between the WTO Members... [s]uch international law applies to the extent that the WTO treaty agreements do not "contract out" from it'.[159]

(v) The DSB and Regional Trading Agreements

The WTO shares its regulatory space with the organizations created through Regional Trade Agreements (RTAs).[160] These agreements create regional trading associations

---

[151] See DSU, Art 22.1.

[152] E.g. in the *EC—Bananas III* dispute the US increased the customs duty on carefully selected EC products to 100%: *EC—Bananas III (Art 21.5—US)*, WTO Doc WT/DS27/RW/USA, 19 May 2008.

[153] Further: DSU, Art 22.4.

[154] *Japan—Alcoholic Beverages II*, WTO Docs WT/DS8/AB/R, WT/DS10/AB/R, WT/DS11/ABR, 4 October 1996, §108; *US—Shrimp (Art 21.5—Malaysia)*, WTO Doc WR/DS58/AB/RW, 22 October 2001, §109.

[155] E.g. DSU, Art 3.2, which requires that the covered agreements be interpreted in accordance with customary international law reflected by the VCLT: *US—Gasoline*, WTO Doc WT/DS2/AB/R, 29 April 1996.

[156] E.g. in *US—Shrimp*, the Appellate Body held that the 'chapeau' of GATT Art XX was an expression of the general principle of good faith: WTO Doc WT/DS58/AB/R, 12 October 1998, §158.

[157] Palmeter & Mavroidis (1998) 92 *AJIL* 398; van den Bossche (2nd edn, 2008) 53–71.

[158] *US—Gasoline*, WTO Doc WT/DS2/AB/R, 29 April 1996, 17.

[159] *Korea—Government Procurement*, WTO Doc WT/DS163/R, 1 May 2000, §7.96.

[160] Generally: Sands, Mackenzie & Shany, *Manual on International Courts and Tribunals* (1999) §C; Mathis, *Regional Trade Agreements in the GATT/WTO* (2002); Ganz, in Bethlehem et al (eds), *The Oxford Handbook of International Trade Law* (2009) 237; Bartels, 'Regional Trade Agreements' (2009) *MPEPIL*.

with internalized privileges between Members and in many cases their own rules-based dispute resolution bodies. Prominent bodies include the European Union, MERCOSUR, ASEAN, CARICOM, and the Andean Community of Nations. With the exception of Mongolia, all WTO Members are presently a party to at least one RTA.

(D) INTERNATIONAL INVESTMENT TRIBUNALS[161]

(i) International investment arbitration

International investment arbitration is conducted between a foreign investor and the 'host' state in which its investment is located, usually pursuant to a dispute resolution clause in a bilateral[162] or multilateral[163] investment treaty concluded between the host state and the 'home' state of the investor. Described as 'arbitration without privity',[164] investment arbitration does not require the intervention of the home state by way of diplomatic protection. The first such agreement was concluded between the Federal Republic of Germany and Pakistan in 1959.[165]

It is also possible for the host state and the investor to include an arbitration clause in an investment contract, or refer a dispute to arbitration after it has arisen. The municipal law of the host state may also require that investor-state disputes be referred to an investment tribunal.[166] But most investment disputes today arise from a BIT or MIT.

An additional layer of complexity is added by the 1965 ICSID Convention.[167] The Convention created an arbitral institution, the International Centre for the Settlement of Investment Disputes (ICSID), to administer investment arbitrations. Most investment treaties give the investor the option of arbitration through ICSID or an ad hoc tribunal, usually under the UNCITRAL arbitration rules.[168] Despite the conclusion

---

[161] Generally: Paulsson (1995) 10 *ICSID Rev-FILJ* 232; McLachlan, Shore & Weiniger, *International Investment Arbitration* (2007); Schreuer, 'Investment Disputes' (2007) *MPEPIL*; Dolzer & Schreuer, *Principles of International Investment Law* (2008); Douglas, *The International Law of Investment Claims* (2009); Schreuer, Malintoppi, Reinisch & Sinclair, *The ICSID Convention* (2nd edn, 2009); Binder, Kriebaum, Reinisch & Wittich (eds), *International Investment Law for the 21st Century* (2009); Sornarajah, *The International Law on Foreign Investment* (3rd edn, 2010); Waibel, Kaushal, Chung & Balchin (eds), *The Backlash Against Investment Arbitration* (2010); Salacuse, *The Law of Investment Treaties* (2010).

[162] There are presently some 3,000 BITs in effect, the majority of which are maintained in an online database by UNCTAD: www.unctadxi.org/templates/docsearch____779.aspx.

[163] Cf NAFTA, 17 December 1992, 32 ILM 289, Ch 11; Energy Charter Treaty, 17 December 1994, 2080 UNTS 100, Part III; Association of South-East Asian Nations Investment Guarantee Agreement, 15 December 1987, 27 ILM 612; Dominican Republic–United States–Central American Fair Trade Agreement, 5 August 2004, ch 20.

[164] Generally: Paulsson (1995) 10 *ICSID Rev-FILJ* 232.

[165] Federal Republic of Germany–Pakistan, Treaty for the Promotion and Protection of Investments, 25 November 1999, 457 UNTS 23. On the wider history of international investment law, see Salacuse (2010) ch 4; Sornarajah (3rd edn, 2010) 19–28.

[166] Schreuer et al (2nd edn, 2010) 190–217.

[167] Convention on the Settlement of Investment Disputes between States and Nationals of Other States, 18 March 1965, 575 UNTS 159. The Convention has 157 parties.

[168] Douglas (2009) 3–6. Generally: Jagusch & Sullivan, in Waibel et al (2010) 79.

of the ICSID Convention, however, investment arbitration pursuant to investment treaties was not popular until 1990, when the first BIT-based arbitration award was handed down.[169]

(ii) Structure and features of investment treaties[170]

Investment treaties follow a basic structure. Aside from the dispute resolution clause, investment treaties offer substantive protections to investors.[171] These may be divided into *absolute* standards, which are not contingent on specified factors or events, and *relative* standards, which are dependent on the host state's treatment of other investors and investments. Examples of the former include guarantees of full protection and security, compensation for expropriation, and fair and equitable treatment. Examples of the latter include most-favoured-nation and national treatment.

Ordinarily, only a breach of these standards will provide a basis of claim; the ordinary breach of an investment agreement will not. The situation may be different where the investment treaty includes a so-called 'umbrella clause', which guarantees the observation of obligations assumed by the host state with respect to the investor.[172] Whether this equates the breach of an investment agreement to a breach of an investment standard—and the scope of the obligation if it does—is uncertain and controversial.[173]

(iii) Jurisdiction of tribunals

Investment treaties ordinarily include several jurisdictional gateways through which the investor must pass in order to bring the dispute before any tribunal. Additional requirements may be imposed if the arbitration is to occur under the ICSID Convention.[174] To provide jurisdiction, the claim must concern (a) an investment within the meaning of the investment treaty and the ICSID Convention (if applicable), (b) made by an investor or national within the meaning of the investment treaty, and (c) within the temporal limits set down by the treaty.[175]

---

[169] *Asian Agricultural Products Ltd v Sri Lanka* (1990) 106 ILR 416.

[170] Salacuse (2010) 37–42.

[171] Generally: McLachlan et al (2007) Part III; Reinisch (ed), *Standards of Protection* (2008); Salacuse (2010) chs 8–13.

[172] E.g. UK Model BIT (2005, amended 2006), Art 2(2) ('Each Contracting Party shall observe any obligation it may have entered into with regard to investments of nationals or companies of the other Contracting Party'). Also: German Model BIT (2005), Art 7(2).

[173] Generally: Sinclair (2004) 20 *Arb Int* 411; Shany (2005) 99 *AJIL* 835; Dolzer & Schreuer (2008) 153–62; Gallus (2008) 24 *Arb Int* 157; Crawford (2008) 24 *Arb Int* 351; Schill (2009) 18 *Minn JIL* 1 with references to the case-law. See also chapter 28.

[174] Generally: Schreuer et al (2nd edn, 2009) 71–347.

[175] Even where jurisdiction is established, the claim may nonetheless be inadmissible. The concept of admissibility is presently relatively poorly defined in investment arbitration literature: Douglas (2009) 146–8, 363–472.

(iv) Challenge and annulment

As a general principle, the awards of investment arbitration tribunals are not subject to appeal. Only under limited circumstances is the review of an award possible.[176] If the claimant opts for ad hoc arbitration, the award will be subject to the rules for enforcement and challenge provided in the New York Convention on the Recognition and Enforcement of Foreign Arbitral Awards,[177] in the same way as any private international arbitration. This will ordinarily be done through the courts of the country where the tribunal had its seat, or in the courts of any country in which enforcement is sought. Article V of the New York Convention lists several narrow grounds on which the recognition and enforcement of an arbitral award may be challenged.[178]

By contrast an ICSID award is not subject to review by national courts; the Convention provides its own self-contained system for review of final awards by way of annulment. Annulment is distinct from appeal, and is concerned only with the process by which the award was rendered, not its substantive correctness. This much is seen by the grounds for annulment provided in Article 52(1) of the ICSID Convention:

(a) that the Tribunal was not properly constituted;

(b) that the Tribunal has manifestly exceeded its powers;

(c) that there was corruption on the part of a member of the Tribunal;

(d) that there has been a serious departure from a fundamental rule of procedure; or

(e) that the award has failed to state the reasons on which it is based.

In the event of annulment, the ad hoc Committee cannot replace the original decision of the tribunal with its own; it can only invalidate it, with the claim then able to be referred to a new tribunal for rehearing.

(v) Remedies and enforcement

Under both the New York[179] and ICSID[180] Conventions a valid arbitral award must be recognized and enforced within any state party jurisdiction, subject to the grounds for challenge described above. The standard remedy for breach of an investment standard in an investment treaty is financial compensation for the loss suffered.[181]

---

[176] Generally: Marboe, in Binder et al (2009) 200; Kalina & Di Pietro, ibid, 221. On the potential for the WTO Appellate Body to act as a model for an ICSID appeals facility: McRae (2010) 1 *JIDS* 371.

[177] 10 June 1958, 330 UNTS 38.

[178] New York Convention, Art V(1), V(2)(b). These grounds are largely replicated in Arts 34 and 36 of the UNCITRAL Model Law (1985, amended 2006), which forms the basis of many national arbitration laws: www.uncitral.org/pdf/english/texts/arbitration/ml-arb/07–86998_Ebook.pdf.

[179] New York Convention, Arts III, IV.

[180] ICSID Convention, Art 54. Further: Alexandrov, in Binder et al (2009) 322.

[181] McLachlan et al (2007) ch 9; Dolzer & Schreuer (2008) 271–7; *Petrobart Limited v Kyrgyz Republic* (2005) 13 ICSID Reports 387, 467–8; *MTD Equity Sdn Bhd & MTD Chile SA v Chile* (2004) 12 ICSID Reports 3, 50; *ADC Affiliate Limited and ADC & ADMC Management Limited v Republic of Hungary* (2006) 15 ICSID Reports 534, 621.

33

THE USE OR THREAT OF
FORCE BY STATES

1. HISTORICAL OVERVIEW 1815–1945[1]

In the practice of states in nineteenth-century Europe, war was sometimes still represented as a last resort, that is, as a form of dispute settlement.[2] However, the prevailing view was that resort to war was an attribute of statehood and that conquest produced title.[3] Thus, the annexation of Alsace-Lorraine by the German Empire was not the object of a policy of non-recognition either by France or by third states.[4] Certain other aspects of nineteenth-century practice are worth recalling. In particular there was a somewhat nebulous doctrine of intervention, which was used, to a certain extent, in conjunction with coercive measures short of a formal 'state of war', such as reprisals or pacific blockade. This evasion was useful both diplomatically and to avoid internal constitutional constraints on resort to war.

The approach adopted under the League of Nations Covenant of 1919 essentially reflected nineteenth-century thinking. The principal innovations were certain procedural constraints on resort to war, but, provided the procedures foreseen in Articles 11 to 17 were exhausted, resort to war was permissible. This was despite Article 10, under which members were obliged to respect and preserve as against external aggression the territorial integrity and existing independence of all members of the League.[5]

---

[1] Generally: Brownlie, *International Law and the Use of Force by States* (1963) 3–50; Bobbitt, *The Shield of Achilles* (2002); Neff, *War and the Law of Nations* (2005); Gray, *International Law and the Use of Force* (3rd edn, 2008); Neff, in Evans (ed), *International Law* (3rd edn, 2010) 3. On earlier practice: Russell, *The Just War in the Middle Ages* (1975); Keane, *Violence and Democracy* (2004).

[2] This notion was given expression by Grotius in *De Iure Belli ac Pacis* (1625, Tuck ed, 2005) I.i.§1, who identified the concept of the 'just' war waged in order to restore order. To this end, Grotius identified three possible sources of a 'just' war—self-defence, reparation of injury, and punishment. Further: von Elbe (1939) 33 *AJIL* 665; Donelan (1983) 12 *Millennium* 233; Tuck, *The Rights of War and Peace* (1999); Brunnée & Toope (2004) 51 *NILR* 363; Neff (2005) ch 3.

[3] Either by way of the subsequent peace treaty (which would, vis-à-vis the defeated state, be compelled) or by reason of the complete defeat and disappearance of a party (*debellatio*), as with the defeat of the South African Republic at the end of the Boer War.

[4] Preliminaries of Peace between France and Germany, 26 February 1871, 143 CTS 37, Art I.

[5] Brownlie (1963) 55–65; and see chapter 1.

Independently of the Covenant, certain states were concerned to establish the illegality of conquest. A recommendation of the International Conference of American States at Washington in 1890 contained the principle that cessions of territory made under threats of war or in the presence of an armed force should be void.[6] After 1919 the effort took the form of attempts to fill what was described as the 'gap in the Covenant'. The Sixth Assembly of the League adopted a resolution on 25 September 1925 which stated that a 'war of aggression' constituted 'an international crime', in accordance with a Spanish proposal.[7] At the Eighth Assembly a Polish proposal for a resolution prohibiting wars of aggression was adopted unanimously.[8] Neither proposal was put forward as representing existing law.

A more important development was the conclusion in 1928 of the General Treaty for the Renunciation of War (the Kellogg–Briand Pact).[9] By Article I the parties 'condemn[ed] recourse to war for the solution of international controversies, and renounce[d] it as an instrument of national policy in their relations with one another'. By Article II they agreed that settlement of all disputes arising among them 'shall never be sought except by pacific means'. The Pact had 63 states parties and is apparently still in force. Only four states in existence before the Second World War were not bound by its provisions.[10]

The Kellogg–Briand Pact was prominent as the foundation of the prosecution case on the count of waging aggressive war at the International Military Tribunals in Nuremberg and Tokyo.[11] The Pact prefigures the legal regime of the Charter of the United Nations, providing a degree of continuity with the law of the interwar period.[12]

The principal parties to the Kellogg–Briand Pact made reservations, accepted by the other parties, relating to self-defence.[13] The system which emerged had four elements: first, the obligation not to resort to war to solve international controversies; secondly, the obligation to settle disputes exclusively by peaceful means; thirdly, the reservation of the right of self-defence including collective self-defence, and fourthly, the reservation of the obligations of the League Covenant. Seen in its context, this was a realistic and comprehensive legal regime, which played a considerable role in practice.[14] Thus, the US invoked the Pact in relation to hostilities between China and the USSR in 1929, in 1931 in relation to the conflict between China and Japan, and

---

[6] Moore, 1 *Digest* 292.

[7] (1925) 6 *LNOJ Sp Supp* 33, Annex 14, 403 (25 September 1925).

[8] (1927) 8 *LNOJ Sp Supp* 51, 155 (24 September 1927).

[9] 27 August 1928, 94 LNTS 57.

[10] Brownlie (1963) 74–111.

[11] Finch (1947) 41 *AJIL* 30; Kelsen (1947) 1 *ILQ* 153; Gallant, *The Principle of Legality in International and Comparative Criminal Law* (2005) 115–16, 128, 144; Lesaffer, 'Kellogg–Briand Pact (1928)' (2010) *MPEPIL*.

[12] On the developments of the period 1920–45: Brownlie (1963) 66–111, 216–50; Neff (2005) part IV.

[13] Brownlie (1963) 235–47. Also: Neff (2005) 303–5, considering the role played by self-defence in the drafting of the Pact.

[14] Brownlie (1963) 74–111; 6 Hackworth 46, 51–2; cf Gallant (2005) 115–16, arguing that the Nuremberg Tribunal overstated the effect of the Pact.

in the context of the Leticia dispute between Peru and Ecuador in 1933. The Pact continued to play a role even in 1939, when it was cited by the League Assembly in condemnation of Soviet action against Finland. Practice was not consistent, however: the Italian conquest of Ethiopia, although subject to ineffective sanctions, was accorded recognition by a number of states including the UK and France (recognition was rescinded in 1941).[15]

2. THE CHARTER PROHIBITION ON USE OR THREAT OF FORCE[16]

(A) ARTICLE 2 IN CONTEXT

The essentials of the Kellogg–Briand regime reappeared in the UN Charter, but subject to the important qualification that the powers of the Security Council were disjoined from the rules relating to the use of force, whereas under the Covenant the powers of the Council had been closely linked to the rubric of 'resort to war' in breach of the Covenant.

Article 2 formulates certain principles applicable both to the Organization and its Members. In particular:

3. All Members shall settle their international disputes by peaceful means in such a manner that international peace and security, and justice, are not endangered.

4. All Members shall refrain in their international relations from the threat or use of force against the territorial integrity or political independence of any State, or in any other manner inconsistent with the Purposes of the United Nations.

...

7. Nothing contained in the present Charter shall authorize the United Nations to intervene in matters which are essentially within the domestic jurisdiction of any State or shall require the Members to submit such matters to settlement under the present Charter; but this principle shall not prejudice the application of enforcement measures under Chapter VII.

Article 2(4) has been described as 'a cornerstone of the United Nations Charter'.[17] It bans the unilateral threat or use of force by states, save in certain limited circumstances.

---

[15] Talmon, *Recognition of Governments in International Law* (1996) 102–3.

[16] 24 October 1945, 1 UNTS 16. E.g. Russell, *A History of the United Nations Charter* (1958); Brownlie (1963); Simma (ed), 1–2 *The Charter of the United Nations* (2nd edn, 2002); Pellet (ed), *La Charte des Nations Unies* (2nd edn, 1991); Gray (3rd edn, 2008) ch 7. Also: Franck, *Recourse to Force* (2002); Gardam, *Necessity, Proportionality and the Use of Force by States* (2004); Stürchler, *The Threat of Force in International Law* (2007).

[17] *Armed Activities on the Territory of the Congo (Democratic Republic of the Congo v Uganda)*, ICJ Reports 2005 p 168, 223. Further: Gray (3rd edn, 2008) 6–24. But cf Tams (2009) 20 *EJIL* 359, 359–60.

But it raises acute questions of interpretation.[18] The first concerns the vital subject of the provision, the 'threat or use of force'. Even the scope of the fundamental notion of 'force' is not undisputed. The prevailing view, however, is that it is confined solely to armed force[19] used directly or indirectly (i.e. state participation in the use of force by another state or by irregulars, mercenaries or rebels).[20] It does not extend to political or economic coercion.[21]

While the term 'use' in the context of armed force is tolerably clear, the term 'threat' remains uncertain.[22] Although the prohibition is clear on its face, the threat of force remains a part of everyday life on the international plane, and state practice has demonstrated a certain tolerance of it, one reason being that some obvious threats—such as the development and stockpiling of weapons—are concomitant to the right of self-defence under Article 51 of the Charter. In addition, the *threat* of force is preferable to the alternative, and may even play a role in the settlement of disputes.[23]

Another disputed phrase in Article 2(4) is 'against the territorial integrity or political independence of any State'. Some writers have relied on this language to propound substantial qualifications on the prohibition of the use of force,[24] and in *Corfu Channel* the UK argued along similar lines in defending its mine-sweeping operation to collect evidence within Albanian waters. However, the preparatory work of the Charter is sufficiently clear: this phrasing was introduced precisely to provide guarantees to small states and was not intended to have a restrictive effect; the Court has consistently so held.[25]

(B) THE RIGHT OF SELF-DEFENCE

The most prominent exception to the prohibition on the use of force is each state's right to defend itself. Article 51 relevantly provides:

Nothing in the present Charter shall impair the inherent right of individual or collective self-defence if an armed attack occurs against a Member of the United Nations, until

---

[18] On restrictive versus extensive interpretations of the prohibition: Corten (2005) 16 *EJIL* 803.

[19] Randelzhofer, in 1 Simma (2nd edn, 2002) 112, 117.

[20] Ibid, 118–20. Also: *Military and Paramilitary Activities in and against Nicaragua (Nicaragua v US)*, ICJ Reports 1986 p 14.

[21] Randelzhofer, in 1 Simma (2nd edn, 2002) 112, 118.

[22] *Corfu Channel (UK v Albania)*, ICJ Reports 1949 p 4; *Nicaragua*, ICJ Reports 1986 p 14; *Legality of the Threat or Use of Nuclear Weapons*, ICJ Reports 1996 p 226. For an eccentric interpretation: *Guyana v Suriname* (2007) 139 ILR 566, 690–7. Generally: Stürchler (2007).

[23] Randelzhofer, in 1 Simma (2nd edn, 2002) 112, 124.

[24] E.g. Bowett, *Self-Defence in International Law* (1958) 152; Stone, *Aggression and World Order* (1958), 43; Higgins, *Problems and Process* (1994) 245–6. Also: Reisman (1984) 78 *AJIL* 642 and Schachter (1984) 78 *AJIL* 642 (in reply).

[25] ICJ Reports 1949 p 4, 35. The Court's famous rejection of the UK argument has been interpreted variously as a complete rejection of narrow interpretation or as a more limited repudiation of the particular UK claim on the facts: Gray (3rd edn, 2008) 32. The Court itself subsequently interpreted the position as a blanket rejection: *Nicaragua*, ICJ Reports 1986 p 14, 106–8. Also: Brownlie (1963) 265–8; Randelzhofer, in 1 Simma (2nd edn, 2002) 112, 123.

the Security Council has taken measures necessary to maintain international peace and security....

Article 51 reserves the 'inherent' right of individual or collective self-defence 'if an armed attack occurs against a Member of the United Nations'. In *Nicaragua* it was recognized that this formulation refers to pre-existing customary law.[26]

A central difficulty in applying Article 51 is the term 'armed attack'.[27] The drafters likely interpreted the term as encompassing the kind of conventional attack characteristic of the Second World War. The evolution of modern weapons, however, makes any rigid typology difficult to maintain.[28] Modern warfare also tends to feature increased participation of irregular forces alongside or instead of state armies. In *Nicaragua*, drawing on the law of state responsibility and the General Assembly's 1974 definition of 'aggression', the Court concluded there was general agreement that armed attack included 'the sending by or on behalf of a State of armed bands, groups, irregulars or mercenaries',[29] 'if such an operation, because of its scale and effects, would have been classified as an armed attack rather than as a mere frontier incident had it been carried out by regular armed forces'.[30]

But it is doubtful whether a state which provides aid and support to rebel groups without actually sending them against another state has committed an 'armed attack'.[31] In *Nicaragua* the Court was not persuaded that the provision of arms and other support to irregular groups demonstrated an armed attack by the US against Nicaragua or by Nicaragua against neighbouring states, although other illegalities (the mining of a harbour, intervention in internal affairs) had been committed.[32] Such assistance may amount to a threat or use of force, or unlawful intervention,[33] but falls short of 'armed attack' triggering the Article 51 right of self-defence.

Another criterion for 'armed attack' focuses on the 'scale and effects' of an attack, distinguishing the 'most grave forms' of force (armed attacks) from 'other less grave forms' (e.g. border skirmishes or 'mere frontier incident[s]').[34] The gravity threshold

---

[26] *Nicaragua*, ICJ Reports 1986 p 14, 94. Further: Gray (3rd edn, 2008) 171–3. For contemporary criticisms of the decision: Franck (1987) 81 *AJIL* 116; D'Amato (1987) 81 *AJIL* 101; Hargrove (1987) 81 *AJIL* 135; Moore (1987) 81 *AJIL* 151.

[27] Generally: Constantinou, *The Right of Self-Defence under Customary International Law and Article 51 of the UN Charter* (2000); Ruys, *'Armed Attack' and Article 51 of the UN Charter* (2010); Zemanek, 'Armed Attack' (2009) *MPEPIL*.

[28] Generally: Schmitt & O'Donnell (eds), *Computer Network Attack and International Law* (2001).

[29] ICJ Reports 1986 p 14, 103, citing GA Res 3314(XXIX), 14 December 1974, Annex, Art 3(g). Higgins considers the Court's adoption of the definition to be 'operationally unworkable': (1994) 251.

[30] ICJ Reports 1986 p 14, 103. This position was reaffirmed in *Armed Activities (DRC v Uganda)*, ICJ Reports 2005 p 168, 222–3. On the legal aspects of the Congo conflict: Okowa (2006) 77 *BY* 203.

[31] ICJ Reports 1986 p 14, 103–4, cf 543 (Judge Jennings, diss). Also Randelzhofer, in 1 Simma (2nd edn, 2002) 788, 801.

[32] ICJ Reports 1986 p 14, 62, 64. Also: Crawford, 'Military and Paramilitary Activities in and against Nicaragua Case (Nicaragua v United States of America)' (2006) *MPEPIL*, §D.

[33] ICJ Reports 1986 p 14, 104.

[34] Ibid, 101, 103.

was reiterated in *Oil Platforms*.[35] There the US alleged that the gravity of an attack on one of its ships was exacerbated because it was part of a pattern of similar incidents; the Court left open whether a series of attacks could cumulatively amount to 'armed attack'.[36] The majority in *Oil Platforms* also found that any attack must be carried out with 'the specific intention of harming'.[37] But the addition of such criteria, based as they are on an *ex post facto* assessment of a state's behaviour, is problematic; it may be difficult for a state to discern if a minor incursion is part of some larger design, or done with harmful intent.[38]

The meaning of 'armed attack' remains controversial, particularly in connection to international responses to terrorism, discussed below. Short of a dedicated resolution on the subject from the General Assembly,[39] it appears that the question will be assessed on a case by case basis.[40]

Although the right to self-defence is established, it is not unconstrained; force used in self-defence must be necessary and proportionate.[41] The International Court has reaffirmed repeatedly that these limitations apply to all forms of self-defence, individual and collective.[42] In this context, necessity has generally been interpreted as meaning that the defending state must have no other option in the circumstances than to act in forceful self-defence,[43] whilst proportionality requires that the size, duration, and target of the response correspond to the attack in question.[44] Thus, self-defence cannot be merely punitive or retaliatory in character.

(i) Collective self-defence

The right of collective self-defence was accepted prior to 1945 and is expressly recognized in Article 51.[45] Following the Iraqi attack on Kuwait, the Security Council referred in the preamble of SC Resolution 661 to the 'inherent right of individual or collective self-defence, in response to the armed attack by Iraq against Kuwait'.[46] In

---

[35] *Oil Platforms (Iran v US)*, ICJ Reports 2003 p 161, 186–7. Generally: Gray (3rd edn, 2008) 143–8.

[36] ICJ Reports 2003 p 161, 190–2.

[37] Ibid, 192.

[38] For criticism of the majority's approach: ibid, 225–40 (Judge Higgins), 246–65 (Kooijmans), and 270–89 (Judge Buergenthal). Further: Taft (2004) 29 *Yale JIL* 259.

[39] Ruys (2010) 535–9.

[40] Higgins (1994) 248–51; Randelzhofer, in 1 Simma (2nd edn, 2002) 794–803; Gray (3rd edn, 2008) 128–48.

[41] Generally: Gray (3rd edn, 2008) 148–56. Some commentators see these limitations as illegitimate, and additional to those imposed by customary international law: Kunz (1947) 41 *AJIL* 872; Gardam (1993) 87 *AJIL* 391; Gardam (2004). The contrarian position is generally not accepted.

[42] *Nicaragua*, ICJ Reports 1986 p 14, 103; *Nuclear Weapons*, ICJ Reports 1996 p 226, 245; *Oil Platforms*, ICJ Reports 2003 p 161, 183; *Armed Activities (DRC v Uganda)*, ICJ Reports 2005 p 168, 223.

[43] Though there is some controversy as to whether it needs to be immediate: Gardam (2004) 149–53; Gray (3rd edn, 2008) 150.

[44] Gray (3rd edn, 2008) 150.

[45] Generally: Bowett (1958) 200–48; Randelzhofer, in 1 Simma (2nd edn, 2002) 788, 802–3; Gray (3rd edn, 2008) 167–92; Dinstein, *War, Aggression and Self-Defence* (5th edn, 2011) 278–302.

[46] SC Res 661 (1990). The operation was actually conducted pursuant to a further express mandate: SC Res 678 (1990) operative §1.

Nicaragua, the Court indicated three conditions for the lawful exercise of collective self-defence. The first is that there must have been an 'armed attack'.[47] The second, procedural condition is that the victim state 'must form and declare the view that it has been so attacked'.[48] The third condition, also procedural, is that the 'use of collective self-defence by the third State for the benefit of the attacked State…depends on a request addressed by that State to the third State'.[49] It did not require (as had sometimes been argued) that the assisting states should themselves have been the subject of an armed attack. So interpreted and so procedurally limited, collective self-defence is a valuable protection for weaker states: it was the legal basis for most of the collective security arrangements of the Cold War period.[50]

(ii) Anticipatory or pre-emptive self-defence

There is a long-standing controversy as to whether the Charter definitively excludes the possibility of anticipatory self-defence,[51] that is, the use of force pre-emptively to avert an imminent armed attack. Since 1945 states using force have preferred to justify their actions as self-defence in response to an armed attack, rather than asserting a right of pre-emptive action.[52] But when pressed, the proponents of anticipatory self-defence rely on two related propositions.[53] The first is that Article 51 reserves a right of self-defence which existed in customary law and included certain anticipatory action. The problem is that the argument is incompatible with the text of Article 51 ('if an armed attack occurs'),[54] as well as the object and purpose of the Charter, which aims to restrict the capacity of states to employ force unilaterally.[55]

The second proposition is that the customary law was formed in the nineteenth century, in particular, as a result of correspondence exchanged by the US and Great

---

[47] *Nicaragua*, ICJ Reports 1986 p 14, 103–4.

[48] Ibid; Dinstein (5th edn, 2011) 296–7.

[49] ICJ Reports 1986 p 14, 104, cf 356 (Judge Schwebel, diss), 544–5 (Judge Jennings, diss); *Oil Platforms*, ICJ Reports 2003 p 161, 186–7. Also: Gray (3rd edn, 2008) 184–6.

[50] E.g. North Atlantic Treaty, 4 April 1949, 34 UNTS 243 (NATO); Southeast Asia Collective Defence Treaty, 8 September 1954, 209 UNTS 28; Declaration relating to the Baghdad Pact, 28 July 1958, 335 UNTS 205; Warsaw Treaty of Friendship, Cooperation, and Mutual Assistance, 14 May 1955, 219 UNTS 3 (Warsaw Pact). Further: Gray (3rd edn, 2008) 167.

[51] Bowett (1958) 188–93; Randelzhofer, in 1 Simma (2nd edn, 2002) 788, 803–4; Hamid (2007) 54 *NILR* 441; Gray (3rd edn, 2008) 160–5; Ruys (2010) 255–67.

[52] Gray (3rd edn, 2008) 160–5.

[53] E.g. Waldock (1952) 81 Hague *Recueil* 451, 497–8; Bowett (1958) 188–9; Schwebel (1972) 136 Hague *Recueil* 411, 479–81; Van den Hole (2003–04) 19 *AUILR* 69. Also Kelly (2003–04) 13 *J Trans LP* 1; Yoo (2003) 97 *AJIL* 563, 571–4; Guiora (2008) 13 *JCSL* 3.

[54] The English and Spanish ('*en caso de ataque armado*') texts seem clear; the French ('*dans le cas où un Membre des Nations Unies est l'objet d'une agression armée*') may be open to a broader reading.

[55] Randelzhofer, in 1 Simma (2nd edn, 2002) 788, 803. Dinstein adds complexity by introducing the concept of 'interceptive' self-defence, whereby an attacking state has 'crossed the Rubicon' by embarking on an irreversible course of action: (5th edn, 2011) 203–5. Higgins argues that, notwithstanding its plain meaning, the right to anticipatory self-defence should be read into Art 51 in order to account for the exigencies of modern warfare (notably the existence of nuclear weapons): (1994) 242–3.

Britain in the period from 1838 to 1842.[56] The cause of the exchange was the seizure and destruction in 1837 in American territory by British armed forces of a vessel (the *Caroline*) used by private persons assisting an armed rebellion in Canada. In protesting against the incident the US Secretary of State Daniel Webster required the British government to show the existence of a

necessity of self-defence, instant, overwhelming, leaving no choice of means, and no moment for deliberation. It will be for it to show, also, that the local authorities in Canada, even supposing the necessity of the moment authorised them to enter the territories of the United States at all, did nothing unreasonable or excessive; since the act justified by the necessity of self-defence, must be limited by that necessity, and kept clearly within it.[57]

Lord Ashburton in his response did not dispute this statement of principle. Webster's formula has been repeatedly cited in support of the doctrine of anticipatory self-defence but the correspondence made no difference to the legal doctrine, such as it was, of the time. Self-defence was then regarded either as synonymous with self-preservation or as a particular instance of it. The statesmen of the period used self-preservation, self-defence, necessity, and necessity of self-defence more or less interchangeably, and the diplomatic correspondence was not intended to restrict the right of self-preservation. Many works on international law both before and after the *Caroline* case regarded self-defence as an instance of self-preservation and discussed the *Caroline* under that rubric.

Reference to the period 1838–42 as the critical date for the customary law said to lie behind the UN Charter is anachronistic and indefensible. Whether or not custom is capable of expanding the prima facie narrow right of self-defence expressed in Article 51,[58] it is also more appropriate to know the state of customary law in 1945, and it is far from clear that in 1945 the customary law was so flexible. Since 1945 the practice of states generally has been opposed to anticipatory self-defence.[59] The Israeli attack on an Iraqi nuclear reactor in 1981 was strongly condemned as a 'clear violation of the Charter of the United Nations' in SC Resolution 487 (adopted unanimously).[60] Although it has never specifically ruled on the subject, the International Court may have impliedly excluded anticipatory self-defence from the ambit of Article 51. In *Armed Activities (DRC v Uganda)*, the Court said:

Article 51 of the Charter may justify the use of force in self-defence *only within the strict confines there laid down*. It does not allow the use of force by a State to protect perceived

---

[56] For the documents: Jennings (1938) 32 *AJIL* 82. Cf Reisman (1999) 22 *Hous JIL* 3 for possible modern applications.

[57] Shewmaker (ed), *The Papers of Daniel Webster* (1983) 62.

[58] In the sense that the right is triggered by an armed attack: Brownlie (1963) 275–80; Randelzhofer, in 1 Simma (2nd edn, 2002) 788, 803; cf Franck (2002) 97–9; Koo (2003) 97 *AJIL* 563, 571.

[59] Gray (3rd edn, 2008) 214; cf Reisman & Armstrong (2006) 100 *AJIL* 525 (an argument based on a somewhat oracular interpretation of *opinio iuris*).

[60] SC Res 487 (1981) op §1. Cf D'Amato (1996) 10 *Temple ICLJ* 259. But no such response occurred in relation to the Israeli bombing of the Deir ez-Zor reactor in Syria in 2007: Gray (3rd edn, 2008) 237.

security interests beyond those parameters. Other means are available to a concerned State, including, in particular, recourse to the Security Council.[61]

The concept of anticipatory self-defence has seen a revival in the literature with the prosecution of the so-called War on Terror. The Bush administration denounced the 'reactive posture' of the past, refusing to wait for enemies such as 'rogue states and terrorists' to strike first and announcing its readiness to act to prevent threats from potential adversaries, even in the face of uncertainty as to the time and place of an attack.[62] This goes further than pre-emptive self-defence into the realm of *preventive* self-defence; it lacks any legal basis and is not generally accepted.[63] It may be noted that when the US Expeditionary Force began military operations against Iraq in March 2003, the letter to the Security Council of 20 March 2003 relied upon Security Council resolutions as the primary putative legal basis of the action, not on any right to pre-emptive or preventive self-defence under general international law.[64]

(iii) Humanitarian intervention[65]

Another debate over the scope of Article 2(4) concerns forcible measures of so-called 'humanitarian intervention'.[66] By the end of the nineteenth century most publicists admitted that a right of humanitarian intervention existed. A state which had abused its sovereignty by brutal and excessively cruel treatment of those within its power was regarded as having made itself liable to action by any state which was prepared to intervene. The action was in the nature of a police measure, and no change of sovereignty could result. Some writers restricted it to action to free a nation oppressed by another; some considered its object to be to put an end to crimes and slaughter; some referred to 'tyranny', others to extreme cruelty; some to religious persecution, and, lastly, some confused the issue by considering as lawful intervention in case of feeble government or 'misrule' leading to anarchy.[67]

---

[61] ICJ Reports 2005 p 168, 223–4 (emphasis added).

[62] *The National Security Strategy of the United States of America*, Washington, September 2002, 1, 15, available at www.au.af.mil/au/awc/awcgate/nss/nss_sep2002.pdf. Also: Farer (2002) 96 *AJIL* 359; Gray (3rd edn, 2008) 209–16.

[63] Gray (2002) 1 *Chin JIL* 437; Duffy, *The 'War on Terror' and the Framework of International Law* (2005) 209–12.

[64] S/2003/351, 21 March 2003 (passing reference to self-defence is made in the final substantive paragraph). The UK and Australian letters rely exclusively upon SC resolutions: S/2003/350, 21 March 2003; S/2003/352, 21 March 2003. Further: Koo (2003) 97 *AJIL* 593. On the UK position: (2003) 52 *ICLQ* 811; (2005) 54 *ICLQ* 767, 768; Weller, *Iraq and the Use of Force in International Law* (2010).

[65] Brownlie (1963) 338–42; Franck (1993) 240 Hague *Recueil* 9, 256–7; Higgins (1994) 245–8; Murphy, *Humanitarian Intervention* (1996); Simma (1999) 10 *EJIL* 1; Chesterman, *Just War or Just Peace?* (2001); Krisch (2002) 13 *EJIL* 323; Randelzhofer, in 1 Simma (2nd edn, 2002) 112, 130–2; Franck (2002) ch 9; Holzgrefe & Keohane (eds), *Humanitarian Intervention* (2003); Kennedy, *The Dark Sides of Virtue* (2004) 235–324; Goodman (2006) 100 *AJIL* 107; Gray (3rd edn, 2008) 32–59.

[66] This is to be distinguished from non-forcible measures of humanitarian assistance, e.g. delivery of food or medical aid, whether with or without the consent of the central government: Randelzhofer, in 1 Simma (2nd edn, 2002) 112, 130.

[67] Brownlie (1963) 338.

Much of the time, however, humanitarian intervention appeared as a cloak for episodes of imperialism, including the US invasion of Cuba in 1898, and the doctrine of humanitarian intervention did not survive the post-1919 era. For example, the Indian intervention in Bangladesh (1971), the Tanzanian action in Uganda (1979), and the Vietnamese invasion of Cambodia (1979) were all possible examples of humanitarian intervention, but in all three cases the belligerents chose to justify their actions under the rubric of self-defence.[68]

The issue was raised once more with the NATO bombing of targets throughout Yugoslavia in March to May 1999. There is a preliminary difficulty in that, beginning in October 1998, the threats of force were linked directly to a collateral agenda, that is, the acceptance by Yugoslavia of various 'demands' concerning the status of Kosovo. This background has been ignored by many commentators.

The UK position was set out in a statement by the Permanent Representative to the United Nations on 24 March 1999. He said:

The action being taken is legal. It is justified as an exceptional measure to prevent an overwhelming humanitarian catastrophe. Under present circumstances in Kosovo there is convincing evidence that such a catastrophe is imminent. Renewed acts of repression by the authorities of the Federal Republic of Yugoslavia would cause further loss of civilian life and would lead to displacement of the civilian population on a large scale and in hostile conditions. Every means short of force has been tried to avert this situation. In these circumstances, and as an exceptional measure on grounds of overwhelming humanitarian necessity, military intervention is legally justifiable. The force now proposed is directed exclusively to averting a humanitarian catastrophe, and is the minimum judged necessary for that purpose.[69]

This statement clearly asserted the action was legal but invoked no specific international law source; in particular, no reference is made to the UN Charter.

The position in 1999, when the operations took place, was that there was little or no authority or state practice to support the right of individual states to use force on humanitarian grounds.[70] The weak legal position was recognized by the UK when it informed the Select Committee on Foreign Affairs of the House of Commons of its aim of establishing in the UN 'new principles governing humanitarian intervention'.[71]

Three months after the NATO action against Yugoslavia had ended, the Foreign Ministers of the G77

stressed the need to maintain clear distinctions between humanitarian assistance and other activities of the United Nations. They rejected the so-called right of humanitarian intervention, which had no basis in the UN Charter or in international law.[72]

---

[68] Gray (3rd edn, 2008) 33–4.

[69] S/PV.3988, 24 March 1999, 12. Also UKMIL (1999) 70 *BY* 387, 571–601.

[70] Brownlie & Apperley (2000) 49 *ICLQ* 878.

[71] House of Commons, Foreign Affairs Committee: Fourth Report—Kosovo (HC 28-I), 7 June 2000, §144. Further: UKMIL (2000) 71 *BY* 517, 649.

[72] Declaration on the Occasion of the Twenty-third Annual Ministerial Meeting of the Group of 77, 24 September 1999, §69 (132 states participated). For its part the Court declined provisional measures on jurisdictional grounds: *Legality of Use of Force (Yugoslavia v US)*, Provisional Measures, Order of 2 June 1999, ICJ Reports 1999 p 916.

Those who espouse the right of humanitarian intervention tend to ignore state practice. Instead, reliance is placed upon a number of ambiguous episodes, which, it is said, either presage or constitute a change in the customary law.[73] In addition, reference is often made to the need to balance human rights against the prohibition of the use of force in the international legal order. Worthy though such an impulse may be, it runs into the same obstacle as the argument for anticipatory self-defence: there is simply no room for it within the regulatory space established by Articles 2(4) and 51 of the Charter.[74]

The material relied upon includes three problematic developments. The first was the Air Exclusion Zone in northern Iraq, created in 1991. This involved using force with the object of excluding Iraqi air power in order to protect the Kurds of northern Iraq. This was, in the view of the British government, justified by 'the customary international law principle of humanitarian intervention'.[75] Again no sources were provided to support this view. The Air Exclusion Zone in southern Iraq, created in 1992, was also controversial but was, unlike its predecessor, purportedly based upon SC Resolution 668 of 1990.[76] The UK position over the life of the no-fly zones was, however, inconstant; on occasion, it claimed that both zones were supported by the resolution; in other instances, it claimed that even without the resolution, both zones could be justified under the supposed principle of humanitarian intervention.[77]

The third episode is the operations authorized by the Economic Community of West African States (ECOWAS) in Liberia in 1990.[78] The operations (by the Economic Community of West African States Monitoring Group) were a regional peacekeeping exercise which, at a certain stage, received the support of the Security Council and the Organization of African Unity.[79] Contemporary observers did not recognize the episode as a case of humanitarian intervention. The practical basis of the action was the need to restore order in a state without an effective government. The 'practice', such as it is, involves a small number of adherent states, and contemporary debates in the Security Council reveal marked divisions of opinion.[80]

(iv) Intervention to rescue nationals[81]

International law in the Charter era contains multiple instances of a state utilizing force within another's territory in order to rescue its nationals. Some writers argue the

---

[73] Greenwood (2000) 49 *ICLQ* 926; Franck (2002) 135–73.

[74] Randelzhofer, in 1 Simma (2nd edn, 2002) 112, 130–1; cf Greenwood (1993) 48 *Europa-Archiv* 93. Also: Gray (3rd edn, 2008) 35–6. Higgins makes the more utilitarian point that 'if it is felt that the erstwhile articulation of norms no longer serves community interests, then those norms can properly be subjected to processes for change… [t]he normal processes for change will include non-compliance': (1994) 252.

[75] Brownlie & Apperley (2000) 49 *ICLQ* 878, 882–3.

[76] Ibid, 906–7. On the air exclusion zones: McIlmail (1994–95) 17 *Loyola LA ICLJ* 35; Lobel & Ratner (1999) 93 *AJIL* 124; Franck (2002) 152–5; Gray (3rd edn, 2008) 36–9, 348–51.

[77] E.g. UKMIL (2001) 72 *BY* 551, 692–5.

[78] E.g. Franck (2002) 155–62.

[79] Brownlie & Apperley (2000) 49 *ICLQ* 878, 907–8; Franck (2002) 162; Gray (3rd edn, 2008) ch 9.

[80] Note the SC debates on 24 March 1999 (S/PV.3988) and 26 March 1999 (S/PV.3989). Further: Chesterman (2001) 211–13.

[81] Eichensehr (2008) 48 *Va JIL* 451; Gray (3rd edn, 2008) 156–60; Dinstein (5th edn, 2011) 255–9.

right to protect nationals by the use of force is an aspect of the customary law right of self-defence,[82] but again this is doubtful.[83] The protection of nationals was one of several justifications invoked by the US in relation to the use of force against Panama in 1989.[84] Further examples abound,[85] including, *inter alia*, the joint US–Belgian operation in the Congo in 1964,[86] the landing of US troops in the Dominican Republic in 1965,[87] the 1976 rescue of Israeli nationals at Entebbe Airport in Uganda,[88] Operation *Eagle Claw*, the aborted attempt to resolve the Iranian hostage crisis in 1980,[89] and the purported rescue of US medical students in Grenada in 1983.[90] France intervened in a variety of central and western African nations from 2002 onwards.[91] More recently, Russia has claimed this right with respect to its 2008 conflict with Georgia.[92]

(v) The 'responsibility to protect'[93]

Less a doctrine of its own than a refocusing of humanitarian intervention, the term 'responsibility to protect' emerged in 2001 in a Report of the International Commission on Intervention and State Sovereignty (ICISS).[94] It was subsequently adopted in several other United Nations documents, most notably the General Assembly's 2005 World Summit Outcome.[95] In essence, it is intended to permit (and even require) international action in the face of the most serious human rights abuses or international crimes, in cases where a state fails in its duty to protect its own citizens.[96] Although originally

---

[82] Bowett (1958) 87–105; Waldock (1952) 81 Hague *Recueil* 451, 466–7; Eichensehr (2008) 48 *Va JIL* 451; Dinstein (5th edn, 2011) 255–9. Also Bowett, in Cassese (ed), *The Current Legal Regulation of the Use of Force* (1986) 39; Franck (2002) 76–96.

[83] Gray (3rd edn, 2008) 88–92. Also: Ruys (2008) 13 *JCSL* 233. Cf UK Ministry of Defence, *Manual of the Law of Armed Conflict* (2004) 2 ('Self-defence may include the rescue of nationals where the territorial state is unable or unwilling to do so').

[84] Wedgwood (1991) 29 *Col JTL* 609; Chesterman, in Goodwin-Gill & Talmon (eds), *The Reality of International Law* (1999) 57–94. On the invasion of Panama: Nanda (1990) 84 *AJIL* 494; D'Amato (1990) 84 *AJIL* 516; Henkin (1991) 29 *Col JTL* 293.

[85] Gray (3rd edn, 2008) 156–60.

[86] Gerard (1967) 3 *RBDI* 242.

[87] Nanda (1966) 43 *Den LJ* 439.

[88] Green (1976) 6 *Is YBHR* 312; Schachter (1984) 82 *Mich LR* 1620, 1630; Dinstein (5th edn, 2011) 257–9.

[89] Eichensehr (2008) 48 *Va JIL* 451, 453–6.

[90] Gilmore, *The Grenada Intervention* (1984); Nanda (1984) 14 *California WILJ* 395.

[91] Notably the Central African Republic, Côte d'Ivoire, and Liberia in 2002–03, and Chad in 2006: Gray (3rd edn, 2008) 159.

[92] E.g. S/2006/555, 20 July 2006 and further Okawa (2008) 3 *Hague JJ* 41. Also *Application of the International Convention on the Elimination of All Forms of Racial Discrimination*, Preliminary Objections, Judgment of 1 April 2011 (dismissed for want of jurisdiction); *Georgia v Russia (No 2)* [2012] ECtHR 38263/08 (2008, pending).

[93] Further: Evans (2004) 98 *PAS* 78; Stahn (2007) 101 *AJIL* 99; Zifcak, in Evans (ed), *International Law* (3rd edn, 2010) 504; Winkelmann, 'Responsibility to Protect' (2006) *MPEPIL*.

[94] A/57/303, 14 August 2002, Annex.

[95] Report of the High Level Panel on Threats, Challenges and Change, A/59/595, 6 December, 2004; Report of the Secretary-General, A/59/2005, 21 March 2005; 2005 World Summit Outcome, GA Res 60/1, 25 October 2005, §§138–9.

[96] Stahn identifies five propositions, attended by increasing levels of controversy: (1) the host state has a duty to protect citizens on its territory; (2) states failing the duty have a weak sovereignty defence; (3) foreign

labelled a 'new approach'[97] or a 'recharacterization of sovereignty',[98] support for the concept gathered speed, to the extent that it was soon considered by some to be an emerging norm of international law.[99] The 2001 Report purported to identify three situations where the 'residual responsibility' of the states to take action was activated: (a) when a particular state is clearly unwilling or unable to fulfil its responsibility to protect; (b) where a particular state is itself the perpetrator of crimes or atrocities; or (c) where people living outside a particular state are directly threatened by actions taking place there.[100] This was rendered more generally in the 2005 World Summit Outcome:[101]

In this context, we are prepared to take collective action, in a timely and decisive manner, through the Security Council, in accordance with the Charter, including Chapter VII, on a case-by-case basis and in cooperation with relevant regional organizations as appropriate, should peaceful means be inadequate and national authorities are manifestly failing to protect their populations from genocide, war crimes, ethnic cleansing and crimes against humanity.

But it remains clear that the responsibility to protect cannot be used within the framework of Articles 2(4) and 51 to justify the unilateral use of force. The various resolutions and statements endorsing the concept do so subject to the crucial qualifier that collective security and the UN system remain the primary forum for military action.[102]

The Security Council has been receptive to the nascent doctrine, highlighting that states have a responsibility to protect their own citizens in relation to the situation in Sudan (though not commenting on the capacity of other states to intervene),[103] and more dramatically, authorizing the collective use of force under Chapter VII against Libya.[104] As such, the concept reflects an evolution in the way the Security Council views its powers under Articles 39 and 42 of the Charter. Thus the 'responsibility to

---

states may intervene non-forcibly; (4) foreign states may intervene forcibly; and (5) foreign entities have a positive duty to act: (2007) 101 *AJIL* 99, 118–20.

[97]   ICISS Report, ch 2.

[98]   Ibid, §2.2.

[99]   Report of the High Level Panel on Threats, Challenges and Change, A/59/595, 6 December 2004, §203; Report of the Secretary-General, A/59/2005, 21 March 2005, §135.

[100]   ICISS Report, §2.31.

[101]   GA Res 60/1, 16 September 2005, §139. This was further condensed into 'three pillars' by the Report of the Secretary-General on the Responsibility to Protect, focusing on: (1) the protection responsibilities of the state; (2) international assistance and capacity building; and (3) a timely and decisive response: Report of the Secretary-General, A/63/677 (2009).

[102]   Report of the High Level Panel on Threats, Challenges and Change, A/59/595, 6 December 2004, §203; Report of the Secretary-General, A/59/2005, 21 March 2005, §135; 2005 World Summit Outcome, GA Res 60/1, 16 September 2005, §139.

[103]   SC Res 1706 (2006), preamble ('[reaffirming] *inter alia* the provisions of paragraphs 138 and 139 of the 2005 United Nations World Summit outcome document').

[104]   SC Res 1973 (2011), preamble ('Reiterating the responsibility of the Libyan authorities to protect the Libyan population and reaffirming that parties to armed conflicts bear the primary responsibility to take all feasible steps to ensure the protection of civilians').

protect' cannot justify the unilateral use of force, but may justify collective measures within the Charter system. This leaves an underlying concern unaddressed. Thus Tomuschat asks:

[M]ust the international community stand idly by whilst millions of human beings are massacred just because in the Security Council a permanent member holds its protective hands over the culprit? Must national sovereignty be understood as the paramount rule of international law that overrides any other value? Giving an affirmative response to these two questions would totally deprive international law of its essential value content.[105]

As a statement about the political landscape this seems persuasive. But the prohibition of the use of force as established in the post-war period was designed to prevent precisely this kind of adventure, and the overall record of high-minded intervention is dismal. At any rate it cannot be said that any new exception to Charter prohibitions has been authoritatively articulated, still less generally accepted.[106]

3. AUTHORIZING THE USE OF FORCE: THE SECURITY COUNCIL

The United Nations presents itself as a comprehensive public order system. Despite persistent weaknesses in multilateral decision-making, the Security Council has primary responsibility for enforcement action to deal with breaches of the peace, threats to the peace or acts of aggression. Individual member states have the right of individual or collective self-defence, but only 'until the Security Council has taken measures necessary to maintain international peace and security'. In the case of regional organizations the power of enforcement is in certain conditions delegated by the Security Council to the organizations concerned.

Enforcement action may involve the use of force against a state. However the practice has evolved of authorizing peacekeeping operations which are contingent upon the consent of the state whose territory is the site of the operations. The roles of peacekeeping and enforcement action have on occasion become confused, with unfortunate results.

Certain corollaries to the legal regime have developed, with significance independently of questions of institutional design. They include: (a) the principle of non-recognition of territorial acquisitions obtained by use or threat of force;[107] and

---

[105] Tomuschat (1999) 281 Hague *Recueil* 9, 224.

[106] Some NATO states argued for a right of unilateral humanitarian intervention to justify the bombing campaign in Kosovo in 1999. For the (predominantly negative) literature: Simma (1999) 10 *EJIL* 1; Kritsiotsis (2000) 49 *ICLQ* 330; Chesterman (2001) 219–36; Holzgrefe & Keohane (eds), *Humanitarian Intervention* (2003); Gray (3rd edn, 2008) 33–55.

[107] Brownlie (1963) 410–23; Brownlie (2002) 1 *Chin JIL* 1, 9. Also: *Legal Consequences of the Construction of a Wall in the Occupied Palestinian Territory*, ICJ Reports 2004 p 136, 171.

(b) the principle that a treaty procured by the threat or use of force in violation of the Charter is void.[108] Certain corollaries are also expressed in the ILC's 2001 Articles on the Responsibility of States for Intentionally Wrongful Acts.[109] The appearance of such corollaries suggests an evolution in the direction of greater consistency, such as one would expect of a public order system at national level. But such great expectations, though long held,[110] have often been frustrated, and it remains true that the legal regime of enforcement has at its heart a broad collective discretion fettered by an unaccountable veto.

(A) THE ROLE OF THE SECURITY COUNCIL[111]

The Security Council is the keystone of the UN system of collective security, bearing 'primary responsibility for the maintenance of international peace and security' under Article 24(1) of the Charter.[112] An essential part of its mandate is its monopoly over the authorization of the use of force, pursuant to Chapter VII.[113] In so doing, the Security Council acts on behalf of the Members, who agree to accept and carry out the decisions of the Security Council (Articles 25 and 48); further, binding decisions of the Council, being obligations under the Charter, prevail over obligations contained in any other agreement (Article 103), though presumably not over peremptory norms.[114]

The Security Council has 15 members, five of them permanent and with a power of veto over any non-procedural decision.[115] This perpetuates the Grand Alliance that emerged victorious from the Second World War: the US, the UK, France, Russia (previously the USSR), and the People's Republic of China. The remaining 10 members are elected from the members of the General Assembly for two-year terms, and may not be immediately re-elected. Every year, five positions on the Security Council become available.

---

[108] McNair, *Treaties* (1961) 209–11, 234–6; Brownlie (1963) 404–5, and see chapter 16.

[109] Appended to GA Res 56/83, 12 December 2001. Cf Arts 39–46, and see chapters 26–7.

[110] Cf Kant, 'Perpetual Peace: A Philosophical Sketch' (1795), reproduced in Reiss (ed), *Kant: Political Writings* (2nd edn, 1992) 93, 105. Also: chapter 1.

[111] Bailey & Daws, *The Procedure of the UN Security Council* (3rd edn, 1998); Simma (2nd edn, 2002); Blokker & Schrijver (eds), *The Security Council and the Use of Force* (2005); Conforti (3rd edn, 2005); Malone, in Weiss & Daws (eds), *The Oxford Handbook on the United Nations* (2007) 117; Gray (3rd edn, 2008) ch 7; Orakhelashvili, *Collective Security* (2011); Wood, 'United Nations, Security Council' (2007) *MPEPIL*.

[112] This responsibility is not exclusive: *Certain Expenses of the United Nations*, ICJ Reports 1962 p 151, 163.

[113] The other substantial portion of its competence is contained in Chapter VI of the Charter, and relates to the peaceful settlement of disputes: Conforti (3rd edn, 2005) 149–69; Orakhelashvili (2011) 26–32.

[114] Thus, the SC could not direct a Member to commit or permit the occurrence of genocide: Genocide Convention, 9 December 1948, 78 UNTS 227, Arts I–II. Further: Orakhelashvili, *Peremptory Norms in International Law* (2006) ch 12; and chapter 27.

[115] Generally UN Charter, Art 27. Art 27(3) requires with respect to non-procedural matters the 'concurring votes' of all permanent members. But the practice of the SC has been to require a 'veto' to be positively exercised; accordingly, abstention by a permanent member will not prevent the adoption of a resolution. This was confirmed by the Court in *Legal Consequences for States of the Continued Presence of South Africa in Namibia (South West Africa) notwithstanding SC Res 276 (1970)*, ICJ Reports 1971 p 16, 22.

The drafters of the Charter intended the Security Council to be the central enforcement organ of the United Nations. The subsequent breakdown of relations between the USSR and the western powers resulted in a deadlock, and the Security Council was largely ineffective until the end of the Cold War.[116] The permanent members of the Security Council co-operated in response to the Iraqi invasion of Kuwait,[117] and the subsequent prosecution of the first Gulf War. The capacity for co-operation has been somewhat variable since then, with the co-ordinated reaction to the 11 September 2001 attacks on the US[118] disintegrating with the US invasion of Iraq in 2003.[119] More recently, the Security Council has demonstrated again its capacity for meaningful action with its intervention in the Libyan insurgency.[120]

(B) DETERMINATION PRIOR TO THE AUTHORIZATION OF FORCE: ARTICLE 39

Within the UN system, the Security Council is the sole body with the capacity to authorize the use of force. The taking or authorizing the use of force is only one of several measures available to the Council under Chapter VII. The starting point is Article 39, which provides:

The Security Council shall determine the existence of any threat to the peace, breach of the peace or act of aggression and shall make recommendations, or decide what measures should be taken in accordance with Articles 41 and 42, to maintain or restore international peace and security.

Only those resolutions that are *intra vires* the Charter acquire binding force on Members under Article 25, which speaks of 'decisions of the Security Council 'in accordance with the present Charter'. To this end, Article 39 functions as the gateway to Chapter VII: before taking action, the Council must first determine the existence of a threat to or breach of the peace, or an act of aggression. But the Council enjoys wide discretion.[121] Article 39 sets no express limits, and it is difficult to think of realistic scenarios in which such determinations would be justiciable.[122]

---

[116] Further: Gray (3rd edn, 2008) 255–63. Such was the deadlock of the Security Council that the Western powers in 1950 contrived the passing of the so-called Uniting for Peace resolution, envisaging the exercise of (recommendatory) competence by the General Assembly, if the Security Council fails to exercise its functions: GA Res 377(V), 3 November 1950 (adopted 50–5 (Czechoslovakia, Poland, Ukraine, USSR, Belorussia): 2 (India, Argentina)). The substance of the resolution was confirmed in *Certain Expenses of the United Nations (Article 17, paragraph 2, of the Charter)*, ICJ Reports 1962 p 151, 164 and *Wall*, ICJ Reports 2004 p 136, 148–9. Further: Binder, 'Uniting for Peace Resolution (1950)' (2006) *MPEPIL*.

[117] E.g. SC Res 660 (1990); SC Res 661 (1990); SC Res 662 (1990); SC Res 664 (1990), SC Res 665 (1990); SC Res 678 (1990); SC Res 686 (1991).

[118] E.g. SC Res 1373 (2001).

[119] SC Res 1441 (2002). Further Weller (2010) ch 5.

[120] SC Res 1970 (2011); SC Res 1973 (2011).

[121] Frowein & Krisch, in 1 Simma (2nd edn, 2002) 717, 719; Conforti (3rd edn, 2005) 171–2; Orakhelashvili (2011) 149–71.

[122] *Certain Expenses*, ICJ Reports 1962 p 151, 168 (holding that in the absence of any specific procedure to clarify the validity of the Organization's institutions, each one must determine its own jurisdiction);

(i) 'Threat to the peace'[123]

The notion of a threat to the peace is mercurial: it raises the possibility of multiple perspectives as to what constitutes a threat,[124] a position which led the International Criminal Tribunal for the Former Yugoslavia (ICTY) in the *Tadić* case to note that declaration of a threat entails a factual and political judgment, not a legal one.[125] A threat to the peace is, practically speaking, the only Article 39 declaration needing to be made by the Security Council.[126]

At its most basic, the concept is intended to enable a response to imminent armed conflict between states.[127] Severe intrastate violence (such as the Balkan War prior to the splintering of Yugoslavia),[128] serious violations of human rights and humanitarian law (such as in Somalia and other east/central African nations during the early 1990s),[129] and terrorism[130] have also been designated as threats to the peace.

The concept has been further expanded to include not only situations in which the use of armed force appears imminent, but those where factors subsist that may *lead* to the use of force. In 1992, the President of the Security Council stated that '[t]he absence of war and military conflicts amongst states does not in itself ensure international peace and security. Non-military sources of instability in the economic, social, humanitarian and ecological fields have become "threats to peace and security"'.[131] The Security Council has yet to expressly utilize this 'expanded' mandate.

(ii) 'Breach of the peace'

A breach of the peace within the meaning of Article 39 is typically characterized by hostility between the armed units of two states.[132] Since the term focuses on the

---

Application of the Convention on the Prevention and Punishment of the Crime of Genocide (Bosnia and Herzegovina v Serbia and Montenegro), Provisional Measures, ICJ Reports 1993 p 325, 439 (Judge ad hoc Lauterpacht); *Questions of Interpretation and Application of the 1971 Montreal Convention arising from the Aerial Incident at Lockerbie (Libya v UK)*, Provisional Measures, ICJ Reports 1992 p 3, 66 (Judge Weeramantry, diss). Cf, however, the decision on jurisdiction in the *Tadić* case, where the Appeals Chamber of the ICTY examined the validity of the ICTY Statute, SC Res 827 (1993): *Prosecutor v Tadić* (1995) 105 ILR 419 (jurisdiction). Also: Gowlland-Debbas (1994) 43 *ICLQ* 55; Gowlland-Debbas (1994) 88 *AJIL* 643; Gardam (1995) 285 *Mich JIL* 285; Akande (1997) 46 *ICLQ* 309; Cronin-Furman (2006) 106 *Col LR* 435.

[123] Frowein & Krisch, in 1 Simma (2nd edn, 2002) 717, 722–6; Orakhelashvili (2011) 149–75.

[124] Kelsen, *The Law of the United Nations* (1950) 737 ('threat to the peace, breach of the peace allow a highly subjective interpretation'); Frowein & Krisch, in 1 Simma (2nd edn, 2002) 717, 722.

[125] (1995) 105 ILR 419, 435 (Jurisdiction). The Chamber attributed these sentiments (apparently falsely) to Judge Weeramantry's dissent in *Lockerbie*.

[126] Frowein & Krisch, in 1 Simma (2nd edn, 2002) 717, 722.

[127] E.g. SC Res 1298 (2000) (continued fighting between Ethiopia and Eritrea considered a threat). Also: SC Res 353 (1974) (on Cyprus); SC Res 1304 (2000) (on the DRC).

[128] E.g. SC Res 713 (1991); SC Res 724 (1991).

[129] SC Res 794 (1992) (on Somalia); SC Res 929 (1994) (on Rwanda); SC Res 1078 (1996) (on Zaire).

[130] SC Res 731 (1992); SC Res 748 (1992) (on Libya's failure to respond fully and effectively to the Lockerbie and UTA Flight 772 bombings). Also: SC Res 1373 (2001) (requiring states to take measures combating the financing of terrorism in response to the 11 September 2001 attacks).

[131] S/23500, 31 January 1992, §3. Further: Talmon (2005) 99 *AJIL* 175, 180.

[132] Frowein & Krisch, in 1 Simma (2nd edn, 2002) 717, 721.

point at which hostilities commence, it accordingly becomes irrelevant if one side is defeated quickly thereafter. In SC Resolution 502, the Security Council considered the Argentine invasion of the Falklands to be a breach of the peace even prior to the UK's counter-offensive.[133] A similar determination was made following the Iraqi invasion of Kuwait in 1990.[134]

(iii) 'Act of aggression'

In 1974 the General Assembly adopted Resolution 3314 on the definition of aggression. It defines 'aggression' broadly as:[135]

the use of armed force by a state against the sovereignty, territorial integrity or political independence of another state or in any other manner inconsistent with the Charter of the United Nations, as set out in this definition.

Article 2 provides that the first use of armed force by a state in contravention of the Charter constitutes prima facie evidence of an act of aggression (though the Security Council may determine otherwise based on relevant circumstances, including the gravity of the alleged act). The substance of the definition is contained principally in Article 3, which lists a series of acts considered instances of aggression. Noteworthy is the final paragraph, which covers:

(g) The sending by or on behalf of a state of armed bands, groups, irregulars or mercenaries, which carry out acts of armed force against another state of such gravity as to amount to the acts listed above, or its substantial involvement therein.

The phrase 'or its substantial involvement therein' indicates that the formulation extends to the provision of logistical support,[136] even if the Court in *Nicaragua* was unwilling to permit such an extension with respect to the definition of 'armed attack' under Article 51.

As a somewhat dated, non-binding resolution, GA Resolution 3314(XXIX) might have been increasingly disregarded.[137] However, the International Criminal Court (ICC) Assembly of States Parties in 2010 adopted a definition of the crime of aggression for the purposes of the Rome Statute of the International Criminal Court.[138] Notably, Article 8*bis*(2) provides that *acts* of aggression which may generate individual criminal responsibility for the *crime* of aggression[139] are the same as those contained in Article 3 of GA Resolution 3314. To this is added the more general perambulatory

---

[133] SC Res 502 (1982), preamble.
[134] SC Res 660 (1990), preamble.
[135] GA Res 3314(XXIX), 14 December 1974, Art 1.
[136] The drafting history of Art 3(g) is examined in *Nicaragua*, ICJ Reports 1986 p 14, 341–7 (Judge Schwebel, diss).
[137] But cf *Armed Activities (DRC v Uganda)*, ICJ Reports 2005 p 168, 223 (referring to the resolution).
[138] 17 July 1998, 2187 UNTS 3, Art 8*bis*.
[139] ICC Statute, Art 8*bis*(1) ('the planning, preparation, initiation or execution, by a person in a position effectively to exercise control over or to direct the political or military action of a State, of an act of aggression which, by its character, gravity and scale, constitutes a manifest violation of the [Charter]').

definition of 'the use of armed force by a State against the sovereignty, territorial integrity or political independence of another State, or in any other manner inconsistent with the Charter of the United Nations', derived from Article 1 of Resolution 3314 and Article 2(4) of the Charter.

(c) RESPONSES TO THE THREATS TO OR BREACHES OF THE PEACE

Following an Article 39 determination, the Security Council may decide that provisional (Article 40), non-forcible (Article 41), or forcible (Article 42) measures shall be taken to maintain or restore international peace or security. In exercising its Chapter VII powers, the Council is subject to certain constitutional limitations.[140] It 'shall act in accordance with the Purposes and Principles of the United Nations' (Article 24(2)), and is presumably bound by peremptory norms (though not international law more generally).[141] In addition, it is limited by strictures of necessity and proportionality.

(i) Provisional measures: Article 40[142]

Before making recommendations or deciding on measures under Article 39, the Security Council may order the imposition of provisional measures under Article 40. Unlike the balance of Chapter VII, Article 40 was used with some regularity during the Cold War period, a situation that has not changed with the dissolution of the USSR.[143]

The relationship between Article 39 and Article 40 is not clearly delineated. The practice of the Security Council, however, supports the notion that an Article 39 determination is a precondition to provisional measures.[144]

Provisional measures leave unaffected the legal position of the parties to the dispute.[145] Thus the Security Council could not call on a Member to acknowledge its own breach of Article 2(4) or its violation of another Member's territorial sovereignty. It can, however, call on Members to observe a ceasefire or withdraw troops from certain areas.[146] Whether measures under Article 40 are binding on Members depends on

---

[140] Gardam (1996) 17 *Mich JIL* 285; Frowein & Krisch, in 1 Simma (2nd edn, 2002) 701, 710–12.

[141] Ibid, 711–12.

[142] Generally: Bailey (1977) 71 *AJIL* 461; Frowein & Krisch, in 1 Simma (2nd edn, 2002) 729; Conforti (3rd edn, 2005) 182–5.

[143] Though what has been seen is an increased willingness to couple measures under Art 40 with the more persuasive means at the disposal of the SC under Arts 41–2: Conforti (3rd edn, 2005) 184.

[144] Frowein & Krisch, in 1 Simma (2nd edn, 2002) 729, 731.

[145] Ibid, 732.

[146] Dinstein (5th edn, 2011) 54–61. E.g. SC Res 27 (1947) (on the Indonesian war of independence); SC Res 50 (1948); SC Res 54 (1948) (on the Arab–Israeli conflict); SC Res 92 (1951) (on the Middle East); SC Res 82 (1950) (on Korea); SC Res 104 (1954) (on Guatemala); SC Res 164 (1961) (on the Franco-Tunisian War); SC Res 209 (1965); SC Res 210 (1965) (on India and Pakistan); SC Res 233 (1967); SC Res 234 (1967); SC Res 235 (1967) (on the Six Day War); SC Res 353 (1974); SC Res 357 (1974) (on Cyprus); SC Res 205 (1982) (on the Falklands War); SC Res 514 (1982); SC Res 582 (1986) (on the Iran–Iraq War); SC Res 812 (1993) (on Rwanda), SC Res 1052 (1996) (on Lebanon); SC Res 1097 (1997) (on eastern Zaire and the Great Lakes region); SC Res 1397 (2002); 1435 (2002) (on Israel and Palestine); SC Res 1484 (2003); 1493 (2003) (on the DRC); SC Res 1497 (2003); 1509 (2003) (on Liberia).

the interpretation of the resolution; certainly they can be.[147] But particularly when considering a provisional measure requiring a ceasefire, compliance vis-à-vis one belligerent is in practice conditioned on the reciprocity of the other, even if the resolution is framed in absolute terms.[148]

(ii) Non-forcible measures: Article 41[149]

The basis for all non-military enforcement measures is Article 41 of the Charter, which empowers the Security Council to 'decide what measures not involving the use of armed force are to be employed to give effect to its decisions'. Such measures may include 'complete or partial interruption of economic relations and of rail, sea, air, postal and telegraphic, radio and other means of communication, and the severance of diplomatic relations'.

The Security Council is not responsible for the direct enforcement of non-forcible measures; rather it obliges Members to implement any measures so ordered,[150] with Articles 25 and 103 of the Charter providing that the obligation to implement takes precedence over any other treaty obligation.[151]

Due to the deadlock within the Security Council, Article 41 was invoked only twice during the Cold War era, both times with limited effect.[152] After 1989, however, it experienced a surge of activity.[153] But it quickly became apparent that economic penalties imposed pursuant to Article 41 could inflict serious harm on citizens of embargoed states without engendering any will to comply in the government in question. An early example concerned Iraq following the invasion of Kuwait: a dire humanitarian situation, due in part to Security Council-imposed sanctions, coincided with the Iraqi government growing ever more obstreperous. Article 41 is a 'blunt instrument'.[154]

---

[147] E.g. SC Res 54 (1948); SC Res 59 (1948) (on Palestine); SC Res 598 (1987) (on the Iran–Iraq War); SC Res 660 (1990) (on the Iraqi invasion of Kuwait). Further: Frowein & Krisch, in 1 Simma (2nd edn, 2002) 729, 734–5; cf Conforti (3rd edn, 2005) 183. The binding character of the measure, however, will be predicated on the use of suitably mandatory wording, e.g., 'orders', 'demands', or 'decides' versus 'calls for' or 'appeals', as is indeed the case with all Chapter VII resolutions. Compare, e.g. the two clauses in SC Res 1593 (2005) op §1 (referring the situation in Darfur to the ICC).

[148] Frowein & Krisch, in 1 Simma (2nd edn, 2002) 729, 734–5.

[149] Kelsen (1946) 12 *Can JEPS* 429; Doxey, *International Sanctions in Contemporary Perspective* (2nd edn, 1996); Frowein & Krisch, in 1 Simma (2nd edn, 2002) 735; Conforti (3rd edn, 2005) 185–9; Gray (3rd edn, 2008) 266–72; Orakhelashvili (2011) 188–220.

[150] But cf Orakhelashvili (2006) ch 14; Tzanakopoulos, *Disobeying the Security Council* (2011).

[151] Some treaty regimes acknowledge this expressly in order to avoid complication: e.g. Marrakesh Agreement establishing the World Trade Organization, 15 April 1994, 1867 UNTS 3, Annex 1A; General Agreement on Tariffs and Trade, Art XXI(c).

[152] E.g. SC Res 232 (1966); SC Res 253 (1986) (against Southern Rhodesia); SC Res 418 (1977) (against South Africa). Further: Conforti (3rd edn, 2005) 187–8.

[153] Gray (3rd edn, 2008) 266. Further: SC Res 661 (1990); SC Res 687 (1991). Also: SC Res 757 (1992) (on the former Yugoslavia); SC Res 841 (1993); SC Res 917 (1994) (on Haiti). For a further overview: Frowein & Krisch, in 1 Simma (2nd edn, 2002) 735, 738.

[154] UN Secretary-General, *Supplement to an Agenda for Peace*, A/50/60, 3 January 1995, §70; cf also the *Millennium Report*, A/54/2000, 27 March 2000, §50. Further: Reisman & Stenvick (1998) 9 *EJIL* 86; Conforti (3rd edn, 2005) 191.

It has been deployed in a number of ways.[155] Despite the apparent constraints on the list of possible measures, these are illustrative only.[156] Although Article 41 measures are often referred to as 'sanctions', they do not have to be directed against the belligerent but may be employed in any manner deemed conducive to international peace and security.[157]

Article 41 measures are usually economic in character. In order to avoid harming civilian populations, the Security Council is now more circumspect in its use of the provision, implementing so-called 'smart sanctions' targeting specific industries or imports, like arms,[158] or individuals.[159] But if these do not work, the only option remaining to the Security Council is to levy more punitive sanctions,[160] or to authorize the collective use of force under Article 42. Diplomatic measures may also be taken with Members called upon to reduce the number or level of staff at the diplomatic and consular missions of the offending state.[161] Where the situation calls for it, the Security Council may also establish international criminal tribunals[162] such as the International Criminal Tribunals for the Former Yugoslavia[163] and Rwanda,[164] and latterly, refer situations to the ICC pursuant to Article 13(b) of the ICC Statute.[165] It has used the provision to create subsidiary investigative panels.[166]

---

[155] Generally: Frowein & Krisch, in 1 Simma (2nd edn, 2002) 735, 740–5.

[156] Cf *Prosecutor v Tadić* (1995) 105 ILR 419, 469–70 (jurisdiction).

[157] Cf the predecessor of Art 41, Art 16(1) of the Covenant of the League of Nations. Further: Frowein & Krisch, in 1 Simma (2nd edn, 2002) 735, 739.

[158] E.g. SC Res 1970 (2011) op §§9–13 (concerning events in Libya preceding the overthrow of Colonel Qaddafi).

[159] E.g. SC Res 1970 (2011) op §§15–16 & Annex I (travel bans placed on certain individuals) and operative §§17–21 & Annex II (freezing certain assets). The practice of targeting individuals with the weight of a Chapter VII resolution has raised human rights concerns: Bulterman (2006) 17 *LJIL* 753; O'Donnell (2006) 17 *EJIL* 945. For the *Kadi* cases: chapter 29.

[160] As in the case of the measures called for against Libya in response to the Lockerbie and UTA Flight 772 bombings: SC Res 731 (1992); SC Res 748 (1992); SC Res 883 (1993); SC Res 1192 (1998); SC Res 1506 (2003). These were in effect for over a decade. Also: SC Res 1033 (1996); SC Res 1054 (1996); SC Res 1070 (1996); SC Res 1372 (2001) (with respect to Sudan following the attempted assassination of President Mubarak of Egypt); SC Res 1189 (1998); SC Res 1214 (1998); SC Res 1267 (1999); SC Res 1333 (2000) (against Afghanistan and the Taliban following attacks against US embassies in Nairobi and Dar-es-Salaam).

[161] E.g. SC Res 748 (1992) op §6.

[162] The SC in the relevant resolutions does not refer to Art 41 specifically, but rather states generally that it is using its powers under Chapter VII. But the power to create international tribunals is interpreted as arising from Art 41: *Prosecutor v Tadić* (1995) 105 ILR 419, 469–70 (jurisdiction). Although once controversial, the capacity of the Security Council to create such tribunals is no longer questioned: ibid; *Prosecutor v Kanyabashi*, ICTR-96-15-T, Trial Chamber, Decision on Jurisdiction, 18 June 1997; Schabas, *The UN International Criminal Tribunals* (2006) ch 2; and further chapter 30.

[163] SC Res 827 (1993).

[164] SC Res 955 (1994). Also: SC Res 1315 (2000), requesting the Secretary-General to start negotiations with Sierra Leone to create the Special Court for Sierra Leone.

[165] SC Res 1593 (2005) (referring the situation in Sudan to the ICC); SC Res 1970 (2011) op §§4–8 (referring to the situation in Libya). The Security Council can also under ICC Statute Art 16 request that the Court delay investigation or prosecution of a matter for up to 12 months. At the urging of the US, this was used *preemptively* to shield all UN-authorized missions from prosecution: SC Res 1422 (2002); SC Res 1483 (2003). Further: Zappalà (2003) 1 *JICJ* 114; Stahn (2003) 14 *EJIL* 85; Schabas, *An Introduction to the International Criminal Court* (3rd edn, 2007) 24–32.

[166] SC Res 1556 (2004); SC Res 1564 (2004); SC Res 1591 (2005) (creating an international commission of inquiry in relation to human rights abuses in Darfur, leading to referral of the matter to the ICC); SC Res

A more controversial development in the practice of the Security Council is the so-called 'legislative' resolution.[167] Such resolutions do not seek to respond to a particular situation but rather to some general phenomenon, and may necessitate the passage of detailed domestic legislation. The first example occurred in response to the events of 11 September 2001. SC Resolution 1373 required Members to introduce measures to combat the financing of terrorism,[168] drawing heavily on the International Convention for the Suppression of the Financing of Terrorism.[169] It created the Counter-Terrorism Committee to oversee implementation of the resolution.[170]

(iii) Forcible measures: Article 42[171]

Article 42 allows the Security Council to 'take such action by air, sea or land forces as may be necessary to maintain or restore international peace or security'. Such action may include 'demonstrations, blockade, and other operations by air, sea or land forces of Members of the United Nations'.

Article 42 was a fundamental innovation of the Charter, representing a break from Article 16(2) of the Covenant under which the League Council could only recommend the application of collective force against an aggressor. It remains incomplete in one important respect, however: Article 43 requires Members to place troops directly at the UN's disposal via 'special agreement', but these agreements never came to pass, preventing the formation of a UN 'standing army' dedicated to the maintenance of international peace and security. The result has been the reliance of the Security Council on volunteer 'coalitions of the willing' to enforce its resolutions.[172] This delegation of enforcement action has been considered controversial,[173] but constitutionally the matter appears to have been settled, with the Security Council apparently capable of such action even where the conditions of Article 43 have not been met. The International Court in *Certain Expenses* rejected the view that the Security Council was unable to take forcible action: the Charter did not require that the Security Council be 'impotent in the face of an emergency situation when agreements under Article 43 have not been concluded'.[174] Even so, the ad hoc formation of coalitions is far from an effective

---

1595 (2005); SC Res 1636 (2005); SC Res 1644 (2005); SC Res 1757 (2007) (creating an international commission of inquiry to investigate the assassination of former Lebanese Prime Minister Rafiq Hariri, leading to the creation of the Special Tribunal for Lebanon).

[167] Further: Lavalle (2004) 41 *NILR* 411; Talmon (2005) 99 *AJIL* 175; Bianchi (2006) 17 *EJIL* 881; Joyner (2007) 20 *LJIL* 489; Hinojosa-Martínez (2008) 57 *ICLQ* 333; Orakhelashvili (2011) 220–2.

[168] Also: SC Res 1540 (2004), addressing the non-proliferation of weapons of mass destruction.

[169] 9 December 1999, 2178 UNTS 197.

[170] Further: Rosand (2003) 97 *AJIL* 333; Donnelly, in Eden & O'Donnell (eds), *September 11, 2001* (2005) 757.

[171] Generally: Frowein & Krisch, in 1 Simma (2nd edn, 2002) 749; Gray (3rd edn, 2008) ch 8; Orakhelashvili (2011) 223–59.

[172] Frowein & Krisch, in 1 Simma (2nd edn, 2002) 749, 751; Franck (2002) 24; Gray (3rd edn, 2008) 327–9.

[173] Sarooshi, *The United Nations and the Development of Collective Security* (1999); Blokker (2000) 11 *EJIL* 541; Gray (3rd edn, 2008) 327–69; Dinstein (5th edn, 2011) 303–35.

[174] Although the Court was here referring to peacekeeping operations, the same line of reasoning applies to more direct uses of force under Art 42: *Certain Expenses*, ICJ Reports 1962 p 151, 167.

solution, with many situations going unaddressed due to a lack of political will on the part of those who ordinarily contribute to Article 42 operations.[175]

Article 42 remained something of a dead letter during the Cold War. Before 1991, the only case of large-scale collective use of force following action by the Security Council was not authorized under Article 42; rather, the UN commitment to the Korean War followed a Security Council recommendation that other nations aid South Korea in repelling the North Korean attack by way of collective self-defence under Article 51.[176] Since 1990, however, Article 42 has been utilized repeatedly (though not expressly) by the Security Council. Operation *Desert Storm*, to repel the Iraqi invasion of Kuwait,[177] represented the high-water mark of such action. Such a co-ordinated, pan-regional response (with over 30 contributing nations) has not been replicated since; rather, smaller coalitions of the willing have formed, often based around regional arrangements.

Nonetheless, the Security Council has been able to achieve a consensus sufficient to authorize the use of force on numerous occasions. A large-scale operation was mounted in Somalia in 1992;[178] the peacekeeping operation itself in 1993.[179] Limited use of force in support of humanitarian operations was authorized with respect to the Balkan War in 1992, expanded to support economic sanctions and a no-fly zone soon afterwards, and finally extended to cover the use of force in the defence of 'safe areas', which led to a prolonged NATO bombing campaign in 1995.[180] In 1994, force was authorized in order to instate the elected president of Haiti.[181] Difficulties encountered in addressing the situations in Bosnia and Somalia, however, caused the Security Council to adopt a more cautious attitude towards Article 42, ordering the use of force only reluctantly and with considerable qualification.[182]

Overhanging all has been the major controversy over the US/UK attempt to justify the invasion of Iraq in 2003 on the ground that SC Resolution 1441 of 2002 'revived' an earlier 'implied' authorization to use force in SC Resolution 678.[183] The better

---

[175] Emblematic of this is the Rwandan genocide, which attracted action by the Security Council only after a considerable time due to unwillingness of members to provide sufficient troops: Frowein & Krisch, in 1 Simma (2nd edn, 2002) 749, 752.

[176] SC Res 83 (1950) ('The Security Council...*[r]ecommends* that the Members of the United Nations furnish such assistance to the Republic of Korea as may be necessary to repel the armed attack and to restore international peace and security to the area'). The authorization of a peacekeeping operation in the Congo in 1961 was based on some elements of Art 42: SC Res 161 (1961); SC Res 169 (1961). Art 42 was also invoked in turning oil tankers away from the embargoed Rhodesia: SC Res 221 (1966). Further: Frowein & Krisch, in 1 Simma (2nd edn, 2002) 749, 751.

[177] SC Res 665 (1990); SC Res 678 (1990); Schachter (1991) 85 *AJIL* 452; Gray (3rd edn, 2008) 327–9.

[178] SC Res 794 (1992).

[179] SC Res 814 (1993).

[180] SC Res 770 (1993); SC Res 787 (1993); SC Res 816 (1993); SC Res 836 (1993). Further: Weller (1996) 56 *ZaöRV* 70.

[181] SC Res 875 (1993); SC Res 917 (1994); SC Res 940 (1994).

[182] Further Frowein & Krisch, in 1 Simma (2nd edn, 2002) 749, 752; Gray (3rd edn, 2008) 327–48 .

[183] (2003) 52 *ICLQ* 811; Greenwood (2003) 4 *San Diego ILJ* 7. On SC Res 1441 (2002) itself: Byers (2004) 10 *GG* 165.

and certainly more widely held view rejects the doctrine of revival after more than a decade;[184] and although the subsequent occupation of Iraq was covered by Chapter VII resolutions, this was done in terms which left the original illegality very much open.[185]

The controversy casts a long shadow. In relation to the 2011 authorization of force in Libya, SC Resolution 1973 confined the use of force to 'protect[ing] civilians and civilian populated areas under threat of attack in the Libyan Arab Jamahiriya, including Benghazi, while excluding a foreign occupation force of any form on any part of Libyan territory' and the support of a no-fly zone.[186] Again there were suggestions that outright support for the rebels went beyond the limited scope of SC Resolution 1973.[187] This may well be true, but the contrast between responses to Iraq and Libya shows the value of a Security Council umbrella—or even a semblance of one.

(D) REGIONAL ARRANGEMENTS: CHAPTER VIII OF THE CHARTER[188]

With the expansion of the role of the United Nations post-1989, the role of regional organizations has expanded as well, raising questions as to the interaction between them. The Secretary-General's 1992 Report, 'Agenda for Peace', was optimistic as to the roles that might be played by such organizations.[189] This was reiterated in a further Report in 1995.[190]

Regional action under the Charter is governed by Chapter VIII. Article 52(1) provides that regional arrangements may deal with matters relating to the maintenance of international peace and security which are appropriate for regional action, provided that such arrangements are consistent with the principles and purposes of the UN. Article 53(1) provides that the Security Council may authorize regional arrangements to undertake enforcement action under its authority, though action may not be taken without Security Council approval. Article 54 provides that any action undertaken by regional arrangements for the maintenance of international peace and security must be brought to the attention of the Security Council. Nothing in Chapter VIII authorizes regional arrangements to undertake the unilateral use of force.

---

[184] E.g. Hofman (2002) 45 *GYIL* 9; Wolfrum (2003) 7 *MPUNYB* 1; Gray (3rd edn, 2008) 354–66; Dinstein (5th edn, 2011) 322–5 (arguing that Coalition action was nonetheless justified as an exercise of collective self-defence).

[185] E.g. SC Res 1472 (2003); SC Res 1476 (2003); SC Res 1483 (2003); SC Res 1490 (2003); SC Res 1500 (2003); SC Res 1511 (2003); SC Res 1518 (2003); SC Res 1537 (2004); SC Res 1546 (2004); SC Res 1557 (2004); SC Res 1619 (2005); SC Res 1637 (2005).

[186] SC Res 1973 (2011) op §§4, 7.

[187] E.g. Henderson (2011) 60 *ICLQ* 767, and more stridently Posner, 'Outside the Law' (*Foreign Policy*, 25 October 2011), www.foreignpolicy.com/articles/2011/10/25/libya_international_law_qaddafi_nato?page=0,0.

[188] Hummer & Schweitzer, in 1 Simma (2nd edn, 2002) 807; Gray (3rd edn, 2008) ch 9; Dinstein (5th edn, 2011) 282–302.

[189] Report of the Secretary-General, A/47/277, 17 June 1992, §VII.

[190] Report of the Secretary-General, A/50/60, 25 January 1995.

Chapter VIII thus gives a certain constitutional role to regional arrangements. Such organizations currently include the Organization of American States (OAS), the League of Arab States, the African Union, the Organization for Security and Cooperation in Europe, the Organization of Eastern Caribbean States, ECOWAS, and, most notably, the EU and NATO. In practice the Security Council has been pragmatic in accepting the status of organizations as regional arrangements for the purpose of using its powers to authorize enforcement action.

The important distinction is between a collective self-defence organization, which hinges on a member being the victim of an armed attack, and the looser concept of a response to a 'threat to the peace of the region'. In the Cuban missile crisis the US justified the blockade of Cuba on the basis of the provisions in the Inter-American Treaty of Reciprocal Assistance which related to the regional peacekeeping function, no doubt because the emplacement of Soviet missiles in Cuba did not plausibly constitute an 'armed attack'.[191]

The surge in peacekeeping operations since 2003 has led to calls for increased UN engagement with regional arrangements.[192] United Nations and regional peacekeeping forces have co-operated in, *inter alia*, Liberia, Georgia, Tajikistan, Sierra Leone, Côte d'Ivoire, and the DRC.[193] In SC Resolution 1464, Members participating in an ECOWAS-led peacekeeping operation under Chapter VIII were authorized 'to take the necessary steps to guarantee the security and freedom of movement of their personnel and to ensure...the protection of civilians immediately threatened with physical violence within their zones of operation, using the means available to them'.[194] The Security Council has also demonstrated that it is willing to permit regional arrangements to take more informal control over enforcement action. Although SC Resolution 1973 permitted Members generally to take enforcement action against Libya, the resultant operation was almost entirely planned and undertaken by NATO forces.[195]

4. CONTINUING SOURCES OF CONTROVERSY UNDER THE CHARTER

Since 1945 there have been significant sources of controversy in the legal regime presented thus far.

---

[191] Akehurst (1967) 42 *BY* 175; R Kennedy, *Thirteen Days* (1968); Chayes, *The Cuban Missile Crisis* (1974). If Soviet missiles in Cuba were an armed attack, then so were US missiles in Turkey. Chayes (1974) Appendices I–III usefully reproduce the key legal advices.

[192] Gray (3rd edn, 2008) 371.

[193] Ibid, 382.

[194] SC Res 1464 (2003) op §9. Also: SC Res 1497 (2003) preamble, op §3; SC Res 1498 (2003) op §1; SC Res 1508 (2003) op §§8, 9; generally SC Res 1509 (2003); SC Res 1521 (2003).

[195] SC Res 1973 (2011) and note particularly op §5, recognizing the potential role of the League of Arab States under Chapter VIII.

(A) HEGEMONIC INTERVENTION ON THE BASIS OF REGIONAL ARRANGEMENTS

Here three episodes may be recalled. The first was the action taken by the OAS in the Cuban missile crisis. On 22 October 1962 President Kennedy announced that the OAS would be asked to invoke Articles 6 and 8 of the Rio Treaty of 1947.[196] Thus, the action taken was not related to Article 3 of the Rio Treaty which is predicated upon the existence of an armed attack and the provisions of Article 51 of the Charter. The point is that the *casus foederis* of the Rio Treaty extends to mere threats to the peace of the region, and is not limited to the concept of self-defence. In the second place there was the crisis in the Dominican Republic in 1965 and the dispatch of an Inter-American Peace Force.[197] In this case the jurisdiction of the Security Council was recognized in principle at least. Lastly, there was the Soviet-led Warsaw Pact invasion of Czechoslovakia in 1968.[198] In this instance the parties to the Warsaw Pact treated it as a regional arrangement, in spite of the fact that the language of the Pact was contingent upon the existence of an armed attack. No armed attack on Czechoslovakia had in fact taken place. The problem presented by this type of action by regional arrangements is that it gives rise to a second-hand and low-level legitimacy without the more objective constraints of Article 51.

(B) FORCIBLE INTERVENTION IN A STATE ON THE BASIS OF CONSENT

A second source of controversy is the incidence of intervention based upon the consent of the territorial sovereign.[199] Consent may be given ad hoc or in advance via treaty:[200] it may always be restricted in scope and—depending on the form of consent—withdrawn unilaterally. A recent example is the Regional Assistance Mission to the Solomon Islands, created by the Pacific Islands Forum and sent to the Solomon Islands at its request with a view to restoring internal security.[201]

The title of such intervention is clear: the consent of states.[202] Thus in the context of a civil war, the recognized government of a state is free to request outside assistance in putting down any rebellion, unless perhaps the conflict gains such scope that the insurgency is granted belligerent status.[203] The lawfulness of such activities, conducted with the full consent of the state in conflict, was acknowledged by the International Court in *Armed Activities (DRC v Uganda)*.[204] The problem is that in many cases the

---

[196] Inter-American Treaty of Reciprocal Assistance, 2 September 1947, 21 UNTS 77.
[197] Nanda (1966) 43 *Den LJ* 439; Fenwick (1966) 60 *AJIL* 64; Nanda (1967) 44 *Den LJ* 225.
[198] Goodman (1969) 4 *Int Lawyer* 2.
[199] Brownlie (1963) 317–27. Also: *Nicaragua*, ICJ Reports 1986 p 14.
[200] Dinstein (5th edn, 2011) 122–3.
[201] Australian Practice in International Law (2005) 24 *AYIL* 337, 426–8.
[202] Abass (2004) 53 *ICLQ* 221, 224 ('Article 2(4) of the UN Charter does not take away the sovereign right of States to permit other states to use force on their territory').
[203] Dinstein (5th edn, 2011) 119.
[204] ICJ Reports 2005 p 168, 198–9.

status of the consenting government is problematic. The worst case scenario is the situation in which competing *de facto* governments sponsor foreign intervention.

Further issues may arise when considering the nature of the consent itself. Any intervention on the basis of state consent is best supported by clear evidence of its genuine character.[205] Thus it is impermissible for a puppet government established by an external power to call for the presence of that power on the territory of the state in question,[206] a point made with respect to the Soviet intervention in Hungary in 1956[207] and its later intervention in Afghanistan in 1979.[208] The US intervention in Panama in 1989 was similarly of dubious validity, predicated in part on the consent of the elected President of Panama, sworn in on an American military base.[209]

(C) FORCIBLE INTERVENTION TO NATIONAL LIBERATION MOVEMENTS

Another source of controversy in the period from 1945 to 1990 was the existence of recognized national liberation movements and the legality of external assistance to such movements.[210] In 1974 the UN General Assembly admitted as observers those liberation movements which were recognized by regional organizations at that time. Such recognition was accorded to the Angolan, Mozambican, Palestinian, and Rhodesian movements.

Many states have recognized the purported legality of wars of liberation in certain conditions and, as a consequence, the putative legality of external assistance. The Friendly Relations Declaration[211] and Article 8 of the 1974 Definition of Aggression[212] are both relevant here. But on the other hand the Court in *Nicaragua* stated that state practice did not support the existence of a customary right of intervention, 'directly or indirectly, with or without armed force, in support of an internal opposition in another State, whose cause [appears] particularly worthy by reason of the political and moral values with which it [is] identified'.[213] It would therefore appear that intervention in support of an insurgency must be in accordance with the provisions of Chapter VII, as was the case with NATO's support of Libya's National Transitional Council against the Qaddafi regime in 2011.

[205] Orakhelashvili (2006) 76 *NJIL* 371, 381.

[206] Dinstein (5th edn, 2011) 121.

[207] Wright (1957) 51 *AJIL* 257, 275.

[208] Reisman & Silk (1988) 82 *AJIL* 459, 472–4, 485.

[209] Chestermann, in Goodwin-Gill & Talmon (1999) 57, 85–6.

[210] Abi-Saab (1979) 165 Hague *Recueil* 353, 371–2; Abi-Saab (1987) 207 Hague *Recueil* 9, 410–16; Cassese, *Self-determination of Peoples* (1995) 150–8; Gray (3rd edn, 2008) 88–92.

[211] GA Res 2625(XXV), 24 October 1970, Annex. On the Friendly Relations Declaration: Rosenstock (1971) 65 *AJIL* 713; Arangio-Ruiz (1972) 137 Hague *Recueil* 419; Sinclair, in Warbrick & Lowe (eds), *The United Nations and the Principles of International Law* (1994) 1; Gray, ibid, 33.

[212] GA Res 3314(XXIX), 14 December 1974.

[213] *Nicaragua*, ICJ Reports 1986 p 14, 110–11.

(D) TERRORISM, NON-STATE ACTORS, AND ARTICLE 51 OF THE CHARTER[214]

The issues that have arisen in the fight against international terrorism since 2001 have centred predominantly on the use of force against non-state actors, and more particularly, whether the activities of such actors can constitute an 'armed attack' within the meaning of Article 51. The Charter itself is silent on the subject. Consideration of the issue by the International Court has been generally unhelpful. In the *Wall* advisory opinion, the majority's consideration of the issue was perfunctory.[215] The Court simply remarked that 'Article 51 of the Charter thus recognizes the existence of an inherent right of self-defence in the case of armed attack *by one State against another State*',[216] thereby apparently excluding non-state actors. In *Armed Activities (DRC v Uganda)*, the majority declined to address the issue,[217] attracting criticism from judges in the minority.[218]

The conclusion appears to be that a state under assault by non-state actors cannot effectively defend itself against them by recourse to Article 51 unless, following the position of the Court in *Nicaragua*, they are under the effective control of a foreign state.[219] Three potential counter-arguments to this exist:

(1) Notwithstanding the *Wall* opinion, Article 51 of the Charter *does* permit the exercise of self-defence against non-state actors.

(2) The criterion in *Nicaragua* for the attribution of the actions of irregular forces to a state should be loosened.

(3) Where non-state actors are taking refuge in a state unable to exert the control necessary to prevent attacks, Article 51 ought to permit action in self-defence.

The first position was taken by Judge Higgins in the *Wall* opinion,[220] arguing that the limitation imposed by the majority derived not from the text of the Charter but from the Court's earlier opinion in *Nicaragua*, itself a flawed appropriation of Article 3(g) of Resolution 3314(XXIX).[221] The upshot is effectively that the right to self-defence must give way to territorial sovereignty unless a state has participated in an armed attack, a position Judge Higgins argues is 'operationally unworkable'. Nonetheless,

---

[214] Byers (2002) 51 *ICLQ* 401; Paust (2002) 35 *Cornell ILJ* 533; Duffy (2005) chs 3, 5; Ruys & Verhoeven (2005) 10 *JCSL* 289; Trapp (2007) 56 *ICLQ* 141; Gray (3rd edn, 2008) ch 6; Tams (2009) 20 *EJIL* 359.

[215] Further: Murphy (2005) 99 *AJIL* 62, 62; Scobbie (2005) 99 *AJIL* 76, 87; Tams (2005) 16 *EJIL* 963.

[216] ICJ Reports 2003 p 3, 194 (emphasis added). The Court here drew a distinction between an entirely external attack, and an attack from within on an occupying power such as Israel. Further: Franck (2002) ch 4; Tams (2005) 16 *EJIL* 293; Gray (3rd edn, 2008) 134–5; Tams (2009) 20 *EJIL* 359.

[217] *Armed Activities (DRC v Uganda)*, ICJ Reports 2005 p 168, 223.

[218] Ibid, 311–5 (Judge Kooijmans); 335–7 (Judge Simma).

[219] Generally: Reisman (1999) 22 *Hous JIL* 39.

[220] ICJ Reports 2003 p 3, 215 (Judge Higgins). Also: ibid, 242–3 (Judge Buergenthal); 229–30 (Judge Kooijmans).

[221] Higgins (1994) 250–1.

Judge Higgins conceded that this was an authoritative statement of the law as it then stood.[222]

Any rebuttal of *Wall* is contingent on the recognition of a shift in state practice that has occurred since 2001. Until this point, unilateral action in response to the activities of non-state actors free of the effective control of a state was frowned upon,[223] primarily due to the infringement of sovereignty it represented, but also because acts of 'self-defence' actually carried out during this period appeared rather to be punitive reprisals. The Israeli bombing of Beirut airport in response to the earlier bombing of an Israeli plane in Athens was condemned by the Security Council.[224] A subsequent Israeli attack on Tunis targeting the headquarters of the Palestine Liberation Organization was similarly censured.[225] The 1986 US bombing of Tripoli in response to the terrorist bombing of a nightclub in Berlin was condemned as disproportionate, though an attempt to express this opprobrium via SC Resolution was promptly vetoed.[226] The Council was similarly divided with respect to the US bombing of the headquarters of the Iraqi secret police in 1993 in response to the attempted assassination of former President Bush Sr,[227] and its 1998 cruise missile attacks on terrorist training camps in Afghanistan and a pharmaceutical plant were the subject of condemnation by the Arab states, the Non-Aligned Movement, Pakistan, and Russia.[228]

Since 2001, however, state practice has, from some perspectives,[229] become more accepting of self-defence abroad with respect to independent non-state actors. The primary evidence of this shift was the attitude of the international community towards Operation *Enduring Freedom*, the invasion of Afghanistan in October 2001,[230] following SC Resolution 1386 identifying terrorism as a threat to the peace under Article 39 of the Charter.[231] The Security Council in Resolution 1373 of 2001 directed states to '[t]ake the necessary steps to prevent the commission of terrorist acts',[232] language which arguably authorized the use of force.[233]

Acceptance of *Enduring Freedom* was conditioned heavily on the manner in which the US linked the Taliban 'government' of Afghanistan to al-Qaeda.[234] International

---

[222] ICJ Reports 2003 p 3, 215.

[223] Byers (2002) 51 *ICLQ* 401, 407–8; Gray (3rd edn, 2008) 195–8.

[224] SC Res 262 (1986).

[225] SC Res 573 (1985).

[226] Gray (3rd edn, 2008) 196.

[227] Ibid, 196–7.

[228] Ibid, 197.

[229] Generally: Franck (2001) 98 *AJIL* 840; Greenwood (2003) 4 *San Diego ILJ* 17; Tams (2009) 20 *EJIL* 359. Also: *Armed Activities (DRC v Uganda)*, ICJ Reports 2005 p 168, 337 (Judge Simma).

[230] E.g. Murphy (2003) 43 *Harv JIL* 41; Jinks (2003) 4 *Chicago JIL* 83; Ruy & Verhoeven (2005) 10 *JCSL* 289; Kammerhofer (2007) 20 *LJIL* 89. Further: Gray (3rd edn, 2008) 200–1.

[231] SC Res 1386 (2001); SC Res 1373 (2001).

[232] SC Res 1373 (2001) op §2(b).

[233] Cf Byers (2002) 51 *ICLQ* 401, 402, 412 and Ruys & Verhoeven (2005) 10 *JCSL* 289, 310–13, both pointing out correctly that were this interpretation adopted, it would in effect authorize the unlimited use of force against terrorism by any state.

[234] Byers (2002) 51 *ICLQ* 401, 406–10.

reaction to other extra-territorial uses of force directed against non-state actors has been more equivocal: it is too much to argue that these instances reflect what would be a major shift in customary international law. As Tams notes, '[r]e-adjustments of the *ius ad bellum* are not deduced from some legal principle, but borne out by the actual practice of states'.[235] To date, the actual practice of states has been notably lacking in clarity.[236]

The second, more nuanced argument for using force against independent non-state actors in the context of Article 51 involves acceptance of the dictum of the majority in *Wall* that self-defence can only be exercised in response to an armed attack by a state, but at the same time arguing for the relaxation of the test of 'effective control' imposed in *Nicaragua* that permits the acts of non-state actors to be attributed to states.[237] This position was foreshadowed in the dissent of Judge Jennings in *Nicaragua*.[238] On this view, an armed attack occurs in situations where a state makes its territory available to non-state actors carrying out the actual attack with a view of facilitating the attack or provides logistical support or safe haven. An obvious parallel in this respect is the concept of aiding or abetting,[239] which has the advantage of being able to take into account a broader range of activities than those contemplated in *Nicaragua*, as well as the intention of the state in question. (Thus, states giving humanitarian aid to private groups would be in a different position, provided they were unaware that their support was being used to commit atrocities abroad.)[240] The criminal law analogy is not a perfect one, however: for example, states that merely sympathize or give 'moral support' to terrorists could not be held responsible for their actions.[241]

This position arguably does not take account of the increased role of the Security Council in the regulation of force between states. A central element in Judge Jennings' reasoning in *Nicaragua* was the ongoing Security Council deadlock that frustrated the effective operation of Chapter VII.[242] With the Cold War barrier removed, it may be better to leave the use of force against non-state actors to the Security Council.

The final argument for the unilateral use of force against independent non-state actors arises in the context of so-called 'failed states', where the central government

---

[235] Tams (2009) 20 *EJIL* 359, 394

[236] Ruys & Verhoeven (2005) 10 *JCSL* 289, 310–13. Further: Sperotto (2009) 20 *EJIL* 1043; Trapp (2009) 20 *EJIL* 1049; Tams (2009) 20 *EJIL* 1057.

[237] E.g. Ranzelhofer, in 1 Simma (2nd edn, 2002) 788, 801–2; Murphy (2003) 43 *Harv JIL* 41; Stahn, in Walter (ed), *Terrorism as a Challenge for National and International Law* (2004) 827; Ruys & Verhoeven (2005) 10 *JCSL* 289; Tams (2009) 20 *EJIL* 359, 385; cf Gray (3rd edn, 2008) ch 6.

[238] *Nicaragua*, ICJ Reports 1986 p 14, 543.

[239] As argued persuasively by Ruys & Verhoeven (2005) 10 *JCSL* 289, 309–15. Also: Tams (2009) 20 *EJIL* 359, 385.

[240] Ruys & Verhoeven (2005) 10 *JCSL* 289, 316.

[241] Ibid, 316–17. An example of how this might work is the process by which the US linked the Taliban to al-Qaeda. Before employing force, the US demanded that the Taliban hand over Osama bin Laden, it ensured that any refusal would be viewed as providing the al-Qaeda leader with shelter and thereby endorsing his acts: Byers (2002) 51 *ICLQ* 401, 408.

[242] ICJ Reports 1984 p 75, 543–4.

is simply unable to control non-state actors operating within its territory. This has led some to argue for a right of self-defence in such circumstances even where the acts in question cannot be attributed to the state.[243] In *Armed Activities (DRC v Uganda)*, Judge Kooijmans referred to

a phenomenon which in present-day international relations has unfortunately become as familiar as terrorism, viz. the almost complete absence of government authority in the whole or part of the territory of a State. If armed attacks are carried out by irregular bands from such territory against a neighbouring State, they are still armed attacks even if they cannot be attributed to the territorial State. It would be unreasonable to deny the attacked State the right to self-defence merely because there is no attacker State, and the Charter does not so require.[244]

In accordance with this line of reasoning, there is an exception to the notion that only inter-*state* violence can constitute an armed attack. Again, however, it may be that the integrity of the international system requires that such matters be left to the Security Council. Certainly, it has demonstrated that it is capable of handling such situations, for example when responding to Somali pirates raiding commercial shipping in the Gulf of Aden from 2008.[245]

---

[243] Randelzhofer, in 1 Simma (2nd edn, 2002) 788, 802.

[244] ICJ Reports 2005 p 168, 314 (Judge Kooijmans), 337 (Judge Simma). Cf Kammerhofer (2007) 20 *LJIL* 89.

[245] Though the actual *use* of force has not been as effective: SC Res 1816 (2008); SC Res 1838 (2008); SC Res 1846 (2008); SC Res 1851 (2008); SC Res 1897 (2009); SC Res 1918 (2010); SC Res 1950 (2010). Further: Guilfoyle (2008) 57 *ICLQ* 690; Treves (2009) 20 *EJIL* 399; Guilfoyle (2010) 59 *ICLQ* 141.

INDEX